CHAMBERS OF HEDLEY MARTEN
11 New Square
Lincoln's Inn
London
WC2A 3QB
Telephone 020 7831 0081

THE
LAW OF
PASSING-OFF

UNFAIR COMPETITION BY
MISREPRESENTATION

AUSTRALIA
Law Book Co.
Sydney

CANADA and USA
Carswell
Toronto

HONG KONG
Sweet & Maxwell Asia

NEW ZEALAND
Brookers
Wellington

SINGAPORE and MALAYSIA
Sweet & Maxwell Asia
Singapore and Kuala Lumper

THE
LAW OF
PASSING-OFF

UNFAIR COMPETITION BY
MISREPRESENTATION

BY

CHRISTOPHER WADLOW

SOLICITOR
SIMMONS & SIMMONS
LONDON

THIRD EDITION

LONDON
SWEET & MAXWELL
2004

First Edition published 1990
Second Edition published 1995

Published in 2004 by
Sweet & Maxwell Limited of
100 Avenue Road
London NW3 3PF
Typeset by YHT Ltd,
1 The Avenue
West Ealing
W13 8NT
Printed and bound in Great Britain
by William Clowes Ltd,
Beccles, Suffolk NR34 9QE

No natural forests were destroyed to
make this product: only farmed timber
was used and replanted.

ISBN 0 421 789204
A CIP catalogue record for this book is
available from the British Library

ISBN 0-421-78920-4

9 780421 789203

PREFACE

In this third edition, the *Law of Passing-off* gains a new subtitle and two major extensions to its coverage. Though the term "passing-off" is familiar enough, it is something of a misnomer. It understates the full extent and importance of the tort, and baffles all but specialists. In the Civil law "unfair competition" has long been recognised as a subject of major importance in its own right, and even in England the phrase is increasingly accepted either as a synonym for passing-off, or as an all-embracing term for that and related causes of action, of which the natural counterpart to passing-off is injurious falsehood. This edition is therefore better described as the *Law of Unfair Competition by Misrepresentation*.

The present edition includes for the first time a chapter on the international law of unfair competition under the Paris Convention for the Protection of Industrial Property, with a detailed account of the drafting and negotiating history of Article 10*bis* of the latter. As related but logically separated developments, there are new sections on the possible impact of the European Convention on Human Rights, the WTO TRIPs Agreement, and on unfair competition in private international law. Although the Paris Convention does not directly affect day-to-day practice it does provide the only international consensus against which national laws of unfair competition may be compared, and any future efforts at harmonisation by the European Community can hardly fail to take it as their starting point. The Community has so far concentrated on consumer protection law rather than unfair competition, but it is not too early for common lawyers to give thought to whether domestic law complies with Paris Convention norms, and to see what can be done, absent legislation, to bring it into conformity where it might be thought to depart. The present edition is to some extent pre-emptive of what can be expected to come.

The three specific categories of misrepresentation which the Paris Convention addresses as unfair competition correspond respectively to classic passing–off, trade libel, and various misdescriptions which are civilly actionable, if at all, under one of the extended forms of passing-off. For this reason, as well as for its affinity with passing-off, I have included in the

v

present edition a treatment of the law of injurious falsehood, principally as it applies between competitors, but drawing on cases between non-competitors where matters of principle are concerned. Injurious falsehood has historically been of secondary importance, but the past decade or so has produced a significant number of decided cases, some dealing specifically with competitive situations such as comparative advertising, while others far removed from commercial competition have important implications for the law in its wider aspects. I have endeavoured to deal with injurious falsehood to the same standard as for passing-off, and with the ultimate aim of presenting an integrated treatment of the two if or when they converge sufficiently.

In addition to these major developments, there has been a steady stream of decided cases from the United Kingdom courts and the major common law jurisdictions—some dealing with issues which could hardly have been anticipated even as recently as the last edition, such as domain names; some restating old principles anew or applying them to new situations; and some requiring my former understanding of the law to be reconsidered, and corresponding sections rewritten. In the result, this edition is approximately 40% longer than the second, despite pruning material which has become obsolete or been superceded. A few decisions might even be thought unduly reactionary, and I have generally been more cautious than in previous editions in predicting how the law might develop in the future.

It is noticeable that many more passing-off cases are going to trial or summary judgment than a decade ago, so that complicated legal issues may now require and receive much more thorough consideration than was usual when most actions were decided on applications for interim injunctions, and *American Cyanamid* prevailed. There is certainly no sign of passing-off being eclipsed by the registered trade mark system, and the Court of Appeal was kind enough to pronounce on the interpretation of my favourite statutory provision just one day before the cut-off date for the present edition: the Trade Marks Act 1994, s.2(2) means precisely what it says: "nothing in this Act affects the law relating to passing off".

Once again, I am immeasurably grateful to Simmons & Simmons, and especially to Kevin Mooney, for their continuing support.

I have endeavoured to state the law at July 31, 2003.

Christopher Wadlow
Simmons & Simmons
CityPoint
One Ropemaker Street
London
EC2Y 9SS

CONTENTS

PLAN OF THE BOOK

New in the present edition

The present edition includes for the first time a treatment of the tort of injurious falsehood in a competitive or near-competitive context. Where possible, this is integrated with the treatment of passing-off so that although there is one whole chapter (chapter 6) devoted to matters of principle which arise in injurious falsehood alone, examples of misrepresentations of both kinds are included in chapter 7 under the title "actionable misrepresentations".

The other major innovation of the present edition is its treatment of unfair competition in international law. A new chapter (chapter 2) deals with the unfair competition provisions of the Paris Convention for the Protection of Industrial Property and the extent to which the subject matter of the present work might be affected by TRIPs. There are also new sections on human rights, in chapter 9, and on unfair competition in private international law in chapter 10.

The book and its coverage

The basic plan of the book is carried over from previous editions, but two chapters are entirely new and others are renumbered, extended, or reordered internally. So far as passing-off is concerned, the structure continues to be defined by the "Classical Trinity" of goodwill, damage and misrepresentation. Each of these three essential elements receives at least one chapter to itself. However, the decided cases do not deal in anything like equal proportion with the theoretical issues into which passing-off may be resolved. The length of the treatment given to each issue has to take into account the size of the relevant body of law and the numerous subsidiary rules, presumptions, exceptions, and even inconsistencies which have evolved. In the case of the element of misrepresentation, this means that three chapters are required for its treatment in passing-off, moving progressively from general principles, through the intermediate level of actionable misrepresentations, to the one particular way in which the most common kind of misrepresentation is most typically made, which is by imitation of the claimant's distinctive sign.

Injurious falsehood also has a Trinity of its own, namely misrepresentation, malice, and damage; but the tort is less important than passing-off by at least an order of magnitude, and the body of decided cases is very much smaller. Malice and other matters which have no direct counterpart in passing-off are dealt with in a chapter (chapter 6) entirely devoted to injurious falsehood, but tracking so far as possible the structure of the corresponding chapter for passing-off, while examples of potentially actionable misrepresentations of every kind are included in a single chapter regardless of whether they are currently thought to constitute passing-off, injurious falsehood, both, or neither. Elsewhere, matters primarily or wholly relevant to injurious falsehood alone have been incorporated at appropriate places within the existing structure.

With peripheral and mostly obvious exceptions, the treatment of the substantive law of unfair competition by misrepresentation in the present work is entirely concerned with the common law torts of passing-off and injurious falsehood. In these two fields the common law is rightly assumed, with surprisingly few necessary provisos, to be essentially uniform no matter wherever it may find itself applied, and by whomsoever it may be expounded. Extensive reference is therefore made, generally without further explanation or qualification, to the decisions of courts in the major common law jurisdictions other than the United Kingdom. Conversely, other bodies of law which may be relevant in specific instances, such as the other common law economic torts, defamation, and the statutory or European regimes for registered trade marks, geographical indications trade descriptions and misleading advertising, receive only peripheral mention. Readers are referred to the appropriate specialist texts.

In the case of trade mark law it would be perverse or impossible to exclude from consideration the many decided cases in which passing-off and trade mark infringement have both played a role, but the present work attempts to describe the law of passing-off in its own terms and almost entirely in reliance on decisions in cases where passing-off was the major issue or one of them, rather than by analogy with the parallel but distinct body of case law on registered trade marks. Likewise, injurious falsehood is treated as far as possible either as a topic in its own right, or as a practical counterpart to passing-off, but never as a distant relative of defamation in the sense of libel and slander.

Passing-off, injurious falsehood, and "unfair competition"

Section A of chapter 1 begins the book with the question of whether "unfair competition" deserves to supercede "passing-off", either as a synonym, or as a more widely embracing term. There follows an overview of passing-off in section B in terms of its "Classical Trinity" of goodwill, misrepresentation and damage, with judicial definitions or summaries of passing-off from some of the leading cases. A corresponding overview of injurious falsehood in terms of misrepresentation, malice and damage follows in section C. Section D provides an extended history of the development of the law, and section E revisits passing-off in its context as a common law tort of unfair competition.

New chapter 2 describes the treatment of unfair competition in international law. Section A distinguishes between the role of international law as defining substantive obligations on states, considered in the present chapter but not yet directly affecting day-to-day practice, and its adjectival effects on defences and enforcement, which are considered at appropriate places in chapters 9 and 10. Sections B and C concentrate on the provisions of the Paris Convention for the Protection of Industrial Property relevant to unfair competition, with section B presenting a commentary on Art.10*bis* of the latter and Section C describing in some detail its drafting and negotiating history, spanning half-a-dozen formal revision conferences from the first years of the twentieth century onwards. The TRIPs Agreement has relatively little to say about mainstream unfair competition law, but its possible implications are considered in section D.

Goodwill and damage

After this introduction, the first substantial chapter on English law as such is chapter 3 which deals with goodwill in terms of its importance as the property right protected by the action for passing-off. Injurious falsehood protects a wider and indeed much vaguer class of pecuniary interests and requires only brief mention in this context. Section A explains the nature of goodwill and its importance as the basis of the action. Goodwill is also contrasted with reputation on the one hand, and statutory rights in registered marks on the other. Only traders may have goodwill, and section B sets out the rather elastic idea of what constitutes being a trader for the purposes of the law of passing-off. Sections C and D elaborate on this and respectively deal with two specific examples of claimants on the margin of trading activities, namely trade and professional associations and non-trading organisations such as charities. Goodwill is normally created by trading, but section E discusses whether goodwill can exist before actual business commences. Sections F and G discuss the inherently territorial nature of goodwill and the circumstances in which a foreign enterprise can be said to have goodwill to protect. Section F presents an orthodox account in terms of the English authorities, and section G gives an international overview for several common law jurisdictions which differ from the English point of view to a greater or lesser extent. The next three sections deal with goodwill as legal property. Section H introduces the question of ownership of goodwill in general terms by reference to a number of cases decided since the previous edition, and section I discusses ownership in a variety of commercially important circumstances in which more than one party might plausibly be said to have a claim to the goodwill, or a share in it. Section J covers dealings with goodwill, their validity effects and incidental consequences. Section K deals with extinction of goodwill, and section L mentions some peripheral sources of law which may be relevant for non-traders.

Chapter 4 deals with damage. Only misrepresentations *really likely* to cause damage are actionable as passing-off, whatever their nature. Damage was the gist of the common law tort of passing-off, and its theoretical importance has been reaffirmed in modern law now that the class of actionable misrepresentations may perhaps be so wide as to be embarrassing if no such restriction is imposed. Section A deals with the theoretical importance of damage in the history of the tort and today. Section B qualifies this, because as a practical matter proof of likelihood of damage was never insisted upon in its own right in the majority of cases. The apparent contradiction may be resolved by saying that the legal burden of proving damage is always on the plaintiff, but that the evidential burden may shift to the defendant. It is on him to disprove damage in certain situations which have occurred so often before that damage may safely be assumed in the absence of proof to the contrary. Damage thus remains the acid test for unusual misrepresentations or unprecedented circumstances, but without requiring wasted effort in the ordinary case. Section C categorises the heads of damage in passing-off which are established or have received judicial consideration, and section D deals with the treatment of damage in injurious falsehood.

The misrepresentation: basic principles

Chapters 5 to 8 all deal with the element of misrepresentation from various standpoints, with chapters 5 and 8 being specific to passing-off, chapter 6 specific to injurious falsehood, and chapter 7 relevant to both.

Chapter 5 is entirely concerned with passing-off and sets out certain common principles which apply whatever the nature of the misrepresentation and however it may be made. Section A deals with the essential importance of the misrepresentation to the cause of action and foreshadows certain situations in which there is no misrepresentation, or one which does not amount to passing-off. Passing-off is not confined to misrepresentations which are false in every conceivable sense, and section B deals with those which are misleading in fact though literally or colourably true. As well as being false, the misrepresentation in passing-off must be a material one, as described in Section C. Section D deals with the contexts in which the claimant's distinctive name, mark or get-up can be used without misrepresentation and therefore without liability for passing-off. The next two sections E and F deal with the defendant's state of mind: innocence is no defence and fraud is not essential, but the latter has evidential value. Section G deals with the status of the defendant as a trader, and Section H with the so-called "common field of activity", which, like fraud, remains of evidential value despite being repudiated as a component of the cause of action in its own right. Section I discusses the classes of person to whom the misrepresentation may be made. Customers and consumers are the obvious candidates but suppliers and others may also be relevant. Any definition of passing-off in terms of misrepresentation would be incomplete without mentioning that there is strict liability for putting deceptive goods into circulation even before any customer or consumer is deceived. This doctrine of "instruments of deception" is introduced in section J as part of the wider topic of who may be liable for passing-off; and discussed in more detail in section K, which includes the treatment of exports and the rather unsatisfactory way in which the original concept has been extended to goods which are incomplete or otherwise not inherently deceptive, and even to intangibles such as company and domain names. The final section, L, discusses the relevant time for determining if the defendant's conduct is actionable.

Chapter 6 is the counterpart chapter for injurious falsehood, and deals with issues of general importance which have no parallel in passing-off, or which receive significantly different treatments in the two bodies of law. With those qualifications, it follows a similar order to chapter 5. Section A deals with the essential importance of the misrepresentation to the cause of action and asks what makes a false representation actionable as injurious falsehood, and in particular whether the misrepresentation need be a disparaging one. As in passing-off, the misrepresentation in injurious falsehood must be a material one, and Section B deals with this and the two related issues of identification of the claimant and the treatment of representations categorised as "puffing". Sections C and D deal with the mental element of malice, which, unlike fraud in passing-off, remains very much an essential element of injurious falsehood to this day. The (mis)representation in injurious falsehood is interpreted in a different manner to that in passing-off, and the application and legal basis of the so-called "single meaning rule" are considered in Section E.

Is the misrepresentation actionable?

Chapter 7 discusses in more detail the categories of misrepresentation which are potentially actionable as passing-off or injurious falsehood, or both, and the manner in which the misrepresentation may be effected. The most common manner, imitation of the claimant's distinctive sign, has the whole of chapter 8 to itself. Since chapter 7 covers both passing-off and injurious falsehood, it begins with a short section A contrasting and attempting to distinguish the two torts. Thereafter, sections B to K deal primarily with misrepresentations capable of amounting to passing-off and sections L to O with those capable of amounting to injurious falsehood, although the boundary is not precise and a damaging misrepresentation may sometimes amount to both, or more often is neither. The most fundamental kind of misrepresentation actionable as passing-off is that the defendant is the claimant, or is so closely associated with the claimant as to make no difference, and this is addressed in section B. More specifically, the earliest kind of misrepresentation recognised as passing-off, and still the most common, is that the goods of the defendant are those of the claimant or an associated enterprise. This provides the subject matter of sections C and D, the latter dealing with passing-off where the defendant's goods are substituted in purportedly fulfilling orders for those of the claimant. In certain circumstances there may be passing-off even though the goods sold by the defendant really do originate from the claimant. Liability in these circumstances is dealt with in section E.

Passing-off need not involve goods. There may be passing-off of businesses or services whether or not goods are also involved, and in broader circumstances than already discussed in Section B. Section F deals with licensing and franchising, and sections G and H discuss the problems of merchandising and endorsement in which real characters, or the creators of fictitious ones, have used or attempted to use the action for passing-off to restrain the unauthorised use of their names or likenesses. Producers of products such as *Champagne*, *Scotch Whisky* and *Advocaat* are recognised as having a cause of action against misuse of those terms for spurious products, so section I deals in general terms with misrepresentations or misdescriptions of this kind, while some of the more important specific products are dealt with individually in section J. Section K deals with what is sometimes called "inverse passing-off", because the misrepresentation is not that the goods or services of the defendant are those of the claimant, but that the claimant's goods or achievements are those of the defendant, who thereby misappropriates the credit due to the claimant.

The next four sections are principally concerned with misrepresentations actionable as injurious falsehood. Section L covers misrepresentations that the claimant has ceased to trade at all, or is under some other material disadvantage. Section M deals with various kinds of outright disparagements which fall more naturally under the head of injurious falsehood rather than defamation, and section N with comparative advertising. Section O addresses various kinds of disparagements relating to intellectual property rights. Section P, the final section, revisits the question of whether or to what extent all or any of these categories can be embraced within a single general rule.

Passing-off as a law of signs

Chapter 8 (under the new heading of "Signs") concentrates on the one particular way in which the misrepresentation in passing-off is most often supposed to have been made. This is by the adoption by the defendant, innocently or otherwise, of a name, mark, get-up or other sign sufficiently close to what is distinctive of the claimant to deceive. The first three sections are of general relevance regardless of the type of mark or sign in issue. Section A discusses the concept of distinctiveness and section B the factors which influence whether a sign is distinctive or not. Section C describes how one approaches the question of whether the defendant's sign is similar enough to that of the claimant for the relevant public to be deceived. Thereafter the chapter is divided up in terms of certain types of sign of recurring importance. Section D covers the related but logically distinct concepts of word marks which may be distinctive though *prima facie* descriptive, and terms which are really the generic name of the goods or services they describe. Section E deals with certain categories of verbal marks which raise specific issues, such as personal and geographical names.

Cases on the titles of publications and the like raise few issues of principle but are sufficiently numerous to have a section to themselves, section F. Sections G and H deal with the distinctiveness of get-up, and the important distinction between the get-up of packaging and the intrinsic appearance of the goods themselves. Get-up is not confined to goods sold: one may have a distinctive get-up for premises or business assets. Section I discusses a broader spectrum of visual marks, which may contribute to get-up or be relevant in their own right. Problems arising from the internet are new to the present edition, and section J now addresses the response of the law to cybersquatting and similar abuses. Finally section K mentions some matters for which distinctiveness had been claimed, but which cannot easily be fitted into the previous categories.

Defences, remedies and procedure

Chapter 9 deals with defences. A brief introduction in section A explains the sources of law and their different degrees of relevance to passing-off and injurious falsehood. New section B deals with the possible impact of the European Convention on Human Rights by reference to unfair competition cases decided by the European Court of Human Rights and admissibility decisions of the European Human Rights Commission. The other potentially relevant body of European law in the form of the Community rules on free movement and competition is dealt with in Section C. The remaining sections deal with defences under national law. Section D deals with misleading or illegal conduct by the claimant, including deceptive marks and unjustified claims to patent or trade mark protection. Section E covers honest use of one's own name, which may perhaps still be a defence when the name is used as the name of a business, though it is no defence when the name is used on goods. Section F covers innocent passing-off in general, innocence being no defence to an injunction but possibly a defence, or a partial defence, to pecuniary remedies. Various situations can arise in which different parties assert mutually incompatible rights and these are the subject of section G. Finally, section H deals with defences which arise when the claimant fails to enforce his rights sufficiently promptly or vigorously.

Chapter 10 is on remedies and procedure. The detailed impact of the Civil Procedure Rules is as yet unclear, and on most issues the pre-CPR authorities are assumed to have been superceded, so the chapter has been simplified accordingly. An outline of the effects of the CPR reforms is given in section A. Section B deals with interim measures, which are still of considerable, if no longer overwhelming, importance. Two topics which are relatively unaffected by the CPR, and for which pre-CPR authorities are assumed still to be of relevance, are evidence and its admissibility in passing-off actions, including trade and survey evidence, and the various kinds of final relief, respectively considered at sections C and D. The private international law of unfair competition is the subject of new section E.

TABLE OF CASES

Table of European Cases

Table of International Cases by Country

Australia

United States of America

1

TABLE OF EUROPEAN LEGISLATION
TREATIES, REGULATIONS AND DIRECTIVES
Paragraph references in **bold** indicate that the Article is reproduced in full.

li

Regulations

Directives

TABLE OF STATUTES

Paragraph references in **bold** indicate that the Article is reproduced in full.

liii

TABLE OF SUPREME COURT RULES AND CIVIL PROCEDURE RULES

INTRODUCTION

1

A. Unfair Competition by Misrepresentation and Otherwise

The name and nature of unfair competition

1–1 The term "unfair competition" may be used in several senses. One is as the collective name for a variety of nominate or emergent torts which have in common their usefulness in protecting traders in their relationships with one another. This is how the term is principally employed in this edition of the present work, which deals the two common law torts which together constitute the law of unfair competition by misrepresentation, namely passing-off and injurious falsehood. The relationship of these two torts to the wider concept of actionable unfair conduct between competitors in trade has been stated by Lord Diplock[1]:

> "Unfair trading as a wrong actionable at the suit of other traders who thereby suffer loss of business or goodwill may take a variety of forms, to some of which separate labels have become attached in English law. Conspiracy to injure a person in his trade or business is one, slander of goods another, but the most protean is that which is generally and nowadays, perhaps misleadingly, described as passing-off. The forms that unfair trading takes will alter with the ways in which trade is carried on and business reputation and goodwill acquired."

Another usage for "unfair competition" is as a synonym for passing-off. It is in this sense that Aldous L.J. has recently referred to "the cause of action traditionally called passing-off, perhaps best referred to as unfair competition".[2]

1–2   Under whatever name, the cause of action for unfair competition or passing-off is now precisely two centuries old, if one takes the decision of Lord Eldon in *Hogg v Kirby*[3] as the first reported decision in point. What is perhaps more surprising, is that unfair competition as a name has a fair claim to be older than passing-off by almost half a century. In *Hogg v Kirby* itself Lord Eldon adjudged the defendant's conduct in representing his magazine as a continuation of a title established by the plaintiff in terms of competition, fair or otherwise: "for if there was fair competition by another original work, really new, be the loss what it may, there is no damage or injury". What made Kirby's conduct unfair and therefore actionable was his misrepresentation that the new work was connected with the old one. The term passing-off itself does not appear in a law report (and then, only at first in a headnote) until half way through the nineteenth century.

Lawyers in the late nineteenth century and early twentieth had little dif-

---

[1] *per* Lord Diplock in *Erven Warnink BV v J Townend & Sons (Hull) Ltd* [1979] A.C. 731; [1979] 2 All E.R. 927; [1980] R.P.C. 31 at 91, HL.
[2] *per* Aldous L.J. in *Arsenal Football Club plc v Reed (No.2)* [2003] EWCA Civ 696; [2003] 2 CMLR 25, CA.
[3] (1803) 32 E.R. 336; 8 Ves. Jun. 215 (Lord Eldon L.C.).

ficulty with the term "unfair competition" (or close variants such as "unfair trade competition"), if not as the name of a cause of action, then at least to describe a loosely defined but easily recognisable set of situations for which the law provided remedies. The first edition of Clerk & Lindsell[4] has marginal sub-titles for "rivalry in business", "unfair interference" and "fair competition"; and the first edition of Salmond[5] says of what is "commonly, but awkwardly, termed ... passing off" that "the law on this matter is designed to protect traders against that form of unfair competition which consists in acquiring for oneself, by means of false and misleading devices, the benefit of the reputation achieved by rival traders." According to *Daniell's Chancery Practice*[6]:

> "The Court will also, as we have seen, interfere by injunction to restrain the infringement of a patent, and the piracy of a copyright, or of trade marks, labels, or names, and to prevent unfair competition in trade."

It is also at the beginning of the twentieth century that unfair competition **1–3** first appeared in international law,[7] in the form of Art.10*bis* of the Paris Convention for the Protection of Industrial Property. In 1911, and again in 1925, the United Kingdom was the sole or principal sponsor for strengthened versions of Art.10*bis* intended to provide effective protection against defined acts of unfair competition. The first two paragraphs of Art.10*bis* now provide, in general terms:

1. The countries of the Union are bound to assure to nationals of such countries effective protection against unfair competition.
2. Any act of competition contrary to honest practices in industrial or commercial matters constitutes an act of unfair competition.

Despite this start, for most of the twentieth century "unfair competition" has been used but rarely in English legal literature, and then mainly by specialists in international or comparative law. One may wonder how a concept orthodox enough for the editors of *Daniell's Chancery Practice* has come to be to be shunned and avoided except by a minority.

In the United States, in contrast to the United Kingdom, the term "unfair **1–4** competition" not only became accepted and established in legal usage, but was also to branch out rapidly in several quite separate directions. A convenient starting point is the publication of the first edition of Harold Nims' textbook *Trademarks and Unfair Competition* in 1909. The first and most familiar usage for unfair competition was as a synonym for passing-off, though it progressively embraced other private-law actions which were felt to be analogous. Quite apart from that, however, the phrase evidently struck a chord with the populist element in American legal and political thought,

---

[4] Clerk & Lindsell, *The Law of Torts* (1st ed., 1889), p.14.
[5] Salmond, *The Law of Torts* (1st ed., 1907), para.150, p.429.
[6] *Daniell's Chancery Practice* (8th ed., 1914) pp.1282, 1388; (6th ed., 1882) pp.1476, 1591.
[7] Under the French name *concurrence déloyale*. The original Art.10*bis* was new with the 1900 (Brussels) revision. See Chapter 2.

because it was applied to the anti-competitive activities of trusts and corporations, whether monopolistic or collusive, and to dumping and other practices in international trade which were thought to abuse the international trading system. By the time of the First World War the phrase "unfair competition" was sufficiently familiar in the United States to have been adopted in an Act of Congress[8] and decisions of the Supreme Court.[9]

In American usage "unfair competition" frequently embraces trade mark law as well as passing-off and other related causes of action.[10] This perhaps reflects the fact that trade mark law in the United States is still not wholly the creature of statute, as it is in the United Kingdom, and retains a common law basis. Be that as it may, the law of registered trade marks is obviously one way in which fairness and honesty in competition are maintained, whether or not one treats unfair competition law as a separate subject or as an all-embracing one:

> "These causes of action[11] are the subject of a great deal of learning, some of which has been deployed in argument during the hearing, but their basic idea is quite simple. It is (and has been for a very long time) the policy of the law to permit and indeed encourage fair competition in trade but to discourage and indeed prevent unfair competition ... The rules as to passing off and trade mark infringement are (in non-statutory and statutory form respectively) a very important part of the law preventing unfair competition. Their basic common principle is that a trader may not sell his goods under false pretences, either by deceptively passing them off as the goods of another trader so as to take unfair advantage of his reputation in his goods, or by using a trade sign the same as, or confusingly similar to, a registered trade mark."[12]

1–5   It might be objected that the name unfair competition is merely an epithet, that unfairness is too imprecise to serve as a definition for legal liability, or that the term describes neither a single cause of action, nor any separate or precisely defined category. But objections such as these, however true, lie awkwardly in the mouth of a common lawyer. One is used to imprecise or inappropriate categories, whose boundaries and terminology (often unhelpful, if not actually misleading) are sanctioned by nothing more than history and usage. One talks without embarrassment about the "economic torts", which from most points of view constitute an even more unsatisfactory and disparate collection. And if the worst that can be said against unfair competition is that it is no more than a synonym for passing-off, then perhaps one may agree with Lord Diplock that "passing off" has

---

[8] The Federal Trade Commission Act, s.5(a)(1); strictly, "unfair methods of competition".

[9] *Hannover Star Milling Co v Metcalfe* (1916) 240 U.S. 403; 36 S.Ct. 357; 60 L.Ed. 713; *International News Service v Associated Press* (1918) 248 U.S. 215; 39 S.Ct. 68; 63 L.Ed. 211.

[10] This is the sense in which it continues to be used in the *Restatement (3d) Unfair Competition* (1995).

[11] Passing-off and registered trade mark infringement.

[12] *per* Robert Walker J. in *United Biscuits (UK) Ltd v Asda Stores Ltd* [1997] R.P.C. 513.

become misleading with the development of the action which it once purported to describe, and with Aldous L.J. that the synonym is the better term.

The English response to problems of unfair competition

For most practical purposes the law of unfair competition as understood in **1–6**
English common law begins and ends with misrepresentation. Passing-off
and injurious falsehood are exclusively concerned with misrepresentations
of one kind or another. As Jacob J. has said about passing-off[13]:

> "I turn to consider the law and begin by identifying what is not the law.
> There is no tort of copying. There is no tort of taking a man's market or
> customers. Neither the market nor the customers are the plaintiff's to
> own. There is no tort of making use of another's goodwill as such. There
> is no tort of competition...
> At the heart of passing off lies deception or its likelihood, deception of
> the ultimate consumer in particular. Over the years passing off has
> developed from the classic case of the defendant selling his goods as and
> for those of the plaintiff to cover other kinds of deception, e.g. that the
> defendant's goods are the same as those of the plaintiff when they are not,
> e.g. *Combe International Ltd v Scholl (UK) Ltd* [1980] R.P.C. 1; or that
> the defendant's goods are the same as goods sold by a class of persons of
> which the plaintiff is a member when they are not, e.g. *Warnink (Erven)
> Besloten Vennootschap v J. Townend Sons Ltd* [1980] R.P.C. 29. Never has
> the tort shown even a slight tendency to stray beyond cases of deception.
> Were it to do so it would enter the field of honest competition, declared
> unlawful for some reason other than deceptiveness. Why there should be
> any such reason I cannot imagine. It would serve only to stifle competition."

Though the language may appear strong, what is perhaps most remarkable
is how little hyperbole is involved in the statement that this tort has never
shown even a slight tendency to stray beyond cases of deception. Superficial
exceptions are not only few in number, but tend to suffer one of three fates:
evolution or absorption into an entirely independent body of law, subsequent rationalisation in orthodox terms, or total oblivion.

Unfair competition by other means, the "economic torts"

The common law also provides remedies for a number of categories of **1–7**
wrongful conduct which go under the name of the economic torts.[14] They
are so called because their primary function is the protection of purely
economic interests. As well as passing-off and injurious falsehood, the
economic torts are normally considered to include the causes of action for
civil conspiracy, inducing breach of contract, intimidation, deceit, and some

---

[13] *Hodgkinson Corby Ltd v Wards Mobility Services Ltd* [1995] F.S.R. 169.
[14] Hazel Carty, *An Analysis of the Economic Torts* (2000).

aspects of negligence. There is also an emergent (but ill-defined) tort of interference with trade. Except for a brief review of the latter, they are not further considered in this work.

B. THE "CLASSICAL TRINITY" OF PASSING-OFF

Goodwill, damage and misrepresentation

1–8 Passing-off is concerned with misrepresentations made by one trader which damage the goodwill of another trader. Misrepresentation, damage and goodwill are therefore the three essential elements of the tort, and are sometimes referred to as its "classical trinity".[15] It is worth adding that liability for passing-off is not affected by the defendant's state of mind. There is no fourth element requiring the defendant to be fraudulent, malicious, or even negligent.

Misrepresentation bears the same meaning in passing-off as in any other branch of law. A representation is false if it is calculated to deceive in fact, even if it is literally true in some sense. Likewise, a representation is false if it will deceive a substantial number of those to whom it is addressed, even if others will not be deceived. Not every type of misrepresentation amounts to passing-off. Misrepresentations which disparage the goods, business or reputation of the claimant fall within the realms of injurious falsehood or defamation. Passing-off was traditionally confined to misrepresentations that the goods, services or business of the defendant were those of the plaintiff or closely connected with him, but this is now recognised as no more than the forerunner of a more general rule. Such misrepresentations are still the most typical by a large margin, but passing-off has expanded to deal with misrepresentations as to quality or nature. The borders of the tort have yet to be fully explored.

1–9 The misrepresentation in passing-off is almost always conveyed by the defendant adopting for his own goods or business some material such as a name, mark, get-up or other sign which is deceptively similar to material distinctive of the claimant. The misrepresentation is deemed to be made as soon as such goods are released into circulation, even if the immediate recipients are traders who are not themselves deceived. To this extent, passing-off is concerned with trade marks and service marks in the widest sense, but it is by no means confined to misrepresentations conveyed through the use of such marks or to matter which would be registrable under the Trade Marks Act 1994. The Act expressly leaves the action for passing-off unaffected.[16] Passing-off and the law of registered trade marks deal with some overlapping factual situations, but deal with them in dif-

---

[15] Variations on the classical trinity are possible, substituting reputation for goodwill, and confusion or deception for misrepresentation.
[16] Trade Marks Act 1994, s.2(2); explained in *Inter Lotto (UK) Ltd v Camelot Group plc* [2003] EWCA Civ 1132; affirming [2003] EWHC 1256; [2003] 3 All E.R. 191 (Laddie J.).

ferent ways and from different standpoints. Passing-off emphatically does not confer monopoly rights in any names, marks, get-up or other indicia, nor does it recognise them as property in their own right.

Damage is essential to passing-off in that for a misrepresentation to be actionable it must be one calculated to cause damage to the claimant's goodwill. Damage is thus one acid test which distinguishes actionable mis-representations from those which are beneath the notice of the law. The claimant need not prove either actual or special damage. A real, tangible probability of damage is sufficient. The two most common heads of damage are that the claimant will lose business to the defendant if the two are in competition, or that the claimant will suffer if, as is often the case, the defendant's goods or services are inferior. Other heads of damage have been recognised and there is no reason to believe that the categories of damage have been closed.

Goodwill is a legal right of property associated with every business. It has **1–10** concisely been described as "the attractive force which brings in custom".[17] It follows that the action for passing-off is only open to traders, because private individuals can have no goodwill. However, the concepts of trader and goodwill are very widely interpreted so as to cover virtually every economic activity. The action for passing-off is therefore open to the liberal professions, entertainers, artists, writers and almost anyone who can be said to derive an income from the provision of goods or services. As legal property, goodwill may be created, owned, assigned and extinguished, and all these operations are governed by the system of law under which the goodwill exists. A foreign business may have goodwill in England if its goods or services are in demand here and that demand is capable of being satisfied, but a foreign business which lacks such goodwill cannot bring an action for passing-off.

Every modern definition of passing-off is complete without reference to the defendant's state of mind. This is a noteworthy fact in itself, both because passing-off was expressly based on fraud until as little as a century ago; and because the common law torts with which passing-off has the closest affinity mostly require some mental element varying from negligence through intent to deliberate malevolence. Intention to deceive has evidential value, but no more. Conversely, *mala fides* cannot render actionable any conduct which would not be passing-off if innocently performed.

Lord Diplock in *Advocaat* and Lord Parker in *Spalding v Gamage*

The leading modern authority on passing-off remains the decision of the **1–11** House of Lords in the *Advocaat* case, *Erven Warnink v Townend*,[18] and the leading speech is that of Lord Diplock:

"*Spalding v Gamage*[19] and the later cases make it possible to identify five characteristics which must be present in order to create a valid cause of

---

[17] *per* Lord Macnaghten in *Inland Revenue Commissioners v Muller & Co's Margarine Ltd* [1901] A.C. 217, HL.
[18] [1979] A.C. 731; [1979] 2 All E.R. 927; [1980] R.P.C. 31 at 93, HL.
[19] (1915) 32 R.P.C. 273, HL.

action for passing-off: (1) a misrepresentation (2) made by a trader in the course of trade, (3) to prospective customers of his or ultimate consumers of goods or services supplied by him, (4) which is calculated to injure the business or goodwill of another trader (in the sense that this is a reasonably foreseeable consequence) and (5) which causes actual damage to a business or goodwill of the trader by whom the action is brought or (in a *quia timet* action) will probably do so."

Lord Diplock was referring to and approving the speech of Lord Parker in *Spalding v Gamage*,[20] which was the first unambiguous definition of the tort by a superior court in its modern form of protecting business goodwill against misrepresentation.

"[T]he basis of a passing-off action being a false representation by the defendant, it must be proved in each case as a fact that the false representation was made. It may, of course, have been made in express words, but cases of express misrepresentation of this sort are rare. The more common case is, where the representation is implied in the use or imitation of a mark, trade name, or get-up with which the goods of another are associated in the minds of the public, or of a particular class of the public. In such cases the point to be decided is whether, having regard to all the circumstances of the case, the use by the defendant in connection with the goods of the mark, name, or get-up in question impliedly represents such goods to be the goods of the plaintiff, or the goods of the plaintiff of a particular class or quality, or, as it is sometimes put, whether the defendant's use of such mark, name or get-up is calculated to deceive. It would, however, be impossible to enumerate or classify all the possible ways in which a man may make the false representation relied on.

There appears to be considerable diversity of opinion as to the nature of the right, the invasion of which is the subject of what are known as passing-off actions. The more general opinion appears to be that the right is a right of property. This view naturally demands an answer to the question property in what? Some authorities say property in the mark, name, or get-up improperly used by the defendant. Others say, property in the business or goodwill likely to be injured by the misrepresentation. Lord Herschell in *Reddaway v Banham*[21] expressly dissents from the former view; and if the right invaded is a right of property at all, there are, I think, strong reasons for preferring the latter view. In the first place, cases of misrepresentation by the use of a mark, name, or get-up do not exhaust all possible cases of misrepresentation."

1–12   Neither of these two extracts can be read as a comprehensive definition of what amounts to passing-off. Rather, they serve to identify the fundamental principles of the law and to provide a framework around which to develop its application to the diverse circumstances of the business world. Lord

---

[20] (1915) 32 R.P.C. 273 at 284, HL.
[21] [1896] A.C. 199; [1895–9] All E.R. 313; 13 R.P.C. 218, HL.

Diplock himself warned of the fallacy of supposing that all situations falling within his five enumerated heads were necessarily actionable examples of passing-off. Lord Diplock's definition is of what is necessary, not what is sufficient, for passing-off to be made out.

"In seeking to formulate general propositions of English law, however, one must be particularly careful to be aware of the logical fallacy of the undistributed middle. It does not follow that because all passing-off actions can be shown to present these characteristics, all factual situations which present these characteristics give rise to a cause of action for passing-off. True it is that their presence indicates what a moral code would censure as dishonest trading, based as it is upon deception of customers and consumers of a trader's wares, but in an economic system which has relied upon competition to keep down prices and to improve products there may be practical reasons why it should have been the policy of the common law not to run the risk of hampering competition by providing civil remedies to every one competing in the market who has suffered damage to his business or goodwill in consequence of inaccurate statements of whatever kind that may be made by rival traders about their own wares."[22]

The only other reasoned speech in *Advocaat*[23] was that given by Lord **1–13** Fraser, for whom the plaintiff had to show:

"(1) That his business consists of, or includes, selling in England a class of goods to which the particular trade name applies; (2) That the class of goods is clearly defined, and that in the minds of the public, or a section of the public, in England, the trade name distinguishes that class from other similar goods; (3) That because of the reputation of the goods, there is goodwill attached to the name; (4) That he, the plaintiff, as a member of the class of those who sell the goods, is the owner of goodwill in England which is of substantial value; (5) That he has suffered, or is really likely to suffer, substantial damage to his property in the goodwill by reason of the defendants selling goods which are falsely described by the trade name to which the goodwill is attached."

Lord Diplock's formulation is of much more general application than that of Lord Fraser, which is much more closely tied to the facts of the case in hand. Passing-off is not confined to the sale of goods, nor to misrepresentations conveyed through the use of misleading trade names. Lord Fraser cannot be taken to have intended to give as comprehensive a definition of the tort as did Lord Diplock.

---

[22] *ibid.*
[23] *Erven Warnink BV v J Townend & Sons (Hull) Ltd* [1979] A.C. 731; [1979] 2 All E.R. 927; [1980] R.P.C. 31, HL.

An alternative trinity: Lord Oliver in *Jif Lemon*

1–14 A decade after *Advocaat*, the House of Lords had the opportunity to restate the essential elements of passing-off in a case in which the misrepresentation was the long familiar one that the defendants' goods were those of the plaintiffs, rather than the extended form of the tort recognised in *Advocaat* itself. What was in issue in *Reckitt & Colman v Borden*[24] was imitation of the get-up of the plaintiffs' *Jif* brand of lemon juice, which was packaged in a plastic container closely resembling a real lemon in shape, size and colour. In the event, Lord Diplock's identification of the three essential elements of passing-off as goodwill, misrepresentation and damage was adopted in the different context without significant modification. In the two reasoned speeches in *Jif* Lord Oliver paraphrased Lord Diplock's speech, and Lord Jauncey quoted from it with approval.

According to Lord Oliver, the elements which the plaintiff has to prove in order to succeed in a passing-off action are three in number:

> "First, he must establish a goodwill or reputation attached to the goods or services which he supplies in the mind of the purchasing public by association with the identifying 'get-up' (whether it consists simply of a brand name or a trade description, or the individual features of labelling or packaging) under which his particular goods or services are offered to the public, such that the get-up is recognised by the public as distinctive specifically of the plaintiff's goods or services. Secondly, he must demonstrate a misrepresentation by the defendant to the public (whether or not intentional) leading or likely to lead the public to believe that goods or services offered by him are the goods or services of the plaintiff. Whether the public is aware of the plaintiff's identity as the manufacturer or supplier of the goods or services is immaterial, as long as they are identified with a particular source which is in fact the plaintff. For example, if the public is accustomed to rely upon a particular brand name in purchasing goods of a particular description, it matters not at all that there is little or no public awareness of the identity of the proprietor of the brand name. Thirdly, he must demonstrate that he suffers or, in a *quia timet* action, that he is likely to suffer damage by reason of the erroneous belief engendered by the defendant's misrepresentation that the source of the defendant's goods or services is the same as the source of those offered by the plaintiff."[25]

The respective values of *Jif* and *Advocaat*

1–15 The concurrent existence of two House of Lords authorities (each comprising two reasoned judgments) is bound to lead to a certain amount of confusion. It is suggested that there is no fundamental difference between *Advocaat* and *Jif* in the law they describe, but that they approach the same

---

[24] [1990] 1 W.L.R. 491; [1990] 1 All E.R. 873; [1990] R.P.C. 340, HL.
[25] *Reckitt & Colman v Borden*, above.

underlying principles from different perspectives, and are useful in different contexts.

Of the two decisions, it must be admitted that *Jif* is definitely the more useful in everyday practice. When one has a contentious factual situation to analyse, whether for a client, colleague, adverse party, or judge, then it is the *Jif*-derived "classical trinity" of reputation, misrepresentation (or confusion), and damage which better corresponds to the central factual and evidential issues in nearly every passing-off case. Is the claimant's name or mark or get-up distinctive, and if so to whom? How extensive is its reputation? What is supposed to be confusingly similar about the defendant's product, and is there any evidence of actual confusion? Is any such confusion damaging? Lord Oliver's formulation leads one directly to these central questions of fact which will determine liability or innocence, avoiding any number of legal issues which will not be relevant in more than one case in a hundred.

It may therefore come as something of a surprise that in the present work **1–16** it is the *Advocaat* decision, and especially the speech of Lord Diplock, that receives far more prominence and is referred to far more pervasively. This is not particularly, nor even primarily, an accident of timing or personal preference. The fundamental reason is that the strengths of *Jif* in the ordinary case are its weakness in the unusual one. *Jif* was primarily concerned with matters of fact and evidence, while *Advocaat* was much more concerned with legal principle. *Jif* rightly assumed that because of *Advocaat* the fundamental legal principles could be taken as read, whereas *Advocaat* itself could not help but address them head on.

If it is to justify its existence, a book such as this one has to deal with the unusual or even pathological case, as well as the run-of-the-mill one, and inevitably devotes a large part of its coverage to issues which few individuals will confront in practice so much as once in a lifetime. When it comes to exploring the furthest and least familiar limits of passing-off, and understanding the theoretical underpinning which ties them together and distinguishes them from situations dealt with by other torts, or not amounting to actionable behaviour at all, then the words of Lord Oliver in *Jif* are found to be inadequate to a task for which they were never intended. It is the formulation of Lord Diplock in *Advocaat* (for all its superficial complexity and difficulty) which probes more deeply into the inwardness of the tort.

No judicial exposition of the law, however, eminent, is to be regarded as **1–17** having the force of an Act of Parliament. "Even a speech of Lord Diplock is not to be construed like a statute"[26] and even the most exemplary statute may require tens or hundreds of sections to define the law to the satisfaction of the draftsman, and still lend itself to commentaries which may be several times longer than the text of the Act itself. There is sometimes a tendency in passing-off to suppose that the law is so simple that whatever the problem in hand one need look no further than the latest encapsulation handed down

---

[26] *per* Slade L.J. in *Metall und Rohstoff AG v Donaldson Lufkin & Jenrette Inc* [1990] 1 Q.B. 391, CA. The speech in question was that in *Lonrho Ltd v Shell Petroleum Co Ltd (No.2)* [1982] A.C. 173, HL.

by a superior court. The law is more complex than that. It would be surprising indeed if a few paragraphs could say all that would ever be needed about the law of passing-off or any other subject.

With that proviso in mind, the best one line summary of the law of passing-off is probably that by Lord Oliver in *Jif*:

"The principle that no man is entitled to steal another's trade by deceit."[27]

The terminology of passing-off

1–18 Passing-off has suffered from the lack of a consistent and precise vocabulary to describe its fundamental legal concepts. Certain recurrent words appear to be used as if they were terms of art, but on closer inspection turn out to bear a variety of inconsistent meanings which are not always correctly distinguished. It does not help that passing-off shares some of its terminology with the law of registered trade marks, without always considering whether it is appropriate in the different context.

The first problem term is **passing-off** itself. As with negligence, for instance, "passing-off" can denote either a state of fact or one of law. The term "passing off" came to be used in litigation in the mid-nineteenth century[28] and meant the actual sale of the defendant's goods under the pretence that they were those of the plaintiff. This being the most common factual situation before the courts, the action to restrain it came to be known as "the action for 'passing-off'" (often with "passing off" in quotation marks) and in due course the original narrow meaning of the term was largely superseded. However, passing off has continued to be used occasionally in the old sense of a state of facts, rather than their legal consequences, even into recent times. Examples are statements to the effect that damage will be assumed if passing off is proved to have taken place, or that the defendant in England is liable for passing off in a foreign country whose legal treatment of unfair competition may know no such term or concept. In the present work the hyphenated form "passing-off" is preferred for the legal concept and the cause of action, and the two separate words for the state of facts giving rise to liability.

1–19 The most seriously misused term is **reputation**. This one word has been made to bear three or four quite separate meanings with the predictable result that different issues are rolled up together and parties who have difficulty substantiating or attacking one of them turn their attention to an easier target and call it by the same name. Even when one uses the word in its popular sense a number of ambiguities immediately arise. Does one mean the reputation of the claimant in general, or of specific goods or services of his, or the reputation associated with a specific name, mark or brand? And by reputation does one mean that the possessor is well-known or that he or it is highly regarded? The two are not the same. A specialist firm may have a very high reputation in a very narrow field and be known to very few; a

---

[27] Above.
[28] The earliest instance appears to be *Perry v Truefitt* (1842) 49 E.R. 749, but only in the headnote. "Put off" is even older.

public utility may be known to the whole population and deprecated by everyone. In addition to its popular meanings of notoriety on the one hand and esteem on the other, reputation has acquired two mutually incompatible uses as a term of art. It is used of marks to denote that they have become distinctive, and it is used as a synonym for goodwill as the legal property protected by the action.

Another problem term is **confusion**. The legitimate use for this word is in the context of comparing the defendant's name, mark or get-up with the distinctive aspects of the claimant's corresponding sign. This may be put in terms of an equation: distinctiveness of name, mark or get-up plus confusing similarity in what corresponds, equals deception. Unfortunately, confusion has come to be used in a number of senses which are at best questionable and at worst fallacious. From the expression in the Trade Marks Act 1938 "deceive or cause confusion",[29] it has come to be supposed that proof of confusion is in some sense an acceptable substitute for proof of deception. This is not so. Deception pre-supposes the existence of a misrepresentation, confusion does not. Then again, the phrase from the Act has been taken out of its context of comparing indicia and used as if it meant that confusion of the parties or their goods or businesses could be treated on the same footing. Confusion of this sort is only relevant if it arises from a misrepresentation and causes damage. It does not give rise to a cause of action in its own right. Confusion frequently arises for reasons for which the defendant ought not to be held liable. Finally, confusion has been invoked as a head of damage in itself, a doctrine which is dubious though probably harmless if the parties are in competition.

C. INJURIOUS FALSEHOOD

Misrepresentation, damage and malice

Like passing-off, injurious falsehood has three essential elements, which in **1–20** its case are misrepresentation, damage, and malice. Unlike passing-off, the defendant's state of mind is therefore central to the existence of liability, and the near-impossibility of proving malice in all but the most blatant cases contributes to the fact that injurious falsehood is infinitely less important as a tort of unfair competition than passing-off.

Unlike passing-off, moreover, the law of injurious falsehood lacks a major restatement of the law from the House of Lords any more recently than the late nineteenth or very early twentieth century. Among more modern authorities, the judgment of Glidewell L.J. in *Kaye v Robertson*[30] is frequently cited, and provides as good a formulation as any:

---

[29] Trade Marks Act 1938, s.4(1); compare Trade Marks Act 1994, s.10.
[30] [1991] F.S.R. 62, CA. Glidewell L.J. calls the tort "malicious falsehood" (as do most recent authorities) but nothing turns on the choice of name.

"The essentials of this tort are that the defendant has published about the plaintiff words which are false, that they were published maliciously, and that special damage has followed as the direct and natural result of their publication. As to special damage, the effect of section 3(1) of the Defamation Act 1952 is that it is sufficient if the words published in writing are calculated to cause pecuniary damage to the plaintiff. Malice will be inferred if it be proved that the words were calculated to produce damage and that the defendant knew when he published the words that they were false or was reckless as to whether they were false or not."

1–21 Whereas passing-off is concerned with certain kinds of misrepresentation by which the defendant unfairly commends himself, his goods, or his business, thereby appropriating to himself a benefit which is in fact due to the claimant; injurious falsehood is concerned with misrepresentations of the opposite kind, made by the defendant about the claimant. Subject to the overriding requirements of malice and damage to an economic interest, the categories of misrepresentation potentially actionable as injurious falsehood are probably even broader than for passing-off. As a practical matter if a misrepresentation is to be actionable as injurious falsehood then it is virtually certain to be a disparaging one, though this is not a matter of principle. In contrast to passing-off, the misrepresentation in injurious falsehood is almost always made expressly or by innuendo, and distinctive signs have only a small role to play.

Damage is essential to injurious falsehood for the same historical reasons as for passing-off, in that both evolved as actions on the case. Prior to the Defamation Act 1952 the need to prove special damage was a major hurdle for the plaintiff, but in the kind of case dealt with in the present work it is no longer seriously problematic in its own right. Damage remains of importance in two respects: first, because only misrepresentations calculated to cause pecuniary damage to the claimant in respect of any office, profession, calling, trade or business are exempted by the 1952 Act from the need to prove special damage; and secondly in so far as the need for damage to an economic interest of some kind distinguishes injurious falsehood from defamation in the sense of libel and slander.

Goodwill does not have the same essential place in injurious falsehood that it has in passing-off. The action for injurious falsehood protects a variety of economic interests, of which business goodwill is only one. Although the present work is only concerned with injurious falsehood in competitive or near-competitive situations, there is no theoretical requirement that either party should be in business.

Malice and the terminology of injurious falsehood

1–22 The importance of malice as the defining characteristic of injurious falsehood is implicit in the tort's alternative title of malicious falsehood. Whether considered as word, a concept, or a requirement, "malice" turns out to be elusive and unsatisfactory:

14

"The tort requires proof of malice, a term which has been subject to a 'regrettable exuberance of definition' and which has caused 'more confusion in English law than any judge can hope to dispel.' Originally malice was 'but the clerk's drawing,' an abusive pleading form meaning simply an intent to disparage the plaintiff's title. Then a stricter form of malice was allowed to rebut a plea of privilege and has come to be required even when no plea of privilege is raised. The arguments against this development are that it is unjustified historically, that it puts the tort out of line with defamation and passing off, that it places too big a burden on the plaintiff, and that false statements are just as harmful to the plaintiff whether innocent or malicious."[31]

Be that as it may, there is no doubt that whatever malice means, it remains an essential pre-condition for liability. The present state of the law is that malice has the same meaning in injurious falsehood (where it is an essential part of the cause of action) as it does in defamation,[32] where it may be relevant to rebut a defence of privilege or fair comment. As a practical matter, malice in its primary sense of a deliberate intention to injure can rarely be made out in cases of commercial competition, so that proof of malice tends to depend on the inference referred to in the final sentence of the quotation from Glidewell L.J.[33]

The tort which the present work describes as **injurious falsehood** goes 1–23 under a number of names: slander of title, slander of goods, trade libel, and malicious falsehood, as well as that preferred here. Of these, the first two are really aspects of the tort applicable to specific situations—but the first is by now of primarily historical interest and neither of them is general enough to be preferred. These two and the third also have the disadvantage of implying that the cause of action is more closely connected than it is with the law of defamation, and for suggesting a distinction between written and spoken misrepresentations which is almost entirely irrelevant. In modern legal literature, the preferred name for the tort is normally taken as "malicious falsehood", which has the advantages of reflecting its generality, identifying two of its three essential elements, and asserting its independence from defamation. The same can be said of "injurious falsehood", and the choice between the two is essentially a personal one.

The term injurious falsehood was originally coined by Sir John Salmond[34] to distinguish it from the tort of deceit. The latter is "the wrong of deceiving the plaintiff, so that he causes harm to himself by his own mistaken act". The former is "the wrong of deceiving other persons, so that they by their mistaken acts cause harm to the plaintiff". In this formulation, the term

---

[31] Heydon, *Economic Torts* (2nd ed., 1978), p.83. Internal quotations are to *British Railway Traffic and Electric Co Ltd v CRC Co Ltd* [1922] 2 K.B. 260 *per* McCardie J.; *Shapiro v La Morta* [1923] All E.R. 378, CA *per* Scrutton L.J.; and *Eberow v Allen* (1623) Cro.Jac. 642; with an acknowledgment to Newark, "Malice in Actions on the Case for Words" (1944) 60 L.Q.R. 366.

[32] *Spring v Guardian Assurance plc* [1993] 2 All E.R. 273, CA.

[33] Above.

[34] Salmond, *The Law of Torts* (1st ed., 1907) p.417.

injurious falsehood was recognised by Salmond as being wide enough to encompass passing-off, which Salmond would have treated as a specialised variety of injurious falsehood, for which malice was not required. In the present work, the preference for "injurious falsehood" over "malicious falsehood" is frankly programmatic. It is to emphasise the similarities between passing-off and injurious falsehood (as that term is now predominantly used), rather than the difference.

D. HISTORY

Introduction

1–24 The history of passing-off is sometimes presented in terms of a seamless progress in which a legal cause of action based on fraud arose by analogy with the tort of deceit and was superseded in equity as early as the mid-nineteenth century by one based on the protection of property rights.[35] The truth is certainly more complex but not easy to unravel. The central problem is that it is only very recently that passing-off has more than occasionally been recognised as a body of law worthy of attention in its own right. Throughout the nineteenth century judges of every temperament agreed that passing-off actions raised no questions of law, but only ones of fact. It is quite plausible that many early passing-off cases went unreported for this very reason, as the earliest known cases of passing-off being dealt with at law do not give the impression that any new legal principles were in issue. Later in the nineteenth century the problem arises in a different form. There are sufficient reported cases to work on, but little conscious analysis of how the law was developing.

The simplified view has several shortcomings and it may be convenient to summarise the development of passing-off in terms of the three essential elements of misrepresentation, damage and goodwill, and the obsolete element of fraud.

1–25 First, if the reported cases are representative, then passing-off was being restrained in equity before any legal cause of action was known. If so, the intervention of equity would have been as part of its original, rather than auxiliary, jurisdiction.[36] On this assumption, the parallel with deceit partly breaks down, and damage may consequently be less fundamental than in that instance or negligence, where damage is the gist of the action because both originated at law as actions on the case.[37] In Lord Eldon's time it

---

[35] The "erudite discussion of the development of the law of passing off" which follows was cited with approval by Laddie J. in *Inter Lotto (UK) Ltd v Camelot Group plc* [2003] EWHC 1256; [2003] All E.R. 191; affirmed [2003] EWCA Civ 1132, CA.

[36] The term "original" is used because distinguishing between the exclusive and concurrent jurisdictions of equity is meaningless in this context.

[37] Compare *Draper v Trist* [1939] 3 All E.R. 513; 56 R.P.C. 429, CA. There is much authority for the proposition that the common law action for passing-off grew out of deceit, but that is not to say that passing-off in equity necessarily had the same origins.

would have been a contradiction in terms to refer to a purely equitable tort or even to an equitable cause of action.

Equitable passing-off, if it may be so called, arose from Lord Eldon's willingness to grant injunctions against conduct which he considered fraudulent, irrespective of whether the plaintiff had a cause of action at law. In equity, damage seems to have been taken for granted; and in any case a *quia timet* injunction could be granted against damage which was only prospective. With isolated exceptions, damage came to be ignored as a separate requirement in passing-off, probably because ordinary passing-off cases fell within a very narrow compass in which it would have been perverse to deny that damage would occur if the rest of the tort was made out. The importance of damage in its own right is a recent discovery.

There can be little doubt that fraud in one sense or another was essential to the very earliest cases, whether in equity or at law. However, the fact that the same word was used by judges in both courts is perhaps misleading. At law, there is little doubt that "fraud" was used in its everyday sense of intentional and dishonest deception. In equity the likelihood is that "fraud" was used in a very much wider sense which defies any definition except the circular one that equity would characterise as fraudulent, conduct which it was prepared to restrain. From at least as early as *Keech v Sandford*[38] equity had used the word "fraud" in other contexts for behaviour which involved neither misrepresentation nor conscious dishonesty. As early as 1838 equity was expressly prepared to enjoin defendants from unintended passing-off, although they had acted honestly.[39] That the common law continued to require fraud for the award of damages mattered little, because defendants were often insubstantial and the injunction was by far the more important remedy. As passing-off came to be understood in terms of property, the importance of fraud waned and eventually disappeared altogether.

However, equity did not initially repudiate the need to prove *mala fides* in **1–26** favour of a doctrine based on property rights, but rather for one to the effect that for the defendant to continue with deceptive behaviour after being put on notice was equivalent to fraud.[40] When Lord Westbury interpreted the law in terms of property rights, he did so by identifying trade marks as the property protected. Goodwill was not identified as the basis of the action until the early twentieth century, and that was after a hiatus of over thirty years during which hardly any judge suggested passing-off defended property rights at all.

Misrepresentation has always been fundamental to passing-off and the main interest under this head is the recognition of new actionable misrepresentations. Apart from *Spalding v Gamage*[41] and a few individual cases, this is largely a new development in which there has been systematic pro-

---

[38] (1726) 25 E.R. 223.
[39] *Millington v Fox* (1838) 40 E.R. 956.
[40] This is the orthodox explanation adopted in the late nineteenth century, following the *Singer* decisions (*Singer Machine Manufacturers v Wilson* (1877) 3 App. Cas. 375, HL and *Singer Manufacturing Co v Loog* (1882) 8 App. Cas. 15, HL). It is doubtful if the pre-1875 cases were either that explicit or that consistent.
[41] (1915) 32 R.P.C. 273, HL.

gress only since the 1960s. Over the whole of its history, however, the law has made steady but unspectacular progress in terms of becoming more and more willing to restrain colourable or equivocal cases of misrepresentation. Examples include recognising new categories of signs, or granting relief where the plaintiff's sign is *prima facie* descriptive, or the parties are not in competition, or the plaintiff's sign has not been precisely copied.

Far from unfolding in a consistent and purposeful manner, passing-off has largely developed through *ad hoc* decisions which were often motivated primarily by a desire not to let an unmeritorious defendant escape liability.[42] The law has advanced on the strength of common sense and judicial instinct, with rationalisation and consolidation following. Despite this, passing-off presents an example of the incremental approach of the common law at its most effective. The law has adapted creditably to changing business conditions, and if it is not as comprehensive as some commentators would like there are others who would decry any major extension to its present scope. Certainly, it has shown itself far more flexible and responsive than the statutory law of registered trade marks or the common law of injurious falsehood. Without much exaggeration, one can adopt the comment Sir Frederick Pollock made with regard to agreements in restraint of trade: "Without any legislation, without express disapproval of a single received authority, the law ... has in our time effected a change of front that has brought it completely into line with business conditions".[43]

Origins and early development

1–27   It was long thought that passing-off might have been recognised by the common law as early as the sixteenth century.[44] In *Southern v How*[45] and *Dean v Steel*[46] Dodderidge J. referred to an unreported case in which the defendant put the mark of an eminent clothier on inferior cloth and sold it.

> "An action upon the case was brought in the Common Pleas by a clothier, that whereas he had gained great reputation for his making of his cloth, and by reason whereof he had great utterance to his great benefit and profit, and that he used to set his mark to the cloth, whereby it should be known to be his cloth, and another clothier perceiving it, used the same

---

[42] Examples might include *Reddaway (Frank) & Co Ltd v George Banham & Co Ltd* [1896] A.C. 199; [1895–9] All E.R. 313; 13 R.P.C. 218, HL; *Bollinger v Costa Brava Wine Co Ltd* [1960] Ch. 262; [1959] 3 All E.R. 800; [1960] R.P.C. 16; *Erven Warnink BV v J Townend & Sons (Hull) Ltd* [1979] A.C. 731; [1979] 2 All E.R. 927; [1980] R.P.C. 31, HL; and most recently *British Telecommunications plc v One in a Million Ltd* [1999] 1 W.L.R. 903; [1998] 4 All E.R. 476; [1999] E.T.M.R. 61; [1999] F.S.R. 1, CA.

[43] *The Genius of the Common Law* (1912).

[44] For a more detailed treatment of the early history of passing-off, and what might be called the pre-history of trade marks back to the middle ages, see F. I. Schechter, *The Historical Foundation of the Law Relating to Trade-Marks* (1925). Marks were originally used either to denote ownership (much as shipping marks today) or for regulatory purposes so that substandard goods could be traced to the trader responsible. The concept of a trade mark as an asset, as opposed to a source of liability, is quite recent.

[45] (1618) Cro. Jac. 468; Poph. 143; 2 Roll Rep. 26 (Dodderidge J.).

[46] (1626) 82 E.R. 339 (Dodderidge J.).

mark to his ill-made cloth on purpose to deceive him, it was resolved that an action did well lie."[47]

Two reports of *Southern v How* differ, with one saying that the action was brought, and won, by the clothier,[48] the other by the defrauded customer.[49] A third denies that Dodderidge J. said by whom the action was brought, but speculates that it was by the customer.[50]

With so many conflicting reports it must have seemed impossible to resolve the issue, but the case Dodderidge J. was referring to has been identified by Professor Baker[51] as *Samford's case*[52] with unexpected results. The record[53] confirms that the case was brought by the established rival clothier rather than the defrauded customer, but no judgment was entered because the Court was evenly divided between plaintiff and defendant. Peryam and Mead JJ. concluded that "anyone may give what mark he will, and it is *damnum absque injuria* to the other; and deceit does not lie against him who does a wholly lawful act for his own profit". Wyndham J. would have found for the plaintiff, but apparently on the narrow ground that the defendant was in breach of a statute regulating the use of marks by clothiers.[54] Only Anderson C.J. was prepared to hold the defendant liable at common law, and it must have been his minority opinion which was recalled by Dodderidge J. so long afterwards. In any event, *Samford's case* is an isolated example and does not appear to have contributed much to the development of passing-off, either then or later.

The next development came with *Blanchard v Hill*[55] in 1742, in which Lord **1–28** Hardwicke L.C. refused to grant an injunction restraining the defendant from using a mark imitating that claimed by the plaintiff, though acknowledging in deference to *Southern v How* that one might issue in the right circumstances: "[I]t was not the single act of making use of the mark that was sufficient to maintain the action but doing it with a fraudulent design to put off bad cloths by this means, or to draw away customers from the other clothier".

Although this was a negative decision, it has been pointed out that the background to the case would have made any other result impossible. The plaintiff claimed exclusive use of the mark *The Great Mogul* on playing cards by virtue of a charter granted to the Cardmakers' Company by Charles I. Not only had such monopolies been declared illegal,[56] but the case

---

[47] This passage was quoted by Lord Halsbury L.C. in *Magnolia Metal Co v Tandem Smelting Syndicate Ltd* (1900) 17 R.P.C. 477, HL to demonstrate the supposed antiquity of passing-off.
[48] Cro. Jac. 468; 79 E.R. 400. *Dean v Steel* also supports the passing-off hypothesis.
[49] Poph. 143; 79 E.R. 1243.
[50] 2 Roll. Rep. 26; 81 E.R. 635.
[51] J. H. Baker, *An Introduction to English Legal History* (3rd ed., 1990) p.522 and J. H. Baker and S. F. C. Milsom, *Sources of English Legal History* (1986) p.615.
[52] *JG v Samford* (1584) (unreported).
[53] Set out, in translation, in Baker and Milsom *op. cit.*
[54] 27 Hen. VIII c.12, see Baker and Milsom *op. cit.* A supposed custom of London was also cited by the plaintiff's counsel.
[55] (1742) 26 E.R. 692, *per* Lord Hardwicke L.C.
[56] *Darcy v Allen* "The Case of Monopolies" (1602) 77 E.R. 1260.

outlawing them had itself been concerned with the much-hated monopoly over playing cards. The subject matter could hardly have been less auspicious. *Blanchard v Hill* appears to have aroused no interest at the time and, like *Southern v How*, it was not until the nineteenth century that its significance came to be appreciated.[57]

1–29   There are indications that what would now be called passing-off actions did continue to occur in the eighteenth century without attracting much attention. In *Singleton v Bolton*[58] the plaintiff's father had invented a medicine and sold it as *Dr Johnson's Yellow Ointment*; and the plaintiff had continued the business. The defendant sold what was presumably an identical medicine under the same name. The plaintiff was non-suited, Lord Mansfield holding that

> "[I]f the defendant had sold a medicine of his own under the plaintiff's name or mark, that would be a fraud for which an action would lie. But here both the plaintiff and the defendant use the name of the original inventor, and no evidence was given of the defendant having sold it as if prepared by the plaintiff."

The court notebooks of Lord Mansfield[59] contain half a dozen instances of actions for passing-off, half of which resulted in damages being awarded. Perhaps equity was less progressive. In *Webster v Webster*[60] the executor of a deceased partner was refused an injunction against the surviving partners continuing to use his name. The claim that this might expose the estate to liability failed and the plaintiff fell back on the argument that it was a fraud on the public. Lord Thurlow L.C. rejected that too, saying "The fraud on the public is no ground for the plaintiff's coming into this court".

Recognition of passing-off in the early nineteenth century

1–30   It was Lord Eldon who established the principle that equity would intervene to prevent a defendant representing his goods or business as those of the plaintiff. In *Hogg v Kirby*[61] the proprietor of a magazine obtained an injunction against the defendant using the same title. In *Byron (Lord) v Johnson*[62] the poet was granted an injunction against the publication of poems not by him under his name. It is interesting that although Lord Eldon justified his decisions in terms of fraud, the law was argued using an analogy with copyright, suggesting that these were indeed treated as cases of first impression. *Hogg v Kirby* itself was an ambiguous case. The defendant had originally published the magazine in question on behalf of the plaintiff, and

---

[57] In *Collins v Brown* (1857) 69 E.R. 1174 Page-Wood V.C. described it as "the true foundation of the jurisdiction in these cases". See also *Farina v Silverlock* (1855) 69 E.R. 560 reversed (1856) 43 E.R. 1214; (1858) 70 E.R. 270.

[58] (1783) 99 E.R. 661, *per* Lord Mansfield.

[59] Adams, John, "Intellectual Property Cases in Lord Mansfield's Court Notebooks" (1987) 8 *Journal of Legal History* 18.

[60] (1791) 36 E.R. 949, *per* Lord Thurlow L.C.

[61] (1803) 32 E.R. 336 (Lord Eldon L.C.).

[62] (1816) 35 E.R. 851 (Lord Eldon L.C.).

the case was argued on the basis of property in the title, contract and trust. The decision might have been dismissed as one turning on the existence of a special relationship between the parties, but in later cases, some of which had nothing to do with passing-off,[63] Lord Eldon more clearly identified its ratio as lying in the fact that the defendant had misrepresented his magazine as a continuation of the plaintiff's series and had thereby taken the credit properly belonging to the originator.

In *Crutwell v Lye*[64] Lord Eldon stated the law in terms which have scarcely dated: "There can be no doubt that the court would interpose against that sort of fraud which has been attempted by setting up the same trade in the same place, under the same sign or name, the party giving himself out to be the same person".[65] The first case in which an injunction was granted to protect a trade mark in the narrow sense of an elaborate device appears to have been *Day v Day*[66] in 1816.

The first unambiguous example of passing-off being dealt with at common law does not occur until 1824, but this may simply be because early cases were not reported.[67] In *Sykes v Sykes*[68] the plaintiff alleged that he marked his shot-belts and powder-flasks with the words *Syke's Patent* and that they enjoyed a great reputation. They had indeed once been patented, but the patent had been declared invalid. The defendant was alleged to have fraudulently marked inferior goods with the same words and sold them "as and for" the goods of the plaintiff. The jury found that the defendant had manufactured similar but inferior goods, marked them with an imitation of the plaintiff's mark, and sold them to retail dealers at a lower price with the intention that the latter should sell them as the goods of the plaintiff, which did happen. The defendant objected that he was entitled to judgment either on the ground that "Sykes" was his own name, or because his immediate customers, the retailers, were not deceived. The judge overruled both objections, the jury brought in a verdict for the plaintiff, and the defendant's application for a new trial was refused. In *Blofeld v Payne*[69] it was decided that the plaintiff could recover nominal damages at law without having to prove that the defendant's goods were inferior, or that special damage had

1–31

---

[63] *Longman v Winchester* (1809) 33 E.R. 987, a copyright case.

[64] (1810) 34 E.R. 129, *per* Lord Eldon L.C.

[65] The defendant was a common carrier plying between Bristol and London. An injunction was actually refused, this being an early anticipation of the rule in *Trego v Hunt* [1896] A.C. 7, HL.

[66] Unreported, mentioned in *Eden on Injunctions* (182.) and *Sebastian's Digest*, p.10. The plaintiff's labels for blacking were imitated.

[67] *Sykes v Sykes*, below is treated as turning on a pleading point and nothing in the report suggests that the court regarded it as raising a novel, or even interesting, point of law. See Adams, *op. cit.*

[68] (1824) 107 E.R. 834.

[69] (1833) 110 E.R. 509.

occurred.[70] At law, passing-off was regarded as analogous to, or even an example of, the law of deceit,[71] and intent to deceive was essential.

1–32 The last important step in this period was taken by Lord Cottenham L.C. in 1838. In *Millington v Fox*[72] he laid down that an injunction could be granted against a defendant who had originally acted innocently, not even knowing of the existence of the plaintiff. The common law continued to require fraud in the original sense.

By 1842 the term "pass off" was in use[73] and the law was defined in terms which are applicable even today.[74]

"I think that the principle on which both the courts of law and of equity proceed, in granting relief and protection in cases of this sort, is very well understood. A man is not to sell his own goods under the pretence that they are the goods of another man; he cannot be permitted to practice such a deception, nor to use the means which contribute to that end. He cannot therefore be allowed to use names, marks, letters, or other indicia, by which he may induce purchasers to believe, that the goods which he is selling are the manufacture of another person. I own it does not seem to me that a man can acquire property in a name or mark; but whether he has or not a property in the name or mark, I have no doubt that another person has not the right to use that name or mark for the purposes of deception, and in order to attract to himself the course of trade, or that custom, which, without the improper act, would have flowed to the person who first used, or was alone in the habit of using the particular name or mark."[75]

The mid-nineteenth century

1–33 From the 1840s onwards there are sufficient reported cases on passing-off for one to be able to trace the development of the law with more certainty. The common law continued to treat the action as one based on fraud and consequently marked little advance on *Blofeld v Payne*[76] except in the application of the settled principle to new sets of facts. Most of the new

[70] See also *Rodgers v Nowill* (1847) 136 E.R. 816. *Edelsten v Edelsten* (1863) 46 E.R. 72 belatedly confirmed that this also applied in equity.
[71] *Crawshay v Thompson* (1842) 134 E.R. 146; *Rodgers v Nowill* (1847) 136 E.R. 816; *Edlsten v Edelsten* (1863) 46 E.R. 72; *Leather Cloth Co Ltd v American Leather Cloth Co Ltd* (1865) 11 E.R. 1435, HL; *Bourne v Swan & Edgar Ltd* [1903] 1 Ch. 211; 20 R.P.C. 105.
[72] (1838) 40 E.R. 956 (Lord Cottenham L.C.). The conclusion for which this case is cited is actually *obiter*, the defendants having submitted to an injunction and the live issue being whether they were liable to an account of profits.
[73] *Perry v Truefitt*, below. Though only in the headnote, not the judgment itself. "Put off" and "palm off" were at least as common but fell into disuse.
[74] This passage (or extracts from it) has been cited with approval many times, from *Leather Cloth Co Ltd v American Leather Cloth Co Ltd* (1865) 11 E.R. 1435, HL to *Erven Warnink BV v J Townend & Sons (Hull) Ltd* [1979] A.C. 731; [1979] 2 All E.R. 927; [1980] R.P.C. 31, HL and *Reckitt & Colman Products Ltd v Borden Inc* [1990] 1 W.L.R. 491; [1990] 1 All E.R. 873; [1990] R.P.C. 340, HL.
[75] *per* Lord Langdale M.R. in *Perry v Truefitt* (1842) 49 E.R. 749.
[76] (1833) 110 E.R. 509.

developments occurred in the courts of equity. One reason for this must have been the much greater importance of injunctions compared to damages, but equity also amplified its doctrine that for the defendant to continue with a deceptive course of conduct after being put on notice was sufficiently fraudulent for an injunction to be granted, even if the conduct has been commenced in ignorance and even if the defendant honestly continued to believe that his behaviour was justifiable. The difference between law and equity may be seen by comparing the common law case of *Crawshay v Thompson*[77] with *Millington v Fox*.[78] In the former, the defendants stamped steel with a mark distinctive of the plaintiffs and continued to do so after being put on notice. The defendants insisted the mark would not deceive, the jury found for them, and a new trial was refused in terms which suggested that fraud was an essential part of the cause of action. In the latter, Lord Cottenham L.C. would have granted an injunction against the use of the plaintiff's mark *Crowley*, also for steel, although the defendants had adopted it in good faith, not knowing of the plaintiff, and believing it to be *publici juris*.[79]

While the common law still required fraud, equity did not confine itself to relaxing the standard of dishonesty required before it would intervene. In a series of cases[80] Lord Westbury L.C. "surprised the profession"[81] by holding that there was a right of property in trade marks which was transmissible and enforceable even against innocent infringement. Perhaps Lord Westbury would also have recognised property in trade names, and if so the whole of the law of passing-off as it was then understood could have been re-interpreted in terms of infringement of property rights as opposed to misrepresentation. That, however, was not to happen. The law of trade marks was put on a statutory basis, the law of passing-off continued in terms of misrepresentation, and the idea of passing-off protecting a property right was largely rejected or forgotten until the twentieth century. In retrospect, passing-off and trade mark infringement may be seen as separate torts which to some extent evolved out of the same historical authorities, just as copyright and breach of confidence cannot always be distinguished in early cases on piracy of unpublished literary works.

Passing-off in law and equity before the Judicature Act

It may be helpful at this point to clarify the respective roles of equity and the **1–34** common law in early passing-off actions. The essential difference to litigants was that injunctions could only be granted by the court of Chancery. In the

[77] (1842) 134 E.R. 146.

[78] (1838) 40 E.R. 956. See *Singer Manufacturing Co v Loog* (1882) 8 App. Cas. 15, HL where Lord Blackburn contrasts the two cases and contemplates that the common law might have accommodated itself to the equitable view with time.

[79] An injunction was conceded by the defendants, but it is clear the Lord Chancellor would have granted one if the bill had been opposed.

[80] Notably *Edelsten v Edelsten* (1863) 46 E.R. 873; *Hall v Barrows* [1863] 46 E.R. 72; *M'Andrew v Bassett* (1864) 46 E.R. 965 and *Leather Cloth Co Ltd v American Leather Cloth Co Ltd* (1865) 11 E.R. 1435, HL.

[81] The expression comes from Fry L.J. in *Newman v Pinto* (1887) 4 R.P.C. 508, CA.

courts of law damages were the only remedy. At its simplest, the auxiliary jurisdiction of equity could be invoked in support of the plaintiff who had established (or would undertake to establish) fraudulent passing-off in an action at law. This was how Lord Cottenham L.C. explained the intervention of equity in *Motley v Downham*[82]:

> "The court, when it interferes in cases of this sort, is exercising a jurisdiction over legal rights; and although sometimes, in a very strong case, it interferes, in the first instance, by injunction, yet, in a general way, it puts the party upon asserting his right by trying it in an action at law. If it does not do that, it permits the plaintiff, notwithstanding the suit in equity, to bring an action. In both cases, the court is only acting in aid of, and is only ancillary to, the legal right."

If a passing-off action in the first half of the century went its full course, it might involve an initial application in equity for an interim injunction, which would be granted in a sufficiently strong case but refused if there was too much doubt about the merits.[83] The practice of requiring the plaintiff to give the defendant the benefit of a cross-undertaking in damages seems to have become established in about the 1840s.[84] The plaintiff would then bring an action at law for damages before a jury, and, if successful, would go back to Chancery to have the interim injunction made final. The procedure, with the additional complication of an interlocutory appeal, is well illustrated by *Farina v Silverlock*.[85] The Common Law Procedure Act 1854 allowed the common law courts to grant interlocutory and final injunctions, but did not result in any noticeable shift of business away from Chancery, presumably because of the continuing need to prove fraud in the strict sense in an action at law. More importantly, the same Act allowed the courts of equity to determine legal rights and award damages,[86] and the practice of requiring the plaintiff to establish his right at law before granting a final injunction became obsolete.[87] The old practice was, in any event, illogical because there were already cases in which equity would grant relief although the plaintiff had no cause of action at law.

1–35   There were conceptual as well as practical difficulties with the *Motley v Downham* approach. The auxiliary jurisdiction of equity is normally described in terms of restraining wrongful conduct which would infringe a

---

[82] (1837) 40 E.R. 824 (Lord Cottenham L.C.).

[83] An order for the defendant to keep an account pending trial was also possible.

[84] In *Chappell v Davidson* (1856) 44 E.R. 289, Knight-Bruce L.J. said that requiring the cross-undertaking had been almost universal practice for the past 12 or 13 years; though 10 years earlier in *Spottiswoode v Clarke* (1846) 41 E.R. 900 Lord Cottenham L.C. had thought it was "utterly impossible" to compensate the defendant if it turned out that the interim injunction should not have been granted.

[85] (1855) 69 E.R. 560 reversed (1856) 43 E.R. 1214; (1858) 70 E.R. 270.

[86] See P.M. McDermott, "Jurisdiction of the Court of Chancery to Award Damages" (1992) 109 L.Q.R. 652; and P.M. McDermott, *Equitable Damages* (1994).

[87] *Chappell v Davidson*, above, must be one of the last cases under the old procedure: Page Wood V.C. had originally granted an interlocutory injunction without requiring the plaintiff to bring an action at law, but was reversed on this point on appeal.

legal right of a proprietary nature. The latter qualification is important, and explains why, for instance, equity would not enjoin libel or trespass to the person. At the time *Motley v Downham* was decided, Lord Cottenham probably did not envisage equity adopting a different standard of liability to that at law, but the very next year, in *Millington v Fox*[88] Lord Cottenham himself indicated that equity would restrain misrepresentations which the common law would not have characterised as fraudulent.

The question of whether the common law passing-off action protected a proprietary legal right seems simply to have been overlooked in the first half of the century, although in *Clark v Freeman*[89] absence of damage to property was given as a ground for refusing an injunction to an eminent surgeon who objected to having a quack medicine sold under his name. An important category of passing-off actions at the time consisted of actions by publishers in respect of the titles of periodicals or single works. These seem to have been relatively numerous, and they were certainly influential to the development of the law.[90] There was undoubtedly a widespread belief (despite judicial *dicta* to the contrary) that publishers had a right of property in the titles of their publications, and it was not until the 1850s or later that property *qua* trade mark in the title was consistently distinguished from property *qua* copyright in the work as such.[91] In this particular group of cases, it may have been taken as self-evident that there was a right of property to protect, and the precedents may have been applied outside the field of publishing without further consideration. Outside the publishing field, it would have been hard to identify a proprietary right as the basis of the action. Specifically, it was not until the time of Lord Westbury that the doctrine of property in trade marks made any progress, and until then the passage from *Perry v Truefitt* quoted above would almost certainly have received unanimous approval. Whether coincidentally or not, it is noticeable that express recognition of property in trade marks only took hold shortly after the important decision in *Emperor of Austria v Day and Kossuth*[92] which reaffirmed the importance of a proprietary right as the basis for granting an injunction in the auxiliary jurisdiction.

Lord Westbury's innovation was to assert that there was a right of **1–36** property in a trade mark which came into existence as soon as the mark was used as such,[93] and which would be enforced in equity even against completely innocent infringement. At first sight this identified a right of property to protect, but even after ignoring the unorthodoxy of the solution, two difficulties remained. One was that the supposed right of property was only

---

[88] (1838) 40 E.R. 956.

[89] (1848) 117 L.J. Ch. 142.

[90] *Hogg v Kirby* (1803) 32 E.R. 336; *Longman v Winchester* (1809) 33 E.R. 987.

[91] *Kelly v Hutton* (1868) LR 3 Ch. App. 703 (Page-Wood L.J.). There was still confusion as late as 1880: *Dicks v Yates* (1880) 18 L.R. Ch. 76, CA

[92] (1861) 45 E.R. 861. The case had nothing to do with trade marks or passing-off, but observations of Stuart V.C. *arguendo* tend towards treating trade marks as a species of property.

[93] Previous case law had required a substantial, but unspecified, period of user: *e.g. London and Provincial Law Life Assurance Society v London and Provincial Joint-Stock Insurance Company* (1847) 11 Jurist 938. (Shadwell V.C.)

25

recognised in the courts of equity, the other that the remedy in equity went far beyond restraining what was wrongful at law. In this respect, the Common Law Procedure Act 1854 probably had the opposite effect to that intended. What began as a power to determine legal rights to save the plaintiff the delay and expense of bringing an action at law rapidly led to equity developing a much wider independent jurisdiction over passing-off or trade mark infringement, which virtually ignored the question of strict legal liability unless damages were claimed. On whatever basis, injunctive relief against passing-off could no longer credibly be explained as part of the auxiliary jurisdiction.

It is quite possible that Lord Westbury was inclined to reject altogether the idea of basing passing-off on fraud and misrepresentation. In *Leather Cloth v American Leather Cloth* he asserted that innocent infringement of a trade mark was actionable and continued:

> "Imposition on the public, occasioned by one man selling his goods as the goods of another, cannot be the ground of private action or suit ...[94] It is indeed true that, unless the mark used by the defendant be applied by him to the same kind of goods as the goods of the plaintiff, and be in itself such, that it may be, and is, mistaken in the market for the trade mark of the plaintiff, the court will not interfere, because there is no invasion of the plaintiff's right; and thus the mistake of buyers in the market under which they in fact take the defendant's goods as the goods of the plaintiff, that is to say, imposition on the public, becomes the test of the property in the trade mark having been invaded and injured, and not the ground on which the court rests its jurisdiction."[95]

If the doctrine of property in trade marks was to some extent a rationalisation of some of the earlier cases, the same is even more true of goodwill. One finds goodwill mentioned in some early passing-off and trade mark cases, but that was because disputes were particularly likely to arise between former partners, or the vendor and purchaser of a business. So in *Crutwell v Lye*[96] an attempt was made to argue that the involuntary transfer of the defendant's goodwill to the plaintiff imposed a general covenant on him not to compete, and in *Hall v Barrows*[97] Lord Westbury L.C. dealt quite separately with ownership of trade marks as such on the dissolution of a partnership and ownership of the goodwill. The idea of passing-off protecting goodwill as a right of property was not to be recognised judicially until much later.

1–37   Extra-judicially, however, there is an impressive and forward-looking

---

[94] Citing *Webster v Webster* (1791) 36 E.R. 949.
[95] (1843) 4 De G. J. and Sm. 1347. Note that this is precisely the reverse of the currently accepted doctrine (*Burberrys v Cording* (1909) 26 R.P.C. 693) to the effect that misrepresentation is the basis of the action and misuse of indicia of purely evidential value. For rather more accommodating attempts by Lord Westbury to reconcile the two threads see *Leather Cloth Co v American Leather Cloth Co* in the House of Lords (1865) 11 HL Cas 523; 11 E.R. 1435 and *Hall v Barrows* (1863) 46 E.R. 72.
[96] (1810) 34 E.R. 129 (Lord Eldon L.C.).
[97] (1863) 46 E.R. 72 (Lord Westbury L.C.).

analysis of the law as it stood in 1862 in *The Law of Trade Marks* by Edward Lloyd.[98] Lloyd was strongly in favour of the emerging doctrine of property in trade marks, both on policy grounds and as a rational basis for the existing body of case law, referring to which he wrote:

> "I think no one who reads their decisions will fail to be struck by a species of timidity in their expressions, by an anxiety to guard against anything like a recognition of property in a trade-mark, although in fact some of these very decisions can only be supported by reference to the general right of a court of equity to interfere for the protection of property against injury."[99]

More importantly, Lloyd seems to have been the first in England to recognise expressly the twofold importance of goodwill. If no trade mark for goods was involved, goodwill itself was the only possible proprietary right to protect, as in the cases on the trading names of service businesses. In the typical trade mark case, property in the goodwill of the business *in nubibus* could be regarded as coexisting with property in the trade mark as such, which took on the aspect of a sort of special goodwill embodied in a name, label, wrapper or other mark; and imitation of this distinctive mark by a rival amounted both to infringement of the right of property in the trade mark and to an attempt to appropriate the goodwill of the established business. This was already the approach of at least one American decision, but in English law the suggestion was half a century ahead of its time:

> "In the case of *Partridge v Menk*[1] the right of a trader in the use of his mark is regarded as a species of goodwill which he acquires in his business (which is undoubtedly a proprietary right); and it is said that by the appropriation to himself of a particular label, sign or mark, indicating that the article is made or sold by him, or by his authority, or that he carries on business at a particular place, he is entitled to protection against one who attempts to pirate upon the goodwill of his friends or customers, or the patrons of his trade or business, by using such label, sign or mark without his authority."[2]

The abolition of common law trade mark infringement

By the beginning of the 1870s there appear to have been at least three **1–38** interconnected bodies of law. There was a common law action for passing-off which was of little practical importance because fraud still had to be proved and damages were the only remedy. There was the corresponding equitable action which would grant an injunction in similar circumstances but without proof of *mala fides*, and there was a more recent and more

---

[98] The work was published in book form and in instalments in the *Solicitor's Journal*.
[99] *op. cit.* p.26. He goes on to cite *Story's Equity Jurisprudence* for confirmation that trade marks were recognised as property in American law.
[1] 2 Sand Ch. 622.
[2] Lloyd, *op. cit.* p.27.

contentious equitable doctrine of property in trade marks, which treated infringement as a wrong irrespective of knowledge or intent. Even left to its own devices, the law of passing-off was evolving quite rapidly by the 1870s, although judges of every persuasion insisted that they were only applying settled principles of law to the facts of each case. On top of this evolution came two revolutionary changes. The first was the substantive fusion of law and equity by the Judicature Act 1873, the second was the passing of the first Trade-Marks Registration Act in 1875.

The 1875 Act did not ostensibly affect the action for passing-off at all, but its indirect effects were considerable. The Act did not create a cause of action for infringement, assuming that one already existed at common law and in equity. Its purpose was to create procedural and evidential advantages for registered marks, and in order to encourage registration it provided that no one was to be entitled to institute proceedings to prevent the infringement of any trade mark as defined in the Act unless and until it had been registered.[3] The definition of trade mark was fairly narrow and an amending Act of 1876 allowed infringement actions to be brought on marks in use before the 1875 Act which had been refused registration.[4]

The courts immediately began to enforce the new registered trade marks, thereby implicitly confirming Lord Westbury's view that an enforceable right of property already existed in them at common law and in equity. It was not until 1905 that the action for infringement was given a statutory basis.[5] The 1905 Act expressly stated that nothing in it affected the action for passing-off,[6] but by the time the courts had spontaneously reached the same conclusion in respect of its predecessors.[7]

1–39   The new regime of registered trade marks presented the courts with problems in respect of passing-off which very few cases addressed expressly. On the one hand, the new system of registration applied only to trade marks as such, and not to trade or business names. Clearly, some form of action was still needed to protect service industries and the trading names of businesses dealing in goods. On the other hand, the policy of the Act was to require post-1875 marks to be registered if they were to be enforced.

In *Singer Manufacturing Co v Loog*[8] the House of Lords defined passing-off in terms of misrepresentation, whether made innocently or fraudulently, and denied that the plaintiffs had any monopoly in a name or mark as such. The closest one comes to a case refusing relief in a passing-off action on the ground that the case turned on the use of an unregistered mark on goods is

---

[3] Trade-Marks Registration Act 1875, s.1.

[4] Trade-Marks Registration Amendment Act 1876, s.1.

[5] Trade Marks Act 1905, s.39. The right to sue for infringement of unregistered marks in use prior to 1875 which had been refused registration was preserved. *ibid.*, s.42.

[6] Trade Marks Acts 1905, s.45.

[7] *Faulder (Henry) & Co Ltd v O & G Rushton Ltd* (1903) 20 R.P.C. 477, CA; see now *Inter Lotto (UK) Ltd v Camelot Group plc* [2003] EWCA Civ 1132, CA, affirming [2003] EWHC 1256; [2003] 3 All E.R. 191 (Laddie J.) in relation to Trade Marks Act 1994, s.2(2).

[8] (1882) 8 App. Cas. 15, HL.

Thorneloe v Hill,[9] where the main reason was that the mark had become deceptive as a result of various dealings with it in gross.[10]

The final result was that the law of passing-off emerged into the last quarter of the nineteenth century with its scope unaffected but one possible theoretical basis destroyed. It could not be said that passing-off protected a right of property in a trade mark, because if it did so it would have been no more than the abolished common law infringement action under another name. By the same token, to have admitted that the action for passing-off had sometimes protected a right of property in a trade name would have confined it for the future to cases not involving the use of marks on goods, which the courts were reluctant to do. Lord Westbury's doctrine of property in trade marks had never enjoyed unanimous support, even among equity lawyers. After 1875, it was probably with some relief that the courts abandoned the idea that passing-off protected a right of property in anything and returned to defining it in terms of an extended concept of fraud. This was possible because from 1875 onwards the power to grant an injunction derived directly from the Judicature Act 1873, and the presence or absence of a proprietary interest to protect lost its former importance. If the courts could now enjoin a mere libel, then what did it matter whether the action for passing-off protected property or not?

Reddaway v Banham and the late nineteenth century

The last quarter of the nineteenth century was the time when passing-off **1–40** came of age. Lord Halsbury may have insisted that every case to come before the House of Lords raised no new issues of law and was all one way on the facts, but this period supplied a series of cases which defined much of the law that still applies today. *Singer v Loog*[11] settled that passing-off is based on misrepresentation rather than trade mark rights as such. *Johnston v Orr-Ewing*[12] is still cited on instruments of deception, liability for exports and the "idea of the mark". *Montgomery v Thompson*[13] confirmed that a place name could be distinctive and that it was no defence that the defendant produced his goods in a place of that name. *Reddaway v Banham*[14] extended this doctrine to *prima facie* descriptive terms of every type and gave us the modern law of "secondary meaning". *Powell v Birmingham Vinegar Brewery*[15] stated expressly that the plaintiff need not be known by name. In the last year of the century *Cellular Clothing v Maxton & Murray*[16] somewhat reluctantly confirmed that *Reddaway v Banham* was good law. Turning to decisions of the Court of Appeal, *Lever v Goodwin*[17] protected

---

[9] [1894] 1 Ch. 569; [1891–4] All E.R. 1263 (Romer J.).
[10] See also *Goodfellow v Prince* [1887] 35 Ch.D. 9, CA; *Great Tower Tea Co v Smith* (1889) 6 R.P.C. 165; *Faulder (Henry) & Co Ltd v O & G Rushton Ltd* (1903) 20 R.P.C. 477, CA.
[11] (1882) 8 App. Cas. 15, HL.
[12] (1882) 7 App. Cas. 219, HL.
[13] [1891] A.C. 217; 8 R.P.C. 361, HL.
[14] [1896] A.C. 199; [1895–9] All E.R. 313; 13 R.P.C. 218, HL.
[15] [1897] A.C. 710; 14 R.P.C. 721, HL.
[16] [1899] A.C. 326; 16 R.P.C. 397, HL.
[17] [1887] 36 Ch.D. 1; 4 R.P.C. 492, CA.

get-up in its own right for the first time and *Payton v Snelling, Lampard*[18] laid down much of the modern law for get-up cases.

These cases are so much a part of the law as we now understand it that with hindsight they may seem to form a natural and even inevitable progression. On the contrary, passing-off was being extended at a time when the higher courts were adopting a policy of detachment and even hostility towards torts of unfair competition in general. The other common law economic torts were being given restrictive interpretations which have sapped their commercial importance to this day. The mirror image of passing-off is injurious falsehood, but at the same time as passing-off was reducing fraud to a legal fiction and going a long way to assuming damage, in the other the courts were insisting on malice and special damage so strictly that the tort ceased to be of much more than academic interest. The same could easily have happened to passing-off if the decision of the Court of Appeal in *Reddaway v Banham* had been upheld, which *Cellular Clothing v Maxton & Murray* suggests could well have happened. Although the general trend in passing-off was progressive, the law did miss one major opportunity. In *Powell v Birmingham Vinegar Brewery*[19] the House of Lords unwittingly introduced the idea of passing-off by misdescription, but when the issue was presented to it expressly in *Magnolia Metal v Tandem Smelting Syndicate*[20] it gave a strong indication that only misrepresentations as to source were actionable.

1–41   All these advances were carried through despite the absence of a really satisfactory theoretical basis for the tort. In particular, there was a vacuum caused by the impossibility of understanding passing-off in terms of property in trade marks after the Act of 1875. It was appreciated that relief against passing-off was only available to businesses,[21] but there are only very isolated instances of it being suggested that the plaintiff had a right of property in his business which was to be protected against certain types of damage. In the absence of a property right to protect, the courts were reluctant to admit that passing-off was effectively becoming a tort of strict liability. They clung to the doctrine that although the defendant might be innocent in adopting a particular name or mark in the first place, he was to be treated as fraudulent if he continued to use it after being put on notice, even if he honestly believed no confusion would result, and even if it took an appeal to the House of Lords to prove him wrong. This rationale for passing-off was more often assumed than expressly stated, but here is an example from as late as 1900:

> "[J]urisdiction [over passing-off] which was formerly vested from a very early date in the Court of Chancery in this country, and has survived to the High Court, is a jurisdiction which has rested on fraud. It is the commonest principle of honesty that no man shall be allowed to sell as the goods of another either his own goods or the goods of some third man-

---

[18] (1900) 17 R.P.C. 48, CA affirmed [1901] A.C. 308; 17 R.P.C. 628, HL.
[19] [1897] A.C. 710; 14 R.P.C. 721, HL.
[20] (1900) 17 R.P.C. 477, HL.
[21] *Du Boulay v Du Boulay* (1869) L.R. 2 P.C. 430, PC.

ufacturer ... For any trader to attempt to sell either his own goods or the goods of a third person as the goods of the complainant is, of course, a fraud. It is quite true that it is not necessary in cases of this kind to prove that the defendant whose conduct is complained of was consciously, or intentionally, doing the acts complained of before the issue of the writ; but, when the facts are brought to his attention, and when the facts are established in a Court of Justice, for him to continue to do that which perhaps he was previously doing unintentionally, or unconsciously before the matter was brought to his attention, constitutes, and is a fraud ...[22]

Spalding v Gamage and the early twentieth century

This doctrine deserved the comment to be made, in another context, by the **1–42** Court of Appeal in *Baume v Moore*[23]: "a man is either honest or dishonest in his motives; there is no such thing, so far as we are aware, as constructive dishonesty".[24] Fraud as a legal fiction was obviously unsatisfactory as the basis of passing-off, but it was to be another decade before it was superseded; and the consequences of understanding passing-off in terms of fraud have survived to some extent even today. Passing-off continued to develop in the early years of the twentieth century, as may be seen from the fact that cases went to the House of Lords about once every two years, a rate only matched in the preceding decade. For the most part, however, decisions were more conservative both in the House of Lords and the Court of Appeal. The main advances had been made, and the law was entering a period of consolidation and filling out of detail.

The one fundamental step forward was that passing-off was finally provided with a satisfactory theoretical basis by Lord Parker. The reported first instance judgments of Parker J. are themselves models of intellectual rigour which have rarely been matched in this field. *Burberrys v Cording*[25] in particular deserves to be remembered as the classic statement of the principles of passing-off in its traditional form. However, it was Lord Parker's speech in *Spalding v Gamage*[26] which gave passing-off its modern basis. The importance of *Spalding v Gamage* was twofold. In the first place, it confirmed passing-off as a tort of misrepresentation but cut it free from the previous restriction to misrepresentations that the goods or business of the defendant were those of the plaintiff. In the second place, it explained passing-off in terms of protection of a property right, the right being the property the plaintiff had in the goodwill of his business. The latter was an inspired innovation. Goodwill had long been recognised as a form of legal property and its description as "the attractive force which brings in custom"[27] meant that it was uniquely liable to be damaged by the type of

---

[22] *per* Lord Davey in *Edge & Sons Ltd v Gallon & Son* (1900) 17 R.P.C. 557 at 566, HL.
[23] [1958] Ch. 907; [1958] 2 All E.R. 113; [1958] R.P.C. 226, CA.
[24] *per* Romer L.J., delivering the judgment of the Court.
[25] (1909) 26 R.P.C. 693 (Parker J.).
[26] (1915) 32 R.P.C. 273, HL.
[27] *per* Lord Macnaghten in *Inland Revenue Commissioners v Muller & Co's Margarine Ltd* [1901] A.C. 217, HL.

misrepresentation which constituted passing-off. The previous suggestion that passing-off protected a right of property in the plaintiff's business as such had neither advantage. With passing-off treated as protecting property, the courts had no difficulty in abandoning the need for fraud even as a legal fiction. Passing-off, alone among the common law economic torts, became a tort of strict liability.

1–43   Although *Spalding v Gamage* was immediately adopted as a comprehensive definition of passing-off, its influence on the way cases were actually decided was slight. Instead of using it as a precedent for including new categories of misrepresentation as circumstances demanded, later courts treated it as having decided that only one exception of precise and limited scope was needed to bring the traditional rule to a standard of perfection. Why one exception to deal with different classes of goods emanating from the plaintiff should be both necessary and legitimate, and all other possible extensions rejected out of hand, was never explained. More seriously, it was not yet realised that *Spalding v Gamage* freed passing-off from being no more than the common law counterpart of trade mark infringement. With goodwill as the right protected and misrepresentations not confined to misuse of the plaintiff's indicia, the way was open to deal with deceptive conduct which had nothing to do with names or marks in any sense.

Disappointingly, in the half-century that followed Lord Parker's identification of goodwill as the right protected, there are hardly more than a handful of cases which would not have been decided precisely the same way if the courts had explicitly treated them in terms of property in the plaintiff's name, mark or get-up as such. The mid-twentieth century was for the most part a time of stagnation, reflected in the fact that no passing-off case went to the House of Lords between 1916[28] and 1946.[29] The reason for this state of affairs may not lie simply in the generally undistinguished record of the courts over this period. Passing off is a form of unfair competition, but at least it is an indication that competitive processes are at work. In the inter-war climate of growing cartelisation and protectionism, fair and unfair competitive practices may have been suppressed together; and recourse to the legal process replaced by the edicts of trade associations governing whole industries.

Indirect influences on passing-off: a retrospective resumé

1–44   The slowing down of developments in the mainstream of passing-off after *Spalding v Gamage*[30] provides an opportunity to take stock and go back in time to notice what had been happening in some other areas of law. What is particularly interesting is the fact that the action for passing-off had survived, and indeed flourished, at a time when liability in the most closely

---

[28] *Horlicks Malted Milk Co v Summerskill* (1916) 34 R.P.C. 63, HL.
[29] *Office Cleaning Services Ltd v Westminster Office Cleaning Association* [1946] 1 All E.R. 320; 63 R.P.C. 39, HL.
[30] (1915) 32 R.P.C. 273, HL.

related torts was being curtailed as a matter of what appears to have been deliberate judicial policy. This applies in particular to injurious falsehood,[31] to liability for innocent but negligently made misstatements,[32] and to the deliberate infliction of economic loss in trade.[33]

For this state of immunity, three reasons may be advanced. First, passing-off was still understood in terms of fraud, so its proponents could claim to hold the moral high ground; and in contrast to cases of reliance on negligent misstatement it could hardly be said that the plaintiff had no-one to blame but himself. Admittedly, the moral argument might not have helped in front of judges of Lord Bramwell's persuasion, but passing-off actions were mostly commenced in the Chancery Division, reflecting the fact that the misrepresentation was likely to be repeated (compared to ones made on a single occasion, as in a company prospectus) and the relative importance of an injunction compared to damages. Secondly, passing-off was recognised as applying only between businesses, so it was not caught up in the political struggle between capital and labour which culminated in *Allen v Flood*. Finally, passing-off could take refuge in its protean or chameleon-like quality. Without any recognised base of underlying principle, it was that much less vulnerable to developments in other, not obviously related, areas of law.

The closest body of law to passing-off is injurious falsehood. In contrast **1–45** to passing-off, the misrepresentation in injurious falsehood is generally a disparaging one directed at the claimant, his goods or business; as opposed to a commendatory one made by the defendant in respect of himself. Put this way, it may seem that there can be no overlap between passing-off and injurious falsehood, and it is conventional to say that an actionable misrepresentation in a business context must fall under one body of law or the other.

However, with the action for injurious falsehood rendered virtually ineffective in the context of business competition by *White v Mellin*[34] and *Royal Baking Powder v Wright Crossley*[35] it is possible that litigants were tempted to see how far passing-off could be made to fill the gap, at least if the misrepresentation complained of was open to more than one interpretation. It is noticeable that it was around the turn of the century that passing-off actions seem to have been brought for the first time against defendants who were not in actual or prospective competition with the plaintiff, and the basis for granting relief was for a time uncertain.[36] Diversion of sales was irrelevant in these cases but damage was still the gist of the action, so plaintiffs were driven to alleging that the inferiority of the defendant's goods would rub off on them; an allegation which is now

---

[31] Principally *White v Mellin* and *Royal Baking Powder v Wright Crossley*, below.

[32] *Derry v Peek* (1889) 14 App. Cas. 337, HL.

[33] *Mogul Steamship Co Ltd v McGregor Gow & Co Ltd* [1892] A.C. 25, HL and *Allen v Flood* [1898] A.C. 1, HL.

[34] [1895] A.C. 154, HL.

[35] (1900) 18 R.P.C. 95, HL.

[36] So in *Walter v Ashton* [1902] 2 Ch. 282 (*Times* Bicycles) the case was treated as one of exposure to liability.

familiar in passing-off but which in different circumstances could well have fallen within the tort of injurious falsehood. If so, the process by which passing-off eventually freed itself from the need to find a "common field of activity" may have begun with the emasculation of the action for injurious falsehood.

The *Drinks Cases* and *Advocaat*

1–46 Apart from a few isolated cases, the next important advance in passing-off after *Spalding v Gamage*[37] occurred in 1960 when *Bollinger v Costa Brava*[38] was decided. Hitherto, passing-off had always been understood in terms of some mark, etc., which was distinctive of the plaintiff alone. Passing off one quality or kind of goods for another was actionable only if both classes of goods originated from the plaintiff. Otherwise, misdescription of goods or misuse of a descriptive term was generally considered to be outside the reach of the civil law. *Bollinger v Costa Brava* decided that the producers of Champagne were jointly and severally entitled to restrain wine not produced in the Champagne region being described and sold as, in that case, "Spanish Champagne". Neither the fact that Champagne was the name of the product as such, nor the fact that over a hundred producers were entitled to use the term, was any reason for allowing the defendants to persist in a deceptive course of conduct.

With the *Champagne* case passing-off at last began to fulfil the promise of *Spalding v Gamage* by ceasing to be confined to misrepresentations conveyed through the use of common law trade marks. The decision in favour of the producers of Champagne was followed by others dealing with *Sherry*,[39] *Harris Tweed*[40] and *Scotch Whisky*,[41] but leaving open the question of how far the law would be allowed to develop. In one case it was suggested that the *Champagne* decision might be outside the scope of passing-off altogether and perhaps the precursor of a generic tort of unfair competition[42]; in others that the only allowable extension to the old law was to protect the names of products named after and owing their quality to a precise geographical area. These doubts were resolved with the decision of the House of Lords in *Advocaat*,[43] with which the history of the tort to date is substantially complete.

Injurious falsehood

1–47 The history of injurious falsehood is much more simply stated. Its origins lie

---

[37] (1915) 32 R.P.C. 273, HL.
[38] [1960] Ch. 262; [1959] 3 All E.R. 800; [1960] R.P.C. 16 (Dankwerts J.) for the preliminary point of law.
[39] *Vine Products Ltd v Mackenzie & Co Ltd* [1968] F.S.R. 625; [1969] R.P.C. 1.
[40] *Argyllshire Weavers Ltd v A Macaulay Tweeds Ltd* [1964] R.P.C. 477 (Court of Session).
[41] *Walker (John) & Sons Ltd v Henry Ost & Co Ltd* [1970] 1 W.L.R. 917; [1970] 2 All E.R. 106; [1970] R.P.C. 489.
[42] *Vine Products Ltd v Mackenzie & Co Ltd* [1968] F.S.R. 625; [1969] R.P.C. 1.
[43] *Erven Warnink BV v J Townend & Sons (Hull) Ltd* [1979] A.C. 731; [1979] 2 All E.R. 927; [1980] R.P.C. 31, HL.

in the late sixteenth and early seventeenth centuries in the action for slander of title to land. As such, it was not yet of any direct relevance as a tort of unfair competition, and even in this original manifestation it fell into disuse. Around the middle of the nineteenth century a number of cases were brought which explored the relationship between defamation and the re-emerging action on the case for damage caused by words published mal-iciously. The separate existence of the latter was recognised in *Evans v Harlow*[44] and *Young v Macrae*,[45] although the plaintiff was successful in neither case.

Most of the development which injurious falsehood has undergone as a tort of unfair competition was packed into the quarter-century following the Judicature Act 1873. Initially, the merger of law and equity encouraged plaintiffs to attempt to restrain publication of alleged falsehoods, which had been impossible under the pre-Judicature Act system because neither defa-mation nor the action on the case protected a property right. After some confusion, the law became settled with the twin propositions that a final injunction could be granted, but that interim relief should be confined to the very clearest cases. Between 1875 and 1900 a series of decisions identified the essential elements of the tort as a falsehood, maliciously made, which was calculated to damage an economic interest of the plaintiff, and which could be proved to have caused special damage.

With the beginning of the twentieth century, the leading cases of *Ratcliffe* **1–48** *v Evans*,[46] *White v Mellin*,[47] *Hubbuck v Wilkinson Heywood*,[48] and *Royal Baking Powder v Wright Crossley*[49] had settled the law in its modern form, and deprived it of very nearly all practical significance. Cases occasionally continued to be brought in the twentieth century, but success was elusive unless one could find an unusually sympathetic judge or jury, or an improbably villainous opponent. A major legislative stimulus may have been intended by the effective abolition of the requirement to prove special damage with the passage of the Defamation Act 1952, but in retrospect it is hard to identify any major impact. The last decade or so of the twentieth century witnessed a number of actions by private individuals in cases which were really ones of defamation, exploiting (with more or less success) the fact that legal aid was available for injurious falsehood though not for libel or slander. Although not strictly within the scope of the present work, some of these have been important in contributing to the modern understanding of the tort.

The most recent chapter in the history of injurious falsehood as a tort of unfair competition was dependent on the passage of the Trade Marks Act 1994. The latter reversed the previous Act by permitting the use of a com-petitor's registered trade marks in comparative advertising, but subject to the use being in accordance with honest practices in industrial or commer-

---

[44] (1844) 5 Q.B. 624; 114 E.R. 1384.
[45] (1862) 122 E.R. 100.
[46] [1892] 2 Q.B. 524, CA
[47] [1895] A.C. 154, HL.
[48] [1899] 1 Q.B. 86, CA.
[49] (1900) 18 R.P.C. 95, HL.

cial matters.[50] This produced a crop of cases either alleging trade mark infringement alone, or trade mark infringement with injurious falsehood as a secondary cause of action on he same facts. The majority of these failed on both heads, with the clear and in some cases express implication that if the statutory cause of action could not be made out, then that at common law was even less likely to succeed.

E. "UNFAIR COMPETITION" AS A NOMINATE OR SUI GENERIS WRONG

What is meant by "unfair competition"?

1–49 The case for adopting "unfair competition" in place of "passing-off" is considered at the start of the present chapter. More generally, unfair competition and cognate terms have been used as terms of art in legal writing in at least two or three other senses[51]:

"The phrase 'unfair competition' has been used in judgments and learned writings in at least three distinct ways, namely: (i) as a synonym of the doctrine of passing-off; (ii) as a generic name to cover the wide range of legal and equitable causes of action available to protect a trader against the unlawful trading activities of a competitor; and (iii) to describe what is claimed to be a new and general cause of action which protects a trader against damage caused either by 'unfair competition' generally or, more particularly, by the 'misappropriation' of knowledge or information in which he has a quasi-proprietary right. The first and second of the above uses of the phrase are liable to be misleading in that they may wrongly imply that the relevant action or actions are restricted to proceedings against a competitor. The second use is also liable to imply that there exists a unity of underlying principle between different actions when, in truth, there is none. The third use of the phrase is, in an Australian context, simply mistaken in that 'unfair competition' does not, in itself, provide a sufficient basis for relief under the law of this country."[52]

Neither English nor Australian law has recognised a general tort of unfair competition in the third sense above, but the formulation in terms of misappropriation of knowledge or information is unduly restrictive. Unfair competition (in a broad sense) can be found in misappropriating more than knowledge or information, and need not be defined in terms of mis-

---

[50] Trade Marks Act 1994, s.10(6) proviso.
[51] A fourth sense might be identified in which it is simply a term of disapproval without legal significance.
[52] *per* Deane J. in *Moorgate Tobacco Co Ltd v Philip Morris Ltd* (1984) 156 C.L.R. 414; 59 A.L.J.R. 77; 56 A.L.R. 193; 3 I.P.R. 545; [1985] R.P.C. 219 (High Court of Australia).

appropriation at all. Broadly speaking, four overlapping theories of unfair competition can be identified.

The first is known in the United States as the *prima facie* tort theory[53] and **1–50** holds that it is actionable deliberately to cause injury to another without just cause. The closest English concept is liability for civil conspiracy when neither the means nor the end are intrinsically unlawful, but the *prima facie* tort theory does not require there to be more than one tortfeasor or any common design. Closely related to this is the concept of general liability for harm caused by unlawful and intentional acts. An Australian court has stated that "a person who suffers harm or loss as the inevitable consequence of the unlawful, intentional, and positive acts of another"[54] may recover damages, but the decision was in a different context and has never been cited except to be distinguished. In England, *Ex p. Island Records*[55] is to much the same effect, but was disapproved in *Lonrho v Shell Petroleum.*[56]

The second theory is that competitive acts which are unfair, or contrary to generally recognised principles of honest commercial practice, will be restrained at the suit of a competitor. The latter is the sense in which the term "unfair competition" is used in the Paris Convention on Industrial Property,[57] and is recognised by many civil law jurisdictions. Compared to the foregoing rule there need be no extraneous element of malevolence or illegality to convert fair into unfair competition.

Next, there is the concept of unfair competition by misappropriation of what are compendiously described as trade values, in particular, the reputation and other benefits created by the industry of the claimant. Some definitions of unfair competition require the misappropriation to be unfair in the sense of deliberately underhand, but it is not necessary to combine the two concepts in this way: unfairness may take a form not involving misappropriation, and even unintentional misappropriation may be regarded as inherently unfair.

The fourth and last theory might be identified as abuse of disproportionate economic power. It corresponds in general terms to the concept of monopolisation under s.2 of the United States Sherman Act or abuse of a dominant position under Art.82 (formerly Art.86) of the EEC Treaty. Unfair competition of this kind can arise from conduct which would be innocent or ineffective if practised by a smaller enterprise, which is why it justifies identification as a separate head.

It will be seen that neither English nor Australian law has recognised a **1–51** general tort of unfair competition in any of the forms described above. However, it is still useful to be able to use terms such as unfair competition to describe a state of affairs and discuss the legal remedies (if any) available

---

[53] The classic example is *Tuttle v Buck* (1909) 107 Minn; 119 N.W. 946, where the plaintiff claimed he had been driven out of business as part of a vendetta by the defendant.
[54] *Beaudesert Shire Council v Smith* (1966) 120 C.L.R. 145; 40 A.L.J.R. 211; [1966] A.L.R. 1175 (High Court of Australia, Full Court).
[55] [1978] Ch. 122; [1978] F.S.R. 505, CA.
[56] [1982] A.C. 173; [1981] 2 All E.R. 456, HL.
[57] Art.10*bis*, see Chapter 2.

to deal with it. Much can still be accomplished within the framework of the existing law.

> "The rejection of a general action for 'unfair competition' or 'unfair trading' does not involve a denial of the desirability of adopting a flexible approach to traditional forms of action when such an approach is necessary in order to adapt them to meet new situations and circumstances. It has not, for example, prevented the adaptation of the traditional doctrine of passing-off to meet new circumstances involving the deceptive or confusing use of names, descriptive terms or other indicia to persuade purchasers or customers to believe that goods or services have an association, quality or endorsement which belongs or would belong to goods or services of, or associated with, another or others."[58]

Unfair competition in Australia...

1–52   The notion of a general common law tort of unfair competition has received the most thorough consideration in Australian law.[59] The starting point is the decision of the High Court of Australia in *Victoria Park v Taylor*.[60] The plaintiffs were the owners and operators of a racecourse near Sydney. The defendant, Taylor, owned land near the course and allowed the second defendants, a radio station, to erect a tower on the land from which the course could be viewed. The defendants broadcast live descriptions of the races and the plaintiffs claimed that attendances at their meetings dropped as a result. The High Court dismissed the case by a majority of three to two. The most influential judgment was that of Dixon J., who adopted the dissenting judgment of Brandeis J. in the American case of *International News v Associated Press*[61] as accurately stating English and Australian law.

> "The fact is that the substance of the plaintiff's complaint goes to interference, not with its enjoyment of the land, but with the profitable conduct of its business. If English law had followed the course of development that has recently taken place in the United States, the 'broadcasting rights' in respect of the races might have been protected as part of the quasi-property created by the enterprise, organisation and labour of the plaintiff in establishing and equipping a racecourse and doing all that is necessary to conduct race meetings. But courts of equity have not in British jurisdiction thrown the protection of an injunction around all intangible elements of value, that is, value in exchange, which may flow from the exercise by an individual of his powers or resources whether in the organisation of a business or the use of ingenuity, knowledge, skill or labour. This is sufficiently evidenced by the history of

---

[58] *per* Deane J. in *Moorgate Tobacco Co Ltd v Philip Morris Ltd*, above.
[59] Apart from the law of the United States, which is outside the scope of this work. South Africa has a general law of unlawful competition, but this is based on Roman-Dutch principles and is inapplicable to common law jurisdictions.
[60] (1937) 58 C.L.R. 479 (High Court of Australia, Full Court).
[61] (1918) 248 U.S. 215; 39 S.Ct. 68; 63 L.Ed. 211.

the law of copyright and by the fact that the exclusive right to invention, trade marks, designs, trade name and reputation are dealt within English law as special heads of protected interests and not under a wide generalisation.

In dissenting from a judgment of the Supreme Court of the United States by which the organised collection of news by a news service was held to give it in equity a quasi-property protected against appropriation by rival news agencies, Brandeis J. gave reasons which substantially represent the English law and he supported his opinion by a citation of much English authority (*International News v Associated Press*).[62] His judgment appears to me to contain an adequate answer both upon principle and authority to the suggestion that the defendants are misappropriating or abstracting something which the plaintiff has created and alone is entitled to turn to value. Briefly, the answer is that it is not because the individual has by his efforts put himself in a position to obtain value for what he can give that his right to give it becomes protected by law and so assumed the exclusiveness of property, but because the intangible or incorporeal right he claims falls within a recognised category to which legal or equitable protection attaches."

The judgment of Sir Owen Dixon has been criticised as too conservative, but even the dissenting minority were not inclined to support a general tort of unfair competition or recognise any new intangible right of property in the plaintiff's business as such. Rich J. would have found for the plaintiffs entirely under the head of nuisance,[63] thereby protecting the oldest and most tangible of all forms of property: land. Evatt J. gave scarcely more attention to competition law. The concern of both was not to create a new tort of unfair competition but to do to the tort of nuisance what *Donoghue v Stevenson*[64] had recently done for negligence.

Unfair competition as a nominate cause of action reappeared in Australian law with *Willard King v United Telecasters*,[65] encouraged by the New South Wales decision in *Henderson v Radio Corporation*[66] and drawing on the judgment of Romer L.J. in *Samuelson v Producers*.[67] In the *Willard King* case itself one television company sued another for broadcasting a television series, *Its Academic*, whose title and content had been copied from them. The decision can be understood in terms of the title, and perhaps presentation, being distinctive in the sense required for passing-off, but the judge was prepared to consider going further: "If one were to simply adopt the principle that no man should be allowed to misappropriate what equitably belongs to a competitor, there would be little doubt that the plaintiff's claim to enjoin the first defendant ought to succeed...".

1–53

---

[62] Above.
[63] With some references to a general right of privacy, but none to unfair competition or anything similar.
[64] [1932] A.C. 562, HL.
[65] (1970) [1981] 2 N.S.W.L.R. 547 (Else-Mitchell J.).
[66] [1960] N.S.W.L.R. 279; [1969] R.P.C. 218 (Full Court).
[67] (1931) 48 R.P.C. 580, CA.

This suggestion was to be taken up in another case on very similar facts. In *Hexagon v Australian Broadcasting Commission*[68] the plaintiffs had invented and popularised the character Alvin Purple in two films. They had negotiated with the defendants to make a television series around him, but on the negotiations breaking down the defendants proceeded on their own. Needham J. held that the plaintiffs had made out a case of passing-off and continued:

"Because of this conclusion, it is perhaps not necessary for me to consider the submissions of the plaintiffs based on the doctrine of 'unfair competition', but the point was fully argued by both sides, and I think I should express my view on the point as it is one of some novelty.

It was argued that passing-off merges into 'unfair competition'. I was referred to a decision of Else-Mitchell J ... *Willard King Organisation v United Telecasters*[69] in which his Honour expressed a view that the United States doctrine of 'unfair competition' might adequately meet the need, recognised in *Samuelson's* case[70] and in *Henderson v Radio Corporation*[71] to apply equitable doctrines to new categories of situations, some arising from 'the evolution of new technical means of communication'. I was also referred to the classic United States cases of *Schechter v United States*;[72] *International News v Associated Press*,[73] especially at 240–2, and three English cases, in which the doctrine of 'unfair competition', as distinct from 'passing-off', has been applied *Bollinger v Costa Brava*;[74] *Vine Products v Mackenzie*[75] and *John Walker v Henry Ost*.[76] These latter cases seem to proceed on the basis that, because the respective plaintiffs were not all of the people involved in the production of the particular beverage concerned, they could not succeed on a passing-off, as the necessary evidence of confusion would be lacking. The cases seem to assent that 'unfair competition' is an extension of the doctrine of passing-off, or, possibly, is a new and independent cause of action. It consists of misappropriation of what equitably belongs to a competitor ...

I think it is correct to say that in all these cases, English and American, the court has found an element of fraud or inequitable conduct on the part of the defendant. The very description of the tort 'unfair competition' leads one to a conclusion that there must be something underhand or sharp in the conduct of the defendant. I do not think that there is any such conduct here.

It seems to me that there is room in our jurisprudence for a concept such as 'unfair competition'."

---

[68] (1975) 7 A.L.R. 233; [1976] R.P.C. 628 (Needham J.).
[69] (1970) [1981] 2 N.S.W.L.R. 547 (Else-Mitchell J.).
[70] (1931) 48 R.P.C. 580, CA.
[71] [1960] N.S.W.L.R. 279; [1969] R.P.C. 218.
[72] (1935) 295 U.S. 495; 55 S.Ct. 837; 79 L.Ed 1570.
[73] (1918) 248 U.S. 215; 39 S.Ct. 68; 63 L.Ed. 211.
[74] [1960] Ch. 262; [1959] 3 All E.R. 800; [1960] R.P.C. 16 (Dankwerts J.).
[75] [1968] F.S.R. 625; [1969] R.P.C. 1 (Cross J.).
[76] [1970] 1 W.L.R. 917; [1970] 2 All E.R. 106; [1970] R.P.C. 489 (Foster J.).

These passages were *obiter*, because in both cases there was passing-off in its recognised form.[77] *Hexagon v Australian Broadcasting Commission*, although going into the matter in more depth than its predecessor, was open to criticism for misunderstanding the authorities and proposing a rule of unworkable vagueness. The cause of action suggested by Needham J. in *Hexagon* was based on three concepts which are all imprecise and unsatisfactory: property in intangible rights not otherwise recognised by any branch of law; equitable ownership of such rights; and underhand or sharp practice by the defendant. In *Cadbury Schweppes v Pub Squash*[78] at first instance Powell J. preferred the view that the English *Drinks Cases* were examples of passing-off and that the *Its Accdemic* and *Hexagon* cases were inconclusive.[79] On appeal, the Privy Council left the question of unfair competition open.

With *Moorgate Tobacco v Philip Morris*[80] the Full Court of the High **1–54** Court of Australia returned to the attitude of Sir Owen Dixon in *Victoria Park v Taylor*[81] and expressly denied that there was any general tort of unfair competition in Australian law. The facts were that Moorgate were the successors to the business of the tobacco division of Loew's Theatres. Philip Morris had enjoyed the benefit of a trade mark licence with Loew's, under which they sold *Kent* cigarettes in Australia. There was discussion about introducing a low tar brand as *Kent Golden Lights*. Shortly after expiry of the licence, Philip Morris applied to register the mark *Golden Lights* in its own name and commenced to sell *Marlboro Golden Lights*. Moorgate claimed for ownership of the mark, breach of fiduciary duty, breach of confidence and unfair competition. They failed in all three courts[82] on all counts.

"The rejection of a general action for 'unfair competition' involves no more that a recognition of the fact that the existence of such an action is inconsistent with the established limits of the traditional and statutory causes of action which are available to a trader in respect of damage caused or threatened by a competitor. Those limits, which define the boundary between the area of legal or equitable restraint and protection and the area of untrammelled competition, increasingly reflect what the responsible Parliament or Parliaments have determined to be the appropriate balance between competing claims and policies. Neither legal principle nor social utility requires or warrants the obliteration of that boundary by the importation of a cause of action whose main char-

---

[77] In *Hexagon* relief was refused because of acquiescence.

[78] [1980] 2 N.S.W.L.R. 865; [1981] 1 All E.R. 213; [1981] R.P.C. 429, PC.

[79] See also *Isaacson (Peter) Publications Pty Ltd v Nationwide News Pty Ltd* (1984) 56 A.L.R. 595 (Federal Court of Australia).

[80] (1984) 56 C.L.R. 414; 59 A.L.J.R. 77; 56 A.L.R. 193; 3 I.P.R. 545; [1985] R.P.C. 219 (High Court of Australia, Full Court).

[81] (1937) 58 C.L.R. 479 (High Court of Australia, Full Court).

[82] At first instance and on appeal in New South Wales, and on appeal to the High Court of Australia.

acteristic is the scope it allows, under high-sounding generalisations, for judicial indulgence of idiosyncratic notions of what is fair in the market place."[83]

... and in England

1–55 English law has been even less willing than Australian to admit the existence of a separate tort of unfair competition. The principle still followed is that stated by Fry L.J. in *Mogul Steamship Co v McGregor Gow*[84]: "[T]o draw a line between fair and unfair competition, between what is reasonable and unreasonable, passes the power of the courts".

In *Vine Products v Mackenzie*[85] Cross J. was at one point minded to understand the Spanish Champagne case as "not passing-off but a new-fangled tort called unlawful competition" but later disclaimed any intention to distinguish the two. It is now settled law that all the *Drinks Cases* are examples of passing-off and that no more general theory of unfair or unlawful competition is required to explain them.[86]

Contemporaneously with the *Drinks Cases*, there was another line of authority starting with *Ex p. Island Records*[87] which at one stage showed signs of developing into a general tort of unfair competition, based on unlawful interference with business, but which proved abortive. In *Ex p. Island Records* itself, a majority of the Court of Appeal held that the contractual rights existing between performers and their recording companies were a form of property, and that equity would enjoin criminal acts which would interfere with those rights. "[A] man who is carrying on a lawful trade or calling has a right to be protected from any unlawful interference with it".[88] The criminal acts in question were breaches of the Performers Protection Acts, which did not create any civil remedies. If this principle had been taken to its logical conclusion, any illegal act might have been civilly actionable by a person whose business was harmed by it. However, in *Lonrho v Shell Petroleum*[89] the House of Lords disapproved *Ex p. Island Records* and denied that any such general principle was part of English law.[90]

There are also a few English passing-off actions since *Advocaat*[91] in which

---

[83] *per* Deane J. (with whom the rest of the Court agreed) in *Moorgate Tobacco Co Ltd v Philip Morris Ltd*, above.

[84] (1889) 23 Q.B.D. 598, CA.

[85] [1968] F.S.R. 625; [1969] R.P.C. 1, *per* Cross J.

[86] *Erven Warnink BV v J Townend & Sons (Hull) Ltd* [1979] A.C. 731; [1979] 2 All E.R. 927; [1980] R.P.C. 31, HL; though a dictum of Aldous L.J. in *Arsenal Football Club plc v Reed (No.2)* [2003] EWCA Civ 696; [2003] 2 CMLR 25, CA revives the possibility of *Vine Products v Mackenzie* being a precursor to a more general tort than classic passing-off.

[87] [1978] Ch. 122; [1978] F.S.R. 505, CA. See also *Carlin Music Corp v Collins* [1979] F.S.R. 548, CA.

[88] *per* Lord Denning, *loc. cit.*

[89] [1982] A.C. 173; [1981] 2 All E.R. 456, HL.

[90] *RCA Corp v Pollard* [1983] Ch. 135; [1982] 3 W.L.R. 1007; [1982] 3 All E.R. 771; [1983] F.S.R. 9, CA confirmed that *Ex p. Island Records* is no longer good law even on its own facts.

[91] *Erven Warnink BV v J Townend & Sons (Hull) Ltd* [1979] A.C. 731; [1979] 2 All E.R. 927; [1980] R.P.C. 31, HL.

plaintiffs have argued that there is a general tort of unfair competition or of deliberate or fraudulent interference with trade or goodwill, but without success. In *Harrods v Schwartz-Sackin*[92] the plaintiffs suggested that there might be actionable unfair competition by appropriating the goodwill of another without any misrepresentation, but Warner J. granted an interlocutory injunction solely on the strength of a contract between the parties.[93] In *Associated Newspapers v Insert Media (No.2)*[94] the plaintiffs in a passing-off action sought leave to amend their statement of claim by pleading three additional grounds for granting an injunction. The first was that the plaintiffs were entitled to restrain any deliberate acts calculated to damage their business and goodwill; the second was that the defendants were liable for "unfair trading" in a wider sense than that recognised as passing-off; the third was that it was just and convenient to grant an injunction on the facts of the case whether or not the plaintiffs had a cause of action. Hoffmann J. refused all the proposed amendments as being unarguable and insufficient in law to justify the grant of an injunction. The latter decision of Hoffmann J. was followed by Harman J. in striking out a claim expressed to be for "fraudulent interference with trade" in *Swedac v Magnet & Southerns*.[95]

Although there may be no general tort of unfair competition in English **1–56** law; there is a recognised tort of unlawful interference with business when is perhaps even more protean than passing-off. Its existence is beyond dispute but its details, and perhaps even its principles have yet to be fully worked out.[96] In *Lonrho v Fayed*[97] the plaintiffs claimed that the defendants had tortiously interfered with their business by making misrepresentations to the Secretary of State for Industry which resulted in the defendants being able to bid successfully for control of a company, House of Fraser plc, for which the plaintiffs also wanted to bid. The claim was framed both as unlawful interference with business and as conspiracy to injure by unlawful means. At first instance[98] the whole statement of claim was struck out but the Court of Appeal[99] and subsequently the House of Lords reinstated it and allowed the action to go to trial.[1]

The Court of Appeal would still have struck out the conspiracy part of the claim, following its own recent decision in *Metall und Rohstoff v Donaldson Lufkin*[2] to the effect that a predominant intention to injure was essential to the tort of conspiracy even in the case of conspiracy to injure by unlawful means. The appeal to the House of Lords was mainly concerned with this issue. The House of Lords deliberately refrained from any general statement of either branch of the law except to overrule the *Metall und Rohstoff*

---

[92] [1986] F.S.R. 490 (Warner J.).
[93] On appeal (1987) [1991] F.S.R. 209, CA the injunction was discharged but the refusal to recognise a cause of action for unfair competition was approved.
[94] [1988] 1 W.L.R. 509; [1988] 2 All E.R. 420 (Hoffmann J.).
[95] [1989] F.S.R. 243 (Harman J.). Also following *Bradford v Pickles* [1895] A.C. 587, HL.
[96] For a detailed discussion see Hazel Carty, *An Analysis of the Economic Torts* (2000), Ch.5.
[97] [1992] A.C. 448, HL.
[98] [1990] 1 Q.B. 490 (Pill J.).
[99] [1990] 2 Q.B. 479, CA.
[1] Though the action was later settled.
[2] [1990] 1 Q.B. 391, CA.

decision on this point. Assuming that the Court of Appeal decision in *Lonrho v Fayed* is still good law on the tort of interference with business, it follows that it is not an essential element of the tort that the tortfeasor's predominant intention should be to injure the victim rather than to further his own interests; nor was it fatal that the defendants might not have committed any tort against the Secretary of State.

CHAPTER 2

UNFAIR COMPETITION IN EUROPEAN AND INTERNATIONAL LAW

45

A. INTRODUCTION AND SCOPE OF CHAPTER

Public and private law; substantive and adjectival law

2–1 Historically, as in the two previous editions of the present work, there was little need to consider the interaction between domestic unfair competition law and international law in any of its manifestations, with the specific exception of defences arising under European Community law. In the present edition, a much more extensive discussion is given to the treatment of unfair competition in international law in several of its other aspects. Specifically, the present chapter deals with the evolution of the substantive law of unfair competition as it is to be found in the Paris Convention for the Protection of Industrial Property, and with the extent to which domestic law might already be affected by the TRIPs Agreement. Defences under the EC Treaty continue to be dealt with in Chapter 9, as are defences under the European Convention on Human Rights which receive consideration for the first time. The extent to which actions for unfair competition are affected by the EC Jurisdiction Regulation and its predecessors, the Brussels and Lugano conventions, is considered in Chapter 10.

In the present state of the law, there is a well-marked, if probably coincidental, distinction to be drawn between international law as it defines substantive rights; and the essentially adjectival effect of international law on defences, enforcement and remedies. Paradoxically, perhaps, it is in its adjectival effects that international law cannot safely be ignored by the practitioner. This has long, and most obviously, been true for European Community law on competition and freedom of movement of goods, where international law may provide an overriding defence for conduct which might be actionable under domestic law. The same is now true of defences under the European Convention on Human Rights. The practical effects of both these bodies of law on the English doctrines of passing-off and injurious falsehood has been and will probably continue to be slight, but there can be no doubt that if a conflict between domestic law and either of these international instruments should arise, then it is the domestic law which must yield.

2–2 So far as substantive law is concerned, it is trite law that international treaties have no effect on private rights except to the extent that they have been incorporated into UK municipal law by legislation, or may legitimately be referred to in interpreting legal obligations arising from a source of law recognised as affecting private rights.[1] To this extent, the relevant provisions

---

[1] *CANADEL TM* [1980] R.P.C. 535 (Registry) dismissing an opposition purportedly based directly on Art.10*bis* of the Paris Convention.

of the Paris Convention have no effect in English domestic law, and the question of whether English law does or does not comply with the United Kingdom's obligations on the international plane is one which may fascinate the specialist, but can still safely be ignored in day to day practice.

It might be thought that the TRIPs Agreement would have provided an opportunity to legislate against unfair competition on a uniform basis and worldwide scale, but at a very early stage a policy decision seems to have been taken to confine the relevant legislative programme of TRIPs to two specific topics at the margin of unfair competition law in even the broadest sense, namely the protection of geographical indications and undisclosed information. If TRIPs does have any binding and relevant effect, which is by no means certain in the present context, then that again is most likely to be found in the adjectival sense of guaranteeing prompt, fair and equitable civil remedies. Finally, the effects of the Brussels and Lugano conventions, and the Jurisdiction Regulation which has superceded them, are again felt in the procedural sphere.

English law and the international norm of "fair competition"

From the scope of the present work it will be apparent that what is still **2–3** called "the action for passing-off" provides much wider coverage against acts of unfair competition than either its name or its nineteenth century origins might suggest. To this extent, "passing off" is well-established in legal usage as a synecdoche for a range of factual situations embraced within a single legal concept. However, it cannot be suggested that the action for passing-off in anything like its present form could ever provide an all-embracing remedy for acts of "unfair competition" of whatever nature.

For present purposes, passing-off has three inherent characteristics which restrict it in comparison with other possible causes of action between competitors. First, passing-off is exclusively concerned with damage caused by a misrepresentation. Damage arising from any other form of "unfair" conduct in competition or otherwise cannot amount to passing-off. Secondly, the types of misrepresentation with which passing-off is concerned are exclusively those which promote or extol the defendant's goods, business or services to the disadvantage of the claimant. Misrepresentations of a disparaging nature are dealt with under the historically separate (and commercially much less significant) heads of injurious falsehood or defamation; and misrepresentations of any other kind are likely to fall into a legal limbo unless they can themselves be passed off as one or the other. Finally, passing-off is a branch of the law of tort, protecting a property right which is the goodwill the claimant has in his business. It has not developed as part of the law of restitution and it does not focus on any enrichment which the defendant may have procured for himself at the notional expense of the claimant—whether or not a competitor. Nor does passing-off have any of the character of an *actio popularis*, allowing a civil action to be brought by a competitor, or another, whose interest may amount to nothing more than seeing that standards of legality and fairness are upheld. Absent actual or threatened damage to the claimant in one of the recognised forms, there can be no right of action for either passing-off or injurious falsehood.

Passing-off is thus relatively narrow by the standards of unfair competition law in many developed countries, and especially in Continental Europe. Even if one takes account of other relevant civil causes of action in English law such as injurious falsehood, interference with contract and breach of confidence, then in aggregate one still has a rather disparate body of law which is much less systematic and comprehensive than the unfair competition laws of, for instance, France, Germany or the Netherlands. On the other hand, the coverage of English law is not much narrower in principle than that of American law as stated in the *Restatement (3rd) Unfair Competition*, even if the actual circumstances in which conduct is actionable differ.

2-4   This relative disparity, at least between English law and many Continental European legal systems, has long raised the question of whether the United Kingdom is significantly out of step with international norms, perhaps even to the extent of being in breach of its obligations in public international law, by failing to have a more comprehensive law of unfair competition. Previously, the question was of no more than academic interest because international treaties are not self-executing in English law. International obligations such as those assumed under successive Acts of the Paris Convention for the Protection of Industrial Property only affect private rights to the extent that they are given effect by Act of Parliament. If Britain were in breach of any of its international obligations, then the remedies for an aggrieved contracting state would have been be confined to diplomatic efforts, or, in the last resort, an action before the International Court of Justice.[2] A private party damaged by non-compliance would have no remedies at all.

This state of affairs can no longer entirely be taken for granted, for several reasons. In particular, there is the 1994 Agreement on Trade-Related Aspects of Intellectual Property Rights (The TRIPs Agreement) which, within its field of application, has a far more effective mechanism for enforcement than the Paris Convention. A member state in breach of TRIPs can be taken before the Dispute Settlement Body of the World Trade Organisation which has power to order remedial legislation, and to authorise retributive sanctions in favour of the aggrieved member state in the event of non-compliance. The procedure before the DSB is relatively quick, and on early indications effective. There was previously the question of whether any of the obligations imposed by TRIPs might have direct effect in the United Kingdom under the Community legal order. However, the European Court of Justice has rejected giving TRIPs direct effect by virtue of implicit incorporation into Community law, while encouraging national courts interpreting Community and national law to comply with TRIPs as far as they can.[3]

---

[2] Under Art.28 of the Paris Convention. No such action has ever been brought in respect of intellectual property rights of any kind.

[3] Cases C-300/98 and C-392/98 *Parfums Christian Dior SA v Tuk Consultancy BV* [2000] E.C.R. I-11307; [2001] E.T.M.R. 26.

UK compliance (or not) with Art.10*bis*

It remains to be seen whether, or to what extent, the Paris Convention or **2–5** any other source of international law does impose international norms in the field of unfair competition, and whether the United Kingdom complies with those norms. After what has been said about the limitations of the action for passing-off, it may come as a surprise to see that the United Kingdom has several times been the instigator or principal supporter of significantly increased protection against unfair competition in successive versions of the Paris Convention, and that the present text of Art.10*bis* is actually much less strict than the United Kingdom would once have favoured.

One key to appreciating this apparent paradox is the official and long-standing British understanding that the "repression" of unfair competition does not necessarily entail civil actionability for damages or even an injunction. "Repression" is hardly employed used in English legal usage except in a pejorative sense, but in French it is used routinely (and more accurately) where English law might use "prevent". English law, as represented at successive revision conferences for the Paris Convention, has tended to regard the first line of defence against acts of unfair competition in general as the Merchandise Marks Acts (and the Trade Descriptions Acts succeeding them) which imposed criminal liability for various forms of dishonest or deceptive conduct, to a much wider extent than the civil actions for passing-off or injurious falsehood. As the United Kingdom delegate formally declared at the 1900 Brussels Conference when the original Art.10*bis* was adopted[4]:

"The Government of the United Kingdom supports the proposition made by the honourable French delegates at the previous Conference, according to which foreign nationals of the Union should enjoy, in matters of unfair competition, the same protection as nationals.	"Le Gouvernement de S.M. Britannique se rallie à la proposition faite par MM. Les honorable Délégués de la France à la dernière Conférence,[5] et d'après laquelle les étrangers unionistes jouiront, en ce qui concerne la concurrence déloyale, de la même protection que les nationaux.
All the same, it wishes to have it understood that Great Britain is not to be obliged to afford any protection beyond that established by the *Merchandise Marks Act* 1887, which is very rigorous and complete.	Toutefois, il désire qu'il soit bien entendu que la Grande-Bretagne ne sera pas tenue d'accorder une protection allant au delà de celle établie par le *Merchandise Marks Act* de 1887, laquelle est très rigoureuse et complète.
Foreigners also enjoy, to the	Les étrangers jouiront d'ail-

---

[4] *Actes de Bruxelles* (1901), p.382 (original in French, translation by the author).
[5] The first Brussels Conference of 1897 which was adjourned to 1900.

same extent as nationals, the full protection afforded by the English common law."	leurs, aussi bien que les nationaux, de toute protection accordée par la loi commune anglaise."

2–6 In the subsequent history of the Paris Convention this interpretation has been maintained and apparently accepted: the Merchandise Marks Acts (and their equivalents elsewhere in the British Empire) have been listed in tabulations of unfair competition laws compiled by the International Bureau; proposals for new or strengthened Convention obligations have been discussed, primarily in terms of whether the Merchandise Marks Acts already complied or would require amendment; and new Convention obligations have been proposed to be implemented by amending the Merchandise Marks Acts. Proposals, by the United Kingdom among others, to require uniform civil or criminal remedies for acts of unfair competition have been defeated.

If this proposition seems surprising, it is partly as a result of late twentieth century preconception equating intellectual property protection with civil actionability: over many periods, and in many countries, wide tracts of intellectual property protection have principally been a matter for the criminal law. It is also notable that the United Kingdom point of view has been accepted in much harmonised European Community law, under which acts of unfair competition as defined in uniform substantive law may be dealt with, according to the internal law of the member state, by almost any combination of civil actionability, criminal liability, administrative action, or even self-regulation.

Factors for change

2–7 Underlying the substantial coverage now given in the present edition to the treatment of unfair competition in public international law is the probability that that an increasing degree of harmonisation *de facto*, if not necessarily *de jure*, is likely even within its expected lifetime.

The most obvious, but perhaps the least immediate, factor for change is explicit harmonisation of unfair competition law by European Community legislation or international agreement. So far as the first is concerned, harmonisation of unfair competition law has been on the agenda of the European Economic Community (as it then was) since the early 1960s, but with few practical results beyond a limited degree of harmonisation of the law of misleading advertising.[6] At the time of writing, the Commission has published a Proposal for a Directive Concerning Unfair Business-to-Consumer Commercial Practices in the Internal Market,[7] but its focus is on consumer protection, rather than unfair competition.

---

[6] Directive 84/450/EEC of September 10, 1984, as amended by Directive 97/55/EC of October 6, 1997.
[7] COM (2003) 356 Final of June 18, 2003.

International harmonisation has a much longer history within the context of the Paris Convention for the Protection of Industrial Property, and although the influence of the latter on English domestic law has been minimal, the Paris Convention provides the obvious and only international standard from which divergences can be measured. There is little immediate prospect of TRIPs addressing unfair competition in any wider aspects than it does at present.

Any increase in European influence is therefore likely to come indirectly, **2–8** if at all. There is already a fairly substantial body of case law from the European Court of Justice, but since this is almost entirely in the context of defences to actions for unfair competition, it does not help very much in defining unfair competition or giving the law any underlying rationale. It is notable that the Court has not yet attempted to define the specific subject matter of unfair competition, as it has for other nominate intellectual property rights. A second avenue for defining "unfairness" in competition is opened up by the incorporation of wording from the Paris Convention into the Trade Mark Directive[8] and Regulation[9] providing immunity for certain non-infringing uses of the trade mark (or collective mark) provided they are in accordance with "honest practices in industrial and commercial matters". A reference from the English High Court to the European Court of Justice is currently pending[10] in the context of Art.6(1)(c) of the Directive.[11]

However, it is suggested that the most important factor is likely to come from the creation of a single European jurisdiction for unfair competition actions. It has always been the case that actions for unfair competition under the 1968 Brussels Convention on Jurisdiction and the Enforcement of Judgments were governed by the latter's general rules, and not by the specific provisions for the registered intellectual property rights, and it is increasing likely that actions for unfair competition will be fought on a multilateral or pan-European basis under the Jurisdiction Regulation,[12] which replaces the Brussels Convention. There is no impediment, therefore, to an action for unfair competition being brought on a pan-European scale in the country of the defendant's domicile or that in which the tort or "harmful event" is deemed to have occurred. A foreign court seized of a claim for unfair competition in several jurisdictions would find its job very much simpler if it could simply assume that all contracting states to the Paris

---

[8] First Council Directive of December 21, 1988 to approximate the law of Member States relating to trade marks (89/104/EEC) Arts 6(1)(c) and 15(2).

[9] Council Regulation (EC) No.40/94 of December 20, 1993 on the Community trade mark, Arts.12 (proviso) and 64(2).

[10] Case C-404/02 *Nichols plc's TM Application* [2003] O.J. C7/15, [2002] EWHC 1424; [2003] E.T.M.R. 15; [2003] R.P.C. 16, asking, *inter alia*, "[W]hat amounts to 'honest practices in industrial and commercial matters;' in particular, does that expression apply where (i) the defendant is not, in practice, deceiving the public by using his own name or (ii) the defendant is merely causing unintentional confusion thereby".

[11] However, the inclusion of the same Paris Convention wording in the proviso to s.10(6) of the Trade Marks Act 1994 (and its consequent relevance in cases of comparative advertising) was a purely domestic initiative.

[12] Council Regulation (EC) No.44/2001 of December 22, 2000 on Jurisdiction and the Recognition and Enforcement of Judgments in Civil and Commercial Matters.

Convention, TRIPs, or just all EU member states, adopted a similar standard of protection. Rather than undertake a detailed comparative analysis of unfair competition law in a score of different jurisdictions, it is almost inevitable that the parties, the court, or both, will seek a rough and ready common standard to apply to all of them.

B. UNFAIR COMPETITION AND THE PARIS CONVENTION

The Paris Convention: relevant provisions

2–9 The main source of international obligations in the field of unfair competition is the Paris Convention for the Protection of Industrial Property of 1883, as revised most recently at Stockholm in 1967. The United Kingdom is bound by the Stockholm Act.[13] The United Kingdom is also a party to the Agreement on Trade-Related Aspects of Intellectual Property Rights (the TRIPs Agreement), but the substantive law of the latter has only peripheral relevance to passing-off or to wider concepts of unfair competition. The TRIPs Agreement itself, and the extent to which the unfair competition provisions of the Paris Convention are incorporated into it, are discussed in Section D.

The Paris Convention provisions of most relevance to passing off are Art.2, establishing the principle of "national treatment" in relation to the protection of all kinds of industrial property, which is defined to include "the repression of unfair competition"; and Art.10*bis* which contains a nonexhaustive list of contraventions of "honest practices in industrial and commercial matters," against all of which member states are required to provide "effective protection".

Other Paris Convention provisions are relevant to unfair competition in at least some of its aspects, depending to some degree on how broadly one draws one's definition. Provisions at the margin of unfair competition, and not further considered here, include those relating to well-known marks (Art.6*bis*); trade names (Art.8); and customs seizure (Arts 9 and 10). Geographical indications (indications of source and appellations of origin) are included in the listing of "industrial property" so as to be subject to the principle of national treatment, and receive a rather limited degree of protection under Arts 10 and 10*ter*. In addition to the Paris Convention, the United Kingdom is a party to the Madrid Arrangement of 1891 Concerning the Prevention of False or Misleading Indications of Source, but not to the 1958 Lisbon Arrangement for the Protection of Appellations of Origin and their International Registration. In view of the separate existence of these two treaty regimes, and the drafting history of Art.10*bis*(3) itself, it is doubtful if geographical indications are entitled to protection under Art.10*bis* as such.

---

[13] Successive versions of the Paris Convention are called "Acts" and named after the city which hosted the revision conference at which they were adopted.

No direct effect in English law

All these provisions are subject, at least in the United Kingdom, to two **2–10**
fundamental qualifications which virtually deprive them of day-to-day
practical effect. First, English law belongs to the dualist system under which
international treaties have no effect in domestic law except to the extent that
their provisions have been enacted into domestic legislation. The Paris
Convention, like any other treaty, is not self-executing.[14] After each revision
conference, consideration has to be given to whether English law requires
amendment to comply with newly undertaken Convention obligations; or
old ones, reconsidered. In the present context, this has resulted from time to
time in amendments to the Merchandise Marks Acts, but not to the common law of passing-off or injurious falsehood. No litigant in an English
court can rely directly on the Paris Convention as such, whether with respect
to provisions of substantive law such as Art.10*bis*, or the principle of
national treatment under Art.2. The most that can be expected is that the
court should attempt to interpret and apply any relevant English law consistently with the United Kingdom's Convention obligations.

If, as some maintain, the United Kingdom is in breach of Arts 10*bis* and
10*ter* by failing to provide a more comprehensive law of unfair competition,
then the only legal remedy is for another state of the Union to pursue a
claim in international law. The Paris Convention itself has, since the
Stockholm Act, conferred jurisdiction on the International Court of Justice
to determine disputes between member states concerning the interpretation
or application of the Convention: Art.28. The provision has never been
used, despite having been supported vigorously (not least by the United
Kingdom) since at least as early as the 1925 Hague Conference. An
aggrieved private party has no legal standing or remedy.

The beneficiaries of Art.10*bis*

Secondly, and as a matter of general Convention law rather than that of the **2–11**
United Kingdom, no one is entitled to be treated as a *ressortissant* of the
Convention in his own state, so nationals of a given contracting state do not
automatically benefit from the provisions of the Convention in the state of
their nationality. States enter into international conventions primarily to
protect their interests—and those of their nationals—abroad. There are
exceptions, such as conventions on human rights, in which states do contract internationally so as to guarantee certain rights to their own nationals,
but there is no reason to believe that the Paris Convention is among them.
In so far as states wish to protect their own (or foreign) nationals at home,
the normal and appropriate route is by domestic legislation. In the case of
those states for which treaties may have direct effect in domestic law, the law
may (and probably will) confer the same benefits on nationals as on foreign

---

[14] In the specific context of the Paris Convention, see G.H.C. Bodenhausen, *Guide to the Paris Convention* (1968), p.14 and commentary on Art.25.

ressortissants,[15] but that is a matter for the internal law of the relevant member state.

The result may be surprising, but is not seriously in doubt[16]: in so far as Arts 10*bis* and 10*ter* create a uniform minimum standard of protection against acts of unfair competition, each member state is obliged to provide the requisite degree of protection to nationals of *other* member states (and any other foreign *ressortissants*) who may suffer from such acts in its territory, but it is *not* obliged to provide that level of protection, or any protection at all, to its own nationals in respect of the same kind of acts.[17] Of course few states will deliberately withhold from their own nationals benefits which they are obliged to confer on foreigners, but that is a matter of domestic policy and legislation, not international obligation.

The principle of national treatment

2–12   Article 1(1) of the Paris Convention declares that "The countries to which this Convention applies constitute a Union for the protection of industrial property" and Art.1(2) defines the latter by enumeration: "The protection of industrial property has as its object ... the repression of unfair competition". Despite what can be mistaken for mandatory language, Art.1 is partly institutional (in so far as it constitutes the Union) and partly definitional. In itself it does not oblige the member states to legislate for, or otherwise protect, any of the categories of industrial property referred to.

The consequences of the breadth of the definition of "industrial property" begin to be felt at Art.2(1), under which the principle of national treatment is declared:

Nationals of any country of the Union shall, as regards the protection of industrial property, enjoy in all the other countries of the Union the advantages that their respective laws now grant, or may hereafter grant, to nationals; all without prejudice to the rights specifically provided for by this Convention. Consequently, they shall have the same protection as the latter, and the same legal	Les ressortissants de chacun des pays de l'Union jouiront dans tous les autres pays de l'Union, en ce qui concerne la protection de la propriété industrielle, des avantages que les lois respectives accordent actuellement ou accorderont par la suite aux nationaux, le tout sans préjudice des droits spécialement prévus par la présente Convention. En conséquence, ils auront la même protection que ceux-ci et le

---

[15] France is an example, details are given in the citations from Bodenhausen and Ladas, below.

[16] For the general principle, see Bodenhausen, above, commentary on Art.2(1), note (e), at the paragraph bridging pp.30–31; Stephen Ladas, *Patents, Trademarks and Related Rights–National and International Protection* (1975) §158, p.256.

[17] This is express in relation to Art.10*ter* (1): "the countries of the Union undertake to assure to *nationals of the other countries of the Union* appropriate legal remedies ..." (emphasis added). The fact the corresponding wording of Art.10*bis* differs slightly is an accident of drafting history, rather than an deliberate distinction.

remedy against any infringement of their rights, provided that the conditions and formalities imposed upon nationals are complied with.	même recours légal contre toute atteinte portée à leurs droits, sous réserve de l'accomplissement des conditions et formalités imposées aux nationaux.

By paragraph (2) "no requirement as to domicile or establishment in the **2–13** country where protection is claimed may be imposed upon nationals of countries of the Union for the enjoyment of any industrial property rights". Paragraph (3) contains important reservations from the principle of national treatment in respect of judicial and administrative procedure, jurisdiction, and the designation of an address for service or the appointment of an agent. Article 3 assimilates to nationals of countries of the Union nonnationals who have real and effective industrial establishments in a member state, though the distinction is of minimal importance now that so few countries remain outside the Paris Union. Collectively, nationals of the Union and those assimilated to national treatment are referred to as *ressortissants*.

The legal effect of Arts 1 and 2 in the context of unfair competition is this: whatever rights and remedies a country confers on its own nationals in the field of unfair competition must equally be made available, without discrimination or any requirement of reciprocity, to nationals of the other countries of the Union and other *ressortissants*, subject to the reservation of Art.1(3) in respect of matters of jurisdiction and judicial procedure. This obligation of national treatment is quite independent from that of Art.10*bis*: the latter provides for certain minimum standards of protection which all *ressortissants* are entitled to claim, but there is nothing to prevent a particular member of the Union legislating more generously than Art.10*bis* requires (whether in terms of substantive law, or in terms of the rights and remedies made available) and in that case the foreign *ressortissant* cannot be denied the more generous protection of national law.

Articles 10*bis* and 10*ter*

The whole substantive law of unfair competition in the Paris Convention is **2–14** to be found in Art.10*bis*, which, in the text of the current (Stockholm) Act, provides:

1. The countries of the Union are bound to assure to nationals of such countries effective protection against unfair competition.	1. Les pays de l'Union sont tenus d'assurer aux ressortissants de l'Union une protection effective contre la concurrence déloyale.
2. Any act of competition contrary to honest practices in industrial or commercial matters constitutes an act of unfair competition.	2. Constitue un acte de concurrence déloyale tout acte de concurrence contraire aux usages honnêtes en matière industrielle ou commerciale.

3. The following in particular shall be prohibited:	3. Notamment devront être interdits:
1 all acts of such a nature as to create confusion by any means whatever with the establishment, the goods, or the industrial or commercial activities, of a competitor;	1° tous faits quelconques de nature à créer une confusion par n'importe quel moyen avec l'établissement, les produits ou l'activité industrielle ou commerciale d'un concurrent;
2 false allegations in the course of trade of such a nature as to discredit the establishment, the goods, or the industrial or commercial activities, of a competitor;	2° les allégations fausses, dans l'exercice du commerce, de nature à discréditer l'établissement, les produits ou l'activité industrielle ou commerciale d'un concurrent;
3 indications or allegations the use of which in the course of trade is likely to mislead the public as to the nature, the manufacturing process, the characteristics, the suitability for their purpose, or the quantity, of the goods.	3° les indications ou allégations dont l'usage, dans l'exercice du commerce, est susceptible d'induire le public en erreur sur la nature, le mode de fabrication, les caractéristiques, l'aptitude à l'emploi ou la quantité des marchandises.

2–15 Article 10*bis* is given practical effect by Article 10*ter* which reads:

1. The countries of the Union undertake to assure to nationals of the other countries of the Union appropriate legal remedies effectively to repress all the acts referred to in Articles 9, 10, and 10*bis*.	1. Les pays de l'Union s'engagent à assurer aux ressortissants des autres pays de l'Union des recours légaux appropriés pour réprimer efficacement tous les actes visés aux articles 9, 10 et 10*bis*
2. They undertake, further, to provide measures to permit federations and associations representing interested industrialists, producers, or merchants, provided that the existence of such federations and associations is not contrary to the laws of their countries, to take action in the courts or before the administrative authorities, with a view to the repression of the acts referred to in Articles 9, 10, and 10*bis*, in so	2. Ils s'engagent, en outre, à prévoir des mesures pour permettre aux syndicats et associations représentant les industriels, producteurs ou commerçants intéressés et dont l'existence n'est pas contraire aux lois de leurs pays, d'agir en justice ou auprès des autorités administratives, en vue de la répression des actes prévus par les articles 9, 10 et 10*bis* dans la mesure où la loi du pays dans lequel la protection est réclamée

far as the law of the country in which protection is claimed allows such action by federations and associations of that country.	le permet aux syndicats et associations de ce pays.

As the awkward numbering suggests, these two Articles were not to be found in the original Paris Convention of 1883, but were introduced by subsequent amendments. Art.10*bis* is not a sub-division of Art.10, but a separate Article inserted after the latter. Likewise Art.10*ter*, which postdates Art.10*bis*. Article 10 itself, dealing with customs seizure in a variety of situations, is of no more than marginal relevance to unfair competition. For further details of the legislative history of both Articles, see the following Section.

The language of Art.10*bis*: "unfair competition" and "*concurrence déloyale*"

Before attempting to interpret the language of Art.10*bis*, one must first **2–16** decide which language one is going to interpret. Like previous Acts, the Stockholm Act of the Paris Convention exists in a single copy in the French language.[18] Prior to the Lisbon Act of 1958, there was no provision for texts or translations in any language other than French. The Lisbon Act made provision, for the first time, for official translations by the International Bureau[19] into other languages, including English; and the Stockholm Act elevated the status of these translations into "official texts", but with the proviso that in case of differences of opinion of interpretation, the French text was to prevail.[20]

Quite apart from the ultimately subordinate status of the English language text, there are the further problems that the conferences at which Art.10*bis* was originally adopted and subsequently amended used French are their sole working language, that their records and *travaux préparatoires* are published only in French,[21] and that in its crafting style and legislative technique the Paris Convention is no less French than its name. Art.10*bis* may have suffered less than some others from the vagaries of translation, but there is more than a risk of misunderstanding it in any language other than the original. In the present work, the relevant texts from the Convention are given in both French and English, and the commentary follows the English text except to the extent that the French text clarifies or removes difficulties of interpretation.

A term which requires special consideration is "unfair competition" itself. **2–17**

---

[18] Art.29(1)(a).
[19] The International Bureau of what is now the World Intellectual Property Organisation (WIPO) was formerly the *Bureau de L'Union Internationale pour la Protection de la Propriété Industrielle*.
[20] Art.29(1)(b) and (c).
[21] The Stockholm conference was the first to have its records published in English, but no amendments to Art.10*bis* were made or even considered.

This phrase attempts or purports to translate the French term *concurrence déloyale* which has appeared in the authentic text of successive Acts of the Paris Convention since the Brussels Act of 1900. Not only was French then the sole language of the Paris Convention itself, but France was the first country to develop what would now be called a law of unfair competition, and before the end of the nineteenth century *concurrence déloyale* was a well-accepted term of art, well in advance of any corresponding term or concept in English law. True, the phrase "unfair competition" (or something like it) may be found in English writing or decided cases around the turn of the Century; but there is little suggestion that a term of art is in the making, and its more widespread adoption was thwarted by the language as well as the reasoning of *Mogul v McGregor Dow*.[22] After *Mogul*, no one was going to formulate a claim as one for "unfair competition" with any hope of success. In any event, "unfair" would have been an inappropriate translation for the French "*déloyale*", since the latter implied a more stringent ethical content than mere unfairness. An accurate translation would need to have been pitched somewhere in the region of "dishonest", "unethical", or even "fraudulent"; with the proviso that French and English concepts of what was ethical in trade were often very much at odds.

Fortunately it will be seen that in interpreting Art.10*bis*, very little actually turns on the precise turn of phrase used in either French or English: "unfair competition" or "*concurrence déloyale*" is used in the body of Art.10*bis*, but is promptly defined for the purposes of the Article in terms of a more precise and seemingly rather different concept, namely contravention of honest practices in trade. As for the title of Art.10*bis*, it is not even part of the text of the Convention, but a harmless interpolation by the International Bureau which has received the sanction of time and convenience. It is only in the context of national treatment under Article 2 that "unfair competition" probably falls to be understood on its own.

Interpreting Art.10*bis*

2–18 The treatment of Art.10*bis* of the Paris Convention in the present work attempts to follow the scheme of the Vienna Convention on the Law of Treaties.[23] First of all, the "general rule" of Art.31(1) of the latter states that any treaty is to be interpreted in good faith in accordance with the ordinary meaning to be given to the terms of the treaty in their context and in the light of its object and purpose. Paragraphs (2), (3) and (4) go on further to define the contextual material; provide for the taking into account of subsequent agreement as to interpretation or application, subsequent practice establishing the agreement of the parties as to interpretation, and relevant rules of international law; and to provide that a special meaning is to be

---

[22] [1892] A.C. 25, HL, affirming (1889) 23 Q.B. 598, CA.

[23] It is not suggested that the Vienna Convention applies in terms to the Paris Convention or any of its Acts, all of which were adopted before the Vienna Convention came into force on January 27, 1980 (see Art.4, non-retroactivity). However Arts 31 and 32 of the Vienna Convention are widely and conveniently taken as being declaratory of pre-existing international law.

given to a term if it is established that the parties so intended. In the second place, Art.32 of the Vienna Convention provides for recourse to supplementary means of interpretation, and specifically what are compendiously called the *travaux préparatoires*, in order to confirm the meaning resulting from the application of Art.31; or to determine the meaning if Art.31 itself leaves the meaning ambiguous or obscure, or leads to a result which is manifestly absurd or unreasonable.

The remainder of the present section therefore attempts to offer an interpretation of Art.10*bis* in the light of the primary or Art.31 material: principally its text, its context, and its purpose, but with forward references to the next Section to confirm that any interpretation proposed is supported or at least not contradicted by the negotiating history. The following Section deals in much greater detail with the history of Art.10*bis* and the records of the conferences at which successive versions were enacted, and might be thought redundant if the Article could be interpreted without their aid. However the division into materials of primary and secondary relevance is much less clear cut than might be supposed. In particular (and after the passage of a full human lifetime since Art.10*bis* took its present shape in 1925 and 1934) its object, purpose and factual matrix, all of which are Art.31 materials, are only likely be ascertained with any degree of accuracy by reference to the published records (at least partly Art.32 materials), other historical materials, and even to sources which are inadmissible as aids to interpretation in their own right, such as the private records of individual contracting states. A similar comment applies to the language of the treaty, especially to the extent that concepts and usages may have changed over time.

Finally, a commentator cannot simply satisfy himself that a particular interpretation based on Art.31 material is correct, and free from ambiguity, obscurity, absurdity, or unreasonableness. Others may legitimately differ in the interpretation itself, or the confidence with which it is asserted. The Art.32 material still needs to be considered, whether to confirm the correctness of one's first conclusion, or to provide the basis from which it can be questioned.

The purpose(s) of Art.10*bis*

With few qualifications, the purpose of Art.10*bis* of the Paris Convention **2–19** might be thought self-evident: it is the repression of unfair competition in international trade between the contacting states, for the benefit of honest traders in those states, and other such traders given the status of *ressortissants*.

This simple conclusion does require some elaboration; first, as to the intended beneficiaries of Art.10*bis*. In English law, unfair competition tends to be regarded as much as a branch of consumer protection law as anything. However, it can be said with confidence that for most of its history Art.10*bis* was intended to protect competing traders. rather than consumers. Consumer protection simply was not considered a suitable topic for an international convention, and it is only with the Lisbon amendments of 1958 that this proposition may have to be qualified. With this possible exception, it is not helpful to attempt to interpret Art.10*bis* as though it belonged to consumer protection law. It is the nucleus of an international law of unfair competition, not one of unfair trading.

2–20 Secondly, there is the question of whether the repression of unfair competition is to be understood as a goal in itself, or as a means to an end—in the sense that Art.10*bis* is intended to promote or protect economically liberal market values in international trade. This might be put rhetorically in terms of whether an isolated and centrally-directed socialist economy, in which imports were discouraged and all kinds of competition repressed alike, would comply with the spirit as well as the letter of Art.10*bis*. The origin of the 1925 version of Art.10*bis* in the work of the League of Nations strongly suggests that the liberal thesis is the correct one. It is the protection and promotion of fair competition in international trade, rather than the repression of unfair competition *per se*, which is the underlying purpose of the Article, in terms of which it falls to be interpreted. The Covenant of the League of Nations contained at Art.23(e) an obligation on the members of the League to "make provision to secure and maintain ... equitable treatment for the commerce of all Members of the League", and Art.10*bis* in the form adopted at the 1925 Hague Conference was based on a programme initiated by the League pursuant to this Article of the Covenant. Art.10*bis* is therefore, by the narrowest of margins, the product of the immediate post-War effort to re-establish international trade on a sound basis, as opposed to the protectionist reaction of a few years' later.

The structure of Art.10*bis*: general part and specific instances

2–21 The structure of Art.10*bis* in its present form comprises what might be called a "general clause" requiring the contracting states to assure to one another's nationals effective protection against unfair competition; followed by a clause defining unfair competition in terms of acts of competition contrary to honest practices in industrial or commercial matters; followed by three specific instances which are required to be prohibited: broadly speaking, classic passing-off, disparagement of competitors, and various specific kinds of misdescription.

For present purposes, an analysis of Art.10*bis* may be broken down into the following issues:

1. What is meant by "effective protection" and the "repression" of unfair competition?

2. What is meant by "competition," and is Art.10*bis* confined to economically competitive situations?

3. What is meant by "fairness," and its definition in terms of "honest practices in industrial or commercial matters"?

4. Is the defendant's subjective intent of any relevance?

5. Taking the enumerated prohibitions of paragraph (3) as self-

explanatory, then do paragraphs (1) and (2) together have any residual role to play as a "general clause".

Effective protection and the "repression" of unfair competition

According to Art.10*bis*, member states of the Union are obliged to provide **2–22** "effective protection" against unfair competition as defined, whether in the general terms of paragraph (2) or the specific examples of paragraph (3) which are to be "prohibited". Art.10*ter* amplifies this by requiring members to assure "appropriate legal remedies effectively to repress" all acts contrary to Art.10*bis*.

Neither Art.10*bis* nor 10*ter* requires in terms that there should be a civil action for an injunction in respect of all, or any, of the acts addressed by Art.10*bis*. What is required is that there should be "effective protection", "prohibition", or "legal remedies effectively to repress" the act of unfair competition, as the case may be. While a civil action for an injunction is perhaps the most obvious and common means of enforcement, its availability is not the only way in which a member state may comply. Criminal sanctions on their own, if effective, not only satisfy the Convention obligations, but might be thought to correspond rather better to the strong language of prohibition and even repression. The conclusion is confirmed by the legislative history of the Article. *A fortiori*, Art.10*bis* does not require member states to provide a civil action for damages, or for restitution, in cases of breach of Art.10*bis*. The obligation is to prohibit or repress unfair competition effectively, not to provide for compensation if the prohibition is defied.[24]

The *travaux préparatoires* for various conferences have noted that the repression of unfair competition in the contracting states involved various combinations of civil, criminal, and administrative law, and this state of affairs was not intended to be affected.[25] Likewise, it is accepted that Art.10*bis* does not create any obligation to enact a specific statute, or an unfair competition law *eo nomine*, if sufficient protection is provided by the general law.[26]

Essential concepts of Art.10*bis*: "competition"

The first essential concept of Art.10*bis* is competition, which is not further **2–23** defined. In both the French and English texts, the requirement of competition is not just something which is implicit in the name or concept of "unfair competition" or *concurrence déloyale*: it is reiterated in the requirement of paragraph (2) that there be an "act of competition" which can be characterised as unfair, and (at least in the contexts of subparagraphs 1 and 2 of paragraph 3) by the respective definitions of confusion

[24] Bodenhausen, above, p.148; *Actes de la Haye* (1926), p.581.
[25] See Section C below, and especially *Actes de la Haye* (1926), pp.478–480; *Actes de Londres* (1934), pp. 421–422. Bodenhausen, above, p.149.
[26] See Section C below, and specifically *Actes de Washington* (1911), pp.255, 305; *Actes de la Haye* (1926), pp.472, 578. Bodenhausen, above, p.143.

or false allegations in relation to the establishment, goods or activities of a competitor. A straightforward and not unduly literal reading of Art.10*bis* would therefore confine its application to the rights and remedies of competitors *inter se*; and this is implicitly confirmed by the fact that Art.10*ter*(2) finds it necessary to confer rights of action in certain circumstances on a certain kind of non-competitor, namely interested trade associations.

Any extension of the general part of Art.10*bis* or the specific instances to non-competitors would therefore have to be justified, if at all, by recourse to secondary means of interpretation. In fact, it will be found that proposals to broaden the Article by deleting or replacing the words "competitor" and "competition" have been tendered and defeated, so the negotiating history confirms that the narrow interpretation is the correct one. The 1925 version of Art.10*bis* was expressly adopted on the basis that it was confined to acts of commercial competition, and an attempt at the 1958 Lisbon Conference to remove this restriction was defeated.[27] In this respect the Convention obligations under Art.10*bis* are considerably narrower than the modern unfair competition laws of many of the contracting states. There is no Convention obligation to protect a *ressortissant* against, for instance, unjustified disparagement by a party who is not a trade competitor.

2–24   Bodenhausen, whose preferred interpretation of Art.10*bis* tends towards the expansive, would not go much further:

> "What is to be understood by 'competition' *will be determined in each country according to its own concepts*: countries *may* extend the notion of acts of competition to acts which are not competitive in a narrow sense, that is, within the same branch of industry or trade, but which unduly profit from a reputation established in another branch of industry or trade and thereby weaken such reputation."[28]

If it be asked what reason there can be for giving a permissive interpretation to Art.10*bis*, when nothing in the Convention prevents the contracting states from legislating against unfair trade practices in wider or more stringent terms without reference to the presence of competition, then the answer may be that the principle of national treatment under Art.2(1) applies to national laws of unfair competition in their entirety, and not just to so much of the law as implements Art.10*bis*.

"Fairness" and "honest practices"

2–25   Secondly, there is the element of fairness or honesty. What Art.10*bis* prohibits in terms is not dishonest or unfair competition *per se*, but acts of competition "contrary to honest practices in industrial or commercial matters." To paraphrase the nine words of the text into a single epithet is tempting, but is itself an act of interpretation requiring better justification than a preference for simplicity over pleonasm. The intended meaning of

---

[27]   *Actes de la Haye* (1926), pp.475–477; *Actes de Lisbonne* (1963), pp.721–722.
[28]   Bodenhausen, above, p.144 at (d), (emphasis added).

Art.10*bis* is to be derived from the complete formula of paragraph (2), which is at risk of being lost if one notionally replaces it with a single word, whether "unfair" or "dishonest." To attempt to use "unfair" as a paraphrase is doubly inadmissible, because the formula which is abbreviated was actually devised as a definition of what is "unfair" in this context.

The requisite standard of fairness or honesty in competition is defined by reference to "honest practices" in "industrial and commercial matters." One is not simply dealing with some abstract standard of ethical conduct approved by a philosopher or moralist, as might be the case if a word such as "unfair" or "dishonest" stood on its own. Nor, on the other hand, is Art.10*bis* a mandate for enforcing objectively dubious practices which traders connive in for their own advantage. "Honest practices" carries with it three further and interrelated implications. First, there is an inference of continuity and consistency in the word "practices", and the standard of honesty must be a realistic one, since otherwise it would merely represent an aspiration rather than a practice. Something done once, rarely, or never at all, cannot amount to a practice. Secondly, the field of reference is trade or commerce, where standards may be less demanding than, say, in the liberal professions (though it is unclear to what extent different standards in different trades are contemplated). Finally, in defining the relevant standard one is principally concerned with what is actually done ("practised") by the generality of honest traders rather than any words of theory, admonishment or undeserved self-congratulation. It is not uncommon for actual market behaviour to be a degree or two rougher than market participants will willingly admit to. The defining practice is what is honestly done by participants in the market, not what is piously enjoined by outsiders.

As Jacobs A-G said (in the context of the Trade Marks Directive) in *Hölterhoff v Freiesleben*.[29]

"The precise delimitation of 'honest practices' is of course not given in the Trade Marks Directive. By its very nature, such a concept must allow of a certain flexibility. Its detailed contours may vary from time to time and according to circumstances, and will be determined in part by various rules of law which may themselves change, as well as by changing perceptions of what is acceptable, however, there is a large and clear shared core concept of what constitutes honest conduct in trade, which may be applied by the courts without great difficulty and without any excessive danger of diverging interpretations."

This is not to say that Art.10*bis*(2) is entirely free from difficulties of **2–26** interpretation. Once one admits that the standard of honesty is a relative one, then the question arises: relative to what? The reference to "honest practices in industrial or commercial matters" only goes part of the way to providing an answer, since it begs the question of where one looks for what is practised.

[29] Case C-2/00 [2002] E.C.R. I-4187; [2002] All E.R. (EC) 665; [2002] E.T.M.R. 79; [2002] F.S.R. 52.

Bodenhausen suggests:

"Any act of competition will have to be considered unfair if it is contrary to *honest practices in industrial or commercial matters*. This criterion is not limited to honest practices existing in the country where protection against unfair competition is sought. The judicial or administrative authorities of such country will therefore also have to take into account honest practices established in international trade."

Bodenhausen's preference for defining the standard of honest practices in terms of international trade is attractive, but not without its problems. It appeals in so far as it promises to provide a uniform and objective standard, and one which is also entirely appropriate since the Paris Convention is an international instrument concerned with promoting fair competition in international trade. Its main problem is that acts of unfair competition occur or have their effects predominantly at the retail level, which is highly variable and sensitive to local factors, whereas international trade is at the wholesale level or higher. It will therefore often be the case that there is no appropriate point of comparison in international trade against which to compare a practice occurring in a particular national retail market.

2–27   The alternative dismissed by Bodenhausen is certainly no more attractive, although in some cases it may turn out to be the only practical one. What benefit is there to the rest of the World if Indonesia, say, or Nigeria, defines "honest practices" entirely according to locally prevailing standards of what one is allowed to get away with? This would reduce Art.10*bis*(2) if not quite to a nullity, then to little more than a re-enactment of the principle of national treatment already found in Art.2(1): foreign *ressortissants* would have a cause for complaint only if they were defrauded even more shamelessly than locals already defrauded one another. The Convention makes more sense if at least a minimal objective standard of reference can be defined.

There is also something of a counsel of perfection about the final sentence of Bodenhausen's proposal: so far as one can tell, neither national laws of unfair competition, nor courts charged with implementing them, do in general look at what is practised outside their own jurisdiction in defining what is or is not unfair. Of course, if the relevant local standard of honest practices is as high or higher than that prevailing in international trade then there is no breach of Art.10*bis* on this account.

The defendant's state of mind

2–28   The definition of fairness in terms of honest practices raises the further question of whether the defendant's state of mind is ever relevant. It is suggested that the full formulation "contrary to honest practices in industrial or commercial matters" implies otherwise. One is directed to the standard adopted by honest traders in general, and if an individual trader personally falls short of these standards, even if in good faith, then it does not affect the standard of liability. This is implicitly confirmed by the three specific instances of Art.10*bis* (3), none of which has any overt mental element or any reservation for *bona fide* conduct.

The negotiating history confirms, with one proviso, that Art.10*bis* is not confined to acts done with some kind of subjective dishonest intent, be that fraudulent or malicious. At the 1925 Hague Conference, Italy would have proposed a text which was explicitly confined to acts done "*dans le but de détourner la clientèle d'un concurrent*".[30] Even the rather modest element of motive in this is was unacceptable, and as Bodenhausen summarises the outcome:

> "At the Revision Conference in the Hague it was understood that national legislation, in providing for effective repression of the acts referred to, may make a difference between provisions allowing claims for damages and those providing for injunctions against the incriminated acts. Whereas it would be possible not to grant damages with respect to acts committed in good faith, the same would not apply to injunctions."[31]

The accepted position is therefore that the contracting states are free to impose damages for the defined acts of unfair competition only in cases of bad faith, but must always provide an effective (civil or, one assumes, criminal) sanction against repetition of the act in the future, regardless of the state of mind with which it was originally done.

The position is even clearer in respect of the treatment of disparaging **2–29** statements under Art.10*bis* (3)(2). At common law, such statements are actionable as injurious falsehood only if they are made maliciously. It is clear from the circumstances in which the original paragraph was adopted at the 1925 Hague Conference that the text is a compromise between French pressure for a wider provision extending to disparaging statements regardless of truth or falsity,[32] and Anglo-American doubts about including any such provision at all. Art.10*bis* (3)(2) as adopted was expressly intended to be free from any requirement of intention to injure: "*la notion de dénigrement ... n'implique pas une intention injurieuse*"; and Art.10*bis* (3)(2) is framed in absolute terms because it was intended to catch all disparaging statements about a competitor, which were contrary to truth, regardless of how or why they came to be made.

The "general clause" of Art.10*bis*

The final question is whether Art.10*bis* (1) and (2) are together intended to **2–30** have some sort of normative effect over and above the individual instances of conduct specifically prohibited under Art.10*bis*(3).

The definition of unfair competition in terms what is "contrary to honest practices in industrial or commercial matters" is potentially rather wider than the specific instances of Art.10*bis* (3), but it is sufficiently precise to be

---

[30] *Actes de la Haye* (1926), p.350.
[31] Bodenhausen, above, p.148.
[32] *Actes de la Haye* (1926), p.477; see also *Actes de Londres* (1934), p.418, at which a French attempt to delete "false" from Art.10*bis* (3)(2) was defeated.

capable of having legal effect, and it contains nothing which need unduly dismay the common lawyer: the standard of fairness or honesty so defined is pragmatic, realistic, adaptable, consensual and above all ascertainable by reference to what is actually practised in the relevant branch of trade or commerce. If only such a practice were sufficiently localised within the United Kingdom, then one would call it a "custom" (in the true sense of the word) and there would be no dogmatic or practical objections to enforcing it. In so far as there is a degree of circularity in defining honest practices by reference to what is done by honest traders, then the objection is no more fundamental than is implicit in the concept of the "reasonable man", and the dependency provides the court with an opportunity to refuse to apply any practices which may appear to be prevalent in an industry, but dishonest in some extrinsic sense.

Where interpretation of Art.10*bis* (1) and (2) becomes more speculative is in the meaning to ascribe to "honest". All the specific prohibitions of paragraph (3) are examples of dishonesty in the sense of misrepresentation, and the more conservative interpretation of Art.10*bis* is that "honest" in paragraph (2) is to be understood in the same sense, so that the residual effect of paragraphs (1) and (2) is essentially interstitial, dealing with misrepresentations in competition which are not among those listed. There is another much broader interpretation of "honest" in the sense of "ethical" or even "honourable", but although national laws of unfair competition may consciously adopt such a standard, as might other international instruments,[33] it is not compelled by a reading of the Paris Convention itself; and it is contradicted by the circumstances in which substantially the present form of Art.10*bis* (2) was adopted at the 1925 Hague Conference in preference to a French proposal.[34]

2–31 It should also be borne in mind from what is said above that Art.10*bis* only applies to situations of commercial competition in the strict sense; that compliance with the Article need not involve civil actionability or any *lex specialis*; and that the standard of liability is defined not by reference to abstract "unfairness" but in terms of honest commercial practices. It will be seen, for instance, that such issues as trade mark dilution and character merchandising have little or nothing to do with Art.10*bis*, because even if the conduct of the defendant may be thought to be "unfair" or "dishonest" (in the sense of being adverse to the claimant's legitimate interests) it is not competitive in the economic sense.

With these reservations in mind, it is suggested that the "general clause" of Art.10*bis* is indeed intended to have the effect of obliging the contracting states to provide a remedy for "unfair competition," as defined, in situations broader than those envisaged by Art.10*bis*(3), albeit with a considerably wider margin of appreciation than under those paragraphs. This is sup-

---

[33] As in Art.20 of the General Inter-American Convention for Trade Mark and Commercial Protection (Washington, 1929): "Every act or deed contrary to commercial good faith or to the normal and honourable development of industrial or business activities shall be considered as unfair competition..."
[34] Under which Art.10*bis* (2) would have read "[T]ous les actes contraires à la loi, aux usages commerciaux, ou a l'équité".

ported by the history of the Article. In the 1911 Washington Act, Art.10*bis* simply comprised an unparticularised obligation in the form "All contracting states undertake to assure to *ressortissants* of the Union effective protection against unfair competition". The practical inadequacies of this were obvious, but it has never been suggested that it was intended as a mere non-binding *voeu*, and the Convention continues to include legally effective provisions which are quite as imprecise.[35] When Art.10*bis* in the precursor of its present form was adopted at the 1925 Hague Conference the language of paragraph (1) was deliberately strengthened,[36] and the debate on whether or not to include a definition of "unfair competition" at all, and if so in what terms, is hardly consistent with paragraphs (1) and (2) being mere surplussage.

C. THE HISTORY OF ART.10*BIS*

The contribution of the United Kingdom to Art.10*bis*

Art.10*bis* in its present form originally owed its existence, and still owes **2–32** much of its content and coverage, to a series of initiatives by the United Kingdom which have long since passed into oblivion on both sides of the English Channel.[37] It was the United Kingdom which made the original proposal for "effective protection against unfair competition" which became Art.10*bis* of the 1911 Washington Act of the Paris Convention, and this was originally intended merely as a preamble to a second and more detailed paragraph prohibiting, in effect, various enumerated acts of passing off or trade mark infringement. In the period 1919 to 1925 the United Kingdom was also the principal advocate for enhanced international protection against unfair competition, initially in the perhaps surprising context of the Versailles Peace Conference and subsequently through the League of Nations and then the International Industrial Property Union. To describe these efforts now is not merely an academic exercise or a belated attempt at claiming credit where it is due. It is essential to understanding Art.10*bis* in its historical context; and in due course it may go some way to reconciling common lawyers to a rather more friendly view of Art.10*bis* than they are used to holding, while reminding their civil law counterparts that the Article is neither wholly of their own making, nor made in the image of their own laws.

The importance of unfair competition to the United Kingdom in this **2–33** period, and the central importance of the United Kingdom in what follows, are exemplified by the several roles played by a senior British civil servant, Sir Hubert Llewellyn Smith. Sir Hubert was permanent secretary of the

---

[35] For example, Arts 6*sexies* (service marks) and 8 (trade names).
[36] From "*s'engagent*" to "*sont tenus*".
[37] Though an account from a transatlantic perspective may be found in Stephen Ladas, *Patents, Trademarks and Related Rights–National and International Protection* (1975), pp.1678–1683.

Board of Trade between 1907 and 1919, and chief economic adviser to the Government between 1919 and 1927. He was the British delegate to the Economic Committee at the Versailles Peace Conference, and a member (and latterly the Chairman) of the Economic Committee of the League of Nations, for whom he prepared the 1922 report on unfair competition which led to draft articles tabled at the 1925 Hague Conference and subsequently to the rewriting of Art.10*bis* in 1925. That it was he (rather than the Comptroller of the Patent Office) who led the British delegation at the Hague Conference reflects the importance of the fight against unfair competition to the United Kingdom at the time. The official brief to the British delegates at the 1925 Conference identified unfair competition as the single most important item on the agenda, and when the Conference was over the British delegation declared itself well pleased with what it had achieved.[38] After 1925, it must be admitted, the attitude of the United Kingdom to further revisions of Art.10*bis* has tended to be conservative, though not invariably so.

There are several consistent themes to the United Kingdom's proposals for attacking unfair competition between 1911 and 1925, whether the international context be that of Versailles, the League of Nations, or the International Union. Most obviously, there is the use of very detailed legislative language (typically derived from the Merchandise Marks Acts); the mandatory imposition of criminal liability, at least in cases of fraud; a tendency to understand the problem almost entirely as one relating to trade in goods, and in terms analogous to passing-off or common-law trade mark infringement (albeit with extensions for all kinds of geographical indications); and above all in the concentration on specific acts and instances of unfair competition rather than any attempt to frame a more general concept akin to the "general clause" of the German UWG[39] or that of *concurrence déloyale* in French law. In addition to these, and in marked contrast to the over-simplified view of the United Kingdom's position as wilfully backwards or obstructive, the United Kingdom consistently attempted to make the relevant Paris Convention obligations enforceable on the international plane by conferring jurisdiction on the International Court of Justice or its predecessors.

2–34   To understand the United Kingdom's position one must bear in mind both its national commercial interests, and the legal philosophy which it brought to bear in its attempts to protect them. The relevant commercial interests of the United Kingdom in the early twentieth century were predominantly in terms of protecting its international trade in manufactured goods. Since the industrial revolution of the eighteenth century, Britain had regarded itself with some justification as the workshop of the world, and even as early as the Parliamentary Committee on the proposed Trade Marks Bill of 1862 there was widespread complaint that British manufacturers and exporters had no adequate protection when they increasingly came into

---

[38] UK Public Record Office file BT 209/706, letter of September 30, 1925; BT 209/712 Report of December 10, 1925.
[39] The *Gesetz gegen den unlauterer Wettbewerb*, 1909.

competition with American or (especially) German rivals in international markets. The main complaints of British industry were about passing-off and counterfeiting of their goods in all the classic forms (especially in markets where registered trade mark protection was unknown, ineffective, or effectively biased against British interests by a requirement for prior registration at home); misuse of British national or local names and indicia such as *Sheffield* steel or *Manchester* cottons; systematic use of short measure so as to give the false appearance of a price advantage; and (towards the end of the period) various ingenious or outrageous abuses of national registered trade mark systems, such as agents registering the marks of their principals in their own names, or local manufacturers registering as their own trade marks what were in fact national emblems, quality marks, or even hallmarks.

The legal philosophy of the United Kingdom in this period was based on the fact that the first line of defence against unfair competition at home was perceived by the Government as being the Merchandise Marks Acts—rather than the civil actions for passing-off and injurious falsehood—and the Merchandise Marks Acts were criminal statutes. It should not be supposed that the Merchandise Marks Acts were originally thought of (as the Trade Descriptions Acts are today) solely or ever primarily as instruments for consumer protection. Businesses, unlike individual consumers, had the means as well the motive to prosecute offenders; and after a shaky start the Merchandise Marks Acts were quite actively enforced both by individual companies and by trade associations. The original ninteenth century decision to attack domestic cases of unfair competition through the criminal law was probably dictated at least in part by the absence of a system of local courts which could offer reasonably quick, cheap and speedy access to civil justice, but it coincided with (or helped to engender) a belief that nothing short of criminal liability was sufficient to stamp out fraud on the international stage. When one is imposing civil liability for acts of "unfair competition", it is perhaps acceptable for the formulation of the standard of liability to be broad and flexible, and its detailed implementation and progressive development left to the good sense of the courts, especially if (as was quite widely accepted during this period) damages were only to be awarded against fraudulent defendants, with innocent transgressors of commercial standards exposing themselves only to a civil *action en cessation*. In contrast, a law which criminalises something as ill-defined as "unfairness" is bound either to be self-defeating (since no court will enforce it except in the clearest cases) or oppressive. If the British proposals for successive conferences read like the drafts for a criminal statute, then that is precisely what they were intended to be.

The successive texts of Art.10*bis*

In the history of the Paris Convention the degree of interest in unfair **2–35** competition follows a Gaussian (or bell-shaped) curve. Unfair competition was prominent and even dominant on the agenda for the 1925 (Hague) and 1934 (London) conferences, was a topic of relatively minor importance in the conferences immediately on either side of this period,[40] and received no consideration at all at the early and late extremes.[41]

The original Paris Convention, as adopted in 1883,[42] contained no provisions expressly dealing with unfair competition, though the Preamble[43] referred to the desire of the contracting states to guarantee *"la loyauté des transactions commerciales"* and Art.8 required (and still requires) trade names to be protected without any requirement for deposit or registration. Efforts were made at revision conferences between 1883 and 1900 to incorporate a general prohibition on acts of unfair competition, analogous to the contemporary French law of *concurrence déloyale*, but these lacked general support and came to nothing.

2–36   The Brussels Conferences in 1897 and 1900 first applied the principle of national treatment to laws of unfair competition by adopting a new Art.10*bis* on the proposal of the French delegation, without opposition and almost without debate[44]:

The *ressortissants* of the Convention (Articles 2 and 3) shall enjoy in all countries of the Union the protection afforded to nationals against unfair competition.	Les ressortissants de la Convention (art. 2 et 3), jouirent, dans tous les États de l'Union, de la protection accordée aux nationaux contre la concurrence déloyale.

The effect of this was to prohibit discrimination in the application of national unfair competition laws, but it did not require any particular level or kind of protection. A country of the Union could comply with Art.10*bis* by having no law of unfair competition of any kind.

At the Washington Conference in 1911, "the repression of unfair competition" (*"la répression de la concurrence déloyale"*) was added to the list of categories of industrial property in Art.2, on the proposal of the International Bureau, so as automatically to be made subject to the general principle of national treatment along with patents, trade marks, designs and the other enumerated industrial property rights. This more elegant solution to the original omission of unfair competition from the scheme of the 1883 Convention rendered the original Art.10*bis* of 1900 redundant, and the International Bureau had proposed simply to delete it, but a new Art.10*bis* was proposed by the United Kingdom. The original United Kingdom proposal had two paragraphs. The first corresponded quite closely to that

---

[40] Brussels in 1900, Washington in 1911 and Lisbon in 1958.

[41] Paris in 1883 and Stockholm in 1967.

[42] The United Kingdom was not one of the original parties, but acceded the following year.

[43] The original Preamble was suppressed from the adoption of the 1911 (Washington) Act onwards and is no longer part of the Convention.

[44] *Actes de Bruxelles* (1901), pp.164 (French proposition), 187 and 310 (*procès-verbaux*), 382 (*procès-verbaux* at resumed conference in 1900), 383 (vote). For a formal declaration by the United Kingdom delegate see above, para.2–05.

actually adopted.[45] A second paragraph[46] would have given a non-exhaustive (and distinctly limited) definition of unfair competition in terms of classic cases of passing off of goods, with special reference to indicia unregistered or unregistrable as trade marks in the strict sense. Several (unspecified) delegations objected to the second paragraph on the ground that by enumerating certain cases of unfair competition, there was a risk of implicitly excluding others from the scope of the Article, and so doing more harm than good,[47] and Austria objected to the inclusion of any special cases because its proposed law was still under discussion. As adopted by the Conference the new Art.10*bis* read[48]:

All contracting states undertake to assure to *ressortissants* of the Union effective protection against unfair competition.	Tous les pays contractants s'engagent à assurer aux ressortissants de l'Union, une protection effective contre la concurrence déloyale.

Art.10*bis* was next amended at the Hague Conference in 1925 to adopt **2–37** what is recognisably its present structure, with a general clause and specific instances of prohibited conduct, though at this stage the latter were still exclusively concerned with goods[49]:

The countries of the Union are bound to assure to nationals of such countries effective protection against unfair competition.	Les pays contractants sont tenus d'assurer aux ressortissants de l'Union une protection effective contre la concurrence déloyale.
Any act of competition contrary to honest practices in industrial or commercial matters constitutes an act of unfair competition.	Constitue un acte de concurrence déloyale toute acte de concurrence contraire aux usages honnêtes en matière industrielle ou commerciale.
The following in particular shall be prohibited.	Notamment devront être interdits:
1 all acts of such a nature as to create confusion by any means	1 tous faits quelconques de nature à créer une confusion par

---

[45] It would have read "Les sujets ou citoyens des pays de l'Union jouiront, dans chacun de ces pays, d'une protection effective contre la concurrence déloyale".

[46] "L'expression 'concurrence déloyale' s'etendra a l'apposition sur les produits, de chiffres, de mots ou de marques, employes soit isolement, soit en forme d'arrangements ou de combinaisons, contendant ou non une marque de fabrique, et pouvant etre consideres commes calcules pour porter le public a croire que les produits ou marchandises proviennent d'une personne autre que celle dont ils sont veritablement les produits ou les marchandises".

[47] *Actes de Washington* (1911), pp.305, 310. This was to be a consistent theme of argument in future conferences. One wonders what extent it was genuine, and to what extent a convenient and politically acceptable excuse for maintaining the *status quo*.

[48] *Actes de Washington* (1911), pp.53 (proposal of International Bureau), 105 (United Kingdom proposal), 254 (*procès-verbaux* and vote), 305 (report of committee), 310 (annex).

[49] For details of the Conference, see para.2–48, below.

whatever with the goods of a competitor;	n'importe quel moyen avec les produits d'un concurrent;
2 false allegations, in the course of trade, of such a nature as to discredit the goods of a competitor.	2 les allégations fausse, dans l'exercice du commerce, de nature à discréditer les produits d'un concurrent.

At the same time, a new Art.10*ter* was added to the Convention, of which paragraph (1) read[50]:

The countries of the Union undertake to assure to nationals of the other countries of the Union appropriate legal remedies effectively to repress all the acts referred to in Articles 9, 10 and 10*bis*.	Les pays contractants s'engagent à assurer aux ressortissants des autres pays de l'Union des recors légaux appropriés pour réprimer efficacement tous les actes visés aux articles 9, 10 et 10*bis*.

2–38   The London conference in 1934 widened the terms of the two numbered sub-paragraphs of Art.10*bis*(3) so as to read, in place of "*les produits d'un concurrent*" ("the goods of a competitor"):

... the establishment, the goods, or the industrial or commercial activities, of a competitor ...	... l'établissement, les produits ou l'activité industrielle ou commerciale d'un concurrent ...

Article 10*ter* was slightly amended at the same time to remove an uncertainty from the categories of commercial associations which could instigate legal proceedings to enforce the substantive obligations of Art.10*bis*.

2–39   Finally, the Lisbon conference in 1958 adopted a third and final sub-paragraph to Art.10*bis*, adding to the list of enumerated prohibited acts:

3 Indications or allegations the use of which, in the course of trade, is liable to mislead the public as to the nature, the manufacturing process, the characteristics, the suitability for their purpose, or the quantity, of the goods.	3 Les indications ou allégations dont l'usage, dans l'exercice du commerce, est susceptible d'induire le public en erreur sur la nature, le mode de fabrication, les caractéristiques, l'aptitude a l'emploi ou la quantité des marchandises.

Article 10*bis* was not further amended at the 1967 Stockholm conference, which was the last occasion on which the Paris Convention has been revised.

---

[50] The second paragraph of the 1925 version of Art.10*ter* is omitted. It extended the principle of national treatment to the *locus standi* of trade associations so as to allow foreign associations recourse to the courts on the same basis as local ones.

The various changes made (and rejected) at the 1925, 1934 and 1958 Conferences are more fully described in the paragraphs which follow.

Prelude to 1925: the Treaty of Versailles

From 1911 to 1925, the only provisions of the Paris Convention relevant to **2–40** unfair competition were those of national treatment, and the entirely unparticularised obligation under Art.10*bis* of the Washington Act for "effective protection against unfair competition". The inadequacy of the existing Paris regime had become apparent in every respect even before the First World War, and became more apparent still during and after the hostilities. Although a comprehensive solution to the problem obviously required coordinated and voluntary international action over many years, the peace settlement with Germany and its allies did provide one opportunity for imposing what were thought to be suitable international obligations on the former enemies. The Versailles Treaty[51] with Germany therefore included (as Ch III of Pt X) two Articles collectively entitled "Unfair Competition".

ARTICLE 274

Germany undertakes to adopt all the necessary legislative and administrative measures to protect goods the produce or manufacture of any one of the Allied and Associated Powers from all forms of unfair competition in commercial transactions.

Germany undertakes to prohibit and repress by seizure and by other appropriate remedies the importation, exportation, manufacture, distribution, sale or offering for sale in its territory of all goods bearing upon themselves or their usual get-up or wrappings any marks, names, devices, or description whatsoever which are calculated to convey directly or indirectly a false indication of the origin, type, nature, or special characteristics of such goods.

ARTICLE 275

Germany undertakes on condition that reciprocity is accorded in these matters to respect any law, or any administrative or judicial decision given in conformity with such law, in force in any Allied or Associated State and duly communicated to her by the proper authorities, defining or regulating the right to any regional appellation in respect of wine or spirits produced in the State to which the region belongs, or the conditions under which the use of any such appellation may be permitted; and the importation, exportation, manufacture, distribution, sale or offering for sale of products or articles bearing regional appellations inconsistent with such law or order shall be prohibited by the German Government and repressed by the measures prescribed in the preceding Article.

---

[51] Treaty of Versailles (June 28, 1919).

Corresponding articles were included in the respective Treaties of Peace with Germany's allies: Austria,[52] Hungary,[53] Bulgaria,[54] and Turkey.[55]

2–41   The drafting history of what became Arts 274 and 275 may be traced in the minutes of the Economic Committee and its sub-committees at the Versailles Peace Conference.[56] The predecessor of Art.274 was in fact originally framed in the context of a proposal for a wide-ranging commercial treaty, which was intended to provide a model for all the new states created under the Versailles settlement, and not only those which had voluntarily aligned themselves with Germany in the war.[57] At the first meeting of the relevant principal sub-committee Britain[58] tabled two relevant proposals: Project A was for the insertion of eight Articles into the treaties of peace with Germany and its allies. Of these, Art.VI addressed unfair competition. Project C was for draft commercial convention of 11 Articles which would govern commercial relations with and between the new states created from the break-up of the pre-war European empires. Article 8 of this addressed unfair competition in very similar terms to that proposed in Project A[59]:

Project A, Article VI (Germany)

Le Gouvernement allemand s'engage à décourager toutes formes de concurrence déloyale, telles que l'emploi dans le commerce de fausses marques, noms, ou descriptions, ou de marques donnant une fausse indication, directement ou indirectement, sur l'origine ou la nature d'une marchandise quelconque, et il s'oblige à prendre les mesures législatives et administratives nécessaires pour sauvegarder les marchandises, produits naturels ou fabriqués des territoires de l'un quelconque des états Alliés ou Associés, contre une concurrence déloyale de cette nature a l'intérieur de l'Allemagne.

[52] Treaty of Saint-Germain (September 10, 1919), Arts 226 and 227.
[53] Treaty of Trianon (June 4, 1920), Art.210(1) and (2).
[54] Treaty of Neuilly (November 27, 1919), Arts 154 and 155. Article 166 obliged Bulgaria to accede to the Washington Act of the Paris Convention.
[55] Treaty of Sevres (August 10, 1920), Arts 266 and 267. The Treaty of Sevres never came into effect, and was superceded by the Treaty of Lausanne (July 24, 1923). The Treaty of Lausanne itself lacked any corresponding Articles, but the Commercial Convention (also of July 24, 1923) which was concluded with the Treaty of Lausanne contained at Arts 12 and 13 provisions which generally corresponded to Arts 274 and 25 of the Versailles Treaty, except that Art.12 (as well as Art.13) was subject to reciprocity, and Art.13 extended to regional appellations in respect of all kinds of "products which derive their special qualities from the soil or the climate" and not just to wines and spirits. Article 14 of the Commercial Convention obliged Turkey to accede to the Washington Act of the Paris Convention.
[56] *Conférence de la Paix* 1919–1920–Recueil des Actes de la Conférence–Partie IV–Commissions de la Conférence–B–Questions Generales–VII–Commission Economique (Paris, 1933). Hereafter "*Actes de Versailles*" vols 1 (main Committee) and 2 (sub-committees).
[57] This proposal made no progress, though there is a late echo in the Commercial Convention with Turkey, which formed part of the 1923 Lausanne peace settlement.
[58] March 12, 1919, *Actes de Versailles* vol. 2, pp.369–370 (Minutes), 371–372 (text of Project A), 373–375 (text of Project B).
[59] The proposals were tabled in English, but only French translations are given in the *Actes*.

Project C, Article 8 (new states)

Les États auxquels s'applique cette Convention conviennent de repousser toute forme de concurrence déloyale, tels que l'usage dans le commerce de fausses marques, fausses dénominations, ou fausses signalements, ou de marques donnant une fausse indication, directe ou indirecte, sur l'origine ou la nature des marchandises, et ils s'engagent à prendre les mesures législatives et administratives nécessaires pour protéger les marchandises, produits ou manufacturées dans les territoires d'un des Etats auxquels s'applique cette Convention contre toute concurrence déloyale a l'intérieur de leur territoire.

These proposals were delegated to a further sub-committee which held eight **2–42** sessions.[60] So far as the treaty with Germany was concerned, Britain reintroduced the proposals of Art.VI of Project A, to which was added an appendix foreshadowing Art.275 as adopted. France proposed a draft Article directed solely to the protection of *appellations d'origine*. After the usual discussions, a joint Anglo-French proposal was adopted for inclusion in the peace treaty with Germany in terms closely foreshadowing Arts 274 and 275. A proposal for corresponding Articles[61] in the proposed commercial convention for the new states was adopted in the sub-committee, but proceeded no further. At this stage, the obligations of what became Art.275 were framed in absolute terms, but when the Plenary Economic Committee adopted the Anglo-French proposal it was subject to a condition of reciprocity being inserted, on the insistence of the American delegation. Article 274 remained without any such condition.

Before dismissing the importance of these two Articles to the development of the Paris Convention, some potential misconceptions should be anticipated and avoided. First, though Germany was a signatory to the Washington Act of the Paris Convention and already had its own wide-ranging unfair competition law in the form of the *Gesetz gegen den unlauterer Wettbewerb* 1909 (the UWG), the Allies obviously felt that in its practical application this law was inadequate to protect non-German interests fairly. The main Allied concern may well have been the protection of certain, especially French, geographical indications (bearing in mind that Germany was not a party to the Madrid Arrangement) but that was certainly not all: "*Les abus de la législation allemande en ce qui touche les marques et les appellations d'origine sont supprimés par les deux articles relatifs aux méthodes déloyales de concurrence*".[62] Secondly, although the perceived need for provisions such as these may have been exacerbated by the War, they were in no way concerned with providing remedies for the

---

[60] The Third sub-Committee (*Methodes Déloyales de Concurrence*), *Actes de Versailles* vol. 2, pp.495–496 (summary of work), 497–500 (minutes of first meeting, UK and French proposals), 501–518 (subsequent proceedings).

[61] *Actes de Versailles* vol. 2, p.515 (Third sub-Committee, minutes of meeting of April 11, 1919). The draft Article corresponding to Art.274 was in less peremptory terms, and subject to reciprocity, but otherwise similar to that proposed for Germany. That corresponding to Art.275 amounted to no more than a declaration of intent with a view to a future Convention dealing generally with regional *appellations* for all products deriving their character from soil or climate.

[62] *Actes de Versailles* vol.1, p.231.

numerous acts of unfair competition which must have taken place during wartime conditions. On the contrary, the European parties to the peace settlement agreed a complete amnesty for infringements of industrial property which had occurred on either side during the hostilities.[63] Articles 274 and 275 looked forwards, not backwards.

Finally, although Germany had no say in the terms of Arts 274 and 275, the first of these especially was by no means simply an example of the Allies exercising the prerogatives of victory. More stringent proposals (such as obliging Germany to accede to the Madrid Arrangement, or making Art.275 independent of reciprocity) had been contemplated and rejected. As for Art.274, it was the model used by the League of Nations when it came to strengthening Art.10*bis* of the Paris Convention, and in due course it provided a stepping stone to the proposals considered (and to some extent adopted) at the 1925 Hague Conference. The imposition of Art.274 on Germany was undoubtedly one-sided, as were the obligations it created in international law, but the standard of commercial morality it imposed was hardly unduly onerous. It could even be argued that what was required under Art.274 went no further than the existing terms of the UWG. On this basis, all that Art.274 added was the formal and explicit international engagement of Germany.

The League of Nations: 1921–1925

2–43 After the Treaties of Peace concluding the First World War, international efforts against unfair competition initially proceeded under the sponsorship of the League of Nations, rather than the International Union. This was again on the initiative of the United Kingdom, but the original reason for proceeding by way of the League is obscure. It may have been that the League was in permanent session, whereas the International Union was formally confined to acting through periodic revision conferences, with the timing of the first post-War conference (at the Hague) being both uncertain and unacceptably distant. The relevant Committee of the League was also smaller, and more amenable than the full Assembly of the International Union. A further reason may have been that from the very beginning these League proposals included mandatory provisions for criminal enforcement, in some cases at the suit of legal persons who would have had no *locus standi* under existing domestic laws, and the International Bureau regarded this as an intrusion into an area traditionally reserved to the individual member states. In due course the consideration which prevailed was that the United States and (until the end of this period) Germany were members of the International Union, but not of the League.[64]

---

[63] Article 309 of the Versailles Treaty. This expressly did not apply as between the United States and Germany.

[64] From December 1921, the exercise was carried forward by the League in cooperation with the International Bureau and with a view to amending the Paris Convention at the Conference originally expected to take place at the Hague in 1922 or 1923. However the International Bureau did not play a central role until shortly before the Hague Conference actually took place in 1925, and the possibility of a freestanding convention remained as an option if that had failed.

The Covenant of the League of Nations (which constituted Pt I of the Versailles Treaty of 1919) contained at Art.23(e) an obligation on the members of the League to "make provision to secure and maintain ... equitable treatment for the commerce of all Members of the League". Basing itself on this provision, one of the first official acts of the Economic Section of the Provisional Economic and Financial Committee of the League was to identify unfair competition in international trade on a shortlist of priorities, and to circulate to the League's member states a questionnaire enquiring about the existing state of their laws with regard to import and export restrictions, monopolies, and unfair competition.[65] On the basis of replies received (and with the comments of Dr Röthlisberger of the International Bureau) the Economic Committee produced a "Report on Unfair Competition, Particularly in Relation to False Marks and Indications" with recommendations for "Rough Heads of Articles of Convention on Unfair Competition".[66] The Economic Committee also confirmed its opinion that the obligation to secure equitable treatment for commerce under Art.23(e) included "an obligation to suppress all forms of fraudulent trade competition by which other members of the League may be prejudiced".[67]

The Report itself[68] began by reciting the Committee's mandate and **2–44** describing the existing international regimes, including those under Arts 274 and 275 of the Versailles Treaty.[69] Of Art.10*bis* of the Paris Convention (in the 1911 Washington Act) it was said that

"[A]lthough it marks a considerable advance in principle, it has not hitherto produced any practical results ... partly because of the extremely vague and general character of the undertaking, the absence of any international jurisdiction to enforce it, and the entire lack of any detailed indications of the precise character of the frauds at which it is aimed and of the legal and administrative remedies which are necessary for their suppression."

Recommendations were made for members of the League to adhere to the Paris Convention (if they were not already members), and for strengthening Art.10*bis* of the latter in six respects: by affording "really effective remedies to persons aggrieved by acts of unfair competition" including official and trade representatives; providing a comprehensive definition of the "unfair"

---

[65] [1921] *League of Nations Official Journal*, p.55 (Report of First Session); p.58 (terms of questionnaire and covering letter).

[66] See below. For adoption of the Report by the Council of the League of Nations, see [1922] *League of Nations Official Journal*, p.618 at (5).

[67] [1922] *League of Nations Official Journal*, pp.624–625, at III (5).

[68] [1922] *League of Nations Official Journal*, pp.625–632. Ladas identifies the author of the Report as Sir Hubert Llewellyn Smith, which is confirmed at [1922] *Propriété Industrielle*, p.98 and [1923] *Propriété Industrielle*, p.191.

[69] The Report's treatment of false indications of origin, especially in relation to the Madrid Arrangement, is omitted here.

practices constituting unfair trade competition[70]; prohibiting the registration of trade marks embodying public emblems and the like; dealing with abusive registration of foreign-owned trade marks and enabling improperly registered marks to be removed from the register; and enabling differences of interpretation or performance of the Convention between member states to be resolved by an international tribunal.

These recommendations were elaborated in the three Rough Heads of Articles of Convention on Unfair Competition which were annexed, with a commentary. Draft Art.1 provided:

"The Contracting States undertake to make effective provision to ensure that persons (including companies) aggrieved by the manufacture, sale, or offering for sale, within the territories of the respective States, or by the importation into or exportation from those territories of goods improperly bearing a trade mark or trade name or bearing a false or misleading indication of geographical or commercial origin, or any figures, words or marks, or arrangement or combination thereof, whether including a trade mark or not, as are calculated to lead persons to believe that the goods are the manufacture or merchandise of some person other than the person whose manufacture or merchandise they really are, shall have an adequate remedy at law against such abuses, and that proceedings may be taken in respect thereof by the duly authorised official or trade representative of the person aggrieved.

The provisions of this article shall extend to written misdescriptions even if not physically attached to the goods."

The second draft Article dealt with the two kinds of trade mark abuses, and the third proposed submission to the Court of International Justice or to arbitration. The Report concluded by recommending that members of the League should strongly support appropriate amendments to the Paris Convention at the proposed Hague Conference.

2–45   Further progress initially depended on members of the League (and the International Bureau[71]) replying to the draft proposals, and when these were more or less complete Japan submitted a request for a meeting of experts in advance of the Hague Conference. This was approved, and revised draft Articles, together with four specific questions, were prepared for the experts' meeting.[72] The revised draft of Art.1 now read:

---

[70] "The definition should embrace the improper use of trade-marks and names and false and misleading indications of geographical or commercial origin, or of the manufacturer of or dealer in the goods. It should also include written misdescriptions even if not physically attached to the goods".

[71] The International Bureau proposed a draft Article on much more expansive lines than the League favoured, prohibiting unfair competition both by way of a general clause ("... *une protection effective contre les actes généralement désignés sous le nom d'actes de concurrence déloyale ...*") and including four specific prohibitions against passing-off, abusive advertising and publicity, denigration, and *débauchage* (or "labour piracy"); but leaving all questions of remedies and enforcement to national law. This draft Article quite closely corresponded to contemporary proposals by the French Group of the AIPPI. See *Actes de la Haye* (1926), p.96.

[72] [1923] *League of Nations Official Journal*, pp.1440; 1443–1444.

"The Contracting States undertake to ensure on their territory an adequate remedy at law to all persons or companies aggrieved by the manufacture, sale, offering for sale, within the territories of the respective States, or by the importation or exportation of goods bearing trade-marks or trade-names to which they have no right, or bearing marks, names, inscriptions or any kind of signs (or combinations of such elements) improperly used, and giving directly or indirectly false indications of the geographical or commercial origin of the said goods or in regard to the identity of the producer or seller, and also to ensure that proceedings may be taken in respect of such abuses by or at the instance of the duly authorised official or trade representative of the person aggrieved. The measures provided in the present article shall extend equally to inaccurate descriptions of the kind referred to therein, even when not physically attached to the goods."

The four specific questions for the experts concerned: better international protection for regional appellations for products deriving their characteristics from soil or climate; the possibility of allowing criminal proceedings to be taken by a representative of a contracting state, in another state, in the general interests of his state's commerce[73]; the possibility of drawing up an illustrative but non-exhaustive list of acts of unfair competition as an annex to the Paris Convention; and the desirability of including a recommendation for states to provide effective remedies against commercial libel.

The meeting of experts took place in Geneva in May 1924, with 22 **2–46** member states of the League sending representatives, and with the Director of the International Bureau also attending as an observer.[74] The terms of reference of the meeting made it clear that it was advisory only: the experts were encouraged to give their personal opinions and had no authority to bind their respective governments. Collectively, the meeting approved the general principles of the previous draft Articles (except for proposed Art.3, conferring international jurisdiction, which they unanimously considered to be outside their remit). Their Report to the Economic Committee of the League recommended separate treatment of trade mark infringement and other acts of unfair competition, so that instead of draft Art.1 there would be two Articles A and B, with the latter being intended to supplement the ineffective and imprecise provisions of the current Art.10*bis*:

"A. The Contracting countries undertake to assure to the nationals of the other Contracting countries legal redress—which shall include penal remedies—in the case of any fraudulent use of the marks of such nationals.

B. 1. The Contracting States undertake to assure to the nationals of other Contracting States in their respective territories effective protection against unfair competition.

[73] Such action for the benefit of specific victims of unfair competition already being contemplated by draft Art.1.
[74] [1924] *League of Nations Official Journal*, pp.946–947; 950–953 (the Experts' Report); [1925] *Propriété Industrielle* pp.99–103 (also listing the individual participants).

More especially, they agree to adopt suitable civil measures and, in cases of fraud, suitable penal measures in regard to the use in commerce of trade designations (names, styles of firms, headings of printed matter and other signs of all kinds, *e.g.* emblems, get-up etc.) intended to distinguish the products or goods of a producer, manufacturer, or merchant, and also in regard to the use of descriptions or pictorial representations, or a combination of the two, or any other indication relating to the origin of the products or the goods, when such use is obviously of a nature to create either confusion with the goods of another person, physical or judicial, or an error as to the real origin of the goods.

Proceedings may be taken by any person or company aggrieved and, in the case of an action for an injunction or of criminal prosecution, by any association or person representing the special industry thus prejudiced.[75]

2. The provisions of the foregoing paragraph shall also apply to colourable initiations of the above-mentioned *designations* or *descriptions* when such imitations, although not in all respects exact copies of the original, are likely to cause confusion or mistakes.

3. The provisions of Article 9 of the [Paris] Convention shall apply to any product or to any goods which directly or indirectly bear a false indication as to the origin of the products or goods, or as to the identity of the producer, manufacturer or merchant."[76]

Other Articles (C and D) dealt with abuses of the registered trade mark system. So far as the four specific questions were concerned, majorities considered it desirable and feasible to draw up an illustrative list of practices to be included under the head of unfair competition, in which commercial libel should be included, but that it was not possible to produce such a list instantly. An international regime for better protecting geographical appellations was regarded as premature, and there was next to no support for the kind of criminal proceedings contemplated by the second of the four questions.

2–47 The final chapter in the involvement of the League of Nations followed the Geneva meeting of the experts. The Economic Committee formulated a series of amendments to the Paris Convention to be tabled by a suitable member state at the forthcoming Hague Conference (the League as such having no official standing) and, it was to be hoped, supported by the other members of the League.[77] The proposals for the new Art.10*bis* corresponded precisely to Art.B paragraphs (1) and (2) of the draft produced at the Geneva Expert's meeting.[78] In addition, a declaration would have been inserted in the final Protocol in the following terms:

---

[75] This sub-paragraph was adopted by a majority, with minorities either preferring a slightly different text, or considering that the whole issue should be left to national law.

[76] This paragraph was also adopted on a majority vote.

[77] [1924] *League of Nations Official Journal*, pp.1472–1474 (Economic Committee), 1479–1484 (proposed amendments); [1925] *Propriété Industrielle*, pp.56–57.

[78] Article B(3) was now to be included in Art.10 of the Paris Convention. The draft provisions on abuse of the registered trade mark system were also proposed for inclusion in the appropriate places.

"In order to avoid doubts it is hereby declared that the term 'unfair competition' mentioned in Articles 2 and 10*bis* of the Convention signed this day is not to be understood as being limited to the particular abuses specified in the second paragraph of Article 10*bis*, but as including all other methods of fraudulent misdescriptions of goods, as, for example, false statements as to material or mode of manufacture, false claims to awards or certificates in respect of goods, in so far as such practices are prejudicial to international commerce."

Although not included in the formal amendments to the Paris Convention, the Committee also supported the earlier proposal for an international institution to adjudicate disputes under the Convention.

The various proposals of the League of Nations were duly included or noted in the *traveaux preparatoires* for the 1925 Hague Conference.[79] It will be seen that they were influential to the drafting of the revised Art.10*bis* proposed by the International Bureau in the Programme, and that the United Kingdom simply adopted the League proposals as its own. After discussion of the new Art.10*bis* was complete, the Conference recorded its appreciation of the League's work.[80]

The 1925 Hague Conference: the Programme and national proposals

The International Bureau's Programme for the 1925 Hague Conference[81]   **2–48** mentioned the efforts of previous conferences to legislate against unfair competition, and evidence for the post-War consensus that the Washington text was completely inadequate. The Programme therefore proposed an almost entirely new Art.10*bis*, drafted so as to give effect to four principles: first, not to disturb the existing structure of the Convention so that, for instance, provisions specifically relating to trade marks or indications of provenance were dealt with in their respective sections rather than as part of a general unfair competition clause; secondly, to attempt to formulate a general definition of unfair competition (though none could ever be complete) followed by a non-exhaustive list of examples; thirdly, to list the typical abuses against which the contracting states were to be required to take appropriate measures; and finally, to establish a uniform standard for the availability of legal proceedings. It will be seen that the first principle was met, though not without opposition; that the second and third also prevailed, though in much more limited form (even today) than the Bureau would have preferred; but that the fourth has made next to no progress.[82]

In detail, the Programme recommended two minor drafting amendments

---

[79] [1925] *Propriété Industrielle*, pp.166–169 (general preview), *ibid.* pp.242–243 (specific to unfair competition). *Actes de la Haye* (1926), pp.97 (the six recommendations of the Economic Committee from 1922), 97–100 (1922 draft Articles, 1924 Expert's meeting, proposed declaration on Art.10*bis*, Council approval of Economic Committee proposals), 253 (background to the Programme of the International Bureau).

[80] *Actes de la Haye* (1926), p.480.

[81] *Actes de la Haye* (1926), Point IX, pp.252–255.

[82] The Programme also raised, but did not pursue, the question of protection for "news of the day", which is outside the scope of the present work.

to the existing Art.10*bis*[83] and the addition of three substantial new paragraphs to it. The new Art.10*bis* would have read[84]:

1. Les pays contractants sont tenus d'assurer aux ressortissants des autres pays contractants une protection effective contre la concurrence déloyale.

2. Constitue un acte de concurrence déloyale tout acte contraire aux usages honnêtes en matière industrielle ou commerciale, par exemple l'apposition sur des produits, marchandises, emballages, papiers d'affaires ou documents commerciaux, de mentions trompeuses de récompenses industrielles (médailles, diplômes, distinctions honorifiques, prix, etc.); les fausses déclarations relatives a la matière première ou a la mode de fabrication des produits; la réclame fausse; le fait de discréditer injustement les produits ou marchandises d'un concurrent, etc.

3. Les pays contractant conviennent, en particulier, de prévoir des mesures appropriées d'ordre civil et, en cas de pratiques frauduleuses, d'ordre pénal, en ce qui concerne l'usage industriel ou commercial, manifestement de nature a créer soit une confusion avec les produits ou marchandises d'autrui, soit une erreur quant a l'origine véritable de ces produits ou marchandises:

   (a) de marques de fabrique ou de commerce;
   (b) emblèmes, armoires, signes ou poinçons officiels de contrôle et de garantie;
   (c) de désignations commerciales servant a distinguer les produits ou marchandises d'un producteur, fabricant, ou commerçant, telles que noms, firmes, titres d'imprimés et autres signes de tout genre comme enseignes, conditionnement, etc.;
   (d) de descriptions ou représentations figuratives ou de leurs combinaisons;
   (e) de toute autre désignation se rapportant a l'origine du produit ou de la marchandise.

4. Toute personne physique ou morale léssée, ainsi que, dans le cas d'actions en cessation du trouble ou actions pénales, les syndicats et associations intéressés régulièrement constitués dans leur pays d'origine, auront le droit d'agir ou d'intervenir en justice à raison de tous les actes de concurrence déloyale.

Draft Art.10*bis* of the Programme may thus be divided into four parts. First, there is the single paragraph carried over from the 1911 Washington version by which the contracting states undertake to provide effective protection against *concurrence déloyale*, but strengthened slightly by the stronger language of "*sont tenus*" and clarified so as not to create any

---

[83] Changing "*s'engagent*" to "*sont tenus*" and "*de Union*" to "*des autres pays contractants*".
[84] The paragraph numbers 1 to 4 are not part of the text, but are inserted for convenience.

obligations of the states towards their own nationals.[85] On its own, this would hardly have remedied the perceived failings of the previous text, so there follows a general definition of *concurrence déloyale* in terms of all acts contrary to honest practices in industrial or commercial matters, followed by a list of representative (but non-exhaustive) examples of these in which there is typically some kind of fraudulent misrepresentation or misdescription, but not one such as to induce confusion in the normal trade mark sense. The third paragraph addresses various malpractices by which confusion with the goods of another, or more generally, mistake as to origin, might be induced and requires the availability of civil remedies in all such cases, and criminal ones in cases of fraud. The fourth and final paragraph is wider still in procedural terms: anyone injured by an act of unfair competition is to have a right of action; and in actions for an injunction, or criminal prosecutions, there is to be a right for trade associations to sue or intervene.

Several national delegations proposed variants on the draft Article of the **2–49** Programme, or drafts of their own. In view of their length, and the fact that many of them more or less followed the programme, these can only be summarised here.

The United Kingdom formally proposed the amendments to Art.10*bis* which had been adopted by the League of Nations.[86] In addition, and also in accordance with the League's recommendations, the United Kingdom would have added a provision to the *Protocol de Clôture* stating that the interpretation of "*concurrence déloyale*" in Arts 2 and 10*bis* was not to be confined to the circumstances of para.2 in the UK numbering (3 in the Programme) of the latter, but extended to other fraudulent or misleading acts in relation to goods, in so far as they adversely affected international trade. The official instructions of the Board of Trade to the British delegation identified unfair competition as their highest priority:

"His Majesty's Government attach special importance to the proposals which have been put forward on behalf of Great Britain in connection with articles 6, 6a, 6b, 9 10 and 10*bis* for securing more effective international protection against unfair competition. As you are aware, these proposals were originally framed by the Economic Committee of the League of Nations who consulted a Conference of Experts which met at Geneva in May, 1924. They received the approval of the League of

---

[85] This clarification, though approved by the Hague Conference in principle, seems subsequently to have been lost in the process of drafting and re-drafting, leaving even the present (1967) version of the Article in its original 1911 form in this respect.

[86] See above, para.2–47. Compared to the Programme, this meant that para.1 was retained with some drafting amendments; para.2 was to be deleted; para.3 retained in general terms, but with the individual instances (a) to (e) deleted; and para.4 substantially retained.

Nations, and every endeavour should be made by you to maintain the measure of international agreement which has thus been obtained, and to secure the incorporation of the League's proposals in the Convention."[87]

In other respects the instructions were restrictive. In the specific context of Art.10bis it was said:

"In dealing with the various texts submitted for this Article, you will aim generally at securing as little divergence as possible from the text agreed at the League of Nations meeting, and embodied in the British proposals, In particular you will resist all amendment designed to bring within the scope of the Article matters of unfair competition (such as the protection of press information, or trade libel, bribery &c.) which are not connected with what is known as industrial property, or which are not well known grievances in international trade."

2–50 France and Germany may be said to have favoured proposals framed in much more general terms than those of the Programme or the League of Nations, rejecting both the excessive detail of the Programme, and the relatively narrow scope of the League's proposals.[88] Those of Germany were the more concise.[89] Paragraphs 1 and 4 of the programme would have been retained (the latter with a drafting amendment); para.2 would have been stripped down to the general proposition defining "*concurrence déloyale*" in terms of acts contrary to honest practices in industrial or commercial matters, with the list of examples deleted[90]; and para.3 would have been replaced in its entirety with three new sub-paragraphs addressing various kinds of false or misleading advertising, confusion, and disparagement. The French proposal[91] was for entirely new Arts 10bis and 10ter, in which "*concurrence déloyale*" was defined to in very broad terms starting with familiar examples and culminating in "*tous les actes contraires à la loi, aux usages commerciaux, ou à l'équité*". More specific articles dealt with false indications of origin and the like, and passing-off, in terms generally consistent the League of Nations proposals. New Art.10ter would have provided for trade associations to have *locus standi*. The proposal of Italy[92] is notable for the simple elegance which with it dealt with the major problems—without limiting itself to cases involving goods and without

---

[87] UK Public Record Office file BT 209/706, letter of September 30, 1925. The instructions went on to say that if agreement could not be reached at all, or reached only on terms which deprived the League of Nations proposals of their value, then the British delegation was authorised to propose a separate Convention dealing specifically with unfair competition, to be considered at a subsequent conference which might be convened by the League of Nations or some other suitable international body.

[88] Both Germany and France also initially addressed as an act of unfair competition, the problem of fraudulently registered trade marks. This does not correspond to the eventual treatment of the issue in the Convention, and is not further considered here.

[89] *Actes de la Haye* (1926), p.349.

[90] As was subsequently adopted.

[91] *Actes de la Haye* (1926), pp.349–350.

[92] *Actes de la Haye* (1926), p.350.

attempting to invoke a general clause. After retaining only the first paragraph of the Programme, it would have read:

"Est coupable de concurrence déloyale celui qui, dans le but de détourner la clientèle d'un concurrent:

    (a) fait usage de noms et signes distinctifs propres à engendrer confusion avec les noms et signes légitimement adoptés par autrui;

    (b) décrie les produits ou les services d'autrui;

    (c) excite les dépendants d'autrui à la violation des devoirs fixés par la loi ou par le contrat;

    (d) fait usage d'indications de provenance fausses, à moins qu'il ne s'agisse de désignations d'usage courant."

The 1925 Hague Conference: the discussions and outcome

At the Hague Conference itself, the change from "*s'engagent ...*" to "*sont* **2–51** *tenus d'assurer*" was readily and unanimously agreed, though being recognised as little more than a gesture. Thereafter, the discussions at the Conference can only readily be followed if the issues are broken down (following the treatment in *Actes de la Haye*) into the following groupings: (1) the terms of any general clause against unfair competition and its intended legal effect; (2) specific kinds of unfair competition against which mandatory protection was considered, namely confusion, disparagement, false advertising, *débauchage*,[93] and misuse of news of the day; and (3) the legal nature of the action against unfair competition, and specifically the extent to which civil and/or criminal sanctions were to be mandatory, the *locus standi* of parties who did not suffer damage (including trade associations), and the desirability of special legislation.[94] In accordance with normal practice, policy decisions were taken in principle by the relevant sub-committee, the resulting texts were edited as necessary by a drafting committee, and finally adopted (if necessary, after further debate and amendment) in plenary session, where unanimity was required. In the case of Art.10*bis* discussions took place both in sub-committee IV itself, and in a smaller *ad hoc* committee or working party which reported to sub-committee IV.

So far as the *general clause* was concerned, there was little opposition in principle to the (truncated) proposition in the Programme, reading "*constitue un acte de concurrence déloyale tout acte contraire aux usages honnêtes en matière industrielle ou commerciale*" except that France would have supported a more far-reaching form of wording in terms of "*tous les actes contraires a la loi, aux usages commerciaux ou a l'équité*". Either of these would apparently have received widespread support, but both were opposed, as being too vague and indeterminate for inclusion in an international convention, by a number of delegations including Italy, Japan, the United Kingdom and the United States. In the result, the Working Party felt

---

[93] Inducing employees of a competitor to break their contracts or legal duties, sometimes translated as "labour piracy".

[94] *Actes de la Haye* (1926), p.472 onwards (Report of sub-committee IV).

unable to propose any general clause against unfair competition, but when the issue was revisited in sub-committee IV, the Dutch delegation revived the proposal of the Programme, and was enthusiastically supported by the French delegate, M. Maillard. The latter even suggested that it would be preferable to leave Art.10*bis* unchanged, rather than degrade its pre-existing generality to a listing of a few specific prohibited acts. M. Maillard's intervention must have been sufficiently inspirational for all delegations to declare themselves in support of the Franco-Dutch proposal,[95] subject only to the United States (supported by the United Kingdom) requesting clarification that only acts in the course of commercial competition were being referred to.[96] With this proviso, and subject to an unimportant reservation entered by Belgium, this was passed unanimously.[97]

2–52   Turning to specific instances of unfair competition, attention was directed in turn to five topics under the names of confusion, denigration, false advertising, *débauchage*, and news of the day.[98] So far as *confusion* was concerned, there was unanimity on the need for a specific provision and the only disagreement was over its terms. The working party rejected the Programme's listing of a number of means of causing confusion, on the basis that enumerations of this kind only lent themselves to restrictive interpretations. There was discussion as to whether confusion was to be understood only in terms of physical products (*marchandises et produits*), or also in terms of the person and establishment of a trader, and in the interests of clarity only the former was addressed.[99] After a discussion initiated by Italy, it was agreed to make it explicit that only confusion with the products *of a competitor* was relevant, but that liability (as opposed to remedies) would not depend on the presence of bad faith.[1] The provision proposed by the working party and adopted by the sub-committee read: "... *tous faits quelconques de nature a créer une confusion par n'importe quel moyen avec les marchandises ou produits d'un concurrent*".

On denigration (*dénigrement*) the sub-committee unanimously adopted the text: "... *les allégations fausse dans l'exercice de commerce, de nature à discréditer les marchandises ou produits d'un concurrent*". Great Britain and the United States had some reservations which they did not press, and France would not have confined the prohibition to disparaging statements which were untrue. In view of the (still-outstanding) question of whether the common law of injurious falsehood complies with the Paris Convention, it is interesting to record how the report of the sub-committee distinguished

---

[95] Unless it be thought that M. Maillard was contemplating vetoing any further and more detailed improvements to the Article; or even (from the second part of his reported intervention) that he might have been hinting that France could re-open the issue of compulsory working of patents, where an accommodation satisfactory to certain other member states had been reached.

[96] "...*qu'il ne s'agit dans les faits visés que de la concurrence commerciale*".

[97] *Actes de la Haye* (1926), p.475, at I.

[98] *Actes de la Haye* (1926), p.475, at II, and onwards: (1) *Confusion* at p.476, (2) *Denigration* at p.477, (3) *Reclame fausse* at p.477, (4) *Le débauchage* at p.478, and (5) *Les informations de presse* (supported only by the Serb-Croat-Slovene state, and not further considered here) at p.478.

[99] This was, of course, to be remedied at the 1934 London Conference.

[1] It is a reasonable inference that some kind of bad faith or fraudulent intent might be a prerequisite for an award of damages.

dénigrement (the concept under discussion) from *diffamation*: "... *la notion du dénigrement est plus large que celle de diffamation, notamment qu'elle n'implique pas une intention injurieuse. Ce qu'on veut frapper c'est le fait de discréditer un concurrent par des affirmations contraires à la vérité*". As with the previous subject, confusion, only disparagement of a competitor's products was addressed and not disparagement of the person or establishment of the competitor himself.[2]

On false advertising or publicity[3] (*réclame fausse*) there was fundamental disagreement as to whether this kind of conduct was an aspect of unfair competition law or consumer protection law, and those in the latter camp objected that it was a matter for national law alone, and was unsuitable for inclusion in an international convention. Since agreement was impossible, no specific proposal was formulated or adopted. A provision dealing with *débuachage* was supported only by France and Italy, and as several delegations found it unacceptable, also went no further.

Finally, on the question of sanctions the sub-committee noted the existing diversity of legal actions and remedies by which unfair competition was sought to be suppressed,[4] and the impossibility of stipulating uniform procedures or remedies. In the event, the only concrete proposal was that adopted as the second paragraph of Art.10*ter*.

The 1934 London Conference

The discussion of unfair competition at the 1934 London Conference was **2-53** quite as extensive as at the 1925 Hague Conference, but it achieved relatively little.

The Programme for the Conference, Point XI, proposed only one substantial change to Art.10*bis*, namely to replace "*les produits d'un concurrent*" in the two specific prohibitions of Art.10*bis* (3) with "*l'établissement, les produits ou les services d'un concurrent*." The commentary very briefly explained that the 1925 text only applied to confusion or denigration relating to goods, and that there was an equal need to protect service businesses, and the enterprise or establishment itself. In due course, this was adopted unanimously.[5]

In addition, numerous proposals for amendment of Art.10*bis* were made by individual member states, and by various non-governmental organisations. The latter are mentioned only to the extent that they were adopted by a national delegation, or specifically debated.[6] Germany proposed a new Art.10*bis* (3)(3) directed to misleading and comparative advertising, which was subsequently considered in tandem with the AIPPI proposal, below.

---

[2] This was also remedied at the 1934 London Conference.

[3] In the sense of various untrue claims about a trader's own goods. The report of the sub-committee notes that the term was neither in general use, nor uniformly interpreted, and in fact there seems to have been little common ground about what was being addressed.

[4] *Actes de la Haye* (1926), pp.478–480.

[5] *Actes de Londres* (1934), p.418.

[6] Proposals relating to news of the day (*informations de presse*) were made by Germany and Czechoslovakia, but are not further considered here. Likewise a proposal by Czechoslovakia for protection of radio transmissions against unauthorised commercial use.

Hungary proposed a new sub-paragraph (3) dealing expressly with the problem of substitution.[7] Italy would have introduced the words "*la personne*" instead of "*les services*" in both sub-paragraphs (2) and (3); and the United States would expressly have made the examples of Art.10*bis* (3) non-exhaustive ("*Seront interdits, entre autres, les actes suivantes ...*"), and would have made drafting amendments to sub-paragraphs (1) and (2). These proposals by Italy and the United States were withdrawn in favour of the text of the Programme.[8]

The United States would also have added a new paragraph 10*bis* (4) reading: "*En l'absence, dans un pays de l'Union, de sanctions spéciales assurant la répression des actes de concurrence déloyale, seront applicables à ces actes les sanctions prévues par la législation sur les marques ou sur le nom commercial*", and this was not withdrawn.

The proposal with the most widespread support was made by Denmark, France, Norway, Sweden and Switzerland, all of which supported the proposal adopted by the AIPPI at its 1932 London conference for the addition of a third sub-paragraph reading: "*Les allégations fausses, dans l'exercice du commerce, de nature à attirer la clientèle, qui se rapportent à l'origine, à la nature, à la fabrication, à la vente des produits ou à la qualité de l'établissement commercial ou à des récompenses industrielles*".

In addition France, alone of these, would have followed the AIPPI in proposing to delete the word "*fausses*" in sub-para.(2), so as to prohibit statements which were disparaging, but true. In sub-committee IV, this was supported by Belgium, which would also have replaced "*discréditer*" with "*nuire*" and by Hungary and Czechoslovakia. The United States objected that truth could never be treated as discrediting, and while Italy accepted that there might be occasions for prohibiting truthful but disparaging statements in competition, it submitted that there was no justification for such an unqualified rule. The Belgian and French propositions were defeated by 13 votes to 10, and by 13 to nine, respectively.

2–54   The remaining discussion in sub-committee IV concerned the proposed addition of new sub-paragraphs to the existing two of Art.10*bis*(3), and the possible addition of a new para.(4) dealing with sanctions. The proposals of the AIPPI and Germany (which were not distinguished at this stage) were approved in principle by a vote of 19 to five, and were remitted to the drafting committee. The latter recommended a version based on one proposed by Switzerland, which would have read "*notamment devront être interdits: ... 3° les allégations fallacieuses par un industriel ou commercent sur son établissement, ses produits et son activité commerciale, si elles sont de nature à nuire un concurrent*". However, in plenary session the only proposals put to the vote, and adopted without debate, were to the opening words of the Article and to sub-paras 3(1) and 3(2), as indicated above.

---

[7] This was eventually defeated by 11 votes to six, and is not further discussed here: *Actes de Londres* (1934), p.419.

[8] As to paras (1) and (2) of Art.10*bis*, the Programme of the International Bureau was accepted unanimously by committee IV, subject to the Drafting Committee being invited to find a more elegant expression for "*services*". In due course this resulted in the present text " ... *l'activite industrielle ou commerciale ...*" *Actes de Londres* (1934), pp.417–418, 469.

The proposal by the United States for acts of unfair competition, in the **2–55** absence of special legislation, to be subject to the same sanctions as provided for by trade mark legislation was vigorously opposed by Italy. Further discussion was curtailed, and the sub-committee voted in favour of the United States proposal by 11 votes to nine. Hungary, recalling (wrongly) that it was 50 years since the Convention had provided for the repression of unfair competition, also proposed a fourth paragraph for Art.10*bis*, which would have provided: "*De leur côté, les pays de l'Union s'engagent à prendre, dans les deux ans qui suivront la ratification de la présente Convention, des dispositions légales spéciales en vue de la répression de la concurrence déloyale, dans le cas où ils n'auraient pas encore pris de telles dispositions*".

The United Kingdom objected that Art.10*ter* was sufficient, and Switzerland recalled that following the 1925 Hague Conference it had been understood that the countries of the Union were not obliged to enact any special legislation for the repression of unfair competition, and that it was sufficient for this to be dealt with by the general law. In the result, Hungary withdrew its proposal, but resubmitted it as a non-binding resolution or *voeu*, which was accepted unanimously by the sub-committee, and after being submitted to the drafting committee was adopted by the plenary session in the following form: "*La Conférence insiste sur la nécessité, pour les pays de l'Union, de prendre le plus tôt possible les dispositions légales afin d'assurer la répression de la concurrence déloyale*".

On the proposal of the United Kingdom, the second paragraph of Art.10*ter* was proposed to be amended by substituting "... *syndicats et associations représentant les industrieles, les producteurs*[9] *ou les commerçants intéressés ...*" for "... *syndicats et associations représentant l'industrie ou le commerce intéressé ...*" and (more significantly) by deleting the words "... *dans le mesure ou la loi du pays dans lequel la protection est réclamée le permet aux syndicats et associations de ce pays*" with which the Article then ended. This was agreed without opposition or debate, although for reasons which are unclear only the first of these amendments was finally adopted.[10]

The 1958 Lisbon Conference: Art 10*bis*(3)(3) and misdescription

The only amendment to Art.10*bis* adopted at the Lisbon Conference was **2–56** not foreshadowed in the Programme of the International Bureau, but one which resulted from a proposal by Austria on lines previously suggested by the International Chamber of Commerce.[11] It would have added to the two enumerated prohibitions of Art.10*bis* (3) a third sub-paragraph: "*L'emploi dans l'exercice du commerce d'indications ou d'allégations susceptible d'in-*

---

[9] In the original proposal, "*fabricants*". The change was proposed by France and was not opposed.
[10] *Actes de Londres* (1934), p.422 (sub-committee IV), p.470 (drafting committee), p.520 (plenary). A minor drafting change was also made, in line with Art.10*bis*, changing "*Les pays contractants ...*" to "*Les pays de l'Union...*".
[11] Paris, 1956. The Austrian proposal also revived, in modified form, a proposal which had failed to find sufficient support at the 1934 London Conference, see above. The 1934 proposal was in one respect wider than that of 1958, since it was not wholly confined to misdescriptions of goods.

duire le public en erreur sur la nature (y compris le mode de fabrication), l'origine, la qualité, l'utilité ou le prix des produits, ou sur les qualités du producteur ou négociant de ces produits".

This was originally debated in sub-committee III, where it was approved in principle by 13 votes to nil, with 14 abstentions, but was transferred to sub-committee IV for further discussion.[12] In the latter, it was accepted in principle without debate by 15 votes to nil, with 14 abstentions. An *ad hoc* sub-committee (chaired by the United Kingdom) produced a revised version which read: *"L'emploi dans l'exercice du commerce d'indications ou d'allégations susceptible d'induire le public en erreur sur la nature, y compris le mode de fabrication, l'origine, les caractéristiques, l'aptitude à l'emploi (ou la quantité) des marchandises".*

This proposal was duly accepted in sub-committee IV, with little further debate, by 15 votes to nil, with 11 abstentions.[13] In plenary session, the United States (which had previously abstained) opposed the new paragraph solely because of the inclusion of the word *"l'origine"*, and despite attracting 24 votes in favour and only one against, with 14 abstentions, the proposal was defeated. It was immediately put to the vote again with *"l'origine"* deleted, and in this form was passed by 17 votes to nil, with 22 abstentions.[14] Australia is reported as having supported the United States position, but this does not entirely bear examination. Australia's express objection was that the Commonwealth Parliament could not legislate on issues of purely domestic importance–but out of all the contemplated subject matter for Art.10*bis* (3)(3) it is only "origin" that seems to have any significant international element, and its deletion would not have met the Australian objection. In the event, Australia abstained twice: both on the original proposal, and on the modified proposal in which the American objection was accepted and "origin" deleted.

After further reconsideration by the drafting committee, the new addition to Art.10*bis* (3) was adopted in the following terms.

The following in particular shall be prohibited.	Notamment devront être interdits:
. . .	. . .
Indications or allegations the use of which, in the course of trade, is liable to mislead the	Les indications ou allégations dont l'usage, dans l'exercice du commerce, est susceptible d'in-

---

[12] *Actes de Lisbonne* (1963), pp.725 (sub-committee III); 852 (sub-committee IV). The proposal probably originally received consideration in sub-committee III (trade marks) rather than sub-committee IV (unfair competition and indications of source) because the former was debating at length a proposal relating to use of marks on dissimilar goods which was capable of affecting either Art.6*bis* or Art.10*bis*, and no other amendments to the latter were included in the Programme.

[13] *Actes de Lisbonne* (1963), p.789.

[14] *Actes de Lisbonne* (1963), pp.726, 790. There is a difference as to the number of votes in favour, with Switzerland being omitted from the list at p.727, so that the count there is 16. Since Switzerland undoubtedly voted for the first version, and is not recorded as having abstained on the second vote, it is to be assumed that the listing of votes in favour, on p.727, is one short.

public as to the nature, the manufacturing process, the characteristics, the suitability for their purpose, or the quantity, of the goods.	duire le public en erreur sur la nature, le mode de fabrication, les caractéristiques, l'aptitude a l'emploi ou la quantité des marchandises.

Well-known marks, dilution and related proposals at the Lisbon Conference

As well as the initiative to add a third category of misrepresentations to **2–57** Art.10*bis*, the 1958 Lisbon conference also considered at length various proposals to protect especially famous marks ("*marques de haute renommée*"[15]) against use on goods which were neither identical nor similar to those for which the mark was famous. Point XX of the Programme of the International Bureau devoted five pages to considering the proposition that there was already an international consensus against parasitic, but possibly non-confusing, use of highly renowned marks, citing cases from a number of jurisdictions.[16] From this discussion, it is clear that the Bureau was principally addressing the problem of the dissimilar goods being taken for those of the trade mark proprietor, with consequent damage; but was also aware of the concept of "dilution" in the modern sense, in which the complaint is not about confusion in even the broadest sense, but a gradual loss of the attractive power of the mark. Moreover, it is clear that the Bureau was considering under the same rubric liability for the actual use of highly renowned marks for dissimilar goods, and preventing the registration of such marks for dissimilar goods by third parties.

From all these factors, the issue might seem to belong principally with the trade mark sections of the Convention, and it was in the Trade Mark subcommittee that it was eventually discussed. However, in the Programme it was introduced by the International Bureau by way of a possible amendment to Art.10*bis*, and the latter possibility was among those debated.[17] After a country-by-country survey, the Bureau asked if the protection of highly renowned marks belonged to Art.6*bis* or to Art.10*bis*. The first option was supported by the AIPPI,[18] who had proposed a new fourth paragraph to Art. 6*bis* reading: "*La protection prévue par le présent article s'étend, sous réserve des droits acquis de bonne foi, même a l'égard de produites non identiques ou similaires, s'il s'ensuit ou bien une possibilité de confusion, ou bien un avantage injustifié, ou bien un affaiblissement réel du caractère distinctif ou du pouvoir attractif de la marque*". However, the Bureau preferred the view that liability for use of highly renowned marks on dissimilar goods

[15] One degree higher than "*marques notoirement connue*'.

[16] *Actes de Lisbonne* (1963), p.705 *et seq*. The United Kingdom took pride of place, apparently by virtue of the 1898 *Kodak* case. Examples from elsewhere, in so far as they can be dated, mostly appear to come from the 1940's onwards, and none are as early as *Kodak*.

[17] All the debate took place in sub-committee III (Trade Marks), rather than sub-committee IV (Unfair Competition and Indications of Source).

[18] The *Association pour la Protection de la Propriété Industrielle*.

belonged to the realm of unfair competition, and that trade mark law properly so called was concerned only with use of the mark on identical or similar goods. In the result, the International Bureau made no proposals of its own for the further protection of highly renowned marks under either Art.6*bis* or 10*bis*, partly because it was of opinion that Art.10*bis* already provided sufficient protection.

2–58 Several such propositions and observations were made by individual member states or non-governmental observers,[19] with those that made any progress being summarised below. In the event, none of these various proposals were adopted, but the debate casts some light on some of the limitations of Art.10*bis* itself, and on the extent to which there was support for extending its protection. In what follows, emphasis is given to aspects of Art.10*bis*, and proposals specifically directed to Art.6*bis* or to a new *sui generis* Article are given much abbreviated treatment. However, it is impossible to avoid reference to them altogether, and the debate on protection of highly renowned marks against use on dissimilar goods was preceded by a lengthy debate on the protection of "*marques notoirement connue*" in the context of Art.6*bis*.

So far as concerns the discussion of Point XX of the Programme in subcommittee III and *marques de haute renommée* properly so called, UNIFAB[20] proposed a slightly extended version of the AIPPI text, the latter also being formally supported by Denmark and Sweden. Iran proposed that the issue should be dealt with by an amendment to Art.10*bis*, and was supported in this by Yugoslavia, the United States and Germany. France opposed amendment to Art.6*bis* or adoption of a separate article, considering that the treatment of "*confusion*" in the existing text of Art.10*bis* was adequate. Japan objected that the concept of confusion in Art.10*bis* was limited by the word "*concurrence*," and that "*d'un concurrent*" should be replaced with "*d'autrui*". This in turn was opposed by Italy, as potentially extending Art.10*bis* too far. The Netherlands basically supported the proposal of the FIIC.[21] Belgium supported the UNIFAB text in principle. The United States thought that the concept of unfair competition already covered use of a well-known mark on different products, but would have supported a new article following Art.6*bis*.

In the result, six propositions were put to a vote[22]: (a) that of Japan, to retain Art.10*bis* but with the word "*concurrent*" in paragraph (3) replaced with "*d'autrui*"–the United Kingdom and Israel[23] supported this proposal; (b) of the Netherlands, to include a new Art.10*bis*(4); (c) of Portugal, to include a new Art.6*bis*(4); (d) of UNIFAB (supported by Germany) and the LICCD[24] to draft a separate Article; (e) of the United States, to extend the benefit of Art.6*bis* to dissimilar goods, in the case of marks with an

[19] *Actes de Lisbonne* (1963), p.709 *et seq.*
[20] *The Union des Fabricants*, present as an observer.
[21] *Federation Internationale des Ingenieurs-Conseils.*
[22] *Actes de Lisbonne* (1963), p.717.
[23] Israel would also have amended "*concurrance déloyale*" to "*practiques commerciales déloyale*" in Art.10*bis*(1). This was opposed by the United States.
[24] The *Ligue Contre la Concurrence Déloyale.*

exceptional reputation; and (f) of Sweden, to adopt the AIPPI draft for a new Art.6*bis* (4).

In this confused state of affairs, a series of votes was taken.[25] The general **2–59** proposition for protection of a mark on dissimilar products attracted 20 votes in favour, three against, and three abstentions. Including such a provision in Art.6*bis* was rejected by six in favour to 16 against, with six abstentions; but introducing it into Art.10*bis* was rejected by a larger margin: one in favour to 10 against, with nine abstentions. Since this implicitly favoured a separate article, votes were taken on its terms. The proposal of the Netherlands received six votes for, three against and 16 abstentions; parts common to the proposals of UNIFAB, Sweden, the AIPPI and the International Chambers of Commerce received 10 for, four against and 11 abstentions.[26] The Portuguese proposal was withdrawn. In the result, the Drafting Committee was asked to prepare the text of a new Article based on the AIPPI, UNIFAB and ICC proposals. This resulted in a further selection of three drafts,[27] which would have created a new Article numbered either as new Art.6*septies* (UNIFAB) or as new Art.1*ter* (Netherlands and a compromise proposal initiated by the Drafting Committee), in the latter case with the existing Art.10*ter* being renumbered as Art.10*quater*.

All three of these drafts were initially opposed by the United Kingdom, on the ground of excessive detail and lack of flexibility.[28] Objections of principle were taken in varying degrees by Italy, but especially by Austria and Yugoslavia. A compromise proposal by the United States and Italy was put to the vote, and attracted 18 votes in favour (including the United Kingdom), three against, and six abstentions. It would have read[29]:

L'enregistrement ou l'usage de la marque ou d'un nom commercial d'un tiers pour des produits dissemblables est interdit comme contraire à la loyauté commerciale, des qu'il est régulièrement démontré que cette marque, en raison de son caractère unique et de sa célébrité, a conquis une telle réputation qu'elle incite ceux qui l'emploient commercialement ou le grand public à établir un lien commercial entre l'utilisateur ou celui qui procède à l'enregistrement de la marque pour des produits dissemblables et le propriétaire de la marque bénéficiant d'une réputation exceptionnelle.[30]

---

[25] *Actes de Lisbonne* (1963), p.710.

[26] Sub-proposals of UNIFAB to provide the same protection to trade names were accepted (16:1:11); but rejected for emblems (nil in favour) and slogans (1:18:7).

[27] *Actes de Lisbonne* (1963), p.721 *et seq.*

[28] In contrast, the United States objected to the UNIFAB-based draft as too imprecise, and resubmitted a draft of its own with the support of Italy.

[29] *Actes de Lisbonne* (1963), p.723–724.

[30] "The registration or use of the trademark or tradename of another party for dissimilar products is prohibited as contrary to commercial loyalty when due proof is given that such mark, by reason of its unique character and its celebrity, has acquired such a reputation that it may induce the belief in the trade or in the general public of establishing a commercial connection between the user or applicant for dissimilar goods and the proprietor of the mark enjoying such exceptional reputation". The English text follows Stephen Ladas, *Patents, Trademarks and Related Rights–National and International Protection* (1975) §684, Ladas being one of the authors of the proposal. The status of this Article as part of the law of trade marks, or unfair competition, was deliberately left undecided (Ladas), and its language would fit either.

In the light of the vote, and continuing opposition by Austria and Yugo-slavia (the third opponent, Belgium, having less fundamental objections which might have been met by redrafting) the Chairman decided that that it was futile to make any formal proposals to the full Conference. This was challenged by the United States and by the Vice-President of the Drafting Committee, who thought that a working party consisting of the two main proponents and the three opponents might still be able to make progress. However, the Chairman disagreed, and neither the Italian-American proposal nor any of its antecedents proceeded any further.[31]

A vote on the Japanese proposal to replace "*concurrent*" with "*autrui*" in Art.10*bis* (3) was passed by 11 votes to three, with 12 abstentions; and on the suggestion of Belgium the drafting committee was also invited to remove the words "*de concurrance*" in paragraph (2).[32] The resulting proposal from the drafting committee would also have removed the words "*de con-currence*" from Art.10*bis* (2) and in Art.10*bis* (3) would have substituted "*d'un concurrent*" with "*d'un tiers*". However, when this proposal returned to the committee, Israel (which had supported the original Japanese amendment) objected that the former amendment would extend the Article too far; and Italy and Austria also announced their opposition. This also made no further progress.[33]

D. UNFAIR COMPETITION AND TRIPS

TRIPs and unfair competition

2–60 The 1994 Agreement on Trade Related Aspects of Intellectual Property Rights (TRIPs or the TRIPs Agreement) has little or no overt impact on the substantive law of unfair competition in general, or passing-off in particular. To a much greater extent than the Paris Convention, TRIPs does contain detailed provisions for the minimum level of protection to be provided in many specific areas of intellectual property law. However, the only provisions of TRIPs touching on the subject matter of the present work are those relating to geographical indications.[34] Article 22(2)(b) provides:

In respect of geographical indications, Members shall provide the legal means for interested parties to prevent—

. . .

---

[31] *Actes de Lisbonne* (1963), p.724.
[32] *Actes de Lisbonne* (1963), p.721.
[33] *Actes de Lisbonne* (1963), p.722.
[34] Arts 22 to 24, constituting Section 3 of Pt II of TRIPs. The main response of the United Kingdom to this and earlier international obligations is in criminal or administrative proceedings under the Trade Descriptions Act 1968, or its predecessors, or more recently by *sui generis* EU legislation. Passing-off provides civil remedies against certain examples of misuse of geographical indications.

any use which constitutes an act of unfair competition within the meaning of Article 10*bis* of the Paris Convention (1967).

TRIPs also contains provisions regarding the protection of confidential or "undisclosed" information, which is treated as part of a general law of unfair competition under some legal systems, though not in the United Kingdom. It is on this basis that Art.30 of TRIPs provides:

> In the course of ensuring effective protection against unfair competition as provided in Art.10*bis* of the Paris Convention (1967), Members shall protect undisclosed information in accordance with paragraph 2 and data submitted to government agencies in accordance with paragraph 3.[35] ...

With these very peripheral exceptions, TRIPs does not purport to affect substantive unfair competition law or to require any minimum standard of protection. There is little doubt that this results from a decision early in the negotiating process, probably reflecting the diversity of existing national laws and their underlying policy considerations and the consequent improbability of consensus.[36]

TRIPs and Art.10*bis* of the Paris Convention

Absent relevant specific provisions, the other way in which laws of unfair **2–61** competition might be affected by TRIPs is by the incorporation into TRIPs of the substantive provisions of the Paris Convention, and specifically Art.10*bis* of the latter. Art.2(1) of TRIPs provides that

> "In respect of Parts II, III and IV of this Agreement, Members shall comply with Articles 1 through 12, and Article 19, of the Paris Convention (1967)."

One must now address an argument, based on the treatment of Art.8 of the Paris Convention in the *Havana Club*[37] decision of the WTO Appellate Body, that any failure to comply with Art.10*bis* of the Paris Convention would also constitute a breach of TRIPs. If correct, this would be important since a member state of the WTO could then invoke the Dispute Settlement Understanding of GATT to compel compliance with pure Paris Convention obligations such as Art.10*bis*, rather than the slower and less effective route of an action before the International Court of Justice under Article 28 of the

---

[35] Remainder of Art.30 omitted.
[36] See Daniel Gervais *The TRIPS Agreement–Drafting History and Analysis* (1998), at note 43 below. The present (non)-treatment of unfair competition in TRIPs was present to a surprising level of detail at least as early as the 1991 "Dunkel Draft" which formed the basis of most of the detailed negotiations. See also Frauke Henning-Bodewig, "International Protection against Unfair Competition–Art. 10*bis* Paris Convention, TRIPS and WIPO Model Provisions" [1999] IIC 166 and Gerald Reger, *Der internationale Schutz gegenden unlauteren Wettbewerb und das TRIPS-Ubereinkommen* (1999).
[37] AB-2001–7 *United States–Section 211 Omnibus Appropriations Act of 1998*.

Paris Convention. It would not affect the substantive content of the respective states' rights and obligations under Art.10*bis* itself.

2–62   However, Art.2(1) of TRIPs in terms only requires compliance with the Paris Convention "in respect of Parts II, III and IV" of TRIPs. Subject to what was said in *Havana Club*, any breach of the Paris Convention which is not "in respect of" any of these Parts of TRIPs would not constitute a breach of Art.2(1), and the remedies for an aggrieved member state would be confined to those provided for by the Paris Convention itself. Part II of TRIPs self-evidently governs unfair competition arising from misuse of geographical indications or undisclosed information, but not unfair competition in any more general sense.[38] Part IV of TRIPs is irrelevant to unfair competition because its subject matter ("Acquisition and Maintenance of Intellectual Property Rights and Related *Inter Partes* Procedures") is inherently inapplicable to unregistered rights. That leaves Pt III as the only possible Part of TRIPs to which Art.10*bis* of the Paris Convention might apply. However, that begs two questions. First, whether Part III applies to unfair competition at all, in view of the definition of "intellectual property" in Art.1(2) by reference to Sections 1 to 7 of Pt II; and secondly, whether a breach of Art.10*bis* of the Paris Convention is capable of being a breach of any relevant Article of Pt III of TRIPs.

Subject to the implications of *Havana Club*, the preferred analysis is that non-compliance with Art.10*bis* of the Paris Convention constitutes a breach of TRIPs if (and only if) the alleged act of unfair competition involves the use of geographical indications or undisclosed information. If the alleged act of unfair competition does not involve either of these sub-categories, then non-compliance with Art.10*bis* entails only the legal consequences provided for in the Paris Convention itself. The non-compliance is no longer "in respect of" any of Pts II, III or IV of TRIPs.

TRIPs and adjectival law in unfair competition cases

2–63   There is a further question as to whether the provisions of TRIPs relating to adjectival law, in particular Enforcement of Intellectual Property Rights (Pt III, Arts 41 to 61), apply to causes of action for passing-off or for unfair competition in a more general sense; and more generally, whether TRIPs obligations expressed to apply in respect of "intellectual property", such as national treatment (Art.3) and most-favoured-nation treatment (Art.4) apply to unfair competition in general, or only in so far as the act of unfair competition involves misuse of geographical indications or undisclosed information.

Perhaps the single most important issue under TRIPS from the point of view of existing United Kingdom unfair competition law is that of com-

---

[38] To avoid repetition, and because geographical indications and the protection of trade secrets are both arguably higher in the taxonomy of intellectual property than mere species of the genus unfair competition, such a proviso is implicit in the references to "unfair competition" which follow.

pliance with the provisions of Art.42, requiring that "Members shall make available to right holders[39] civil judicial procedures concerning the enforcement of any intellectual property right covered by this Agreement". Previous United Kingdom practice has assumed that the sole availability of criminal (or administrative, or even self-regulatory) measures against certain residual acts of unfair competition other than passing-off, injurious falsehood, and misuse of trade secrets was sufficient compliance with Art.10*bis* of the Paris Convention.

Article 41 (enforcement procedures to be both fair and equitable, and effective) raises the same issues of applicability to unfair competition as does Art.42, but compliance by the United Kingdom is less controversial. Litigation procedure and remedies in the United Kingdom so far as passing-off is concerned almost certainly comply with Pt III on any understanding of the latter, but the question is not without interest for other aspects of unfair competition and for practitioners litigating in countries with relatively ineffective legal systems, since breach of Pt III would provide an opportunity for a friendly member state to initiate enforcement proceedings at the WTO.

Article 1(2) of TRIPs states that "For the purposes of this Agreement, **2–64** 'intellectual property' refers to all categories of intellectual property that are the subject of Sections 1 through 7 of Part II".[40] However, Sections 1 to 7 do not have any general relevance to unfair competition or passing-off, and only apply (in terms, to the former) to the limited extent that they deal with geographical indications (Section 3) or undisclosed information (Section 7). TRIPs does not attempt to incorporate or cross-refer to definitions such as that of "industrial property" in the Paris Convention or "intellectual property" in the WIPO Convention,[41] either of which would have included protection against unfair competition; and this is consistent with the fact that some aspects of intellectual property, of which unfair competition is perhaps the most conspicuous example, were simply excluded from the later stages of the negotiations leading up to TRIPs.[42] As Gervais[43] comments:

> "It is also important to note that contrary to the Paris Convention, TRIPS does not cover protection from unfair competition. While efforts were made to agree norms in this field, the result of the negotiation is a truncated text on undisclosed information."

---

[39] Footnote to Art.42 reads "For the purpose of this Part, the term 'right holder' includes federations and associations having legal standing to assert such rights".

[40] These are (1) copyright and related rights, (2) trademarks, (3) geographical indications, (4) industrial designs, (5) patents, (6) topographies of integrated circuits, and (7) protection of undisclosed information. This definition by enumeration has not changed since the 1991 Dunkel Draft, or even earlier. See Gervais *op. cit.*

[41] Convention Establishing the World Intellectual Property Convention (Stockholm, 1967).

[42] There are other intellectual property rights which are only mentioned in passing in TRIPs: for instance, plant variety rights (see Art.27(3)(b) proviso) and moral rights (Art.9(1) proviso); and some minor rights are not mentioned at all.

[43] *Op. cit.* at para.2.14.

2–65   On the definition of "intellectual property" in Art.1(2), those provisions of TRIPs employing that term do not to apply to passing-off or unfair competition, except to the limited extent that issues provided for under Sections 1 to 7 of Pt II may arise. In the case of Arts 3 and 4 (national treatment and most-favoured-nation treatment), the obligations are stated in terms of "intellectual property", which was defined in Art.1(2). Articles 41 (general obligations in relation to enforcement) and 42 (fair and equitable procedures) are both expressed to apply to "intellectual property rights covered by this Agreement" which is even more explicit, as well as contemplating the existence of intellectual property rights not so covered.[44] Article 50 (provisional measures) is simply in terms of "intellectual property right[s]" and Sections 4 and 5 (border measures and criminal procedures respectively) are mandatory only in relation to trade mark and copyright infringement, though some residual permissive provisions are in terms of "intellectual property rights" again.

It follows that, outside the context of Sections 3 and 7 and subject to *Havana Club*, there is no obligation in TRIPs to provide civil judicial procedures or specific remedies in relation to acts of unfair competition in general, whether directly under Art.42 *et seq* or by virtue of Arts 10*bis* and 10*ter* of the Paris Convention in conjunction with TRIPs Art.2.

The *Havana Club* case

2–66 The relatively simple conclusion that TRIPs has no application to situations of alleged unfair competition not involving geographical indications or undisclosed information does require to be reconsidered in the light of the Report of the WTO Appellate Body in AB-2001-7 *United States–Section 211 Omnibus Appropriations Act of 1998* (the *Havana Club* case). That decision did not directly concern unfair competition, but it does proceed on the basis that a breach of TRIPs could be committed in relation to industrial property rights which are provided for under the Paris Convention, but which are not the subject of any of Pts II, III and IV of TRIPs in the sense of being among the rights expressly provided for in any of the Sections of Pt II.

The facts of *Havana Club* are complicated, and their details are fortunately not relevant for present purposes. In general terms, complaint was made by the European Union against the United States in respect of Section 211 of the Omnibus Appropriations Act of 1998, which effectively denied protection under United States law to trade marks and trade names associated with businesses expropriated by the Castro regime in Cuba following the revolution of 1963. TRIPs contains no provisions so much as mentioning trade names *eo nomine*, so the case in respect of trade names involved one preliminary issue and two substantive ones: first, did TRIPs have any application to trade names at all; and if so then could the case of the European Union be based either on the general principles of national treatment or most favoured nation treatment; or on the incorporation of the

---

[44] And so, by implication, the remaining provisions of Sections 1 and 2 of Pt III.

substantive law of Art.8 of the Paris Convention into the obligations which members of TRIPs assumed *vis à vis* one another.

The first instance Panel decided the preliminary issue against the EU. **2–67**

"The initial focus of the analysis is the examination of the definition of the term 'intellectual property' which is defined in Article 1.2 of the TRIPS Agreement as follows:

> For the purposes of this Agreement, the term 'intellectual property' refers to all categories of intellectual property that are the subject of *Sections 1 through 7 of Part II.* (emphasis added)

Sections 1 through 7 of Part II of the TRIPS Agreement deal with the following categories of intellectual property: copyright and related rights; trademarks; geographical indications; industrial designs; patents; layout-designs (topographies) of integrated circuits; and protection of undisclosed information. The categories of related rights covered by Article 14 are protection of performers, producers of phonograms and broadcasting organizations.

Categories of protectable subject matters not dealt within Sections 1 to 7 of Part II of the TRIPS Agreement are not included in the definition of 'intellectual property' in Article 1.2. That is, Sections 1 to 7 of Part II do not contain any reference to trade names as a category that comes within the definition of the term 'intellectual property'.

We interpret the terms 'intellectual property' and 'intellectual property rights' with reference to the definition of 'intellectual property' in Article 1.2 of the TRIPS Agreement. The textual reading of Article 1.2 is that it establishes an inclusive definition and this is confirmed by the words 'all categories': the word 'all' indicates that this is an exhaustive list. Thus, for example, the national and most-favoured-nation treatment obligations contained in Articles 3 and 4 of the TRIPS Agreement that refer to the 'protection of intellectual property' would be interpreted to mean the categories covered by Article 1.2 of the TRIPS Agreement. We consider the correct interpretation to be that there are no obligations under those Articles in relation to categories of intellectual property not set forth in Article 1.2, e.g., trade names, consistent with Article 31 of the Vienna Convention.

Based on these reasons, we can provisionally conclude that trade names are not covered by the TRIPS Agreement "

The conclusion of the Panel was reversed by the Appellate Body.[45] To the **2–68** Appellate Body, the overriding consideration was that there was an explicit obligation to comply with Art.8 of the Paris Convention which could not be ignored, and any interpretation of Arts 1(2) and 2(1) of TRIPs which reduced that obligation to a nullity could not be supported.

---

[45] Both the European Union and the United States agreed that the Panel erred in this respect. That TRIPs applied to trade names had been common ground below, and the Panel had reached the opposite conclusion on its own initiative.

"We disagree with the Panel's reasoning and with the Panel's conclusion on the scope of the *TRIPS Agreement* as it relates to trade names.

To explain, we turn first to the Panel's interpretation of Article 1.2 of the *TRIPS Agreement*, which, we recall, provides:

> For the purposes of this Agreement, the term 'intellectual property' refers to all categories of intellectual property that are the subject of Sections 1 through 7 of Part II.

The Panel interpreted the phrase ' "Intellectual property" refers to all categories of intellectual property that are the *subject* of Sections 1 through 7 of Part II' (emphasis added) as if that phrase read 'intellectual property means those categories of intellectual property appearing in the *titles* of Sections 1 through 7 of Part II.' To our mind, the Panel's interpretation ignores the plain words of Article 1.2, for it fails to take into account that the phrase 'the subject of Sections 1 through 7 of Part II' deals not only with the categories of intellectual property indicated in each section *title*, but with other *subjects* as well. For example, in Section 5 of Part II, entitled 'Patents', Article 27(3)(b) provides that Members have the option of protecting inventions of plant varieties by *sui generis* rights (such as breeder's rights) instead of through patents. Under the Panel's theory, such *sui generis* rights would not be covered by the *TRIPS Agreement*. The option provided by Article 27(3)(b) would be read out of the *TRIPS Agreement*.

Moreover, we do not believe that the Panel's interpretation of Article 1.2 can be reconciled with the plain words of Article 2.1. Article 2.1 explicitly incorporates Article 8 of the Paris Convention (1967) into the *TRIPS Agreement*.

The Panel was of the view that the words 'in respect of' in Article 2.1 have the effect of 'conditioning' Members' obligations under the Articles of the Paris Convention (1967) incorporated into the *TRIPS Agreement*, with the result that trade names are not covered. We disagree...

Thus, in our view, the Panel's interpretation of Articles 1.2 and 2.1 of the *TRIPS Agreement* is contrary to the ordinary meaning of the terms of those provisions and is, therefore, not in accordance with the customary rules of interpretation prescribed in Article 31 of the *Vienna Convention*. Moreover, we do not believe that the negotiating history confirms, within the meaning of Article 32 of the *Vienna Convention*, the Panel's interpretation of Articles 1.2 and 2.1.

For all these reasons, we reverse the Panel's finding in paragraph 8.41 of the Panel Report that trade names are not covered under the *TRIPS Agreement* and find that WTO Members do have an obligation under the *TRIPS Agreement* to provide protection to trade names."

How does *Havana Club* apply to Art.10*bis* and unfair competition?

2–69 Supposing *Havana Club* to be correctly decided and of precedential value, bearing in mind that the relevant finding was uncontested, then does it follow that any breach of Art.10*bis* by a TRIPs member state; or any breach of the principles of national and most-favoured-nation treatment in relation to unfair competition, would also constitute a breach of TRIPs and therefore be within the jurisdiction of the WTO DSB? Whatever the correctness of the *Havana Club* decision, the conclusion to the opposite effect, proposed above, probably remains unchanged.

The dilemma posed on the facts of *Havana Club* was of the all-or-nothing kind. On the reasoning of the Panel, the purported obligation of TRIPs members to comply (*inter alia*) with Art.8 of the Paris Convention "in respect of Parts II, III and IV" of TRIPs created no obligations at all: indeed, it was simply meaningless. Since this conclusion was unacceptable to the Appellate Body, the latter found itself obliged to disregard the apparent limitations of Arts 1(2) and 2(1) of TRIPs:

"Article 8 of the Paris Convention (1967) covers only the protection of trade names; Article 8 has no other subject. If the intention of the negotiators had been to exclude trade names from protection, there would have been no purpose whatsoever in including Article 8 in the list of Paris Convention (1967) provisions that were specifically incorporated into the *TRIPS Agreement*. To adopt the Panel's approach would be to deprive Article 8 of the Paris Convention (1967), as incorporated into the *TRIPS Agreement* by virtue of Article 2.1 of that Agreement, of any and all meaning and effect. As we have stated previously:

'One of the corollaries of the general rule of "interpretation" in the *Vienna Convention* is that interpretation must give meaning and effect to all the terms of a treaty. An interpreter is not free to adopt a reading that would result in reducing whole clauses or paragraphs of a treaty to redundancy or inutility.' "

However, no such fatal dilemma arises in the case of unfair competition. **2–70** The TRIPs agreement was negotiated and drafted on the basis that some acts of unfair competition within Art.10*bis* of the Paris Convention were to be subject to specific TRIPs provisions (namely acts of unfair competition involving misuse of geographic names, or undisclosed information) and that other acts of unfair competition were not. This is precisely the sort of case for which the words "in respect of" make perfect sense. Breaches of Art.10*bis* of the Paris Convention are to be treated as breaches of TRIPs itself to the extent that the breach of Art.10*bis* involves a kind of intellectual property which is the subject matter of Part II, but not otherwise. In fact, unfair competition is a paradigm example of why the limitations of Arts 1(2) and 2(1) were necessary in the first place, and on the reasoning of *Havana Club* it may be the only one.

It follows (whatever the correctness of *Havana Club*) that there is no inconsistency between the substantive obligations undertaken by TRIPs members in relation to Art.10*bis*, and the restrictions on the scope of those obligations arising from the definition of "intellectual property" in Art.1(2) and the language of Art.2(1). On the contrary, to extend TRIPs obligations to the whole of unfair competition would be to commit precisely the solecism of "reducing whole clauses or paragraphs of a treaty to redundancy or inutility" which the Appellate Body sought to avoid in *Havana Club*.

What if *Havana Club* applies?

2–71 It remains to consider what would happen if *Havana Club* (contrary to the analysis above) applies to the whole extent of Art.10*bis* of the Paris Convention, exactly as it has been held to apply to Art.8. In this case, the results are very simply stated. The definition of "intellectual property" in Art.1(2) of TRIPs must be deemed to include some such wording as "... and the repression of unfair competition" (lifted, in this case, from Art.1(2) of the Paris Convention); and the introductory words to Art.2(1) of TRIPs might just as well be omitted: members of TRIPs must comply with Art.10*bis* of the Paris Convention, without qualification.

The consequences are that any breach of the principle of national treatment in relation to unfair competition would be a breach of TRIPs Art.3.1 as well as Paris Art.2(1), and any breach of the principle of most favoured nation treatment would be a breach of TRIPs Art.4, there being no provision for most favoured nation treatment in the Paris Convention. The detailed provisions of Pt III of TRIPs would apply in relation to actions for unfair competition, and any breach of Part III in this context could be brought before the WTO DSB. So, most importantly, could any failure to comply with the provisions of Art.10*bis* of the Paris Convention, although the substantive law of the latter would remain unaffected by TRIPs.

Havana Club criticised

2–72 However, before leaving *Havana Club*, it is by no means clear that it is rightly decided in relation to the point addressed here.

The central thesis of the Appellate Body in *Havana Club* was that "Article 2.1 explicitly incorporates Article 8 of the Paris Convention (1967) into the *TRIPS Agreement*". If this is accepted, then there is indeed a fatal inconsistency between the apparent intention of Art.2(1) with regard to Art.8, and the limitations imposed or implicit from the introductory words of Art.2(1) and the definition of "intellectual property" in Art.1(2). But what Art.2(1) actually provides is that "in respect of Parts II, III and IV of this Agreement, Members shall comply with Articles 1 through 12, and Article 19, of the Paris Convention (1967)". So far as the Paris Convention is concerned, the Appellate Body treated this as equivalent to a listing *seriatim* of the individual provisions of the Paris Convention from 1 to 12, plus 19: one so to speak unpacks the compendious listing into its individual component articles, one of which is Art.8. But applying the logic in this case reveals a flaw: Members are supposed to comply with Arts 1 through 12 of Paris, in respect of Pts II, III and IV of TRIPs. But when one comes to perform the same unpacking exercise on TRIPs, one discovers that Pt II of TRIPs begins with a whole Section, comprising six Articles, dealing with "Copyright and Related Rights". Now it is elementary that the Paris Convention has no application at all to copyright or copyright-related rights, which since 1886 have been the subject of an entirely separate international regime under the Berne Convention. But applying the language of *Havana Club*, Art.2(1) of TRIPs seems "explicitly" to require compliance with the Paris Convention, in respect of no fewer than six Articles of TRIPs to which the Paris Convention simply does not and cannot apply. The answer can only be that the draftsman of TRIPs was not sufficiently precise or pedantic to identify the individual Articles of Pt II in respect of which compliance with Paris was required. In effect, he was leaving the reader to exercise his or her common sense as to whether certain Articles of Pt II were (or were not) capable of being relevant to compliance with Paris Convention obligations, and *vice versa*.

CHAPTER 3

GOODWILL

105

A. THE IMPORTANCE OF GOODWILL

Damage to goodwill the basis of the action for passing-off

The essential elements of passing-off have long been recognised as a mis- **3–1** representation causing damage to the business or goodwill of the claimant[1]:

> "There appears to be considerable diversity of opinion as to the nature of the right, the invasion of which is the subject of what are known as passing-off actions. The more general opinion appears to be that the right is a right of property. This view naturally demands an answer to the question, property in what? Some authorities say property in the mark, name, or get-up improperly used by the defendant. Others say property in the business or goodwill likely to be injured by the misrepresentation. Lord Herschell in *Reddaway v Banham*[2] expressly dissents from the former view; and if the right invaded is a right of property at all, there are, I think, strong reasons for preferring the latter view."[3]

> "Whatever doubts there may have previously been as to the legal nature of the rights which were entitled to protection by an action for 'passing-off' in courts of law or equity, these were laid to rest more than 60 years ago by the speech of Lord Parker of Waddington in *Spalding v Gamage* ... with which the other members of the House of Lords agreed. A passing-off action is a remedy for the invasion of a right of property not in the mark, name or get-up improperly used, but in the business or goodwill likely to be injured by the misrepresentation made by passing off one person's goods as the goods of another."[4]

---

[1] *Spalding (AG) & Bros v A W Gamage Ltd* (1915) 32 R.P.C. 273, HL; *Star Industrial Co Ltd v Yap Kwee Kor* [1976] F.S.R. 256, PC; *Erven Warnink BV v J Townend & Sons (Hull) Ltd* [1979] A.C. 731; [1979] 2 All E.R. 97; [1980] R.P.C. 31, HL; *Cadbury Schweppes Pty Ltd v Pub Squash Co Pty Ltd* [1981] 1 All E.R. 213; [1981] R.P.C. 429, PC; *Reckitt & Colman Products Ltd v Borden Inc* [1990] 1 W.L.R. 491; [1990] 1 All E.R. 873; [1990] R.P.C. 340, HL.

[2] [1896] A.C. 199; [1895–9] All E.R. 313; 13 R.P.C. 218, HL.

[3] *per* Lord Parker in *Spalding (AG) & Bros v A W Gamage Ltd* (1915) 32 R.P.C. 273, 284, HL.

[4] *per* Lord Diplock in *Star Industrial Co Ltd v Yap Kwee Kor* [1976] F.S.R. 256, 269, PC. See also Lord Diplock's formulation in *Advocaat: Erven Warnink BV v J Townend & Sons (Hull) Ltd* [1979] A.C. 731; [1979] 2 All E.R. 927; [1980] R.P.C. 31, HL.

It follows that if the claimant has neither a business nor any goodwill in the jurisdiction then a passing-off action brought by him cannot succeed,[5] even if there is a clear misrepresentation by the defendant.

Explanation and definitions of goodwill

3–2 The nature of goodwill is more easily understood than defined, but "no one, judge or jurist, has yet improved on Lord Macnaghten's description of goodwill"[6] in *Inland Revenue Commissioners v Muller & Co's Margarine Ltd*:

> "What is goodwill? It is a thing very easy to describe, very difficult to define. It is the benefit and advantage of the good name, reputation, and connection of a business. It is the attractive force which brings in custom. It is the one thing which distinguishes an old-established business from a new business at its first start. The goodwill of a business must emanate from a particular centre or source. However widely extended or diffused its influence may be, goodwill is worth nothing unless it has power of attraction sufficient to bring customers home to the source from which it emanates."[7]

> "Goodwill regarded as property has no meaning except in connection with some trade, business, or calling. In that connection I understand the word to include whatever adds value to a business by reason of situation, name and reputation, connection, introduction to old customers, and agreed absence from competition, or any of these things, and there may be others which do not occur to me. In this wide sense, goodwill is inseparable from the business to which it adds value, and, in my opinion, exists where the business is carried on. Such business may be carried on in one place or country or in several, and if in several there may be several businesses, each having a goodwill of its own."[8]

Judicial opinions have differed as to precisely what may be included in the term goodwill. There is no doubt that for some purposes at least goodwill includes the benefit of a particular site, for instance of a retail shop or public house. It has also been suggested that goodwill includes the benefit of valid covenants in restraint of trade.[9] Fortunately, for the purposes of passing-off one need only be concerned with those components of goodwill which are capable of being damaged by misrepresentation. Natural advantages of the claimant's business, such as its situation, are not likely to be so damaged,

---

[5] *Anheuser-Busch Inc v Budejovicky Budvar NP* [1984] F.S.R. 413, CA.
[6] *per* Sir Stephen Browne P. in *Scandecor Development AB v Scandecor Marketing AB* [1999] F.S.R. 26, CA.
[7] *per* Lord Macnaghten in *Inland Revenue Commissioners v Muller & Co's Margarine Ltd* [1901] A.C. 217, 223, HL.
[8] *ibid.*, *per* Lord Lindley at 235.
[9] *per* Lord Lindley in *Inland Revenue Commissioners v Muller & Co's Margarine Ltd* [1901] A.C. 217, HL. Compare *Churton v Douglas* (1859) 70 E.R. 385, a classic definition by Page-Wood V.C. which excludes them. The benefit of such covenants certainly passes with the goodwill: *Jacoby v Whitmore* (1883) 49 L.T. 335, CA.

nor are the benefits of existing contracts with customers or potential competitors.

Goodwill in England is personal property.   3–3

"It is very difficult, as it seems to me, to say that goodwill is not property. Goodwill is bought and sold every day. It may be acquired, I think, in any of the different ways in which property is usually acquired. When a man has got it he may keep it as his own. He may vindicate his exclusive right to it if necessary by process of law. He may dispose of it if he will—of course under the conditions attaching to property of that nature."[10]

Goodwill is to be considered as a whole. Passing-off requires only that damage should be caused to the goodwill of the claimant's business as a result of the defendant's misrepresentation. It is therefore unnecessary to attempt to sever the claimant's goodwill into its various components: damage of any recognised kind to the whole or any part of the goodwill is sufficient. "It is the injury to the goodwill rather than the precise method of inflicting that injury that matters".[11] Components which are obviously incapable of being damaged by misrepresentation, such as the advantage of being in a busy shopping street, are inapplicable to passing-off and may be disregarded.

"Goodwill is composed of a variety of elements. It differs in its composition in different trades and in different businesses in the same trade. One element may preponderate here and another element there. To analyse goodwill and split it up into its component parts ... seems to me to be as useful for practical purposes as it would be to resolve the human body into the various substances of which it is said to be composed. The goodwill of a business is one whole, and in a case like this it must be dealt with as such."[12]

Distinction between goodwill and rights in names or trade marks

Since the right of property protected by the action for passing-off is the   3–4
goodwill of the claimant's business as a whole, passing-off does not directly protect marks, get-up or other signs and indicia[13]; nor does it recognise them as forms of property in their own right. There is no such thing as an action for infringement of a common-law trade mark.[14] Of course, trade marks in the widest sense are of the greatest importance in passing-off because the

---

[10] Above at n.7.
[11] *per* Megarry V.C. in *British Broadcasting Co v Talbot Motor Co Ltd* [1981] F.S.R. 228.
[12] *per* Lord Macnaghten in *Inland Revenue Commissioners v Muller & Co's Margarine Ltd* [1901] A.C. 217, 223, HL, at 224 (a stamp duty case). Compare *HFC Bank plc v Midland Bank plc* [2000] F.S.R. 176.
[13] *Payton & Co v Snelling, Lampard & Co* (1899) 17 R.P.C. 48 affirmed [1901] A.C. 308; 17 R.P.C. 628; *Burberrys v J C Cording & Co Ltd* (1909) 26 R.P.C. 693; as well as the cases cited at n.1 above.
[14] Trade Marks Act 1994, s.2(2); and see *Inter Lotto (UK) Ltd v Camelot Group plc* [2003] EWHC 1256; [2003] 3 All E.R. 191, (Laddie J.), affirmed [2003] EWCA Civ 1132, CA.

essential element of misrepresentation often depends on whether the claimant's alleged indicia have trade mark significance. If they do, then use of a deceptively similar sign by the defendant is likely to constitute a misrepresentation. But it is still "a right of property in the business or goodwill in connection with which the mark was being used"[15] which the action is protecting, not any goodwill in the mark itself.

> "On the one hand, apart from the laws as to trade marks, no one can claim monopoly rights in the use of a word or name. On the other hand, no one is entitled by the use of any word or name, or indeed in any other way, to represent his goods as being the goods of another to that other's injury. If an injunction be granted restraining the use of a word or name, it is no doubt granted to protect property, but the property, to protect which it is granted, is not property in the word or name, but property in the trade or goodwill which will be injured by its use."[16]

3–5 Because passing-off normally turns on the misuse by the defendant of some name, mark, get-up or other sign distinctive of the claimant, it is tempting to regard the claimant as having a specific goodwill in that sign which is protected by the action for passing-off. However, passing-off is not confined to such cases, and the misrepresentation need not take the form of misuse of a distinctive sign to which goodwill might be said to attach:

> "Cases of misrepresentation by the use of a mark, name, or get-up do not exhaust all possible cases of misrepresentation. If A says falsely, 'These goods I am selling are B's goods,' there is no mark, name, or get-up infringed unless it be B's name, and if he falsely says, 'These are B's goods of a particular quality,' where the goods are in fact B's goods, there is no name that is infringed at all."[17]

It should also be remembered that goodwill is a form of legal property and is only valuable to the extent that it can be protected through the courts. Although it is possible to speak of the goodwill attached to a mark, or the goodwill in a mark, this can mean no more than the mark as legal property: the right to protect the mark against infringement.[18] A "common law trade mark" may be property in a limited sense, since under certain circumstances it can be assigned,[19] but the right to bring an action for its infringement is excluded by statute.[20] If passing-off were based on the protection of the goodwill in a specific mark, as opposed to the goodwill of the business as a

---

[15] per Lord Diplock in *Star Industrial Co Ltd v Yap Kwee Kor* [1976] F.S.R. 256, 271, PC.

[16] per Parker J. in *Burberrys v J C Cording & Co Ltd* (1909) 26 R.P.C. 693.

[17] per Lord Parker in *Spalding (AG) & Bros v A W Gamage Ltd* (1915) 32 R.P.C. 275, 284, HL.

[18] Compare the passage from the judgment of Lord Evershed M.R. in *Adrema Maschinenbau GmbH v Custodian of Enemy Property* [1957] R.P.C. 49, CA, set out below.

[19] Trade Marks Act 1994, s.24(6).

[20] Trade Marks Act 1994, s.2(2).

whole, it would be indistinguishable from the abolished common law infringement action.[21]

Distinction between goodwill and reputation

Goodwill as a form of legal property is also to be distinguished from mere **3-6** reputation, which is primarily a matter of fact. In so far as reputation may be a legally protected interest, it is a non-proprietary one. It is true that the two are very closely related, and a business with goodwill (at least in the sense in which it is used in passing-off) can hardly fail to have a reputation in some sense. The converse, however, is not true, and the existence of a reputation associated with a person, product, name or mark does not necessarily imply the existence of goodwill:

> "[T]hat, as it seems to me, is to confuse goodwill, which cannot exist in a vacuum, with mere reputation which may, no doubt, and frequently does, exist without any supporting local business, but which does not by itself constitute a property which the law protects."[22]

Reputation may be relevant to the passing-off action in three respects. The most important is that proof of misrepresentation often turns on the reputation of the claimant's mark in the sense of its being recognised as distinctive by a sufficiently large proportion of the public. The other two are that the claimant's reputation, in a somewhat different sense, will suffer if the goods passed off by the defendant are inferior; and that the existence of reputation (in either preceding sense) may go some way to proving the existence of goodwill. It is unfortunately not uncommon to find the word "reputation" used interchangeably in the various senses of widespread repute, perceived high quality, trade mark distinctiveness, and goodwill in the strict sense. Likewise "goodwill" is quite often used when reputation in some sense is meant.

The interest protected after *Harrods*

It would be hard to imagine names of higher reputation—in every sense—in **3-7** their respective fields than *Harrods*[23] or *Mercedes-Benz*[24] or *Elvis Presley*,[25] but the majority judgments of the Court of Appeal in *Harrods v Harrodian School*[26] emphasise that even a name of exceptionally high inherent and acquired distinctiveness, and one which could be described without exaggeration as "world-famous" and "a household name" is not protected in its own right: the defendants were free to use the adjectival form as the name of

---

[21] Compare *Thorneloe v Hill* [1894] 1 Ch. 569; [1891–4] All E.R. 1263.

[22] per Oliver L.J. in *Anheuser-Busch Inc v Budejovicky Budvar NP* [1984] F.S.R. 413, CA.

[23] *Harrods Ltd v Harrodian School Ltd* [1996] R.P.C. 597. CA.

[24] *Daimler Chrysler AG v Alavi* [2001] E.T.M.R. 98; [2001] R.P.C. 42 (Pumfrey J.).

[25] *Elvis Presley Trade Marks* [1999] R.P.C. 567, CA.

[26] [1996] R.P.C. 697, CA.

their school, because the goodwill of the plaintiffs in their business of a department store did not stand to be damaged.[27]

> "It is well settled that (unless registered as a trade mark) no one has a monopoly in his brand name or get up, however familiar these may be. Passing off is a wrongful invasion of a right of property vested in the plaintiff but the property which is protected by an action for passing off is not the plaintiff's proprietary right in the name or get up which the defendant has misappropriated but the goodwill and reputation of his business which is likely to be harmed by the defendant's misrepresentation.
> It is this fundamental principle of the law of passing off which leads me to reject the main way in which the Plaintiffs have put their case before us. ... The name 'Harrods' may be universally recognised, but the business with which it is associated in the minds of the public is not all-embracing. To be known to everyone is not to be known for everything."

3–8 Notwithstanding a last-minute argument that its reputation would suffer because of an alleged adulterous affair between the Headmistress and the English Master at the defendant school, it is noticeable that *Harrods* actually prospered over a decade in which it was at the centre of litigation and controversy in which far more serious allegations were traded. It was in one of these cases (an action for conspiracy to injure by lawful means, in which pecuniary damage is the gist of the action), that Dillon L.J. observed[28]:

> "To prove loss of orders and loss of trade is another matter that is recognisable pecuniary damage. Such loss of orders, for example, would involve injury to the goodwill of a business which may be one of the most important assets of the business. But goodwill in that sense must have the meaning put on that word in *Trego v Hunt* [1896] A.C. 7: see especially, *per* Lord Herschell, at pp.17–18, and *per* Lord Macnaghten, at p.24. It cannot mean some airy-fairy general reputation in the business or commercial community which is unrelated to the buying and selling or dealing with customers which is the essence of the business of any trading company."

On an application to strike out the statement of claim, the damage which allowed the re-amended statement of claim to stand was to Lonrho's various trading interests. Claims by Lonrho and individual plaintiffs for conspiracy to damage their reputation were struck out as sounding in defamation or not at all.

---

[27] The status of *Harrods* as a household name lessened, but did not eliminate, the significance of the absence of any common field of activity, according to Millett L.J., speaking for the majority. Even the protection afforded to household names such as *Marks and Spencer* in *British Telecommunications plc v One in a Million* [1999] 1 W.L.R. 903; [1998] 4 All E.R. 476; [1999] E.T.M.R. 61; [1999] F.S.R. 1, CA was expressly predicated on an actual, or threatened, fraudulent misrepresentation of some kind.

[28] *Lonrho plc v Fayed (No.5)* [1993] 1 W.L.R. 1489, CA.

Whether goodwill may exist without business

The form of words used by both Lord Parker in *Spalding v Gamage*[29] and by **3–9**
Lord Diplock in *Star*[30] and *Advocaat*[31] contemplates that the damage which
is the basis of the action for passing-off may be caused either to the business
or to the goodwill of the claimant. This raises the question of whether the
two can ever be separate. May the claimant in a passing-off action have a
business but no goodwill, or goodwill without a business? To appreciate the
significance of this it must be remembered that the English tort of passing-
off only protects a business or goodwill so far as it exists in England.[32]
Although goodwill can probably only be created as a result of trading
activities it does not follow that a trader must have a business in England for
goodwill to exist here.

The simpler case concerns businesses which have ceased to trade without
their goodwill being extinguished. It is well established[33] that a passing-off
action may succeed if the goodwill of the former business still exists, even if
the business itself ceased several years ago. It is not even essential that there
should be definite plans to recommence it. Subsisting goodwill arising from
a formerly subsisting business is therefore a sufficient basis for a passing-off
action.

Actions by foreign traders are another example of goodwill in England
being protected in the absence of a business here.[34] A foreign claimant with
customers in England may have a goodwill in this country capable of being
protected by a passing-off action even if his business is wholly carried on
abroad, for instance because his goods are handled by a third party or are
imported by individual end users.

Goodwill itself as the right protected

Although the passages cited above[35] speak in terms of damage being caused **3–10**
either to the claimant's business or to his goodwill, the two are not strictly
speaking comparable. Goodwill is undoubtedly legal property and its nature
is reasonably well understood. A business, however, is something rather
broader and would not normally be thought of as a form of property at all.
This may account for Lord Parker's caution in accepting that passing-off
necessarily protects a proprietary right. English law has tended to understand passing-off primarily in terms of damage to goodwill, partly because

---

[29] (1915) 32 R.P.C. 263, HL.

[30] *Star Industrial Co Ltd v Yap Kwee Kor* [1976] F.S.R. 256, PC.

[31] *Erven Warnink BV v J Townend & Sons (Hull) Ltd* [1979] A.C. 731; [1979] 2 All E.R. 927;
[1980] R.P.C. 31, HL.

[32] *Anheuser-Busch Inc v Budejovicky Budar NP* [1984] F.S.R. 413, CA.

[33] *Kark (Norman) Publications Ltd v Odhams Press Ltd* [1962] R.P.C. 163.

[34] *SA des Anciens Etablissements Panhard et Levassor v Panhard Levassor Motor Co Ltd* [1901]
2 Ch. 513; [1900–3] All E.R. 477; 18 R.P.C. 405.

[35] From *Spalding (AG) & Bros v A W Gamage Ltd* (1915) 32 R.P.C. 73, HL; *Star Industrial
Co Ltd v Yap Kwee Kor* [1976] F.S.R. 256, PC and *Erven Warnink BV v J Townend & Sons
(Hull) Ltd* [1979] A.C. 731; [1979] 2 All E.R. 927; [1980] R.P.C. 31, HL.

goodwill has not always been distinguished from the claimant's reputation in the indicia taken by the defendant.

It is sometimes said that goodwill itself is the essential basis of the action for passing-off. This is an attractive point of view. First, it deals with the question of why damages for passing-off are not recoverable by every business in the chain of distribution from manufacturer to retailer. In general, only one business in the chain is likely to have any relevant goodwill with the consuming public and it is only that business which can complain of passing-off. However, if damage to business generally were sufficient, then each party from manufacturer to retailer would apparently be able to sue, since an order lost is a loss to all. Secondly, goodwill is undoubtedly a form of legal property. It has a clearly understood meaning, and is particularly liable to be damaged by the misrepresentations recognised in passing-off. The concept of "business" is wide and indeterminate in comparison.

Business with little or no goodwill

3–11 It has been suggested that some businesses may be of such a nature that they are incapable of having any goodwill. In principle, this might be true of a travelling hawker who never visited the same address twice, but such a business is hardly likely to be damaged by the sort of misrepresentation with which passing-off is concerned. If damage to either the business as such or to its goodwill is a sufficient basis for the action then the question is probably academic. In any event, the courts are very unwilling to assume that a business can have customers but no goodwill.

The mere fact that the claimant's business is very small does not prevent it having a goodwill. In *Stacey v 2020 Communications*[36] an individual working from home certainly had a goodwill to protect, though he failed to obtain an interlocutory injunction on the balance of convenience. Likewise, in *Teleworks v Telework Group*[37] the reason for the claimant's failure was not that it was too small to have goodwill to protect, but that its reputation was too slight to conclude that the defendant's use of a similar name in a non-competitive field would deceive. In a somewhat comparable Scottish case, interim interdict was granted in favour of a sole trader with an annual turnover of about £250,000 and a record of trading since 1983: *Thistle Communications v Thistle Telecom*.[38]

3–12 The acceptable limit is probably represented by *Stannard v Reay*[39] in which an interlocutory injunction was granted to the proprietor of a mobile fish and chip van in a holiday resort. Given the transient nature of most of the plaintiff's custom the element of goodwill must have been small.

In *Hart v Relentless Records*[40] the claimant had unsuccessfully tried to promote a record company under the name *Relentless Recordings* over a

---

[36] [1991] F.S.R. 49 (Millett J.).
[37] [2002] R.P.C. 27 (Christopher Floyd Q.C., Deputy Judge). The claimant's turnover was a little less than £250,000 in its best year, representing about 0.001 per cent of the overall market.
[38] 2000 S.L.T. 262 (Lord Hamilton, O.H.).
[39] [1967] R.P.C. 589 (Buckley J.).
[40] [2002] EWHC 1984; [2003] F.S.R. 36 (Jacob J.).

period of three years before the defendants adopted a similar name, but he had never got any further than issuing four promotional tracks to DJs and receiving some ephemeral mention in specialist magazines and perhaps on radio. Jacob J. held that he had no goodwill. There had been no trading, the name never came before the public, and no recordings had been released on a commercial basis.

In *Aubanel and Alabaster v Aubanel*[41] the parties competed in the cork trade where the number of suppliers and trade customers was so small and other circumstances such that it was said to be normal for a purchaser to seek quotations from all suppliers and buy from the cheapest. The defendant's argument that the plaintiffs had no goodwill because of these factors was rejected.

In *Austen v Boys*[42] it was suggested that a solicitor's business could not have any goodwill because of the degree of personal trust and confidence involved. This is either obsolete, or correct only in so far as it means that the goodwill does not become attached to the premises of the solicitor as opposed to the firm itself. In general, professional practices may have goodwill capable of being protected. In *Burchell v Wilde*[43] the Court of Appeal treated a solicitors' practice as having goodwill.

In most cases it is sufficient to ask if the claimant has a goodwill here. If **3–13** the answer is in the affirmative then it does not matter whether the goodwill results from the claimant actually carrying on a business here or not. If the answer is negative then there are two reasons why passing-off is unlikely even if the claimant can be said to have a business. One is that no misrepresentation of the sort which can amount to passing-off is likely to damage the business of a trader who, ex hypothesi, has no goodwill to bring in more business. The other is that since goodwill and reputation tend to go together it is equally unlikely that any but the most express misrepresentation would be taken as referring to the claimant.

An anomaly when passing-off occurs abroad

Passing off occurring in foreign countries is the one context in which a **3–14** claimant may clearly base his action on damage to an English business whether or not it has an English goodwill. It is well established that there may be passing-off actionable under English law even though both parties compete solely in the export trade. In such a case the nature of the goods and the mark under which they are sold are likely to be specific to a particular foreign market and the claimant may have no customers in England for those goods.[44] In some cases the claimant may have no domestic retail business at all. Misrepresentations by the defendant, whether made in England or abroad, would not thereby be actionable under English law if the only property damaged were the claimant's goodwill in the foreign market. Since the claimant need have no relevant goodwill in England it can

---

[41] (1949) 66 R.P.C. 343 (Dankwerts J.).

[42] (1858) 44 E.R. 1123 (Lord Chelmsford L.C.).

[43] [1900] 1 Ch. 551, CA. See also *Neumgen v Neumgen & Co* [1998] 3 N.Z.L.R. 311, CA of NZ.

[44] For example *Johnston v Orr-Ewing* (1882) 7 App. Cas. 219, HL.

only be the damage to the claimant's business in England which is the basis of the action for passing-off. Like much of the law relating to "instruments of deception" in the export trade the result is an anomaly which it is difficult to reconcile with purely domestic law. There is even an early example of passing-off abroad being restrained purely on the basis of personal jurisdiction over the defendant, the plaintiff having no business or goodwill of any sort in England,[45] but the same decision could not now be reached without express consideration of private international law principles.

Distinction between "personal" and "local" goodwill

3–15 Although the goodwill of a business falls to be considered as a whole, there is one important component which is irrelevant for the purposes of passing-off. This is the goodwill which attaches to the premises in which the business is carried on, rather than to the proprietor of the business. It has been said[46] that in its original sense goodwill was always appurtenant to land and that the concept of personal goodwill was a later development.

"It is quite plain that the goodwill of a public house passes with the public house. In such a case the goodwill is the mere habit of the customers resorting to the house. It is not what is called a personal goodwill."[47]

"A division of the elements of goodwill was referred to during the argument and appears in Mr Merlin's book as the 'cat, rat and dog' basis. The cat prefers the old home ... though the person who has kept the house leaves. The cat represents that part of the customers who continue to go to the old shop, though the old shopkeeper has gone; the probability of their custom may be regarded as an additional value given to the premises by the tenant's trading. The dog represents that part of the customers who follow the person rather than the place; these the tenant may take away with him if he does not go too far. There remains a class of customer who may neither follow the place nor the person, but drift away elsewhere. They are neither a benefit to the landlord nor the tenant, and have been called 'the rat' for no particular reason except to keep the epigram in the animal kingdom. I believe my brother Maugham has introduced the rabbit, but I will leave him to explain the position of the rabbit. It is obvious that the division of the customers into 'cat, rat and dog' must vary enormously in different cases and different circumstances."[48]

Passing-off is concerned with "dog" goodwill, because it is the dog in this example who is loyal to the person carrying on the business. In modern conditions, trade, and consequently goodwill, need not be associated with

[45] *Collins v Brown* (1857) 69 E.R. 1174.
[46] *Arguendo* in *Inland Revenue Commissioners v Muller & Co's Margarine Ltd* [1901] A.C. 217, HL.
[47] *per* Jessel M.R. in *Re Kitchin Ex p. Punnett* (1880) 16 Ch.D. 226, CA.
[48] *per* Scrutton L.J. in *Whiteman Smith Motor Co v Chaplin* [1934] 2 K.B. 35 at 42, CA.

specific premises at all. "Cat" goodwill is irrelevant to passing-off. Customers represented by the cat do business with the claimant only because of the location of his premises. They are therefore unlikely to be wooed to another location by a misrepresentation that the person trading there is connected with the claimant.

Goodwill which is local in the sense of benefiting and belonging to a piece of land (as opposed to the business carried on there) is to be distinguished from goodwill belonging to a business which is local in the sense that the customers of the business are to be found in a limited geographical area.

When goodwill has to be considered

In the normal passing-off case there is little doubt that the claimant is a **3–16** trader with a business and goodwill and it is not necessary to deal specifically with the point at trial. However, there are certain types of case in which the existence or absence of goodwill may be the major issue. If the claimant has no goodwill or business in the jurisdiction then the action must fail as a matter of law. In particular, no saving inference can be drawn from the behaviour of the defendant even if it amounts to deliberate fraud. For the defendant to have copied the indicia claimed by the claimant proves, at most, that those indicia enjoy a reputation. It does not prove that there is any goodwill attached to them in the legal sense, still less that any such goodwill is owned by the claimant.[49]

The cases in which the existence of goodwill may be a major issue tend to fall into six categories: non-traders as claimants; foreign claimants; mis-identification of the proper claimant; defective title, in particular reliance on an assignment in gross; business which have been abandoned; and businesses for which preparations have been made but which have not yet commenced trading. All except the first and last may be illustrated in two Privy Council decisions.

In *Star Industrial v Yap Kwee Kor*[50] the defendants closely copied the brand name and get-up previously used by the plaintiffs for their toothbrushes in Singapore. The plaintiffs had abandoned their trade some years previously and had assigned their goodwill to another company. The Privy Council held that the plaintiffs' claim was bound to fail even though the defendants' conduct raised an irresistible inference that reputation and goodwill still attached to the get-up.

In *Ullman v Leuba*[51] the Privy Council allowed an appeal by the defendants and held that the plaintiffs should have been non-suited even though the question of title had hardly been disputed at trial. The plaintiffs as Swiss manufacturers were held to have no goodwill in Hong Kong on their own account and an agreement on which they relied was held to be an ineffective attempt to assign trade marks in gross.

---

[49] *Star Industrial Co Ltd v Yap Kwee Kor* [1976] F.S.R. 256, PC; *Bernadin (Alain) et Cie v Pavilion Properties Ltd* [1967] R.P.C. 581. Both were cases of obvious fraud in which injunctions were refused.
[50] [1976] F.S.R. 256, PC.
[51] (1908) 25 R.P.C. 673, PC.

The interest protected by the action for injurious falsehood

3–17 The action for injurious falsehood protects the pecuniary or economic interests of the claimant (thereby distinguishing itself from defamation, which protects honour and reputation) but is not confined to protecting goodwill in the sense recognised in passing-off. So, for instance, actions for injurious falsehood have successfully been brought by private individuals in respect of damage to their employment prospects,[52] or other economic interests not amounting to trading goodwill,[53] and a foreign company with no goodwill in the jurisdiction is not precluded from suing for injurious falsehood despite being unable to maintain an action for passing-off.[54]

B. The Meaning of "Business" and "Trader"

The general principle

3–18 According to Lord Diplock in *Advocaat*,[55] the second of the "five characteristics which must be present in order to create a valid cause of action for passing-off" is that the misrepresentation should be one "made by a trader in the course of trade . . .". The fourth and fifth refer to damage to the "business or goodwill of the trader" by whom the action is brought. In previous editions it has been assumed that the single word "trader" has the same extended meaning in respect of both claimant and defendant, and this gave rise to little or no practical difficulty. However, the increasing tendency towards protection and concomitant liability when one or both parties are obviously not traders in any normal sense requires reconsideration of this assumption from first principles. As Robert Walker J. remarked in *British Diabetic Association v The Diabetic Society*[56] "[T]he wider the scope of passing off, the more caution is needed in applying principles which may have been formulated with reference to a totally different set of facts".

It is now suggested that the necessary status of the claimant and defendant as traders derives from two different elements in the "classical trinity" of goodwill, misrepresentation and damage. In the case of the claimant, his status as a trader is almost synonymous with the fact that he must have goodwill to protect, since goodwill is defined in terms of trading activities:

---

[52] *Joyce v Sengupta* [1993] 1 W.L.R. 337; [1993] 1 All E.R. 897, CA. In *Spring v Guardian Assurance plc* [1993] 2 All E.R. 273; [1993] ICR 412, CA (on appeal without reference to this issue [1995] 2 A.C. 296, HL) the claim failed on the facts.
[53] *Kaye v Robertson* [1991] F.S.R. 62, CA. The plaintiff (a popular actor) obtained an interlocutory injunction against injurious falsehood but was held not to have sufficient status as a trader to support an action for passing-off.
[54] *Anheuser-Busch Inc v Budejovicky Budvar NP* [1984] F.S.R. 413, CA. The injurious falsehood claim failed on the facts, but unlike that for passing-off it was not dismissed *in limine*.
[55] *Erven Warnink BV v J Townend & Sons (Hull) Ltd* [1979] A.C. 731; [1979] 2 All E.R. 927; [1980] R.P.C. 31, HL.
[56] [1996] F.S.R. 1 (Robert Walker J.).

"Passing-off is a remedy which is designed to protect some form of property—usually the goodwill of the plaintiff in his business or his goods or his services or in the work which he produces or something of that kind."[57] In the case of the defendant, on the other hand, it arises from the kind of misrepresentations with which passing-off is concerned, which are those that tend to misappropriate the benefit of the claimant's goodwill, so that misrepresentations actionable as passing-off may be distinguished from those in injurious falsehood or defamation, as well as those which are not actionable at all. If different factors underlie the respective requirements that the claimant and defendant must both be traders, then it may follow that a purposive interpretation of Lord Diplock's speech can result in the word receiving a slightly different meaning or nuance in each context.[58]

The boundaries of trading activity

There has never been any doubt that the concept of trader for the purposes **3–19** of passing-off is extremely wide. No general definition exists and to give one would risk excluding unusual businesses for no good reason. However, it seems that any person who derives an income from the provision of goods or services can be said to be a trader. "[T]he word 'trade' is widely interpreted and includes persons engaged in a professional, artistic or literary occupation."[59]

Examples have included professional writers (from *Aunt Naomi* to James Joyce)[60]; a greyhound racing tipster and the promoters of a lottery[61]; a newspaper cartoonist and a crossword puzzle setter[62]; pop groups and a classical musician[63]; a professional motor racing driver,[64] and, in Australia, professional ballroom dancers.[65] In the very early case of *Archbold v Sweet*[66] a barrister recovered nominal damages in his capacity as the author of a legal textbook (but not for alleged damage to his professional practice as such) and in *Clark v Associated Newspapers* the well-known politician, historian and diarist Alan Clark was successful in his capacity as an

---

[57] *per* Buckley L.J. in *Kean v McGivan* [1982] F.S.R. 119, CA; quoted with approval by Brooke L.J. in *Burge v Haycock* [2001] EWCA Civ 900; [2002] R.P.C. 28, CA.

[58] For the trading status of the defendant, see Chapter 3 Section G.

[59] *per* Ackner L.J. in *Kean v McGivan* [1982] F.S.R. 119, CA.

[60] Respectively *Landa v Greenberg* (1908) 24 T.L.R. 441 and *Sweeney v Macmillan Publishers Ltd* [2002] R.P.C. 35.

[61] *Shallis v Freeman and Stirling Press Ltd* (1931) 48 R.P.C. 370 and *Inter Lotto (UK) Ltd v Camelot Group Plc* [2003] EWHC 1256; [2003] 3 All E.R.

[62] *Marengo v Daily Sketch & Sunday Graphic Ltd* [1948] 1 All E.R. 406; 65 R.P.C. 242, HL and *Lovatt v Consolidated Magazines* (1988) 12 I.P.R. 26 (Wilcox J., Federal Court of Australia).

[63] *Sutherland v V2 Music Ltd* [2002] EWHC 14; [2002] E.M.L.R. 28 (affirmed [2003] EWCA Civ 1132, CA) and (Sir Thomas) *Beecham v British Lion* (1951) 68 R.P.C. 111.

[64] *Irvine v Talksport Ltd* [2002] EWHC 367, [2002] 1 W.L.R. 2355, [2002] 2 All E.R. 414, [2002] E.M.L.R. 32, [2002] F.S.R. 60 (Laddie J.), affirmed (as to liability) [2003] EWCA Civ 423, [2003] 2 All E.R. 881, [2003] E.M.L.R. 26, CA.

[65] *Henderson v Radio Corporation Pty Ltd* [1960] N.S.W.L.R. 279; [1969] R.P.C. 218.

[66] (1832) 1 M. & Rob. 162; 5 Car. & P. 219. *Archbold's Pleading and Practice.*

author.[67] The oldest profession of all is represented, albeit only as a defendant, by the escort agency in *Annabel's v Schock*.[68]

To an increasing extent *locus standi* has also been asserted and acknowledged in cases brought by clubs, various kinds of associations, charities, churches, and even political parties or interest groups.

3–20 The cases which follow on public bodies, charities, churches, clubs, political parties, and (to some extent) associations all raise the same issue, which is whether a body can be said to enjoy a goodwill when it does not carry on any business with the public in the normal sense, but still benefits from voluntary membership, subscriptions, donations or support so as to be capable of being damaged by a misrepresentation in the nature of passing-off. The modern tendency is to recognise that bodies of this kind do have goodwill capable of being protected, so that it is increasingly unhelpful simply to ask whether the claimant can be said to carry on any trade. But whatever the claimant may do by way of trading or otherwise, it is in his capacity as a trader that he must suffer damage. To this extent, the old authorities are still relevant, even if their language has been superceded. In some of the cases which follow, the claimant suffered nothing more serious than a degree of inconvenience or embarrassment which might not have been recognised as legal damage even if he had been a trader.[69] There is still no reason to doubt that private individuals, in their capacity as such, have no *locus standi* in passing-off.

Public bodies

3–21 Bodies discharging public or official functions are protected by the action for passing-off in so far as their activities generate goodwill in the normal sense, by trading, and presumably in the extended sense recognised for charities, associations, and the like. In accordance with general principles, It is not necessary for the claimant to aim to trade at a profit,[70] nor does it matter that the trade may be carried on for public or altruistic reasons. The proprietors of the Royal Albert Hall may have failed on the facts,[71] but their action was maintainable in principle. The British Broadcasting Corporation has been a successful plaintiff,[72] as has a statutory totalisator board.[73] In *BBC Worldwide v Pally Screen Printing*[74] a merchandising subsidiary of the

---

[67] [1998] 1 W.L.R. 1558; [1998] 1 All E.R. 959; [1998] R.P.C. 261 (Lightman J.).

[68] [1976] R.P.C. 838, CA; as explained by Lord Denning M.R. in *Miss World (Jersey) Ltd v James St Productions Ltd* [1981] F.S.R. 309, CA.

[69] Compare *Street v Bank of Spain and England* (1885) 30 Ch.D. 156 with *Day v Brownrigg* (1878) 10 Ch.D. 295, CA. In both the respective plaintiffs had to suffer the inconvenience caused by identical telegraphic or postal addresses. Street was a trader, Day was not. Both were refused injunctions.

[70] Dictum in *Lagos Chamber of Commerce Incorp v Registrar of Companies and Association of Merchants and Industrialists* (1955) 72 R.P.C. 263, PC, not strictly a passing-off case.

[71] *Corporation of the Hall of Arts and Sciences v Albert Edward Hall* (1934) 51 R.P.C. 398. The defendant promoted and conducted a dance band as *The Albert Hall Orchestra*.

[72] *British Broadcasting Co v Talbot Motor Co Ltd* [1981] F.S.R. 228; *BBC v Talksport Ltd* [2001] F.S.R. 6.

[73] *Totalizator Agency Board v Turf News Pty Ltd* [1967] V.R. 605; [1972] R.P.C. 570.

[74] [1998] F.S.R. 665 (Laddie J.).

BBC failed to obtain an interlocutory injunction in respect of unlicensed use of the *Teletubbies* characters, but the determinative issue was absence of any misrepresentation. For successful passing-off actions brought by the Law Society, a private body which discharges public functions, see *Law Society of England and Wales v Griffiths*[75] and *Law Society of England and Wales v Society of Lawyers*.[76]

In *Borough of Morecambe and Heysham v Mecca*[77] the plaintiff local authority, "possessed of a spirit of enterprise", promoted a beauty contest which became known as *Miss Great Britain*. There was a charge for admission to the finals but they made no profit from the contest themselves and their motive was to draw holidaymakers to Morecambe and so to benefit local businesses. The defendants, after a period of collaboration with the plaintiffs, started a rival contest as *Miss Britain*. The plaintiffs were refused an interlocutory injunction (mainly on the ground of delay) and failed at trial to prove significant confusion between the two contests. Otherwise, Buckley J. would have allowed as damages any increased financial burden to the council in running the contest which might have arisen from confusion with the defendants' contest: "[The council] do not run this contest for profit, but that does not mean that they would not suffer any damage if the contest became less popular, for they do to a large extent finance the contest". However, although the contest was ultimately conducted for the benefit of the ratepayers of Morecambe, any effect on the trade of the borough as a whole, as opposed to damage to the council itself, would have been irrecoverable.[78]

Nice and Safe Attitude v Flook[79] is inconclusive as to whether the scientific activities of the American National Aeronautics and Space Administration (*NASA*) were relevant to an action for passing-off, since it had little presence in England, and in any event they were too remote from the field of fashion clothing. A licence from NASA (USA) to the defendant's suppliers did not avail the defendant against a plaintiff who had actually used *NASA* for clothing.

Clubs

A proprietary club such as a night club is a business like any other and **3–22** requires no special treatment in the law of passing-off. Injunctions have been granted in favour of proprietary clubs in *Annabel's v Schock*[80] and

---

[75] [1995] R.P.C. 16 (Aldous J.).

[76] [1996] F.S.R. 739 (Rimer J.).

[77] [1962] R.P.C. 145 (interlocutory); [1966] R.P.C. 423 (trial). Compare *Derbyshire CC v Times Newspapers* [1993] AC 534, HL, holding that a local authority could sue in injurious falsehood, though not in libel.

[78] A similar distinction was drawn in *Artistic Upholstery v Art Forma (Furniture)* [1999] 4 All E.R. 277; [2000] F.S.R. 311 between the interest of the representative plaintiff as member of a trade association which promoted exhibitions, and its interest as a manufacturer of furniture.

[79] [1997] F.S.R. 14 (Robert Walker J.).

[80] [1976] R.P.C. 838, CA.

Ad-Lib Club v Granville.[81] Professional sports clubs such as *Arsenal*[82] also require no special analysis.

The position of a private members' club such as a sports or social club is more difficult. In general, one would not necessarily think of such a club as being a trader or as carrying on a business in the normal sense of those words. However, in *British Legion v British Legion Club (Street) Ltd*[83] an injunction was granted against a social club of about 500 members in a small village. The action for passing-off lies only against traders, and if the criteria for claimant and defendant are comparable, then this would suggest that such a club could itself sue for passing-off in an appropriate case.

3–23   The position of a members' club somewhere between the private and proprietary extremes did arise obliquely in *Harrods v Harrodian School.*[84] The defendants' school was on the site of the former *Harrodian Club*, but the club probably had little or no goodwill *vis-a-vis* the public at large since most of its former members were Harrods employees, and any goodwill it might ever have had in its own right must have been abandoned when the club closed. Millett L.J. observed:

> "The Plaintiffs rightly point out that the operation of a club for the benefit of employees is a trading activity, and that it would not matter if it were not—non-trading organisations such as clubs and charities are as much entitled to protection from passing-off as any one else. The Plaintiffs also submit that the Judge was wrong to disregard the separate but material reputation which the club acquired in Barnes as the staff club of *Harrods*.
>
> In my view these criticisms are misplaced. The Judge was not distinguishing between trading and non-trading activities but between the use of the name 'Harrods' in relation to goods or services supplied to customers, that is to say in the course of a trading activity calculated to generate goodwill, and the use of the name 'Harrodian' in connection with a club provided as a facility for employees. The use of the club's name when hiring out its premises to members of the public was a minor and incidental extension of the latter usage. But in any case the Plaintiffs have neither pleaded nor established a reputation for running a club, and if the club acquired any goodwill of its own in the name *Harrodian* it was abandoned when the business of the club was discontinued."

The implication seems to be that a private members' club is in much the same position as a trade association or a charity founded for mutual support: what goodwill it has exists principally with respect to its own membership, actual and prospective, and to the extent that such goodwill may be damaged it may have *locus standi* in a passing-off action.

---

[81] [1971] 2 All E.R. 300; [1972] R.P.C. 673 (Pennycuick V.C.).

[82] *Arsenal Football Club Plc v Reed* [2001] E.T.M.R. 77; [2001] R.P.C. 46 (Laddie J.). The passing-off claim failed for absence of misrepresentation, but the *locus standi* of the claimant club was not in doubt.

[83] (1931) 48 R.P.C. 555 (Farwell J.).

[84] [1996] R.P.C. 697, CA.

What is true for small clubs applies *a fortiori* to similar but larger asso- **3–24**
ciations, especially if they carry on trading activities of a more conventional
kind. In *Royal Automobile Association of South Australia v Hancock*[85] the
plaintiff association authorised certain garages to describe themselves as
"RAA" garages. Authorised garages performed breakdown services and the
like for members. A permanent injunction was granted against a defendant
who used this description without authority. In *RAC Motoring Services v
RAC (Publishing)*[86] the successful plaintiffs were a legally distinct entity to
the *Royal Automobile Club* itself, but nothing turned on the distinction.

Personalities: entertainers, sportsmen, etc.

The definition of "trader" for the purposes of the law of passing-off is quite **3–25**
wide enough to embrace those who make their living in entertainment, the
performing arts, professional sport, writing and the like. The issue of the
locus standi of such claimants has arisen in two main contexts: ownership of
pen names or stage names, and merchandising and endorsement. In *Irvine v
Talksport*[87] the professional motor racing driver Eddie Irvine obtained
damages of £25,000 (increased from £2,000 at first instance) for the use of
his photograph in a promotional mailshot in a way which implied that he
endorsed the defendants' radio station. Other illustrations are provided by
the conductor Sir Thomas Beecham in *Beecham v British Lion*[88] and the
professional boxer in *Serville v Constance*.[89] The latter failed for reasons
which are now partly obsolete, but there would have been no reason to
doubt his capacity to sue if he had been an English champion. The decision
of the Court of Appeal in *Kaye v Robertson*[90] illustrates that a distinction has
to be drawn between the private and professional lives of such individuals,
but is not necessarily the last word on where the line ought to be drawn.

Even sportsmen who are nominally amateurs more than arguably may
have goodwill in so far as they can attract sponsorship, grants or other
financial benefits, although the few authorities are not entirely satisfactory.[91]
In the Australian case of *Honey v Australian Airlines*[92] Northrop J. decided
that the plaintiff long jumper was technically an amateur, despite the fact
that he received financial benefits as a result of his athletic activities,
including being paid for endorsing *Nike* products. He had competed with
conspicuous success in the Olympic and Commonwealth Games which were

[85] [1939] S.A.S.R. 60 (Clelland J.).
[86] [1988] R.P.C. 321 (Browne-Wilkinson V.C.).
[87] [2003] EWCA Civ 423; [2003] 2 All E.R. 881; [2003] E.M.L.R. 26, CA affirming [2002]
EWHC 367; [2002] 1 W.L.R. 2355; [2002] All E.R. 414 [2002] E.M.L.R. 32; [2002] F.S.R. 60
(Laddie J.) as to liability and reversing [2003] EWHC 539 [2003] E.M.L.R. 6 (Laddie J.) on
quantum of damages.
[88] (1951) 68 R.P.C. 111. The defendants offered an undertaking.
[89] (1954) 71 R.P.C. 156 (Harman J.).
[90] [1991] F.S.R. 62, CA.
[91] The reasoning of *British Diabetic Association v The Diabetic Society* [1996] F.S.R. 1 is
applicable by analogy.
[92] (1990) 18 I.P.R. 185 (Federal Court of Australia) *affirming* (1989) 14 I.P.R. 264 (Northrop
J.).

perceived as amateur events. Although a passing-off action by him was unsuccessful on the facts, his claim would probably not have failed *in limine*. His recognised amateur status was said to be relevant to the conclusion that he would not have been perceived as having endorsed, for reward, the use made of his photograph by either of the two defendants, but this seems dubious. The distinction between amateur and professional sport was admittedly fine, and the public might either have supposed that he had changed status or that the endorsement in question was compatible with his continuing to be an amateur. The reasoning, if not perfect, is much preferable to that in another Australian decision, *Wickham v Associated Pool Builders*.[93]

Personal and family matters

3–26 It is not passing-off, nor otherwise actionable, to adopt a family name or title which is not one's own, nor even to impersonate a specific individual. Thomas Castro, the "Tichborne Claimant", was guilty of perjury and worse,[94] but would not have been liable for passing off. In *Du Boulay v Du Boulay*[95] the plaintiffs were a distinguished family on St Lucia and the defendant was the illegitimate son of a former slave of theirs who had adopted their name after emancipation. Although the proper law of the case was French law as it applied in St Lucia, the Privy Council made it clear that there would have been no remedy under English law: "[T]he mere assumption of a name, which is the patronymic of a family, by a stranger who had never before been called by that name, whatever cause of annoyance it may be to the family, is a grievance for which our law affords no redress".

In *Earl Cowley v Countess Cowley*[96] the House of Lords refused to restrain the divorced former wife of the Earl of Cowley from continuing to use the title Countess Cowley after her remarriage to a commoner.

Nor is it passing-off for one private individual to adopt the same name for his house as another, even though this may result in confusion and inconvenience.[97]

3–27 An action formerly lay to restrain a person from falsely claiming to be married to the plaintiff. The cause of action was not in passing-off but under an older and unconnected cause of action known as jactitation of marriage, which was abolished by the Family Law Act 1986, s.61. The *locus classicus* is *Hawke (Lord) v Corri*[98] in 1820 where it was already described as "a proceeding not very usually adopted of late years; but it has, I presume, a legal existence." A ceremony of marriage apparently took place, but:

"[T]he description given of the marriage certainly insinuates something of

---

[93] (1988) 12 I.P.R. 567 (Spender J., Federal Court).
[94] *R. v Castro* (1880) 5 Q.B.D. 490, CA.
[95] (1869) L.R. 2 P.C. 430, PC, *per* Lord Chelmsford.
[96] [1901] A.C. 450, HL.
[97] *Day v Brownrigg* (1878) 10 Ch.D. 292, CA.
[98] (1820) 161 E.R. 743 (Sir William Scott).

a doubt respecting its canonical regularity; for it in some degree appears to authorise a suspicion that the licence was a forged instrument, and the officiating minister a mere pretender to Holy Orders ... Lord Hawke ... asserts that [Corrie] was a married woman with a husband living during his cohabitation with her; and taking that to be an undisputed fact, there is an end to any legal consequence belonging to this marriage, if it did pass and in what manner it might."

In the event, the plea that the parties were validly married was withdrawn, but the action failed because Lord Hawke had cohabited with Mrs Corrie for several years and had held her out as his lawful wife to everyone from foreign governments to his own children by a previous marriage:

"It is too much to expect that, if a person imposes false characters of this nature upon the world, the Ecclesiastical Court is to interpose in his behalf, as soon as the consequences of such unfortunate conduct begin to assail him."

C. TRADE AND PROFESSIONAL ASSOCIATIONS

Trade and professional associations: introduction

Actions for passing-off have been allowed where the claimant has been an **3–28** association formed to represent the members of a particular trade or profession, or representing traders with some other interest in common.[99] It is not essential that the association should carry on any sort of trade with the public in its own right, nor that the damage suffered or expected should relate to such trading activities, if any. Such associations, even if non-profit making, have been said to stand in the same position as trading companies.[1] It does not matter whether the association is incorporated or not.[2]

There is ample authority that such an association may, in its own capacity, obtain relief for passing-off in the following circumstances:

1. Against a person who misrepresents himself as a member of the claimant association or as having a particular status or qualification conferred by it;

---

[99] The present section is not concerned with passing–off actions by associations whose members are not traders themselves, as in *British Legion v British Legion Club (Street) Ltd* (1931) 48 R.P.C. 555.
[1] *Lagos Chamber of Commerce Incorp v Registrar of Companies and Association of Merchants and Industrialists* (1955) 72 R.P.C. 263, PC. Strictly, not a passing-off case but one under the (Nigerian) Companies Ordinance.
[2] *Artistic Upholstery Ltd v Art Forma (Furniture)* [1999] 4 All E.R. 277; [2000] F.S.R. 311.

2. Against a competing association which misrepresents itself as the claimant association or claims the right for its members to use a designation distinctive of the claimant; and

3. More generally, against any other person misrepresenting himself as connected with the claimant association in such a way as to cause damage to its goodwill.

The status of the defendant as a trader is relevant as a separate issue: a solicitor or accountant misrepresenting himself as a member of a professional body would be liable for passing-off; and *a fortiori* if he had no such qualifications at all; but a private individual misrepresenting himself as a member of the *British Legion*, the *British Diabetic Association* or the *Countryside Alliance* probably would not.

3–29   Although the relevant decided cases have been concerned with actions brought by the associations themselves, it would also seem that in appropriate circumstances an individual member of the association might have a several right of action on his own behalf, or as a representative of other members, provided he could prove damage in his or their capacity as a trader. *Artistic Upholstery v Art Forma*[3] may be such a case, but is complicated by the fact that the aggrieved party was an unincorporated association. The Australian case of *Scott v Tuff-Kote*[4] in which an individual member of a Lloyd's syndicate successfully sued a business which misrepresented itself as being insured at Lloyd's may also be comparable.

An association may have *locus standi* in theory but it must still prove all the essential elements of passing-off. Cases brought by associations have failed because their name,[5] or their initials,[6] were not distinctive, or because the defendants adequately distinguished themselves,[7] or because they did not stand to suffer sufficiently proximate damage.[8]

Examples

3–30   In *Society of Accountants and Auditors v Goodway*[9] the plaintiffs were an incorporated association. It was proved that the term *Incorporated Accountant* was distinctive of accountants who had joined the association and passed its exams. Injunctions were granted both against an individual accountant who described himself as "Incorporated Accountant", and

---

[3] [1999] 4 All E.R. 277; [2000] F.S.R. 311 (Lawrence Collins Q.C., Deputy Judge).
[4] [1975] N.S.W.L.R. 537; [1976] 2 Lloyd's Rep. 103.
[5] *British Association of Aesthetic Plastic Surgeons v Cambright Ltd* [1987] R.P.C. 549 (Scott J.). In *An Bord Trachtala v Waterford Foods* [1994] F.S.R. 316 (Keane J., Ireland) *Food Ireland* was not found not to be distinctive of the plaintiff Board.
[6] *AG v Barret Proprietaries Ltd* (1932) 50 R.P.C. 45 where the letters "BP" for "British Pharmacopoeia" were not recognised by the public; *Society of Architects v Kendrick* (1910) 26 T.L.R. 433.
[7] *Workman and Persson v Johns* [1960] R.P.C. 89; *Lagos Chamber of Commerce Incorp v Registrar of Companies* (1955) 72 R.P.C. 263, PC.
[8] *Motor Manufacturers' & Traders' Society v Motor Manufacturers' and Traders' Insurance Co* [1925] All E.R. 616; 42 R.P.C. 307, CA.
[9] [1907] 1 Ch. 489; 24 R.P.C. 159 (Warrington J.).

against a rival incorporated association to which he belonged which claimed for its members the right to use the term. Similarly in *Society of Incorporated Accountants v Vincent*[10] the defendant was restrained from using the initials *FSAA* so as to misrepresent that he was a fellow of the plaintiff society[11] and an enquiry as to damages was granted. An injunction was granted by the Court of Appeal in *Institute of Chartered Accountants v Hardwick*[12] where the defendant had passed the examinations of the plaintiffs but had been excluded from membership on his bankruptcy. In *Institute of Electrical Engineers v Emerson*[13] an interlocutory injunction was granted against the defendant using the initials *MIEE* in his business as an electrical contractor. He was not a member of the plaintiff institute.

Society of Architects v Kendrick[14] is contrary to the mainstream of authority. An injunction (in default of appearance) was refused, ostensibly because the matter was too trivial, but more probably because the judge did not believe that the initials in question were distinctive.

Toms and Moore v Merchant Service Guild[15] was an action brought on behalf of all members of an unincorporated association, the *Imperial Merchant Service Guild*, which represented the interests of officers in the Merchant Navy. It was apparently a trade union in all but name. The defendants were a recently founded incorporated association with the same objectives. An injunction was granted. An injunction was also granted in *British Medical Association v Marsh*.[16] The defendant carried on business as a retail chemist and sold imitations of patent medicines made up according to analyses which had been published by the BMA. He used the initials "BMA" on his shops very conspicuously and so as to give the impression to the public that he was in some way associated with the plaintiffs.

The Law Society has been a successful plaintiff in two cases. In *Law* **3–31** *Society of England and Wales v Griffiths*[17] the plaintiffs were awarded an interlocutory injunction to protect the freephone number of their *Accident Line* referral service against the use of a similar number by the defendant firm of solicitors. Not only would member firms of the plaintiffs' scheme lose business, but confidence in the scheme would be undermined and member firms would become disaffected with it. In *Law Society of England and Wales v Society of Lawyers*[18] the defendants were in reality a commercial organisation which purported to offer membership, for a fee, to natural or legal persons who were not necessarily lawyers properly so-called but who might have various quasi-legal qualifications or practical experience. A larger fee (of £2,000 upwards) bought the right to call oneself an Area

[10] (1954) 71 R.P.C. 325 (Vaisey J.).
[11] Apparently the same one as in the previous case.
[12] (1919) 35 T.L.R. 342, CA.
[13] (1950) 67 R.P.C. 167 (Dankwerts J.).
[14] (1910) 26 T.L.R. 433.
[15] (1908) 25 R.P.C. 474 (Neville J.).
[16] (1931) 48 R.P.C. 565 (Maugham J.). From *Pratt v British Medical Association* [1919] 1 K.B. 244 it would seem that the spirit of a trade union burned beneath the veneer of a professional association.
[17] [1995] R.P.C. 16 (Aldous J.).
[18] [1996] F.S.R. 739 (Rimer J.).

Secretary and receive commission on new members recruited. Membership criteria were so lax as to be a sham, certain individuals in important positions were unfit to exercise their purported roles, and the defendant society did not exercise any of the normal functions of a *bona fide* professional association.[19] Rimer J. granted the Law Society an interlocutory injunction.

In *Artistic Upholstery v Art Forma*[20] an unincorporated association of furniture manufacturers whose main activity was holding bi-annual exhibitions under the name *Long Point* obtained a permanent injunction against a former member company which had been expelled for organising a rival exhibition under the same name.

The problem of *locus standi*

3–32 In all the foregoing cases the claimant association sued in its own right in respect of a misrepresentation whose truth or falsity was determined, both in fact and in the public estimation, by the association itself. The association therefore had goodwill in the activity of conferring or withholding that endorsement, and stood to suffer damage if the endorsement was misappropriated by a non-member or someone without the relevant qualifications. An individual accountant or engineer may have qualifications or personal attributes as good as or better than those required for admission to the relevant professional body, but unless he is a member of that body then it is passing-off for him to claim whatever additional prestige or benefit comes from membership.

Such cases are to be distinguished from those in which the association is made a party to an action in which the real complaint is that the defendant is misrepresenting his goods, services or business as those of one or more of the members of the association, or as having some quality which is in fact possessed by the members of the association or their products, whether or not by them alone. In this case, it is the members who are the real victims of the passing-off and the association as such has no *locus standi* to sue for passing-off in either a personal or representative capacity.[21] As Bowen L.J. put it in *London Association of Shipowners and Brokers v London and India Docks Joint Committee*[22]:

> "If a number of individuals are injured, all of them may sue. In some cases one or more of them may sue as representing the rest. But the individuals cannot, before they are injured, form themselves into a joint stock company for the purpose of bringing actions on their own behalf, or give to such an incorporated body a legal *locus standi* to sue for them."

---

[19] The chairman of the "accreditation committee" was not without practical experience of the legal system himself: he had been convicted of obtaining property by deception and sentenced to two years' imprisonment.

[20] [1999] 4 All E.R. 277; [2000] F.S.R. 311 (Lawrence Collins Q.C., Deputy Judge).

[21] *Chocosuisse Union des Fabricants Suisse de Chocolat v Cadbury Ltd* [1999] E.T.M.R. 1020; [1999] R.P.C. 826, CA. See para.3–34 below.

[22] [1892] 3 Ch. 242, CA, not a passing-off case.

Though many cases on geographical indications have involved actions by trade associations as well as individual traders, the *locus standi* of those claimants who were actually traders did not depend on their being members of the association. Non-members who met the relevant objective criteria would have had exactly the same cause of action. On the present understanding of the law the relevant trade associations probably had no cause of action for passing-off at all: the only proper claimants were individual suppliers of the products in question, suing in either their personal, or representative, capacities. The process by which the law has reached this conclusion is convoluted.

The first relevant decision came with the *Parma Ham* case, *Consorzio del* **3–33** *Prosciutto Di Parma v Marks & Spencer*[23] in which the Court of Appeal held that an association of producers, the *Consorzio*, could not bring a representative action on behalf of its members because its capacity to sue for passing-off was dependent on a different category of damage to that suffered by them, so that the association and its members lacked a common interest. In *Parma Ham* itself it was conceded that the *Consorzio* could sue in a non-representative capacity, but in *Scotch Whisky Association v JD Vintners*[24] Scott V.C. was to cast doubt on the *locus standi* of the plaintiff trade association to sue in its personal capacity at all. In the latter case the three plaintiffs (a trade association suing in its personal, rather than representative, capacity, and two whisky distillers and blenders) sued for passing-off and breach of European Community law[25] by the sale of a spirit as "Light Canadian Rye". This had a strength of 30 per cent alcohol, compared to a minimum strength of 40 per cent for whisky. It was alleged that the name "Light Canadian Rye" implicitly misrepresented the product as whisky properly so called. On an application to strike out part of the statement of claim Scott V.C. agreed with the defendants that the first plaintiff had no cause of action in passing-off, distinguishing the cases where the *locus standi* of similar trade associations had not been challenged:

> "I cannot see on what basis a trade association can maintain a passing off action based upon conduct which constitutes a passing off by the defendant of its products for those of the members of the trade association. The trade association, if it sues in a representative capacity, can perhaps maintain such an action but that would be to base the action on the combined causes of action of its members. Such an action would not be based upon a cause of action vested in the Association itself."

At this point, the two possible bases on which an association might be able to sue for passing-off in similar circumstances were contradicted by different, and inconsistent, authorities. The Court of Appeal in *Parma Ham* had ruled out a representative action, but did not exclude an action by an association in its personal capacity. Scott V.C., apparently unaware of the

[23] [1991] R.P.C. 351, CA.
[24] [1997] Eu. L.R. 446 (Scott V.C.).
[25] Council Regulation 1576/89.

implications of *Parma Ham*, had ruled out the latter while tentatively permitting the former. In *Chocosuisse v Cadbury*[26] the contradiction between the authorities was resolved by the Court of Appeal, but with the result that trade associations now have no *locus standi* in either capacity when the complaint is not that the defendant is liable for passing himself off in the "classic" sense as being a member of the association or otherwise associated with it, but in the "extended" sense of having some quality which the members of the association in fact share.

Capacity to sue in *Chocosuisse v Cadbury*

3–34 The first plaintiff in *Chocosuisse v Cadbury*[27] was a trade association for Swiss chocolate manufacturers, and the two individual plaintiffs (*Suchard* and *Lindt*) were members of it. Both at first instance and on appeal it was held that the defendants were liable under the "extended" form of passing-off for selling a chocolate confectionary bar under the name *Cadbury's Swiss Chalet* and with a Swiss theme to the get-up, so as to misrepresent as Swiss chocolate, chocolate which was in fact made in England to lower standards than those used or permitted in Switzerland.

At first instance,[28] Laddie J. very briefly accepted that Chocosuisse could bring proceedings on its own behalf to prevent the reduction of its membership which might supposedly be caused if the designation "Swiss chocolate" became unprotectable in England, but it was conceded[29] that it could not sue in a representative capacity in respect of the damage likely to be caused to its members if cheaper and inferior chocolate was passed off as Swiss chocolate. On appeal, both parties challenged what had been accepted or decided below: Chocosuisse argued that it did have the right to sue in a representative capacity and Cadbury argued that Chocosuisse had no right of action even in its personal capacity, because it had no goodwill or reputation in England and because there was no likelihood of damage actually occurring under the one head relied on, which was the potential reduction in its membership.

3–35 Chadwick L.J. (with whom the other members of the court agreed) first decided that the case advanced by Chocosuisse was not within the category of representative actions permitted under the former R.S.C.[30]

"The ability to sue in a representative capacity is conferred by Order 15, rule 12 of the Rules of the Supreme Court 1965. Rule 12(1) provides:

'Where numerous persons have the same interest in any proceedings, not being such proceedings as are mentioned in rule 13, the proceedings may be begun, and, unless the court otherwise orders, continued, by or

---

[26] [1999] E.T.M.R. 1020; [1999] R.P.C. 826, CA.

[27] [1999] E.T.M.R. 1020; [1999] R.P.C. 826, CA.

[28] [1998] R.P.C. 117 at 149.

[29] On the authority of *Consorzio del Prosciutto Di Parma v Marks & Spencer* [1991] R.P.C. 351, CA.

[30] Now C.P.R. 19.6. There are no material differences in wording.

against any one or more of them as representing all or as representing all except one or more of them.' ...

The requirement under Order 15, rule 12 is that the representative plaintiff should have the same interest in the proceedings as the person that he purports to represent. That, as it seems to me, requires a consideration of two factors: first, does the plaintiff have any interest which would entitle him to bring proceedings; and secondly, if he has some interest, is that interest the same interest as those that he seeks to represent?"

After approving the opinion of Scott V.C. in *Scotch Whisky Association v JD Vintners*,[31] quoted above, Chadwick L.J. cited the *Parma Ham* case[32] and continued:

"The position, therefore, on this first question is that it seems to have been accepted, both by Morrit J. and by this Court in the *Parma Ham* case (but without argument) that a trade association has locus to sue in its own right; but that contention was expressly rejected by the Vice-Chancellor in *The Scotch Whisky Association* case. For my part, I adopt the reasoning of the Vice-Chancellor on this point. I am unable to identify any business interest or goodwill which the trade association, Chocosuisse, is entitled to protect in an action in England for passing-off against a trader ... If there is no individual right, then it seems to me that Order 15, rule 12 can be of no assistance. But, even if there were an individual right, it is not the same right as the right of the Swiss Chocolate Manufacturers whom the association seeks to represent."

Although Scott V.C. appeared to have taken the opposite view in *Scotch Whisky Association v JD Vintners*, there were indications that this was not a concluded opinion, and perhaps that it was unduly influenced by the desirability of the outcome:

"I respectfully agree with the Vice-Chancellor's view that it would be convenient if a trade association were permitted to sue in a representative capacity on behalf of its members. But I find it impossible to reach the conclusion that that is permitted under the language of Order 15, rule 12(1) in circumstances where, as will usually be the case, the trade association either has no interest of its own capable of founding a cause of action; or, if it has any interest of its own, that is not the same interest as that interest of its members. The remedy lies in an alteration to the Rules of Court. It does not lie in bending those Rules to allow a representative action in circumstances which, as drawn, they were not intended to cover.

For those reasons I take the view that Chocosuisse does not have *locus* to sue in these proceedings, whether in its own right or as a representative of the Swiss chocolate manufacturers."

[31] [1997] Eu. L.R. 446 (Scott V.C.).
[32] *Consorzio del Prosciutto Di Parma v Marks & Spencer* [1991] R.P.C. 351, CA.

Goodwill and *locus standi* for associations after *Chocosuisse*

3–36 The *Chocosuisse* case[33] need not be taken as casting doubt on the many cases in which trade or professional associations have sued for passing-off in their own right, but it does re-open the question of whether all those cases were rightly decided (or, at least, adequately reasoned); and it emphasises that a distinction must be drawn between cases in which the association sues in its own capacity, typically against a rival association or a non-member holding himself out as a member, and cases in which the association has really been trying to vindicate some right vested in its members in their individual capacity. There is also a relevant distinction to be drawn between the kind of association which exists simply to promote or protect the collective interests of its members in some respect, and trade or professional associations in which the narrow interests of the members are subordinated to the good name of the trade or profession as a whole.

As always, an association's cause of action for passing-off depends on there being a misrepresentation causing damage to its goodwill. The first question is therefore whether the association may be said to have any goodwill, and if so how that goodwill is defined and how it is capable of being damaged. Given that a charity, a church, and even the *Countryside Alliance*, can be said to have goodwill, the answer to the first half of the question may appear to be open and shut in favour of the association. However, the nature of this goodwill needs to be more carefully defined because of its interaction with the issues of misrepresentation and damage.

3–37 Any voluntary non-charitable association attracts and retains members by offering services to its members which are otherwise unobtainable, or at least are more effectively or economically provided by the association rather than by its members acting individually or collectively though ordinary contractors on a commercial basis. To this extent, at least, the association enjoys goodwill with respect to its members, actual and potential, in respect of the services it provides or offers to them, as has implicitly been recognised since as early as *Society of Accountants and Auditors v Goodway*.[34] In *Chocosuisse v Cadbury*[35] the association co-ordinated activities against counterfeiters of Swiss chocolate, and other than suing in its own name (where local law permitted) many of its activities could have been performed by a Swiss law firm and its overseas correspondents. Associations may, or may not, also provide services to non-members or to the general public and enjoy a wider goodwill from these operations. Different considerations (with which the present section is not concerned) arise when an association actually sells to the public goods or services produced by its individual members, on their collective behalf. Then it falls into a completely different legal categorisation: something akin to a producers' co-operative or a trading partnership.

---

[33] *Chocosuisse Union des Fabricants Suisse de Chocolat v Cadbury* [1999] E.T.M.R. 1020; [1999] R.P.C. 826, CA.
[34] [1907] 1 Ch. 489; 24 R.P.C. 159 (Warrington J.).
[35] [1999] E.T.M.R. 1020; [1999] R.P.C. 826, CA.

In the *Chocosuisse* case itself, it is only the beginning of the analysis to say that "Chocosuisse does not, itself, manufacture or sell Swiss chocolate".[36] Chocosuisse was a provider of services to Swiss chocolate manufacturers, and there was no suggestion that it provided any relevant services except to its members. The goodwill of Chocosuisse, as with any other putative trader, was defined by reference to its customers and the services it provided to them. More to the point is the comment that "if anything, Cadbury's activities are of benefit to the business which *Chocosuisse* carries on; in that these activities tend to reinforce the perception that there is a need for an active trade association".[37] In this respect *Chocosuisse* was in a rather similar position to the AA or the RAC—a breakdown or accident suffered by a member of one or the other may cause significant damage to the member, but neither harms nor benefits the association: it simply provides an occasion for the latter to provide the services for which the individual member has contracted and paid. It is more than arguable that Chocosuisse provided its services wherever Swiss chocolate was eaten or counterfeited, and that its goodwill extended correspondingly widely. But such goodwill as it may have had in England was of a very narrow character and was not at risk of being damaged by what Cadbury were doing.

Trade and professional associations: misrepresentation

When it comes to the issue of misrepresentation, a distinction typically needs **3–38** to be drawn between two extremes which may conventionally be represented by trade associations and professional ones. Professional associations exist because it is in the interest of their members for the public to have a reliable indication and assurance of a consistent level of professional competence and integrity. This means that a professional association may function and even flourish although the only service it appears to offer its members for their subscriptions is the negative one of expelling them (or refusing admission) if they fail to meet the standards it imposes. Conversely, trade associations typically exist to promote the collective interests of their members in some more direct sense such as organising exhibitions or promotions, suing counterfeiters, or lobbying governments. This is not to say that professional associations do not provide their members with other, more tangible, benefits; or that the functions of trade associations may not involve maintaining public confidence in the members of the trade and their products, but the two extremes provide a useful comparison for analysis.

In the case of a professional association in the sense used above, it is indispensable for the association to be known to the relevant public and for the public to rely on membership as a guarantee of professional suitability, otherwise the very reason for the existence of the association would be frustrated. In this state of affairs it is a material misrepresentation for anyone who is not a member to represent himself as such, and this is damaging both to the association (whose whole *raison d'être* is undermined)

---

[36] *ibid, per* Chadwick L.J.
[37] *ibid, per* Chadwick L.J.

and to the individual members. In this respect the analysis in *Society of Accountants and Auditors v Goodway*[38] is indisputable, and just as valid as a century ago. However, membership of a relevant professional association may be less important in some cases than is assumed in the analysis above. The strict regulation of solicitors, for instance (by the Law Society, but under statutory powers applicable to members and non-members alike) means that consumers of legal services have no reason to attach any further significance to membership of the Law Society as such. Doctors are regulated by the (statutory) General Medical Council, not by the British Medical Association. If the association is not known to the relevant public—the consumers of the services provided by its members—then there can be no reliance on the fact of membership and any action on this basis must fail.[39]

3–39   In contrast, in *Chocosuisse v Cadbury*[40] there was never any suggestion that Cadbury were misrepresenting themselves as members of Chocosuisse, nor that it would have mattered in the slightest to the public if they were. In the first place, the existence and activities of Chocosuisse seem to have been unknown to the chocolate-buying public in the United Kingdom, but what is more fundamental is that though members of the public bought Swiss chocolate in preference to other kinds of chocolate, and paid more for it, they did not rely (even unconsciously) on the chocolate manufacturers' membership of Chocosuisse as guaranteeing the quality or "Swiss-ness" of the chocolate. If any member of the public had actually bothered to enquire, he would have found out that anyone could manufacture and sell perfectly genuine Swiss Chocolate without being a member of Chocosuisse, and that the obligations of membership did not preclude a member (in the instant case, Lindt) from making and selling non-Swiss chocolate under its brand name, provided it did not misrepresent the product's origin.

There is at least a theoretical possibility that in a suitable case members of the public might regard the "seal of approval" of a body such as Chocosuisse as conferring value over and above the brand name of the manufacturer and the use of a protected and strictly defined term. In such a case Chocosuisse or their counterpart might be said to have goodwill capable of being damaged by misrepresentation, but the relevant misrepresentation would be that the chocolate had been approved or endorsed by them, and such a misrepresentation would not be inherent simply in the use of the description *Swiss Chocolate*, whether accurately or inaccurately. The closest to a decided case on this situation appears to be *An Bord Trachtala v Waterford Foods*[41] in which the plaintiffs were an Irish statutory body established to promote the export of Irish foods, for which they used a logo incorporating the words *Food Ireland*. Keane J. in the Irish High Court accepted that the nature of the plaintiffs did not prevent them from having goodwill, but refused to accept that the *Food Ireland* logo was distinctive of them. Customers abroad relied on it to identify the products to which it was

---

[38] [1907] 1 Ch. 489; (1907) 24 R.P.C. 159 (Warrington J.).
[39] *British Association of Aesthetic Plastic Surgeons v Cambright* [1987] R.P.C. 549 (Scott V.C.).
[40] [1999] E.T.M.R. 1020; [1999] R.P.C. 826, CA.
[41] [1994] F.S.R. 316 (Keane J., Ireland).

applied as being Irish food products from a clean and pollution-free environment, not as sponsored by the Board.

Trade and professional associations: damage

The issue of damage is closely tied up with that of goodwill, and from an **3–40** early stage the law has been prepared to assume the prospect of loss to the association of actual or prospective members, and therefore their subscriptions, if the defendant is not restrained. This was originally put forward in *Society of Accountants and Auditors v Goodway*[42] where the question was new to English law. Warrington J. found that membership of the plaintiffs conferred a valuable status, that it was in the plaintiffs' pecuniary interest to maximise their membership, and that the value of membership and the incentive to join the plaintiff association and pass its examinations would be reduced if non-members could describe themselves in the same terms as members. In *British Medical Association v Marsh*[43] it was suggested that the doctors would abstain from joining the BMA, or would resign from membership, if the general public supposed that their professional body had lent its name to a retail chemist.

A problem with this approach is that although it may be justified in some cases, in others, such as *BMA v Marsh* itself, it takes *a priori* reasoning far beyond the bounds of credibility. In *Scotch Whisky Association v JD Vinters*[44] Scott V.C. described the same argument (in a related context) as "a fanciful and unacceptable basis" for allowing the Association to sue for a breach of Community law; and in *Artistic Upholstery v Art Forma*[45] Lawrence Collins Q.C. said that "The relevant damage is that to the Guild's members as such, which (as I have said) is somewhat artificially regarded as a potential loss of actual or prospective membership, but more realistically as a loss of direct income from the promotion of the exhibition (and not loss of sales by the individual members)". In *Chocosuisse v Cadbury*[46] it is implicit that the unlawful activities of Cadburys and others elsewhere made it more, not less, likely that Swiss chocolate manufacturers would rally behind the efforts of their trade association, unless those were wholly unavailing. The argument of *BMA v Marsh* is inapplicable if membership of the relevant association is compulsory, or if the association finances itself by charges or levies which do not depend on membership.

In the case of the Law Society, for instance, no separate charge is made **3–41** for membership and the Society finances itself from fees which are paid by all solicitors with practising certificates, whether members or not. So in *Law Society v Griffiths*[47] Aldous J. focused on the Society's activities in running a personal injuries panel and referral service rather than on its general

[42] [1907] 1 Ch. 489; 24 R.P.C. 159 (Warrington J.).
[43] (1931) 48 R.P.C. 565 (Maugham J.).
[44] [1997] Eu. L.R. 446 (Scott V.C.).
[45] [2000] F.S.R. 311; [1999] 4 All E.R. 277 (Lawrence Collins Q.C., Deputy Judge). Note that the Guild was an unincorporated association, with no legal personality.
[46] [1999] E.T.M.R. 1020; [1999] R.P.C. 826, CA.
[47] [1995] R.P.C. 16 (Aldous J.).

functions for the membership at large. In *Law Society v Society of Lawyers*[48] Rimer J. was rather more troubled with the *locus standi* of the Society but held that they had at least an arguable case. In the first *Law Society* case, the proposition was not that solicitors would resign from the Society itself, as hypothesised in *BMA v Marsh*, but the more plausible one that the panel and referral service would be jeopardised. In the second case, the defendant *Society of Lawyers* was such a sham or scam that damage to the plaintiffs could reasonably be asserted under the head of "injurious association" without needing to ask if the Law Society would immediately be injured in any more material sense. In such extreme cases the activities of the defendant may also be likely to expose the claimant association to liability within the rule in *Routh v Webster*.[49] This was alluded to in *British Medical Association v Marsh*,[50] but was not essential to the decision.

Where the association does provide services to non-members on a commercial basis then damage to it in its capacity as such presents no problem, but this head of damage is logically separate from loss of membership and requires separate factual analysis.[51]

> "Although a commonly advanced justification for allowing trade associations to maintain a claim in passing off is the prospect of loss to the association of actual or prospective members (as it was also, in a different context, in the *British Legion*), there is no reason in principle why an association which carries on some form of limited trade may not rely on damage to that trade. In the present case, there is evidence that the Guild generates a surplus in the promotion of the Long Point exhibition, and if there were confusion in the trade, there is every reason to believe that exhibitors would be deterred from exhibiting at the exhibition, and the Guild would thereby lose a contribution to its expenses in hiring the exhibition centre, and a break even position or surplus might be turned into a loss."

Unincorporated associations

3-42   There is no difference in principle between an association which is incorporated and one which is not, although there are procedural differences reflecting the fact that an unincorporated association has no legal existence and so cannot hold property or sue in its own name. Nothing turned on the unincorporated nature of the *Imperial Merchant Service Guild* in *Toms and Moore v Merchant Service Guild Ltd*[52] and in *British Legion v British Legion Club (Street) Ltd*[53] Farwell J. expressly rejected the submission that a change in the status of the *British Legion* from an unincorporated associa-

---

[48] [1996] F.S.R. 739 (Rimer J.).
[49] (1847) 50 E.R. 698 (Langdale M.R.).
[50] (1931) 48 R.P.C. 565 (Maugham J.).
[51] *Artistic Upholstery v Art Forma (Furniture)* [1999] 4 All E.R. 277; [2000] F.S.R. 311 (Lawrence Collins Q.C., Deputy Judge).
[52] (1908) 25 R.P.C. 474 (Neville J.).
[53] (1931) 48 R.P.C. 555 (Farwell J.).

tion to an incorporated one made any difference, even though the defendant had started the conduct complained of before the plaintiff was incorporated.[54]

In *Artistic Upholstery v Art Forma*[55] the claimant sued in a representative capacity on behalf of itself and all other members of the *Long Eaton Guild of Furniture Manufacturers*. The Guild was an unincorporated association which had organised furniture exhibitions for almost 20 years under the name *Long Point*. The defendant had been a founder member, but had been expelled after organising a rival exhibition under the same name and, subsequently, asserting ownership and control of the *Long Point* name by virtue of a trade mark registration.

Lawrence Collins Q.C. held that the action was properly constituted as a representative action. "The goodwill [of the association] is held by the members as their property in that capacity in accordance with the constitution and rules". However:

"Since the Guild itself has no standing to sue in its own name, it can only sue through its members, and in the present case one of its members sues in a representative capacity. In my judgment that is the appropriate course, since the claimant and those whom it represents have the same interest in the proceedings, namely to protect the reputation and goodwill which they have as members of the Guild. They are not suing in respect of damage to their own businesses, but in respect of the activity which they carry on as members of the Guild."

On the facts, there was no doubt that *Long Point* was distinctive of the furniture exhibitions organised by the Guild, that the defendants had no right to use it in respect of their own exhibition, and that its use by them would damage the Guild by reducing its income from the exhibition. A permanent injunction was granted.

D. OTHER NON-TRADING ORGANISATIONS

Introduction: charities

In contrast to trade and professional associations, charities do not neces- **3–43** sarily or typically provide their members, subscribers, or supporters with tangible benefits so as to be said to enjoy any goodwill in the provision of services to their members for value. However charities, and other non-profit or non-trading organisations such as churches, political parties and interest groups, do depend on the financial contributions of their members and the

---

[54] Both these cases were followed and approved in *Artistic Upholstery v Art Forma (Furniture)*, below. The reservations expressed by Russell J. in *Workman and Persson v Johns* [1960] R.P.C. 89 may probably now been consigned to history, both as regards charitable status and the relevance or otherwise of incorporation.

[55] [1999] 4 All E.R. 277; [2000] F.S.R. 311 (Lawrence Collins Q.C., Deputy Judge).

general public, and to that extent they may be said to have something corresponding sufficiently closely to the goodwill of trading organisations in so far as they are able to attract money (or money's worth) which would otherwise have been kept, spent, or bestowed elsewhere. It has now been decided that even a non-trading charity may maintain a passing-off action against another similar charity,[56] and it is much more certain that it would be protected against exploitation of its reputation by a non-charitable commercial organisation. Although the claimant in that case was principally a self-help charity (analogous in some ways to a members' club or even a motoring organisation) the implications of the decision extend to every kind of charity, regardless of the extent to which selflessness is combined with self-interest. What is true for charities may be applied with suitable caution to other non-trading organisations dependant on public financial support.

It is common for charities to raise money by trading as well as by seeking donations. The activities for which a charity exists may also involve carrying on a trade or business even though it makes no profit on them. Many public schools, for instance, are run by charities and a charity might charge the public for admission to an historic building it was responsible for preserving. There is no doubt that in its capacity as a trading concern a charity, whether incorporated or not, has as much *locus standi* in a passing-off action as any other business.

Actions by charities against one another

3–44 It is now clear that a passing-off action lies at the suit of one charity even against another *bona fide* charity, and *a fortiori* against a non-charitable defendant holding itself out as the claimant charity. In *British Diabetic Association v The Diabetic Society*[57] Robert Walker J. held that the tort of passing-off was wide enough for the plaintiff charity to be granted relief against three defendants: a much smaller break-away charity with similar objectives, and its two founders. The plaintiff charity had a trading subsidiary but this was not the basis of the decision. It was more relevant was that the plaintiff charity was, perhaps unusually, one where both benefactors and beneficiaries were largely drawn from the same class of the population and to that extent had some of the character of a self-help association, but it would be wrong to assume that charities such as the NSPCC or RNLI (the examples given by the judge) would fail in otherwise comparable circumstances.

Referring to Lord Diplock's speech in *Erven Warnink v Townend*,[58] Robert Walker J. concluded:

"The wider the scope of passing-off, the freer has to be the interpretation of some of Lord Diplock's requirements, especially the reference to 'prospective customers of [a trader] or ultimate consumers of goods or

---

[56] *British Diabetic Association v The Diabetic Society* [1996] F.S.R. 1 (Robert Walker J.).
[57] [1996] F.S.R. 1 (Robert Walker J.). The principle was also stated, *obiter*, in *Harrods Ltd v Harrodian School Ltd* [1996] R.P.C. 697, CA.
[58] [1979] A.C. 731, 740; [1979] 2 All E.R. 927; [1980] R.P.C. 31, 91, HL.

services supplied by him'. It is obvious that in the case of many charities, their benefactors are likely to be a class of the public quite different from that of their beneficiaries. In the case of—for instance—the NSPCC or the RNLI the 'prospective customers ... or ultimate consumers' of the charity's services will, with rare exceptions, be different from those whose generosity funds the services.

By contrast the Association (like the average church congregation) seems to be a charity which for its financial needs depends to a high degree on self-help: the evidence suggests that diabetics and their families and friends are a major source (though not, of course, the only source) of subscriptions, legacies, *in memoriam* gifts (in lieu of flowers) and fund-raising activities. That reinforces my conclusion that (whatever may be the position with charities of a different character) passing-off can provide a remedy in a situation such as the present, if misrepresentation is established."

On the facts, the plaintiffs failed to make out that they had a *de facto* exclusive reputation in the name *The (British) Diabetic Society* but the defendants' name was confusingly similar to the plaintiffs' official name and a final injunction was granted. Another charity run by the defendants as *The Diabetes Foundation* was not objected to. It concentrated on supporting scientific research into a cure for diabetes, was much more substantial than the defendant Society, and had co-existed for many years with the plaintiff with no more evidence of confusion than was likely from occasional mistakes. The jurisdiction of the court under the law of passing-off was not displaced by the concurrent statutory jurisdiction of the Charity Commissioners under s.6 of the Charities Act 1993 to order a registered charity to change its name if confusingly similar to that of another.

In Australia, the Court of Appeal of New South Wales had already sta- **3–45** ted: "We see no reason why an element essentially indistinguishable from commercial goodwill should not be attributed to a charitable organisation and be equally entitled to protection from the law".[59] Three American decisions to this effect were cited with approval, in addition to the older of the English cases on charities and other associations discussed in the present work. In the result, the defendant, a church, was ordered to change its name. More recently, the Federal Court of Australia treated an action between competing charities for the help and support of blind people as turning purely on its facts: *Guide Dog Owners & Friends Association v Guide Dogs Association of NSW and ACT*.[60] *Seeing Eye* and *Seeing Eye Dogs* were held to be generic terms for guide dogs for blind people, and the plaintiff charity had no right to prevent two other charities using them to advertise their

---

[59] *The Holy Apostolic and Catholic Church of the East (Assyrian) Australia NSW Parish Association v Attorney General Ex p. Elisha* (1989) 16 I.P.R. 619. This case, and those cited in it, were approved by Robert Walker J. in *British Diabetic Association v The Diabetic Society*, above.

[60] [1999] FCA 316; 43 I.P.R. 531 (Federal Court of Australia). At first instance (1998) 42 I.P.R. 481 Sackville J. had specifically confirmed that an action for passing-off could be brought by one charity against another, while questioning the wisdom of such litigation.

services. It is of interest that the relevant state of mind was not defined by reference to blind people themselves (as consumers or recipients of the charities' guide dog services) who understood the terms as denoting the plaintiff charity specifically, but of the general public who used and understood them in the generic sense.

In the South African case of *Williams v Life Line*[61] a charity which had promoted fund-raising concerts under the title *Last Night of the Proms* was not entitled to prevent the organiser of the concerts using the same title, conductor and orchestra for fund-raising concerts on behalf of another charity. It was assumed that the charity had sufficient trading status to bring the action, but the concerts were not regarded as being of the charity's sole provenance, so the latter had no exclusive rights to the name as against the organiser, the orchestra, the conductor, or even the prominent corporate sponsor.

3–46   In the light of these decisions, as well as that in *Artistic Upholstery v Art Forma*,[62] the difficulties caused by some *obiter* remarks of Russell J. in *Workman and Persson v Johns*[63] may probably be regarded as past history, though without casting doubt on the correctness of that decision on its facts. The plaintiffs brought a representative action on behalf of the council of an unincorporated charity, the *National Canine Defence League*, against a former employee who had been dismissed and had founded his own movement with similar objectives as the *World Dog Defence Campaign*. Russell J. refused an interlocutory injunction, holding that the rival names were distinct, that there was no evidence of the defendant causing confusion, and that it was improbable that any members of the plaintiff League would subscribe to the defendant in error.

Fraudulent or sham "charities"

3–47 In *British Diabetic Association v The Diabetic Society*[64] (where the defendant charity was entirely *bona fide*) Robert Walker J. observed:

> "If a so-called charity is set up as a sham or a scam, and uses a large part of its funds for private gain under the guise of administration and fund-raising, it is right that it should be stopped—either by the Charity Commissioners in exercise of their statutory powers, or by the Court at the instance of the Attorney-General or the Charity Commissioners, or (if the bogus charity is diverting funds from an established and properly-run charity in circumstances amounting to passing-off) by the Court at the instance of that charity. There would be nothing deplorable about a genuine charity suing a bogus charity in those circumstances."

---

[61] 1996 (3) S.A. 408 (Appellate Division).
[62] [1999] 4 All E.R. 277; [2000] F.S.R. 311 (Lawrence Collins Q.C., Deputy Judge), where the *locus standi* of a non-charitable unincorporated association was recognised.
[63] [1960] R.P.C. 89 (Russell J.).
[64] [1996] F.S.R. 1 (Robert Walker J.).

Actions by charities against non-charities

In *British Legion v British Legion Club (Street) Ltd*[65] the plaintiffs had come **3–48** into existence as an unincorporated association to provide for the welfare of ex-servicemen. Subsequently they had become incorporated as a charity under Royal Charter. There were many local *British Legion* clubs which were legally independent of the plaintiffs but which acknowledged its ultimate authority. The defendants were a company operating as a social club primarily, but not exclusively, for ex-servicemen. Farwell J., granting an injunction, held that the defendants were bound to be taken as connected with the plaintiffs and that the plaintiffs would be damaged if any misfortune befell the defendants. As a charity, it was particularly important for the plaintiffs to be above any suspicion of impropriety.

In *Dr Barnardo's Homes v Barnardo Amalgamated Industries*[66] the plaintiffs were an incorporated charity so well known that Vaisey J. was prepared to take judicial notice of their national reputation. The plaintiffs were "publishers on a large scale", although it is unclear to what extent the published material was sold and to what extent it was distributed free to solicit contributions. The defendants were commercial publishers of romantic fiction, and, in addition to the use of their corporate name, prominently used the slogan *This is a Barnardo Publication* on their books. There was no evidence of actual confusion but an interlocutory injunction was granted.

Although the defendant's choice of name or trading style may be inappropriate and even misleading, it may still fall short of causing confusion with the plaintiff, and in that case there is no liability for passing-off. In *British Association of Aesthetic Plastic Surgeons v Cambright*[67] the motives of the defendants in calling themselves *The Association of Aesthetic Plastic Surgery* were not above suspicion, since they were an ordinary trading company and not an association at all, but the plaintiff association produced little evidence of reputation and none of confusion, and an interlocutory injunction was refused. If evidence of confusion and damage had been forthcoming, it would not apparently have mattered that the plaintiffs were a registered charity and did not carry on any trade.

Churches

In the South African case of *Old Apostolic Church of Africa v Non-White Old* **3–49** *Apostolic Church of Africa*[68] relief was granted to the plaintiff on the basis of passing-off. The judge reasoned that the plaintiff church received subscriptions and was in an analogous position to associations such as the plaintiff in *British Medical Association v Marsh*.[69] In Australia, the Court of Appeal of New South Wales has also said that a church may be entitled to

---

[65] (1931) 48 R.P.C. 555 (Farwell J.).
[66] (1949) 66 R.P.C. 103 (Vaisey J.).
[67] [1987] R.P.C. 549 (Scott J.).
[68] 1975 (2) S.A. 684.
[69] (1931) 48 R.P.C. 565 (Maugham J.).

relief under the law of passing-off by analogy with the cases on charitable associations.[70] On the facts, the defendant (appellant) church was enjoined from calling itself the *Ancient Church of the East*. The action was one by the Attorney-General rather than by the church actually entitled to use the name, but the court expressly dismissed arguments that the relator church could have no goodwill because it was not in business. Both these cases were approved by Robert Walker J. in *British Diabetic Association v The Diabetic Society*.[71]

In *Honey v Australian Airlines*[72] the second defendant, the *House of Tabor*, was a non-profit-making non-denominational charismatic teaching centre predominantly for members of the Pentecostal Church. The plaintiff, an Olympic long jumper and practising Roman Catholic, unsuccessfully objected to a photograph of himself in a magazine and on the cover of a book published by the centre. The status of the House of Tabor as a defendant does not seem to have been in doubt.

Political parties; interest and pressure groups

3–50 The *locus standi* of a political party in an action for passing-off was originally considered in *Kean v McGivan*,[73] in which the plaintiffs claimed the exclusive right to the name *Social Democratic Party*. Although the plaintiff party was local and very little known, the Court of Appeal apparently based its refusal of an interlocutory injunction on the more fundamental ground that neither party was engaged in any commercial activities[74]:

> "The situation is simply that a non-commercial activity—a political party—is seeking to use the same name, the same initials, as a very small other such party with, so we are told, somewhat similar values and ideals. It does not provide a situation, in my judgement, in which there is any basis for contending that a tort has occurred."

For most practical purposes, any practical problems this decision may have given rise to were addressed by Parliament in the Registration of Political Parties Act 1998, which is now replaced by the Political Parties, Elections and Referendums Act 2000.[75] Section 23 of the 2000 Act provides for the replacement of the Register of political parties formerly kept under the 1998 Act. Section 28 provides for the registration of political parties and their names, and that a party may not be registered if the proposed name would

---

[70] *The Holy Apostolic and Catholic Church of the East (Assyrian) Australia NSW Parish Association v Attorney General Ex p. Elisha* (1989) 16 I.P.R. 619.

[71] [1996] F.S.R. 1 (Robert Walker J.).

[72] (1990) 18 I.P.R. 185 (Federal Court of Australia) affirming (1989) 14 I.P.R. 264 (Northrop J.).

[73] [1982] F.S.R. 119, CA.

[74] *per* Ackner L.J. in *Kean v McGivan* [1982] F.S.R. 119, CA.

[75] In *Sanders v Chichester* (1995) 92(3) L.S.G. 37, (1995) 139 S.J.L.B. 15 an election petition by an unsuccessful *Liberal Democrat* candidate failed, despite the rival candidate (who described himself on the ballot as a *Literal Democrat*) attracting an implausibly large number of votes.

be the same as that of another party already registered,[76] or likely to result in the party's being confused by electors with a party which is already registered for the relevant part of the United Kingdom.[77] There is provision for co-pending applications[78] and for registration of parties' emblems.[79] Section 22 provides that in the more important categories of elections, candidates may only stand in the name of a party registered under the Act or as an independent. However, the relevant provisions do not (and did not) apply to parish or community elections.

In *Burge v Haycock*[80] the claimants were the Chief Executive and Deputy **3–51** Chief Executive of the *Countryside Alliance*. The defendant was a private individual who was standing for election to a town council, purportedly in the name of the Countryside Alliance. The Countryside Alliance itself was non-party-political and never put up candidates for election. The defendant, apart from not being authorised to stand in the name of the Alliance, was not even a member of it and was publicly associated with the British National Party. At first instance the judge held that he was bound by *Kean v McGivan*[81] and refused an interim injunction. The Court of Appeal distinguished *Kean v McGivan* as turning on the very slight reputation of the plaintiff in that case, rather than on any legal principle, and granted an interim injunction against the defendant representing that he was a member of the Countryside Alliance, was supported as a candidate by it, or was otherwise associated with it.

Cases in other common law jurisdictions prior to *Burge v Haycock* had already tended away from *Kean v McGivan*. In the Canadian case of *Polsinelli v Marzilli*[82] the official Liberal candidate in a provincial election failed to restrain the defendant from describing himself as a *Trudeau Liberal*. The defendant had recently been expelled from the Liberal Party and was campaigning against the plaintiff. However, although the first instance judge would have followed *Kean v McGivan*, the Ontario Divisional Court affirmed him purely on the ground that there was insufficient evidence of confusion, and indicated that they were inclined to disagree with the view that the law of passing-off was inapplicable in principle to political affairs.[83] In Australia, the Court of Appeal of New South Wales refused to follow *Kean v McGivan* in a case between rival churches.[84] Noting that the plaintiff in *Kean v McGivan* had appeared in person, the Court suggested that the line of cases in which charities were admitted to have *locus standi* must have been overlooked in the latter case.

An earlier example of a misrepresentation on the borderline of passing-off **3–52**

---

[76] Political Parties, Elections and Referendums Act 2000, s.28(4)(a)(i).
[77] s.28(4)(a)(ii).
[78] s.28(7).
[79] s.29.
[80] [2001] EWCA Civ 900; [2002] R.P.C. 28, CA. The defendant did not appear and was not represented.
[81] [1982] F.S.R. 119, CA.
[82] (1987) 60 O.R. (2d) 713; 21 C.P.R. (3d) 140 (Ontario, Campbell J.).
[83] (1987) 21 C.P.R. (3d) 145.
[84] *The Holy Apostolic and Catholic Church of the East (Assyrian) Australia NSW Parish Association v Attorney General Ex p. Elisha* (1989) 16 I.P.R. 619.

is to be found in *Pryce v Pioneer Press*[85] where it was treated as defamation. The plaintiffs, who printed posters for one political party, successfully objected to the issue of posters on behalf of a rival party imitating the form of the plaintiffs' posters and carrying their imprint. In *Kennard v Lewis*,[86] the *Campaign for Nuclear Disarmament* sued for copyright infringement in respect of a pamphlet *Thirty Questions and Honest Answers about CND* which imitated the layout of their pamphlet *Thirty Questions and Answers about CND*. They were refused an interlocutory injunction by analogy with the practice in defamation actions with Warner J. observing: "interlocutory injunctions should not in general be used to restrain free speech and in particular should not be used to restrain political controversy".

The limits of protection for non-traders

3–53 The judgment of Robert Walker J. in *British Diabetic Association v The Diabetic Society*[87] illustrates that there is no completely satisfactory policy answer to whether one charity should be able to sue another for passing-off. An action between two charities properly so called was "on the face of it a deplorable, even a scandalous thing" because funds intended for charitable purposes were diverted into litigation.[88] An exception would be an action against a so-called charity which was really "a sham or a scam a bogus charity diverting funds from an established and properly-run charity in circumstances amounting to passing-off" but in the instant case there was no allegation that the individual defendants were motivated by private gain. None the less, the judge accepted that an action for passing-off lay in principle and granted a permanent injunction.

In the first edition of the present work, it was suggested that the action for passing-off was an inappropriate way of resolving disputes between the likes of churches, charities or political parties. However, the courts cannot avoid entertaining such disputes altogether. Schismatic churches, for instance, may litigate over entitlement to trust funds or rival charities may dispute the meaning of an ambiguous bequest in a will. If litigation is unavoidable, it is probably best to accept as a matter of policy that the courts should be able to grant the fullest relief that the situations justifies, which must include injunctive relief against a misleading choice of name. Given the extremely broad meaning which the terms "trader" and "goodwill" were already capable of bearing, even before the *British Diabetic Association* case, it is suggested that this need not do undue violence to the nature of passing-off as a tort protecting traders in their goodwill.

3–54 However there is an important distinction to be drawn between the

---

[85] (1925) 42 T.L.R. 29. Finlay J. (*obiter*) would have granted relief on the basis of improper use of the plaintiffs' name, but the only authority he cited was *Cowley (Earl) v Cowley (Countess)* [1901] A.C. 450, HL which is hardly in point.
[86] [1983] F.S.R. 346 (Warner J.).
[87] [1996] F.S.R. 1 (Robert Walker J.).
[88] A sentiment amply confirmed by the facts of *Guide Dog Owners & Friends Association v Guide Dogs Association of NSW and ACT* [1999] FCA 316; 43 I.P.R. 531 affirming (1998) 42 I.P.R. 481.

interest a charity, church, or campaigning organisation has in attracting
financial contributions by way of subscriptions, donations or legacies, or by
fund-raising trading activities; and the interest it has in attracting sympathy,
assistance, or other kinds of public support for its cause or those it cares for,
let alone the interest a church has in attracting converts. It is only the first
which can properly be regarded as goodwill in the sense in which the term is
used in passing-off:

> "I conclude, therefore, that the scope of a passing-off action is wide
> enough to include deception of the public by one fund-raising charity in a
> way that tends to appropriate and so damage another fund-raising
> charity's goodwill—that is, the other charity's 'attractive force' (see Lord
> Macnaghten in *IRC v Muller's Margarine* [1901] AC 217, 223) in
> obtaining financial support from the public."[89]

This important proviso was overlooked when the principle of the *British
Diabetic Association* case was purportedly applied to a non-charitable, non-
political, interest group in *Burge v Haycock*.[90] One may agree with the Court
of Appeal that the *Countryside Alliance* was within the category of associations deemed to have sufficient interest to sue, if only because of the
goodwill it had with regard to its 95,000 subscribing members; but there was
no threat or even possibility of the defendant attracting or diverting any of
that goodwill to himself. The most he could be said to be misappropriating
from the claimants were the votes which an authorised *Countryside Alliance*
candidate might have attracted in Bromyard and Winslow; but it is very
dubious to suggest that electoral support of this kind falls within even the
most extended definition of goodwill, and in any event the *Countryside
Alliance* neither fielded nor endorsed individual candidates in any elections.
There was certainly a misrepresentation by the defendant, and one which
was capable of causing serious damage to the Alliance, but not all misrepresentations implying that one enjoys the support or endorsement of
someone else amount to passing-off, even when both parties are traders in
the everyday sense.[91] The real complaint of the Alliance was that as a result
of his conduct they would be tarred (or bloodied) with same the brush as the
British National Party—but to that extent their remedy should have been in
libel, slander, or injurious falsehood alone.

E. CREATION OF GOODWILL

Is actual trading necessary?

Goodwill is normally created by trading, and very slight trading activities **3–55**

---

[89] *per* Robert Walker J. in *British Diabetic Association v The Diabetic Society* [1996] F.S.R. 1.
[90] [2001] EWCA Civ 900; [2002] R.P.C. 28, CA.
[91] *Harrods Ltd v Harrodian School Ltd* [1996] R.P.C. 697, CA.

have been held to suffice.[92] There is some uncertainty as to whether a passing-off action can be brought in respect of a business which is about to commence trading and for which a demand has been created by advertising. In England, recent cases have allowed that the claimant in such circumstances has at least an arguable case which should not be struck out,[93] and which may support an application for an interlocutory injunction.[94] In Australia the law is clearly in the plaintiff's favour, and the leading case carries the authority of Sir Owen Dixon.[95] However, an early English authority held that trading must actually have commenced before there was any cause of action,[96] so that a defendant who entered the market before the plaintiff could do so with impunity, even if it was the plaintiff's advertising that had spurred him to take that step. The more recent English authorities are also less conclusive than may appear.

Despite these reservations, it is suggested that advertising directed at a specific market in actual preparation for trading does generate sufficient goodwill to support the action. Lord Macnaghten's description of goodwill as "the attractive force which brings in custom"[97] is consistent with goodwill existing because advertising has created a demand for the claimant's business before it commences, even if it be thought that the following passage "[i]t is the one thing that distinguishes an old established business from a new one at its first start" points the other way. The increasing importance of advertising in creating goodwill has been recognised by the highest authority[98]:

"The forms that unfair trading takes will alter with the ways in which trade is carried on and business reputation and goodwill acquired. Emerson's maker of the better mousetrap, if secluded in his house built in the woods, would today be unlikely to find a path beaten to his door in the absence of a costly advertising campaign to acquaint the public with the excellence of his wares."

3–56 In the Australian case of *Turner v General Motors*[99] the only plaintiffs (respondents) were a newly incorporated Australian subsidiary of the well known American motor manufacturers, established to assemble cars in Australia. The American company had previously traded through another

---

[92] Foreign claimant cases provide many examples. For instance *Sheraton Corp of America v Sheraton Motels Ltd* [1964] R.P.C. 202; *Globelegance BV v Sarkissian* [1974] R.P.C. 603; *JC Penney Co Inc v Penneys Ltd* [1975] F.S.R. 367, CA; *Metric Resources Corp v Leasemetrix Ltd* [1979] F.S.R. 571; *Jian Tools for Sales v Roderick Manhattan Group* [1995] F.S.R. 924.

[93] *My Kinda Bones Ltd v Dr Pepper's Stove Co Ltd* [1984] F.S.R. 289.

[94] *Allen (WH) & Co v Brown Watson Ltd* [1965] R.P.C. 191; *British Broadcasting Co v Talbot Motor Co Ltd* [1981] F.S.R. 228; *Labyrinth Media v Brave World* [1995] E.M.L.R. 38 (in the latter there was insufficient reputation in fact).

[95] *Turner v General Motors (Aust) Pty Ltd* (1929) 42 C.L.R. 352.

[96] *Maxwell v Hogg* (1867) L.R. 2 Ch. 307 (L.JJ.).

[97] *Inland Revenue Commissioners v Muller & Co's Margarine Ltd* [1901] A.C. 217 at 224, HL.

[98] *per* Lord Diplock in *Erven Warnink BV v J Townend & Sons (Hull) Ltd* [1979] A.C. 731 at 740; [1979] 2 All E.R. 927; [1980] R.P.C. 31 at 91, HL.

[99] (1929) 42 C.L.R. 352 (High Court, Full Court).

subsidiary which imported complete cars, but–as the court fully appreciated–neither that company nor its parent was a party and there had been no assignment of the goodwill of either. Heavy advertising of the new manufacturing company inspired the defendant to set up a second-hand car business as *General Motors* before the plaintiffs had begun to trade. The High Court of Australia, affirming the Supreme Court of New South Wales, granted an injunction.

Existence of goodwill was not in issue in *Terrapin v Ariston Buildings*[1] but an *obiter dictum* of Harman L.J. equates advertising with actual sales: "[The plaintiff's] goods, *either as advertised or as actually sold and bought*, must mean to the public and to the trade the plaintiff's goods and nobody else's".[2]

The opposite point of view draws on the *Budweiser* case[3] to say that there **3-57** can be no goodwill, even in the presence of demand, if the demand is incapable of being fulfilled. However, in *Budweiser* the plaintiffs did not direct any advertising at England and had no intention of serving the English market. Authorities on temporary discontinuance of businesses show that goodwill can exist in similar circumstances provided the claimant intends to make his goods or services available in the not too distant future. Alternatively, it can be said that passing-off only protects goodwill which the claimant has earned for himself by the excellence of his wares, and that if they are not on the market their excellence cannot be judged. This was the approach which commended itself to Slade J. in *My Kinda Bones v Dr Pepper's Stove Co*,[4] but it is too narrow. In *Trego v Hunt*[5] Lord Macnaghten said that goodwill "may have been built up by years of honest work or gained by lavish expenditure of money". Provided the claimant is actually on the market, it has never been suggested that he has to prove why the public buys his goods. If there is a demand for the claimant's goods it ought not to matter whether it has arisen from their inherent qualities, their cheapness, the dictates of fashion, advertising, press comment, personal recommendation, or for no good reason at all.

The nineteenth century: *Maxwell v Hogg*

The earliest decision in point is from the nineteenth century, and adopted a **3-58** strict approach. In *Maxwell v Hogg*[6] the plaintiff extensively advertised a new magazine to be known as *Belgravia*. Before the first issue appeared, the defendant hastily brought out a magazine of his own under that name, using material originally intended for other magazines of his. The Court of Appeal held that the plaintiff could have no rights to the name until the first issue of his magazine appeared, and that he had been successfully pre-empted by the

---

[1] [1964] F.S.R. 218, CA.
[2] Emphasis added. *Allen (WH) & Co v Brown Watson Ltd* [1965] R.P.C. 191 was roughly contemporaneous, but as the latter case is undated in the report one cannot be certain that Harman L.J. was approving it.
[3] *Anheuser-Busch Inc v Budejovicky Budvar NP* [1984] F.S.R. 413, CA.
[4] [1984] F.S.R. 289.
[5] [1896] A.C. 724, HL.
[6] (1867) L.R. 2 Ch. 307 (L.JJ.).

defendant. The fact that the defendant acted dishonestly (he had even accepted advertising for the plaintiffs' magazine without disclosing his own intentions) was only relevant to defeat his counterclaim.

Maxwell v Hogg was decided before it was appreciated that the property protected by the action for passing-off was the goodwill in the plaintiffs' business rather than in the word or other mark used. It was said that here would be enormous inconvenience in deciding what degree of advertising would suffice, but this rested on the erroneous proposition in *Hall v Barrows*[7] that if a mark had been used at all then a right of property arose in it irrespective of whether it had acquired a reputation and become distinctive. The question of distinctiveness must be answered in all conventional passing-off actions and it is commonplace to take account of advertising as well as sales. *Hall v Barrows* itself favoured protecting the plaintiff at what had seemed to Romilly M.R. to be the earliest possible moment, precisely because malicious rivals might otherwise forestall him. *Maxwell v Hogg* is also open to strong criticism on other grounds. It rests on the proposition, presumably derived from patent law, that the plaintiff who had not begun to trade had failed to give any consideration for the property right he claimed. No such concept is relevant in passing-off or trade mark law, and *Maxwell v Hogg* seems to be the only case in which it has been advanced.[8]

3–59   In *Chivers v Chivers*[9] the plaintiffs' actual trade was confined to a limited area within England but advertisements were circulated more widely. Farwell J. refused to take the latter into account:

> "Advertisement, distinguished from trade, is nothing. No doubt if you have the trade the advertisement assists the trade, but to say that a man can by advertising along make his name known in connection with particular goods so as to assist him in obtaining a monopoly of those goods seems to be untenable as a proposition."

However, *Chivers v Chivers* cannot very well be reconciled with the decision of the Court of Appeal in *Chelsea Man Menswear v Chelsea Girl*,[10] so its current status is open to doubt.

Maxwell v Hogg was considered inconclusively by the Court of Appeal in *Marcus v Hutton-Wild*[11] but the highly descriptive magazine title in question, *Leisure News*, cannot have become distinctive on the strength of minimal pre-publication use, and the abstract legal question did not need to be decided.

---

[7] (1863) 32 L.J. Ch. 548 (Romilly M.R.); (1863) 46 E.R. 873 (Westbury L.C.).

[8] The idea of there being a consideration for trade marks in the same sense as for patents, designs and copyright was demolished by W. Hindmarch in his evidence to the 1862 *Select Committee on Trade Marks*, 129 (Q2772) in a passage quoted in Sherman and Bentley, *The Making of Modern Intellectual Property Law* (1999), p.171.

[9] (1900) 17 R.P.C. 420 (Farwell J.).

[10] [1987] R.P.C. 189, CA. Nor, perhaps, with *Faulder (Henry) & Co Ltd v O & G Rushton Ltd* (1903) 20 R.P.C. 477, CA.

[11] [1990] R.P.C. 576, CA.

Trade preceded by advertising

The more recent English authorities begin with *Allen v Brown Watson*.[12] The **3–60** autobiography of Frank Harris had been published in an expurgated edition as *My Life and Adventures*. The plaintiffs proposed to publish an unexpurgated version as *My Life and Loves*. They had advertised it widely and had arranged for pre-publication reviews to appear. The defendants obtained the right to publish the original expurgated version but advertised it as *My Life and Loves* in terms which suggested it was the unexpurgated version and which acknowledged that great public interest had been created. The defendants' first advertisement apparently appeared before either party had published its book, but by the time the motion for an interlocutory injunction came to be heard the plaintiffs' book had been published, though the defendants' had not. Pennycuick J. accepted that the title *My Life and Loves* had come to denote the unexpurgated edition published by the plaintiffs and granted an interlocutory injunction.

Allen v Brown Watson was followed by Megarry V.C. in *BBC v Talbot*[13] in which he granted the BBC an interlocutory injunction restraining the defendants from using the term *Carfax* for a motor parts business. The BBC intended to use the word for a broadcast motoring information service and although the service had not commenced there was widespread public awareness of it under that name. In *My Kinda Bones v Dr Pepper's Stove Co.*[14] Slade J. refused to strike out the statement of claim in a case in which the plaintiff had advertised, but not yet opened, a restaurant to be called *The Chicago Rib Shack*.

Allen v Brown Watson has been accepted as authority for the proposition **3–61** that a passing-off action can be brought on the strength of goodwill generated by advertising even before trade has commenced. However, in *My Kinda Bones v Dr Pepper* Slade J. correctly pointed out that it did not necessarily go any further than to show that with heavy pre-launch publicity a very short time on the market might be sufficient to support an action.[15] The same cannot be said of *BBC v Talbot*, but that case may have misunderstood the earlier authority. It is implicit in this approach that Brown Watson's own advertisement when first published would not have been actionable: there was not yet any goodwill to be damaged. This is a distinction with important consequences. Suppose A and B both adopt and advertise the same new brand, with B issuing his advertisements after A's but before A launches. Even if A's goods are the first to be sold, he may find that the distinctiveness of his mark has already been destroyed by B's advertisements which he could not prevent.[16] The reason the latter problem

---

[12] [1965] R.P.C. 191 (Pennycuick J.).
[13] [1981] F.S.R. 228 (Megarry V.C.).
[14] [1984] F.S.R. 289 (Slade J.).
[15] In *MINERVA TM, Reed Consumer Books Ltd v Pomaco Ltd* [2001] E.T.M.R 92; [2000] F.S.R. 734 (Jacob J.) three weeks' use of *Minerva* as a new publisher's imprint, with considerable launch publicity, gave the opponents prior rights (in respect of literary matter) under the Trade Marks Act 1994, s.5(4)(a).
[16] Compare *Elida Gibbs Ltd v Colgate-Palmolive Ltd* [1983] F.S.R. 95.

did not arise in *Allen v Brown Watson* turns on the unusual nature of the misrepresentation, which was essentially one of quality, rather than source. The terms of the defendants' advertisements were such that they would not have prevented the title becoming distinctive of the unexpurgated version. In fact, the publicity put out by the defendants probably reinforced public awareness of *My Life and Loves* as the name of the full text.

In reality, neither *Allen v Brown Watson* nor *BBC v Talbot* actually turned on the existence of goodwill. It is irrelevant to ask whether either advertising or actual use generated goodwill in the title or name itself, because the right protected by passing-off is not a right of property in a particular name or mark, but the goodwill in the claimant's business as a whole. W. H. Allen was a long established business with ample goodwill. So was the BBC. Suppose that the defendants Brown Watson had expressly misrepresented their book as published by W. H. Allen. That would have been passing-off and would have damaged the plaintiffs' goodwill in their business even, and perhaps especially, if the latter had no intention of publishing such a book at all.[17] The only significance of the pre-launch advertising in *Allen v Brown Watson* was that it identified the new title with a particular text and, incidentally, with its publisher. Without the advertising, the defendants would not have been guilty of any misrepresentation.

Examples

3–62   In the Canadian case of *Windmere v Charlescraft*[18] it was held that extensive promotion of a novel razor, the *Vibra Shave*, had generated both goodwill and distinctiveness by the time the defendant attempted a hurried launch of a rival product in an attempt to forestall the plaintiffs. The American plaintiffs began promoting their razor in Canada at trade fairs and to dealers in March 1988 and took advance orders, with delivery to retailers commencing in August. Promotional material for the defendants' razor was first issued in August and the razor was on the market in September. The generation of goodwill was taken to have started in March, when a concerted effort to promote the razor had begun: "it would not make commercial sense to conclude that the plaintiff's actions, integrally linked as they were to the receipt of large numbers of orders for the product bearing the trade mark, did not build up substantial goodwill in the trade mark which accrued solely to the benefit of the plaintiff".

In *Marcus v Hutton-Wild*[19] the parties were both on the point of launching rival magazines under the name *Leisure News* with next to no advance publicity in either case. An interlocutory injunction was granted in favour of the defendants at first instance but discharged on appeal. The attitude the Court of Appeal displayed to *Maxwell v Hogg*[20] is ambiguous, and confused

---

[17] The plaintiffs in *Totalizator Agency Board v Turf News Pty Ltd* [1967] V.R. 605; [1972] R.P.C. 570 had no intention of publishing a tip-sheet, any more than *Annabel's* night club intended to branch out into escort agency.

[18] (1988) 23 C.P.R. (3d) 60 (Rouleau J., Federal Court).

[19] [1990] R.P.C. 576, CA.

[20] Above.

by the fact that no distinction was made between the existence of goodwill as such, and acquisition of secondary meaning for a very descriptive title. There is no doubt that the decision is right on its facts, since *Leisure News* could not possibly have become distinctive of either party with such minimal use.

The distinction between reliance on pre-trading activities to generate goodwill as such, and their relevance to the existence of a misrepresentation by the defendant is also illustrated by *Law Society v Griffiths*.[21] The plaintiffs were awarded an interlocutory injunction to protect the freephone number of their *Accident Line* service although the use by the defendants of a confusingly similar number narrowly anticipated the date of actual commencement of the former. The defendants' principal submission that there was no misrepresentation to restrain failed on the facts, the time factor notwithstanding.

The proposition that pre-launch publicity can support a passing-off **3–63** action was also approved in principle by Blackburne J. in *Labyrinth Media v Brave World*,[22] although on the facts the publicity relied on fell far short of the necessary standard. The plaintiffs and defendants both intended to launch videos of real-life police car chases under the title *Police America* with the plaintiffs' video being second on the market. The plaintiffs obtained an *ex parte* injunction on the strength of a certain amount of pre-launch publicity but it was discharged at the *inter partes* hearing. Blackburne J. was prepared to say that he could see "no good reason why in an appropriate case a plaintiff may not establish his reputation in a product in advance of its release to the public simply by pre-launch publicity sufficient to enable it to mount a claim in passing-off". The decision of the Court of Appeal in *Marcus Publishing v Hutton-Wild Communications*[23] did not preclude this and there were passages in all three judgments consistent with the possibility. However the only pre-launch publicity to have come to the attention of the general public was a single inconspicuous paragraph in *The Sun*, and although publicity to the trade had been more extensive there was no possibility of traders being deceived.

In *Pontiac Marina v CDL Hotels*,[24] the plaintiffs had not yet opened to the public at their new *Millenia* development in Singapore, consisting of office blocks, a shopping mall and the *Ritz Carlton Millenia Hotel*; but the Court of Appeal of Singapore held that there had already been sufficient publicity and trading for the complex and the hotel alike to have the necessary goodwill to support a passing-off action at the date on which the defendants announced their intention to rebrand themselves as *Millennium*, and to incorporate *Millennium* into the names of three of their existing Singapore hotels, which in the meantime would be known as *Millennium Partner Hotels*. Promotion and marketing of the *Millenia* complex had already cost the plaintiffs S\$1 million, numerous tenants had signed up for space in the office blocks and shopping mall, and hotel bookings for 2,840 room-nights

---

[21] [1995] R.P.C. 16 (Aldous J.).
[22] [1995] E.M.L.R. 38 (Blackburne J.).
[23] [1990] R.P.C. 576, CA.
[24] [1998] F.S.R. 839 (CA, Singapore) affirming [1997] F.S.R. 725.

had already been taken.[25] These amounted to trading activities, rather than mere preparations. Though much of this goodwill was in the plaintiff's capacity as property developers rather than hoteliers, that goodwill was not entirely irrelevant, and they also had sufficient goodwill specifically in relation to the *Ritz Carlton Millenia Hotel*, of which they were the owners and principals.

In Malaysia, pre-launch promotion of the plaintiffs' remote control car immobiliser under the name *Stopcard* was held to have generated sufficient goodwill and reputation to justify a finding of passing-off against the defendants' *Stopcar*, which was launched a few days' later: *Electro CAD Australia v Mejati*.[26]

Mere preparations for trading

3-64 The existence of preparations in advance of commencing business is insufficient in itself to generate goodwill. In the early case of *Lawson v Bank of London*[27] the plaintiff was the promoter of a bank to be known as the *Bank of London*. He had issued a prospectus and found premises, but the bank had not been formed or begun to trade. His action against a rival bank which had started business under the same name was dismissed. In *Hart v Relentless Records*[28] the claimant had unsuccessfully tried to promote a record company under the name *Relentless Recordings*, but had never got any further than issuing four promotional tracks to DJs. No recordings had been released on a commercial basis and Jacob J. held that there was no goodwill. Several actions by foreign claimants have failed despite the existence of preparations to enter the English market. In *Amway v Eurway*[29] a foreign plaintiff had started seeking premises and employees; in *Athlete's Foot v Cobra Sports*[30] the plaintiffs were seeking an English franchisee, and one potential franchisee had ordered goods and stationery. In both cases interlocutory injunctions were refused.

Difficulties are caused by the Australian case of *Fletcher Challenge v Fletcher Challenge*.[31] The plaintiff was incorporated in New Zealand on November 10, 1980 to act as holding company for three existing companies. The merger had been announced in October, and the individual defendants had immediately reserved the name "Fletcher Challenge Pty. Ltd." in New South Wales for a company they subsequently formed. Powell J. was prepared to hold that the few hours which had elapsed between announcement of the merger and the defendants' reservation of the name was sufficient, and granted an interlocutory injunction. The reasoning seems doubtful. There may have been a reputation for the proposed holding company, but

---

[25] The figure is at the date of the writ, October 15, 1995, but that was only a week after the *quia timet* cause of action was held to have accrued. The plaintiff's first hotel reservation was placed in May 1995, and the hotel was to open in February 1996.

[26] [1999] F.S.R. 291 (HC Malaysia).

[27] (1856) 139 E.R. 1296.

[28] [2002] EWHC 1984; [2003] F.S.R. 36 (Jacob J.).

[29] [1974] R.P.C. 82 (Brightman J.).

[30] [1980] R.P.C. 343 (Walton J.).

[31] [1981] 1 N.S.W.L.R. 196; [1982] F.S.R. 1 (Powell J.).

as the plaintiff company was not even in existence at the relevant time, it can hardly have had any goodwill of its own. The best justification for *Fletcher Challenge* is probably to regard the plaintiff company as the *de facto* successors to the goodwill of the three predecessor companies and their accrued rights of action.[32]

What is true of preparations to start trading at all, is true *mutatis mutandis* of preparations by an existing business to enter a new, especially if unrelated, field.[33]

Trading with other traders; goodwill as a purchaser

The goodwill of a business does not only exist in relation to the sale of goods **3–65** or the provision of services to the consuming public, whether directly or indirectly through other traders further down the chain of distribution. Several cases acknowledge that a business may have goodwill in its capacity as a purchaser, and of course a newly established business must typically purchase before it can have anything to sell.

In a domestic context such goodwill was important in *Pullman (R & J) Ltd v Pullman*,[34] as well as *Chelsea Man Menswear v Chelsea Girl*,[35] where it justified an injunction extending beyond the places in which the plaintiffs' shops actually traded. In the international context, *Penney v Penney's*[36] and *Penney v Punjabi Nick*[37] were both decided in the plaintiffs' favour solely on the basis of purchasing activities in Hong Kong; and purchasing was important in the corresponding English *Penney's* case[38] and in *Woolworth v Woolworths (Australasia)*.[39] In all such cases care has to be taken to ensure that damage to the claimant's goodwill as a purchaser is really at risk from the defendant's conduct, bearing in mind that suppliers are typically more careful than consumers: and that any mistakes they make may not be damaging to the claimant to the same extent as mistakes by consumers.

An unusual situation arose in *Scandecor Development v Scandecor Marketing*[40] in so far as it was common ground that although the parties' posters were sold by retailers to members of the public, nonetheless the only relevant goodwill owned by either party was in relation to the retail trade. The qualities which distinguished one supplier of posters from another mattered to retail traders, but not to consumers, who simply bought whatever posters they fancied without reference to the identity or brand name of the publisher or supplier.

---

[32] See also *Glaxo plc v Glaxowellcome Ltd* [1996] F.S.R. 388 (Lightman J.) where no such problem arose.

[33] *Teleworks Ltd v Telework Group plc* [2002] R.P.C. 27 (Christopher Floyd Q.C., Deputy Judge).

[34] (1919) 36 R.P.C. 240.

[35] [1987] R.P.C. 189, CA.

[36] [1979] F.S.R. 29 (Huggins J., Hong Kong).

[37] [1979] F.S.R. 26 (Leonard J., Hong Kong).

[38] *J C Penney Co Inc v Penney's Ltd* [1975] F.S.R. 367, CA.

[39] (1930) 47 R.P.C. 337.

[40] [1999] F.S.R. 26, CA. The issue was whether goodwill was owned by the Swedish publisher of the posters, or the English distributor.

F. Territorial Scope of Goodwill

The problem and national differences in approach to it

3–66 The problem of the foreign claimant whose goods or business may be known in a particular jurisdiction although he has no business there is one of the most intractable in the law of passing-off. It is one of the very few topics where it is impossible to say that the underlying substantive law is essentially uniform throughout the common law world; and there are differences in national case law which are too great to dismiss as the inevitable result of different judges using different words in applying the law to differing factual situations. The Australian courts have gone furthest in departing from the law as it is understood in England. It is now common ground, however, that the claimant need not have a branch, agent or business operation as such in the country where he sues, and decisions critical of any such former rule are no longer controversial.

In the worst case, an international company seeking to expand into a new territory may find itself blocked by a small business already trading under the same name or style, perhaps on a miniscule scale; and perhaps having been set up for the very purpose of blocking anticipated expansion by the claimant or being bought out for a large sum. On the other hand, a rule of law dealing with this situation has to avoid the opposite scenario of *bona fide* domestic traders finding themselves open to litigation at the suit of unknown or barely-known claimants from almost anywhere in the world. Some of the more radical proposals for changing the law to assist foreign claimants ignore the need for this balancing exercise, without which the opportunities for abuse are simply increased, and further uncertainty created.

The remainder of the present section attempts to state the law in a way consistent with the English Court of Appeal decision in the *Budweiser* case, *Anheuser-Busch v Budejovicky Budvar*,[41] drawing on other common law authorities to the extent that the various bodies of law are reconcilable. Many decisions which are radical on their face can equally well be understood in more orthodox terms. In the following section the current position in each of the major common law jurisdictions outside England is summarised, with the emphasis being on departures from the Court of Appeal decision in the *Budweiser* case. This section also includes a further commentary on one English case, *Pete Waterman v CBS*,[42] because of its affinities with Australian, Canadian and New Zealand case law.

Goodwill and national boundaries

3–67 The nature of goodwill as legal property with no physical existence means that where a business is carried on in more than one country or jurisdiction there must be a separate goodwill in each.[43] For this purpose "country"

---

[41] [1984] F.S.R. 413, CA.
[42] [1993] E.M.L.R. 27 (Browne-Wilkinson V.C.).
[43] *Star Industrial Co Ltd v Yap Kwee Kor* [1976] F.S.R. 256, PC.

means the territory whose legal system protects the goodwill in question. As goodwill is protected by the common law it follows that goodwill exists separately in England and Scotland, and in the various Australian states and Canadian provinces.

"However you attempt the difficult task of defining goodwill for the purpose of English law ... the proprietary rights which it involves and confers are rights, no more and no less, to come to the English courts to prevent the goodwill being damaged or infringed by others. Goodwill in England is only of value and of practical existence insofar as these rights of invocation of the courts' powers can be asserted; and the nature and value of goodwill in other countries will, I assume, in like manner exist or not exist, and be of value or not be of value, to the extent to which, according to the laws of those countries, like rights can be asserted and enforced there."[44]

If a business is carried on in several such territories, then a separate goodwill attaches to it in each notwithstanding that the business may not be carried on by different legal entities. Similarly, a business carried on in one territory but exporting to others will have a separate goodwill in each. In the extreme, but illustrative, case of a business which exports all its products to a single foreign market the goodwill of the business is best regarded as being wholly situate in that foreign territory, where all its customers are to be found.

"Supposing that the products of the manufactory [in Germany] were all exported to England and sold to English customers, I should find it difficult to hold that the goodwill was out of England merely because the manufactory was."[45]

The existence of relevant goodwill in England

The test for whether a foreign claimant may succeed in a passing-off action **3–68** is normally stated in terms of whether his business has a goodwill in England.[46] This criterion is broader than obsolete statements that the claimant must have a business or place of business in England. Provided there are customers or ultimate consumers for the claimant's goods or services in England then the claimant stands in the same position as a domestic trader. It is of no importance whether the foreign claimant conducts his English business directly or through intermediaries of whatever legal status, nor

[44] *per* Lord Evershed M.R. in *Adrema Maschinebau GmbH v Custodian of Enemy Property* [1957] R.P.C. 49, CA.

[45] *per* Lord Robertson in *Inland Revenue Commissioners v Muller & Co's Margarine Ltd* [1901] A.C. 217, HL.

[46] *Anheuser-Busch Inc v Budejovicky Budvar NP* [1984] F.S.R. 413, CA; *Erven Warnink BV v J Townend & Sons (Hull) Ltd* [1979] A.C. 731; [1979] 2 All E.R. 927; [1980] R.P.C. 31, HL (especially, *per* Lord Fraser); *Oertli (T) AG v E J Bowman (London) Ltd* [1959] R.P.C. 1, HL; affirming [1957] R.P.C. 388, CA.

whether his terms of trade provide for his goods to be sold in England in the sense of property in them passing to the buyer here.

In *Anheuser-Busch v Budejovicky Budvar*[47] Oliver L.J. put the question in terms of the foreign business having customers, directly or indirectly, in the jurisdiction.

"The principle was expressed by Walton J.[48] ... as follows:

'[A]s a matter of principle, no trader can complain of passing-off as against him in any territory ... in which he has no customers, nobody who is in a trade relation with him. This will normally shortly be expressed by stating that he does not carry on any trade in that particular country ... but the inwardness of it will be that he has no customers in that country: no people who buy his goods or make use of his services (as the case may be) there.'

This is, I think, a helpful statement, but needs, in the light of the authorities, to be approached with the caveat that 'customers' must not be read as confined to persons who are in a direct contractual relationship with the plaintiff, but includes persons who buy his goods in the market."[49]

3-69   The law had been stated in very similar terms in the Australian case of *Taco Bell v Taco Co of Australia*[50]:

"In order to succeed in an action for passing-off in relation to the Sydney metropolitan area a plaintiff must show that it has a goodwill here. This can usually be established by proof that there has been some prior business activity here involving the use of the name or mark or get-up in question in relation to the plaintiff's goods or services. The nature and degree of business activity will differ from case to case. It does not follow from what Walton J.[51] said that a single transaction will always suffice. In some cases it may. Nor is it necessary that the plaintiff has an established place of business here. Its goods may have been imported and sold here under the relevant name or mark by another. It may have licensed people to use its name or mark on products which are sold there. It may have advertised here to solicit orders by post from the public or to encourage the public to travel to do business at its premises in another country...

A business has goodwill attached to it in a particular place if there is an attraction among people there to do business with it. Even if it has no place of business there people residing there may, nevertheless, be attracted to do business with it. For example, by buying goods which it produces and are sold there by importers, or by ordering goods from it by

[47] [1984] F.S.R. 413, CA.
[48] In *Athlete's Foot Marketing Associates Inc v Cobra Sports Ltd* [1980] R.P.C. 343.
[49] *per* Oliver L.J. in *Anheuser-Busch Inc v Budejovicky Budvar NP* [1984] F.S.R. 413, CA.
[50] *per* Elliott J. (1981) 60 F.L.R. 60; 40 A.L.R. 153, affirmed (1982) 2 T.P.R. 48; 42 A.L.R. 177.
[51] In *Athlete's Foot Marketing Associates Inc v Cobra Sports Ltd* [1980] R.P.C. 343.

mail or by travelling from their residence to its place of business in an adjoining country. . . . However, one thing, in my opinion is clear, namely knowledge by people in Sydney that a successful business is being conducted in the United States under a distinctive name does not give that business a reputation or goodwill here unless people in Sydney are attracted to do business with it despite the distance separating them. Only then could it be said that there existed in Sydney 'the attractive force which brings in custom.' In many cases distance or the nature of the business will make it highly unlikely that anyone could be so attracted."

If the claimant has English customers in this sense then he has at least **3–70** some goodwill in England and is entitled to be treated in the same way as an English claimant. It does not follow, however, that the claimant's English goodwill will be sufficient to support a passing-off action. In normal trading conditions, only one trader in the chain of distribution has any relevant goodwill in the sense of being identified by the public with the character or quality of the goods they buy. This will often be the manufacturer, but it may be an importer, distributor or even a retailer. Other traders are likely to have only a very limited goodwill or no relevance because it is restricted to their relationship with their immediate customers.[52] If the public does not attribute the goods to the claimant, then he has no goodwill in relation to them, and cannot bring a passing-off action whether he is a domestic trader or a foreign one.

For the claimant trading in England on his own account, even quite a small amount of business is sufficient to establish a goodwill. There may be sufficient goodwill even if the business has been intermittent, very recent in commencement, localised, or confined to a few customers. In these respects, a foreign business setting up in England for the first time is in the same position as any other small-scale or newly established business here.[53] However, proof of the existence of goodwill in England is merely the first step in a successful passing-off action. Liability ultimately depends on proof of likelihood of damage to that goodwill arising from a misrepresentation made by the defendant. If the claimant is barely known here and has very little business in England, then it may reasonably be doubted if any but the most blatant misrepresentation would be likely to deceive anyone, or damage such goodwill as the claimant might have. In some of the cases which follow, one wonders if the unsuccessful defendants may not have set themselves too high a target by arguing that their respective claimants had no goodwill at all.

The claimant represented in or exporting to England

Rather than establishing a branch or subsidiary of his own in a foreign **3–71** territory, a trader may appoint another independent trader to represent him there. In the decided cases such representatives are normally described as

---

[52] As in *Ullman (J) & Co v Cesar Leuba* (1908) 25 R.P.C. 673, PC.
[53] *Weingarten Bros v Bayer & Co* [1904–7] All E.R. 877; (1903) 22 R.P.C. 341, HL; *Penney (JC) Co Inc v Penneys Ltd* [1975] F.S.R. 367, CA.

agents, although it may be doubted whether they were agents in the legal sense with power to bind their principals rather than distributors trading on their own account. The latter seems more likely in most cases, but the precise form of the legal relationship is of secondary importance. Whatever the status of the representative, provided that the goods handled by him are identified with the foreign supplier rather than the agent or importer, then the supplier will have goodwill in the territory into which the goods are imported.

Thus, in *White Hudson v Asian Organisation*[54] the plaintiffs' trade was through "agents" in Singapore. In *Johnston v Orr-Ewing*[55] the plaintiffs had three successive "agents" in Bombay. In *Manus v Fullwood & Bland*[56] the defendants were "the agent (in the commercial sense) in importing the plaintiffs' machines and marketing them ... in the English market." The machines were shipped FOB Swedish port, so even the sales to the defendants themselves took place outside England. In all three cases the plaintiffs were successful, notwithstanding that all sales to the trade or general public in the relevant markets had been made by others. In *Standard Ideal v Standard Sanitary Manufacturing Co*[57] the plaintiffs were an American company which sold goods in Quebec through an agent who took orders. The Privy Council held that it was not carrying on a business in Quebec so as to contravene a statute requiring registration. They discharged an injunction solely on the ground that *Standard* was not distinctive.

3–72 Whether the foreign supplier, the importer, or some other party is the owner of the goodwill is a question of fact in every case.[58] The inference that the foreign supplier is the owner is strengthened the more he enjoys control over the selection of the importer and his conduct, or if there is more than one importer at a time or in succession, though none of these factors is necessary or conclusive. Conversely, all the relevant goodwill may be owned by the importing business to the exclusion of the supplier if it is the importer who is seen as responsible for the goods.

In *Ullman v Leuba*[59] the plaintiffs were Swiss watch manufacturers with an export business to Hong Kong. Their claim that the marks in question were distinctive of them in Hong Kong was rejected as resting on a disguised assignment in gross. The action for passing-off was dismissed by the Privy Council:

"Their Lordships are of opinion that the respondents, the plaintiffs in the suit, ought to have been non-suited for want of title ... That Hong Kong business of selling watches to the public belongs now, not to the respondents, but to a certain Madame Bovet; and the relation in which the respondents stand to Madame Bovet is simply that of manufacturers

---

[54] [1964] 1 W.L.R. 1466; [1965] 1 All E.R. 1040; [1965] R.P.C. 45, PC.
[55] (1882) 7 App. Cas. 219, HL.
[56] (1949) 66 R.P.C. 71, CA.
[57] [1911] A.C. 78, PC.
[58] *Scandecor Development AB v Scandecor Marketing AB* [1999] F.S.R. 26, CA See Sections H and I below.
[59] (1908) 25 R.P.C. 673, PC, *per* Lord Robertson.

to a customer ... It results that the only person who could be deceived, so far as they are concerned, is Madame Bovet, and that is not their case at all. Their case consists in ignoring the contractual relation of manufacturers to dealer, by which they are connected with, and are separated from, Madame Bovet, and identifying themselves with the trade which belongs to her..."

Foreign claimants with identifiable customers in England

The most difficult cases for the foreign claimant are those in which he does 3–73 not carry on any business in England, does not have an agency or distributor, and does not actively export. Even if none of these conditions are met, however, it does not follow that the claimant can have no goodwill in England. Depending on the circumstances of the trade, English customers may be prepared to seek out the claimant and avail themselves of his goods or services. If this occurs on a more than trivial scale, then the claimant will have goodwill in England.

In *SA des Anciens Etablissements Panhard et Levassor v Panhard Levassor Motor Co*[60] the plaintiffs were a French car manufacturing company who deliberately refrained from selling cars directly to England because of a risk of patent infringement. However, an English company and private individuals bought their cars in France and imported them into England. England was therefore one of the plaintiff's markets. A permanent injunction was granted.

In *Grant v Levitt*[61] a Liverpool business trading as the *Globe Furnishing* 3–74 *Company* obtained an injunction against use of the same name in Dublin. Advertisements by the plaintiff reached Ireland, mail order was an important part of its business and there were Irish customers.

In *Globelegance v Sarkissian*[62] the plaintiff *Valentino* was a couturier with a salon in Rome. Buyers from England attended his shows, which were favourably commented on in the English press. Some clothes to his patterns were made up and sold in England under his name. He had held two fashion shows of his own in England. An interlocutory injunction was granted. In *Poiret v Jules Poiret*[63] an earlier case by a French couturier on similar, but stronger, facts a permanent injunction was granted after trial.

In *C & A Modes v C & A (Waterford)*[64] the plaintiffs operated a chain of 3–75 clothes stores throughout the UK, including one in Northern Ireland, but none in the Irish Republic where the defendants traded.

"[A] very substantial and regular custom from the Republic of Ireland was enjoyed by this [the Belfast] store ... an excursion train travelled each Thursday from Dublin to Belfast, and so great was the influx of customers from the Republic as a result of that excursion that the store ordinarily

[60] [1901] 2 Ch. 513; [1900–3] All E.R. 477; 18 R.P.C. 405 (Farwell J.).
[61] (1901) 18 R.P.C. 361 (Porter M.R., Ireland).
[62] [1974] R.P.C. 603 (Templeman J.).
[63] (1920) 37 R.P.C. 177 (P. O. Lawrence J.).
[64] [1976] I.R. 198; [1978] F.S.R. 126 (Irish S.C.).

employed extra part-time staff on Thursdays on the same basis as it did on Saturdays which were normally the busiest shopping days."

Advertising in English publications and on television was also widely received in Ireland. An injunction was granted at trial (the defendants did not give evidence) and upheld by the Irish Supreme Court.

In *Nishika Corp v Goodchild*[65] the plaintiffs were manufacturers of a three-dimensional camera and the first defendants were their distributors in America. The plaintiffs had no customers to speak of in the UK until the defendants imported and sold a supply of the plaintiffs' cameras. The goodwill so generated accrued to the plaintiffs, not least because the defendants had actually held themselves out as being authorised distributors. Knox J. granted an interlocutory injunction[66] against the defendants misrepresenting themselves as more than mere unlicensed importers.

Borderline cases: to infer goodwill or not?

3–76 If the claimant can prove as a matter of fact that he has more than a trivial number of customers in England then the question of whether he owns goodwill is resolved in his favour. Often, however, the existence of English goodwill is to some extent a matter of inference. There are then three particularly important matters of evidence to be taken into account. These are the practical ease or difficulty of obtaining the claimant's goods or services from a foreign territory where they are available; the nature and value of the goods in question, especially whether they are such that customers would put themselves out to obtain them from abroad; and the extent to which the claimant's goods or services are known and sought after, whether as a result of advertising, press comment, personal recommendation or for any other reason.

In *Metric Resources v Leasemetrix*[67] the plaintiffs hired out electronic equipment in the USA and Canada. There was a little evidence of trade with English customers:

"On the facts, the plaintiff's case is thin. There are many difficulties in a hiring business, particularly when much of the hiring is on a short term basis: for the goods have to be returned at the end of the hire, and the Atlantic lies between the point of hire and the point of use in this country. ... There seems, however, to be some attraction for customers outside North America in the range of instruments which are available from the plaintiff company and are not readily available elsewhere, and in the option to purchase instruments that have been hired."

An interlocutory injunction was granted.

In *Jian Tools for Sales v Roderick Manhattan Group*[68] Knox J., after an

---

[65] [1990] F.S.R. 371 (Knox J.).
[66] In similar terms to *Sony KK v Saray Electronics (London) Ltd* [1983] F.S.R. 302, CA.
[67] [1979] F.S.R. 571 (Megarry V.C.).
[68] [1995] F.S.R. 924 (Knox J.).

extensive review of the authorities, held that the American plaintiffs had sufficient English goodwill in relation to their business plan software to obtain an interlocutory injunction. 127 sales, including review copies, were not *de minimis* and sales in England generated by foreign sources such as advertisements in American computer magazines should not be ignored. *Budweiser* was distinguished as a case where the plaintiffs' sales to PX customers and the American embassy were in a watertight compartment compared to the public at large, who could not buy the plaintiffs' beer however hard they tried. This is another case where the defendant had been in abortive negotiations to represent the plaintiff and suffered as a result, especially on the balance of convenience. They took a calculated risk with their eyes open.

However, in the absence of any evidence of actual customers in England, **3–77** there may be no reason to suppose that the claimant has any goodwill here.

In *Amway v Eurway*[69] the first plaintiffs were an American company selling cleaning materials direct to the American public. They had incorporated a subsidiary in England (the second plaintiffs) which had acquired premises but had not commenced to trade. An interlocutory injunction was refused.

In *Athlete's Food v Cobra Sports*[70] the plaintiffs carried on a retail shoe franchising business, mainly in the USA. They had a prospective franchisee in England but trade had not commenced. There was considerable evidence of public knowledge of the plaintiff's business, but none of any person in this country having bought anything from one of the plaintiffs' franchised shops abroad. The plaintiffs' advertisements in American publications reached England, but did not solicit postal trade. An interlocutory injunction was refused.

In *Nice and Safe Attitude v Flook*[71] such presence as the American National Space and Aeronautics Administration (*NASA*) had in England by virtue of scientific collaboration projects was too remote from the field of young persons' fashion for a licence by them to be effective as a defence against a company with actual goodwill in relation to *NASA* for clothing.

Several cases in which relief has been refused involve restaurants, which **3–78** by their nature have a fairly localised trade. In *Taco Bell v Taco Co of Australia*[72] a American chain of Mexican-style restaurants was refused relief in Australia. In *Wienerwald v Kwan, Wong, Tan and Fong*[73] a Swiss company controlling 420 restaurants in Europe, the United States, South Africa and Japan granted a franchise for Hong Kong and discovered the name had already been reserved by the defendants. Leonard J. refused an interlocutory injunction, describing it as "a lamentable conclusion" to which he was driven. An injunction in default of defence was granted in England in *Maxim's v Dye*.[74]

---

[69] [1974] R.P.C. 82; [1972] F.S.R. 213 (Brightman J.)
[70] [1980] R.P.C. 343 (Walton J.).
[71] [1997] F.S.R. 14 (Robert Walker J.).
[72] (1981) 60 F.L.R. 60; 40 A.L.R. 153, affirmed (1982) 2 T.P.R. 48; 42 A.L.R. 177.
[73] [1979] F.S.R. 381 (Leonard J., HK).
[74] [1977] 1 W.L.R. 155; [1978] 2 All E.R. 55; [1977] F.S.R. 364 (Graham J.).

In the majority of decided cases in which foreign claimants have been unsuccessful the goods were relatively commonplace and of low value, such as fast food, drinks, footwear, or cleaning materials, and the claimant very far removed from the forum. It is not surprising that retail shoe stores or fast food restaurants based in America should have no goodwill in England, Australia or Hong Kong. No one would be prepared to travel that far to patronise them. Conversely, there may be goodwill in England if there are customers here prepared to take whatever trouble is necessary to obtain the claimant's goods from abroad. This may be more readily believed when the goods are expensive, prestigious or without a satisfactory local substitute. The Haute Couture creations of leading international designers clearly stand in a different position to mass-produced sports footwear; likewise *Maxim's* to the *Taco Bell* or *Wienerwald* chains. A three star rating for a restaurant in the *Guide Michelin* means "*vaut le voyage*", and *Wienerwald* itself draws attention to the fact that *Maxim's* was extensively patronised by English residents and that tables were booked from England.[75] If the inconvenience to which customers are put in crossing a national border to obtain the claimant's goods is slight, as between England and Scotland, Ulster and the Irish Republic, or two Australian states, then even the most mundane business may enjoy goodwill across the border.

Foreign claimants with only reputation in England

3–79 Reputation as such is a state of fact rather than a form of property capable of being protected by the law of passing-off. If the claimant has or has had no significant number of customers in England, in the broad sense identified by Oliver L.J. in *Budweiser*,[76] then he has no goodwill here which no amount of reputation can replace.

> "[T]he plaintiffs' name *Budweiser* was well known to a substantial number of people in this country ... as a name associated with the beer brewed by the plaintiffs in the United States. The plaintiffs can thus legitimately claim that before the defendants' entry into the market here, they had a reputation as the brewers of a beer, *Budweiser*, with a substantial section of the public. The question is whether this reputation associated with a beer which, for practical purposes, nobody could buy here, constituted a goodwill in any relevant sense."

In *Budweiser* the plaintiffs' reputation in England was acquired without any advertising directed at the English market. Even such advertising, however, is no substitute for goodwill. In the *Athlete's Foot* case American press advertising which reached the UK was not shown to have generated any custom and even in *Conagra v McCain Foods*[77] the Federal Court of Australia attached very little importance to advertisements in American publications circulating in Australia, despite adopting a view of the law very

[75] Compare *Ten-Ichi Co Ltd v Jancar Ltd* [1990] F.S.R. 151.
[76] *Anheuser-Busch Inc v Budejovicky Budvar NP* [1984] F.S.R. 413, CA.
[77] (1992) 23 I.P.R. 193 (Federal Court of Australia).

much more favourable to the plaintiffs than that of Walton J. in *Athlete's Foot*[78] or the English Court of Appeal in *Budweiser*.

In the *Crazy Horse* case, *Bernadin v Pavilion Properties*,[79] the plaintiffs' night club in Paris had distributed promotional literature to English tourist organisations and hotels. Pennycuick J. held that this was insufficient to constitute user in this country, and that the reputation the plaintiffs had in the wider sense was insufficient to found a passing-off action. Two of the central propositions in the Crazy Horse case are undoubtedly correct: advertising on its own does not amount to carrying on a trade and reputation is not a sufficient basis for a passing-off action. However, it is suggested that Pennycuick J. was wrong to impose the further requirement that the foreign plaintiff should actually carry on business in the jurisdiction, and that the distinction purportedly drawn with the *Poiret*[80] and *Sheraton*[81] cases was made on the wrong basis. Applying the reasoning of *Budweiser* to the facts of *Crazy Horse*, one finds that the plaintiffs had customers in England and could quite easily have been recognised as having at least some English goodwill.

Service businesses

The definition of goodwill in terms of the presence or absence of customers **3–80** in the jurisdiction raises few problems when the business in question relates to the production or supply of goods, which can physically be traced from their place of origin to the place where they are eventually consumed or put to use by customers. However, the definition may not lend itself to service businesses without further explanation and perhaps adaptation: in what circumstances can a service business located in one jurisdiction claim to have customers in another?

Services may be grouped at least approximately into the following categories, according to whether the place for the provision of the services is defined in terms of the location of the supplier, the customer, both or neither. First, the services may be such that they can only be provided at the supplier's fixed place of business; for example, an hotel, restaurant, theme park or hospital. Secondly, there are those that can only be supplied at the customer's premises, such as pest control. Thirdly, services may be provided in a suitable but arbitrary place provided supplier and the customer or customers are there together, for example, live entertainment, personal tuition or osteopathy. Fourthly, and of increasing importance, the nature of the services provided may make no demands on the relative locations of customer and supplier, as with the provision of legal or professional advice. As a variation on the final category, the services may simultaneously be received in many different places, as with broadcast entertainment. In parallel with this categorisation there exists a continuous spectrum between services for which the supplier is consciously chosen by the customer, who

---

[78] *Athlete's Foot Marketing Associates Inc v Cobra Sports Ltd* [1980] R.P.C. 343 (Walton J.).
[79] [1967] R.P.C. 581 (Pennycuick J.).
[80] *Poiret v Jules Poiret Ltd* (1920) 37 R.P.C. 177 (P. O. Lawrence J.).
[81] *Sheraton Corp of America v Sheraton Motels Ltd* [1964] R.P.C. 202 (Buckley J.).

may attach great importance to his choice, and those for which the supplier is selected at random or taken for granted.

An analysis of goodwill in terms of the location of the customers of a service business needs to take account of these underlying factual differences. After all, an international hotel does not only draw guests and bookings from the city in which it is actually located, so it is unrealistic to regard more than a proportion of its total goodwill as being situated there. The same is true for businesses such as car hire which will be used mainly by visitors. The majority of the reported cases on service businesses have concerned businesses in the first category, those providing services at or from fixed premises abroad, and if these cases seem to present the greatest conceptual difficulty that is at least partly the result of the obsolete tendency to associate the goodwill of a business uniquely with the place or places where the business is carried on. This has been repudiated in the case of businesses dealing in goods, and it is now suggested that a service business operating from a place or places abroad has customers and therefore goodwill in England to the extent that persons from England consciously seek out and make use of its services in preference to those available from competitors, in England or elsewhere. So the foreign business has goodwill here if English residents are prepared to go to it (literally or figuratively) to avail themselves of its services, or if the availability of those services abroad is a material factor in their travelling to wherever the services can be acquired or experienced.

3–81   This formulation would go a long way to resolving the concern voiced by Browne-Wilkinson V.C. in *Pete Waterman v CBS*,[82] where the question arose of whether a New York recording studio could be said to have an English goodwill:

> "In my view, the law will fail if it does not try to meet the challenge thrown up by trading patterns which cross national and jurisdictional boundaries due to a change in technical achievement.
>
>   The problem is particularly acute with service industries. A first division recording studio is catering to a market which treats crossing the Atlantic as an everyday incident. Similar problems arise in relation to professional and other services. For example, an internationally famous hospital in Paris or Boston, Massachusetts draws its patients from worldwide. Is it unable to protect its goodwill otherwise than in its home country?"

On the foregoing analysis, the recording studio and hospital would have English goodwill, and in the case of the studio at least it would be highly relevant that actual and potential English customers regarded crossing the Atlantic as a minor inconvenience. Likewise, even a single foreign restaurant of the calibre of *Maxim's* in Paris or Tokyo's *Ten-Ichi* may have goodwill far outside its actual place of operation, while mass-market fast food chains probably do not. Browne-Wilkinson V.C. was inclined to doubt the cor-

---

[82] *Pete Waterman Ltd v CBS United Kingdom Ltd* [1993] E.M.L.R. 27 (Browne-Wilkinson V.C.).

rectness of the decision in the *Crazy Horse* case, *Bernadin v Pavilion Properties*,[83] and it is suggested that he was right to do so. The admitted existence of English customers should have been recognised as more important than the absence of bookings actually made in or from England.

Conversely, it should not matter either way whether the contract for the provision of the services is made or performed inside or outside the jurisdiction: "[s]uch narrow distinctions are unsatisfactory".[84] This has never been regarded as relevant in the case of goods. Nor ought it to be sufficient that persons can be found in the jurisdiction who may have availed themselves of the services of the foreign business *nolens volens*: it is not to be supposed that the shops, bars or taxi services at a foreign international airport have an English goodwill, simply because many English residents may have used them. More tentatively, it is suggested that a foreign business may still have an English goodwill if English residents who happen to go abroad for wholly unconnected reasons none the less systematically patronise it in preference to other competitive local services. If no one willingly goes to Ruritania but travellers who cannot avoid doing so favour a particular hotel or airline, then it is probably still reasonable to speak of those as having an English goodwill. However, this extension to the basic principle needs to be treated with caution and common sense if it is not to lead to unreasonable results in some cases.

Examples

In *Home Box Office v Channel 5 Home Box Office*[85] the plaintiff company **3–82** operated a cable television service in America. It produced programmes itself, and had sold eight to television companies in England. It had some other activities in England. Peter Gibson J. held that there was an arguable case, but refused an interlocutory injunction on the balance of convenience.

In *Orkin v Pestco*[86] the plaintiffs were an American pest control company and one of the largest in the world. They did not do business in Canada, but their reputation extended there and there were Canadian residents who used their services for properties in the USA. The defendants adopted the same name dishonestly. The Ontario Court of Appeal granted a permanent injunction.

In *Pebble Beach Co v Lombard Brands Ltd*,[87] the owners of a Californian golf course of World-wide reputation complained about use of the same name for a brand of Scotch malt whisky. They were refused an interim interdict on the ground that there was no prospect of confusion. Since golfers from Scotland and the rest of the United Kingdom patronised the pursuers' course, and since *Pebble Beach* licensed merchandise to the value of US$ 250,000 p.a. was sold in the United Kingdom, the case is best

---

[83] [1967] R.P.C. 581.
[84] *per* Browne-Wilkinson V.C. in *Pete Waterman v CBS* [1993] E.M.L.R. 27.
[85] [1982] F.S.R. 449 (Peter Gibson J.).
[86] [1985] 19 D.L.R. (4th) 90, 50 O.R. (2d) 726; 5 C.P.R. (3d) 433.
[87] 2002 S.L.T. 1312 (Lord Menzies, OH).

regarded as turning on the remoteness of the parties' respective fields of business rather than the foreign status of the pursuer.

Businesses having goodwill as purchasers

3–83 The action for passing-off is also capable of protecting the goodwill the claimant has *vis-à-vis* his suppliers in his capacity as purchaser. In the present context this means that a foreign business may have goodwill in the jurisdiction although the only business it transacts consists of purchasing goods or services, or it may strengthen a case based on the existence of customers in the normal sense by relying also on the business it conducts with its suppliers. The two Hong Kong cases of *Penney v Penney's*[88] and *Penney v Punjabi Nick*[89] were both decided in the plaintiffs' favour solely on the basis of purchasing activities in Hong Kong. In England, purchasing was important in the corresponding English *Penney's* case[90] and in *Home Box Office v Channel 5 Home Box Office*.[91] However, the existence of goodwill is not sufficient in the abstract. If there is to be liability for passing-off on this basis then there must be a misrepresentation by the defendant which is damaging to the plaintiff's goodwill as a purchaser, and this is inevitably harder to make out than when one is dealing with misrepresentations made to customers or the public at large.

Regional goodwill

3–84 The nature of goodwill means, as a matter of law, that it cannot extend over national boundaries. The converse is not automatically true, in that goodwill does not necessarily extend right up to the boundaries at which it must stop. Goodwill may be localised in a specific region within a state. If all the claimant's customers come from that region, it cannot very well be said that the claimant's goodwill is of any greater extent. In practice, the courts are reluctant to confine the claimant's remedy to a limited geographical area in all but the clearest cases, and a fairly thin spread of goodwill outside the claimant's main centre of operations is likely to suffice. In *Chelsea Man v Chelsea Girl*[92] the plaintiffs operated retail menswear shops in Leicester, Coventry and London's Oxford Street. The defendants argued that any injunction should be confined to around those areas, but the Court of Appeal granted one with nationwide effect. In *Brestian v Try*[93] the plaintiff had hairdressing salons in London and Brighton. The Court of Appeal found in his favour against a hairdresser based in Tunbridge Wells and did not qualify the scope of the final injunction.[94]

Some businesses are so inherently localised that the geographical extent of

[88] [1979] F.S.R. 29 (Huggins J., Hong Kong).
[89] [1979] F.S.R. 26 (Leonard J., Hong Kong).
[90] *J C Penney Co Inc v Penney's Ltd* [1975] F.S.R. 367, CA.
[91] [1982] F.S.R. 449 (Peter Gibson J.).
[92] [1987] R.P.C. 189, CA.
[93] [1958] R.P.C. 161, CA.
[94] See also *Faulder (Henry) & Co Ltd v O & G Rushton Ltd* (1903) 20 R.P.C. 477, CA.

their associated goodwill can be defined with reasonably precision. If so, any injunction should preferably be confined to that area. In *Clock v Clock House Hotel*[95] the Court of Appeal granted a road house a permanent injunction against an hotel some five miles away, but the injunction was confined to those specific premises. A restaurant in the London suburb of Kingston-upon-Thames was refused an interlocutory injunction against one in central London in *Clouds Restaurant v Clouds Hotel.*[96] In *Bushbury Land Rover v Bushbury Ltd*[97] a Land Rover dealership in Wolverhampton failed to obtain an interlocutory injunction against a Suzuki dealership in Sheffield and the Court of Appeal refused to interfere with the judge's award of defendants' costs in any event. The extremely localised goodwill and reputation of two high street dentists who practised as *Smilecare* was noted in *Harding v Smilecare*,[98] but the main reason for deciding against them was that there was no prospect of confusion with the dentists' credit administration scheme of the defendant.

In the Canadian case of *Blades Enterprises v Thibault*[99] an injunction was refused to one restaurant against another 30 miles away, the plaintiffs having only a few months' priority, and the nature and customers of the parties' restaurants differing.

Department stores have been awarded interlocutory injunctions restricted **3-85** to the towns in which they were situated in *Cavendish House v Cavendish-Woodhouse*[1] and *Levey v Henderson-Kenton.*[2] In both cases the defendants were already established outside those towns. In many similar cases, particularly the older ones, it is difficult to say whether the claimant's difficulty was lack of goodwill outside his home area or lack of distinctiveness.[3] The two are likely to go together, but in theory a business could be known in a remote area of the country without there being any possibility of its having any customers there. The *Levey* case was applied in *Associated Newspapers v Express Newspapers*,[4] but the latter is better regarded as exemplifying the converse of the previous situation. The claimants' newspapers the *Daily Mail* and the *Mail on Sunday* enjoyed national goodwill, but because of the existence of various unconnected regional *Mail* newspapers the abbreviation *The Mail* was only unambiguously distinctive of them in the London area.

[95] (1936) 53 R.P.C. 269, CA.
[96] Unreported, cited in *Chelsea Man Menswear Ltd v Chelsea Girl Ltd* [1987] R.P.C. 189, CA.
[97] [1997] F.S.R. 709, C.A., on appeal from Rattee J.
[98] [2002] F.S.R. 37 (P.W. Smith Q.C., Deputy Judge).
[99] (1975) 65 D.L.R. (3d) 378; 24 C.P.R. (2d) 288.
[1] [1970] R.P.C. 234, CA.
[2] [1974] R.P.C. 617 (Foster J.).
[3] For example, *Chivers (S) & Sons v S Chivers & Co Ltd* (1900) 17 R.P.C. 420; *Thorne & Co Ltd v Sandow* (1912) 29 R.P.C. 440.
[4] [2003] EWHC 1322. (Laddie J.).

G. Foreign Claimants: an International Overview

Australia

3–86 Of all the common law jurisdictions considered here, Australia has gone furthest in repudiating the need for the foreign claimant to have goodwill in the jurisdiction, and has provided the largest number of cases offering alternative formulations of the law. The problem is particularly acute in Australia, because it was recognised at a fairly early stage that Australia's federal legal system meant, for instance, that a Queensland-based business suing for passing-off in New South Wales had to be treated according to the same body of law as one from New Zealand, America or the United Kingdom.

The authoritative statement of Australian law may now be taken to be that of the Federal Court of Australia in *Conagra v McCain Foods*[5] in which the Federal Court preferred to follow a body of predominantly Australian authorities which ultimately led it to a conclusion openly inconsistent with the English *Budweiser*[6] decision. The facts were that Conagra marketed in the United States a range of frozen meals under the name *Healthy Choice* with an emphasis on nutritional claims to be low in fat, cholesterol and salt. Conagra had appointed a licensee for Australia but had terminated the licence before it was acted upon and intended to enter the Australian market itself in due course. However, McCain were first to the market in Australia with a *Healthy Choice* range which was undoubtedly inspired by the success of Conagra in America, and in some respects was a copy. McCain's range was sold in Australia under its own name as *McCain Healthy Choice*. An interlocutory injunction was granted but at trial the passing-off claim was dismissed, despite a finding of fraud, on the ground that Conagra had no business in Australia. On appeal, all three members of the Full Court favoured protecting reputation as such (rather than goodwill) as a sufficient business interest susceptible to damage. Lockhart J. concluded from a review of Australian and foreign authorities:

"I am of the opinion that it is not necessary in Australia that a plaintiff, in order to maintain a passing-off action, must have a place of business or a business presence in Australia; nor is it necessary that his goods are sold here. It is sufficient if his goods have a reputation in this county amongst persons here, whether residents or otherwise, of a sufficient degree to establish that there is a likelihood of deception among consumers and potential consumers and of damage to his reputation."

3–87 The first sentence is not necessarily inconsistent with English law, since a foreign business can still be said to have customers here even if they buy the goods abroad and import them. The second half of the passage is more radical and must be intended to contradict *Anheuser-Busch v Budejovicky*

---

[5] (1992) 23 I.P.R. 193 (Federal Court of Australia).
[6] *Anheuser-Busch Inc v Budejovicky Budvar NP* [1984] F.S.R. 413, CA.

Budvar. On the facts, however, *Conagra* still failed because they had no sufficient reputation in Australia. From the absence of reputation, it followed that there was no misrepresentation to restrain, no interest to protect, and nothing to suffer damage, The *McCain* product was also adequately distinguished. Nor, in the absence of reputation, did the finding of fraud assist Conagra; and since the intention of McCain was to appropriate a good idea rather than to deceive the Australian public it was probably inappropriate to accuse them of fraud in any relevant sense.

In finding that the plaintiffs had only minimal reputation in Australia, the Court allowed next to no weight to evidence of occasional advertisements in US magazines reaching Australia or to the evidence of travellers to and from the United States. Interestingly, one of the reasons given for this was that Australian readers of American magazines or tourists shopping in American supermarkets would pay little or no attention to brands of goods they could not buy back home. In this respect the reasoning of Oliver L.J. in *Budweiser*–rejected in the context for which it was actually intended—seems to have been reintroduced as relevant in another.

Following *Conagra v McCain Foods* earlier Australian cases[7] are now **3–88** interesting mainly to the extent that they are reconcilable with English law, as the majority are, or they illustrate particular factual situations. Modern Australian case law can be said to begin with *BM Auto Sales v Budget Rent A Car*.[8] This was not, in fact, a case involving a foreign business in the normal sense since the separate jurisdictions in question were the Northern Territory, where the defendants had commenced business, and the other Australian states in which the plaintiffs were already well established. The High Court held that the business activities of the plaintiffs in the Northern Territory by way of taking bookings, though slight, and the fact that many prospective customers would be visitors from other parts of Australia, were sufficient to justify an injunction. *Taco Bell v Taco Co of Australia*[9] is dealt with above. *Contal v Szozda*[10] was another inter-state action where a Melbourne plaintiff obtained an injunction against a New South Wales defendant. Bryson J. affirmed that a plaintiff had goodwill where he had customers, to whom state boundaries would not be of much significance. An actual office or establishment in New South Wales was not necessary. In *Merv Brown v David Jones*[11] slight pre-trading activities were sufficient to generate goodwill in favour of a foreign clothing designer. In *TV-AM v Amalgamated TV*,[12] the last case prior to *Conagra*, the British television company *TV AM* failed to prove it had either reputation or business presence in Australia, but the principal ground for the decision was that there was no misrepresentation. In contrast to the *TV-AM* case, the defendants in *Jelly's Music Hall v Triple-M Broadcasting*[13] were restrained from using the

---

[7] *Conagra v McCain Foods* itself contains a comprehensive overview.
[8] (1976) 12 A.L.R. 363; 51 A.L.J.R. 254.
[9] (1981) 60 F.L.R. 60; 40 A.L.R. 153, affirmed (1982) 2 T.P.R. 48; 42 A.L.R. 177.
[10] (1986) 7 I.P.R. 373; (1986) A.I.P.C. 90–317 (Bryson J.).
[11] (1988) 10 A.T.P.R. 40–858 (Federal Court of Australia, Full Court).
[12] (1988) 12 I.P.R. 85 (Einfeld J.).
[13] (1993) 26 I.P.R. 127 (Einfield J.).

name *Radio Free* on the application of the American plaintiffs who already used that name for a service broadcast in Hawaii. There was barely any reputation in Australia, but the defendants were perceived to have stolen a march from some abortive discussions to licence the name and format to them.

The publishers of an internationally-known Arabic language newspaper, *Al Hayat*, were granted an interlocutory injunction although it was not distributed in Australia: *Al Hayat Publishing v Sokarno*.[14] The defendant had taken part in abortive negotiations to publish the paper in Australia, and had applied to register *Al Hayat* in his own name, so there was a clear implicit concession that the name was valuable.

3-89   The normal analysis was reversed with a vengeance in *TGI Friday's Australia v TGI Friday's Inc*.[15] Although the international *TGI Friday's* chain of bars and restaurants had only two branches in Australia (out of 400 worldwide) the trial judge was prepared to hold that they had sufficient goodwill and reputation to maintain a passing-off action against a hotel and tavern in Sydney trading as *TGI Friday*. On appeal, the Full Court dismissed the action: *TGI Friday's* was so well known internationally not only by name, but also for the design and layout of their premises, that the very different appearance of the defendants' hotel would actually serve to dispel any initial confusion caused by the choice of name.

The Australia–New Zealand relationship

3-90 Several decisions from both Australia and New Zealand have been particularly willing to protect the interests of parties trading across the Tasman Sea. In *Fletcher Challenge v Fletcher Challenge*[16] Powell J. in the Supreme Court of New South Wales granted an injunction in favour of a New Zealand company very recently incorporated for the merger of three well-known predecessors. The plaintiff as such had never traded in Australia, or at all, but this was not true of all of the companies which were in the process of being amalgamated into it. Whether *Fletcher Challenge* can be regarded as consistent with English law depends on how one reacts to Powell J.'s conclusion that it was "not illegitimate for it [the plaintiff company] to be treated as entitled to the combined goodwill of the three". Conversely, in *Chase Manhattan Overseas v Chase Corp*[17] Wilcox J. relied on *Fletcher Challenge* in contemplating that an established New Zealand company might have sufficient reputation in Australia to provide a defence to a passing-off action, although it had never traded there.

Fletcher Challenge has been followed several times in New Zealand, and in some cases reliance has also been placed on the Australia-New Zealand

---

[14] (1996) 34 I.P.R. 214 (Tamberlin J., Federal Court).
[15] [1999] FCA 304; 45 I.P.R. 43 (Federal Court of Australia, Full Court)
[16] [1981] 1 N.S.W.L.R. 196; [1982] F.S.R. 1 (Powell J., New South Wales).
[17] (1985) 6 I.P.R. 59; 63 A.L.R. 345 (Wilcox J).

Closer Economic Relations Agreement.[18] To the extent that these cases simply recognise and give effect to a state of facts they are undoubtedly correct. When one is dealing with a relatively small and isolated country such as New Zealand which has long-standing business, cultural and historical relations with Australia, then it is very easy to conclude that an Australian business has customers and goodwill in New Zealand, or *vice versa*, even if it has not actually conducted business there. However, once the decisions go further they are open to criticism. There is no rule of law that allows claimants (or defendants) to be treated more favourably simply because they come from states with which relations have been particularly close, and as treaties are not self-executing in the common law any obligations they impose on the contracting states in public international law can hardly affect private rights.

Canada

In *Orkin v Pestco*[19] the plaintiffs were an American pest control company. **3–91** Although they did not do business in Canada their "outstanding reputation for reliability and competence" extended there They had some thousands of Canadian customers in the sense that Canadian residents used their services for pest control at properties they owned in the United States. There were well-advanced plans to expand into Canada. The defendants fraudulently adopted the plaintiffs' name by putting an entry in the telephone directory as *Orkin Exterminating Co* although apart from that they continued to trade simply as *Pestco*. Customers phoning the *Orkin* number were served by *Pestco* employees but the plaintiffs' logo was used with that of *Pestco* on the invoices. The Court of Appeal of Ontario affirmed the grant of a permanent injunction.

Orkin v Pestco has been influential inside Canada and out. It was followed by the Federal court in *HQ Network v HQ Systems*.[20] In *Walt Disney v Triple Five*[21] the Alberta Court of Appeal upheld a permanent injunction against use of the name *Fantasyland* for an indoor amusement park at West Edmonton Shopping Mall. However, in *Walt Disney v Fantasyland Hotel*[22] the same plaintiffs failed in respect of the same name for an hotel at the same shopping mall. The Alberta Court of Appeal held that liability of the hotel was not *res judicata* as a result of the successful action against the amusement park, and that passing-off was not made out. In terms which are rather closer to English law than the previous decision, the court held:

---

[18] *Essanda Ltd v Essanda Finance Ltd* [1984] F.S.R. 96; (1983) 2 I.P.R. 182; *Crusader Oil NA v Crusader Minerals NZ Ltd* (1984) 2 I.P.R. 171; *Vicom (New Zealand) Ltd v Vicomm Systems Ltd* [1987] 2 N.Z.L.R. 606; *Midas International Corp v Midas Autocare Ltd* (1988) 2 N.Z.B.L.C. 102 and *Dominion Rent a Car Ltd v Budget Rent a Car Systems (1970) Ltd* [1987] 2 N.Z.L.R. 395 (CA, New Zealand).
[19] [1985] 19 D.L.R. (4th) 90; 50 O.R. (2d) 726; 5 C.P.R. (3d) 433 (CA of Ontario).
[20] (1990) C.P.R. (3d) 558 (Reed J., Federal Court).
[21] (1994) 53 C.P.R. (3d) 129 (Alberta CA) affirming 43 C P.R. (3d) 321; 93 D.L.R. (4th) 739.
[22] (1996) 67 C.P.R. (3d) 444 (Alberta CA).

"The appellant says the respondent in using the name *Fantasyland* for its hotel, is creating the false impression that it is authorized or connected with the appellant, in other words, the respondent is, 'cashing in' on the appellant's goodwill.

The appellant's theory of the law of passing-off contains a fatal weakness. Even the 'more common type of passing-off' referred to requires proof of the essentials of goodwill misrepresentation or confusion, which the trial judge found, as a fact, did not exist in this case. In other words, the allegation or even the belief that the respondent is benefiting from the use of the name *Fantasyland* is not enough to found the tort of passing-off. The British Columbia cases cited do not support a modification in the requirements for the tort of passing-off."

3-92 In *Enterprise Rent-A-Car Co. v Singer*[23] an American car hire company were the first to have goodwill in relation to the name *Enterprise* in Canada and obtained an injunction at trial against a Canadian company using the same name. Canadians had used its services on visits to the United States and it had conducted some leasing transactions in Canada. One reason from dismissing the Canadian company's cross-action was that they came to the Court with unclean hands, having adopted the name knowing of the plaintiffs and their plans to expand.[24] The defendants' use was also too small-scale and too late, since the plaintiffs had begun to generate Canadian goodwill by the time it started.

However, though the Canadian courts may have relaxed the need for goodwill or reputation in the jurisdiction, the latter at least has not been abandoned altogether. In *Business Depot v Canadian Office Depot*[25] the problem arose in its opposite form since the defendants attempted to rely on their own reputation in the United States, but they had not shown significant goodwill or reputation in Ontario and mere use of a name in a foreign country was not enough. An interlocutory injunction was granted. *Stink Inc. v Venditti*[26] is reminiscent of some of the earlier Canadian cases in the weakness of the plaintiffs' case on the facts. A single San Francisco restaurant called *The Stinking Rose*, in reference to its stress on garlic on the menu, had neither goodwill nor reputation in Vancouver and the defendants were not liable for passing-off by opening an Italian restaurant with the same name. *Orkin v Pestco* and *Walt Disney v Triple Five* were distinguished for the overwhelming evidence in those cases of reputation in the Canadian market through massive advertising or acknowledged international reputation.

---

[23] (1996) 66 C.P.R. (3d) 543 (Federal Court, McKeown, J.).
[24] Following *Brewster Transport v Rocky Mountain Tours* [1931] 1 D.L.R. 713 (S. Ct. of Canada).
[25] (1993) 49 C.P.R. (3d) 230 (Rouleau J., Federal Court).
[26] (1994) 53 C.P.R. (3d) 24 (Houghton J., British Columbia).

Hong Kong

In *Ten-Ichi v Jancar*[27] Sears J. expressed a willingness to follow *Orkin v* **3–93**
Pestco[28] and *Dominion Rent a Car v Budget Rent a Car*[29] in accepting that a
Japanese business had an international goodwill extending to Hong Kong.
However, the case is somewhat erratic in its reasoning. *Anheuser-Busch v*
Budejovicky Budvar[30] was not cited at all and *Star Industrial v Yap Kwee*
Kor[31] was misunderstood. *Ten-Ichi v Jancar* need not be doubted on its facts,
but in its wider sense the judgment probably does not represent settled law
even in Hong Kong.[32]

India

In *Apple Computer v Apple Leasing*[33] the High Court at Delhi refused to **3–94**
follow *Anheuser-Busch v Budejovicky Budvar*,[34] though principally on the
ground that sales of the plaintiff's beer at US bases and diplomatic establishments should not have been ignored. The actual result is still consistent
with *Budweiser*: *Apple Computer* had sufficient goodwill in India by virtue of
sales of small quantities of computers through distributors (there were
import restrictions) and it was not relevant that they did not actually carry
on business in India themselves. An interlocutory injunction was granted.
Further Indian cases adopting the "soft" line of authority are *William Grant*
v McDowell,[35] *Calvin Klein v International Apparel Syndicate*,[36] and
WHIRLPOOL TM,[37] although the first two, at least, were probably strong
enough on the facts to have been decided the same way in England. In the
third, there may have been some overspill of the plaintiffs' reputation into
India (for instance by advertising in international magazines) and this may
conceivably have generated some distinctiveness for a mark which had never
otherwise been used there, but the only source of the plaintiffs' *Whirlpool*
washing machines in the general Indian market was though occasional
second-hand sales by American diplomatic personnel.

---

[27] [1990] F.S.R 151 (Sears J., Hong Kong).
[28] [1985] 19 D.L.R. (4th) 90; 50 O.R. (2d) 726; 5 C.P.R (3d) 433 (CA of Ontario).
[29] [1987] 2 N.Z.L.R. 395 (CA, New Zealand).
[30] [1984] F.S.R. 413, CA.
[31] [1976] F.S.R. 256, PC.
[32] See also *Wienerwald Holding AG v Kwan, Wong, Tan and Fong* [1979] F.S.R. 381 and the
trade mark case of *Hong Kong Caterers Ltd v Maxim's Ltd* [1983] H.K.L.R. 287.
[33] (1991) 22 I.P.R. 257 (Narain J., High Ct. Delhi). Other Indian decisions to similar effect
(some unreported) are cited in *Apple*.
[34] [1984] F.S.R. 413, CA.
[35] [1994] F.S.R. 690 (Mahinder Narain J., Delhi).
[36] [1995] F.S.R. 515 (Mrs Justice Ruma Pal, Calcutta)
[37] [1997] F.S.R. 905 (HC at Delhi and SC of India): a passing-off action, despite the heading
given in the report and the prevalence of trade mark reasoning. An interlocutory injunction was
granted and upheld on appeal.

Ireland

3–95 The leading case is *C & A Modes v C & A (Waterford)*[38] which is normally taken as aligning Ireland with the camp supporting the so-called "soft line" of English cases. In fact, it hardly deserves this description even though the plaintiffs did obtain an injunction against the use of C & A for a retail clothes store in the Republic. Their closest store was in Belfast, but this enjoyed substantial custom from the other side of the border. Beyond this, the reasoning of the Supreme Court is unsatisfactory. Kenny J. sought to distinguish *Oertli v Bowman*[39] by drawing a distinction between goodwill attaching to a trade name, which did not require actual user in the jurisdiction, and that attaching to a mark or get-up, which did. This is a distinction without a difference and it cannot be supposed to have been intended by Jenkins L.J. The confusion was perpetuated in *Adidas v O'Neill*[40] where the majority of the Supreme Court refused protection for the "three-stripe" mark of Adidas. If this was because the three-stripe mark had not become distinctive in Ireland then it is reasonable, but O'Higgins J., for the majority, expressly adopted Kenny J.'s distinction between name and get-up to the extent that he would have allowed Adidas' appeal—notwithstanding the lack of use or reputation in Ireland—if it had been the *Adidas* name, as opposed to the get-up, which had been in issue. The dissenting opinion of Henchy J. is much preferable.

An unusual situation arose in *Guinness Ireland Group v Kilkenny Brewing Co*,[41] in which it was said that the plaintiffs' relatively recent goodwill in the Irish market for *Kilkenny Irish Beer* was strengthened by much longer use abroad: since 1987 in Germany, and progressively through Benelux, mainland Europe and the United Kingdom. In fact, there was probably more than sufficient Irish goodwill on a conventional analysis. The beer was only launched in Ireland in 1995, but that was with heavy advertising, six months before the defendant company was even incorporated, and the defendant had not commenced trading.

In *DSG Retail v PC World*[42] the *PC World* chain of the plaintiffs was acknowledged to have had goodwill in Ireland, even before they opened a computer superstore in Dublin, but an interlocutory injunction was refused (subject to undertakings) on the balance of convenience.

Jamaica

3–96 In *McDonald's Corp v McDonald's Corp Ltd*[43] the worldwide McDonald's chain were refused an interlocutory injunction against a local restaurant that had been trading since 1971 (the first McDonald's franchise in Jamaica dating only from 1994) but in terms which followed the more liberal English

---

[38] [1976] I.R. 198; [1978] F.S.R. 126 (Irish SC).
[39] [1959] R.P.C. 1, HL; affirming [1957] R.P.C. 388, CA.
[40] [1983] F.S.R. 76 (Irish Supreme Court).
[41] [2000] F.S.R. 112 (Laffoy J., HC Ireland).
[42] [1998] E.T.M.R. 321 (Laffoy J., Ireland).
[43] [1997] F.S.R. 760 (CA, Jamaica).

authorities and acknowledged that the worldwide McDonald's probably had reputation and goodwill in Jamaica.

Malaysia

In *Compagnie General des Eaux v Compagnie General des Eaux Sdn Bhd*[44] **3–97** injunctions were granted against the defendant, a shell company, at the suit of the French plaintiffs. The latter did a substantial amount of business in Malaysia by way of a joint venture with local partners. The defendants had no credible reason for choosing the name, and appeared to have incorporated the company solely to inconvenience the plaintiffs. Likewise, in *Dun & Bradstreet (Singapore) v Dun & Bradstreet (Malaysia)*[45] the Singapore members of the well-known international credit reference agency obtained an interlocutory injunction against an unconnected local company. The business of the plaintiff company already extended to Malaysia, where it had 31 subscribers.

New Zealand

In *Dominion Rent a Car v Budget Rent a Car*[46] Cooke P. denied that any **3–98** distinctively New Zealand approach to the problem of the overseas plaintiff had emerged. This is perhaps too modest,[47] but the *Rent a Car* case itself was sufficiently unrepresentative of more typical factual situations for it to lend itself more to a wide-ranging review of the law, rather than a definitive statement of it. In the result, the judgments tend towards accepting the concept that goodwill may transcend territorial boundaries, provided there is a sufficient, but unspecified, business connection with the forum. However, *Anheuser-Busch v Budejovicky Budvar*[48] was not actually disapproved, and the case is consistent with those in which relatively slight trading activities were sufficient to generate goodwill.

The facts of the case were of "outstanding complexity". From 1977 Dominion were exclusive New Zealand licensees of *Budget Australia*, who were in turn licensed by *Budget USA*. Dominion offered a full-service car rental service throughout New Zealand under the name and trading style of the American *Budget* business. Mutual, the effective defendants, were licensees of Avis and since 1971 had operated a small no-frills car rental business in Auckland under the name "Budget" with the express intention of forestalling Budget USA, who at that time were unconnected with Budget Australia. Budget Australia acquiesced in this. In separate actions, each party sued the other for passing-off and each obtained injunctions. There followed a second passing-off action by the international Budget group

---

[44] [1993] 1 M.L.J. 55; [1997] F.S.R. 610 (HC, Malaysia).
[45] [1994] 1 M.L.J. 32 (HC Malaysia).
[46] [1987] 2 N.Z.L.R. 395 (CA, New Zealand.).
[47] The judgment of Chillwell J. in *Gallaher Ltd v International Brands Ltd* (1976) 1 N.Z I.P.R. 43 was particularly thorough and ahead of its time, but unfortunately it was not reported for more than a decade. See also *Essanda Ltd v Essanda Finance Ltd* [1984] F.S.R. 96; 2 I.P.R. 182 and *Crusader Oil NL v Crusader Minerals NZ Ltd* (1984) 3 I.P.R. 171.
[48] [1984] F.S.R. 413, CA.

against Mutual, which resulted in a finding of passing-off against Mutual and dismissal of Mutual's counterclaim. The Court of Appeal held that both Mutual and the international Budget group were entitled to use the name for their respective businesses.

In the context of the rights of the Australian Budget company prior to the arrangement with Dominion in 1977 Cooke P. stated:

> "I think that an Australian company's reputation and goodwill can extend to New Zealand (and vice versa) and, at least if there is sufficient business connection with this country, will be entitled to protection here. Except in special cases ... it seems to me artificial to analyse such a state of affairs by saying that the company has one goodwill in Australia and another in New Zealand. Rather the goodwill transcends territorial boundaries."

It followed that in 1977, Budget Australia already possessed goodwill in New Zealand which it was entitled to exploit and develop further. Subsequent to 1977, the differences between the operations of Mutual and Dominion meant that any confusion which occurred probably benefited Mutual on balance. Since Mutual suffered no damage from the use of the Budget name by Dominion, it could not complain of passing-off.[49] However, by 1977 Mutual had an established right to trade as *Budget* which could not be overridden by subsequent events, and the injunction against it could not be upheld.

3–99   In *Green v Broadcasting Corp. of New Zealand*[50] there was a claim by the entertainer Hughie Green, based on the broadcasting in New Zealand of a television talent spotting programme under the name *Opportunity Knocks* which copied some of the features introduced by him in his United Kingdom programme of the same name. The Court of Appeal dismissed the action both because Mr Green had no goodwill in New Zealand, and because there was no misrepresentation. So far as the existence of goodwill was concerned, English television programmes were not received in New Zealand and Mr Green had not performed there or had his programmes shown there. The only basis on which the existence of goodwill was argued was that visitors to England from New Zealand, or English immigrants, might have seen the show; but their numbers and significance were inadequate. It was not passing-off for the defendants to have copied features of the presentation of the show when the plaintiff had no goodwill in New Zealand to protect, and it was unreasonable to suppose that any one watching the defendants' show would suppose it even to have been authorised by him.

---

[49] Casey J. dissented on the issue of whether Dominion had been guilty of passing-off between 1977 and 1983, when it went into liquidation.

[50] [1988] 2 N.Z.L.R. 490; [1989] R.P.C. 469 (CA, New Zealand). The appeal to the Privy Council [1989] 2 All E.R. 1056; [1990] R.P.C. 700, PC was concerned only with copyright infringement.

Singapore

Star Industrial v Yap Kwee Kor[51] was a decision of the Privy Council on **3–100** appeal from Singapore, and Singapore has tended to continue to adopt a strict approach to foreign businesses claiming to have goodwill in Singapore without actual local trading activities, although the latest decision in point[52] shows a willingness to follow the lead set by Canada in *Orkin v Pestco*[53] and Australia in *Conagra v McCain Foods*.[54]

In *Tan Gek Neo Jessie v Minister for Finance*[55] the applicant applied for registration of *JC Penney Collections* as a business name. Registration was initially refused because of the worldwide reputation of the American JC Penney Company and their (expired) local trade mark registrations, but on appeal it was held that the American company would not have been able to maintain an action for passing-off or trade mark infringement in Singapore and that registration should therefore be permitted.

The more recent Singapore cases have involved the reverse situation of a foreign defendant (or an associated local company) claiming to have a defence against a local Singapore company, by virtue of usage abroad sufficient to generate independent or antecedent goodwill in Singapore. A relatively strict approach to a claim to ownership of goodwill by a foreign party (in effect, the defendant) was adopted in *Jumbo Seafood v Hong Kong Jumbo Seafood Restaurant*.[56] The local plaintiffs had operated seafood restaurants in Singapore under variants of the name *Jumbo* since 1987 and 1994, including a *Jumbo Garden* restaurant which had traded between 1993 and 1996, when it was wound up. The site of the latter was acquired by the defendants, who commenced business under the name *Hong Kong Jumbo Seafood Restaurant* and purported to be connected with the famous *Jumbo* floating restaurant in Hong Kong. An injunction was granted. The connections of the defendant with the Hong Kong restaurant were tenuous, the plaintiffs had not acted with unclean hands in adopting the name, and in any event the Hong Kong *Jumbo* restaurant was held to have no goodwill in Singapore under which it could confer any immunity on the defendants. A similar result had previously been reached by the Singapore Court of Appeal in *Pontiac Marina v CDL Hotels*[57] in which it did not avail the defendants that they had previously used the contested *Millennium* name for three hotels in the United States and New Zealand. In *Jet Aviation v Jet Maintenance*[58] the international group to which the defendant belonged was held to have no goodwill in Singapore, even on the more flexible analysis of the *Conagra* and *Orkin* cases, but the action failed on other grounds.

---

[51] [1976] F.S.R. 256, PC.
[52] *Jet Aviation (Singapore) Pte Ltd v Jet Maintenance Pte Ltd* [1998] 2 S.L.R. 287, below.
[53] [1985] 19 D.L.R. (4th) 90; 50 O.R. (2d) 726; 5 C.P.R. (3d) 433 (CA of Ontario).
[54] (1992) 23 I.P.R. 193 (Federal Court of Australia).
[55] [1991] 2 M.L.J. 301. Compare *RH Macey & Co Inc v Trade Accents* [1992] 1 S.L.R. 581, decided in favour of the American retailer solely on trade mark grounds.
[56] [1998] 1 S.L.R. 860 (HC of Singapore).
[57] [1998] F.S.R. 839 (CA, Singapore).
[58] [1998] 3 S.L.R. 287.

South Africa

3–101 South Africa was formerly the only major jurisdiction outside the United Kingdom in which the so-called "hard line" of English cases prior to *Budweiser*[59] was followed. An authoritative restatement of the law for a foreign plaintiff bringing a passing-off action in South Africa has now been given by the Supreme Court of Appeal in *Caterham Car Sales v Birkin Cars*,[60] producing what is effectively a synthesis of the classic English and South African authorities with the more liberal influence of *Conagra v McCain*,[61] so that it can now be said that there is no need for actual trade in South Africa provided that there is sufficient reputation among actual or prospective customers there:

> "The correct question can be distilled from the judgments of this Court ... and from *Conagra* ... In general terms it appears to me to be whether the plaintiff has, in a practical and business sense, a sufficient reputation amongst a substantial number of persons who are either clients or potential clients of his business. As far as the 'location' of the reputation is concerned, it must subsist where the misrepresentation complained of causes actual or potential damage to the drawing power of the plaintiff's business. Otherwise the misrepresentation would be made in the air and be without any consequences. The locality of the plaintiff's business is not hereby rendered irrelevant. Obviously, it must be an important consideration in determining whether the plaintiff has potential clients and whether the alleged misrepresentation causes his business any harm. Likewise, the extent of a business's reputation and the scope of its activities are relevant to the probability of deception and damages—the smaller the reputation, the smaller the likelihood of deception and of damage, and *vice versa*."[62]

The facts of *Caterham Car Sales v Birkin Cars*[63] were that both Caterham and Birkin made replicas of the Lotus Super Seven Series III sports car, Caterham in Britain and Birkin in South Africa. At first instance, Caterham relied on being the assignee of the goodwill of Lotus. However, Lotus had not sold any Series III cars anywhere in the World since 1973, so that at the date of the purported assignment in 1988 there could have been no residual South African goodwill to assign. On appeal, the Supreme Court of Appeal overruled the previous South African cases requiring an actual local trading presence, but still held that Caterham were bound to fail: they were not successors to whatever goodwill Lotus might have had, and their own relevant reputation in South Africa was entirely dependent on passing themselves off as the authorised distributor of Lotus.

3–102 Earlier South African cases may now be regarded as superceded by

---

[59] *Anheuser-Busch Inc v Budejovicky Budvar NP* [1984] F.S.R. 413, CA.
[60] 1998 (3) S.A. 938 (SCA).
[61] (1992) 23 I.P.R. 193 (Federal Court of Australia).
[62] *per* Harms JA.
[63] 1998 (3) S.A. 938 (SCA).

Caterham Car Sales v Birkin Cars but are not entirely without interest. In *Slenderella v Hawkins*[64] the plaintiffs failed to prove that they had any goodwill in South Africa on the strength of use overseas, press advertising possibly circulating in South Africa, or the fact that they were contemplating expanding to South Africa. In the Dallas case, *Lorrimar v Sterling*,[65] the unsuccessful plaintiffs were held to have no goodwill in South Africa (unless in the field of entertainment) but the decision could equally well be explained in terms of the judge's attachment to the need for a "common field of activity" and the difficulties confronting any plaintiff in a character merchandising case at that time. However, in *Tie Rack v Tie Rack*[66] the problem of the overseas plaintiff recurred in its pure form and *Slenderella* was again followed. The plaintiffs, owners of a chain of retail shops in the United Kingdom and elsewhere, may have been known in South Africa, but they had no South African customers and no goodwill to be damaged.

Actions have also been based on the South African law of unlawful competition which is part of Roman-Dutch law, but with no more success.

United Kingdom

Although the *Budweiser* case, *Anheuser-Busch v Budejovicky Budvar*,[67] is **3–103** binding authority in England, one subsequent High Court case shows a willingness to prefer the line of authority represented by *Dominion Rent A Car v Budget Rent A Car*[68] in denying that goodwill is necessarily split along national boundaries. In *Pete Waterman v CBS*[69] Browne-Wilkinson V.C. had to decide whether the defendants' licensors, the owners of a New York recording studio known as the *Hit Factory*, had goodwill in England so as to be able to make out a defence of concurrent user. He concluded:

"A.   As a matter of principle, the existence of a severable English goodwill attached to a place of business in this country is not the basis of a right to complain of passing-off in this country. What is necessary is for the plaintiffs to show they have a trade connection here which will normally consist of customers forming part of their goodwill, wherever that goodwill is situate, which goodwill is being invaded by the acts of the defendant in this country;

B.   The approach which I have set out at A above is not open to me as there is binding authority to the effect that the basis of [the] plaintiff's claim must be a goodwill locally situate in England; but

C.   The presence of customers in this country is sufficient to constitute the carrying on of business here whether or not there is otherwise a place of business here and whether or not the services are provided here. Once it

---

[64] 1959 (1) S.A. 519 (W).
[65] 1981 (3) S.A. 1129; [1982] R.P.C. 395 (Van Djikhorst J.).
[66] 1989 (4) S.A. 427 (Kriegler J., Transvaal).
[67] [1984] F.S.R. 413, CA.
[68] [1987] 2 N.Z.L.R. 395 (CA. New Zealand).
[69] [1993] E.M.L.R. 27 (Browne-Wilkinson V.C.).

is found that there are customers, it is open to find that there is business here to which the local goodwill is attached;

    D. To the extent that the *Crazy Horse*[70] case is authority to the contrary, I prefer not to follow it."

The rejection of *Crazy Horse* is explicit and by now almost uncontroversial. The best that can be said for *Crazy Horse* is that it may be justified on its facts, but much of its reasoning is too restrictive and the requirement of a business actually carried on in England obsolete. The implicit criticism of *Budweiser* is relatively muted, especially in comparison to *Conagra v McCain Foods*,[71] and Browne-Wilkinson V.C. would agree with the Court of Appeal that the claimant must have customers in the jurisdiction, though he departs from them on the question of whether it is right to speak of the need for damage to goodwill in the jurisdiction. This leads to the final issue, which is whether passing-off actions by foreign claimants are better understood in terms of damage to goodwill which has no national *situs* at all, or which is situated abroad.

    The reason why goodwill is territorial is that it is a legal proprietary right, existing or not in any jurisdiction according to whether the laws of that jurisdiction protect its putative owner. Goodwill in the legal sense is therefore something more than bare reputation or the totality of the relations a business has with its customers. The distinction between goodwill in the legal sense and reputation in the everyday sense is like that between copyright and the underlying literary work. It may be surprising, and even inconvenient, that at the moment a literary work is reduced to writing tens or hundreds of legally distinct copyrights may simultaneously come into existence all over the world, but the nature of copyright as a legal right of property arising in any given jurisdiction from national legislation, common law or self-executing treaty means that it must be wrong to speak as if there were a single international copyright. In the same way, one can only speak of international goodwill in a non-technical sense. The legal situation is that even the most internationally renowned business owns not one goodwill, but a bundle of many different national ones.

H. Ownership of Goodwill

Problem and principle stated

3–104 Ownership of goodwill has been a central issue in three or four comparatively recent cases, two of them in the Court of Appeal, a high number in such a short period of time for a topic which has previously tended to be taken for granted and dealt with as a subsidiary issue, if specifically

---

[70] *Bernadin (Alain) et Cie v Pavilion Properties Ltd* [1967] R.P.C. 581.
[71] (1992) 23 I.P.R. 193 (Federal Court of Australia).

addressed at all.[72] What these cases have in common is their emphasis that, in the absence of agreement, ownership of goodwill is ultimately a question of fact to be decided in the light of all the relevant circumstances, and that arbitrary presumptions or rules of thumb (including some canvassed in previous editions of the present work) provide illusory assistance and are best avoided.

With a well-known and widely used mark such as *Dulux* or *St Michael*, for example,[73] it is often obvious who owns the goodwill in the business in respect of which it is used. Two interchangeable items may stand side-by-side on the supermarket shelf, and may even have been made in the same factory. It is self-evident that the goodwill for the supermarket "own brand" belongs to the retailer, and that of the nationally advertised market leader to the manufacturer. However, passing-off is not confined to misuse of household names. All that is necessary for a mark to be capable of being protected is that the public should rely on the mark as denoting that the quality or character of the goods so marked is the responsibility of some one trader.[74] The public need not be able to identify him by name, and they need not even know the capacity in which he stands in relation to the goods. Verbal marks such as brand names may provide a clue as to who is responsible for applying them if they correspond to the name of a trader, but more than one competing trader may have a name incorporating the mark. Many marks, such as get-up, most visual marks and many arbitrary words coined for specific lines of goods may not correspond to the name of any trader involved. Hence there is a need for objective criteria from which ownership of the goodwill may be determined, irrespective of the way the goods are marked. The question is sometimes put in terms of whether a mark is a manufacturer's mark, an importer's mark, a retailer's mark, etc. There is no magic in these terms, which simply re-state the problem in different words.

The problem in one of its manifestations, and the general principles to **3–105** apply in all kinds of situation in which the ownership of goodwill is not effectively stipulated for by contract, were recently explained by Sir Stephen Browne (delivering the judgment of the court) in *Scandecor Development v Scandecor Marketing*:[75]

"The effects of the expansion of international trade, the globalisation of markets and the growth of multi-national corporate conglomerates are all reflected in this and similar disputes. A company incorporated outside the United Kingdom and carrying on business in a number of other countries may expand into the United Kingdom market in a number of different

---

[72] *Gromax Plasticulture Ltd v Don & Low Nonwovens Ltd* [1999] R.P.C. 367; *Scandecor Development AB v Scandecor Marketing AB* [1999] F.S.R. 26, CA and *MedGen Inc v Passion for Life Products Ltd* [2001] F.S.R. 30. *Dawnay Day & Co Ltd v Cantor Fitzgerald International* [2000] R.P.C. 669, CA is less relevant in the present context, and is considered in more detail in Chapter 7.

[73] Examples given in *Gromax Plasticulture Ltd v Don & Low Nonwovens Ltd* [1999] R.P.C. 367.

[74] *Powell v Birmingham Vinegar Brewery Co* [1897] A.C. 710; 14 R.P.C. 721, HL.

[75] [1999] F.S.R. 26, CA.

ways. It may establish a branch or form a subsidiary company to manufacture or to trade in its products or services in the United Kingdom; or it may appoint an unconnected company to act as the sole or exclusive distributor of its products or the supplier of services in that local territory for a fixed term or until terminated on notice or other specified events; or it may enter into an agreement with a local company to make and sell its products under licence. The local company may use the same marks in the territory as the foreign company uses in other territories both in its corporate name and in relation to its products and services. No problems are likely to occur while the local subsidiary, distributor, agent or licensee company is a member of the same group or is bound by a contractual arrangement containing provisions governing the use of the mark. Difficulties, like those in the present case, are likely to arise when the corporate or the contractual connection is severed and there are no express post-termination contractual provisions designed specifically to regulate the future use of the mark in the local territory. Who is then entitled to use the mark in relation to goods or services or in the corporate or trading name?

The legal response is that this problem, if not solved by agreement, is ultimately soluble only by a factual inquiry with all the disadvantages of the length of its duration, the cost of its conduct and the uncertainty of its outcome. There are no quick, cheap or easy answers to be found in hard and fast legal rules, in binding precedents or in clear cut factual and legal presumptions."

3–106 Accepting the statement of principle from *Scandecor*, there remain two problems which cannot be ignored. The first is that ownership of goodwill is not a primary or directly observable fact. Ownership has to be deduced by applying legal reasoning to facts extracted from the mass of evidence and identified as relevant, and in the process there is scope for mistakes of law as well as ones of fact to be made: As Sir Stephen Browne acknowledged: "Error may, however, occur in the interpretation of the facts and in the conclusions drawn from them".

The second is that identifying the owner of goodwill is really a two-stage process because of the dual character of goodwill as a reflection of a public state of mind on the one hand, and as legal property on the other. It is in its latter capacity that any agreement or special relationship between the parties becomes relevant. The two aspects are easily reconciled by saying that the initial vesting of goodwill in one trader or another is always a matter of fact; but that having vested there on its creation it may be transferred to another trader by prior or subsequent agreement, or by operation of the general law, always provided that the transfer does not offend against the rule prohibiting assignments in gross. In this respect goodwill is little different to any other proprietary intellectual property right, such as copyright.

Initial or *prima facie* ownership

Goodwill is legal property. It can be assigned by the owner, dealt with in **3–107** other ways, and protected against damaging misrepresentations by the action for passing-off. Goodwill is created by trading activities, but it often happens that more than one business is involved in the sequence which results in goods or services being made available to the consuming public. If so, then the question arises of which of those businesses is the owner of goodwill which the law recognises as damaged when a person passes off his goods or business as those with which the public is acquainted. The problem arises in two main contexts. One is where two or more businesses which have previously worked together fall out. The other is where a passing-off action is brought by a claimant who considers himself damaged by the activities of the defendant but who is not, in law, the owner of any relevant goodwill.[76]

The factors which influence the ownership of goodwill were encapsulated by Lord Reid in *Oertli v Bowman*[77]:

"Bowmans made and marketed the *Turmix* machines without the appellants [plaintiffs] having controlled or having had any power to control the manufacture, distribution or sale of the machines, and without there having been any notice of any kind to purchasers that the appellants had any connection with the machines."

There are two distinct, and not necessarily consistent, standards in this passage. One is to ask who is in fact most responsible for the character or quality of the goods; the other is to ask who is perceived by the public as being responsible. The latter is (perhaps surprisingly) the more important,[78] but it does not provide a complete answer to the problem because in many cases the relevant public is not concerned with identifying or distinguishing between the various parties who may be associated with the goods. If so, actual control provides a less decisive test, but one which does yield a definite answer.

To expand, the following questions are relevant as to who owns the **3–108** goodwill in respect of a particular line of goods, or, *mutatis mutandis*, a business for the provision of services:

1. Are the goods bought on the strength of the reputation of an identifiable trader?

2. Who does the public perceive as responsible for the character or

---

[76] To avoid problems such as those in *Star Industrial Co Ltd v Yap Kwee Kor* [1976] F.S.R. 256, PC it is normal to join as claimants every company with a plausible claim to the goodwill affected.

[77] [1959] R.P.C. 1 at 7, HL.

[78] *Vokes (CG) Ltd v Evans* (1931) 49 R.P.C. 140; *Scandecor Development AB v Scandecor Marketing AB* [1999] F.S.R. 26, CA; *MedGen Inc v Passion for Life Products Ltd* [2001] F.S.R. 30.

quality of the goods? Who would be blamed if they were unsatisfactory?

3. Who is most responsible in fact for the character or quality of the goods?

4. What circumstances support or contradict the claim of any particular trader to be the owner of the goodwill? For example, goodwill is more likely to belong to the manufacturer if the goods are distributed through more than one dealer, either at once or in succession. If more than one manufacturer supplies goods to a dealer and they are indistinguishable, the dealer is more likely to own the goodwill.

3–109 So in *Gromax v Don & Low*[79] Lindsay J. said of the situation in 1990 (the date immediately before a distributorship agreement was entered into):

"Reverting, as I therefore have to, to the 7th June 1990, I find different factors pointing in different directions. I notice that 'Gro-Shield' had then been used as a name for less than 8 months and for only one growing season, between February and May 1990. The name had been agreed between the two sides and both had promoted it; Gromax by contact with growers, by the early advertisements and, perhaps, by leaflets and DLN by its part in the drafting of, by featuring on and contributing substantially towards the cost of the brochures which promoted the product as made by it as an arm of Shell. Whilst, over a time, the Gromax team gained a reputation amongst growers as knowledgeable and helpful in their advice as to use of plastics in horticulture such as to lead to a perceived connection between 'Groshield' and no-one but Gromax, I have no evidence that such was at all widely seen to be the case in the very earliest days. Although the technical specification of the fleece was DLN's yet it was Mr Crame [of Gromax] who pushed to ensure that the product was made in a way that suited growers' needs. It cannot be said that Gromax alone was in fact looking to quality; DLN was checking and sampling during the production runs. So far as concerns public perception of who was responsible for the character and quality of the goods (I have in mind Wadlow's helpful summary at para 2.53[80]) I have no evidence of what that perception was at June 1990 but would surmise, given the promotion of the fleece as having a British manufacturer and a connection with Shell, that no-one would then have thought that such matters were exclusively the province of Gromax, then a small undertaking incorporated only 9 months earlier and hardly likely to have been regarded as the owner or operator of the most modern equipment to which Gromax's early literature drew attention. As to whether, at the time, the 'Gro-Shield' fleece was bought on the strength of an identifiable trader, Gromax was then an infant company and whilst Mr Crame

---

[79] [1999] R.P.C. 367 (Lindsay J.), decided before *Scandecor Development AB v Scandecor Marketing AB* [1999] F.S.R. 26, CA. The reasoning is consistent with the latter, though the result might not have been approved of.
[80] Corresponding to the preceding paragraph.

brought to it experience gained with other employers, he was prudently content to point, as DLN were content that he should, to DLN and its connection with Shell. I have to have in mind, too, that Mr Crame proposed the name and that no 'Gro-Shield' was sold, even then, other than through Gromax and to its order. In some cases it was not manufactured but only cut, glued, packaged and labelled by DLN.

I have not found any one factor as determinative but having regard as best I can to all of them I do not see the goodwill as at the 7th June 1990 as belonging wholly to either side; rather I hold that as at that date the goodwill and the business associated with the 'Gro-Shield' name was vested in DLN and Gromax jointly."

Contracts as to prospective ownership of goodwill

The bleak conclusion of *Scandecor Development v Scandecor Marketing*[81] **3–110** (from the point of view of those who have to pay their lawyers' fees) is alleviated for the prudent by the thought that in *Scandecor* itself, as in the other recent cases, a properly drawn agreement could and should have made it clear who was entitled to the relevant goodwill during the currency of the relationship and afterwards, and unless the agreement offended the rule against transactions in gross, its terms would have been given effect. Of the four, in *Gromax* and *MedGen* there were only simple distributorship agreements lacking any provisions for ownership of goodwill in the relevant names; in *Scandecor* the parties had attempted to delineate their respective rights after falling out but had been unable to do so with sufficient precision or completeness; and in *Dawnay Day* a term had to be implied into the relevant joint venture agreement to give effect to the common intent of the parties.

Though there is a role for implied terms, there is a limit to what can be implied under the name of business efficacy, and the legal position in the absence of express agreement may be precisely the opposite to what the parties would have agreed if left to their own devices. In *MedGen v Passion for Life*[82] the goodwill was held to belong to the distributor, but if the issue had been addressed at the start of the relationship then MedGen's ownership would surely have been conceded, or MedGen would have looked elsewhere.

Notwithstanding the rule against assignments in gross, the terms of a voluntary agreement deserve to be given effect in full when it serves to reinforce what would have occurred at common law or when ownership at common law would be uncertain. There are many situations in which, in the absence of agreement, the goodwill could almost equally well be said to belong to one party or the other, and to give effect to the choice of the parties avoids a difficult, pointless and unreliable enquiry. If so, it follows that the party agreed to own the goodwill is the only proper claimant in a passing-off action during the course of the agreement, that he alone is

---

[81] [1999] F.S.R. 26, CA, quoted above.
[82] [2001] F.S.R. 30 (Kevin Garnett Q.C., Deputy Judge).

entitled to use the names or marks with which the goodwill is associated, and that on termination of the agreement it is he who immediately has the right to sue third parties, or even his former colleague, for passing-off.

Scandecor

3–111 The facts of *Scandecor Development v Scandecor Marketing*[83] were exceptionally complicated, but before dealing with them it is essential to note one unusual feature of the case, which is that the goodwill attached to the name in question in the United Kingdom existed solely in relation to retailers. Despite the fact that all the goods in question were destined for ultimate retail sale on a very substantial scale to individual consumers, no company on either side claimed to have any goodwill *vis-à-vis* the general public. As the Court of Appeal noted:

> "It is common ground that:
> (1) A valuable goodwill in the mark 'Scandecor' exists in the United Kingdom in connection with posters, calendars, art prints, cards and related products.
> (2) The relevant section of the public among whom that goodwill exists is the United Kingdom retail trade. There is no relevant goodwill in the mark 'Scandecor' with the general public. As the judge said
>
>> 'It is not suggested that the general public knows the name "Scandecor" or is influenced by it in deciding whether to buy any poster or calendar. The goodwill attached to the name affects only the retailers who choose whether to stock posters or calendars from Scandecor or from any of a number of other suppliers.'"

3–112 Though not further explained, it is not difficult to see why this was rightly taken as common ground on the appeal. Members of the general public buy posters, calendars and the like almost entirely on aesthetic grounds, and they satisfy themselves by eye at the time of purchase that the goods they select are of the character and quality that they want, at a price they are prepared to pay. There is no reliance on the identity of any business involved in producing, publishing or distributing those goods. The identity of the company which published or supplied the poster is no more relevant to the decision to buy than the identity of the printer or the paper mill, and receives scarcely more publicity at the point of sale.

It is otherwise with the retailers. Given the diversity of posters and similar goods that a shop has to stock to satisfy the whims of all potential customers, they rely on a publisher or intermediary such as one of the Scandecor companies to supply a comprehensive and well-chosen range of posters to a consistent and satisfactory level of artistic and technical quality. A corollary of this is that the success of the supplier in meeting the expectations of its

---

[83] [1999] F.S.R. 26, CA. An appeal to the House of Lords, and reference to the European Court of Justice, only involved questions of registered trade mark law.

trade customers—in other words, its goodwill—may crucially depend on its ability to understand and anticipate the tastes of different national groups of retail consumers. Retailers are also interested in factors which do not concern the general public, such as satisfactory copyright and trade mark clearances, without which they may find themselves in court.

The relevance of the service aspect of the Scandecor business in the United Kingdom was explained by the trial judge[84]:

"Scandecor Ltd [the defendant] provides to retailers a standard assortment of posters which is reviewed and changed every three months or thereabouts with a wide range of designs in different sizes and formats and a regular turnover. The retailer is offered a sales service which includes providing display cabinets and units to retailers for the display of the products which are made available generally free on loan to the retailer for as long as he has an agreement for Scandecor to supply goods. The Scandecor sales representative calls on customers on a regular basis to see what lines are selling well, which need restocking and which are selling badly and need replacing. ... The defendants' case is that, even though the plaintiff was the publisher for most (though not all) of the posters sold in the United Kingdom, Scandecor Ltd was responsible for selecting the range of posters offered, and that is part of the basis on which it claims to have the local goodwill in the name Scandecor."

Turning to the facts; two friends from Uppsala University set up the **3–113** Scandecor poster business in 1967, and in 1971 the second defendant (Scandecor Ltd) was set up in the United Kingdom. The two founders fell out, and the business of distributing the posters was divided up on a geographical basis with Continental Europe in one camp and the UK, Scandinavia and North America in the other. The Swedish company which actually published the posters remained under joint control for the time being, but went into administration in 1994 and was effectively bought up by the Continental side of the distribution business. There were attempts at delimitation agreements from time to time, but none expressly governed ownership of the United Kingdom goodwill or the right to use the name. The action in the United Kingdom was framed as one for passing-off and trade mark infringement, with the plaintiffs ("Development") being the Swedish publisher which owned the relevant United Kingdom trade mark registrations, and the defendants ("Limitec") being the United Kingdom distribution company and its parent company in Sweden. There was also a counterclaim.

So far as passing-off is concerned, the *Scandecor* dispute effectively resolves itself into the question of whether the relevant goodwill vested in the Swedish plaintiffs, as publishers of the posters; or the British second defendants, as distributors of those posters and other goods sold under the *Scandecor* name but not necessarily sourced from the plaintiffs' group.

Because of the complexity of the factual background, it is difficult to **3–114**

---

[84] [1998] F.S.R. 500 (Lloyd J.), reversed [1999] F.S.R. 26, CA.

extract useful short quotations from *Scandecor* or to summarise its conclusions at all concisely. With that reservation, the Court of Appeal gave a critical review of the judgment below, which had held that the goodwill was shared by both parties. In the course of tracing the history of the parties' relationship the Court of Appeal concluded that the goodwill in the mark *Scandecor* in the United Kingdom had belonged to "Limited" (the defendants) in the period up to 1979, and that the parties' subsequent dealings had confirmed this state of affairs. Finally, the court concluded:

"In relation to the disputed goodwill what matters is the identity of the person carrying on the trading activities in the local territory with the retailers: with whom do they associate the mark Scandecor? Mr Wyand emphasised the presentation of the image of the unified world-wide group, in preference to publicising and highlighting the divisions occurring within it. He relied on the publicity to the outside world (the 'one face to the world' policy) and the claims by Limited to international connections. However, the commercial reality in the market place (and that is what really counts on this issue of entitlement to goodwill) is that International neither had a business in the United Kingdom nor did it ever exercise control over any relevant business activities in the United Kingdom to which its goodwill could attach. The judge referred ... to the evidence of the retailers called by the Defendants who all associated the name Scandecor with Limited, the company with which they dealt and with whose service they were satisfied. Although some knew that the products or some of them were made in Sweden, they were more interested in the quality, price and service offered by the supplier than in the original source or publisher of the product. He also referred in the same paragraph to the evidence given by one of the Plaintiff's witnesses ... that the name and logo were used to distinguish products placed on the market by Limited from other companies' products, whether posters or calendars."

In the result the decision of the trial judge that the goodwill was jointly owned by both parties was reversed, and the goodwill was held to be owned by the defendants alone.

After *Scandecor*

3–115 In view of the factual complexity of *Scandecor Development v Scandecor Marketing*[85] it may be useful to quote from *MedGen v Passion for Life*[86] at greater length than one would normally do for a first instance judgment expressly applying a recent Court of Appeal decision to different facts. The facts of *MedGen* were simplicity itself in comparison to *Scandecor*. The American claimant, MedGen, had developed a snoring preventative which was sold as *Snorenz*—being distributed in the United Sates by MedGen themselves; and in the United Kingdom by the defendant *Passion for Life*

---

[85] [1999] F.S.R. 26, CA.
[86] [2001] F.S.R. 30 (Kevin Garnett Q.C., Deputy Judge).

("PfL"), under the latter's own name, with no mention of MedGen, and with the benefit of an written exclusive distributorship agreement which was silent on ownership of the name.

"1. The key question is: Has MedGen proved that the name Snorenz, and the packaging in which Snorenz was sold, are associated in the minds of a substantial number of the relevant persons (in this case, the purchasing public and purchasing retailers) specifically and exclusively with it and with its products?...

...

7. In *Scandecor*, the Court of Appeal concluded that the judge had correctly appreciated the local nature of the relevant goodwill acquired by the company actually carrying on the business in the UK and to goods marketed by that company in the UK. According to the Court of Appeal, however, he fell into error in assigning a separate goodwill to the foreign publisher who had not carried on any trading or marketing activities in this country. He was wrong to assign such goodwill to it based on the trading activities of a wholly-owned subsidiary or an authorised agent or distributor. This was so even though the UK company had taken certain steps to emphasise its connection with the foreign publisher."

And the Deputy Judge continued: **3–116**

"Applying these general principles to the facts of this case, in my judgment the goodwill in the name 'Snorenz' belonged exclusively to PfL, for the following reasons:

1. MedGen carried on no business in the United Kingdom.
2. The packaging in which the product was sold carried no reference to MedGen nor any reference to the product having been developed by or produced for MedGen.
3. In contrast, the whole business of the marketing and sale of the product was carried out by PfL. The references on the label packaging and in advertisements were exclusively to PfL.
4. Self-evidently, and as confirmed by the limited evidence, the wholesale or retail trade would only know PfL as the source for the product. It was to PfL that such traders would go for further product. In the event of any defect or problem, it would have been to PfL and not to MedGen that the wholesaler or retailer would have turned. There is no evidence that retail traders either:

  i.   Knew that MedGen was the developer of the product or responsible for its manufacture; or
  ii. Cared who had developed it or who was responsible for its manufacture.

5. Similar remarks, with perhaps even greater force, can be made about the purchasing members of the ordinary public. So far as they were concerned, their reasons for buying the product would either have been:

 i. The advertisements or product references effected by PfL, which for the most part carried PfL's name; or

 ii. Their satisfaction with the product, which again carried PfL's name. I think it is reasonable to infer that members of the public who made successive purchases would only be concerned that the next bottle which they purchased would be of the same quality as the last. In order to obtain further supplies, they would either contact PfL using the contact details on the package, or look for it in the shops by reference to the name Snorenz and the packaging.

In either case, there is no evidence that they would be concerned as to who had been responsible for the original development of the product or as to who had manufactured the product. On the contrary, I think it can be inferred that they would be indifferent to these things. If the product failed to live up to their expectations they would have blamed PfL. There is no evidence that anyone actually took up PfL's 'Money back guarantee', but if they had done so, it would only have been to PfL that they could have looked for their money."

An introduction to the older decided cases

3–117 The Section which follows this one presents the older decided cases, categorised in terms of certain common and recurrent factual situations. The recent cases dealt with at length in the present Section are also briefly noted where appropriate as examples of their facts. After *Scandecor Development v Scandecor Marketing*,[87] it might be supposed that these older cases are of no more than historical interest, and it is certainly true that the reader will be better served by analysing any given factual situation in all its detail, rather than seeking the closest factual analogy in the reported cases. Even the most trivial glance shows that two cases on superficially indistinguishable facts can easily be decided in diametrically opposite ways. The cases which do not depend on public recognition (or express agreement) are particularly difficult to reconcile with one another, despite the fact that they are relatively few in number. Several in which ownership of goodwill was the crucial issue lack proper reasoning and treat the final result as self-evident.

However *Scandecor* itself strictly deserves no more prominent treatment than any of the older cases which follow. The aphorism that every passing-off case turns on its own facts, and that precedents are of no more than analogical value, applies with a vengeance to a case whose facts were especially unusual and whose stated *ratio decidendi* is that "there are no quick, cheap or easy answers to be found in hard and fast legal rules, in binding precedents or in clear cut factual and legal presumptions". And with unconscious irony, *Scandecor* itself is thoroughly pervaded by two such presumptions of its own. First, there is the Court of Appeal's obvious determination to reach a clear-cut finding in one favour of one party or the other, and to avoid the compromise reached by the trial judge. Secondly, there is the court's instinctive reluctance to believe that local English

---

[87] [1999] F.S.R. 26, CA, reversing [1998] F.S.R. 500 (Lloyd J.).

goodwill could really be owned by a foreign company which the relevant United Kingdom public dealt with only through intermediaries. The latter was not unreasonable on the facts, given that the relevant public consisted of retailers who treated *Scandecor* essentially as denoting a provider of business services, rather than imported goods, but one hopes its inappropriateness would be self-evident if one were talking about *Saab* cars.

Scandecor Development v Scandecor Marketing[88] is by no means alone in **3–118** treating English businesses more favourably than foreign ones, whatever their nature. This is not just the case for the English subsidiaries, licensees or distributors of foreign enterprises. The doctrine of instruments of deception and the appellate jurisdiction of the Privy Council have meant that English law contains many decisions in favour of English manufacturing businesses where the passing off took place abroad. Few of these even seem to contemplate that the relevant overseas goodwill might not have belonged to the English claimant, but to a local trader. Yet when tables are turned, as in *Scandecor*[89] or *MedGen v Passion for Life*,[90] it is the United Kingdom distributor who turns out to own the local goodwill, and not his foreign principal.

In deference to *Scandecor*,[91] the commentary in the following Section has been edited to remove, as far as possible, almost all previous attempts to deduce quick and easy answers from inadequate and contradictory materials, while preserving what are believed to be uncontroversial statements of general validity in respect of employees and fiduciaries. To this there is one minor exception, and one striking one. The first concerns authors' pen names and the like, for which the authorities may now be sufficiently numerous and self-consistent to constitute a body of law in their own right, regardless of the dubious compatibility of some of them with basic principles. The major exception is the proposition that goodwill accrues to the licensor of a name or mark rather than the licensee. Properly explained and suitably qualified, it is maintained that this is an inherent consequence of the licensor-licensee relationship, notwithstanding the criticism it received in *Gromax v Don & Low*,[92] and, less expressly, in *Scandecor* itself.[93]

---

[88] above.
[89] above.
[90] [2001] F.S.R. 30 (Kevin Garnett Q.C., Deputy Judge).
[91] [1999] F.S.R. 26, CA.
[92] [1999] R.P.C. 367 (Lindsay J.), decided before *Scandecor Development AB v Scandecor Marketing AB* [1999] F.S.R. 26, CA. The reasoning is consistent with the latter, though the result would not have been approved of.
[93] [1999] F.S.R. 26, CA; this specific criticism is rather more marked in the first instance judgment of Lloyd J. [1998] F.S.R. 500.

I. Ownership in Common Situations

Licensor and licensee: trade marks

3–119   If the commercial purpose of an agreement is to license the use of a distinctive name or mark in respect of which the licensor has (or is agreed to have) goodwill, to a licensee with no such goodwill, and in circumstances where the licensee's use would otherwise be actionable as passing-off, then in the absence of agreement to the contrary or other supervening factors, the goodwill in the business so carried on by the licensee under the licensed name or mark will accrue to the licensor rather than the licensee. The licence may be express or implied, provided always that it does not offend against the prohibition on transactions in gross. The licensee acquires no interest in the licensed name or mark, and must cease using it on termination of the licence. Examples are to be found in *Coles v Need*,[94] *Roberts v Davis*,[95] *Manus v Fullwood & Bland*,[96] *Bostitch*[97] and *Dawnay Day v Cantor Fitzgerald*[98]. It is irrelevant whether the goodwill in the licensed business would otherwise have accrued to the licensee, the licensor, or both. It is the parties' contractual agreement, not some extrinsic legal fiction or equitable doctrine, which operates to vest the goodwill in the licensor, unless otherwise agreed, because no other outcome is consistent with the ordinary licensor-licensee relationship. An agreement which is not a trade mark licence in the foregoing sense cannot be assumed to affect ownership of goodwill in this, or any other, predetermined way.

3–120   In a previous formulation the preceding paragraph was criticised by Lindsay J. in *Growmax v Don & Low*,[99] and it has been reformulated in the present edition to meet the substance of that criticism, and to explain its basis and limitations. An extended treatment is also required in the light of the more fundamental criticisms which might be levelled at it on the strength of *Scandecor Development v Scandecor Marketing*:[1]

> "Mr Purvis relies on a passage in Wadlow's 'The Law of Passing Off' 2nd Edition 1995 where at para 2.62 one finds:
>
> > 'If a valid licence of a name or mark is in operation then the goodwill in respect of the business so carried on accrues to the licensor rather than the licensee ... the licensee acquires no interest in the name or mark, and must cease using it on termination of the licence. ... Provided the licence is valid, it does not matter that the licensee may be held out as

---

[94] [1934] A.C. 82; 50 R.P.C. 379, PC.
[95] (1935) 53 R.P.C. 79 (Luxmoore J.).
[96] (1949) 66 R.P.C. 71, CA.
[97] *Bostitch TM* [1963] R.P.C. 183 and *Bostitch Inc v McGarry and Cole Ltd* [1964] R.P.C. 173.
[98] [2000] R.P.C. 669, CA.
[99] [1999] R.P.C. 367 (Lindsay J.).
[1] [1999] F.S.R. 26, CA, judgment in *Gromax* having been delivered before the decision of the Court of Appeal in *Scandecor*, and without citing the first instance judgment of Lloyd J.

the provider of the goods in question and may in fact be primarily responsible for their character or quality'.

Whilst I recognise that the Courts would not wish to undermine the utility of distributorship agreements (and exclusive distributorship agreements would be the most vulnerable) I am loth in this area, which is to some extent one of fact and degree, to endorse a proposition which is, as framed, so inflexible, so free of regard to the terms of the particular licence, to the state of affairs when the licence was made and to whether the licensee has, for example, promoted the name in ways beyond such as may have been incidental to his obligations under the agreement or beyond preservation or enhancement of such interests as he acquires under the agreement. I would, however, be content for present purposes with a proposition which stated that subject to special circumstances being proved to the contrary and to the terms of the particular licence, as between licensor and licensee as competitors for the ownership of the goodwill at the termination of a licence, the position of the licensor should not be taken to be weakened nor that of the licensee enhanced by such activity on the licensee's part or such his contractual position during the currency of the licence as was respectively either required of him or conferred upon him by the licence or, as to activity of his known to the licensor, was such as could be fairly regarded by the licensor as no more than reasonably incidental to the maintenance or promotion of such commercial interest in the name as the licence had conferred upon the licensee."

The criticisms fall into two overlapping categories: that the original proposition was too general, in so far as one can imagine licences, or circumstances, for which it does not apply; and that it was too dogmatic, especially in so far as it took too little account of an admittedly sensible and desirable *prima facie* rule being displaced by express agreement or other overriding factors. Both deserve to be answered, although the first especially may have been based on a misunderstanding as to the kind of agreements to which the original proposition was intended to apply.

So far as the first criticism is concerned, one can indeed imagine licences **3–121** which the original proposition superficially fitted, but without the stated consequence being necessary, intended, or even desirable. For example, a trade mark delimitation agreement between two parties with genuine interests in the same mark, perhaps in different fields, might involve cross-licensing, but be perfectly consistent with each licensee retaining the goodwill in its own area of activity. Again, a licence may simply be intended to recognise or legitimate a situation under which the licensee has ample goodwill of his own in a business which marginally trespasses on the rights of the licensor; or a licence may be sought, and obtained, more from caution or courtesy than legal necessity. A licence need not even be contractual. It may be added that the proposition of the previous edition was never intended to apply to agreements which were not licence agreements at all, whether expressly or by necessary implication. In particular, it is hard to see how even the original formulation fits the agreement in *Gromax v Don &*

Low itself, which was on its face a simple distributorship agreement, entirely silent as to whether the name *Gro-Sheild* was being licensed at all, and if so whether from Gromax to Don & Low, or *vice versa*. The preferred analysis for a distributorship agreement is that unless the relationship is one of such trust and confidence as to create fiduciary obligations (which is unusual in a commercial context, but not entirely impossible) then one simply cannot generalise.

The reason one can state the proposition with some confidence for trade mark licence agreements as such is that in this case alone the consequence is inherent to the licensor-licensee relationship in a way that need not be true for other kinds of contract. Two specific situations are contemplated. First, where the agreement is what one would normally think of as a trade mark licence in that its principal commercial purpose is to enable a person, the licensee, to use a name, mark, or other sign in a manner which the licensor could otherwise prohibit by virtue of his pre-existing goodwill in relation to the matter licensed. In this situation, any other consequence than that stated would destroy the licensor-licensee relationship as inevitably as allowing a tenant under a lease to claim adverse possession against his landlord, and cannot be assumed to have been the intention of the parties unless so stated in absolutely clear language. Secondly, the proposition applies to similar agreements when there is no pre-existing goodwill, or when ownership of such goodwill as already exists is uncertain or controversial. For the same reasons as previously, by identifying themselves respectively as licensor and licensee the parties have specified which of them is actually to own the goodwill generated in performance of the agreement, and which is to enjoy it on terms, and their decision should be given effect. This situation may again be compared to that on the facts of *Gromax v Don & Low*. In 1990, each party had a tenable but inconclusive claim to what goodwill already existed in relation to the name *Gro-Sheild*. If the distributorship agreement signed that year had identified one party as the licensor of the name and the other as the licensee (which it did not, and which is quite unrelated to which party manufactured the goods and which marketed them) then at the very least there would have been an estoppel by convention as to which party owned the goodwill in the name.

3–122   That the benefit of the licence may inure to the licensor in actions against third parties may be seen from *Dawnay Day v Cantor Fitzgerald*[2] as well as *Dunhill v Sunoptic*[3] and *News Group Newspapers v Rocket Record Co*,[4] in both of which interlocutory injunctions were granted largely on the strength of licensing activities well outside the claimants' core businesses.

An unusual situation arose in the South African case of *Caterham Car Sales v Birkin Cars*[5] which concerned the Lotus Super Seven Series III sports car and replicas of it. Caterham claimed that their own trade in replicas, as licensees of Lotus, had enured to the benefit of Lotus and had subsequently been assigned by Lotus to them. The argument failed, because Caterham

[2] [2000] R.P.C. 669, CA.
[3] [1979] F.S.R. 337, CA.
[4] [1981] F.S.R. 89 (Slade J.).
[5] 1998 (3) S.A. 938 (SCA).

had never been licensees of Lotus at all, but had been passing themselves off as such.

Licensor and licensee: technology

The licensing of patent or similar rights, and even the provision of know- **3–123** how and technical assistance, do not result in the licensor having any interest in the goodwill of the business carried on by the licensee. Such agreements, in which the licensee traded on its own account with the assistance of the licensor but not under its control, are to be found in *Oertli v Bowman*,[6] *Sturtevant v Sturtevant Mill Co of USA*,[7] and perhaps *Jaeger v Jaeger & Co*.[8] In all of these the goodwill was held to belong exclusively to the licensee, and in the last two the former licensor was prevented from using its own name in competition with the licensee. If the licensor of technology wishes to obtain the benefit of the goodwill in the licensed field for himself, he should therefore reserve and exercise control over how the licensed technology is used and ensure that customers have notice of the fact. If the licensee uses the name of the licensor or any of his marks it should be made clear that this is under a revocable licence.

In *Freeman v Sharpe*[9] the plaintiffs had licensed the defendants to manufacture water closets under a patent. The defendants sold some on their own account under the mark *Capstan* and some to the plaintiffs who sold them under the mark *Turrit*. The plaintiffs terminated the licence and the defendants continued to use *Capstan* for a new design outside the scope of the patent. North J. refused an interlocutory injunction, rejecting an argument that *Capstan* denoted closets constructed under the plaintiffs' licence.

In *Frankau v Pflueger*[10] the defendant had invented an absorbent cartridge for use in tobacco pipes. He granted an exclusive licence for the life of the patent to the plaintiffs, and manufactured and packed some cartridges for them under contract. On the patent expiring he claimed to be entitled to sell cartridges on his own account using the same get-up as the plaintiffs. Eve J. held that he had no such joint interest in the get-up and granted an interlocutory injunction against him.

Foreign businesses and their representatives

A foreign business may have a goodwill in the jurisdiction even though it **3–124** may not trade here in its own right. As the Court of Appeal acknowledged in *Scandecor Development v Scandecor Marketing*[11]:

---

[6] [1959] R.P.C. 1, HL; affirming [1957] R.P.C. 388, CA.
[7] [1963] 3 All E.R. 137; 53 R.P.C. 430. The licensor provided "every assistance" including drawings and experts.
[8] (1927) 44 R.P.C. 437, CA. It is unclear just what was licensed.
[9] (1899) 16 R.P.C. 205 (North J.).
[10] (1910) 28 R.P.C. 130 (Eve J.).
[11] [1999] F.S.R. 26, CA.

"We accept that, in an appropriate case, it is legally and factually possible for a business based overseas to acquire a goodwill in this country by the supply of its products or services through a subsidiary, agent or licensee. Whether or not that occurs must depend on the facts of the particular case."

It is sufficient that customers for its goods are to be found here, whether or not the foreign business is in direct contractual relations with them.[12] In particular, if the foreign business is represented by a legally distinct person of whatever capacity then the goodwill will in general belong to the foreign business rather than its local representative *provided* that the foreign business is recognised as the ultimate source of the goods.[13] It is not necessary, or common, for the relationship to be one of agency in the strict legal sense.

3–125   Problems have arisen when an English business imports and sells the goods of a foreign business. Several authorities have held the goodwill to belong to the English business, apparently on the assumption that a foreign business can have no goodwill in England unless it trades here in its own right or through an agent as such. This is certainly wrong,[14] and the goodwill is more likely to belong to the foreign business as the recognised ultimate source of the goods unless there are circumstances to displace this presumption. No one suggests that the eponymous owner of *Quine's Diner* in Canterbury ever had any interest in the United Kingdom goodwill in relation to American *Budweiser* beer, although he was once the first and only source of supply in this country. The same question may arise, though less frequently in the decided cases, where all the traders concerned are domestic. Whether the manufacturer of the goods is abroad or not is irrelevant if they have a market in this country, and ownership of goodwill as between the various parties in the chain ought to be decided in the same way irrespective of national boundaries.

This section discusses the problem mainly in terms of foreign and English businesses because most of the authorities do so.[15] The relevant English goodwill most clearly belongs to the foreign business if the foreign business is in fact predominantly responsible for the character or quality of the goods and the English business is held out as representing the foreign one, either expressly or by implication. On general principles it is unnecessary for the foreign business to be known by name, provided its existence is known or assumed. The most important factor would appear to be the state of the public mind, so that if the public attributes the goods to the foreign business then it may not matter that the foreign business does not manufacture them,

---

[12] *Anheuser-Busch Inc v Budejovicky Budvar NP* [1984] F.S.R. 413, CA.

[13] This sentence, with justified emphasis on word "provided", and recognising the possibility of exceptions to it, was approved in *MedGen Inc v Passion for Life Products Ltd* [2001] F.S.R. 30.

[14] *SA des Anciens Etablissements Panhard et Levassor v Panhard Levassor Motor Co Ltd* [1900–3] All E.R. 477; 18 R.P.C. 405.

[15] *Thorne (R) & Sons Ltd v Pimms Ltd* (1909) 26 R.P.C. 221 is nearly a domestic case, as is *Gromax Plasticulture Ltd v Don & Low Nonwovens Ltd* [1999] R.P.C. 367. In both cases the only "foreign" element was the Scottish origin of the goods.

and may exercise less control over the local business or the goods themselves than the public may suppose.

Examples

In *Roberts v Davis*[16] the plaintiffs were an American manufacturer of **3–126** numbering machines. They appointed the defendant as their exclusive distributor in England and he carried on business under their name, effectively being held out as a branch of the American business. The defendant was obliged to deal only in the plaintiffs' machines. On the plaintiffs terminating the agreement, the defendant continued to use their name and had identical goods made for him with the name on them. Luxmoore J. held that the plaintiffs had a business in England, that the name was distinctive of them, and that the defendant had only a revocable licence to use their name, which had been withdrawn when the agreement was terminated. An injunction was granted against him.[17]

In *Manus v Fullwood & Bland*[18] the plaintiffs manufactured milking machines in Sweden. The defendants were their English distributors and known as such. The Second World War interrupted imports and the defendants started to manufacture themselves, initially under licence but subsequently independently. After the War the defendants argued that the mark, if ever distinctive of the plaintiffs, had become distinctive of them. The Court of Appeal found for the plaintiffs.

In *Bostitch TM*[19] and *Bostitch v McGarry and Cole*[20] the facts were similar except that even after the War had ended the American plaintiffs continued progressively to transfer manufacture of their stapling machines and staples to the defendants in England. On the relationship being terminated the defendants claimed to be entitled to continue to use the name *Bostitch* on staples and staplers of their manufacture. Lloyd-Jacob J. held that the connection of the plaintiffs with the goods sold in England had been advertised to the public and it was irrelevant that the goodwill had been "focused" on the defendants as named distributors. The change in status of the defendant from selling finished goods to manufacturing in England under sub-contract to the plaintiff did not affect matters.

In the Canadian case of *Tricom Automotive Dealer Systems v Tricom* **3–127** *Vehicle Maintenance Systems*[21] the plaintiffs were a United States corporation. The defendants had acted as their Canadian distributor under an agreement which had been terminated. Apart from this, the plaintiffs did not trade in Canada. The agreement provided for the Canadian company to cease using the names and marks in issue on the distributorship terminating,

---

[16] (1935) 53 R.P.C. 79 (Luxmoore J.).
[17] See also *Reuter (RJ) Co Ltd v Mulhens* (1953) 70 R.P.C. 235, CA.
[18] (1949) 66 R.P.C. 71, CA.
[19] [1963] R.P.C. 183 (Lloyd-Jacob J.).
[20] [1964] R.P.C. 173 (Cross J.). Ownership was initially decided in terms of a registered trade mark; but the same conclusion was applied in a subsequent passing-off case between the same parties.
[21] (1987) 14 C.P.R. (3d) 22.

but it continued to use them. Each applied for an interlocutory injunction against the other. The Ontario High Court found for the American plaintiffs. Their trade with Canada through distributors (of which the defendants were the second) was sufficient to generate goodwill, and the defendants had only a revocable licence.

An elegant application of the principle that goodwill accrues to the identified foreign supplier of imported goods rather than to the importer occurs in *Nikisha Corp. v Goodchild.*[22] The plaintiffs were manufacturers of a three-dimensional camera and the first defendants were their distributors in America. They had no distributors as such in the United Kingdom, but the defendants imported a supply of the plaintiffs' cameras and represented themselves as being closely associated with the plaintiffs. Knox J. granted an interlocutory injunction in similar terms to *Sony v Saray.*[23] For the defendants simply to import and sell the plaintiffs cameras was lawful and the goodwill so generated had accrued to the plaintiffs, not least because the defendants had actually held themselves out as the authorised distributors for a foreign manufacturer. What was unlawful was for the defendants to misrepresent that they had any closer connection with the plaintiffs than that of unauthorised importers of their goods.

In *Guangdong Foodstuffs v Tung Fook*[24] the plaintiffs exported two brands of rice wine from the Chinese mainland to Hong Kong, where they had been distributed by the second defendant under the names *Super Mellow Mijiu* and *Shiwan Mijiu*. The defendants changed their source of supply, and issued press advertisements and letters to customers stating that they had changed the plaintiffs' *Pearl River Bridge* house mark to *Zu Miao*, and implying that rice wine sold under the two trade marks (and others used by the plaintiffs) was only genuine if it also carried the *Zu Miao* mark. The court held that the goodwill in Hong Kong belonged to the plaintiffs, who were responsible for the character of the rice wine in both fact and repute, and that the defendants were liable for passing-off and injurious falsehood.

From *Bostitch* and *Manus* it appears that once a business becomes identified with a foreign principal the goodwill may continue to accrue to the foreign business rather than the local one for as long as the latter is held out as representing the former, even if the balance of control shifts to the local business.

Goodwill owned by representative of foreign business

3–128 Conversely, circumstances may point to the goodwill being owned by the English business to the exclusion of the foreign manufacturer. This is particularly likely if the foreign origin is concealed and the English company held out as the ultimate source of the goods[25].

---

[22] [1990] F.S.R. 371 (Knox J.).
[23] [1983] F.S.R. 302, CA.
[24] [1999] 3 H.K.L.R.D. 545 (Cheung J., CFI).
[25] As in *Adrema Ltd v Adrema Werke GmbH* [1958] R.P.C. 323; *MedGen Inc v Passion for Life Products Ltd* [2001] F.S.R. 30.

In *Sturtevant v Sturtevant Mill Co of USA*[26] the plaintiffs were an English company which had once distributed the machines of an American manufacturer. For twenty years past, however, they had manufactured themselves using patents and know-how licensed from the Americans under an agreement which prevented the Americans selling in England. On this agreement terminating the Americans incorporated the defendants as their English subsidiary. Farwell J. found for the English plaintiffs.

In *Jaeger v Jaeger & Co*[27] Professor Jaeger, a German, devised a system of clothing and granted the defendants the sole right to use his name in England, apparently in perpetuity and without power of revocation. The defendants could buy the clothing from the Professor's concessionaires in Germany or pay a royalty on items from other sources. It is unclear what quality control was exercised over clothing not supplied from Germany. By 1914 only one quarter of the defendants' supplies were German, and on the outbreak of war the contract was terminated and the defendants continued their business but ceased to pay royalties. In 1924 the plaintiffs, the successors of Professor Jaeger, opened a shop in London and renewed a claim that the defendants had no title to the *Jaeger* name. The Court of Appeal found for the defendants.

Jaeger is the more telling of these cases. The professor had carried on no **3–129** trade in England before granting the licence, and his system had been known here only to a few aficionados, who required "considerable moral courage" to wear it. His licence was therefore a bare endorsement of the defendants rather than a licensing of any subsisting legal rights. The terms of the licence would not be acceptable even today, and when the plaintiffs finally came to assert their rights there was a long history of uncontrolled use of the name by the defendants. Even so, the case is not as clear cut as the Court of Appeal assumed. They seem to have regarded it as self-evident that the defendants had the goodwill in the name *Jaeger* perhaps even before 1914, and that neither the existence nor the termination of the agreement affected matters.[28]

Sturtevant v Sturtevant Mill Co of USA[29] may be distinguished from *Roberts v Davis*[30] and *Bostitch*[31] but in terms of general approach the latter are to be preferred. The decision may be right on its facts, but much of the reasoning is suspect. It assumes that the American company could have had no goodwill in England prior to 1911 because their goods were sold by a distributor rather than through a branch or agent, and could have no

[26] [1936] 3 All E.R. 137; 53 R.P.C. 430 (Farwell J.).
[27] (1927) 44 R.P.C. 437, CA. For subsequent proceedings see (1929) 46 R.P.C. 336.
[28] But in 1927 any licensing of trade marks was still anathema. *Bowden Wire Ltd v Bowden Brake Ltd* (1914) 31 R.P.C. 385, HL was yet to be superseded by *Coles (JH) Pty Ltd v Need* [1934] A.C. 82; 50 R.P.C. 379, PC.
[29] [1936] 3 All E.R. 137; 53 R.P.C. 430 (Farwell J.).
[30] (1935) 53 R.P.C. 79.
[31] *Bostitch TM* [1963] R.P.C. 183 and *Bostitch Inc v McGarry and Cole Ltd* [1964] R.P.C. 173.

goodwill thereafter because they had bound themselves not to trade in England.[32] Both propositions are inconsistent with the *Panhard*[33] case, which was not cited. Nor was *Coles v Need*.[34] An alternative analysis is that the American company had a goodwill in 1911, had granted a valid revocable licence to use their name on goods manufactured to their designs, and that the goodwill continuing to be created accrued to them.

3–130   In *Scandecor Development v Scandecor Marketing*,[35] the plaintiff group published posters in Sweden, and the defendants distributed them in the United Kingdom. The trial judge held that both parties owned goodwill in relation to the *Scandecor* mark in the United Kingdom, the plaintiffs as publishers and the defendants as distributors, but the Court of Appeal held that it belonged to the defendants alone. The case is unusual in that neither party claimed any goodwill among ordinary customers (who purchased the posters without regard to their trade source), and retailers treated the defendants primarily as providers of a service, rather than goods. The *Scandecor* case may have been unusual, but it is not entirely unprecedented, since the successful defendants' arguments were as foreseen by Lord Phillimore in *Imperial Tobacco v Bonnan*.[36]

In *MedGen v Passion for Life Products*[37] the American claimant had developed a snoring preventative (*Snorenz*) for which it appointed the defendant as exclusive distributor in the United Kingdom, under a contract with no other express terms. After the defendants had marketed the product for 18 months, the parties fell out and each claimed to be the owner of the goodwill in relation to the name, and corresponding registered trade mark applications. The defendants discontinued selling *Snorenz* in favour of a new formulation of their own, to which they gave the name *Snoreeze*. MedGen sued for passing-off, claiming that *Snoreeze* and the get-up of its packaging was confusingly similar to *Snorenz*, and that MedGen owned the goodwill in relation to the latter.

Applying *Scandecor Development v Scandecor Marketing*,[38] the Deputy Judge held that the goodwill belonged to the defendant: *Snorenz* had not been sold by the claimants in the United Kingdom prior to the appointment of the defendants as distributors; it had been marketed under the name of Passion for Life and without use of MedGen's name; its packaging (except for an early batch of product in the original American packaging) also identified Passion for Life rather than MedGen; and press coverage treated it as a Passion for Life product. Except for one batch of 5,000 bottles in American packaging, there was nothing to connect the product in the public eye with anyone other than the defendants.

---

[32] The successful Swedish plaintiffs in *Manus (A/B) v R J Fullwood & Bland Ltd* (1949) 66 R.P.C. 71, CA gave their distributors, the defendants, the benefit of a similar covenant.
[33] *SA des Anciens Etablissements Panhard et Levassor v Panhard Levassor Motor Co Ltd* [1901] 2 Ch. 513; [1900–3] All E.R. 477; 18 R.P.C. 405.
[34] [1934] A.C. 82; 50 R.P.C. 379, PC.
[35] [1999] F.S.R. 26, CA, reversing [1998] F.S.R. 500 (Lloyd J.).
[36] [1924] A.C. 755, 760; 41 R.P.C. 441, PC.
[37] [2001] F.S.R. 30 (Kevin Garnett Q.C., Deputy Judge).
[38] [1999] F.S.R. 26, CA.

Manufacturers, importers, dealers and retailers

It is possible for a business which imports to have a goodwill in its capacity **3–131** as an importer, and likewise for any business which is known to obtain its goods from third parties to have a goodwill which reflects public trust in its ability to select or handle goods to a particular standard.[39] *Scandecor Development v Scandecor Marketing*[40] is now the prime example. This goodwill can co-exist with the goodwill of another business such as that of a manufacturer in the sense that the public may prefer goods manufactured by A and imported or otherwise handled by B to goods known to be manufactured by A but handled by another. This, however, is rare.

> "It is possible for an importer to get a valuable reputation for himself and his wares by his care in selection or his precautions as to transit and storage, or because his local character is such that the article acquires a value by his testimony to its genuineness; and if therefore goods, though of the same make, are passed off by competitors as being imported by him, he will have a right of action."[41]

The important point is that for the dealer, importer, etc. to have a cause of action in his capacity as such there must be a misrepresentation that the goods are his goods in some sense, and the misrepresentation must be a material one in that the public attach importance to who has imported, handled or otherwise dealt with the goods as opposed to who was responsible for their manufacture. If this is not the case, then the importer or dealer cannot be said to have any goodwill *quoad* the public and he can therefore have no *locus standi* to sue when goods are passed off as those he is accustomed to deal in, even if he suffers damage. This is so notwithstanding the fact that he may have handled all the goods of the proper claimant or that he may have the benefit of an exclusive agreement with the proper claimant.[42]

That there must be a particular close connection between the claimant **3–132** and the cause of action may be expressed in various ways, all of which lead to much the same result. One of these is to say that although every business handling goods has a goodwill with respect to those in a direct contractual relationship with it, the claimant in a passing-off action must be a business whose goodwill fulfils two essential requirements:

1. The goodwill supposed to be injured should relate specifically to the goods or services in question; and

2. It should be goodwill *vis-à-vis* the relevant public for those goods,

---

[39] *Hirsch v Jonas* (1876) 3 Ch. 584; *Dental Manufacturing Co Ltd v C de Trey & Co* [1912] 3 K.B. 76; 29 R.P.C. 557, CA.

[40] [1999] F.S.R. 26, CA.

[41] *per* Lord Phillimore in *Imperial Tobacco Co of India Ltd v Bonnan* [1924] A.C. 755, 760; 41 R.P.C. 441, PC. The importer's claim failed on the facts.

[42] As in *Poister Ltd v Marcel Fenez Ltd* [1965] R.P.C. 557, CA.

whether or not the public are the immediate customers of the claimant.

This may be illustrated by a simple example. An English trader well-known to the public by name instructs a foreign manufacturer to make goods to its specification and mark them with its name. The manufacturer ships them to England, where they need not even pass through the possession of the trader. They are distributed to retailers who sell them to the public. Quite clearly, the proper claimant is the named trader, the company with whose name the goods are marked. Every retailer selling the goods has a goodwill of his own, but although this is a goodwill which brings the custom of the public to his shop, rather than another shop round the corner, it has little or no relation to any of the specific lines of goods he sells. The foreign manufacturer may well have an English goodwill, but so far as it relates to these goods his goodwill extends to one customer only, the trader who commissioned the goods, and he has no goodwill with respect to the public at large. Even the carrier of the goods to the retailers has a goodwill as a carrier, but that neither relates specifically to the goods nor to the consuming public.

3–133   As Buckley L.J. observed in *Dental Manufacturing v de Trey*[43]:

"The plaintiff's goods need not be goods manufactured by the plaintiff. They may be goods which he purchases, or which he imports, or otherwise acquires, and which he sells under some 'get-up' which conveys that they are goods which, whether made, imported, or sold by him, carry with them the advantage of the reputation that the plaintiff's well-known firm are responsible for their quality or their character. I do not doubt that a person dealing with the goods of another may have a goodwill in the business of dealing with them. A carrier who carries the goods of others may have a goodwill in his business of carrier. An agent who is the agent for the sale of goods of others may have a goodwill in his agency business, and, as such agent, may have a 'get-up' whose reproduction may entitle him to succeed in a passing-off action."

If passing off occurs in the previous example then every business in the chain will be damaged, but it is only the named trader who has the right to sue. Conversely, if the goods had been marked with the name of a chain store, the only claimant would have been the retailer.

3–134   The South African case of *Premier Trading v Sportopia*[44] is inconclusive as to whether the goodwill in *Bladeline* for inline roller skates belonged to the Australian company which had originated the name, but in any event it did not belong to the local plaintiffs. The claim that *Bladeline* was distinctive of the latter rested on a predecessor, Jokari, having imported into South Africa from Taiwan a number of batches of counterfeit *Bladeline* skates with the name *Jokari* equally prominent. The Supreme Court of Appeal acknowledged that Jokari were not simply an inactive link in the chain through

---

[43] [1912] 3 K.B. 76, 88; 29 R.P.C. 557, CA.
[44] 2000 (3) S.A. 259 (SCA)

which the goods reached the public, and that they had their own stamp of identity for the goods, but at most this suggested that the *Jokari* component of the get-up was an importers' or distributors' mark which was being used coextensively with *Bladeline* as the manufacturers' mark. That gave Jokari no exclusive rights in *Bladeline*, and there was therefore no cause for complaint in the second defendant distributing what were in fact the *Bladeline* skates of the Australian manufacturer.

Manufacturer to retailer: examples

In *Richards v Butcher*[45] the plaintiffs had an exclusive contract with Heid- **3–135** sieck, a well-known champagne house, to sell their wine in England. The relevant marks were registered in the name of the producer and had been in use before the exclusive agreement was introduced. It was not alleged that the marks specifically denoted wine sent by Heidsieck to the English plaintiffs. Kay J. held as a preliminary point of law that even if the defendants were guilty of fraud in selling their wine as Heidsieck's the plaintiffs had no right to restrain them.[46]

In *Dental Manufacturing Co v de Trey*[47] the defendants to a claim for libel counterclaimed for passing-off. The defendants had been the exclusive agents for a patented American product and the plaintiffs had been their exclusive distributors. On expiry of the patent and the agreements the plaintiffs marketed a similar product not obtained from the American company or through the defendant. The Court of Appeal held that the get-up of the product was, at most, distinctive of the American manufacturer, that there was nothing to identify it with the defendants, and that on the facts the defendants had no cause of action for passing-off.

Dental Manufacturing Co v de Trey[48] was followed in the Canadian case of *Sheres v Texpol*.[49] The plaintiffs had imported sewing boxes from Poland to a design which had been modified to their requirements. The defendants commenced to import exact replicas. The Exchequer Court refused an interlocutory injunction. There was no reason to believe that the public identified the appearance of the boxes with any trade source at all, still less with the plaintiffs as importer. In South Africa a similar result was reached on the same authority in *Rusmarc v Hemdon*.[50] The plaintiffs had an exclusive distributorship for *Win* cigarette lighters in the Republic. The defendants imported lighters with an identical get-up. Despite admitting survey evidence to the effect that the get-up was distinctive, Coetzee J. refused relief.

When goods are manufactured to the order of a trader it is rather easier to **3–136**

---

[45] [1891] 2 Ch. 540; 8 R.P.C. 249 (Kay J.).
[46] And see *Goodfellow v Prince* (1887) 35 Ch.D. 9, CA where the point is obscured by the fact that there was insufficient use of the mark in England to make it distinctive of anyone. See also *Van Zeller v Mason, Catley & Co* (1907) 25 R.P.C. 37.
[47] [1912] 3 K.B. 76; 29 R.P.C. 557, CA.
[48] Above.
[49] (1969) 58 C.P.R. 136.
[50] 1975 (4) S.A. 625.

conclude that the goodwill belongs to that trader rather than to the actual manufacturer. If so, then the former can change his source of supply whilst continuing to use the same marks for the goods from the new source, and the manufacturer cannot use those marks in dealing with third parties during or after termination of the relationship.[51]

In *Defries v Electric & Ordnance*[52] the American plaintiffs had made lamps to the special order of the defendants' predecessors in business, who had sold them under their own name. The defendants kept the name but changed their source of supply, and the plaintiffs entered the English market under the same brand name. The plaintiffs' action was dismissed and an injunction granted to the defendants on their counterclaim.

The opposite result is likely to be reached if the manufacturer alone is held out as the source of the goods. In *Hirsch v Jonas*[53] the plaintiff, a cigar dealer, had a label designed for him and instructed Genir, his supplier, to use it on the cigars consigned to him. Genir did so, but in such a way as to identify the cigars as being of his own manufacture with no reference to the plaintiff. For some time Hirsch was the only customer for cigars with that label. Genir then supplied the same cigars under the same label to the defendant. Jessel M.R. refused an interlocutory injunction. There was nothing in the mark to displace the impression it created that it denoted cigars manufactured by Genir and show instead that it denoted ones selected by Hirsch.

Parent and subsidiary; corporate groups

3–137 Corporate groups for present purposes are groups of companies ultimately under common ownership or control which are held out to the public in such a way as to emphasise that the group is a single enterprise. Groups of companies also exist, for instance in the consumer goods, tobacco and spirits trades, in which the individuality of the different trading companies is emphasised and the fact that they form part of a larger group is more or less suppressed. This paragraph is of little relevance to them, nor to diverse conglomerates trading in many fields or under many distinct names or brands.

Corporate groups are no exception to the rule that goodwill as legal property must necessarily be owned by some identifiable person. It is meaningless to speak of legal property which is not owned by anyone, or which is supposed to be distributed among a group of persons who do not own it individually, as joint tenants or as tenants in common. It is not often necessary to decide how goodwill is divided between the companies in the group, because intra-group disputes are unlikely to arise and in suing third parties it is normal to join as claimants every company with a plausible stake in the goodwill infringed.

The Court of Appeal has recently reasserted the importance of the dis-

---

[51] *Vokes (CG) Ltd v Evans* (1931) 49 R.P.C. 140.
[52] (1906) 23 R.P.C. 341 (Joyce J.).
[53] (1876) 3 Ch. D. 584 (Jessel M.R.).

tinction between parent and subsidiary in *Scandecor Development v Scandecor Marketing*:[54]

> "There is no rule of law or presumption of fact that the goodwill generated by the trading activities of a wholly owned subsidiary company belongs to the parent company or is the subject of an implied, if not an express, licence in favour of the subsidiary. It may happen, as observed by Oliver L.J. in *Habib Bank Ltd v Habib Bank AG Zurich*, that the goodwill in a mark is 'shared' in the sense that an internationally known business based abroad, which establishes a branch in this country as part of that international organisation, does not cease to be entitled to its existing goodwill because there is also a goodwill in the local branch. In that situation it would be correct to assert that the international organisation retains its existing 'international' goodwill and that the newly created branch or subsidiary company has a local goodwill in the business carried on by it in this country, at the very least for the purpose of protecting it against injury by third parties."

Rights of parent and subsidiary *inter se*

Subsidiaries are frequently given virtually the same name as their parents **3–138** and sister companies. This confuses the issue of ownership of goodwill, because although the public may identify the source of goods as X, they are unlikely to distinguish by name between the parent X Inc or X plc, and its subsidiary X Ltd. By establishing a subsidiary under a particular name the parent self-evidently confers rights of some kind on it. What is questionable are conclusions such as those sometimes previously reached that the rights of the subsidiary automatically prevail over those of the parent, or, conversely, that the goodwill generated by the trading activities of the subsidiary automatically belongs to the parent. Conclusions such as these cannot be deduced from the parent-subsidiary relationship as such. If the use of the name by the subsidiary is pursuant to a contract term, whether express or implied, then one must look to the contract to see whether the right to use the name is conditional or unconditional, permanent or revocable, exclusive or non-exclusive.[55] Otherwise, one must look to all the relevant facts.

Early cases involving parents and their subsidiaries gave full effect to the doctrine of the corporate veil. The subsidiary was treated as a legally separate entity to the parent which could acquire goodwill in its own name and even assert that goodwill against its parent in a passing-off action. Whether it was the subsidiary or the parent which owned the relevant goodwill depended on the same factors as for businesses in separate ownership, in particular the capacity in which the subsidiary was held out, and what contribution it made to manufacturing.

It may be doubted whether this strict approach entirely corresponds to **3–139**

---

[54] [1999] F.S.R. 26, CA.

[55] *Dawnay Day & Co Ltd v Cantor Fitzgerald International* [2000] R.P.C. 669, CA.

reality. Parent and subsidiary do not simply stand in an arm's length relationship with one another as if they were totally separate businesses. Although the principle remains that either the subsidiary or the parent may be the legal owner of the relevant goodwill, the consequences of this may have to be qualified. In *Habib Bank v Habib Bank AG Zurich*[56] Oliver L.J. observed:

"Where an internationally known business establishes a branch in this country through a limited company, either incorporated here or abroad, it may be that technically the goodwill and reputation of that business 'belongs' to the limited company in the sense that the company may be the proper and only plaintiff in an action taken here to protect it. But it does not cease to be the goodwill and reputation of the international business because it is also the goodwill and reputation of the local branch. And that reputation inures, as it seems to me, equally in any other local branch which the international business may set up in the same place...

[T]here lies the notion [in the plaintiff's arguments] that even in the case of an international group in the sense used above, once there has been established here a corporate entity making use of their goodwill, the goodwill becomes a localised asset forming part of the exclusive property of the corporate entity, and can be attached to another corporate entity established by the international body only by some transfer from the original user in this country, for instance, by assignment or licence express or implied. For my part I think that that displays an unduly and unjustifiably formalist approach to the matter and to be an approach which ignores both substance and reality."

This now has to be read in the light of *Scandecor Development v Scandecor Marketing*,[57] and *Dawnay Day v Cantor Fitzgerald.*[58] As a matter of common sense one might expect the situation epitomised in the latter, especially, to be more common than that found to exist in *Habib Bank v Habib Bank AG Zurich* itself.

3–140   So far as the older cases are concerned, in *Adrema*[59] the English subsidiary of a German office equipment company had acted mainly as the importer of goods manufactured by its parent but had concealed, as far as possible, their German origins and its own status. At first instance in an action by the German company against the Custodian of Enemy Property Lloyd-Jacob J. held that it was the subsidiary that had always owned the English goodwill. On appeal, the Court of Appeal found it unnecessary to decide the point because even if the German company had previously owned the goodwill, it had been appropriated. In a passing-off action brought by the English company (under its new owners) against the German company the German

---

[56] [1981] 1 W.L.R. 1265 at 1278; [1981] 2 All E.R. 650; [1982] R.P.C. 1, CA.
[57] [1999] F.S.R. 26, CA.
[58] [2000] R.P.C. 669, CA.
[59] *Adrema Machinebau GmbH v Custodian of Enemy Property* (1954) 71 R.P.C. 197; affirmed [1957] R.P.C. 49, CA; *Adrema Ltd v Adrema Werke GmbH* [1958] R.P.C. 323.

company admitted that the goodwill had always belonged to its subsidiary. Although the point was therefore not in issue Dankwerts J. clearly agreed.

Conversely, in *Reuter v Mulhens*[60] the parent company had apparently owned the goodwill in England because it, rather than its subsidiary, was identified as responsible for the quality of the goods. Before the Second World War the defendant, the German proprietor of the old-established *4711* Eau de Cologne business, had carried on business in England through the plaintiffs, an almost wholly-owned subsidiary company. As well as importing finished products the subsidiary had carried out certain manufacturing operations (in a factory owned, but not operated, by the Germans) using essences imported from Germany, where they were made up according to a secret formula. The German connection was emphasised. All the English assets of the defendant were seized under wartime legislation and the shares in the plaintiffs were assigned to a third party. On a counterclaim for passing-off the Court of Appeal held that the defendant had no English goodwill. It was not strictly necessary to decide whether the goodwill had been owned by the German parent or its subsidiary, but Romer L.J. was prepared to say that the German defendant had possessed a goodwill in England before 1939 and could have sued for passing-off.

The facts were comparable in the Australian case of *Bayer v Henry Yorke*.[61] The plaintiffs were formerly the Australian subsidiary of the famous German Bayer group, but since the War had been owned by Sterling Drug. Both before the War and after they had traded on the worldwide reputation of the original Bayer company to a degree which amounted to systematic misrepresentation once the connection with the German company had ceased. The defendants imported a medicine made by the German company and marked with the Bayer cross. Myers J. held for the defendants on the ground that the Bayer cross had been distinctive of the German company before the War and the plaintiffs' way of trading since then had reinforced that state of affairs. In terms of goodwill, the parent rather than the subsidiary was the owner prior to the War. Although the goodwill must therefore have been enemy property, it does not appear to have been confiscated or assigned to the plaintiffs.[62]

Multinational groups and parallel imports

It is common for a multinational group to have at least one subsidiary in **3–141** every country in which it trades on a sufficiently large scale. Whether the goodwill in a particular country belongs to the local subsidiary, its immediate parent, or a company further up in the hierarchy, is primarily a matter of fact. If the local subsidiary imports and is known simply as a dealer, the likelihood is that it will not own any material goodwill. Within certain limits, however, there is much the group can do to ensure that the company of choice owns the goodwill in any particular country, whether by

---

[60] (1953) 70 R.P.C. 235, CA.
[61] [1964] F.S.R. 143 (Myers J., NSW).
[62] It is notable that these three cases, and *Habib Bank Ltd v Habib Bank AG Zurich* [1981] 1 W.L.R. 1265; [1981] 2 All E.R. 650; [1982] R.P.C. 1, CA, involved expropriation.

influencing the public state of mind, or by arranging for the contractual reassignment of goodwill within the group. Only that company will have the right to sue third parties for passing-off.[63]

Although goodwill is in principle owned by individual companies in the group, and can be transferred from one to another, reputation is normally of the group as a whole. Reputation is a state of fact. It is wholly dependent on the state of the public mind. Unlike goodwill, it is not the subject of ownership or capable of voluntary transfer. The public is unlikely to know or care how the group allocates its business internally: so far as they are concerned there might just as well be one single company. The house marks used by the group are unlikely to be recognised as denoting any single company within it. They are distinctive of the group as such.

One consequence of this is that there is nothing deceptive in the group arranging and re-arranging the functions and ownership of its trading companies as it chooses. "No purchaser knows or cares whether REVLON FLEX is made in Wales by a Venezuelan company or in New York by a Delaware corporation."[64] What matters to the customer is that the product originates from somewhere in the group.

3–142   Although the group may validly have arranged for its English subsidiary to own the English goodwill corresponding to the business it does in England, it does not follow that there will be passing-off if goods produced by another company in the group are imported without the authority of the English subsidiary. In general, the law of passing-off prevents parallel imports (in the wider sense) only when the imported goods are inferior to those normally on the local market or differ from those in a significant way which would not be apparent to the uninstructed purchaser. The purchaser generally wants the goods of the group itself, rather than a particular company within it, so there is no misrepresentation inherent in supplying goods which have indeed come from the group.

There are cases in which parallel imports have gone unrestrained because proceedings were brought by independent distributors or local subsidiaries with no interest in the relevant goodwill at all. In strict logic, such claimants could not even have sued counterfeiters.[65] This should not obscure the fact that even if such companies do own the goodwill, there must also be a material misrepresentation to restrain. Conversely, the fact that parallel imports may have been allowed in a particular case does not necessarily mean that the claimant had no goodwill.

In *Imperial Tobacco Co of India v Bonnan*[66] the world-wide business of the former Imperial Tobacco Group had been divided, with the plaintiffs taking over the Indian market but continuing to act simply as distributors for the United Kingdom company. There was an agreement to assign the Indian business to the plaintiffs, although no assignment as such had been executed. The defendant imported into India cigarettes manufactured by the

---

[63] *Imperial Tobacco Co of India Ltd v Bonnan* [1924] A.C. 755; 41 R.P.C. 441, PC; *Habib Bank Ltd v Habib Bank AG Zurich* [1981] 1 W.L.R. 1265; [1981] 2 All E.R. 650; [1982] R.P.C. 1, CA.
[64] *per* Templeman L.J. in *Revlon Inc v Cripps & Lee Ltd* [1980] F.S.R. 85, CA.
[65] *Star Industrial Co Ltd v Yap Kwee Kor* [1976] F.S.R. 256, PC.
[66] [1924] A.C. 755 at 763; 41 R.P.C. 441, PC.

English company and originally sold to the British Army. The Privy Council found for the defendant. That the decision turned on the absence of any material misrepresentation rather than on *locus standi* may be seen from the following:

"It is not as if the Respondents were attempting to pass off as *Wills' Gold Flake* cigarettes stuff not manufactured by the lawful successors in title of W.D. & H.O. Wills. Any such attempt would be at once restrained at the suit of the lawful successors; and in India and for India the Appellant company would be the lawful successors."

Fiduciary relationships

A person who stands in a fiduciary relationship to another cannot benefit **3–143** himself at the expense of the person to whom he owes fiduciary obligations. In particular, any property he wrongfully acquires will be held on trust, including the goodwill in a business carried on by him in breach of this obligation.

In *New Zealand Netherlands Society "Oranje" v Kuys*[67] the plaintiff (respondent), while the secretary of the defendant association, founded a newspaper called the *Windmill Post* directed at the expatriate Dutchmen in New Zealand who made up the defendants' membership. On leaving the employment of the defendants he continued to publish it but the defendants started a competing paper themselves. The Privy Council held that the defendants had specifically consented to the plaintiff starting the paper as a venture of his own and that this displaced the fiduciary duty which would otherwise have resulted in the plaintiff holding the paper on trust.

Apart from *New Zealand Netherlands Society "Oranje" v Kuys* there is **3–144** very little express authority on fiduciary obligations in the context of passing-off, if only because such relationships are comparatively rare in a commercial context. In *Accumulator Industries v Vandervell*[68] the plaintiffs were refused an interlocutory injunction restraining the defendants from making use of testimonials received while they had been exclusive distributors of the plaintiffs' goods. Eve J. asked whether the relationship was a fiduciary one, and concluded that it was not so because the defendants were not agents as such. In *Fleetwood Mac v Clifford Davis*[69] the manager of a pop group was treated as having broken fiduciary obligations to the plaintiffs, but the grant of the injunction did not depend on this.

Allegations of unfair competition and breach of fiduciary duties failed in the Australian case of *Moorgate Tobacco v Philip Morris*.[70] Still in Australia, Lehane J. held in *C-shirt v Barnett Marketing and Management*[71] that the

---

[67] [1974] R.P.C. 272, PC.
[68] (1911) 29 R.P.C. 391 (Eve J.).
[69] [1975] F.S.R. 150 (Goff J.).
[70] (1984) 156 C.L.R. 414; 59 A.J.L.R. 77; 56 A.L.R. 193; 3 I.P.R. 545; [1985] R.P.C. 219 (High Court of Australia). See also *Hospital Products Ltd v US Surgical Corp* (1984) 156 C.L.R. 41 (High Court of Australia).
[71] (1996) 37 I.P.R. 315 (Lehane J.).

distributor of the plaintiffs' sun-protective clothing for children had not owed any fiduciary obligations to the latter. That the defendant had lied to the plaintiff about secret plans to introduce a rival product of its own, and had thereby kept the distributorship contract going until its own product was well-established, was only relevant to the claim for deceit.

Employer and employee

3–145　In general, an employee does not acquire any interest in the goodwill of the business in which he is employed. The goodwill accrues solely to the business as such, not to the individuals who work for it.

The personal defendant in *Asprey & Garrard v WRA (Guns) Ltd and Asprey*[72] was a member of the Asprey family which had owned the claimant until 1995, and had previously worked for the claimant company, but in neither capacity did he have any right to share in the claimant's goodwill:

> "The goodwill generated by the previous six generations of Aspreys previous to William Asprey, trading for two centuries and more, unquestionably belongs to the claimants. No doubt that was reflected in the price paid in 1995 to the Asprey family for their shares in the claimant. Any goodwill resulting from William Asprey's work for the claimant as its employee also belongs to the claimant and he cannot properly seek to associate any business in which he is now interested with the claimant's goodwill. Of course the fact that he has established personal contacts whilst so employed cannot be taken from him and in the absence of a restrictive covenant restraining him from making use of such contracts he is free to do so. But what he cannot do by reason of the law of passing off is to present any business in which he is now interested as in some way associated with that of the claimant."[73]

3–146　To the same effect, in *Kingston Miller v Kingston (Thomas) & Co. Ltd*[74] Thomas Kingston had left the employment of the plaintiffs and founded a rival company of which he became managing director. He claimed (as a precondition to making out the own-name defence as then understood) that as a result of his employment with the plaintiffs he had a goodwill which he could assign to the defendant company. Warrington J. found for the plaintiffs:

> "[H]e had nothing in the nature of a goodwill. So far as his exertions and his skill have contributed to the success of the business of the plaintiff company, the advantage of that is theirs. The goodwill, or that part of their goodwill, which is made up of the reputation of Thomas Kingston, is their goodwill and not his."

[72] [2001] EWCA Civ 1499; [2002] E.T.M.R. 47; [2002] F.S.R. 31, CA.
[73] *per* Peter Gibson L.J. (delivering the judgment of the Court).
[74] [1912] 1 Ch. 575, 582; 29 R.P.C. 289 (Warrington J.).

The principle applies even to a "one-man" business. In *Globelegance v Sarkissian*[75] the proper plaintiff was one such company which employed the designer known as *Valentino*, not Valentino himself, even though the goodwill of the company depended entirely on his talent and reputation.[76] In *Irvine v Talksport*[77] the defendants' argument that the merchandising activities of the claimant racing driver were carried out entirely through companies was met by joining them as additional claimants.

The principle stated is capable of leading to hard results. In *Balden v* **3–147** *Shorter*[78] the plaintiff had been a salesman with the defendant's predecessor in business, but had left when the former company went into liquidation and the defendant bought the name and goodwill. Maugham J. held that there was no liability for injurious falsehood when customer of the old company placed an order with the defendant on the express understanding that the plaintiff was still employed by them and would receive the commission. The mistake was a careless but honest one, so there was no malice. Passing-off was not argued, and although the customer in question completely relied on the plaintiff as an individual, it could not be said that the latter had any goodwill. *Joyce v Sengupta*[79] confirms that an employee or prospective employee has sufficient pecuniary interest in his capacity as such to maintain an action for injurious falsehood, but this is not to say that the employee has any goodwill in the technical sense, and it applies irrespective of whether the employer (in *Joyce's* case a member of the Royal Family) is a trader with goodwill or not.

Writers and publishers; artists and impresarios

An exception to the foregoing rule may exist in the case of writers, artists, **3–148** performers and the like. The goodwill associated with the name, real or assumed, under which the individual produces his work has been said *prima facie* to belong to the individual,[80] rather than to any publisher, impresario or even employer through whom the work reaches the public. This rule was originally developed in the context of authors and performers who were independent contractors rather than employees, and in that connection is satisfactory. Its application to pen names or performing names used by employees is more questionable, and seems to have occurred without recourse to basic principles. The cases are presented here as an internally consistent but partly anomalous collection.

In *Franke v Chappel*[81] Chitty J. dismissed as absurd a claim that *Richter Concerts* meant concerts produced by the plaintiff, as opposed to concerts

---

[75] [1974] R.P.C. 603 (Templeman J.).
[76] See also *Oranje v Kuys* [1974] R.P.C. 272, PC; *Frankau (Adolph) & Co v Pflueger* (1910) 28 R.P.C. 130.
[77] [2003] EWCA Civ 423; [2003] 2 All E.R. 881; [2003] E.M.L.R. 26, CA affirming [2002] EWHC 367; [2002] 1 W.L.R. 2355; [2002] All E.R. 414; [2002] E.M.L.R. 32; [2002] F.S.R. 60 (Laddie J.) as to liability.
[78] [1933] Ch. 427 (Maugham J.).
[79] [1993] 1 W.L.R. 337, CA.
[80] *Landa v Greenberg* (1908) 24 T.L.R. 441 (Eve J.).
[81] (1887) 57 L.T. 141; 3 T.L.R. 524 (Chitty J.).

conducted by Dr Richter. Dr Richter was free to transfer his services to the defendants under the same name. In *Landa v Greenberg*[82] the plaintiff contributed a column to the *Jewish Chronicle* under the name *Aunt Naomi*. Eve J. held that it was she who was entitled to it on her contract being terminated. She does not appear to have been an employee, although her duties went beyond those of a normal contributor into performing some editorial and managerial functions. In *Hepworth v Ryott*[83] the Court of Appeal dealt with a dispute between a film actor and his former employers by striking down a term preventing him from using his performing name *Stewart Roome* without their permission as being in unreasonable restraint of trade. Astbury J. at first instance would also have refused to enforce the contract as "tyrannous and oppressive". The House of Lords granted an injunction to a newspaper cartoonist in *Marengo v Daily Sketch*.[84] The defendants published the work of another cartoonist with a similar signature.[85]

3–149   The plaintiff in *Hines v Winnick*[86] was employed[87] by the defendant as the conductor of a band which had broadcast on the BBC as *Dr Crock and his Crackpots*. He obtained an injunction against the defendant producing programmes with another conductor billed as *Dr Crock*. *Dr Crock* meant the plaintiff personally, not the conductor of the band for the time being. In *Modern Fiction v Fawcett*[88] there were cross actions by an author and his publisher as to who could use the pseudonym *Ben Sarto*. Romer J. found for the author, and granted an injunction against the publisher using the name for books by any other author. The publisher had suggested and perhaps commissioned the series, but the relationship was not one of master and servant.

Employed journalists have prevailed against their newspaper proprietors in *Forbes v Kemsley Newspapers*[89] and *Sykes v John Fairfax*.[90] In the former case, the *Sunday Times* published a weekly series of articles written by the plaintiff over a period of five years under the pseudonym *Mary Delane*. Wynn-Parry J. held that the plaintiff was *prima facie* entitled to ownership of the pseudonym in the absence of agreement to the contrary, and an attempt by the newspaper to find an implied term in its favour in her contract of employment failed. The few weekly articles in the series not written by Mrs Forbes had been published under other names. However, in *Sykes v John Fairfax* the plaintiff journalist was successful although his investment column *Pierpont Speaking* in the *Australian Financial Review* had continued to be published under the pseudonym *Pierpont* on several occasions when it

---

[82] (1908) 24 T.L.R. 441 (Eve J.).

[83] [1920] 1 Ch. 1, CA.

[84] [1948] 1 All E.R. 406; 65 R.P.C. 242, HL.

[85] "*Kem*" and "*Kim*".

[86] [1947] Ch. 708; [1947] 2 All E.R. 517; 64 R.P.C. 113 (Vaisey J.).

[87] The word seems to be used in the sense of "retained". The plaintiff personally was held to own the copyright in his sketches, an unlikely result if he was employed under a contract of service.

[88] (1949) 66 R.P.C. 230 (Romer J.).

[89] (1951) 68 R.P.C. 183 (Wynn-Parry J.).

[90] [1977] 1 N.S.W.L.R. 415: [1978] F.S.R. 312.

had not been written by him. This happened once during a four-month period when he had worked on another newspaper and the column had been written by fellow employees; and during several shorter periods when he had been on leave and he had nominated another journalist (not an employee of the defendants) to take his place. *Pierpont,* the invention of the plaintiff, was depicted as an elderly, portly, rich bon vivant, airing his views with a crusty humour. In welcome contrast to some of the English authorities, Helsham C.J. in Eq. approached the issue of ownership by asking if the *nom-de-plume* was associated by readers with a particular author, even though they might be unaware of his real identity. The plaintiff was helped by the fact that the defendants had published a caricature of the plaintiff as that of Pierpont, in one case with the caption "Pierpont, alias Tony Sykes". Once again, an attempt by the publishers to find an implied contractual term in their favour failed.

Similar considerations apply when one is dealing solely with the title of a **3–150** feature rather than the name or pen name under which it is written, but the inference is more readily drawn that the title does not denote any particular author. In *Lovatt v Consolidated Magazines*[91] the compiler of a crossword puzzle and the publisher of the magazine in which it regularly appeared each claimed to be entitled to exclusive use of its title *Colossus.* Wilcox J. said:

> "A pseudonym is a direct reference to the author, so that continuity in the use of a pseudonym tends to suggest continuity in the identity of the author. In contrast, the title given to a regular feature of a magazine or of a newspaper is a reference to that feature. Members of the public are familiar with the notion that the authorship of particular features in a magazine or in a newspaper changes from time to time. During his or her incumbency a particular author, or editor, of a feature may become well known to readers; but the readers would not normally expect that the feature will close down, or the title will be changed, if someone else takes over responsibility for it."

On the facts, the title of the crossword puzzle had not come to denote either party.

Partnership and joint ventures

Cases in which the owner of goodwill was a firm were familiar in the **3–151** nineteenth century, before incorporation became common. The House of Lords in *Leather Cloth Co v American Leather Cloth Co*[92] accepted that partners might succeed one another without affecting the firm's ownership of its name and trade marks:

> "[B]y the usage of trade, the name of a firm is understood not to be confined to those who first adopted it, but to extend to and include

[91] (1988) 12 I.P.R. 261 (Wilcox J., Federal Court).
[92] (1865) 11 E.R. 1435, HL.

213

persons who have afterwards been introduced as partners, or persons to whom the original partners have transferred their business. The name of the firm continues to be used in many cases long after all the original traders have died, or ceased to have any interest in the concern, as in the great banking houses of *Child* and of *Coutts*, and many other mercantile houses .... For the same reason, the use of the old trade mark of the firm by the new partners, or their successors ... is no fraud upon the public; it is only a statement that the goods are the goods of the firm whose trade mark they bear."

The Court of Appeal in *Pinto v Badman*[93] rejected as unduly technical an objection by the defendant that only one of two (or more) partners had sued, although they found for the defendant on other grounds. In *Trego v Hunt*[94] the House of Lords gave effect, as between the parties themselves, to a provision in a partnership deed providing that the goodwill of the firm was to be the sole property of one of the partners.

3–152   Pop groups and the like may have legal status as companies,[95] but if not, they are likely to constitute a partnership between the performers.[96] In *Byford v Oliver*[97] Laddie J. held that the heavy metal pop group *Saxon* had originally been a partnership at will when founded in the late 1970s. Since that time, members had come and gone, with Mr Byford being the only founder member still performing in it. The two defendants, Oliver and Dawson, had left and joined other bands. The goodwill in relation to the name *Saxon* was an asset of the partnership as such, and the former members had no continuing right to use it, still less to claim a right to its exclusive use against the current band by virtue of a trade mark application.

Professional partnerships and pop groups apart, true joint ownership of goodwill is uncommon. Joint ventures are normally carried on through *ad hoc* companies, which will own the goodwill in the relevant business, as in *Dawnay Day v Cantor Fitzgerald*.[98] The fact that more than one enterprise may be involved in the process by which goods or services reach the public does not mean that the goodwill in that business is shared between them. Such a result was reached (with some reluctance) by Lindsay J. in *Growmax v Don & Low*,[99] and by Lloyd J. at trial in *Scandecor Development v Scandecor Marketing*,[1] but in the latter the Court of Appeal noted its inconvenience and discouraged it for the future.

A possible example of a joint venture as such is to be found in *Shell-Mex*

[93] (1891) 8 R.P.C. 181, CA.
[94] [1896] A.C. 7, HL.
[95] As in *Fleetwood Mac Promotions Ltd v Clifford Davis Management Ltd* [1975] F.S.R. 150.
[96] See also *Wright v Morris* (1990) [1997] F.S.R. 218, CA (*Paper Lace*—reported solely on striking out for want of prosecution; [1999] E.M.L.R. 233, CA (*The Smiths*). In *Sutherland v V2 Music Ltd* [2002] EWHC 14; [2002] E.M.L.R. 28 (*Liberty*) the two groups were entirely unrelated.
[97] [2003] EWHC 295; [2003] E.M.L.R. 20 (Laddie J.), distinguishing *Burchell v Wilde* [1900] 1 Ch. 551, CA.
[98] [2000] R.P.C. 669, CA.
[99] [1999] R.P.C. 367 (Lindsay J.).
[1] [1999] F.S.R. 26, CA, reversing [1998] F.S.R. 500 (Lloyd J.).

& *BP and Aladdin Industries v Holmes*[2] in which an oil manufacturer and a lamp manufacturer set up jointly to supply paraffin oil under the mark already used by the second plaintiffs for their lamps and heaters. In reality, the arrangement seems to have been more in the nature of a licence from the second plaintiffs to the first, in which the second plaintiffs provided the pink dye and exercised quality control. The two successfully sued together for passing-off, their *locus standi* being conceded by the defence at trial.

Two cases from the nineteenth century show a willingness to allow actions **3–153** by one of several independent owners of a business, formerly under common ownership, which has had its goodwill severed.

In *Dent v Turpin*[3] EJ Dent, a watchmaker, died and left two of his three places of business to his stepson Frederick and the third to his stepson Richard. The administratrix of the estate of Frederick sued a third party who marked his watches "*Dent, London*". A demurrer arguing that the action could not succeed without Richard Dent joining as co-plaintiff was rejected by Page-Wood V.C. The one plaintiff could sue in her own right for an injunction and delivery up, and for an apportioned account of profits on the infringing articles.

In *Southorn v Reynolds*[4] two brothers manufactured tobacco pipes independently in the village of Broseley where their father had founded the business and made the name *Southorn's Broseley Pipes* famous. The defendant, a pipe manufacturer in London, took into his employment another man of the name of Southorn who came from Broseley and on the strength of that marked his pipes "Reynolds' purified clay pipes, made by Southorn, from Broseley". Page-Wood V.C. granted one brother an injunction, although the other brother (who had apparently taken over the father's factory) had not joined in the suit.

The *Drinks Cases* and actionable misdescriptions

Dent v Turpin[5] and *Southorn v Reynolds*[6] are of greater importance because **3–154** they provided authority for the first of the *Drinks Cases, Bollinger v Costa Brava*[7] in which Dankwerts J. held that every Champagne exporting company had a joint and several right to sue for misuse of the term *Champagne*. This was followed in the *Sherry*[8] and *Whisky*[9] cases, and approved by the House of Lords in *Advocaat*.[10]

---

[2] (1937) 54 R.P.C. 287 (Luxmoore J.).
[3] (1861) 70 E.R. 1003 (Page-Wood V.C.), applied in *Bollinger v Costa Brava Wine Co Ltd* [1960] Ch. 262; [1959] 3 All E.R. 800; [1960] R.P.C. 16. as was the following case.
[4] (1865) 12 L.T. 75 (Page-Wood V.C.).
[5] (1861) 70 E.R. 1003 (Page-Wood V.C.).
[6] (1865) 12 L.T. 75 (Page-Wood V.C.).
[7] [1960] Ch. 262; [1959] 3 All E.R. 800; [1969] R.P.C. 16 for the preliminary point of law. At trial [1961] 1 W.L.R. 277; [1961] 1 All E.R. 561; [1961] R.P.C. 116 (Danckwerts J.).
[8] [1967] R.P.C. 193; [1966] F.S.R. 426 (Cross J.).
[9] *Walker (John) & Sons Ltd v Henry Ost & Co Ltd* [1970] 1 W.L.R. 917; [1970] 2 All E.R. 106; [1970] R.P.C. 489; *John Walker & Sons Ltd v Douglas McGibbon & Co* [1975] R.P.C. 506.
[10] *Erven Warnink BV v J Townend & Sons (Hull) Ltd* [1979] A.C. 731; [1979] 2 All E.R. 927; [1980] R.P.C. 31, HL.

It has been conventional to say that all those entitled for the time being to use terms such as *Champagne, Sherry, Whisky* or *Advocaat* for their products share in the goodwill attaching to those terms. To this extent the goodwill might be said to be held in common, though with the proviso that such goodwill cannot in any meaningful sense be severed and no existing user can prevent any number of newcomers sharing in it if they satisfy certain objective criteria. However, this analysis is only necessary because of the historical tendency to view passing-off as protecting the goodwill associated with a particular name or mark. With passing-off recognised as protecting the claimant's goodwill in his business as such, there is no conceptual difficulty in finding the other essential element of misrepresentation in the defendant's use of a name or mark which is not exclusive to the claimant. This would be consistent with *Chocosuisse v Cadbury*[11] in which a cause of action was denied to the trade association of Swiss chocolate manufacturers, although two individual manufacturers, Lindt and Suchard, succeeded on the facts.

J. DEALINGS WITH GOODWILL

Transmissibility of goodwill

3–155 Goodwill is personal property and can pass by voluntary assignment, under a will or intestacy, or by operation of law. English goodwill is the creature of English law and has no more independent existence than a patent or copyright. It can therefore only be dealt with according to transactions recognised by English law.[12] The most important restriction is that goodwill cannot be assigned or otherwise dealt with in gross, but must remain in the same ownership as the business to which it relates.

> "[A]ssuming ... that the Plaintiff company had a goodwill in England ... that goodwill was a piece or species of property locally situate here, and could be dealt with effectively only by some transaction which, according to our law, the English Courts must recognise."[13]

An assignment of goodwill does not have to be in writing or any particular form, and need not mention goodwill by name. A transaction intended to assign a business as a whole necessarily passes the goodwill to the assignee. A transaction which purports to deal with specific brands or marks may be interpreted as dealing with the goodwill of the business in which they are used. It should be remembered that in construing commercial agreements the golden rule is to give effect to the common intention of the parties as

---

[11] [1999] E.T.M.R. 1020; [1999] R.P.C. 826, CA.
[12] *per* Lord Macnaghten in *Inland Revenue Commissioners v Muller & Co's Margarine Ltd* [1901] A.C. 217, HL.
[13] *per* Lord Evershed M.R. in *Adrema Maschinenbau GmbH v Custodian of Enemy Property* [1957] R.P.C. 49, CA.

expressed in the words they have chosen to use, and to that extent words such as "goodwill" may be used in a variety of ways at variance with their strict legal meaning. For an example of the meaning of "goodwill" in a will see *Re Jacobson (dec'd)*.[14]

In *Wood v Hall*[15] the defendant, a wine and spirit merchant, assigned his **3–156** business and property (including the goodwill) to a trustee for the benefit of his creditors and the trustee sold the brands and trade marks to the plaintiff. The goodwill was not mentioned by name. After being employed by the plaintiff for a period the defendant set up in business on his own account again and claimed he was entitled to use his old trading name because the plaintiff had only purchased specific marks and not the goodwill in the former business as a whole. Younger J. found for the plaintiff.

In view of the fact that living writers undoubtedly have a cause of action in respect of work not of their own authorship being passed off as theirs, and that goodwill survives death and is transmissible by will or on intestacy, it was surely right for Lloyd J. to treat with a certain amount of scepticism submissions to the effect that the trustees of the estate of the late James Joyce had no goodwill or *locus standi* in relation to the novel *Ulysses*, though in the event he found for the defendants on other grounds: *Sweeney v Macmillan Publishers*.[16] The argument that the trustees did not make or sell any books themselves is misconceived: Alan Clark (like almost every other author) did not print or publish his own works, but it was he who was responsible for their literary content, and it was he (rather than his publishers) who could sue the *Evening Standard*.[17]

Assignments in gross

An assignment in gross can take two forms. The more common is for the **3–157** owner of goodwill to purport to grant to a third party the bare right to use a mark which is distinctive of the assignor, there being no connection between the two which would justify its use by the assignee.[18] The less common is for the assignor to purport to assign his goodwill in whole or in part without the assignee taking over any relevant interest in the business to which the goodwill related. An example is to be found in *Barnsley Brewery Co Ltd v RBNB*[19] in which the goodwill and name of the former *Barnsley Bitter* were purportedly assigned to the plaintiffs 20 years after the relevant business had been discontinued. Both categories of transaction are regarded at common law as being inherently deceptive. They are consequently ineffective to

---

[14] [1970] V.R. 180.
[15] (1915) 33 R.P.C. 16 (Younger J.).
[16] [2002] R.P.C. 25 (Lloyd J.).
[17] *Clark v Associated Newspapers* [1998] R.P.C. 261; [1988] 1 W.L.R. 1558; [1998] 1 All E.R. 959 (Lightman J.).
[18] As in *Pinto v Badman* (1891) 8 R.P.C. 181, CA; *Thorneloe v Hill* [1894] 1 Ch. 569; [1891–4] All E.R. 1263.
[19] [1997] F.S.R. 462 (Robert Walker J.). See also *Warwick Tyre Co Ltd v New Motor & General Rubber Co Ltd* [1910] 1 Ch. 248; 27 R.P.C. 161.

confer any rights on the assignee as against the world at large,[20] and are likely to result in the relevant goodwill becoming unprotectable. The same principle applies to transactions such as licences which are not assignments as such but which have similar effects.

Deceptiveness aside, some authorities have defined goodwill in terms which suggest it is inherently incapable of being separated from the business to which it relates.[21] Likewise, and subject to s. 24(6) of the Trade Marks Act 1994, it must be doubted whether a "common law trade mark" is a right of property capable of assignment at all. However, this in itself is not conclusive, because if otherwise unobjectionable a purported assignment could be given effect in equity as an exclusive licence. The rule against assignments in gross is therefore better understood as one founded at least in part on policy.

3–158 *Pinto v Badman* was an action for trade mark infringement and passing-off in which the mark relied on by the plaintiff had become distinctive of the cigars of a certain manufacturer in Mexico. The manufacturer sold the mark without any of the business to which it related, and the purchaser took the plaintiff into partnership with himself. The defendant had obviously copied the whole of the plaintiff's label. The Court of Appeal held that the assignment of the mark, even if valid under Mexican law,[22] was ineffective to confer any rights on the plaintiff or his partner.

> "[C]an a trader, who has used a brand upon a particular article, alienate that brand to another person so as to give that alienee any right whatever? It appears to me that, upon first principles, he can have no such right. The brand is an indication of origin, and if you transfer the indication of origin, without transferring the origin itself, you are transferring a right, if any right at all, to commit a fraud upon the public..."[23]

In *Thorneloe v Hill*[24] a firm purchased the business and goodwill of a deceased watchmaker. It effectively discontinued the business, but granted another watchmaker the exclusive right to use the trade mark for seven years. After expiry of this agreement the mark fell out of use again, and it was ultimately assigned to the plaintiff. Romer J. held that the seven year licence had rendered the mark deceptive, but even if that had not been so the subsequent assignments were only of the mark in gross and were also ineffective. The plaintiff, therefore, had no title on which to sue.

The rule against assignments in gross was at one time stated in terms of ownership of the mark becoming separated from the premises at which the business was carried on, but this may be regarded as obsolete.[25] More

[20] *Ullman (J) & Co v Cesar Leuba* (1908) 25 R.P.C. 673, PC; *Barnsley Brewery Co Ltd v RBNB*, above.
[21] *per* Lord Lindley in *Inland Revenue Commissioners v Muller & Co's Margarine Ltd* [1901] A.C. 217, HL.
[22] Apparently the proper law of the contract.
[23] *per* Fry L.J. in *Pinto v Badman* (1981) 8 R.P.C. 181, CA.
[24] [1894] 1 Ch. 569; [1891–4] All E.R. 1263 (Romer J.).
[25] *Globelegance BV v Sarkissian* [1974] R.P.C. 603.

generally, the rule may be expected to respond to changing business conditions and the liberalising tendency to be found in recent trade mark legislation.

Severance of goodwill

There are a number of ways in which a composite business may be divided **3–159** between new owners. It may be split geographically along national frontiers, or locally within one country. It may be divided according to fields of business, classes of customers, or brands in use. This was not uncommon in the nineteenth century, when a partnership might be broken up or the business of a sole trader split between his children on death. That there are few recent cases probably reflects the fact that distinct parts of a composite business are more likely to be owned by a number of different subsidiaries. If a business owned by one legal person is divided, then as long as each of the new owners can fairly be said to own a severable part of the old business and the goodwill corresponding to that part[26] there is no reason for the validity of transaction to be called into question at common law. Cases on registered trade marks may appear to contradict this but are best regarded as turning on the wording or policy of the trade marks act in question. In passing-off it is always a defence that there has been no material misrepresentation, and this deals effectively with artificial schemes such as that in *Lacteosote v Alberman*[27] without inhibiting genuine transactions simply because they do not preserve a business intact. In *Boot Tree Ltd v Robinson*,[28] the plaintiff was held to have an arguable case, although he claimed under an assignment not dissimilar to that in *Lacteosote*.

The common law accommodated transactions which resulted in the goodwill of a business being split. It was even possible for the goodwill to be divided between new owners to the extent that each of them was entitled to use the old name, in the same field of business, in the same place and at the same time. *Dent v Turpin*[29] and *Southorn v Reynolds*[30] are examples of plaintiffs being successful in passing-off actions, although in each case the goodwill of the founder of the business had been divided after his death. An extreme illustration is provided by *Burchell v Wilde*.[31] The Court of Appeal there held that on the expiry of a solicitors' partnership, with no provision for the sale of the business or goodwill and in the absence of agreement to the contrary, each partner in the firm was entitled to enjoy his severed share of the goodwill previously held in common. Each, therefore, was entitled to carry on business in his own right under the old firm name, although the Court expressed the hope that the defendant would voluntarily distinguish himself.

---

[26] *Star Industrial Co Ltd v Yap Kwee Kor* [1976] F.S.R. 256, PC.
[27] (1927) 44 R.P.C. 211.
[28] [1984] F.S.R. 545.
[29] (1861) 70 E.R. 1003 (Page-Wood V.C.).
[30] (1865) 12 L.T. 75 (Page-Wood V.C.).
[31] [1900] 1 Ch. 551, CA; explained in *Byford v Oliver* [2003] EWHC 295; [2003] E.M.L.R. 20 (Laddie J.).

Effect of assignment

3–160 Between the parties to an assignment of the goodwill in a business, the effect is to confer on the assignee the exclusive right to carry on the business assigned and to represent himself as carrying on that business. Consequently, the assignee has the right to sue the assignor for damages and an injunction if he infringes the rights assigned.[32] In this respect, the assignor is in the same position as a third party. He has no additional rights or immunities arising from the fact that the business was once his.[33]

> "[W]hen you are parting with the goodwill of a business you mean to part with all that good disposition which customers entertain towards the house of business identified by the particular name or firm, and which may induce them to continue giving their custom to it. You cannot put it anything short of that. That the name is an important part of the goodwill of a business is obvious, when we consider that there are at this moment large banking firms and brewing firms and others in this metropolis, which do not contain a single member of the individual name exposed in the firm. That being so, it appears to me that, when the defendant parted with the goodwill of this business to the plaintiffs, he handed over to them all the benefit that might be derived from holding themselves out as the persons interested in that particular business, which business had been identified as being carried on by the particular firm."[34]

3–161 As against the world at large, the effect of an assignment of goodwill with the business to which it relates is to put the assignee in the position formerly enjoyed by the assignor, notwithstanding that the public may to some extent have associated the business assigned with the former owner personally.

> "The only way in which the goodwill of business can be preserved in the hands of a purchaser is by inducing the public to believe that the purchaser is still carrying on the business which the transferor owned and carried on, and that the public may, therefore, expect to receive the same attention and satisfaction and the same type and quality of goods. This, as I remarked in the course of the argument, is lawful deception.[35] .. It is, in my view, in the absence of special circumstances, perfectly legitimate for the purchaser of the goodwill of the business to use the get-up and appearance of the goods previously sold ...."[36]

---

[32] *Walker v Mottram* (1881) 19 Ch.D. 355, CA.

[33] *Allen v Original Samuel Allen & Sons Ltd* (1915) 32 R.P.C. 33.

[34] *per* Page-Wood V.C. in *Churton v Douglas* (1859) 70 E.R. 385 at 391; cited by Parker J. in *Mrs Pomeroy Ltd v Scalé* (1906) 24 R.P.C. 177.

[35] Citing *Lewis v Langdon* (1885) 58 E.R. 899.

[36] *per* Dankwerts J. in *Reuter (RJ) Co Ltd v Mulhens* (1953) 70 R.P.C. 102, affirmed (1953) 70 R.P.C. 235, CA.

Competition and solicitation of old customers

In the absence of agreement to the contrary, which may be express or **3–162** implied, the vendor of goodwill is immediately free to set up in business in direct competition with the purchaser and may continue to deal with his former customers as well as new ones. This is the result reluctantly accepted by the House of Lords in *Trego v Hunt*[37] (following *Leggott v Barrett*[38] and disapproving a *dictum* of Jessel M.R. in *Ginesi v Cooper*)[39] as being too well established to reverse. It is therefore strongly desirable for the purchaser to obtain an express covenant against competition by the vendor. The benefit of such a covenant passes with the goodwill (arguably it forms part of the goodwill)[40] without express mention.[41]

On a voluntary assignment of goodwill there is implied as a matter of law an obligation that the vendor will not solicit the former customers of the business. He is not precluded from competing with the purchaser or dealing with his old customers if they seek him out,[42] or are influenced by advertisements directed to the public at large.

"I do not think that 'a person not a lawyer', to use the Vice-Chancellor's phrase, would suppose that a man might sell the goodwill of his business and then set to work to withdraw from the purchaser the benefit of his purchase. However authorities, which it is now too late to question, undoubtedly show that a man who has sold the goodwill of his business may do much to regain his former position, and yet keep on the windy side of the law ... And so it has resulted that a person who sells the goodwill of his business is under no obligation to retire from the field. Trade he undoubtedly may, and in the very same line of business. If he has not bound himself by special stipulation, and if there is no evidence of the understanding of the parties beyond that which is to be found in all cases, he is free to carry on business wherever he chooses. But then, how far may he go? He may do everything that a stranger to the business, in ordinary course, would be in a position to do. He may set up where he will. He may push his wares as much as he pleases. He may thus interfere with the custom of his neighbour as a stranger and an outsider might do; but he must not, I think, avail himself of his special knowledge of the old customers to regain, without consideration that which he has parted with for value."[43]

---

[37] [1896] A.C. 7, HL.
[38] (1880) 15 Ch.D. 306, CA.
[39] (1880) 14 Ch.D. 596 (Jessel M.R.).
[40] *per* Lord Lindley in *Inland Revenue Commissioners v Muller & Co's Margarine Ltd* [1901] A.C. 217, HL.
[41] *Townsend v Jarman* [1900] 2 Ch. 698; 17 R.P.C. 649.
[42] *Leggott v Barrett*, above, n.38, approved in *Trego v Hunt*, above.
[43] *per* Lord Macnaghten in *Trego v Hunt* [1896] A.C. 7 at 24, HL.

3–163 In *Labouchere v Dawson*[44] the defendant sold his interest in a brewing company to the plaintiff, including its goodwill, but without a covenant not to compete. The plaintiff complained that the defendant then set up in business on his own account and solicited its customers. Lord Romilly M.R. held that he could not be allowed to depreciate the value of the goodwill he had sold, and that although he could compete with the plaintiff for the custom of the public at large he could not approach the customers of the old firm and invite them to transfer their custom. *Labouchere v Dawson* was doubted by the Court of Appeal in *Pearson v Pearson*[45] where the transaction was termination of a partnership rather than an assignment as such, but it was reinstated and *Pearson v Pearson* overruled in *Trego v Hunt*.

In *Trego v Hunt*[46] itself the plaintiff and defendant were partners for a term of years which was about to expire. The plaintiff alone owned the goodwill of the firm. The defendant admitted copying lists of the firm's customers for the purpose of soliciting them in his own right as soon as the partnership terminated. The House of Lords held that the principle to apply was the same as upon an assignment of goodwill and declared that the plaintiff was entitled to an injunction against the defendant's soliciting the customers of the old firm once the partnership had expired.

The obligation not to solicit is treated as a collateral implied term rather than an inherent consequence of the assignment of the goodwill. Consequently, on an involuntary assignment, an obligation not to solicit cannot be imposed on the assignor if there is no power to commit him to personal obligations.[47]

It has been held that the obligation not to solicit is binding on an executor responsible for selling the business of a deceased trader.[48] For a case involving a sale by a receiver under a court order see *Re Irish*.[49]

Other rights and obligations under assignments

3–164 An assignment of goodwill does not in itself confer on the purchaser the right to use the name of the vendor in such a way as to expose him to liability. Nor does it operate to waive whatever right (if any) the vendor would have against the world at large to carry on business honestly in his own name. Whether or not there is a general covenant against the vendor competing with the assigned business, it is desirable for the vendor to undertake not to trade under the former name. A general non-competition covenant might be vulnerable as being in restraint of trade, and there is always some possibility that assumed names used for trading purposes will

---

[44] (1872) L.R. 13 Eq. 322 (Romilly M.R.).
[45] (1884) 27 Ch.D. 145, CA.
[46] [1896] A.C. 7, HL.
[47] *Walker v Mottram* (1881) 19 Ch.D. 355, CA.
[48] *Boorne v Wicker* [1927] 1 Ch. 667; [1927] All E.R. 388. This was despite the fact that the soliciting had nothing to do with the defendant's capacity as an executor.
[49] (1888) 40 Ch.D. 49.

become the normal name of the individual.[50] Although exposure to liability is less of an issue now, it is also desirable to obtain express consent to use the vendor's name in whatever way is needed for the assigned business. Both types of obligations are binding on the vendor, transmissible with the goodwill,[51] and enforceable at the suit of a subsequent purchaser.

In *Mrs Pomeroy v Scalé*[52] the defendant traded as a beautician on her own account but then assigned her business and goodwill, with the exclusive right to use her assumed name, to a company controlled by her. The company went into voluntary liquidation and its assets were sold to the plaintiff company, with which the defendant had no connection. She started business again in competition with the plaintiffs under her assumed name. Parker J. held that by the first assignment the defendant had precluded herself from trading under the name *Pomeroy* even assuming that to have been for all practical purposes her own name. The plaintiffs had succeeded to the rights of the first company and were therefore entitled to an injunction. To similar effect there is now *Asprey & Garrard v WRA (Guns) Ltd and Asprey.*[53] The Asprey family had sold their business to the claimant company in 1995, and the personal defendant (though an Asprey himself) had no right to trade off what was now the company's goodwill.

In the South African case of *Nino's Coffee Bar & Restaurant v Nino's Italian Coffee and Sandwich Bar*[54] a company controlled by the sons of the vendor of the original *Nino's* in Johannesburg was not entitled to restrain the purchasers or their franchisees from opening *Nino's* establishments in Cape Town. Though the company associated with the vendors had been the first to trade as *Nino's* in Cape Town, and there might be confusion, they could not set up their own wrongful use against the purchasers.

Assignment of business premises

The sale of business premises or their reversion to their landlord on the **3–165** expiry of a lease does not normally carry with it the goodwill of the business formerly carried on there unless the business and premises are inseparable, as in the case of a public house.[55] The vendor or tenant takes the goodwill of his business with him to his new premises.[56] In the absence of express agreement, the purchaser of premises is not obliged to remove any name or mark which forms part of their fabric; and if a name is the address of the premises, or is distinctive of the premises themselves rather than the

---

[50] In Chapter 9 it is doubted if the "own name" defence really exists, but that is no reason for failing to make one's position certain on the terms of the contract. See *Rael-Brook Ltd v Head Shirts Ltd* [1963] R.P.C. 6.

[51] By analogy with non-competition covenants it would seem the benefit need not be assigned expressly: once taken they pass with the goodwill.

[52] [2001] EWCA Civ 1499; (1906) 24 R.P.C. 177 (Parker J.).

[53] [2002] E.T.M.R. 47; [2002] F.S.R. 31, CA.

[54] 1998 (3) SA 656 (CPD).

[55] An example given by Lord Lindley in *Inland Revenue Commissioners v Muller & Co's Margarine Ltd* [1901] A.C. 217, HL. See also *Re Kitchin Ex p. Punnett* (1880) 16 Ch.D. 226, CA.

[56] An early example of the defendant setting up in the former premises of the plaintiff is to be found in *Wotherspoon v Currie* (1872) L.R. 5 H.L. 508, HL.

vendor's business, the purchaser may continue to use the name in that limited sense. These apart, nothing entitles the purchaser to use the trading name or trade marks of the vendor for his own goods or business. It is a matter of fact whether a name, if distinctive at all, denotes the premises themselves or the business of the vendor. In modern circumstances the presumption is more likely to be that it denotes the vendor.[57]

In *Berkeley Hotel v Berkeley International*[58] the plaintiffs' hotel had been situated in Berkeley Street since it opened in 1870. The owners sold the site and the building was demolished. A new *Berkeley Hotel* was under construction for them elsewhere. The defendants bought the old site and proposed to build a hotel on it and call it the *Berkeley International Hotel*. Pennycuick J. granted an interlocutory injunction. Similarly, in *Ad-Lib Club v Granville*[59] the same judge granted an interlocutory injunction against the defendant opening a night club under the name *Ad-Lib* in the premises formerly used by the plaintiffs. There was evidence of express misrepresentations that it was the old club reopening. In *Harrods v Harrodian School*[60] the defendants admitted adopting the name *Harrodian* from the *Harrodian Club* (a sports and social club for the plaintiffs' employees) formerly on the premises which it had purchased from the plaintiffs. It could not be said that this entitled his school to use the name or gave any immunity from suit, but it was relevant to rebut a charge that the defendants' owner had chosen the name with intent to deceive, and the passing-off claim failed. The plaintiffs had left a large signboard for *The Harrodian Club* in their house script and colours on the site, and the defendants would have probably been liable to an injunction to remove it, had they not done so voluntarily before trial. In the Singapore case of *Jumbo Seafood v Hong Kong Jumbo Seafood Restaurant*[61] the fact that the defendants had purchased the site of one of the plaintiffs' *Jumbo* restaurants, which had gone into liquidation, did not entitle them to trade as the *Hong Kong Jumbo Seafood Restaurant* themselves. On the contrary, it increased the risk of confusion.

3–166 In *Townsend v Jarman*[62] a company which had carried on business in two towns under the surname of the defendant was put into voluntary liquidation and sold in lots. The plaintiff bought the business, premises and goodwill except for the small branch shop which was bought by the defendant. When the branch had to close the defendant moved his business close to the plaintiff's. He was sued for passing-off and counterclaimed that the plaintiff was in breach of covenant, was exposing him to liability by the use of his name, and was holding himself out as the sole successor of the old business. Farwell J. found for the plaintiff on all issues. The defendant had objected to the presence of his name and initials carved in stone over the door of the plaintiff's shop, which had been done for the former before the

---

[57] See also *Barnsley Brewery Co Ltd v RBNB* [1997] F.S.R. 462.
[58] [1972] R.P.C. 237 (Pennycuick J.).
[59] [1971] 2 All E.R. 300; [1972] R.P.C. 673 (Pennycuick J.).
[60] [1996] R.P.C. 697, CA.
[61] [1998] 1 S.L.R. 860 (HC of Singapore).
[62] [1900] 2 Ch. 698; 17 R.P.C. 649 (Farwell J.).

shop was sold to the company. Farwell J. held that the plaintiff could not be obliged to remove it from the building but was not allowed to use the name and initials (as opposed to the surname itself) as his trading name.

In *Rickerby v Reay*[63] the defendant's parents had carried on business as agricultural engineers. The plaintiff bought the business from the executors as a going concern and took a lease of the premises. The trade marks were the word *Crown* and the device of a crown. At some stage the premises became known as the *Crown Works*. On the lease ending the plaintiff moved and the defendant started a similar business there, claiming that he was exclusively entitled to the marks because the goodwill in the business had not been assigned and had continued to accrue to the reversioner. Byrne J. granted an injunction against use of either mark in relation to goods, and against use of the device at the premises. He held that the goodwill in the original business had been assigned despite the absence of express words. Even if that had not been the case, the goodwill generated since then had belonged to the plaintiff as the person carrying on the business and not to the landlord. However, the plaintiff had allowed the premises to become known as the *Crown Works* and the defendant could not be obliged to change the name of the place, although he would not be allowed to exploit it for passing-off.

In contrast, the decision in *Nicholson v Buchanan*[64] is at best dubious and turns on a factor which would no longer be considered very relevant. The plaintiffs were the assignees of the goodwill of the business of a firm of gin distillers who had occupied premises known as the *Black Swan Distillery* and had used a black swan as their mark. The defendant, who had a whisky distillery in Scotland, separately purchased the freehold of the premises and used them as storage and offices. He used *Black Swan Distillery* prominently in advertisements for whisky distilled at his Scottish premises. Stirling J. treated the lack of competition between the parties as virtually conclusive evidence that there would be no confusion, even in respect of the use of the name in the advertisements as opposed to the use on the premises themselves.

In *Boussod Valadon v Marchant*[65] the plaintiffs were an international firm **3–167** of art dealers. Until 1901 they ran a picture gallery in London which was known as the *Goupil Gallery, Goupil* being their previous firm name. The defendant had been the manager of the London gallery and in 1901 he bought the business and the lease of the premises under an agreement which allowed him to hold himself out as the London agent of the plaintiffs for five years, during which the plaintiffs were not to trade in the United Kingdom on their own account or through another agent. The plaintiffs co-operated in issuing a circular notifying the transfer of ownership. They alleged but failed to prove two collateral agreements reserving ownership of the name and goodwill. Despite his description as agent the defendant predominantly

[63] (1903) 20 R.P.C. 380 (Byrne J.).
[64] (1902) 19 R.P.C. 321 (Stirling J.).
[65] (1907) 24 R.P.C., CA.

traded on his own account. The Court of Appeal, affirming Parker J., found for the defendant and granted him a declaration on his counterclaim.

Cozens-Hardy M.R. was much influenced by the fact that *Goupil Gallery* was the name fixed to the premises, but this seems of little relevance except as to acquiescence. The name was undoubtedly distinctive of the business, much dependent upon personal skill, rather than the premises themselves, which had moved three times in a few years. The better reasoning (that of Fletcher Moulton L.J.) is that for five years past the name had meant the business of the defendant in both fact and repute. Far from reserving any control over him, his business or the name itself, the plaintiffs had told the public that the business was no longer theirs. Even Cozens-Hardy M.R. *arguendo* drew a distinction between assigning the right to trade as *Goupil* and the right to leave the name in position on the premises.

Mortgages

3–168 Goodwill may be charged or mortgaged, as is commonly done by a company's debentures.[66] In *Kelly v Hutton*[67] a mortgage of a share in the "copyright" of a newspaper (the *Sporting Life*) was interpreted as effective to charge the mortgagor's interest in the title and goodwill. However, mortgages form no exception to the rule that goodwill cannot be separated from the business to which it relates. A mortgagee cannot purport to enforce mortgaged goodwill by a passing-off action when it is the mortgagor or his successor who is actually carrying on the old business.[68]

Licences

3–169 The owner of the goodwill in a business may *prima facie* license another business to do any act which but for the licence would amount to passing off. To this extent it is permissible to speak of licensing goodwill, although what is licensed is not properly the goodwill as such but the right to do something which would otherwise infringe the licensor's rights in it. This normally takes the form of licensing the use of a name, mark or get-up which is distinctive of the licensor. Provided there is no inherent deception of the public the existence of one or many licences will not compromise the goodwill of the licensor or his right to bring a passing-off action against a former licensee, a licensee exceeding the scope of his licence, or a third party. It may even strengthen his position.[69]

In *Coles v Need*[70] the plaintiffs licensed the defendant to use their name for a retail shop which was obliged to sell only their goods. Owing to difficulties with suppliers, they temporarily allowed the shop to purchase

---

[66] *Dictum* of Lord Evershed M.R. in *Reuter (RJ) Co Ltd v Mulhens* (1953) 70 R.P.C. 235, CA.
[67] (1868) L.R. 3 Ch. App. 703 (Page-Wood L.J.).
[68] *Beazley v Soares* (1882) 22 Ch.D. 660.
[69] See also *Gromax Plasticulture Ltd v Don & Low Nonwovens Ltd* [1999] R.P.C. 367; *Scandecor Development AB v Scandecor Marketing AB* [1999] F.S.R. 26, CA; and *Dawnay Day & Co Ltd v Cantor Fitzgerald International* [2000] R.P.C. 669, CA; and the commentary on those cases in Sections H and I above.
[70] [1934] A.C. 82; (1933) 50 R.P.C. 379, PC.

most of its goods elsewhere. The supply agreement and licence were terminated, but the defendant claimed to be entitled to continue to use the name. The Privy Council found for the plaintiffs. The licence had been properly granted and had been continued by the plaintiffs in good faith, in the belief that they would again be able to resume full supplies. Even if the manner of trading had ever been deceptive, there was no reason for allowing the defendant to practise a more serious deception without limit of time.

In *British Legion v British Legion Club (Street) Ltd*[71] the plaintiffs were a **3–170** charity for ex-servicemen. As well as providing benefits in their own right, they allowed local clubs to use the name *British Legion* on condition that they abided by the rules of the plaintiffs and submitted to its ultimate authority. The right to use the name could be withdrawn. Apart from this, the clubs appear to have been independent in terms of ownership and management. The plaintiffs had offered such arrangements to the defendant club, but when its membership failed to agree they sued for passing-off and were granted an injunction. It was inevitable that the defendant club would be taken as "under the supervision of the plaintiff association or for which the plaintiff association had in some way made itself responsible".

The plaintiffs in *Dunhill v Sunoptic*[72] and *News Group Newspapers v Rocket Record Co*[73] had respectively made their names in smokers' goods and publishing. They had licensed the marks *Dunhill* and *Page Three* on a wide scale in quite unrelated fields of business. Their success in obtaining interlocutory injunctions against defendants using those marks for sunglasses and pop records largely depended on the extent of those licensing programmes.

A licence in gross, however, is ineffective at common law. In *Warwick* **3–171** *Tyre v New Motor & General Rubber Co*[74] the plaintiffs had once carried on business in their own right but had purported to assign the exclusive right to manufacture and sell *Warwick* tyres to another company (Dunlop) for a term of years while retaining ownership of the goodwill in the mark. The benefit of the licence appears to have been their sole remaining asset. The precise terms and nature of the agreement are unclear. The plaintiffs sued to restrain use of the mark by the defendants without joining Dunlop as co-plaintiffs. Neville J. granted an injunction, but the Privy Council in *Star Industrial v Yap Kwee Kor*[75] condemned his reasoning as based on the fallacy that passing-off protected a right of property in the mark itself.[76]

Nationalisation and expropriation

Foreign expropriatory legislation cannot affect the ownership of English **3–172** goodwill. This does not depend on the legislation being of a penal char-

---

[71] (1931) 48 R.P.C. 55 (Farwell J.).
[72] [1979] F.S.R. 337, CA.
[73] [1981] F.S.R. 89 (Slade J.).
[74] [1910] 1 Ch. 248; 27 R.P.C. 161 (Neville J.).
[75] [1976] F.S.R. 256, PC.
[76] See also *Thorneloe v Hill* [1894] 1 Ch. 569; [1891–4] All E.R. 1263.

acter,[77] the reason being that goodwill is property locally situated in England and is therefore outside the jurisdiction of the foreign legislature.[78] It makes no difference that the owner may owe personal allegiance to the foreign state. Conversely, the English courts are bound to give effect to English legislation affecting the ownership of goodwill, and at common law cannot enquire into its justice.[79]

In *Lecouturier v Rey* the Order of Carthusian monks at *La Grande Chartreuse* in France produced a liqueur which had a world-wide reputation. A French statute and a court order made under it confiscated the French assets, and the monks moved to Spain where they set up a rival company. The House of Lords held that the French court order had not purported to dispose of property outside France, but had it done so it would have failed to transfer the English trade marks.

"To me it seems perfectly plain that by the very nature of things a law of a foreign country, and a sale by a foreign court under that law, cannot affect property not within the reach of the foreign law, or the jurisdiction of the foreign court charged with its administration."[80]

In *Ingenohl v Wing-On*[81] American legislation in the First World War had confiscated the assets of the plaintiff as a supposed German national. The assets included a cigar factory in the Philippines, which was under American jurisdiction, and the goodwill of the business which extended to China. The Privy Council agreed that the legislation could not transfer property in China. Much more questionably, it treated the involuntary assignment as creating something in the nature of a personal estoppel in the defendants' favour.

3–173 When the English goodwill is owned by a company and it is the shares in the company which have been appropriated (or the shares in a parent) the goodwill itself remains the property of the company and the effect and validity of the appropriation depend on company law principles.[82]

Goodwill almost certainly qualifies as "possessions" for the purposes of Art. 1 of the First Protocol to the European Convention on Human Rights, and to that extent may now be protected from unjustified expropriation under the Human Rights Act 1998.[83]

---

[77] *Ingenohl v Wing-On & Co (Shanghai) Ltd* (1927) 44 R.P.C. 343, PC.
[78] *Lecouturier v Rey* [1910] A.C. 262; 27 R.P.C. 268, HL.
[79] *Reuter (RJ) Co Ltd v Mulhens* (1953) 70 R.P.C. 235, CA; *Adrema Maschinenbau GmbH v Custodian of Enemy Property* (1954) 71 R.P.C. 197.
[80] *per* Lord Macnaghten in *Lecouturier v Rey* [1910] A.C. 262; R.P.C. 268 at 276, HL.
[81] (1927) 44 R.P.C. 343, PC.
[82] *Williams & Humbert Ltd v W & H Trade Marks Ltd (Jersey) Ltd* [1986] A.C. 368, HL; *Habib Bank Ltd v Habib Bank AG Zurich* [1981] 1 W.L.R. 1265; [1981] 2 All E.R. 650; [1982] R.P.C. 1, CA; *Reuter (R J) Co Ltd v Mulhens* (1953) 70 R.P.C. 235, CA; *Adrema Maschinenbau GmbH v Custodian of Enemy Property* (1954) 71 R.P.C. 197.
[83] *Van Marle v Netherlands* (8543/79 and others), Series A/101, (1986) 8 E.H.R.R. 483, ECHR.

Insolvency

On the bankruptcy of a trader the goodwill of his former business vests in **3–174** his trustee in bankruptcy who may confer a good title to it on the purchaser of the business. However, although the trustee can dispose of the bankrupt's property he is not empowered to give personal covenants binding on him. Consequently, the normal implied covenant not to solicit customers of the old business does not apply, nor, *a fortiori*, is there a general covenant not to compete, which would require express inclusion or necessary inference even in a voluntary assignment. It does not make any difference that the bankrupt could be compelled to join in the conveyance by the trustee.[84]

> "[T]he assignee under an involuntary assignment fails to obtain those benefits which require the covenant of the assignor, namely the covenant, normally given by a vendor on a voluntary sale, not personally to compete with the business sold or to solicit in his own name his old customers. Nothing in those cases qualifies the right of an assignee under an involuntary assignment to enjoy the benefits properly flowing from an assignment of goodwill... "[85]

The same principle was applied in *Green v Morris*[86] in which an insolvent individual had made a voluntary arrangement with his creditors to avoid formal bankruptcy. However, the reasoning is suspect in failing to draw a distinction between a sale under compulsion of law and one made reluctantly because of external circumstances: "There is all the difference in the world between the case of a man who sells what belongs to himself, and receives the consideration, and a man whose property is sold without his consent by his trustee in bankruptcy..."[87]

The Court of Appeal in *Farey v Cooper*[88] took *Green v Morris* as settled law and held that a covenant in a voluntary deed of assignment under which the debtor undertook to do the utmost to aid the realisation of his property for the benefit of his creditors would not prevent him subsequently canvassing his former customers. This seems questionable, but presumably effect would be given to an express undertaking by the debtor, the giving of which could be made a pre-condition to accepting the voluntary arrangement instead of bankruptcy. It is to be noted that the wording of the covenant was taken *verbatim* from the Debtors Act 1869, under which *Walker v Mottram* had been decided. Both *Farey v Cooper* and *Green v Morris* are better explained as turning on the trustee having been given insufficient authority to bind the assignor, rather than on a rule of law that no such authority could be given.

---

[84] *Walker v Mottram* (1881) 19 Ch.D. 355, CA, following *Crutwell v Lye* (1810) 34 E.R. 129.
[85] *per* Evershed M.R. in *Reuter (RJ) Co Ltd v Mulhens* (1953) 70 R.P.C. 235, CA explaining *Green & Sons (Northampton) Ltd v Morris* [1914] 1 Ch. 562; [1914–15] All E.R. 942 and *Walker v Mottram* (1881) 19 Ch.D. 355, CA.
[86] [1914] 1 Ch. 562 (Warrington J.).
[87] *per* Lord Macnaghten in *Trego v Hunt* [1896] A.C. 7 at 23, HL.
[88] [1927] 2 K.B. 384; [1927] All E.R. 311, CA.

3-175   These problems do not normally arise in corporate insolvencies[89] because of the practice of dissolving the insolvent company after its assets have been disposed of.

In *Dawany Day v Cantor Fitzgerald*[90] a 50 per cent subsidiary of the claimants which operated an inter-dealer Eurobond broking business under the name *Dawnay Day Securities* became deadlocked and was put into administration by the court. The defendants purchased the business formerly operated by the company from the administrator. The Court of Appeal held that they were entitled to hold themselves out as carrying on the former business (and, conversely, that the claimants could not do so) but that they were not entitled to trade under the former name or any other name incorporating *Dawnay Day*.

De facto assumption: "adverse possession"

3-176   It may happen that what appears to the public to be one continuous business has in fact been carried on by two or more unconnected persons in succession. This may happen by agreement, by coincidence, or as a result of passing-off going unrestrained. If the succession is by consent, then it may be reasonable to infer an assignment of the goodwill in the old business. If not, then although there appears to be no express authority,[91] there is no reason to believe that any surviving goodwill of the old business accrues to the new one. The new business may generate goodwill of its own, but the goodwill of the old business is simply extinguished.

In *Barnsley Brewery Co Ltd v RBNB*[92] the name *Barnsley Bitter* had been used from 1883 to 1976 for beer brewed at the Oakwell Brewery in Barnsley, by a company unconnected with either of the parties, and had acquired a high reputation. "But after 1976 the reputation and goodwill attaching to Barnsley Bitter evaporated and became merely a memory . . .". The plaintiffs had obtained a purported assignment of goodwill from the original company in 1996, but this was irrelevant to their title, as being an assignment in gross. The plaintiffs' case therefore rested entirely on their own use of the same name for beer brewed at a different brewery (also near Barnsley) since 1994. At the end of 1996 (the relevant date being that on which the defendants withdrew an undertaking not to use the name) their annual turnover was £400,000 and advertising expenditure £25,000 p.a., but the theme of this had been to invoke the original *Barnsley Bitter*. The defendants (or an associated company) were proposing to reopen the old brewery and sell its beer as *Barnsley Bitter*. Robert Walker J. held that the plaintiff's case based on its own trade and advertising was arguable, though not strong, but that it was undesirable to grant an interlocutory injunction which would have the

---

[89] Such as *Mrs Pomeroy Ltd v Scalé* (1906) 24 R.P.C. 177.

[90] [2000] R.P.C. 669, CA.

[91] Other than *Barnsley Brewery Co Ltd v RBNB* [1997] F.S.R. 462, discussed here, the closest appears to be *Pink v Sharwood (JA) & Co Ltd* (1913) 30 R.P.C. 725. If the original proprietor cannot revive his own defunct goodwill, then there seems even less reason to allow a stranger to do so. See also *dicta* of Laddie J. in *Byford v Oliver* [2003] EWHC 295; [2003] E.M.L.R. 20.

[92] [1997] F.S.R. 462 (Robert Walker J.).

effect of giving the plaintiffs a near-conclusive advantage in what was then an unfinished race to see who (if either of the parties) would be successful in appropriating the legendary reputation of a beer which was no longer made.

"It is, if you like, similar to a variation on the facts of the *Stone Ales* case. If in that case the original Stone Brewery which had been there for 100 years had closed overnight and its goodwill had suddenly vanished, it is doubtful whether Mr. Montgomery, the unsuccessful appellant in that case, could have appropriated for himself the original brewery's residual goodwill simply by being first in the field with his Stone Brewery in different premises. The field would, it seems to me, have been open to any number of competitors and if competition had ensued it is quite likely that no one would have succeeded in establishing himself for passing off purposes as exclusively entitled to reputation attaching to the geographical name Stone Ale in such a way as to be entitled to have the use of that description by competitors enjoined as unfair competition."[93]

Ineffective or colourable transactions

It is not uncommon, even today, to come across transactions which are on **3–177** their face assignments or licences by established businesses, but which are in fact fraudulent in that their purpose is to give a colourable title to someone wanting to use a name likely to bring in business because of its use by another. Whatever the effect between their parties, such transactions confer no rights or immunities on the assignee or licensee as against a person with real goodwill associated with the name in question.

In *Morrall v Hessin*[94] the plaintiffs dealt in needles on a large scale under the names *Morrall's* and *Moggs* which were admittedly distinctive of them. Needle manufacture was still, to some extent, a cottage industry with many small subcontractors. The defendants found two such individuals named Morrall and Mogg who had very small businesses in making or packing needles and purported to buy their respective businesses and goodwill. Morrall also ran a beerhouse, Mogg a tobacco shop. The Court of Appeal held that these were colourable transactions which gave the defendants no right as against the plaintiffs to use the names.[95]

In *Dunhill v Sunoptic*[96] the first defendants entered into an agreement with the second defendant, Christopher Dunhill, under which he would act as a consultant and allow his name to be used on spectacle frames and sunglasses. He had no expertise in this field. The Court of Appeal granted an interlocutory injunction.

---

[93] *per* Robert Walker J. *ibid.*
[94] (1903) 20 R.P.C. 429, CA.
[95] See also *Valentine Meat Juice Co v Valentine Extract Co Ltd* (1900) 17 R.P.C. 673, CA.
[96] [1979] F.S.R. 337, CA.

K. Extinction and Revival of Goodwill

Goodwill may survive cessation of business

3–178 The goodwill in a business is not necessarily extinguished immediately if the owner ceases to trade. This has been recognised by the Privy Council,[97] and there are numerous cases of claimants succeeding in passing-off actions even though they may have been out of business for several years.

In an early trade mark case[98] it was suggested by analogy with the law of easements that an intention to abandon goodwill was essential if it was to be extinguished, but this has subsequently been denied.[99] The better view is that if a business is deliberately abandoned in circumstances which are inconsistent with its ever being recommenced then the goodwill in it is destroyed unless contemporaneously assigned to a new owner. Otherwise, the goodwill in a discontinued business may continue to exist and be capable of being protected, provided the claimant intended and still intends that his former business should resume active trading. It is not necessary that the prospect should be imminent, but the mere possibility of resumption if circumstances should ever change in the claimant's favour is not enough.[1] The claimant's intention to resume business may the more readily be believed where the original cessation was forced on him by external circumstances, but this factor is not conclusive either way.

This analysis would be consistent with a minor aspect of *Harrods v Harrodian School*[2] where the plaintiffs' *Harrodian Club* was discontinued and the site sold off (to the defendants) without any apparent attempt to preserve or transfer any separate goodwill the club may have had. The time interval (three years) between closure of the club and the opening of the defendants' school is not self-evidently long enough to have destroyed the goodwill simply by passage of time. Conversely, in *Barnsley Brewery Co. Ltd v RBNB*[3] cessation of business 20 years previously meant that in 1996 there was no goodwill which could be assigned to the plaintiffs by the dormant company which had formerly brewed *Barnsley Bitter*, even though the beer retained a local reputation which both parties were attempting to exploit.

Examples

3–179 In *Pink v Sharwood*[4] the plaintiff, who had carried on the business of jam manufacturer, became insane and in 1908 a receiver was appointed for the

---

[97] *Star Industrial Co Ltd v Yap Kwee Kor* [1976] F.S.R. 256, PC, citing *Mouson v Boehm* (1884) 26 Ch.D. 398. It was the principle which was approved: the reasoning of the later case remains flawed in its detail.

[98] *Mouson v Boehm* (1884) Ch.D. 398.

[99] *Kark (Norman) Publications Ltd v Odhams Press Ltd* [1962] R.P.C. 163.

[1] *Kark (Norman) Publications Ltd v Odhams Press Ltd* [1962] R.P.C. 163. *Poiret v Jules Poiret Ltd* (1920) 37 R.P.C. 177 is barely consistent, but the defendant was fraudulent and the plaintiff had ceased business to join the colours.

[2] [1996] R.P.C. 697, CA.

[3] [1997] F.S.R. 462 (Robert Walker J.)

[4] (1913) 30 R.P.C. 725 (Eve J.).

business. The receiver failed to sell the business as a going concern, and in 1910 the business was discontinued, its assets split up and sold by auction, and the books destroyed. Pots and labels bearing the plaintiff's mark were bought and used by competitors. Eve J. held that the goodwill of the business had come to an end in 1910 and that an action, brought in 1913, failed. The facts were inconsistent with there having been any intention by those responsible ever to resume the business or retain the goodwill, but even such an intention would have been insufficient given the way the former business had been abandoned.

In *Poiret v Jules Poiret*[5] the plaintiff was successful notwithstanding an interruption in his business as a couturier between 1914 and 1919, when he had served in the French Army and his factory had been converted to other uses. In the Second World War, the plaintiffs in *Manus v Fullwood & Bland*[6] were unable to export their milking machines from Sweden to England. As an interim measure to keep their name before the public they authorised the defendants, their former distributors, to use their mark on goods made in England, but this was held not to invalidate it. The plaintiffs in *Music Corporation of America v Music Corporation (Great Britain)*[7] found their English Agency uneconomical and decided to shut it down for the duration of the war. All three plaintiffs were held to have retained their goodwill.

In *Ballarat v Farmers Smallgoods*[8] the plaintiffs closed the branch of their **3–180** business (which dealt in ham and bacon under the name *Farmers*) in July 1949 because it had become uneconomic. They retained the necessary factory and plant and a senior employee and kept the possibility of reopening under review. In 1956 the plaintiffs were on the point of concluding a joint venture which would resume the old business. The defendant company was also incorporated in 1956. The Supreme Court of Victoria held that the plaintiffs had satisfied the onus of proving that they had not abandoned the business, that there was a real possibility of use resuming, and that *Farmers* still had a valuable reputation.

In the Canadian case of *Nissan Motor Co of BC v Nissan Automobile Co (Canada)*[9] the defendants were a wholly owned subsidiary of the Japanese car manufacturers and had replaced the plaintiffs as Nissan agents in British Columbia. On an application for an interlocutory injunction the Supreme Court of British Columbia held that the plaintiffs had no arguable case. They no longer had a business in selling Nissan vehicles, the agency agreement had been terminated, only a few cars and trucks remained in stock, and there was no prospect of business recommencing.

In *Ad-Lib Club v Granville*,[10] *Berkeley Hotel v Berkeley International*[11] and **3–181** *Levey v Henderson-Kenton*[12] the businesses of the plaintiffs had been closed

---

[5] (1920) 37 R.P.C. 177 (P. O. Lawrence J.).
[6] (1949) 66 R.P.C. 71, CA.
[7] (1947) 64 R.P.C. 48 (Wynn-Parry J.).
[8] [1957] V.R. 104.
[9] (1965) 53 W.W.R. 44; 31 Fox P.C. 149; 49 C.P.R. 134.
[10] [1971] 2 All E.R. 300; [1972] R.P.C. 673 (Pennycuick V.C.).
[11] [1972] R.P.C. 237 (Pennycuick V.C.).
[12] [1974] R.P.C. 617 (Foster J.).

for five, three and two years respectively, in all three cases because the premises from which they had traded had become unavailable. The Ad-Lib Club was still seeking suitable premises, the other plaintiffs were about to recommence business. All obtained interlocutory injunctions. Conversely, in *Harrods v Harrodian School*,[13] any goodwill attaching to the plaintiffs' former *Harrodian Club* had been abandoned when the club closed in 1990, three years before the defendants' school was launched. Other goods or services for which the plaintiffs had used the word *Harrodian* as well as some education-related services provided under the *Harrods* name, had been discontinued long before.

An argument that the allegedly wrongful expulsion of the defendants from a trade association or guild had caused the latter to cease to exist and its goodwill to dissolve, so that the plaintiffs could not sue in a representative capacity on behalf of its remaining members, was dismissed as absurd in *Artistic Upholstery v Art Forma*.[14]

In *Sutherland v V2 Music*[15] the members of the original pop group *Liberty* were found to have sufficient residual goodwill surviving from the period up to about 1995, to justify judgment at trial against an unconnected group adopting the same name in 2001. The original group had faded from the public eye, but they still had a significant body of admirers and had never entirely ceased operating. The former, without the latter, might not have been sufficient. In *Barnsley Brewery Co Ltd v RBNB*[16] it would have required more than fond memories of the original *Barnsley Bitter,* brewed from 1883 to 1976, for goodwill still to have existed in the 1990s.

But goodwill cannot survive loss of distinctiveness

3–182 Once the claimant's business has been discontinued then, even though he may intend to resume it at some time, it is a matter of fact and degree at what point he should be treated as no longer having any goodwill in that business or in respect of any name attached to it.[17] The question is normally equivalent to that of whether use of a particular mark by the defendant any longer conveys a misrepresentation that his goods or business are those of the claimant or connected with him. In turn, this depends on whether the mark is still distinctive of the claimant after the lapse of time since it was last used.

In *Kark v Odhams*[18] the plaintiffs had published a magazine entitled *Today* until 1953 when it was discontinued and nominally incorporated into another magazine of the plaintiffs' called *Courier*. In 1960 the defendants renamed an existing magazine of theirs *Today*. Wilberforce J. gave judgment for the defendants. He rejected the plaintiffs' contention that their goodwill remained in existence unless deliberately abandoned. They had made no

---

[13] [1996] R.P.C. 697, CA.
[14] [1999] 4 All E.R. 277; [2000] F.S.R. 311 (Lawrence Collins Q.C., Deputy Judge).
[15] [2002] EWHC 14; [2002] E.M.L.R. 28 (Laddie J.).
[16] [1997] F.S.R. 462 (Robert Walker J.).
[17] *Ad-Lib Club Ltd v Granville* [1971] 2 All E.R. 300; [1972] R.P.C. 673.
[18] [1962] R.P.C. 163 (Wilberforce J.).

effort to preserve the reputation of *Today*, and by 1969 the name had ceased to be distinctive of them and its use by the defendants was not misleading.

If one treats publication of the original *Today* as a business in its own right, then *Kark v Odhams* may be regarded as a case in which the plaintiffs' business ceased altogether, although the plaintiffs were still in business as the publisher of *Courier* the word *Today* still received some very inconspicuous usage, and the incorporation of *Today* into *Courier* might be taken as the equivalent of an assignment of its goodwill.

Cases in which a business has altogether ceased trading raise similar issues **3–183** to those in which a claimant who is still actively trading complains of the use by the defendant of a mark which the plaintiff no longer uses.

In *Thermawear v Vedonis*[19] there was no doubt that the plaintiffs were in business on a large scale, but their case rested on the defendants' mark *Thermawarm* as being confusingly similar to the plaintiffs' *Thermawear* which they had not used (except as part of their corporate name) for five years. Whitford J. found for the plaintiffs.

In Australia, the former *Western Mining* company and a subsidiary obtained a permanent injunction in 1997 against another mining company using the same name,[20] despite having dropped *Western Mining* from their names in 1995 or 1996. They were still very well known under the old name: *WMC v Westgold Resources*.[21]

Kark v Odhams[22] may be compared with *EMAP National Publications v* **3–184** *Security Publications*,[23] where the plaintiffs' former *Popular Classics* motoring magazine had been discontinued as a separate publication for about a year, though the title was still used (in a subordinate position) on the cover of *Practical Classics* magazine, into which it had been merged. The retention of *Popular Classics* and its distinctive "badge" format assisted the plaintiffs' case against *Classics* presented in a similar format.

Abandoned goodwill cannot be revived

If the goodwill in a business is abandoned, and the former business is then **3–185** recommenced, is it possible for the abandoned goodwill to be brought back into life? What authority there is suggests that it is not.[24]

"If, hereafter, the plaintiff should recover and resume business, he will resume with the benefit of his former reputation, but the goodwill which he will then assume will be a goodwill he will then start to create, and not the goodwill of the old business revived and resuscitated."

---

[19] [1982] R.P.C. 44 (Whitford J.).
[20] The second defendant, Western Mining NL.
[21] (1997) 39 I.P.R. 319 (North J, Federal Court of Australia).
[22] [1962] R.P.C. 163 (Wilberforce J.).
[23] [1997] F.S.R. 891 (Lloyd J.).
[24] *Pink v Sharwood (JA) & Co Ltd* (1913) 30 R.P.C. 725 per Eve J. See also *Barnsley Brewery Co Ltd v RBNB* [1997] F.S.R. 462, where the attempt to revive the goodwill was by a stranger.

L. Remedies for Non-Traders

Injurious falsehood

3–186 Damage to some kind of pecuniary interest is the gist of the action for injurious falsehood, but the interest damaged does not have to be goodwill. The action for injurious falsehood may therefore be brought by persons who are not traders in any sense, as well as by traders who for any reason have no relevant goodwill.

In the *Budweiser* case, *Anheuser-Busch v Budejovicky Budvar*,[25] a passing-off claim was dismissed *in limine* because the American plaintiffs had no goodwill in the United Kingdom, but a claim for injurious falsehood failed only because it was not made maliciously.[26] In *Kaye v Robertson*[27] the plaintiff, an actor, was held not to be a trader in respect of a claim for passing-off against a newspaper purporting to publish an interview with him while an injured patient in hospital, but a claim for injurious falsehood on the same facts and in the same capacity was sufficiently arguable to support an interlocutory injunction. In *Joyce v Sengupta*,[28] *Khodaparast v Shad*[29] and *Spring v Guardian Assurance*[30] private individuals were able to sue for damage to their employment prospects.

Exposure to liability: *Routh v Webster*

3–187 A person, whether a trader or a private individual, is entitled to restrain any unauthorised use of his name that would expose him to liability. The origin of this rule is *Routh v Webster*[31] in which Lord Langdale M.R. granted an injunction restraining the publication of a prospectus for a new company in which the plaintiff was named as a trustee without his authority. Though the cause of action is old and obscure, a new lease of life for it might be predicted in countering the modern problem of "identity theft".

When partnership was more common than incorporation, it was important for non-partners, especially former partners, to be able to restrain any unauthorised use of their names that would make them liable for the debts of the firm. In *Gray v Smith*[32] the Court of Appeal held that a partner who had retired from a firm without agreeing to assign his share of the goodwill was entitled to restrain all use of his name that might expose him to further liabilities. Consequently, the remaining principal was not allowed to con-

---

[25] [1984] F.S.R. 413, CA.
[26] Though Oliver L.J. also doubted whether the plaintiffs could prove damage.
[27] [1991] F.S.R. 62, CA.
[28] [1993] 1 W.L.R. 337, CA.
[29] [2000] 1 W.L.R. 618, CA.
[30] [1993] All E.R. 273, CA. The latter action failed on the facts for lack of malice.
[31] (1847) 50 E.R. 698 (Langdale M.R.).
[32] (1889) 43 Ch.D. 208, CA distinguishing *Levy v Walker* (1879) 10 Ch.D. 436; [1874–80] All E.R. 1173, CA.

tinue to use the name of the former partner in the firm name, although he was allowed to dispose of existing stock with the old name on it.[33]

It has been doubted whether this cause of action is distinct from passing- **3–188** off, and if the claimant is a trader the question may be considered academic because exposure to liability or even the possibility of litigation is a recognised head of damage in passing-off.[34] However, in terms of being exposed to liability, no logical distinction can be drawn between claimants in business on their own account, those who have retired, and those who were never in business at all. In *Cundey v Lerwill and Pike*[35] Parker J. recognised this cause of action (in a somewhat narrower formulation) as being distinct from passing-off and injurious falsehood:

"It is not every false representation that a firm has a right to restrain, though if the public is deceived, the Attorney-General may take civil or criminal proceedings; but to entitle a private person to an injunction something further is required. Roughly, the cases divide into three heads: where the false statement tends to a passing off of one man's goods or business as another's; where it amounts to a holding out of the plaintiff as a partner and exposes him to liability; and where it tends to disparage his goods and causes special damage."

Although holding out as a partner may have been the most common **3–189** occasion on which this right of action was needed, it is not confined to that situation and appears to exist whatever the context in which the claimant's name is used, and whatever the source of the potential liability. It is no defence that the claimant is entitled to an indemnity,[36] from which it would seem to follow that it is not essential that the claimant should ultimately be responsible in law for meeting the claims to which he may be exposed. Even to defend oneself successfully involves trouble and irrecoverable expense.[37]

In *Hodges v London Trams Omnibus*[38] the plaintiff, as manager of the defendant company, was issued with statutory licences in his own name and was liable for the company's compliance. On his ceasing to be manager, he attempted to have the licences transferred but could not do so without the consent of the company. The Court of Appeal granted an injunction restraining the defendants from continuing to use the plaintiff's name as licensee.

---

[33] Followed in *Thynne v Shove* (1890) 45 Ch.D. 577; [1886–90] All E.R. 874 where there had been an express assignment of goodwill.
[34] *Walter v Ashton* [1902] 2 Ch. 282; *Illustrated Newspapers Ltd v Publicity Services (London) Ltd* [1938] Ch. 414; [1938] 1 All E.R. 321; 55 R.P.C. 172.
[35] (1908) 99 L.T. 273; 24 T.L.R. 584 (Parker J.).
[36] *Routh v Webster* (1847) 50 E.R. 698; *Hodges v London Trams Omnibus Company* (1883) 12 Q.B. 105, CA.
[37] *Illustrated Newspapers Ltd v Publicity Services (London) Ltd* [1938] Ch. 414; [1938] 2 All E.R. 321; 55 R.P.C. 172.
[38] (1883) 12 Q.B. 105, CA.

Restitution

3–190 In *Newsweek v British Broadcasting Corporation*[39] the defendants proposed to broadcast a current affairs programme with the same name as the plaintiffs' news magazine. One of the arguments advanced for the plaintiffs was that a television reporter introducing himself simply as from *Newsweek* might be thought by the source of information to represent them. At first instance on an application for an interlocutory injunction Walton J. refused to accept that this would be passing-off, even if the deception were deliberate.[40] However, he suggested that the reporter in those circumstances would be a constructive trustee of the information received which he would hold on behalf of the plaintiffs.[41]

It is doubtful that a constructive trust would be of any benefit to the plaintiffs in the circumstances contemplated by Walton J. However, as a general rule it is correct to say that if a person receives property knowing it to be intended for another then he can be compelled to account for it. A remedy exists at law as well as in equity. A charity, for instance, would have a remedy in restitution against a person fraudulently collecting money in its name but for his own benefit, quite independently of the law of passing-off. The restitutionary cause of action would not depend on either the plaintiff or defendant acting as traders in any sense, nor on the charity being able to prove damage.

---

[39] [1979] R.P.C. 441, CA.
[40] Questionable, given the cases on businesses having goodwill as purchasers. The Court of Appeal affirmed him on narrower, factual grounds.
[41] On the principle of *Phipps v Boardman* [1967] 2 A.C. 46; [1966] 3 All E.R. 721, HL.

DAMAGE

A. THE IMPORTANCE OF DAMAGE IN PASSING-OFF

The principle stated

4–1 The action for passing-off protects the claimant's right of property in his business or goodwill.[1] It is therefore essential that the defendant's misrepresentation should be such as to be really likely to cause substantial damage to that property. If there is no damage or prospect of damage to the claimant's business or goodwill then there can be no cause of action for passing-off. The original reason for this may lie deep in the history of the tort, but the importance of damage has been confirmed in the modern definitions of passing-off given by the House of Lords in both the *Advocaat* and *Jif Lemon* cases. The fourth and fifth of Lord Diplock's heads in *Advocaat* are as follows:

> "(4) Which [misrepresentation] is calculated to injure the business or goodwill of another trader (in the sense that this is a reasonably foreseeable consequence) and (5) which causes actual damage to a business or goodwill of the trader by whom the action is brought or (in a *quia timet* action) will probably do so."[2]

The importance of damage was emphasised even more clearly by Lord Fraser who said that the claimant must show

> "That he has suffered, or is *really likely* to suffer, substantial damage to his property in the goodwill."[3]

4–2 These restate the proposition, accepted since at least as early as *Spalding v Gamage*,[4] that passing-off protects the right which the claimant has in his goodwill or business, and that the basis of the action is damage to this right of property.

The principle was affirmed once again by Lord Oliver in *Reckitt & Colman v Borden*[5]:

> "[H]e must demonstrate that he suffers or, in a *quia timet* action, that he is likely to suffer damage by reason of the erroneous belief engendered by the defendant's misrepresentation that the source of the defendant's

---

[1] *Spalding (AG) & Bros v A W Gamage Ltd* (1915) 32 R.P.C. 273, HL; *Star Industrial Co Ltd v Yap Kwee Kor* [1976] F.S.R. 256, PC; *Erven Warnink BV v J Townend & Sons (Hull) Ltd* [1979] A.C. 731; [1979] 2 All E.R. 927; [1980] R.P.C. 31, HL; *Reckitt & Colman Products Ltd v Borden Inc* [1990] 1 W.L.R. 491; [1990] 1 All E.R. 873; [1990] R.P.C. 340, HL.
[2] *Erven Warnink BV v J Townend & Sons (Hull) Ltd* [1979] A.C. 731, 742; [1979] 2 All E.R. 927; [1980] R.P.C. 31, HL.
[3] *ibid.*, italics (in the R.P.C.s) are Lord Fraser's.
[4] (1915) 32 R.P.C. 273, HL.
[5] *Reckitt & Colman Products Ltd v Borden Inc* [1990] 1 W.L.R. 491; [1990] 1 All E.R. 873; [1990] R.P.C. 340, HL.

goods or services is the same as the source of those offered by the plaintiff."

And by Lord Jauncey in the same case:

"It is also a prerequisite that the misrepresentation has deceived or is likely to deceive and that the plaintiff is likely to suffer damage by such deception. Mere confusion which does not lead to a sale is not sufficient."

The two kinds of damage to goodwill

As with many kinds of property, the claimant's interest in his goodwill is **4–3** capable suffering from two fundamentally different kinds of damage, which might be labelled respectively as *destruction* and *diversion*. In the first case, the goodwill as such is destroyed, damaged, or depreciated. This is likely to happen, for instance, when dangerous or unsatisfactory counterfeit goods are sold under the claimant's name. Customers will no longer rely on the name, or may even avoid it, and the goodwill will cease to have any attractive power at all. In the second and probably more common type of case, the goodwill as such may not initially be damaged to any measurable extent, but the claimant is just as certainly deprived of its benefit: the "attractive force" which is the goodwill may draw in custom as powerfully as before, but draw it to the defendant and not to the claimant. These two situations are conveniently elided to go under the description of damage to the claimant's property in his goodwill, which may be further simplified to damage to the goodwill, although strictly speaking it is only in the first case that the goodwill as such is damaged. In the second, the claimant is damaged by being deprived of its benefit. As Laddie J. observed in *Irvine v Talksport*[6]:

"[T]he purpose of a passing off action is to vindicate the claimant's exclusive right to goodwill and to protect it against damage. When a defendant sells his inferior goods in substitution for the claimant's, there is no difficulty in a court finding that there is passing off. The substitution damages the goodwill and therefore the value of it to the claimant. The passing off action is brought to protect the claimant's property. But goodwill will be protected even if there is no immediate damage in the above sense. For example, it has long been recognised that a defendant cannot avoid a finding of passing off by showing that his goods or services are of as good or better quality than the claimant's. In such a case, although the defendant may not damage the goodwill as such, what he does is damage the value of the goodwill to the claimant because, instead of benefiting from exclusive rights to his property, the latter now finds that someone else is squatting on it."

[6] [2002] EWHC 367, [2002] 1 W.L.R. 2355, [2002] 2 All E.R. 424, [2002] E.M.L.R. 32, [2002] F.S.R. 60 (Laddie J.), affirmed in part [2003] EWCA Civ 423, [2003] 2 All E.R. 881; [2003] E.M.L.R. 26; [2003] F.S.R. 35, CA.

Of course, the two kinds of damage may and frequently do coexist in the same case, and one may merge into the other with the passage of time.

History: an action on the case

4–4 Passing-off is relatively new for a common-law tort, and because it was not within one of the nominate medieval forms of action it evolved as an action on the case. As with all actions on the case, no cause of action originally accrued until the plaintiff had suffered damage:

> "The action is one of that class which is known as an action on the case, akin to an action of deceit. In an action on the case, the cause of action is the wrongful act or default of the defendant. The right to bring the action depends on the happening of damage to the plaintiff. A man, for instance, may be negligent: and the consequences of his negligence may not cause damage for twelve months. The cause of action is the breach of duty: the right to bring the action depends upon the happening of the damage. But this class of case, forms an exception, or an apparent exception, to the ordinary action of deceit; because, in an ordinary action of deceit, the plaintiff's cause of action is false representation, but he cannot bring an action until the damage has accrued to him by reason of that false representation.
>
> In passing-off cases, the true basis of the action is that the passing off by the defendant of his goods as the goods of the plaintiff injures the right of property in the plaintiff, that right of property being his right to the goodwill of his business. The law assumes, or presumes, that, if the goodwill of a man's business has been interfered with by the passing off of goods, damage results therefrom. He need not wait to show that damage has resulted. He can bring his action as soon as he can prove the passing off; because it is one of the class of cases in which the law presumes that the plaintiff has suffered damage.
>
> It is in fact, I think, in the same category in this respect as is an action for libel."[7]

Of these comparisons the most relevant is probably the last. Passing-off and libel have in common the fact that it is possible for deception, and consequently damage, to occur on a wide scale without the claimant being able to point to any particular example. Members of the public who continue to be deceived will not, *ex hypothesi*, be aware of the fact, and those who were once deceived may not come forward to give evidence.[8] The practical difficulty of proving damage probably explains why in both torts it came to be sufficient to prove that the defendant's misrepresentation was one calculated to cause damage. However, in both cases this seems to have developed to the point where the tort may be complete even though no damage can have

---

[7] *per* Goddard L.J. in *Draper v Trist* [1939] 3 All E.R. 513 at 525; 56 R.P.C. 429, CA.

[8] The rationale is very similar to that given by Bowen L.J. in *Ratcliffe v Evans* [1892] 2 Q.B. 524, CA, where the context was injurious falsehood; but passing-off has gone much further than the latter, and without statutory intervention.

occurred. Thus, in libel, nominal damages may be awarded even though the statement may have been published only to one person, who knew the true facts and was not deceived. In passing-off substantial damages have been awarded although no customer could apparently have acted upon the misrepresentation complained of.[9]

Damage as the "acid test" for passing-off

Advocaat[10] and the preceding *Drinks Cases* threw wide open the question of **4–5** what categories of misrepresentations were to be actionable as passing-off. It was no longer possible to define the tort as one of misrepresenting one's goods or business as those of the claimant, with a few extensions of precise and limited scope. In principle, almost any misrepresentation might be considered actionable. Part of the answer has been found to lie in a much more rigorous investigation into whether damage to the claimant is really likely to result from the misrepresentation in issue. Faced with sets of facts which would hardly have fitted within the traditional notion of the tort, likelihood of damage provides one acid test to distinguish those misrepresentations which amount to passing-off from those of which the claimant cannot complain. In several cases subsequent to *Advocaat* the test of likelihood of damage has been applied with a degree of strictness unfamiliar since *Borthwick v Evening Post*.[11]

The former requirement that there be a common field of activity between claimant and defendant may now be regarded as discredited.[12] Now that there is no such convenient rule, the question of whether the defendant's misrepresentation will cause damage to a particular claimant is all the more important.[13] Conversely, there may be a common field of activity without any damage being caused to the claimant. In exceptional circumstances, there may be no damage though the parties provide the same goods or services under the same mark.[14]

The plaintiffs in *Anheuser-Busch v Budejovicky Budvar*[15] were American **4–6** brewers, and their claim to goodwill in England rested principally on sales to American servicemen at United States bases. The majority of the Court of Appeal doubted if this generated any relevant goodwill at all. All were agreed that such goodwill as the plaintiffs enjoyed in this special market was incapable of being damaged by the defendants, and that the action therefore failed.

In *Harrods v Harrodian School*[16] the difference in trading fields between

---

[9] As in *Spalding (AG) & Bros v A W Gamage Ltd* (1915) 32 R.P.C. 273, HL, where one of the main submissions for the defence was that no damage had accrued before issue of the writ.

[10] *Erven Warnink BV v J Townend & Sons (Hull) Ltd* [1979] A.C. 731; [1979] 2 All E.R. 927; [1980] R.P.C. 31, HL.

[11] (1883) 37 Ch. D. 449, CA.

[12] *Harrods Ltd v Harrodian School Ltd* [1996] R.P.C. 697, CA.

[13] *Annabel's (Berkeley Square) Ltd v Schock* [1972] R.P.C. 838, CA.

[14] *Anheuser-Busch Inc v Budejovicky Budvar NP* [1984] F.S.R. 413, CA; *Habib Bank Ltd v Habib Bank AG Zurich* [1981] 1 W.L.R. 1265; [1981] 2 All E.R. 650; [1982] R.P.C. 1, CA.

[15] [1984] F.S.R. 413, CA.

[16] [1996] R.P.C. 697, CA.

the plaintiffs' department store and the defendants' preparatory school meant that confusion would be non-existent or minimal, and unlikely to damage the plaintiffs to the limited extent it might occur. An attempt to argue that the reputation of *Harrods* would suffer because of an alleged adulterous affair between the Headmistress and the English Master at the defendant school was dismissed as fanciful; the remaining alleged heads of damage (none of which depended on confusion) are considered below.

Damage assumed

4–7 The converse doctrine is that damage will be assumed if the other elements of passing-off are present. The high water mark of this point of view is the decision of the Full Court of New South Wales in *Henderson v Radio Corporation*.[17] The defendants in that case issued a record of music for ballroom dancing and used a photograph of the plaintiff dancers on its sleeve without their authority. The Full Court rejected the trial judge's finding of actual damage as speculative, but found for the plaintiffs on the ground that a misappropriation of their professional reputation was sufficient damage in itself. The plaintiffs had been deprived on the fee they could have charged for their endorsement as effectively as if the defendants had handed over the money and then stolen it back.

If *Henderson v Radio Corporation* was intended to state a general rule for passing-off actions[18] it is not only inconsistent with English law, but with a subsequent decision of the Federal Court of Australia on appeal from New South Wales. In *Taco Bell v Taco Co of Australia*[19] the defendants and counterclaimants were an American company which operated a chain of Mexican-style restaurants under the name *Taco Bell*. On expanding into Australia they found themselves in conflict with a restaurant already trading under that name. The trial judge found against the Americans on the ground that they had no goodwill in New South Wales at the relevant time. On appeal, the Federal Court of Australia, following *Advocaat*,[20] came to the same conclusion on what it described as a narrower and surer ground. There was no probability of the opening of the plaintiffs' restaurant doing any damage to whatever reputation, goodwill or business the defendants[21] might already have had in Australia. *Taco Bell* may be seen as anticipating the decision of the Court of Appeal in *Anheuser Busch v Budejovicky Budvar*.[22] Unlike *Henderson*, it is consistent with the English doctrine that damage to goodwill is an essential requirement in its own right. However, *Henderson* has continued to be applied by Australian courts in the context of character merchandising and endorsement, notably in the two *Crocodile Dundee*[23]

---

[17] [1960] N.S.W.L.R. 279; [1969] R.P.C. 218.
[18] As opposed to ones based on the "right of publicity".
[19] (1982) 2 T.P.R. 48; 42 A.L.R. 177.
[20] *Erven Warnink BV v J Townend & Sons (Hull) Ltd* [1979] A.C. 731; [1979] 2 All E.R. 927; [1980] R.P.C. 31, HL.
[21] Counterclaimants.
[22] [1984] F.S.R. 413, CA.
[23] *Hogan v Koala Dundee* (1988) 12 I.P.R. 508 (Pincus J.) and *Hogan v Pacific Dunlop* [1989] A.T.P.R. 50,325 (Fed. Ct. of Australia).

cases, and the conclusion is unavoidable that they are resorting to a legal fiction.

Outside Australia, the reasoning of *Henderson v Radio Corp* has not gone **4–8** unchallenged. In a case in which character merchandising rights were asserted in the *Buzzy Bee* toy a New Zealand judge has observed:

"The other problem[24] concerns the damage alleged to have been suffered by the plaintiff. It is axiomatic that damage must be proved or presumed as one of the ingredients of passing-off. It has never been sufficient for plaintiffs to fill the gap by arguing that their loss is the right to charge the defendant for a fee for continuing conduct the lawfulness of which is the subject currently under enquiry. To accept that proposition would be to deny that damage is an essential and independent ingredient of the tort. And if the defendant's conduct is otherwise lawful, it cannot be rendered unlawful upon the ground that it might induce others to act in a similar way without the plaintiff's permission. Yet in *Crocodile Dundee*[25] and similar decisions, the damage relied upon has been the prejudice to the opportunity to license the merchandising 'right' to the defendant and others. The plaintiff has a right to extract a fee for character merchandising only if he has an enforceable right to prevent others from using his image without his permission. In the present context he has a right to prevent them only if he can sue them in passing-off. He can sue them in passing-off only if he can show a loss. The only loss he can point to is the loss of the right to insist upon a fee for the character merchandising. So the argument is circular. Unless there is some damage other than the loss of potential character merchandising rights, one might think that the action would fail on that ground."[26]

Damage and *quia timet* actions

There may still be a degree of uncertainty as to whether actual damage must **4–9** have occurred for the cause of action in passing-off to have accrued. In other words, can nominal damages be awarded if a misrepresentation calculated to cause damage has been made but no damage can yet have been caused? Lord Diplock's choice of words in *Advocaat*[27] suggests that in such circumstances any action is *quia timet*, but there are reasons for believing that his formulation is, for once, too narrow. Lord Parker, in *Spalding v Gamage*, preferred the view that there was a *prima facie* right to at least nominal damages upon the misrepresentation being made: "It is sufficient to say that the misrepresentation being established, and being in its nature calculated to produce damage, the plaintiffs are *prima facie* entitled both to

---

[24] The first being whether there was a misrepresentation.
[25] The reference is to *Hogan v Koala Dundee* (1988) 12 I.P.R. 508.
[26] *per* Fisher J. in *Tot Toys v Mitchell* (1992) 25 I.P.R. 337 (HC of NZ).
[27] *Erven Warnink BV v J Townend & Sons (Hull) Ltd* [1979] A.C. 731; [1979] 2 All E.R. 927; [1980] R.P.C. 31, HL.

an injunction and to an inquiry as to damage, the inquiry, of course, being at their own risk in respect of costs".[28]

Passing-off actions are often *quia timet*, or at least are brought so early that actual damage is hard to prove and likely to be slight. A claimant who obtains an injunction, especially an interlocutory one, is often prepared to forego damages, and until the early twentieth century would not have asked for damages unless he had been able to prove fraud. Even on very careful examination, it is hard to say of many early precedents whether they were *quia timet* or whether the cause of action was thought to be complete.

4–10   It is likely that the law has developed on the basis that acts which were originally only restrained *quia timet*, or under the equitable protective jurisdiction, subsequently came to be regarded as actionable *per se*. For the award of an injunction, it never mattered whether the cause of action was complete or not, as long as there was a subsisting right to protect against a threatened infringement. If there was a precedent for granting an injunction, then there may have seemed to have been one for granting first nominal damages, and later substantial damages or profits. This can be no more than conjecture, but it would explain the unconscious progress the law has made from giving nominal damages when there was passing off in fact,[29] to giving substantial damages merely for offering deceptive goods for sale.[30] It would also explain why damages or profits have come to be awarded simply for disposing of "instruments of deception" to middlemen,[31] even though on a traditional view of the tort the cause of action would not be complete until much later.

The result is anomalous: damage remains an essential element of the tort in that it is only misrepresentations calculated to cause damage which are actionable. On the other hand, the cause of action for passing-off appears to be capable of arising before any actual damage can have been caused to the claimant. In this respect passing-off has parted company with deceit and negligence.

B. The Requirement to Prove Damage in Practice

What the claimant has to prove

4–11 The claimant does not have to prove actual damage (still less special damage) in order to succeed in an action for passing-off. Likelihood of damage is sufficient.

> "[I]t is well established that a court of equity will protect the business reputation enjoyed by any person or corporation against tangible risk or

---

[28] *Spalding (AG) & Bros v A W Gamage Ltd* (1915) 32 R.P.C. 273, HL, *per* Lord Parker.
[29] *Blofeld v Payne* (1833) 110 E.R. 509.
[30] *Spalding (AG) & Bros v A W Gamage Ltd* (1918) 35 R.P.C. 101, CA.
[31] *Lever v Goodwin* [1887] 36 Ch.D. 1; [1900] 4 R.P.C. 492, CA; *Draper v Trist* [1939] 3 All E.R. 513; 56 R.P.C. 429, CA.

probability of injury, just as it will protect any other property of such person or corporation against any such risk or probability. One of the ways in which a business reputation may be injured is by the appropriation by a stranger of part of such reputation. Such appropriation may be brought about by the adoption of a name which suggests that the person or corporation adopting it is in some way connected or associated with the person or corporation enjoying the reputation.

Damage or likelihood of damage is the gist of all such actions, and unless a plaintiff can prove that his credit or business reputation has suffered damage or that there is a tangible risk or probability of his credit or business reputation suffering damage, no action will lie.

In cases of fraud the court will readily assume that the defendant has succeeded or will succeed in accomplishing that which he has set himself to accomplish,[32] and in such a case the onus of proof of damage or of likelihood of damage is, speaking generally, not heavy."[33]

"It is well settled that the plaintiff in a passing-off action does not have to prove that he has actually suffered damage by loss of business or in any other way. A probability of damage is enough, but the actual or probable damage must be damage to him in his trade or business, that is to say, damage to the goodwill in respect of that trade or business."[34]

The action must therefore fail if no damage to the claimant's goodwill is reasonably likely to occur, even if the facts of the case correspond to the typical passing-off action in every other respect.[35]

In *Borthwick v Evening Post*[36] the plaintiff was the publisher of the **4–12** *Morning Post* newspaper. The defendants commenced to publish an evening newspaper as the *Evening Post*. Apart from the titles, the papers were dissimilar. The Court of Appeal held that despite examples of actual deception and evidence of fraudulent intent there would be no damage to the plaintiff. Although the *Evening Post* might be taken for an evening edition of the *Morning Post* the papers were not in competition. Purchasers of the evening paper would not buy the morning one any less often, whatever they thought, so no sales would be lost directly. The argument that the *Morning Post's*

---

[32] This is probably in deference to *Harrods Ltd v R Harrod Ltd* (1924) 41 R.P.C. 74, CA, in which Pollock M.R. came close to saying that damage was unnecessary if there was fraud. But even the fraudulent defendant never means to damage the claimant, but to benefit himself.

[33] *per* Lawrence J. in *Motor Manufacturers' & Traders' Insurance Society v Motor Manufacturers' & Traders' Insurance Co* [1925] Ch. 675 at 686; [1925] All E.R. 616; 42 R.P.C. 307 affirmed *ibid.*, CA. But there was no likelihood of deception, nor of any damage if deception did arise.

[34] *per* Buckley L.J. in *Bulmer (H P) Ltd v J Bollinger SA* [1978] R.P.C. 79; [1978] 2 C.M.L.R. 625, CA. However, the majority of the Court of Appeal (Buckley and Goff L.JJ., Waller L.J. dissenting) found for the defendants to the counterclaim because there was no proof of deception or damage in fact despite the length of time they had been on the market.

[35] The fact that profits are damaged does not give *locus standi*: *Dental Manufacturing Co Ltd v C de Trey & Co* [1912] 3 K.B. 76; 29 R.P.C. 557, CA; *Bulmer (H P) Ltd v J Bollinger SA* [1978] R.P.C. 79; [1978] 2 C.M.L.R. 625 CA, *per* Buckley L.J. at 99; *Poister Ltd v Marcel Fenez Ltd* [1965] R.P.C. 187.

[36] (1888) 37 Ch.D. 449, CA.

readers might disapprove of the quality, contents or politics of the new paper and cease buying the former was also rejected. Differences of that sort would simply disabuse readers of the thought that there was any connection between the papers.[37]

Circumstances in which damage may be assumed

4–13 For many years passing-off actions were decided with little or no express consideration of whether the plaintiff would suffer actual damage, or in what form. This may be explained by the very restrictive view of the tort generally observed between *Spalding v Gamage*[38] and *Advocaat*.[39] A misrepresentation that the defendant's goods or business are those of the claimant is intrinsically likely to damage the claimant if the fields of business of the claimant and defendant are reasonably close. The fact that virtually every successful passing-off action for half a century fell into this category meant that an inquiry as to damages could be granted as a matter of routine if the other elements of the tort were made out.

Some difficulties may apparently be caused by *dicta* to the effect that damage will be assumed if passing off is proved or admitted to have occurred. In *Draper v Trist*[40] the defendant admitted passing off and submitted to an order for an inquiry as to damages. On the inquiry he attempted to argue that the plaintiff had suffered no damage. The Court of Appeal rejected this contention. The decision has sometimes been used to support the argument that damage is not a necessary independent element of the tort, in that it will be inferred if the other elements are present. The better conclusion is the opposite one. By admitting liability for passing-off the defendant had implicitly admitted all its essential elements, one of which is damage. He therefore could not be heard to say that no damage had been caused.

4–14 The term "passing off" was not originally a legal term of art. It meant the actual sale to a customer of goods which were not those he wanted or expected. "Passing off" has continued to be used occasionally in this sense long after the "action for passing-off" ceased to require that any identifiable person should actually have been deceived into buying the defendant's goods for those of the claimant.

> "My Lords, the action in which this appeal arises is what is known as a passing-off action, and having regard to the arguments which have been addressed to your Lordships, I think it well to say a few words as to the principle on which such actions are founded. This principle is ... the

[37] See also *Walter v Emmot* (1885) 54 L.J. Ch. 1059; 54 L.T. 437, CA (*The Mail, The Morning Mail*) and *Oughtram v London Evening Newspapers Co* (1911) 28 R.P.C. 308 (London, Glasgow); but compare *Associated Newspapers Ltd v Express Newspapers* [2003] EWHC 1322.
[38] *Spalding (A G) & Bros v A W Gamage Ltd* (1915) 32 R.P.C. 273, HL.
[39] *Erven Warnink BV v J Townend & Sons (Hull) Ltd* [1979] A.C. 731; [1979] 2 All E.R. 927; [1980] R.P.C. 31, HL.
[40] [1939] 3 All E.R. 513; 56 R.P.C. 429, CA.

proposition that nobody has any right to represent his goods as the goods of somebody else. It is also sometimes stated in the proposition that nobody has the right to pass off his goods as the goods of someone else. I prefer the former statement, for whatever doubts may be suggested in the earlier authorities, it has long been settled that actual passing off of the defendant's goods for the plaintiff's need not be proved as a condition precedent to relief in equity either by way of an injunction or of an inquiry as to profits or damages."[41]

This ambiguity should be borne in mind when considering statements[42] to the effect that damage to the claimant is to be inferred if passing off is proved to have taken place. Such statements are not circular, as long as the term "passing off" is understood in its older and narrower sense. Nor are they redundant, since strict proof of damage to the claimant might require more than proof of the fact that a real customer was deceived.

Confusion, deception and damage

The existence of confusion, especially in the popular sense of the public **4–15** sometimes failing to distinguish the goods or businesses of the claimant and defendant, does not mean that there is actionable passing-off. "There must be deception, whether intentional or unintentional. If there is no deception, mere confusion or the likelihood of confusion is not sufficient to give a cause of action".[43] Confusion may arise without any misrepresentation,[44] and even if the confusion is the result of a misrepresentation it may not necessarily be damaging to the claimant. In the typical case between trade competitors it is fairly safe to assume (at least as a starting point) that confusion is either inherently damaging, or a sufficient indication of damage, but there are exceptions. Occasional inconvenience does not amount to damage. As Lord Greene M.R. put it in *Marengo v Daily Sketch*[45]:

"No one is entitled to be protected against confusion as such. Confusion may result from the collision of two independent rights or liberties and where that is the case neither party can complain; they must put up with the results of the confusion as one of the misfortunes which occur in life. The protection to which a man is entitled is protection against passing-off which is quite a different thing from mere confusion."

In *HFC Bank v Midland Bank*[46] there was some confusion between the **4–16** claimants and the defendants when the latter rebranded themselves as

[41] *per* Lord Parker in *Spalding (A G) & Bros v A W Gamage Ltd* (1915) 32 R.P.C. 273, 283, HL
[42] Such as that of Goddard L.J. in *Draper v Trist*, above.
[43] *per* Robert Walker J. in *Barnsley Brewery Co Ltd v RBNB* [1997] F.S.R. 462. See also the quotation from the speech of Lord Jauncey in *Reckitt & Colman Products Ltd v Borden Inc* [1990] 1 W.L.R. 491; [1990] 1 All E.R. 873; [1990] R.P.C. 340, HL, quoted above.
[44] *County Sound plc v Ocean Sound Ltd* [1991] F.S.R. 367, CA.
[45] (1946) [1992] F.S.R. 1 reversed (on the facts) by (1948) 65 R.P.C. 242, HL.
[46] [2000] F.S.R. 176 (Lloyd J.).

HSBC, but much of this was due to the relatively low level of brand recognition which the claimants enjoyed for their name, and none of it was such as to amount to passing-off. The evidence only went to show "that people make assumptions, jump to unjustified conclusions, and put two and two together to make five".[47] This passage from *HFC Bank v Midland Bank* was quoted with approval by the Court of Appeal in *Premier Luggage and Bags v Premier Co*[48] where Chadwick L.J. (also referring to the judgment of Millett L.J. in *Harrods v Harrodian School*) observed:

> "The relevant question, in the context of an action for passing off, is not whether there is a risk of confusion because the defendant's name is similar to the plaintiff's name; the relevant question is whether the defendant's use of his name in connection with his goods or his business will be taken as a representation that his goods or business are, or have some connection with, the goods or business of the plaintiff—so giving rise to harm, or the risk of harm, to the goodwill and reputation which the plaintiff is entitled to protect. A risk of confusion is not enough."

The relevance of actual confusion

4–17 Even the fact that members of the public can be shown to have been deceived into believing that the defendant's goods or business were those of the claimant does not quite prove that the claimant must have suffered damage. Customers may have bought the defendant's goods in the belief that they were the claimant's, but this does not mean that they bought them because they thought they were the claimant's. Customers frequently buy whatever is available, irrespective of the brand. "[I]f a customer asks for a tin of black shoe polish without specifying any brand and is offered the product of A which he mistakenly believes to be that of B, he may be confused as to what he has got but he has not been deceived into getting it. Misrepresentation has played no part in his purchase".[49] In some fields of business brand loyalty is probably the exception rather than the rule, in others customers may have a preferred brand but will not put themselves to any inconvenience to obtain it.

Evidence of actual confusion is cogent evidence that damage is likely, but not always any more than that.

> "I am satisfied that both these witnesses, when they purchased the respondents' lipstick, thought that they were purchasing lipstick manufactured by the appellants. I cannot help thinking that Bennett J. approached the consideration of the evidence under a misapprehension as to its real significance. He seems to have thought that, but for their belief that the lipstick was the appellants', they would not have bought it. I

---

[47] *per* Lloyd J., above.
[48] [2002] EWCA Civ 387; [2002] E.T.M.R. 69; [2003] F.S.R. 5, CA *per* Chadwick L.J. (delivering the judgment of the Court).
[49] *per* Lord Jauncey in *Reckitt & Colman Products Ltd v Borden Inc* [1990] 1 W.L.R. 491; [1990] 1 All E.R. 873; [1990] R.P.C. 340, HL.

agree that they do not establish this fact. But this does not, as Bennett J. seems to have thought, dispose of their evidence. It is true that the deception may not have induced the purchases, but it was there all the same, and the evidence is valuable as showing that the respondents' goods were sold in a manner calculated to lead to the belief that they were the goods of the appellants."[50]

Damage and "instruments of deception"

It has generally been accepted that the tort of passing-off is complete when **4–18** the defendant disposes of goods which are calculated to deceive, even if the immediate recipient is a trader who is not himself deceived. This is despite the fact that no actual damage can normally be said to accrue until the infringing goods are sold to a customer who had intended to buy the goods of the claimant, which often will not be until the goods are purchased by the ultimate consumer. In particular, the numerous cases on "instruments of deception" being exported by the defendant to foreign markets are only consistent with the proposition that a cause of action for an injunction and for damages accrues on the disposal to a middleman (or even a carrier) in England, notwithstanding that the actual passing off (in the factual sense of the term) occurs abroad. Indeed, no misrepresentation can really be said to be made and acted upon until the goods are put on the market in the foreign country, which is where the damage to the claimant's goodwill occurs.

Similarly, a defendant is liable to account for his illegitimate profits on all instruments of deception disposed of by him, notwithstanding that not all of them may subsequently be disposed of in such a way as to deceive.[51] The magnitude of his liability to damages depends on an estimate of how the goods will subsequently be marketed, but the principle remains that the tort is complete and the right to at least nominal damages accrues as soon as the goods leave his hands.

Fraud

The courts have generally not insisted on proof of damage in cases where **4–19** fraudulent intent has been made out,[52] even if the respective fields of business of the parties differed widely. The reason normally given is that if the defendant clearly intended to appropriate the benefit to the claimant's reputation, he is not to be believed if he pretends to have failed in his object.[53] So far as the issue is one of whether there has been a mis-

---

[50] *per* Lord Greene M.R. in *Saville Perfumery Ltd v June Perfect* (1941) 58 R.P.C. 147, CA affirmed *ibid.*, HL. See also *Asprey & Garrard v WRA (Guns) Ltd and Asprey* [2002] F.S.R. 30 (Jacob J.) affirmed [2001] EWCA Civ 1499; [2002] E.T.M.R. 47; [2002] F.S.R. 31, CA, where evidence of actual examples of confusion (in the popular sense) were persuasive although none of them amounted to examples of passing-off in fact.
[51] *Lever v Goodwin* [1887] 36 Ch.D. 1; 4 R.P.C. 492, CA.
[52] *Lloyd's & Dawson Bros v Lloyds, Southampton Ltd* (1911) 29 R.P.C. 433, CA; *Harrods Ltd v R Harrod Ltd* (1924) 41 R.P.C. 74, CA.
[53] *Motor Manufacturers' & Traders' Society v Motor Manufacturers' & Traders' Insurance Co* [1925] Ch 675; [1925] All E.R. 616; [1900] 42 R.P.C. 307, CA.

representation, this is reasonable. Fraud ought, for instance, to be very nearly conclusive as to whether any differences in the defendant's mark are material.[54] However, it must be accepted that there are circumstances in which an otherwise actionable misrepresentation causes no damage.[55] The intention of the fraudulent defendant is always to benefit himself, not to damage the claimant. Damage in terms of lost business is only a necessary consequence of the defendant's intention to deceive if the parties are in actual competition.

There are two other reasons which can be advanced for not requiring proof of damage in cases of fraud. One is that the defendant who deliberately deceives his customers as to the origin of his goods or the identity of his business is likely to be no more scrupulous in the rest of his dealings. He is likely to have or deserve a bad reputation, which may rub off on the claimant. The other is that by intentionally taking the benefit of the claimant's reputation, the defendant has indicated that he would, if honest, have been willing to pay for a licence, however improbable the granting of one might otherwise have seemed.[56]

Damage in the *Harrods* case

4–20 The conflicting views on the importance and nature of damage in the modern law of passing-off are well illustrated by the judgments of the Court of Appeal in *Harrods v Harrodian School.*[57] Harman J. dismissed the action at trial, holding that there was no likelihood of confusion, but did not deal separately with the issue of damage. The majority in the Court of Appeal[58] affirmed him in terms consistent with the treatment of damage in *Stringfellow v McCain.*[59]

Beldam L.J. explained the majority view of the interrelation between the extent of any confusion, and the likelihood that confusion would be damaging. On the facts, and given the very distinct fields of activity of the parties, the plaintiffs had failed to prove their case.

"The risk of significant damage to the appellant's goodwill and reputation from the activities of the defendant depends not only on the nature and strength of the connection made by the public who perceive a link in the name notwithstanding the different spheres of activity, but also on how many of those persons would in consequence regard shortcomings in the running of the school as reflecting adversely on the quality of the goods and services offered in the department store and on its reputation as a supplier of such goods and services and so whether any customer or

---

[54] *Slazenger & Sons v Feltham & Co* (1889) 6 R.P.C. 531, CA.
[55] *Stringfellow v McCain Foods (GB) Ltd* [1984] R.P.C. 501, CA.
[56] Compare *Stringfellow v McCain Foods (GB) Ltd* [1984] R.P.C. 501, CA, where importance was attached to the fact that the defendant had acted innocently and gained no benefit from the endorsement which the public might suppose to exist.
[57] [1996] R.P.C. 697, CA.
[58] Millett and Beldam L.JJ.
[59] [1984] R.P.C. 501; [1984] F.S.R. 199, C.A.

potential customer is likely to withhold, withdraw or reduce his custom or consider the appellant's reputation for excellence to be diminished."

In a dissenting judgment,[60] Sir Michael Kerr would have allowed the **4–21** plaintiffs' appeal. He would have held that:

"Loss of distinctiveness causes damage to a reputation for excellence, and loss of trade will ultimately follow. The authorities show two relevant propositions in this regard. First, a debasement or dilution of the plaintiffs' reputation, as the result of the action of the defendant, is a relevant head of damage. Secondly, if the act which constitutes the passing-off has the effect of raising in people's minds the mistaken belief of a connection between the defendant and the plaintiff, but which is in fact non-existent, then the court will have regard to the fact that the plaintiff has, to that extent, lost control of his reputation, and that he has therefore suffered damage to his goodwill by a potentially injurious association with the defendant against which the court will protect him by injunction."

From the words "potentially injurious association" as well as other passages it is clear that to Sir Michael Kerr, the mere loss of exclusivity or control of the name *Harrods* was damage enough: it was irrelevant that the defendants might not be taken as having any connection at all with the plaintiffs, or that there was nothing currently or foreseeably disreputable or discreditable about their business.[61] Citing but distinguishing *Taittinger v Allbev*[62] where (to quote Bingham M.R.) the defendants' conduct would "debase or cheapen" the plaintiffs' reputation for *Champagne* he went on:

"In fairness to the defendants, it cannot of course be said in the present case that a similar consequence would necessarily follow, and indeed it is greatly to be hoped that this would not be the case. But that is not the test. The crucial point, as stated in the second of the foregoing propositions, is the plaintiff's inevitable loss of control of his reputation and the consequent risk of damage to it."

As a third head of damage Sir Michael Kerr alluded to the argument that the plaintiffs would have to abandon their proposed use of *Harrodian* in relation to various facilities at the *Harrods House Hotel* which they planned to open.

The problem with a strong dissenting judgment is that it gives expression **4–22** to the very arguments which have been rejected by the majority. If any of the heads of damage identified below as reputation in defendant's hands, restriction on expansion, loss of exclusivity, or dilution were sufficient to

---

[60] The dissent of Sir Michael Kerr was cited in *EasyJet Airline Co Ltd v Dainty* [2002] F.S.R. 6 as if it were part of the *ratio*.

[61] The former distinguishes *Harrods* from *Dawnay Day & Co Ltd v Cantor Fitzgerald International* [2000] R.P.C. 669, CA, where confusion was likely and loss of control of the name was therefore a relevant head of damage.

[62] [1993] 2 C.M.L.R. 741; [1993] F.S.R. 641, CA.

support a passing-off action in their own right, then Harrods should have won.[63] That they did not, confirms that damage is still an independent and essential element of the tort alongside misrepresentation and goodwill, and that the damage relied on must arise from the misrepresentation as the cause of confusion.[64] Millett L.J. in the majority noted the inconsistency of relying on one specific head of damage, erosion of distinctiveness, which arose independently of one of the other essential elements of the tort:

"I have an intellectual difficulty in accepting the concept that the law insists upon the presence of both confusion and damage and yet recognises as sufficient a head of damage which does not depend on confusion."

The same applies to the other heads relied on by Sir Michael Kerr: they can arise independently of any misrepresentation, the interest protected is not the claimant's goodwill, and they potentially debase the element of damage to a mere circularity, a legal fiction.

A rule of reason

4–23 There is a difference in emphasis, to say the least, between two lines of authority on the importance of damage as an independent element of the tort. The more rigorous[65] requires proof of likelihood of damage in every case and is quite prepared to hold that the senior user suffers no damage although the junior user is using the same name, in the same business, for the same narrowly defined class of customers, at an address a few hundred yards away.[66] The other line[67] is prepared to go a long way to assuming likelihood of damage once deception (or even confusion) has been proved. Without understating the importance of damage as the acid test in cases on the borderline of the tort this seems to be the more realistic approach in the

---

[63] Though not "confusion *per se*", it being common ground to the trial judge and all three members of the Court of Appeal that probability of confusion in the normal sense had not been made out.

[64] It is notable that the *Merc* case, *Daimler-Chrysler AG v Alavi* [2001] R.P.C. 42 was argued and decided without any mention of dilution.

[65] Represented in comparatively recent times by *Unitex Ltd v Union Texturising Co Ltd* [1973] F.S.R. 181; [1973] R.P.C. 119, CA; *Hayter (John) Motor Underwriting Agencies Ltd v RBHS Agencies Ltd* [1977] F.S.R. 285, CA; the majority in *Bulmer (H P) Ltd v Bollinger SA* [1978] 2 C.M.L.R. 625; [1978] R.P.C. 79, CA; *Habib Bank Ltd v Habib Bank AG Zurich* [1981] 1 W.L.R. 1265; [1981] 2 All E.R. 650; [1982] R.P.C. 1, CA; *Stringfellow v McCain Foods (GB) Ltd* [1984] R.P.C. 501, CA; *Anheuser-Busch Inc v Budejovicky Budvar NP* [1984] F.S.R. 413, CA; and the majority in *Harrods Ltd v Harrodian School Ltd* [1996] R.P.C. 697, CA.

[66] The facts of *Habib Bank Ltd v Habib Bank AG Zurich* [1981] 1 W.L.R. 1265; [1981] 2 All E.R. 650; [1982] R.P.C. 1, CA, though lack of damage was not the most important issue.

[67] Represented by *Brestian v Try* [1958] R.P.C. 161, CA; the dissenting judgment of Waller L.J. in *Bulmer (H P) Ltd v J Bollinger SA* [1978] 2 C.M.L.R. 625; [1978] R.P.C. 79, CA; *Chelsea Man Menswear Ltd v Chelsea Girl Ltd* [1987] R.P.C. 189, CA; *McDonalds Hamburgers Ltd v Burger King (UK) Ltd* [1987] F.S.R. 112, CA; *Taittinger SA v Allbev Ltd* [1993] 2 C.M.L.R. 741; [1993] F.S.R. 641, CA; the dissenting judgment of Sir Michael Kerr in *Harrods Ltd v Harrodian School Ltd* [1996] R.P.C. 697, CA; and *Dawnay Day & Co Ltd v Cantor Fitzgerald International* [2000] R.P.C. 669, CA.

typical passing-off action, especially given the increasing pressure (under the Civil Procedure Rules) on trial duration and the fact that the measure of any damages will be evaluated separately in the inquiry. "It is the injury to the goodwill rather than the precise method of inflicting that injury that matters".[68] It may be hard to pin down what damage the claimant will suffer or when, but it is sometimes even harder to believe that in the long term he will suffer none at all.

Most of the authorities may perhaps be reconciled with the proposition that the risk of damage is sufficiently real if:

1. Confusion between the parties will be widespread and inevitable, even though there may be no immediate reason to believe that actual damage in any particular form will occur, or

2. There will be some confusion of the parties, and the defendant's business poses a special risk to the claimant because of the way it is currently conducted or because of future developments which can actually be expected.

If confusion with the claimant is slight and tangible damage speculative then there is no liability for passing off.

The best short formulation of the test to apply is probably that of Lord Fraser in *Advocaat*[69]: is there a misrepresentation which is *really likely* to cause substantial damage to the claimant's goodwill? If there is fraud or the claimant stands to lose sales to the defendant then damage will normally be inferred. If not, the major head of damage to consider is general damage to goodwill. The legal burden of proving damage is always on the claimant, but the evidential burden is not. In practice, damage still tends to be assumed unless the case is on the borderline of what would traditionally have been regarded as passing-off[70]; or the defendant's conduct has persisted openly for such a length of time that actual damage, had any occurred, would be easy to prove.[71]

Recognised, emergent and parasitic heads of damage

The following section lists the various heads of damage which have been **4-24** considered sufficiently often in the context of passing-off for there to be a reasonably sized body of law on which to comment. That is not to say that all these heads ought to be regarded as recognised as established in every

---

[68] *per* Megarry V.C. in *British Broadcasting Co v Talbot Motor Co Ltd* [1981] F.S.R. 228; *Ewing v Buttercup Margarine Co Ltd* [1917] 2 Ch. 1; [1916–17] All E.R. 1012; 34 R.P.C. 232, CA.
[69] *Erven Warnink BV v J Townend & Sons (Hull) Ltd* [1979] A.C. 731; [1979] 2 All E.R. 927; [1980] R.P.C. 31, HL.
[70] *Stringfellow v McCain Foods (GB) Ltd* [1984] R.P.C. 501, CA; *Anheuser-Busch Inc v Budejovicky Budvar NP* [1984] F.S.R. 413, CA.
[71] *Bulmer (H P) Ltd v J Bollinger SA* [1978] 2 C.M.L.R. 625; [1978] R.P.C. 79, CA; *Habib Bank Ltd v Habib Bank AG Zurich* [1981] 1 W.L.R. 1265; [1981] 2 All E.R. 650; [1982] R.P.C. 1, CA.

context or applicable in every case. They are presented according to an informal ranking in which the first five enumerated heads are fully established, and the remainder need to be treated with varying degrees of caution. The common problem with all but the last of the remaining heads is that if damage under one of these were sufficient to support an action for passing-off, then there would be no genuine need to prove damage as an essential element of the tort in its own right: it could be assumed almost regardless of the facts of the case. This would deprive damage of its value as the acid test for distinguishing actionable misrepresentations from those outside the scope of the law. The final head, dilution, is different in that relatively few claimants could invoke it at all, because it assumes that the mark in question is exclusive to an exceptional degree. It is placed last because it is inherently a form of damage which does not arise from misrepresentation and so has little or no relevance to passing-off.

It is suggested that there may be a distinction to be drawn between heads of damage which are sufficient to support a passing-off action in their own right, and those which may be taken into account in some circumstances, but only if the damage under one of the heads in the first category can be proven or presumed. To this extent, the situation is analogous to negligence, where pure economic loss is not, in general, actionable in its own right although economic loss can be recovered if damage to physical property has occurred. One has, so to speak, a category of recoverable parasitic damages.

C. Heads of Damage in Passing-Off

Direct loss of sales

4–25 The earliest actions for passing-off were between traders who were in actual competition for the same customers in the same market, and despite the extent to which the law has developed this remains the most common factual situation to this day. It has long been recognised that damages could be awarded for: "depriving [the plaintiff] of the profit he might have made by the sale of the goods which, *ex hypothesi*, the purchaser intended to buy",[72] irrespective of the quality of the defendant's own goods.

> "The original foundation of the whole law is this, that when one knowing that goods are not made by a particular trader sells them as and for the goods of that trader, he does that which injures that trader. At first, it was put upon the ground that he did so when he sold inferior goods as and for the trader's; but it is established (alike at law: *Blofeld v Payne*,[73] and in equity: *Edelsten v Edelsten*,[74]) that it is an actionable injury to pass off

---

[72] *per* Lord Cranworth L.C. in *Seixo v Provezende* (1866) 1 Ch. App. 192.
[73] (1833) 110 E.R. 509.
[74] (1863) 46 E.R. 72 (Lord Westbury L.C.).

goods known not to be the plaintiff's as and for the plaintiff's, even though not inferior."[75]

Direct loss of sales is the major head of damage in most cases in which the parties are in actual competition. Normally, its existence is so obvious as to require no express mention, and examples are almost superfluous.[76] The parties need not appeal to the same classes of customer for there to be damage under this head. If the claimant deals in expensive goods of high quality and the defendant in cheaper ones then there may be no competition in the sense that any purchaser would consciously buy from the defendant rather than the claimant, but an unwary customer may still buy the defendant's goods under the impression that they are those of the claimant.[77] The loss may be indirect, as in *Hoffman-La Roche v DDSA*[78] where the plaintiffs lost sales to pharmacists as a result of patients being misled.

In *Unik Time Co v Unik Time*[79] the plaintiffs used *Unik Time* as the brand **4–26** name for their watches, the defendants as the name of their wholesale business. On an inquiry as to damages by consent, the defendants argued that because they did not deal in watches bearing the mark *Unik Time* itself, the plaintiffs would suffer damage only in the rare case of a trader approaching the defendants for *Unik Time* watches and either consenting to buy another brand, or buying no watches at all from either party. Warner J. disagreed. Traders might have heard that a company called *Unik Time* made good watches, without knowing what brand name they were sold under. They might buy the defendants' watches under the impression those were the watches of whose reputation they had heard.

In *Warnink v Townend*[80] the defendants used the name *Advocaat* for a drink which was based on sherry rather than *Brandewijn* and were able to undercut the plaintiffs by 50 p per bottle. They admitted that the plaintiffs had lost some business, although they thought the less successful Dutch brands had suffered more. "In this class of case there are ... two types of damage to be considered: direct loss of sales through the defendants' illegitimate competition, and a more gradual damage to the plaintiffs' business through depreciation of the reputation their goods enjoy".[81]

Inferiority of defendant's goods or services

The damage the claimant suffers by having inferior goods passed off as his is **4–27** the oldest recognised head of damage in passing-off.[82] When the claimant

---

[75] *per* Lord Blackburn in *Singer v Loog* (1882) 8 App. Cas. 15, HL.
[76] They might include *Powell v Birmingham Vinegar Brewery Co* [1897] A.C. 710; 14 R.P.C. 721, HL; and *Reddaway (Frank) & Co Ltd v George Banham & Co Ltd* [1896] A.C. 199; [1895–9] All E.R. 313; 13 R.P.C. 218, HL.
[77] *Chelsea Man Menswear Ltd v Chelsea Girl Ltd* [1987] R.P.C. 189. CA.
[78] [1969] F.S.R. 416, CA.
[79] [1983] F.S.R. 121, (Warner J.).
[80] [1979] A.C. 731; [1979] 2 All E.R. 927; [1980] R.P.C. 31, HL.
[81] *per* Goulding J at first instance. Neither Lord Diplock nor Lord Fraser, though affirming that damage was essential to the tort, found it necessary to go into even this much detail.
[82] See the quotation from Lord Blackburn in *Singer v Loog* (1882) 8 App. Cas. 15, HL, above.

and defendant are in actual competition this head of damage is not essential to the cause of action, but it may still be relevant as strengthening the balance of convenience in favour of the claimant on an application for an interlocutory injunction. If the claimant and defendant do not compete, it shades into the broader idea of "injurious association"[83] with the claimant.

There is one category of case in which it is essential that the goods offered by the defendant should be of a recognisably different quality to those of the claimant. That is where the defendant is dealing in goods which really are those of the claimant, but is passing off one quality for another. In theory, all that is necessary is that there should be two distinct categories of goods, but in practice this form of passing-off is only likely to occur in the form of inferior goods being passed off as the superior.[84]

In *Bollinger v Costa Brava Wine Co*[85] Dankwerts J. quoted a witness's comment on Spanish Champagne with apparent approval: "That is enough to put anybody off wine-drinking for life. They will drink it, think it nasty, and never drink any more wine".

Similar reasoning may be implicit in the other drinks cases, especially those such as *Bulmer v Bollinger*[86] in which the defendant's goods were so inferior to those of the plaintiff as hardly to be in the same market.

In *Chelsea Man v Chelsea Girl*[87] the plaintiffs used the mark *Chelsea Man* on a fairly small scale for high quality leather jackets and similar clothing meant for comparatively older and wealthier customers. The defendants intended to use it for cheap and ephemeral fashion garments for the teenage market. This was bound to damage the plaintiffs over and above direct loss of sales.

4–28 Damage arising from the defendant's goods being inferior to those of the claimant is particularly important on applications for interlocutory injunctions. It is harder to quantify than simple loss of sales, and damages are less likely to compensate the claimant adequately.

> "The damage that may be done to the plaintiffs, if inferior work is put out as being the work of *Rolls-Royce*, is quite incalculable and of very great financial harm to *Rolls-Royce*. On this aspect of the case they are certainly in a very unusual position, in that a large part of the goodwill of *Rolls-Royce* does depend on their reputation for immaculate finish and engineering."[88]

In *Combe v Scholl*[89] the defendants implicitly misrepresented that their

---

[83] The expression is that of Megarry J. in *Unitex Ltd v Union Texturising Co Ltd* [1973] R.P.C. 119.

[84] *Spalding (A G) & Bros v A W Gamage Ltd* (1915) 32 R.P.C. 273, HL; *Wilts United Dairies Ltd v Thomas Robinson Sons & Co Ltd* [1958] R.P.C. 94, CA. Compare *Hunt, Roope, Teague & Co v Ehrmann Bros.* [1910] 2 Ch. 198 and *Harris v Warren & Phillips* (1918) 35 R.P.C. 217.

[85] *Bollinger v Costa Brava Wine Co Ltd* [1960] Ch. 262; [1959] 3 All E.R. 800; [1960] R.P.C. 16.

[86] *Bulmer (H P) Ltd v Bollinger SA* [1976] R.P.C. 97 (reversed as to one defendant [1978] R.P.C. 79; [1978] 2 C.M.L.R. 625, CA).

[87] [1987] R.P.C. 189, CA.

[88] *per* Browne-Wilkinson J. in *Rolls-Royce Motors Ltd v Zanelli* [1979] R.P.C. 148.

[89] [1977] F.S.R. 464; [1980] R.P.C. 1 (Fox J.).

insoles were as effective in suppressing odours as those of the plaintiffs. The absorbency of the defendants' product was actually inferior to that of plaintiffs'. One reason for granting an interlocutory injunction was that the plaintiffs' reputation would suffer if the public bought the defendants' goods and believed them to be the plaintiffs'.

"Injurious association" with the claimant

If the claimant and the defendant are not in actual competition then any **4–29** business done by the defendant is unlikely to be at the expense of the claimant. However, it does not follow that there can be no damage in those circumstances:

> "To induce the belief that my business is a branch of another man's business may do that other man damage in all kinds of ways. The quality of goods I sell; the kind of business I do; the credit or otherwise which I might enjoy–all those things may immensely injure the other man who is assumed wrongly to be associated with me."[90]

This is expressed in terms of one business being mistaken for another, but the same principles apply when the misrepresentation is that the defendant's goods are those of the claimant in some sense.[91]

If the defendant is an honest trader of good repute carrying on a reputable business to the satisfaction of those who deal with him then there is no immediate prospect of damage to the claimant on this ground.[92] So in *Harrods v Harrodian School*[93] the majority in the Court of Appeal entirely dismissed arguments based on the possibility of the defendant school going bankrupt or suffering at some future time from a sex or drugs scandal. In *Daimler-Chrysler v Alavi*[94] the fact that "mods, skinheads and casuals" predominated among customers for the defendant's *Merc* brand of fashion clothing was not enough to damage the claimants' goodwill in relation to *Mercedes-Benz* cars.

For the claimant to succeed under this head it is necessary to bring the **4–30** case within one of the following examples:

1. The defendant's business may be of a sort which is generally held in low regard, in which case the claimant's reputation is likely to suffer whether or not the defendant himself deserves the public's disapproval[95];

---

[90] *per* Warrington L.J. in *Ewing v Buttercup Margarine Co Ltd* [1917] 2 Ch. 1, 13; [1916–17] All E.R. 1012; 34 R.P.C. 232, CA.
[91] *Bulmer (H P) Ltd v J Bollinger SA* [1978] R.P.C. 79; [1978] 2 C.M.L.R. 625, CA.
[92] *Hayter (John) Motor Underwriting Agencies Ltd v RBHS Agencies Ltd* [1977] F.S.R. 285; [1977] 2 Lloyd's Rep. 105, CA.
[93] [1996] R.P.C. 697, CA.
[94] [2001] R.P.C. 42 (Pumfrey J.).
[95] For example, a moneylender in *Harrods Ltd v R Harrod Ltd* (1924) 41 R.P.C. 74, CA; an escort agency in *Annabel's (Berkeley Square) Ltd v Schock* [1972] R.P.C. 838, CA.

2. Conversely, although the defendant's chosen trade may be reputable, the defendant personally may have, and perhaps deserve, a bad reputation for other reasons[96];

3. In particular, the defendant may provide goods or services of poor quality;

4. Or may break the law;

5. There may be a real likelihood of the defendant's business failing or getting into difficulties with consequent damage to the claimant's own credit.

Under the last head one has to consider the nature and seriousness of the risks to which the claimant is allegedly being exposed and how probable it is that those risks will become reality. If the worst happens to the defendant, then what sector of the public, in terms of numbers and importance, will visit the defendant's misfortunes on the claimant, and with what consequences? The issue partly depends on whether deception is a remote possibility or a virtual certainty.

Examples

4–31 In *Annabel's v Schock*[97] the plaintiffs were the proprietors of a well known night club. The defendant started an escort agency under the name *Annabel's*. The Court of Appeal granted an interlocutory injunction. Escort agencies in general had "but an indifferent public image". Without suggesting that the defendant personally deserved criticism, it was inevitable that his agency and the club would be tarred with one and the same brush. Although there was no immediate likelihood of the plaintiffs' club losing members or turnover, the association would damage their general goodwill to an unquantifiable extent.

In *Sony v Saray*[98] the defendants were dealers in consumer electronics, including "grey imports" of the plaintiffs' goods. They impliedly misrepresented themselves as authorised dealers of the plaintiffs and as empowered to give guarantees on their behalf. They had a bad trading reputation, having twice been the subject of unfavourable comment in a BBC consumer affairs programme "revealing a very unpleasant way of trading", and had been obliged to give undertakings to the Office of Fair Trading. The Court of Appeal granted an interlocutory injunction. In *Nationwide Building Society v Nationwide Estate Agents*[99] an individual associated with the defendants was under suspicion of mortgage fraud, and in *Law Society of England and Wales v Society of Lawyers*[1] the chairman of the defendants' "accreditation committee" not only lacked any legal or

---

[96] *Sony KK v Saray Electronics (London) Ltd* [1983] F.S.R. 302, CA.
[97] [1972] R.P.C. 838, CA.
[98] [1983] F.S.R. 302, CA.
[99] [1987] F.S.R. 579 (Browne-Wilkinson V.C.).
[1] [1996] F.S.R. 739 (Rimer J.).

professional qualifications for the role, but had been convicted of obtaining property by deception and sentenced to two years' imprisonment. The defendant society itself seems to have differed from a classic pyramid selling scheme only in so far as nothing tangible was actually bought and sold: a payment of £2,000 to £12,000 bought the right to call oneself an Area Secretary, with the promise of commission of up to £50,000 per year from introducing new members.

In *Totalizator Agency Board v Turf News*[2] the plaintiffs were a statutory corporation with a monopoly of off-course betting. Their name was habitually abbreviated to *The TAB*. The defendants published a racing tip-sheet under the same name. Smith J. in the Victoria Supreme Court found damage in the fact that the plaintiffs would be identified as the publishers of the paper, and would be branded as "[P]ersons lacking in taste and scruple; for the selling line of the publication will be an obvious and slangy appeal to greed and simplicity in the reader". The defendants had been in trouble with the police, and were careless and inaccurate even in giving basic factual information. Readers would suppose the plaintiffs were giving deceptive advice to improve their takings. In *Rumcoast Holdings v Prospero Publishing*[3] the plaintiffs' goodwill in a regional up-market lifestyle magazine would have been damaged by the defendants using the same title for a national magazine of vulgar and pornographic content.

Exposure to liability or risk of litigation

If it is passing-off to cause the claimant to be associated with a business **4–32** which is held in low public esteem, then the claimant's case is all the stronger if the defendant's conduct is such as to expose the claimant to liability or even to the mere risk of litigation. The law recognises that the claimant in these circumstances may suffer damage even if the liability is successfully repudiated or the litigation defended.[4] There is a great deal of overlap between this head of damage in the law of passing-off, and the cause of action under the rule in *Routh v Webster*[5] in which a plaintiff who need not be a trader may restrain the use of his name in a manner calculated to expose him to liability.

In *Illustrated Newspapers v Publicity Services*[6] one of the reasons given for the plaintiffs suffering damage from the defendants putting advertising inserts in copies of their publications was said to be that "[T]hey run a reasonable risk of being exposed to litigation—not successful litigation, but litigation which may none the less be very annoying and possibly cause them considerable expense".[7]

Many cases on passing oneself off as an authorised dealer fall under this **4–33**

---

[2] [1967] V.R. 605; [1972] R.P.C. 570.
[3] [1999] W.A.S.C. 176; 48 I.P.R. 75 (Templeman J., SC of Western Australia).
[4] *Walter v Ashton* [1902] 2 Ch. 282 was criticised in *Harrods Ltd v R Harrod Ltd* (1924) 41 R.P.C. 74, CA, for assuming that the plaintiff need be exposed to actual liability.
[5] (1847) 50 E.R. 698.
[6] [1938] Ch. 414; [1938] 1 All E.R. 321; 55 R.P.C. 172, *per* Crossman J.
[7] See also *Clerke v Motor Car Co (1905) Ltd* (1905) 49 Sol. J. 418.

head. In *Sony v Saray*,[8] for example, the defendants impliedly mis-represented themselves as authorised agents of the plaintiffs and as empowered to give guarantees on their behalf. It is doubtful if the plaintiffs could have been obliged to honour these guarantees in law, but refusing to do so could seriously have damaged their goodwill, even assuming that claims by customers of Saray's could have been distinguished from those who had bought through authorised dealers.

In *Associated Newspapers v Insert Media*[9] one of the reasons given for supposing that the plaintiffs would suffer damage from the defendants placing unauthorised advertising inserts in their newspapers was that there was a risk of the advertisements not complying with statutes such as the Financial Services Act. In addition, the defendants did not subscribe to either the Mail Order Protection Scheme or to the British Code of Advertising Practice.

Damage to reputation within the trade

4–34 Passing-off is primarily concerned with the relationship between a trader and the public as consumers of his goods or services. However, the concept of goodwill is wide enough to embrace the trader's connection with suppliers, business customers, and others.[10] This wider goodwill may also be damaged by passing-off.

In *Spalding v Gamage*[11] the defendants obtained a stock of discontinued footballs of the plaintiffs and advertised them at very low prices as if they were the latest model. On the inquiry as to damages[12] the Court of Appeal awarded substantial damages for the damage the plaintiffs suffered from their normal trade customers thinking that the plaintiffs had treated them unfairly by giving a specially favourable deal to the defendants.[13]

In the Canadian case of *Lee's Food Products v Shaffer-Hargart*[14] the defendants obtained a consignment of imported tinned mushrooms which had been ordered by the plaintiffs and printed with the plaintiffs' mark. They sold them with the mark inadequately covered with labels of their own which came loose. The Ontario High Court found for the plaintiffs. The plaintiffs had been unable to fulfil their own obligations because the order had not arrived. The defendants were not liable for this as such, but damage included loss arising from customers of the plaintiffs thinking that they were being poorly treated and the defendants unfairly favoured at their expense.

4–35 In *Chelsea Man Menswear v Chelsea Girl*[15] the Court of Appeal relied on damage to the plaintiffs' goodwill with its suppliers to justify a geographically unrestricted injunction. As well as misdirected correspondence,

---

[8] [1983] F.S.R. 302, CA.
[9] [1991] F.S.R. 380, CA.
[10] *Home Box Office Inc v Channel 5 Home Box Office Ltd* [1982] F.S.R. 449.
[11] (1915) 32 R.P.C. 273, HL.
[12] (1918) 35 R.P.C. 101, CA.
[13] A similar head of damage was treated as injurious falsehood in *Rima Electric Ltd v Rolls Razor Ltd* [1965] R.P.C. 4.
[14] (1984) 81 C.P.R. (2d) 204 (Ontario, Van Camp J.).
[15] [1987] R.P.C. 189, CA.

telephone calls and deliveries there had been an example of the plaintiffs being blamed for an unpaid debt incurred by the defendants. The plaintiffs themselves were extremely prompt payers.

One of the heads of damage relied on in *Provident Financial v Halifax Building Society*[16] turned on the fact that the plaintiff insurance company dealt exclusively through brokers whereas the defendants proposed to deal directly with the public. The goodwill the plaintiffs had with their broker customers would have been damaged if the latter had been led to believe that the parties were connected and that the plaintiffs were, in effect, cutting the brokers out.

Confusion *per se*

There are numerous examples of passing-off actions failing despite the **4–36** existence of confusion in some sense between the goods or businesses of the parties. "Mere confusion which does not lead to a sale is not sufficient".[17] Some of these turn on the confusion being caused by factors for which the defendant ought not to be held responsible, for instance the choice by the claimant of a descriptive name[18] or the breaking of the claimant's former monopoly.[19] Others support the conclusion that confusion *per se* is neither a recognised ground of damage nor a sufficient reason for supposing that damage will occur.[20]

There are also authorities to the opposite effect. In *Brestian v Try*[21] Jenkins L.J. said:

"In an action such as this the plaintiff in order to succeed must show first that he has a proprietary interest in the name, or perhaps it is more accurate to say in the goodwill attaching to the name, and, secondly, that the adoption of [the] name by the defendant brings about a tangible risk of damage whether in the form of diversion of customers or confusion of the plaintiff's and defendant's businesses or both. To that one must add that confusion in itself is held to import a sufficient risk or [*sc* of] damage to maintain the action."

Similarly, in the *Chelsea Man* case[22] Slade L.J. identified the relevant heads **4–37** of damage thus:

"(a) by diverting trade from the plaintiffs to the defendants;

[16] [1994] F.S.R. 81 (Aldous J.).
[17] *per* Lord Jauncey in *Reckitt & Colman Products Ltd v Borden Inc* [1990] 1 W.L.R. 491; [1990] 1 All E.R. 873; [1990] R.P.C. 340, HL.
[18] *Office Cleaning Service Ltd v Westminster Office Cleaning Association* [1946] 1 All E.R. 320; 63 R.P.C. 39, HL.
[19] *My Kinda Town Ltd v Soll* [1983] R.P.C. 407, CA.
[20] *Unitex Ltd v Union Texturising Co Ltd* [1973] R.P.C. 119; [1973] F.S.R. 181, CA; *Hayter (John) Motor Underwriting Agencies Ltd v RBHS Agencies Ltd* [1977] F.S.R. 285; [1977] 2 Lloyd's Rep. 105, CA. In the latter there was not even a triable issue.
[21] [1958] R.P.C. 161, CA.
[22] *Chelsea Man Menswear Ltd v Chelsea Girl Ltd* [1987] R.P.C. 189, CA.

(b) by injuring the trade reputation of the plaintiffs whose men's clothing is admittedly superior in quality to that of the defendants; and

(c) by the injury which is inherently likely to be suffered by any business when on frequent occasions it is confused by customers or potential customers with a business owned by another proprietor or is wrongly regarded as being connected with that business."

Taken as general statements of principle these *dicta* can hardly be reconciled with decisions of greater authority. The better way of putting the question is to ask whether confusion as such is so inherently likely to cause damage to the claimant, that further proof of damage will not be required. This must depend on the facts of each case, and, in particular, how widespread and serious the confusion will be. It is suggested above that although the legal burden of proving damage must always be on the claimant, the evidential burden may shift to the defendant. This may occur when the parties are in actual competition or very close to one another in their respective fields of business.

Licensing opportunity or income

4–38 The misrepresentation that one business is licensed by another is potentially actionable as passing-off but the law does not assume that such a misrepresentation is inherently damaging.[23] As well as showing the existence of the misrepresentation, the claimant must prove the real likelihood of actual damage. The main heads of damage are likely to be that the claimant or an existing licensee has lost sales to the defendant as putative licensee; that the assumed existence of the licence is damaging to the claimant's goodwill, for instance because the defendant is of bad repute; or that someone in the position of the defendant would voluntarily have paid for a licence from the claimant. The present section is mainly concerned with the latter head, which may also be relevant although the misrepresentation is not on its face one to the effect that the defendant is licensed at all.

It might be said that the misrepresentation in passing-off could always have been sanctioned by the claimant for payment; and, therefore, that the claimant has automatically been damaged by the unauthorised making of the misrepresentation.[24] This does not represent English law. If right, it would mean that there would never be any independent need to prove likelihood of actual damage in passing-off. As an argument it is circular, because a misrepresentation which causes no damage is not actionable and needs no licence.

4–39 It now seems that in some circumstances at least a claimant may recover damages on a royalty basis for the unauthorised use of his name (etc.), or for actual lost profits if greater. The following factors appear to be relevant, although none of them need be conclusive:

---

[23] *Ormond Engineering Co Ltd v Knopf* (1932) 49 R.P.C. 634.
[24] *Henderson v Radio Corp Pty Ltd* [1960] N.S.W.L.R. 279; [1969] R.P.C. 218.

1. Is the claimant already in the business of granting licences;

2. If not, is licensing a potentially profitable activity for the claimant;

3. Does the claimant have any rights to license other than the bare right to use his name;

4. Does the reputation or personal recommendation of the claimant carry weight in the defendant's field;

5. What benefit, if any, does the defendant obtain from the claimant's name;

6. Is the claimant's actual or prospective licensing business damaged by the belief that the defendant is licensed?

In *Dunhill v Sunoptic*[25] the plaintiffs, originally famous for tobacco and smokers' goods, had diversified into a range of luxury goods for men. The defendants started to advertise sunglasses and spectacle frames under the name *Christopher Dunhill*. The plaintiffs had no existing trade in these goods but they had been conducting negotiations to enter that market themselves or by licensing their name, and there was impressive evidence of third parties wanting to use the *Dunhill* name under licence for those goods. The defendants' motives were suspect. The Court of Appeal granted an interlocutory injunction.[26]

In *Stringfellow v McCain*[27] the Court of Appeal refused a final injunction in a case where no damage was likely. They found that a television advertisement for the defendants' potato chips might have misled some people to believe there was a connection of some sort with the plaintiff's nightclub. However, the plaintiff had no subsisting licensing business and had been alerted to the possibility only by the defendants' activities. The defendants had acted innocently and had not derived, or intended to derive, any benefit from such confusion as arose. They would not, therefore, have been in the market for a licence themselves, and the argument that there were prospective licensees who might have been discouraged by the association with potato chips was speculative.

Conversely in *Irvine v Talksport*[28] the motor racing driver Eddie Irvine was already active and successful in the business of endorsing products of various kinds. He recovered £25,000 damages (increased from £2,000 on appeal) for the conspicuous and recognisable use of his photograph in a promotional mailshot for the defendant's radio station. Recipients would assume that Mr Irvine was endorsing the defendants, and the latter were therefore making unauthorised use of his goodwill. Because Mr Irvine was already active in granting endorsements and had goodwill in relation to that

[25] [1979] F.S.R. 337, CA.
[26] Followed in *News Group Newspapers Ltd v Rocket Record Co Ltd* [1981] F.S.R. 89.
[27] [1984] F.S.R. 175, CA.
[28] [2002] EWHC 367, [2002] 1 W.L.R. 2355, [2002] 2 All E.R. 424, [2002] E.M.L.R. 32, [2002] F.S.R. 60 (Laddie J.). affirmed in part [2003] EWCA Civ 423, [2003] 2 All E.R. 881; [2003] E.M.L.R. 26; [2003] F.S.R. 35, CA.

activity, there was no circularity involved in awarding him damages on the basis of what he could have charged.

Reputation in defendant's hands

4–40 It is clear that if the defendant's business is currently being conducted in such a way as to discredit the claimant then there is sufficient damage to support an action for passing-off.[29] A more difficult question arises if the activities of the defendant are perfectly innocuous and there is no reason to believe that the situation will change.[30] If the businesses are likely to be confused, then can an injunction be granted on the basis that the claimant would otherwise be entrusting his reputation against his will to a third party over whom he has no control? In principle this seems dubious, and if it were true, damage would no longer be useful as the acid test for passing off: any form of association with any defendant would put the claimant's reputation at risk. The law requires there to be at least a real tangible risk of substantial damage. If that risk is absent, then there is no passing-off. Even a *quia timet* action requires more than fear on the claimant's behalf. The Court of Appeal in *Habib Bank v Habib Bank AG Zurich*[31] was invited to say there was a danger of malpractice by the defendants rubbing off on the plaintiffs and dismissed the argument as "two-way traffic" and pure speculation.

Despite this, there are several cases in which injunctions have been said to be justified, at least in part, on the basis that the claimant would be injured if some unforeseeable evil were to befall the defendant at some time or other. In *Warwick Tyre Co v New Motor & General Rubber Co*[32] Neville J. said that use of the plaintiff's name put "the reputation of the plaintiffs in the hands of persons over whom they have no control whatever", but the decision was doubted by the Privy Council in *Star Industrial v Yap Kwee Kor*.[33] In two cases[34] Farwell J. held that there was a likelihood of damage to the plaintiffs if the defendants got into financial or legal trouble, although conceding that this was not actually likely to happen to either. The damage which would be caused by an accident or epidemic at the defendants' holiday camp was given as justification for an interlocutory injunction in *Hulton Press v White Eagle Youth Holiday Camp*,[35] where the plaintiffs were publishers of a boys'

[29] *Annabel's (Berkeley Square) Ltd v Schock* [1972] R.P.C. 838, CA, where the defendant's business was an escort agency. It is sufficient for the defendant (or the class to which he belongs) to have a bad reputation, whether or not he deserves it personally. See also *Nationwide Building Society v Nationwide Estate Agents* [1987] F.S.R. 579 where a person connected with the defendants had been accused, perhaps unjustly, of mortgage fraud.
[30] As in *Hayter (John) Motor Underwriting Agencies Ltd v RBHS Agencies Ltd* [1977] F.S.R. 285; [1977] 2 Lloyd's Rep. 105, CA.
[31] [1981] 1 W.L.R. 1265; [1981] 2 All E.R. 650; [1982] R.P.C. 1, CA.
[32] [1901] 1 Ch. 248; 27 R.P.C. 161.
[33] [1976] F.S.R. 256, PC.
[34] *Woolworth (F W) & Co Ltd v Woolworths (Australia) Ltd* (1930) 47 R.P.C. 337 and *British Legion v British Legion Club (Street) Ltd* (1931) 48 R.P.C. 555.
[35] (1951) 68 R.P.C. 126 (Wynn-Parry J.). Compare *Harrods Ltd v Harrodian School Ltd* [1996] R.P.C. 697, CA where the supposed possibility of the defendant school going bankrupt, or suffering from a sex or drugs scandal, was entirely discounted by the majority.

magazine. In *Dawnay Day v Cantor Fitzgerald*[36] Scott V.C. in the Court of Appeal identified as one of two possible heads of damage[37] that "the Dawnay Day members, collectively and individually, have no control over the activities of the proprietors of Dawnay Day Securities. The Dawnay Day reputation will suffer if those activities become in any respect reprehensible. The Dawnay Day companies will be unable to prevent that happening".

Injunctions (whether final or interlocutory) have often been granted on **4–41** weaker facts than these without this head of contingent damage being referred to, which suggests that it may not have been essential to the final result. It is suggested that speculation of this sort does not improve the claimant's case if there is no present likelihood of the defendant's business getting into difficulties, but that in the typical passing-off case it is in fact unnecessary. If the parties are using the same name in closely similar fields it can be said that the evidential burden of proving damage is taken off the claimant's shoulders.

On an application for an interlocutory injunction it is not enough for the claimant to allege that he would be damaged if the defendant failed in his business or got into other difficulties. For the balance of convenience to be affected, he must show that there is a real likelihood of this happening in the relatively short period before the action can be tried.[38]

Restriction on expansion

If the defendant's chosen field of business is a natural extension of that in **4–42** which the claimant trades then, as a practical matter, damage is likely to be inferred even if the claimant has no present intention of expanding into that field.[39] The only relevance of such an intention would be on the balance of convenience on an application for an interlocutory injunction.[40] Restriction on expansion as a head of damage was rejected as speculative by the Court of Appeal in *Newsweek v British Broadcasting Corporation*.[41] It is unlikely that intention to expand into an unrelated field can create a cause of action where one would not otherwise exist.[42]

"[T]his court would never restrain the use of a trade name at the instance of a trader merely because that trader might at some future indefinite date

---

[36] [2000] R.P.C. 669, CA.

[37] The other was loss of exclusivity in the name.

[38] *Unitex Ltd v Union Texturising Co Ltd* [1973] R.P.C. 119; [1973] F.S.R. 181, CA; *Home Box Office Inc v Channel 5 Home Box Office Ltd* [1982] F.S.R. 449.

[39] *Eastman Photographic Materials Co Ltd v Griffiths (John) Cycle Corp Ltd* (1898) 15 R.P.C. 105 somewhat implausibly treated bicycles as a natural field of expansion for a camera manufacturer; likewise *Hulton Press Ltd v White Eagle Youth Holiday Camp Ltd* (1951) 68 R.P.C. 126 (publishing, holiday camps).

[40] As in *Nationwide Building Society v Nationwide Estate Agents* [1987] F.S.R. 579 where the plaintiff had actual plans to expand into estate agency. An injunction was refused on other grounds. See also *Ten-Ichi v Jancar* [1990] F.S.R. 151 (Hong Kong), discussed below.

[41] [1979] R.P.C. 441, CA.

[42] See also *Teleworks Ltd v Telework Group plc* [2002] R.P.C. 27 in which Christopher Floyd Q.C. (Deputy Judge) dismissed the argument that the claimant could protect so-called "future goodwill" in a field it had not yet entered.

want to start a new business and use that name in connection with such business."[43]

"It is true that a merchant who has sold one kind of goods, sometimes finds himself driven to add other 'lines' in order to hold or develop his existing market; in such cases he has a legitimate present interest in preserving his identity in the ancillary market, which he cannot do, if others make his name equivocal there. But if the new goods have no such relation to the old, and if the first user's interest in maintaining the significance of his name when applied to the new goods is nothing more than the desire to post the new market as a possible preserve which he may later choose to exploit, it is hard to see any basis for its protection. The public may be deceived, but he has no claim to be its vicarious champion; his remedy must be limited to his injury and by hypothesis he has none."[44]

4–43 Similar issues may arise when the matter is one of expansion into a broader market in geographical, as opposed to economic, terms, but the authorities are more favourable to the claimant.[45] In the Hong Kong case of *Ten-Ichi v Jancar*[46] the plaintiffs operated a chain of restaurants in Japan. They had actual plans to open a restaurant in Hong Kong, but were narrowly forestalled by the defendants. The decision is open to criticism on several grounds, and it is circular to argue that sufficient damage to support a cause of action for passing-off arose from the plaintiffs being prevented from expanding their Japanese operation to Hong Kong under their chosen name. However, once it is allowed that they had a cause of action independently of this, the fact that they had a genuine intention to operate a restaurant in Hong Kong in the immediate future and were making active preparations to that end was very relevant to the balance of convenience. The defendants, who admitted copying, did not do their case any good by asserting a right to prevent the plaintiffs trading in Hong Kong under the very name the defendants had taken from them.

Loss of exclusivity; erosion or swamping of distinctiveness

4–44 As passing-off was traditionally understood, the claimant had to prove that in the field in which he and the defendant traded, the name or mark relied on was distinctive of him and him alone. To that extent, exclusivity was a precondition to success in a passing-off action, and the remedy of an

---

[43] *per* Lawrence J. in *Motor Manufacturers' & Traders' Society v Motor Manufacturers' & Traders Insurance Co* [1925] Ch. 675 at 688; [1925] All E.R. 616; 42 R.P.C. 307 affirmed *ibid.*, CA. To the same effect see *Corporation of the Hall of Arts and Sciences v Albert Edward Hall* (1934) 51 R.P.C. 398 where the argument was rejected in the context of the defendants' *Albert Hall Orchestra*. The Hall had at one time maintained an orchestra of its own.

[44] *per* Learned Hand J. in *Johnson (S C) & Son Inc v Johnson* (1940) 116 F 2d 427. This seems equally true of English law.

[45] *Brestian v Try* [1958] R.P.C. 161, CA; *Chelsea Man Menswear Ltd v Chelsea Girl Ltd* [1987] R.P.C. 189, CA. Compare *Thompson (D C) & Co Ltd v Kent Messenger Ltd* [1975] F.S.R. 485; [1975] R.P.C. 191.

[46] [1990] F.S.R. 151 (Sears J., Hong Kong).

injunction restored or maintained that exclusivity. Conversely, failure to enforce the claimant's rights resulted in their destruction: "the very life of a trade mark depends on the promptitude with which it is vindicated".[47] Perhaps because of this, loss of exclusivity has tended not to be regarded as a head of damage in its own right, but rather as a state of affairs arising when passing-off goes unchecked.

Considered as a head of damage in its own right, loss of exclusivity in a name, mark or get-up needs to be treated with caution. It lends itself to circular arguments, thereby undermining the importance of damage as an essential element of passing-off, and it leads easily to the fallacy that the property which is being protected is the name or mark or get-up itself, rather than the goodwill in the claimant's business. In the normal course of events there is little to be gained by enumerating loss of exclusivity as a separate head of damage, since it overlaps with, or is an intermediate cause of, several other heads of damage which are better established. Loss of exclusivity in the word *Lego* was treated as damaging in *Lego v Lego M Lemelstrich*[48] (where the defendants proposed to use it on garden sprinklers) but it was not the only head of damage relied on, and much of the reasoning of *Lego* is unconvincing. *Lego* was considered inconclusively in *Pete Waterman v CBS*[49] where Browne-Wilkinson V.C. dismissed as unrealistic various specific forms of damage which would supposedly arise from the defendants operating a recording studio under the name *The Hit Factory*, but found it unnecessary to decide whether the plaintiffs' loss of exclusivity in the name could in itself support an action for passing-off. There was no evidence on the issue. The *Lego* case was also referred to by the Court of Appeal of New Zealand in *Taylor Bros v Taylor Group*[50] in concluding: "We think that in some cases it is legitimate to infer damage from a tendency to impair distinctiveness". The facts were stronger than *Lego*, since although the parties were not in direct competition they both operated in the textile cleaning field in Wellington.

In *Dawnay Day v Cantor Fitzgerald*[51] Scott V.C. in the Court of Appeal identified (as the second of two heads of damage) that "the use of Dawnay Day as a trading style by a company that is not a member of the Dawnay Day group will dilute and, potentially, may destroy the distinctiveness of the name".[52] Once again, however, the parties traded in very closely related fields and the claimants even had a subsidiary which actually competed with the relevant business of the defendants. A conclusion that the claimants

---

[47] *per* Lord Blackburn in *Johnson v Orr-Ewing* (1882) 7 App. Cas. 219, HL.
[48] [1983] F.S.R. 155 (Falconer J.).
[49] [1993] E.M.L.R. 27 (Browne-Wilkinson V.C.).
[50] [1988] 2 N.Z.L.R. 1 (CA of NZ).
[51] [2000] R.P.C. 669, CA.
[52] Citing the judgment of Peter Gibson L.J. in *Taittinger SA v Allbev Ltd*; [1993] 2 C.M.L.R. 741; [1993] F.S.R. 641, CA, and implicitly distinguishing *Harrods Ltd v Harrodian School Ltd* [1996] R.P.C. 697, CA. That the name *Dawnay Day* was highly unusual was mentioned, but can hardly have been determinative since the same was obviously even more true of *Harrods*. The other head of damage was that the claimant's reputation in the name would be in the defendants' hands, see above.

would suffer no damage at all from this state of affairs would have been plainly contrary to common sense.

4-45   There are, however, occasional cases in which the issue of damage is most realistically approached on the basis that the most serious effect of the defendant's misrepresentation would be to destroy the very ability of the claimant's name or mark to denote the claimants' business. This can arise, in particular, if the defendant is very much larger or better known that the claimant, a situation which shades over into liability for "inverse" passing-off.

The situation can be demonstrated in an extreme form by reference to an American case[53] where the defendants launched a massive national advertising campaign for a new brand of tyres under the name *Bigfoot*, which was already in use by the plaintiffs on a smaller but not insubstantial scale. The Court accepted that the continuing use of the name by the plaintiffs for their own business implied that they would wrongly be branded as pirates cashing in on Goodyear's campaign. A mark which had previously been a modest asset had been turned into a major liability. No English decision appears to have gone so far but one can imagine this head of damage occurring on the facts of *Chelsea Man v Chelsea Girl*[54] even if the decision did not address it specifically. If the defendants had gone ahead with the launch of hundreds of *Chelsea Man* boutiques, then a shopper entering one of the plaintiffs' *Nickelby* retail shops in London's Oxford Street and picking up a *Chelsea Man* branded jacket could very easily conclude that it was the plaintiffs, rather than the defendants, who were guilty of passing-off.

A less extreme situation is represented by *Provident Financial v Halifax Building Society*.[55] The plaintiffs had a well established motor insurance business under the name *Halifax Insurance* which had co-existed with the various non-competitive businesses of the defendant. They obtained an interlocutory injunction against the defendants expanding into the field of motor insurance under the proposed name *Halifax Motor Extra*. One of four reasons given by Aldous J. for concluding that damages would not be an adequate remedy for the plaintiffs was that "the defendant is so large that I anticipate that its reputation will tend to swamp that of the plaintiff. Any goodwill the plaintiff has at the moment will be subsumed into the defendant's goodwill". Indeed, on the balance of convenience, this appeared to be the single most important factor.[56]

Sutherland v V2 Music[57] provides a further example. The residual goodwill of the claimant pop group *Liberty* would have been completely overwhelmed if the defendant group had been allowed to go ahead under the same name, with the benefit of having come second in the popular television contest *Popstars*.

---

[53] *Big O Tire Dealers Inc v Goodyear Tire & Rubber Co* (1977) 561 F.2d 1365 (C.A. 10th Circuit) affirming (1976) 408 F. Supp. 1219 (District Ct, Colorado).
[54] [1987] R.P.C. 189, CA.
[55] [1994] F.S.R. 81 (Aldous J.).
[56] The defendants subsequently bought out the rights to the name for £2 million: *Halifax Building Society v Urquart-Dykes & Lord* [1997] R.P.C. 55.
[57] [2002] EWHC 14; [2002] E.M.L.R. 28 (Laddie J.).

Dilution: damage without confusion

A mark is likely to be strongest in commercial terms if it is used by one **4–46** trader to the exclusion of all others without exception, in no matter what fields of business. It is necessary to emphasise the universality of this, because in passing-off one is used to speaking of "exclusive" use as a precondition for distinctiveness, when in reality one means exclusive use within a fairly narrowly defined field of activity. Should another trader use the same mark for wholly different goods or services then the attractive power of the mark may become diminished, even though the public do not consciously or unconsciously associate the latter goods with the first user. "Dilution" is the name given to this head of damage. The term is taken from American law, where it is well understood as being, as a matter of definition, a form of damage which arises despite the absence of any confusion between the parties, their goods or services. Even in America, dilution is unknown to the common law and is only actionable by virtue of legislation.[58]

Since this is a technical meaning to attribute to an ordinary English word, it is not surprising that several English and common law decisions are to be found in which "dilution" of reputation, distinctiveness or goodwill is accepted as a recognised and uncontroversial head of damage. In the context, however, it will almost always be seen that the word is being used where there is actual or potential confusion in the normal sense; that the damage suffered or foreseen can be attributed to a misrepresentation; and is of the same nature as that discussed above under the headings of confusion *per se* and erosion of distinctiveness. Seen in this light, the cases need not be interpreted as meaning that dilution in the American sense is a recognised head of damage in the English law of passing-off. Passing-off always depends on the existence of a misrepresentation, and dilution in its strict sense occurs despite the absence of confusion, or, *a fortiori*, deception.

The cases which come closest to recognising dilution as a head of damage are both to do with *Champagne*. An observation of Buckley L.J. in *Bulmer v Bollinger*[59] does suggest that dilution even in the strict sense may be known to the common law: "[T]he exclusivity of the association of the name, mark or get-up with A's business might, perhaps, be shown to be a valuable asset as a powerful means of bringing A's goods to the notice of the public, thus maintaining and promoting A's competitive position in the market".

In *Taittinger v Allbev*[60] the defendants sold as *Elderflower Champagne* a **4–47** non-alcoholic, carbonated, fruit-flavoured soft drink in a bottle with a Champagne-like get-up. At trial, Mervyn Davies J. held that there was a misrepresentation, but that the plaintiffs had failed to prove that there was any real prospect of damage to them as producers of Champagne. On appeal, all three members of the Court of Appeal were prepared to hold that there was ample evidence of prospective damage to the plaintiffs' goodwill

---

[58] The conclusion is taken from the *Restatement (3rd), Unfair Competition* (1995) §25. There are numerous state anti-dilution statutes. See Martino, *Trademark Dilution* (1996).
[59] [1978] 2 C.M.L.R. 625; [1978] R.P.C. 79, CA.
[60] [1993] 2 C.M.L.R. 741; [1993] F.S.R. 641, CA.

both as a result of undiscerning purchasers confusing *Elderflower Champagne* with the French wine and from the distinctiveness of *Champagne* being eroded by its inappropriate use on the defendants' goods. In a passage reminiscent of that of Buckley L.J. above, Bingham M.R. stated:

"The first plaintiffs' reputation and goodwill in the description *Champagne* derive not only from the quality of their wine and its glamorous associations, but also from the very singularity and exclusiveness of the description, the absence of qualifying epithets and imitative descriptions. Any product which is not Champagne but is allowed to describe itself as such must inevitably, in my view, erode the singularity and exclusiveness of the description *Champagne* and so cause the first plaintiffs damage of an insidious but serious kind."

If this is a recognition of dilution it is *obiter*, because the Master of the Rolls was emphatic that there was confusion as well as damage. Indeed, in deciding to grant an injunction under EEC law he adverted to the fact that Regulation 823/87 treated confusion, rather than damage, as the critical issue. But whether this passage represents judicial approval of dilution at all depends on what Bingham M.R. meant by "any product". The paragraph from which the quotation is taken concludes by saying that if the defendants were correct, then any other fruit cordial diluted with carbonated water could be sold as *Champagne*, which suggests that Bingham M.R. was not directing his mind to products beyond the broad category of beverages. Peter Gibson L.J. gave a more extended treatment of damage to distinctiveness entirely in the context of the *Drinks Cases* while Mann L.J. referred to the plaintiffs' contention that *Champagne* had an exclusiveness which would be impaired if used in relation to "a product (particularly a potable product) which is neither *Champagne* nor associated or connected with the businesses which produce *Champagne*". All this suggests that the majority was principally concerned with erosion of distinctiveness in the familiar sense.

If the passage quoted from the judgment of Bingham M.R. is given the widest meaning then it is open to two objections: one is the apparent lack of positive evidence that *Champagne* was not already used in fact in various contexts for a variety of products, because in that case maintaining its exclusivity outside the beverage field would already be a lost cause. The Court of Appeal apparently ignored the fact, appreciated by Dankwerts J., that *Champagne* is a known and legitimate term in relation to Cognac. The other is that there was not and is not any legal remedy to prevent this kind of use, because even if the Champagne houses could invoke *Taittinger v Allbev* on the issue of damage they would still have to prove misrepresentation, which was scarcely an issue in the *Elderflower* case because of the transparency of the defendants' intentions. One is driven back to the conclusion that a form of damage which cannot be attributed to misrepresentation can only be relevant to passing-off as a sort of legitimated head of parasitic damages. It can never be sufficient in its own right.

Dilution compared to descent to generic status

This relatively narrow interpretation of the *Elderflower Champagne* case[61] **4–48** was confirmed by the Court of Appeal in *Harrods v Harrodian School*[62] where Millett L.J., for the majority, rejected an argument that *Harrods* department store would suffer a similar kind of damage from the existence of the *Harrodian School*, even in the absence of confusion between the plaintiffs' store and the defendants' school.[63]

> "In *Taittinger SA v Allbev Ltd* the court appears to have recognised a different head of damage.[64] If the defendants were allowed to market their product under the name *Elderflower Champagne*:

> > 'there would take place a blurring or erosion of the uniqueness that now attends the word "champagne", so that the exclusive reputation of the champagne houses would be debased' (per Peter Gibson L.J.).

> It is self-evident that the application of the plaintiff's brand name to inferior goods is likely to injure the plaintiffs' reputation and damage his goodwill if people take the inferior goods to be those of the plaintiff. That is a classic head of damage in cases of passing-off. But Peter Gibson LJ may have had more in mind than this. He referred without disapproval to the submission of Counsel for the plaintiffs that if the defendants were allowed to continue to call their product *Elderflower Champagne*:

> > 'the effect would be to demolish the distinctiveness of the word champagne, and that would inevitably damage the goodwill of the champagne houses.'

> Erosion of the distinctiveness of a brand name has been recognised as a form of damage to the goodwill of the business with which the name is connected in a number of cases, particularly in Australia and New Zealand but unless care is taken this could mark an unacceptable extension to the tort of passing off. To date the law has not sought to protect the value of the brand name as such, but the value of the goodwill which it generates and it insists on proof of confusion to justify its intervention. But the erosion of the distinctiveness of a brand name which occurs by reason of its degeneration into common use as a generic term is not necessarily dependent on confusion at all. The danger that if the defendant's product was called champagne then all sparkling wines would eventually come to be called champagne would still exist even if no one was deceived into thinking that such wine really was champagne. I have an intellectual difficulty in accepting the concept that the law insists upon the presence of both confusion and damage and yet recognises as suffi-

---

[61] *Taittinger SA v Allbev Ltd* [1993] F.S.R. 641; [1993] C.M.L.R. 741, C.A.
[62] [1996] R.P.C. 697, CA.
[63] Sir Michael Kerr dissented, see above.
[64] As compared to *Lego v Lego M. Lemelstrich* [1983] F.S.R. 155, treated by the Court of Appeal as a case where there was a real risk of the defendant's goods, though non-competitive, being taken for those of the plaintiffs.

cient a head of damage which does not depend on confusion. Counsel for the Plaintiffs relied strongly on the possibility of damage of this nature, but it is in my opinion not necessary to consider it further in the present case. There is no danger of 'Harrods' becoming a generic term for a retail emporium in the luxury class, and if such a danger existed the use of a different name in connection with an institution of a different kind would not advance the process."

It is implicit in this treatment of *Taittinger v Allbev* that the result depended on the very close proximity of the fields of business of the parties. Self-evidently, *Champagne* is severely at risk of losing its distinctiveness and suffering a descent to merely generic status if the term is used for sparkling wines in general, and the same risk exists to some extent if it is used for other sparkling beverages, even fruit-flavoured water. The term sometimes used in American law is "genericide". However, use of *Champagne* for wholly unrelated goods, such as perfume or soap, cannot possibly affect the question of whether *Champagne* is at risk of becoming generic in relation to sparkling drinks any more than the distinctive quality of *Scotch* for whisky is at risk because Scotch eggs and *Scotch* brand adhesive tape do not come from Scotland. In reality, this head of damage in *Taittinger v Allbev* was not dilution in the American sense at all, but simply an aspect of the relatively familiar one of loss of distinctive character.

D. DAMAGE IN INJURIOUS FALSEHOOD

The principle stated

4–49 Of the fairly numerous and substantially identical summaries of the essential elements of the action for injurious falsehood, one of the most frequently cited in the context of unfair competition is that of Glidewell L.J. in *Kaye v Robertson*[65]:

> "The essentials of this tort are that the defendant has published about the plaintiff words which are false, that they were published maliciously, and that special damage has followed as the direct and natural result of their publication. As to special damage, the effect of section 3(1) of the Defamation Act 1952 is that it is sufficient if the words published in writing are calculated to cause pecuniary damage to the plaintiff. Malice will be inferred if it be proved that the words were calculated to produce damage and that the defendant knew when he published the words that they were false or was reckless as to whether they were false or not."

This restates the requirement of damage as it has been understood since the nineteenth century, subject to the qualifications introduced by statute in

[65] [1991] F.S.R. 62, CA.

1952. Prior to the Defamation Act 1952, the position was of course more severe. As Nicholls V.C. stated in *Joyce v Sengupta*[66]:

"[I]t is well settled that at common law proof of 'special damage' is an essential ingredient in this cause of action. At common law if such damage is not established the action will fail. Lord Robertson emphasised this in *Royal Baking Powder Co. v Wright Crossley & Co.*:

'Unless the plaintiff has in fact suffered loss which can be and is specified, he has no cause of action. The fact that the defendant has acted maliciously cannot supply the want of special damage, nor can a superfluity of malice eke out a case wanting in special damage.'"

It had previously been decided by the House of Lords in *White v Mellin*[67] that not only was special damage necessary to support an action for damages, but that an action for an injunction would only lie if the statement complained of, as well as being false and malicious, was calculated to cause damage with the same degree of certainty as was required at law:

"But it was said [by the plaintiffs] that although an action for damages could not be sustained, an injunction in equity could be obtained. It would certainly be a strange and novel chapter of equity if a party could get a perpetual injunction to restrain an act which is not an illegal act."[68]

The Defamation Act 1952

Like passing-off, the action for injurious falsehood is an action on the case **4–50** and damage is therefore the gist of the action. Unlike passing-off, however, the degree of proof of damage required is now governed by statute in the form of the Defamation Act 1952. Although the Act does not apply to all allegations of injurious falsehood in the widest sense, it is unlikely that any misrepresentations of the kind dealt with in the present work would fall outside it.

Section 3(1) of the Defamation Act 1952 provides:

In an action for slander of title, slander of goods or other malicious falsehood, it shall not be necessary to allege or prove special damage—

(a) if the words upon which the action is founded are calculated to cause pecuniary damage to the plaintiff and are published in writing or other permanent form; or

(b) if the said words are calculated to cause pecuniary damage to the plaintiff in respect of any office, profession, calling, trade or business held or carried on by him at the time of the publication.

As a practical matter, and in the context of the present work, one or both **4–51**

---

[66] [1993] 1 W.L.R. 337, CA.
[67] [1895] A.C. 170, HL.
[68] *ibid.*, *per* Lord Morris.

of subsections (a) or (b) are almost bound to apply, and in that case the existence of sufficient pecuniary damage to support the action is likely to be uncontroversial. Whether quantum of damage will require proof at trial is likely to depend on whether the action is brought in the Chancery Division or (as is not uncommon) in the Queen's Bench. In the first relevant case in modern times, *De Beers v General Electric*,[69] Walton J. noted that a claim in respect of special damage was "wholly irrelevant" since the passing of the Act, and that "no such averment is now necessary in a claim for slander of goods or injurious falsehood or what ever label one choose to put upon this particular tort". Of the relatively few cases of injurious falsehood between competitors subsequent to 1952, most make little more than passing reference to the 1952 Act, either directly or by way of citing the brief summary of the requirements for the action for injurious falsehood from the judgment of Glidewell L.J. in *Kaye v Robertson*.[70] In cases of injurious falsehood damage tends to be the last issue addressed, and few get to the point at which it needs to be addressed at all.

Slightly more attention to the issue of damage is to be found in *DSG Retail v Comet Group*[71] in which Owen J. stated:

> "It was submitted on behalf of Currys that the whole purpose of the posters was to lure potential customers from Currys to Comet at the most crucial time of the year for sales of electrical and electronic goods. That was undoubtedly the case. As Jonathan Parker J. put it in *Emaco v Dyson Appliances*, a passage cited with approval by Morland J. in *Jupiter v Johnson Fry*:
>
> > 'Comparative advertising is by its nature calculated (in the sense of likely) to cause pecuniary damage to suppliers of the competing product, if only by reducing the market share of the competing product whilst increasing that of the product which is the subject of the comparative advertising. That after all is the purpose of comparative advertising.'
>
> In those circumstances Currys have plainly established a likelihood of actual damage. Counsel for Comet did not seek to persuade me otherwise."

4–52   For completeness, reference may be made to cases of injurious falsehood subsequent to 1952 where the parties were not in competition. In *Calvet v Tomkies*[72] the Court of Appeal held that where the plaintiff relied on the section and had not pleaded special damage, then she was precluded from introducing proof of special damage at trial, and would not be obliged to give discovery of documents relating to her income. In *Feilding v Variety*[73] it was implicitly conceded (by default of defence) that the untrue description

---

[69] [1975] F.S.R. 323 (Walton J.).
[70] [1991] F.S.R. 62, CA.
[71] [2002] EWHC 116; [2002] F.S.R. 58 (Owen J., QBD).
[72] [1963] 1 W.L.R. 1397, CA.
[73] [1967] 2 Q.B. 841, CA.

of the plaintiff's musical *Charlie Girl* as a "disastrous flop" was calculated to cause pecuniary damage, but on appeal damages for injurious falsehood were reduced from £10,000 to a nominal £100: "that which was published, though at the time it was published might have been a very damaging thing, has been proved by the passage of time not to have had that result at all".[74] In *Bestobell Paints v Bigg*[75] the mere statement that the defendant's house was painted with *Carson's* paint was true but disingenuous, since the innuendo was that Carson's paint was unsatisfactory and subject to fading or changes in colour, and that was clearly calculated to cause pecuniary damage to the plaintiffs in their trade.

In *Kaye v Robertson*[76] the defendant newspaper proposed to publish what purported to be an interview with the plaintiff actor who was in hospital. Although the Court of Appeal held that the plaintiff did not have sufficient trading status to sue for passing-off, the deprivation of the fee he might have charged for an authorised interview was sufficient damage for the law of injurious falsehood:

"As to damage, I have already recorded that Mr. Robertson appreciated that Mr. Kaye's story was one for which other newspapers would be willing to pay 'large sums of money.' It needs little imagination to appreciate that whichever journal secured the first interview with Mr. Kaye would be willing to pay the most. Mr. Kaye thus has a potentially valuable right to sell the story of his accident and his recovery when he is fit enough to tell it. If the defendants are able to publish the article they proposed, or one anything like it, the value of this right would in my view be seriously lessened, and Mr. Kaye's story thereafter be worth much less to him."

In *Joyce v Sengupta*[77] a former maid to Princess Anne had a claim to damages, which might be more than nominal, in so far as accusations of theft and disloyalty made it more difficult for her to obtain future employment.

---

[74] *ibid., per* Harman L.J.
[75] [1975] F.S.R. 421 (Oliver J.). An interim injunction was refused by analogy with *Bonnard v Perryman* [1891] 2 Ch. 269, CA.
[76] [1991] F.S.R. 62, CA.
[77] [1993] 1 W.L.R. 337, CA. Similar cases are *Khodaparast v Shad* [2000] 1 W.L.R. 618, CA, and *Spring v Guardian Assurance plc* [1993] All E.R. 273, CA. The latter action failed on the facts for lack of malice.

CHAPTER 5

THE MISREPRESENTATION IN PASSING-OFF

A. The Essential Misrepresentation

Misrepresentation: the basis of the action

The essence of the tort of passing-off is a misrepresentation made by the **5–1** defendant which is calculated to cause damage to the business or goodwill of the claimant[1]:

> "My Lords, *Spalding v Gamage*[2] and the later cases make it possible to identify five characteristics which must be present in order to create a valid cause of action for passing-off: (1) a misrepresentation (2) made by a trader in the course of trade, (3) to prospective customers of his or ultimate consumers of goods or services supplied by him, (4) which is calculated to injure the business or goodwill of another trader ... and (5) which causes actual damage to a business or ... will probably do so."[3]

Although Lord Fraser did not use the term misrepresentation in his five enumerated heads he agreed with its central importance to the tort and used it in the context of treating misuse of the term *Advocaat* as an actionable misrepresentation. Likewise, in *Reckitt & Colman v Borden*[4] Lord Oliver gave misrepresentation as the second in his list of three essential elements:

> "[The plaintiff] must demonstrate a misrepresentation by the defendant to the public (whether or not intentional) leading or likely to lead the public to believe that goods or services offered by him are the goods or services of the plaintiff. Whether the public is aware of the plaintiff's identity as the manufacturer or supplier of the goods or services is immaterial, as long as they are identified with a particular source which is in fact the plaintiff. For example, if the public is accustomed to rely upon a particular brand name in purchasing goods of a particular description, it matters not at all that there is little or no public awareness of the identity of the proprietor of the brand name."

Lord Diplock expressly had in mind the speech of Lord Parker in **5–2** *Spalding v Gamage* which also identified a false representation as the basis of the action:

> "[T]he basis of a passing-off action being a false representation by the

---

[1] *Spalding (AG) & Bros v A W Gamage Ltd* (1915) 32 R.P.C. 273, HL; *Erven Warnink BV v J Townend & Sons (Hull) Ltd* [1979] A.C. 731; [1979] 2 All E.R. 927; [1980] R.P.C. 31, HL; *Cadbury Schweppes Pty Ltd v Pub Squash Co Pty Ltd* [1981] R.P.C. 429; [1981] 1 All E.R. 213, PC; *Reckitt & Colman Products Ltd v Borden Inc* [1990] 1 W.L.R. 491; [1990] 1 All E.R. 873; [1990] R.P.C. 340, HL.
[2] (1915) 32 R.P.C. 273, HL.
[3] *per* Lord Diplock in *Erven Warnink BV v J Townend & Sons (Hull) Ltd* [1979] A.C. 731; [1979] 2 All E.R. 927; [1980] R.P.C. 31, 93, HL.
[4] [1990] 1 W.L.R. 491; [1990] 1 All E.R. 873; [1990] R.P.C. 340, HL. The factual context is that of passing-off in its classic pre-*Advocaat* form.

defendant, it must be proved in each case as a fact that the false representation was made. It may, of course, have been made in express words, but cases of express misrepresentation of this sort are rare. The more common case is, where the representation is implied in the use or imitation of a mark, trade name, or get-up with which the goods of another are associated in the minds of the public. In such cases the point to be decided is whether, having regard to all the circumstances of the case, the use by the defendant in connection with the goods of the mark, name, or get-up in question impliedly represents such goods to be the goods of the plaintiff, or the goods of the plaintiff of a particular class of quality, or, as it is sometimes put, whether the defendant's use of such mark, name or get-up is calculated to deceive."[5]

The proposition that "nobody has any right to represent his goods as the goods of someone else"[6] grew imperceptibly out of the rather different one that "a man is not to sell his goods under the pretence that they are the goods of another man".[7] The difference was alluded to by Lord Parker at the start of his speech,[8] and the importance is that the law had come to recognise that damage to the plaintiff could flow from the very act of making a false representation (such as by issuing a misleading advertisement) even before there were any sales. In *Spalding v Gamage* itself the defendants relied heavily on the defence that the writ had been issued prematurely, that no customer had bought the defendant's goods and no damage could have been caused. This would not have prevented a *quia timet* action, but they claimed to have offered an adequate undertaking. The House of Lords rejected these arguments, and on the subsequent enquiry as to damages[9] the Court of Appeal awarded a substantial sum for general damage to goodwill caused by the advertisements themselves.

No monopoly or property in name, mark or get-up

5–3 The action for passing-off does not confer monopoly rights, and there is no property in a name as such, even one as well-known and distinctive in its field as *Harrods, Mercedes* or *Elvis Presley*.[10] In particular, passing-off differs from the law of registered trade marks in that the use of a particular mark is only actionable if in all the circumstances of the case it is calculated to mislead. Passing-off recognises no "exclusive right" to any name, mark or

---

[5] (1915) 32 R.P.C. 273, HL *per* Lord Parker.

[6] *per* Lord Parker in *Spalding (AG) & Bros v A W Gamage Ltd* (1915) 32 R.P.C. 273, HL, quoting and very slightly amending Lord Halsbury L.C. in *Reddaway (Frank) & Co Ltd v George Banham & Co Ltd* [1896] A.C. 199; [1895–9] All E.R. 313; 13 R.P.C. 218, HL.

[7] *per* Lord Langdale in *Perry v Truefitt* (1842) 49 E.R. 749.

[8] In which he used "pass off" in the old sense.

[9] *Spalding (AG) & Bros v A W Gamage Ltd* (1918) 35 R.P.C. 101, CA.

[10] *Harrods Ltd v Harrodian School Ltd* [1996] R.P.C. 697, CA; *Daimler-Chrysler AG v Alavi* [2001] R.P.C. 42; *Elvis Presley Trade Marks* [1999] R.P.C. 567, CA. Even the protection afforded to "household names" such as *Marks and Spencer* in *British Telecommunications plc v One in a Million Ltd* [1999] 1 W.L.R. 903; [1998] 4 All E.R. 476; [1999] E.T.M.R. 61; [1999] F.S.R. 1, CA, was predicated on an actual, or threatened, misrepresentation of some kind.

get-up[11]; and, in theory, the defendant is always free to use such material if he can effectively distinguish his own goods or business,[12] or if circumstances are such that there is no need to take active steps to distinguish it in the first place. The fact that there is or would be infringement of a registered trade mark under the Trade Marks Act 1994 (or a previous Act) does not mean that there is passing-off. Passing-off does not prevent accurate comparative advertising; nor is there any question of a purchaser requiring an implied licence, or of a vendor being able to impose restrictions running with the goods.

As Millett L.J. observed in *Harrods v Harrodian School*[13]:

"It is well settled that (unless registered as a trade mark) no one has a monopoly in his brand name or get up, however familiar these may be. Passing off is a wrongful invasion of a right of property vested in the plaintiff but the property which is protected by an action for passing off is not the plaintiff's proprietary right in the name or get up which the defendant has misappropriated but the goodwill and reputation of his business which is likely to be harmed by the defendant's misrepresentation...

It is this fundamental principle of the law of passing off which leads me to reject the main way in which the Plaintiffs have put their case before us ... The name 'Harrods' may be universally recognised, but the business with which it is associated in the minds of the public is not all-embracing. To be known to everyone is not to be known for everything."

In *Harrods* as in every other case, liability depends on whether in all the circumstances of the case the defendant's conduct is calculated to deceive. That is why the success of the defendants on the facts of that case does not imply that they would be have been allowed to call their school *Harrods' School* or use the plaintiffs' distinctive script or livery. A sufficiently explicit or outrageous representation of a connection with Harrods would have overcome the effect of the parties' very different fields of activity. Conversely, it did not follow that an "enterprising trader" would have been allowed to set up a retail shop under the name *The Harrodian*.

In *Singer Manufacturing Co v Loog*,[14] the defendants had published price **5–4** lists using the name *Singer* in respect of sewing machines not manufactured by the plaintiffs, but said to employ the same system of operation. There was a finding against the defendants at first instance which they accepted in part, but they appealed against the form of the order which would effectively have prevented them from using the word Singer at all. The price lists

---

[11] *Burberrys v J C Cording & Co Ltd* (1909) 26 R.P.C. 693; *Payton & Co v Snelling, Lampard & Co* [1901] A.C. 308; 17 R.P.C. 628, HL.
[12] Although this may be impossible in practice—*Montgomery v Thompson* [1891] A.C. 217; 8 R.P.C. 361, HL and the pair of cases over *Yorkshire Relish: Powell's TM* [1894] A.C. 8; 11 R.P.C. 4, HL and *Powell v Birmingham Vinegar Brewery Co* [1897] A.C. 710; 14 R.P.C. 721, HL.
[13] [1996] R.P.C. 697, CA.
[14] (1882) 8 App. Cas. 15, HL.

were only circulated to the trade. The House of Lords rejected the proposition that there was property in the mark which entitled the plaintiffs to restrain competitors from using it at all; and held that only use calculated to deceive could be restrained:

> "[N]o one has a right to use the word [*Singer*] for the purpose of passing off his goods as theirs, or, even when he is innocent of that purpose, to use it in any way calculated to deceive or aid in deceiving the public. None of the numerous authorities cited at the bar by the appellants' counsel carry the exclusive right of a trader to a particular name, beyond that limit. There is no authority, and, in my opinion, no principle for giving the trader any higher right. If he cannot allege and prove that the public are deceived, or that there is a reasonable probability of deception, he has no right to interfere with the use of his name by others."[15]

Passing-off is not a general tort of misappropriation or of "unfair copying". The claimant may have expended money, time, effort and ingenuity on introducing or popularising new goods or services; or an original way of promoting them. It may be the "custom of the trade" to allow him to reap the benefit without close competition, but so far as the law of passing-off is concerned all these may be copied wholesale if no misrepresentation results.[16]

Examples of actionable misrepresentations

5–5 In *Spalding v Gamage*[17] Lord Parker said that it would be impossible to enumerate or classify all the possible ways in which a man might make the false representation relied on. It is clear that the class of misrepresentations is wide, but not unlimited. Misrepresentations which have been recognised as actionable in passing-off are categorised and described in detail in the next chapter. What follows is a summary of some of the forms of misrepresentation which are most often encountered or are particularly valuable in illustrating the boundaries of the tort. It is assumed that all the other elements of the tort are present, and in particular, that the claimant is really likely to suffer substantial damage to his business or goodwill from the misrepresentation in question. No misrepresentation, whatever its nature, is actionable if this is not made out.

The earliest misrepresentation to be recognised as passing-off was that the goods of the defendant were those of the claimant. The misrepresentation may be made expressly, by offering the defendant's goods without explanation when the claimant's are asked for, or by adopting some distinguishing sign distinctive of the claimant such as his name, trade mark or get-up sufficiently closely to deceive. The misrepresentation may relate to goods in the defendant's hands which do in fact come from the claimant, provided

---

[15] *per* Lord Watson.
[16] *Payton & Co v Snelling, Lampard & Co* [1901] A.C. 308; 17 R.P.C. 628, HL; *Cadbury Schweppes Pty Ltd v Pub Squash Co Pty Ltd* [1981] R.P.C. 429; [1981] 1 All E.R. 213, PC.
[17] (1915) 32 R.P.C. 273, HL.

that the effect of the representation is to make the goods seem different to what they really are. Thus, it is passing-off to represent the claimant's goods of one type or quality as those of another, or to represent substandard, altered or second-hand goods as new. It is also passing-off to misuse the claimant's own goods to sell others, for instance by refilling the claimant's containers.

The misrepresentation need not relate to goods, but may be to the effect that the businesses of the claimant and the defendant are the same, or have merged, or that one is a branch, agency or subsidiary of the other; or, more generally, that the defendant has any connection with the claimant that is likely to cause damage. It may therefore be actionable to misrepresent oneself as the licensee of another business, although this is an area where the English courts have been reluctant to conclude that damage will result. Misrepresentations as to business connection are especially relevant to businesses supplying services, but the same principles apply where one or both businesses deal in goods (of the same or different kinds) whether or not there is also passing-off of the goods themselves.

Since the 1960s it has become recognised that actionable representations **5–6** are not confined to those suggesting a non-existent connection with a particular claimant. It is actionable to misrepresent that goods are produced in a particular place, or according to a particular process or from particular ingredients. Although the law is not entirely clear, it may potentially be passing-off to claim any desirable attribute that the claimant has (or can confer) and the defendant lacks, such as the endorsement of a third party. Misleading comparative advertising may therefore amount to passing-off.

Recognition of even wider categories of misrepresentation makes some progress, albeit slowly. In *SDS Biotech v Power*[18] both parties marketed a fungicide with a MAFF[19] number denoting it had been approved for use by the Government. In the case of the defendants, such approval had not been given and they were not entitled to use the MAFF number. Applications by the plaintiffs for summary judgment under former RSC Ord. 14, and by the defendants to strike out the statement of claim were both refused. Difficult points of law arose which were inappropriate to determine on motion. *SDS Biotech v Power* was considered in *Hodge Clemco v Airblast*[20] where the defendants sold replacement lenses as "to suit" or as "suitable for" for the plaintiffs' sand-blasting helmets. The replacements were safe, but their use would be illegal because they did not have the necessary approval under the COSHH Regulations.[21] Jacob J. held that it was at least arguable that stating that the defendants' lenses were "to suit" the plaintiffs' helmets, or simply selling them for that purpose, amounted to an implicit misrepresentation that their use would be legal for that purpose and that although the plaintiffs' standing to complain about such a misrepresentation as passing-off was arguable either way, the necessary standard for an

---

[18] (1989) [1995] F.S.R. 797 (Aldous J.).
[19] Ministry of Agriculture Fisheries and Food.
[20] [1995] F.S.R. 806 (Jacob J.).
[21] Control of Substances Hazardous to Health.

interlocutory injunction had been met. However, the balance of convenience favoured the defendants and an injunction was refused.

Liability for passing-off is not confined to traders who deal directly with the public. Actions are frequently brought against manufacturers, importers, dealers and others under the doctrine of "instruments of deception". In effect, there is deemed to be a misrepresentation as soon as deceptive goods are released into circulation.

Misrepresentations not actionable as passing-off

5–7 Historically, passing-off was for many years concerned only with one category of misrepresentation, and with only a limited number of variations on the way that misrepresentation was conveyed: identity or close similarity of name, mark or get-up conveyed, or did not, the message that the goods or business of the defendant were those of the plaintiff, or closely associated with him. If that was not the message conveyed, then it was hardly ever necessary to delve any more deeply into questions of interpretation. Whatever the message may have meant, if anything, it could not amount to passing-off. To this extent, and only to this extent, passing-off formerly had something akin to a "single meaning" rule of its own.

When the class of potentially actionable misrepresentations was expanded in *Advocaat*,[22] both Lord Diplock and Lord Fraser acknowledged that not all misrepresentations would be actionable as passing-off at the suit of a trader damaged by them. Lord Diplock gave the example of one trader "puffing" his goods at the expense of one more scrupulous: this had been permitted at common law and although higher standards of commercial morality are now expected and enforced there is still a grey area between actionable passing-off and exaggerated but venial claims.

As a separate matter, misrepresentations about the goods or business of the claimant would still seem to be actionable, if at all, only as injurious falsehood[23] which requires proof of malice and special damage.[24] It is true that a misrepresentation which is *prima facie* one in the nature of injurious falsehood may also satisfy Lord Diplock's criteria, but he warned against the fallacy of supposing that all factual situations presenting those characteristics gave rise to the action for passing-off. In the *Budweiser* case[25] both passing-off and injurious falsehood were in issue. The Court of Appeal expressly followed *Advocaat* in respect of passing-off but treated a misrepresentation that the plaintiffs required the licence of the defendants for their business as potentially injurious falsehood only, which gave rise to no cause of action because it was not made maliciously.

[22] *Erven Warnink BV v J Townend & Sons (Hull) Ltd* [1979] A.C. 731; [1979] 2 All E.R. 927; [1980] R.P.C. 31, HL.
[23] Or, infrequently, as defamation proper, as in *Linotype Co Ltd v British Empire Typesetting Machine Co Ltd* (1899) 81 L.T. 331; 15 T.L.R. 524, HL.
[24] Subject to the Defamation Act 1952, s.3.
[25] *Anheuser-Busch Inc v Budejovicky Budvar NP* [1984] F.S.R. 413, CA.

Some discarded misconceptions

Over the past century or so, the law of passing-off has evolved so as to **5–8** discard some former restrictions as to which misrepresentations are actionable and which are not. Since these still occasionally recur, it may be useful to summarise and dismiss some of the most persistent. Most importantly, the misrepresentation in passing-off need not be made fraudulently or with any intention to deceive: "calculated" in Lord Diplock's speech in *Advocaat*[26] means *likely* rather than *intended*. The only continuing importance of fraud is for its evidential value.

The misrepresentation need not be to the effect that the defendant's goods or business are those of the claimant; and as two partial corollaries of this, passing-off is not confined to misrepresentations in the nature of common law trade mark infringement, and the misrepresentation may be such as to be actionable by a potentially large but determinate class of claimants. Finally, the oddly durable fallacy that the claimant and defendant must in some sense share a common field of activity may be regarded as obsolete. The presence or absence of a common field is no more than a matter of degree and inference.

B. WHAT MAKES A REPRESENTATION FALSE?

Objective truth as the standard

It is well settled that the test for whether a representation is true or not is the **5–9** objective one of the effect it will have on the mind of the relevant public: "[E]ven a description of goods which is literally true may be so framed as to mislead".[27] If it will deceive a substantial number in fact, then it is no defence that it may be literally true, nor that some may not be deceived, nor that the defendant may have made it honestly. As usual, the claimant's case is strengthened if the defendant's motives were fraudulent, but this is not essential.

> "[T]he falsity of a representation does not depend (at any rate in the absence of fraud) on the meaning which the maker of the representation intended or believed it to have or upon the construction which the court itself puts upon it, but upon the way in which it would reasonably be understood by the persons to whom it is addressed. In this respect there is no difference between the law in passing-off actions and the law in any other action based on misrepresentation."[28]

---

[26] *Erven Warnink BV v J Townend & Sons (Hull) Ltd* [1979] A.C. 731; [1979] 2 All E.R. 927; [1980] R.P.C. 31, HL.
[27] *per* Lord Davey in *Grand Hotel Co of Caledonia Springs v Wilson* [1904] A.C. 103; 21 R.P.C. 117, PC.
[28] *per* Lord Devlin in *Parker-Knoll Ltd v Knoll International Ltd* [1962] R.P.C. 265, 289, HL; dissenting in the result, but not on this point.

"[I]f a man makes a statement which is true, but which carries with it a false representation and induces the belief that his goods are the plaintiff's goods, he will be restrained by injunction. He cannot rely on the fact that his statement is literally and accurately true, if, notwithstanding its truth, it carries with it a false representation."[29]

In *Iron-Ox Remedy Co v Co-op Wholesale Society*[30] the plaintiffs introduced Iron Oxide tablets in competition with the plaintiffs' *Iron-Ox*. The name of the latter was fanciful: it contained no iron oxide, which was useless as a drug. The defence that the defendants were doing no more than satisfying a public demand for iron oxide as a useful medicine was rejected. The name would lead to confusion with the plaintiffs' product and that was why it had been chosen.

Strict truth not a defence if misleading

5–10 The source of the proposition that a defendant may be restrained from making a representation which is literally true in one sense but calculated to deceive in another is generally taken to be the decision of the House of Lords in *Reddaway v Banham*[31] in 1896. The House of Lords had already decided in two cases that a place name could become distinctive of a manufacturer, and that a person setting up business in the same place could not use that name so as to pass off his goods as those of the plaintiff: *Wotherspoon v Currie*[32] and *Montgomery v Thompson*.[33] There was also a line of cases in which defendants had been restrained from trading dishonestly under their own name, although the rationale for this was, and remains, uncertain. *Reddaway v Banham* itself began as a normal passing-off action in which the plaintiffs' mark was thought by all to be completely arbitrary,[34] but in the course of the trial it turned out that it was accurately descriptive of both the plaintiffs' and the defendants' goods:

"The action was launched on the footing that the expression '*Camel Hair Belting*' was a fanciful term. But in the course of the trial it was proved, partly by the evidence of experts and partly by an exhibit collected from a living animal in the Zoological Gardens at Manchester, that the camel hair of commerce, of which many bundles were produced, was really and truly, for the most part, composed of genuine camel hair. This evidence seems to have come as a revelation to *Reddaway* and his advisers. However, they accepted the situation, and forbore to contest the point further. And so it was established that *Reddaway's* trade designation,

---

[29] *per* Buckley L.J. in *Brinsmead (John) & Sons Ltd v Brinsmead & Waddington & Sons Ltd* (1913) 30 R.P.C. 493, CA.
[30] (1907) 24 R.P.C. 425 (Parker J.).
[31] [1896] A.C. 199; [1895–9] All E.R. 313; 13 R.P.C. 218, HL.
[32] (1872) L.R. 5 H.L. 508, HL.
[33] [1891] A.C. 217; 8 R.P.C. 361, HL.
[34] See *Reddaway (F) & Co Ltd v Bentham Hemp Spinning Co Ltd* [1892] 2 Q.B. 639; 9 R.P.C. 503, CA.

instead of being, as everybody supposed, a fanciful term, was nothing more nor less than a substantially accurate description of the material of which this belting was composed...

The learned counsel for the respondents maintained that the expression '*Camel Hair Belting*' used by *Banham* was 'the simple truth'. Their proposition was that 'where a man is simply telling the truth as to the way in which his goods are made, or as to the materials of which they are composed, he cannot be held liable for mistakes which the public may make.' That seems to me to be rather begging the question. Can it be said that the description '*Camel Hair Belting*', as used by *Banham*, is the simple truth? I will not call it an abuse of language to say so, but certainly it is not altogether a happy expression. The whole merit of that description, its one virtue for *Banham's* purposes, lies in its duplicity ... I venture to think that a statement which is literally true, but which is intended to convey a false impression, has something of a faulty ring about it; it is not sterling coin; it has no right to the genuine stamp and impress of truth."[35]

The importance of *Reddaway v Banham*[36] may be seen from the fact that the Court of Appeal[37] had found in favour of the defendants despite self-confessed fraud; the reluctance of Lord Morris to concur in a decision which, he said, "establishes, and in my opinion for the first time, the proposition that a trader is not permitted to merely tell truthfully and accurately the material of which his goods are made"; and comments made on it by a differently constituted House of Lords in *Cellular Clothing Co v Maxton & Murray*.[38] *Reddaway v Banham* was not entirely unprecedented, but it is one of the landmark cases in passing-off. Like *Advocaat*,[39] it took a rule which had previously been recognised only for geographical terms and established it as applying to *prima facie* descriptive terms of every nature.

"Misrepresentations" which deceive no one

Since passing-off is concerned with misrepresentations which are material in **5–11** the sense of being really likely to cause damage; and since it is always permissible, and indeed obligatory, to take into the account the whole of the surrounding circumstances, there is no contradiction in terms in the concept of a misrepresentation which does not deceive. On the contrary, there is a serious risk or falling into error if one jumps to the conclusion that a statement which appears to be untrue on its face must necessarily be false in any relevant and material sense. The risk is exacerbated if one deliberately excludes from consideration everything except a bare comparison of the respective names, marks or signs of the parties, or substitutes some kind of notional use for what is known to happen in fact—both exercises which may

[35] *per* Lord Macnaghten at 232.
[36] [1986] A.C. 199; [1895–9] 2 All E.R. 313; 13 R.P.C. 218, HL.
[37] [1892] 2 Q.B. 639; 9 R.P.C. 503, CA.
[38] [1899] A.C. 326; 16 R.P.C. 397, HL
[39] *Erven Warnink BV v J Townend & Sons (Hull) Ltd* [1979] A.C. 731; [1979] 2 All E.R. 927; [1980] R.P.C. 31, HL.

be entirely appropriate for trade mark infringement, but certainly not for passing-off.

In *Consorzio del Prosciutto di Parma v Marks & Spencer*[40] the Court of Appeal held that it was not passing-off to sell as "genuine 'Parma ham'" pre-packed slices of Parma ham which met all the objective requirements of Italian law except for the fact that the latter only permitted sliced Parma ham to be sold as such if the slices were actually cut in the presence of the consumer. The ham did not cease to be Parma ham when it was sliced and packed, and the defendants could not be prevented from identifying it for what it really was. The Court of Appeal, reversing Morritt J. on this point, also held that there was not even an arguable case that sliced and packaged Parma ham was so affected by the processing as to become goods of a different category or quality. The conclusion on appeal was assisted by the amendment to the relevant law to allow Parma ham to be so described if sliced and packed in the Parma Region under the supervision of the Consorzio, and the fact that most of the differences identified by the plaintiffs' expert were either irresolvable matters of subjective opinion, or attributable to non-traditional but legitimate industrial processes (de-boning, chilling, and forming into a "brick") which members of the *Consorzio* also practised and of which they could not complain. There was not even an arguable misrepresentation of either provenance or quality.

5–12   The primary reason for the decision in *Parma ham* is so obvious (at least to common lawyers) that it is easy to overlook a second and more subtle aspect to the decision which has not always been noticed in subsequent cases on similar facts.[41] Nourse L.J., especially, was prepared to assume that there was indeed a section of the public for whom "Parma ham" was synonymous with "a whole ham bearing the crown sliced in the presence of the ultimate purchaser". However this class of customer would be no more confused or deceived than those whose instinctively acquired understanding of "Parma ham" was entirely consistent with what was being offered by the defendants. It was perfectly obvious to anyone buying Marks & Spencer "Parma ham" in its flat plastic pack that it lacked the one property which was relied on as differentiating it from Parma ham as defined by Italian law and the Consorzio. For this well-informed category of consumers one could say either that there was no misrepresentation at all (because what was otherwise implicit in the description "Parma ham" was explicitly contradicted by the goods themselves); or that if there was a misrepresentation, it was an immaterial one, because it could not have been relied on. Both are equally well summed up by saying of this particular class of the public that "they will know that Marks & Spencer's Parma ham cannot be the real thing and

---

[40] [1991] R.P.C. 351, CA. A subsequent case *Consorzio del Prosciutto di Parma v Asda* [2001] UKHL 7, [2001] 1 C.M.L.R. 43; [2001] E.T.M.R. 53; [2002] F.S.R. 3, HL and (on reference to the European Court of Justice) Case C-108/01 [2003] 2 C.M.L.R. 21 was concerned solely with Regulation 2081/92 and did not raise any issues of passing-off.

[41] Such as *Scotch Whisky Association v Glen Kella Distillers Ltd* [1997] Eu.L.R 455. The one material difference between the defendants' *White Whisky* and "genuine" whisky was that the colouring materials in the latter had been removed; but this was the unique selling point of the defendants' product and could not possibly have been overlooked by the purchaser.

may decide to buy it or not as they choose". An analogous conclusion could be reached for the much larger category of consumers whose knowledge and experience of Parma ham came from eating it in restaurants or buying it from delicatessens, in neither of which cases was it typically cut in the presence of the consumer. Again, either there was no misrepresentation, or it was an immaterial one. The consumer could not be said to rely on the precise details of an Italian law of which he was wholly ignorant, which was inconsistent with his personal experience and expectations, and which was plainly contradicted by the form in which he bought the Marks & Spencer's product.

Advocaat cases and actionable misdescriptions

Cases of alleged misdescription such as *Erven Warnink v Townend*[42] or **5–13** *Consorzio del Prosciutto di Parma v Marks & Spencer*[43] require a definite meaning to be attached to the term in issue if one is to answer two essential questions: is the defendant using it accurately or misleadingly, and is the claimant one of those entitled to sue to restrain misuse? Despite the fundamental importance of the question there has been relatively little discussion of how one sets about defining terms such as *Advocaat* or *Champagne*. In *Warnink v Townend* itself the public was familiar with *Advocaat*, but had only a very rudimentary idea of what distinguished it from similar drinks. There was widespread misconception that brandy was an essential component of Advocaat, which had probably arisen from mistranslation of the Dutch word "brandewijn". This misconception had been fostered, albeit innocently, by the plaintiffs in their advertising. The defendants' *Olde English Advocaat* contained brandy, the plaintiffs' did not. By finding for the plaintiffs the House of Lords implicitly adopted an objective test: the defendants' *Advocaat* was not what the public was used to, although the public would not have been able accurately to define what real *Advocaat* was.

The practical result of *Warnink v Townend* was that *Advocaat* meant, in England, the same as it meant under Dutch law. However, it is clear that one cannot simply import and enforce a suitable definition from the relevant foreign legal system, even if one is to be found. In *Consorzio del Prosciutto Di Parma v Marks & Spencer*[44] the plaintiffs alleged that according to Italian law Parma ham could only be sold as such if it was sliced in the presence of the purchaser, and that the defendants were not entitled to sell pre-sliced and packaged ham as Parma ham even though it came from the Parma region. The allegation was struck out as untenable.

The converse situation in one respect arose in *Chocosuisse v Cadbury*,[45] **5–14** with the result that the definition of "Swiss chocolate" finally adopted for the purposes of passing-off was actually more restrictive than under the

---

[42] [1979] A.C. 731; [1979] 2 All E.R. 927; [1980] R.P.C. 31, HL.
[43] [1991] R.P.C. 351, CA.
[44] [1991] R.P.C. 351, CA.
[45] [1999] E.T.M.R. 1020; [1999] R.P.C. 826, CA, on appeal from [1998] E.T.M.R. 205; [1998] R.P.C. 117 (Laddie J.).

relevant Swiss (and EC) legislation, but once again in accordance with the way the term was actually used in the English market. In *Chocosuisse v Cadbury* the plaintiffs (a trade association and two individual chocolate manufacturers, Lindt and Suchard) sued Cadbury in respect of a chocolate confectionery bar named *Swiss Chalet* which was made by Cadbury in England. At first instance, Laddie J. held that "Swiss chocolate" was not merely descriptive: to a substantial part of the public Swiss chocolate was perceived as distinctive premium product. It made no difference that there was no public unanimity as to what distinguished Swiss chocolate, nor that chocolate indistinguishable in taste and quality could be made outside Switzerland. Laddie J. went on to define "Swiss chocolate", for the relevant purposes under *Advocaat*, as being chocolate made in Switzerland under the relevant Swiss food regulations. It followed that the two manufacturers (but not the association) had *locus standi* to sue, and that the Cadbury's were liable for misrepresentation, since their Swiss Chalet bar complied with neither of these requirements. On appeal, the Court of Appeal imposed a narrower definition of Swiss chocolate by adding the requirement that it should contain no added vegetable fat or "cocoa butter equivalent". The latter, CBE, was permitted by Swiss legislation in small quantities but in fact none of the Swiss chocolate manufacturers used it and it was considered detrimental to quality. Real Swiss chocolate consumed in the United Kingdom was made without CBE, and this contributed to its characteristic smoothness.

5–15   The situation is particularly confused with regard to *Champagne*, where courts outside England have looked at the meaning generally attributed to the term in their respective jurisdictions and come to diametrically opposite conclusions. In the English "Spanish Champagne" case, *Bollinger v Costa Brava*,[46] the defendants argued that the term could only deceive a trifling minority of ignorant persons. Dankwerts J. cautioned that: "[W]hen the case is tried in an atmosphere of educated persons, many of whom are well acquainted with the qualities of various wines, it may seem absurd that persons should be deceived by what may appear to be a transparent impersonation" and found for the plaintiffs.[47] However, in more recent cases in other common law countries, the increasing knowledgability of purchasers has implicitly been recognised, especially where there has been a history of locally produced wines being sold as *Champagne*. In Australia the French Champagne producers admitted the legitimacy of *Australian Champagne* and failed to obtain an interlocutory injunction under the Trade Practices Act in respect of *Spanish Champagne*.[48] In Canada there was no misrepresentation by selling *Canadian Champagne*.[49] In the *Australian*

---

[46] [1961] 1 W.L.R. 277 [1961] R.P.C. 116; [1961] 3 All E.R. 561 (Danckwerts J.).

[47] See also the *Champagne Cider* case *Bulmer (HP) Ltd v J Bollinger SA* [1978] 2 C.M.L.R. 625; [1978] R.P.C. 79, CA reversing in part [1976] R.P.C. 97 and compare the different approaches of Whitford J. and the Court of Appeal.

[48] *Comité du Vin de Champagne v N L Burton Pty Ltd* (1981) 57 F.L.R. 434; 1 T.P.R 128; 38 A.L.R.J. 664 (Franki J., Federal Court).

[49] *Institut National des Appellations D'Origine des Vins v Andres Wines Ltd* (1987) 60 O.R. (2d) 316; 14 C.I.P.R. 138; 16 C.P.R. (3d) 385; 40 D.L.R. (4th) 239 (Dupont J., Ontario).

Champagne case in New Zealand, *Comité Interprofessionel du Vin de Champagne v Wineworths Group*[50] the trial judge regretted that the case law did not provide much assistance in how to set about ascertaining the degree to which *Champagne* had kept or lost its original meaning, but found on the facts that to New Zealand customers it still meant exclusively the French product.

Standards of truth and plausibility in other contexts

Outside the context of misdescription, somewhat similar issues were dealt **5-16** with inconclusively in *Kelly v Byles*[51] in which *Post Office* for a directory was said to be a true description of the defendant's but not of the plaintiffs' book, and *Brock's "Crystal Palace" Fireworks v James Pain.*[52] In the former, relief was refused on the basis that the term was not distinctive. The latter case avoided the broader issue by treating *Crystal Palace* as wholly arbitrary. Had the court recognised it as denoting that the user was under contract to give the celebrated firework displays at the Crystal Palace then it would have been true of the defendant alone. In general, the issue is only likely to arise under the extended form of passing-off which recognises misuse of descriptive or generic terms as actionable. Where the misrepresentation is supposedly that the defendants' goods or business are those of the claimant the only difficulty lies in deciding if such a representation has in fact been made. If so, its truth or falsity is not normally hard to judge.

It may happen that an alleged misrepresentation is so inherently implausible that no one will believe it. If so, it cannot be material and there will be no passing-off. More commonly, the representation may be open to more than one interpretation, and the court may lean towards giving it an innocent one because the surrounding circumstances make that far more credible than the one argued for by the claimant. It has, for instance, been said that one small business cannot be confused with a large one of many branches,[53] but that begs the question. Large businesses also trade through small local branches and the customer may believe he is dealing with one of these. There is always a danger that when all the facts of the case have been discussed at length, it will seem scarcely credible that anyone could be confused. But real customers are not in such a position. They make sudden decisions on the basis of a few prominent indications and their pre-existing knowledge, such as it is.

In *Cochrane v Macnish*[54] the defendant argued that the plaintiff was disentitled to relief, having himself been guilty of misrepresentation by putting "manufactured ... by letters patent" on his soda water labels. However, no one could conceivably suppose soda water itself to be patented, and the

---

[50] [1992] 2 N.Z.L.R. 327 (CA of NZ).
[51] (1880) 13 Ch.D. 682, CA.
[52] (1911) 28 R.P.C. 697, CA.
[53] *Hammond (Marc A) Pty Ltd v Papa Carmine Pty Ltd* (1976) 15 A.L.R. 179; [1976] 2 N.S.W.L.R. 124; [1978] R.P.C. 697 (Wootten J., New South Wales).
[54] [1896] A.C. 225; 13 R.P.C. 100, PC.

statement was justified by the fact that the plaintiff used patented machinery.

In *Miss World v James Street*[55] the plaintiffs complained of the showing of a satirical X-rated film called *The Alternative Miss World* on the same night as the *Miss World* contest took place. The Court of Appeal rejected as equally absurd the suggestions that the plaintiffs would be thought to be involving themselves in X-rated films or that they would be putting on a rival show on the very same night. No one would be confused.

C. THE MATERIALITY OF THE MISREPRESENTATION

The misrepresentation must be material

5–17 The misrepresentation in passing-off must be a material one if it is to be actionable. That is to say it must be such as to create a real, tangible risk of damage to the claimant. In practice, this almost invariably means that the misrepresentation must be believed by those to whom it is addressed, and that the addressees must act in reliance upon it. If the supposed misrepresentation does not actually influence the prospective customer then it is most unlikely to be a material one, whether or not the customer is deceived by it. The general rule is that expressed by Lord Oliver in the *Jif Lemon* case, *Reckitt & Colman v Borden*, where he said[56]:

> "Thirdly, [the plaintiff] must demonstrate that he suffers or, in a *quia timet* action that he is likely to suffer, damage *by reason of the erroneous belief engendered by the defendant's misrepresentation* that the source of the defendant's goods or services is the same as the source of those offered by the plaintiff."

And more briefly by Lord Jauncey in the same case:

> "It is also a prerequisite that the misrepresentation has deceived or is likely to deceive and that the plaintiff is likely to suffer damage *by such deception*."

In the light of both principle and authority, doubts must therefore be expressed about those few cases in which misrepresentation and damage have been regarded as somehow independent, so that the damage relied on need not arise from any member of the relevant public either believing or relying on the misrepresentation. There are valid exceptions to the general rule in which damage has occurred without any addressee having acted upon

---

[55] [1981] F.S.R. 309, CA.
[56] [1990] 1 W.L.R. 491; [1990] 1 All E.R. 873; [1990] R.P.C. 340, HL. Emphasis added in both quotations. The context is that of the traditional, rather than extended, category of misrepresentations.

the misrepresentation, but they are comparatively rare and tend to involve misrepresentations which are likely to damage goodwill in the long term by virtue of being believed and perhaps remembered; though without being acted upon for the time being.[57]

Irrelevant or self-induced assumptions

The distinction between material and immaterial misrepresentations is **5-18** particularly important in three fields: licensing; character merchandising; and the get-up or intrinsic appearance of goods. In the first two, the public may be led to believe that the goods or business of the defendant are in fact licensed or authorised by the claimant, but that in itself does not necessarily constitute a material misrepresentation. The public is unlikely to be influenced merely by the thought that a percentage of the price is going to a third party. Hence, the importance of quality control in licensing and merchandising. If the public believes the licensor to exercise quality control over licensed products then it becomes more plausible that a misrepresentation that the defendant is licensed will influence their choice. This is the most common argument advanced for such a misrepresentation being material, but others can exist. For instance, if the defendant's business is disreputable then the very fact of its being associated with the claimant can be damaging.[58] So far as the appearance of goods is concerned, the public may assume that all goods with the same external appearance emanate from one source. However, if the goods are bought for their appearance alone, as with ornaments,[59] or furnishings,[60] then any such belief is immaterial. The customers are not relying on the appearance to denote a supposedly common trade source.

It can also happen that the customer makes his choice on the basis of some misconception for which the defendant ought not to be held liable. This occurs quite commonly when a former monopoly is broken.[61] A part of the public is always inclined to suppose that the defendant's goods or services are those of the claimant in a new guise, simply because the claimant's are the only ones with which they have been familiar till then.[62] As Slade L.J. had said in the Court of Appeal in *Reckitt & Colman v Borden*[63] itself. "They [the defendants] were under no duty to guard against self-induced misapprehensions on the part of potential consumers who failed to exercise the degree of perspicacity which the law of passing off expects of such consumers".

---

[57] See *Spalding (AG) & Bros v A W Gamage Ltd* (1918) 35 R.P.C. 101, CA, above.
[58] As in *Annabel's (Berkeley Square) Ltd v Schock* [1972] R.P.C. 838, CA.
[59] *British American Glass Co Ltd v Winton Products (Blackpool) Ltd* [1962] R.P.C. 230.
[60] *Jarman & Platt Ltd v I Barget Ltd* [1977] F.S.R. 260, CA.
[61] *Compatibility Research Ltd v Computer Psyche Co Ltd* [1967] R.P.C. 201; *My Kinda Town Ltd v Soll* [1983] R.P.C. 407, CA.
[62] *per* Lord Oliver in *Reckitt & Colman Products Ltd v Borden Inc* [1990] 1 W.L.R. 491; [1990] 1 All E.R. 873; [1990] R.P.C. 340, HL.
[63] [1990] R.P.C. 340, CA; affirmed without reference to this point in the House of Lords, above.

In *Philips v Remington*[64] the Federal Court of Australia commented that any such confusion arising on the introduction of *Remington* electric shavers with three rotary cutting heads into a market previously entirely dominated by Philips would not amount to passing-off, provided the Remington product was clearly branded as such:

"But arguments of this kind could always be raised when an incoming competitor seeks to break a monopoly. Of course, some people might, probably unjustifiably, and probably transiently, associate the new product in some way with the only product of that sort previously available. However, if anyone were misled as a result, it would not be by the conduct of the intruder upon the monopoly, but by virtue of an inherent problem of the situation. Nor is such a difficulty to be attributed to passing off, provided the goods in question are appropriately and clearly branded."

5–19 This is true *a fortiori* where the supposed misrepresentation by the defendant is in fact the consequence of misrepresentations made by the claimant. In the South African case of *Caterham Car Sales v Birkin Cars*,[65] the trial judge had held that "for many years, Caterham had been sedulously passing off its product as that of Lotus", and consequently benefited from a reputation in relation to replicas of the Lotus Seven Series III sports car which they did not deserve. On appeal to the Supreme Court of Appeal Harms J.A. observed:

"Whether a passing-off action can be used to protect a misapprehension or a false reputation appears to me to open to serious doubt but since it was not argued it need not be decided. However, to the extent that a reputation is founded on a conscious falsehood, public policy demands that legal protection should be withheld."

5–20 Even if competition already exists, some members of the public may be familiar only with the claimant's goods or business. Customers unfamiliar with what makes the claimant distinctive in the market may conclude that the defendant's goods or business are those of the claimant, by virtue of the defendant using indicia which are in fact open to use by all, but which those customers in their ignorance associate only with the claimant. It has long been settled that there is no liability for passing-off in those circumstances.[66] It is not the defendant who has deceived the customer, but the customer who has deceived himself.

As Chadwick L.J. observed in *Premier Luggage v Premier Co*[67]:

"Mr Justice Lloyd was right, if I may say so, to point out in *HFC Bank Plc v Midland Bank Plc* ... that even actual confusion does not show that

---

[64] [2000] FCA 876; 48 I.P.R. 257, (Federal Court of Australia).
[65] 1998 (3) SA 938 (SCA).
[66] *Payton & Co v Snelling, Lampard & Co* [1901] A.C. 308; 17 R.P.C. 628, HL.
[67] [2002] EWCA Civ 387; [2002] E.T.M.R. 69; [2003] F.S.R. 5, CA *per* Chadwick L.J. (delivering the judgment of the Court); reversing [2001] E.T.M.R. 6, [2001] F.S.R. 29.

there has been misrepresentation by anyone; all that it shows is 'that people make assumptions, jump to unjustified conclusions, and put two and two together to make five'."

In particular, the test sometimes formerly employed under s.11 of the Trade **5–21** Marks Act 1938 of whether any customer would have "cause to wonder" whether the goods or businesses of the parties were connected (or would "entertain a reasonable doubt" on that score) is self-evidently less demanding than that contemplated for passing-off, as is clear from the speech of Lord Upjohn in *Berlei v Bali Brassiere Co*[68] from which the phrase is taken:

"It is not necessary in order to find that a mark offends against section 11 to prove that there is an actual probability of deception leading to a passing off or (I add) an infringement action. It is sufficient if the result of the registration of the mark will be that a number of persons will be caused to wonder whether it might not be the case that the two products come from the same source."

Misrepresentations not operative at time of purchase

Problems are caused by misrepresentations which for one reason or another **5–22** are not operative on the mind of the purchaser at the time of purchase. These may be divided into two categories: misrepresentations which were made at some point in the past but which may have been corrected, forgotten or otherwise nullified prior to purchase; and those which are of such a kind as to act on the mind of the purchaser, if at all, only after completion of the transaction.

The first situation is exemplified by switch selling, discussed below. It is suggested that if misrepresentation was a material factor in obtaining the customer's business and the claimant suffered damage in consequence then there may still be liability for passing-off, either on the basis that the misrepresentation was inherently damaging[69] or that in the typical situation in which switch selling takes place the customer may not be given a *bona fide* opportunity to evaluate the alternative on offer. In the context of substitution, it is well established that presenting the customer as a *fait accompli* with a product which is recognisably not what he wanted may still amount to passing-off. On the other hand, a superficial misrepresentation which catches the attention but is otherwise wholly transient, such as those in *Newton-John v Scholl-Plough*,[70] or *Ciba-Geigy v Parke Davis*[71] probably cannot amount to passing-off.

---

[68] [1969] 1 W.L.R. 1306; [1969] 2 All E.R. 812; [1969] F.S.R. 288; [1969] R.P.C. 472, HL. The Trade Marks Act 1994, s.5(4)(a) expressly requires the opponent to establish that use of the mark would have amounted to passing-off.

[69] As in *Rima Electric Ltd v Rolls Razor and Rolls Appliances Ltd* [1965] R.P.C. 4, although the latter was treated as a case of injurious falsehood.

[70] (1986) 11 F.C.R. 233.

[71] [1994] F.S.R. 8 (Aldous J.).

Various pre- and post-sale misrepresentations were alleged without success in the Australian case of *Dr Martens Australia v Rivers*[72] in an attempt to circumvent findings that although the defendants' boots were closely similar in appearance to *Doc Martens* products, they were adequately distinguished by brand name so that there was no substantial risk of deception or confusion at the time of purchase. It was irrelevant that purchasers might initially be attracted to the defendants' footwear before realising that it was not the plaintiffs', or that people in the street might think that persons wearing the defendants' boots were actually wearing *Doc Martens*.

5–23   So far as the second situation is concerned, the general rule must be that there cannot be passing-off solely as a result of a misrepresentation which comes to the attention of the customer after completion of a purchase which was not influenced by that misrepresentation or any other. In particular, the claimant cannot rely on the defendant supposedly using distinctive indicia such as a name or get-up if they are hidden prior to sale. In *Bostik v Sellotape*[73] the claimants did not even have an arguable case from the defendants having copied the blue colour of their *Blu-tack* adhesive putty. The defendants' product was clearly distinguished both by the brand name *SelloTak* and by its get-up. The blueness of the claimants' product did not form the "crucial point of reference" for any customer making a repeat purchase, and the colour of the defendants' putty would only be apparent after purchase.

However, this is not to say that features invisible at the time of sale are always irrelevant. The main area of concern is in passing-off by substitution, where the misrepresentation may be implicit in tendering goods which are not those asked for, even, or especially, if there is nothing to show what they really are. Copying features of the claimant's goods which are only apparent when they are consumed or put to use may well be necessary from the point of view of a fraudulent defendant if the counterfeit substitute goods are not to be detected. If this is part of a scheme to defraud then goods with such features may properly be regarded as "instruments of deception" even if the deceptive features are hidden at the time of sale. Marks applied to corks in bottles provide a ready example. It is relatively easy to print counterfeit labels and apply them to bottles of inferior quality. Marks on corks are more secure and are relied on by consumers of fine wines as confirmation of the producer's or bottler's identity.

5–24   An example analogous to post-sale misrepresentation occurs in connection with the get-up of pharmaceutical preparations. It is well established that imitation of the distinctive get-up of capsules or tablets may amount to passing-off, although health care professionals would not be deceived.[74] The patient (who is a consumer, though not, in law, a purchaser) is unlikely to look at his tablets or capsules before opening the container at home, but would have the strongest possible motivation to return them if he suspected the wrong ones had been dispensed.

---

[72] [1999] FCA 1655; 47 I.P.R. 499, (Federal Court of Australia). Claims for passing-off were combined with ones under the Trade Practices Act 1974.
[73] [1994] R.P.C. 556 (Blackburne J.).
[74] *Hoffman La Roche & Co AG v DDSA Pharmaceuticals Ltd* [1969] F.S.R. 410, CA.

Relationship of the misrepresentation to *locus standi* to sue

The final respect in which the misrepresentation must be material concerns **5–25** the claimant's capacity to sue. The nature of the misrepresentation in the traditional form of passing-off meant that what was an actionable misrepresentation when made by the defendant would necessarily have been true if made by the claimant about his own goods or business, but with the recognition of extended forms of passing-off this formerly implicit relationship has been stated expressly. In *Erven Warnink v Townend*[75] Lord Fraser emphasised that the right to restrain the misuse of terms such as *Champagne* or *Advocaat* was confined to those businesses which owned English goodwill in respect of the products properly so called:

> "In the *Champagne* case, as in this case, the class, membership of which gives the plaintiff the right to sue, consists of all those who sell the genuine product in England under the distinctive name by which it is known here, and who together are the owners of the goodwill or reputation attaching to the name in England ... In either case the class is open to new members provided they qualify themselves by acquiring the necessary goodwill, which they can do by selling, in the one case under the name 'Champagne' a wine made in Champagne by the correct process from grapes grown there, and in the other case under the name 'Advocaat' a liqueur made according to the Dutch recipe. But although membership of the class can change, it must be definite and ascertainable at any particular time if it is to carry a right to sue in an action for passing-off."

In other words, precise definitions of *Champagne* or *Advocaat* were necessary not only in order to judge whether the defendant was making a misrepresentation, but also so as to be able to ascertain whether any given prospective plaintiff was a member of the class entitled to sue to restrain it. If the plaintiff could not justify use of either name in respect of goods of his own, then he could not sue for passing-off even if he suffered damage from the fact that the defendant was using the name inaccurately.

An aspect of *Consorzio del Prosciutto Di Parma v Marks & Spencer*[76] is **5–26** that if the plaintiffs' definition of "Parma ham" had been adopted, then retail sales of pre-sliced or pre-packed ham (even if from Parma) would have to have been excluded when it came to defining the members of the Consorzio who had goodwill by virtue of selling Parma ham in England. Since hardly any Parma ham sold in England was actually sliced in the presence of the consumer as Italian law required, it would have been difficult or impossible to say of any Italian Parma ham producer that he had goodwill at the retail level in England at all.

---

[75] [1979] A.C. 731; [1979] 2 All E.R. 927; [1980] R.P.C. 31, HL.
[76] [1991] R.P.C. 351, CA.

D. Use of Name or Mark Without Misrepresentation

Introduction: when may use be legitimate?

5–27 From the foregoing sections, it follows that the defendant may use any aspect of the claimant's name, mark or get-up (even precisely) if he does so in a manner which will not deceive. This is of importance in three main areas and one minor one. One is where the defendant makes fair use of the claimant's name or mark to denote the purpose or suitability of accessories, consumables, spare parts and the like intended for use with the claimant's goods. The second is where the defendant uses the claimant's name, mark or get-up to draw a comparison between his goods or business and the claimant's or to state that his are an alternative. The third is where the defendant truthfully refers to a former or subsisting relationship with the claimant.[77] Lastly, the use may be in a satirical, parodic or disparaging sense. Ambiguous or colourable use purportedly in any such manner, will, of course, still be restrained as passing-off and is likely to be taken as indicating an intention to deceive. An example is the case of *Burberrys v Raper*,[78] in which the defendant's advertisement headed "Burberry's Slip-on Coats" went on to say in smaller type and equivocal terms that theirs were identical in appearance and material. Even without any intention to deceive, an otherwise legitimate comparison may overstep the mark by over-estimating the acuity of the purchasing public, as in *Kimberley-Clark v Fort Sterling*.[79]

Accessories, consumables, spare parts, etc.

5–28 When the defendant claims to be using a term supposedly distinctive of the claimant to denote that his goods are suitable for use in connection with goods of the claimant the issues are whether the term is indeed distinctive of the claimant in that context, and whether the manner of use by the defendant is calculated to deceive. It is possible for a term to be distinctive in relation to the principal article, but to have an essentially descriptive character in respect of accessories for it.[80] Even if the term is *prima facie* distinctive in both contexts, it may be used by the defendant if his manner of use does not deceive. In *IBM v Phoenix*[81] there was an arguable defence, which should not be struck out, that the defendants were making no misrepresentation by selling as "IBM Manufactured" IBM computer memory cards which had been reworked by a third party by the addition of additional memory modules made by IBM and removed from other cards. The truth or falsehood of the representation was not self-evident but depended on what would be understood by the expression by those in this very spe-

---

[77] As in *Pompadour Laboratories Ltd v Frazer* [1966] R.P.C. 7.
[78] (1906) 23 R.P.C. (Warrington J.). See also *Bechstein v Barker & Barker* (1910) 27 R.P.C. 484, below.
[79] [1997] F.S.R. 877 (Laddie J.).
[80] *Gledhill (GH) & Sons Ltd v British Perforated Toilet Paper Co* (1911) 28 R.P.C. 714, CA.
[81] [1994] R.P.C. 252 (Ferris J.).

cialised market. In *Hodge Clemco v Airblast*[82] there was arguably passing-off by selling accessories for the plaintiffs' sand-blasting helmets whose use would be illegal.

In *Yost Typewriter Co v Typewriter Exchange Co*[83] an interlocutory injunction was refused against the defendants using *Palmer's Yost Pads* for their own replacements:

> "What do the words '*Yost Pads*' convey as a matter of fact? Do they convey the meaning of an article manufactured by, or for whose quality the plaintiffs give a guarantee; or do they mean pads manufactured for use upon the *Yost* typewriting machine? Supposing that question should be answered that they convey the meaning of a pad manufactured by, or guaranteed by, the plaintiffs, then the question would arise: does the use of the word 'Palmer', in the connection '*Palmer's Yost Pad*', sufficiently distinguish the defendants' article from the plaintiffs' article."

Buckley J. concluded that the evidence favoured the defendants on both points, especially as they and other traders had used the expression for substitute pads for several years.

On the other hand, in *Kodak v London Stereoscopic*[84] the defendants failed **5–29** to make good a claim to be entitled to sell film not of the plaintiffs' manufacture in response to orders for "Kodak film" or "Brownie film" on the basis that the terms simply denoted the size of the film or the type of camera it was intended for. The evidence was that they meant films manufactured by the plaintiffs. In *Neostyle Co v Ellam's Duplicator Co*[85] the plaintiffs failed to restrain use of *Neostyle* for paper, ink and accessories for their duplicating machine. The defendants used expressions such as "ink for the *Neostyle*" and their get-up was distinct, although they had not always put their own name on the goods. In *Gledhill v British Perforated Toilet Paper Co*[86] the plaintiffs claimed that the words *Gledhill Coils* were distinctive of them in respect of rolls of paper for their cash registers. The trial judge[87] considered that *Gledhill Coils* had been distinctive of the plaintiffs before 1902 but had become descriptive as a result of use by the defendants after that date. The Court of Appeal held that the way the defendants had used *Gledhill* was fair and descriptive and doubted if it would have been actionable even before 1902.

A few cases have dealt with part numbers.[88] In *Purefoy Engineering Co v* **5–30** *Sykes Boxall*[89] the Court of Appeal allowed the defendants to fill orders from existing customers with their own parts, but held there was passing-off

---

[82] [1995] F.S.R. 806 (Jacob J.).
[83] (1902) 19 R.P.C. 422 (Buckley J.).
[84] (1903) 20 R.P.C. 337 (Swinfen Eady J.)
[85] (1904) 21 R.P.C. 569, CA.
[86] (1911) 28 R.P.C. 714, CA.
[87] Eve J.
[88] As well as those that follow, see *Broad & Co Ltd v Graham Building Supplies Ltd* [1969] F.S.R. 153; [1969] R.P.C. 285 and *Broad & Co Ltd v Cast Iron Drainage Co Ltd* [1970] F.S.R. 363.
[89] (1955) 72 R.P.C. 89, CA.

when they supplied new customers with such parts without enquiring whether it was the plaintiff's parts they wanted. The respective defendants were allowed to use the plaintiff's part numbers for equivalent parts of their own in *Hilti v Ucan Development*[90] and *British Northrop v Texteam Blackburn*.[91]

Get-up may raise different issues to names and word marks. It can rarely be necessary to copy the claimant's get-up in addition to using his name or mark in order to denote that the goods to which it is applied are an accessory or substitute. If the defendant takes the claimant's name or mark and fails to distinguish his own goods adequately in terms of get-up or in some other respect then it is to be doubted if he is acting fairly. "It is clear that the defendants are entitled to sell paper and ink, manufactured by them, described as being 'for the *Neostyle*' provided that by the get-up of those goods the defendants do not represent such goods as having been made by the plaintiffs".[92]

Legitimate comparative advertising

5–31 As passing-off was formerly understood, it could not be actionable for the defendant to make use of the claimant's name or mark to draw an explicit comparison with his own goods or business.[93] Such use could hardly lead to confusion in the traditional sense, because the comparison both assumed and proclaimed that the two businesses were separate and unconnected. As the law is now understood, it might be actionable as passing-off to make an express and sufficiently material representation that one's goods or services were the same as, or similar to, those of the claimant if that were not the case. It remains the law, however, that there is no passing-off by way of misrepresentation of source if the defendant makes use of the claimant's name or mark at the same time as making it unambiguously clear that the goods or services he will be supplying are not connected in any way with the claimant.

In *Ciba-Geigy v Parke Davis*[94] there was no serious issue to be tried when the defendants prominently used a picture of an apple with a bite taken out of it in advertisements for their cheaper generic substitute for the plaintiffs' drug *Diclomax*. The plaintiffs' own advertisements made extensive use of a picture of an apple to denote their brand, *Voltarol*, but any doctor reading the defendants' advertisement would realise they were drawing attention to the cost advantages of their own different product.

5–32 In the normal comparative advertising case the possible existence of

---

[90] [1964] R.P.C. 206 (Ungoed-Thomas J.).
[91] [1974] R.P.C. 57 (Megarry J.).
[92] *per* Buckley L.J. in *Neostyle Manufacturing Co v Ellam's Duplicator Co* (1904) 21 R.P.C. 569, CA. Get-up was particularly important because the defendants did not put their own name on all their goods.
[93] Though untruthful comparative advertising may amount to injurious falsehood: for example *Compaq Computer Corp v Dell Computer Corp Ltd* [1992] F.S.R. 93 (Aldous J.). Examples of comparative advertising actionable as passing-off or injurious falsehood are considered in Chapter 7.
[94] [1994] F.S.R. 8 (Aldous J.).

members of the public who mistake the defendants' material for that of the claimants through carelessness or indifference is irrelevant, because any misrepresentation which is not acted on is at most an immaterial one. Any doctors mistaking the defendants' advertisements in *Ciba-Geigy v Parke Davis* for ones issued by the plaintiffs would not as a result be any more likely to prescribe the defendants' product, or less likely to prescribe the plaintiffs', and no other head of damage was plausible.

Where, less usually, the comparison involves the actual use of the claimant's brand name on the defendant's goods themselves, the scope for damage arising directly from this kind of confusion is much increased. In *Kimberley-Clark v Fort Sterling*[95] the slogan "Softness guaranteed (or we'll exchange it for Andrex®)" on promotional packs of the defendants *Nouvelle* brand of toilet tissue was actionable by the manufacturers of *Andrex* on proof that significant numbers of consumers would simply notice the prominent use of *Andrex*, and would pay little or no attention either to the implication that *Nouvelle* and *Andrex* were rival brands, or to a disclaimer in very small type. There was no suggestion that a supporting television advertising campaign (which referred anonymously to the "number one brand") amounted to passing-off.

Examples

In *Singer Manufacturing Co v Loog*[96] the defendant sold sewing machines **5–33** copying the manner of operation of the plaintiffs'. The House of Lords allowed him to describe the machines as *Singer System* in his trade price lists. He had rightly been enjoined from putting *Singer* prominently on the machines themselves, despite other wording which might have informed the careful purchaser that the plaintiffs were not the manufacturer. *Armstrong Pattern* was allowed in *Armstrong Oiler Co v Patent Axelbox and Foundry*[97] on the basis that customers knew the defendants would supply their own goods. Whether *Armstrong* on its own was distinctive or descriptive was left undecided. Two exceptions to the usual run of cases occur in *Vacuum Oil Co v Gooch & Tarrant*[98] and *Bechstein v Barker & Barker*[99] in which *Vacuum Quality* for oil and *Bechstein model* for pianos were restrained. In the latter case, there was trade evidence that "X model" for pianos meant a piano manufactured by X, and the defendant was dishonest. In *A.V. Roe v Aircraft Disposal Co*[1] aeroplanes to the design of the plaintiffs had been manufactured by others in the course of the war. The defendants claimed *Avro* simply denoted the design. Although they failed on this head they were allowed to use "*Avro* type" and like expressions but not *Avro* on its own. *Alligator Pattern* was restrained as trade mark infringement in *Stone v*

[95] [1997] F.S.R. 877 (Laddie J.).
[96] (1882) 8 App. Cas. 15, HL.
[97] (1910) 27 R.P.C. 362 (Joyce J.).
[98] (1909) 27 R.P.C. 76 (Neville J.).
[99] (1910) 27 R.P.C. 484 (Eve J.).
[1] (1920) 37 R.P.C. 249 (Peterson J.).

Steelace Manufacturing Co[2] but the action was held to have been rightly dismissed as regarded passing-off. In two related cases the respective defendants were allowed "as *Broadstel*" in *Broad v Graham Building Supplies*[3] and "similar to *Broadstel*" in *Broad v Cast Iron Drainage Co*[4] In both they had made it clear they would supply their own goods.

Business relationship with the claimant

5–34 It cannot be passing-off truthfully to advertise a subsisting or former connection with the claimant because there is no element of misrepresentation in doing so. A business which wants to prevent its sub-contractors, employees or agents basking in its reflected glory should insist on a contractual term to that effect.[5] In a case between *Harrods* and the business which had previously operated its fine art department Bingham L.J. said[6]:

> "The defendant wishes to advertise the fact that for 15 years it operated the plaintiffs' fine art department. That is agreed to be a true statement. The fact that a statement is true does not of course mean that it is lawful to make it: to do so may, for instance, be an unlawful breach of confidence or involve disclosure of an official secret or amount to a criminal libel. But the right to freedom of speech does at least mean that a person may say or write what he likes unless there is some legal reason why he should not. Four legal reasons were advanced before the judge why the defendant should not be allowed to make this statement. Three of these (passing-off, infringement of trade mark and unfair competition) he comprehensively and in my view unarguably rejected."

However, this principle does not entitle former employees, partners, subcontractors and the like to make equivocal or excessively conspicuous use of the claimant's name or indicia. Such use may ostensibly appear to be legitimate, but it will be restrained if the manner of use is calculated to deceive.[7] The same principle applies to the vendor of a business. He may advertise his former connection with the business sold (in the absence of express or implicit agreement to the contrary) but he is not entitled to

---

[2] (1929) 46 R.P.C. 406, CA.

[3] [1969] R.P.C. 285; [1969] F.S.R. 152 (Graham J.). The plaintiffs' equivalent part number was also used.

[4] [1970] F.S.R. 363 (Whitford J.).

[5] As in *Harrods Ltd v Schwartz-Sackin & Co Ltd* [1986] F.S.R. 490; reversed (1987) [1991] F.S.R. 209, CA. Care should be taken that the covenant is not invalid as being in restraint of trade.

[6] *Harrods Ltd v Schwartz-Sackin & Co Ltd* (1987) [1991] F.S.R. 209, CA.

[7] *Wheeler & Wilson Manufacturing Co v Shakespear* (1869) 39 L.J. Ch. 36; *Henderson v Munroe* (1905) 7 S.C. 636; *Asprey & Garrard v WRA (Guns) Ltd and Asprey* [2001] EWCA Civ 1499; [2002] E.T.M.R. 47; [2002] F.S.R. 31, CA.

represent himself as the current proprietor,[8] or his business as a continuation of the old,[9] and still less as the only original business.[10]

Examples

In *Hookham v Pottage*[11] a partnership business carried on by the plaintiff **5–35** and the defendant was wound up by court order which provided for the business to belong in future to the plaintiff. The defendant set up in business on his own account very near the plaintiff under a sign reading "S. Pottage, from Hookham and Pottage" with the words "from" and "and" in small letters. The Court of Appeal held that although the defendant was entitled to make use of the reputation accruing from having formerly been a partner, he had done so in such a way as to misrepresent that his business was that of the partnership.[12]

In *Pompadour Laboratories v Frazer*[13] the defendants had formerly been the plaintiffs' subcontractors. On their goods and advertising they put the message "Frazer Chemicals have manufactured hair lacquer for Pompadour Laboratories Ltd. for several years". Plowman J. held that this was not passing-off. Somewhat surprisingly, the plaintiffs did not argue that this statement would be read as implying that the defendants still did manufacture for the plaintiffs. On the assumption that it only denoted the former connection it was legitimate. Otherwise it would have been actionable.

In *Harrods v Schwartz-Sackin*[14] the defendants had formerly operated the fine arts department at Harrods under an agreement by which the defendants were held out as part of Harrods. They subsequently proposed to open a showroom in their own name and advertise the former connection. Warner J. held that under the law of passing-off there was nothing to prevent the defendants truthfully stating that they had operated the fine arts department for Harrods, and on that head the plaintiffs had no arguable case. He was prepared to enjoin the defendants on the ground that a contractual term preventing them from advertising their connection with Harrods had survived termination of the agreement, but the Court of Appeal held that the term in question had ceased to apply when the agreement came to an end, and discharged the injunction. Bingham L.J. would have agreed with Warner J. that a perpetual undertaking not to advertise a former business connection was *prima facie* unenforceable as being in restraint of trade, but that it might be justified as being reasonable with regard to the interests of the parties and the public.

---

[8] *Mrs Pomeroy Ltd v Scalé* (1906) 24 R.P.C. 177; *May v May* (1914) 31 R.P.C. 325, DC.
[9] *Churton v Douglas* (1859) 70 E.R. 385 (Page-Wood V.C.); *Dawnay Day & Co Ltd v Cantor Fitzgerald International* [2000] R.P.C. 669, CA.
[10] *Allen v Original Samuel Allen & Sons Ltd* (1915) 32 R.P.C. 33 (Sargant J.).
[11] (1872) L.R. 8 Ch. 91, CA.
[12] *Glenny v Smith* (1865) 62 E.R. 701 is an earlier case of an injunction being granted on very similar facts, except that the defendant's business was not so close to that of the plaintiff. *Rickett, Cockerell & Co Ltd v Nevill* (1904) 21 R.P.C. 394 and *Cundey v Lerwill & Pike* (1908) 99 L.T. 273; 24 T.L.R. 584 failed on the facts.
[13] [1965] R.P.C. 7 (Plowman J.).
[14] [1986] F.S.R. 490 (Warner J.), reversed (1987) [1991] F.S.R. 209, CA.

5–36   In *Dawany Day v Cantor Fitzgerald*[15] the defendants Cantor Fitzgerald International ("CFI") had purchased from the administrator the inter-dealer Eurobond broking business formerly operated by a 50 per cent subsidiary of the claimants under the name *Dawnay Day Securities* ("DDSL"). Lloyd J. and the Court of Appeal held that they were entitled to hold themselves out as carrying on the former business (and, conversely, that the claimants could not do so) but that they were not entitled to trade under the former name or any other name incorporating *Dawnay Day*. The general injunction against the defendants using the *Dawnay Day* name was expressly qualified to allow them to state that they were carrying on the former business of Dawnay Day Securities; but the defendants' counter-claim was dismissed because the claimants had done nothing to represent that the broking business which they had set up subsequently as *Dawnay Day REPOs*[16] was a continuation of the old one. Scott V.C. said:

"CFI appeals also against the judge's dismissal of its counterclaim. CFI's case in this regard is a simple one. CFI is the proprietor of the business formerly carried on by DDSL. CFI is entitled to represent itself as the successor of DDSL in carrying on that business. Both these propositions are correct. They were recognised by the judge in adding to the injunction he granted against CFI an express proviso 'That the Defendant may state to any person that it is conducting the business formerly conducted by Dawnay, Day Securities Limited'. CFI contends that DDE, in carrying on an inter-dealer broking business under the style Dawnay, Day Repos, is representing that its business is the former business of DDSL or is otherwise connected or associated with the former business of DDSL.

For DDE to trade in inter-dealer broking under the name Dawnay, Day Repos carries with it the representation that the proprietor of the business is a member of the Dawnay, Day group. That representation is true. It carries with it also the representation to all those who knew of Dawnay Day Securities that Dawnay Day Repos is taking the place of Dawnay Day Securities as the style under which a member of the Dawnay, Day group is trading in inter-dealer broking. That representation also is true. The only representation of which CFI can legitimately complain is a representation that the Dawnay, Day Repos business is the same business as was formerly carried on under the style Dawnay, Day Securities. That would not be true. There is a very narrow line between, on the one hand, a representation that Dawnay, Day Repos is taking the place of Dawnay, Day Securities as the Dawnay, Day inter-dealer broker—which is true—and a representation that Dawnay, Day Repos is continuing the inter-dealer broking business formerly carried on by Dawnay Day Securities—which is not true.

The judge held that none of the documents emanating from the Dawnay, Day group contained any representation that DDE was carry-

[15] [2000] R.P.C. 669, CA.
[16] As part of Dawnay Day Equities ("DDE").

ing on the same business that DDSL had carried on. I agree ... In my judgment, the judge was right to dismiss the counterclaim."

Satire and parody

A further example of use of the claimant's name or mark without mis- **5–37** representation, rare in commerce, is where the defendant uses it in a satirical manner or to disparage the claimant. This cannot be passing-off and an action for injurious falsehood would require proof of malice. In *Miss World v James St. Productions*[17] an application for an interlocutory injunction to restrain the showing of a satirical film *The Alternative Miss World* failed, *inter alia* because no one would have supposed it had any connection with the plaintiffs. In *Kennard v Lewis*,[18] the *Campaign for Nuclear Disarmament* sued for copyright infringement in respect of a pamphlet *Thirty Questions and Honest Answers about CND* which imitated the layout of their pamphlet *Thirty Questions and Answers about CND*. They were refused an interlocutory injunction by analogy with the practice in defamation actions.

The comparative willingness of Australian courts to restrain unauthorised personality and character merchandising has obliged them to recognise that use of a real or artificial character in satire or parody may not be actionable as passing-off, but attempts to raise the defence have so far failed and its scope and even its basis remain undefined.[19]

Since the action for passing-off is by definition confined to the repression of damaging misrepresentations, and lies only at the suit of one trader against another, one would like to conclude that it is inherently incapable of being used to suppress any legitimate form of free expression and that no issues under Art.10 of the European Convention on Human Rights are capable of arising. While undeniably true in theory, the proposition is not entirely borne out in practice.

A justly deprecated example at the extreme boundary of what ought to **5–38** amount to passing-off, if not well beyond, is provided by *Clark v Associated Newspapers*.[20] Alan Clark, the politician, historian and diarist, was the subject of a spoof diary column in the London *Evening Standard*. Lightman J. found for the plaintiff on his claims for passing-off and false attribution of authorship under s.84 of the Copyright, Designs and Patents Act 1988. While the abstract statements of the law are unobjectionable, their purported application to the facts is unconvincing. Even allowing that the use of Mr Clark's photograph and the title "*Alan Clark's Secret Election* [or *Political*] *Diary*" constituted "an unequivocal false statement attributing their authorship to the plaintiff", then the misrepresentation could amount to passing-off only if it was a material one. But it was not alleged that there was anything inherently damaging to Mr Clark's goodwill as a serious author merely in people supposing, on the strength of a casual glance, that

---

[17] [1981] F.S.R. 309, CA.
[18] [1983] F.S.R. 346 (Warner J.).
[19] *Hogan v Koala Dundee* (1988) 12 I.P.R. 508 and *Hogan v Pacific Dunlop* (1988) 12 I.P.R. 225; affirmed (1989) 14 I.P.R. 398.
[20] [1988] 1 W.L.R. 1558; [1998] 1 All E.R. 959; [1998] R.P.C. 261, (Lightman J).

he contributed a column in the form of a dairy to the *Evening Standard*. The suggested damage could only arise from the content of the "diaries", but that argument supposed the existence of a substantial number of readers so credulous or humourless as to read the column from end to end without realising that it was not of Mr Clark's authorship.

The proper analysis is that passing-off reaches substantially the same result as that established (for libel) in *Charleston v News Group Newspapers*,[21] albeit by a different route. In passing-off, there is no "single meaning" rule and it may be necessary to examine the state of mind of different categories of reader: careful readers could not possibly be deceived, and though casual readers of the *Evening Standard* might (just) be the victims of whatever misrepresentation was implicit in the heading, in their case any such misrepresentation would be immaterial and therefore not actionable. There was no credible intermediate class.[22] It is strictly speaking unnecessary to go any further and ask if any of the supposed damage suffered by Mr Clark was truly in his professional authorial capacity, or sounded in passing-off at all. Of course Mr Clark would prefer not to have his inflated self-importance pricked or his personal and political foibles ridiculed; but if his reputation as a serious historian could survive the image he deliberately promulgated for himself in his genuine *Diaries*, it was hardly likely to be damaged by the spoof ones.

As a not entirely trivial counterexample the defendants in *McIlhenny Co v Blue Yonder Holdings*[23] were not liable for passing-off by making express allusions to the plaintiffs' *Tabasco Sauce* in an advertisement for their own services in designing and constructing stands for exhibitions. There was no misrepresentation of any connection between the parties, and the advertisement would simply be understood as a cheeky invocation of "hot" associations.

Disclaimers and distinguishing matter

5–39 In theory, it is always open to the defendant to use indicia which are distinctive of the claimant in conjunction with a disclaimer which indicates that there is no connection. In practice this may be difficult, whether or not the disclaimer is honestly meant. In *Montgomery v Thompson*[24] the defendant was restrained in absolute terms from calling his beers by the plaintiff's name *Stone Ales*. "Any attempt to distinguish the two, even if it were honestly meant, would have been perfectly idle. Thirsty folk want beer, not explanations". More recently, in *Asprey & Garrard v WRA (Guns) Ltd and Asprey*[25] the Court of Appeal observed of an express disclaiming notice that

---

[21] [1995] 2 A.C. 65, HL.

[22] The correct analysis may be seen (on very different facts, but raising the same underlying issue) in the judgment of Aldous J. in *Ciba-Geigy plc v Parke Davis & Co Ltd* [1994] F.S.R. 8.

[23] (1997) 39 I.P.R. 187 (Lehane J, Federal Court of Australia). Their original trading name *Tabasco Design* had been discontinued.

[24] [1891] A.C. 217; 8 R.P.C. 361, HL, *per* Lord Macnaghten.

[25] [2002] F.S.R. 30 (Jacob J.) affirmed [2001] EWCA Civ 1499; [2002] E.T.M.R. 47; [2002] F.S.R. 31, CA. Compare *Arsenal Football Club plc v Reed* [2001] R.P.C. 46 (Laddie J.), below.

Jacob J. "was entitled to draw on his considerable experience in this field to say that such disclaimers hardly ever work".

In *Scandecor Development v Scandecor Marketing*[26] the Court of Appeal (having found that the United Kingdom goodwill was owned by the defendants ("Limited") and not by the plaintiffs, or the parties jointly) went on to address the only remaining defence of a company proposing to distribute the plaintiffs' products:

> "The only substantial submission of Mr Wyand on this point was that the use of 'Panther' in the corporate name is sufficient to distinguish the businesses and goods of the parties. We disagree. Both sides have fought hard and long for the right to use the mark Scandecor on the basis that it is distinctive and that its use by the other is likely to be deceptive and damaging. Prefacing Scandecor with 'Panther +' in the corporate name does not remove or diminish the likelihood of deception and damage to the goodwill of Limited in the UK, any more than prefacing the use of Scandecor by 'Huldtgren' in the corporate name of Limited would avert passing off by Limited if, contrary to our view, Scandecor was distinctive of Development in the UK. Relief for passing off is appropriate."

On the other hand, in *Sony Music Australia v Tansing*[27] there was no serious issue to be tried because the unauthorised *Michael Jackson* recording issued by the defendants was clearly identified as such and there was very little else the defendants could have done to make the position clear. A similarly clear and express disclaimer was used in similar circumstances by the defendant in *Arsenal v Reed*,[28] who traded in (predominantly) unlicensed *Arsenal* souvenirs and memorabilia from a stand near the Arsenal football ground. Laddie J. acknowledged that such disclaimers were rarely perfectly effective, but concluded that the risk of confusion was already so slight that a notice that the defendant's goods were not "official" could contribute to the finding that there was no passing-off.

Two modern cases further illustrate the difficulties which can face **5–40** defendants in attempting to distinguish their goods or business from the claimant. In *Associated Newspapers v Insert Media*[29] Mummery J. and the Court of Appeal held that confusion would not be obviated by an express disclaimer which the defendants offered to print on the advertising inserts which they intended to place in the plaintiffs' newspapers. In part this was because the disclaimer was inconspicuous, but an additional reason given was that the public would suppose that the plaintiffs had given their consent to the inserts on condition that the disclaimer was printed. This may have been justified on the facts; but if a disclaimer is accurate, prominent, credible and sincerely meant then it seems unduly harsh to enjoin the defendant

---

[26] [1999] F.S.R. 26, CA. An appeal to the House of Lords, and reference to the European Court of Justice, only involved questions of registered trade mark law.
[27] (1994) 27 I.P.R. 649 (Federal Court of Australia).
[28] [2001] E.T.M.R. 77; [2001] R.P.C. 46 (Laddie J.), the claim for passing off was not pursued on appeal and might have received different treatment if it had been: [2003] EWCA Civ 696.
[29] [1990] 2 All E.R. 803 (Mummery J.), affirmed CA.

because members of the public suspect the plaintiff of duplicity and conniving in deception.

In the *Jif Lemon* case, *Reckitt & Colman v Borden*[30] Lord Bridge, reluctantly concurring with the majority of the House of Lords in the result, dwelt on the near impossibility of the defendants distinguishing their goods without abandoning the use of a plastic lemon altogether.

"The idea of selling preserved lemon juice in a plastic container designed to look as nearly as possible like the real thing is such a simple, obvious and inherently attractive way of marketing the product that it seems to me utterly repugnant to the law's philosophy with respect to commercial monopolies to permit any trader to acquire a *de jure* monopoly in the container as such. But, as Mr Jacob for the respondents, quite rightly pointed out, the order made by the trial judge in this case does not confer any such *de jure* monopoly because the injunction restrains the appellants from marketing their product 'in any container so nearly resembling the plaintiffs' Jif lemon-shaped container as to be likely to deceive *without making it clear to the ultimate purchaser that it is not of the goods of the plaintiff.*' [Emphasis added.] How then are the appellants, if they wish to sell their product in plastic containers of the shape, colour and size of natural lemons, to ensure that the buyer is not deceived? The answer, one would suppose, is by attaching a suitably distinctive label to the container. Yet here is the paradox: the trial judge found that a buyer reading the labels proposed to be attached to the appellants' Mark I, II or III containers would know at once that they did not contain Jif lemon juice and would not be deceived; but he also enjoined the appellants from selling their product in those containers because he found, to put it shortly, that housewives buying plastic lemons in supermarkets do not read the labels but assume that whatever they buy must be *Jif*. The result seems to be to give the respondents a *de facto* monopoly of the container as such which is just as effective as *de jure* monopoly."

5–41 Conversely, the defendant may use his own name or mark so prominently as to distinguish his goods, but may rely on similarity of get-up to convey the subliminal message that his goods are equivalent to those of the claimant or are a substitute for them. *Fisons v Godwin*[31] is one such case, in which Brightman J. would have found for the plaintiffs on get-up but for the different brand names. *Tetrosyl v Silver Paint & Lacquer Co*[32] and *Cadbury Schweppes v Pub Squash Co*[33] may be others, although it is an open question whether the aspects of the plaintiffs' get-up taken by the defendants were sufficiently distinctive for any further obligation to distinguish to arise. If the get-up copied is not so overwhelmingly distinctive as to outweigh the differences in brand or other names then this may be legitimate. *A fortiori*, when the shared aspects of get-up are essentially descriptive or common to

[30] [1990] 1 W.L.R. 491; [1990] 1 All E.R. 873; [1990] R.P.C. 340, HL.
[31] [1976] R.P.C. 653 (Brightman J.).
[32] [1980] F.S.R. 68, CA.
[33] [1981] 1 All E.R. 213; [1981] R.P.C. 429, PC.

the trade, as with the packaged gravy mixes in *RHM Foods v Bovril*[34] or the frozen chips in *McCain v Country Fair*.[35]

Labels on visibly similar goods

In the *Jif Lemon*[36] case itself what was in issue was packaging for lemon **5–42** juice, rather than the product itself; and the members of the majority in the House of Lords were prepared to tolerate a *de facto* monopoly of an attractive packaging concept in the interest of preventing customer deception. Where the issue is a *de facto* monopoly in an article of commerce in its own right different priorities ought to apply, and it is suggested that the South African Supreme Court erred in its decision in *Weber-Stephen Products Co v Alrite Engineering*[37] where the plaintiffs alleged that the defendants had broken a qualified interim interdict against selling a copy of their allegedly distinctive kettle-type barbecue. The defendants' barbecue bore a label saying that it had no connection with that of the plaintiffs, who were identified by name. The plaintiffs argued successfully that this was inadequate, because their name was unknown to most purchasers and their barbecue was identified by its appearance alone.

It is suggested that the granting of the injunction at all was questionable, but in any event the first instance judgment of Stegmann J. is to be preferred on the issue of the effect of the disclaimer. As with highly descriptive marks,[38] a degree of confusion is the price the claimant has to pay for failing to adopt genuinely distinctive indicia, and he has only himself to blame if the courts refuse to allow him the benefit of an undeserved monopoly. In *Parkdale v Puxu*,[39] a case under the Australian Trade Practices Act, Gibbs C.J. stressed the importance of labels for distinguishing goods of similar appearance:

"Speaking generally, the sale by one manufacturer of goods which closely resemble those of another manufacturer is not a breach of s. 52 if the goods are properly labelled. There are hundreds of ordinary articles of consumption which, although made by different manufacturers and of different quality, closely resemble one another. In some cases this is because the design of a particular article has traditionally, or over a considerable period of time, been accepted as the most suitable for the purpose which the article serves. In some cases indeed no other design would be practicable. In other cases, although the article in question is the product of the invention of a person who is currently trading, the suitability of the design or appearance of the article is such that a market has

---

[34] [1983] R.P.C. 275, CA.

[35] [1981] R.P.C. 69, CA.

[36] *Reckitt & Colman Products Ltd v Borden Inc* [1990] 1 W.L.R. 491; [1990] 1 All E.R. 873; [1990] R.P.C. 340, HL.

[37] 1992 (2) S.A. 489; [1992] R.P.C. 549.

[38] *Office Cleaning Services Ltd v Westminster Office Cleaning Association* [1946] 1 All E.R. 320; 63 R.P.C. 39, HL.

[39] (1982) 149 C.L.R. 191; see also *Koninklijke Philips Electronics NV v Remington Products Australia Pty Ltd* [2000] FCA 876; 48 I.P.R. 257.

become established which other manufacturers endeavour to satisfy, as they are entitled to do if no property exists in the design or appearance of the article. In all of these cases, the normal and reasonable way to distinguish one product from another is by marks, brands or labels. If an article is properly labelled so as to show the name of the manufacturer or the source of the article its close resemblance to another article will not mislead an ordinary reasonable member of the public."

E. The Defendant need not Act Fraudulently

History: law and equity

5–43 At common law passing-off is considered to have evolved out of the tort of deceit, and intention to deceive was therefore an essential component of the cause of action. From 1838[40] equity adopted the doctrine that it was equivalent to fraud for an otherwise innocent defendant to continue in a deceptive course of conduct after being put on notice, and equity would therefore grant an injunction (but not an account of profits) irrespective of the defendant's initial state of mind. In the latter part of the nineteenth century this doctrine was superseded, at least in equity, by one to the effect that the action protected a right of property, initially identified as the plaintiff's trade mark and subsequently as his goodwill.

Lord Westbury's doctrine that passing-off protected a common law right of property in a trade mark never enjoyed wholehearted support and needed qualification after the passing of the Trade-Marks Registration Act of 1875, which restricted actions for the infringement of unregistered marks. In the last quarter of the nineteenth century the doctrine that it was effectively fraudulent to practice deception after being put on notice again became adopted as the only common explanation of why the action for passing-off lay against an innocent defendant, and the word "fraud" sometimes came to be used in this technical sense. It was not until the twentieth century that Lord Parker[41] conclusively identified the plaintiff's goodwill as the right protected by the action. Once passing-off was recognised as protecting a property right it was no longer necessary to impute any mental element to the defendant.

The fusion of law and equity and the fact that passing-off actions are mainly fought over injunctions have obscured the relevance of fraud at common law. To all intents and purposes the modern form of the tort derived from that recognised by the courts of equity. The preferable view[42] is that there is now a single tort of passing-off actionable both at law and in equity, that it protects a right of property in the claimant's goodwill, and

---

[40] *Millington v Fox* (1838) 40 E.R. 956 (Lord Cottenham L.C.).
[41] Especially in *Burberrys v JC Cording & Co Ltd* (1909) 26 R.P.C. 693 and *Spalding (AG) & Bros v A W Gamage Ltd* (1915) 32 R.P.C. 273, HL.
[42] That of Oliver L.J. in *Habib Bank Ltd v Habib Bank AG Zurich* [1981] 1 W.L.R. 1265; [1981] 2 All E.R. 650; [1982] R.P.C. 1, CA.

that the defendant's state of mind is—with one possible exception for "instruments of deception"—wholly irrelevant to the existence of the cause of action. Although neither equity nor the common law would award pecuniary remedies against a wholly innocent defendant, it is doubtful if this partial defence has survived to any useful extent in modern law.[43]

Mental element irrelevant to cause of action

Any lingering doubts as to whether fraud is either relevant or essential to **5–44** liability for passing-off must have been laid to rest by *Reckitt & Colman v Borden*.[44] The trial judge found two of the defendants guilty of fraudulent passing-off, which was expressly pleaded. On appeal, they were acquitted of having intended to deceive, but the finding of passing-off and the *quia timet* injunction remained. On a further appeal to the House of Lords, the plaintiffs' cross-appeal on the issue of fraud was not pursued and all the other findings of the Court of Appeal were upheld in terms which made no reference to the tort having any mental element. If fraud was not essential, it seems to have been of even less relevance that the defendants' commercial objective was not to make a profit from the sale of lemon juice in lemon-shaped containers similar to those of the plaintiffs, but rather to force down the plaintiffs' prices and so prevent them subsidising the price of their bottled lemon juice which competed directly with the defendants' main product.

The defendant's state of mind is wholly irrelevant to the existence of the cause of action for passing-off.[45] Neither fraud, recklessness, negligence, nor knowledge of the existence of the claimant's business are necessary. Nor is it any defence that the defendant honestly believes that no confusion will result from his conduct, or that he has an independent claim to use the name or mark in question.[46] In this respect passing-off is unique among the common law economic torts, all of which otherwise require a mental element varying from negligence,[47] through malice to malevolence in the sense of a deliberate intention to injure coupled with an improper motive.[48] This may be thought to bear harshly on the defendant who has no reason to be aware of the likelihood of confusion with the claimant's business, especially in such circumstances as the claimant trading in a very different field of activity, or abroad, or having temporarily discontinued his business without

---

[43] *Gillette (UK) Ltd v Edenwest* [1994] R.P.C. 279.

[44] [1990] 1 W.L.R. 491; [1990] 1 All E.R. 873; [1990] R.P.C. 340, HL.

[45] *Spalding (AG) & Bros v A W Gamage Ltd* (1915) 32 R.P.C. 273, HL; *Office Cleaning Services Ltd v Westminster Office Cleaning Association* [1946] 1 All E.R. 320; 63 R.P.C. 39, HL; *Parker-Knoll Ltd v Knoll International Ltd* [1962] R.P.C. 265, HL. Neither Lord Diplock nor Lord Fraser included any mental element in his formulation of the tort in *Erven Warnink BV v J Townend & Sons (Hull) Ltd* [1979] A.C. 731; [1979] 2 All E.R. 927; [1980] R.P.C. 31, HL. There is one possible exception for instruments of deception. See the following paragraph.

[46] Both illustrated by *Asprey & Garrard v WRA (Guns) Ltd and Asprey* [2001] EWCA Civ 1499; [2002] E.T.M.R. 47; [2002] F.S.R. 31, CA.

[47] *Hedley Byrne & Co Ltd v Heller & Partners Ltd* [1964] A.C. 465.

[48] Compare injurious falsehood, the various forms of conspiracy, and intimidation. See Heydon, *Economic Torts* (1978); Carty, *An Analysis of the Economic Torts* (2001).

extinguishing his goodwill. These would be examples of cases where damages or an account of profits might be withheld, if *Gillette v Edenwest*[49] is reconsidered, but the right to an injunction would undoubtedly remain.

In logic, innocence is only relevant to establish one of two specific defences or to rebut a charge of fraud. The fact that the defendant may have acted innocently does not create any presumption in his favour corresponding to the presumption in favour of the claimant if fraud is proved. If fraud is not alleged, then, strictly speaking, the defendant has no business asserting his own innocence at all.[50] However, claimants have not always been held to the rule that fraud must be pleaded specifically, and it is therefore wise for the innocent defendant to come to court able to prove the fact. It also cannot be denied that some judges have treated the presence or absence of fraud practically as the one decisive issue, and many more have been swayed in favour of innocent defendants when objective factors were inconclusive.

Fraud and instruments of deception

5–45 There is one possible exception to the rule that the defendant's state of mind is irrelevant to the existence of the cause of the action for passing-off. It has been suggested that defendants may be liable for passing-off by supplying another trader with goods which are not inherently deceptive, knowing or intending that they would be used in a deceptive manner.[51] It is clear that if the goods do not tell a lie about themselves, then an innocent supplier is not liable simply because his purchasers or others may use them for passing-off.[52] The damage is too remote to attribute to him. This cause of action has sometimes been treated as analogous to passing-off by supplying inherently deceptive "instruments of deception", for which no mental element is needed.

The imposition of liability on the defendant in these circumstances is better understood on the basis of joint tortfeasorship with the subsequent trader who commits passing-off in dealing with the public. This would not require an exception to the general rule that state of mind is irrelevant in passing-off, and it is therefore more consistent with the basic principles of the tort.

The plaintiffs in *Cadbury v Ulmer*[53] sold bars of flaked chocolate under the name *Flake*. One market was among ice-cream vendors who sold the bars inserted into cones of soft ice-cream. The defendants supplied bars which were visually indistinguishable. The plaintiffs claimed that vendors used these for passing off. Falconer J. struck out the whole of the statement of

---

[49] [1994] R.P.C. 279.
[50] *Parker-Knoll Ltd v Knoll International Ltd* [1962] R.P.C. 265, HL.
[51] Likewise "instruments of deception" which are not goods at all, such as the Internet domain names in *British Telecommunications plc v One in a Million Ltd* [1999] 1 W.L.R. 903; [1998] 4 All E.R. 476; [1999] E.T.M.R. 61; [1999] F.S.R. 1, CA, where the whole judgment is predicated on the defendants' dishonesty.
[52] *Payton & Co v Snelling, Lampard & Co* [1901] A.C. 308; 17 R.P.C. 628, HL.
[53] [1988] F.S.R. 385 (Falconer J.).

claim. The appearance of the plaintiffs' chocolate bars was not distinctive,[54] so there was nothing inherently deceptive in the defendants copying it. For there to have been liability on the basis of joint tortfeasorship the defendants would have had to have done more than merely facilitate wrongdoing by the retailers, but there was no such common design.

Although the legal integrity of passing-off is best preserved by insisting **5–46** that the defendant's state of mind can never be an essential element of the cause of action, it has to be admitted that not all the cases are easily reconcilable with the view that there is no middle ground between the "common design" required for joint tortfeasorship on the one hand and strict liability for the supply of instruments of deception which are inherently likely to deceive on the other. In particular, if the goods are exported, then liability as a joint tortfeasor should be governed by the law of the place in which they are ultimately marketed, but what authority there is suggests that the tort does not depend on foreign law in this way. The latter is probably no more than oversight of an esoteric point of private international law. The tort may also perhaps be complete when the defendant knowingly parts with the potentially deceptive goods, as is the case with ordinary instruments of deception, whereas liability for joint tortfeasorship would not occur until actual passing-off by a subsequent recipient occurred. Finally, liability sometimes seems to be stricter than for joint tortfeasorship. For a secondary tortfeasor to be liable there must be a common design with the primary tortfeasor: it is not sufficient that the secondary party facilitates what he knows to be tortious. Liability for passing-off by supplying goods which lend themselves to deceptive use perhaps exists if there is knowledge, or even if the defendant merely turns a blind eye.

This branch of the tort has developed in an irrational way and would benefit from restatement. The law of instruments of deception already extends the concepts of misrepresentation and damage in a necessary if rather artificial manner. It would be logical to say that a person who supplies goods which are not inherently deceptive to a person who is not deceived makes no misrepresentation, and does not thereby commit passing-off, whatever the state of his mind. Joint tortfeasorship would deal adequately with deliberate collaboration in fraud, as in other torts.

The continuing influence of fraud

Despite the rule that fraud is not essential to the cause of action, the pre- **5–47** sence of an intention to deceive has greatly influenced the development of passing-off and continues to be important in many individual cases. The real and ostensible reasons are explained with candour by Lord Devlin in *Parker-Knoll v Knoll International*[55]:

"[W]hile proof of intent to deceive is unnecessary to the proof of falsity of a representation, it is not immaterial. The materiality is said to lie in the

---

[54] Following *Williams (JB) Co v H Bronnley & Co L'd* (1909) 26 R.P.C. 765, CA.
[55] [1962] R.P.C. 265 290, HL.

fact that where the object is to deceive, 'the court will be very much more ready to infer that its object has been achieved.' That is the way it is put in Buckley, L.J.'s second proposition.[56] It is not easy to see why the defendant's own estimate of the effect of his representation should be worth more than anybody else's. It seems probable that the rule is steeped in history rather than in logic and that it is the attenuated remains of the original doctrine, which prevailed until the intervention of equity, that fraud was an essential element in the tort. It is a wholesome rule which I for one have no wish to disturb."

Wholesomeness notwithstanding, the rule does have some less welcome tendencies. If the existence of fraud is not self-evident then a trial within a trial may develop in which the defendant's motives are investigated. If the defendant emerges with his reputation intact the case ought to be left in much the same state as if fraud had never been in issue, but even a finding of *mala fides* is not conclusive against him. In either event, this is not much return for an investigation which is likely to be prolonged, expensive and acrimonious. Cases exist in which the trial court has apparently found passing-off solely as a result of a successful attack on the defendant's honesty, though on appeal the same defendant has been acquitted of passing-off and perhaps of dishonest intention as well. Examples are *Lever Bros v Beddingfield*,[57] *Oertli v Bowman*[58] and *Jarman & Platt v Barget Ltd*.[59] As long as this can occur there is a temptation to rescue objectively weak cases with arguments *ad hominem*. Finally, rules of law developed to deal with fraudulent defendants inevitably come to be applied with equal severity to honest ones, with results which may seem harsh when the defendant is guilty of nothing worse than bad luck or bad judgment.[60]

F. Effect of Fraud where Shown

Evidential value of fraud

5–48 There is ample authority that is does not lie in the mouth of a fraudulent defendant to say that his fraudulent purpose has failed.[61] An intention to deceive the public is strong evidence that deception will occur. However, this is not a rule of law[62] but one of common sense: every element of the tort must still be made out.

---

[56] In *Brinsmead (John) & Sons Ltd v Brinsmead & Waddington & Sons Ltd* (1913) 30 R.P.C. 493, CA.
[57] (1898) 16 R.P.C. 3, CA.
[58] [1959] R.P.C. 1, HL.
[59] [1977] F.S.R. 260, CA.
[60] Compare, for instance, *Harrods Ltd v R Harrod Ltd* (1924) 41 R.P.C. 65, CA with *Lego System AS v Lego M Lemelstrich Ltd* [1983] F.S.R. 155.
[61] *Slazenger & Sons v Feltham & Co* (1889) 6 R.P.C. 531, CA.
[62] *per* Lord Blackburn in *Johnston & Co v Orr-Ewing & Co* (1882) App. Cas. 219, HL.

"No court would be astute when they discovered an intention to deceive, in coming to the conclusion that a dishonest defendant had been unsuccessful in his fraudulent design. When once you establish the intent to deceive, it is only a short step to proving that the intent has been successful, but it is still a step, even though it be a short step. To any such charge there must be, however, two conditions. The first is that it ought to be pleaded explicitly so as to give the defendant the opportunity of rebutting the accusation of intent. The second is that it must be proved by evidence."[53]

"The rule that if a mark or get-up for goods is adopted for the purpose of appropriating part of the trade or reputation of a rival, it should be presumed to be fitted for the purpose and therefore likely to deceive or confuse, no doubt, is as just in principle as it is wholesome in tendency. In a question how possible or prospective purchasers will be impressed by a given picture, word or appearance, the instinct and judgment of traders is not to be lightly rejected, and when a dishonest trader fashions an instrument or weapon for the purpose of misleading potential customers he at least provides a reliable and expert opinion on the question whether what he has done is in fact likely to deceive. Moreover he can blame no one but himself..."[64]

"Confusion innocently caused will yet be restrained. But if the intention to deceive is found, it will be readily inferred that deception will result. Who knows better than the trader the mysteries of his trade?"[65]

Fraud is most relevant where the issue is whether the defendant's name, **5-49** mark or get-up is confusingly similar to that of the claimant. On this issue the existence of an intention to deceive will readily and rightly be taken as proving that the resemblance is close enough [66] The evidential value of fraud was acknowledged in *Harrods v Harrodian School*[67] but the plaintiffs failed in a concerted attack on the *bona fides* of the defendants' proprietor. The trial judge found that his intention was not to deceive the public or to exploit the name and reputation of *Harrods*, but to take legitimate advantage of the name of the site of the former *Harrodian Club* as such. Collateral attacks on his conduct in negotiations which eventually led to the purchase of the site of the *Harrodian Club* and in enforcing an order for costs against the plaintiffs by writ of *fi. fa.* after trial also failed.

On the issue of the distinctiveness of the claimant's name, mark or get-up fraud is less conclusive. It is not sufficient to prove that the defendant

---

[63] *per* Lord Loreburn L.C. in *Ash (Claudius) & Sons Ltd v Invicta Manufacturing Co Ltd* (1911) 28 R.P.C. 465 at 475, HL.
[64] *per* Dixon and McTiernan JJ. in *Australian Woollen Mills v Walton* (1937) 58 C.L.R. 641.
[65] *per* Lord Simonds in *Office Cleaning Services Ltd v Westminster Office Cleaning Association* [1946] 1 All E.R. 320; 63 R.P.C. 39, 42, HL.
[66] *Johnston & Co v Orr-Ewing & Co* (1882) 7 App. Cas. 219, HL; *Slazenger & Sons v Feltham & Co* (1889) 6 R.P.C. 531, CA: *Demon* and *Demotic*.
[67] [1996] R.P.C. 697, CA.

deliberately copied whatever is claimed by the claimant, because if it is not distinctive he is free to do so.[68] Several of the leading get-up cases from the turn of the century disregarded evidence of deliberate copying, such as "Size, shape and colour as Williams" in *Williams v Bronnley*.[69] Intention to copy would have been relevant only if the plaintiffs had established some rights in that combination. In *Reckitt & Colman v Borden*[70] the trial judge (Walton J.) was reversed in the Court of Appeal in so far as he had equated an (admitted) intent to introduce a "facsimile" plastic lemon with intent to deceive. However, if it can be proved not only that the defendant copied, but that he did so with the intention of passing his goods off as those of the claimant, then that is effectively close to an admission that what was copied was distinctive.[71]

5–50   If the claimant and defendant are in competition, then the defendant's fraudulent intent to benefit himself can hardly fail to damage the claimant. If the parties do not compete, damage may still be more readily inferred in cases of fraud, but it should be remembered that the defendant's intention is always to benefit himself, and in some circumstances this may be fulfilled without damage to the claimant.

Fraud is of little weight on the issue of whether the claimant has a goodwill in the jurisdiction. Reputation can exist without goodwill, and a fraudulent defendant is satisfied if there is a reputation to exploit. There may be no goodwill at all, or it may not belong to the claimant.[72] There are also circumstances in which an existing reputation may be appropriated by a third party without the latter being guilty of anything more culpable than opportunism, as was true of both plaintiff and defendant in *Barnsley Brewery Co Ltd v RBNB*.[73] Proof of the defendant's intention to benefit himself, even at the expense of another, is not the same as proving that the claimant actually before the court owns any relevant goodwill.

What must be shown

5–51 The intention which must be pleaded and proven is one to deceive the public in a manner likely to damage the claimant. Any other form of deception is relevant only to the credibility of the defendant's evidence. Fraud in this sense is not to be inferred from the fact that the defendant can be proved to have copied what was in fact open to the public,[74] even if he did so covertly or in the belief that he was doing wrong.[75] If fraud is to assist the claimant's

---

[68] *Jarman & Plat Ltd v I. Barget Ltd* [1977] F.S.R. 260, CA; *Cadbury Schweppes Pty Ltd v Pub Squash Co Pty Ltd* [1981] R.P.C. 429; [1981] 1 All E.R. 213, PC.
[69] (1909) 26 R.P.C. 765, CA.
[70] [1990] R.P.C. 340, CA; affirmed without reference to this point *ibid.*, HL.
[71] As in *Reddaway (Frank) & Co Ltd v George Banham & Co Ltd* [1896] A.C. 199; [1895–9] All E.R. 313; 13 R.P.C. 218, HL.
[72] *Star Industrial Co Ltd v Yap Kwee Kor* [1976] F.S.R. 256, PC.
[73] [1997] F.S.R. 462 (Robert Walker J.).
[74] *Singer v Loog* (1882) 8 App.Cas. 15, HL; *Goya Ltd v Gala of London Ltd* (1952) 69 R.P.C. 188.
[75] *Cadbury Schweppes Pty Ltd v Pub Squash Co Pty Ltd* [1981] 1 All E.R. 213; [1981] R.P.C. 429, PC.

case there must be evidence of it beyond what is self-evident from the defendant's choice of name, mark or get-up. It may be legitimate to infer fraud from close similarities, but if they are that strong the cause of action would be complete anyway and the inference unnecessary. It is inevitably circular to deduce the presence of fraud from inconclusive resemblances in mark (etc.), and use the finding of fraud to conclude that the resemblances are close enough to deceive.

In *Lever Bros v Bedingfield*[76] Kekewich J. allowed the fact the defendant had copied features of the plaintiffs' get-up to outweigh the lack of any objective evidence that deception was likely or intended and concluded that in granting an injunction he was giving effect to *Reddaway v Banham*.[77] The Court of Appeal reversed him.

"There is no proof that the defendant intended to do more than use the wrapper complained of; and if that wrapper does not in fact deceive and is not calculated to deceive, there is no ground for granting an injunction against the defendant who uses it. No injunction can properly be granted to restrain a man from doing that which, if done, will not infringe the plaintiff's rights. The defendant no doubt wanted an ornamental wrapper which would attract the public. The designer took the plaintiffs' wrapper as the best to start from, and he adapted it to what he thought would meet the defendant's wants and not infringe the plaintiffs' rights. There is always a danger in this mode of procedure, and the first design made for the defendant was thought to go too far, and we think it did, but it was altered before action. The defendant refused to alter it further, and although it is obvious he could easily have done so without detriment to his own business we are unable to say that in point of law he was bound to do so."[78]

In *Cadbury-Schweppes v Pub Squash Co*[79] the plaintiffs introduced a soft **5–52** drink *Solo* which was unusual in being specifically aimed at the adult male market. The defendants produced a rival drink, distinguishable on sale from that of the plaintiffs but advertised using similar themes. They denied having copied the plaintiffs in any respect but were proved to have deliberately copied the taste of the drink and to have concealed the fact from the court. The trial judge found for the defendants and was upheld by the Privy Council. The defendants had copied, but what they had copied was open to the public.

"When an intention to deceive is found, it is not difficult for the court to infer that the intention has been, or will be, effective[80] ... But in dealing with the issue of deception the learned judge directed himself correctly and made the comment, which is also good law, that 'the court must be on

---

[76] (1898) 16 R.P.C. 3, CA.
[77] [1896] A.C. 199; [1895–9] All E.R. 313; 13 R.P.C. 218, HL.
[78] *per* Lindley M.R. However, the Court of Appeal refused him the costs of the action itself.
[79] [1981] R.P.C. 429; [1981] 1 All E.R. 213, PC.
[80] *Slazenger & Sons v Feltham & Co* (1889) 6 R.P.C. 531, CA, approved.

its guard against finding fraud merely because there has been an imitation of another's goods, get-up, method of trading or trading style (see, for example, *Goya Ltd. v Gala of London Ltd.*[81])'

The intention was not to pass off the respondent's goods as those of the appellants but to take advantage of the market developed by the advertising campaign for *Solo*."

5–53   In the *Jif Lemon* case, *Reckitt & Colman v Borden*[82] the trial judge (Walton J.) found two of three defendants guilty of fraudulent intent on the strength of three pieces of evidence or impression: a letter stating that they intended to produce a "facsimile" of the plaintiffs' plastic lemon; an admission by one of the defendants' managers (Mr Merckx) that he expected some confusion to result on the launch of the defendants' lemon; and a finding that this witness was untrustworthy. Walton J. treated the issue of fraudulent intent as synonymous with the defendants deliberately pressing ahead with their product, knowing that confusion would result. On appeal, the finding of fraud was reversed. "Fraudulent intention in the present context, in my judgment, involves the intention to mislead" said Slade L.J., observing that there was no express or implicit admission or finding of fraud in this sense. The defendants were under no obligation to guard against self-induced misapprehensions on the part of careless consumers; and if they had misjudged the perspicacity of the typical consumer or the effectiveness of their efforts to distinguish themselves then their mistake did not convict them of fraudulent intentions, even though it could not absolve them of liability for passing-off.

"On the authorities there can be no doubt that a trader who contemplates putting a new product on the market in competition with another trader, who has already entered the market, is entitled, when devising the get-up of his new product to assume that members of the public will exercise a certain (if limited) degree of perspicacity in distinguishing the two products. Later in this judgment I will have to revert to the question of the degree of perspicacity which he is entitled in law to expect. If he erroneously overestimates this degree he may well find himself in law liable for passing off, since fraudulent intent is not part of the cause of action for this tort. If, however, his overestimate was a genuine one and he genuinely considers that those members of the public who exercised the relevant degree of perspicacity would not be deceived, I do not think he can fairly be said to have had a fraudulent intention.

The learned judge appears to have overlooked this point in the course of finding fraudulent intention on the part of Mr. Merckx and, through him, on the part of Suzy. Very significantly, though he took a poor view of Mr. Merckx as a witness and indeed of the defendants' conduct generally, at no place in his judgment did he make any explicit finding that there had been any intention to deceive on the part of Mr. Merckx or any

[81]   (1952) 69 R.P.C. 188 (Lloyd-Jacob J.).
[82]   [1990] 1 W.L.R. 491; [1990] 1 All E.R. 873; [1990] R.P.C. 340, HL.

of the defendants. All he found was that the defendants decided to proceed with the launch of their lemons well knowing that persons would purchase them under the belief that they were JIF lemons. Neither this finding nor his general conclusion that 'beyond his own admissions ... Mr. Merckx is far from being a normally honest person' would suffice to justify a finding that Suzy intended by the get-up of their lemons to induce potential purchasers to believe that their lemons were the products of the manufacturers of JIF lemons."[83]

The "badges of fraud"

It is unusual for a fraudulent defendant to be as candid in his evidence as the **5–54** one in *Slazenger v Feltham*,[84] who admitted he had used a dictionary to find the closest possible word to the plaintiff's mark *Demon*, and had settled on *Demotic*. A similar if unacknowledged *modus operandi* seems to have guided the defendants' suppliers in the New Zealand case of *Yves St Laurent Parfums v Louden Cosmetics*,[85] where (allowing also for the effect of get-up) *Kosmos, Java* and *Paradise* were too close to the plaintiffs' *Kouros, Jazz* and *Paris* brands; but ingenuity (or courage) failed when it came to *Optimism*, which was too distinct from *Opium* to confuse.

Fraud must be proven by evidence,[86] and the evidence normally consists of circumstances which are inconsistent with any honest intention and inexplicable except as part of a scheme to deceive. These are conventionally known as "badges of fraud",[87] and are most commonly found in the objectionable name or mark itself. If the defendant has no plausible reason for adopting it, and especially if resemblances with the claimant's seem deliberately close, intention to deceive may be inferred. However, the importance of badges of fraud has diminished now that fraud itself is of no more than evidential value. If the evidence proves that deception is objectively likely, then it is of little importance that it may also suggest that the deception was intended. Inexplicable resemblance of marks as a badge of fraud may still be important in cases of "instruments of deception", as providing evidence of the necessary intention that the goods supplied should be passed off in the retail market.

Badges of fraud need not be obvious, nor even calculated to deceive in **5–55** their own right. Like the reverse countersink in *LB Plastics v Swish Products*,[88] they may be insignificant in themselves but able to cast "a flood of light" on the defendant's motives and manner of doing business. If the claimant's mark is the name of a particular place, then for the defendant to set up business there excites suspicion. If the claimant's name or mark

---

[83] *per* Slade LJ [1990] R.P.C. 340, CA; affirmed (without reference to this point *ibid*, HL).
[84] (1889) 6 R.P.C. 531, CA.
[85] (1997) 39 I.P.R. 11, HC of NZ.
[86] *Ash (Claudius) & Sons Ltd v Invicta Manufacturing Co Ltd* (1911) 28 R.P.C. 597, HL.
[87] The expression is used in a somewhat different sense in *Cadbury Ltd v Ulmer GmbH* [1988] F.S.R. 385 as meaning a feature of name, mark or get-up which is calculated to deceive.
[88] [1979] F.S.R. 145; [1979] R.P.C. 551, HL, a copyright case. The reverse countersink was a minor feature of the plaintiffs' design of plastic drawer, whose presence in the defendants' corresponding design could only be ascribed to deliberate copying.

happens to be a personal name it was once quite common to recruit an individual of that name and name the business after him in purported exercise of the right of every person to trade under his own name. Examples of this being restrained are numerous.[89] The two occur together in *Southorn v Reynolds*[90] and in the hypothetical example of a Mr Bass setting up as a brewer in Burton-on-Trent.[91] In general, the defendant who goes out of his way to give colourable truth to a representation which is misleading in fact only provides evidence against himself. "The defendant was actually manufacturing starch at Glenfield, having gone thither for the purpose of enabling him to say that he was manufacturing it at Glenfield" is how James L.J. in *Massam v Thorley's Cattle Food Co*[92] summarised the facts of *Wotherspoon v Currie*.[93]

In *Metzler v Wood*[94] the plaintiff was the publisher of *Hemy's Piano Tutor*. The defendant retained the same Hemy to revise an obsolete book by another author and was restrained from publishing it with the name of *Hemy* prominent: "[W]e find this defunct work started into life with the name of *Hemy* prominently put on the outside. Why was that done, but for the purpose of passing off the defendant's book as that of the plaintiffs?"[95]

5–56   False claims to prizes, testimonials and the like have sometimes been invoked as badges of fraud but have tended to be treated more leniently than they deserve.[96] It is suggested that they are relevant both to intention and credibility, and that they may be actionable in their own right as "inverse" passing-off. Other badges of fraud include suggestions that the defendant is larger,[97] or longer-established than is really the case,[98] or that he also trades in a place of business of the claimant.[99] Setting up in business near the address of the claimant has sometimes been invoked as a badge of fraud, but in *British Vacuum Cleaner Co v New Vacuum Cleaner Co*[1] Parker J. treated it as legitimate. Occupying the plaintiff's former premises excited suspicion in *Wotherspoon v Currie*,[2] but in modern conditions the premises the claimant vacates may well be suitable for use only by someone in the same line of business. The situation may increase the risk of confusion, but

---

[89] *Croft v Day* (1843) 49 E.R. 994; *Valentine Meat Juice Co v Valentine Extract Co Ltd* (1900) 17 R.P.C. 673, CA; *Morrall (Abel) Ltd v Hessin & Co* (1903) 20 R.P.C. 429, CA; *Rodgers (Joseph) & Sons Ltd v W N Rodgers & Co* (1924) 41 R.P.C. 277; *Alfred Dunhill Ltd v Sunoptic SA* [1979] F.S.R. 337, CA.

[90] (1865) 12 L.T. 75 (Page-Wood V.C.).

[91] *Massam v Thorley's Cattle Food Co* (1880) 14 Ch. D. 748, CA, *per* James L.J.

[92] (1880) 14 Ch.D. 748, CA.

[93] (1872) L.R. 5 H.L. 508, HL.

[94] (1878) 8 Ch.D. 606, CA.

[95] *per* Cotton L.J.

[96] Examples are *National Starch Manufacturing Co v Munn's Patent Maizena & Starch Co* [1894] A.C. 275; 11 R.P.C. 281, PC and *King (F) & Co v Gillard & Co* [1905] 2 Ch. 7; 22 R.P.C. 327, CA.

[97] *Rodgers (Joseph) & Sons Ltd v W N Rodgers & Co* (1924) 41 R.P.C. 277 (Romer J.). But it is possible to take this too far. Many small businesses adopt trappings appropriate to a larger concern and are guilty of nothing worse than harmless puffing.

[98] *Estcourt v Estcourt Hop Essence Co* (1875) L.R. 10 Ch. 276, CA.

[99] *Van Oppen & Co Ltd v Van Oppen* (1903) 20 R.P.C. 617.

[1] [1907] 2 Ch. 312; 24 R.P.C. 641 (Parker J.).

[2] (1872) L.R. 5 H.L. 508, HL.

need not indicate fraud.[3] Fraudulent intent has sometimes been inferred from copying matter which is not distinctive *per se*, such as printed forms,[4] literature,[5] or a slogan.[6] Of course, if what is copied is distinctive alone or in combination, and the similarities are such as to deceive, then passing-off is established without the need to invoke fraud.

Fraud and two defences

It may be a defence to an action for passing-off that the defendant is making   **5–57** *bona fide* use of his own name or should be absolved from paying damages or profits because of his complete innocence. Neither is of practical importance, and their continuing existence in modern law is open to doubt. To the extent they still exist, both these defences are clearly lost if there is fraud, but the standard of dishonesty needed to rebut the defences is very much lower that what is understood by fraud at common law. They are considered in Chapter 9.

G. The Trading Status of the Defendant

The defendant must be a trader

The action for passing-off lies only against a trader in his capacity as such,[7]   **5–58** as Lord Diplock stated in the passage quoted at the start of the present Chapter. Lord Fraser in the same case does not use the word "trader" in his definition, but does contemplate that the defendant will be selling goods of his own. The reasoned speeches of Lord Oliver and Lord Jauncey in *Reckitt & Colman v Borden*[8] both contemplate that the defendant (as well as the claimant) will be a trader, supplying goods (or services) of his own. It is the essence of passing-off as it is normally understood that the defendant is making a misrepresentation about his own goods or business, which directly benefits himself and indirectly harms the claimant. Though the test for whether a party is a trader may not be exactly the same for the defendant as for the claimant, it is probably sufficiently close for one to say that in both contexts the term "trade" is to be construed widely as covering any business

---

[3] Compare *Berkeley Hotel Co Ltd v Berkeley International (Mayfair) Ltd* [1972] R.P.C. 237 in which an interlocutory injunction was granted with *IDW Superstores Ltd v Duncan Harris & Co Ltd* [1975] R.P.C. 178; [1974] F.S.R. 114 in which one was refused.

[4] *Van Oppen & Co Ltd v Van Oppen* (1903) 20 R.P.C. 617.

[5] *Masson, Seeley & Co Ltd v Embossotype Manufacturing Co* (1924) 41 R.P.C. 160.

[6] *Harrods Ltd v R. Harrod Ltd* (1924) 41 R.P.C. 74, CA and perhaps *Ideal General Supply Co Ltd v Edelson* [1957] R.P.C. 252.

[7] *per* Lord Diplock in *Erven Warnink BV v J Townend & Sons (Hull) Ltd* [1979] A.C. 731; [1979] 2 All E.R. 927; [1980] R.P.C. 31, HL.

[8] [1990] 1 W.L.R. 491; [1990] 1 All E.R. 873; [1990] R.P.C. 340, HL.

activity for which there can be said to be customers, but no action lies against a private individual in his capacity as such.

In the majority of passing-off actions, the trading status of the defendant is hardly in doubt, but there are some situations in which the issue is not entirely trivial. These may be categorised as:

1. Actions against defendants so fraudulent that their whole operation is no more than a sham or scam;

2. Actions against ordinary trading companies in respect of something done outside the course of any existing trade;

3. Actions against non-trading shell or dormant companies[9]; and

4. Actions where the activities of one party or both are on the margins of what is recognised as trading, for example because both are charities, churches or political organisations.

In all but the last of these the claimant will typically be a normal trader and the status of the defendant arises as a completely separate issue. In the last, it is tempting to suppose that once the status of the claimant has been assimilated to that of a trader, then the defendant's trading status follows automatically unless the defendant is in no sense a competitor. That, however, may be one degree too simple, and consideration of that case perhaps helps to understand the others.

"Trader" probably does not mean the same for both parties

5–59 The action for passing-off protects the right of property the claimant has in the goodwill of his business. Damage is the gist of the action, and if there is no damage to any business or goodwill then an action for passing-off cannot succeed. Although definitions of passing-off may expressly require the claimant to be a trader,[10] this is strictly speaking redundant, because unless one is a trader one can have no business or goodwill to suffer damage.

The analysis is rather different for the defendant. No definition of passing-off requires the defendant to have, or even to be in the process of creating, any relevant goodwill of his own. Passing-off all too often has to deal with outright fraud or counterfeiting, and the counterfeiter is a rare example of the trader who neither has, nor deserves, any goodwill at all. Quite apart from the illegality of his trade, there is the more fundamental point that no member of the public deliberately buys his goods in preference to those of anyone else.[11] This leads to one of two conclusions: either the requirement for the defendant to be a trader is something extraneous to the "classical trinity" of goodwill, misrepresentation and damage as the three

---

[9] Raising similar issues to unused or inactive internet domain names, addressed at Section K.

[10] As in Lord Diplock's formulation in *Erven Warnink BV v J Townend & Sons (Hull) Ltd* [1979] A.C. 731; [1979] 2 All E.R. 927; [1980] R.P.C. 31, HL, above.

[11] Though wholesale counterfeiters might, but for illegality, have a goodwill of sorts with respect to dishonest retail traders in the counterfeit goods. Even counterfeiters and their counterfeits have graduations of (un)desirability.

essential elements of passing-off—which is not necessarily to say that it is merely arbitrary or wrong—or it is derived from them by a different route to that requiring the claimant to have goodwill.

The question is not entirely an academic one. If one tries to apply to **5–60** "cybersquatters," or even to shell companies, the same criteria for trading status as one applies to claimants then it is perfectly obvious that one is often dealing with defendants who cannot properly be called traders at all, even in the most extended sense recognised for claimants in Section D of Chapter 3. If the illegitimate *Glaxowellcome* company[12] had attempted to sue anyone for passing-off, then the action would have been hopeless from the start: the company merely existed as a name on the Register, it had no business or assets, it carried on no trade, and had no customers or goodwill—irrespective of any other factors that might come to mind. However, there is now a quite substantial body of cases in which passing-off actions have succeeded against non-trading companies and their owners, and unless all these are to be treated as wholly *quia timet*, or based on causes of action other than passing-off, or dismissed as wrongly decided, then it is necessary to reconcile the results with the concept of the defendant as a trader, as is expressly or implicitly required by the leading authorities.

No way out of the impasse is provided by invoking the doctrine of "instruments of deception", since that is simply one aspect of passing-off, to which all the essential elements of the tort continue to apply. What can be said, perhaps, is that where the instruments of deception are shares in shell companies or unused names of some kind, then all that is required is that the defendant owner of the company should be a trader in intangibles of that kind. It was providential that the individual defendant in *Glaxowellcome* was a small-time company registration agent, and shell companies were his stock in trade.

It is now suggested that the concept of a trader is not precisely the same **5–61** for claimant and defendant, and that the question of the defendant's trading status must be understood in terms of the type of misrepresentation with which passing-off is typically and perhaps solely concerned, namely a misrepresentation calculated (in the objective sense) to attract to the defendant some advantage of an economic or pecuniary nature which would otherwise flow to the claimant by virtue of the attractive force which is the latter's goodwill. This is most unlikely to happen unless the defendant is, or is holding himself out as, a trader in the same sense in which the term is used for the claimant, but it does not necessarily require that the defendant should be a trader in actual fact. If the advantage in question is simply money, as opposed to custom, then the defendant can benefit from the misrepresentation, and the claimant suffer, even if the former is not in business at all.

---

[12] *Glaxo plc v Glaxowellcome Ltd* [1996] F.S.R. 388.

Fraudulent non-traders

5-62 The proposition advanced above is most obviously useful in dealing with a particularly blatant form of passing-off, in which the defendant solicits payment in the name of the claimant for goods or services which it has no intention of providing at all. Examples are to be found in *Blacklock v Bradshaws Publishing Co*[13] in which the defendants solicited payment for advertisements or subscriptions for a *Bradshaws Directory*,[14] and *RAC Motoring Services v RAC (Publishing)*[15] where the defendants were committed for breach of an interlocutory injunction requiring them to repay money obtained from hoteliers under the pretence that it was in payment for entries in the *RAC Handbook*. Likewise, in *Law Society v Society of Lawyers*[16] the defendant society was little more than a pyramid selling scheme, offering nothing substantial in return for members' subscriptions. Needless to say *Bradshaws Directory* did not exist, and the *RAC Handbook* owed nothing to *RAC (Publishing) Ltd*; but is the proper legal analysis that the activities of the defendants amounted to a trade of some kind (albeit an entirely dishonest one), or that it did not matter whether they were actually trading or not? It is suggested that it was sufficient that the respective defendants were holding themselves out as traders of some kind, whether or not they could be said to traders in fact.

Conduct outside any existing trade

5-63 Cases in which ordinary trading companies are accused of passing-off in respect of activities outside any existing trade are rare, and the analysis inconclusive. The fact that an interlocutory injunction was granted in *Elida Gibbs v Colgate Palmolive*[17] is of some interest because although the defendant was undoubtedly a trader the misrepresentation was not made in the course of any existing trade. It was purely intended to protect an area of business the defendant might one day want to enter. A somewhat comparable case from South Africa is *Searles Industrials v International Power Marketing*[18] in which the advertisement complained of was only intended to test the market and no trade was imminent. However, the issue did not fall to be decided because there was no prospect of confusion.

Shell and dormant companies: introduction

5-64 In several cases the names of dormant or non-trading companies have been ordered to be changed for the benefit of someone with an existing goodwill in relation to a business carried on under that name or a close variant. Of

---

[13] (1926) 43 R.P.C. 97 (Astbury J.).
[14] Canvassers for the defendants actually collected money owed to the plaintiffs, who published *Bradshaws Railway Guide*.
[15] [1988] R.P.C. 321 (Browne-Wilkinson V.C.).
[16] [1996] F.S.R. 739 (Rimer J.).
[17] [1983] F.S.R. 95 (Goulding J.).
[18] 1982 (4) S.A. 123 (Transvaal.).

course, where the defendant company is actually trading (or is threatening to trade) under a name and in a field of business which would cause damaging confusion with the claimants' established business, then liability for passing-off is clear and does not depend on the mere fact of registration. In such a case, an order for the corporate name of the defendant to be changed may be likened to an order for delivery up, in the sense that its purpose is essentially to strengthen the normal prohibitory injunction to which the claimant is entitled, by removing a source of temptation from the defendant's possession. As with an order for delivery up, it need not imply that the claimant has any proprietary interest in the thing ordered to be surrendered, or that the mere possession of it would be unlawful. The cases fall into three main groups: the older English cases, *SA des Anciens Etablissements Panhard et Levassor v Panhard Levassor Motor Co*[19] and *Suhner & Co v Suhner*;[20] a couple of persuasive authorities from abroad; and a recent batch of decisions represented by *Glaxo plc v Glaxowellcome Ltd*,[21] *Direct Line Group Ltd v Direct Line Estate Agency Ltd*[22] and *British Telecommunications v One in a Million*.[23] First, however, it is necessary to look at the former provisions of the Companies Acts, and their relevance to the older decided cases.

The Companies Acts

In the decided cases against companies which were not actually or pro- **5–65** spectively trading, care needs to be taken to identify whether any cause of action was (or was thought to be) under the general law of passing-off, the relevant companies legislation then in force, or some other body of law altogether.[24] So the familiar *Manchester Brewery*[25] and *Aerators*[26] cases were actually decided under the now-repealed provisions of s.20 of the Companies Act 1862, but the same cannot be said for the *Panhard*[27] or *Suhner*[28] cases, since in both of those there was no registration for the foreign plaintiff to rely on, and the relevant Companies Act was applicable only in so far as it was the underlying cause of the plaintiff's grievance.

Until the mid-nineteenth century incorporation was rare and the problem of companies with identical or similar names was not addressed in legislation. In 1862, when the Companies Acts were amended and consolidated, a new provision, s.20, was inserted providing that "no company shall be registered under a name identical with that by which a subsisting company is

---

[19] [1901] 2 Ch. 513; [1900–3] All E.R. 477; 18 R.P.C. (Farwell J.).
[20] [1967] F.S.R. 319 [1967] R.P.C. 336 (Plowman J.).
[21] [1996] F.S.R. 388 (Lightman J.).
[22] [1997] F.S.R. 374 (Laddie J.).
[23] [1999] 1 W.L.R. 903; [1998] 4 All E.R. 476; [1999] E.T.M.R. 61; [1999] F.S.R. 1, CA.
[24] For example, s.6 of the Charities Act 1993, alluded to by Robert Walker J. in *British Diabetic Association v The Diabetic Society* [1996] F.S.R. 1.
[25] *North Cheshire & Manchester Brewery Co v Manchester Brewery Co* [1899] A.C. 83, HL.
[26] *Aerators Ltd v Tollitt* [1902] 2 Ch 319; 19 R.P.C. 418.
[27] *SA des Anciens Etablissements Panhard et Levassor v Panhard Levassor Motor Co* [1901] 2 Ch. 513; [1900–3] All E.R. 477; 18 R.P.C. (Farwell J.).
[28] *Suhner & Co AG v Suhner Ltd* [1967] F.S.R. 319; [1967] R.P.C. 336.

already registered, or so nearly resembling the same as to be calculated to deceive". There was already a body of cases in which registered or chartered companies, as well as unincorporated businesses such as sole traders or partnerships, had attempted to protect their corporate or trading names against confusingly similar ones, although most appear to have failed on the facts. In the confused taxonomy of mid-nineteenth century unfair competition law, the action to restrain use of a trade name was probably regarded as separate from the actions for trade mark infringement or passing-off strictly so called, but governed by the same equitable principles as the latter. The changes made by the 1862 Act were twofold. First, the rights of the originally registered company to exclusive use of its name would apparently derive directly from the fact of registration without need for proof of acquired distinctiveness through user, contrary to the position at common law and in a manner reminiscent of some unsuccessful contemporary proposals for a register of trade marks. Secondly, the section was inherently pre-emptive and self-enforcing to a large degree, and unlikely to require more than occasional intervention from the courts. With hindsight, an uncertainty can be identified in the operation of s.20: was the comparison of names intended to be a purely abstract one, and if not then what surrounding circumstances were to be taken into account?

5-66   The well-known *Manchester Brewery* case in the House of Lords,[29] is easily read and sometimes misunderstood as an application of the law of passing-off, but the judgments in the Court of Appeal, and in particular that of Lindley M.R., make it clear that it was brought under s.20 of the 1862 Act. On the facts, the result might have been no different at common law,[30] but some unguarded generalisations by way of *obiter dicta* were made in the House of Lords which obviously went too far if they implied that passing-off actions in general could be decided simply by comparison of the parties' respective corporate names without regard to how (if at all) they would be used in practice. Shortly afterwards, in *Aerators v Tollit*,[31] Farwell J. explained the *Manchester Brewery* case so as to take account of the fields of business of the parties as well as the bare names, with the practical result that the action under the statute (assuming the names were not identical) became very similar in actual effect to a *quia timet* action for passing-off, except that the plaintiff's *locus standi* was derived from the fact of registration rather than reputation through actual use. Throughout this period, it could be assumed that the intended field of business of the defendant company would be defined with precision in its memorandum of association, if it was not already implicit from the choice of name. There is also no

---

[29] *North Cheshire and Manchester Brewery Co Ltd v Manchester Brewery Co Ltd* [1899] A.C. 83, HL affirming [1898] 1 Ch. 539, CA.

[30] Although the trial judge (Byrne J.) had refused relief under the Act on the ground that the names were not so close as to lead to the defendants' beer being passed off as that of the plaintiffs in retail trade.

[31] [1902] Ch. 319; 19 R.P.C. 418 (Farwell J.). This is another case which has been subsumed into the general law of passing-off, although the cause of action was very clearly under s.20 of the Companies Act 1862 alone.

doubt in either of these cases that both parties traded or genuinely intended to trade.

Section 20 of the 1862 Act was re-enacted in successive Companies Acts through to that of 1929,[32] but in the Companies Act 1948 it was replaced with s.17 which provided that "no company shall be registered by a name which in the opinion of the Board of Trade is undesirable". From 1948 to 1981 the Registrar adopted a consistent and well-documented practice under s.17 of refusing registration to companies with names confusingly similar to those already registered,[33] and under s.18 had the power, within six months of registration, to require a company to change its name. The latter power was sometimes invoked on the application of existing companies and in simple cases which the Registrar had overlooked it could be quick, cheap and effective, especially in comparison to a full-scale passing-off action. Under the Companies Acts 1981 and 1985, the discretionary power to refuse registration of a name was virtually removed, so that as far as original registration is concerned, the 1985 Act provides only that companies cannot have names identical to any of those on the Registrar's index of company and corporate names,[34] and in considering identity of names a few very common words are excluded from the comparison.[35] However the position after registration is closer to that under the 1948 Act, since s.28(2) gives the Secretary of State the power, within 12 months of registration, to require a company to change its name if it is the same as, or too like, a name which appeared or should have appeared on the Registrar's index at the time of registration.

Shell and dormant companies: *Panhard* to *Fletcher Challenge*

The *Panhardt* and *Suhner* cases were both ones in which an attempt was **5–67** being made by the defendants to misuse the provisions of the Companies Act to prevent the registration by a foreign plaintiff of a branch or subsidiary in England under its own name, the foreign plaintiff itself having no prior registration on which it could rely.

In the first of these, *SA des Anciens Etablissements Panhard et Levassor v Panhard Levassor Motor Co*,[36] the plaintiffs were a French car manufacturing company which had no place of business in England, and which refrained from selling cars directly to England because of a risk of patent

---

[32] The Companies Act 1929, s.17 is mentioned, although it was not the cause of action, in *Office Cleaning Services Ltd v Westminster Office Cleaning Association* (1944) 61 R.P.C. 133, CA; affirmed [1946] 1 All E.R. 320; 63 R.P.C. 39, HL.

[33] This was the section under which the Swiss plaintiffs in *Suhner & Co AG v Suhrer Ltd* [1967] F.S.R. 319; [1967] R.P.C. 336 found that their attempt to incorporate a local subsidiary had been blocked.

[34] Companies Act 1985, s.26(1)(c) and s.714. The index is not confined to companies incorporated under the 1985 Act or its predecessors but includes (for instance) Oversea Companies with branches registered under Pt XXIII of the Act.

[35] Companies Act 1985, s.26(3): principally the definite article at the start of the name; and "company," "limited", "public limited company" and the like, and their abbreviations and Welsh equivalents.

[36] [1901] 2 Ch. 513; [1900–3] All E.R. 477; 18 R.P.C. (Farwell J.).

infringement. There would therefore have been no need (or occasion) for them to have registered under the Companies Act as a branch of a foreign company. The two defendant companies,[37] and the seven individuals who had promoted them, were sued before any trading by either had commenced, and the defendants gave undertakings until trial not to trade under either of the names complained of. It was admitted (and indeed asserted) that the reason for setting up the defendant companies was to place an obstacle in the way of the plaintiffs, in the event of their ever attempting to trade or establish a branch or subsidiary in England, and thereby to improve the competitive position of another company which was not directly involved in the action.

Farwell J. held that the case was a plain one, and that the court would intervene to protect a foreign trader, which had a market for its products in England, against having its name annexed by a third party without justification. The case against the individual defendants caused him more trouble, but he found against them on the basis of a fraudulent conspiracy.[38] In the result, two final injunctions were awarded: first, against any of the defendants using the names in connection with the motor car business; and secondly against the individual defendants allowing the company to remain on the Register under its name. It may be noted that the second injunction did not issue against the company as such, and that the first injunction would not have been breached by the company merely continuing to exist under its name, provided it did not attempt to trade in motor cars.

Panhardt was followed in *Suhner & Co AG v Suhner Ltd*[39] in which the main issue was again whether the foreign company had any local goodwill. The electrical components of the Swiss Suhner company had formerly been distributed in the United Kingdom by Trans-Radio Ltd,[40] but when the distributorship agreement was terminated the Swiss company found itself unable to form a subsidiary in England under its own name because the defendant company had already been incorporated at the instigation of Trans-Radio, the two individual defendants being employees of Trans-Radio's solicitors and the sole subscribers to the memorandum of association. Holding that there was a *prima facie* case that the Swiss plaintiff did own goodwill, Plowman J. granted an interlocutory injunction against the two individual defendants requiring them, in effect, to change the corporate defendant's name or to remove it from the Register.

5–68   Is there a common *ratio decidendi* for *Panhardt* and *Suhner*? *Panhard* was treated in part as a *quia timet* action in which it was assumed that the defendant company would or might trade, and the individual signatories to the memorandum of association were made liable for conspiracy to injure by procuring its incorporation for that purpose. *Suhner* is unambiguously a

---

[37] The corporate defendant in a second action was called the *Panhard Company Ltd*.

[38] It may be doubted if this part of the judgment is consistent with civil conspiracy as it is now understood: there is more to conspiracy than seven office juniors signing on the dotted line because they have been told to do so.

[39] [1967] F.S.R. 319; [1967] R.P.C. 336. (Plowman J., not Lloyd-Jacob J. as stated at the head of the F.S.R. report).

[40] Background is to be found in *Suhner & Co AG v Transradio* [1967] R.P.C. 329.

blocking case pure and simple, since an interlocutory undertaking not to trade under the disputed name had been offered, and the only issue remaining on motion was the continued existence of the defendant company under the name. It is interesting that in both cases the injunction effectively requiring the company to change its name was issued against the subscribers, and not against the company itself. In part, this may reflect purely practical considerations, but in *Suhner* there was an application for an injunction against the company itself, which Plowman J. refused. This is consistent with the underlying reasoning of *Panhard*, which is that the complaint justifying the change of name is essentially one of conspiracy to injure, rather than passing-off as generally understood: the individuals are deemed to be liable for conspiracy as well as for passing off; the company is liable *quia timet* for passing-off but not for conspiracy, it being the instrument, rather than the instigator, of the latter.

It might be suggested that since the company in each case was no more that a man of straw, an injunction against it alone would easily be circumvented, but that is to treat both cases entirely as ones of real or threatened passing-off. The purpose for registration of the company in either case was to secure for the defendants (or their principals) priority for the relevant name on the Register and to block the respective plaintiffs. Take the shell company away, and the tables are turned. The plaintiffs can proceed with their registration unhindered, and any attempt thereafter by the individual defendants to promote another company under a similar name would be futile, being blocked by the relevant section of the Companies Act itself.

The English *Panhard* and *Suhner* cases were followed in the Australian **5–69** case of *Fletcher Challenge v Fletcher Challenge*,[41] and as in those two cases the question of the defendants non-trading status (though specifically raised) was subordinated to that of the plaintiffs' *locus standi*. The plaintiff company was incorporated in New Zealand on November 10, 1980 to act as holding company for three existing companies and their subsidiaries. The merger had been announced in October, and the individual defendants had immediately reserved the name "Fletcher Challenge Pty Ltd" in New South Wales for a company which they subsequently formed. Powell J. first held that the few hours which had elapsed between announcement of the merger and the defendants' reservation of the name was sufficient to generate goodwill and reputation in Australia, and granted an interlocutory injunction on reasoning which appears to treat the passing-off case as entirely *quia timet*, but the cause of action for conspiracy as complete.

The New Zealand case of *Esanda Ltd v Esanda Finance Ltd*[42] may be cited in this context but is comparable only in respect of the plaintiffs' status as a recently merged foreign holding company. The interlocutory injunction granted by Casey J. does not seem to have extended to requiring the defendant company to change its name, and there was no claim for conspiracy. That the defendant was not trading was relevant only to the *status quo*. Both *Fletcher Challenge and Essanda* were followed at trial in *Crusader*

---

[41] [1982] F.S.R. 1 [1981]; 1 N.S.W.L.R. 196 (Powell J.).
[42] [1984] F.S.R. 96; [1984] 2 N.Z.L.R. 748.

Oil v Crusader Minerals,[43] another classic case of threatened passing-off which would have been open-and-shut for the plaintiffs but for the international element. The plaintiffs were a Queensland-based oil exploration company which had been active in Australia since about 1970, although so far as New Zealand was concerned its activities prior to the defendants' date of incorporation in 1982 were rather slight, being confined low-key prospecting activities in partnership with other companies, on which it had spent about AUS$300,000. It also had shareholders resident in New Zealand. Jeffries J. held that although its reputation and goodwill would have been sufficient as at November 1982, when the defendant company was incorporated, the relevant date was in fact June 1983, when the defendants entered the public arena by converting to a public company and issuing a prospectus. By this date, the plaintiffs' case was strengthened by the existence of active negotiations to sell gas concentrate to New Zealand, which had started in April. there is no doubt that the defendant company did intend to trade, albeit only in the related field of mineral exploitation, and there is not suggestion that it had been formed to block the plaintiffs' expansion or to be bought out.

Shell and dormant companies: recent examples

5–70 More recent cases illustrate the practical and analytical problem of companies being registered under a particular name, not with any intention of trading but simply in the hope of being bought out for an inflated amount by a business with a genuine commercial interest in the name. In *Glaxo plc v Glaxowellcome Ltd*[44] Glaxo announced (on the morning of January 23, 1995) an unsolicited takeover bid for Wellcome plc, with the proposal to name the merged company Glaxo-Wellcome plc if the bid was successful. The following day, the individual defendants, a company registration agent and his mother, filed an application to register a company under the name Glaxowellcome Ltd. The Glaxo bid was initially opposed by Wellcome, but was accepted by the Wellcome board on March 7. On March 13 Glaxo's solicitors noticed the existence of the defendant company on the Register and offered to buy it for the defendants' standard fee of £1,000. The personal defendants demanded (in purportedly "without prejudice" correspondence) £100,000 to sell it. Lightman J. described the defendants' conduct as "A dishonest scheme to appropriate the goodwill of the two plaintiffs and to extort from the plaintiffs a substantial sum as the price for not damaging the plaintiffs' goodwill in the names Glaxo and Wellcome" and granted mandatory interlocutory injunctions to change the first defendants' company name.

Although *Glaxowellcome* is reported (and has come to be regarded) as if it were a passing-off case, this is by no means explicit in the judgment. Passing-off is not mentioned until after liability had been established, and then by way of comparison and to provide precedents for the mandatory inter-

---

[43] (1984) 3 I.P.R. 171 (Jeffries J., HC of NZ).
[44] [1996] F.S.R. 388 (Lightman J.).

locutory injunction to change the company's name, at which point the Judge may be taken as referring to the *Panhard* and *Suhner* cases. Up to that point, the reasoning seems to be based on company law principles, with the implication that the case was not one of passing-off:

"The court will not countenance any such pre-emptive strike of registering companies with names where others have the goodwill in those names, and the registering party then demanding a price for changing the names. It is an abuse of the system of registration of companies' names. The right to choose the name with which a company is registered is not given for that purpose.

There is a statutory procedure under the Companies Act enabling the registrar of companies to require names to be changed, but a party prejudiced by this course is not obliged to have recourse to this procedure, which can be protracted. In an action for passing off in just this scenario, in a series of cases the courts have granted relief requiring the registered name of the company to be changed, with the requisite injunctions to that effect being granted against the company and its subscribers. This course will be adopted irrespective of whether the registered company has traded or not."

In *Direct Line Group Ltd v Direct Line Estate Agency Ltd*[45] companies incorporated as Direct Line Estate Agency Ltd, Direct Line Will's Ltd and Direct Line Estates Ltd were ordered to change their names at the suit of various companies in the Direct Line group which was best known for its *Direct Line* insurance business. The two individual defendants had made a practice of incorporating companies under various well known names, and in at least one case the relevant *Direct Line* defendant company had commenced trading, if only on a small scale.

The results in *Glaxowellcome* and *Direct Line*, as well as *Panard* and **5–71** *Suhner*, have been approved by the Court of Appeal (in the context of internet domain names) in *British Telecommunications v One in a Million*,[46] under the explanation that in all four cases the defendants were assumed to be arming themselves, or third parties, with "instruments of fraud" which would sooner or later be used for actual passing off. But beyond that point the analysis of *One in a Million* confuses an already unsatisfactory situation, since in almost the same breadth *One in a Million* accepted the proposition that the mere entry of the defendants as proprietors of the relevant names in a register open to public inspection amounted to passing off:

"The placing on a register [of domain names] of a distinctive name such as 'marksandspencer' makes a representation to persons who consult the register that the registrant is connected or associated with the name registered and thus the owner of the goodwill in the name. Such persons would not know of One in a Million Ltd. and would believe that they

---

[45] [1997] F.S.R. 374 (Laddie J.).
[46] [1999] 1 W.L.R. 903; [1998] 4 All E.R. 476; [1999] E.T.M.R. 61; [1999] F.S.R. 1, CA.

were connected or associated with the owner of the goodwill in the domain name they had registered. Further, registration of the domain name including the words 'Marks & Spencer' is an erosion of the exclusive goodwill in the name which damages or is likely to damage Marks & Spencer Plc."[47]

If this be so for the Register of Companies as well as for registers of internet domain names, then these four cases are retrospectively provided with yet another possible rationale, or at least with an argument which should have been advanced and decided in preference to ones less conclusively determinative of liability. Yet neither judge nor advocate in any of these cases, nor in the far more numerous ones of companies being registered with misleading names in preparation for actually trading under them, has suggested that the mere existence of an entry on the Register made the cause of action for passing off complete. And if liability for passing-off in *Glaxowellcome*, say, was complete from the date of registration (by parity of reasoning with the passage from *One in a Million* quoted above) then what becomes of the argument that *Glaxowellcome* and the others can be identified as cases whose unstated *ratio* was to prevent the dissemination of "instruments of fraud"?

5–72   In contrast to *Glaxowellcome*, in *Ben & Jerrys Homemade Inc v Ben & Jerrys Ice Cream Ltd*[48] the American plaintiffs, an ice-cream company, found on attempting to establish a subsidiary in the United Kingdom that there was already a shelf company on the Register with a similar name. The defendants did not attempt to extort any money and the plaintiffs did not seek a mandatory injunction for a change of name but only a *quia timet* interlocutory injunction against the defendant company commencing to trade in the ice-cream market under its registered name. Since the proprietors of the company expressly had no such intention, and there was delay, Ferris J. refused the injunction.

Dormant company names: analysis and conclusions

5–73 The treatment of shell and non-trading companies in the present section cannot avoid the question of whether such a defendant can be said to be a trader for the purposes of passing-off, especially in the terms in which it was defined by Lord Diplock in the *Advocaat* case. Can a company which does not trade at all be liable for passing-off, or is its unexplained existence on the Register simply a more or less equivocal threat of passing-off to come?

It is suggested that this is not the most helpful point from which to start the analysis, not least because it encourages resort to the convenient but entirely unconvincing legal fiction that the likes of Messrs McCloud, Pyatt and Joseph, Conway and Nicholson,[49] ever really intended to carry on a

---

[47] *per* Aldous L.J.
[48] (1995) 33 I.P.R. 157 (Ferris J.).
[49] Respectively the third defendant in *Glaxo plc v Galxowellcome Ltd*, the fourth and fifth in *Direct Line Group Ltd v Direct Line Estate Agency Ltd*, and the second and third in *British Telecommunications plc v One in a Million Ltd*.

trade on even the most miniscule or tentative basis, whether in pharmaceuticals or financial services—or indeed in anything other than the shares of the shell companies themselves, and their valuable names. If the contrary be suggested at all seriously, unless as an admission against interest by the defendant, then there are limits to authorial—as well as judicial—credulity. The timely opportunism of the first of these individuals and the sheer number and variety of the companies or domain names registered by the others were cogent evidence of their bad faith, but equally so for the irresistible inference that none of them ever intended to carry on any kind of proper business at all. Rather, one should ask whether the three essential components of goodwill, misrepresentation and damage are present; and treat the trading status of the defendant not as a separate requirement in its own right, but as an issue which may or may not be relevant under one of those heads.

The preferred analysis is that if the defendant company is indeed making **5–74** a representation that it is the claimant, or associated with the claimant in one of the ways capable of amounting to passing-off, and if that misrepresentation is really likely to cause damage to subsisting goodwill of the claimant, then there ought to be liability for passing-off even though the defendant is not actually or prospectively engaged in any trade. The question is not whether the defendant company is a trader in fact, but whether it is making a representation of the kind which real traders make in the course of trade, whether to their customers, or to members of the other classes (such as suppliers) who may be relevant for these purposes. On this analysis, it cannot be said *a priori* that no passing off action can lie (unless on a *quia timet* basis) against a dormant or shell company—but its non-trading status may be highly relevant to whether the tort of passing-off is already considered to be complete as soon as incorporation occurs or is officially published. In the normal course of events the likelihood is that a successful action against a dormant company will more usually be better understood as being either *quia timet* or as based on the equitable protective jurisdiction.

As a matter of principle, there are two fundamental difficulties which always arise in trying to treat the existence of a non-trading company on the Register as actionable passing-off in its own right. First, the mere existence of a company on the Register under a particular name cannot easily be regarded as an actionable misrepresentation (whether or not as one made by a trader in the course of trade) even if it does not go wholly unnoticed. If it were otherwise, then any passing-off action between two English companies with similar corporate names would (at least to that extent) be open and shut in favour of the claimant, even if, for instance, they traded in such disparate fields or geographical regions that no confusion was possible in reality.

To the extent that the existence of a shell company under a particular **5–75** name may be noticed by a few interested company registration agents, accountants, or solicitors, then there is at most an immaterial misrepresentation for the purposes of passing-off, causing no damage because no one relies on it in any relevant sense. No one consults the Register of Companies in order to buy an ice cream, a cold cure, or even an expensive motor car—one does so in order to serve a writ or a statutory notice, and it is not passing-off if these go astray.

In this respect there is an important distinction to be drawn with the cases on internet domain names, since a company is known on the internet only (to the public) by its domain name, and the latter is actually used by the public to direct communications and custom to the owner of the name. In this respect too, *Glaxowellcome* is atypical because there had been intense media speculation about imminent consolidation in the pharmaceutical industry, in which even the most obscure or insubstantial suggestion of the identity of prospective bidders and targets was likely to be seized on. In fact, Glaxo partly refrained from pre-emptively registering a company under the name Glaxo-Wellcome for the very good reason that it would have prematurely disclosed their intention to bid.[50]

5–76 Secondly, the non-availability of a preferred corporate name is, at best, a weak head of damage to rely on, and it is hard to see what other damage the claimant inherently suffers. Even if it is allowed that the blocking effect of the registration causes damage in this or some other legally recognised form, then such damage cannot be said to be caused because of any misrepresentation: it arises from the fact of the prior registration *per se*, regardless of whether anyone is deceived by it or not.

There is a third difficulty which will sometimes arise but is not inevitable. Since the object of the defendant is to forestall the claimant in its choice of name, it may happen that the claimant will have no goodwill in the jurisdiction, either because one is dealing with an overseas claimant expanding as in *Ben & Jerry's* or with a totally new venture. This was not a problem in *Glaxowellcome* because the existing Glaxo and Wellcome companies (rather than a newly formed merged body, as in the Australian *Fletcher Challenge* case) were plaintiffs. In this context, the meritorious claimant may actually be put at a disadvantage if it is suggested that the defendant's liability for passing-off is to be evaluated at the date of incorporation, since if a later date is chosen then the claimant is in less danger of being forestalled.[51]

5–77 Before condemning the practical consequences of a strict application of the law, two further points need to be borne in mind. The first is that a company which merely exists on the Register without trading acquires no rights, so far as the law of passing-off is concerned, to prevent another company or person trading under even precisely the same name in any line of business. Passing-off protects a trader's goodwill, and a shell company which has never traded can by definition have no goodwill. Its rights, such as they are, are confined to blocking the registration of another company with an identical name.

The second point is that even if the shell company were to begin to trade under its registered name, its prior registration would not confer any immunity from suit. A defence of antecedent user would require actual (and *bona fide*) use of the name in trade, so as to generate goodwill. If the defence of use of one's own name exists at all for a company, it too requires *bona*

---

[50] See the letter from their solicitors, Clifford-Chance, at [1997] 19(12) E.I.P.R. 736.
[51] Compare *Crusader Oil NA v Crusader Minerals NZ Ltd* (1984) 2 I.P.R. 171.

fides. A defence of acquiescence would not arise until the claimant had an opportunity to sue, and in any event would be precluded by putting the defendant on notice, or defeated, again, by the defendant's own inequitable conduct.

One may readily agree with Lightman J. that these practices are "an abuse of the system of registration of company names" and if so, it may be in company law that the remedy should be sought. Unlike Panhard, Suhner and Ben & Jerry's, all of whom were unregistered foreign companies, Glaxo, Wellcome and Direct Line were UK registered companies and could have invoked the procedure of s.28(2) of the Companies Act 1985. Since there may assumed to be a statutory right of some kind underlying the statutory remedy, those cases are susceptible to the explanation that all the court was doing was to grant an interim remedy in support of a right which was ultimately required to be pursued in a different forum, a not uncommon situation.

Both parties at margin of trading activity

Cases dealing with the claimant's trading status are considered in detail in **5–78** Chapter 3, Section B. The cases dealt with there fall into three categories. The first category consists of cases where the only live question was that of the claimant's *locus standi* to sue, with the defendant's status as a trader *a fortiori* not being in doubt: for example the *Barnado*[52] case where the plaintiff was a charity and the defendant a commercial publisher. Secondly, there are those in which the claimant and defendant were in all relevant respects in the same situation. Both, for instance, were churches, or charities, or members' clubs; and it could have made little or no difference in principle that the claimant was typically longer established, larger, and better known than the defendant. Once the trading status of the claimant had been acknowledged then that of the defendant might seem to follow almost automatically, although what is now the leading case rightly acknowledged that a separate analysis of the defendant's trading status was necessary.[53]

A third category of case has not received sufficient express attention, which is where neither party is obviously a trader, and the process of reasoning which acknowledges the claimant's trading status cannot fairly be applied to the defendant either *a fortiori* or at all.[54] So one may agree with the Court of Appeal that the *Countryside Alliance*[55] was within the extended category of associations deemed to have sufficient trading interest to sue— but by what possible stretch of the imagination could the defendant Haycock also be said to be a trader? He was not sued as an officer, member or representative of any rival party or association which might be deemed to

---

[52] *Dr Barnardo's Homes v Barnardo Amalgamated Industries* (1949) 66 R.P.C. 103 (Vaisey J.).
[53] *British Diabetic Association v The Diabetic Society* [1996] F.S.R. 1 (Robert Walker J.).
[54] For example, *Honey v Australian Airlines* (1990) 18 I.P.R. 185 (Federal Court of Australia) affirming (1989) 14 I.P.R. 264 (Northrop J.) where the plaintiff was an amateur athlete and the second defendant (the *House of Tabor*) a religious organisation.
[55] *Burge v Haycock* [2001] EWCA Civ 900; [2002] R.P C. 28, CA.

have comparable trading status. Such evidence as there was, was that he was no longer even a member of the British National Party, and his public support for that party in the past was relevant only to damage to the Countryside Alliance by association with an unpopular cause. He did not engage in any of the kind of activities which might have given the Countryside Alliance trading status in the narrow sense, such as selling promotional merchandise or offering holidays or insurance. Even a full-time professional politician such as Alan Clark is not considered to be a trader in his capacity as such, and Haycock was simply a private individual, politically active on the small stage of Bromyard and Winslow, and on the larger one of the national press.

Private individuals as defendants

5–79 No action for passing-off lies against a private individual in his capacity as such, as distinguished from an individual being liable as a joint tortfeasor, or as a sole trader or partner. There are very few examples of such actions being brought at all, the only apparent exception to the rule being the early case of *Upmann v Forester*[56] where the defendant, a china merchant, unwittingly imported 5,000 counterfeit cigars for his personal and family use. Liability (except for costs) was conceded, and the case is better regarded as an over-zealous application of the equitable protective jurisdiction, or as turning on trade mark infringement, with the size of the consignment being crucial to the result in either case.

The modern state of the law is represented by *Rolls-Royce v Zanelli*[57] in which a motor dealer was restrained from using a car got-up as a *Rolls-Royce Corniche* in the course of trade but was allowed to use it for private purposes. An unqualified injunction was granted in *Rolls-Royce v Dodd*.[58] The defendant was a trader, and the decision seems to rest on the proposition that any use of the car would in effect have been an advertisement. In *Charles Church Developments v Cronin*[59] it was alleged that three private individuals (as well as a builder) were liable for passing-off by building and offering for sale a house copied from one of the plaintiffs' designs, but the action was struck out on other grounds and the point was never considered.

5–80 A private individual therefore commits no tort by using, giving away, or even selling—if not in the course of trade—goods in circumstances which would amount to passing-off if done by a trader. It may be reprehensible, but it is not passing-off to economise by telling ones' guests that cheap sparkling wine is *Champagne* or by re-filling an empty spirits bottle with a cheaper brand. Nor is it passing-off for a private individual to seek to impress with known counterfeit versions of expensive and prestigious goods. More importantly, there is consequently no liability on the basis of joint tortfeasorship against a trader who encourages or facilitates this sort of

---

[56] (1883) 24 Ch.D. 231 (Chitty J.).
[57] [1979] R.P.C. 148, CA.
[58] [1981] F.S.R. 517 (Whitford J.).
[59] [1990] F.S.R. 1 (Edward Nugee Q.C.).

conduct without making any misrepresentation himself or through another trader.

In the Australian case of *Dr Martens Australia v Rivers*[60] it was unsuccessfully argued that people in the street might think that persons wearing any of the various defendants' look-alike boots or shoes were actually wearing *Doc Martens*. The former were close copies, but were adequately distinguished at point of sale by their respective brand names. The allegation seems to have been pursued solely under the Trade Practices Act 1974, and it is suggested that there could have been no liability for passing off in these circumstances, even if the appearance or "trade dress" of the plaintiffs' footwear had been sufficiently distinctive.

H. THE DEFENDANT NEED NOT COMPETE WITH THE CLAIMANT

Common field of activity unnecessary...

The earliest cases of passing-off were fought between trade rivals in direct **5–81** competition with one another. Towards the end of the nineteenth century it came to be recognised that damage did not depend on the defendant actually taking business from the plaintiff, and actions were progressively allowed in which the fields of business of the plaintiff and defendant were more and more remote.[61] In practice, cases where the plaintiff was successful against a defendant in a totally unconnected field of business were almost all, until quite recently, ones in which the defendant was obviously fraudulent, but this was never put as a rule of law.

It has sometimes been said that there can be no passing-off unless the claimant and the defendant are engaged in a "common field of activity". The expression was coined by Wynn-Parry J. in *McCulloch v May*[62] in which a broadcaster known as "Uncle Mac" unsuccessfully sued the manufacturers of a breakfast cereal called *Uncle Mac's Puffed Wheat*. The case was opened as one of deliberate fraud but this allegation was dropped in the course of the trial. In dismissing the action Wynn-Parry J. made the remark that "[T]here is discoverable in all those cases in which the court has intervened this factor, namely, that there was a common field of activity in which, however remotely, both the plaintiff and the defendant were engaged and that it was the presence of that factor that accounted for the jurisdiction of the court". He went on to consider whether the plaintiff would suffer any damage and concluded that the risk of litigation was "visionary and illusory" and that the prospect of damage to his professional reputation as a broadcaster or to his ability to make his living was not real or tangible.

This notorious dictum has now been repudiated by the Court of Appeal in

---

[60] [1999] FCA 1655; (1999) 95 F.C.R. 136; 47 I.P.R. 499, (Federal Court of Australia, Full Court).
[61] Jeremy Phillips and Allison Coleman, "Passing off and the Common Field of Activity" (1985) 101 L.Q.R. 242.
[62] [1947] 2 All E.R. 845; 65 R.P.C. 58 (Wynn-Parry J.).

Harrods v Harrodian School[63] as discredited and contrary to authority: "There is no requirement that the defendant should be carrying on a business which competes with that of the plaintiff or which would compete with any natural extension of the plaintiff's business".[64] The absence of a common field of activity between the plaintiffs' department store and the defendants' preparatory school was therefore not fatal as a matter of law, but was highly relevant to the conclusion that there was no risk of confusion. As in *Stringfellow v McCain*,[65] the burden of proving confusion and damage was a heavy one when there was no overlap, or only a tenuous overlap, in the parties' respective fields of activity. Customers of *Harrods* would be incredulous if they were told that *Harrods* had opened a preparatory school: "The question is whether there is a real risk that members of the public will be deceived into thinking that a school called *The Harrodian School* (not written in the distinctive *Harrods* script or livery) is owned or managed by *Harrods* or under *Harrods'* supervision or control".[66]

5–82   *McCulloch v May* had previously been criticised in Australia on the ground that "If deception and damages are proved, it is not easy to see the justification for introducing another factor as a condition of the court's power to intervene".[67] In England, *McCulloch v May* had been explained to similar effect by Oliver J. in *Lyngstad v Annabas*[68] and by Falconer J. in *Lego System v Lego M Lemelstrich*,[69] but its reasoning was roundly condemned (in a situation much closer to the original context) by Laddie J. in *Irvine v Talksport*.[70]

As the law stands, the presence or absence of a common field of activity may be relevant to the issues of misrepresentation and damage, but is no more than a rule of thumb which may be a convenient starting point for analysis in particular cases. There is no rule of law that a claimant cannot succeed in the absence of a common field. *A fortiori* there need not be actual competition for the same customers. On the other hand, neither is there any rule of law to the effect that particularly famous marks receive any greater protection than normal in fields distant to that in which their fame was earned. As well as the example of *Harrods*, there is that of *Mercedes-Benz*, whose owners failed to restrain the use of *Merc* for a retail clothing store in Carnaby Street.[71] The case was advanced and decided on entirely orthodox principles: the claimants had more than ample goodwill and reputation in relation to *Mercedes* and *Mercedes-Benz* for cars, for which *Merc* was a widely used abbreviation, but the defendant had been trading for many

---

[63] [1996] R.P.C. 697, CA.
[64] *per* Millett L.J.
[65] [1984] F.S.R. 199; [1984] R.P.C. 501, C.A.
[66] *per* Millett L.J.
[67] *Henderson v Radio Corporation Pty Ltd* [1960] N.S.W.L.R. 279; [1969] R.P.C. 218 (High Court of New South Wales, Full Court; *per* Evatt C.J. and Myers J.).
[68] [1977] F.S.R. 62 (Oliver J.).
[69] *Lego System A/S v Lego M Lemelstrich Ltd* [1983] F.S.R. 155.
[70] [2002] EWHC 367; [2002] 1 W.L.R. 2355; [2002] 2 All E.R. 424; [2002] E.M.L.R. 32; [2002] F.S.R. 60 (Laddie J.), affirmed in part [2003] EWCA Civ 423; [2003] 2 All E.R. 881; [2003] E.M.L.R. 26; [2003] F.S.R. 35, CA.
[71] *Daimler-Chrysler AG v Alavi* [2002] R.P.C. 42 (Pumfrey J.).

years with no evidence of confusion, and had established his own independent reputation and goodwill. Limited use by the claimants of *Mercedes-Benz* (with the equally famous three-pointed star) on clothing did not assist since this was "T-shirt use", intended to advertise the mark in relation to motor vehicles, rather than to identify a brand of clothing.

...but common field may be relevant

This is not to say that the common field of activity has no relevance. In the **5–83** first place, the misrepresentation in passing-off is hardly ever an express one. Instead, the court has to decide whether in all the circumstances of the case the use by the defendant of a particular name, mark or get-up is likely to deceive. Clearly, the similarity or dissimilarity of the parties' respective fields of business is one important factor to consider.[72] In general, the closer they are the more likely it is that the public will assume there to be a connection. Secondly, if the existence of a misrepresentation may be inferred, then the similarity of the fields of activity may again become relevant on the logically separate question of likelihood of damage.

The "common field of activity" has different degrees of relevance on the two issues. Where it is the existence of a misrepresentation which is in issue the matter is entirely one of degree: in a blatant case there need be no common field in any real sense at all, but even competition between the parties will not outweigh such factors as strong dissimilarities in the respective marks. On the issue of damage a more important criterion than the common field is the existence or absence of actual competition. If the claimant stands to lose sales to the defendant then damage will normally be inferred. If not, then similarities in the respective fields of business are still of some weight in deciding whether damage in one of the other forms recognised by law will occur, and on what scale.

The residual, but not unimportant, relevance of the common field was **5–84** described by Millett L.J. in *Harrods v Harrodian School*[73]:

"What the plaintiff in an action for passing off must prove is not the existence of a common field of activity but likely confusion among the common customers of the parties. The absence of a common field of activity, therefore, is not fatal; but it is not irrelevant either. In deciding whether there is a likelihood of confusion, it is an important and highly relevant consideration '... whether there is any kind of association, or could be in the minds of the public any kind of association, between the field of activities of the plaintiff and the field of activities of the defendant': *Annabel's (Berkeley Square) Ltd. v G. Schock per* Russell L.J.

In the *Lego* case Falconer J. likewise held that the proximity of the defendant's field of activity to that of the plaintiff was a factor to be taken into account when deciding whether the defendant's conduct would cause the necessary confusion. Where the plaintiff's business name is a house-

[72] *Annabel's (Berkeley Square) Ltd v Schock* [1972] R.P.C. 838, CA.
[73] [1996] R.P.C. 697, CA.

hold name the degree of overlap between the fields of activity of the parties' respective businesses may often be a less important consideration in assessing whether there is likely to be confusion, but in my opinion it is always a relevant factor to be taken into account. Where there is no or only a tenuous degree of overlap between the parties' respective fields of activity the burden of proving the likelihood of confusion and resulting damage is a heavy one."

The presence of a common field of activity is by no means a conclusive reason to believe that misrepresentation and damage will result, even if the two parties are using the same name or mark. In *Unitex v Union Texturising Co*[74] both companies used the mark *Unitex* and both were involved in the building industry in Yorkshire, though one as a manufacturer and the other as a contractor. There was some evidence of confusion but on closer analysis this would have occurred even "if the defendants carried on the business of chocolate manufacture"[75] and was therefore irrelevant to the issue of damage. The remaining evidence of damage was insufficient to justify an interlocutory injunction. In *Anheuser-Busch v Budejovick Budvar*[76] the parties both sold lager under the name *Budweiser*. The plaintiffs' trade in England was virtually confined to United States Air Force Bases where the defendants' beer would never be available. Even assuming, therefore, that the plaintiffs had a goodwill to protect, they stood to suffer no damage to this trade from the defendants.

Illustrations of degree—claimant successful

5–85 In *Eastman Photographic Materials Co v John Griffiths*[77] the plaintiff camera manufacturers restrained the use by the defendants of *Kodak* for bicycles and in the name of their company. In *Dunlop Pneumatic Tyre Co v Dunlop Lubricant Co*[78] there was passing-off by the defendants using the name of a tyre company for oils, but in a case by the same plaintiffs against a retail garage the House of Lords found for the defendants.[79] In *Walter v Ashton*[80] the proprietor of *The Times* newspaper restrained the defendant from advertising *Times* cycles as if endorsed by the newspaper. Byrne J. treated the case as one of exposure to liability[81] rather than as passing-off, but the Court of Appeal in *Harrods v R. Harrod*[82] said it was decided on too narrow a ground. In *Lloyd's & Dawson Bros. v Lloyds, Southampton*[83] the Court of Appeal granted an injunction against a firm of yacht brokers at the suit of Lloyd's of London and their agents in Southampton. In this and the fol-

[74] [1973] F.S.R. 181; [1973] R.P.C. 119, CA.
[75] *per* Russell L.J.
[76] [1984] F.S.R. 413, CA.
[77] (1898) 15 R.P.C. 105 (Romer J.).
[78] (1898) 16 R.P.C. 12 (Romer J.).
[79] *Dunlop Pneumatic Tyre Co Ltd v Dunlop Motor Co* [1907] A.C. 430; 24 R.P.C. 527, HL.
[80] [1902] 2 Ch. 282 (Byrne J.).
[81] *Routh v Webster* (1847) 50 E.R. 698.
[82] (1924) 41 R.P.C. 74, CA.
[83] (1912) 29 R.P.C. 433, CA.

lowing case, interlocutory relief had been refused at first instance because of the dissimilarities in fields of business.

In *Harrods v R. Harrod*[84] itself the Court of Appeal granted an interlocutory injunction at the suit of the famous department store against a moneylender who had assumed the name "R. Harrod". The plaintiffs operated a bank but their Articles of Association prohibited trading as a moneylender. The British Medical Association restrained the use of their initials by a retail chemist: *British Medical Association v Marsh*[85]. In *Dr Barnardo's Homes v Barnardo Amalgamated Industries*[86] the plaintiff charity restrained the use of their name by a publisher of pulp fiction. In *Treasure Cot Co v Hamley Bros.*[87] the goods were respectively babies' cots and cots for dolls. A declaration was granted. In *Hulton Press v White Eagle Youth Holiday Camp*[88] the publishers of a children's magazine *Eagle* prevented the use of *White Eagle* for a children's holiday camp, there supposedly being a possibility of the plaintiffs opening one in the future.

The modern law may be said to begin with *Annabel's v Schock*[89] where the **5–86** plaintiffs owned a night club and the defendant an escort agency. The Court of Appeal found a common field of activity in the provision of night life, but more importantly based their judgment on the likelihood of confusion and the damage which the unsavoury reputation of escort agencies would cause. Note that the common field of activity test is mutually applicable, but the test of likeliness of damage is not. It does not follow that an escort agency would be damaged by a nightclub using the same name, common field notwithstanding.

In *LRC International v Lila Edets Sales Co*[90] an interlocutory injunction was granted to restrain the use of *Marigold* for toilet paper, the plaintiffs using it for rubber gloves and plastic pants. Interlocutory injunctions were also granted in *Computervision Corp v Computer Vision*[91] where the defendants intended to use the name for electronic check-out equipment in supermarkets and the plaintiffs made a variety of non-competing electronic instrumentation; and in *Ames Crosta v Pionex International*[92] which involved two companies whose areas were protective clothing and pollution control. In *John Walker v Rothmans International*[93] an interlocutory injunction was refused on discretionary grounds but there was said to be a strongly arguable case that use of *Red Label* for cigarettes would be passing-off actionable by the distillers of *Red Label* whisky. In *Alfred Dunhill v Sunoptic*[94] an interlocutory injunction was granted by the Court of Appeal (reversing the judge at first instance) where the defendant's goods were sunglasses and the

---

[84] (1924) 41 R.P.C. 74, CA.
[85] (1931) 48 R.P.C. 565 (Maugham J.)
[86] (1949) 66 R.P.C. 103 (Vaisey J.).
[87] (1950) 67 R.P.C. 89 (Harman J.).
[88] (1951) 68 R.P.C. 126, the more notable for being a decision of Wynn-Parry J.
[89] [1972] R.P.C. 838, CA.
[90] [1973] R.P.C. 560 (Whitford J.).
[91] [1975] R.P.C. 171; [1974] F.S.R. 206 (Plowman J.).
[92] [1977] F.S.R. 46 (Walton J.).
[93] [1978] F.S.R. 357 (Brightman J.).
[94] [1979] F.S.R. 337, CA.

plaintiffs, who had made their name in tobacco and smokers' goods, had diversified into a variety of luxury goods for men.

5–87   Cases subsequent to *Advocaat*[95] have applied criteria at least as generous. In *British Broadcasting Co v Talbot Motor Co*[96] the British Broadcasting Corporation obtained an interlocutory injunction against use of *Carfax* for car parts, confirming that a service industry can prevent use of a name on goods.[97] The BBC intended to use the name for a motoring information service by radio. In *Home Box Office v Channel 5 Home Box Office*[98] an American cable television station failed to obtain an interlocutory injunction against a video cassette hire shop, but on the balance of convenience only. In *News Group Newspapers v Rocket Record Co*[99] the proprietors of *The Sun* newspaper obtained an interlocutory injunction against the producers of a pop record. In *NAD Electronics v NAD Computer Systems*[1] it was said that there was little separation between the parties' respective fields of hi-fi audio equipment and computers, and the two were converging to an increasing degree. A permanent injunction was granted.

In *Easyjet v Dainty*[2] the claimants operated a budget airline, a chain of internet cafés, and a car hire business under various names beginning *easy-*. They obtained summary judgment against a cybersquatter who had registered the domain name *easyRealestate.co.uk* and copied the claimants' get-up for an online estate agency service, but the broader proposition that the claimants had prior rights to the word "easy" regardless of field of business was rejected. In *Reed Executive v Reed Business Information*[3] there had never been any question of passing off between the claimants' recruitment agency and the defendants' stable of business and professional magazines, notwithstanding the recruitment advertising carried by the latter, but the defendants inadvertently went too far in using the name *Reed* on the pages and metatags of a web site *totaljobs.com* which aimed to match job applicants to vacancies.

The case which has probably gone furthest in England is still *Lego System v Lego M. Lemelstrich*[4] in which the makers of the well-known children's building bricks were granted a permanent injunction at trial against the admittedly *bona fide* use of the name for garden irrigation equipment. Falconer J. adopted the explanation of *McCulloch v May*[5] given by Oliver J. in *Lyngstad v Annabas Products*[6] and held that there was no rule of law requiring a common field of activity if deception and damage were proven.

---

[95] *Erven Warnink BV v J Townend & Sons (Hull) Ltd* [1979] A.C. 731; [1979] 2 All E.R. 927; [1980] R.P.C. 31, HL.
[96] [1981] F.S.R. 228 (Megarry V.C.).
[97] *Hulton Press Ltd v White Eagle Youth Holiday Camp Ltd* (1951) 68 R.P.C. 126 shows the reverse happening.
[98] [1982] F.S.R. 449 (Peter Gibson J.).
[99] [1981] F.S.R. 89 (Slade J.).
[1] [1997] F.S.R. 380 (Ferris J.).
[2] [2002] F.S.R. 6 (Bernard Livesey Q.C., Deputy Judge).
[3] [2002] EWHC 1015; [2003] R.P.C. 12 (Pumfrey J.).
[4] [1983] F.S.R. 155 (Falconer J.).
[5] [1947] 2 All E.R. 845; 65 R.P.C. 58. (Wynn-Parry J.).
[6] [1977] F.S.R. 62 (Oliver J.).

Whether the evidence justified finding for the plaintiffs on the facts is another matter. There may have been a degree of confusion but none of the arguments advanced for supposing this would cause any tangible damage to subsisting goodwill carries conviction.

McCulloch v May first received explicit criticism in Australia,[7] so it is not **5–88** surprising that Commonwealth courts have granted injunctions despite the absence of any common field of activity in the strict sense. In *Henderson v Radio Corp* itself two ballroom dancers obtained relief at trial against a record company.[8] A bus operator was granted an injunction at trial against a car and truck company in Canada: *Greyhound Corp v Greyhound Car and Truck Rental*.[9] An automobile sales company likewise obtained an injunction against a taxi business: *Paris Investments v Davis Taxis*.[10] The owners of a sports resort in British Columbia enjoyed the use of their name by a nearby motel: *Mountain Shadows v Pemsall*[11] In *VISA International Service Association v Visa Motel Corp*.[12] the plaintiffs were a consortium of banks issuing credit cards. The defendants supplied portable buildings to construction sites. An injunction and damages were granted by the British Columbia Court of Appeal. In South Africa the Appellate Division refused to follow *McCulloch v May* in *Capital Estate & General Agencies v Holiday Inns*[13] and granted a chain of hotels an injunction against the operators of a shopping centre. In one respect the plaintiffs' case was strengthened by the absence of a common field. *Holiday Inn* might plausibly be descriptive for an hotel, but there can only be one possible explanation for using it for a shopping centre. In Canada an insurance company successfully restrained the use of *Sunlife* for fruit juice: *Sun Life Assurance Co of Canada v Sunlife Juice*.[14]

In Australia, a mortgage lender trading as *Aussie Home Loans* was granted a final injunction against the use of *Aussie Home Builders* in *Australian Home Loans v Phillips*.[15] The defendant had previously briefly acted as an agent for the plaintiffs, the plaintiffs' "house device" mark had been copied almost precisely, and the defendant intended to arrange home loans as well as constructing houses. In *Campomar v Nike International*[16] the marketing by the defendants in Australia of *Nike Sport Fragrance* was restrained as passing off and under the Trade Practices Act 1974. The Spanish defendants' original use outside Australia of *Nike* for perfumes considerably pre-dated that of the American plaintiffs' use for sports footwear and clothing, but the former were effectively unknown in Australia and

---

[7] In *Henderson v Radio Corp Pty Ltd* [1960] N.S.W.L.R. 279; [1969] R.P.C. 218.
[8] Followed in *Totalizator Agency Board v Turf News Pty Ltd* [1967] V.R. 605; [1972] R.P.C. 579.
[9] [1962] 35 D.L.R. (2d) 13; [1962] O.R. 988; 23 Fox, P.C. 63; 40 C.P.R. 131 (Schatz J. Ontario High Court).
[10] (1969) 70 W.W.R. 674; 8 D.L.R. (3d) 775; 61 C.P.R. 178.
[11] (1973) 9 C.P.R. (2d) 172; 40 D.L.R. (3d) 231.
[12] (1984) 1 C.P.R. (3d) 109 (British Columbia Court of Appeal).
[13] 1977 (2) S.A. 916 (Appellate Division).
[14] (1988) 22 C.P.R. (3d) 244 (MacFarland J., Ontario).
[15] (1998) 40 I.P.R. 392 (Lehane J., Federal Court of Australia).
[16] [2000] HCA 12; 46 I.P.R. 481 (High Court of Australia).

there was no doubt that their *Nike Sport Fragrance* would be taken for a brand extension by the American company. Wider injunctions directed to any future use for perfumes and cosmetics of *Nike* on its own, regardless of surrounding circumstances, were discharged without prejudice to what would happen if any such products were launched.

Defendant successful

5–89 Early cases in which relief was refused are now of little more than historical interest. Examples are *Turner's Motor v Miesse Petrol Car Syndicate*,[17] where the difference was between petrol and steam powered motor cars and *Joseph Lucas v Fabry*[18] which involved motor accessories and tyres. Many turned predominantly on the *bona fides* of the defendant, which would now be given little weight. In modern cases in the defendant's favour it may be difficult to separate the absence of a common field from other factors. Most of the recent cases in which the absence of a common field of activity has contributed to relief being refused are in the fields of licensing and character merchandising and are discussed in Chapter 7, Sections F and H. Ironically, the case which has gone furthest in recognising character merchandising in English law would have caused least concern to Wynn-Parry and Walton JJ., since in *Mirage Studios v Counter-Feat Clothing*[19] (the *Teenage Mutant Ninja Turtles*) the parties were, for once, in direct competition as licensors.

In *McCulloch v May*[20] a broadcaster failed to prevent use of his performing name for a breakfast cereal. Similarly, in *Sim v Heinz*[21] an actor failed to prevent an advertisement for food being broadcast in an imitation of his voice, though the possibility of relief being given at trial was not ruled out. In Canada, an entertainer failed to prevent use of his name by a cleaning company: *Young v Scot Young*.[22] In *Stringfellow v McCain*[23] the owner of a night club failed to restrain use of his name for frozen chips. There was an example of implicit misrepresentation but no probability of damage.

In *Rolls Razor v Rolls Lighters*[24] the plaintiff razor manufacturers failed to restrain *Rolls* for cigarette lighters. It did not matter that they had once manufactured lighters themselves, because the fact had not been known to the public. In *Ronson Products v James Ronson*[25] it was the plaintiffs' mark which was used for cigarette lighters. The defendants adopted the same

---

[17] (1907) 24 R.P.C. 531 (Warrington J.).
[18] (1905) 23 R.P.C. 33 (Warrington J.).
[19] [1991] F.S.R. 145 (Browne-Wilkinson V.C.).
[20] [1947] All E.R. 845; 65 R.P.C. 58 (Wynn-Parry J.). The decision is now discredited, see above.
[21] [1959] 1 W.L.R. 313; [1959] 2 All E.R. 547; [1959] R.P.C. 80, CA.
[22] (1972) 29 D.L.R. (3d) 146 (Moorhouse J., Ontario High Court). A very backward case in its reasoning: *Krouse v Chrysler Canada Ltd* (1971) 25 D.L.R. (3d) 49 reversed (1973) 40 D.L.R. (3d) 15 (not cited, though also from Ontario) had been decided at first instance the previous year.
[23] [1984] R.P.C. 501, CA.
[24] (1949) 66 R.P.C. 299, CA.
[25] [1957] V.R. 731 (Supreme Court of Victoria, Full Court).

mark for car polish and cleaning fluid. The Supreme Court of Victoria (Full Court) found for the defendants. The differences in fields of activity were such that there was no tangible probability of either deception or damage. In another Australian case *FMC Engineering v FMC.* there was some confusion but no probability of injury to the plaintiffs' business of food machinery manufacturers from the use by the defendants of the same initials *FMC* in a different field of engineering.[26]

In *Unitex v Union Texturising Co*[27] the Court of Appeal refused an **5–90** interlocutory injunction, although there was undoubtedly a common field. In *Granada Group v Ford Motor Co*[28] the television and cinema company Granada failed to obtain an interlocutory injunction against the use of the name for a motor car, the evidence being inadequate. In *Newsweek Inc v BBC*[29] the Court of Appeal refused the proprietors of a news magazine an interlocutory injunction to restrain the same name being used for a television current affairs programme. There was little prospect of damage, although it can hardly be denied there was a common field.

There was a sufficient overlap of businesses for there to be an arguable case in *Stacey v 2020 Communications Ltd*[30] where both parties were in the business of supplying telephone equipment, though the fact that most of the plaintiff's business was not directly competitive with that of the defendants was one reason for refusing an interlocutory injunction on the balance of convenience. In *Blazer v Yardley*[31] the much greater difference between the plaintiffs' business as a chain of retail menswear shops and that of the defendants as manufacturers of toilet goods again meant that the balance of convenience was against the grant of an interlocutory injunction. In *Fortnum & Mason v Fortnam*[32] the fact that the plaintiffs' business was that of high-class retailers (principally for food) in England and the defendants dealt in various cheap wholesale goods which they imported from the far East and re-exported to Europe meant that there was most unlikely to be any relevant confusion. An interlocutory injunction was refused. A credit administration scheme for dentists marketed under the name *Smilecare* did not infringe the rights of two high street dental practitioners who already traded under that name. There was no prospect of confusion either among dentists, or the public: *Harding v Smilecare.*[33] In Scotland, the owners of a Californian golf course and resort named *Pebble Beach* were refused an interim interdict against use of the name for a brand of malt whisky.[34] The pursuers had an extensive licensing programme internationally and in the United Kingdom, but the closest licensed goods were hip flasks, glassware and decanters.

A drinks manufacturer obtained an interlocutory injunction against a **5–91**

[26] [1966] V.R. 529.
[27] [1973] R.P.C. 119; [1973] F.S.R. 181, CA.
[28] [1973] R.P.C. 49. (Graham J.).
[29] [1979] R.P.C. 441, CA.
[30] [1991] F.S.R. 49 (Millett J.).
[31] [1992] F.S.R. 501 (Aldous J.).
[32] [1994] F.S.R. 438 (Harman J.).
[33] [2002] F.S.R. 37 (P.W. Smith Q.C., Deputy Judge).
[34] *Pebble Beach Co v Lombard Brands Ltd* 2002 S.L.T 1312 (Lord Menzies, OH).

restaurant in the Australian case of *Cinzano v Ruggiero (No.1)*,[35] but at trial it was discharged as there was no possibility of deception.[36] It was not conclusive that the defendants had intended to derive some benefit from the choice of the name of an internationally famous drink. By way of contrast to the English *Lego*[37] case, one in Australia under the (wider) Trade Practices Act 1974 failed: *Lego Australia v Paul's*.[38] In South Africa, the device of a horse's head for jeans was not likely to cause deception when the plaintiffs used it for shoes, the word marks differing: *Searles Industrials v International Power Marketing*.[39] In Australia again, a dress shop and a restaurant were too dissimilar for there to be damage in *Cue Design v Playboy Enterprises*.[40] In *San Remo Macaroni v San Remo Gourmet Coffee*[41] an interlocutory injunction was refused, although pasta and coffee were not so far apart that the passing off case was unarguable. In Hong Kong, an American computer company failed to obtain an interlocutory injunction against a group proposing to rename itself eSun.com Holdings Ltd on expanding from hotel management and ownership into the fields of television and internet entertainment: *Sun Microsystems v Lai Sun Hotels International Ltd*.[42]

I. To Whom may the Misrepresentation be Made?

Prospective customers and ultimate consumers

5–92 The misrepresentation in passing-off is normally made to customers or ultimate consumers[43] of the goods or services in question. It is an interesting question whether the customers to consider are those of the claimant or the defendant. The relevant public is normally stated to consist of the actual or potential customers of the claimant, and this is consistent with the fact that only misrepresentations directed to them are likely to damage the claimant's goodwill. The claimant is much less likely to suffer from a misrepresentation made to a person who would never be likely to deal with him. Indirect customers, who buy the claimant's goods from intermediaries, are the claimant's customers just as much as those with whom the claimant actually deals. Ultimate consumers are important in cases such as *Hoffman-La-Roche v DDSA*,[44] where the only persons deceived were patients as opposed to doctors, pharmacists, or the NHS itself.

---

[35] (1979) 25 S.A.S.R. 321 (Supreme Court of South Australia, Full Court).
[36] *Cinzano (Francesco) & Cia (Australia) Pty Ltd v Ruggiero (No.2)* (1980) 25 S.A.S.R. 341 (Matheson J.).
[37] *Lego System A/S v Lego M Lemelstrich Ltd* [1983] F.S.R. 155 (Falconer J.).
[38] (1982) 60 F.L.R. 465; 2 T.P.R. 7; 42 A.L.R. 344.
[39] 1982 (4) S.A. 123 (Transvaal).
[40] (1982) 65 F.L.R. 383; 2 T.P.R. 412; 45 A.L.R. 535.
[41] [2000] F.C.A. 1842, 50 I.P.R. 321 (Goldberg J., Federal Court of Australia).
[42] [2000] 2 H.K.L.R.D. 616.
[43] *per* Lord Diplock in *Erven Warnink BV v J Townend & Sons (Hull) Ltd* [1979] A.C. 731; [1979] 2 All E.R. 927; [1980] R.P.C. 31, HL.
[44] [1969] F.S.R. 416, CA.

Conversely, though the relevant customers are normally retail customers or members of the consuming public, that is not essential. There is no reason in principle why liability for passing-off should not arise when goods are sold from one trader to another. This may be by virtue of the trade purchaser actually being deceived, or under the doctrine of instruments of deception which applies even (or perhaps especially) if the trade purchaser knows that the goods are counterfeit. Occasionally, as in *Scandecor Development v Scandecor Marketing*[45] no relevant misrepresentation occurs except in the transaction between wholesaler and retailer. In that case, the goods in question (posters) were purchased by consumers without any regard to their publisher, but retailers relied on the range and service provided by the defendants, who therefore owned the relevant goodwill in the name.

The definition of passing-off given by Lord Diplock in *Advocaat*[46] refers to the misrepresentation being made to prospective customers or consumers of the defendant's goods or services, rather than those of the claimant. There may, of course, be a large common pool of customers for whom the parties compete, and in that case the misrepresentation is necessarily made to potential customers of both. Nevertheless, there is a difference in emphasis, with Lord Diplock giving a slight restitutionary emphasis and reminding one that the defendant in a passing-off case is always concerned to benefit himself, so that misrepresentations to the claimant's customers are only made because they are potentially customers of his. In the typical case the question is probably academic. The misrepresentation is normally broadcast to the world at large.

In *Harrods v Harrodian School*[47] the trial judge was criticised in argument **5–93** for supposedly looking for evidence of confusion only among those members of the public who had enquired about sending their children to the defendants' school. The Court of Appeal[48] rejected the criticism on the facts, and put the question in terms of whether there would be "confusion among the common customers of the parties"—the broad section of the public for whom both parties catered in their different fields of business:

"In the course of argument before us the Judge was criticised for having considered only those members of the public who had made enquiry of the school with a view to sending their children there. It was submitted that he wrongly allowed himself to be influenced by the consideration that the choice of a fee-paying school for one's children is not an impulse purchase, and that a parent who was considering the Defendants' school for his children would be likely to make sufficient enquiries to eliminate any potential confusion that might otherwise occur. This would have been wrong, for the relevant public is not confined to parents who take up places at the school. The Plaintiffs and the Defendants appeal to a common section of the public—affluent members of the middle class who

---

[45] [1999] F.S.R. 26, CA.
[46] *Erven Warnink BV v J Townend & Sons (Hull) Ltd* [1979] A.C. 731; [1979] 2 All E.R. 927; [1980] R.P.C. 31, HL.
[47] [1996] R.P.C. 697, CA.
[48] Millet and Beldam L.JJ., Sir Michael Kerr dissenting.

live in London, shop at Harrods and wish to send their children to fee-paying schools. They are the persons who must be kept in mind when considering the likelihood of confusion."

Customers who do not pay for goods or services

5–94 There may be passing-off even though the retail customer or ultimate consumer does not pay for the goods or services in question, provided the claimant can still be said to suffer damage in some respect. In *OT v Cumming*[49] there was passing-off by substitution of one drink flavouring for another, both normally being given to the customer free on request. the substitution indirectly damaged the pursuers, because their trade customers would have purchased less from them.

National Health Service patients are not legally purchasers of the medicines they consume,[50] whether or not they pay a prescription charge. Nonetheless, an interlocutory injunction was granted in *Hoffman-La Roche v DDSA*[51] although it was common ground that doctors and pharmacists would not be deceived. It was sufficient that patients would be misled by the defendants' choice of get-up into supposing that the defendants' capsules were from the same reliable source that they were used to. Canadian law long insisted that in pharmaceutical get-up cases health care professionals were the only relevant consumers. However, in *Ciba-Geigy v Apotex*[52] the Supreme Court of Canada preferred *Hoffman-La Roche v DDSA* to a line of Ontario decisions and held that patients were to be included among the customers of pharmaceutical laboratories. They could influence the choice of drug prescribed or dispensed to them, and had a legitimate interest in knowing what they were being given.

5–95 Several cases have concerned newspapers and magazines which are distributed free, either door-to-door in the case of many local papers or on a controlled circulation basis for magazines. In this instance, the primary customers of the publication might be said to be advertisers, since it is from them that the publisher derives all his income. However, readers are consumers, and deception of them may also be relevant, not least because advertising rates depend on the size and quality of readership or circulation. The Court of Appeal has accepted that there is no difference in principle between periodicals funded wholly by advertising and those relying on sales or a mix of advertising and sales, with the proviso that advertisers are likely to exercise greater care and so are less likely to be confused than the general public.[53] As with all cases on titles of publications, the main issue tends to be lack of sufficient distinctiveness and the following cases are cited only to show that the absence of a cover price on either side or both is not a conclusive factor in its own right.

---

[49] (1915) 32 R.P.C. 69 (Lord Anderson, Court of Session).
[50] *Pfizer Corp v Ministry of Health* [1965] A.C. 512; [1965] 1 All E.R. 450; [1965] R.P.C. 284, HL.
[51] [1969] F.S.R. 416, CA.
[52] (1992) 95 D.L.R. (4th) 385; 44 C.R.R. (3rd) 289; 24 I.P.R. 652.
[53] *Management Publications Ltd v Blenheim Exhibitions Group plc* [1991] F.S.R. 550, CA.

Neylan v Toison[54] concerned confusion between competing local "throwaway" newspapers distributed free and in *Tamworth Herald v Thomson Free Newspapers*[55] the dispute was between an established paid title and a new free one in the same town. In *Management Publications v Blenheim Exhibitions Group*[56] and *Morgan-Grampian v Training Personnel*[57] the publications (which did not compete in either case) were controlled circulation magazines. In all these cases the plaintiffs might have lost advertising revenue, and were at least theoretically exposed to adverse comment or worse.

Similarly, television and radio broadcasting may not be charged for, but individual programs, and whole stations, have been the subject of passing-off actions. In *British Broadcasting Co v Talbot Motor Co*[58] the plaintiffs would not, apparently, have charged the public for the radio broadcasts they intended to make under the name *Carfax* but commercial support for it would have been placed in jeopardy. For passing-off by choice of a free-phone telephone number see *Law Society v Griffiths*.[59] In *Jian Tools for Sales v Roderick Manhattan Group*[60] Knox J. refused to disregard instances in which the plaintiffs' software had been given away free for review, since though these could not be described as sales to consumers, they were relevant to whether the plaintiffs had goodwill in the jurisdiction.

A fortiori, it cannot be conclusive that although the claimant charges for **5–96** his goods or services, the defendant gives his away for nothing,[61] provided the defendant can still be said to be a trader and damage results. In *Illustrated Newspapers v Publicity Services*[62] the defendants distributed free of charge to hotels copies of the plaintiff's magazines with their own advertisement supplement bound in. The plaintiffs may have gained a few sales but they stood to lose advertising revenue and might have been exposed to blame and even litigation in respect of what was advertised. Similar arguments prevailed in *Associated Newspapers v Insert Media*[63] where the defendants proposed to place advertising inserts in newspapers delivered to (and paid for by) individual subscribers at home. The latter decision is also interesting for holding that the relevant public consisted not only of the subscribers as such, but all readers of the papers in question including, for instance, family members. In *Associated Newspapers v Express Newspapers*[64] the publishers of the *Daily Mail* and the *Mail on Sunday* were awarded *quia timet* injunctions at trial against a giveaway London evening newspaper proposed to be launched as *The Mail*, the *Evening Mail*, or the *London Evening Mail*.

---

[54] [1983] 1 Qd. 600 (Williams A.J.).
[55] [1991] F.S.R. 337 (Aldous J.).
[56] [1991] F.S.R. 550, CA.
[57] [1992] F.S.R. 267 (Mummery J.).
[58] [1981] F.S.R. 228 (Megarry V.C.).
[59] [1995] R.P.C. 16 (Aldous J.).
[60] [1995] F.S.R. 924 (Knox J.).
[61] As in *Tamworth Herald Co Ltd v Thomson Free Newspapers Ltd*, above.
[62] [1938] Ch. 414; [1938] 1 All E.R. 321; 55 R.P.C. 172 (Crossman J.).
[63] [1991] F.S.R. 380, CA.
[64] [2003] EWHC 1322, (Laddie J.).

There may also be passing-off though the goods in question never pass to the customer, for instance because they are consumed in the provision of services. Such a case was *Sales Affiliates v Le Jean*[65] in which passing-off took place by substituting the defendants' hairdressing materials for those of the plaintiffs. The materials in question were cartridges which were heated by a chemical reaction to give a permanent wave and were then disposed of. As well as loss of sales to hairdressers, there was evidence that the defendants' product was inferior and could hurt the user's head.

Suppliers and the world at large

5–97 A trader may have goodwill with respect to his suppliers and others with whom he does business, although they are not his customers.[66] This goodwill is also protected by the action for passing-off against misrepresentations made to or received by suppliers and other non-customers. In many cases it is unnecessary to distinguish misrepresentations directed at customers and those directed at suppliers.[67] If, for instance, the misrepresentation arises from the defendant's choice of trading name then there is some potential for deception of anyone who deals with the business in any capacity, although it is to be expected that members of the general public will be less careful and more easily misled than other businesses.

There are also instances of misrepresentations being restrained, although they were only made to suppliers. The question first arose in its pure form in *Pullman v Pullman*[68] in which the parties competed in the leather trade. The defendant innocently but carelessly issued a circular to suppliers of raw skins in terms which suggested that his was the plaintiffs' business. Damage was particularly likely because the skins were in short supply. Lawrence J. found for the plaintiff but granted a declaration in lieu of an injunction as the defendant did not intend to continue. In *Woolworth v Woolworths (Australasia)*[69] the plaintiffs were the well-known chain stores. The defendants were associated with Australian chain stores of the same name, but their only activity in England was to purchase goods for the Australian company. They had no retail trade of their own here and they were accepted to have acted in good faith. Farwell J. granted a permanent injunction. The plaintiff and defendant were virtually in direct competition as purchasers, there was likely to be confusion between them, and damage might result. Similar conclusions were reached in the Hong Kong cases of *Penney v Penneys*[70] and *Penny v Punjabi Nick*.[71]

An argument that the House of Lords in *Advocaat*[72] had defined passing-

---

[65] [1947] Ch. 295; [1947] 1 All E.R. 287; 64 R.P.C. 103 (Evershed J.).
[66] *Home Box Office Inc v Channel 5 Home Box Office Ltd* [1982] F.S.R. 449 (Peter Gibson J.).
[67] *Ewing v Buttercup Margarine Co Ltd* [1917] 2 Ch. 1; [1916–17] All E.R. 1012; 34 R.P.C. 232, CA; *Chelsea Man Menswear Ltd v Chelsea Girl Ltd* [1987] R.P.C. 189, CA.
[68] [1919] 36 R.P.C. 240 (Lawrence J.).
[69] (1930) 47 R.P.C. 337 (Farwell J.).
[70] [1979] F.S.R. 29.
[71] [1979] F.S.R. 26.
[72] *Erven Warnink BV v J Townend & Sons (Hull) Ltd* [1979] A.C. 731; [1979] 2 All E.R. 927; [1980] R.P.C. 31, HL.

off in terms which excluded misrepresentations made to persons other than customers or consumers was rejected by the Court of Appeal in *Chelsea Man v Chelsea Girl*,[73] without citing any of the above cases. In that case the defendants' choice of name was mainly calculated to mislead retail customers, but deception of trade suppliers was relied on to justify a nationwide injunction.

Miscellaneous cases

Misrepresentations made to customers, ultimate consumers and suppliers do **5–98** not exhaust the categories recognised by passing-off. In *Music Corporation of America v Music Corp (Great Britain)*[74] the competing businesses were entertainment agencies. The misrepresentees were said to include artistes, impresarios and producers, rival agencies, writers of material and suppliers of props. In *Reed Executive v Reed Business Information*[75] competition between the claimants' traditional High Street recruitment agency and the defendants' website *totaljobs.com* existed both in respect of applicants for jobs ("candidates") and businesses with vacancies to fill ("clients", or advertisers on the website). Both services were free to candidates, and funded by charges to clients or advertisers. The claim for passing-off succeeded, even though evidence of actual or probable confusion and deception was effectively confined to candidates.

In *Morcambe & Heysham v Mecca*[76] the plaintiffs as organisers of the *Miss Great Britain* contest were unsuccessful on the facts, but the relevant misrepresentees would apparently have included entrants to beauty contests and spectators.

In *Newsweek Inc v British Broadcasting Corp*[77] one of the plaintiffs' arguments was that interviewees and other sources of news might mistake reporters from the defendants' programme for those of the plaintiffs. Walton J. refused to accept that this would be passing-off even if deliberate, but the Court of Appeal found for the defendants on purely factual grounds.

In *Law Society v Griffiths*[78] the relevant misrepresentees were victims of accidents or injuries who wished to contact the plaintiffs' referral scheme which had the telephone number 0500 192939. The defendant firm of solicitors were restrained from using the number 0800 192939. Both numbers were free to callers, and in the case of the Law Society the result of a call was that the caller was referred to a member of the Society's personal injury panel.

In *Irvine v Talksport*[79] a publicity flier distributed to potential advertisers on the defendants' radio station gave the false impression that the station

---

[73] [1987] R.P.C. 189. CA.
[74] (1947) 64 R.P.C. 48 (Wynn-Parry J.).
[75] [2002] EWHC 1015, [2003] R.P.C. 12 (Pumfrey J.).
[76] [1966] R.P.C. 423 (Buckley J.).
[77] [1979] R.P.C. 441. CA.
[78] [1995] R.P.C. 16 (Aldous J.).
[79] [2002] EWHC 367; [2002] 1 W.L.R. 2355; [2002] 2 All E.R. 424; [2002] E.M.L.R. 32; [2002] F.S.R. 60 (Laddie J.), affirmed in part [2003] EWCA Civ 423; [2003] 2 All E.R. 881; [2003] E.M.L.R. 26; [2003] F.S.R. 35, CA.

was to be publicly endorsed by the claimant, Eddie Irvine, a motor racing driver. Damages of £2,000 were awarded, increased to £25,000 on appeal.

J. WHO IS LIABLE FOR PASSING-OFF?

Primary liability and "instruments of deception"

5–99 Primary liability for passing-off can accrue only to traders in their capacity as such,[80] but there has been very little express discussion as to what capacity a trader must fill in order to be liable. The classic definition of passing-off in terms of a misrepresentation made to customers or consumers is applicable without difficulty only to retailers. Businesses higher up the chain of distribution, such as manufacturers or importers, are, however, liable for passing-off in their own right under a doctrine known as "instruments of deception".[81] In its most basic form, this states that primary liability for passing-off attaches to the business actually responsible for goods which are inherently likely to deceive ultimate purchasers or consumers. The tort is complete when the defendant parts with possession of the deceptive goods, although actual deception of customers with consequent damage to the claimant may not occur until later, or not at all. The fact that the liability of the manufacturer or importer of deceptive goods arises independently of the possible existence of passing-off at retail level demonstrates that the doctrine is independent of that of joint tortfeasorship.

The doctrine of instruments of deception potentially has to deal with all the various parties who may be involved in the chain by which goods reach the consuming public. Working backwards, it is clear that the doctrine normally has no implications for the retailer selling direct to the public. He is liable, or not, according to whether his own customers are deceived. Goods may be inherently deceptive, but if he can dispose of them without misrepresentation he does not commit the tort of passing-off. This may not be likely in practice, but in theory a prominent and credible disclaimer could suffice.[82] At the other end of the chain, there has been little express discussion of what capacity the defendant must fulfil in order to be liable. It is suggested that at the very least liability without fault attaches to the person responsible for first putting the inherently deceptive goods into circulation, whether a manufacturer or an importer, and, in all probability, to distributors, wholesalers[83] and others through whom the goods reach the retailer. Traders performing essentially ministerial functions such as printers, carriers and warehousemen are probably not liable in the absence of a

---

[80] *per* Lord Diplock in *Erven Warnink BV v J Townend & Sons (Hull) Ltd* [1979] A.C. 731; [1979] 2 All E.R. 927; [1980] R.P.C. 31, HL. See Section G above.
[81] See Section K below.
[82] *Draper v Trist* [1939] 3 All E.R. 513; 56 R.P.C. 429, CA.
[83] *Omega, Louis Brandt et Frere SA v African Textile Distributors* 1982 (1) S.A. 951 (Transvaal).

common design, but they can be compelled to surrender deceptive goods under the equitable protective jurisdiction.

Liability as joint tortfeasor

As part of the general law of tort, liability for passing-off is not confined to **5–100** whoever is directly responsible for committing the offending act. Anyone of whom it can be said that he procured the wrongful act, or that he was engaged in a common design with the primary wrongdoer, may be liable as a joint tortfeasor. However, it is not sufficient to prove that the latter merely facilitated the commission of the tort by the former. The leading cases (both of them in the context of copyright infringement) are now *CBS v Amstrad*[84] and *MCA Records v Charly Records*,[85] with the latter also re-stating the position of directors and controlling shareholders. Liability as joint tort-feasor should be distinguished from that for civil conspiracy, which is a nominate tort in its own right.[86]

The general law of joint tortfeasorship does require one qualification in relation to passing-off. In the context of patent infringement, for instance, it is settled law that even knowingly selling materials which will be used to infringe does not make the vendor liable for infringement, unless there is a closer relationship giving rise to liability as a statutory contributory infringer or as a common law joint tortfeasor.[87] However, in passing-off there is strict liability for supplying inherently deceptive "instruments of deception" even in the absence of any intention that they will be used to mislead. This source of liability, which may co-exist with that as joint tortfeasor, or under the "equitable protective jurisdiction," is discussed in the following Section.

Individual defendants: directors, officers and proprietors

Relatively few modern passing-off cases deal expressly with the personal **5–101** liability of individual defendants such as the directors and proprietors of corporate defendants, so it is probably safest to follow decisions in respect of other intellectual property torts or from the general law, the leading authority now being *MCA Records v Charly Records*.[88] After a lengthy review of the authorities, Chadwick L.J. proposed the following four-point analysis governing liability as a joint tortfeasor, with particular regard to the liabilities of company directors:

> "First, a director will not be treated as liable with the company as a joint tortfeasor if he does no more than carry out his constitutional role in the governance of the company—that is to say, by voting at board meetings.

---

[84] [1988] 1 A.C. 1013; [1988] R.P.C. 567, HL.
[85] [2001] EWCA Civ 1441; [2002] E.M.L.R. 1; [2002] F.S.R. 26, CA, see below.
[86] For unsuccessful allegations of conspiracy in a passing-off action see *Jarman & Platt Ltd v I Barget Ltd* [1977] F.S.R. 260, CA.
[87] *Townsend v Haworth* (1879) 48 L.J. Ch. 770, CA.
[88] [2001] EWCA Civ 1441; [2002] E.M.L.R. 1; [2002] F.S.R. 26, CA.

That, I think, is what policy requires if a proper recognition is to be given to the identity of the company as a separate legal person. Nor, as it seems to me, will it be right to hold a controlling shareholder liable as a joint tortfeasor if he does no more than exercise his power of control through the constitutional organs of the company—for example by voting at general meetings and by exercising the powers to appoint directors. Aldous L.J. suggested in *Standard Chartered Bank v Pakistan National Shipping Corporation (No. 2)* ... that there are good reasons to conclude that the carrying out of the duties of a director would never be sufficient to make a director liable. For my part, I would hesitate to use the word 'never' in this field; but I would accept that, if all that a director is doing is carrying out the duties entrusted to him as such by the company under its constitution, the circumstances in which it would be right to hold him liable as a joint tortfeasor with the company would be rare indeed. That is not to say, of course, that he might not be liable for his own separate tort, as Aldous L.J. recognised at paragraphs 16 and 17 of his judgment in the *Pakistan National Shipping* case.

Second, there is no reason why a person who happens to be a director or controlling shareholder of a company should not be liable with the company as a joint tortfeasor if he is not exercising control though the constitutional organs of the company and the circumstances are such that he would be so liable if he were not a director or controlling shareholder. In other words, if, in relation to the wrongful acts which are the subject of complaint, the liability of the individual as a joint tortfeasor with the company arises from his participation or involvement in ways which go beyond the exercise of constitutional control, then there is no reason why the individual should escape liability because he could have procured those same acts through the exercise of constitutional control. As I have said, it seems to me that this is the point made by Aldous J. (as he then was) in *PGL Research Ltd v Ardon International Ltd* ...

Third, the question whether the individual is liable with the company as a joint tortfeasor—at least in the field of intellectual property—is to be determined under principles identified in *C.B.S. Songs Ltd v Amstrad Consumer Electronics Plc* ... and *Unilever Plc v Gillette (U.K.) Limited* ... In particular, liability as a joint tortfeasor may arise where, in the words of Lord Templeman in *C.B.S. Songs v Amstrad* ..., the individual 'intends and procures and shares a common design that the infringement takes place'.

Fourth, whether or not there is a separate tort of procuring an infringement of a statutory right, actionable at common law, an individual who does 'intend, procure and share a common design' that the infringement should take place may be liable as a joint tortfeasor. As Mustill L.J. pointed out in *Unilever v Gillette*, procurement may lead to a common design and so give rise to liability under both heads.

In the light of the authorities which I have reviewed I am satisfied that no criticism can be made of the test which the judge applied. But, in my view, the test can, perhaps, be expressed more accurately in these terms: in order to hold Mr Young liable as a joint tortfeasor for acts of copying, and of issuing to the public, in respect of which CRL was the primary infringer and in circumstances in which he was not himself a person who committed or participated directly in those acts, it was necessary and sufficient to find that he procured or induced those acts to be done by CRL or that, in some other way, he and CRL joined together in concerted action to secure that those acts were done."

MCA Records v Charly Records[89] was followed by the Court of Appeal in **5–102** the passing-off case of *Premier Luggage and Bags v Premier Co*,[90] with the result that the individual defendant would not have been a joint tortfeasor had the finding of passing-off not been reversed. *Asprey & Garrard v WRA (Guns) Ltd and Asprey*[91] was decided without citation of *MCA Records v Charly Records* but is probably consistent with its reasoning, The second (individual) defendant was a joint tortfeasor with the first (corporate) defendant, even though it could not be said that the latter was merely his *alter ego*: he had set the company up, owned 70 per cent of its shares, was its chairman and managing director, and had expressly chosen the name *Asprey* (which was subsequently changed) to identify himself as its boss. He was enjoined from procuring or procuring the company to engage in passing off. A *quia timet* injunction against the personal defendant trading on his own account was discharged, ostensibly because the circumstances in which he might do so were inadequately defined. The injunctions against the company and the individual director as joint tortfeasor were upheld.

A special category of case exists in which the defendant company is no more than a shell, entirely under the control of the individuals who caused it to be incorporated. In *Glaxo v Glaxowellcome*[92] Lightman J. granted interlocutory mandatory injunctions requiring the promoters of the defendant company to change its name, and Laddie J did likewise in *Direct Line Group Ltd v Direct Line Estate Agency Ltd*.[93] Both decisions were approved by the Court of Appeal in *British Telecommunications v One in a Million*.[94]

K. INSTRUMENTS OF DECEPTION

Introduction

It is passing-off for a trader to put into circulation goods which are inher- **5–103** ently likely to deceive ultimate purchasers or consumers, even though the immediate purchasers may be middlemen who are not themselves deceived and even though the middleman may ultimately dispose of the goods in a

---

[89] [2001] EWCA Civ 1441; [2002] E.M.L.R. 1; [2002] F S.R. 26, CA.
[90] [2002] EWCA Civ 387, [2002] E.T.M.R. 69; [2003] F.S.R. 5, CA.
[91] [2002] F.S.R. 30 (Jacob J.) affirmed [2001] EWCA Civ 1499; [2002] E.T.M.R. 47; [2002] F.S.R. 31, CA.
[92] [1996] F.S.R. 388 (Lightman J.).
[93] [1997] F.S.R. 374 (Laddie J.).
[94] [1999] 1 W.L.R. 903; [1998] 4 All E.R. 476; [1999] E.T.M.R. 61; [1999] F.S.R. 1, CA.

manner which does not deceive anyone at all. The tort is complete when the defendant parts with possession of the deceptive goods, though actual damage to the claimant may not occur until later, if at all. However, a defendant is not responsible for additional misrepresentations made by dishonest dealers unless he knew or intended that those misrepresentations would be made. If the goods tell a lie about themselves then liability is absolute. If they do not, then liability depends at the very least on the defendant's knowledge or intention that they will be used deceptively.

> "[N]o man is entitled to represent his goods as being the goods of another man; and no man is permitted to use any mark, sign or symbol, device or other means, whereby, without making a direct false representation himself to a purchaser who purchases from him, he enables such purchaser to tell a lie, or to make a false representation to somebody else who is the ultimate consumer ... [H]e must not, as I said, make directly, or through the medium of another person, a false representation that his goods are the goods of another person."[95]

5–104   The doctrine of instruments of deception has to distinguish the following situations:

1. Goods which are inherently deceptive in that they carry indicia so close to what is distinctive of the claimant that they are bound to deceive unless specific remedial measures are taken. There is strict liability on the part of the supplier, even if he acted innocently and even if no passing-off at retail level actually takes place. The tort is complete when the inherently deceptive goods are put into circulation, with the consequence that the supplier is immediately liable to an injunction, an account of profits, and at least nominal damages.

2. Goods which would not deceive unless the retailer was responsible for a further misrepresentation of his own, but which are still close enough to those of the claimant in their distinctive features for this to be facilitated. It may be assumed that if the defendant supplies goods which just fall short of being inherently deceptive intending that they will be passed off by retailers then he will be liable, but it is unclear whether this is under the doctrine of instruments of deception or that of joint tortfeasorship. Logically, the latter is to be preferred.

3. Liability for supplying deceptive labels, wrappers, packets and the like seems to depend on the degree of initiative and complicity on the part of the supplier. Whether any liability is under the doctrine of instruments of deception or that of joint tortfeasorship is unclear. Logically, the latter is again to be preferred. As a separate matter, the supplier of such deceptive materials is subject to a number of equi-

---

[95] *per* James L.J. in *Singer v Loog* (1880) 18 Ch.D. 395, CA affirmed (1882) 8 App.Cas 15, HL, and approved by Lord Macnaghten in *Reddaway (Frank) & Co Ltd v George Banham & Co Ltd* [1896] A.C. 199; [1895–9] All E.R. 313; 13 R.P.C. 218, HL.

table duties under a doctrine known as the "equitable protective jurisdiction". The latter has an entirely separate legal basis to liability for passing off, but in its practical application partially overlaps with that of instruments of deception.

4. There is no primary liability for passing-off arising from supplying staple commercial products even if it is known that they will be used for passing off. These are not instruments of deception. There will be secondary liability for joint tortfeasorship if the supplier has a common design with a person actually liable for passing off as such.

5. Finally, the doctrine has been extended to "instruments of deception" which are not tangible goods at all such as company names and internet domain names.

The theory and its applicability

Without the doctrine of instruments of deception, the tort of passing-off **5–105** goods would hardly ever be committed except by a retailer. The doctrine is therefore at the heart of almost every action brought against a manufacturer, importer or wholesale dealer in infringing goods. Despite this, the doctrine has received specific consideration in relatively few cases and is not well integrated with the theoretical basis of the tort. Two problems always arise. The first is that a disposal of deceptive goods to a trade purchaser does not cause any immediate damage to the claimant unless the trade purchaser himself was deceived, which is not normally the case. The Court of Appeal in *Draper v Trist*[96] attempted to justify this by saying that the very prospect of spurious goods entering the market is damage enough, but this seems contrived and would cause complications in other areas. The second is that no misrepresentation is necessarily involved in the transaction between the two traders. Dishonest traders may deliberately buy counterfeit goods: if so, they are not deceived. Honest traders may be taken in by counterfeit goods, but are likely to be too experienced and astute to be deceived by less comprehensive imitations of mark or get-up which the general public would not distinguish from the claimant's. This may even reach the point where a trader can distinguish the defendant's goods from the claimant's so readily that he honestly but wrongly believes the public would not be confused.

Even if it can be said that the goods are making a misrepresentation about themselves (which is not always the case), the misrepresentation is an immaterial one if the purchaser is not deceived, and one returns to the objection that actual damage to the claimant is no more than a contingent possibility. In due course it may be assumed that the deceptive goods will be exposed to the public, but it is well established that in this context the tort of passing-off may be complete long before the deceptive goods are offered for retail sale. Thus, a defendant may be compelled to account for his profits on all deceptive goods supplied to trade customers, notwithstanding that a proportion of the goods would have been disposed of subsequently in a

[96] [1939] 3 All E.R. 513; 56 R.P.C. 429, CA.

manner which did not deceive the ultimate customers. There is also passing-off in England if deceptive goods are exported, even though any misrepresentation and consequent damage occurs abroad.

The doctrine of instruments of deception therefore requires the definitions of passing-off given by Lord Diplock or Lord Fraser in *Advocaat*[97] to be read in the light of two qualifications. The tort of passing-off may be complete even though no damage has yet occurred and no misrepresentation has yet been made. It is easy to understand what the problem is and how the common law has approached it, but difficult to define the solution in a few simple words. Part of the answer lies in defining passing-off in terms of a misrepresentation calculated to cause damage, rather than treating cases where damage has yet to occur as *quia timet*. As well as that, the putting into circulation of inherently deceptive goods is effectively deemed to be a misrepresentation in its own right, even before any purchaser is deceived.

5–106   Because liability for issuing inherently deceptive goods is immediate and absolute, the doctrine of instruments of deception cannot be regarded merely as the general law of joint tortfeasorship applied to passing-off, although the two are often likely to go together. However, in all that follows it should be borne in mind that invocation of the doctrine of joint tortfeasorship by the claimant is a relatively modern innovation, roughly dating from the 1970s.[98] Until 1935,[99] the doctrine was highly disadvantageous to the plaintiff, since obtaining judgment against one joint tortfeasor released all the others, even if the judgment was never satisfied—and potential defendants in passing-off actions tend both to be numerous, and more likely than most to be insubstantial, or skilled at hiding their assets. It is therefore not surprising that plaintiffs chose to emphasise that different defendants in the chain of distribution were committing separate torts, for which they were individually liable, and that judges should not have questioned this, if only because of the unfamiliarity of regarding the doctrine as a sword rather than a shield. Now that the former disadvantages of alleging joint tortfeasorship have long since been removed, and the doctrine is well established in all branches of intellectual property law, it is suggested that it provides, albeit retrospectively, a means of bringing a certain amount of coherence to the various cases not involving complete and inherently deceptive goods.

Goods inherently deceptive

5–107 The law regarding inherently deceptive goods is clear. There is strict liability for putting into circulation goods which bear indicia sufficiently close to those distinctive of the claimant for deception to take place when those goods reach the market. It is no defence that the supplier may act honestly and innocently, nor that his immediate customers may not be deceived.

---

[97] *Erven Warnink BV v J Townend & Sons (Hull) Ltd* [1979] A.C. 731; [1979] 2 All E.R. 927; [1980] R.P.C. 31, HL.
[98] The evolution of the doctrine in traced in *MCA Records Inc v Charly Records Ltd* [2001] EWCA Civ 1441; [2002] E.M.L.R. 1; [2002] F.S.R. 26, CA.
[99] Law Reform (Married Women and Tortfeasors) Act 1935, s.6.

"It has long ago been pointed out in decided cases that it is not upon the *mala mens* towards the first purchaser that the decision of these cases rests. The first purchaser buys the goods cheaper for the very purpose of being able to sell them as *Glenfield Starch*, the means of doing so being put in his hands by his being furnished with goods with this label—I will not say in order that he will deceive, but it is a necessary consequence that he is enabled to deceive others by this means.[1]

"[N]o man, however honest his personal intentions, has a right to adopt and use so much of his rival's established trade mark as will enable any dishonest trader, into whose hands his own goods may come, to sell them as the goods of his rival."[2]

The doctrine was taken to its logical conclusion (and perhaps beyond) in a **5–108** series of cases on liability when goods bearing the plaintiff's name, mark or get-up were sold to middlemen. The cases that follow show the consequences of treating passing-off either in terms of property in a trade mark as such, or in terms of fraud. Both are obsolete, but the results have undoubtedly survived into modern law.[3] *Sykes v Sykes*[4] had decided that the defendant was liable for marking power flasks and shot-belts *Sykes Patent* and selling them to dealers for resale as the plaintiff's goods. In *Edelsten v Edelsten*[5] and *Ford v Foster*[6] the respective defendants were ordered to account for all their profits on goods carrying the plaintiff's mark sold to middlemen.[7] In *Lever v Goodwin*[8] the defendant was found liable for imitating the get-up, but not the name, of the plaintiff's soap. The Court of Appeal, following *Edelsten v Edelsten*, rejected an argument that the account of profits claimed by the plaintiff should be limited by reference to the proportion of soap eventually sold to those customers who thought it was the plaintiff's:

"[T]he whole gist of the complaint against [the defendant] is 'you have sold a weapon calculated to be used fraudulently by the middlemen'; and the profit for which they must account is the profit which they have made by the sale of soap in that fraudulent dress to the middlemen. It is immaterial how the latter deal with it. If they find it to their benefit not to use it fraudulently, but to sell the soap to the purchasers from them, as *Goodwin's*, that cannot affect the question whether the sale by the

---

[1] *per* Lord Hatherley L.C. in *Wotherspoon v Currie* (1872) L.R. 5., H.L. 508, HL.
[2] *per* Lord Watson in *Johnston v Orr-Ewing* (1882) 7 App.Cas., HL.
[3] *My Kinda Town Ltd v Soll* [1983] R.P.C. 15 on the account of profits; *British Telecommunications plc v One in a Million Ltd* [1999] 1 W.L.R. 903; [1998] 4 All E.R. 476; [1999] E.T.M.R. 61; [1999] F.S.R. 1, CA.
[4] (1824) 107 E.R. 834 (Abbott C.J.).
[5] (1863) 46 E.R. 72 (Lord Westbury L.C.).
[6] (1872) L.R. 7 Ch. 611, CA.
[7] Note that in *Ford v Foster*, above, the mark had largely ceased to be distinctive in the trade.
[8] [1887] 36 Ch.D. 1; 4 R.P.C. 492, CA.

defendants to those middlemen of this soap in a fraudulent dress was a wrongful act."[9]

5–109 References to fraud and similar expressions in the preceding cases should be taken in their historical context. This was before passing-off was recognised as protecting a property right in the plaintiff's goodwill. In *Weingarten v Bayer*[10] the House of Lords awarded an account of profits on all corsets disposed of by the defendants to the trade in boxes bearing the plaintiff's distinctive "scroll", although there can be no doubt that the vast majority of retail sales were made on the strength either of the defendants' own enormous reputation or that of the descriptive term *Erect Form* which they were free to use. More recently still, *Lever v Goodwin* was followed by the Court of Appeal in *Draper v Trist*.[11] Lord Greene confirmed that the tort was complete when the offending goods were sold to the middleman.

> "The defendant in a passing-off action has in the normal case, the simple case, sold a quantity of deceptive goods. Those goods he may have sold direct to a member of the public, the ultimate purchaser, or he may have sold them to a middleman who is himself going to sell them to members of the public, or perhaps to some other trader who, in turn, deals directly with the public. The defendant has therefore put upon the market and sent into the market a quantity of goods which on the face of them, and *ex hypothesi*, are saying something about themselves which is calculated to mislead. That is the very gist of the conception of passing-off."

Lord Greene went on to identify three categories of middlemen: those who did not realise confusion was likely and who would therefore take no special precautions to prevent it; those who would foresee confusion and take steps to make sure it did not take place; and those who would fail to do so because they intended to benefit from the possibility of confusion. The defendant's liability did not, in principle, depend on which category his trade customers fell into. What happened after the goods left his hands was relevant only to the measure of damages, and that would be the same whether a particular dealer fell into the first category or the third.

Goods potentially deceptive

5–110 It is important, though not always easy, to draw a line between goods which are calculated to deceive—those which tell a lie about themselves—and those which may lend themselves to dishonest use but which require a "little additional lever" of falsehood if they are to be passed off.[12] Normally, in the latter case, the situation is that the defendant's indicia are not close enough to those of the claimant to deceive in their own right, but are close enough

---

[9] *per* Cotton L.J. in *Lever v Goodwin* [1887] 36 Ch.D. 1; 4 R.P.C. 492, CA.
[10] [1904–7] All E.R. 877; (1903) 22 R.P.C. 341, HL.
[11] [1939] 3 All E.R. 513; 56 R.P.C. 429, CA.
[12] The phrase comes from *Brinsmead (John) & Sons Ltd v Brinsmead & Waddington & Sons Ltd* (1913) 30 R.P.C. 493, CA, where it was coined by Buckley L.J.

for there to be passing-off by substitution or express misrepresentation if retailers are so minded. The "additional lever" can take other forms. In South Africa there was passing-off by selling watches marked *HOMEGAS*[13] with the clear intention that retailers should open the glass and obliterate the first and last letters.

There are hardly any goods in existence which cannot be used in a deceptive manner by someone determined to do so. Where the claimant relies on the possibility of dealers deliberately passing the defendant's goods off as his it is necessary for him to prove at least:

1. That such deception by dealers is likely to occur on a significant scale in practice: "I cannot assume all vendors to be knaves, any more than I can assume all purchasers to be simpletons"[14];

2. That the defendant is contributing to it in some way beyond merely supplying goods which could equally well be used innocently; and

3. That he intended, or at least knew, that his goods were to be used dishonestly.

The cases make it clear that there is at least a risk of liability if these are **5–111** made out. What is less clear is whether the liability is as a primary tortfeasor responsible for passing-off in one's own right, or as a secondary infringer jointly liable under the doctrine of joint tortfeasorship for the acts of passing-off committed by the retailers. The authorities are inconsistent and neither explanation fits them all. The problem with the first is that, if true, it would create an exception to the rule that the cause of action in passing-off never depends on the defendant's state of mind. An anomaly of this magnitude is to be avoided if at all possible. It would be more logical to say that if goods are not inherently deceptive then their ultimate supplier is liable as a joint tortfeasor or not at all. This would be consistent with the most recent authority, which is *Cadbury v Ulmer*,[15] but the cases as a whole do not consciously adopt joint tortfeasorship as the test and some appear to set the standard of liability rather lower.

Examples

In *Payton v Snelling Lampard*[16] the House of Lords, affirming the Court of **5–112** Appeal, rejected the plaintiffs' argument that although the coffee tins of the

---

[13] *Omega, Louis Brandt et Frere SA v African Textile Distributors* 1982 (1) S.A. 951 (Transvaal). The defendant was a wholesaler, and his liability was treated in the same way as for a manufacturer. *Singer Manufacturing Co v Loog* (1882) 8 App.Cas. 15, HL and *John Walker & Sons Ltd v Henry Ost & Co Ltd* [1970] 1 W.L.R. 917; [1970] 2 All E.R. 106; [1970] R.P.C. 489 followed.
[14] *per* Joyce J. in *Horlicks Malted Milk Co v Summerskill* (1915) 33 R.P.C. 1 affirmed (1916) 34 R.P.C. 63, HL.
[15] [1988] F.S.R. 385 (Falconer J.). The test applied is that there is absolute liability if and only if the goods carry a "badge of fraud", but it is clear that the term is used in the sense of a feature of name, mark or get-up inherently likely to deceive.
[16] [1901] A.C. 308; 17 R.P.C. 628, HL.

parties could readily be distinguished, dishonest retailers could substitute the defendants' when the plaintiffs' coffee was asked for. It was said of the defendants' tin that the grocer "could wrap it up in paper and put his hand over it" but there was no reason to suppose retailers would be fraudulent in this way, and, if any were, it was through no fault of the defendants who had done all that could reasonably be expected to prevent it.

In *Brinsmead v Brinsmead and Waddington & Sons*[17] the plaintiffs were well known piano manufacturers. The personal defendant was a member of the same family and went into the business himself, but his pianos were inferior, cheaper, and aimed at a different market. He marked his pianos with his full name in a different style of lettering to that used by the plaintiffs. Despite this, there was evidence that they were passed off as those of the plaintiffs by dishonest dealers. The Court of Appeal held that he was not liable for the fact that his goods were being used to deceive. Vaughan Williams L.J. said that it was the lies of the dealers which had caused the passing-off, and that the fraud was committed not because, but in spite of, his name being on the pianos. The other two members of the Court did not disagree in principle but found for the defendant on the narrow ground that he had not been fixed with notice of the frauds being carried out by retailers. *Brinsmead v Brinsmead* is therefore inconclusive as to what element is required to make the defendant liable for supplying goods which are passed off by dishonest customers. The answer may well depend on how close the goods come to being inherently deceptive in their own right. It is clear that the Court of Appeal would have found against the defendant if he had intended his pianos to be passed off as those of the plaintiff and it is possible that mere notice that they were being used in that way would have sufficed.

In *Lee Kar Choo v Lee Lian Choon*[18] the defendant copied the plaintiff's labels closely enough to enable substitution, but not so closely that the labels on their own were liable to deceive. The differences were such that a claim for infringement of the plaintiff's registered trade mark failed. Two retailers admitted deliberately passing the goods off to less astute customers. There was no doubt that the defendant had acted dishonestly and the Privy Council found against him on the issue of passing-off.

5–113   The doctrine of instruments of deception is clearly inapplicable if the goods will only come to the attention of the public in a form which has no deceptive significance at all. In *Apollinaris Co v Duckworth*[19] the defendants sold salts from which an imitation of *Apollinaris Water* could be prepared. The plaintiffs argued that the salts reconstituted with water could be passed off as *Apollinaris Water*, but the Court of Appeal held that the defendants were not liable for this possibility. Even if the label on the defendants' goods could be said to be deceptive, it would never come to the attention of the customer buying made-up water. *In Star Cycle v Frankenbergs*[20] *Star* for cycles was distinctive of the plaintiffs. They argued that by selling *Midland Star* cycles to retailers the defendant was putting an instrument of fraud in

[17] (1913) R.P.C. 493, CA.
[18] [1967] 1 A.C. 602; [1966] 3 All E.R. 1000, PC.
[19] (1906) 23 R.P.C. 540, CA.
[20] (1907) 24 R.P.C. 405, CA.

their hands. However, the defendant's cycles were not marked with those words, which would never come to the attention of the public. The defendant used them only in his price lists, which circulated in the trade, and trade advertisements. Retailers could not be deceived. His motives were not beyond suspicion but there was no liability for passing-off.

> "[The defendant] does not attach to the articles which he sells to the trade anything by way of description of mark which in any way assists his purchaser to mislead the public as to the articles they are buying from the person who has bought from the defendant. I agree that if he makes misrepresentations to the purchaser, or if he puts into the hands of the purchaser a weapon to enable him to mislead the public there is a ground for an injunction. Neither of those circumstances exists here."[21]

Exports of deceptive goods

When deceptive goods are exported from England liability can arise under **5–114** two heads. Under the doctrine of instruments of deception the tort of passing-off is complete when deceptive goods are exported from or disposed of in England, even though they may be destined for a foreign market. It is necessary to prove that the goods are such as would deceive ultimate purchasers in that market. The claimant must therefore prove that his mark (*etc.*) is distinctive in that market and that the defendant's conduct is calculated to deceive there. These are purely relevant as matters of fact: the claimant does not have to prove that the defendant's conduct infringes any local law. As an entirely separate matter, there may also be liability under the relevant foreign law, as the applicable law for the purposes of the Private International Law (Miscellaneous Provisions) Act 1995.[22]

The origin of liability for exporting instruments of deception in modern law may be taken as the decision of the House of Lords in *Johnston v Orr-Ewing*.[23] The plaintiffs were a firm with a considerable business in exporting yarn to India and Aden. The defendants copied the plaintiffs' label for yarn exported by them to the same market. The House of Lords granted an injunction and an account of profits. That the goods of both parties were exported was significant only in that the plaintiffs had to prove distinctiveness and likelihood of deception in the relevant foreign markets. There was no mention of local law or of private international law principles. The case was treated as raising exactly the same legal issues as in cases such as *Wotherspoon v Currie*,[24] in which a manufacturer disposed of deceptive goods to retailers within the jurisdiction.

Following *Johnston v Orr-Ewing*, cases involving the export of goods **5–115** marked or got up in a deceptive manner became so routine that many refer

[21] *per* Buckley L.J.
[22] See Chapter 10.
[23] (1882) 7 App. Cas. 219, HL. *The Collins Co v Brown, Collins v Cohen* (1857) 69 E.R. 1174 are earlier but their reasoning, based solely on fraudulent intent, is obsolete and they contributed little to how the law developed.
[24] (1872) L.R. 5 H.L. 508, HL.

only in the most incidental manner to the fact that England was not the relevant market. Examples are *Wilkinson v Griffith*[25] where French polish was exported to India; *Reddaway v Banham*[26] where the plaintiffs' industrial belting was apparently exported to many countries, but the crucial evidence of fraud related to India; candles exported to Morocco in *Price's Patent Candle Co v Ogston & Tennant*[27]; pens to various South American markets in *Perry v Hessin*[28] and sweets to the United States in *Tavener Rutledge v Specters.*[29] In *George Ballantine v Ballantyne*[30] passing-off of whisky was found in England, but not, on the facts, abroad. The rationale behind these cases, though not often stated explicitly, is that liability for passing-off is complete at the latest upon the defendant exporting from England goods which will deceive in the foreign market. The tort has been committed by the time the goods leave England, and English law therefore governs.

In Scotland, confirmation that liability for the export of deceptive goods arises under the law of the place from which the goods are exported is to be found in *William Grant v Glen Catrine Bonded Warehouse.*[31] On an interim motion to strike out the part of the claim dealing with exports Lord Abernethy rejected the defenders' argument that liability arose, if at all, under the former double actionability rule of *Phillips v Eyre*[32]; and ruled that the pursuers did not have to plead or prove that the defenders' conduct would have been actionable in any of the numerous jurisdictions to which they exported and where the pursuers claimed, in general terms, to have a goodwill to protect. At trial, the Lord Ordinary found that the defenders were liable for passing off their gin and vodka as the produce of the pursuers both in Scotland and abroad, and these findings of fact were not challenged on appeal. Before the Inner House, the defenders renewed the argument that they should not be interdicted from exporting to any countries where the applicable law did not prevent them from passing off their sprits as those of the pursuers. The Inner House dismissed the argument quite briefly[33]: interdicts in this form had been granted for over a century, and there were no cogent reasons for departing from the practice. The legal basis for the complaint was not that the defenders were passing off their goods in overseas territories that might know no such law, but that a tort had been committed in Scotland which was complete even before the goods were exported. There was no need to consider whether a wrong would have been

---

[25] (1891) 8 R.P.C. 370 (Romer J.).

[26] [1896] A.C. 199; [1895–9] All E.R. 313; R.P.C. 218, HL.

[27] (1909) 26 R.P.C. 797 (Lord Johnston, Court of Session).

[28] (1912) 29 R.P.C. 509, CA. The action failed on the facts.

[29] [1959] R.P.C. 355, CA.

[30] [1959] R.P.C. 273, CA.

[31] *William Grant v Glen Catrine Bonded Warehouse (No.1)* was an unsuccessful interim application to strike out the claim in so far as it related to exports: 1995 S.L.T. 936 (Lord Abernethy, Outer House); *(No.2)* at trial (Lord Cameron, August 18, 1999, unreported); *(No.3)* on reclaiming motion to the Inner House 2001 S.C. 901; 2001 S.L.T. 1419 (Inner House).

[32] (1870) L.R. 6 Q.B. 1.

[33] Citing the second edition of the present work and approving the interim judgment of Lord Abernethy, 1995 S.L.T. 936.

committed in the foreign market. An argument that the interdict contravened Art.29 (formerly 34) of the EC Treaty (in so far as exports to the European Union were affected) was also dismissed.

Incautious printers, suppliers and agents

The doctrine of instruments of deception as it is normally understood **5–116** imposes liability on traders who release deceptively marked goods into circulation. The question then arises of whether the concept is wide enough to cover not just complete merchandise as it will be sold to end users, but labels, packages and the like which carry indicia which will eventually deceive. Relatively few passing-off actions have involved printers, packaging suppliers or similar third parties who find themselves involved in passing-off directed by another. Although the authorities are not entirely consistent, it is suggested that the concept of instruments of deception only covers goods which are substantially complete and ready to be released into circulation. Wrappers, labels, containers and packaging, even if they carry the claimant's marks, ought not to be regarded as instruments of deception in their own right. On this analysis, the supplier of such items is not liable for passing-off as such but only for joint tortfeasorship with his customer if he knew of the use of which the material would be put and shared with him a common design to infringe. As a separate matter, even innocent possessors of such material may be compelled to surrender it under the equitable protective jurisdiction. *A fortiori*, there should be no primary liability in passing-off for supplying goods such as the salts in *Apollinaris Co v Duckworth*[34] which may perhaps be used for passing-off irrespective of any indicia they may bear.

The best starting point is probably the decision of the Court of Appeal in **5–117** *Paterson Zochonis v Merfarken.*[35] Printers were instructed by a fraudulent third party to make up cartons and leaflets in imitation of those used by the plaintiffs for their *Venus de Milo* skin cream. The third party must have been guilty of passing-off. As against the defendant printers the plaintiffs claimed for copyright infringement and for negligence in that the defendants supposedly owed a duty of care to the plaintiffs which had been broken by failing to enquire as to the purpose to which the cartons and labels would be put. The plaintiffs claimed to be able to recover, as damages under one or both of these heads, the loss they had suffered from the passing off committed by the third party. The Court of Appeal struck out all of the statement of claim except for the bare allegation of copyright infringement. On the claim that the defendants were liable in damages for the passing off committed by the third party, the Court held that to supply materials for incorporation into an infringing article was tortious only in extreme cases, not including the present one. There was no general obligation upon a trader to satisfy himself that goods supplied by him would not be used to facilitate some dishonest purpose.

---

[34] (1906) 23 R.P.C. 540, CA.
[35] [1983] F.S.R. 273, CA.

Paterson Zochonis v Merfarken was followed by Falconer J. in *Cadbury v Ulmer*[36] where the defendants successfully applied to strike out a statement of claim based on their supplying to middlemen bars of chocolate which retailers could pass off as *Cadbury's Flake* bars. It is also consistent with dicta of Harman J. in *Saper v Specter's*[37] in which he doubted if the manufacturers of sweet boxes said to resemble those of the plaintiffs would have been liable even if the first defendants, their customers, had not won the action on the issue of confusion. In *Stringfellow v McCain*[38] at first instance Whitford J. dismissed the action against the first defendants' advertising agents, saying he was at a loss to understand why they had been joined. The justification advanced was that they were said to have acted as principals in booking television time for a deceptive advertisement. The Court of Appeal did not address the issue because they found for the first defendants on the merits.

Printers, suppliers and agents (2)

5–118   There are some cases which might have imposed more stringent liability on the suppliers of deceptive labels or containers. Most of these have involved the practice of exporting Scotch whisky to countries where it will be mixed with local spirit and sold as genuine Scotch. However, it is convenient to begin with a dictum of Cotton L.J. in quite different circumstances.

"[I]f a man does that, the necessary consequence of which (although it does not deceive the person with whom he deals, and is therefore no misrepresentation to him) is to enable that other person to deceive and pass off his goods as somebody else's, for that he is answerable. But this is confined to those things which in their necessary or natural uses accompany the things sold. For instance, the corks of *Champagne* marked '*Moet & Chandon*' must be in the bottles sold, and must accompany the bottles. They must necessarily accompany the thing to the retail buyer, and so must labels to be put on the bottles. The very reason for their existence is that they must be put on the bottles, and, if they are deceptive and fraudulent, then the person who prepares them is answerable for it."[39]

This was cited in *John Walker v Douglas McGibbon*[40] as if it meant that the suppliers of the corks or labels were liable in their capacity as such, but it is doubtful if this is what Cotton L.J. intended. His purpose must have been to compare the behaviour of *Loog* to a familiar and uncontroversial situation,[41] and it is suggested he had in mind the liability of the person who caused the

[36] [1988] F.S.R. 385 (Falconer J.).
[37] (1953) 70 R.P.C. 173 (Harman J.), distinguishing *Farina v Silverlock* (1855) 69 E.R. 560 reversed (1856) 43 E.R. 1214; (1858) 70 E.R. 270.
[38] [1984] R.P.C. 501 reversed *ibid.*, CA.
[39] *Singer Manufacturing Co v Loog* (1880) 18 Ch.D. 395 affirmed (1882) 8 App.Cas. 15, HL *per* Cotton L.J., distinguishing the facts of the case before him in which the defendant used the name *Singer* only on his trade price lists which would never come to the attention of the public.
[40] [1975] R.P.C. 506 (Lord Avonside, Court of Session).
[41] As James L.J. did in the passage quoted above.

labels to be printed, the bottles to be filled and corked, and the whole assemblage to be released into circulation. This was the interpretation implicitly given to the passage in *John Walker v Henry Ost*[42] where Foster J. quoted it and went on to say that none of the cases cited to him had dealt with liability arising before the mark was affixed to the article sold.

Of the older cases, the few express authorities which would have imposed **5–119** liability do not take the matter much further. In *Guinness v Ullmer*[43] (which is very briefly reported) an injunction was granted against the engravers of blocks from which counterfeit labels had been printed.[44] The defendants appear to have been innocent. In *Farina v Silverlock*[45] a complicated series of cases ended with an injunction being granted against a printer who had printed copies of the labels on the plaintiff's *Eau de Cologne* bottles and offered them to all and sundry. There was a slight legitimate market for re-labelling genuine bottles which had lost their labels, but the case probably turned on the fact that the defendant asserted a right to continue doing so despite knowing that they would be used fraudulently. In *British Telecommunications v One in a Million* Aldous L.J. approved and explained the reasoning of the latter:

> "Trade mark infringement and passing off was alleged in *Farina v Silverlock* (1855) 1 K. & J. 509. Sir William Page Wood V.C. explained the law on trade marks and passing off. He went on to point out that the defendants, when they sold the offending Eau de Cologne labels, had made it clear to the purchasing retailers that they were produced by them and not by the plaintiff. Thus no misrepresentation was made to the retailers; they were not deceived. However an injunction was granted against the defendants. Sir William Page Wood V.C. said, at p. 516:
>
> > 'But if it be stated that the defendant is manufacturing that which is known to be the trade mark which the plaintiff alone has the right to use, and the use of which on the goods of a third party would be a fraud upon the plaintiff; and that the defendant is selling such labels to anyone who asks for them, and is thus scattering over the world the means of enabling parties to commit frauds upon the plaintiff, and that such frauds have been committed; that is, I think, a sufficient averment to entitle the plaintiff to an injunction. The ground of the jurisdiction being fraud, if the defendant be committing fraud, either by selling goods under the plaintiff's trade mark, or enabling others to do so by

---

[42] [1970] 1 W.L.R. 917; [1970] 2 All E.R. 106; [1970] R.P.C. 489 (Foster J.).

[43] (1847) 10 L.T. O.S. 127.

[44] In *British Telecommunications plc v One in a Million Ltd* [1999] 1 W.L.R. 903; [1998] 4 All E.R. 476; [1999] E.T.M.R. 61; [1999] F.S.R. 1, CA, Aldous L.J. treats *Guinness v Ulmer* as an early case of unregistered trade mark infringement, rather than passing-off in the modern sense. Another old case, *Jameson v Johnston* (1901) 18 R.P.C. 259 (Ireland), is hard to understand. The short judgment lacks proper reasoning and may have turned on infringement of the plaintiff's registered marks. It is so treated in *British Telecommunications v One in a Million*.

[45] (1855) 69 E.R. 560 reversed (1856) 43 E.R. 1214; (1858) 70 E.R. 270. Page-Wood V.C. granted an interlocutory injunction but it was discharged on appeal by Lord Cranworth L.C. until the plaintiff established his right at law. He obtained nominal damages from a jury and the defendant was refused a new trial. Finally, Page-Wood V.C. granted a permanent injunction.

distributing the means of doing so, it cannot be said that this court has no power to interfere by injunction to arrest the evil at its source, without compelling the plaintiff to wait until the whole fraud is brought to a completion by the sale of the goods.'

The defendant might have been a joint tortfeasor with the retailers, but Sir William Page Wood V.C. indicated that an injunction was appropriate even where the fraud was to be committed by another person. He said the jurisdiction was based on fraud and an injunction would be granted to, *inter alia*, prevent the defendant from enabling passing off.

The injunction in *Farina's* case was dissolved on appeal ((1856) 6 De G.M. & G. 214), but was followed by a trial at which the jury found for the plaintiff. The plaintiff renewed his application for an injunction before Sir William Page Wood V.C. and the injunction was granted in its original form."

5–120   *John Walker v Henry Ost*[46] itself involved the supply by one defendant to Ecuador of malt whisky, bottles, labels and cartons, knowing the whisky would be adulterated with local spirit and sold in the deceptive containers. Before turning to the argument that there was any breach of Ecuadorian law, Foster J. held that a tort had been committed in England by selling those goods knowing the whisky would be adulterated and sold in those containers as Scotch. No tort under English law would have been committed if the same goods had been sold for export without the supplier knowing they would be used deceptively. This cannot be joint tortfeasorship, because Foster J. had yet to decide that a tort had been committed in Ecuador. The reasoning is that the established doctrine of complete goods as instruments of deception should be extended to fit the facts of the case, but at the cost of making the defendant's state of mind an essential element of the cause of action.

John Walker v Douglas McGibbon[47] virtually duplicated the facts and result of the previous case. It is reported on what would have been, in England, an application to strike out the statement of claim as disclosing no cause of action. This was rejected but the reasoning does not mark any advance on *John Walker v Henry Ost*. It amounts to saying that it is tortious under Scottish law to do any acts in Scotland which result in another party doing in Honduras what would be passing-off if done in Scotland, but is not even alleged to be illegal where done. *White Horse Distillers v Gregson*[48] did go one step further, but that step has subsequently been disapproved.[49] The plaintiffs argued that the defendants were liable, as a matter of the English law of passing-off, for exporting bulk malt whisky to Uruguay without taking precautions to see that it was not used deceptively in the country of destination. Nourse J. rejected such a wide submission, but described the bulk whisky as an "inchoate instrument of deception" for the export of

---

[46] [1970] 1 W.L.R. 917; [1970] 2 All E.R. 106; [1970] R.P.C. 489 (Foster J.).
[47] [1975] R.P.C. 506 (Lord Avonside, Court of Session).
[48] [1984] R.P.C. 61 (Nourse J.).
[49] In *British Telecommunications plc v One in a Million Ltd*, below.

which the defendant could be made liable in appropriate circumstances. If the defendant not only supplied the goods, but played a part in their deceptive marketing abroad, he had committed a tort in England.

"Suppose, for example, a case where the English exporter has told the foreign importer exactly how to set up deceptive sales of the admixture. It cannot be the law that the English exporter will escape liability simply because he does nothing except export the Scotch whisky. If he exports if with the intention that the admixture shall be sold in a deceptive manner, it is immaterial that he has been responsible neither for the printing and production of the deceptive labels and cartons, nor for their actual implication in the sale of the liquor in the foreign country. In that state of affairs the whisky, being intended to facilitate the deceptive sales, is itself, if you like, an inchoate instrument of deception."

There are two possible explanations for the short line of authorities from **5–121** *John Walker v Henry Ost* to *White Horse Distillers v Gregson*. One is that *mala fides* on the part of the supplier can turn goods of any description into instruments of deception in the eyes of the law, even if the goods cannot deceive on their own and require a major intervention by a third party if there is ultimately to be passing off in fact. Not only that, but the so-called "passing off" for which the supplier is thus made liable need not be illegal where it takes place. This, however, is so inconsistent with the general law of passing-off that it is suggested that it cannot be correct. The better view is that liability in these circumstances depends on the supplier being a joint tortfeasor with his customer. This is how *White Horse Distillers v Gregson* was understood, and its wider invocation of "inchoate" instruments of deception rejected, by the Court of Appeal in *British Telecommunications v One in a Million*[50]:

"The conclusion reached by Nourse J. in the *White Horse Distillers* case was probably based upon his view that the defendants were part of a common design to pass off and therefore were joint tortfeasors. It would be wrong to hold that the whisky as such was an instrument of fraud and therefore its sale to Ecuador could be restrained."

Likewise, the decision of Chitty J. in *Lever v Goodwin*[51] was to be understood in the same way[52]:

"I believe, when Chitty J. referred to the 'means of deceiving the ultimate purchaser,' he had in mind a name or a get-up which made a false representation. That was the instrument of fraud. He could not have contemplated that a manufacturer of goods which did not themselves make a false representation was liable for the fraud of a retailer. For

[50] [1999] 1 W.L.R. 903; [1998] 4 All E.R. 476; [1999] E.T.M.R. 61; [1999] F.S.R. 1, CA.
[51] (1887) 4 R.P.C. 492, affirmed [1887] 36 Ch.D. 1; 4 R.P.C. 492, CA.
[52] *per* Aldous L.J., above.

example a wine producer cannot be liable for passing off if a waiter covers a bottle with a cloth and serves it as champagne when it is not."

Intangibles as instruments of deception

5–122   In the general law of passing-off, it is suggested above that the doctrine of instruments of deception in its classic form unambiguously applies in one situation only, namely to finished merchandise which is ultimately destined to be released into retail trade and which bears indicia which are inherently likely to deceive. If this be thought too restrictive, then a similar doctrine may also apply (though much more uncertainly) to two further situations: first, to the supply of components for such merchandise which bear deceptive indicia, but which are not yet in a marketable state; and secondly, to the supply of goods which require a "little additional lever of deception" if they are to deceive. The former category covers liability for supplying incomplete but deceptive goods or counterfeit labels and the like which have not yet been applied to goods. In all these cases the "instruments of deception" are tangible things which will in due course pass to the purchaser, who is justifiably assumed to buy them by mistake for the goods of the claimant. In both the latter cases, but not in the first, liability depends to some undefined extent on the defendant's state of mind.

Following the decision of the Court of Appeal in *British Telecommunications v One in a Million*,[53] there now appears to exist another branch to the doctrine, under which the "instrument of deception" or "instrument of fraud" may be something entirely abstract or intangible, provided that it possesses a sufficiently proprietary character to be capable of assignment, at least in an informal sense, and provided also that it embodies matter which is distinctive of the claimant, so that its use by a third party would or might amount to passing-off. Such distinctive matter is most likely to consist of a name or trade mark, though there is no theoretical reason to confine the discussion to such cases.

It will be noticed that the original doctrine had little or no application to something, such as the benefit of an internet domain name, or even a company name, which was not tangible, and which never passed to the ultimate customer or consumer. Registration and transfer of such a name may be the means by which a fraud is carried out or facilitated, but if the name is to be treated as an "instrument of deception" or an "instrument of fraud" then this is in an extended sense rather than the established one. It may also be noted that the two doctrines contemplate entirely different life cycles for the alleged instrument of deception: in the classic form the goods which constitute the instrument of deception ultimately pass to a purchaser or consumer who may be assumed to have bought them because he had been deceived by the name or get-up they bear. In the extended form, the intangible instrument of deception may pass from one trader to another but is never an object of retail commerce in its own right. Like a brass plate

---

[53] [1999] 1 W.L.R. 903; [1998] 4 All E.R. 476; [1999] E.T.M.R. 61; [1999] F.S.R. 1, CA.

bearing a false name, it is simply one means under which a deceptive trade may be conducted.

Internet domain names and *One in a Million*

The facts of *British Telecommunications v One in a Million*[54] were that the **5–123** defendants[55] made a practice of registering internet domain names corresponding to the corporate names or trade marks of well known companies, and subsequently offering those names for sale to the same companies at an extortionate price, with the implicit (and in some cases explicit) threat that they would otherwise be offered for sale on the open market. Six plaintiffs in all[56] sued for passing-off (and trade mark infringement) and obtained summary judgment.[57]

The defendants appealed, without success. In the Court of Appeal, Aldous L.J. concluded his review of the authorities:

"In my view there can be discerned from the cases a jurisdiction to grant injunctive relief where a defendant is equipped with or is intending to equip another with an instrument of fraud. Whether any name is an instrument of fraud will depend upon all the circumstances. A name which will, by reason of its similarity to the name of another, inherently lead to passing off is such an instrument. If it would not inherently lead to passing off, it does not follow that it is not an instrument of fraud. The court should consider the similarity of the names, the intention of the defendant, the type of trade and all the surrounding circumstances. If it be the intention of the defendant to appropriate the goodwill of another or enable others to do so, I can see no reason why the court should not infer that it will happen, even if there is a possibility that such an appropriation would not take place. If, taking all the circumstances into account the court should conclude that the name was produced to enable passing off, is adapted to be used for passing off and, if used, is likely to be fraudulently used, an injunction will be appropriate.

It follows that a court will intervene by way of injunction in passing off cases in three types of case. First, where there is passing off established or it is threatened. Second, where the defendant is a joint tortfeasor with another in passing off either actual or threatened. Third, where the defendant has equipped himself with or intends to equip another with an instrument of fraud. This third type is probably a mere *quia timet* action."

The remainder of the present section examines the theoretical justification **5–124** for treating internet domain names as "instruments of fraud" or "instruments of deception" and the potential consequences of this development for

---

[54] above.

[55] The company One in a Million Ltd, the two individuals who controlled it, and two other firms (Global Media Communications and Junic) through which they conducted business.

[56] British Telecommunications plc and Telecom Securicor Cellular Radio Ltd, Virgin Enterprises Ltd, J Sainsbury plc, Marks and Spencer plc and Ladbroke Group plc.

[57] [1998] F.S.R. 265 (Jonathan Sumption Q.C., Deputy Judge).

the tort in general.[58] For present purposes the result in *British Tele-communications v One in a Million* is assumed to be based on the finding that that in all five cases the defendants' attempts at extortion were only credible, and the charges asked for the domain name registrations only worth con-templating paying, on the assumption that the defendants were willing to dispose of the names to fraudulent third parties who would use them for actual passing off.

From this point of view, the *One in a Million* case demonstrates what might be thought of as a development or synthesis of two separate doctrines which have been known individually since the late nineteenth century. The first is the classic doctrine of "instruments of deception", considered above, with the proviso that the latter had never unambiguously been applied to intangibles, nor even to tangible things which would not ultimately pass to the consumer. The company name cases are at most ambiguous exceptions to the first of these propositions, and to the second not at all. The appli-cation of the old doctrine to the new situation was expressly conceded by counsel for the defendants in the *One in a Million* case itself, thereby reducing the authority of that decision in its most wide-ranging aspect. Secondly, under an entirely separate nineteenth century doctrine known as the "equitable protective jurisdiction" a person in possession of goods which would infringe the rights of another if they were released, might be enjoined from parting with possession of them except to the rightful owner or right-holder. In the twentieth century, the latter doctrine had been extended to compel innocent holders of information to disclose it in order to allow right-holders to pursue infringers or notify purchasers or counterfeit goods.[59]

Unfortunately, the synthesis attempted in the *One in a Million* case is an incomplete one, and important practical consequences turn on precisely which of these doctrines accounts for what parts of the actual result. It may be noted that although the two doctrines may overlap in fact, they have entirely separate legal bases: the classic doctrine of instruments of deception was and is an integral and essential part of the tort of passing off in both its legal and equitable aspects; whereas that of the equitable protective jur-isdiction is a purely equitable doctrine, giving rise to no remedy in damages, and existing independently of any specific intellectual property right which might be infringed.

The problems of *One in a Million* ...

5–125 Taking *British Telecommunications v One in a Million*[60] at face value, two sets of problems arise. The first are purely practical: how far does the decision apply beyond its actual facts—a certain kind of intangible (internet domain names highly distinctive of third parties) being offered to sale to all

[58] For the specific context of "cybersquatting" and a more detailed treatment of the facts see Chapter 8, section J. There was also a finding of actual passing off by registration of ownership of the names, which the present section does not address.

[59] The leading case is *Norwich Pharmacal Co v Customs and Excise Commissioners* [1974] A.C. 133; [1973] 2 All E.R. 943; [1973] F.S.R. 365; [1974] R.P.C. 101, HL.

[60] [1999] 1 W.L.R. 903; [1998] 4 All E.R. 476; [1999] E.T.M.R. 61; [1999] F.S.R. 1, CA.

and sundry by unscrupulous and hypocritical defendants? The second set of questions is theoretical: to what extent did liability in that case depend on any of four possible bases: actual passing off arising from the registration as such; actual or incomplete passing off by making, keeping and offering "instruments of fraud"; *quia timet* liability under one of the previous headings; or the equitable protective jurisdiction? Joint tortfeasorship might have been relevant in other circumstances, but may be eliminated on the facts of *One in a Million* since none of the names concerned had been transferred to any third party.

The major theoretical question left open by *One in a Million* is the standard of liability to apply to defendants who are honest, but who through ignorance, carelessness, or inadvertence engage in practices which are objectively equivalent to those practised by the *One in a Million* defendants, though without being so thoroughly and obviously tainted with fraud and extortion. It is a recurring problem for passing-off that since the cause of action is supposed to be entirely independent of the defendant's state of mind, there is rarely any opportunity to apply different standards to fraudulent, negligent, or entirely innocent defendants.

A second major question is that once the concept has been recognised, the **5–126** categories of intangible instruments of deception are potentially very much broader than internet domain names. The reasoning in *One in a Million* incorporated a short series of cases on corporate names, retrospectively providing them with a previously unstated and perhaps unrecognised rationale. These decisions on company names provided the only category of supposed "instruments of fraud" which did not involve tangible goods, and to that extent their importance to the reasoning of *One in a Million* is considerable. The problem of internet domain names may be a recent one, but company names are as old or older than passing-off itself, and at first sight the principle of *One in a Million* might equally well seem applicable to such things as old-fashioned telegraphic addresses, phone numbers, and registered business names, and above all to registered trade marks or service marks.

Related to both these questions is whether the *One in a Million* doctrine applies only to household names of supposedly universal distinctiveness, or to those and a scarcely less distinctive second tier, or to every kind of name, mark or sign with which passing-off may be concerned, provided that it is distinctive in fact.

These three problems and others may be illustrated by asking whether the **5–127** lead plaintiff in the *One in a Million* case might itself have been liable for passing off in the following situations, neither of which is hypothetical. In *Law Society v Griffiths*[61] it was British Telecom who provided the defendant with the telephone number 0800 192939 which was confusingly similar to the plaintiffs' number 0500 192939. In *Easyjet v Dainty*[62] the offending domain name *easyRealestate.co.uk* had been obtained by the defendant from British Telecom who also "made available"—it is not clear in precisely

---

[61] [1995] R.P.C. 16 (Aldous J.).
[62] [2002] F.S.R. 6 (Bernard Livesey Q.C., Deputy Judge).

what sense—the individual web page designer who was responsible for the offending get-up of the defendant's site. In the first case, British Telecom certainly had the means of knowing that the defendant's 0800 number might deceive, though they would have been unusually alert to notice that it would do so in fact. In the second, British Telecom can hardly have been ignorant of the existence of the *easyJet* group and its diversified businesses, and might be thought rather naïve not to have foreseen a least the possibility of a claim.

Whether as a matter of justice or social policy, it hardly seems appropriate to impose liability on the likes of British Telecom in either of these two cases, but if the number 0800 192939 and the domain name *easy-Realestate.co.uk* are calculated to deceive, as they are, then are they not both "instruments of deception" in the extended sense of the *One in a Million* case?–And if suppliers of such instruments of deception are to be liable for passing off without any requirement of knowledge or intent (which is undeniably the case in the general law, so far as tangible complete instruments of deception are concerned) then why not British Telecom in these cases?

... and the "instruments of fraud" approach

5–128 A possible answer to this conundrum is that the Court of Appeal contemplated a distinction between fraudulent suppliers of "instruments of fraud" and innocent suppliers of deceptive matter to be categorised under another name and in less pejorative terms. If so, then by calling the case one of "instruments of fraud", the Court of Appeal gave itself two superficial but essentially specious benefits. First, once the domain names in question had been assimilated to tangible instruments of fraud, and once it had been accepted that the defendants intended them as marketable commodities, then there may have seemed to be an almost entirely orthodox route to holding that the tort of passing-off was indeed made out on at least a *quia timet* basis even though the domain names had not yet been used in any trade, had deceived no one, and had not yet (nor would perhaps ever) cause damage to the relevant plaintiff. Though the Court of Appeal was prepared to go much further, there was no logical need for it to do so: treat a domain name in the same way as a bottle of Ecuadorian whisky labelled *Scotch* and the rest follows. Secondly, in a case described and analysed as one of "instruments of fraud" it may seem self-evident that the defendant's subjective intent is, exceptionally for passing-off, highly relevant.

There are serious problems with this analysis. First, for the reasons given above, it requires a major extension of the doctrine of instruments of deception so as to apply to intangibles of any kind, a rule of liability which had previously only attached to tangibles of a particular kind. Secondly, it misunderstands what is meant by "instruments of fraud." These were originally so called in the nineteenth century either because their ultimate disposal would (or might) constitute a fraud on the public, or because certain pre-Judicature Act authorities turned on the defendant persisting in his conduct after notice. However, by the end of the nineteenth century neither the name nor the nature of the doctrine required that any party higher up the chain of distribution than the retailer should be motivated by fraudulent intent. The doctrine applied with equal severity to the fraudulent and the innocent: "[N]o man, *however honest his personal intentions*, has a right to adopt and use so much of his rival's established trade mark as will enable any dishonest trader, into whose hands his own goods may come, to sell them as the goods of his rival".[63] It is a complete *non sequitur* to equate liability under the doctrine with fraud in the sense of personal dishonesty of the person made liable.

A distinction which might conceivably be invoked at this point is between **5–129** *complete* instruments of deception, for the supply of which liability is absolute and independent of intent; and *incomplete* ones, for which it might be said that liability depends on the intention that they should be used or completed in such a way as to deceive. Incomplete instruments are represented both by complete goods which require a little additional lever of deception to deceive, and by deceptive components such as counterfeit labels not yet made up into marketable goods. It is only in the case of incomplete instruments of deception (in either sense) that there is scope for a mental element to enter. If one supposes that a domain name is more analogous to an incomplete instrument of deception, then one may have a basis for saying that the supplier of the name is liable only if fraudulent. However it is very far from certain that there is a doctrine of liability for fraudulently intended incomplete instruments of deception at all. If there is, it is an anomalous one, based on a small number of inadequately reasoned and barely compatible decisions, which are susceptible to more satisfactory explanations.

Unfortunately, the judgment of the Court of Appeal does not expressly distinguish between the categories of instrument, referring to them equally as "instruments of fraud". In logic, there are two criteria by which domain names might be analogised to tangible instruments of deception. On one analysis, deceptive domain names would always be assimilated to incomplete instruments of deception because the existence of the name in the abstract requires at least one more intervention to turn a threat of passing-off into passing off in fact, namely activating a website under the disputed name. On the other analysis, the question is whether there is a legitimate alternative use for the domain name, other than by the claimant: if so, then one examines the state of mind of the holder of the name, so as to render him liable if he intends to use the name in a deceptive manner or to permit another to do so; if there is no such alternative then liability is strict. The analysis is confused by two factors: the conclusion that in the case of the *marksandspencers* names at least mere registration amounted to actual passing off irrespective of whether the names were up for sale or not, and the obvious untenability of the defence of aggrieved innocence for any of the *One in a Million* examples.

This attempt by the *One in a Million* defendants at invoking what might have been a perfectly valid distinction on appropriate facts obscures a more fundamental question, which is whether an intangible such as a domain

---

[63] *per* Lord Watson in *Johnston v Orr-Ewing* (1882) 7 App.Cas., HL, emphasis added.

name (or, to give more familiar examples, a registered company name or a registered trade mark) can ever be an "instrument of deception" in the technical sense at all. Since the point was expressly conceded by the defendants the Court of Appeal can hardly be blamed for proceeding on that basis, but it is perhaps the least satisfactory aspect of the decision.

Conclusion: what are "instruments of deception"?

5–130   It is suggested that the only unambiguous application of the doctrine of instruments of deception is to complete goods which are inherently deceptive in their own right, and that the supplier of those goods is strictly liable for putting them into circulation, regardless of his state of mind. In the more authoritative of the older cases on instruments of deception the defendant always issued or dealt in complete and fully packaged goods. Deception was always likely to arise from a name, mark or get-up which was already emblazoned on the goods when they left the defendant's hands.

In the case of goods which require that "little additional lever" of falsehood if they are to deceive, it is clear that the supplier is not liable if he acted innocently. Rather than create an exception to the rule that the defendant's state of mind cannot influence *prima facie* liability for passing-off, it is suggested that such goods are better not regarded as instruments of deception at all. If the supplier intended them to be passed off at retail level and that occurs in fact then liability can be attributed to him on the basis of joint tortfeasorship.

5–131   Difficult questions arise when the alleged instruments of deception in the state in which they leave the defendant are far from being ready to put on the market in a form which will inevitably deceive. This can involve labels, containers and the like bearing the claimant's indicia, or unmarked goods which could equally well be used innocently. The issue is not just that of the defendant's customers possibly making an additional misrepresentation when the goods are retailed: it is those customers who assume responsibility for making marketable goods up in a deceptive manner in the first place. It is suggested that the two situations may raise different issues. Where labels or containers are concerned there may seem to be an obvious analogy with inherently deceptive instruments of deception, but that would be inconsistent with the best modern authority, which is *Paterson Zochonis v Merfarken*.[64] The most satisfactory approach to cases of this kind would probably be to treat them as an aspect of the equitable protective jurisdiction, meaning that the claimant would have a right to delivery up of the deceptive materials regardless of the defendant's state of mind, but that no damages would be awarded except on the basis of actual passing off or joint tortfeasorship.

When it comes to materials which have no inherent capacity to deceive, such as the bulk whisky in *White Horse Distillers v Gregson*, it is suggested that Aldous L.J. was correct to say in *British Telecommunications v One in a*

---

[64] [1983] F.S.R. 273, CA.

Million[65] that the doctrine of instruments of deception is wholly inapplicable. The answer to the rhetorical question put by Nourse J. is that if the scheme is illegal where it is carried out there will be liability on the basis of joint tortfeasorship.

So far as intangibles such as domain names are concerned, and not- **5–132** withstanding *British Telecommunications v One in a Million*,[66] it is submitted that the doctrine is once again inapplicable. The doctrines of joint tortfeasorship and the equitable protective jurisdiction provide adequate protection without requiring any unorthodox and potentially dangerous extension to the scope of passing-off as such. Under the doctrine of joint tortfeasorship, a defendant who knowingly participates in passing off by others will be jointly liable with those others. Under that of the equitable protective jurisdiction, even an innocent defendant may be compelled to surrender tangibles or intangibles to the extent necessary to prevent or redress infringement of the claimant's rights. There is neither any need, nor any legitimate basis, for extending the doctrine of instruments of deception to this case.

A final point on "instruments of deception" is that the phrase is a term of art. In its classic usage, the "instrument" invariably consists of compete goods (or, more questionably, components for such goods) which will in due course pass to the consumer. In either case, it is essential that the "instrument" should be released into channels of commerce so that the relevant "deception" is the actual passing off which occurs at the final retail sale. A business which is carried on fraudulently will very probably make extensive use of other things, tangible or intangible, which are useful or essential in practising the fraud or evading detection. Some of them, such as printing plates, may even embody the claimant's name, mark or sign. All these might be said to be instrumental to the success of the deception which is ultimately practised on the consumer, and all of them may properly be the subject of an order for destruction or delivery up, but they are not "instruments of deception" in the technical sense.

L. THE TIME FACTOR

Start of conduct complained of

As a matter of law, the relevant date for deciding whether the conduct of the **5–133** defendant amounts to passing-off is the date on which that conduct commenced.[67] The claimant must therefore prove that on that date he had goodwill in the jurisdiction and that the defendant was guilty of making (or

---

[65] [1999] 1 W.L.R. 903; [1998] 4 All E.R. 476; [1999] E.T.M.R. 61; [1999] F.S.R. 1, CA.
[66] above.
[67] *Cadbury Schweppes Pty Ltd v Pub Squash Co Pty Ltd* [1981] R.P.C. 429; [1981] 1 All E.R. 213, PC; *Anheuser-Busch Inc v Budejovicky Budvar NP* [1984] F.S.R. 413, CA; *Chocosuisse Union des Fabricants Suisses de Chocolat v Cadbury Ltd* [1999] R.P.C. 826, [1999] E.T.M.R. 1020, CA.

threatening) a misrepresentation which would cause damage. In the normal passing-off action this means that the name or mark relied on by the claimant must have become distinctive of the claimant—or as it is often put, have a reputation—before the date on which the defendant commences the conduct complained of.

Needless to say, the conduct complained of must mean the whole course of the defendant's conduct and not just that of which the claimant was aware or chose to plead. In *Daimler Chrysler v Alavi*,[68] the claimants failed to prove that the defendant's trade in fashion clothing under the name *Merc* was recently commenced (or a recent revival of a sporadic, discontinuous business from the past), with Pumfrey J. holding that trading under the *Merc* name had been continuous since at least as early as 1985, without there being any misrepresentation then or subsequently, so that the action was bound to fail.

5–134   If any of these criteria is not met, then it cannot matter that at a later date the claimant may have generated goodwill or that the claimant may have rendered the mark distinctive of himself.[69] In particular, it is not sufficient for the claimant to have goodwill and reputation at the date the writ is issued if those came into existence too late. *Dicta* giving importance to the date of commencement of proceedings must be taken as overruled by *Cadbury-Schweppes v Pub Squash Co* and being inconsistent with basic principles.[70] *A fortiori*, there is no room for any concept by the name of "future goodwill", meaning the goodwill the claimant might generate as a result of what is supposed to be legitimate and logical expansion of the existing business.[71] That is not to say that a claimant cannot succeed in relation to activity by the defendant in a field in which he does not presently trade, but his cause of action depends entirely on whether such goodwill as he already has stands to suffer damage, and it is irrelevant whether he would or might expand into the field of the controversy, or would avoid it completely.

It would not appear to be necessary for the conduct complained of to cause immediate damage, as, in any case, it would immediately be actionable *quia timet*. More difficult questions arise as to whether even a *quia timet* action can ever lie before the claimant has generated the necessary goodwill and reputation. On general principles the answer would appear to be no.[72] The claimant must have a subsisting right to protect, and the defendant must be threatening conduct which would be actionable if started immediately.

5–135   In *Barnsley Brewery Co Ltd v RBNB*[73] a dispute arose as to whether the

---

[68] [2001] R.P.C. 42 (Pumfrey J.).

[69] *Licensed Victuallers Newspaper Co v Bingham* (1888) 38 Ch.D. 139, CA.

[70] Except in *quia timet* actions. In *Saville Perfumery Ltd v June Perfect* (1941) 58 R.P.C. 147, HL the writ was taken as the date, but nothing turned on it.

[71] *Teleworks Ltd v Telework Group plc* [2002] R.P.C. 27 (Christopher Floyd Q.C., Deputy Judge).

[72] *Teleworks Ltd v Telework Group plc* [2002] R.P.C. 27 (Christopher Floyd Q.C., Deputy Judge). *Elida Gibbs Ltd v Colgate Palmolive Ltd* [1983] F.S.R. 95 may be an exception, but it is hard to account for the result.

[73] [1997] F.S.R. 462 (Robert Walker J.).

relevant date was in March 1995 (when the defendants' solicitors notified the plaintiffs that they intended to market *Barnsley Bitter* at some indeterminate time in the future) or at the end of 1996 when launch of the defendants' beer was imminent. Robert Walker J. held that a *quia timet* action in 1995, relying only on the letter and two trade mark applications, would have been premature. The relevant date was late 1996, and the plaintiffs were therefore entitled to rely on an additional 20 months trading and advertising. This is preferable to the Irish *Kilkenny*[74] case in which the date of incorporation of the non-trading defendant was taken as determinative, but the plaintiffs had ample (if predominantly recent) trade to support goodwill even at the earliest date.

In *Teleworks v Telework Group*[75] the business of the claimant company was small (having 0.001 per cent of the market), local to North London, and largely confined to the activities of domain name registration, web site and email hosting, computer network infrastructure and general IT support, mostly for small businesses. An argument that it could pray in aid future expansion which would have made it more directly competitive with the defendant in terms of technical field (internet and computer telephony) and type of customer was rejected by the Deputy Judge. The defendant's liability could take into account conduct threatened for the future, but the claimant's rights depended entirely on its goodwill and reputation at the date of the conduct complained of.

In *Rugby Football Union v Cotton Traders*[76] Lloyd J. confirmed that in **5–136** principle the relevant date was that of the start of the conduct complained of, but there was a further dispute as to what that date was. The defendant had started selling the "classic" English rugby jersey in 1987, but between 1991 and 1997 had stopped selling this in favour of newly designed official strip licensed to them by the claimants. After termination of the licence agreement, the defendants had reverted to selling the classic version. Lloyd J. held that the relevant date was 1997 and not 1987 (nor the date of commencement of proceedings in 2000). What happened on expiry of the licence in 1997 was the commencement of a new business, not a revival of the pre-1991 one.

In *Pontiac Marina v CDL Hotels*,[77] the relevant date was that on which the defendants publicly announced their intention to rebrand themselves and their hotels under the name *Millennium* (the plaintiffs being the developers of the *Millenia* complex of offices, shops and hotels), not the date on which they had applied to register *Millennium* as a service mark. The date of the announcement was the earliest on which the plaintiffs could have brought a *quia timet* action. Nor was it relevant that four of the defendants' hotels in the United States and New Zealand already used *Millennium* in their name.

---

[74] *Guinness Ireland Group v Kilkenny Brewing Company Ltd* [2000] F.S.R. 112 (HC Ireland). The action was principally concerned with making the defendant change its corporate name.
[75] [2002] R.P.C. 27 (Christopher Floyd Q.C., Deputy Judge).
[76] [2002] EWHC 467; [2002] E.T.M.R. 76 (Lloyd J.).
[77] [1998] F.S.R. 839 (CA, Singapore) affirming [1997] F.S.R. 725 (Chao Hick Tin J.).

Other relevant times

5–137 Although the most important date is the start of the conduct complained of, other dates may be relevant. If the claimant delays in enforcing his rights they are vulnerable to being lost altogether. If the claimant's mark has ceased to be distinctive of him at the date of the writ then the defendant's conduct will no longer be actionable at all, irrespective of delay and acquiescence. The claimant may be said to have an accrued cause of action, but not a continuing one. In this case damages should be awarded so far as not statute barred, but the claimant will have irretrievably lost the right to an injunction.[78]

In *International Scientific Communications v Pattison*[79] Goulding J. refused an injunction because although the defendant's behaviour had originally involved passing-off,[80] there was no longer any prospect of confusion. This may be given as an example of a general rule that equity will not restrain conduct which is no longer wrongful, even if it was tortious when commenced and when the writ was issued. Another example might occur if the plaintiff's mark had ceased to be distinctive, other than as a result of the conduct complained of, during the course of the action. In such a case, damages should be awarded down to the date at which the defendant's conduct ceased to deceive, but no injunction should be granted.

In *Siegert v Findlater*[81] the defendant argued that the plaintiff himself was guilty of a misrepresentation which had commenced after the action was brought. Fry J. held there was no material misrepresentation, but also said that for a misrepresentation to disentitle the plaintiff to equitable relief it would have to be such as to bar the legal claim to damages. The better view is that equity may refuse relief to a plaintiff without clean hands in wider circumstances than would bar the action altogether at common law. Moreover, equitable relief has been given to plaintiffs formerly guilty of misrepresentations who have repented before trial. The better view is that a misrepresentation by the plaintiff which was current at the time the defendant started the passing-off will not permanently disentitle the plaintiff to all relief if it is discontinued, but that a misrepresentation which the plaintiff refuses to abandon will disentitle him to equitable relief whenever it may have been started.

---

[78] Compare *Daimler-Chrysler AG v Alavi* [2001] R.P.C. 42 (Pumfrey J.).
[79] [1979] F.S.R. 429 (Goulding J.).
[80] For which damages were awarded.
[81] (1878) 7 Ch.D. 801 (Fry J.).

CHAPTER 6

THE MISREPRESENTATION IN INJURIOUS FALSEHOOD

A. THE ESSENTIAL MISREPRESENTATION

Misrepresentation the basis of the action

6–1 Misrepresentation is one of the three essential elements of the tort of injurious falsehood, the other two being malice and damage. These three elements were identified by Glidewell L.J. in the Court of Appeal in *Kaye v Robertson*,[1] which is the short formulation of the tort most often cited in the field of intellectual property:

> "The essentials of this tort are that the defendant has published about the plaintiff words which are false, that they were published maliciously, and that special damage has followed as the direct and natural result of their publication. As to special damage, the effect of section 3(1) of the Defamation Act 1952 is that it is sufficient if the words published in writing are calculated to cause pecuniary damage to the plaintiff. Malice will be inferred if it be proved that the words were calculated to produce damage and that the defendant knew when he published the words that they were false or was reckless as to whether they were false or not."

This convenient summary by Glidewell L.J. is amply supported by previous authorities. As Bowen L.J. observed in the late nineteenth century in *Ratcliffe v Evans*[2]:

> "That an action will lie for written or oral falsehoods, not actionable *per se* nor even defamatory, where they are maliciously published, where they are calculated in the ordinary course of things to produce, and where they do produce, actual damage, is established law."

6–2 The two House of Lords cases which defined injurious falsehood in its present form around the turn of the nineteenth and twentieth centuries also assert the central importance of the misrepresentation. In *White v Mellin*[3] Lord Shand compared the situation in that case, in which the plaintiffs failed, to some which might have been actionable:

> "If there had been in this case an imputation of intentional misrepresentation for the purpose of misleading purchasers, or a statement that Mellin's food was positively injurious, or that it contained deleterious ingredients, and would be hurtful if it were used, I think there would have been a good ground of action ... ."

---

[1] [1991] F.S.R. 62, CA. Glidewell L.J. calls the tort "malicious falsehood" (as do most of the recent authorities) but nothing turns on the choice of name.
[2] [1892] 2 Q.B. 524, CA.
[3] [1895] A.C. 154, HL.

And Lord Watson explained more fully the kind of representations which may be actionable as injurious falsehood, in terms which are still relevant:

"The wrong complained of being the slander of goods, the fact that the representations made by the defendant in the label already referred to might be calculated to disparage the food manufactured by the plaintiff and to interfere with its sale can afford no cause of action. Every extravagant phrase used by a tradesman in commendation of his own goods may be an implied disparagement of the goods of all others in the same trade; it may attract customers to him and diminish the business of others who sell as good and even better articles at the same price; but that is a disparagement of which the law takes no cognizance. In order to constitute disparagement which is, in the sense of law, injurious, it must be shewn that the defendant's representations were made of and concerning the plaintiff's goods; that they were in disparagement of his goods and untrue; and that they have occasioned special damage to the plaintiff. Unless each and all of these three things be established, it must be held that the defendant has acted within his rights and that the plaintiff has not suffered any legal *injuria*."

In the other of these two leading cases, *Royal Baking Powder Co v Wright Crossley*,[4] Lord Davey said:

"To support such an action it is necessary for the plaintiffs to prove: (1) that the statements complained of were untrue; (2) that they were made maliciously—i.e., without just cause or excuse; (3) that the plaintiffs had suffered special damage thereby."

Of the more recent authoritative restatements of the essential elements of **6–3** the tort in the general law (and the features which distinguish it from defamation) probably the most useful in the present context is that Nicholls V.C. in *Joyce v Sengupta*[5]:

"Before turning to the issues raised by the appeal I should comment briefly on the difference between defamation and malicious falsehood. The remedy provided by the law for words which injure a person's reputation is defamation. Words may also injure a person without damaging his reputation. An example would be a claim that the seller of goods or land is not the true owner. Another example would be a false assertion that a person has closed down his business. Such claims would not necessarily damage the reputation of those concerned. The remedy

---

[4] (1901) 18 R.P.C. 95, HL. This passage was quoted by McCardie J. in *British Railway Traffic and Electric Co Ltd v The CRC Co Ltd* [1922] 2 K.B. 260, and has obviously influenced other formulations.

[5] [1993] 1 W.L.R. 337, CA. For the distinction between injurious falsehood and defamation properly so called see also *South Hetton Coal Company Ltd v North-Eastern News Association Ltd* [1894] 1 Q.B. 133, CA, and *Linotype Co Ltd v British Empire Type-Setting Machine Co Ltd* (1899) 81 L.T. 331; 15 T.L.R. 534, HL.

provided for this is malicious falsehood, sometimes called injurious falsehood or trade libel. This cause of action embraces particular types of malicious falsehood such as slander of title and slander of goods, but it is not confined to those headings.

Falsity is an essential ingredient of this tort. The plaintiff must establish the untruth of the statement of which he complains. Malice is another essential ingredient. A genuine dispute about the ownership of goods or land should not of itself be actionable. So a person who acted in good faith is not liable. Further, since the object of this cause of action is to provide a person with a remedy for a false statement made maliciously which has caused him damage, at common law proof of financial loss was another essential ingredient. The rigour of this requirement was relaxed by statute. I shall have to return to the question of damages at a later stage. For present purposes it is sufficient to note that if a plaintiff establishes that the defendant maliciously made a false statement which has caused him financial damage, or in respect of which he is relieved from proving damage by the Defamation Act 1952, the law gives him a remedy. The false statement may also be defamatory, or it may not. As already mentioned, it need not be defamatory. Conversely, the fact that the statement is defamatory does not exclude a cause of action for malicious falsehood, although the law will ensure that a plaintiff does not recover damages twice over for the same loss."

What makes a representation actionable as injurious falsehood?

6–4 From the foregoing extracts, it will be apparent that the defendant's representation must fulfil several criteria if it is to be actionable as injurious falsehood. In addition to the obvious requirement of objective falsity (and the extrinsic one of malice) the misrepresentation must relate to the claimant's goods, or, more generally, his person, business, establishment or services; and it must be of such a kind as to cause damage of a pecuniary nature, as opposed to damage to the claimant's honour and reputation in the sense protected by the law of defamation. Of these requirements, only that of damage corresponds at all closely to passing-off, reflecting the fact that both originated as actions on the case, although a combination of judicial and parliamentary intervention have caused the torts to follow different paths in terms of what proof of damage is now required.[6]

At first glance, the kinds of misrepresentation which may be actionable as injurious falsehood are very widely defined. In a competitive or near-competitive context they include allegations that the goods or services of the claimant are spurious or counterfeit[7]; that they are inferior to those of the

---

[6] Unlike passing-off, the action for injurious falsehood insisted quite strictly on proof of special damage until this was removed (for all practical purposes connected with the present work) by s.3(1) of the Defamation Act 1952.

[7] *Thorley's Cattle Food Co v Massam* (1880) 14 Ch. D. 463, CA; *McManus v Beckham* [2002] EWCA Civ 939; [2002] 1 W.L.R. 2982; [2002] 4 All E.R. 497; [2002] E.M.L.R. 40, CA.

claimant,[8] or more expensive[9]; that they are unsatisfactory, inadequate or dangerous[10]; or that they lack official approval[11]; that they infringe intellectual property rights of the defendant or a third party[12]; or that the defendant's newspaper outsells the plaintiff's by a factor of 20.[13] Other misrepresentations held actionable include saying that the claimant has gone away,[14] is unavailable for the time being,[15] does not deal in a certain line of goods,[16] or has ceased trading altogether.[17]

In its wider aspects[18] the tort is wide enough to include statements that the claimant is not the true owner of goods or land, or that his title is encumbered[19]; that the house he has for sale is haunted,[20] or that his shop premises were the setting for an adulterous affair between his wife and the local parson.[21] Misrepresentations bordering on, or overlapping with, defamation properly so called include statements that the claimant had behaved dishonestly in a position of trust,[22] involved herself in advertising for the sex industry,[23] or has given an exclusive interview to a sleazy national newspaper[24]; but the misrepresentation does not have to be defamatory or even disparaging to be actionable.

All these examples may give the impression that injurious falsehood is of much greater importance than it is. The reality is very different. Often the supposed existence of a whole genus of actionable misrepresentations turns out to depend on one or two decided cases, or even *dicta*, perhaps reported only in a minor series, and probably turning in fact on a successful appeal to the sympathy of the judge or jury, the latter being an important and unpredictable factor in many injurious falsehood cases up to the mid-twentieth century.

6–5

---

[8] *De Beers Abrasive Products Ltd v International General Electric Co of New York Ltd* [1975] 1 W.L.R. 972; [1975] 2 All E.R. 599; [1975] F.S.R. 323.

[9] *Compaq Computer Corp v Dell Computer Corp Ltd* [1992] F.S.R. 93; *British Airways plc v Ryanair Ltd* [2001] E.T.M.R. 24; [2001] F.S.R. 32 (where the claim failed on the facts); *DSG Retail Ltd v Comet Group Ltd* [2002] EWHC 116; [2002] F.S.R. 58 (where it succeeded).

[10] *Alcott v Millar's Karri & Jarrah Forests Ltd* (1904) 91 L.T. 722; 21 T.L.R. 30, CA; *London Ferro-Concrete Co v Justicz* (1951) 68 R.P.C. 261, CA; *dictum* of Lord Denning M.R. in *Drummond-Jackson v British Medical Association* [1970] 1 W.L.R. 688, CA.

[11] *Ucan Products Ltd v Hilti (Great Britain) Ltd* [1968] F.S.R. 248 (Cross J.).

[12] *Greers Ltd v Pearman & Corder Ltd* (1922) 39 R.P.C. 406, CA.

[13] *Lyne v Nicholls* (1906) 23 T.L.R. 86, but compare *MacMillan Magazines Ltd v RCN Publishing Co Ltd* [1998] F.S.R. 9.

[14] *Joyce v Motor Surveys Ltd* [1948] 1 Ch. 252.

[15] *Shapiro v La Morta* [1923] All E.R. 378, CA.

[16] *Jarrahdale Timber Co Ltd v Temperley & Co* (1894) 11 T.L.R. 119 (QB Div.).

[17] *Ratcliffe v Evans* [1892] 2 Q.B. 524, CA.

[18] Not considered further in the present work.

[19] *Green v Button* (1835) 150 E.R. 299 (lien over timber for sale); *Steward v Young* (1870) L.R. 5 C.P. 122 (bill of sale).

[20] *Barrett v Associated Newspapers Ltd* (1907) 23 T.L.R. 666, CA.

[21] *Riding v Smith* (1876) 1 Ex. D. 91 (Divisional Court).

[22] *Joyce v Sengupta* [1993] 1 W.L.R. 337; [1993] 1 All E.R. 897, CA; *Spring v Guardian Assurance plc* [1993] 2 All E.R. 273, CA (where the claim failed on the facts).

[23] *Khodaparast v Shad* [2000] 1 W.L.R. 618; [2000] 1 All E.R. 545; [2000] E.M.L.R. 265, CA; *dictum* in *O'Shea v MGN Ltd* [2001] E.M.L.R. 40.

[24] *Kaye v Robertson* [1991] F.S.R. 62, CA.

Must the misrepresentation be disparaging?

6–6 It may be asked if the misrepresentation in injurious falsehood need be a disparaging one. There is some authority to this effect, and the proposition has some instinctive appeal as defining an appropriate dividing line between injurious falsehood and passing-off. In *White v Melllin*[25] Lords Herschell, Watson and Shand all spoke entirely in terms of disparagement, as did Lindley M.R. in *Hubbuck v Wilkinson Heywood*,[26] but neither case necessarily stands for any wider proposition than that "puffing" representations, even if false, about the defendant's own goods do not amount to injurious falsehood. In the New Zealand case of *Bell-Booth v Attorney General*[27] Cooke P. said "The duty in injurious falsehood may be defined as a duty not to disparage goods untruthfully and maliciously", and the passage in which this appears has been quoted with approval in the Court of Appeal and House of Lords[28]—but Cook P. was dealing with a case of alleged negligence, not injurious falsehood, and he is not to be supposed to have been attempting a quasi-statutory definition of the latter.

Schulke & Mayr v Alkapharm[29] was a case of alleged injurious falsehood and passing-off, in which Jacob J. said about the former[30]:

> "Its whole origin is therefore based on some kind of disparagement of the plaintiffs: 'knocking', to use the advertisers' jargon. I can see nothing in any of the authorities to which I was taken which suggest that the tort goes further than disparaging statements about the plaintiff or his goods."

However, *Schulke & Mayr v Alkapharm* may equally well be regarded as turning, like *White v Mellin*, on the fact that the defendant was, at most, making misrepresentations about his own goods, rather than those of the plaintiff. What Jacob J. said is really true only with qualifications whether one is speaking about the origins of the tort, or its manifestations since; and certainly not to the point where it can be said that a misrepresentation which is not disparaging cannot ever amount to injurious falsehood. It is hardly disparaging to say of a woman that she is married, but the development of

---

[25] [1895] A.C. 154, HL.

[26] [1899] 1 Q.B. 86, CA.

[27] [1989] 3 N.Z.L.R. 148, CA of NZ.

[28] *Lonrho plc v Fayed (No. 5)* [1993] 1 W.L.R. 1489, CA; *Spring v Guardian Assurance plc* [1995] 2 A.C. 296, HL.

[29] [1999] F.S.R. 161 (Jacob J.).

[30] Partly in reliance on a passage in the then current (17th) edition of *Clerk and Lindsell on Torts*, but the current edition (18th ed., 2000) para.23–08 denies that the misrepresentation need involve disparagement or denigration, as does the same author elsewhere: Hazel Carty, *An Analysis of the Economic Torts* (2001), p.155. *Gatley on Libel and Slander* (9th ed., 1998) at para.20–3 even contemplates, by reference to *Kelly v Partington (No. 2)* (1834) 5 B. & Ad. 645; 110 E.R. 929, that a misrepresentation may be actionable as injurious falsehood although its tendency is to improve the reputation of the plaintiff in the eyes of sensible people.

the law from slander of title to malicious falsehood in the more general sense is sometimes traced to just such a case.[31]

In part, the correctness of the Jacob J.'s approach depends on what one **6–7** means by disparagement. Is it disparaging to say that *Ratcliffe* has ceased trading, or that *Joyce* has gone away and left no forwarding address?[32] And is it really disparaging to suggest that there is nothing actually wrong with *Compaq* computers, but that they are not such good value as those of *Dell*; or that *Currys* charge a few pounds more for an electrical appliance than *Comet*?[33] Such representations might be described as unfavourable or disadvantageous to the claimant, but to describe them as disparaging is to stretch its natural meaning by perhaps more than it will bear.

Disparagement is a strong word, but it is probably not a term of art, and although it appears in many of the leading nineteenth century authorities, its use in the twentieth century and more recently tends to be confined to quoting or tracking the language of those cases. There are three possible explanations for its omission from so many of the leading definitions of injurious falsehood: first, that the disparaging nature of the representation is such an obvious pre-condition to the action for injurious falsehood that the need to state it expressly has been overlooked; secondly, that disparagement is already inherent in the requirements of damage, falsity, materiality and malice; and finally that the action is not so confined. It is suggested that there is more than a grain of truth in each of these. So far as the first is concerned, it is a common fault of definitions of both passing-off and injurious falsehood that although the distinction between them is well recognised, definitions purportedly directed to one tend to embrace at least some aspects of the other. The second and third may be addressed together: is it conceivable that a non-disparaging misrepresentation about the claimant might be made maliciously and so as to be calculated to damage him, without constituting injurious falsehood? A relative or comparative disparagement is certainly sufficient to support the action. As a practical matter, a misrepresentation which is not on its face disparaging, at least in a relative sense, is unlikely to meet these criteria, but that is no warrant for the specific requirement that the representation must be a disparaging one.

There are certainly some exceptions in the decided cases. It is actionable **6–8** as injurious falsehood to say of a professional musician that he is unable to

---

[31] *Shepheard v Wakeman* (1662) 1 Sid. 79; 83 E.R. 1052 concerned a letter written by the defendant saying that the plaintiff was already married to him. Although this might have carried the innuendo that she was an intending bigamist, the economic rationale is that she lost an advantageous marriage.

[32] Respectively *Ratcliffe v Evans* [1892] 2 Q.B. 524 and *Joyce v Motor Surveys Ltd* [1948] 1 Ch. 252, both classic cases. In the latter, "disparaging" was used, but that looks like an attempt to make the facts fit an inappropriate statement of the law.

[33] Respectively *Compaq Computer Corp v Dell Computer Corp Ltd* [1992] F.S.R. 93 and *DSG Retail Ltd v Comet Group Ltd* [2002] EWHC 116; [2002] F.S.R. 58.

perform because of a prior engagement,[34] or illness[35]; although in the former the obvious implication is that the plaintiff is in demand, and in the latter the actual terms of the statement by his English agent that "Stephane Grappelli is very seriously ill in Paris and I would be surprised if he ever toured again" are calculated to excite our sympathy, rather than our censure. The Court of Appeal disallowed an innuendo which would have converted a neutral statement of purported fact into an accusation of malingering. In *Shapiro v La Morta*,[36] the plaintiff Mrs Shapiro was billed as the piano accompanist for a vocalist she had accompanied on five previous occasions, although she had in fact turned the engagement down. The action failed because the manager had issued the offending posters in good faith, but if malice had been present she could have recovered for any engagements lost as a result. As a hypothetical example, it would be the opposite of disparaging to say of a successful barrister that he was about to be promoted to the bench—but if the consequence was that he ceased to receive instructions, and if the statement was made maliciously, then there seems no reason in principle why it should not be actionable.

To whom may the misrepresentation be made?

6–9 The action for injurious falsehood (even in a competitive context) is not confined to misrepresentations made to customers or ultimate consumers of the products of either party, although that is overwhelmingly the most common situation in fact. The misrepresentation may be actionable even though it is material and damaging only in so far as the relevant audience consists of the claimant's trade customers (as opposed to the consuming public), as in *Rima Electric v Rolls Razor*,[37] and in the various cases of unfounded assertion of infringement of intellectual property rights such as *Greers v Pearman & Corder*.[38] In part, this reflects the fact that the action for injurious falsehood protects a range of pecuniary and economic interests which are considerably wider than business goodwill in the sense recognised for passing-off. So, for example, several cases have allowed personal claimants to recover for damage to their employment prospects.[39]

In a competitive context, there is no reason to doubt that the class of potential representees for injurious falsehood is at least as wide as for passing-off (so that it includes, for instance, suppliers as well as customers)

---

[34] *Shapiro v La Morta* [1923] All E.R. 378, CA. Lush J. had expressly stated at first instance that the statements complained of were neither defamatory nor disparaging, and there was no appeal from this.

[35] *Grappelli v Derek Block (Holdings) Ltd* [1981] 1 W.L.R. 822; [1981] 2 All E.R. 272, CA. The case is reported on a pleading point but the existence of the cause of action for injurious falsehood was accepted by Lord Denning M.R.

[36] Above.

[37] [1965] R.P.C. 4 (Wilberforce J.). The gravamen of the plaintiffs' complaint was that their trade customers would have thought they were undermining resale price maintenance by offering specially favourable terms to the defendants.

[38] (1922) 39 R.P.C. 406, CA.

[39] *Joyce v Sengupta* [1993] 1 W.L.R. 337, CA; *Khodaparast v Shad* [2000] 1 W.L.R. 618, CA; *Spring v Guardian Assurance plc* [1993] All E.R. 273, CA (the latter action failed on the facts for lack of malice).

and that it ought to include anyone whose actions might be influenced by the defendant's misrepresentation so as to damage some pecuniary or economic interest of the claimant.[40] In *Joyce v Motor Surveys*[41] express misrepresentations that the plaintiff had ceased business were made to all inquirers, but the most serious damage was suffered when they were made to the plaintiff's suppliers and the trade association to which he belonged. In cases of allegedly inflated comparisons of newspaper or magazine circulation figures, the relevant audience consists of potential advertisers to a much greater extent than readers.[42] In *Fielding v Variety*[43] it was argued that the description of the plaintiff's musical *Charlie Girl* as a "disastrous flop" damaged him under two heads: by discouraging attendance at the London production, and by making it more difficult to find backers for an adaptation for Broadway. Neither was made out on the facts and only nominal damages of £100 were awarded for injurious falsehood, but both seem equally recoverable in principle.

The trading status of the defendant and the relevance of competition

Unlike passing-off, it has never been suggested that the action for injurious **6–10** falsehood lies only against traders acting in their capacity as such. While the present treatment of injurious falsehood as an aspect of the law of unfair competition gives prominence to such cases, they are by no means exhaustive of the situations that can arise, whether or not the claimant is a trader. So, for example, actions have been held to lie against disgruntled customers or consumers publicly venting their dissatisfaction with the claimant's products or services,[44] private individuals in their personal capacity,[45] newspapers and individual journalists,[46] the claimant's former employer,[47] a firm of solicitors,[48] and so on. The apparent breadth of the action in this respect is, however, offset in practice by the requirement that the misrepresentation must be made maliciously if it is to be actionable.

However, the kind of misrepresentations with which the present work is concerned are particularly likely to be made between trade competitors.

---

[40] An extreme case is represented by *Stewart-Brady v Express Newspapers* [1997] E.M.L.R. 192, QBD; see also *Stewart-Brady v United Kingdom* (1997) 24 E.H.R.R. CD38, ECHR; in which the relevant representees were the management of the secure hospital at which the claimant (one of the Moors murderers) was detained, who had the power to terminate a regular but discretionary allowance paid to him.

[41] [1948] Ch. 252 (Roxburgh J).

[42] *MacMillan Magazines Ltd v RCN Publishing Co Ltd* [1998] F.S.R. 9.

[43] [1967] 2 Q.B. 841, CA. The plaintiff obtained judgment in default of defence and the case is reported on the enquiry as to damages.

[44] *Crest Homes Ltd v Ascott* [1980] F.S.R. 396, CA; *Bestobell Paints Ltd v Bigg* [1975] F.S.R. 421 (interlocutory injunctions were refused in both cases).

[45] *Khodaparast v Shad* [2000] 1 W.L.R. 618, CA. The defendant was the plaintiff's former lover.

[46] *Ratcliffe v Evans* [1892] 2 Q.B. 524, CA; *Fielding v Variety Inc* [1967] 2 Q.B. 841, CA; *Kaye v Robertson* [1991] F.S.R. 62, CA; *Joyce v Sengupta* [1993] 1 W.L.R. 337, CA.

[47] *Balden v Shorter* [1933] Ch. 427; *Spring v Guardian Assurance plc* [1993] All E.R. 273, CA (both actions failed on the facts for lack of malice).

[48] *CHC Software Care Ltd v Hopkins & Wood* [1993] F.S.R. 241.

Examples are numerous, but by way of example include such well-known sparring partners as *McDonald's* and *Burger King* for hamburgers,[49] *Compaq* and *Dell* for personal computers,[50] *Vodafone* and *Orange* for mobile telephony,[51] *Electrolux* and *Dyson* for vacuum cleaners,[52] *British Airways* and *Ryanair* for air passenger transport,[53] and *Currys* and *Comet* for domestic electrical goods.[54]

6–11   It goes without saying that the action for injurious falsehood lies at the suit of one trader against a competitor, but the existence of a competitive relationship does have two substantial implications. First, there is the question of whether a misrepresentation which at first sight simply extols the defendant's goods, indirectly disparages those of the claimant. Unless the comparison is explicit, it is always difficult to turn a floating comparison of this kind into an actionable disparagement, but the exercise obviously lacks any factual support at all unless the parties are actually competitors, and may be strengthened to the extent that rivalry between them is particularly intense or acrimonious.

On the other hand, the element of malice is much more difficult to establish against competitors than against intermeddlers and the world at large. The fact that the defendant is a trade competitor creates a *prima facie* presumption that any such representations are made with the legitimate objective of increasing his own sales, rather than the illegitimate one of harming the claimant for the sake of it. As Lindley M.R. said in *Hubbuck v Wilkinson Heywood*,[55] where the defendants had issued a circular purporting to prove that their paint was almost as good as the plaintiff's, at half the price:

"It is not necessary to consider how the case would have stood, if the defendants had not been rival traders simply puffing their own goods and comparing theirs with those of the plaintiffs. If the defendants had made untrue statements concerning the plaintiffs' goods beyond saying that they were inferior to, or, at all events, not better than, those of the defendants, or if the defendants were not rivals in trade and had no lawful excuse for what they said, it would not have been right summarily to strike out the statement of claim as shewing no reasonable cause of action."

This is not to say that malice can never be made out against a trade competitor, but unless the statement complained of is self-evidently and incontrovertibly false to the mind of any reasonable and well-informed person, then the exercise is bound to be a difficult and unpredictable one.

---

[49] *McDonald's Hamburgers Ltd v Burger King Ltd* [1986] F.S.R. 45, CA.
[50] *Compaq Computer Corp v Dell Computer Corp Ltd* [1992] F.S.R. 93.
[51] *Vodafone Group plc v Orange Personal Communications Services Ltd* [1997] F.S.R. 34.
[52] *Emaco Ltd v Dyson Appliances Ltd* [1999] E.T.M.R. 903.
[53] *British Airways plc and Ryanair Ltd* [2001] F.S.R. 32.
[54] *DSG Retail Ltd v Comet Group plc* [2002] F.S.R. 58.
[55] [1899] 1 Q.B. 86, CA,

Truth of representation

It is a complete defence to an action for injurious falsehood that the alleged **6–12**
misrepresentation is in fact true. So, for example, in *Vodafone v Orange*[56]
Jacob J. was satisfied of the truth of an advertised claim that users of *Orange*
would save on average £20 per month compared to *Vodafone,* even on the
interpretation which Vodafone proffered; and in *British Airways v Ryanair*[57]
that Ryanair had not exaggerated the relative cost of fares to various
advertised destinations: "in my view the use was honest comparative
advertising. I suspect the real reason BA do not like it is precisely because it
is true".[58]

In *Compaq v Dell*[59] Aldous J. emphasised that the grant of an interlocutory injunction would not prevent the defendants making accurate price
comparisons in press advertisements:

> "Further, price comparisons can be made, but making it clear that the
> comparison is between the plaintiffs' suggested retail price and that
> charged by the defendants. Further, pictures of the systems can be
> properly chosen which, together with appropriate wording, can make a
> fair and proper comparison. I believe it is possible for the defendants to
> compare their systems with the plaintiffs' without using misleading pic-
> tures and making any false statement. Such advertisements should enable
> the defendants to continue with their stated purpose of comparing the
> prices and quality of their systems with that of the plaintiffs. I also cannot
> understand why the defendants wish to continue with the advertisements
> of which complaint is made. They accept that, in some instances, their
> machines shown cannot be purchased at the prices quoted. Further, they
> know that end-users will not, in many cases, pay the suggested retail price
> of the plaintiffs as stated in the 'Spot The Flaw' advertisement.
>
> I also do not believe that an appropriate injunction would interfere with
> the right to freedom of speech. The defendants wish to compare their
> systems with the plaintiffs' both as to price and quality. As I have said, I
> believe they can do that by changes in the advertisements to indicate that
> the price comparison is between their prices and the suggested retail prices
> of the plaintiffs. They can also accurately compare their systems with
> those of the plaintiffs. That shows that this case is very different from the
> *Bestobell* case, in which an injunction would have prevented the defendant
> from saying what he believed to be true, namely that the plaintiff's paint
> caused the mess on his house."

In comparison with defamation properly so called, the burden of proof in **6–13**
injurious falsehood is on the claimant to prove the falsity of the representation complained of, as well as malice and (subject to the Defamation

---

[56] [1997] F.S.R. 34 (Jacob J.).
[57] [2001] F.S.R. 32 (Jacob J.).
[58] *per* Jacob J., in the context of registered trade mark infringement.
[59] [1992] F.S.R. 93 (Aldous J.).

Act 1952) damage. In cases in which interlocutory relief is sought the burden is much higher. If the defendant intends to justify the statement complained of then an interlocutory injunction may only be granted if the court is satisfied that no reasonable jury could find at trial that the statement was true.[60] The practical result is that any ambiguity in the representation, or any uncertainty in the criteria against which its truth or falsity is to be judged, is likely to be fatal to the interlocutory application.[61]

B. The Materiality of the Misrepresentation

Materiality, reliance and damage

6–14 As in passing-off, if a misrepresentation is to be actionable as injurious falsehood it must be material in the sense of being calculated to cause damage to the claimant (taking into account the application of s.3(1) of the Defamation Act 1952); and it is likely to be material only if it is relied on by those to whom it is addressed. The present section also deals with the related propositions that the misrepresentation must be made about the claimant— as opposed to one the defendant makes about himself, as in passing-off— and that certain kinds of misrepresentation dismissed as "mere puffing" are deemed to be beneath the notice of the law.

The misrepresentation must be "of and concerning the claimant"

6–15 The first requirement under materiality is that the misrepresentation must be made about the claimant, or "of and concerning the plaintiff" to use the language of nineteenth century pleadings. Though this may appear to be a fairly simple issue, it actually breaks down into several sub-issues which are not particularly well defined. Perhaps the first to take is whether the public, or a relevant part of them, can in fact identify the claimant from the publication complained of, taking due account of surrounding circumstances. If not, then the publication can hardly cause any relevant damage to the claimant even if that was its intended effect. Conversely, the public may (wrongly) identify the claimant as the intended target, although the defendant may have intended to attack someone else entirely, or no one in particular.

Cases of pure disparagement depend on the target being identifiable, although for one reason or another the target may not be identified by name. Cases of comparative advertisement, on the other hand, may involve hanging or anonymous comparisons with reference to one or more competitors, who may or may not be identifiable. As a practical matter, few such cases are brought, and fewer still succeed, except in the case of one-to-one

---

[60] As was made out in *Compaq v Dell*, above; *Kaye v Robertson* [1991] F.S.R. 62, CA, and *DSG Retail Ltd v Comet Group plc* [2002] F.S.R. 58.
[61] *Bestobell Paints Ltd v Bigg* [1975] F.S.R. 421; *Crest Homes Ltd v Ascott* [1980] F.S.R. 396, CA; *MacMillan Magazines Ltd v RCN Publishing Co Ltd* [1998] F.S.R. 9.

comparisons in which there is no doubt as to the identify of the comparator. Finally, there are cases in which the defendant is at first sight simply making an assertion about himself or what purports to be his property, without reference to any third party—but there are enough of these to conclude that in an appropriate case the claimant may be sufficiently referred to simply by virtue of the fact that he is the only person of whom the relevant statement would in fact be true.

Identifying the claimant

If the claimant or the claimant's product is recognisably identified, by name **6–16** or by some other designation, then there is normally no difficulty under this head. So, for example, in *De Beers v General Electric*,[62] the plaintiffs' *Debdust* was unfavourably compared to the defendants' competitive *MBS-70*. In *McDonalds v Burgerking*,[63] the defendants' advertising for its *Whopper* burger used the slogan *Its Not Just Big, Mac* with the associated copy stating "[u]nlike some burgers, it is 100 per cent. pure beef, flame-grilled never fried, with a unique choice of toppings". The alleged implication that the plaintiffs' *Big Mac* burger was not 100 per cent pure beef failed on the facts. In *British Airways v Ryanair*[64] there was no doubt that advertisements headed EXPENSIVE BA ... DS or EXPENSIVE BA would be taken as referring to the plaintiff airline, though the action failed on other grounds. In *DSG v Comet*[65] the action related to a poster campaign with the message "The Comet price is lower than competitors' 10% off promotions and £10 price cuts. That's Comet sense". There was no doubt that the competitor in question was Currys:

> "In my judgment there can be no doubt that the posters in question were directed at Currys. They make clear reference to the two promotions then being mounted by Currys, the 10 per cent promotion and the £10 off promotion. Secondly Mr Pugh, Comet's head of Brand Marketing, says in terms in his written statement that a decision was made on December 10, to direct Comet stores to use the Bedford poster and to attach Currys' advertisements at its foot. Thirdly Mr Pugh exhibited to his witness statement a sequence of e-mails sent from the central management team to Comet stores. The subject line of that dated November 17, 2001 reads 'Anti Currys weekend activity' and of that dated November 24 'Anti Currys promotion'. The e-mail of December 15 had as its subject 'Anti competition weekend promotion'; but its text contained specific reference to Currys' prices and gave the instructions necessary to implement the decision taken by Mr Pugh and his management team on December 10 to which I have already made reference."

However, cases such as these are not the only ones, nor even the most

---

[62] [1975] 1 W.L.R. 972; [1975] 2 All E.R. 599; [1975] F.S.R. 323 (Walton J.).
[63] [1986] F.S.R. 45 (Whitford J.)
[64] [2001] F.S.R. 32 (Jacob J.).
[65] [2002] F.S.R. 58 (Owen J., QBD).

common. Before 1995, when s.4(1)(b) of the Trade Marks Act 1938 was repealed, comparative advertising by reference to a Part A registered trade mark was effectively prohibited and any comparisons had to be anonymous. Whether before 1938 or after 1995, some traders have been willing to attack their rivals in more or less express terms, while others have been more circumspect.

6–17   For the purposes of injurious falsehood, the claimant need not be identified by name, provided that identification is possible in fact. In *Joyce v Sengupta*[66] the newspaper article complained of clearly referred to the plaintiff, although it came no closer to identifying her than by certain circumstantial statements about her position as a maid in the Royal Household. As an extreme example, in *O'Shea v MGN*[67] it was contemplated that the deliberate publication of a recognisable look-alike photograph of the claimant in an "squalid and degrading" advertisement for a pornographic website would have amounted to injurious falsehood. Compare *Rima Electric v Rolls Razor*,[68] in which a real photograph of the plaintiffs' *Magicair* hair dryer was included in the defendants' promotional catalogue of goods supposedly sold at cost price to purchasers of their washing machines. In fact, the *Magicair* was not kept in stock and the price quoted for it was below its normal wholesale price. Although neither the plaintiffs nor the dryer were identified by name, the latter could be recognised from its appearance. Wilberforce J. held that there was an actionable malicious falsehood in so far as the plaintiffs' trade customers might conclude that the latter were unfairly favouring the defendants, and undermining their normal retail outlets.

As rather more representative examples, in *Thorley's Cattle Food v Massam*[69] the plaintiff company was not identified by name, but there can have been no doubt that they were the target of the defendant's circulars and advertisements. Likewise in *Thomas v Williams*[70] the implication that spurious *Thomas* and *Holyoake* needles were on the market could only be taken as referring to the plaintiffs. In *White v Mellin*[71] there was a difference of opinion in the House of Lords as to whether affixing the defendant's advertisements to the plaintiff's goods before they were sold turned an otherwise perfectly general statement of superiority into an attack on the plaintiffs: Lord Herschell L.C. was prepared to accept that this was the case, at least for the purposes of argument; Lord Watson was not. In *Alcott v Millar's Karri and Jarrah Forests*[72] the defendants were liable for stating that paving blocks made from American red gum wood had rotted after six to 12 months. The plaintiff, though not identified by name, was the importer and agent for American red gum blocks.

---

[66] [1993] 1 W.L.R. 337; [1993] 1 All E.R. 897, CA.
[67] [2001] E.M.L.R. 40 (Morland J., QBD).
[68] [1965] R.P.C. 4 (Wilberforce J.).
[69] (1879) 14 Ch. D. 763, CA.
[70] (1880) 14 Ch. D. 864 (Fry J.).
[71] [1895] A.C. 154, HL.
[72] (1904) 91 L.T. 722; 21 T.L.R. 30, CA.

In *Danish Mercantile Co v Beaumont*[73] a claim by the defendant that a **6–18** company formed by him was the sole importer and distributor of a certain brand of Danish sugar beet harvester was actionable at the suit of the plaintiffs, who were in fact the sole importers of the machinery in question. Although there was no specific reference to them by name or otherwise, Roxburgh J. described the defendant's letters as "the plainest possible trade libel upon the first Plaintiff". A similar result had previously been reached, with rather more hesitation and on much weaker facts, in *Jarrahdale Timber v Temperley*.[74] Both parties imported *Jarrah* timber from Australia, as did many others, but only the defendants also imported *Karri* timber, and the latter issued advertisements saying that they were the only firm to import both *Jarrah* and *Karri*. The plaintiffs complained that this would be understood as meaning that Temperley were the sole importers of *Jarrah*, an interlocutory injunction was granted, and an appeal dismissed because the two-judge Divisional Court could not agree.

In *Serville v Constance*[75] the defendant's baseless claim to be the welterweight boxing champion of Trinidad failed to amount to passing-off because the plaintiff was completely unknown in England, but Harman J. had no doubt that it would have amounted to injurious falsehood if the plaintiff had been able to prove malice. In the instant case the defendant knew perfectly well that he was not the welter-weight champion of Trinidad, but he does not seem to have known that the plaintiff was, and to that extent his claim was not malicious.[76] In *Ucan v Hilti*[77] the plaintiffs had an arguable claim for injurious falsehood, subject again to proving malice, in respect of a published claim by Hilti that their tools were the only ones approved to a certain official standard. Ucan were not named, but they and Hilti were bitter rivals and the Ucan tools had been approved before the Hilti advertisement had been published.

In *Customglass Boats v Salthouse*[78] advertisements issued by the plaintiffs asserted that two models of yacht had been designed by them, when in fact they had been designed by the second defendant. Damages of NZ$500 were awarded on his counterclaim, with the judge finding that although the misstatement had originally been issued carelessly rather than maliciously, the plaintiffs had failed to withdraw it promptly once they had been made aware of its falsity.

Whether representation to be taken seriously

There is a category of misrepresentations which are deemed not to be **6–19** material, and which are therefore not actionable as injurious falsehood, which comprises those which, though untrue, are so obviously false, unsubstantiated, imprecise or exaggerated that the relevant public would

---

[73] (1950) 67 R.P.C. 111 (Roxburgh J.).
[74] (1894) 11 T.L.R. 119 (QB Div.).
[75] [1954] 1 W.L.R. 487 (Harman J.).
[76] This is probably too strict a view of what is required by way of malice.
[77] [1968] F.S.R. 248 (Cross J.).
[78] [1976] R.P.C. 589 (Mahon J., HC of NZ).

not take them at face value. Where such a representation is made by the defendant about his own goods or services, it is conventional to describe it as "puffing".

The treatment of "puffing" allegations goes back to the nineteenth century, but a convenient starting point for their treatment in modern law is provided by the judgment of Walton J. in *De Beers v General Electric*[79]:

> "What precisely is the law on this point? It is a blinding glimpse of the obvious to say that there must be a dividing line between statements that are actionable and those which are not; and the sole question upon a dry point of law such as we are discussing here is: where does that line lie? On the one hand, it appears to me that the law is that any trader is entitled to puff his own goods, even though such puff must, as a matter of pure logic, involve the denigration of his rival's goods. Thus in the well known case of the three adjoining tailors who put notices in their respective windows reading: 'The best tailor in the world,' 'The best tailor in this town,' and 'The best tailor in this street,' none of the three committed an actionable wrong...
>
> Where, however, the situation is not that the trader is puffing his own goods, but turns to denigrate those of his rival, then, in my opinion, the situation is not so clear cut. Obviously the statement: 'My goods are better than X's' is only a more dramatic presentation of what is implicit in the statement: 'My goods are the best in the world.' Accordingly, I do not think such a statement would be actionable. At the other end of the scale, if what is said is: 'My goods are better than X's, because X's are absolute rubbish,' then it is established by dicta of Lord Shand in the House of Lords in *White v. Mellin* [1895] A.C. 154, 171, which were accepted by Mr. Walton as stating the law, the statement would be actionable.
>
> Between these two kinds of statements there is obviously still an extremely wide field; and it appears to me that, in order to draw the line, one must apply this test, namely, whether a reasonable man would take the claim being made as being a serious claim or not."

6–20　Walton J. preferred this test, going to the materiality of the misrepresentation, to a possible alternative formulation:

> "A possible alternative test is to ask whether the defendant has pointed to a specific allegation of some defect or demerit in the plaintiff's goods. This is, I think, the test favoured by the editors of the last few editions of *Salmond on Torts*. My difficulty in accepting this test is simply that I feel that there might conceivably be such an allegation which, for some reason—perhaps the light-hearted way in which it was expressed or perhaps, on the contrary, the extremely vituperative way in which it was expressed (cf. *per* Lord Blanesburgh in *Tolley v J. S. Fry B Sons Ltd.* [1931] A.C. 333, 346)—was nevertheless not one which any reasonable man would take seriously."

[79] [1975] 1 W.L.R. 972; [1975] 2 All E.R. 599; [1975] F.S.R. 323 (Walton J.).

Under whatever rationale, there is no doubt that the decision to characterise a statement as "puffing" (or worse still, "mere puffing") remains fatal to the success of any claim in relation to it. As Jacob J. said in *Vodaphone v Orange*[80]:

"But I must add a general comment. This is a case about advertising. The public are used to the ways of advertisers and expect a certain amount of hyperbole. In particular the public are used to advertisers claiming the good points of a product and ignoring others, advertisements claiming that you can 'save ££££ ...' are common, carrying with them the notion that 'savings' are related to amount of spend, and the public are reasonably used to comparisons—'knocking copy' as it is called in the advertising world. This is important in considering what the ordinary meaning may be. The test is whether a reasonable man would take the claim being made as one made seriously, *De Beers Abrasive Products Ltd v International General Electric Co. of New York Ltd* [1975] 1 W.L.R. 972: the more precise the claim the more it is likely to be so taken—the more general or fuzzy the less so."

Puffing in the nineteenth century cases

The leading authorities from the end of the nineteenth century may not **6–21** attribute any consistent rationale to the treatment of puffing allegations, but they agree that they are not actionable. In *White v Mellin*[81] Lord Shand said:

"It appears to me that in order to constitute a libel of the class here complained of there must be a statement in disparagement of the plaintiff's goods, and that the statement must be false and injurious. But, then, I do not think that disparagement in a popular sense would be enough for the plaintiff's case. It is a disparagement of one man's goods to say that they are inferior to the goods of another; but such a statement cannot, I think, be the ground of a claim of damages or a claim for injunction such as the plaintiff here asked. If there had been in this case an imputation of intentional misrepresentation for the purpose of misleading purchasers, or a statement that Mellin's food was positively injurious, or that it contained deleterious ingredients, and would be hurtful if it were used, I think there would have been a good ground of action; and if the authorities have not settled the law otherwise, I should even say that an averment of special damage ought not to be necessary. But when all that is done is making a comparison between the plaintiff's goods and the goods of the person issuing the advertisement, and the statement made is that the plaintiff's goods are inferior in quality or inferior, it may be, in some special qualities, I think this cannot be regarded as a disparagement of which the law will take cognizance."

[80] [1997] F.S.R. 34 (Jacob J.).
[81] [1895] A.C. 154, HL.

399

And in the same case Lord Herchell had drawn attention to the policy implications of any other result:

"The allegation of a tradesman that his goods are better than his neighbour's very often involves only the consideration whether they possess one or two qualities superior to the other. Of course 'better' means better as regards the purpose for which they are intended, and the question of better or worse in many cases depends simply upon one or two or three issues of fact. If an action will not lie because a man says that his goods are better than his neighbour's, it seems to me impossible to say that it will lie because he says that they are better in this or that or the other respect. Just consider what a door would be opened if this were permitted. That this sort of puffing advertisement is in use is notorious; and we see rival cures advertised for particular ailments. The Court would then be bound to inquire, in an action brought, whether this ointment or this pill better cured the disease which it was alleged to cure—whether a particular article of food was in this respect or that better than another. Indeed, the Courts of law would be turned into a machinery for advertising rival productions by obtaining a judicial determination which of the two was the better."

6–22 *White v Mellin* itself was followed in *Hubbuck v Wilkinson Heywood*,[82] in which Lord Lindley M.R. said:

"We will now consider the circular in its other aspect, namely, as a disparagement of the plaintiffs' goods ... The defendants in this case give the results of some experiments with the two sorts of paint, and in paragraph 5 of the statement of claim the plaintiffs say that the report of the experiments is untrue, and that the trials were not fairly made. But, supposing this to be the case, the result is not altered. Paragraph 5 merely states more particularly what has been already stated before in paragraph 3, where the general charge of falsehood is made. Even if each particular charge of falsehood is established, it will only come to this—that it is untrue that the defendants' paint is better than or equal to that of the plaintiffs, for saying which no action lies. The particular reasons for making that statement are immaterial if the statement itself is not actionable. The statement of claim, then, as it stands, shews no reasonable cause of action; and the only other question is whether the plaintiffs should have liberty to amend by stating special damage as distinguished from general damage...

Lord Herschell expressed himself very emphatically to the same effect in *White v Mellin*, and he expressed his clear opinion that it could make no difference whether a defendant said that his goods were better than the plaintiff's generally, or whether the particulars in which the plaintiff's goods were said to be inferior were specified. He pointed out with great force that, if actions in such cases were held to lie, the Courts would be constantly engaged in trying the respective merits of the goods of rival

[82] [1899] 1 Q.B. 86, paragraph break supplied.

traders, and the pernicious practice of bringing actions for mere purposes of advertising would be greatly encouraged."

Mere puffing—criteria for liability

These cases suggest that the treatment of "puffing" really has several logi- **6–23** cally separate legal justifications, which may overlap in practice. One starting point would be that no amount of uncomparative praise of one's own goods or business, whether or not justified, necessarily constitutes a representation of any kind about one's competitors.[83] Such representations are not made "of or concerning" any potential claimant, unless there is an express or implicit element of comparison or denigration. Even if an element of comparison is present, it may be so imprecise that no individual competitor can be identified. From this fairly secure starting point, one moves to the second, and logically independent justification, which is that the public is supposedly too used to exaggeration and hyperbole in advertisements of every kind to take them seriously. This may mean either that they interpret the representation in a less than literal sense which removes its sting, or that they simply ignore it. On its face these are further reasons for saying that a "puffing" misrepresentation cannot be a material one, but in reality there is also an element of public policy in so far as the courts do not regard themselves as providing a service for determining–let alone advertising—the comparative merits and demerits of rival brands of goods. Allowing some kinds of misrepresentation to go unchecked is the price which has to be paid for this policy of judicial abstention. Finally, malice is difficult or impossible to prove once the representation has been characterised as mere puffing: the inference sometimes drawn from falsity is hardly relevant if the statement is of such a kind that no one will believe it at all; and malice in the sense of intention to injure another is inconsistent in the eyes of the law with a predominant or exclusive desire to promote one's own goods or business, by means fair or not so fair. The end result is something akin to a constitutional right to impart not information, but misinformation—although no one has any corresponding interest in receiving it.

The separate legal existence of at least some of these rationales may be seen by comparing *Hubbuck v Wilkinson Heywood*[84] with *De Beers v General Electric*.[85] In *De Beers*, Walton J. proposed a useful but possibly incomplete criterion to distinguish an actionable misrepresentation from mere puffing, which was whether the relevant public would take it seriously, and on the facts of that case he concluded:

"After this brief review of the relevant authorities I see no inconsistency between any of them; and I therefore now proceed to ask the question: can I be so certain that nobody would have taken the results of Tech-Data/1 seriously that I should grant the relief sought by the defendants and strike out the statement of claim? I do not feel able to do so in any

[83] See *Schulke & Mayr UK Ltd v Alkapharm UK Ltd* [1999] F.S.R. 161.
[84] [1899] 1 Q.B. 86, CA.
[85] [1975] 1 W.L.R. 972; [1975] 2 All E.R. 599; [1975] F.S.R. 323 (Walton J.).

way at all. It appears to me that, where the interested parties are presented with what purports to be a proper scientific test, properly carried out by the 'application laboratory'—whatever that is—they must be intended by the persons who furnished them with this information to take it all very seriously indeed. Such a report framed as the present report is framed cannot be dismissed in any way as a mere idle puff. It may well be of course that that is all in fact it is; but, if so, then the defendants have only themselves to blame for having dressed up a stupid old moke as a thoroughbred Arabian stallion.

If traders take the time and trouble to dress up their advertising material in this manner, then I think they must stand by it; and, if it contains, as in the case here, statements in disparagement of the plaintiffs' goods and if, further, on investigation those statements prove to be false and the plaintiff can show malice, the precise constituents of which for present purposes I think it is better not to investigate, it appears to me that they must answer for it."

However, *Hubbuck v Wilkinson Heywood* was also a case in which the relevant comparison was purportedly supported by proper experimental evidence, as were some of the previous cases.[86] *De Beers* therefore cannot be distinguished from *Hubbuck* on that ground, nor on the ground that the tradesmen to whom the contested circular was addressed would completely ignore the statement that the defendant's paint was as good as the plaintiff's, at half the price. *Hubbuck* does seem to be explicable only on the ground that there is a difference between unjustified praise of oneself and unjustified disparagement of a rival, and that the statement complained of must cross the line between them if it is to be actionable. This is not inconsistent with *De Beers*, but it means there are two criteria to be applied cumulatively: is the "puff" a disparaging one at all in point of law, and if so is it one which would be taken seriously. Conversely, unambiguous self-praise does become actionable, even if untrue, in proportion to the amount of circumstantial detail lavished on it.

C. MALICE, THE MENTAL ELEMENT

Malice as an essential element

6–24 As its alternative title indicates, one of the essential elements of the tort of injurious falsehood or malicious falsehood is "malice", and there are few terms in the law of torts which give rise to greater difficulties of interpretation. What was said by Bowen L.J. about "special damage" in *Ratcliffe*

---

[86] *Young v Macrae* (1862) 3 B. & S. 264; 122 E.R. 100, decided against the plaintiff; *Wesern Counties Manure Co v Lawes Chemical Manure Co* (1874) L.R. 9 Exch. 218 (Divisional Court), decided for the plaintiff on a demurrer.

v Evans,[87] would remain true *mutatur matantur* if "malice" were to be substituted:

"[A] term which, intelligible enough in particular contexts, tends, when successively employed in more than one context and with regard to different subject-matter to encourage confusion in thought. The question to be decided does not depend on words, but is one of substance."

The central importance of malice was established in the second half of the **6–25** nineteenth century. In *Steward v Young*[88] the defendant effectively frustrated an auction by claiming to hold a bill of sale over the goods on offer, but this was held not to be actionable:

"It is admitted ... that it is not enough in slander of title to shew that the claim set up is unfounded or invalid, but that it must further be shewn that the defendant was actuated by a malicious feeling against the plaintiff. The doctrine as to the onus of proof is put in a very plain way by Maule, J., in *Pater v. Baker*,[89] where he says:

'Slander of title ordinarily means a statement of something tending to cut down the extent of title, which is injurious only if it is false. It is essential, to give a cause of action, that the statement should be false. It is essential also that it should be malicious; not, as Lord Ellenborough observes in *Pitt v. Donovan*, malicious in the worst sense, but with intent to injure the plaintiff ... Unless he shews falsehood and malice, and an injury to himself, the plaintiff shews no case to go to the jury.'"

In this respect, injurious falsehood has developed in the opposite direction to passing-off, which was formerly based on fraudulent intent, but which no longer has any mental element at all. Be that as it may, there is no room for doubt that malice (whatever that word means) is an independent and essential element of the tort.

What is malice? Older cases

Numerous attempts to define malice in the context of injurious falsehood **6–26** have been attempted, and although the following may mostly be regarded as superceded by the decision of the Court of Appeal in *Spring v Guardian Assurance*[90] some are still of at least historical interest, if not more. Several of the earlier authorities were gathered together by Scrutton L.J. in *Shapiro v La Morta*[91]:

---

[87] [1892] 2 Q.B. 524, CA.
[88] (1870) L.R. 5 C.P. 122.
[89] (1847) 3 C.B. 831; 136 E.R. 333.
[90] [1993] All E.R. 273, CA, below.
[91] [1923] All E.R. 378, CA.

"The terms 'malice' and 'malicious' have caused more confusion in English law than any judge can hope to dispel. Malice is sometimes said to be 'where any person wilfully does an act injurious to another without lawful excuse': per Blackburn J. in *R. v Pembliton*. This is applied to cases similar to slander of title by Bowen L.J. in *Ratcliffe v Evans* as a statement of 'damage wilfully and intentionally done without just cause or excuse,' in which definition it is not clear what 'wilfully' adds to 'intentionally,' or what is 'just cause or excuse.' Lord Davey in *Royal Baking Powder Co v Wright Crossley* again defines 'maliciously' simply as 'without just cause or excuse.' In neither of these cases was it necessary to define 'malice', and neither definition explains what is a just cause or excuse."

And in *Greers v Pearman & Corder*[92] Scrutton L.J. said:

"The only question in this case is—is there evidence on which the jury could find that the statements were made maliciously? 'Maliciously', not in the sense of illegally, but in the sense of being made with some indirect or dishonest motive. Honest belief in an unfounded claim is not malice; but the nature of the unfounded belief may be evidence that it is not honestly believed."

6–27   After consideration of these and other cases in *Wilts United Dairies v Robinson*[93] Stable J. summarised their effect:

"As I understand it the law is this, that if you publish a defamatory statement about a man's goods which is injurious to him, honestly believing that it is true, your object being our own advantage and no detriment to him, you obviously are not liable. If you publish a statement which turns out to be false but which you honestly believe to be true, but you publish that statement not for the purpose of protecting your own interests and achieving some advantage for yourself but for the purpose of doing him harm, and it transpires, contrary to your belief, that the statement which you had believed to be true has turned out to be false, notwithstanding the bona fides of your belief because the object that you had in mind was to injure him and not to advantage yourself, you will be liable for an injurious falsehood.

The third proposition that I derive from the cases is this, that if you publish an injurious falsehood which you know to be false, albeit that your only object is your own advantage and with no intention or desire to injure the person in relation to whose goods the falsehood is published, then provided it is clear from the nature of the falsehood that it is intrinsically injurious—I say 'intrinsically', meaning not deliberately aimed with intent to injure but as being inherent in the statement itself, the defendant is responsible, the malice consisting in the fact that the fact that what he published he knew to be false."

---

[92] (1922) 39 R.P.C. 406, CA.
[93] [1957] R.P.C. 220 (Stable J., QBD), affirmed [1958] R.P.C. 94, CA.

What is malice? *Spring v Guardian Assurance*

The most recent decision of a superior court attempting to define malice in **6–28** the context of injurious falsehood is *Spring v Guardian Assurance*,[94] in which the Court of Appeal stated that the test for malice in the tort of injurious falsehood was the same as for rebutting a defence of qualified privilege in libel or slander. While this may appear to be conclusive, it will be seen that it is actually of rather less assistance than it seems.

The plaintiff in *Spring v Guardian Assurance* was a former life insurance salesman who had been dismissed when it became apparent that he was planning to join a rival firm. Under the code of conduct of Lautro (the Life Insurance and Unit Trust Regulatory Organisation) his new prospective employers obtained a reference from the defendants. The reference was so unfavourable as to make the plaintiff all but unemployable in the life insurance industry. Mr Spring sued for malicious falsehood, negligence, and breach of a supposed implied term in his contract of employment.

So far as the claim for injurious falsehood was concerned, the judge at first instance held that the terms of the reference were the result of the relevant persons at the defendant company believing that a serious incident of mis-selling for which the plaintiff had been responsible rendered him unfit for future employment. The judge also found that the incident was an honest mistake rather than an attempt to generate commission from an entirely unsuitable proposal, but that the relevant individuals at the defendants had honestly thought otherwise. The Court of Appeal upheld the dismissal of the injurious falsehood claim.

> "The test adopted by the judge as to what constitutes malice in the tort of malicious falsehood was derived from the speech of Lord Diplock in *Horrocks v Lowe* ...
>
> Having decided, as he did, that both Messrs Dixon and Siderfin honestly believed that what they said about the plaintiff was true, the judge acquitted both of malice ...
>
> In our judgment, the test of what constitutes malice in the tort of malicious falsehood is the same as the test in relation to the torts of libel and slander. In this case the learned judge directed himself entirely properly in adopting the guidance given in Lord Diplock's speech."

According to *Spring v Guardian Assurance*,[95] therefore, "malice" in the **6–29** present context means the same as it does in defamation, and for its meaning and rationale in defamation the Court of Appeal referred to the speech of Lord Diplock in *Horrocks v Lowe*[96]:

> "So, the motive with which the defendant on a privileged occasion made a statement defamatory of the plaintiff becomes crucial. The protection

---

[94] [1993] 2 All E.R. 273, CA.
[95] above.
[96] [1975] A.C. 135, HL.

might, however, be illusory if the onus lay on him to prove that he was actuated solely by a sense of the relevant duty or a desire to protect the relevant interest. So he is entitled to be protected by the privilege unless some other dominant and improper motive on his part is proved. 'Express malice' is the term of art descriptive of such a motive. Broadly speaking, it means malice in the popular sense of a desire to injure the person who is defamed and this is generally the motive which the plaintiff sets out to prove. But to destroy the privilege the desire to injure must be the dominant motive for the defamatory publication; knowledge that it will have that effect is not enough if the defendant is nevertheless acting in accordance with a sense of duty or in *bona fide* protection of his own legitimate interests.

The motive with which a person published defamatory matter can only be inferred from what he did or said or knew. If it be proved that he did not believe that what he published was true this is generally conclusive evidence of express malice, for no sense of duty or desire to protect his own legitimate interests can justify a man in telling deliberate and injurious falsehoods about another, save in the exceptional case where a person may be under a duty to pass on, without endorsing, defamatory reports made by some other person.

Apart from those exceptional cases, what is required on the part of the defamer to entitle him to the protection of the privilege is positive belief in the truth of what he published or, as it is generally though tautologously termed, 'honest belief.' If he publishes untrue defamatory matter recklessly, without considering or caring whether it be true or not, he is in this, as in other branches of the law, treated as if he knew it to be false. But indifference to the truth of what he publishes is not to be equated with carelessness, impulsiveness or irrationality in arriving at a positive belief that it is true … But despite the imperfection of the mental process by which the belief is arrived at it may still be 'honest,' that is, a positive belief that the conclusions they have reached are true. The law demands no more.

Even a positive belief in the truth of what is published on a privileged occasion—which is presumed unless the contrary is proved—may not be sufficient to negative express malice if it can be proved that the defendant misused the occasion for some purpose other than that for which the privilege is accorded by the law. The commonest case is where the dominant motive which actuates the defendant is not a desire to perform the relevant duty or to protect the relevant interest, but to give vent to his personal spite or ill will towards the person he defames. If this be proved, then even positive belief in the truth of what is published will not enable the defamer to avail himself of the protection of the privilege to which he would otherwise have been entitled. There may be instances of improper motives which destroy the privilege apart from personal spite. A defendant's dominant motive may have been to obtain some private advantage unconnected with the duty or the interest which constitutes the reason for the privilege. If so, he loses the benefit of the privilege despite his positive belief that what he said or wrote was true."

Applying *Horrocks* and *Spring* to commercial competition

Following *Spring v Guardian Assurance*,[57] the application of *Horrocks v* **6–30**
Lowe[98] to injurious falsehood may be abbreviated to the following propositions:

1. *Prima facie*, "malice" means a desire to injure, and the desire to injure must be the defendant's dominant purpose for there to be liability;

2. Conversely, malice is absent if the defendant is acting in accordance with a sense of duty or in *bona fide* protection of his own legitimate interests;

3. Motive is a matter of inference, and lack of belief in the truth of what is published is generally conclusive evidence of malice (since neither duty nor interest can justify telling deliberate and injurious falsehoods);

4. Malice is rebutted by honest belief in the statement complained of, though deliberate falsity and recklessness are treated alike. However, honest belief is not contradicted by carelessness or even irrationality in forming or holding that belief;

5. Honest belief does not negate malice if the occasion is misused for a collateral purpose or to give vent to spite.

Of these heads, numbers (3) and (4) go together. Subject to one problem, the **6–31**
test of honest belief as a surrogate for malice is one which is workable in the
context of commercial competition, although it cannot be taken as governing all cases. Lord Diplock's words suggest, and it is probably the case in
fact, that there is an element of legal fiction in treating case (3) simply as an
aspect of case (1), intention to injure. If so, so much the better. The facts in
Kaye v Robertson[99] might better be described as showing extreme callousness
rather than any degree of real malice, but they hardly disclose a situation
which the law ought to protect.

Beyond this point, the problems of applying *Horrocks v Lowe* in a commercial context are substantial. The first problem is that to attribute malice
to a company (unless it is so small or so closely controlled as to have an
identifiable moving spirit) is little more than a legal fiction. In *Spring* this
made no difference, since it was common ground that the issue of malice was
to be addressed by reference to the state of mind of the few individuals who
were actually responsible for giving the reference, and Mr Spring's case did
not stop short of alleging that one of those individuals had quite deliberately
told lies which he must have known would ruin Mr Spring's career for ever.
This problem is obviously most severe when one is dealing with aspects of
malice which involve personal motives; but the problem arises even when the

---

[97] [1993] 2 All E.R. 273, CA.
[98] [1975] A.C. 135, HL.
[99] [1991] F.S.R. 62, CA.

question is the less emotive one of truth or falsity, and the relevant knowledge is distributed around a committee, a department, or the business as a whole.

6–32 Secondly, the heads numbered (2) and (5) above require consideration of whether the defendant is acting in the course of performing a duty or protecting a legitimate interest, or for some extraneous purpose. When the issue of malice arises in rebuttal of a defence of qualified privilege then it always falls to be decided in relation to a specific context and purpose (both defined by the privilege in question), and nearly always in relation to a specific audience who have an interest in the receipt of the information in question, corresponding to the duty of the defendant to report it. The defence of fair comment may be an exception, but injurious falsehood is hardly ever concerned with mere statements of opinion. *Spring* itself is typical of this: the Lautro rules required Mr Spring's new employers to seek, and his former employers to give, a reference–for the benefit of the public, the industry and the parties themselves. If the case had been one of libel, there would been a defence of qualified privilege, and all that would have changed would have been the burden of proof. By way of contrast, the (mis)representations with which the present work is concerned are typically broadcast to the world at large, or at least to a large and indeterminate section of the public: the medium may be personal communication or a mailshot, or it may equally be press advertising in national newspapers or magazines, television advertising, posters, and so on. Cases of this kind do not lead to a comfortable analogy with defamation.

D. MALICE AND COMPETITION

Introduction

6–33 The whole body of decided cases on injurious falsehood in all its aspects is not large, and a large proportion of those are on facts of no direct relevance to competitive situations. Of the cases brought by businesses against competitors, most have failed for reasons connected with the absence of any sufficiently explicit or material misrepresentation, or absence of damage. Very few (to which might be added a few more decisions in a non-competitive business context) have gone so far as having to decide the issue of malice, and fewer still have actually decided malice against the defendant.

For present purposes, there are three possible meanings of "malice" in the modern law which need to be considered, and if possible reconciled. In what lawyers call its ordinary and natural meaning, malice denotes (at the very least) a desire or intention to injure someone, with perhaps the further implication that harm is being inflicted for harm's sake alone, out of spite or malevolence. Malice of this kind will rarely be capable of proof in a competitive situation, not least because such situations are in fact likely to be rare. In a capitalist market economy, it is rightly assumed that every individual enterprise is striving to better its competitive position for the benefit of its shareholders. If its competitors suffer in the process, then all that means is that the game is one that produces losers as well as winners. What is true of the enterprise is equally true of those who direct it, or perform ministerial acts on its behalf. Their motivation is presumed to lie in the profits gained for their company, not in the losses suffered by its less successful rivals. Of course, this form of purely economic competition may be enlivened or embittered by personal rivalry or animosity, or by unedifying displays of satisfaction at the discomfiture (or worse) of a particular opponent, but in the eyes of the law all this falls well short of malice. Malice in this sense requires a dominant intention to injure, and the businessman who puts the humiliation of his rivals before the well-being of his own company is, economically speaking, acting just as irrationally as one who puts the well-being of his rivals above or on a par with that of his own.

This leads to the second problem with malice as malevolence, which is that even if a businessman does let personal animosity towards a competitor get the better of him (and there probably are such cases) then from the outside his conduct is not at all easy to distinguish from an extreme case of the sometimes ruthless cut and thrust of legitimate competition. The law starts with a strong *de facto* presumption that acts legitimately done in the course of competition ought not to be actionable, and it ought not to be difficult for anyone really actuated by malice to cover his tracks effectively enough, whether before or after the event. Even if one allows that such a person is bound to be found out in the end (which probably overestimates the infallibility of the legal process) it still requires a considerable degree of faith on the part of the injured claimant to commence proceedings without the sort of proof of malice which is likely to be forthcoming (if at all) no earlier than disclosure or cross-examination.

Finally, in the present context, malice of this kind presupposes some **6–34** individual driving personality, or perhaps a conspiracy of like-minded malicious persons. Again, it cannot be denied that such situations probably do exist and that the law is right to address them as and when they do. But when *Dell* comes to blows with *Compaq*, or *Ryanair* with *British Airways*, it is almost always futile as well as artificial to try to find some individual whose mind or motives can be dissected for evidence of malice or innocence. In all but a few cases of this kind, the representations complained of can only realistically be regarded as the product of the enterprise itself, not of any identifiable individuals within it. True, one may be able to point to some one person who set the objectives and parameters for an advertising campaign or gave the go-ahead for it to run, but he will typically have relied on a pile of information and advice gathered from many diverse sources.

The more typical situation is represented by *Emaco v Dyson*[1]: both parties published disparaging and inaccurate statements about one another's products, but in every case the inaccuracies were the result of "mistakes" which may well have been grossly negligent, but which fell well short of proven malice when examined in detail. The result was that both were liable for

---

[1] [1999] E.T.M.R. 903 (Jonathan Parker J.), the report omits the passages of the judgment dealing with this point.

trade mark infringement, since their conduct fell short of the objective standard of "honest practices in industrial or commercial matters", but not for injurious falsehood. If the latter phrase means the same in Article 10*bis*(3)(2) of the Paris Convention as it does in s.10(6) of the Trade Marks Act 1994, then the non-compliance of the United Kingdom with the former is well illustrated.

Since malice in the sense of malevolence is likely to be either non-existent—or all but incapable of proof–as between competitors, two alternative concepts dominate the decided cases.[2] As a practical matter, malice seems capable of being found only in two situations which are sufficiently repeatable even to begin to be of practical importance: when some specific and unjustified purpose can be identified which is quite unrelated to the normal cut and thrust of competition; or where a disparagement or comparison is so indisputably false and damaging that the defendant cannot be believed if he says he thought otherwise. But much depends on the susceptibility to shock of the individual judge or (previously) the jury: for every successful case in one of these categories, more than one unsuccessful one will be found in which the inference of malice seems no less persuasive.

Malice and untruthfulness

6–35 There is no doubt that inferences of malice may be drawn (in two stages) when the statement complained of is in fact false, and is calculated to damage the claimant. Of course if neither of these conditions are met, then the issue of malice is likely to be a theoretical one. First, depending on its flagrancy, the falsity of the statement may have the practical effect of putting the evidential burden of proof on the defendant so as to require positive evidence that the statement was one which was honestly believed by the person responsible. However this is probably a statement of common sense rather than a rule of law. Both the general law as stated in *Horrocks v Lowe*, and individual cases, confirm that it is always open to the defendant to satisfy the court that the statement corresponded to an honestly held belief, no matter how wrong, careless or even irrational that belief might be.

Rather more strongly, if it is proved that the defendant knew that a damaging statement was false (or was reckless or indifferent as to its truth or falsity) then the inference or malice is very much stronger, and may as a practical matter be irrebuttable. As Glidewell L.J. said in *Kaye v Robertson*[3]:

> "The essentials of this tort are that the defendant has published about the plaintiff words which are false, that they were published maliciously, and that special damage has followed as the direct and natural result of their publication ... Malice will be inferred if it be proved that the words were calculated to produce damage and that the defendant knew when he published the words that they were false or was reckless as to whether they were false or not."

[2] See Hazel Carty, *An Analysis of the Economic Torts* (2000), p.161 *et seq.*
[3] [1991] F.S.R. 62, CA.

And as Atkin L.J. had previously said in *Shapiro v La Morta*[4]:

> "I shall assume that a statement made by a man who knows that it is likely to injure and knows that it is false is made maliciously and I shall make the same assumption if he knows that it is likely to injure and has no belief whether it is true or false, and makes it recklessly, not caring whether it is true or false."

The law may sometimes go even further. In *Joyce v Sengupta*[5] the Court of Appeal refused to strike out a claim in which the inference of malice was even more indirect, but the reasoning may depend on the unusual seriousness of the allegations in that case:

> "Essentially, the plaintiff's case on malice is that the defendants went ahead and published the police suspicions as though they were fact and did so without taking any steps to check or verify them. This showed a calculated, reckless indifference to the truth or falsity of the allegations. Malice is to be inferred from the grossness and falsity of the assertions and the cavalier way they were published In my view the pleading raises an arguable issue, and it does so in terms sufficient to inform the defendants of the case against them."[6]

However, objective falsity, tendency to damage, and malice are inde- **6–36** pendent elements of the tort and one of them cannot be made to stand in for another. What is required to establish malice is actual knowledge of the falsity of an inherently damaging statement, or reckless disregard as to its truth. So in *Balden v Shorter*[7] (in which the defendant had wrongly stated that the plaintiff was still employed by his former company) Maugham J. concluded "I think that in the present case the statements were, at the worst, careless statements made without any indirect motive and without any intention of injuring the plaintiff, and I find that Mr. Bensted believed them to be true". And as *Emaco v Dyson*[8] illustrates, attempts to prove malice from the existence of incontestable falsehoods may still unravel because the source of the inaccuracies cannot be pinned down with sufficient precision. The inference of malice from falsity would be altogether more important if more cases were decided at the interlocutory stage, but this raises entirely separate problems for the claimant, and successful examples are few.

Examples

In *Wilts United Dairies v Robinson*[9] one question was whether the defen- **6–37**

---

[4] [1923] All E.R. 383, CA. Though expressly *obiter* in its original context, this is generally taken as stating the law.
[5] [1993] 1 W.L.R. 337, CA.
[6] *per* Nicholls V.C.
[7] [1933] Ch. 427 (Maugham J.).
[8] [1999] E.T.M.R. 903 (Jonathan Parker J.).
[9] [1957] R.P.C. 220 (Stable J., QBD), affirmed [1958] R.P.C. 94, CA.

dants were liable for injurious falsehood by selling, without explanation, condensed milk prepared by the plaintiffs which had deteriorated to the extent of being unpalatable, though not actually unfit for consumption. Stable J., after summarising the law[10] concluded:

> "I have come to the conclusion here that the representation was that this [milk] was what I may call the Plaintiffs' current milk, which the Defendants knew perfectly well that it was not; that their intention or object in selling the milk, making these representations and all the rest of it, was their own advantage and nothing else ...; but the fact that they knew that what they were saying was intrinsically injurious and they knew it was not true constitutes malice and therefore they are liable at the suit of the Plaintiffs under the heading of injurious falsehood."

In *Danish Mercantile Co v Beaumont*[11] the defendant's claim that a company formed by him was the sole importer and distributor of a certain brand of sugar beet harvester was plainly false when it was made: the company did not then exist; the plaintiffs, and not the defendants, had the benefit of a sole distributorship agreement from the manufacturers, and the defendants had none. The plaintiffs, who were in fact sole importers of the machinery in question, obtained an interlocutory injunction. It did not matter that by the time of the hearing the defendant claimed to believe that the plaintiffs' agreement had been terminated and one in favour of his company substituted. Whatever his state of mind at that point, the legal analysis did not begin to support that conclusion.

6–38 It is probably no coincidence that this and the following two cases involve the grant of interlocutory injunctions. Following *American Cyanamid v Ethicon*,[12] the rule of practice adopted for cases of alleged injurious falsehood was that the claimant had to prove the falsity of the representation complained of beyond any possibility of a hypothetical jury upholding a defence of justification[13]; but that the separate issue of malice was subject to the normal *Cyanamid* standard of there being a serious issue to be tried. Given the rare finding that one was dealing with a misrepresentation which was false beyond any possibility of contradiction, then there could be little residual difficulty in persuading the judge that the allegation of malice was at least not bound to fail. *Kaye v Robertson*[14] is just such an example.

So in *Compaq v Dell*,[15] Aldous J. held that a number of comparisons between the parties' computers in terms of specification and price were so false as to be incapable of justification. That, and consideration of the balance of convenience, were sufficient to justify granting an interlocutory

---

[10] See above, para.6–27.
[11] (1950) 67 R.P.C. 111 (Roxburgh J.).
[12] [1975] A.C. 396; [1975] F.S.R. 101; [1975] R.P.C. 513, HL.
[13] *Bestobell Paints Ltd v Bigg* [1975] F.S.R. 421; *Crest Homes Ltd v Ascott* [1980] F.S.R. 396, CA.
[14] [1991] F.S.R. 62, CA.
[15] [1992] F.S.R. 93 (Aldous J.).

injunction on the reasoning of *Kaye v Robertson*.[15] In *DSG v Comet Group*[17] Owen J. posed the question "were the statements published maliciously" and replied:

> "Malice for the purpose of the tort of malicious falsehood consists of knowledge of falsity or recklessness as to the truth of the statement. If it is made clear to a defendant in the course of proceedings that the statement complained of is false, any further dissemination will be malicious and an injunction may be granted on that basis.
>
> As will be clear from the conclusions at which I have already arrived, I am satisfied that Comet were well aware of the falsity of the statements contained in the offending posters."

It is also noticeable that these two cases were concerned with price comparisons, either between identical brands of household appliances (*DSG v Comet*), or between computers which the defendants *Dell* expressly described as "basically and essentially the same" as those of *Compaq*, when they were not. With price comparisons of these kinds there is little scope for doubt as to whether they are true or false, and still less doubt that they are material.

If the statement complained of is not indisputably false, then there is little **6–39** or no scope for deducing the presence of malice from its supposed falsity. Since truth or falsity tends to be dealt with as one of the first issues, this means that many cases may be disposed of without malice ever becoming a live issue. Many more are decided on the basis that the defendant is at most puffing his own goods: a ground which has no real independent existence but which conflates issues of justification, materiality and public policy with that of malice.

In *McDonald's v Burgerking*[18] the plaintiffs complained of an advertising campaign under the slogan *It's Not Just Big, Mac*, with copy stating that the defendants' *Whopper* "unlike some burgers" was 100 per cent pure beef. The defendants undertook not to repeat the advertisements, but the plaintiffs' claim for damages and costs was refused:

> "Passing off lies close very often to trade libel, but whereas in passing off motive may be quite immaterial, to succeed in trade libel, that is, to succeed in the allegation that there has been a publication of a malicious falsehood, malice must be established. So much Mr. Jacob has accepted. Having heard Mr. Scott and Mr. Kyle Craig, I am entirely satisfied that they were never for one moment intending to suggest that McDonald's hamburgers were not 100 per cent. pure beef, and Mr. Jacob did not attempt to impugn their evidence or to suggest that any other conclusion should be reached on their evidence. He said, however, that although if Burgerking had been saying no more than that the 'Whopper' was better

---

[16] Above.
[17] [2002] EWHC 116; [2002] F.S.R. 58 (Owen J., QBD).
[18] [1987] F.S.R. 112. CA, affirming Whitford J.

than other people's he would not be entitled to complain and although he was not suggesting that what was done here was done with some sort of improper motive, that his clients ought to be entitled to succeed so far as malice is concerned upon the basis of reckless indifference. He referred me to a well known passage in *Gatley on Libel and Slander* (8th Edition) in this particular regard. He did not proceed to elaborate on any way in which it could be suggested that there had been some reckless indifference. I am quite satisfied that no case has been made out under this head at all and the action, in so far as it seeks relief in respect of malicious falsehood, accordingly fails."[19]

6–40 A rare case in recent times of malice being the subject of separate determination at trial is *Vodafone v Orange*,[20] which illustrates how far a claimant may have to go in attempting to prove malice, and the improbability of success in all but the clearest cases:

"To my mind Vodafone's case on malice is hopeless. Mr Hartley did not shrink from accusing Mr Gardner, Mr Harris and Mr Davie of deliberate perjury. The perjury consisted of saying that they believed the statement to be true. I reject that accusation as preposterous. There is not a shred of foundation in it. I found all three witnesses fair and careful. Mr Gardner in particular was cross-examined for a full day—far longer than would have been enough if it was to be shown that the claim was made knowing it to be false or recklessly without regard to its truth or falsity. Mr Gardner explained how the campaign was devised. A wholly independent organisation called Profundus had carried out an exercise of tariff comparison using notional users. It showed that Orange was cheaper. The exercise received some publicity but Vodafone never complained. Profundus' notional users were not typical (they had too high a usage). But the idea of comparison came from the article, but using the actual Orange users. This is a wholly credible account of events.

Mr Hartley submitted that malice was established by two matters. First he said that because the ordinary meaning was so obviously false, malice should be inferred. If and to the extent that any witness said he thought the statement true, he must be lying ... Now I can see that there may be cases where a man makes a statement which is so self-evidently false that if he says he believed it, one does not believe him. But this case is miles from that.

The second submission related to a particular incident in the run up to approval by BACC.[21] ... I reject the malice allegation."

Malice and motive

6–41 The second approach is to equate malice not with intention to injure for the

---

[19] *per* Whitford J. above.
[20] [1997] F.S.R. 34 (Jacob J.).
[21] The allegation was that calculations justifying the comparison had been concocted after the event.

sake of it, but with some collateral object in mind (the "by or sinister purpose" contemplated by Harman J. in *Serville v Constance*[22]) which does not justify the freedom to publish information which may or may not be honestly believed by the defendant, but which *ex hypothesi* is both false and damaging to the claimant. The problem in the present context is that this leads inevitably to the very problem which the courts consistently refuse to answer—that of drawing the line between fair and unfair conduct in competition—and as long as this remains the case it can have no more than marginal significance between competitors.

Although "motive malice" either in the sense of a deliberate intention to injure, or the pursuit of some collateral purpose, is recognised in the decided cases and the literature, it is anything but straightforward to find clear and unambiguous examples in a competitive context which cannot equally well be explained as ones in which the defendant was very well aware of the untruth of what he published. A further problem with many of the older cases is that malice would have been left to the jury, whose reasons for the verdict are sometimes inscrutable to the point of being incomprehensible. At first sight a promising example is the first instance decision in *London Ferro Concrete v Justicz*,[23] where Vaisey J. used some very harsh words about the motives of the individual defendant in stating that the plaintiffs' proposed method of construction was inadequate; but the whole of the judgment is undermined by the assumption that the defendant's pursuit of the contract for himself turned an otherwise innocent statement into an actionable one. "If the defendant had been a mere busybody, I think this action would have failed. [But] the defendant was a busybody with an eye to his own advantage, seeking to serve his own ends ...". Virtually every other decided case on the liability of competitors *inter se* proceeds on precisely the opposite assumption, and Vaisey J. did also hold that the disparagement exceeded what the defendant really believed. On appeal, the issue of malice was treated solely as one of fact and evidence, on which the judge's findings should not be upset.

Perhaps the clearest example of motive malice in a business (though not a **6–42** competitive) situation occurs in *Joyce v Motor Surveys*,[24] where the plaintiff carried on business as a motor tyre agent. To obtain tyres at a trade discount, he had to be registered with the relevant trade association and have suitable premises, which consisted of a lock-up garage which he rented from the defendants. The defendants told the trade association, tyre manufacturers, and casual enquirers that the plaintiff was no longer a tenant of theirs, and they returned his letters to the Post Office with an explanation that he had gone away. All this was done in an attempt to drive him out after the defendants had purported to terminate his tenancy so they could sell the whole premises with vacant possession. There was a concurrent dispute, ultimately resolved in favour of the plaintiff, as to whether the tenancy was one at will or for a fixed term.

---

[22] [1954] 1 W.L.R. 487; [1954] 1 All E.R. 662; (1954) 71 R.P.C. 146 (Harman J.).
[23] *London Ferro-Concrete Co v Justicz* (1951) 68 R.P.C. 261, CA, affirming (1951) 68 R.P.C. 65 (Vaisey J.).
[24] [1948] Ch. 252 (Roxburgh J.).

"There now remains the most difficult question, the question of malice. My view of the evidence as a whole is this: Miss Hammett, on behalf of the defendants, may have believed that the plaintiff was only a weekly tenant ... However, whether she really ever believed that he was a weekly tenant or not, she certainly knew that he was disputing her contention and, with that knowledge, she devised a series of correlated steps designed to drive him out of business and so destroy his will to resist the notice to quit if perchance he should manifest any such a will ... A landlord who, in such circumstances, embarks upon such a scheme is, in my judgment, actuated by an improper motive. He is, in my judgment, pursuing an improper objective and, if he publishes falsehoods, he, in my judgment, publishes them maliciously."

However, the defendants cannot possibly have failed to notice that the plaintiff was still in occupation, so the case may equally well be regarded as one in which the statements were made in the knowledge that they were false.

A possible further example of motive malice is *Bestobell v Bigg*[25] in which the motive of the defendant, a dissatisfied trade customer, was indisputably to put pressure on the claimants so that they would settle a claim for supplying allegedly defective paint. However, in this case, as in *Crest Homes v Ascott*[26] interlocutory injunctions were refused because the respective defendants intended to justify their complaints and the issues of malice and motive were not further examined.

E. Interpreting the Representation; the "One Meaning" Rule

The "one meaning" or "single meaning" rule stated ...

6–43 In defamation properly so called, there is undoubtedly a rule that that a single meaning has to be attributed to the allegedly defamatory statement for the purposes of deciding whether it is true or false in relation to the claimant.[27] There is no room for speculating, or even admitting evidence,[28] that the statement might be understood in one way by one part of the public, and in a different way by others. The rule for defamation may be regarded as an aspect of the related but logically separate rule that the alleged

---

[25] [1975] F.S.R. 421 (Oliver J.).

[26] [1980] F.S.R. 369, CA. The defendant, a disgruntled purchaser of a new house, was criticised for taking matters into his own hands instead of taking legal proceedings.

[27] Though not necessarily for all other purposes, in particular that of rebutting qualified privilege by proving malice: *Bonnick v Morris* [2002] 3 W.L.R. 820, PC. The single meaning rule does apply for calculation of damages in defamation.

[28] Absent a legal innuendo, in the true sense of extrinsic factual circumstances which could result in the statement convening a different meaning to some, compared to what it appeared to say on its face.

defamatory statement must be read as a whole,[29] and as justified, at least in part, by the need to define an issue in a suitable form to put to a jury. This is in marked contrast to the situation for passing-off and trade mark infringement, where it is accepted that different categories of the public may understand the defendant's use of the claimant's indicia in different ways, especially if the imitation is not precise; and where there is no presumption that the "antidote" almost invariably found in minuscule type somewhere on the back of the package will receive anything like equal attention to the "bane" emblazoned all over the front.

The rule for defamation is an ancient one, and its tenuous connection with reality was noted, even in its established context, by Lord Nicholls in the leading modern authority, which is *Charleston v News Group Newspapers*.[30] Two well-known television actors complained of the publication in the *News of the World* of composite photographs which appeared to show them in attitudes suggestive of pornography:

"At first sight one would expect the law to recognise that some newspaper readers will have seen only the banner headline and glanced at the picture. They will not have read the text of the accompanying article. In the minds of these readers, the reputation of the person who is the subject of the defamatory headline and picture will have suffered. He has been defamed to these readers. The newspaper could have no cause for complaint if it were held liable accordingly. It has chosen, for its own purposes, to produce a headline which is defamatory. It cannot be heard to say that the article must be read as a whole when it knows that not all readers will read the whole article.

To anyone unversed in the law of defamation that, I venture to think, would appear to be the common sense of the matter. Long ago, however, the law of defamation headed firmly in a different direction. The law adopts a single standard for determining whether a newspaper article is defamatory: the ordinary reader of that newspaper. I leave aside cases where some readers may have special knowledge of facts which would cause them to give the words a different meaning.

In principle this is a crude yardstick, because readers of mass circulation newspapers vary enormously in the way they read articles and the way they interpret what they read. It is, indeed, in this very consideration that the law finds justification for its single standard. The consequence is that, in the case of some publications, there may be many readers who understand in a defamatory sense words which, by the single standard of the ordinary reader, were not defamatory. In respect of those readers a plaintiff has no remedy. The converse is equally true. So a newspaper may find itself paying damages for libel assessed by reference to a readership many of whose members did not read the words in a defamatory sense."

[29] Defamation lawyers refer to "bane and antidote" by reference to *Chalmers v Payne* (1835) 2 C.M. & R. 156; 150 E.R. 67; see *per* Lord Bridge in *Charleston v News Group Newspapers Ltd* [1995] A.C. 65, HL.

[30] [1995] A.C. 65, HL.

...and applied in injurious falsehood cases

6-44 The question then arises of whether the single meaning rule applies to injurious falsehood, or, to put the question slightly differently, whether for present purposes injurious falsehood has more in common with libel and slander than with passing-off and trade mark infringement.

The question was addressed by Jacob J. in *Vodafone v Orange*,[31] although what follows is entirely *obiter* for two separate reasons. First, the parties agreed to the single meaning rule being applied for the purposes of injurious falsehood; and secondly, when Jacob J. applied the open-ended trade mark and passing-off approach to the trade mark infringement issues under s.10(6) of the Trade Marks Act 1994 he found that it made no difference what interpretation one gave to the advertisement in question. On any interpretation it could credibly bear it was true.

> "The meaning of the words concerned is the first matter to be considered, for their truth or falsity is to be tested against that meaning. The meaning is for the court to determine when a judge sits without a jury. Evidence of the meaning to others is inadmissible. The question:
>
>> 'is not one of construction in the legal sense. The ordinary man does not live in an ivory tower and he is not inhibited by the rules of construction. So he can and does read between the lines in the light of his general knowledge and experience of worldly affairs ... What the ordinary man would infer without special knowledge has generally been called the natural and ordinary meaning of the words. But that expression is rather misleading in that it conceals the fact that there are two elements in it. Sometimes it is not necessary to go beyond the words themselves, as where the plaintiff has been called a thief or a murderer. But more often the sting is not so much in the words themselves as in what the ordinary man will infer from them, and that is also regarded as part of their natural and ordinary meaning, *per* Lord Reid in *Lewis v. The Daily Telegraph*.'
>
> That case was one of libel but the principle must be the same for malicious falsehood: for the question both in libel and malicious falsehood is, 'what is the meaning to the ordinary man?'
>
> The legal construct of the ordinary man—'Joe Soap', 'Joe Punter' and 'Joe Public' as he was variously called during the case—may in reality take a given set of words in different ways. Different people may react in different ways to a statement—and in particular may draw different 'stings' from it. But it is settled, as was accepted by both sides, that I must look for the single natural and ordinary meaning. In *Charleston v. News Group Newspapers Ltd* Lord Bridge (with whom the other members of the House agreed) referred ... to 'two principles which are basic to the law of libel':

---

[31] [1997] F.S.R. 34 (Jacob J.).

'The first is that, where no legal innuendo is alleged to arise from extrinsic circumstances known to some readers, the "natural and ordinary meaning" to be ascribed to the words of an allegedly defamatory publication is the meaning, including any inferential meaning, which the words would convey to the mind of the ordinary, reasonable, fair-minded reader. This proposition is too well established to require citation of authority. The second principle, which is perhaps a corollary of the first, is that, although a combination of words may in fact convey different meanings to the minds of different readers, the jury in a libel action, applying the criterion which the first principle dictates, is required to determine the single meaning which the publication conveyed to the notional reasonable reader and to base its verdict and any award of damages on the assumption that this was the one sense in which all readers would have understood it.'[32]

As a comparative stranger to this branch of the law I find the 'one meaning rule' strange, particularly for malicious falsehood. Without authority, I should have thought it would be enough to satisfy the criterion of falsity for the plaintiff to prove that the defendant made a statement which was false to a substantial number of people. That, for instance, is the position in passing off (a tort also concerned with false representations): for that tort it is enough to show that the representation fools some of the people, even if not most of them."

It may be noted that in *Vodafone v Orange* the application of the single meaning rule was only explained by reference to cases of defamation in the strict sense, and was almost certainly prompted by the recent decision of the House of Lords in *Charleston v News Group Newspapers*.[33] Subsequently, in *British Airways v Ryanair*,[34] Jacob J. again applied the rule in the context of injurious falsehood, but without attempting to amplify the reasoning of *Vodafone*. Since the latter is *obiter* the fundamental question remains: putting aside the imperfect analogy between injurious falsehood and defamation, then can support for the mandatory application of the single meaning rule to the former be justified by principle, authority, or expediency? So far as the latter is concerned, the single meaning rule savours rather too much of rough justice. Passing-off copes very well without a single meaning rule and the continuing imposition of the latter in cases of libel and slander seems to be justified mainly by the right to trial by jury, which is hardly relevant in the present context. None the less, it will be suggested that the application of the single meaning rule in injurious falsehood is supported by unimpeachable authority, and that there is a relevant if not entirely conclusive distinction in principle with passing-off and trade mark infringement. **6–45**

---

[32] A quotation from Diplock L.J. in *Slim v Daily Telegraph Ltd* [1968] 2 Q.B. 157, CA, omitted here, is set out below.
[33] [1995] A.C. 65, HL.
[34] [2001] F.S.R. 32 (Jacob J.).

The comparison with passing-off and other torts

6–46 So far as principle is concerned, in comparing injurious falsehood to other torts one cannot simply deduce the single meaning rule from the proposition that the relevant addressee in both cases is the ordinary man. That the relevant meaning of a representation is ascertained by asking how it will be understood by the ordinary man is equally true for passing-off and registered trade mark infringement, neither of which apply the single meaning rule. And passing-off and trade mark law really do allow the evidence of the ordinary man to be heard, unlike defamation where it is rigorously excluded. As often as not, the "ordinary and natural meaning" adopted for defamation or injurious falsehood is one which could only be imagined by a lawyer. Conversely, the single meaning rule in its wider aspect applies with most rigour where the understanding of the ordinary man is least relevant: patent claims, court orders and Acts of Parliament can only have one meaning, but that is not because any of them are to be construed according to the cannons of Joe Soap.

In *British Airways v Ryanair*[35] Jacob J. followed his own decision in *Vodafone v Orange*[36] and held that the single meaning rule applied to the injurious falsehood claim (though not to that for trade mark infringement) while acknowledging that the "average consumer" standard for the latter[37] was "no different to that which our law has traditionally applied in cases of passing off and trade mark infringement" and that "it is the same average consumer who is relevant when one comes to consider malicious falsehood". So one has the situation that the same "average consumer" or "ordinary man" is relevant for injurious falsehood, trade mark infringement (whether under United Kingdom or European law) and passing-off; but that the single meaning rule applies only to the first. This being the case, one cannot simply reason, as Jacob J. did in *Vodafone*, that "[*Lewis v Daily Telegraph*] was one of libel but the principle must be the same for malicious falsehood: for the question both in libel and malicious falsehood is, 'what is the meaning to the ordinary man?'".

It is suggested, however, that as a practical matter the single meaning rule must stand or fall with the rejection or admission of evidence of how ordinary men and women actually understood the statement in issue. Absent such evidence, it is hard to see how the adjudicator can avoid treating the statement as it if meant only one thing to everyone.

6–47 A better starting point for a four way comparison of injurious falsehood with defamation, passing-off, and registered trade mark infringement is that in injurious falsehood (as in libel and slander) the representation is almost always conveyed by words, and is therefore susceptible to semantic inter-

---

[35] [2001] F.S.R. 32 (Jacob J.).
[36] [1997] F.S.R. 34 (Jacob J.).
[37] Under the case law of the European Court of Justice, specifically Cases C–220/98 *Estee Lauder Cosmetics GmbH & Co OHG v Lancaster Group GmbH* [2000] E.C.R. I-117; [2000] All E.R. (EC) 122; [2000] 1 C.M.L.R. 515 and C-210/96 *Gut Springenheide GmbH v Oberkreisdirektor des Kreises Steinfurt–Amt fur Lebensmitteluberwachung* [1998] E.C.R. I-4657; [1999] 1 C.M.L.R. 1383.

pretation in the same way as any other written or oral statement.[38] The relevant meaning of the representation may be perfectly clear on its face, it may be obscure or ambiguous, or it may be ascertainable only by reference to external facts, in which case one speaks of a legal innuendo. As Diplock L.J. observed in *Slim v Daily Telegraph*[39] (in a passage quoted by Jacob J. in *Vodafone v Orange*):

"Everyone outside a court of law recognises that words are imprecise instruments for communicating the thoughts of one man to another. The same words may be understood by one man in a different meaning from that in which they are understood by another and both meanings may be different from that which the author of the words intended to convey; but the notion that the same words should bear different meanings to different men, and that more than one meaning should be 'right', conflicts with the whole training of a lawyer. Words are the tools of his trade. He uses them to define legal rights and duties. They do not achieve that purpose unless there can be attributed to them a single meaning as the 'right' meaning. And so the argument between lawyers as to the meaning of words starts with the unexpressed major premise that any particular combination of words has one meaning, which is not necessarily the same as that intended by him who published them or understood by any of those who read them, but is capable of ascertainment as being the 'right' meaning by the adjudicator to whom the law confides the responsibility of determining it ... Where, as in the present case, words are published to the millions of readers of a popular newspaper, the chances are that if the words are reasonably capable of being understood as bearing more than one meaning, some readers will have understood them as bearing one of those meanings and some will have understood them as bearing others of those meanings. But none of this matters. What does matter is what the adjudicator at the trial thinks is the one and only meaning that the readers as reasonable men should have collectively understood the words to bear. That is 'the natural and ordinary meaning' of words in an action for libel ..."

By way of contrast, passing-off (like registered trade mark infringement) **6–48** typically deals not with statements whose meaning is defined by their *words*, but with *signs* which may not consist of words at all. The sign may be a composite phrase (The *Daily Telegraph, Camel Hair Belting, British Airways*), a single word (*Orange, Advocaat, Ryanair*), or something entirely or predominantly non-verbal such as a logo, device or get-up; but in no case can the meaning (or significance) of the sign simply be ascertained by a process of semantic interpretation. Signs in general are not the tools of the lawyer's trade, he has no special expertise in interpreting them, and he starts with no preconception or major premise that what is claimed to be a sign (a

---

[38] Misrepresentation by conduct (or even silence) is possible, but rare. *Wilts United Dairies Ltd v Thomas Robinson Sons & Co Ltd* [1958] R.P.C. 94, CA, is an example.

[39] [1968] 2 Q.B. 157, CA.

solid red triangle, say, or a container in the shape of a plastic lemon) means anything at all, still less that it conveys or even ought to convey a single and uniform meaning to everyone to whom it is exposed. Unless the sign is so well known that judicial notice may be taken of its significance, then evidence is not only admissible, but essential, in order to prove what, if anything, it means, and to whom.

This is the exercise one implicitly undertakes when one asks if the sign is distinctive, or, as it is sometimes put, has a reputation. As a matter of semantic interpretation, *Camel Hair Belting* can only mean belting made from the hair of the camel, but that (though not irrelevant) is not remotely decisive. In actual usage, it can be proved that *Camel Hair Belting* means belting made by the firm of *Reddaway*, whether from camel hair or anything else.[40] Likewise, whether *Oven Chips* was indeed "an ungrammatical aggregate of two English nouns ... nonsensical without an explanation"[41] was utterly irrelevant in *McCain v Country Fair*.[42] What mattered was whether it meant the plaintiffs' potato chips, or simply potato chips prepared for cooking in the oven. It actually meant the latter, but evidence could have proved that it meant the former, or (as in the *Corona* case[43]) both usages could have coexisted together. It is, of course, more than possible that terms such as *Camel Hair Belting, Yorkshire Relish*, or *Oven Chips*, will be understood by some in their primary or descriptive sense, and by others as distinctive of some particular trader. They mean one thing to some, and something else to others. They have (or may have) a "secondary meaning", which may co-exist with the original or primary meaning or may wholly supercede it.

The fact that injurious falsehood is typically concerned with words rather than signs does not prove that it is either necessary or desirable that the single meaning rule should apply, but it goes some way to explaining why it does, and why it has never applied to trade mark infringement or passing-off.

Authority supporting *Vodafone*: *Royal Baking Powder v Wright Crossley*

6–49 In terms of authority, the starting point for the application of the single meaning rule to injurious falsehood ought to be the decision of the House of Lords in *Royal Baking Powder Co v Wright Crossley*.[44] The plaintiffs, an American company, had not opposed applications by the defendants for revocation of their two registered trade marks for *Royal Baking Powder*. Soon after rectification of the Register, the defendants issued a circular setting out the order of the court, and threatening to take unspecified legal

---

[40] *Reddaway (Frank) & Co Ltd v George Banham & Co Ltd* [1896] A.C. 199; [1895–9] All E.R. 313; 13 R.P.C. 218, HL.

[41] *per* Jeremiah Harman Q.C., quoted by Templeman L.J., in *McCain International Ltd v Country Fair Foods Ltd* [1981] R.P.C. 69, CA.

[42] [1981] R.P.C. 69, CA.

[43] *Havana Cigar and Tobacco Factories v Oddenino* [1924] 1 Ch. 179; 41 R.P.C. 47, CA.

[44] (1900) 18 R.P.C. 95, HL, affirming (1899) 16 R.P.C. 217, CA.

proceedings against anyone selling American baking powder in cans bearing either of the two revoked marks. The defendants had no proprietary claim to the marks themselves,[45] but use of one of the marks might have contravened s.105 of the Patents, Designs and Trade Marks Act 1883.[46] The plaintiffs were not identified by name.

The trial judge, Romer J., admitted extensive evidence as to the meaning of the circular and found for the plaintiffs. The Court of Appeal, and House of Lords, found for the defendants. In the Court of Appeal, the case was principally treated as one in which misrepresentation was absent: the circular meant precisely what it said, and it was not legitimate to treat it (as the trial judge had done) as if it meant that the plaintiffs could not legally sell their *Royal Baking Powder* under that name in England. Lindley M.R. cited *Daines v Hartley*[47] as deciding that the only relevant material was the language of the circular, which was plain and unambiguous: "The case has been conducted in the most extraordinary way by introducing evidence of what this man and the other understood by this circular. That evidence is absolutely inadmissible". The other two members of the court agreed. In the House of Lords, there was disagreement as to what the circular meant. Lord James and Lord Morris agreed with the Court of Appeal both as to the interpretation of the circular, and on the exclusion of evidence as to how it was understood in fact. Lords Davey and Robertson agreed with Romer J. that the circular was an unveiled assertion that the plaintiffs had no right to sell *Royal Baking Powder* in England at all. However, both of them reached this conclusion solely from the face of the document, and neither would have allowed the admission of evidence as to its meaning any more than the Court of Appeal would have done: "[T]he circular ... is a document of unusual clearness and precision. It contains no term which is either ambiguous or technical. Accordingly the construction of the circular is to be found within itself, and cannot be made to depend on the meaning assigned to it by the witnesses who read it".[48] Lord Halsbury did not address the issue of interpretation, and the whole House agreed in dismissing the appeal for lack of proof of special damage.

There can be no doubt that *Royal Baking Powder Co v Wright Crossley* is **6–50** a case of injurious falsehood pure and simple,[49] and it remains a leading case to this day. It is clear authority that unless the allegedly false statement cannot be properly understood at all without evidence, or an innuendo is alleged, then the statement is to be interpreted by the court by reference to its contents alone; and in any event without evidence from those who

---

[45] Their own product was *The Original Royal Baking Powder—Lion Brand* and they conceded they had no exclusive rights to *Royal* on its own.

[46] Making it an offence falsely to represent a mark as registered. The defendants had in fact taken proceedings under the section. There was a tenuous and ultimately irrelevant argument that use of the other mark might have contravened the Merchandise Marks Act 1887.

[47] (1848) 3 Exch. 200; 154 ER 815. *Daines v Hartley* is described as an action for slander of the plaintiffs in their trade, and was undoubtedly what would now be understood as an action for injurious or malicious falsehood, not for defamation.

[48] *per* Lord Robertson.

[49] An attempt to present it on appeal as one of libel, made barely possible by the fact that there had been no pleadings, was rejected out of hand.

received it as to how they understood it. The conclusion is ironically rein-forced by the extreme divergence of judicial opinion as to what this parti-cular instance of "perfect lucidity ... and business-like phraseology"[50] actually meant. To Romer J. and Lords Davey and Robertson the defen-dants were unambiguously and unjustifiably asserting that the plaintiffs had no right to use the trade mark *Royal* for baking powder in England at all; to the whole Court of Appeal and to Lords James and Morris it meant no more than that anyone using the precise form of label whose registration had been revoked would find themselves in court, under one pretext or another. Plainly, the circular could and did mean different things to dif-ferent people, but when it came to the opinion of the kind of businessman who actually received it, read it, and took notice of it—that was simply irrelevant and inadmissible.

Royal Baking Powder Co v Wright Crossley is also clear authority for the less controversial proposition that the meaning of the statement is to be ascertained objectively, so that the meaning ascribed to it by the author is not relevant at this point.[51]

---

[50] *per* Lord Robertson.
[51] The separate question of malice cannot be addressed without reference to what the author intended. If the author honestly intended an innocent meaning, he can hardly be convicted of malice because he failed to foresee the "ordinary and natural" meaning which the court would attribute to it. Compare *Bonnick v Morris* [2002] 3 W.L.R. 820, PC (defamation).

ACTIONABLE MISREPRESENTATIONS

A. Introduction

Passing-off and injurious falsehood compared

The present chapter attempts to deal with the various kinds of mis- **7–1**
representations which are actionable at common law either as passing-off or
as injurious falsehood. In most sections, this means that a category of
misrepresentation is treated wholly or predominantly as one or the other. It
does not attempt to deal with other torts of misrepresentation which may
occasionally occur in a competitive business context, such as defamation in
the sense of libel or slander, or with competitive torts in which misrepresentation is not an essential element.

The fundamental distinction between passing off and injurious falsehood
concerns the kind of misrepresentation with which each tort purports to
deal, with greater or lesser effectiveness. The tort of injurious falsehood is
the easier to define. To be actionable as injurious falsehood, the misrepresentation must be made about the claimant, or his goods, services, or
business, and be such as to damage him in his economic capacity. In strict
point of law, definitions of injurious falsehood do not require the misrepresentation to be one of disparagement or denigration, but (with a few
exceptions) it is hard to imagine any other kind of misrepresentation about
the claimant either being made maliciously, or being such as to cause
damage in a form recognised by law. One does not maliciously damage ones'
competitors by over-praising them.

As a practical matter, the misrepresentations addressed by injurious fal- **7–2**
sehood are always negative ones, at least in a relative sense, and are always
made by the defendant about the claimant, or his goods, business or services: for instance that the claimant has gone out of business, or lacks
independence or authority, or provides goods or services which are unsatisfactory, or infringes someone's intellectual property rights. A misrepresentation which impugns the personal or moral character of the
claimant is likely to be actionable not as injurious falsehood but as libel or
slander, although the two may overlap and it is possible for a single statement to give rise to liability under more than one head. A claim for injurious
falsehood need not fail because one for libel or slander would equally well lie
on the facts.

In comparison, it is easy to distinguish passing-off from injurious false-hood, but less easy to provide a comprehensive explanation of where its boundaries lie. The fundamental distinction is that passing-off concerns itself with misrepresentations which the defendant makes about himself, his goods services or business; but always with the proviso that although the misrepresentation need not expressly identify the claimant, and is not made "of or concerning the claimant" in the same sense as for injurious falsehood, it must still relate to the claimant in one of a number of defined ways. Of these, the most important in both theory and practice is the mis-representation that the defendant's goods, services, or business are in fact those of the claimant or are connected with the claimant in a sense which is material to those to whom the misrepresentation is addressed. How much further passing-off can be considered to go is addressed in the final section of this chapter, but two necessary (though probably not sufficient) elements are that the misrepresentation must be a positive one made by the defen-dants about his own goods, services, or business, and that the defendant's representation must be one which would be true if made by or with the authority of the claimant.

The importance of the distinction

7–3 At first sight, what could be simpler or more logical than a division between telling lies about oneself (passing-off) and telling lies about a competitor (injurious falsehood)? The problems that arise are threefold: first, passing-off and injurious falsehood by no means exhaust all the kinds of damaging misrepresentation which can be made in the course of commerce and competition; secondly, the misrepresentations which competitors make in the real world do not really fall so neatly into the two categories; and thirdly, the decision to categorise a misrepresentation as passing-off or injurious falsehood has an altogether disproportionate effect on the pro-spects of success in the action and the relief obtainable. It is scarcely an exaggeration to say that if a misrepresentation made in the course of competition can properly be categorised as passing-off, then the common law can be relied on to deal with it quickly and effectively; that if it must be categorised as injurious falsehood, then only the most outrageous cases are worth pursuing; and that if it falls into neither category, then it is unlikely to be civilly actionable at all, and the injured party must look to criminal or administrative law, or to the self-regulatory system for such relief as they respectively offer.

Both in theory and in practice, it is a great deal easier to succeed in an action for passing-off than in one for injurious falsehood. Predictably, this has two consequences: claimants try to present cases which are really ones of injurious falsehood as if they were ones of passing-off; and defendants say that the claim, if actionable at all, is really one for injurious falsehood. It is, of course, possible for one and the same misrepresentation to constitute both passing-off and injurious falsehood, as in *Worsley v Cooper*,[1] in which

---

[1] [1939] 1 All E.R. 290 (Morton J.).

the defendants issued a circular creating the impression that the plaintiff company had gone out of business and that the defendants were their successors. Morton J. held that the circular was actionable as passing off, without evidence of malice, and that on the facts it constituted a malicious falsehood of the *Ratcliffe v Evans*[2] kind.

In formal legal analysis, the main differences between passing-off and **7–4** injurious falsehood concern the presence or absence of a mental element. Over a century ago passing-off freed itself from the need to prove fraud, which had in any event been reduced to little more than a legal fiction, and proclaimed itself as a cause of action protecting a property right against infringers witting or unwitting. This development never happened for injurious falsehood, in which malice remains an essential element. In fact, the divergence is even more marked than this, since at about the same time that passing-off was dispensing with fraud as its basis, the element of malice in injurious falsehood was being elevated from a factor which might rebut a claim of privilege, into an essential element in every case. Until 1952, the requirement to prove special damage was also a significant deterrent.

Although the action for injurious falsehood formerly had some procedural advantages over that for defamation these never made it a preferred cause of action compared to passing-off, even in the comparatively rare cases where the plaintiff was an individual: the action for injurious falsehood does not abate on death, but neither does that for passing-off; legal aid, never available for defamation, was formerly available for passing-off as well as for injurious falsehood; the limitation period for injurious falsehood was previously longer than that for defamation, but has now been reduced to one year whereas that for passing-off remains at six years. So far as actual practice is concerned, perhaps the most important distinction between passing-off and injurious falsehood has been the rule, for injurous falsehood alone, that no interlocutory injunction would be granted unless the misrepresentation complained of was self-evidently false beyond any possibility of contradiction. This is of less conclusive importance under the Civil Procedure Rules, because trial in a few months can frequently be arranged in both classes of cases.

However the main reason for claimants avoiding injurious falsehood as a cause of action is an entirely justified perception of judicial hostility towards the tort, which can be traced, with few exceptions, from the leading cases in the late nineteenth century right down to the present day.

---

[2] [1892] 2 Q.B. 524, CA.

B. DECEPTION AS TO IDENTITY OR BUSINESS CONNECTION

The general principle

7–5   It is passing-off to misrepresent that one's business is that of the claimant, or connected with that of the claimant in any way likely to cause damage.[3] Such a misrepresentation may be implicit in selling goods as and for the goods of the claimant, or may be made by a business trading in goods whether or not any question of passing-off on account of the name, mark or get-up used for the goods arises.[4] However, this aspect of the action for passing-off is most relevant when one or both of the parties provides services rather than goods.

So, for example, in *British Telecommunications v Nextcall Telecom*[5] it was never in dispute that the defendant was liable for passing-off as a result of various express misrepresentations made by its salesmen, and the only question was whether the final injunction against them should be in qualified or absolute form:

"There is no dispute that when Nextcall started, a number of salespersons told lies to persuade consumers to change. Not surprisingly, consumers are conservative, so that persuading them to sign up to a new and unknown company is more difficult than persuading them on the basis that the new company is really BT by another name. Some salespersons represented that Nextcall was part of BT or that Nextcall was taking over BT's billing, or even that BT were paying the salespersons to transfer customers to Nextcall. These lies undoubtedly involve a variety of legal wrongs, including infringement of a number of BT's registered trade marks and passing off."

The connection must be material...

7–6   In principle, any form of alleged or implied connection with the claimant may be actionable as passing-off, but always provided that it is a material one in the sense of being really likely to cause damage. This in turn normally requires that the representation should be one on which the relevant public are likely to rely. As Millett L.J. explained in *Harrods v Harrodian School*:[6]

"In its classic form the misrepresentation which gave rise to an action for passing off was an implied representation by the defendant that his goods were the goods of the plaintiff, but by the beginning of the present century the tort had been extended beyond this. As Lord Diplock explained in the *Advocaat* case [1979] A.C. 731 at pages 741–2, it came to include the case

---

[3] *Ewing v Buttercup Margarine Co Ltd* [1917] 2 Ch.1; [1916–17] All E.R. 1012; 34 R.P.C. 232, CA; *Clock Ltd v Clock House Hotel Ltd* (1936) 53 R.P.C. 269, CA.
[4] *Chelsea Man Menswear Ltd v Chelsea Girl Ltd* [1987] R.P.C. 189, CA.
[5] [2000] F.S.R. 679 (Jacob J.).
[6] [1996] R.P.C. 687, CA.

'where although the plaintiff and the defendant were not competing traders in the same line of business, a false suggestion by the defendant that their businesses were connected with one another would damage the reputation and thus the goodwill of the plaintiff's business.'

In a written summary of the plaintiffs' points in reply which was prepared by their junior counsel and presented to us at the conclusion of the argument, and to the excellence of which I would like to pay tribute, it was submitted:

'In this case the belief engendered [in the minds of the public] is probably that Harrods sponsor or back the school. Obviously not every connection will found an action for passing off ... but where the representation is to the effect that the plaintiff is *behind* the defendant in some way, that is a classic case.'

This is too widely stated. In my judgment the relevant connection must be one by which the plaintiffs would be taken by the public to have made themselves responsible for the quality of the defendant's goods or services ...[7]

It is not in my opinion sufficient to demonstrate that there must be a connection of some kind between the defendant and the plaintiff, if it is not a connection which would lead the public to suppose that the plaintiff has made himself responsible for the quality of the defendant's goods or services."

... but need not be specific

If there is damaging confusion between the businesses of the claimant and   **7–7** the defendant as a result of a misrepresentation by the defendant then it is immaterial that the misrepresentation may not imply the existence of any particular connection between the parties. It is unreasonable to expect those confused to have any precise opinion as to the legal nature of the connection they suppose to exist, or to expect unanimity among those who hold more definite views. The simplest misrepresentation is that the defendant's business is the claimant's, but even if the relevant public appreciate that the claimant and the defendant are different legal persons they may believe or assume that in dealing with the defendant they are dealing with a part of the claimant's enterprise in the broadest sense, and therefore that they can rely on the claimant being ultimately responsible for the defendant's integrity.

"The principle is this, that no man is entitled to carry on his business in such a way or by such a name as to lead to the belief that he is carrying on the business of another man or to lead to the belief that the business which he is carrying on has any connection with the business carried on by another man."[8]

---

[7] Quotations from *British Legion v British Legion Club (Street) Ltd* (1931) 48 R.P.C. 555 *per* Farwell J.; and *Bulmer (HP) Ltd v J Bollinger SA* [1978] R.P.C. 79; [1977] 2 C.M.L.R. 625, CA *per* Buckley and Goff L.JJ. are omitted.

[8] *per* Romer L.J. in *Clock Ltd v Clock House Hotel Ltd* (1936) 53 R.P.C. 269, CA.

A similar statement by the same judge (then Romer J.) is to be found in *Joseph Rodgers v Rodgers*:[9]

"It is the law of this land that no man is entitled to carry on his business in such a way as to represent that it is the business of another, or is in any way connected with the business of another."

These formulations were made at a time when it could be assumed that passing-off actions would only occur between close competitors, and in the modern law need to be qualified by the requirement that the supposed connection should be a material one, such as to cause damage.

7–8   In the typical case the question is best approached without attempting to analyse precisely what connection with the claimant's business is claimed by the defendant. The representation may be vague or ambiguous, whether made inadvertently, or deliberately by a defendant trying to sail close to the wind. The relevant questions are whether there is a misrepresentation that the businesses are connected in some way, and if so whether it is calculated to cause real damage to the claimant. Sometimes the representation may be express or made in such circumstances that some particular connection between the parties is implied. The nature of the connection suggested can then be identified and may be directly relevant to whether there is any cause of action for passing-off.

In *Ewing v Buttercup Margarine*[10] the plaintiffs traded as the *Buttercup Dairy Company* in Scotland and the North of England and had a substantial retail trade in margarine. The defendants intended to manufacture margarine in London and sell it wholesale under a mark other than *Buttercup*.

"I can see no principle for holding that a trader may not be injured, and seriously injured, in his business as a trader by a confusion which will lead people to conclude that the defendants are really connected with the plaintiffs or a branch of the plaintiffs' business, or in some way mixed up with them."[11]

7–9   The judgment of Farwell J. in the *British Legion* case is to the same effect:[12]

"No one supposes for a moment that a person entering into Street and seeing 'British Legion Club (Street) Limited' over the doorway of the defendant company's premises is going to suppose that it is the head-quarters of the British Legion; no one supposes that for one moment; but that is not an answer to the plaintiff association's claim, which is that in my judgment it is perfectly plain and inevitable that persons coming

---

[9] (1924) 41 R.P.C. 277.
[10] [1917] 2 Ch. 1; [1916–17] All E.R. 1012; 34 R.P.C. 232, CA.
[11] *per* Cozens-Hardy M.R.
[12] *per* Farwell J. in *British Legion v British Legion Club (Street) Ltd* (1931) 48 R.P.C. 555. The conclusion of this passage was quoted with approval by Millett L.J. in *Harrods Ltd v Harrodian School Ltd* [1996] R.P.C. 687, CA.

across 'British Legion Club (Street) Limited' either by seeing the name over the door of the club or by seeing it on the notepaper of the defendant company or hearing it spoken of will inevitably come to the conclusion unless they are well instructed to the contrary that the defendant company is connected in some way with the British Legion. In my judgment this is the inevitable conclusion to which any ordinary minded person will come. Seeing the name of the defendants there, such a person would think it was either a branch of the plaintiff association or at any rate that it was a club in some way amalgamated with or under the supervision of the plaintiff association for which the plaintiff association had in some way made itself responsible."

The same business

It is passing-off to represent that one's business is the business of the clai-   **7–10**
mant if damage is likely to result. The misrepresentation is particularly likely to arise in cases where goods or services are known to be provided by a definite person whose identity is unknown, but is not confined to that situation.

In *Edge v Nicholls*[13] the plaintiffs supplied laundry blue under a distinctive get-up but without any name or other form of identification on the goods. The defendants imitated the get-up but labelled their goods with their own name. The House of Lords found there was passing-off. The public had not known the identity of the plaintiffs and might suppose that the defendants were the original manufacturers disclosing their name for the first time.[14]

In *AGS Manufacturing Co v Aeroplane General Sundries*[15] the plaintiffs were the larger and better known business but the initials "AGS" were not distinctive of them. The defendants advertised that the initials "AGS", stood for or were another name of their company. The Court of Appeal held that this amounted to an actionable representation that they and the plaintiffs were one and the same company.

In *Worsley v Cooper*[16] a circular representing that the plaintiff company had gone out of business, and that the defendants were its successors, was held to be actionable both as injurious falsehood and as passing-off.

In the South African case of *Truth Verification Testing Centre v PSE Truth Detection*[17] the personal defendant arranged for her home telephone number to be inserted in the telephone directory against the name of the plaintiff. The result was that calls and business intended for the plaintiff were diverted to her. A final interdict was granted.

This kind of misrepresentation is also likely as a result of one or both   **7–11**
parties being known by trading names rather than their full corporate

---

[13] [1911] A.C. 693; 28 R.P.C. 582, HL.
[14] See also *Copydex Ltd v Noso Products Ltd* (1952) 69 R.P.C. 38, where goods were demonstrated anonymously on television. This would now be regarded as an example of "inverse" passing-off, which often depends on the claimant not being known by name.
[15] (1918) 35 R.P.C. 127, CA.
[16] [1939] 1 All E.R. 290 (Morton J.).
[17] 1998 (2) SA 689 (Witwatersrand).

names. In *Brestian v Try*[18] both parties were hairdressers who traded as *Charles of London*, though in different areas. There was evidence that some customers would think the defendant's shop was a newly opened branch of the plaintiff's, and that the trade might take references to the defendant under that name as referring to the plaintiff. In *Chelsea Man v Chelsea Girl*[19] the Court of Appeal justified an injunction extending outside the three towns in which the plaintiffs had retail shops by the fact that the *Chelsea Man* business of the defendant was bound to be confused with that of the plaintiffs among the trade at large. The Court treated the case as one in which the defendants had held themselves out as the plaintiffs.

On the other hand, it is hardly ever necessary to ask if the public would really believe that the parties are one and the same, because any form of damaging association is sufficient. Cases in which this is the natural tenor of the misrepresentation are simply one particular application of the general rule.

7–12 A particularly blatant example of passing-off by representing oneself as the claimant occurs when the defendant solicits payment for goods or services actually supplied by the claimant. In some cases the defendant may intend to supply supposedly comparable goods or services of his own, in others, the money may buy nothing at all. Either way it is clearly passing-off.[20]

In *Blacklock v Bradshaws Publishing Co*[21] the publishers of *Bradshaws Railway Guide* obtained an interlocutory injunction, *inter alia*, against the defendants soliciting advertisements or subscriptions for a *Bradshaws Directory* which did not exist. The case was one of gross fraud, with canvassers for the defendants actually collecting money owed to the plaintiffs.

In *RAC Motoring Services v RAC (Publishing)*[22] the defendants were committed for breach of an interlocutory injunction requiring them to repay money obtained from hoteliers under the pretence that it was in payment for entries in the *RAC Handbook*.

The plaintiffs in *Tele-Direct (Publications) v Intra Canada Telecommunications*[23] were the Canadian publishers of the *Yellow Pages* telephone directories. The defendants took clippings of advertisements in the directories and sent them to the advertisers with an account similar to that on which the plaintiffs would ask for renewal payments. They obtained an injunction and damages.

Member of same group

7–13 In modern conditions, the most plausible explanation for two companies trading under very similar names (and especially in related fields of business)

---

[18] [1958] R.P.C. 161, CA.
[19] [1987] R.P.C. 189, CA.
[20] The plaintiffs in *Intercontex v Schmidt* [1988] F.S.R. 575 failed on facts supposedly similar to the following cases because the misrepresentations took place abroad and they failed to prove the relevant foreign law.
[21] (1926) 43 R.P.C. 97 (Astbury J.).
[22] [1988] R.P.C. 321 (Browne-Wilkinson V.C.).
[23] (1986) 9 C.I.P.R. 129; 13 C.P.R. (3d) 529 (Quebec Superior Court).

may be that they are part of the same corporate group. In *Dawnay Day v Cantor Fitzgerald*[24] the situation and the legal consequences were summarised thus by Scott V.C. in the Court of Appeal:

"In the present case the misrepresentation is that the business conducted under the name 'Dawnay Day Securities' is being carried on by a member of the Dawnay Day group of companies. A misrepresentation to that effect is, in my judgment, sufficient. I do not think it is necessary for the representation to suggest any particular degree of control that the group, or the holding company of the group, might have over the quality of services offered by Dawnay Day Securities. Different corporate groups exercise different degrees of control over their members. Some are closely controlled; some have almost complete autonomy. The vice of the misrepresentation in a case such as the present is, in my judgment, that the proprietor of the defendant's business, a party unconnected with the Dawnay Day group, is being held out as a member of the group. I do not think anything more is needed."

The main issue was whether the joint venture company Dawnay Day Securities had ever had, and was able to pass on, an unconditional right to use the *Dawnay Day* name once its membership of the Dawnay Day group ceased. Applying *Coles v Need*,[25] the Court of Appeal held that it had no such right, that its trading as *Dawnay Day Securities* while part of the group had not generated any independent reputation or compromised that of the Dawnay Day group itself, and that the defendants' use of the name undeniably rendered them liable for passing themselves off as a member of the group.

Other examples: branch, agency, merger, etc.

Although the majority of cases on passing-off by misrepresentation of **7–14** business connection treat the issue simply as whether there will be damaging confusion of an unspecified nature, it occasionally happens that a more precise connection is stated or can be implied.

In *Wheeler & Wilson Manufacturing v Shakespear*[26] the defendant had formerly been an agent for the sale of the plaintiffs' sewing machines. His agency was terminated, and he claimed to be entitled to use the plaintiffs' name to describe other sewing machines made upon the same, formerly patented, system of operation. He also continued to use advertisements in the same terms as before, expressly and implicitly representing that he was still the plaintiffs' agent and still dealing in their machines in exactly the same manner as before. An injunction was granted.

In *North Cheshire & Manchester Brewery Co v Manchester Brewery Co*[27]

---

[24] [2000] R.P.C. 669, CA.
[25] [1934] A.C. 82; 50 R.P.C. 379, PC.
[26] (1869) 39 L.J. Ch. 36 (James V.C.).
[27] [1899] A.C. 83, HL. The case was not strictly one for passing-off, but under the Companies Act 1862, s.20.

the plaintiffs, respondents in the House of Lords, had traded as the *Manchester Brewery Company* for some years. The defendants had purchased the business of the *North Cheshire Brewery Company* and incorporated themselves as *The North Cheshire and Manchester Brewery Co Ltd.* The House of Lords held that the natural interference was that there had been an amalgamation of the two old-established companies, and that the name was therefore calculated to deceive.

7–15   In *Lloyd's and Dawson Bros v Lloyds, Southampton*[28] the defendants set up a yacht agency in Southampton under the name *Lloyd's*. The form of injunction granted by the Court of Appeal was to restrain the defendants from carrying on business under any name "calculated to lead to the belief that the defendants' business is the business of, or an agency, branch, or department of the business of the plaintiffs Lloyd's".

In *Woolworth v Woolworths (Australasia)*[29] one of the natural inferences from the defendants' choice of name was that they would be taken for a subsidiary of the plaintiffs.

In *Pontiac Marina v CDL Hotels*[30] it was inevitable that if the defendants were allowed to re-brand their three existing Singapore hotels as the *Millennium Orchard Hotel*, *Millennium King's Hotel* and *Millennium Harbour View Hotel*, then there would be more than a risk of their being thought to be in the same chain, or under the same management, as the plaintiffs' much superior *Ritz-Carlton, Millenia Singapore Hotel*. The latter had not yet opened for business, but had already generated sufficient pre-launch goodwill to support the action.

7–16   The converse situation of a misrepresentation to the effect that the claimant is a branch of the defendant is less common but in principle there is no reason why it should not be actionable. In *Dominion Rent-a-Car v Budget Rent-a-Car*[31] Cooke P. observed:

"In principle a misrepresentation by the defendant that the plaintiff's business is a branch of the defendant's can support a passing-off action, provided that damage to the plaintiff is shown—for instance, to take one obvious illustration, by way of damage to his reputation by associating him with inferior quality."

This latter type of misrepresentation might also amount to injurious falsehood.

Authorised dealership service and support

7–17   It is passing-off to represent oneself as an agent of the claimant,[32] in either the legal or popular sense, or as an authorised dealer in the claimant's

---

[28] (1912) 29 R.P.C. 433, CA.
[29] (1930) 47 R.P.C. 337 (Farwell J.).
[30] [1998] F.S.R. 839 (CA, Singapore) affirming [1997] F.S.R. 725 (Chao Hick Tin J.).
[31] [1987] 2 N.Z.L.R. 395 (CA of NZ).
[32] *Wheeler & Wilson Manufacturing Co v Shakespear* (1869) 39 L.J. Ch. 36. The defendant was described as an agent but one wonders if he was not trading on his own account.

goods. The latter misrepresentation may be implicit merely in selling the claimant's goods without a disclaimer. The cases on second-hand motor vehicles[33] are illustrations of a wider proposition that it is passing-off for a business to misrepresent that it is an author sed dealer of another business or competent to give guarantees on its behalf, even if the representation is not made expressly. In fields of business where it is universal for goods to be supplied to the public exclusively through authorised dealers then selling the goods of a particular manufacturer without a disclaimer may amount to such a misrepresentation. For these purposes it does not matter that the goods may be new in both the popular and trade sense of the word.

In *Sony v Saray's*[34] the defendants, who were not authorised *Sony* dealers, sold *Sony* goods and purported to give *Sony* guarantees to customers. Some of the goods were "grey" imports and had been modified by the defendants to work in England. The Court of Appeal accepted that the plaintiffs had raised an arguable case that members of the public expected sellers of *Sony* goods to be *Sony* authorised dealers and to be able to give *Sony* guarantees. Interlocutory injunctions were granted ordering the defendants to mark all *Sony* goods with labels stating that *Saray's* were not authorised Sony dealers and that the goods were not guaranteed by *Sony*; and to mark the imported goods with a notice that they had been modified. A similar but stronger case is *Microsoft v Computer Future Distribution*[35] in which the defendant sold copies of Microsoft computer programs or "licence packs" in circumstances in which the purchaser obtained no licence to use the software. The outer packaging was entirely removed, so that the purchaser could not see that they were in fact unlicensed imports from the North American market, and in some cases only authorised for academic use. In *Musical Fidelity v Vickers*,[36] the defendant, a hi-fi retailer, registered the domain name *musicalfidelity.co.uk* for his business and placed a statement on the "welcome" page that he was one of the claimants' oldest retailers. He had in fact ceased to be one of their authorised distributors a few months previously. The Court of Appeal upheld an injunction granted on an application for summary judgment.

In *United States Surgical v Downs Surgical Canada*[37] the plaintiffs claimed **7–18** that by selling reconditioned equipment of a discontinued design the defendants were holding themselves out as an authorised dealer and passing off the old products as current stock obtained through normal sources. The old products were safe and merchantable. An interlocutory injunction was granted requiring the defendants to notify customers that they were not authorised dealers, that the plaintiffs' guarantee did not apply, that the products had been obtained through various sources and that they had been

[33] *Morris Motors Ltd v Lilley* [1959] 1 W.L.R. 118; *Morris Motors Ltd v Phellan* [1960] 1 W.L.R. 566.
[34] [1983] F.S.R. 302, CA.
[35] [1998] E.T.M.R. 597 (Rimer J.).
[36] [2002] EWCA Civ 1989 CA.
[37] (1982) 67 C.P.R. (2d) 140 (White J., Ontario).

reconditioned.[38] Likewise, in *Sharp Electronics of Canada v Continental Electronic Info*[39] a parallel importer of fax machines was required to give notice that it was not an authorised dealer and that they were not guaranteed. In *Sony du Canada v Multitronic Stereo*[40] and *Sony du Canada v Impact Electronique*[41] the defendants were restrained from holding themselves out as *Sony* authorised dealers and were ordered to identify refurbished, imported *Walkmans* as such. They had previously marketed them without notice that they were used, refurbished and imported from an American distributor.

There was nothing unlawful in the defendants importing the plaintiffs' cameras into the United Kingdom without authorisation in *Nishika Corp. v Goodchild*,[42] but they were restrained from purporting to offer guarantees or franchises in the name of the plaintiffs and from making express misrepresentations that they were the authorised dealers of the plaintiffs, or perhaps the plaintiffs themselves. Note that the existence of goodwill in the jurisdiction rested solely on these imports, and in the circumstances the goodwill accrued to the plaintiffs.

7–19   Cases such as *Sony v Saray's* depend on the qualifications of the retailer or some other party in the chain of supply from the manufacturer being important to the consumer, or on the consumer relying on the retailer having a particular trade connection with the claimant. If there is no reliance on such a connection then any misrepresentation is likely to be an immaterial one: it is not sufficient that the customer may have expected there to be a trade connection which does not in fact exist. It does not follow that there is passing-off in every case where the consumer obtains the claimant's goods through unfamiliar trade channels which the claimant would prefer did not exist.[43]

In *Paquin v John Barker*[44] the plaintiff couturiers sold a dress as a pattern for copying and objected when some 14 weeks later the defendants who had bought it from the original purchaser advertised it for sale as "an exclusive *Paquin* model" at a greatly reduced price. The plaintiffs failed in their claims that this implied misrepresentations that the defendants had purchased the dress directly from the plaintiffs or through normal trade channels; and that the dress was in fashion when it was supposedly outdated. They could not argue that "exclusive" meant "unique".

---

[38] In not preventing the defendants from dealing in the goods altogether this decision is consistent with the subsequent decisions of the Supreme Court of Canada in *Seiko Time v Consumers Distributing Co* [1984] 1 S.C.R. 583; 3 C.I.P.R. 223, 10 D.L.R. (4th) 161; 1 C.P.R. (3d) 1 and the English Court of Appeal in *Sony KK v Saray Electronics (London) Ltd* [1983] F.S.R. 302, CA.

[39] (1988) 23 C.P.R. (3d) 330 (Melnick J., British Columbia).

[40] (1991) 42 C.P.R. (3d) 53 (Quebec CA).

[41] (1991) 39 C.P.R. (3d) 414 (LeBel J., Quebec). But failure to notify customers that the goods were not under guarantee did not amount to passing-off.

[42] [1990] F.S.R. 371 (Knox J.).

[43] See *Richards v Butcher* [1891] 2 Ch. 540; 8 R.P.C. 249 and *Imperial Tobacco Co of India Ltd v Bonnan* [1924] A.C. 755; 41 R.P.C. 441, PC.

[44] (1934) 51 R.P.C. 431 (Clauson J.).

In *Seiko Time Canada v Consumers Distributing Co*[45] the defendants imported genuine *Seiko* watches and sold them in circumstances which made the normal guarantee inoperative. They submitted to an injunction in similar form to that in *Sony v Saray's*, but the trial court also enjoined them from selling or advertising *Seiko* watches at all, on the ground that the product the plaintiffs supplied was a composite package including not just the watch itself but also point-of-sale service, guarantee and after-sales support. The Supreme Court of Canada discharged the wider injunction. The narrower injunction was sufficient to dispel confusion and protect the plaintiffs from consequent damage, and the wider one created without justification a monopoly contrary to the public interest and the common law. Canadian decisions on similar facts falling between the first instance decision in *Seiko* and the appeal to the Supreme Court are not necessarily wrong, but are to be treated with caution. The first instance decision led to a number of cases being brought against parallel importers, some of which went too far.

Member of association

It is passing-off to misrepresent oneself as a member of a particular asso- **7–20** ciation,[46] or as having some qualification conferred by it, or as being connected with it in some way calculated to cause damage.[47] An action may certainly be brought by the association itself, which stands in the same position as an ordinary trading company.

C. DECEPTION AS TO TRADE SOURCE OF GOODS

The general principle

The most common form passing off takes is of a representation by the **7–21** defendant that goods are of the claimant's manufacture or merchandise when this is not the case. Such a representation is normally made by the adoption of features of a name, mark or get-up distinctive of the claimant, but the tort is in no way limited by the form the misrepresentation takes.

> "[T]he basis of a passing-off action being a false representation by the defendant, it must be proved in each case as a fact that the false representation was made. It may, of course, have been made in express words, but cases of express misrepresentation of this sort are rare. The more common case is, where the representation is implied in the use or imitation of a mark, trade name, or get-up with which the goods of another are associated in the minds of the public, or of a particular class of the public.

[45] Above.
[46] *Society of Accountants & Auditors v Goodway* [1907] 1 Ch. 489; 24 R.P.C. 159.
[47] *British Medical Association v Marsh* (1931) 48 R.P.C. 565.

In such cases the point to be decided is whether, having regard to all the circumstances of the case, the use by the defendant in connection with the goods of the mark, name or get-up in question impliedly represents goods to be the goods of the plaintiff, or goods of the plaintiff of a particular class or quality, or, as it is sometime put, whether the defendant's use of such mark, name or get-up is calculated to deceive. It would, however, be impossible to enumerate or classify all the possible ways in which a man may make the false representation relied on."[48]

7–22   As with misrepresentations as to identity, it is not necessary to prove that the defendant's goods will actually be mistaken for those of the claimant. This may be true for counterfeits and other close imitations, but legal liability is not confined to such situations. By analogy with *Harrods v Harrodian School*,[49] the best formulation of the question is probably whether the relevant public would take the defendant's product as something for which the claimant had made himself responsible. In *United Biscuits v Asda*[50] Robert Walker J. summarised the evidence of fact as showing that the defendants' *Puffin* bar was unlikely to be mistaken for the plaintiffs' *Penguin* bar, but that some form of association would be assumed:

"From this evidence as a whole...I draw three conclusions which largely confirm my own first impressions. First, although occasional mistakes may be made for unaccountable reasons, it is unlikely that a significant proportion of supermarket shoppers would fail to distinguish between Puffins and Penguins if both are on sale next to each other, as they usually are. ... Secondly, that a substantial number of shoppers would suppose, or assume, or guess at an association (in the form of a common manufacturer) between the Puffin and the Penguin. Thirdly, that the great majority of shoppers would not know who manufactures Penguins (the McVities logo having appeared on them only quite recently) and that what they are concerned with is taste and quality (which depends primarily on the manufacturer) and cost (which depends on the supermarket retailer and on the supermarket's influence or 'clout' with even the largest manufacturers)."

On the authorities, this was sufficient for there to be liability for passing-off:

"The next point that calls for consideration is the witnesses' general acceptance, under Mr. Pollock's questioning, that their belief that Puffins were made by the same manufacturer as Penguins was supposition, or assumption, or a guess. For one trader to induce the belief, by deceptive suggestion, that his goods are made by another trader with an established reputation can amount to actionable passing off: *Ewing v Buttercup Margarine Co Ltd* (1917) 34 R.P.C. 232; *Wagamama Ltd v City Centre*

---

[48] *per* Lord Parker in *Spalding (A G) & Bros v A W Gamage Ltd* (1915) 32 R.P.C. 273, HL.
[49] [1996] R.P.C. 687, CA.
[50] [1997] R.P.C. 513 (Robert Walker J.).

Restaurants Ltd [1995] F.S.R. 713. In the *Harrods* case Millett L.J. (at page 712), approving what was said by Farwell J. in *British Legion v British Legion Club (Street) Ltd* (1931) 48 R.P.C. 555, characterised the connection rather more widely, as a suggestion that the plaintiff was in some way responsible for the defendant's goods or services. Plainly that includes the manufacturer of a supermarket's own-brand product, even if the supermarket shares that responsibility through its own-brand commendation."

The remainder of this section deals with some categories of misrepresentation as to the origin of goods which fall on the border of or altogether outside the common case of imitation of a distinctive name, mark or get-up.

Direct misrepresentation

In the light of the quotation from Lord Parker above,[51] it can hardly be **7–23** doubted that an express misrepresentation as to the source of goods or as to business connection would be actionable. In *British Telecommunications v Nextcall Telecom*[52] door-to-door salesmen employed by the defendant told existing BT customers a variety of deliberate lies in order to induce them to transfer their telephone subscriptions: that Nextcall was part of BT, that it was taking over BT's billing, and even that BT were paying them to transfer customers to Nextcall. A perpetual injunction in unqualified form was granted. In *British Telecommunications v One in a Million*,[53] one of numerous misrepresentations made by the defendants was that large and reputable companies, including BT itself, were among their clients.

There are also a few reported cases in which an express misrepresentation contributed to passing-off by substitution or imitation of indicia, but otherwise, cases of express misrepresentation rarely seem to come before the courts. One such is *Byron v Johnson*,[54] in which a book of poetry was misrepresented as being by Byron. Otherwise, cases of express misrepresentation are likely either to be open-and-shut, as in *BT v Nextcall*, or to go undetected. An express misrepresentation went unrestrained in *Ainsworth v Walmsley*,[55] but it is suggested that the decision, if ever right, is now obsolete. In *Wheeler & Wilson v Shakespear*[56] an express misrepresentation that the defendant was still the agent of the plaintiffs was restrained. Conversely in *Worsley v Cooper*[57] a circular representing that the plaintiff company had gone out of business, and that the defendants were its successors, was held to be actionable both as injurious falsehood and as passing-off.

---

[51] From *Spalding (A G) & Bros. v A W Gamage Ltd* (1915) 32 R.P.C. 273, HL.
[52] [2000] F.S.R. 679 (Jacob J.).
[53] [1999] 1 W.L.R. 903; [1999] 4 All E.R. 476, [1999] E.T.M.R. 61; [1999] F.S.R. 1, CA.
[54] (1816) 35 E.R. 851.
[55] (1866) L.R. 1 Eq. 518 (Page-Wood V.C.).
[56] (1869) 39 L.J. Ch. 36 (James V.C.).
[57] [1939] 1 All E.R. 290 (Morton J.).

Use of claimant's containers

7–24 In some industries containers such as bottles are re-usable and the empty containers of one manufacturer may come into the hands of another trader who may wish to be able to re-use them for his own goods. It is passing-off to use the claimant's own containers for other goods if they are still recognisable as such and the contents would be taken as the claimant's. This may be so even if some of the claimant's normal indicia are removed and the defendant's name or mark substituted. Even if the bottles or containers are not susceptible to being re-used, there can be passing-off by re-filling them with a different or inferior product so as to assist in a scheme of fraudulent substitution, as in *Hennessy v Neary*[58] and similar cases on substitution in bars and restaurants.

In *Sodastream v Thorn Cascade*[59] the plaintiffs and the defendants both dealt in refillable cylinders of carbon dioxide gas which were interchangeable with one another. The defendants were prepared to accept the plaintiffs' empty cylinders from customers in part-exchange for full cylinders of their own, and proposed to refill them with their own gas and sell them under their own label. The Court of Appeal found, on application for an inter-locutory injunction, that the grey colour of the plaintiffs' cylinders was arguably distinctive of them and held that the defendants should be restrained from supplying their gas in the plaintiffs' cylinders without repainting them as well as removing the plaintiffs' label and replacing it with one of their own.

The foregoing examples suppose either that the re-filling is part of a scheme for passing-off by substitution, or that the refilled containers may be sold on to the public and taken for the claimant's original goods. However, if the customer is an end user then it cannot be passing-off to refill marked containers in his possession (whether or not they are his property) with his knowledge and consent because there is no element of misrepresentation. In *New Zealand Industrial Gases v Oxyman*[60] the plaintiffs were suppliers of compressed gases who supplied customers with gas in cylinders marked with their trade mark, under terms that the cylinders were on loan and only the plaintiffs could replenish them. The defendants were not liable for passing-off by refilling these cylinders with their own gas, but were arguably liable for interference with contractual relations.

Claimant's goods as Trojan horse

7–25 Although it is not normally passing-off to sell the claimant's goods under the claimant's name or mark, a trader is not allowed to make colourable use of the claimant's goods so as to misrepresent the origin of his own. It is passing-off to use an otherwise legitimate reference to genuine goods of the claimant so as to represent that other goods also originate from the claimant

---

[58] (1902) 19 R.P.C. 36 (Chatterton V.C., Ireland).
[59] [1982] R.P.C. 459, CA.
[60] (1992) 24 I.P.R. 161 (Fisher J.).

when they do not. This may be regarded as a more extreme version of the case where the claimant's goods are altered by the inclusion of other goods.[61]

In *Richards v Williamson*[62] Bacon V.C. restrained the defendants from selling carbines assembled from various components, including locks bearing the plaintiff's name and mark. These were genuine, though second-hand. There was evidence that the name on the lock plate was taken as identifying the manufacturer of the gun as a whole.

In *Newton Chambers v Neptune Waterproof Paper*[63] passing-off was found where the defendants marked their lavatory paper "medicated with IZAL", which was literally true but likely to lead to the belief that the paper itself was made by the manufacturers of *Izal* because the words "medicated with" were much less prominent than the brand name.

7–26 If goods are offered or supplied as part of a package then prominence given to the manufacturer of part only of the goods may suggest that the goods as a whole are his.

In *Morny v Ball & Rogers*[64] the defendants (who did not appear on the motion for an interlocutory injunction) were restrained from selling cheap scent packaged together with genuine *Morny* foambath. The packaging and get-up would lead to the belief that the plaintiffs had authorised the scent to be sold in that manner, even though no one would suppose the scent had actually been made by *Morny*.

An interlocutory injunction was also granted in Canada in *Time/System International v Custom Planner*.[65] The defendants acquired boxed time planning systems of the plaintiffs and replaced the out-of-date calendars with ones of their own manufacture. The defendants' advertising showed the plaintiffs' calendar. It was no adequate defence that the defendants claimed to explain the true facts to telephone customers.

7–27 Passing-off may also occur because a defendant who is known as a representative of the claimant introduces goods of his own without making their origin clear.[66] In *International Scientific Communications v Pattison*[67] the defendant acted as the United Kingdom representative of the plaintiffs, who published magazines for advertising laboratory equipment. He launched his own magazine but did not copy any mark or get-up distinctive of the plaintiffs or suggest that his magazine was the same as the existing magazines. Goulding J. still held that there was passing-off. He had misappropriated the plaintiffs' goodwill because it was inevitable that the new magazine would be taken as published by or under the authority of the plaintiff.

---

[61] See *Illustrated Newspapers Ltd v Publicity Services (London) Ltd* [1938] Ch. 414; [1938] 1 All E.R. 321; 55 R.P.C. 172.
[62] (1874) 30 L.T. 746 (Bacon V.C.).
[63] (1935) 52 R.P.C. 399 (Luxmoore J.).
[64] [1978] F.S.R. 91 (Goulding J.).
[65] (1986) 12 C.P.R. (3d) 441 (Campbell J., Ontario).
[66] *Wheeler & Wilson Manufacturing Co v Shakespear* (1869) 39 L.J. Ch. 36.
[67] [1979] F.S.R. 429 (Goulding J.).

D. Substitution and Switch Selling

The general principle

7–28 It is passing-off to supply other goods or services in response to a request for those of the claimant unless the recipient voluntarily accepts them in place of those asked for. It is no defence that the goods could, with diligence, have been distinguished from those requested if no such examination would be likely to be made in practice. The loss of the custom of an incautious purchaser is as damaging to the claimant as the loss of a careful one.[68] The general proposition is that if the name under which the customer requests the goods is distinctive of the claimant then it is passing-off to substitute other goods without informing the customer and obtaining, at least implicitly, his consent. This general rule applies irrespective of whether a sufficiently astute customer would have realised what was happening.

> "The customer expects to receive a given product when he asks for it and should not be deceived. It often happens that products are interchangeable and that a substitution will have little effect. However, the customer may count on having a specific product. There are many reasons for such a choice: habit, satisfaction, another person's recommendation, the desire for change, and so on. I have no hesitation in using the classic saying, taken from popular imagery: 'the customer is always right'. Merchants must respect his wishes, choices and preferences as far as possible. Where this is simply not possible, no substitution should be made without his knowledge. This is the minimum degree of respect which manufacturers and merchants, who we should remember depend on their customers, should show."[69]

7–29 If goods are supplied by the defendant in the course of trade then it is no defence to an action for passing-off by way of substitution that they are provided free of charge, which often means no more than that the customer is not charged for them separately.[70] Nor is it a defence that property in the goods does not pass to the customer but they are consumed in connection with the provision of services.[71] In both cases the claimant may still have lost trade, and if the goods are inferior that will rebound to his disadvantage. In principle, it is no defence that the substitution occurs on the initiative of junior staff without the knowledge or consent of the proprietor,[72] although courts have sometimes overlooked this if satisfied that the substitution was an isolated occurrence.

[68] *Johnston & Co v Orr Ewing & Co* (1882) 7 App.Cas. 219, HL, *per* Lord Blackburn.

[69] *per* Gonthier J. in *Ciba-Geigy Canada Ltd v Apotex Inc.* (1992) 95 D.L.R. (4th) 385; 44 C.P.R. (3rd) 289; 24 I.P.R. 652.

[70] *OT Ltd v Cumming & Co* (1915) 32 R.P.C. 69; *Illustrated Newspapers Ltd v Publicity Services (London) Ltd* [1938] Ch. 414; [1938] 1 All E.R. 321; 55 R.P.C. 172.

[71] *Sales Affiliates Ltd v Le Jean Ltd* [1947] Ch. 295; [1947] 1 All E.R.

[72] *Cusenier (E) Fils, Aine et Cie v Gaiety Bars & Restaurant Co Ltd* (1902) 19 R.P.C. 357 (Buckley J.).

Proof of substitution is heavily dependent upon trap orders, which must be scrupulously fair. If the trap orders result in substitution with the express prior permission of the customer then there is no passing-off. However, it is no defence that the person placing the trap order was not himself deceived, because the relevant question is whether a genuine customer in the same position would have been. If the trap orders result in unexplained substitution then the court is unlikely to be sympathetic to claims that they must have been unrepresentative or isolated instances of what the defendant is already trying to prevent: if so, then an injunction will do his business no harm.[73]

Examples

In *British Leather Cloth Manufacturing v Dickens & Cooper*[74] the defendant **7–30** bookbinders were awarded a government contract to bind 20,000 books in the plaintiff's *Rexine*. Without permission they bound most of them in another material. The defence that this was entirely a matter between them and their customers was rejected and they were held liable for passing-off.

In *Bovril v Bodega*[75] the defendants systematically supplied *Oxo* in their restaurants without explanation when *Bovril* was asked for. The cups of *Oxo* were made from a clearly labelled bottle, but in the majority of cases the customer would not have seen this used and would not have appreciated that *Oxo* rather than *Bovril* was being served. Eve J. granted an injunction, commenting that even as regarded the part of the restaurant from which the bottle was visible:

"[I]t is not everybody who assumes that he is going to be defrauded when he calls for a cup of *Bovril*, and probably a large percentage of the customers would never think of watching the barmaids, and ascertaining from what receptacle they took the commodity."

In *Pearson Bros v Valentine*[76] the plaintiffs complained of the defendants supplying their own goods in response to orders for the plaintiffs' *Mattamac* raincoats. The defence was that all the orders had referred to newspaper advertisements of the plaintiffs, in which readers were warned that coats without the word *Mattamac* on the label were not genuine, and therefore that the purchaser would easily be able to see that the goods supplied were not the plaintiffs'. Not surprisingly this was rejected:

"In this case orders were given for '*Mattamac*' coats. The defendants replied by sending goods which were not '*Mattamac*' without any explanation that they were not '*Mattamac*'; and therefore represented directly that they were '*Mattamac*'. It is idle to suggest that the Defendants are entitled to do that in the expectation that the customer will, by

---

[73] *Bostich Inc. v McGarry and Cole Ltd* [1964] R.P.C. 173 (Cross J.).
[74] (1914) 31 R.P.C. 337 (Serjant J.).
[75] (1916) 33 R.P.C. 153 (Eve J.).
[76] (1917) 34 R.P.C. 267 (Peterson J.).

an examination of the goods, have an opportunity of discovering that they do not bear the name '*Mattamac*'."

Customer aware of substitution

7–31 It is not passing-off to substitute goods with the knowledge and consent of the person placing the order.[77] It has been argued that there may be a breach of contract if the person accepting the substitute goods is not authorised to consent to a variation[78] but this is irrelevant to the action for passing-off. It is also insufficient that he may be enabled to pass off the substitute goods to customers of his own, as a trader is not responsible for the frauds of his customers unless he acts in concert with them or the goods he supplies are inherently deceptive.[79]

Passing-off by substitution depends on an implied misrepresentation that the goods tendered are those requested, and the consequences are the same as if the defendant had initiated the transaction by offering the goods under the claimant's name or mark.[80] The authorities[81] are better understood if it is assumed that such a misrepresentation is always to be implied whenever substituted goods are tendered without explanation, even if the discrepancy ought to be immediately apparent to the recipient. On this basis there is always a misrepresentation, but one which is not material if it is obvious to the customer. If the customer willingly accepts goods other than those he had first intended to buy, the claimant has no cause for complaint.

7–32 The distinction is important in those cases in which the defendant relies on the customer retaining goods which are recognisably not those ordered, not because he is satisfied with them, but because it is more troublesome to return them. If the transaction is initiated by the customer, without the defendant representing that he is willing to supply the claimant's goods, then it is otherwise difficult to identify the misrepresentation which is the root of passing-off. The loss of custom to the claimant may be as serious as in the cases represented by *Pearson Bros v Valentine*[82] however, and there is authority that the practice is actionable.

In *Purefoy Engineering v Sykes Boxall*[83] the defendants offered a range of goods designed to be equivalent to and interchangeable with the plaintiffs'.

---

[77] *Silicate Paint Co, J R Orr & Co Ltd v Smith* (1905) 23 R.P.C. 143; *Lever Bros Ltd v Masbro Equitable Pioneers Society Ltd* (1912) 29 R.P.C. 225, CA; *Broad & Co Ltd v Cast Iron Drainage Co Ltd* [1970] F.S.R. 363; *Broad & Co Ltd v Graham Building Supplies Ltd* [1969] F.S.R. 153; [1969] R.P.C. 285.

[78] *Silicate Paint Co, J R Orr & Co Ltd v Smith* (1905) 23 R.P.C. 143.

[79] *Broad & Co Ltd v Graham Building Supplies Ltd* [1969] F.S.R. 153; [1969] R.P.C. 285. A contractor agreed to accept the defendants' goods in place of those of the plaintiffs as specified by his customer.

[80] *Jacques (John) & Son Ltd v Chess* [1940] 2 All E.R. 285; 57 R.P.C. 77, CA.

[81] Especially *Purefoy Engineering Co Ltd v Sykes Boxall & Co Ltd* (1954) 72 R.P.C. 89, CA.

[82] (1917) 34 R.P.C. 267 (Peterson J.).

[83] (1954) 72 R.P.C. 89, CA.

They supplied their own goods in response to orders for goods by reference to the plaintiffs' reference numbers,[84] and sometimes by reference to the plaintiffs' name, in each case enclosing a copy of their own catalogue with the goods. The Court of Appeal identified two classes of transactions. Where the order had been placed as a result of a visit from a representative of the defendants there was no passing-off, because the customer knew with whom he was contracting and whose goods he would receive, however he identified them. Where the orders were unsolicited the defendants were liable. The Court rejected the opinion of the trial judge that the inclusion of the catalogue negated deception and was prepared to hold that even if the catalogue had

"[I]nformed, or should have sufficed to inform, the recipient that the goods in fact despatched were the defendants' goods and not the plaintiffs', still in the ordinary course, it would have been too late for practical purposes; the goods would have been despatched without any further enquiry or explanation, and the damage to the plaintiffs would already inevitably have been done."[85]

Similarly, in *Procea Products v Evans*[86] the defendants were found liable for passing-off by supplying *Nutrex* bread without explanation when *Procea* was asked for. The substitution would have been obvious to the customer when the bread was unwrapped at home, but no-one was likely "to kick up a fuss over a 4^d loaf which was to all intents and purposes the same as what they wanted."

Customer's implicit consent

On the other hand, the circumstances of the order may suggest that the customer would prefer to receive equivalent goods if necessary, rather than none at all, and the law recognises that an open and honest attempt to oblige the customer in this respect is not passing-off. This is perhaps most likely where the customer is another trader, rather than a consumer. **7–33**

"The test of passing-off is supplying the defendants' goods under such circumstances that there is a representation either explicit or implied that they are the plaintiffs' goods. In some cases that may be done by substitution in the most effective way. Suppose, for instance, a customer comes and asks for a glass of *Otard's* brandy, and a glass of brandy is handed to him, and it happens to be of another brand, the fact that in response to asking for one thing he got another would be the best possible example of passing-off ... On the other hand, I can understand a

---

[84] In general, cases based on the defendant using the plaintiff's reference numbers to identify equivalent parts have failed if there is no additional element of passing-off: *Hilti AG v Ucan Development Ltd* [1964] R.P.C. 206; *British Northrop Ltd v Texteam Blackburn Ltd* [1974] R.P.C. 57.
[85] *per* Evershed M.R.
[86] (1951) 68 R.P.C. 210, *per* Roxburgh J.

wholesale grocer receiving, from a small grocer in the country who regularly trades with him, a long list of orders. He supplies those goods which he has got, and for those goods which he has not got he supplies the best substitute he can, because he thinks that the customer is more anxious to get goods which will be of the nature of the ones he asks for, than to get no goods if he cannot get the actual specific ones. I think such a case would furnish the very weakest basis for a charge of passing-off."[87]

Circumstances of the sale

7–34 If the customer orders goods in person then it is strongly desirable for the supplier to draw his attention there and then to the fact that the goods tendered are not those requested. In cases where the fact of substitution is not self-evident only this will suffice to avoid passing-off, and if the matter is in any doubt then systematic failure to do so may be taken as showing a lack of bona fides. However, if the defendant's goods are very readily distinguishable from the claimant's there is not necessarily passing-off if this is not done; provided the dissimilarities between the goods are immediately apparent to the purchaser taking no special precautions. This depends upon three factors: the degree of resemblance between the two kinds of goods; whether the goods are likely to be inspected by the customer with sufficient care, or at all; and whether the claimant's goods are so well known by sight that the customer could hardly fail to recognise that the substituted goods are not those asked for.[88] If, for instance, there was substantial demand for the claimant's goods on recommendation then differences in get-up, however marked, would be irrelevant because the customer would not know what get-up to expect.

In general, defences based on the likelihood of the substituted goods being readily distinguished without the need for any express disclaimer by the defendants have tended to fail. Cases in which injunctions have been granted in respect of over-the-counter substitution include *Procea v Evans*,[89] where the goods were distinguishable by the brand names on them, but customers were unlikely to inspect them before they were wrapped up; *French v Rhind*,[90] in which the substituted goods were shown to the customer on a trap order without explanation that they were not those asked for; *Goddard v Watford Co-Op Society*,[91] where the get-up of the substituted goods was distinct and the suppliers to the defendants had successfully defended an action brought against them by the same plaintiffs; and various cases brought by *Showerings*, summarised below.

7–35 Again, if the transaction is with the customer in person then there is no

---

[87] *per* Fletcher Moulton L.J. in *Lever Bros Ltd v Masbro Equitable Pioneers Society Ltd* (1912) 29 R.P.C. 225, CA.

[88] These conditions were met in *Lever Bros Ltd v Masbro Equitable Pioneers Society Ltd* (1912) 29 R.P.C. 225, CA.

[89] (1951) 68 R.P.C. 210 (Roxburgh J.).

[90] [1958] R.P.C. 82 (Dankwerts J.).

[91] (1924) 41 R.P.C. 218 (Astbury J.).

difficulty in principle in ascertaining if he is using an ambiguous word in its descriptive or trade mark sense.

In *Havana Cigar & Tobacco Factories v Oddenino*[92] it was found that to most members of the public the word *Corona* in relation to cigars meant a cigar of the plaintiffs' brand, but that a substantial minority of the public used it as descriptive of a cigar of a certain size and shape which could be made by any manufacturer. The defendant restaurateur was restrained from supplying cigars not of the plaintiffs' brand in response to an order for a Corona cigar unless he had first ascertained that the plaintiffs' brand was not required. On appeal the injunction was varied so as to add a second proviso allowing the defendant to make clear that the cigar was of another brand, but otherwise, the appeal was dismissed with costs.

In *Showerings v Mecca*[93] the defendants submitted to an interlocutory injunction against substituting other perry for the plaintiffs' *Babycham*. In *Showerings v Cheltenham & Hereford Breweries*[94] a contested interlocutory injunction was granted against similar acts on the strength of trap orders. In *Showerings v Fern Vale Brewery*[95] the personal defendant (a publican) was found liable for breaching undertakings to similar effect by supplying a perry called *CuVee* in response to orders for *Babycham*. The substitution proved on the motion to commit had been done by two part-time employees of low intelligence acting contrary to instructions from the defendant. The defendant was ordered to pay solicitor and client costs but was not committed.

In *Showerings v Blackpool Tower*[96] the same plaintiffs were granted interlocutory injunctions against substitution of *Baby Bubbly* and *Cherry Red* for *Babycham* and *Cherry B* despite a defence that the get-up of the bottles differed and that bar staff were under instructions to place all drinks so that the customer could see they were what he had ordered. Once again, the trap purchases were fair despite the fact that they were not immediately notified to the defendants. Goff J. also granted an interlocutory injunction on very similar facts in *Showerings v Entam*[97] and refused to accept a qualified undertaking which would have protected the defendants against committal for substitution by staff acting contrary to instructions, subject to the defendant displaying a notice that *Babycham* was not stocked.

If goods are supplied in response to a written order then the general rule is **7–36** the same:

"[The defendants] are not entitled to supply a corresponding ... article without first making it perfectly clear to the enquirer that they cannot

---

[92] [1924] 1 Ch. 179; 41 R.P.C. 47, CA.
[93] [1957] R.P.C. 217 (Roxburgh J.).
[94] [1958] R.P.C. 446 (Lewes J., Vacation judge).
[95] [1958] R.P.C. 484 (Dankwerts J.).
[96] [1975] F.S.R. 40 (Goff J.).
[97] [1975] F.S.R. 45 (Goff J.), followed in *British Telecommunications plc v Nextcall Telecom plc* [2000] F.S.R. 679 (Jacob J.).

supply him with the article which he wants, and leaving him an interval to decide what he is going to do."[98]

In this case if the defendant first obtains the customer's consent then there is no passing-off.[99] If goods are supplied without prior explanation in the expectation that they will be accepted then there is passing-off, whether or not the difference ought to be apparent to the customer.[1]

Switch selling

7–37 Switch selling or "bait-and-switch" is the name given to the practice of deliberately advertising particular goods as being available when they are not, often upon advantageous terms, so as to attract customers in the expectation that they can be persuaded to buy other goods. In a variant the goods advertised may actually be available, with the advertiser relying on high-pressure sales techniques to divert customers to less attractive and more profitable lines. Although the practice is dishonest and damaging, the few authorities most directly in point are reluctant to treat it as passing-off. The conceptual difficulty presented by switch selling is that although there is a misrepresentation it is no longer operative on the mind of the customer when the sale is made, and he is under no misapprehension that he is getting the claimant's goods rather than those of the defendant.

In the early case of *Ajello v Worsley*[2] it was held that it was neither passing-off nor injurious falsehood for the defendants honestly to have advertised the plaintiffs' pianos at low prices, even though they had none to sell at the time the advertisements were placed.

7–38 In *Rima Electric v Rolls Razor*[3] the defendants ran a sales promotion scheme under which purchasers of their washing machines were entitled to buy other domestic goods from a catalogue at wholesale prices. Among the goods illustrated in the catalogue was a hair drier of the plaintiffs. On a trap order the defendants had no such driers in stock and the purchaser was offered other makes. Wilberforce J. granted an interlocutory injunction against injurious falsehood, on the basis that it was damaging to the plaintiffs' relations with their normal trade customers for the defendants to suggest that they enjoyed a particularly privileged relationship with the plaintiffs, but he refused to treat the case as one of passing-off. The case was factually weak, because the drier was not identified by brand name, no prominence was apparently given to it in the catalogue, and the defendants were prepared to obtain that particular drier if the customer insisted.

In the South African case of *Willie Welgemoed Mini-Gym v Kloppers*

---

[98] *per* Cross J. in *Bostich Inc. v McGarry and Cole Ltd* [1964] R.P.C. 173.
[99] *Silicate Paint Co, J R Orr & Co Ltd v Smith* (1905) 23 R.P.C. 143; *Broad & Co Ltd v Cast Iron Drainage Co Ltd* [1970] F.S.R. 363; *Broad & Co Ltd v Graham Building Supplies Ltd* [1969] R.P.C. 285; [1969] F.S.R. 153.
[1] *Pearson Bros v Valentine & Co* (1917) 34 R.P.C. 267; *Purefoy Engineering Co Ltd v Sykes Boxall & Co Ltd* (1954) 72 R.P.C. 89, CA.
[2] [1898] 1 Ch. 274 (Stirling J.).
[3] [1965] R.P.C. 4 (Wilberforce J.).

Discount Houses[4] the defendants advertised the plaintiffs' mini-gym at a low price to attract customers. They then attempted to sell them a competing product. An interim interdict was granted but it is impossible to tell from the headnote (the only part of the report in English) whether this was on the basis of passing-off or the Roman-Dutch law of unlawful competition. Likewise, the Canadian case of *Sony of Canada v Multitech Warehouse*[5] occupies the uncertain frontier between the common law of passing-off and the civil law of unfair competition applicable in Quebec. An interlocutory injunction was granted, but the order that the defendants were not to stock or advertise Sony products would arguably have gone too far, but for suspicions about the defendants' willingness to comply, and illustrates the difficulty of framing an injunction in this sort of case which is effective, enforceable, and not disproportionate to the wrongful conduct.

In the absence of better express modern authority switch selling has to be **7–39** approached from basic principles. First, *Spalding v Gamage*[6] decided that there can be passing-off with liability for substantial damages[7] merely by advertising goods for sale, even if none are in fact sold. Secondly, the basis of passing-off is a misrepresentation causing damage to the claimant's goodwill and there are few *a priori* limits on what the misrepresentation may be or how the damage may arise: the case in which the defendant's goods are sold as and for the goods of the claimant is now recognised as no more than a special instance of a more general rule. In deliberate switch selling there is necessarily a misrepresentation and the question ought therefore to be whether it is material in the sense that damage arises from it.

"[A] representation made by advertisements that the articles sold at a particular shop are articles manufactured by A.B. (if that is the legitimate effect of the advertisements, which is a separate question) must, in my opinion, be as imperious in principle and may possibly be quite as injurious in operation, as the same representation made upon the articles themselves."[8]

The success of switch selling as a business practice depends on a potential customer for the claimant's goods being sold the defendant's by a process in which the making of the misrepresentation is an essential step, and damage may therefore be said to arise from the misrepresentation even though the customer has ceased to be misled by the time the transaction is concluded. The general principle is that if the defendant successfully induces the public to do business with him by making a misrepresentation then it ought not to matter that the falsity of the representation would become apparent at some stage. This would be consistent with the decision of an Australian Court in

---

[4] 1978 (4) SA 105 (Flemming R.).
[5] (1993) 49 C.P.R. (3d) 348 (Tellier J., Quebec).
[6] *Spalding (A G) & Bros v A W Gamage Ltd* (1915) 32 R.P.C. 273, HL.
[7] *ibid.* (1918) 35 R.P.C. 101, CA.
[8] *per* Lord Cairns in *Singer Machine Manufacturers v Wilson* (1877) 3 App.Cas. 376, HL. Note that the goods themselves could be distinguished.

Westinghouse Electric v Thermopart[9] where one issue was whether the defendants could be liable for passing-off by using *Laundromat* on the outside of their premises, when it would be obvious to anyone going inside that they did not use the plaintiffs' machinery. Wolff C.J. dismissed that argument: "Once inside, the person may see the difference in the machine but come to the conclusion that he or she might just as well have the service offered as go in search of another place".

7–40   Similar reasoning was expressed by Swinfen Eady J. in *W & G Du Cross v Gold*:[10]

> "In my opinion these [taxi] cabs of the defendant are got up in such a manner as to be calculated to deceive, and they have in fact deceived and taken in persons of intelligence and persons who are very familiar with the plaintiffs' cabs. They were deceived then, and they have got into them under the impression that they were the plaintiffs' cabs. In my opinion that is quite sufficient to entitle the plaintiffs to an injunction. It may be that before they arrived at the end of their journey these people found out the deception ... They cannot really be expected to stop on these occasions, and have an altercation with the cabman, and discharge the cab, and then look about for another cab wherever they happen to be."

Cases of switch selling may also involve an actionable misrepresentation that the defendant is an authorised dealer of the claimant.

E. Goods Originating from the Claimant

Introduction

7–41 The general principle that there is no passing-off of goods without a misrepresentation as to their origin is subject to a well established exception in cases where the defendant passes off goods as one quality for goods of another quality, even though both classes of goods are indeed the goods of the claimant. The situation may arise because the claimant markets or has marketed goods of more than one level of quality, because the defendant has obtained incomplete or reject goods that the claimant would not normally have sold under his own name; or because the goods are no longer of the same level of quality as when they were marketed by the claimant, perhaps because they have deteriorated (in which case there may also be a cause of action for injurious falsehood), or are second-hand, or have been altered. Similar issues can arise when the defendant deals in imported goods which are not identical to those on the home market. Several aspects of this cause of action are illustrated together in the relatively early case of *Richards v*

---

[9] [1968] W.A.R. 39 (Wolff C.J.).
[10] (1912) 30 R.P.C. 117 (Swinfen Eady J.).

Williamson.[11] Rifles made by the plaintiff had been withdrawn from service by the Army, dismantled and sold as scrap. The defendants took parts of the mechanism which bore the plaintiffs' name and trade mark and fitted them to unsuitable barrels of another manufacturer, cut down from rifle barrels to the length of carbines, for export to South Africa. Bacon V.C. granted an injunction.

This exception is generally thought to have been established by the decision of the House of Lords in *Spalding v Gamage*[12] but it is in fact much older. *Spalding v Gamage* is therefore less radical than is often supposed, and the defence in that case did not seriously dispute that the alleged misrepresentation was actionable in principle. In English law, Swinfen Eady J., in *Teacher v Levy*,[13] had granted an injunction and damages a decade previously when the plaintiffs' second grade of whisky was passed off as their best, without treating any novel issue of law as being involved. In Ireland a similar result had been reached a few years earlier still in *Jameson v Clarke*,[14] and in Australia as early as 1869: *Hennessy v Hogan*[15] and *Hennessy v White*.[16] Two more Australian cases affirming the principle are *Kirker Greer v Mayman*[17] in 1901 and *Ingram v India Rubber, Gutta Percha, and Telegraph Co*[18] in 1902.

Goods not endorsed by claimant

It is for the claimant to decide what goods are placed on the market bearing **7–42** his name or mark, or which name or mark if he has more than one in use. In general, once goods have been marketed by the claimant or on his behalf there can be no passing-off as a result of another trader simply dealing in those goods even if it is in a way not intended or welcomed by the claimant.[19]

Conversely, if the claimant has not consented to the goods being marketed under his name or mark, or at all, then it is no defence to an action for passing-off that the defendant has applied the claimant's name or mark to goods which are objectively the same as those of the claimant.

In *Defries v Electric & Ordnance Accessories*[20] the plaintiffs were the foreign suppliers of goods made to order for the predecessors in title of the defendants. They claimed that they alone could sell such goods under the name *Stewart*. Joyce J. held that they had no right to use the name them-

---

[11] (1874) 30 L.T. 746 (Bacon V.C.).
[12] (1915) 32 R.P.C. 273, HL.
[13] (1905) 23 R.P.C. 117 (Swinfen Eady J.).
[14] (1902) 19 R.P.C. 255 (Chatterton V.C.).
[15] (1869) 6 W.W. & a'B. (E) 225.
[16] (1869) 6 W.W. & a'B. (E) 216; 1 A.J.R. (N.C.) 4 (Supreme Court of Victoria, Full Court).
[17] [1901] 1 S.R. N.S.W. (Eq) 73 (Simpson C.J. in Eq.).
[18] (1902) 29 V.L.R. 172 (A Beckett J.).
[19] *Imperial Tobacco Co of India Ltd v Bonnan* [1924] A.C. 755; 41 R.P.C. 441, PC; *Champagne Heidsieck et Cie v Buxton* (1929) 47 R.P.C. 28; *Paquin Ltd v John Barker & Co Ltd* (1934) 51 R.P.C. 431; *Revlon Inc v Cripps & Lee Ltd* [1980] F.S.R. 85, CA.
[20] (1906) 23 R.P.C. 341 (Joyce J.); see also *MedGen Inc v Passion for Life Products Ltd* [2001] F.S.R. 30.

selves, any more than they could prevent the defendants using it for goods obtained from other sources. The defendants were granted an injunction on their counterclaim.

7–43   In *Vokes v Evans*[21] the plaintiffs obtained their supplies of windscreen wipers from a third party which also supplied the defendants directly with identical goods. The defendants were found liable for passing-off by selling the wipers under the plaintiffs' name notwithstanding that they were "precisely the same in every respect" and that the plaintiffs did not perform any additional operations on them or even examine the goods they received from the contractor. *Vokes v Evans* was followed and summary judgment granted in *Primark Stores v Lollypop Clothing*[22] where the defendants claimed that goods sold by them under the claimants' marks *Primark* and *Denim Co* had been sourced from one of the claimants' own suppliers and might have been made to the claimants' specifications. Even assuming the facts to be correct, there was no arguable defence. The claimants only allowed their clothes to be sold in their own retail outlets, and had never had an opportunity to assess the quality of the goods sold by the defendants.

In *Lee's Food Products v Shaffer-Hagart*[23] the defendants innocently obtained a consignment of imported tinned mushrooms ordered by the plaintiffs and printed with the plaintiffs' mark. They sold them with the mark inadequately covered with labels of their own, which came loose. The Ontario High Court found for the plaintiffs. The goods were precisely what the plaintiffs would have sold themselves, and the fact that the mushrooms had been diverted even meant that the defendants took no trade from them.

7–44   *Vokes v Evans* leaves open the question of whether the cause for action for passing-off turned on the goods having been made for the plaintiffs by a third party. There is no express English authority as to whether it can be passing-off to use the name or mark of the claimant in respect of goods in fact made by him to his usual standard of quality but which he chose not to market under his own name. It is suggested that the claimant alone ought to be the arbiter of what goods enter the market under his name or mark and that the cases including *Spalding v Gamage*, involving goods rejected as incomplete or defective, can also be justified under a wider principle that the claimant is entitled to withhold his consent to goods being sold as his in the first place without having to show why he chose not to market them under his name. This would be consistent with the reasoning of *Vokes v Evans* that passing-off depended on the mere possibility of the plaintiff rejecting the goods for which he would have been held responsible, even though in fact the goods were of the normal quality and the plaintiff took no special precautions. It is the claimant's reputation which is at stake, whether he is careless or over-cautious, and if he prefers to reject a whole batch of goods on finding that a few are defective it is hardly for a third party to decide which might have been retained, and sell them under the claimant's name.

Two early Australian cases did address the question of whether there need

---

[21] (1931) 49 R.P.C. 140 (Farwell J.).
[22] [2001] F.S.R. 37 (John Martin Q.C., Deputy Judge).
[23] (1984) 81 C.P.R. (2d) 204 (Van Camp J., Ontario).

be any objective difference between the two classes of goods. In *Kirker Greer v Mayman*[24] the plaintiffs sold whisky to Australia both in bottles and as bulk whisky in casks. The bottled whisky was considered superior and commanded a higher price. The defendants bottled some of the plaintiffs' bulk whisky and sold it under imitations of the plaintiffs' labels. The defendant claimed the two were practically identical in quality, and the Court agreed that any differences were barely detectable, but he was still restrained. The true test was not by how much the two qualities differed, but whether the public distinguished the two. Likewise, in *Ingram v India Rubber, Gutta Percha, and Telegraph Co*[25] the plaintiffs obtained an injunction when the defendants purchased their cheaper, unbranded enemas and sold them in packaging imitating the more expensive branded item. The two were identical, and the plaintiff had told the defendants as much. A'Beckett J. also rejected the argument that by selling identical goods at two prices and advertising that the higher priced one was superior the plaintiffs had disentitled themselves to equitable relief. Nominal damages were also awarded.

Goods not intended for immediate retail sale

Where the claimant's goods are sold as such in bulk and intended for re-sale **7–45** as his then there can be no misrepresentation by labelling them with his name or a mark appropriate for them to bear, but there is passing-off if one class of goods is represented as another.

A stricter standard of liability should apply when the goods are neither intended, nor suitable, for immediate resale without some further treatment or processing which might affect their final quality; or where skill and judgment are required as to whether they are suitable to be released at a given point in time, or under a given designation. Several Scottish cases (all decided on application for interim interdict) have held that there was *prima facie* liability for passing-off when raw malt whisky sold only for blending was bottled and sold under the name of the distillery:[26] *Macallan-Glenlivet v Speymalt Whisky Distributors*,[27] *Highland Distilleries v Speymalt Whisky Distributors*,[28] and *William Grant v William Caldenhead*.[29] In all three of these cases, the quality of the defenders' whisky was said to be inferior to, or at least different from, that which had undergone the normal maturation and processing employed by the respective pursuers for their branded whisky sold in bottle under the relevant distillery name.[30] That might have been relevant to the balance of convenience, but so far as liability is con-

---

[24] [1901] 1 S.R. N.S.W. (Eq.) 73 (Simpson C.J. in Eq.).
[25] (1902) 29 V.L.R. 172 (A'Beckett J.).
[26] See also *James Burrough Distillers plc v Speymalt Whisky Distributors Ltd* [1991] R.P.C. 130; 1989 SLT 561 (Lord Coulsfield, OH).
[27] 1983 SLT 348 (Lord Cameron, OH).
[28] 1985 SLT 85 (Lord Ross, OH).
[29] 1985 SLT 291 (Lord Ross, OH). Interim interdict was refused for delay and on the balance of convenience.
[30] Respectively *Macallan*, *Bunnahabhain* and *Glenfiddich*.

cerned it is probably best to regard the decisions as applications of *Vokes v Evans*[31] in so far as the respective pursuers had never consented to their raw whisky being matured, processed, and sold retail under their names at all.

In *Alllied Domecq v Murray McDavid*[32] it was conceded that there was no suggestion of any passing off arising from the defenders' practice of buying whisky from the *Laphroaig* Distillery which was surplus to the requirements of blenders to whom it had been sold for blending, and selling it unblended in bottles with the label "Islay single malt Scotch whisky from the LAPH-ROAIG DISTILLERY" with *Laphroaig* most prominent. An *ex parte* interim interdict based only on alleged trade mark infringement was discharged as the balance of convenience did not justify it.

Incomplete, reject or superseded goods

7–46 It is passing-off to sell without notice goods of the claimant which have been rejected as incomplete or substandard, whether they have never been marketed by the claimant or whether they have been marketed previously but withdrawn.

In *Spalding v Gamage*[33] the plaintiffs were manufacturers of footballs. The defendants had obtained from a firm of waste rubber merchants a stock of moulded rubber balls made by the plaintiffs to a design (the *Orb*) which they had rejected as unsatisfactory in favour of sewn balls which they sold as *Improved Sewn Orb*. The defendants issued advertisements in which they implicitly and in some cases specifically claimed that the moulded balls they were selling were the *Improved Sewn Orb*. They were held liable for passing-off by the House of Lords.

In *Britains v Morris*[34] the defendants were restrained from supplying in response for an order for *Swoppets* toys which were apparently unfurnished rejects of the plaintiffs which the plaintiffs would never have sold under their *Swoppets* mark.

7–47 Although it is uncertain to what extent the cause of action is based on the absence of the claimant's consent to marketing, and to what extent on the objective inferiority of the goods, the action will fail if the claimant is to be regarded as having consented to the marketing of the goods, if there is no express misrepresentation that the goods are of a particular nature or quality, and if any differences in nature or defects in quality would be apparent.

In *Revlon v Cripps & Lee*[35] the plaintiffs discontinued sales of their anti-dandruff shampoo after it had been on sale for over a year and donated some of their stocks to a charity on condition that it was not re-sold. By so doing the plaintiffs obtained tax advantages. Other stocks had been sold cheaply to a wholesaler, and other wholesalers and retailers still had the goods in stock from when it was part of the current range. The shampoo was

---

[31] (1931) 49 R.P.C. 140 (Farwell J.).
[32] [1997] F.S.R. 864; 1999 SLT 157 (Lord MacFadyen, OH).
[33] (1915) 32 R.P.C. 273, HL.
[34] [1961] R.P.C. 217 (Lloyd-Jacob J.).
[35] [1980] F.S.R. 85, CA.

not objectively inferior to the types which remained on the market under the *Revlon* name, and was readily identifiable as being medicated. In these circumstances the Court of Appeal treated the plaintiffs as having consented to the marketing of the goods and refused to restrain the defendants from importing and selling the old stock. *Revlon v Cripps & Lee* may be distinguished from *Spalding v Gamage*[36] in that in *Spalding's* case the goods were specifically withdrawn because of their unsatisfactory nature, were sold as scrap, and were expressly misrepresented by the defendants as being the current model.

Goods of different quality

More generally, if the claimant has goods in two or more categories which **7–48** are clearly distinguishable as to nature or quality then it is passing-off to misrepresent goods in one category as being in the other. Although the cause of action originally arose in respect of inferior goods being passed off for superior it is not confined to cases where the goods passed off are worse than those they are represented to be. The principle applies also where the two classes of goods are equally desirable but have different properties or appeal to different consumers. Thus, it would be passing-off to sell medicated anti-dandruff shampoo as unmedicated shampoo, even if both were made by the same firm to the same high level of quality [37]

In *Teacher v Levy*[38] the defendants were found liable for passing-off by filling empty bottles of Teachers' superior *Highland Cream* whisky with the cheapest bulk whisky sold by Teachers and serving it in response to orders for Highland Cream. This was historically one of the commoner forms taken by this head of passing-off. See also the two Australian *Hennessy* cases,[39] *Kirker Greer v Mayman*,[40] and the Irish case of *Jameson v Clarke*.[41]

It is suggested that the true test is that stated in the two Australian cases of *Kirker Greer v Mayman*[42] and *Ingram v India Rubber, Gutta Percha, and Telegraph Co*[43] There is passing-off if the public distinguish two different categories and one is sold as the other, even if objectively there are no differences between the two. Conversely, there is no passing-off if the public do not distinguish two categories of goods, even if the claimant can point to objective differences between them. Even if there can be said to be a misrepresentation, it is not a material one if the public are ignorant of the differences which exist.

For a passing-off action to succeed it is necessary for the claimant to **7–49** establish that the different categories of goods are reasonably well defined either through his own actions or through recognisable objective differences

---

[36] (1915) 32 R.P.C. 273, HL.
[37] The example is based on *Revlon Inc v Cripps & Lee Ltd* [1980] F.S.R. 85, CA.
[38] (1905) 23 R.P.C. 117 (Swinfen Eady J.).
[39] *Hennessy v Hogan* (1869) 6 W. W. & a'B (E) 225 and *Hennessy v White* [1869] 6 W. W. & a'B (e) 216; 1 A.J.R. (N.C.) 4.
[40] [1901] 1 S.R. N.S.W. (Eq.) 73 (Simpson C.J. in Eq.).
[41] (1902) 19 R.P.C. 255 (Chatterton V.C.).
[42] [1901] 1 S.R. N.S.W. (Eq.) 73 (Simpson C.J. in Eq.).
[43] (1902) 29 V.L.R. 172 (A'Beckett J.).

which are appreciated by the public. If the existence of the two or more categories is known to the consuming public and they are clearly identified, for instance by different brand names, then the claimant's appropriation of goods to one class or another ought to be taken as conclusive and it ought not to matter to what extent the goods in one class are better or worse then those in another. More difficult questions arise when the claimant has not systematically differentiated between classes of goods of supposedly different quality. The traditional view was that the plaintiff had to be able to identify a well defined class of goods for which those of the defendant were being passed off.[44] This is readily justifiable in most circumstances on the modern view of the law because in its absence there would normally be no misrepresentation and no damage. All the same, it is suggested that in cases of a sufficiently express misrepresentation as to quality this need not be conclusive, or one has the absurdity that the bigger the lie the less the liability. If the public is led to believe that a category of goods exists when it does not, then self-evidently there is a misrepresentation in saying goods fall into that category.

In *Hunt, Roope, Teague v Ehrmann*[45] the plaintiffs sold port of two qualities, vintage and non-vintage, almost always by the cask. The defendants purchased non-vintage port of the plaintiffs' which had been bottled by third parties and matured. They sold it as "Hunt, Roope's Grand Old Crusted Port. Over six years in bottle ... Usual credit price per doz 60s. Now offered by us at per doz 34s" with a fictitious story of how they had obtained it at an undervalue. The plaintiffs' vintage port, unmatured in bottle, would also have sold for about 60s. Warrington J. held that the plaintiffs had no separate and distinct class of wine to which the defendants should be taken as referring, and that the defendants' wine could not be mistaken for the plaintiffs' vintage port.

In *Consorzio del Prosciuitto Di Parma v Marks & Spencer*[46] an allegation that pre-sliced Parma ham could not be sold as "genuine Parma ham" because it was of a different and inferior quality as a result of the way in which it was sliced and packed was struck out as untenable.

Quality without fixed categories; works of creative individuals

7–50 When one is dealing with articles of commerce, quality is normally susceptible to fixed categorisation: satisfactory or reject in the case of footballs; medicated or non-medicated for shampoo; chocolate which originates in Switzerland, or in Birmingham. In principle, at least, the action for passing-off also protects those in the literary and artistic professions from having genuine but inferior work passed off as work of their normal standard. The practical difficulties of proof may, however, be formidable unless the case borders on one of false attribution of authorship.

The problems which can arise are well illustrated in *Harris v Warren and*

---

[44] *Hunt, Roope, Teague & Co v Ehrmann Bros* [1910] 2 Ch.198, below.
[45] [1910] 2 Ch. 198 (Warrington J.).
[46] [1991] R.P.C. 351, CA.

Phillips[47] in which one of the plaintiffs, a songwriter, claimed an injunction to restrain the owners of the copyright in one of her early compositions from passing it off as one of her recent works. The case was originally pleaded on the basis that the defendants had expressly represented that the old song was new, but the evidence failed to support this allegation. The plaintiff had also pleaded that she held a low opinion of the merit of the early piece and that it had enjoyed little commercial success, but what she had not pleaded was that there was any line of demarcation between the earlier and later works or that the earlier works generally were artistically or commercially inferior. Eve J. held that the plaintiff had failed to lay the necessary foundation for the action by showing the existence of two classes of work, and that the undoubted right of the defendants to publish the early song and represent it truthfully as her work prevailed.

In *Beecham v British Lion*[48] the conductor Sir Thomas Beecham objected to the issue of records of a film sound track conducted by him, on the grounds that they were inferior to records of a concert performance and his reputation would suffer. The defendants gave an interlocutory undertaking not to sell or advertise the records without indicating their source. Compare *Sony Music Australia v Tansing*[49] where an interlocutory injunction was refused against a bootleg recording of a *Michael Jackson* concert which was prominently labelled to show it was unauthorised and of a lower than usual recording standard.

Somewhat similar issues to *Harris v Warren and Phillips* arose in *Sweeny v* **7–51** *Macmillan Publishers*,[50] though the case was treated as one of first impression.[51] James Joyce's *Ulysses* had originally been published in 1922, but the 1922 text had never been accepted as definitive. The second defendant produced, and the first defendant published, a new version of *Ulysses* compiled from the 1922 text and various other authentic sources, which they called a "Reader's Edition". The trustees of Joyce's estate alleged that the Reader's Edition was so different to what Joyce had intended that it could not properly be described as his *Ulysses* at all, or at least not without further explanation. Lloyd J. held that the action failed because the trustees were unable to distinguish any clearly defined category of "products" to which the defendants' edition did not equally well belong. There were several existing variant editions of *Ulysses* in circulation; supposed academic or literary criteria for distinguishing the Reader's Edition from those authorised or tolerated by Joyce or the trustees were controversial, subjective and vague; and there was no adequate evidence that members of the public attributed any importance to the approval of Joyce himself or the *imprimatur* of his estate. There was no way a class could be objectively defined of which it could be said: all these existing editions are within it, but the

---

[47] (1918) 35 R.P.C. 217 (Eve J.).
[48] (1951) 68 R.P.C. 111.
[49] (1994) 27 I.P.R. 649 (Federal Court of Australia).
[50] [2002] R.P.C. 35 (Lloyd J.).
[51] There are also similarities with the *Frank Harris* case, *W H Allen v Brown Watson* [1965] R.P.C. 191; but in that case there were only two editions, they were identified by different titles, and one of them was seriously incomplete.

Reader's Edition is not. When one is dealing with a "class of goods" case, the definition of the class must either be entirely objective, or by reference to the public state of mind, but the only definition the claimants were able to formulate was circular and self-serving: the relevant class consisted of editions which Joyce or the estate had approved, and excluded all others.

Deteriorated goods

7-52 Even if goods were originally placed on the market by the claimant it may be passing-off, injurious falsehood, or both, to sell them without warning if they have deteriorated below the standard expected by the customer.

In *Wilts United Dairies v Thomas Robinson*[52] the defendants obtained supplies of condensed milk manufactured by the plaintiffs and canned in their normal containers but which was at least 20 months' old compared to the normal shelf life of about six months, and which had therefore deteriorated significantly. The Court of Appeal held that the old milk, "a discoloured and gelatinous substance, sprinkled with what a consumer might mistake for pieces of glass", was of a different quality to the "fresh looking wholesome product" the customer was used to, and that by selling the stale milk without warning in tins indistinguishable from those containing fresh the defendants were liable for both passing-off and malicious falsehood.

Although goods may not actually have deteriorated they may have been superseded and it will then be passing-off to sell the old goods as and for the new ones.[53]

Second-hand goods

7-53 Selling second-hand goods as such cannot amount to passing-off,[54] but if the circumstances of the sale are such as to lead them being taken for new goods then there is an actionable misrepresentation. The simpler case is that in which the goods have deteriorated through use or passage of time so that the goodwill of the manufacturer would be damaged if the purchaser thought they were representative of the quality of his unused products. The question in such cases is primarily one of fact: are the circumstances such that the customer would have expected to have received new goods? Since there is a second-hand trade in most durable goods the burden on the claimant is not easy.

In *General Electric v Pryce's Stores*[55] the defendant had obtained a large number of second-hand light bulbs of the plaintiffs' manufacture as a result of properties having their electricity supply voltage changed. The bulbs had been cleaned and were sold in a small general shop in a poor area at a price

---

[52] [1958] R.P.C. 94, CA.

[53] *Spalding (A G) & Bros v A W Gamage Ltd* (1915) 32 R.P.C., HL; but compare *Revlon Inc v Cripps & Lee Ltd* [1980] F.S.R. 85, CA.

[54] *Consumers Distributing Co v Seiko Time Canada Ltd* [1984] 1 S.C.R. 585; 3 C.I.P.R. 223; 10 D.L.R. (4th) 161; 1 C.P.R. (3d) 1.

[55] (1933) R. P.C. 232 (Maugham J.).

well below that for new bulbs.[56] The plaintiffs objected to any trade in second-hand bulbs because their life expectancy was unpredictable. Maugham J. found that in all the circumstances purchasers would not have expected to get new bulbs and that as the defendant's trade was honest it should not be restrained.

In *Gillette Safety Razor v Franks*[57] and *Gillette Safety Razor v Diamond Edge*[58] the defendants re-sharpened old *Gillette* razor blades, put them in *Gillette* envelopes, and sold them as "genuine". Both were treated as cases of obvious fraud on the public. Selling refurbished, second-hand goods as new was restrained in *Sony du Canada v Multitronic Stereo*[59] and *Sony du Canada v Impact Electronique*.[60] Text indicating that they were refurbished had been removed from their packaging.

Different questions arise in cases where the misrepresentation is not **7–54** essentially as to the quality of the goods in the sense of whether or not they have been used, but as to the connection between the claimant and the defendant. In a number of industries it is common for manufacturers to appoint a limited number of retailers to handle their goods and provide the necessary service and support. If a trader not so selected sells those goods as new then there may be a twofold misrepresentation that the defendant has satisfied whatever requirements are set by the claimant for its authorised dealers; and that the customer will receive the expected level of support from the seller, authorised dealers generally, or from the claimants themselves. In such cases it is irrelevant that the goods may indeed be new in the sense that they are unused by any consumer.

There is authority that in the motor industry the unqualified word "new" is inapplicable to a vehicle which has been sold and registered, as the manufacturer's obligations are (or were) owed only to the first purchaser. In *Morris Motors v Lilley*[61] it was held that it was therefore passing-off for a dealer to sell as "new" a vehicle purchased by him from an authorised retail dealer, or elsewhere, even if it was in fact unused.

Altered, repaired or modified goods

When goods are sold as new then it is passing-off to have modified them **7–55** without notice to the consumer.[62] More generally, it is passing-off to represent as goods of the claimant goods which have been altered, modified

---

[56] For low price putting customers on notice see also *Paquin Ltd v John Barker & Co Ltd* (1934) 51 R.P.C. 431.

[57] (1924) 41 R.P.C. 499 (Astbury J.).

[58] (1926) 43 R.P.C. 310 (Romer J.). In the latter case an interlocutory injunction was granted despite four years apparent delay.

[59] (1991) 42 C.P.R. (3d) 53 (Quebec CA).

[60] (1991) 39 C.P.R. (3d) 414 (LeBel J., Quebec).

[61] [1959] 1 W.L.R. 118 (Wynn-Parry J.). See also *Morris Motors Ltd v Phelian* [1960] 1 W.L.R. 566. Since these depend on trade usage, it should not be assumed that they are necessarily current.

[62] *Sony KK v Saray Electronics (London) Ltd* [1983] F.S.R. 302, CA.

or added to without consent where the representee would not appreciate this.[63] Whether this has occurred or not is ultimately a matter of fact, which may require evidence from those in the trade. In *IBM v Phoenix*[64] there was an arguable defence, which should not be struck out, that the defendants were making no misrepresentation by selling as *IBM Manufactured* refurbished IBM computer memory cards which had been reworked by a third party by the addition of additional memory modules made by IBM and removed from other cards. The truth or falsehood of the representation was not self-evident but depended on what would be understood by the expression by those in this very specialised market.

In *Illustrated Newspapers v Publicity Services*[65] the defendants supplied hotels, free of charge, with bound copies of popular magazines into which they had inserted advertising supplements of their own following the style of each magazine. Crossman J. found that readers would be likely to take the supplement as being part of the magazine as published by the plaintiff; that advertising business would be diverted from the plaintiffs to the defendants; and that the plaintiffs might be exposed to the risk of litigation. More recently, the defendants in *Associated Newspapers v Insert Media*[66] were restrained at trial and on appeal from inserting advertising supplements into the *Daily Mail* and *Mail on Sunday*. The placing of the inserts in the newspapers constituted a misrepresentation that they were connected with the plaintiffs and their publications, and a proposed disclaimer was inadequate.

7–56   In *Westinghouse Brake & Signal v Varsity Eliminator*[67] the defendants were restrained (in default of defence) from selling as the plaintiffs' goods rectifiers which had been dismantled and re-assembled with a reduced number of genuine parts so that ten genuine rectifiers could be "stretched" to twelve.

It has been suggested that it may be passing-off to sell repaired or reconditioned goods incorporating essential parts not of the claimant's manufacture.[68] As a general principle this is doubtful because the practice of using spare parts from independent suppliers must be well known to purchasers and there would be no element of misrepresentation. However, if in specific cases the purchaser would expect or was led to believe that only the claimant's parts had been used then there might be passing-off.[69]

Parallel imports

7–57 In general it is not passing-off to import goods marketed abroad by the claimant (or an associated business) and sell them under the name or mark

[63] See also two Canadian cases: *Time/System International v Custom Planner* (1986) 12 C.P.R. (3d) 441 and *United States Surgical Corp. v Downs Surgical Canada Ltd* (1982) 67 C.P.R. (2d) 140.
[64] [1994] R.P.C. 252 (Ferris J.).
[65] [1938] Ch. 414; [1938] 1 All E.R. 321; 55 R.P.C. 172 (Crossman J.).
[66] [1991] F.S.R. 380, CA.
[67] (1935) 52 R.P.C. 295 (Luxmoore J.).
[68] *Hoover Ltd v Air-way Ltd* (1936) 53 R.P.C. 369.
[69] *Richards v Williamson* (1874) 30 L.T. 746.

applied by the claimant because there is no misrepresentation as to the origin of the goods.[70] In modern circumstances the consuming public is unlikely to know or care whether the goods of the claimant are normally imported or not. The arguments which may be raised on behalf of a claimant, and the difficulties in making them out, can be seen from the judgment of Templeman L.J. in the Court of Appeal in *Revlon v Cripps & Lee*:[71]

> "[T]he Revlon plaintiffs submitted that there were misrepresentations by the defendants about the origin, class and quality of the *Revlon Flex* anti-dandruff medicated shampoo and hair conditioner offered for sale by the defendants in the United Kingdom. As to origin, no purchaser knows or cares whether *Revlon Flex* is made in Wales by a Venezuelan company or in New York by a Delaware corporation. As to class, the defendants truly represent that the products they sell are shampoos and hair conditioners of the same class as all *Revlon Flex* products, save that these particular products are intended for hair affected by dandruff whereas other Revlon Flex products are intended for normal or greasy or dry hair, according to the label on the bottle. As to quality, the *Revlon Flex* anti-dandruff products are of a quality equal to other *Revlon Flex* products and are included in the range of *Revlon Flex* products advertised together in the United States."

If the imported goods have come from the claimant or a connected **7–58** enterprise a successful passing-off action depends on showing that the imported goods are not of the class or quality that consumers would expect from the use of the claimant's name or mark. The fact that the imported goods do not precisely correspond in nature or quality to goods already on the home market is not of itself sufficient for there to be passing-off if the imported goods are distinguishable by the consumer, or if the difference is irrelevant or *de minimis*.

> "There is nothing to prevent a tradesman acquiring goods from a manufacturer and selling them in competition with him, even in a country into which hitherto the manufacturer or his agent has been the sole importer. It is not likely to be a successful business operation, unless in some exceptional case. ... The claim of the appellant company is that it can stop a trader, to whom goods have been lawfully sold under a particular trade description ... from reselling them under the same description. Such a claim sounds extravagant. It might, however, possibly be maintained, if it could be shown that the time, place or circumstances of the resale imported some representation that the goods were other than what they were. But in this case there is no such time, place or circumstance."[72]

---

[70] *Imperial Tobacco Co of India Ltd v Bonnan* [1924] A.C. 755; 41 R.P.C. 441, PC.
[71] [1980] F.S.R. 85, CA.
[72] *per* Lord Phillimore in *Imperial Tobacco Co of India Ltd v Bonnan* [1924] A.C. 755; 41 R.P.C. 441, PC.

7-59   In *Champagne Heidsiek v Buxton*[73] the plaintiffs objected to the importation into England and sale of Champagne sold by them in France and
tasting different to the *Champagne* sold by them in England. The English
and Continental bottles were distinguishable without difficulty. An action
for trade mark infringement and passing-off was dismissed, Clauson J.
holding that there could be no case against a defendant who had sold the
Continental *Champagne* under the very marks which the plaintiffs had
thought proper to distinguish it from the English and which did distinguish
it in fact. *Obiter* the judge would also apparently have refused relief if
confusion between the English and Continental products had arisen from
the plaintiffs failing to distinguish them from one another although knowing
that the Continental wine was being imported.

7-60   The same principle applies where the claimant and the foreign manufacturer are associated companies in a group.

In *Revlon v Cripps & Lee*[74] the third plaintiffs manufactured and the
fourth plaintiffs distributed *Revlon* products in the United Kingdom. The
first plaintiffs were the ultimate holding company of both, and also manufactured and distributed similar *Revlon* products in the United States. The
defendants imported into England *Revlon Flex* shampoo manufactured and
sold in the United States by the first plaintiffs. The Court of Appeal refused
to draw any distinction between the companies in the Revlon group and
treated the mark in question as denoting the goods of the group as a whole
rather than any particular company in it. The Court also rejected arguments
that the imported goods were of a different class to those already on the
market, because this was apparent from their labelling; or that they were of
an inferior quality.

That the public knew the plaintiffs' goods were made in the United
Kingdom was allegedly made out in *Colgate-Palmolive v Markwell
Finance*,[75] although it is less clear that they attached any importance to this.
A clear misrepresentation as to quality was also present and did not depend
on the fact that the defendants' goods were imported.

Imports not the same as goods for home market

7-61 It is clear that there is no passing-off by the sale of imported goods of the
claimant if they are the same as his domestic goods; if the domestic market is
already accustomed to distinguishing the imports and able to do so; or if the
nature of the difference between the imports and the domestic goods is
readily apparent to the customer. This leaves two cases where there may be
passing-off without any representation by the defendant other than is
implicit in selling the goods: the imports may be indistinguishable externally
although materially different in nature or quality; or the customer may be
able to recognise that the imported goods differ externally in some way, but
without being able to appreciate in advance of purchase that they are

[73] (1929) 47 R.P.C. 28 (Clauson J.).
[74] [1980] F.S.R. 85, CA.
[75] [1988] R.P.C. 283, CA, on appeal from Falconer J. On appeal, only the misrepresentation of
quality was relevant.

inferior or unsuitable. The latter case is illustrated by *Wilkinson Sword v Cripps & Lee*[76] in which Falconer J. refused to strike out an action based on the importation of inferior quality razor blades sold by the plaintiffs in America under the same mark as in England but with a different get-up. The same judge found for the plaintiffs at trial in *Colgate-Palmolive v Markwell Finance*[77] which concerned parallel imports of toothpaste from Brazil.

It is passing-off to sell imported goods which have been modified to attempt to make them correspond to those on sale in the home market without giving notice to the purchaser.[78] Conversely, selling unmodified imported goods may equally be passing-off, if they are unsuitable for local conditions. In *Star Micronics v Five Star Computers*[79] it was actionable to sell computer printers designed to work on 220 V in Australia, where the mains supply was at 240 V. There was an implicit misrepresentation that the printers were suitable for the local voltage, as well as an explicit mis-representation that they were guaranteed by the plaintiffs. Likewise in *Pioneer Electronics v Lee*[80] DVD players imported by the defendant were of a Japanese model which had not been released in Australia, did not comply with local electrical safety regulations, and had been subjected to unau-thorised and potentially dangerous modifications. An interlocutory injunc-tion was granted. Even if the imported goods are identical to those on the home market, it may be passing-off to sell them without notice when they do not have all necessary regulatory approvals, as with the fax machines imported into Canada from the United States in *Sharp Electronics of Canada v Continental Electronic Info.*[81]

Re-packaged or re-labelled goods

Where the claimant's goods are imported by the defendant it may be diffi-   7–62
cult or impossible for him to sell them in this country in their original packaging, for instance because of instructions and descriptive matter being in a foreign language. The question then arises of whether it is passing-off to re-package or re-label the goods so as to correspond more closely to what the home market expects, subject to any defence under European Com-munity law. In principle the packaging of goods may be important to the consumer in a number of ways: the goods may be liable to deteriorate if inadequately packed or the consumer may wish to be assured for reasons such as hygiene or purity that the goods have not been interfered with since leaving the known manufacturer. Although there is no express authority that re-packaging in such cases may constitute passing-off there is some authority for the proposition that the quality of packaging may be relevant.

In *Yardley v Higson*[82] the defendants imported *English Lavender* soap

[76] [1982] F.S.R. 16 (Falconer J.).
[77] [1988] R.P.C. 283 (Falconer J.) affirmed [1989] R.P.C. 497, CA.
[78] *Sony KK v Saray Electronics (London) Ltd* [1983] F.S.R. 302, CA.
[79] (1990) 18 I.P.R. 225 (Davies J., Federal Court).
[80] [2000] FCA 1936; 51 I.P.R. 291 (Sundberg J, Federal Court of Australia).
[81] (1988) 23 C.P.R. (3d) 330 (Melnick J., British Columbia).
[82] [1984] F.S.R. 304, CA.

which the plaintiffs had sold abroad without the wrapping of individual tablets which the plaintiffs considered essential for the English market if the soap were not to deteriorate. An interlocutory injunction was granted on the basis that the wrapped and unwrapped soaps were goods of different quality. In two respects *Yardley v Higson* is an atypical case, because the imported goods had not been interfered with and because the plaintiffs themselves had even sold goods with the allegedly unsatisfactory packaging in England. If the defendant had been wholly responsible for any deficiencies in the packaging the plaintiffs' case ought to have been no less strong. In *Microsoft v Computer Future Distribution*[83] there was passing off by selling various Microsoft computer programs or "licence packs" with the outer packaging entirely removed, so that the purchaser could not see that they were in fact unlicensed imports from the North American market, and in some cases only intended for academic use. In *Glaxo Group v Dowelhurst (No.2)*[84] Laddie J. very briefly held that a claim for passing-off in relation to imported, repackaged, pharmaceuticals could be no stronger than that for registered trade mark infringement: the blister packs of the products had not been interfered with, and the their quality and integrity had not been compromised.

7–63   It is suggested that an action for passing-off based on re-packaging ought to be entertained if the claimant can show that the quality of the packaging or the identity of the person applying it would be regarded by consumers as significant, and that the defendant had interfered with the packaging applied to the goods by the claimant in a way inconsistent with the expectations of the consumers and without giving adequate notice. If the defendant has done so, then the question of whether or not he has done as good a job of re-packaging as the claimant would have done may be relevant to damages or to any defence of exhaustion of rights, but should not prevent there being a *prima facie* cause of action for passing-off.

The significance of original containers as a guarantee of quality or purity shades over into cases on adulterated goods, such as *John Walker v Henry Ost*;[85] as well as cases in which bulk spirits actually of the claimant's manufacture have been passed off as having been bottled by him. On the other hand, in *Consorzio del Prosciuitto Di Parma v Marks & Spencer*[86] an allegation that pre-sliced and packaged Parma ham could not be sold as "genuine Parma ham" was struck out as untenable. It was irrelevant that Italian law required that Parma ham sold as such always had to be carved from the bone, in the customer's presence.

7–64   Different questions arise if the defendant has left the essential parts of the claimant's packaging intact but has re-labelled the goods or placed them in new outer containers. This is actionable if the effect is to pass off one quality of goods for another. In *Champagne Heidsiek v Scotto and Bishop*[87] there was passing-off where Champagne of the plaintiffs' Continental quality,

---

[83] [1998] E.T.M.R. 597 (Rimer J.).
[84] [2002] E.T.M.R. 415; [2000] F.S.R. 529 (Laddie J.).
[85] [1970] 1 W.L.R. 917; [1970] 2 All E.R. 106; [1970] R.P.C. 489 (Foster J.).
[86] [1991] R.P.C. 351, CA.
[87] (1926) 43 R.P.C. 101 (Tomlin J.).

different in taste and get-up to the English quality, was sold in England under labels which were forgeries of the English labels.

There is generally no passing-off by removing or obliterating the name or mark of the claimant so that the goods are no longer identifiable as originating from him, as in the final situation dealt with by Laddie J. in *Glaxo Group v Dowelhurst (No. 2)*,[88] unless there is liability for "inverse" passing-off. In *Consorzio del Prosciutto Di Parma v Marks & Spencer*, above, there was no liability for passing-off by removing the Ducal Crown which Italian Law required to be stamped on all whole Parma hams. *Microsoft v Computer Future Distribution*[89] is an entirely different case, since the goods were expressly sold as *Microsoft* products, despite the packaging being reduced to a plain brown box. Nor is there passing-off by the addition of another person's name or mark, or matter clearly not emanating from the claimant. Indeed, in *Sony v Saray*[90] the Court of Appeal effectively ordered the defendants to mark the plaintiffs' goods sold in their shop with their own name and a disclaimer.

F. Licensing and Franchising

Introduction

The class of actionable misrepresentations in passing-off is not confined to **7–65** those from which it might be supposed that the goods or businesses of the claimant and defendant are one and the same. It is potentially actionable to claim any connection with the claimant which is untrue and calculated to cause damage. One form such a misrepresentation may take is that the defendant personally, or his goods or business, is licensed by the claimant, so that the public would rely on the claimant's reputation in doing business with the defendant.

"Clearly the concept of connection is more readily understandable and appropriate in the case of businesses where one gets groups of subsidiary and associated companies and trading arrangements, but in my view it is correct and necessary for completeness in the case of goods also, provided one is careful not to allow the concept too wide a meaning.

Not every kind of connection claimed will amount to passing-off; for example if one says one's goods are very suitable to be used in connection with the plaintiff's. On the other hand in my view there can be a passing-off of goods without representing that they are actually the well-known goods which the plaintiff produces or a new line which he is supposed to have started. It is sufficient in my view if what is done represents the defendant's goods to be connected with the plaintiff in such a way as

---

[88] [2002] E.T.M.R. 415; [2000] F.S.R. 529 (Laddie J.).
[89] [1998] E.T.M.R. 597 (Rimer J.).
[90] [1983] F.S.R 302, CA.

would lead people to accept them on the faith of the plaintiff's reputation. Thus for example it would be sufficient if they were taken to be made under licence, or under some trading arrangement which would give the plaintiff some control over them, and I think Harman J. had such ideas in his mind as appears from the passage at page 93 of the *Treasure Cot* case[91] when he spoke of 'something for which the plaintiffs were responsible'."[92]

A misrepresentation that the defendant's goods, or his business as a whole, are licensed by the claimant is therefore actionable as passing-off if the other criteria of the tort are met. Of these, the most important is that the misrepresentation must be really likely to cause damage to the claimant. The requirement to prove damage applies to all misrepresentations, but the English courts have in general been more reluctant to infer that damage will occur when it is clear to the public that the goods or business of the defendant are not actually those of the claimant even in a broad sense. A representation, express or implied, that the defendant's goods or business are licensed or endorsed by the claimant is not assumed to be inherently damaging.

7–66   This quotation from the judgment of Goff L.J. in *Bulmer v Bollinger*, and another by Buckley L.J. to the same effect, were approved by Millett L.J. in the Court of Appeal in *Harrods v Harrodian School*,[93] with the intention of distinguishing those cases in which the claimant was being held out as making himself responsible for the work of the defendant, from those in which there was merely an immaterial misrepresentation that the defendant enjoyed the claimant's sponsorship or support:

"A belief that the plaintiff has sponsored or given financial support to the defendant will not ordinarily give the public that impression. Many sporting and artistic events are sponsored by commercial organisations which require their name to be associated with the event, but members of the public are well aware that the sponsors have no control over and are not responsible for the organisation of the event. Local teams are often sponsored in similar fashion by local firms, but their supporters are well aware that the sponsors have no control over and are not responsible for the selection or performance of the players.

Schools and colleges are not normally sponsored or promoted in the same way, but they are often financially supported by commercial and professional organisations. Scholarships and professorial chairs are increasingly established by professional firms which stipulate that their name is publicly associated with the endowment. But it is generally recognised that those who provide financial support to such institutions do not expect to have any control over or to be held responsible for the institution or the quality of the teaching. Many ancient schools still bear the names of the guilds which founded them, not as part of their trading

---

[91] *Treasure Cot Co Ltd v Hamley Bros. Ltd* (1950) 67 R.P.C. 89.
[92] *per* Goff L.J. in *Bulmer (HP) Ltd v J Bollinger SA* [1978] R.P.C. 79; [1977] 2 C.M.L.R. 625, CA.
[93] [1996] R.P.C. 687, CA.

activities, but as charitable institutions for the benefit of children of their members. The connection is now largely if not entirely historical; but it was probably never one which was capable of adversely affecting the goodwill and business reputation of the founder."

Licensing is of particular interest in three contexts which may overlap: **7–67**

1. Where the defendant was formerly the claimant's licensee or acts outside the scope of a subsisting licence;[94]

2. Where the claimant and defendant are in very different fields of business, so that the most natural and plausible relationship to infer (if one is to be inferred at all) is that of a licence; and

3. In the field of merchandising, where the public cannot be supposed to believe that the claimant and defendant are one and the same business in any sense.

The misrepresentation

The misrepresentation made by the defendant in passing-off is not often **7–68** express. The use of a name or mark supposedly distinctive of the claimant can be interpreted in various ways. Depending on the circumstances it may be thought that the defendant is the claimant, or a branch or subsidiary of the claimant, a member of the claimant's corporate group, the licensee of the claimant, or connected in some indeterminate manner. The same applies when the name is used for goods. Different members of the public may interpret the misrepresentation in different ways and there is no "single meaning rule" in passing-off. On the other hand, there may be no implicit misrepresentation at all, for instance because of sufficient differences in the parties' respective marks or fields of business. The first question to answer is whether there can be said to be a misrepresentation at all. If so, the next question is not what interpretation to put on the misrepresentation, but whether damage to the claimant is likely to occur. It is almost always a mistake to attempt to construe the misrepresentation as if it were a legal document.

Licensing is closely bound up with the issue of the common field of activity. If the businesses of the parties are close then use of similar names, marks or get-up will normally be taken as the familiar misrepresentation that the two businesses are to all intents and purposes one and the same, notwithstanding that a licensing arrangement might provide an even more plausible explanation. If the fields of business are remote then licensing is often the only connection that can be advanced, but in that case the supposed existence of any sort of connection between the parties is itself very dubious. The result is that the concept of licensing in passing-off is subject to a vicious circle: licensing is an argument of last resort in factually weak cases, and the unsurprising failure of many of these makes the argument

---

[94] *Dawnay Day & Co Ltd v Cantor Fitzgerald International* [2000] R.P.C. 669, CA.

seem less attractive still. Despite this, there are sufficient examples of passing-off being found for one to say with confidence that it is actionable for one business to misrepresent itself as the licensee of another if damage will result.

There is no significance in the public believing that the defendant must be licensed by or connected with the claimant because of an erroneous belief that the claimant enjoys a legal monopoly that does not in fact exist.[95]

Licensing of names and marks

7–69 In strict point of law, an unregistered trade mark is not a species of property, so that what may be licensed is actually the right to use the mark in a manner which the action for passing-off would otherwise prevent. As Scott V.C. put it in *Dawnay Day v Cantor Fitzgerald*[96]:

> "[I]n English law, there is no right of property in an unregistered trademark. In *Star Industrial Co Ltd v Yap Kwee Kor* the Privy Council was faced with an argument that a passing-off action could be brought to protect an unregistered mark whether or not there existed some business or goodwill in connection with which the mark was being used. Lord Diplock firmly rejected the argument. Millett L.J. in *Harrods Ltd v Harrodian School Ltd* did the same. ... So there is no right of property in the name. There are rights of property only in the goodwill associated with the name. Nonetheless, the right to use an unregistered mark can be, and often is, conferred as a contractual right. Franchising agreements are an example in point."

The name or trade mark (whether or not registered) of an established business may be sufficiently valuable for it to be worthwhile licensing the use of it in related, or even wholly different, fields.[97] Especially if this already happens, it is quite likely that the public will recognise that use of the name or mark on goods other than those of the licensor himself denotes a trade connection with the licensor. Although licensing of this sort is not confined to prestigious marks originally used for luxury goods,[98] the value of the licence does depend on the reputation of the licensor helping to sell the goods of the licensee. To that extent, a licensing program without quality control is self-defeating; and the fact that businesses are willing to pay for licences may be taken as implying that consumers will rely to some extent on the licensed mark as an indication of origin or quality. The inference is weakened if what is licensed has some intrinsic appeal unconnected with its function as a trade mark.

---

[95] *My Kinda Town Ltd v Soll* [1983] R.P.C. 407, CA; *Parkdale Custom Built Furniture v Puxu* (1982) 42 A.L.R. 1; 149 C.L.R. 191; *Ciba-Geigy plc v Parke Davis & Co Ltd* [1994] F.S.R. 8.

[96] [2000] R.P.C. 669, CA.

[97] See also Chapter 3 Section I. Licensing of know-how, patents and the like raises entirely different issues.

[98] *News Group Newspapers Ltd v Rocket Record Co Ltd* [1981] F.S.R. 89 and *Alfred Dunhill Ltd v Sunoptic SA* [1979] F.S.R. 337, CA, define the opposite ends of the spectrum.

A case based on licensing is strongest if: **7–70**

1. The claimant already has a licensing business;

2. There is public reliance on the licensed mark as an indication of origin or quality;

3. The licensed mark is strongly distinctive;

4. The defendant's goods suggest a connection with the claimant, which may be because of a connection with the claimant's core business or the goods of an existing licensee;

5. Or even because of the very diversity of the goods really licensed;

6. There is evidence of willingness to take licences from the claimant in the defendant's chosen field;

7. The defendant benefits financially from the supposed existence of the licence; and

8. The defendant's motives as suspect.

However, these are all matters of evidence and none are essential individually or in combination.[99]

In *British Legion v British Legion Club (Street)*[1] the plaintiffs were a **7–71** charity providing for the welfare of ex-servicemen. There were many local British Legion clubs which were legally independent of the plaintiff but acknowledged its ultimate authority. The defendant was a company operating as a social club for ex-servicemen. Farwell J., granting an injunction, held that the defendant were bound to be taken as connected with the plaintiffs and that damage would result.

In *Royal Automobile Association of South Australia v Hancock*[2] the plaintiffs authorised certain garages to describe themselves as *RAA* garages. Authorised garages performed breakdown services and the like for members. The defendant used this description without authority. A permanent injunction was granted.

In *Alfred Dunhill v Sunoptic*[3] the plaintiffs were known originally for tobacco and smokers' goods but had diversified into a wide range of luxury goods for men, partly on their own account and partly through licensing. The range did not include sunglasses or spectacle frames, which were the goods intended to be dealt in by the defendants. The Court of Appeal was impressed by the efforts already being made by third parties to obtain licences to use the *Dunhill* name on these goods and granted an interlocutory injunction. The motives of the defendants were not above suspicion.

---

[99] These heads are predominantly derived from *Alfred Dunhill Ltd v Sunoptic SA* [1979] F.S.R. 337, CA, and *Stringfellow v McCain Foods (GB) Ltd* [1984] R.P.C. 501, CA, with the proviso that the latter case failed on the facts.
[1] (1931) 48 R.P.C. 555 (Farwell J.).
[2] [1939] S.A.S.R. 60 (Cleland J.).
[3] [1979] F.S.R. 337, CA.

7–72   The plaintiffs in *News Group Newspapers v Rocket Record*[4] published *The Sun* newspaper, one of the most popular features of which was that page three always carried a picture of a topless girl. A range of merchandise was sold by the plaintiffs or their licensees under the names *Page Three* or *Page 3*, but this did not include records. The defendants proposed to issue records consisting of an album and a single both including a song called *Page Three*, that also being the title of the single. The defendants sought permission from the plaintiffs and it was refused. Slade J. held that in respect of the album the use of *Page Three* as the title of one of the songs was legitimate. However, the use of the term prominently on the sleeve of the single was likely to lead to a belief that it was licensed by the plaintiffs, the very diversity of the goods already licensed supporting that conclusion. The quality and content of the record were such as to damage the plaintiffs' general goodwill, and an interlocutory injunction was granted.

Though not expressly a licensing case, mention may be made of *Easyjet v Dainty*,[5] especially with reference to the claimants' diversity of business (an airline, internet cafés and car hire) and the defendant's disingenuous attempt to engage the claimants in a partnership or joint venture to provide a cut-price online estate agency under the domain name *easyrealestate.co.uk*.

In contrast, all the factors enumerated above were missing in *Stringfellow v McCain*.[6] The plaintiff was the proprietor of a well-known night club, but had not previously attempted to license his name, which was a reasonably common surname in some parts of England. The defendants made potato chips, for which they adopted the same name innocently and without any intention to benefit from the plaintiff's reputation. The Court of Appeal held that the use of the name for the chips conveyed no misrepresentation in itself. One television advertisement which used a "disco theme" could be interpreted as implying a connection, but not such as to damage the plaintiffs.

Passing-off by actual or former licensee

7–73 If the defendant has voluntarily submitted to taking a licence from the claimant then although there may be no formal estoppel in the sense recognised in patent or leasehold law, it is not difficult to conclude that he will be guilty of passing-off if he continues to use the licensed name or mark outside the scope of the licence or after permission has been withdrawn.[7] It is not necessary that the licence should be an express one, if it is reasonable to infer its existence from the relationship of the parties. Thus, in *Coles v Need*[8] the defendant operated a retail shop predominantly selling the goods of the plaintiffs and with their permission held his shop out as a branch of the plaintiffs' business. In *Roberts Numbering Machine v Davis*[9] the defendant

---

[4] [1981] F.S.R. 89 (Slade J.).
[5] [2002] F.S.R. 6 (Bernard Livesey Q.C., Deputy Judge).
[6] [1984] R.P.C. 501, CA.
[7] See Chapter 3 Section I.
[8] [1934] A.C. 82; 50 R.P.C. 379, PC.
[9] (1936) 53 R.P.C. 79 (Luxmoore J.).

was the distributor in England for the plaintiffs' machines, but with the consent of the plaintiffs used their name as his business name. In both cases the defendants needed no licence to use the plaintiffs' name in respect of the plaintiffs' goods, but the defendant in *Coles v Need* benefited from being able to use the name for goods from other sources, and both needed a licence to use the plaintiffs' trade name as their own. On termination of the respective trading arrangements the defendants in both cases were restrained from passing-off by continuing to use the formerly licensed names.

A similar common sense principle to that stated above may apply if the defendant has indicated his willingness to take a licence from the claimant, but has been refused,[10] or changed his mind.[11] However, a defendant is not prejudiced by a request which is a matter of courtesy only.[12]

Licence terminated: *Dawnay Day v Cantor Fitzgerald*

The continuing relevance of *Coles v Need*[3] in modern law has been con-   **7–74** firmed by the Court of Appeal in *Dawnay Day v Cantor Fitzgerald*.[14] The facts were that the Dawnay Day group and three individuals had set up a joint venture company under the name *Dawnay Day Securities* ("DDSL") to carry on inter-dealer broking in Eurobonds. The individuals fell out with Dawnay Day and left to work for Cantor Fitzgerald International ("CFI"), the joint venture company itself was put into administration, and its assets and goodwill sold to CFI. The latter intended to continue the former business under the old name *Dawnay Day Securities*, while Dawnay Day themselves set up a new operation in the same field as *Dawnay Day REPOs*. It was common ground that only CFI were entitled to represent themselves as carrying on the former business of DDSL, but beyond that each party claimed the right to use the *Dawnay Day* name for its business, and to prevent the other party from doing so. An interim injunction was initially granted to Dawnay Day and at the full trial Lloyd J. found for Dawnay Day both on their claim and on Cantor Fitzgerald's counterclaim.

The Court of Appeal upheld both findings. Continuing use of the *Dawnay Day* name by CFI was plainly a misrepresentation once the connection with the Dawnay Day group had been severed:

> "I find it very easy to conclude, indeed impossible not to conclude, that for CFI to trade as Dawnay Day Securities in the field of inter-dealer broking, or in any other field, constitutes a plain misrepresentation. It is a representation to anyone who is aware of the existence of the Dawnay Day group of companies that 'Dawnay Day Securities' is a member of the group or, at the least, is closely associated with the group. This was true

---

[10] *News Group Newspapers Ltd v Rocket Record Co Ltd* [1981] F.S.R. 89; *IPC Magazines Ltd v Black & White Music Corp* [1983] F.S.R. 348; *Miller v Britt Allcroft (Thomas) LLC* [2000] FCA 1724, 52 IPR 419.
[11] *British Legion v British Legion Club (Street) Ltd* (1931) 48 R.P.C. 555
[12] *Harrison & Starkey v Polydor Ltd* [1977] F.S.R. 1.
[13] [1934] A.C. 82; 50 R.P.C. 379, PC.
[14] [2000] R.P.C. 669. CA.

while the business was being carried on by DDSL. It ceased to be true when the business was sold to CFI.

Mr Miller QC, counsel for CFI, sought in two ways to meet the problem created for his case by this obvious misrepresentation.[15] First, he pointed out that the inter-dealing broking business and its goodwill was an asset of DDSL. The right to trade as Dawnay Day Securities was an important part of that asset. The asset, like any other asset belonging to DDSL, was capable of being sold and it would be wrong to emasculate the asset at the point of sale by hiving off the right to use the trading name. I follow the point but, in my opinion, it begs the question. The question is whether a purchaser of the business from DDSL is entitled to use the trading name, Dawnay Day Securities, that DDSL had used. If to do would constitute passing-off, then the answer is that the purchaser cannot use the name."

7-75   The question then was whether DDSL had had an unconditional and transmissible right to use the *Dawnay Day* name, or only a conditional one. During its existence as part of the Dawnay Day group, DDSL had benefited from an express contractual right to hold itself out as part of the group, and (as Scott V.C. held) an implied contractual right to use the *Dawnay Day* name. However, a purposive construction of both the express term and the implied one led to the conclusion that it could represent itself as part of the Dawnay Day group only as long as that was in fact the case. Once DDSL ceased to be part of the group it would have had no continuing licence, and would have been vulnerable to a passing-off action if the requirements of the latter were met. It was in the same position as a franchisee whose franchise had come to an end, and it could pass on to CFI no better rights to the name than it possessed itself.

Other than a continuing licence, the only possible defences to the passing-off action were that the *Dawnay Day* name might have ceased to be distinctive of the plaintiffs and come to denote DDSL specifically, as had been contemplated in *Coles v Need* itself; or that the reputation of the Dawnay Day group was insufficient (or in too remote a field) for them to sustain a passing-off action against any interloper adopting the name for inter-dealer broking:

"As to the first question, the answer I would give is the same as that which was given by Dixon J. and then by Lord Wright in *Need v J. H. Coles Proprietary Ltd*. In a case in which a licensor's trading style has been used by a licensee under a licence and the licence has come to an end, the ex-licensee, if he wants to continue to use the trading style, and is not contractually barred from doing so, must, in my judgment, show that his use of the style has had the effect that the style has ceased to be distinctive of the licensor. Lord Wright referred to the finding in the courts below that 'the appellant's trade names had not lost their distinctive character'. He

---

[15] The second (unsuccessful) argument being based on evidence that there were some bond dealers who had never heard of the Dawnay Day group.

then, after referring to the revocable character of the respondent's licence to use those trade names, continued:

'from these conclusions it follows that prima facie the appellant is entitled on well known principles to an order restraining the respondent from the unauthorised use of the appellant's trade names after the licence was revoked, since the continuance thereafter of such user necessarily involves a passing-off by the respondent of his business as being a business in which the appellant has at least an interest, and in this way there would be practised a deception of the public to the prejudice of the appellant's business reputation and goodwill'.

These remarks apply fully, in my judgment, to the present case."

On the facts the Court of Appeal affirmed that during the existence of the **7–76** joint venture DDSL's use of the *Dawnay Day* name had always clearly and expressly been as part of the Dawnay Day group. It had never been such as to generate any distinct or separate reputation for itself. The only relevant reputation it had acquired was in its capacity as part of the group. Finally, the right of Dawnay Day to sue CFI for passing-off was so clear that any other conclusion would have been an affront to common sense. This was not a case such as *Harrods v Harrodian School*[16] in which the very existence of any supposed connection was speculation: the vice of the misrepresentation was that the defendants' business, though unconnected with the Dawnay Day group, was being held out as part of it. Every company in the group, and not just the holding company, had an interest in restraining such a misrepresentation, which was inherently likely to cause damage. It also followed that CFI's counterclaim would be dismissed.

Franchising: introduction

Franchising is used in English commercial practice to describe a relationship **7–77** in which numerous legally independent businesses trade under a common style and to common standards as if they were branches of one larger enterprise. The franchisor invariably specifies the manner in which each franchised business is to trade, often in great detail, although the day-to-day running is left to the franchisee. This element of operational control typically distinguishes franchising from simple licensing arrangements. The success of any franchising operation depends on the public relying on the individual outlets of the franchise to provide goods or services of a uniform degree of quality. The public may frequently be unable to distinguish franchised businesses from those run as branches of a single business, and in some cases there may be a mixture of franchised outlets and branches owned and operated by the franchisor.

Although not strictly a franchising case, the nature of the obligations under the franchising relationship, both during its existence and after ter-

[16] [1996] R.P.C. 687, CA.

mination, were described by Scott V.C. in the Court of Appeal in *Dawnay Day v Cantor Fitzgerald*[17]:

"The franchisor grants to the franchisee the right to sell the franchisor's goods and to use for that purpose the name of the franchisor as, or as part of, the franchisee's trading style. The contract is likely to prohibit the use by the erstwhile franchisee of the franchisor's trading style after the franchise has come to an end. The prohibition may be express or it may be implied. But, contract apart, the ex-franchisee's ability to continue to use the trading style will depend upon whether to do so would constitute passing-off. The use of the style while the franchise lasted may have had the result that the style has ceased to be sufficiently distinctive of the business of the franchisor. It may, indeed, have become distinctive of the business of the franchisee. These considerations are dealt with in the dissenting judgment of Dixon J in the High Court of Australia in *Need v J. H. Coles Proprietary Ltd* and in the Privy Council judgment which allowed an appeal from the High Court. In the Privy Council Lord Wright said this:

'... all the right that the respondent ever had in regard to the user of the appellants' trade names was a revocable licence to use these names so long as the business arrangement continued between the appellant and the respondent ...'."

Somewhat different legal issues arise where the so-called franchise is really a licence of real or prospective rights to a single licensee, especially if the franchisor has no antecedent goodwill or reputation in the franchised territory and is essentially conferring a bare endorsement on the licensee, perhaps with the additional benefit of know-how and copyright licences.[18]

Locus standi of franchisor

7-78   The conceptual problem posed by franchising in its most general form is that the franchisor need not, and in general does not, compete with his franchisees.[19] The franchisees provide goods or services to the public. The franchisor provides services of a quite different nature (and sometimes also goods) to the franchisees. Can it therefore be said that the franchisor is a trader with a goodwill to protect, that it is an actionable misrepresentation for a business to hold itself out as franchised, and that the franchisor can be said to suffer damage?

The traditional approach to ownership of goodwill might have been to say that each individual franchised business owned a goodwill of its own,

---

[17] [2000] R.P.C. 669, CA.

[18] See *Athlete's Foot Marketing Associates Inc v Cobra Sports Ltd* [1980] R.P.C. 343; *Amway Corp v Eurway International Ltd* [1974] R.P.C. 82; [1972] F.S.R. 213 and *Wienerwald Holding AG v Kwan, Wong, Tan and Fong* [1979] F.S.R. 381, in which prospective arrangements of this kind did not avail overseas plaintiffs with no goodwill of their own.

[19] For a rare exception where the defendant actually purported to offer franchises in the name of the plaintiff see *Nishika v Goodchild* [1990] F.S.R. 371 (Knox J.).

and that the goodwill of the franchisor related solely to the granting of franchises to businesses. This would be wrong. The public may or may not know that a franchising relationship exists, but they do appreciate that one person is responsible for the standards of every franchised outlet. That person is in fact the franchisor, who therefore owns the relevant goodwill *quoad* the public. It is only if the franchisor is perceived to have abandoned control of the business, or surrendered it to the franchisee(s), that the situation contemplated in *Coles v Need* arises and the franchised name or format may become *publici juris*, or distinctive of someone other than the franchisor. This is not to say that individual franchised outlets can have no goodwill of their own, but their position is roughly equivalent to that of a tied public house or a retail shop selling nationally advertised brands of goods.

It follows that under a properly drafted and managed franchise operation the franchisor is the owner of the goodwill relating to the name of the franchised business and whatever else may be distinctive of it, such as the characteristic get-up of premises. Damage to the franchisor's goodwill may take a number of forms. The argument that the franchisor is deprived of the income he would have received had the defendant taken a franchise is legitimate in this case, because granting franchises is the actual business of the franchisor rather than a hypothetical possibility. If the defendant were not passing off, the franchisor might have found a willing franchisee for that territory. If the defendant is in competition with an existing franchisee then the franchisor will lose income and sales, and ultimately the benefit of the franchise itself if the franchisee is not protected. Finally, the franchisor has no control over the defendant's goods or business and will be damaged if they are inferior.

Posing as franchisee after termination

Many franchise businesses involve the supply of goods to the public either as **7–79** their main function or incidentally to the provision of services. If it can fairly be said that the goods disposed of through the franchised outlets are the franchisor's goods, in the sense that they were supplied by him or from a source selected by him, then for the defendant to pose as a franchisee necessarily involves passing-off in the ordinary sense.

In *Coles v Need*[20] the plaintiffs operated two fancy goods stores in Melbourne. They advertised their willingness to fit up and stock a number of suburban and country stores along the same lines as their own. The defendant responded and agreed to purchase a shop in his own name, to bear the cost of having it fitted out in the style directed by the plaintiffs, to stock it with the plaintiffs' goods and to obtain all supplies from them. The plaintiffs agreed to paint and fit up the shop in the same way as theirs, with the name *J H Coles 3d, 6d and 1/- Stores*, and to supply the defendant with

---

[20] [1934] A.C. 82; 50 R.P.C. 379, PC; on appeal from the High Court of Australia (1931) 46 C.L.R. 470. The following summary is taken from the latter report, which is very much fuller than that of the Privy Council hearing.

the goods normally sold in its own shops at cost price plus 5 per cent. The agreement was not reduced to writing and much was left unresolved.

After eight months' successful operation the plaintiffs found themselves unable to supply all the goods the defendant needed. They agreed to allow him to purchase from third parties on paying a royalty. Within a few more months the plaintiffs had almost ceased to supply the defendant altogether. The plaintiff company went into liquidation and three years after the shop had opened the liquidator gave notice to terminate the agreement and to require the defendant to cease using the name. The trial judge held that the plaintiffs had given and validly withdrawn a revocable licence to use the name and was upheld by the Supreme Court of Victoria (Full Court). The High Court of Australia allowed an appeal by a majority[21] on the grounds that the name had been used in such a way that it did not denote the plaintiffs' business, and that the plaintiffs' conduct was misleading and debarred them from relief. The Privy Council restored the injunction.

7-80   Even if it is not the case that franchisees deal in the claimants goods, it is still a material misrepresentation for the defendant to hold himself out as a franchised outlet. It implies not just that he is licensed by the franchisor to use the names and marks in question, but that the franchisor is responsible for the conduct of the business of the defendant to a much greater degree than an ordinary licence would entail. So far as the element of misrepresentation is concerned, the franchisor is in a stronger position than licensors generally and it can hardly be doubted that there is passing-off if the other conditions of the tort are met.

In *Body Shop v Rawle*[22] an interlocutory injunction was granted against the defendant continuing to trade as *The Body Shop* after various franchise agreements for six shops in five towns in Southern England had been repudiated by her. The personal defendant had started behaving very strangely, had expressed great hostility to the plaintiffs, had dismissed experienced staff, closed the shops and reopened them using untrained staff, allowing them to fall into a deplorable condition which was highly damaging to the plaintiffs' goodwill. Even allowing for the fact that a high burden of proof was appropriate since the motion was likely to be final, the plaintiffs had made out a strong prima facie case of passing-off.

7-81   Several successful cases have been brought in Canada[23] by plaintiffs operating a franchise of about 60 sandwich bars under the name *Mr Submarine* with a distinctive get-up for the premises: interlocutory injunctions were granted in *Mr Submarine v Bikas*[24] and *Mr Submarine v Emma Foods*;[25] and a final injunction and profits against a former franchisee (who had himself franchised the offending format to another defendant as well as using it in his own right) in *Mr Submarine v Voultsos*.[26]

---

[21] Rich, Evatt and McTiernan JJ., Starke and Dixon JJ. dissenting.
[22] (1993) 27 I.P.R. 255 (Sir Peter Pain, QBD).
[23] All the following cases are from Ontario.
[24] (1975) 24 C.P.R. (2d) 135 (Cory J.).
[25] (1976) 34 C.P.R. (2d) 177 (Estey C.J., H.C.).
[26] (1977) 36 C.P.R. (2d) 270 (Ostler J.).

In *Goliger's Travel v Gilway Maritimes*[27] the plaintiffs were granted an interlocutory injunction against the defendants, a former franchisee, continuing to use the same telephone number as when it had been franchised. The ordinary and Yellow Pages telephone directories listed the number under the name of the franchisor, and there would be passing-off if a proportion of prospective customers of the franchisor were misled.

In the Australian case of *Ariaans v Hastings*[28] the defendant's franchise for *Excel Carpet Dry Cleaning* was terminated, but he continued to trade as *Excel Carpet Dry Cleaning* as well as *Extra Dry Carpet Dry Cleaning*, to use the same get-up for his van and advertising, and generally to hold himself out as still connected with the plaintiffs. An injunction against the use of *Excel* or *Extra Dry* was granted, and upheld on appeal.

G. PERSONALITY MERCHANDISING AND ENDORSEMENT

Introduction: merchandising and endorsement distinguished

The suggestion that goods or services are endorsed by or otherwise asso- **7–82** ciated with a real person has tended in the past to be treated as an aspect of character merchandising. However, a distinction is increasingly drawn between pure character merchandising, which involves fictitious or artificial characters; personality merchandising in which the characters are real persons; and endorsement, in which real persons are asserted or assumed to endorse the product in question. As Laddie J. stated in *Irvine v Talksport*[29]:

"[T]his case is concerned with endorsement. When someone endorses a product or service he tells the relevant public that he approves of the product or service or is happy to be associated with it. In effect he adds his name as an encouragement to members of the relevant public to buy or use the service or product. Merchandising is rather different. It involves exploiting images, themes or articles which have become famous. To take a topical example, when the recent film, *Star Wars Episode 1*, was about to be exhibited, a large number of toys, posters, garments and the like were put on sale, each of which bore an image of or reproduced a character or object in the film. The purpose of this was to make available a large number of products which could be bought by members of the public who found the film enjoyable and wanted a reminder of it. The manufacture and distribution of this type of spin-off product is referred to as merchandising. It is not a necessary feature of merchandising that members of the public will think the products are in any sense endorsed by the film makers or actors in the film. Merchandised products will

---

[27] (1987) 17 C.P.R. (3d) 380 (Hall L.J.S., Nova Scotia).
[28] (1996) 36 IPR 211 (SC of Western Australia).
[29] [2002] EWHC 367; [2002] 1 W.L.R. 2355; [2002] 2 All E.R. 414; [2002] E.M.L.R. 32; [2002] F.S.R. 60 (Laddie J.), affirmed (as to liability) [2003] EWCA Civ 423; [2003] 2 All E.R. 881; [2003] E.M.L.R. 26; [2003] F.S.R. 35, CA.

include some where there is a perception of endorsement and some where there may not be, but in all cases the products are tied into and are a reminder of the film itself. An example of merchandising is the sale of memorabilia relating to the late Diana, Princess of Wales. A porcelain plate bearing her image could hardly be thought of as being endorsed by her, but the enhanced sales which may be achieved by virtue of the presence of the image is a form of merchandising."

As Laddie J. noted, terms such as sponsorship, endorsement and merchandising are frequently used imprecisely or interchangeably, both in the authorities and in commercial parlance. The primary legal distinction is between endorsement as such, and any other kind of merchandising. The theoretical distinction, however, is not so easy to apply in practice: endorsement is frequently implicit rather than express; but (as Laddie J acknowledged) mere use of the name or image of a real person need not and frequently does not imply endorsement. In the *Eddie Irvine* case it did, in the (actual) example of *Elvis Presley*[30] and the (then) hypothetical one of Princess Diana it would not.[31]

7–83   Endorsement raises somewhat different legal issues to merchandising as such, and in the present section it is treated separately to the extent that state of the authorities permits. A specific section on character merchandising then follows. However both character merchandising (in relation to characters real or fictitious) and merchandising (predominantly by real ones) have this in common: that there is no *sui generis* "merchandising right" or "character right" or "right of publicity" known to English common law. Liability for passing-off, if it is to be established, depends as in any other action on the "classical trinity" of goodwill, reputation and damage, each of which must be established on the evidence and without the benefit of any special presumptions, legal fictions or other shortcuts. In this respect, English law differs from that of some other common law jurisdictions, which may be treading a path towards free-standing character or personality rights by discarding or modifying some or all of the requirements of the traditional passing-off action.

Historically, the first cases to merit discussion are ones to do with real personalities, as are the most recent and definitive, and it is convenient to examine these before dealing with character merchandising in the narrow sense. Of course, there are borderline cases such as those involving *Kojak* or *Crocodile Dundee* where the identification of a person with a specific role is so complete that it can almost equally well be said that one is dealing with a real person, the actor, or the fictitious character he plays. Cases (such as *Elvis Presley*) in which the character has been dead for many years also arguably have more in common with fictitious character merchandising, in so far as any supposed endorsement *post mortem* is really an endorsement by an anonymous corporation, rather than an identifiable living individual.

---

[30] *Elvis Presley TMs; Elvis Presley Enterprises Inc v Sid Shaw Elvisly Yours* [1999] R.P.C. 567, CA.
[31] *Diana, Princess of Wales TM* [2001] E.T.M.R. 25 (Registry).

Endorsement: the principle stated

A person who can be described as a trader has a cause of action for passing- **7–84** off if he suffers damage to the goodwill in a business carried on by him from a misrepresentation, express or implied, that he has endorsed another business or its products. As always in passing-off, the terms "business" and "trader" are very widely defined and would include artists, all kinds of performers, professional sportsmen and the like. All these have goodwill in relation to their paid professional performances, and those who have an income from merchandising or endorsement have goodwill in relation to those activities as well. However, there is in principle no remedy in passing off for a private individual in his capacity as such, whether famous or unknown. Nor is there any remedy for even the most famous public figure unless the use by the defendant of his name, image or personal attributes is calculated to deceive in a material sense. Passing-off, at least in English law, does not provide rights of privacy or publicity

In the words of Simon Browne L.J. in *Elvis Presley TMs*[32]:

"On analysis, as it seems to me, all the English cases upon which Enterprises seeks to rely (*Mirage Studios* not least) can be seen to have turned essentially upon the need to protect copyright or to prevent passing off (or libel). None creates the broad right for which in effect Mr Prescott contends here, a free standing general right to character exploitation enjoyable exclusively by the celebrity. As Robert Walker L.J. has explained, just such a right, a new 'character right' to fill a perceived gap between the law of copyright (there being no copyright in a name) and the law of passing off was considered and rejected by the Whitford Committee in 1977. Thirty years earlier, indeed, when it was contended for as a corollary of passing off law, it had been rejected in *McCulloch v Lewis A. May* [1947] 2 All E.R. 845. I would assume to reject it. In addressing the critical issue of distinctiveness there should be no *a priori* assumption that only a celebrity or his successors may ever market (or licence the marketing of) his own character. Monopolies should not be so readily created."

Merchandising is not confined to artificial characters or real personalities, **7–85** individually or in combinations such as pop groups; although most of the reported cases fall into these categories. In relation to sport, for instance, merchandising rights might also be asserted (with more or less success) in relation to notable events,[33] sports teams as such,[34] national or international

---

[32] [1999] R.P.C. 567, CA.

[33] The *Melbourne Cup* yacht race of the Victoria Racing Club in *Nicholas v Borg* (1987) AIPC 90–366 (Supreme Court of South Australia).

[34] *Arsenal Football Club plc v Reed* [2001] E.T.M.R. 23, [2001] R.P.C. 46 (Laddie J); on appeal [2003] EWCA Civ 696; [2003] 2 C.M.L.R. 25, CA.

associations responsible for the sport as a whole,[35] famous locations[36] and the like.

Early English decisions

7–86 Until the *Eddie Irvine* case[37] in 2002, there appears to have been no reported instance in the United Kingdom of false endorsement (in the modern sense) being held actionable as passing off. In the mid-nineteenth century case of *Clark v Freeman*[38] the eminent physician Sir James Clark was refused an interim injunction against a quack patent medicine being sold as *Sir James Clarke's Consumption Pills*. Sir James was Physician in Ordinary to HM Queen Victoria, and an acknowledged specialist in consumptive diseases. The advertisements complained of began: "BY HER MAJESTY THE QUEEN'S PERMISSION. SIR J. [or JAMES] CLARKE'S [*sic*] CONSUMPTION PILLS". The law of passing-off was then in its infancy, and Lord Langdale M.R. considered it fatal to the claim that Sir James himself had no business in selling pills to protect, and that damage to his professional practice or reputation as a physician had not been established in an action at law.

Even in its own time *Clark v Freeman*, was not popular. In *Springhead Cotton Spinning Company v Riley*[39] Malins V.C. said of it:

> "I confess myself wholly unable to coincide in the reasoning of Lord Langdale in that case, and the decision may now, I think, be considered as erroneous, for the reasons stated by Lord Cairns in *Maxwell v Hogg*, where he says: 'It always appeared to me that *Clark v Freeman* might have been decided in favour of the Plaintiff, on the ground that he had a property in his own name.' And I must say that it is perfectly clear to my mind, at all events, that a man has a sufficient property in his own name to prevent another from falsely passing off, injuriously to his reputation, medicines as personally prescribed by him, which might cause a total destruction of his professional character."

The references to "property" in a name would now be regarded as inaccurate or obsolete, but no more so with regard to the name of a professional person than in any ordinary trade mark or trade name case of about the same time. The reason for their presence is that (in theory at least)

---

[35] *Rugby Football Union v Cotton Traders* [2002] EWHC 467; [2002] E.T.M.R. 76 (Lloyd J.), see below.

[36] *Pebble Beach Co v Lombard Brands Ltd* 2002 S.L.T. 1312 (Lord Menzies, OH), in which a World-famous Californian golf course failed to obtain an interim interdict against use of the same name for a brand of Speyside malt whisky.

[37] *Irvine v Talksport Ltd* [2002] EWHC 367; [2002] 1 W.L.R. 2355; [2002] 2 All E.R. 414; [2002] E.M.L.R. 32; [2002] F.S.R. 60 (Laddie J.), affirmed (as to liability) [2003] EWCA Civ 423; [2003] 2 All E.R. 881; [2003] E.M.L.R. 26; [2003] F.S.R. 35, CA.

[38] (1848) 50 E.R. 759 (Lord Langdale M.R.).

[39] (1868) L.R. 6 Eq. 561(Malins V.C.) and to the same effect see *Dixon v Holden* (1869) L.R. 7 Eq. 493 (Malins V.C.). Both these were cases of injunctions being granted to restrain defamatory statements (and were overruled in that context by *Prudential Assurance Co v Knott* (1875) L.R. 10 Ch. 145), but the criticism of *Clark v Freeman* survives.

jurisdiction to grant an injunction prior to the Judicature Act 1873 depended on the protection of something which could be described as a property right.

By the end of the nineteenth century, *Clark v Freeman* might be regarded **7–87** as almost entirely discredited: "That case has seldom been cited but to be disapproved. Could not a professional man be injured in his profession by having his name associated with a quack medicine?"[40] In due course *Clark v Freeman* was distinguished and disapproved one final time by Maugham J. in *British Medical Association v Marsh*,[41] where the supposed endorsement was by the Association, rather than by any individual doctor.

Although *Clark v Freeman* may be regarded as having received its long-deserved quietus in *British Medical Association v Marsh*, this was without any visible effect outside the special area of actions by professional associations. In the libel case of *Tolley v Fry*[42] the use of a caricature of a famous golfer to advertise chocolate was held to have carried the implicit misrepresentation that he had compromised his amateur status by accepting payment for it, but no false endorsement case appears to have been framed in passing-off until *McCulloch v May*[43] in 1947. In that case, the presenter of the radio programme *Children's Hour*, whose performing name was *Uncle Mac*, sued the manufacturers of a brand of breakfast cereal sold under the same name. Opinions may differ as to whether the claim was always hopeless on its facts, or simply half a century ahead of its time, but in any event it failed completely. *McCulloch v May* came to be remembered for its invention of the need for a "common field of activity," and for as long as the latter doctrine held sway any passing off claim based on a supposed endorsement was as certain to fail as in the days of Lord Langdale, almost precisely a century before.

Endorsement in Australian law (1): *Henderson* and *Hogan*

Between *McCulloch v May*[44] in 1947, and the *Elvis Presley*[45] and *Eddie* **7–88** *Irvine*[46] cases on either side of the new millennium, the focus of attention shifts to Australia and a series of decisions which are necessary to understanding the development and present state of English law, and its limitations. It is in Australia that the common law first allowed celebrities or

---

[40] *per* Lord Selborne L.C. *arguendo* in *Riviere's TM* (1884) 26 Ch. D. 56, CA. Subsequently *Clark v Freeman* was followed with undisguised reluctance in *Williams v Hodge* (1887) 4 T.L.R. 175 (Kay J.) where the name of another eminent doctor was used without his consent to promote a piece of surgical equipment; though no criticism was made of it in *Dockrell v Dougall* (1899) 80 L.T. 536; 15 T.L.R. 333, CA, in which another doctor was held out as having prescribed, and benefited from taking, the defendant's gout curative.

[41] (1931) 48 R.P.C. 565 (Maugham J.).

[42] [1931] A.C. 333, HL.

[43] [1947] 2 All E.R. 845, 65 R.P.C. 58 (Wynn-Parry J.).

[44] Above.

[45] *Elvis Presley TMs; Elvis Presley Enterprises Inc v Sid Shaw Elvisly Yours* [1999] R.P.C. 567, CA.

[46] *Irvine v Talksport Ltd* [2002] EWHC 367; [2002] 1 W.L.R. 2355; [2002] 2 All E.R. 414; [2002] E.M.L.R. 32; [2002] F.S.R. 60 (Laddie J.), affirmed (as to liability) [2003] EWCA Civ 423; [2003] 2 All E.R. 881; [2003] E.M.L.R. 26; [2003] F.S.R. 35, CA.

personalities a cause of action in passing-off for the commercial use of their names or likenesses without permission, and it is there that the action has subsequently exhibited the most far-reaching developments.

In *Henderson v Radio Corporation*[47] the plaintiffs were well-known professional ballroom dancers. The defendants issued a record of strict tempo music for ballroom dancing and used a photograph of the plaintiffs on the sleeve. The impact of this photograph is easily exaggerated. It served purely as the background for two much more prominent photographs, one recognisably that of another professional dancer, Henry Kingston, who was identified as having endorsed the record. The choice of photograph was innocent and accidental, and the plaintiffs were not named, but some of their fellow dancers were able to recognise them. The plaintiffs had some experience of performing in advertisements or promotions, but had not endorsed any records. The High Court of New South Wales found for the plaintiffs at trial and on appeal but on different grounds. The trial judge found damage in the fact that in the future a record producer might be deterred from producing a record under the plaintiffs' sponsorship. The Full Court on appeal rejected this as too speculative. However, they said that the wrongful appropriation of the plaintiffs' professional or business reputation was in itself sufficient damage to found the action. The plaintiffs had been deprived of the fee they could have charged for the endorsement as effectively as if the defendants had handed over the money and then stolen it back.

7-89   Apart from its treatment of damage, the decision in *Henderson v Radio Corp* was ambiguous. Did it mean that use of the plaintiffs' photograph in the circumstances was unlawful *per se*, or did it depend on finding that there was a misrepresentation of sponsorship as opposed to simple misappropriation? Subsequent Australian cases prior to the first of the two *Crocodile Dundee* cases in 1988 still seemed to require misrepresentation, though continuing to give effect to the decision in *Henderson* by not requiring separate proof of damage: *Moorgate Tobacco v Philip Morris*,[48] *10th Cantanae v Shoshana*[49] and *Honey v Australian Airlines*.[50] In *10th Cantanae*, Pincus J. identified the "real complaint" of the unsuccessful plaintiff as "not the falsity of the advertisement, but that the name was used other than pursuant to an 'endorsement' agreement involving a fee".

The facts of *Hogan v Koala Dundee*[51] were that the actor Paul Hogan had played the title role in the extremely successful film *Crocodile Dundee* and in a sequel. In the film, Hogan wore a sleeveless leather vest, a bush hat with crocodile teeth in the band, and carried a large knife. The defendants operated two small shops under the name *Dundee Country* and used as their emblem a picture of a koala bear wearing a sleeveless leather vest and a bush

[47] [1960] N.S.W.L.R. 279; [1969] R.P.C. 218.
[48] (1984) 156 C.L.R. 414; 3 I.P.R. 545; [1985] R.P.C. 219. Not a character merchandising case, but one repudiating the existence of a cause of action for unfair competition.
[49] (1987) 10 I.P.R. 289 (Federal Court).
[50] (1990) 18 I.P.R. 185 (Federal Court of Australia) affirming (1989) 14 I.P.R. 264 (Northrop J.).
[51] (1988) 12 I.P.R. 508 (Pincus J.).

hat with teeth in the band, and carrying a large knife of the same type as in the film. The evidence was that many members of the public associated the shops with the *Crocodile Dundee* film and character, but that very few supposed that the images from the film were used under any sort of commercial arrangement with Paul Hogan, and none with any of the other plaintiffs. Pincus J. concluded from the survey evidence that:

"The answers illustrate the incongruity of basing this sort of suit on the issue of whether the public has been misled about licensing arrangements; in practice, the ideas of the public as to licensing arrangements are very much in the back of their minds and necessarily vague and inaccurate. They have no reason to be interested in the question of licensing. Unlike a representation as to the origin or quality of goods, use of mere images in advertising, although presumably effective to generate sales, does not necessarily do so by creating, or relying on, any specific conclusions in the mind of the public."

In other words, there was probably no misrepresentation and if there was, it was not one to which the public paid much attention. However, for Pincus J. that did not conclude the matter because he decided that in Australia, though probably not in England, there was an extended form of passing-off which protected images of characters from appropriation even in the absence of any misrepresentation. Damage was necessary to support the claim to an injunction, but could be found in the fact that the plaintiffs had lost the fees they could have charged. Damages were refused on the facts because the defendants had not acted fraudulently.

In the second *Crocodile Dundee* case, *Hogan v Pacific Dunlop*,[52] the Full **7-90** Court of the Federal Court of Australia reverted to a definition of passing-off in terms of misrepresentation, expressly requiring a significant proportion of the public to be misled into believing that there was a commercial arrangement between the plaintiff and defendant. The action concerned a television advertisement for shoes which parodied a scene in the film. In the film, Hogan turned the tables on a New York mugger by producing his own knife, which was far more impressive than the knife wielded by the mugger. In the advertisement, a character dressed in similar clothing to *Crocodile Dundee*, but obviously not Paul Hogan, was also attacked by a mugger and got the better of him thanks to his superior *Grosby Leatherz* shoes. At first instance Gummow J. held that a substantial number of persons seeing the advertisement would, "as a matter of real likelihood", have responded to the advertisement on the basis that permission for it had been sought from Mr Hogan or the film makers or both, and that the plaintiffs had some sort of commercial association with the advertisement. The conclusion was not displaced by the nature of the advertisement as a "spoof" of the scene from the film. In the result, the plaintiffs were entitled to an injunction and to an election between damages and an account of profits, not limited to the period after the defendants had been put on notice. On appeal, Sheppard J.

[52] (1989) 14 I.P.R. 398 (Federal Ct., Full Ct.) affirming (1988) 12 I.P.R. 225 (Gummow J.).

would have found for the defendants on the ground that viewers of the advertisement could not reasonably have concluded that the plaintiffs had authorised or consented to it. The majority, Beaumont and Birchett JJ., upheld Gummow J. on the basis that there had been a misrepresentation of an association of some sort, and it did not matter that the association suggested was vague. Confirmation that liability was based on misrepresentation is to be found in the fact that the injunction was qualified to allow the advertisements to continue with an appropriate disclaimer.

7–91 Since *Hogan v Pacific Dunlop* as a decision of the Full Court is more authoritative than *Hogan v Koala Dundee* the current position in Australian law appears to be this. Following *Henderson*, a personality who can be said to be in business–and the term is very broadly understood–is always free to grant or withhold his endorsement, and therefore any unauthorised claim to such endorsement damages him by depriving him of the fee he could otherwise have insisted on. It is irrelevant that the plaintiff may have no existing licensing business or may prefer not to grant such licences. Nor does it matter that the defendant may have derived no benefit from the supposed endorsement, and would not voluntarily have paid a fee. Misrepresentation must still be shown, and the misrepresentation can be found in the public supposing there to be some sort of commercial arrangement of an unspecified kind between the plaintiff and defendant. Given the existence of such a misrepresentation, it does not appear to have to be one on which the public actually rely or to which they attach any importance, and by the same reasoning it does not have to be calculated to cause damage over and above the loss of a licensing fee. To this extent, the reasoning of *Hogan v Koala Dundee* cannot be regarded as good law, even in Australia, but despite its questionable justification either in public policy or in authority, *Hogan v Koala Dundee* does at least strike one as facing the issue of the distinction between misrepresentation and misappropriation with greater realism and intellectual honesty than *Hogan v Pacific Dunlop* or some of the other Australian cases.

Australian law (2): whether endorsement to be presumed

7–92 Even under the comparatively generous provisions of Australian law, there are occasions on which it is not to be supposed that the plaintiff has endorsed the goods or business of the defendant despite the apparent presence of his or her name or likeness in advertisements or even on the goods themselves. Two questions arise: is the plaintiff referred to at all, and does the reference imply endorsement? If the answer to either of these is in the negative, then it is unlikely that there can be said to be any misrepresentation to restrain. If there is to be liability in these circumstances, it would not be under the law of passing-off as generally understood but under a wider concept giving effect to rights of privacy or publicity in the American sense.

The first situation is illustrated by *10th Cantanae v Shoshana*.[53] The

---

[53] (1987) 10 I.P.R. 289 (Federal Court).

effective plaintiff, a well-known television presenter named Sue Smith, failed in claims under Sections 52 and 53 of the Trade Practices Act 1974 and at common law in respect of an advertisement showing a picture of a young woman watching television in bed, with the text "Sue Smith just took control of her video recorder". The model for the advertisement and the plaintiff were both brunettes, but otherwise their appearances were dissimilar. The trial judge held that the defendants had not known of the real Sue Smith, but found against them on the ground that there was some resemblance between her and the woman shown on the television in the advertisement, and that some readers might suppose the latter to be the plaintiff. On appeal, all three members of the Federal Court agreed that Ms Smith was engaged in business in the relevant sense, and that there would be liability for passing-off if the advertisements contained a representation that she had endorsed the *Blaupunkt* video recorder advertised. On the facts the majority (Wilcox and Pincus JJ.) held that the supposed resemblance to the screaming or grimacing woman actually shown on the television set in the photograph was speculative and irrelevant, and that the plaintiff was too different in appearance to the model for readers to suppose there was any association: "It cannot be enough ... merely to hold that a person who had forgotten what the [plaintiff] looks like might mistake the viewer depicted for her".[54] Gummow J., dissenting, treated the case as one of the defendants persisting in an initially innocent misrepresentation after being put on notice, and would have been prepared to find for the plaintiff on the strength of the presence of her name in the prominent headline.

Even if the name or photograph used is recognisably and uniquely that of **7–93** the plaintiff, it may be clear either expressly or from the context in which the use is made that there is no endorsement. In *Newton-John v Scholl-Plough*[55] the actress Olivia Newton-John objected unsuccessfully to the use of a photograph of a "look-alike" model (specially chosen for her resemblance to her) in an advertisement headed "Olivia? No. Maybelline". Burchett J. held that there was no misrepresentation and hence no liability for passing-off or under s. 52 of the Trades Practices Act 1974. The advertiser had indeed used Olivia Newton-John's reputation to the extent of gaining attention, but not to the extent of suggesting an association. Even the most casual reader could see at first glance that it was not Olivia Newton-John in the advertisement.

English cases between *Uncle Mac* and *Elvis Presley*

English decisions between *McCulloch v May*[56] and *Elvis Presley TMs*[57] are **7–94** not entirely to be ignored, and if they contain no lasting statements of principle, then it is equally true that none have seriously been doubted on their facts.

---

[54] *per* Pincus J.
[55] (1986) 11 F.C.R. 233.
[56] [1947] 2 All E.R. 845; 65 R.P.C. 58 (Wynn-Parry J.).
[57] [1999] R.P.C. 567, CA.

In *Sim v Heinz*[58] the famous actor Alastair Sim complained of an imitation of his characteristic voice being used in the voiceover for some television advertisements. An application for an interim injunction failed (mainly because the plaintiff had initially framed his case in libel) and though the judgement of the Court of Appeal is sceptical as to the merits, its reasoning is considerably less dogmatic than that of Wynn-Parry J. in *McCulloch v May*.

The plaintiffs in *Lyngstad v Annabas*[59] were the members of the pop group *ABBA*. They complained that the defendants advertised and sold T-shirts, pillow cases, badges and other goods bearing the name and photograph of the group. The plaintiffs had no English licensees in these fields, their only licence being for jigsaw puzzles, and that had been granted after the acts which were the subject of the complaint. Oliver J. refused an interlocutory injunction, primarily on the balance of convenience in that the plaintiffs had no existing trade which would be prejudiced, whereas serious damage would be caused to the defendants. However, he also doubted if the plaintiffs had made out that there was any misrepresentation.

"I do not think that anyone reading the advertisements of which complaint is made or indeed receiving the goods described in them could reasonably imagine that all the pop stars named in the advertisements were giving their approval to the goods offered or that the defendants were doing anything more than catering for a popular demand among teenagers for effigies of their idols."

7–95   Similar reasoning is implicit in *Merchandising Corporation of America v Harpbond*[60] where there was neither misrepresentation nor damage in the defendants putting out a picture of a pop star (*Adam Ant*, the second plaintiff) in relation to whom the first plaintiffs had contractual merchandising rights.

In *Harrison & Starkey v Polydor*[61] the plaintiffs were two of the *Beatles*. All four of the *Beatles* had given interviews to a journalist, and the defendants intended to release a record of these interviews, interspersed with *Beatles* songs, under the title of *The Beatles Tapes* with pictures of the Beatles on the sleeve. There was no copyright infringement or breach of confidence. Two of the *Beatles* objected to this, and sued for passing-off. Walton J. refused an interlocutory injunction. It was quite clear to anyone buying it that the record was called *The Beatles Tapes* because of what it contained; and there was no reason for anyone to suppose that it was put out by or on behalf of the *Beatles* themselves.[62]

7–96   The differences between English and Australian law emerge most clearly (for this period) in *Stringfellow v McCain Foods*[63] where the individual

[58] [1959] 1 W.L.R. 313; [1959] 2 All E.R. 547; [1959] R.P.C. 80, CA.
[59] [1977] F.S.R. 62 (Oliver J.).
[60] [1983] F.S.R. 32, CA.
[61] [1977] F.S.R. 1 (Walton J.).
[62] See also the *Neighbours* case, *Grundy Television Pty Ltd v Startrain Ltd* [1988] F.S.R. 581.
[63] [1984] F.S.R. 175; [1984] R.P.C. 501, CA.

plaintiff was the proprietor of a London night club which could fairly be said to have a national reputation. The defendants introduced a new type of long, thin frozen potato chip and adopted the name *Stringfellows* for them in good faith. A television advertisement for the chips used the theme of a kitchen turning into a discotheque. At trial, Whitford J. found for the plaintiffs, holding that there was evidence that some people, seeing *Stringfellows* on the chip packages, had assumed there to be a connection between the plaintiff and the defendants by way of a joint venture or licence of the name; and that the association of the name with chips was likely to damage the plaintiff's reputation of a high-class night club. The defendants' appeal was successful. The Court of Appeal held that too few people seeing the packets had been confused for one to conclude that use of the name constituted a misrepresentation in its own right; but allowed that the theme of the advertisements might cause some viewers to make the mental jump necessary to associate chips with the plaintiff's club, and to that extent the element of misrepresentation was present. However, it was not proved that any damage had been caused to the plaintiff in fact, nor that damage was inherently likely, and the action therefore failed. The mere showing of the television advertisement had not prejudiced the plaintiff's chances of profitably exploiting his merchandising rights, and had in fact alerted him to a possibility he had not previously considered. On the facts, the onus on the plaintiff to prove damage was a heavy one, and had not been discharged.

Personality merchandising: *Elvis Presley*

Against this background, the decision of the Court of Appeal in the *Elvis Presley*[64] case confirms that there is no *sui generis* protection for merchandising in English law outside passing-off and the other nominate intellectual property rights, and that the application of passing-off principles to merchandising depends on the existence of a misrepresentation and consequent damage to goodwill, both of which are highly dependent on the facts of the individual case.

Applications by Elvis Presley Enterprises Inc of Memphis for registration of ELVIS, ELVIS PRESLEY and a signature mark for various toilet preparations and cosmetics were opposed on grounds including lack of distinctiveness and conflict with an earlier mark *Elvisly Yours* (in script) belonging to a Mr. Sid Shaw. The applications were accepted in the Trade Marks Registry, but were refused on appeal to the High Court[55] and the Court of Appeal.

Although the *Elvis Presley* case was directly concerned only with the application of the Trade Marks Act 1938,[66] the observations of the Court of Appeal on character (or personality) merchandising are not necessarily

7–97

---

[64] *Elvis Presley TM; Elvis Presley Enterprises Inc v Sid Shaw Elvisly Yours* [1999] R.P.C. 567, CA.

[65] [1997] R.P.C. 543 (Laddie J.), affirmed [1999] R.P.C. 567, CA.

[66] Now repealed and replaced by the Trade Marks Act 1994. The applications, having originally been made while the 1938 Act was in force, proceeded under the transitional provisions of Sch.3 of the 1994 Act.

obiter dicta. Of the three applications, that for ELVIS PRESLEY was for registration in Part B, so that it became relevant "whether other traders are likely, in the ordinary course of their business and without any improper motive, to desire to use the same mark ... upon or in connection with their own goods."[67] Since it could not very well be denied that other traders, not least Mr Shaw and his company, did indeed want to continue to use *Elvis* and *Elvis Presley* in connection with Elvis Presley memorabilia and merchandise, the applicants had to argue that any such use without the licence of the applicants would not be legitimate. Indeed, they attempted to turn the argument to their advantage by submitting that both the ELVIS and ELVIS PRESLEY marks should be considered to be sufficiently distinctive in law by virtue of the fact that no one else could legitimately use either of them.

7–98   In the leading judgment, Robert Walker L.J. reviewed the principal English and Australian merchandising cases and the arguments of the parties in relation to them, but like Laddie J below he agreed that neither the ELVIS or ELVIS PRESLEY marks had sufficient inherent distinctiveness to proceed to registration, there being no evidence of distinctiveness in fact. Though the signature mark might be said to have greater inherent distinctiveness than either of these, it was too similar to Mr Shaw's earlier registration of *Elvisly Yours*, also in a cursive script and with a similar initial Greek E. In the result, he would have dismissed the appeal, and all three applications would be refused, without needing to decide the more general arguments related to merchandising rights.

> "[T]his appeal is not an appropriate occasion on which to attempt to define precisely how far the law of passing off has developed in response to the growth of character merchandising, still less to express views as to how much further it should develop or in what direction."

Elvis Presley: no general or free-standing merchandising right

7–99   However, such matters were not entirely irrelevant because they were the basis of two subsidiary arguments depending on whether the applicant ("Enterprises") would have had a cause of action in passing off or otherwise in respect of unlicensed commercial use of the name *Elvis* or *Elvis Presley* for the kind of goods in question. The arguments, and the breadth of their implications, were summarised by Simon Browne L.J.:

> "There are thus two central strands to the appellant's [Enterprises'] argument: one that the public's awareness of merchandising practices means that they will always assume that products of famous personalities or fictitious characters come from a particular 'genuine' source, namely the person himself or his estate or someone granted the relevant rights (and in the case of fictitious characters the creator or his successors); the other that it would be wrong to deny registration of a celebrity's name by reference to Lord Parker's test in the *W & G* case–that the rights 'should

---

[67] *Registrar of Trade Marks v W & G Du Cross* [1913] A.C. 624, *per* Lord Parker.

largely depend on whether other traders are likely, in the ordinary course of their business and without any improper motive, to desire to use the same mark ... in connection with their own goods' because, although other traders doubtless want to use Elvis Presley's name(s) to market their own goods, their motive for doing so would be improper: it would be to exploit a commercial value in the name that properly belongs only to the character and his successors.

This, it will readily be perceived, is a very wide argument indeed. It applies virtually irrespective of the nature of the products to be marketed (exceptions being made only for non-consumable souvenirs and bio-graphical material), irrespective of when registration is applied for (unless only it is sought for truly historical characters), irrespective of whether it is sought by the personality himself or by his legal successors, and irre-spective of what if any trading in the relevant products has previously been effected either by whoever seeks registration or by competing tra-ders. If, of course, it is sound, then it will greatly enhance the role played by trade mark registration in the promotion and protection of character merchandising. But its difficulty is that both its limbs depend ultimately upon the general proposition that character merchandising is already established and accepted in the public mind as properly the exclusive preserve of the character himself, and that, to my mind, represents an altogether too simplistic view of the effect of the many authorities in this field and discounts utterly the well-established principle that all these cases ultimately must turn upon their own facts."[68]

If either of these arguments had succeeded to any significant extent, then **7–100** the case for the applicants would have been transformed from one in which the burden was upon them to prove distinctiveness in fact, to one in which there would have been a strong *prima facie* assumption that they and only they had any legitimate right to use the marks. Both Morritt L.J. and Simon Brown L.J. (who agreed with both Robert Walker and Morritt L.JJ, but delivered a short judgment of his own) did expressly address the wider issues beyond pure registered trade mark law and concluded that the applicants had no exclusive common law rights to the name of Elvis Presley:

"In a sustained criticism of the judge's conclusion counsel for EPEI [Enterprises] submitted that the fame of Elvis Presley in fact confirmed the conclusion [that ELVIS and ELVIS PRESLEY were distinctive] because of the effect of what has now come to be known as 'character merchan-dising'. That activity is one in which a notable public figure lends his name to a particular product or range of products so as, apparently, to endorse that product. The consequence relied on is that that the consumer comes to regard goods bearing that name as having the approbation of or licence from his or her 'idol'. EPEI relied on a number of reported cases so as to suggest that over the last 20 years the court has come to conclude, without the need for affirmative evidence on the point, that such endorsement

[68] *per* Simon Brown L.J..

does distinguish the goods he or she endorses from those he or she does not...

I do not accept that conclusion. First, the judge concluded that there was no evidence of use by EPEI of ELVIS or ELVIS PRESLEY in the United Kingdom. There is no appeal from that conclusion. Second, Mr Shaw has sold in the United Kingdom quantities of his products by reference to Elvis, which the public would generally appreciate, was a reference to Elvis Presley. For example his brand of soap was called Elvis Soap because it was impregnated with 'an image [of Elvis which] remains right up to the end'. It is not suggested that Mr Shaw has ever claimed any connection with EPEI. Third, the fame of Elvis Presley was as a singer. He was not a producer of soap. There is no reason why he or any organisation of his should be concerned with toiletries so as to give rise to some perceived connection between his name and the product. In these circumstances I do not accept without evidence to that effect that the mark ELVIS PRESLEY would connote to anyone a connection between EPEI and Elvis soap so as to distinguish their soap from that of Mr Shaw's soap."[69]

In the final analysis, all that *Elvis Presley*[70] does in the present context is to reject the twin propositions that merchandising can be addressed outside the confines of passing-off, or without regard to the facts of the individual case. *Elvis Presley* is clear authority that use of the name or image of a celebrity is not actionable *per se*, but it leaves open the possibility of a celebrity establishing as a matter of fact that unauthorised use of his name or likeness implies an endorsement which does not in fact exist.

Eddie Irving: endorsement as passing-off

7–101 Just such a misrepresentation as is contemplated above was made out in *Irvine v Talksport*.[71] Edmund (Eddie) Irvine was a highly successful motor racing driver, who in 1999 had come a close second in the Formula 1 World Championship. The defendants operated a commercial radio station which was in the process of re-branding itself from *Talk Radio* to *TalkSport*, to correspond to a change in content. Shortly before the British Grand Prix, they distributed a promotional pack or brochure to about 1000 individuals who might be influential in placing advertisements. On the front of the pack, there was a conspicuous photograph of Mr Irvine, in his racing clothing, apparently holding and listening to a radio marked *Talk Radio*. This was obtained by altering a real press photograph which showed him using a mobile phone. Mr Irvine was not identified by name, but his appearance was sufficiently familiar to him to be recognised.

---

[69] *per* Morritt L.J.
[70] *Elvis Presley TM; Elvis Presley Enterprises Inc v Sid Shaw Elvisly Yours* [1999] R.P.C. 567, CA.
[71] [2002] EWHC 367; [2002] 1 W.L.R. 2355; [2002] 2 All E.R. 414; [2002] E.M.L.R. 32; [2002] F.S.R. 60 (Laddie J.); affirmed (as to liability) [2003] EWCA Civ 423; [2003] 2 All E.R. 881; [2003] E.M.L.R. 26; [2003] F.S.R. 35, CA.

Laddie J. held that the action succeeded.

"[T]here is nothing which prevents an action for passing off succeeding in a false endorsement case. However, in order to succeed, the burden on the claimant includes a need to prove at least two, interrelated, facts. First, that at the time of the acts complained of he had a significant reputation or goodwill. Second, that the actions of the defendant gave rise to a false message which would be understood by a not insignificant section of his market that his goods have been endorsed, recommended or are approved of by the claimant."

On the facts, Mr Irvine had ample goodwill and reputation, both in his **7–102** capacity as a racing driver, and (through companies controlled by him, who were joined as claimants by amendment) in the business of giving endorsements, which contributed a significant part of his income.[72]

Turning to the element of misrepresentation, it was conceded that the claimant could not succeed merely on proof of use of his image for commercial purposes. The question was whether a significant proportion of those to whom the brochure was sent would think that Mr Irvine had endorsed or recommended *TalkSport*. This was answered in favour of the claimant. The argument that the photograph would not be recognised (except by enthusiasts) was dismissed for several reasons: Eddie Irvine was at that time the most successful and most widely publicised British Formula 1 driver; his face had frequently appeared in print and on television, and not only in sports coverage; it was well known that he drove for Ferrari, whose distinctive racing clothing he was pictured wearing; and the promotion was timed to correspond to the British Grand Prix. He would be identified by sight by a significant part of the general public, and by an even larger proportion of those professionally involved in the business of endorsement by sporting personalities, including the target audience for the *Talksport* promotion. There was evidence of a recipient who drew precisely this conclusion, and the acknowledged objectives of the promotion were entirely consistent with it having this effect, even if unintentionally.

The Court of Appeal upheld the finding of liability (the only issue being **7–103** whether there had been a misrepresentation of endorsement in fact) and increased the award of damages from £2,000 to £25,000.[73] The increase is logical given the nature of the misrepresentation. Mr Irvine's (supposed) endorsement of the mailshot itself was relatively unambiguous but hardly very material: its 1000-odd recipients were hard-headed business men, not gullible members of the public. The real gravamen of the complaint was that Mr Irvine would have been supposed to be endorsing the defendant's radio station itself, and that in due course his endorsement of it would be made public. It may transcend rationality for the general public to listen to

---

[72] Details of Mr Irvine's endorsement activities, and their relevance as a component of his goodwill, emerge more clearly from the judgment on the inquiry as to damages: [2002] EWHC 539; [2002] E.M.L.R. 6 (Laddie J.), reversed as to quantum [2003] EWCA Civ 423, [2003] 2 All E.R. 881, [2003] E.M.L.R. 26; [2003] F.S.R. 35, CA.
[73] Above.

Talksport because Eddie Irvine is supposed to have endorsed it (knowing perfectly well that he had been paid handsomely for any such endorsement) but it is entirely rational for advertisers to pay heavily to trade on this irrationality.

Endorsement in present day English law

7–104 Despite the general reluctance of English courts to entertain passing-off actions in respect of merchandising in the past, it has been recognised that there is a difference between real and fictitious characters in that the former really can give or withhold their approval, and reliance on that approval or endorsement by the public is more readily to be inferred. The unauthorised use of the name or picture of a real person is therefore very much more likely to result in an implied but material misrepresentation than with fictitious characters, especially if the person is qualified to recommend the goods or business in question.

> "The business of what he [Counsel for the licensees] calls character merchandising has become very well known in our present times and everyone who has a character, whether real or fictional, to exploit, does so by the grant of licences to people who wish to use the name of the real or fictional character. I think one must leave real persons out of it because, when one deals with a real person one has a person with real qualities and, therefore, his endorsement or the use of his name may undoubtedly suggest, or may suggest in proper circumstances, an endorsement which may or may not exist. ..."[74]

To similar effect, the judgment of Morritt L.J. in *Elvis Presely TMs*[75] distinguishes between representations of endorsement, and use of the contested name or image in a context which for one reason or another does not imply any relevant trade connection:

> "Pre-eminent amongst the facts here are, first, that there is no connection whatsoever between the class of products in question (toiletries) and the things for which Elvis Presley was and remains famous (this is as far as could be from a case, such as was instanced in the course of argument, of a third party seeking, for example, to market Geoffrey Boycott cricket bats); second, that such marketing of this class of products as has taken place in the United Kingdom since Elvis Presley's death has been effected not by Enterprises but rather by the respondent himself (who, moreover, so far from claiming any endorsement for his products from Enterprises has on the contrary made plain his differences with them); and third, that the Elvis Presley legend is such as would inevitably attract a wide demand for memorabilia, little of which (at any rate (a) in the United Kingdom,

---

[74] *per* Walton J. in *Tavener Rutledge Ltd v Trexapalm Ltd* [1975] F.S.R. 479; [1977] R.P.C. 275.
[75] *Elvis Presley TM; Elvis Presley Enterprises Inc v Sid Shaw Elvisly Yours* [1999] R.P.C. 567, CA.

and (b) following his death) would the general public suppose to be officially licensed and approved."

Hitherto, the essential difference between English and Australian law has **7–105** been that in English law there has been no presumption that a person suffers damage from being wrongly identified as having endorsed the goods or business of another. After *Irvine v Talksport*,[76] the question arises of how far English law has gone in the direction of *Henderson v Radio Corporation*,[77] which held that a personality who could be said to be a trader is always free to grant or withhold his endorsement, and therefore that any unauthorised use is deemed to damage him by depriving him of the fee he could otherwise have insisted on. It is interesting that the judgment of Laddie J. identifies damage to goodwill with misappropriation of goodwill, thereby following the *Henderson* line of authority, but drawing back from the latter's wider implications with a reassertion of the separate need for misrepresentation:

"If someone acquires a valuable reputation or goodwill, the law of passing off will protect it from unlicensed use by other parties. Such use will frequently be damaging in the direct sense that it will involve selling inferior goods or services under the guise that they are from the claimant. But the action is not restricted to protecting against that sort of damage. The law will vindicate the claimant's exclusive right to the reputation or goodwill. It will not allow others to so use goodwill as to reduce, blur or diminish its exclusivity. It follows that it is not necessary to show that the claimant and the defendant share a common field of activity or that sales of products or services will be diminished either substantially or directly, at least in the short term. Of course there is still a need to demonstrate a misrepresentation because it is that misrepresentation which enables the defendant to make use or take advantage of the claimant's reputation."

Consistently with *Irvine v Talksport*,[78] it is now suggested that there are **7–106** three relevant situations which have to be distinguished. In English law, damage to goodwill is still the gist of the action and a misrepresentation which causes no damage is not actionable. If a professional sportsman or entertainer already has a substantial income from granting endorsements or similar kinds of licence, then he has a goodwill in relation to his business as a licensor or endorser, as well as that in relation to the sporting or entertainment activities from which his fame and popularity originally derive. In this case, unauthorised use of his name or likeness in such as way as to imply endorsement will rightly be taken to have deprived him of the royalty he would otherwise have received, whether or not he would actually have endorsed the defendant in fact and whether or not the defendant competes with any existing or prospective endorsee. If the defendant's goods or ser-

---

[76] [2002] EWHC 357; [2002] 1 W.L.R. 2355; [2002] 2 All E.R. 414; [2002] E.M.L.R. 32; [2002] F.S.R. 60 (Laddie J.); affirmed (as to liability) [2003] EWCA Civ 423; [2003] 2 All E.R. 881; [2003] E.M.L.R. 26; [2003] F.S.R. 35, CA.
[77] [1960] N.S.W.L.R. 279; [1969] R.P.C. 218.
[78] Above.

vices, or the nature of the implied connection, are such as to debase the claimant's reputation, then that is a further head of damage, though not one which is essential in its own right. On the other hand, if the claimant's only relevant trading activity consists of his professional sporting or artistic performances then it is probably illegitimate to rely on loss of purely hypothetical licensing income as a head of damage, and the damage which is the gist of the action must be sought elsewhere. Finally, if the celebrity cannot be said to be a trader with goodwill in any relevant sense, then the action must fail.[79]

Merchandising and sports: *Arsenal* and *English Rugby*

7–107 Two recent cases have dealt with merchandising by sports teams. In the first, *Arsenal v Reed*,[80] Laddie J held at trial that there was no passing-off involved in the defendant's operation of a stall outside the Arsenal football ground in North London at which he sold unlicensed or unauthorised merchandise, such as scarves, bearing the names *Arsenal* and *The Gunners* and (in some cases) one or both of the two crests or badges used by the club. The result was doubted by Aldous L.J. in the Court of Appeal,[81] by reference to *Vine Products v Mackenzie*,[82] but since the passing off claims had been abandoned by that stage it is uncertain to what extent the judgment below was thought to be wanting by reference to classic passing-off principles, and to what extent the Court of Appeal regretted being deprived of an opportunity to uncover further unknown pieces of common law or equity in the search for a general remedy against "unfair trading" or "unlawful competition".

On behalf of Arsenal it was argued at first instance that the issue could be disposed of easily: Arsenal and the "Arsenal signs" were so famous that a significant number of members of the public would see the same signs used by Mr Reed, and would conclude that his goods were produced by Arsenal or were licensed by them, so that purchasing them from Mr Reed would contribute to Arsenal's resources. For Mr Reed it was contended that any purchasers who cared about the origin or provenance of the goods would know that the goods on his stand had no connection with Arsenal at all; and that most purchasers were only concerned to own and display products which proclaimed their support for their football team. Scarves bearing the "Arsenal Signs" were garments bearing badges of allegiance and no more.

7–108 Having dismissed Arsenal's supposed argument of principle by reference to the speeches of Lord Diplock and Lord Fraser in *Warnink v Townend*,[83] Laddie J. went on to examine the facts. Mr Reed had been trading openly (and originally without objection from the club) for over 30 years–long

---

[79] As in *Stringfellow v McCain Foods*, [1984] F.S.R. 175; [1984] R.P.C. 501, CA.

[80] [2001] E.T.M.R. 77; [2001] R.P.C. 46 (Laddie J.). Subsequent proceedings on the registered Community trade marks, including a reference to the European Court of Justice as Case C–206/01, did not involve passing-off.

[81] [2003] EWCA Civ 696, CA.

[82] [1968] F.S.R. 625; [1969] R.P.C. 1 (Cross J.).

[83] [1979] A.C. 731; [1979] 2 All E.R. 927; [1980] R.P.C. 31, HL.

before the club had any substantial merchandising programme of its own; there was no evidence of actual confusion in all this time; Arsenal themselves ensured that their authorised merchandise was very clearly identified as such; and the distinction was conspicuously brought to the attention of their fans. On the facts, there could be no doubt that anyone purchasing from Mr Reed knew (if indeed he cared) that he was simply buying an *Arsenal* souvenir or memento of indeterminate trade origin, rather than an "official" product endorsed or licensed by the club:

"It seems to me that the use of the Arsenal Signs on Mr Reed's products carries no message of trade origin. Although I accept that some fans will want to purchase official Arsenal memorabilia so as to support their club, it is a *non-sequitur* to say that this means all Arsenal memorabilia or memorabilia displaying one or more of the Arsenal Signs will be taken by them to have come from or be licensed by AFC. Choosing to give your custom to one company by buying goods from it does not mean that that type of goods only comes from that company. What is necessary is some additional sign or circumstance of trading which says to the customer that the goods come from or are commercially connected with the source he likes and not some other source."

A similar result to *Arsenal v Reed* was reached by Lloyd J. at trial in *Rugby Football Union v Cotton Traders*[84] in which the governing body for Rugby Union in England complained of sales by the defendants of the "classic" English rugby jersey (as opposed to the current official strip of the England team). The classic jersey, in white with a red rose on the left breast, had been worn by the English team for over a century, with examples being sold to the public by many traders, the defendants included. All this had been without any licence, or any sustained complaint, from the claimants. The red rose itself was not distinctive of the Union in the trade mark sense, and there was no evidence that anyone had purchased the defendants' jerseys under the misapprehension that they were officially licensed by the claimants.

The return of South Africa to international sports provided the back- **7–109** ground to *FIFA v Bartlett*[85] where better evidence allowed the *Dallas*[86] case to be distinguished. The defendant had had the foresight to register *World Cup* as a trade mark when sanctions were in force and there seemed to be no prospect of South Africa competing internationally. During the 1994 football World Cup in America he not only launched his own unlicensed range of sports clothing but demanded royalties (of 12½ per cent) from South Africa FIFA sponsors and licensees. As in *Mirage Studios v Counter-Feat Clothing*,[87] which Joffe J. followed, this was a rare case of a defendant actually holding himself out as entitled to grant licences.

---

[84] [2002] EWHC 467; [2002] E.T.M.R. 76 (Lloyd J.)
[85] 1994 (4) SA 722 (Joffe J., TPD).
[86] *Lorimar Productions v Sterling Clothing* 1981 (3) SA 1129; [1982] R.P.C. 395 (Van Dijkhorst J., Transvaal).
[87] [1991] F.S.R. 145 (Browne-Wilkinson V.C.).

A mild example of "ambush" marketing comes from New Zealand. In *New Zealand Olympic and Commonwealth Games Association v Telecom New Zealand*[88] an advertisement which said that you could take the defendants' mobile phones to the (Atlanta) Olympics was unlikely to be taken as representing that the advisers was connected with or a sponsor of the Olympic Games. The device of using the word "RING" five times and in five colours in the manner of the Olympic symbol was more likely to cause amusement than confusion. There might be a marginally arguable case but the balance of convenience favoured the defendants.

Rights of privacy and publicity; injurious falsehood

7–110 In Canada the courts have recognised a "right of publicity" similar to that existing in many American states. This does not depend on there being passing-off in the sense recognised by English, or even Australian, law.

The plaintiff in *Athans v Canadian Adventure Camps*[89] was a professional water skier. He exploited his reputation commercially, and used as his "trademark" a specific photograph of himself in action. The defendants operated a summer camp for children where water skiing was an activity. They illustrated an advertisement and brochure with a drawing unintentionally but recognisably derived from the plaintiff's photograph. The Court found against the plaintiff on the issue of passing-off because the photograph was distinctive of him only to water-skiing enthusiasts, and would mean nothing to readers of the brochure and advertisement. However, the judge found that there had been an invasion of the plaintiff's "exclusive right to market his own personality" for which he recovered damages.

7–111 In contrast, there were no problems of identification for the English plaintiff in *Kaye v Robertson*,[90] but the law of passing-off afforded no relief for a particularly blatant commercial invasion of his privacy. Gordon Kaye was a popular television actor who suffered serious head injuries when a piece of wood fell on his car during a storm. Journalists employed by a "lurid and sensational" newspaper, the *Sunday Sport*, photographed and purported to interview him while he was in hospital recovering from surgery. Mr Kaye was demonstrably incapable of managing his own affairs, but the defendants intended to publish the interview and photographs as an exclusive scoop to which Mr Kaye had given his agreement. An argument that publication of the purported interview without Mr Kaye's consent was passing-off was curtly dismissed as hopeless by the Court of Appeal: "I only need say ... that the plaintiff is not in the position of a trader in relation to his interest in his story about his accident and his recovery, and thus fails from the start to have a right of action under this head".[91]

---

[88] [1996] F.S.R. 757 (McGechan J., High Court of New Zealand). The report at (1996) 35 I.P.R. 55 reproduces the advertisement.
[89] (1977) 17 O.R. (2d) 425; 34 C.P.R. (2d) 126; 80 D.L.R. (3d) 583 (Henry J., Ontario High Court). See also *Krouse v Chrysler Canada Ltd* (1973) 40 D.L.R. (3d) 15.
[90] [1991] F.S.R. 62, CA.
[91] *per* Glidewell L.J.

The cause of action for passing-off may ultimately have been likely to fail on the facts, but it did deserve to be considered more fully than this. It is true that an individual may be a trader for some purposes and not for others, and the dictum quoted does not necessarily contradict the established principle that performers and entertainers may be traders for the purposes of a passing-off action. So was the interview more closely related to Mr Kaye's professional or private life? It is unrealistic to suppose that an actor is only practising his craft when he is actually on stage or in front of the cameras, and the giving of interviews is one way in which entertainers simultaneously exploit and sustain their popularity. On an application for an interlocutory injunction it should not have been too difficult to conclude that there was an arguable case in Mr Kaye's favour. The Court of Appeal was prepared to treat the publication of the interview as a malicious falsehood and libel, and granted an interlocutory injunction under the former head. The Court rejected arguments based on trespass to the person and general rights of privacy or publicity.

H. CHARACTER MERCHANDISING

Introduction

Character merchandising is the name given to the practice of licensing the **7–112** name or likeness of a character, generally a fictitious one, for use on or in the promotion of goods or services with which the character has little or no intrinsic connection. The essence of character merchandising is that goods or services can be made more attractive in the market by associating them with an appropriate and popular character.[92] Despite the prevalence of character merchandising there are still relatively few English decisions on the question of whether (or under what circumstances) it might be passing-off to use the name or likeness of a well-known character without the licence of the originator of the character or his successor, in the case of a fictitious character, or the character himself if real.

What can now be said on the strength of the *Elvis Presley*[93] and *Eddie Irvine* cases, is that there is no *sui generis* character merchandising right known to English common law, and that liability for passing off depends, as always, on the three elements of goodwill, a misrepresentation which must be a material one, and consequential damage to the goodwill. In the case of real and living characters, the elements of misrepresentation and materiality may sometimes be found in the implication that the character has endorsed the goods or services in question, as in the *Eddie Irvine* case. With fictitious

---

[92] See the example given by Laddie J. in *Irvine v Talksport* [2002] EWHC 367; [2002] 1 W.L.R. 2355; [2002] 2 All E.R. 414; [2002] E.M.L.R. 32; [2002] F.S.R. 60 (Laddie J.); affirmed (as to liability) [2003] EWCA Civ 423; [2003] 2 All E.R. 881; [2003] E.M.L.R. 26; [2003] F.S.R. 35, CA, quoted at para.7.82 above.

[93] *Elvis Presley TM; Elvis Presley Enterprises Inc v Sid Shaw Elvisly Yours* [1999] R.P.C. 567, CA.

characters, there cannot be any question of the character as such giving or withholding its endorsement to anything, and the endorsement of the putative owner of whatever rights attach to the character is much less likely to be material, even if such endorsement is to be implied in the first place.

Historically, the majority of English cases would not have regarded the licensors (or potential licensors) of characters as having any cause of action, although the reasons for refusing relief have varied. Some are unquestionably obsolete, for example arguments that the licensors were not in business at all, or did not share a common field of activity with the defendant. In 1975 Walton J. refused an interlocutory injunction over the use of the word *Wombles* for rubbish skips in *Wombles v Wombles Skips*[94] and in *Tavener Rutledge v Trexapalm*[95] granted one against the licensed user of *Kojak* for lollipops at the suit of an unlicensed business which had started first. Oliver J. refused the pop group *ABBA* an interlocutory injunction in *Lyngstad v Annabas*.[96] In South Africa, the producers of the television series *Dallas* were refused interim interdicts against use of the name for clothing and a restaurant: *Lorimar Productions v Sterling Clothing Manufacturers*.[97] The Court of Appeal in *Stringfellow v McCain Foods*[98] refused final relief in a case in which the name of a night club proprietor was used for frozen chips. In *Grundy Television v Startrain*[99] the producers of the television series *Neighbours* were refused an interlocutory injunction against a magazine called *Neighbours Who's Who*.

Merchandising in Australia

7–113 Over the same period, however, the Australian courts were showing much more sympathy to plaintiffs. In *Henderson v Radio Corporation*[1] two well-known professional ballroom dancers recovered for the use of their photograph on the sleeve of a record of music for ballroom dancing. The wrongful appropriation of the plaintiffs' professional or business reputation was said to be sufficient damage to found the action. In *Children's Television Workshop v Woolworths*[2] the defendants sold soft toys which were quite clearly copied from the *Muppet* characters on the plaintiffs' television programme *Sesame Street*. Helsham C.J. held that the public were aware of the practice of character merchandising and would assume that the defendants' toys were licensed. On the authority of *Henderson v Radio Corporation* that was sufficient for there to be passing-off.

In *Hutchence v South Sea Bubble*[3] the pop group *INXS* was able to restrain the sale of unlicensed T-shirts. Items of clothing were also at issue in

---

[94] [1975] F.S.R. 488; [1977] R.P.C. 99 (Walton J.).
[95] [1975] F.S.R. 479; [1977] R.P.C. 275 (Walton J.).
[96] [1977] F.S.R. 62 (Oliver J.).
[97] 1981 (3) SA 1129; [1982] R.P.C. 395 (Van Dijkhorst J., Transvaal).
[98] [1984] R.P.C. 501, CA.
[99] [1988] F.S.R. 581 (Millett J.). In *BBC v Celebrity Centre* (1988) 15 I.P.R. 333 Falconer J. granted an interlocutory injunction against the *A to Z of EastEnders*.
[1] [1960] N.S.W.L.R. 279; [1969] R.P.C. 218.
[2] [1981] 1 N.S.W.L.R. 273; [1981] R.P.C. 187 (Helsham C.J.).
[3] (1986) 64 A.L.R. 330; 6 I.P.R. 473 (Wilcox J.).

Fido Dido v Venture Stores,[4] where an interlocutory injunction was refused on the balance of convenience, although the plaintiffs had an arguable case. In *Hogan v Koala Dundee*[5] and *Hogan v Pacific Dunlop*[6] the actor who played the film character *Crocodile Dundee* obtained injunctions against a retail shop displaying pictures of a koala bear with a bush hat and a crocodile tooth necklace; and a television advertisement for shoes which parodied a scene from the film.

Character mechandising is not confined to the characters as such, but can **7–114** extend to their props, which in the case of the television series *The Simpsons* included the imaginary brand of beer which was drunk by Homer Simpson and his friends. In *Twentieth Century Fox Film v South Australia Brewing*[7] the producers of *The Simpsons* were granted an interlocutory injunction against a real brand of beer being launched as *Duff Beer* without their licence. They had consistently refused to grant licences in relation to alcoholic drinks.

In *Miller v Britt Allcroft*[8] an injunction was granted against a shop trading as *The Thomas Shop*. Its name, get-up, publicity material, and the fact that it dealt almost entirely in *Thomas the Tank Engine* merchandise of the plaintiffs were all likely (and had been intended) to lead to the mistaken conclusion that that the shop was either owned or licensed by the producers of the merchandise. Passing-off was alleged, but the case was decided principally as one of "misleading or deceptive conduct" under the (South Australia) Fair Trading Act 1987, s.56. It was not suggested that the defendant could be prevented from selling licensed *Thomas the Tank Engine* merchandise, even if she sold nothing else.

The *Teenage Mutant Ninja Turtles* case

At first sight the English and Australian lines of authority may seem to have **7–115** been reconciled by the decision of Browne-Wilkinson V.C. in the *Teenage Mutant Ninja Turtles* case, *Mirage Studios v Counter-Feat Clothing*,[9] where the plaintiffs were the creators of the cartoon characters *Leonardo, Donatello, Michelangelo* and *Raphael*:

"The nature of the beast is a humanoid turtle, usually but not invariably green in colour, heavily muscled according to human muscularity, they have bare, aggressive, old-fashioned weapons; their general demeanour is at once jolly and aggressive. They wear, I imagine derived from the Ninjitsu tradition, coloured masks over their eyes, they have coloured scarves on their elbows and wrists and their knees. Each of the four Ninja Turtle characters has a belt surrounding its midriff with an initial on the buckle for his name–L, D, M or R as the case may be."

[4] (1988) 12 I.P.R. 508.
[5] (1988) 12 I.P.R. 225; affirmed (1989) 14 I.P.R. 398.
[6] (1988) 16 I.P.R. 365 (M. L. Foster J.).
[7] (1996) 34 I.P.R. 225 (Tamberlin J., Federal Court)
[8] [2000] FCA 1724; 00 I.P.R. 419 (Federal Court of Australia).
[9] [1991] F.S.R. 145 (Browne-Wilkinson V.C.).

The *Turtles* had become extremely popular in comics and on television and the release of a film was imminent. There were some 150 licensees for *Turtle* merchandise in the United Kingdom. The defendants produced artwork depicting muscular humanoid turtles in various sporting poses and licensed garment manufacturers to use them on T-shirts and jogging clothes. On an application for an interlocutory injunction against passing-off and copyright infringement, the Vice-Chancellor held that the balance of convenience was so finely poised that it was proper to take into account the respective strengths of the parties' cases on the merits. Customers were aware that when characters were reproduced on goods, it was done under licence. To sell unlicensed goods involved a misrepresentation, since the defendants' turtles were confusingly similar to those of the plaintiffs and the public would assume them to be licensed. On the evidence, it was more likely than not that the plaintiffs would prevail at trial on the issue of passing-off.

7–116   In Canada the distributors of *Crocodile Dundee* were awarded C$15,000 and an injunction at trial in respect of unlicensed T-shirts in *Paramount Pictures v Howley*.[10] Although the two Australian *Crocodile Dundee* cases and *Ninja Turtles* were cited and described as helpful, the decision acknowledged that the public were unlikely to have bought the defendant's clothing because of any confusion with the plaintiffs', and the quality was not inferior or unsatisfactory. However, the relevant public included trade customers as well, and retail stores probably bought the defendant's clothing on the assumption that it was licensed by the plaintiffs and that they could look to them for some assurance as to quality and delivery.

Is there a misrepresentation ...

7–117   For the authorised use of a character to constitute passing-off there must be a misrepresentation which causes damage to the goodwill of the claimant, who is normally the licensor or an existing licensee with whom the defendant is competing. The existence of a material misrepresentation is crucial. If the claimant is the licensor, the only misrepresentation which can plausibly be inferred is that the defendant's goods are produced under his licence. Moreover, the implicit misrepresentation must be one on which the public rely if it is to be material. Otherwise, all that can be said is that the public buy the goods under the misconception that a royalty is paid to the licensor, a misconception which is hardly likely to influence their choice.

There are many contexts in which use of the name or picture of a real or fictional character may occur without implying that there is any licensing or similar relationship between the claimant and the defendant. The majority of the following cases fall into that category. However, this does not mean that all merchandising involving fictitious characters falls outside the scope of passing-off. In *Tavener Rutledge v Trexapalm*[11] Walton J. treated *Kojak* as having trade mark significance in relation to lollipops, although it was the unlicensed plaintiff who was the owner. If the licensees had been first on the

---

[10] (1992) 39 C.P.R. (3d) 419 (Van Camp J., Ontario). The *Turtles* were also successful in Australia: *Surge Licensing Inc. v Pearson* (1991) 21 I.P.R. 228 (Einfeld J.).
[11] [1975] F.S.R. 479; [1977] R.P.C. 275; (Walton J.).

market they would have prevailed, but by virtue of their own use, not their licence. In respect of lollipops *Kojak* was treated as an arbitrary or fancy word, and it could therefore be distinctive of one manufacturer and protected by the action for passing-off. If one and the same mark is in use by a number of different businesses for a variety of goods, as in the *Dunhill*[12] and *Page 3*[13] cases, then the natural inference may be that some one person (whose identity need not be known) is ultimately responsible for the character or quality of all of them. In this respect, a name or other mark may develop trade mark significance and become distinctive of the licensor quite independently of the fact that it started as the name of a real or fictitious character. But if the name is recognised, then the natural inference may well be that even the first user of the name is doing so under the control of the inventor of the character, and that may be so whether that user is licensed or not.

Examples

In *Universal City Studios v 309848 Ontario*[14] the plaintiff film producers were **7–118** refused an interlocutory injunction in Canada in respect of unlicensed *Jaws* T-shirts, posters and pillows. Even the wide s.7(e) of the (Canadian) Trade Marks Act 1970, which gives effect to the Paris Convention by prohibiting any act "contrary to honest industrial or commercial usage in Canada" was not contravened.[15] The same plaintiffs obtained an English *Anton Piller* order in *Universal City Studios v Mukhtar*[16] in similar circumstances, but the judgment of Templeman J. does not state whether passing-off was among the causes of action.

The plaintiffs in *Wombles v Wombles Skips*[17] were the assignees of copyright in works depicting fictional characters called *Wombles* who were supposed to inhabit Wimbledon Common and keep it tidy. The creator of the *Wombles* was not herself a party. The *Wombles* had been made the subject of a series of television programmes as well as the book in which they had originally appeared, and licences to use portrayals of the *Wombles* had been granted for goods as diverse as magic slates and yogurt. The defendants hired out skips for clearing rubbish and used *Wombles Skips* as their trading name and on the skips. They did not use pictures of any of the *Wombles*. Walton J. refused to believe that anyone seeing one of the defendants' skips would think there was any connection with the plaintiff. If wrong, the plaintiffs existed only to exploit rights for money and would be adequately compensated by an award of damages.

Similar reasoning as to public recognition of the relationship between

---

[12] *Alfred Dunhill Ltd v Sunoptic SA* [1979] F.S.R. 337, CA.
[13] *News Group Newspapers Ltd v Rocket Record Co Ltd* [1981] F.S.R. 89 (Slade J.).
[14] (1975) 24 C.P.R. (2d) 278 (Addy J., Federal Court, Trial Division).
[15] It is now doubted if the subsection is constitutional: *Macdonald v Vapour Canada Ltd* [1977] 2 S.C.R. 134; 66 D.L.R. (3d) 1; 22 C.P.R. (2d) 1 (Supreme Court of Canada).
[16] [1976] 1 W.L.R. 568; [1976] 2 All E.R. 330; [1976] F.S.R. 252 (Templeman J.).
[17] [1975] F.S.R. 488; [1977] R.P.C. 99 (Walton J.).

licensor and licensee was applied by the same judge in *Tavener Rutledge v Trexapalm*,[18] except that the position of the parties was reversed and an interlocutory injunction was granted to the first, unauthorised, user of *Kojak* for lollipops. The unsuccessful defendants held a licence from the producers of the television series of that name.

The plaintiffs in *IPC Magazines v Black & White Music*[19] published a science fiction magazine in which a prominent character was *Judge Dredd*. The defendants were about to issue a record entitled *Judge Dredd* including a song about him. They had approached the plaintiffs for a licence but had been refused. Goulding J. was prepared to accept that the title would be taken as implying to many that the record had been approved or authorised by the plaintiffs. However, although there might be a misrepresentation, the fact that the plaintiffs were thought to have approved the record would not in itself cause them damage since the quality and content of the record were unobjectionable. If the plaintiff succeed at trial then damages on a royalty basis would probably be adequate. The balance of convenience was in favour of the defendants and an interlocutory injunction was refused.

7–119 *Nice and Safe Attitude v Flook*,[20] though not a character merchandising case, is reminiscent of *Tavener Rutledge v Trexapalm*[21] in that a licence from the American National Aeronautics and Space Administration to the defendant's suppliers for use of *NASA* on T-shirts did not justify varying an injunction granted in favour of the plaintiffs who had been the first in England to use a similar logo for clothing, though without having any connection with NASA (USA).

In *BBC Worldwide v Pally Screen Printing*[22] Laddie J. refused to grant the BBC summary judgment in respect of T-shirts printed with pictures of characters from their children's television series *Teletubbies*. It was impossible to say at that stage whether the public would take the T-shirts as being made with the BBC's approval, or whether they would simply buy them for the artwork, without regard to whether they were sanctioned by the BBC.

...and is it a material one?

According to Walton J. in *Taverner Rutledge v Trexapalm*[23] the plaintiff has
7–120 to show not only that the public are aware of the practice of granting licences but

> "[T]hat it had also become so well known that people in the situation of licensors of these names exercised quality control over any product bearing their name, so that as soon as anybody in the street came to the conclusion that a product was licensed by the owners of some series, such as the '*Kojak*' series, he would say to himself not only 'This must be

---

[18] [1975] F.S.R. 479; [1977] R.P.C. 275 (Walton J.).
[19] [1983] F.S.R. 348 (Goulding J.).
[20] [1997] F.S.R. 14 (Robert Walker J.).
[21] [1975] F.S.R. 479; [1977] R.P.C. 275 (Walton J.).
[22] [1998] F.S.R. 665 (Laddie J.).
[23] [1975] F.S.R. 479; [1977] R.P.C. 275 (Walton J.).

licensed by them,' but also: 'and that is a guarantee of its quality.' That point we are miles from reaching and there is really not a shred of evidence in front of me to that effect."

The reasons for attaching significance to quality control are twofold. One is that if the circumstances postulated by Walton J. are met then the customer may prefer licensed goods to unlicensed on account of the implicit "guarantee" of quality, though there is no guarantee in the legal sense. Licensors are almost certainly not responsible for their licensees' liabilities. The other is that if the goods of the defendant are in fact inferior, then the claimant may be blamed. In the early English cases, the plaintiffs failed to prove that character merchandising was sufficiently well known for the public to infer the existence of a licence when a business used the name or likeness of a well-known character, still less that the use of the character was understood as implying that the quality of the product was guaranteed by the plaintiff. These are both matters of fact and evidence. In Australia especially, plaintiffs have succeeded in proving the first, and the second and more stringent requirement has not been insisted on. The fundamental distinction between the English and Australian authorities is whether a mis-representation that one business is licensed by another is conclusively assumed to damage that other, or whether likelihood of damage must be proved in its own right. On the authority of *Harrods v Harrodian School*[24] there can be little doubt that English law still adopts the latter approach.

Although claimants have generally failed to prove that the existence of a licence would be presumed by customers, it does not follow that evidence of **7–121** such a belief would have been enough. There must not only be a mis-representation, but it must be a material one. For there to be passing-off in the context of character merchandising the name or representation of the character must have trade mark significance in respect of the goods in which complaint is made. It is not sufficient that the public should believe that there is some sort of connection between the defendant and the licensor: the public must select the defendant's goods in reliance upon the assumed connection. Evidence that the public believe the licensor to exercise quality control over the goods of his licensees only goes half way towards what the claimant has to prove. The perceived existence of quality control is only relevant if the public actually rely on the control supposedly exercised by the licensor.

It does not follow that this is always the case. Character merchandising is frequently used by identifiable traders with ample reputation of their own. The customer buying a T-shirt at a branch of a retail chain selling only its own brand of goods is likely to rely entirely on their quality control, not on that hypothetically exercised by a merchandisor whose principal expertise may lie in providing entertainment rather than making clothing. He may believe, and may believe correctly, that the merchandisor has satisfied itself as to the quality of the article but that is not likely to influence his purchase in those circumstances. If the T-shirt were on sale by a street trader or at a

---

[24] [1996] R.P.C. 687, CA.

market stall then reliance by the customer on the licensor's quality control would be rather more plausible, unless the customer was prepared to trust to luck or his own judgment. The licensor would be the only person of known reputation believed to be associated with the goods.

Materiality in the Australian cases

7–122 Australian law is different because it has been widely accepted since *Henderson v Radio Corporation*[25] that, in this context at least, the plaintiff does not have to show reliance on the alleged misrepresentation. The reasoning of *Henderson* was applied in the context of fictitious characters in *Children's Television Workshop v Woolworths*[26] where the defendants sold soft toys which were quite clearly copied from the *Muppet* characters on the plaintiffs' television programme *Sesame Street*. The *Muppets* were very well known on Australian television and sales of licensed merchandise, mainly for children, were running at A$ 10 million per annum. There had been licensed *Muppet* soft toys on the market, but the company which had enjoyed the licence was not a party. None of the plaintiffs were engaged in actual trade in *Muppet* merchandise. Strict quality control was exercised over the licensed products, but the defendants' toys were cheaper and inferior, especially in terms of accuracy. Helsham J. held that the public were aware of the practice of character merchandising and would assume that the defendants' toys were licensed. On the authority of *Henderson* that was sufficient for there to be passing-off.

While Helsham C.J. in *Children's Television Workshop v Woolworths* seemed to attach importance to finding that the public knew the plaintiffs by name as the originators of the Muppet Show, this was strictly unnecessary. In *Fido Dido v Venture Stores*[27] M. L. Foster J. held, following *Powell v Birmingham Vinegar Brewery*, that provided the characters had reputation and goodwill in Australia then it was sufficient for there to be an awareness that the characters had been created by someone who had a business interest in putting them on the market. *Fido Dido* clothing had recently been launched in Australia when the defendants started to promote a rival range *Who Me, You Too*, which the plaintiffs claimed to be so basically similar as to lead to the belief that it was part of the *Fido Dido* range, or produced under licence. Although the defendants had not copied and did not reproduce the *Fido Dido* characters as such, there was a serious issue to be tried; but the balance of convenience favoured refusing an interlocutory injunction.

Although *Fido Dido* followed *Muppets* and was purportedly followed in its turn in *Teenage Mutant Ninja Turtles*[28] it is both more conservative and more sophisticated in its reasoning than either. Unlike either of those two cases, the central issue is identified not as confusion of the characters in some abstract sense, but in the specific context of a purchaser wanting to

[25] [1960] N.S.W.L.R. 279; [1969] R.P.C. 218.
[26] [1981] 1 N.S.W.L.R. 273; [1981] R.P.C. 187 (Helsham C.J.).
[27] (1988) 16 I.P.R. 365 (M. L. Foster J.).
[28] *Mirage Studios v Counter-Feat Clothing Ltd* [1991] F.S.R. 145.

buy what are in fact the claimants' licensed goods, though he may not identify them as such:

"The most significant factual question, in my view, is whether a customer wishing to buy a *Fido Dido* garment would, at the time of purchase, be satisfied that one of the *Who Me, You Too* range of garments, was in fact, a genuine *Fido Dido* garment. Apart from the appearance of the *Fido Dido* garments ... it must be noted that they are also clearly labelled as *Fido Dido* and, generally speaking, have the *Credo*[29] sewn on as a patch or appearing on a swing tag.

I am very much of the view, at this stage, despite the evidence to which I have made reference, that a reasonable customer when seeking to purchase a *Fido Dido* garment would not be misled by the appearance of the *Who Me, You Too* garments into purchasing one of them as a *Fido Dido* product. ... Nevertheless, with some considerable hesitation. I have come to the view that I must find that there is a serious issue to be tried."

Fictitious characters: conclusions

Unauthorised character merchandising can amount to passing-off only if **7–123** there is a misrepresentation by the defendant calculated to cause damage to the goodwill of the claimant. Analysed in these fundamental terms, it need not be conclusive that the claimant and defendant do not share a common field of activity, nor that the only misrepresentation to be implied is that the defendant is licensed, nor that the main head of damage to the claimant can be reduced to a loss of royalty income. These are essentially matters of fact and degree, no more.

The first essential question is whether there has been a misrepresentation, and this depends on whether the name or likeness of the character is used in a trade mark sense or not. It is this failure to distinguish that which serves as an indication of trade source from that which adds to the value of the goods in its own right which undermines the judgment of Browne-Wilkinson V.-C. in *Mirage Studios v Counter-Feat Clothing*.[30] Passing-off deals entirely with the first, copyright with some aspects of the second. In this respect the *Wombles*,[31] *Kojak*[32] and *Dallas*[33] cases are, perhaps, surprisingly, among those in which the merchandisor's case was strongest. In each of them the defendant[34] was clearly using the term in a trade mark sense in relation to his own goods or business, and indeed that was why the piratical plaintiff in *Kojak* himself obtained an injunction. A *Wombles* skip has no attributes to distinguish it from any other skip, except that it is a skip provided by someone who claims the right to identify himself by the name *Wombles*. The

---

[29] The *Fido Credo*, that is.
[30] [1991] F.S.R. 145 (Browne-Wilkinson V.C.).
[31] *Wombles Ltd v Wombles Skips Ltd* [1975] F.S.R. 488; [1977] R.P.C. 99 (Walton J.).
[32] *Tavener Rutledge Ltd v Trexapalm Ltd* [1975] F.S.R. 479; [1977] R.P.C. 275 (Walton J.).
[33] *Lorimar Productions Inc. v Sterling Clothing Manufacturers Pty Ltd* 1981 (3) SA 1129; [1982] R.P.C. 395 (Van Dijkhorst J., Transvaal).
[34] Plaintiff in *Kojak*, where the roles were reversed.

only two questions were, therefore, whether in relation to skips the word *Wombles* denoted some connection with the plaintiffs, and whether damage would result. It was on the facts that neither was made out to the satisfaction of Walton J. Yet one need have no difficulty in imagining Walton J. finding for the plaintiffs on the facts of *Fido Dido v Venture Stores*,[35] at least if the resemblances had been closer or deliberate. *Fido Dido* was not just a character in the abstract, but a brand used by an identifiable trader for a specific range of clothing which the public might want for any number of reasons, including style and quality, and identify by that name. There was more to the *Fido Dido* range than mere depiction of the character.

7–124   These cases are in contrast to the *Muppets*,[36] *Jaws*[37] and *Ninja Turtles*[38] cases, and to those brought by *ABBA*[39] and *INXS*.[40] The appearance of a soft toy, or the design on a T-shirt, are appreciated for their own sakes and not as the vehicle for any information as to who provided those goods. They are not trade marks at all. In the *ABBA* case what customers wanted was effigies of their idols. The purchasers of pop memorabilia such as T-shirts, badges and even soap buy them to indulge or display their fondness for the group in question, and this is likely to be as well served by unlicensed goods as by those on which a royalty may have been paid. In contrast to the *Wombles* skip considered above, a *Wombles* soft toy is physically different to other soft toys in that it must resemble one of the characters in the *Wombles* books. *Wombles* in this example, just as *Elvis* in the case of soap,[41] is capable of being used legitimately in a purely descriptive sense. In *ABBA*[42] the defendants issued goods bearing photographs of the group before any licensee was on the market, but in contrast to *Kojak*[43] there can have been no question of their obtaining any sort of exclusive rights as a result.

In the majority of the decided cases, therefore, there was no misrepresentation, either because the defendant did not make use of the name or likeness of the character in a trade mark sense, or because, although he did so, the court refused to conclude that the public would infer a connection with the claimant. If a misrepresentation can be inferred, the second essential question is whether it is calculated to cause damage, as otherwise it is immaterial. Here belief that the licensor exercises quality control, coupled with reliance on such belief, is one ground on which it could be supposed that the fact of licensing would influence the purchaser. However, knowl-

[35] (1988) 16 I.P.R. 365 (M. L. Foster J.).

[36] *Children's Television Workshop Inc v Woolworths (NSW) Ltd* [1981] 1 N.S.W.L.R. 273; [1981] R.P.C. 187 (Helsham C.J.).

[37] *Universal City Studios Inc v 309848 Ontario Ltd* (1975) 24 C.P.R. (2d) 278 (Addy J., Federal Court, Trial Division) and *Universal City Studios Inc v Mukhtar & Sons Ltd* [1976] F.S.R. 252 (Templeman J.).

[38] [1991] F.S.R. 145 (Browne-Wilkinson V.C.).

[39] *Lyngstad v Annabas Products Ltd* [1977] F.S.R. 62 (Oliver J.).

[40] *Hutchence v South Sea Bubble Co Pty Ltd* (1986) 64 A.L.R. (Wilcox J.). Though the latter two cases involve real persons they raise the same issue in this context.

[41] *Elvis Presley TM; Elvis Presley Enterprises Inc. v Sid Shaw Elvisly Yours* [1999] R.P.C. 567, CA.

[42] *Lyngstad v Annabas Products Ltd* [1977] F.S.R. 62 (Oliver J.).

[43] *Tanever Rutledge Ltd v Trexapalm Ltd* [1975] F.S.R. 479; [1977] R.P.C. 275 (Walton J.).

edge of the practice of merchandising, belief in the existence of quality control, and reliance on that belief are three entirely separate matters.

Character merchandise may be bought in the belief that there is a licen- **7–125** sing or similar relationship with the inventor of the character, but it does follow that any such belief contributed to the decision to purchase. If not, then the most that can be said is that there has been a misrepresentation, but one which was immaterial, and the erroneous public belief might better be described as a misunderstanding, rather than the result of any misrepresentation. The weakness in the reasoning of the *Muppets*[44] case may be seen by imagining that the plaintiffs had actually made soft toys themselves. In that event, if would have been on all fours with *British American Glass v Winton Products*[45] in which an injunction was refused although the plaintiffs' ornamental dogs were copied precisely. The purchaser of a *Cookie Monster* soft toy wants, quite simply, a soft toy depicting the *Cookie Monster*. He may believe that it is licensed by the Children's Television Workshop, but it is the appearance of the toy and not its origin which is uppermost in his mind and dictates his choice. One of *Oscar the Grouch* would be no substitute, notwithstanding that he may assume both to be made under the licence or even control of the same company. The best argument on which to justify *Children's Television Workshop v Woolworths*[46] is that there was implicitly a material misrepresentation as to quality. The Woolworths toys were similar enough to the *Muppets* characters to deceive an incautious parent into buying them in the belief that they were accurate replicas, but they were inaccurate enough to disappoint the children for whom they were presumably intended.

The final word on the Australian character merchandising cases[47] may be **7–126** given to Fisher J. in his judgment at trial in the High Court of New Zealand in *Tot Toys v Mitchell*[48] where the appearance of the *Buzzy Bee* toy was sought to be protected, *inter alia* on the basis of character merchandising rights:

"More fundamentally, however, I am not sure that all the implications of a passing-off approach to artificial character merchandising have yet been fully explored. As I see it, the basic problem is this. The essence of passing-off is deception which damages the plaintiff. Whether there is either deception or damage in the majority of unauthorised artificial character merchandising cases might be questioned. In many (certainly not all) cases of artificial character merchandising, the presence of any deception would be fortuitous because the point may be to project an association with the beneficial image *per se*; not a commercial connection with the persons responsible for creating or licensing it or even their goods. ...

---

[44] *Children's Television Workshop Inc v Woolworths (NSW) Ltd* [1981] 1 N.S.W.L.R. 273; [1981] R.P.C. 187 (Helsham C.J.).
[45] [1962] R.P.C. 230 (Pennycuick J.).
[46] [1981] N.S.W.L.R. 273; [1981] R.P.C. 187 (Helsham C J.).
[47] And, by implication, *Mirage Studios v Counter-Feat Clothing Ltd* [1991] F.S.R. 145, although it does not appear to have been cited.
[48] (1992) 25 I.P.R. 337 (Fisher J., HC of NZ).

There need not be any representation of consequence for present purposes except perhaps the somewhat theoretical implication that the advertiser is not using the image unlawfully. To say that the deception is the false representation that the defendant has an association with the image may be no more than a complicated way of saying that the defendant has no right to use the image. Unless the image is the plaintiff's property for other reasons (e.g. due to copyright, registered trade mark or registered design), it would beg the question to say that the defendant's use of the image is deceptive upon the ground that it is unlawful. And as to damage, the problem may be that frequently the only damage the plaintiff can point to is loss of the right to exploit exclusive character merchandising rights the very existence of which is under enquiry."

In the result, Fisher J. concluded that absent genuine deception such as a false claim to endorsement, "reliance upon passing-off to protect character merchandising rights becomes possible only if the court is willing to entertain a legal fiction".

I. DECEPTION AS TO ORIGIN OR NATURE

Introduction

7–127 A misrepresentation that goods are the product of a particular geographical area or have a particular character or composition is actionable as passing-off if it is material in the sense of being likely to influence customers and cause damage to another trader. The claimant may be any trader likely to suffer damage to the goodwill he enjoys in the business of supplying the public with goods from that area or having that character or composition. It is not necessary for the claimant to produce goods in that area himself, provided that on general principles he is the owner of such goodwill. So, in the various *Scotch Whisky* cases, the successful claimants have included blenders and exporters of Scotch, despite an argument in *John Walker v Henry Ost*[49] that if anyone was entitled to sue at all if would only have been the distillers. It was the blenders, not the distillers, who were recognised by the consuming public as responsible for the quality of the product in that case. There may be one or many suitably qualified traders, and each has a several right of action. Where the product is of foreign origin, only those producers who ship to the English market have a relevant goodwill. However, it has now been decided that bodies with a collective interest in maintaining the integrity of designations of origin are not proper claimants in an action for passing-off in either their personal, or representative, capacities.[50]

This cause of action is to be distinguished from that in which a place name

---

[49] [1970] 1 W.L.R. 917; [1970] 2 All E.R. 106; [1970] R.P.C. 489 (Foster J.).
[50] *Chocosuisse Union des Fabricants Suisse de Chocolat v Cadbury Ltd* [2000] R.P.C. 826, CA.

has become distinctive of the claimant's business. In the latter case the misrepresentation is that the goods are those of a particular trader, the claimant, and it is no defence that the defendant may carry on business at a place of that name, or that the claimant may not do so.[51] As Robert Walker J. explained in the context of geographical names for beer:[52]

> "[A] geographical name for a beer or ale may indicate either (1) that it is brewed in a particular place or (2) that it is of a particular type associated with that place and so likely to appeal to a particular taste, or (3) that it is the product of one particular brewery at that place. If it be said that that the mere information that a beer was made at a particular place is of no interest to anyone, the answer to that may be that there is, as I have noted, a traditional view that certain centres are, because of their water supply and other reasons, likely to produce particularly good beer...
>
> The three possible connotations I have mentioned–place of origin, type and identity of brewer–are not of course clear cut or mutually exclusive. It seems to me that all three may and often do coexist in a rather vague way in the mind of the average beer drinker."

Cases in the mould of *Advocaat*[53] and the earlier *Drinks Cases* are **7–128** sometimes described as ones of "extended" passing-off to distinguish them from "classic" passing-off in which the defendant represents his goods as those of the claimant. This can be convenient, although the purported distinction can obscure the fact that the "classic" passing-off case of *Spalding v Gamage*[54] itself incorporated one extension which is now settled orthodoxy, and that there are other possible extensions of the tort to situations quite distinct from the *Drinks Cases*. These ought not to be ruled out in advance by the implication that the tort can only evolve or extend itself in one direction only.

Misuse of geographic term; the *Drinks Cases*

Although it has origins in the nineteenth century, the modern law dates from **7–129** the *Spanish Champagne*[55] case in 1960, and most of the important cases in its development since then are concerned with the names of alcoholic drinks: *Champagne, Sherry, Scotch Whisky* and finally *Advocaat*. In the *Spanish Champagne* case itself the defendants sold a Spanish sparkling wine as *Spanish Champagne*. The 12 plaintiffs were French Champagne houses who claimed to sue on behalf of all Champagne producers who shipped to England. Dankwerts J. first decided as a preliminary point of law that there

---

[51] *Wotherspoon v Currie* (1872) L.R. 5 HL 508, HL; *Siegert v Findlater* (1878) 7 Ch.D. 801; *Montgomery v Thompson* [1891] A.C. 217; 8 R.P.C. 361, HL.
[52] *Barnsley Brewery Co Ltd v RBNB* [1997] F.S.R. 462 (Robert Walker J.).
[53] *Erven Warnink BV v J Townend & Sons (Hull) Ltd* [1979] A.C. 731; [1979] 2 All E.R. 97; [1980] R.P.C. 31, HL.
[54] (1915) 32 R.P.C. 273, HL.
[55] *Bollinger v Costa Brava Wine Co Ltd* [1960] Ch. 262; [1959] 3 All E.R. 800; [1960] R.P.C. 16 for the preliminary point of law. At trial [1961] 1 W.L.R. 277; [1961] 1 All E.R. 561; [1961] R.P.C. 116.

was in principle a cause of action vested in each Champagne house individually, the representative nature of the action being unnecessary. At the trial itself, the same judge found that the term *Spanish Champagne* would be likely to mislead "persons whose life or education had not taught them much about the nature and production of wine, but who from time to time want to purchase Champagne, as the wine with the great reputation" and granted an injunction.

> "There seems to be no reason why such licence should be given to a person, competing in trade, who seeks to attach to his product a name or description with which it has no natural association, so as to make use of the reputation and goodwill which has been gained by a product genuinely indicated by that name or description. In my view, it ought not to matter that the persons truly entitled to describe their goods by the name and description are a class producing goods in a certain locality, and not merely one individual."[56]

Bollinger v Costa Brava Wine Co was followed by Cross J. in the *Sherry* case, *Vine Products v Mackenzie*,[57] although the Court found in favour of the producers of *British Sherry* on the ground of acquiescence. However *Sherry* on its own still meant only the product of Jerez of Spain and a qualified injunction was granted.

7–130 In the *Champagne*[58] and *Sherry*[59] cases the goods in question were natural products of a limited area and could be said to owe much of their excellence to the advantages of their place of origin. It is now clear that these are not essential requirements. For the misrepresentation to be material the customer must to some degree prefer goods from the place in question, but it does not matter why that preference should exist. The area may be large or small, the goods need not be derived from local natural products, and they may owe their desirability to factors which could easily be reproduced elsewhere.[60]

In the first *Scotch Whisky* case, *John Walker v Henry Ost*[61] the defendants were restrained from selling as *Scotch Whisky* a mixture of Scotch malt whisky and locally distilled spirit. The plaintiffs successfully argued that *Scotch Whisky* denoted whisky distilled in Scotland and blended in Scotland or England. Although Scotch malt whiskies may owe some of their quality to the location of the distillery, it can hardly be said that the whole of Scotland is particularly suitable for whisky production, especially once it is admitted that the term "whisky" properly includes grain whisky distilled in

---

[56] *per* Dankwerts J. in *Bollinger v Costa Brava Wine Co Ltd* [1961] 1 W.L.R. 277; [1961] 1 All E.R. 561; [1961] R.P.C. 116.

[57] [1968] F.S.R. 625; [1969] R.P.C. 1 (Cross J.).

[58] *Bollinger v Costa Brava Wine Co Ltd*, above.

[59] *Vine Products Ltd v Mackenzie & Co Ltd*, above.

[60] See, in addition to the cases which follow, the *Swiss Chocolate* case, *Chocosuisse Union des Fabricants Suisse de Chocolat v Cadbury Ltd* [2000] R.P.C. 826, CA.

[61] [1970] 1 W.L.R. 917; [1970] 2 All E.R. 106; [1970] R.P.C. 489 (Foster J.). The same reasoning is implicit in *John Walker & Sons Ltd v Douglas McGibbon & Co* [1975] R.P.C. 506 (Court of Session) and *White Horse Distillers Ltd v Gregson* [1984] R.P.C. 61.

a patent still from imported cereals. For the whisky to be blended in Scotland or England was important only because that was where all the skilled blenders happened to be. Similarly in the *Harris Tweed*[62] case what distinguished tweed made on the Isle of Harris from tweed made on the mainland was that the islanders still made the tweed wholly by hand in their own crofts, whereas the mainland tweed was mass-produced in factories. In *Lang v Goldwell*[63] there was an arguable case[64] that the defenders were guilty of passing-off by selling a mixture of Scotch Whisky and English ginger wine under the name *Wee McGlen* and a tartan label. Consumers might suppose it to be a wholly Scottish product, but ginger wine is hardly part of Scotland's spiritous heritage.

Actionable misdescriptions defined in *Advocaat*

The cases on passing-off by the misuse of geographic terms are illustrations **7–131** of a wider principle that it may be passing-off to misuse any sufficiently significant descriptive or generic term in relation to goods, services or a business for which it is inappropriate. For the misrepresentation to be a material one the descriptive or generic term must have a reasonably definite meaning and some attraction for the customer, or no one would ever rely on it and any misrepresentation would be immaterial. In other words, it must have some drawing power in its own right The misrepresentation is actionable by a person damaged in the goodwil he has in relation to goods or services to which the term is properly applicable. There is a tendency to deny that terms like *Champagne* are descriptive or generic at all, reflecting the former dichotomy under which the only terms that could be protected were those which could be called "distinctive". For the purposes of passing-off it is better to say that they are generic terms with well-defined meanings, which may consequently be protected despite the fact that they are not distinctive in the traditional sense of denoting a specific producer.

In all the *Drinks Cases* prior to *Advocaat*[65] the origin of the goods in a specific geographical area was a necessary, but not sufficient, condition for them to be entitled to carry the name in question. It can hardly be doubted that it would be passing-off to describe an artificially carbonated sparkling wine as *Champagne* even if it came from the Champagne region. In the *Advocaat* case itself, *Erven Warnink v Townend*, the House of Lords affirmed the *Drinks Cases* and extended the tort to cases where there was no geographical element at all. The plaintiffs were producers and shippers of *Advocaat*. *Advocaat* was always made according to a specific formula but did not have to be made in any particular place. The defendants found that by making a similar drink fortified with sherry they could save on excise

---

[62] *Argyllshire Weavers Ltd v A Macaulay Tweeds Ltd* [1964] R.P.C. 477 (Lord Hunter, Court of Session).

[63] 1982 SLT 309; [1983] R.P.C. 289 (Court of Session, Inner House), reversing [1977] F.S.R. 353.

[64] The Outer House had held that there was no case for the defence to answer.

[65] *Erven Warnink BV v J Townend & Sons (Hull) Ltd* [1979] A.C. 731; [1979] 2 All E.R. 97; [1980] R.P.C. 31, HL.

duty. It was properly an Egg Flip, but they sold it as *Advocaat*. They did not suggest any connection with Holland. At first instance, Goulding J. granted an injunction. The Court of Appeal dissolved it, holding, on the authority of *Native Guano Co v Sewage Manure Co*[66] that when a name was purely descriptive the inaccurate use of it by one trader was not actionable at the suit of another who used it correctly. The House of Lords reversed the Court of Appeal and reinstated the injunction. Lord Diplock said:

"If a product of a particular character or composition has been marketed under a descriptive name and under that name has gained a public reputation which distinguishes it from competing products of different composition, I can see no reason in principle or logic why the goodwill in the name of those entitled to make use of it should be protected by the law against deceptive use of the name by competitors, if it denotes a product of which the ingredients come from a particular locality, but should lose that protection if the ingredients of the product, however narrowly identified, are not restricted as to their geographical provenance."

7–132 Lord Fraser agreed:

"In the *Champagne* case, as in this case, the class, membership of which gives the plaintiff the right to sue, consists of all those who sell the genuine product in England under the distinctive name by which it is known here, and who together are the owners of the goodwill or reputation attaching to the name in England. In that case, as in this, membership of the class may vary from time to time. An existing trader who discontinues sales of the genuine product of England would cease to belong to the class and the class would thereby be reduced. Conversely, a new trader who begins to sell the genuine product would become a member of the class when he had become well enough established to have acquired a substantial right of property in the goodwill attaching to the name. In either case the class is open to new members provided they qualify themselves by acquiring the necessary goodwill, which they can do by selling, in the one case under the name '*Champagne*' a wine made in Champagne by the correct process from grapes grown there, and in the other case under the name '*Advocaat*' a liqueur made according to the Dutch recipe. But although membership of the class can change, it must be definite and ascertainable at any particular time if is it to carry a right to sue in an action for passing-off."

The antecedents of *Advocaat*

7–133 The decision in *Advocaat* was not entirely unprecedented. In *Siegert v Findlater*[67] (the *Angostura Bitters* case) Fry J. granted an injunction restraining the use of the term, although *Angostura Bitters* was the name of the product as such and was apparently not distinctive of the plaintiff, who had called

---

[66] (1891) 8 R.P.C. 125, HL.
[67] (1878) 7 Ch.D. 801 (Fry J.).

his product *Aromatic Bitters*. The bitters were made according to a secret formula. The defendant's bitters did not have the same composition as the plaintiff's, so they could not accurately be described as *Angostura Bitters* at all. The distinction is illustrated by the fact that Fry J. accepted that if the defendant were to discover the plaintiff's formula, then he would be entitled to use the name *Angostura Bitters* provided he did nothing to encourage confusion with the plaintiff's goods. *Siegert v Findlater* may therefore be regarded as an early example of a defendant being restrained from misusing a generic term at the suit of a plaintiff (admittedly then the only plaintiff) who was using the term accurately.

A similar result was reached in the *Yorkshire Relish case, Powell v Birmingham Vinegar Brewery Co.*[68] The House of Lords found that *Yorkshire Relish* was distinctive of the plaintiff's goods in the normal way, but several Lords were also prepared to allow the action on the broader ground that the defendants' product was not *Yorkshire Relish* even in the generic sense because it was not made according to the formula used by the plaintiff. This distinction between the two causes of action, both of which they would have allowed, perhaps emerges most clearly from the speech of Lord Shand:[69]

> "The first objection to the proceedings of the defendants is that they called the article manufactured by them '*Yorkshire Relish*', when, in point of fact, it was not that article at all, as an article of commerce, that had been known in the market; and I think the plaintiff had a right of action to put a stop to an article, which could not possibly or reasonably be called '*Yorkshire Relish*', being sold under that name, on the ground of its being detrimental and injurious to him, as depriving him of a source of profit.
>
> But then, *in addition to that*, it humbly appears to me that there really was *de facto* representation here that the goods sold by the defendants were the goods of the plaintiff."

This interpretation of *Powell v Birmingham Vinegar Brewery* in terms of a misrepresentation of quality in addition to one of source seems to have occurred to some contemporary practitioners, but was too much for the House of Lords itself to tolerate. It was at the forefront of the plaintiffs' argument in *Magnolia Metal v Tandem Smelting Syndicate*[70] and recurred occasionally until *Horlicks Malted Milk v Summerskill*.[71] The House of Lords consistently disowned having had any such radical intention in the earlier case, and treated it, whether sincerely or disingenuously, as no more than an orthodox application of settled law to the facts.

---

[68] [1897] A.C. 710; 14 R.P.C. 721, HL.
[69] In a passage omitted from the Law Reports (emphasis added). See Anthony Walton, "A Pervasive but not Often Explicitly Characterised Aspect of Passing-off" [1987] E.I.P.R. 159.
[70] (1900) 17 R.P.C. 477, HL.
[71] (1916) 34 R.P.C. 63, HL.

Other predecessors of the *Drinks Cases*

7-134 There are other precursors of the *Drinks Cases* from as early as the nineteenth century, in a series of cases in which the defendant was using a geographical name which was in fact the name of the place where the plaintiff carried on business, and which the plaintiff claimed to be distinctive of him. In *Braham v Beachim*[72] the plaintiff owned and worked all the collieries in the parish of Radstock and used *Radstock* as part of the trade name of the business. The defendants adopted the name *Radstock Colliery Proprietors* and sold coal which was extracted at a colliery outside the parish. The coal came from the same seam and was similar in quality. Fry J. granted an injunction with the proviso that it was not to apply if the defendants were to obtain coal from a colliery within the parish. In *Free Fishers of Whitstable v Elliott*[73] Stirling J. granted an injunction against selling as *Whitstable Natives* oysters which had been spawned in France and imported to Whitstable to be raised. These could properly be described as *Whitstable* oysters but not as natives. At first, he seems to have treated the case correctly as raising the novel issue of passing-off by misdescription, but in the reserved judgment it is somewhat unconvincingly treated as one in which *Whitstable Native* was the trade name of the plaintiffs.

In *Rugby Portland Cement Co v Rugby & Newbold Portland Cement Co*,[74] *Whitstable Oyster Fishery Co v Hayling Fisheries*,[75] *Grand Hotel Co of Caledonia Springs v Wilson*[76] and *Hopton Wood Stone Firms v Gething*[77] the respective plaintiffs failed to prove that the place names in issue were distinctive of them; and in each case the defendant was only making fair and accurate use of the name to describe his own goods. These cases are therefore inconclusive as to whether misdescriptive use would have been restrained, but it is striking that in all these cases[78] the court went to some length to decide, not that the term was *publici juris*, but that it had some definite descriptive meaning which was equally applicable to the goods of the two parties.

"The plaintiffs sold their water as '*Caledonia Water*' at a time when they had no competitors in the sale of natural mineral waters from the place called Caledonia Springs, but in giving it that name they ran the risk of other persons discovering other springs in the same locality, and being entitled to sell other water as coming from the springs in that locality."[79]

---

[72] (1878) 7 Ch.D. 848 (Fry J.).
[73] (1888) 4 T.L.R. 273 (Stirling J.).
[74] (1892) 9 R.P.C. 46, CA.
[75] (1901) 18 R.P.C. 434, CA.
[76] [1904] A.C. 103; 21 R.P.C. 117, PC.
[77] (1910) 27 R.P.C. 605 (Parker J.).
[78] Except perhaps *Rugby Portland Cement Co Ltd v Rugby & Newbold Portland Cement Co Ltd* (1892) 9 R.P.C. 46, CA, where the defendants' right to use the term was self-evident.
[79] *per* Lord Davey in *Grand Hotel Co of Caledonia Springs v Wilson* [1904] A.C. 103; 21 R.P.C. 117, PC.

In *Smith v Fieldhouse*[80] the plaintiffs were the only company to quarry **7-135**
sand at Brereton in Cheshire. Another village called Brereton in Stafford
also produced sand. The defendants sold sand quarried elsewhere as Brereton Sand. Pennycuick J. granted an interlocutory injunction but qualified it
so as not to prevent the defendants from stating that their sand had come
from either Brereton if that were the case. Although *Smith v Fieldhouse* came
to be regarded as an example of passing-off by misdescription, Pennycuick
J. seems to have treated the defendants as implicitly misrepresenting their
sand as sand of the plaintiffs. However, he does not seem to have required
proof that *Brereton* had become distinctive of the plaintiffs in the normal
sense, and if it had been distinctive the proviso to the injunction would have
been inappropriate. In truth, *Smith v Fieldhouse* is halfway between passing-
off by misrepresentation of source and passing-off by misdescription.

Advocaat applied

The circumstances in which the allegedly untruthful use of a geographical **7-136**
name may be restrained as passing-off have been considered in a number of
decisions in the Court of Appeal subsequent to *Advocaat*.

In *Consorzio del Prosciutto di Parma v Marks & Spencer*[81] the Court of
Appeal decided that it was not passing-off to sell as "genuine 'Parma ham'"
pre-packed slices of Parma ham which met all the objective requirements of
Italian law except for the fact that the latter only permitted sliced Parma
ham to be sold as such if the slices were actually cut in the presence of the
consumer. The relevant Law was in fact being amended to allow Parma ham
to be so described if sliced and packed in the Parma Region under the
supervision of the *Consorzio*. The Court of Appeal held that ham did not
cease to be Parma ham when it was sliced and packed, and the defendants
could not be prevented from identifying it for what it really was. There was
not even an arguable misrepresentation of either provenance or quality.

In *Taittinger v Allbev*[82] the cause of complaint was a non-alcoholic drink
of flavoured carbonated water sold as *Elderflower Champagne* in bottles
with a similar get-up to that used for Champagne. The plaintiffs succeeded,
both on the narrow ground that the bottles and labels actually used would
be mistaken for a Champagne sold under the name *Elderflower*, and on the
broader one that the distinctiveness of the term *Champagne* would be eroded
if it were permitted to be used as the defendants proposed.

In *Chocosuisse v Cadbury*[83] the plaintiffs (a trade association and two **7-137**
individual Swiss chocolate manufacturers) complained of the sale by Cadbury of chocolate confectionery bars under the name *Swiss Chalet*, using get
up which included a representation of the Matterhorn, with a Swiss-style
chalet in the foreground. At first instance, Laddie J. held that the term

---

[80] [1961] R.P.C. 110 (Pennycuick J.).
[81] [1991] R.P.C. 351, CA. A subsequent case, *Consorzio del Prosciutto di Parma v ASDA*
[2001] UKHL 7; [2001] 1 C.M.L.R. 43; [2001] E.T.M.R. 53; [2002] F.S.R. 3; C–108/01 [2003] 2
C.M.L.R. 21 was concerned solely with Regulation 2081/92.
[82] [1994] 4 All E.R. 75; [1993] 2 C.M.L.R. 741; [1993] F.S.R. 641, CA.
[83] [2000] R.P.C. 326, CA.

"Swiss chocolate" was not merely descriptive but was perceived as distinctive premium product by a substantial proportion of the public. Laddie J. went on to define "Swiss chocolate", for the relevant purposes under *Advocaat*, as being chocolate made in Switzerland under the relevant Swiss food regulations. It followed that the two manufacturers had *locus standi* to sue, and that Cadbury were liable for misrepresentation, since their *Swiss Chalet* bar was made in England and complied with neither of these requirements. The Court of Appeal imposed a narrower definition of Swiss chocolate (without affecting the final result) by adding the requirement that it should contain no added vegetable fat or "cocoa butter equivalent". The latter, CBE, was permitted by Swiss legislation in small quantities but in fact none of the Swiss chocolate manufacturers used it and it was considered detrimental to quality. Real Swiss chocolate consumed in the United Kingdom was made without CBE, and this contributed to its characteristic smoothness.

It may be noted that it made little or no difference to Laddie J. or to the Court of Appeal that there was no agreement among the relevant public as to what made *Swiss chocolate* special, compared to chocolate in general. It is, in fact, a common feature of these cases that the objective definition of the product in question fails to correspond to the public state of mind, and it may even be said that success often depends on this mismatch. If the public knew, for instance, that *Champagne* was made exclusively from grapes gathered in the *Champagne* region of France then there would be no possibility of anyone being deceived by straightforward use of obviously self-contradictory terms such as *Spanish Champagne, Champagne Cider* or *Elderflower Champagne*. Success depends on there being at least a substantial minority of *Champagne* buyers confused enough as to what makes *Champagne* different. Taking *Taittinger v Allbev* at face value, does one have the paradoxical situation that Champagne's reputation for social exclusivity is protected precisely because it is undeserved?

Misuse of non-geographic descriptive or generic terms

7–138 The *Advoccat* case apart, there is relatively little authority to illustrate how far the reasoning of *Advocaat*[84] can be taken outside the field of geographical indications. It may therefore be helpful to take some examples from cases decided against the respective plaintiffs which would probably now be decided differently if appropriately pleaded. The House of Lords was able to distinguish the *Native Guano*[85] case in *Advocaat* because the former was decided on a pleading point, as was the *Magnolia*[86] case. Despite this, there can be little doubt what would have happened in those cases if the pleadings had been different.

In *Native Guano v Sewage Manure*[87] the plaintiffs had been the patentees

---

[84] *Erven Warnink BV v J Townend & Sons (Hull) Ltd* [1979] A.C. 731; [1979] 2 All E.R. 927; [1980] R.P.C. 31, HL.
[85] *Native Guano Co v Sewage Manure Co* (1891) 8 R.P.C. 125, HL.
[86] *Magnolia Metal Co v Tandem Smelting Syndicate Ltd* (1900) 17 R.P.C. 477, HL.
[87] (1891) 8 R.P.C. 125, HL.

for a process of producing fertiliser which they called *Native Guano*. The name may already have been in use, but in any event it became the generic name of the product. The defendants used the same name in relation to manure apparently produced by a different process. The plaintiffs sued for passing-off and inevitably failed to prove that the name denoted them. At a late stage they attempted to argue that misuse of the generic name was a fraud on the public, but it was held that no such argument was open on the pleadings and leave to amend was refused.

Similarly, in *Magnolia Metal v Tandem Smelting Syndicate*[88] the plaintiffs had used *Magnolia* as the name of a patented alloy. They claimed that the defendants used it in respect of another composition and that they had wrongly stated that their *Tandem* metal was the same as *Magnolia* metal. The case was again pleaded only in the traditional form that the defendants were passing off their goods as those of the plaintiffs. Counsel for the defendants were not called upon to argue the appeal to the House of Lords, although Lord Halsbury in the only judgment ostensibly left open the question of whether any such causes of action existed.

The plaintiff in *Fels v Christopher Thomas*[39] sold a soap as *Fels-Naptha* in which naptha was an important and novel ingredient. The defendants used the word *Naptha* for soap which according to the plaintiffs' expert evidence contained a different substance. The Court of Appeal held that "naptha" was a descriptive term, that the plaintiffs had failed to prove it had become distinctive of them, and that the presence or absence of naptha in the defendant's soap was immaterial.

J. Specific Products and Indications

Introduction

The majority of the decided cases on misuse of terms of geographical origin **7–139** concern drinks, specifically *Champagne, Sherry* and *Scotch Whisky*. The logical process by which this category of misrepresentation has come to be recognised as actionable is described above. The present section deals with individual instances in more detail, with the emphasis being on whether there has been an actionable misrepresentation on the facts of each case.

The law of passing-off does not create monopoly rights in names, marks, geographical indications or *appellations d'origine*, no matter how distinctive or prestigious. Success depends on proof that use of the term in question by the defendant constitutes a misrepresentation and is damaging to those having a goodwill in relation to the article properly so called, which generally means that consumers must rely on the misrepresentation in purchasing the defendant's product. Conversely, it is possible for there to be liability for passing-off without the defendant using one of these geo-

---

[88] (1900) 17 R.P.C. 477, HL.
[89] (1903) 21 R.P.C. 85, CA.

graphical terms at all, for instance because get-up or other indicia sufficiently indicate the goods' supposed origin.

Champagne

7–140 The very first of the English *Drinks Cases* concerned *Champagne*, with Dankwerts J. first deciding the preliminary point of law in favour of the *Champagne* houses and then holding on the facts that the term *Spanish Champagne* was misleading and damaging.[90] In *Bulmer v Bollinger*[91] the terms *Champagne Cider* and *Champagne Perry* were restrained by the trial judge, but on appeal by one plaintiff–the action being for a declaration–the Court of Appeal held by a majority that in the absence of evidence of actual confusion or deception it was not to be supposed that the Champagne Houses would have suffered any damage from the sale of the appellants' *Babycham* under the description *Champagne Perry*. It may have been relevant that the get-up of *Babycham* was very dissimilar to that used for *Champagne*, and *Babycham* was consciously aimed at a different and very specific market. In contrast, the get-up of Bulmer's *Pomagne* brand of *Champagne Cider* had deliberately imitated *Champagne* bottles, and Bulmer did not appeal. In *Taittinger v Allbev*[92] the plaintiffs initially obtained an interlocutory injunction[93] against a non-alcoholic drink of flavoured carbonated water sold as *Elderflower Champagne* in bottles imitating the typical *Champagne* get-up, lost at trial on the issue of damage, but succeeded on appeal.

In contrast to the situation in England, the Champagne houses have generally been less successful in the wine-growing common law countries, where, delay and acquiescence aside, consumers are more likely to be familiar with locally produced "Champagne" and to understand that not everything sold as *Champagne* is French. In the Australian case of *Comité du Vin de Champagne v Burton*[94] the plaintiffs failed to obtain interlocutory injunctions under s.52 of the Trade Practices Act 1974 against the use of *Champagne* or *Imported Champagne* for wines imported from countries other than France. The use of the terms was not misleading. The plaintiffs admitted they could not object to Australian wine being called *Champagne* and in fact wine from countries other than France had also been so called. In the Ontario case of *Institut des Appellations d'Origine v Andres*[95] the decision of the House of Lords in *Advocaat*[96] was followed both in allowing

---

[90] *Bollinger v Costa Brava Wine Co Ltd* [1960] Ch. 262; [1959] 3 All E.R. 800; [1960] R.P.C. 16 for the preliminary point of law. At trial [1961] 1 W.L.R. 277; [1961] 1 All E.R. 561; [1961] R.P.C. 116.
[91] [1977] 2 C.M.L.R. 625; [1978] R.P.C. 79, CA.
[92] [1993] F.S.R. 641, CA.
[93] [1992] F.S.R. 647 (Robert Reid Q.C., Deputy Judge).
[94] (1981) 57 F.L.R. 434; A.T.P.R. 128; 38 A.L.R. 664 (Franki J., Federal Court).
[95] (1987) O.R. (2d) 316; 14 C.I.P.R. 138; 16 C.P.R. (3d) 385; 40 D.L.R. (4th) 239 (Dupont J.); affirmed (1990) 30 C.P.R. (3d) 279 (Ontario Court of Appeal). The judgment on appeal is very brief.
[96] *Erven Warnink BV v J Townend & Sons (Hull) Ltd* [1979] A.C. 731; [1979] 2 All E.R. 927; [1980] R.P.C. 31, HL.

the concept of shared goodwill in a descriptive term, and in defining the three essential elements of passing-off as goodwill, misrepresentation and damage. However, there was no misrepresentation because *Canadian Champagne* (of which term the plaintiffs complained) was a distinct product and recognised as such by consumers. It had been produced since the 1920s with little evidence of any confusion. The intention of the Canadian producers to benefit from the reputation of French Champagne did not in itself amount to passing-off as long as there was no association of *Canadian Champagne* with the French product. The latter's high reputation had not suffered. The plaintiffs had not acquiesced, but delay would have barred them from an injunction.

In comparison to the Australian and Canadian decisions, and more consistently with *Taittinger v Allbev*,[97] the Court of Appeal of New Zealand found for the Champagne houses against imported Australian "Champagne" in *Comité Interprofessionel du Vin de Champagne v Wineworths Group*[98] under both the law of passing-off and s.9 of the New Zealand Fair Trading Act. Although some New Zealand sparkling wine had been sold as *Champagne*, none had remained on the market for long, and imports of "Australian Champagne" as such had been very slight until duties were reduced a year or so before commencement of the action. The trial judge concluded on the evidence that *Champagne* had not become generic for sparkling white wine in New Zealand and that it still denoted wine from the Champagne region in France.[99] "Australian Champagne" did not have a concurrent independent reputation in New Zealand and it was irrelevant that its sale as such would have been lawful in Australia.[1] While the trial judge had treated the action as virtually *quia timet*, the Court of Appeal was prepared to hold that damage could be inferred from erosion of distinctiveness of the term *Champagne*, following in this respect its own decision in *Taylor Bros v Taylor Group*.[2]

Sherry

In the first *Sherry* case, *Vine Products v Mackenzie*,[3] Cross J. held that **7–141** *Sherry* standing alone ordinarily meant wine from the Jerez district of Spain, although he went on to find in favour of the producers of *British Sherry* and the like on the ground of acquiescence. In the result, the (British) plaintiffs were granted declarations that they were entitled to use any of the expressions *British Sherry*, *English Sherry*, *South African Sherry*, *Cyprus Sherry*, *Australian Sherry* and *Empire Sherry*. However *Sherry* on its own still meant only the product of Jerez of Spain and an injunction was granted restraining

[97] Above.
[98] [1992] 2 N.Z.L.R. 327 (CA of NZ). Brendan Brown, "Generic Term or Appellation of Origin–Champagne in New Zealand" [1992] E.I.P.R. 176.
[99] [1991] 2 N.Z.L.R. 432 (Jeffries J.).
[1] *cf. Testut Freres v J E Lightbourne & Co Ltd* [1981] F.S.R. 458 (CA of Bermuda) deciding that the meaning of *Chablis* in countries outside Bermuda was irrelevant to a passing-off action there.
[2] [1988] 2 N.Z.L.R. 1 (CA of NZ).
[3] [1968] F.S.R. 625; [1969] R.P.C. 1 (Cross J.).

the plaintiffs from using the word other than for wine from Jerez, except as part of one of the permitted composite phrases.

In *Consejo Regulador de las Denominaciones "Jerez-Xeres-Sherry" y "Manzanilla de Sanlucar de Barrameda" v Mathew Clark & Sons*[4] Mervyn Davies J. granted an interlocutory injunction against a mixture of British Wine with a small amount of Spanish Sherry being sold as *Stones Original Pale Cream* with the explanation "Classic Aperitif–a select blend of Premium British Sherry and Fino Sherry from Spain" or "Classic Aperitif–a select blend of Premium British Sherry and Fine Fortified Wines from Spain" in much smaller type. There was at least an arguable case that the product would be taken as sherry, the balance of convenience and *status quo* favoured the plaintiffs, and deletion of the word "sherry" in the second version of the label did not affect liability for passing-off. The defendants' own marketing documents admitted that *Original Pale Cream* was "a sherry term" strongly associated with *Crofts* sherry, giving the relatively unusual situation that passing-off by generic misdescription was implicit in the choice of an otherwise unobjectionable brand name. Crofts were one of the plaintiffs, but the decision does not appear to rest on *Original Pale Cream* being distinctive of them in the normal sense.

Scotch whisky

7–142 The majority of cases on *Scotch Whisky* as such–as opposed to individual brands–have involved passing-off abroad and the doctrine of instruments of deception. The first *Scotch Whisky* case was *John Walker v Henry Ost*[5] in which the defendants were effectively restrained from selling bulk Scotch malt whisky with bottles and labels to Ecuador in the knowledge that it would be blended with locally distilled spirit and sold as *Scotch Whisky*. On similar facts the Court of Session found for the pursuers over the sale of whisky bottles and labels to Honduras in *John Walker v Douglas McGibbon*[6] and Nourse J. did the same over the sale of bulk whisky alone to Uruguay in *White Horse Distillers v Gregson.*[7] In *Lang Bros v Goldwell*[8] there was an arguable case that the defenders committed passing-off by selling a mixture of Scotch Whisky and English ginger wine under the name *Wee McGlen* and a tartan label.

In England, rather more equivocal misrepresentations have attracted the attention of the Scotch Whisky producers and the courts, and none of the

[4] [1992] F.S.R. 525 (Mervyn-Davies J.).
[5] [1970] 1 W.L.R. 917; [1970] 2 All E.R. 106; [1970] R.P.C. 489 (Foster J.).
[6] [1975] R.P.C. 506 (Lord Avonside, Court of Session). What was in issue was whether the pleadings stated a cause of action.
[7] [1984] R.P.C. 61 (Nourse J.). The reasoning must now be read in the light of *British Telecommunications plc v One in a Million Ltd* [1999] 1 W.L.R. 903, [1999] 4 All E.R. 476, [1999] E.T.M.R. 61; [1999] F.S.R. 1, CA.
[8] 1982 SLT 309; [1983] R.P.C. 289 (Court of Session, Inner House), reversing [1977] F.S.R. 353.

three cases which follows is entirely satisfactory. In *Scotch Whisky Association v J D Vintners*[9] the plaintiffs sued for passing-off and breach of European Community law[10] by the sale of a spirit as "Light Canadian Rye". This had a strength of 30 per cent alcohol, compared to a minimum strength of 40 per cent for whisky. It was alleged that the name "Light Canadian Rye" implicitly misrepresented the product as whisky properly so called. On an application to strike out part of the statement of claim Scott V.-C. agreed with the defendants that the first plaintiff had no cause of action in passing-off, though assuming–there being no argument to the contrary at that stage–that the alleged misrepresentation was actionable as passing-off at the suit of one of the other plaintiffs. In *Scotch Whisky Association v Glen Kella Distillers*[11] the defendants sold under the brand name *Glen Kella Manx Whiskey* and the description "white whiskey" a clear spirit drink which was prepared in the Isle of Man by re-distilling mature blended Scotch Whisky so as to remove all of the colouring, and some of the taste. Rattee J. held that the resulting product was not "whisky" as defined in Regulation 1576/89 and that its sale constituted passing-off. In *Gloag & Son v Welsh Distillers*[12] the defendants sold as "*SWY Y MOR* Welsh whisky" what was in fact a blend of Scotch whisky with various herbs, and which was a product of Wales only in the sense that Wales was where the final mixing and bottling took place. On an application by the defendants to strike out the statement of claim Laddie J. refused to do so, his reasoning being that the defendants' conduct was arguably within the emergent doctrine of reverse passing-off in that they were misrepresenting as Welsh whisky, what was really not Welsh at all but Scotch. It was conceded that the product was rightly called whisky.

In South Africa, two cases have dealt with the use of characteristically **7–143** Scottish indicia for whisky-based drinks not wholly from Scotland. Both were argued principally under the general law of unlawful competition which South Africa derives from Roman-Dutch law, but English passing-off authorities were among those applied.[13] In *William Grant v Cape Wine and Distillers*[14] the name *Macleans Gold Label Whisky* for a blend of Scotch with local spirit was considered deceptive in itself, and advertising material with a Scotsman in full Highland dress and the slogan *Ten years in Scotland Makes all the Difference* removed any doubt of what the defendants' intentions must have been, even before the story behind the choice of name emerged. The plaintiffs enjoyed the rare advantage of calling a witness who had attended the board meeting at which the crucial decision to market a predominantly South African whisky as *Macleans Gold Label Whisky* had been taken. *Maclean* was the family name of the witness, and he raised no

---

[9] [1997] Eu. L.R. 446 (Scott V.C.). The first plaintiff was a trade association suing in its personal, rather than representative, capacity. The two other plaintiffs (*Justerini & Brookes Ltd*, and *William Grant & Sons Ltd*) were whisky distillers and blenders.
[10] Regulation 1576/89.
[11] [1997] Eu.L.R 455; [1997] E.T.M.R. 470 (Rattee J.).
[12] [1998] F.S.R. 718 (Laddie J.).
[13] See Andrew Domanski, "Scotch Whisky and Unlawful Competition" (1991) 3 S.A. Merc. L.J. 89.
[14] 1990 (3) SA 897 (Berman J., CPD).

objection to its being used, but as his own given names (*Pieter Christiaan*) were unsuitable "for obvious reasons", his father's and son's name *William Henry Maclean* was adopted for the company responsible for the product, which duly changed its name from *Franschoeck Valley Wines Ltd* to *William H Maclean & Sons Ltd*. W. H. Maclean *fils* was appointed a director of the latter, but never attended a single board meeting.

Likewise, in *Long John International v Stellenbosch Wine Trust*[15] a product called *Ben Nevis Scotch Whisky Liqueur* with a Scottish theme to the label was enjoined. It apparently consisted of Scotch whisky diluted with water from its normal strength of 43 per cent alcohol to 30 per cent and sweetened with sugar.

K. INVERSE PASSING-OFF

The principle

7–144 The classic example of passing-off takes place when one trader represents his goods or business to be those of another trader with a better reputation. Inverse passing-off (or reverse passing-off) is the name sometimes given to the situation where the defendant takes the benefit of the claimant's reputation is a less direct way, by claiming that goods or services for which the claimant properly deserves the credit were in fact his. This assumes that the public do not know the claimant by name, but no problem arises on that score. The common law was for long ambivalent in its treatment of inverse passing-off but it is now established that inverse passing-off is indeed tortious and that it can be accommodated within the wider form of passing-off recognised since Advocaat. Inverse passing-off is not, therefore, a nominate tort in its own right but a further example of an actionable misrepresentation to which the normal principles of passing-off apply.[16]

Historically, the leading common-law example of inverse passing-off is probably the decision of the United States Supreme Court in *International News Service v Associated Press*[17] The plaintiffs (Associated Press) were a news agency with a monopoly of reports from the Allied Forces in the First World War. The defendants, a rival news agency reported this news by copying from the published bulletins of the Associated press and transmitting the news to their own subscribers, who published it without acknowledging its original source. No question of copyright infringement arose, because American requirements for registration and notice were not met. The Supreme Court was split in its decision. For present purposes the most relevant judgment is that of Justice Holmes with whom Justice McKenna concurred. He would have found in the plaintiffs' favour solely

---

[15] 1990 (4) SA 136 (Booysen J., Durban).
[16] It is so treated by W. L. Morison in "Unfair Competition and 'Passing-off': The Flexibility of a Formula" (1956) 2 Sydney Law Review 50. See also Anthony Walton, "A Pervasive But Not Often Explicitly Characterised Aspect of Passing-off" [1987] E.I.P.R. 159.
[17] (1918) 248 U.S. 215; 39 S.Ct. 68; 63 L.Ed. 211 (United States Supreme Court).

on the grounds that there had been no acknowledgement of the source of the news. Holmes J. rejected the idea of a general tort of misappropriation or unfair competition and based his judgment on an analogy with the law of passing-off, which still corresponded closely to English common law.

"The ordinary case is a representation by device, appearance, or other indirection that the defendant's goods come from the plaintiff. But the only reason why it is actionable to make such a representation is that it tends to give the defendant an advantage in business and it is thought undesirable that an advantage should be gained that way. Apart from that the defendant may use such unpatented devices and uncopyrighted combinations of words as he likes. The ordinary case, as I say, is palming off the defendant's product as the plaintiff's but the same evil may follow from the opposite falsehood from saying, whether in words or by implication, that the plaintiff's product is the defendant's, and that, it seems to me, is what has happened here.[18]

The falsehood is a little more subtle, the injury a little more indirect, than in ordinary cases of unfair trade, but I think that the principle that condemns the one condemns the other."

An intriguing anticipation of *International News* nearly occurred in **7–145** England. In *Walter v Steinkopff*[19] the defendant, publisher of *The St James' Gazette*, made a practice of publishing large extracts from other papers, including *The Times*. The proprietor of the latter sued for copyright infringement, but North J. referred to the fact that the defendant had acknowledged his sources in terms which suggested there would otherwise have been what could at least colloquially be called passing-off:

"A man cannot justify the taking of what he has no right to take by stating whence he has taken it, though he may thereby avoid the additional dishonesty of passing off as the product of his own labour what is really cribbed from another."

Inverse passing-off in English law: *Bristol Conservatories*

Any treatment of inverse passing-off in English law previously faced the **7–146** problem of attempting to reconcile two bodies of case law: the one refusing as a matter of principle to recognise inverse passing-off as actionable; the other being prepared to grant relief in what were in fact cases of inverse passing-off, but without expressly recognising them as such. However, the Court of Appeal has now come down in favour of recognising "inverse" passing-off in terms as explicit as those of Holmes J. in *International News* and to confirm that it falls within the tort of passing-off as such.

In *Bristol Conservatories v Conservatories Custom Built*[20] one of the

---

[18] This might almost have been written with the facts of *AGS Manufacturing Co Ltd v Aeroplane General Sundries Ltd* (1918) 35 R.P.C. 127, CA, in mind.
[19] [1892] 3 Ch. 489 (North J.).
[20] [1989] R.P.C. 455, CA.

individual defendants had worked for the plaintiffs as a salesman and had kept a book of photographs showing conservatories designed and built by the plaintiffs. On his joining the defendants, who were a newly established business, he and other salesmen used the photographs to show to prospective customers as examples of conservatories which the defendants had supposedly supplied. The plaintiffs successfully appealed from a decision of a Deputy High Court judge striking out the statement of claim as disclosing no reasonable cause of action. In a judgment with which the other members of the Court of Appeal concurred, Ralph Gibson L.J. preferred to follow the line of authorities comprising *Samuelson v Producers Distributing*,[21] *Plomien Fuel Economiser v National School of Salesmanship*[22] and *Henderson v Munroe*[23] and rejected the line of first instance cases to the opposite effect.[24] A final argument that Lord Fraser in *Advocaat* and the members of the House who agreed with him had confined passing-off to its classic form and one specific extension to cover the *Drinks Cases* was also rejected.

"I do not intend to decide whether there is a form of the tort to be known as reverse passing-off. It is sufficient, I think, to hold that the facts alleged can properly be regarded as within the tort of passing-off...

[T]he claim in passing-off is not ... ruled out because it is not alleged that any member of the public, looking at any of the photographs, would associate any conservatory with the plaintiffs. No person affected by the misrepresentation in *Samuelson's* case, or in the *Plomien* case, or in the *Henderson* case would have known who the plaintiff in any of those cases was. That did not stop the plaintiff being injured in his property rights in the business or goodwill. Nor would it matter if there was nothing in any photograph to link the conservatory there depicted with the plaintiffs in any way. Next, it would not matter that there was no allegation that there would be any confusion in the minds of the public. The concept of confusion, in my view, is irrelevant when the misrepresentation leaves no room for confusion. The prospective customer here is not left to perceive the difference between the two allegedly similar products, he is told simply and untruthfully that *Custom Built* designed and constructed the conservatories which provide the evidence for the experience, skill and reputation of the plaintiffs."[25]

Claim to credit due to claimant

7–147 Before *Advocaat*[26] the common law was inconsistent in how it treated cases in which the defendant claimed the benefit of prizes, testimonials or

---

[21] (1931) 48 R.P.C. 580, CA.

[22] (1943) 60 R.P.C. 209, CA.

[23] (1907) 7 F. 636 (Court of Session, Inner House).

[24] They were *Browne v Freeman* (1864) N.R. 476; *Batty v Hill* (1873) 1 H.&M. 268; *Tallerman v Dowsing Radiant Heat* [1900] 1 Ch. 1; *Cambridge University Press v University Tutorial Press* (1928) 45 R.P.C. 335 and *Serville v Constance* (1954) 71 R.P.C. 156.

[25] *per* Ralph Gibson L.J.

[26] *Erven Warnink BV v J Townend & Sons (Hull) Ltd* [1979] A.C. 731; [1979] 2 All E.R. 927; [1980] R.P.C. 31, HL.

recommendations properly belonging to the claimant. Apart from a few argued as injurious falsehood, the earlier cases largely depended on whether it could be said that this led to the passing-off of the defendant's goods or business for those of the claimant in the traditional sense, or whether it was a sufficient "badge of fraud" to justify finding for the claimant. This may now be seen to be an unduly narrow and artificial test. Those authorities decided in the claimant's favour can be justified on wider grounds and some decided for the defendant ought to be reconsidered.

In *Franks v Weaver*[27] an injunction was granted against the defendant misappropriating the plaintiff's testimonials, but this was treated as part of a wider scheme to pass off the defendant's goods as the plaintiff's. In *Chappell v Sheard*[28] and *Chappell v Davidson*[29] untrue claims by the respective defendants that songs published by them under the titles *Minnie Dale* and *Minnie, dear Minnie* had been sung with great success by a certain celebrated popular singer contributed to findings of passing off based mainly on the title *Minnie*, which was the name of the song she had actually performed.[30] In *National Starch Manufacturing Co v Munn's Patent Maizena & Starch Co*[31] the Privy Council extracted from the defendants in the course of the argument an undertaking to discontinue showing on their labels medals which had been won by the plaintiffs, but in the judgment this was dismissed as an advertising trick which had done the plaintiffs no harm:[32]

"[T]he statement in question would have demanded more serious consideration, and probably very different treatment, if, in their lordships' opinion it had formed part of a scheme designed with a view of appropriating the Appellants' custom, instead of being 'an advertising trick' as Owen J. describes it, not indeed very creditable to its authors, but yet one which could not, in the circumstances, deceive anybody into buying the Respondents' '*Maizena*' in the place of the Appellants."[33]

More recent cases have taken a more serious view of such advertisements. **7–148** In *Samuelson v Producers Distributing Co*[34] the plaintiff was the author under his stage name *Lawrie Wylie* of a humorous sketch, *The New Car*, which had been performed successfully before the King and Queen at a Royal Command Performance and had attracted favourable reviews. The defendants retained the principal comedian from the sketch to write and

---

[27] (1847) 50 E.R. 596.

[28] (1855) 69 E.R. 717 (Page Wood V.C.).

[29] (1855) 69 E.R. 719 (Page Wood V.C.), order varied (1856) 44 E.R. 289 (L.JJ.).

[30] All three songs were based on the same traditional American air, *Lillie Dale*, but the words and arrangements differed. The plaintiffs and both defendants published pictures of the singer in question on the title pages of their songs.

[31] [1894] A.C. 275; 11 R.P.C. 281, PC. See also *MedGen Inc v Passion for Life Products Ltd* [2001] F.S.R. 30.

[32] It had even less impact in *King (F) & Co v Gillard & Co* [1905] 2 Ch. 7; 22 R.P.C. 327, CA, where the defendants claimed they were entitled to decorate their soup mix packets with medals won for other goods.

[33] *per* Lord Ashbourne.

[34] (1931) 48 R.P.C. 580, CA.

perform a film version, which emerged as totally different to the original. The defendants used misleading quotations from newspaper reviews of the Command performance to advertise their film as if it was the sketch which had pleased the King and Queen. They argued that this was not passing-off but Lord Hanworth M.R. did not agree:

"It appears to me idle to say that this is not a passing-off. What was the purpose of what I have described as a moulding of the observations contained in *The Daily Telegraph*? To leave out *Lawrie Wylie* and refer to '*His First Car*' and not '*The New Car*'. '*His First Car*' was the title of the film of the defendants and they were adducing its success as appropriate to and belonging to their film '*His First Car*' when in truth and in fact it belonged to the plaintiff and his sketch '*The New Car*'. That seems to me to amount to a notice or invitation: 'Come and see our film and when you have seen our film you will have seen the sketch which has been spoken of in the manner which is stated in the passages which appear in the advertisement.' It appears to me quite clear that this was an attempt to pretend that the defendants' sketch was the same as the sketch which had made Her Majesty the Queen laugh."

Plomien Fuel Economiser v National School of Salesmanship[35] provides an even clearer example, with the following passage being taken from the judgment of Greene M.R.:

"[The defendants] represented that certain tests which had been made were tests in connection with the defendants' economiser, whereas in fact they were tests in connection with the plaintiffs' economiser. They represented that certain economisers which had been fitted for a number of purchasers, and which were in fact the plaintiffs' economisers, were the defendants' economisers, and in the correspondence which took place when they were negotiating for an order or had obtained an order for a trial, they then repeated in the most barefaced and dishonest manner those suggestions, stating that a number of customers, said to be satisfied customers, were customers for their article, whereas in fact they were customers who had ordered, and were satisfied with, the plaintiffs' article. . . .

If that is not passing-off, I really do not know what is. It is perfectly true, and I am willing to assume, that not one single customer who went to the shop . . . had ever heard of the plaintiffs or ever heard that they had put on the market an economiser. That, to my mind, matters not one bit when it is realised that those customers were coming with the intention of getting goods from a particular source, namely, the same source as those from which the satisfied customers had got their goods."

[35] (1943) 60 R.P.C. 209, CA.

Claimant's work used to promote defendant

A further example of inverse passing-off occurs when the defendant uses the **7–149**
claimant's work as an example of what he is capable himself. The definitive
example is now to be found in *Bristol Conservatories v Conservatories
Custom Built*.[36] The foregoing cases in which the defendant has misappropriated specific testimonials or recommendations may be regarded as
particularly blatant examples of this. However, it is not necessary for third
parties to have endorsed the claimant's goods or business for this form of
passing-off to have occurred. The defendant may expressly represent that he
was responsible for some achievement which may be expected to impress the
customer, or he may do so implicitly, for instance, by marking the claimant's goods with his own name or submitting them as samples of his own
work.

In *Bullivant v Wright*[37] the plaintiffs and defendants were competing
manufacturers of aerial cableways. The defendants issued advertisements
showing various installations they claimed to have supplied, but which in
fact had been made by the predecessors in title of the plaintiffs. Kekewich J.
admitted that an action lay in principle to restrain this, but refused relief
because it was not the plaintiffs themselves who could claim to have provided the installations shown.

The pursuers and defenders in *Henderson v Munro*[38] competed in drilling
artesian wells. The defenders hired the former manager of the pursuers and
issued advertisements referring to his personal experience, but also giving a
list of wells drilled by him for his former employers in terms which suggested
they had been drilled by the defenders. The Court of Session granted an
interdict.

In *Masson, Seeley v Embossotype*[39] the plaintiffs supplied machines and
materials for producing cardboard and paper lettering for use in displays.
The machines required special type and card or paper which the plaintiffs
selected from various sources as the best available. In the case of the type
they had an exclusive contract with a foreign manufacturer. They issued a
catalogue and samples showing these typefaces and materials. The defendants copied the plaintiffs' catalogue and samples, and used them to sell
inferior goods.[40] Tomlin J. held that there was passing-off and granted an
injunction restraining the defendants from "representing or acting by means
of the issue of catalogues, samples or otherwise in such a way as to induce
the belief that the goods being supplied by them are in origin and character
the same as the goods supplied by the plaintiffs".

The plaintiff in *Dwarkadas v Lachland*[41] had a monopoly in the sale in **7–150**

---

[36] [1989] R.P.C. 455, CA, above.
[37] (1897) 13 T.L.R. 201 (Kekewich J.).
[38] 7F (Ct. of Sess.) 636; 42 Sc. L.R. 530, 13 S.L.T. 57 (Scot.).
[39] (1924) 41 R P.C. 160 (Tomlin J.).
[40] They may also have used actual samples of the plaintiffs: the judgment is not entirely clear
on this point. There was passing-off by using vouchers of the plaintiffs in *Fairest (Arthur) Ltd v
Fairest* (1949) 66 R.P.C. 275.
[41] [1932] All Ind. Re. Sind 222, cited in Morison *op. cit.* from which this summary is taken.

India of certain cloth from Manchester. The defendant bought some of the plaintiff's cloth, cut off the plaintiff's mark, and sold it to wholesalers who concluded that the defendant had direct connections with the manufacturers. This was held to be actionable.

In the Canadian case of *Therapeutic Research Corp. v Life Aid Products*[42] the defendants issued a leaflet containing photographs of an oxygen mask which was stated to be the defendants' product and obtainable from no one else. It was also incorrectly claimed that the defendants had applied for patents on it. In fact, it was a mask of the plaintiffs' with the defendants' label stuck over theirs. The Exchequer Court granted an injunction under s. 7(e) of the Trade Marks Act 1952–3 which is derived from Art. 10*bis* of the revised Paris Convention and prohibits "any act or ... any other business practice contrary to honest industrial or commercial usage in Canada". Despite the apparent breath of these words they had been construed as *ejusdem generis* with subsections which effectively give Federal statutory recognition to the traditional form of passing-off. It is suggested the decision could now be justified under the general law of passing-off.

7–151   Now that inverse passing-off is well accepted in principle, attention can turn to the question of whether or not there is a sufficiently material misrepresentation in a given case to create liability. For there to be passing-off there must be a misrepresentation, and it must be a material one in the sense that the customer relies on it to the claimant's disadvantage. For there to be inverse passing-off the misrepresentation must relate to the capacity of the defendant to produce the goods or services in question. This would apply, for instance, if the re-labelled goods were submitted as samples to a trade buyer. If the general public are simply presented in a shop with goods bearing the defendant's name they are unlikely to conclude that he must have been the actual manufacturer: subcontracting is far too prevalent for that. Nor, if they did, would the sale of the claimant's goods to the general public under the defendant's name necessarily damage the claimant.

In *Chater v Rose*[43] the use of the slogan *It's Back* for the defendants' production of *Peter Pan* might have amounted to passing-off, if it had suggested that the defendants' pantomime in 1993 was the same as or associated with the plaintiffs' production of the pantomime at the same theatre in 1991, but the offending material was withdrawn and the point was not decided. In the Singapore case of *John Robert Powers School v Tessensohn*,[44] the use of the plaintiffs' lecture notes at the defendants' self-development school did amount to inverse passing-off, but statements in the defendants' literature to which the plaintiffs objected were merely "puffing" rather than an attempt to misappropriate credit properly due to the plaintiffs. The emergent doctrine of reverse passing-off was invoked by Laddie J. to justify refusing to strike out the statement of claim in *Gloag & Son v Welsh Distillers*,[45] but it is doubtful if the case really bears that description. True, the defendants' *Welsh Whisky* was in fact made from Scotch, but it is

---

[42] [1968] 2 Ex. C.R. 605 (Can.).
[43] [1994] F.S.R. 491 (Jacob J.).
[44] [1995] F.S.R. 947 (CA, Singapore).
[45] [1998] F.S.R. 718 (Laddie J.).

not obvious that this was either material or damaging. In *BBC v Talksport*[46] the BBC held the sole right to provide live radio broadcasts of the European Football Championships 2000. The defendants broadcast commentary from watching live television broadcasts, with the addition of spurious ambient sound effects to give the impression that their broadcasts were live from inside the stadium. Certain undertakings were given, but a more extensive interlocutory injunction was refused.

Claim to be "original" or "patented"

Two instances of inverse passing-off which deserve specific mention are false **7-152** claims to be the "original" business or product and false claims to patent protection. In the early case of *Brown v Freeman*[47] the plaintiff failed to show that anyone had been deceived by the defendant's false description of his medicine as *Original Chlorodyne* (*Chlorodyne* probably being generic) and an interlocutory injunction was refused, but to the extent that the case stood for a wider principle it was disapproved of by the Court of Appeal in *Bristol Conservatories v Conservatories Custom Built*.[48] In *Cocks v Chandler*[49] the defendant was restrained from describing his imitation of the plaintiff's sauce as *The Original Reading Sauce, Reading* Sauce itself being the generic name of the article. The case was expressly argued on the basis that there were two misrepresentations: one depending on the composite phrase being distinctive of the plaintiff in the normal sense and the other on its simply being factually inaccurate as used by the defendant.[50]

The frequency with which plaintiffs in the nineteenth century misrepresented their products as patented suggests that customers at that time were influenced by such a claim.[51] It may be doubted if this is any longer the case, but in principle a claim by the defendant that his goods were patented when in fact this was true only of the claimant ought to be actionable as passing-off provided that damage can be proved. *Ormond Engineering v Knopf*,[52] sometimes cited as authority to the contrary, turned on the lack of damage to the plaintiffs but is still too restrictive in its reasoning. For a case in which the defendants misrepresented their goods as manufactured under a specific patent actually worked by the plaintiffs one need look no further than *Spalding v Gamage*,[53] but this misrepresentation was obscured by more material ones.

In *Chub v Priest*[54] an injunction was granted against a defendant who had

---

[46] [2001] F.S.R. 6 (Blackburne J.).
[47] (1864) 12 W.R. 305 (Page-Wood V.C.).
[48] [1989] R.P.C. 455, CA.
[49] (1871) L.R. 11 Eq. 446. See the comments in *Jacques (John) & Son Ltd v Chess* [1940] 2 All E.R. 285; 57 R.P.C. 77, CA.
[50] See also *James v James* (1872) L.R. 13 Eq. 421.
[51] The Patent Act 1835 (5 & 6 Wm 4 c. 83) s.6 (repealed) prescribed a penalty, recoverable in a common informer action, for misrepresenting goods as patented or produced under the licence of the patentee. See *Myers v Baker* (1858) 157 E.R. 691.
[52] (1932) 49 R.P.C. 634.
[53] (1915) 32 R.P.C. 273, HL. The patent number was actually misidentified.
[54] (1843) 1 L.T. (O.S.) 142.

advertised and sold his own safes as *Chub's Patent Fire-Proof Safe*. In *Lawrie v Baker*[55] the defendant was restrained from supplying his own goods in response to orders for "patent cups", but an alternative explanation is that the term had acquired secondary meaning.[56] A slightly clearer example is to be found in *Pneumatic Rubber Stamp Co v Lindler*[57] where nominal damages were awarded for a misrepresentation that the defendant's goods were licensed under the plaintiffs' patent, although a conventional allegation of passing-off had failed. In *Post Card Automatic Supply v Samuel*[58] Stirling J. allowed the defendants in a patent infringement action to treat a licence to them as repudiated and to challenge the validity of the patent, but ordered them to remove the words "manufactured under licence ..." from their goods.

L. Denial of Existence, Business Connection or Independence

Assertion that claimant does not exist or does not trade

7–153 It is actionable as injurious falsehood to misrepresent that a trader has ceased to trade or has completely ceased to exist, provided the other elements of the tort are present. The same principle applies where the misrepresentation is that the trader does not trade in a particular line of goods,[59] or is unavailable at a particular time,[60] or address.[61] The misrepresentation may be made expressly, or by implication.

In the leading case of *Ratcliffe v Evans*[62] a newspaper published a report that the plaintiff firm *Ratcliffe & Sons* had ceased to trade as engineers and boiler makers, and no longer existed. At trial the jury found that the statement was not made *bona fide* and awarded £120 damages. The case is reported in the Court of Appeal solely on the point of whether evidence of a general dropping off of trade was sufficient proof of special damage, but there seems no reason to doubt the correctness of the rest of the decision, which has been applied since.

In *Jarrahdale Timber v Temperley*[63] both parties imported *Jarrah* timber from Australia, as did many other firms, but the defendants were the only

---

[55] (1885) 2 R.P.C. 213.
[56] *Spratt's Patent v Ward* (1879) L.R. 11 Ch.D. 240 clearly distinguishes the two potential misrepresentations, but is only reported on a procedural point. The very early case of *Sykes v Sykes* (1824) 107 E.R. 834 is normally understood in terms of *Sykes Patent* having acquired secondary meaning.
[57] (1898) 15 R.P.C. 525.
[58] (1889) 6 R.P.C. 560 (Stirling J.).
[59] *Jarradale Timber Co Ltd v Temperley & Co* (1894) 11 T.L.R. 119, below; *Danish Mercantile Co v Beaumont* [1950] R.P.C. 111.
[60] *Shapiro v La Morta*, CA, below.
[61] *Joyce v Motor Surveys Ltd* [1948] Ch. 252, below.
[62] [1892] 2 Q.B. 524, CA.
[63] (1894) 11 T.L.R. 119 (QB Divisional Court).

importers of *Karri* timber. The defendants issued advertisements saying that they were the only firm to import both *Jarrah* and *Karri*. The plaintiffs complained that this would be understood as meaning that Temperley were the sole importers of *Jarrah*, with the implication that it could be obtained from no one else. An interlocutory injunction was granted, and an appeal dismissed because the two-judge Divisional Court could not agree.

In *Worsley v Cooper*[64] the defendants left the employment of the plaintiff to set up a competing business. The first defendant had been the sales director of the plaintiff company, and he issued a circular creating the impression that the plaintiff company had gone out of business and that the defendants were their successors. Morton J. held that the circular was actionable as passing off, without evidence of malice, and that on the facts it constituted a malicious falsehood of the *Ratcliffe v Evans* kind. A similar misrepresentation was also conveyed by the wording of a business card.

Ratcliffe v Evans[65] was also applied in *Joyce v Motor Surveys*[66] where the **7–154** plaintiff carried on business as a motor tyre agent. To obtain tyres at a trade discount, he had to be registered with the relevant trade association, and to qualify for registration he had to have suitable premises, which consisted of a lock-up garage he rented from the defendants. The defendants also took in his letters and answered telephone calls for him. The defendants purported to terminate his tenancy so they could sell the whole premises with vacant possession, and while the validity of the notice to quit was in issue and the plaintiff was still in occupation[67] they took a number of steps to drive him out: tyre manufacturers were notified that he was no longer a tenant of theirs; his letters were returned to the Post Office with an explanation that he had gone away; and telephone callers (including the local secretary of the tyre manufacturers' association) were told that he and his son were unavailable. All this had the effect that the plaintiff was removed from the association's register, and was unable to buy tyres, or communicate with customers or suppliers. Roxburgh J. found for the plaintiff.

On the other hand, in *Plant Location International v Yaseen*[68] statements made by the defendants to the effect that the plaintiff company had closed down, though inaccurate and self-evidently likely to cause it damage, had been made through carelessness rather than any improper motive and had subsequently been corrected. An interlocutory injunction was refused.

The same principle applies when the supposed reason for the claimant not **7–155** being available for business is temporary. So it may be actionable as injurious falsehood to say of a professional musician that she has a non-existent prior engagement, with the implication that she is unable to perform for anyone else during its currency. Such were the facts of *Shapiro v La Morta*[69] in which the plaintiff was billed as the piano accompanist for a week's concerts by a vocalist whom she had accompanied on five previous

---

[64] [1939] 1 All E.R. 290 (Morton J.).
[65] Above.
[66] [1948] Ch. 252 (Roxburgh J.).
[67] The issue was subsequently decided in the his favour.
[68] [1964] R.P.C. 345 (Buckley J.).
[69] [1923] All E.R. 378, CA.

occasions, although she had in fact turned the engagement down. The action failed because the manager had issued the offending posters in good faith, but the Court of Appeal accepted that if malice had been present she could have recovered damages for any engagements lost as a result. Loss of one engagement was proved, but it was the consequence of the original *bona fide* publication.

In *Grappelli v Derek Block*[70] the defendants, who represented the plaintiff jazz violinist and his trio, accepted bookings for a tour of England without his authority. When the engagements had to be cancelled, the agent invented the excuse that "Stephane Grappelli is very seriously ill in Paris and I would be surprised if he ever toured again". Lord Denning M.R. accepted that this was actionable as injurious falsehood.

> "Mr. Grappelli says that that was an entirely false statement about his health: it was known by the agents to be false. They put it forward as an excuse to get themselves out of the unauthorised engagements. If it was a false statement, maliciously made, which would cause damage, it would give rise to a cause of action for injurious falsehood. A cause of action has been brought accordingly."[71]

However, a claim for defamation based on a supposed innuendo that the plaintiff was malingering to evade his contractual commitments was struck out.

7–156   An allegation that the claimant is insolvent might appear at first sight to be one degree less damaging than an allegation that he has actually ceased business altogether, but it is in fact more insidious and may be defamation properly so-called.[72] While the kind of allegation of *Ratcliffe v Evans*[73] or *Joyce v Motor Surveys*[74] is inherently self-defeating unless the claimant is so small, vulnerable, or inconspicuous as to go unnoticed, an allegation that even a large and flourishing business is in financial difficulties is not inherently implausible, and may become self-fulfilling if it is not restrained.

In the South African case of *Abakor v Crafcor Farming*[75] there was actionable unlawful competition (*semble* both injurious falsehood and defamation) by the defendants issuing a circular letter to local farmers and landowners stating that the plaintiffs' abattoir faced imminent closure, as a prelude to applying for planning permission for building an abattoir of their own. The recipients would take the reference to imminent closure as implying that the plaintiffs were in a desperate financial situation.

---

[70] [1981] 1 W.L.R. 822; [1981] 2 All E.R. 272, CA.
[71] *per* Lord Denning M.R.
[72] See the cases reviewed in *Aspro Travel Ltd v Owners Abroad Group* [1996] 1 W.L.R. 133, CA, in which an allegation that the plaintiff company had been trading while insolvent was pursued by the individual plaintiffs, its directors, on the basis that it was defamatory to accuse them of causing or permitting it to do so. The action by the company settled.
[73] [1892] 2 Q.B. 524, CA.
[74] [1948] Ch. 252 (Roxburgh J.).
[75] 2000 (1) SA 973 (Natal).

Denial of business connection

A misrepresentation, express or implicit, that the claimant lacks some **7–157** advantageous connection with the defendant or a third party may amount to injurious falsehood, *Joyce v Motor Surveys*[76] being one such a case in so far as the plaintiff was at all times the tenant of the defendant. In *Danish Mercantile Co v Beaumont*[77] the defendant falsely claimed that a company formed by him (which did not even exist) was the sole importer and distributor of a certain brand of sugar beet harvester. The plaintiffs, who were in fact sole importers of the machinery in question under a contract with the Danish company, obtained an interlocutory injunction.

Conversely, in *Balden v Shorter*[78] the plaintiff had been a salesman with the defendant's predecessor in business, but had left for other employment when the former company went into liquidation and the defendant bought up the name and goodwill. A customer of the former business placed an order after expressly having it confirmed to him that the plaintiff was still an employee and would receive the commission on it. The action failed because the false statement had been made carelessly and as a result of a mistake. Maugham J. would have held that if the speaker had known the plaintiff had left for good, then the case would have been one to justify the inference that knowledge of falsity was sufficient proof of malice.

In *Hong Kong Wing On v Hong Thai Citizens Travel*[79] the defendants had **7–158** in fact been appointed as "exclusive agents" in respect of packaged visits to a pop concert on the Chinese mainland, but overstepped the mark by issuing an advertisement stating that rival tours offered by the plaintiffs were unauthorised and that their ticket holders risked being refused admission. The tickets had in fact been legitimately purchased. The defendants knew that the allegation was false (or were recklessly indifferent), and were also malicious in the sense of having the predominant purpose of injuring the plaintiffs. Damages of HK$30,000 were awarded.

> "In the round, therefore, the Announcement is false. It is false insofar as it suggests that the plaintiff required but did not have permission or authority to organise packaged tours to attend the Concerts and that the organisers were in a position to refuse to allow the plaintiff's tour group members who held valid tickets to attend the concert."[80]

Assertion that claimant lacks independence

In principle, a false assertion that the claimant lacks independence from the **7–159** defendant (or a third party) should be actionable as injurious falsehood if the other elements of the cause of action are met. In practice, injurious falsehood is likely to be the preferred cause of action only if the assertion is

---

[76] [1948] Ch. 252 (Roxburgh J.).
[77] [1950] R.P.C. 111 (Roxburgh J.).
[78] [1933] Ch. 427 (Maugham J.).
[79] [2001] H.K.L.R.D. 481 (Chu J.).
[80] *per* Chu J.

unusually explicit and the cause of action cannot be framed as one for passing-off. Since almost any unspecified allegation of a connection between the parties is capable of amounting to passing-off, and since the latter action is very much easier to succeed in than that for injurious falsehood, it is not surprising that examples are rare.

In *Anheuser Busch v Budejovicky Budvar*[81] there were claims both for passing off and for injurious falsehood. The passing off claim raised the question of whether the American plaintiffs or the Czech defendants, if either, had exclusive rights to the name *Budweiser* for beer in the United Kingdom when sales by either party had been at a very low level. The claim for injurious falsehood was based on the third defendants distributing to the trade some leaflets in which it was stated

"There is a very marginal awareness of the use of the Budweiser name for an American beer, brewed in the U.S.A. under Czechoslovak licence. It is limited to those who have been to the U.S.A. or have regular contact with Americans. This connotation, to the very minor extent to which it exists, in no way adversely affects or creates difficulties for the acceptance of the Czechoslovakian derivation of the original and true product, a strong beer brewed in a traditional way."

The statement that the American beer was brewed under Czechoslovakian licence was plainly false, and the individual responsible for making it had no reason to believe it was true and was unable to explain how he came to have made it. However Whitford J. dismissed the injurious falsehood claim because the statement had not been made maliciously, and was upheld in the Court of Appeal.

M. Outright Disparagement and Denigration

Assertion that claimant's goods or services unsuitable or inadequate

7–160 Untrue statements that the claimant's goods or services are significantly defective or deficient in some way are *prima facie* actionable as injurious falsehood, provided that the other requirements of the tort are met. Practical complications are likely to include proof of malice, though this may be inferred if the statement was known to be false; proof that the statement referred to the claimant; the near-impossibility of obtaining an interlocutory injunction if there is a defence of justification;[82] and, in older cases, the need for proof of special damage.

Unequivocal statements disparaging the claimant's goods in absolute terms or by reference to some objective or extrinsic standard are to be distinguished from those which compare them unfavourably, and perhaps

---

[81] [1984] F.S.R. 413, CA.
[82] *Bestobell Paints Ltd v Bigg* and *Crest Homes Ltd v Ascott*, both below.

unfairly, to those of the defendant or a third party, which are not so readily actionable.[83]

In *Alcott v Millar's Karri and Jarrah Forests*[84] the parties were competitors **7–161** in providing wooden blocks for street paving, the plaintiffs being the importers and agents for American red gum blocks. The defendants wrote to the local council responsible for paving Oxford Street, saying that American red gum blocks laid elsewhere in London had gone rotten after six to 18 months. The plaintiffs' tender was still accepted, but with a retention from the contract price. The jury found for the plaintiffs, and the verdict was upheld on appeal. One may compare *Griffiths v Benn*[85] in which an action responding to intemperate and politically motivated attacks on the safety and cost-effectiveness of the plaintiffs' patented tramway system succeeded at first instance but failed on appeal. The underlying (if unstated) distinction may have been the court's greater concern for freedom of expression in the political arena.

In *Gaskell & Chambers v Hudson Dodsworth*[86] the allegation alleged to constitute injurious falsehood was that the plaintiffs' apparatus for serving beer was "obsolete and anti-hygienic", but the case is only reported for the proposition that the defendants were not committing a contempt of court by describing the statement of claim as a "cock and bull" story by their "rabidly jealous" competitors, and copying it to their own customers.

In *London Ferro Concrete v Justicz*[87] the parties were competing sub- **7–162** contractors for a building project. After the plaintiffs' tender had been accepted, the defendant wrote to the main contractor saying that the plaintiffs' proposed method of construction was not adequate. At trial, Vaisey J. found for the plaintiffs:

"To say that the method which involved the use of the scarf-joint was inadequate, or not adequate, is, in my judgment, as disparaging a statement as can well be imagined. To say that something is 'adequate' means that it will serve its purpose, though not necessarily in the best or most approved way; to say it is 'inadequate' is equivalent to saying that it will not do at all. When applied to a particular engineering process, the word would signify, as it appears to me, that the process would be rejected and ruled out by any experienced or reputable engineer. It has a far stronger connotation than words indicating inferiority, or the second-rate, or a capacity for improvement."

The evidence was that similar buildings had been built with the plaintiffs' construction without problem, that the defendant's expressed view was not representative of professional opinion, and that although he believed his own form of construction to be preferable, he did not sincerely doubt the suitability of that proposed by the plaintiffs.

---

[83] *Schulke & Mayr UK Ltd v Alkapharm UK Ltd* [1999] F.S.R. 161. See para.7–174 below.
[84] (1904) 91 L.T. 722; 21 T.L.R. 30, CA.
[85] (1911) 27 T.L.R. 346, CA.
[86] [1936] 2 K.B. 595 (Divisional Court).
[87] (1951) 68 R.P.C. 65, affirmed (1951) 68 R.P.C. 261, CA.

7–163   In principle, the supposed inadequacy or unsuitability of the claimants' products may be inferred from the terms in which the defendant advertises his own, even if the claimant is not identified, although this is inevitably harder to make out. In *Ucan v Hilti*[88] the plaintiffs had an arguable claim for injurious falsehood, subject to proving malice, in respect of an advertisement by Hilti claiming that their tools were the only ones approved to an official British Standard. Ucan and Hilti were bitter rivals, and the competitive Ucan tools had been approved before the Hilti advertisement had been published. However, an interlocutory injunction was refused because malice had not been established, and the defendants had undertaken not to repeat the advertisement.

7–164   In *Bestobell Paints v Bigg*[89] the defendant property developers painted a house with the plaintiffs' *Carson* brown paint, but after six months the paint turned green in patches, producing a multicoloured camouflage-like effect, so that "what the building gained in originality it lost in aesthetic appeal" and presumably also in market value. There was a difference of opinion and evidence as to whether this was the result of a defect in the paint, or poor workmanship. The house was very near a busy main road, and to put pressure on the plaintiffs to settle their demand for compensation the defendants erected on it a sign reading "This house is painted with <u>CAR-SON'S</u> paint". Oliver J. agreed that the gravamen of the sign was that Carson's paint was inferior and liable to change colour, that the accusation was made maliciously and that it was likely to cause pecuniary damage, but refused an interlocutory injunction because the defendants intended to justify the innuendo.

Likewise, in *Crest Homes v Ascott*[90] a dissatisfied purchaser of a new house from the plaintiffs removed its front door (which had begun to shrink and crack, and from which the paint was peeling off), repainted it in red and yellow with an inscription critical of their workmanship and after-sales service, and attached it to the front of his Rolls-Royce. The Court of Appeal discharged an interlocutory injunction restraining him from "publishing or displaying a door with painted markings on it referring to the plaintiffs".

Assertion that claimant's goods not "genuine"

7–165   Statements that the claimant's goods are spurious, counterfeit or otherwise not the genuine article are generally speaking more serious than mere allegations that they infringe an intellectual property right of some kind, and may shade into libel or slander as well as injurious falsehood.[91] Cases in which the claimant was successful against blatant and unequivocal misrepresentations of this kind tend to come from the late nineteenth century,

---

[88] [1968] F.S.R. 248 (Cross J.).
[89] [1975] F.S.R. 421 (Oliver J.).
[90] [1980] F.S.R. 396, CA.
[91] For "threats actions" and the modern treatment of false allegations of infringement in general, see Section O below. See also *Easycare Inc v Lawrence* [1996] F.S.R. 597, at para.7–203 below.

while the law was still in the process of development and the boundaries of what was or was not permissible were unclear.[92]

In *James v James*[93] the formerly secret recipe of *Lieutenant James' Horse Blister* (an ointment for horses) came into the possession of the defendant, who competed with the original business carried on by the plaintiff. The defendant's advertisements stated that his was the only genuine item, and any others spurious. Lord Romilly M.R. held that although the defendant was entitled to make and sell *Lieutenant James' Horse Blister* he should distinguish himself by the use of his full name, and should not assert that his was the only one, or that the plaintiff's product was not genuine.

In *Thorley's Cattle Food v Massam*[94] the executors of the late Joseph Thorley, after being refused an interlocutory injunction against alleged passing off, published newspaper advertisements and circulars stating that they alone possessed the secret of manufacture of *Thorley's Food for Cattle*, and warning that that a company which could be identified as the plaintiffs was selling an inauthentic imitation. The Court of Appeal subsequently held in the passing-off action that *Thorley's* was not a generic name and that the plaintiff company (in the action for injurious falsehood) was liable for passing-off by selling cattle food under that name, and with confusingly similar get-up. However there was no longer any question of any secret or proprietary recipe, the company's cattle food was no different in composition to that sold by the executors, and the latter had overstepped the mark in issuing a circular in which they accused the company of "seeking to foist upon the public an article which they pretend is the same as that manufactured by the late Joseph Thorley", as well as an advertisement asserting that the executors alone possessed the secret of compounding the food.

In *Thomas v Williams*[95] Fry J. granted an injunction against the dis- **7–166** tribution in Australia, by the English defendant, of a circular stating that the defendant had made arrangements to represent the needle-making firms of *Holyoake* and *Millward* in the export trade. There had been several *Holyoake* and *Millward* businesses, to some of which the plaintiffs were the legitimate successors. The sting of the circular lay in its opening words: "Knowing the number of spurious makes of needles extant, we have made arrangements with the original firm of *Thomas*, the original and only manufacturers of the name of *Holyoake*, etc". The implication that spurious *Thomas* and *Holyoake* needles were on the market could only be taken as referring to the plaintiffs.

"These being the facts, the question arises what is the meaning of this circular, and how would it be understood by a person having a knowledge of the Australian trade corresponding with the facts which I have just

---

[92] A rare example in modern law is *McManus v Beckham* [2002] EWCA Civ 939; [2002] 1 W.L.R. 2982; [2002] 4 All E.R. 497; [2002] E.M.L.R. 40, CA, in which the defendant was alleged to have complained publicly that autographed memorabilia sold in the claimants' shop were fake.
[93] (1872) L.R. 13 Eq. 421 (Lord Romilly M.R.).
[94] (1879) 14 Ch. D. 763, CA.
[95] (1880) 14 Ch. D. 864 (Fry J.).

stated? It appears to me that it can mean nothing else than this, that the needles of *Samuel Thomas & Sons* sold under their name are not an honest, independent make of needles, but are intended to imitate the needles of *J. Thomas & Sons*–that they are a spurious make of needles; and in like manner I think that it is intended to affirm that the needles sold by the Plaintiff under the names of *George Holyoake* and *Holyoake* are not a *bona fide* and original make of needles, but are imitations of the make of *Edmund Holyoake*. For such a suggestion it appears to me that there is no justification; and further, it appears to me clear that the effect of the circular is directly and clearly to work all injury to the Plaintiff's trade; and, as such, the circular appears to me to be a ground of action, subject to the various objections which were made on the part of the Defendants, and which I am now about to consider."

7–167 In *Hatchard v Mège*[96] the plaintiff's claim in injurious falsehood was based on a circular summarised by Day J. as "substantially a warning not to buy *Delmonico* Champagne because it is not genuine." It was allowed to proceed, notwithstanding the plaintiff's death and the fact that a libel action would have abated. But at the end of the nineteenth century the Court of Appeal in *Hubbuck v Wilkinson Heywood*[97] took a dim view of an attempt to convert an otherwise legitimate comparative advertisement into an allegation that the plaintiff's paint was something spurious, simply because the defendants alone called their paint "genuine".

Both parties carried on business as safe makers in *Thomas Withers v Samuel Withers*[98] and the businesses, which shared a common founder, had co-existed uneasily for many years. Whenever the plaintiffs advertised an auction of their stock of surplus safes, the defendants would insert advertisements in the same local papers to the effect that they were the only makers of the genuine *Withers* safe. Wright J. observed that "...this method of advertising...strikes me as not only somewhat indelicate and in bad taste, but as crude and unfair competition..." but held that neither injurious falsehood nor libel was made out on the facts.

7–168 In *Reuter v Muhlens*[99] the German defendant had engaged in correspondence with the plaintiffs' export agents and with *Vogue* magazine in which he asserted that the plaintiffs' product was not the genuine *4711* eau de Cologne, and that they were not entitled to use the *4711* trade mark in certain markets. Prior to the Second World War the defendant's predecessors had undoubtedly owned the relevant trade mark and goodwill in the United Kingdom and the rest of the World (the plaintiffs being their sole UK concessionaires, and under their ownership) but the shares in the plaintiff company, and the UK trade marks and goodwill, had been appropriated and reassigned by the Custodian of Enemy Property. Dank-

---

[96] (1887) 18 Q.B.D. 771, Divisional Court.
[97] [1899] 1 Q.B. 86, CA.
[98] (1926) 44 R.P.C. 19 (Wright J., KBD).
[99] (1953) 70 R.P.C. 102 (Dankwerts J.), affirmed (1953) 70 R.P.C. 235, CA. The relevant first instance findings were not challenged on appeal, except in so far as the plaintiffs attempted (unsuccessfully) to obtain a declaration.

werts J. allowed the company's claims for trade mark infringement, but refused those for injurious falsehood.[1] One of the defendant's assertions was that eau de Cologne exported to Eritrea infringed his trade mark registrations there and was not "genuine" in the specific sense that the plaintiffs did not have access to the authentic secret formula. The latter was true, infringement or not of the Eritrean registrations could not be decided, and in any event the defendant was not acting maliciously in defending what he (or rather the writer of the letter) honestly perceived to be his legitimate interests. So far as the *Vogue* correspondence was concerned the action for injurious falsehood also failed. Once again the defendant was only trying to protect his own interests rather than maliciously injure the plaintiffs, and statements that his was the "genuine and original" *4711* brand, and that it had regained its pre-War position in various foreign markets, were substantially true. References in the letter to the "non-genuine" Reuters product simply meant, in context, that the latter was not made according to the old secret formula, not that it was spurious in any opprobrious sense.

In *New Musical Express v Cardfont Publishers*[2] the parties published **7–169** competing weekly music journals, each with a list of the top ten records from the previous week. The plaintiffs complained of a statement in the defendants' *Record Mirror* that the latter's *Top Tens* were the most authentic, but Harman J. refused an interlocutory injunction. There might have been a cause of action for injurious falsehood (depending on the precise interpretation put on the claim) but the defendants had already published a retraction in terms stipulated by the plaintiffs, there was no prospect of the statement being repeated, and no need for an interlocutory injunction pending trial.

In the *Harris Tweed* case, *Argyllshire Weavers v Macaulay*[3] the pursuers were refused a declarator (declaration) that they were entitled to use "Harris Tweed" for cloth woven in the Hebrides but spun and finished on the mainland, and their claims for injurious falsehood fell with it. Assertions by the defenders that so called Harris Tweed not bearing their certification mark was "not genuine" or "of doubtful origin and quality" may not have been not totally accurate (since some genuine Harris Tweed did not bear the mark) but they had not been made maliciously, and if made in relation to the pursuers' tweed they were not untrue.

Disparagement distinguished from abuse

In *Fielding v Variety*[4] the producers of the highly successful musical *Charlie* **7–170** *Girl* recovered damages of £100 for injurious falsehood[5] (in default of

---

[1] A counterclaim for passing-off was dismissed, the defendant's former goodwill in the United Kingdom having validly been transferred to the plaintiffs.
[2] [1956] R.P.C. 211 (Harman J.).
[3] [1964] R.P.C. 477 (Lord Hunter, OH).
[4] [1967] 2 Q.B. 841, CA.
[5] And £1,500 for libel. By agreement, the damages for injurious falsehood were awarded to the corporate plaintiff and the libel damages to the individual. The level of damages was much reduced on appeal (from £10,000 and £5,000 respectively).

defence on the merits) against a trade newspaper which had described it as a "disastrous flop".

However, abuse, no matter how offensive, is only likely to be actionable if in all the circumstances it is likely to be taken seriously.[6] In *Compaq v Dell*[7] it was not the eye-catching headlines *It Doesn't Compute* and *Spot the Flaw in Compaq's Logic* which were actionable, but the detailed price comparisons for supposedly identical computer systems. In *British Airways v Ryanair*[8] Jacob J. said about the defendants' advertising headline EXPENSIVE BA...DS! "Nor is it a malicious falsehood, amounting as it does to no more than vulgar abuse." It was accepted that "BA...DS!" stood for "BASTARDS!" and the advertisement had been the subject of a successful complaint to the Advertising Standards Authority on the grounds that the headline "was likely to cause serious or widespread offence".

Disparagement as defamation

7–171 Disparaging misrepresentations may also or alternatively amount to defamation in the sense of libel or slander. The earliest authority of any continuing relevance is *Harman v Delaney*,[9] still occasionally cited for the *dictum* that:

> "[T]he law has always been very tender of the reputation of tradesmen, and therefore words spoken of them in the way of their trade will bear an action, that will not be actionable in the case of another person..."[10]

As Lord Esher M.R. observed in *South Hetton Coal v North Eastern News*[11]:

> "Suppose the plaintiff was a merchant who dealt in wine, and it was stated that wine which he had for sale of a particular vintage was not good wine; that might be so stated as only to import that the wine of the particular year was not good in whosesoever hands it was, but not to imply any reflection on his conduct of his business. In that case the statement would be with regard to his goods only, and there would be no libel, although such a statement, if it were false and were made maliciously, with intention to injure him, and it did injure him, might be made the subject of an action on the case. On the other hand, if the statement were so made as to import that his judgment in the selection of wine was bad, it might import a reflection on his conduct of his business, and shew that he was an inefficient man of business. If so, it would be a libel. In such a case a jury would have to say which sense the libel really bore; if they thought it related to the goods only, they ought to find that it was not

---

[6] See *Heriot v Stuart* (1796) 170 E.R. 411; 1 Esp. 437.
[7] [1992] F.S.R. 93 (Aldous J.).
[8] [2001] F.S.R. 32 (Jacob J.).
[9] (1731) 93 E.R. 925; 2 Stra. 898.
[10] *per curiam.*
[11] [1894] 1 Q.B. 133, CA.

a libel; but, if they thought that it related to the man's conduct of business, they ought to find that it was a libel."

In *Linotype Co v British Empire Typesetting Machine Co*[12] the plaintiffs **7–172** complained of a draft for a newspaper article (written by the defendants, but not published by the two papers to which it was submitted) which disingenuously stated that they had suffered a very serious blow because five of their printing machines had been installed at the New York *Evening Sun*, but shortly afterwards removed. This much was literally true, but they had been removed because of opposition from a trade union and not because they were unsatisfactory. The plaintiffs' claim for libel was upheld at all three instances: the imputation was not just that the machines were unsatisfactory, but that the plaintiffs were knowingly foisting worthless machines on a customer. Likewise, in *Bendle v United Kingdom Alliance*[13] criticisms of the terms in which *Bendle's Meat-Port Nutrient* wine was advertised "were such as to impute either dishonesty or fraudulent incapacity to the plaintiffs in the way of conducting their business"[14] and were not proved to be justified. While decisions such as these are still technically good law, the lack of similar cases in more recent times probably reflects a change in judicial attitudes as to where the dividing line lies.[15]

In *Drummond-Jackson v British Medical Association*[16] the plaintiff, a **7–173** dentist, had pioneered an anaesthetic technique which was severely criticised in the defendants' *British Medical Journal* as "having serious detrimental physiological effects, which may well have been the cause of the reported deaths". The plaintiff was identified by name in the article. The Court of Appeal (by a majority) refused to strike out a claim for libel. Lord Denning M.R. (dissenting) would have struck out the libel claim and required the plaintiff to sue, if at all, in injurious falsehood.

In *McManus v Beckham*[17] the Court of Appeal held that the defendant, the wife of a famous footballer and a celebrity in her own right, might be liable in slander[18] for the foreseeable republication in newspapers of remarks she had supposedly made in the claimants' shop, accusing them of selling fake autographed memorabilia.

---

[12] (1899) 81 L.T. 331; 15 T.L.R. 524, HL.
[13] (1915) 31 T.L.R. 403, CA.
[14] *per* Swinfen Eady L.J.; Phillimore L.J. dissented.
[15] Compare *Thomas Withers & Sons Ltd v Samuel Withers & Co Ltd* (1926) 44 R.P.C. 19, KBD.
[16] [1970] 1 W.L.R. 688, CA.
[17] [2002] EWCA Civ 939; [2002] 1 W.L.R. 2982; [2002] 4 All E.R. 497; [2002] E.M.L.R. 40, CA.
[18] Malicious falsehood was also pleaded, but was not separately addressed in the judgments.

N. COMPARATIVE ADVERTISING

Introduction

7–174 The present section deals with comparative advertising from the point of view of injurious falsehood. In principle, comparative advertising might also involve passing-off, but the way the law has developed makes it no less difficult to frame a successful action in passing-off than in injurious falsehood.[19] As passing-off was formerly understood, it could not be actionable for the defendant to make use of the claimant's name or mark to draw an explicit comparison with his own goods or business. Such use could hardly lead to confusion in the traditional sense, because the comparison both assumed and proclaimed that the two businesses were separate and unconnected. Passing-off has extended to cover at least some situations in which the defendant may be making an untrue claim about himself which the claimant has a right to restrain, for instance by misuse of certain kinds of descriptive terms, or by "inverse" passing-off, but these are very far from providing anything like a complete code for cases of comparative but non-disparaging misrepresentation.[20]

Although an explicit head-to-head comparison may seem to provide a relatively favourable context in which to bring an action for injurious falsehood, the majority of the reported cases point the other way, and are probably more representative of how future actions would fare. A particular burden on the claimant has historically been the unwillingness of the courts to grant interim relief where there is any uncertainty as to the truth or falsehood of the statements complained of, meaning that if the representation is at all obscure or ambiguous then the only option is to go to trial.[21] The principle still holds, but its practical effect is mitigated now that it is possible to obtain a full trial within a matter of months, rather than years.

7–175 Another problem facing the claimant in a comparative advertising case is that exaggerated praise by the defendant of his own goods or services is frequently dismissed as mere "puffing".[22] This is most often shorthand for saying that the misrepresentation is not a material one, for instance because it is obviously too imprecise or exaggerated to have any effect on the consumer. "The public are used to the ways of advertisers and expect a certain amount of hyperbole"[23]–though there is another school of thought that standards of truthfulness in advertising have risen sufficiently since the nineteenth century for the public to have a legitimate expectation of substantial accuracy in at least some cases.[24] There is a second and perhaps more fundamental aspect to puffing, in so far as exaggerated praise of one's

---

[19] See Chapter 5, Section D, above.

[20] For the treatment of comparative advertising under Directive 97/55/EC see Ansgar Ohly and Michael Spence; *The Law of Comparative Advertising* (2000).

[21] *Bestobell Paints Ltd v Bigg* [1975] F.S.R. 421.

[22] For "puffing" and materiality generally, see Chapter 6 Section B, above.

[23] *per* Jacob J. in *Vodafone Group plc v Orange Personal Communications Services Ltd* [1997] F.S.R. 34.

[24] *Ciba-Geigy plc v Parke Davis & Co Ltd* [1994] F.S.R. 8.

own goods or services is not in principle actionable as injurious falsehood at all, even if knowingly false, unless it can realistically be characterised as an implicit disparagement of the claimant's goods or services. For no very obvious reason this seems easier to make out in the case of price comparisons for identical or equivalent goods; and difficult or impossible to make out for comparisons of quality alone, or mixed comparisons of quality and price.

Many of the more recent cases which follow raise issues of registered trade mark infringement (not further discussed here) as well as injurious falsehood, with the latter frequently being treated as the subordinate cause of action. Historically, s.4(1)(b) of the Trade Marks Act 1938 provided an effective remedy against any comparative advertising employing the plaintiff's registered Part A trade mark, and although this could be circumvented, it probably contributed to comparative advertising being relatively rare in practice before 1994. The reforms introduced by s.10(6) of the Trade Marks Act 1994 permitted use of a competitor's registered trade marks in comparative advertising, but subject to a newly-introduced concept of "honest practices in industrial or commercial matters" which seems to be derived from Art. 10*bis* of the Paris Convention.[25]

Leading cases and development

The leading cases on injurious falsehood in the present context come from **7–176** the late nineteenth century, with the final pair, *White v Mellin*[26] and *Hubbuck v Wilkinson Heywood*[27] still being authoritative. The earliest reported comparative advertising case in the present sense appears to be *Young v Macrae*[28] in which the patentee of an invention for obtaining paraffin (or "paraffine oil") complained of a circular in which the importers of some American paraffin published the report of a professor of chemistry comparing their oil favourably to his in terms of colour, odour, and lighting power. On a demurrer, the Divisional Court dismissed the action.[29]

"I am far from saying that if a man falsely and maliciously makes a statement disparaging an article which another manufactures or vends, although in so doing he casts no imputation on his personal or professional character, and thereby causes an injury, and special damage is averred, an action might not be maintained. For although none of us are

[25] The first such case under the 1994 Act, *Barclays Bank plc v RBS Advanta* [1996] R.P.C. 307 was pleaded solely as one of registered trade mark infringement. Arguments relating to injurious falsehood were relevant only in so far as the defendants argued that *Bestobell v Bigg*, above, should be applied by analogy, but it was unnecessary to decide this point.
[26] [1895] A.C. 154, HL.
[27] [1899] Q.B. 86, CA.
[28] (1862) 3 B. & S. 264; 122 E.R. 100. *Harman v Delaney* (1731) 93 E.R. 925; 2 Stra. 898 and *Evans v Harlow* (1844) 114 E.R. 1384; 5 Q.B. 624 are older, but in neither case is the defendant actually identified as a trade competitor.
[29] With a parting shot from Cockburn C.J.: "You can bring another action, and perhaps get another professor to make a report in favour of your oil".

familiar with such actions still we can see that a most grievous wrong might be done in that way, and it ought not to be without remedy.

But then comes the question: assuming that such an action would lie, does this declaration allege acts to support it? All that appears is that, falsely and maliciously, the defendant has made representations and instituted a comparison between the plaintiff's oil and that of someone else. But it may be that all the falsehood consists in this, that the defendant has alleged what is true of the plaintiff's oil, and what is false of the oil of some other man .... . But it may be that the falsehood here consists in a false representation of the superior quality in respect of colour and odour of the oil which the defendant advertised. The action therefore cannot be maintained."[30]

Young v Macrae was distinguished in *Western Counties Manure v Lawes Chemical Manure.*[31] The parties competed in the sale of artificial manure, and the defendants published a chemical analysis which purported to show that the plaintiff's product was inferior to that of the defendants and two others, and only deserved to be sold at about 5/8 the price of the defendants' manure. The Exchequer (Bramwell and Pollock BB.) held for the plaintiffs on a demurrer. *Western Counties Manure v Lawes Chemical Manure* turned out not to be representative of the way the law actually developed, although express disapproval of it was muted.

7–177 The direction of the law for most of the twentieth century was set in *White v Mellin,*[32] in which the plaintiff (respondent in the House of Lords) was the proprietor of *Mellin's Food for Infants*, and the defendant a retail chemist in Portsmouth who bought bottles of *Mellin's* food wholesale. Before selling them to the public, the defendant attached to the bottles a paper reading:

"Notice. The public are recommended to try Dr. Vance's prepared food for infants and invalids, it being far more nutritious and healthful than any other preparation yet offered ... Local agent, Timothy White, chemist, Portsmouth."

Mellin sued, originally relying on a supposed implied contract (or "custom of the trade") that the bottles would be sold on to the consumer without any further addition or alteration to the wrappers. When this case collapsed, the plaintiff was left with an allegation of injurious falsehood which the trial judge (Romer J.) held could not be made out on the evidence: there was scientific evidence that Mellin's food was superior to Vance's for some kinds of infant; but none of malice, loss of sales, or other special damage. Romer J. dismissed the action without calling on the defendants, the Court of Appeal held that he should have heard both sides' evidence, and ordered a new trial, but the House of Lords reinstated the decision of Romer J.

7–178 There are three aspects to *White v Mellin*[33]: the decision on the facts,

---

[30] *per* Cockburn C.J.
[31] (1874) L.R. 9 Exch. 218, also decided on a demurrer.
[32] [1895] A.C. 154, HL.
[33] Above.

which was unremarkable almost to the point of being inevitable; its restatement of the law, which is also conventional; and the direction it pointed to in terms of its *dicta*. In terms of the decision on the facts. Lord Herschell L.C. pointed to the weakness and inadequacy of the plaintiff's evidence: there was expert evidence that *Mellin's* food was preferable for infants younger than six months, but the same evidence suggested that it was less suitable for those over six or 12 months. Infancy itself could not be precisely defined, but taking the term as meaning the first two years of childhood then it could not be said that the claim made for Vance's food had been shown to be false, let alone disparaging of the plaintiff's food. There was no evidence of damage, and it would be wrong to infer it from an anonymous and unsubstantiated advertising puff which no one would take seriously. The original wrappers, which were not removed, carried a similarly extravagant puff for *Mellin's* food. Finally, evidence of malice was absent, and there was nothing to suggest that the defendant disbelieved his own claims, or that his object was anything other than selling his own goods.

Finally, and most importantly, *dicta* in *White v Mellin* removed any doubts that similar actions, even on stronger facts, would be any more favourably received in the future. In reply to an argument that an distinction could be drawn between mere statements of personal opinion and purported statements of fact, Lord Herschell L.C. observed:

"The allegation of a tradesman that his goods are better than his neighbour's very often involves only the consideration whether they possess one or two qualities superior to the other. Of course 'better' means better as regards the purpose for which they are intended, and the question of better or worse in many cases depends simply upon one or two or three issues of fact. If an action will not lie because a man says that his goods are better than his neighbour's, it seems to me impossible to say that it will lie because he says that they are better in this or that or the other respect. Just consider what a door would be opened if this were permitted. That this sort of puffing advertisement is in use is notorious; and we see rival cures advertised for particular ailments. The Court would then be bound to inquire, in an action brought, whether this ointment or this pill better cured the disease which it was alleged to cure—whether a particular article of food was in this respect or that better than another. Indeed, the Courts of law would be turned into a machinery for advertising rival productions by obtaining a judicial determination which of the two was the better."

White v Mellin[34] was followed in *Hubbuck v Wilkinson Heywood*.[35] In the **7–179** latter, the plaintiff complained of the issue by the defendant of a circular, to tradesmen in China and Japan, reporting on a experiment from which the conclusion was drawn that the defendants' white zinc paint had a "slight advantage" over the plaintiffs', but that "for all practical purposes they can

[34] [1895] A.C. 154, HL.
[35] [1899] Q.B. 86, CA.

be regarded as equal being in every respect". The defendants' paint was much cheaper. There was no plea of special damage.

"The truth is that the defendants' circular when attentively read comes to no more than a statement that the defendants' white zinc is equal to, and, indeed, somewhat better, than the plaintiffs'. Such a statement, even if untrue and the cause of loss to the plaintiffs, is not a cause of action. Moreover, an allegation that the statement was made maliciously is not enough to convert what is *prima facie* a lawful into a *prima facie* unlawful statement. It is not unlawful to say that one's own goods are better than other people's; and *Allen v Flood* shews that malice in such a case is immaterial . . .
    We will now consider the circular in its other aspect, namely, as a disparagement of the plaintiffs' goods. From this point of view the case is undistinguishable from *Evans v Harlow* and *Young v Macrae*, where malice, falsehood, and damage were all alleged, and yet it was held that what the defendant there published was not actionable. The ground of the decision in both cases was that for a person in trade to puff his own wares and to proclaim their superiority over those of his rivals is not actionable. The principle laid down in these cases has never been questioned, and it has been emphatically approved in *White v Mellin*. The defendants in this case give the results of some experiments with the two sorts of paint, and in paragraph 5 of the statement of claim the plaintiffs say that the report of the experiments is untrue, and that the trials were not fairly made. But, supposing this to be the case, the result is not altered. Paragraph 5 merely states more particularly what has been already stated before in paragraph 3, where the general charge of falsehood is made. Even if each particular charge of falsehood is established, it will only come to this–that it is untrue that the defendants' paint is better than or equal to that of the plaintiffs, for saying which no action lies. The particular reasons for making that statement are immaterial if the statement itself is not actionable."

With *White v Mellin* and *Hubbuck v Wilkinson, Heywood* the application of injurious falsehood to advertising was effectively defined for the twentieth century. Unequivocal disparagement of the goods of a competitor might be actionable as injurious falsehood–provided the requirements of falsity, malice and special damage were met. However, a mere comparison favourable to the defendant's products at the expense of those of the plaintiff would be treated, at most, as unjustified praise of the former rather than unjustified denigration of the latter.

Head-to-head comparisons: claimant successful

7–180   Published head-to-head comparisons of the products of the defendant with those of the claimant (inevitably to the disadvantage of the latter) ought to provide a relatively straightforward situation to which the law of injurious falsehood may be applied, since there is generally little doubt as to the identity of the party whose goods or services are at the unfavourable end of the comparison. In fact, cases in which the claimant has prevailed are in the minority, but it is these which provide the most useful starting point for analysis because a finding for the claimant necessarily means that every relevant issue has had to be addressed *seriatim*; whereas those decided in favour of the defendant often offer an analysis which is less thorough and complete because a single point was conclusive against the claimant.

Modern law may be said to begin with the decision of Walton J. in *De Beers v International General Electric*.[36] The parties competed in the market for diamond-based abrasive materials, made from natural diamonds in the case of the plaintiffs and synthetic diamonds in the case of the defendants. The defendants prepared and circulated to prospective customers a pamphlet reproducing the results of tests at their "Applications Laboratory" which appeared to show that the plaintiffs' materials were inferior. De Beers sued for injurious falsehood (nominally for slander of their goods, the abrasive *Debdust*)[37] and the defendants applied to have the action struck out. Walton J. held that the pamphlet could not be said to fall on the innocuous side of the line between mere puffing and implicit denigration of a rival's goods. There were two possible tests to distinguish mere puffing from actionable falsehood, namely whether a reasonable man would take the claim as a serious one or not, and whether the defendant had gone beyond mere generalities to assert some specific defect or demerit in the plaintiff's goods. The first was more persuasive, but in the present case there was no need to choose between them, since both were met. What was in issue was not just typical advertising copy, but what purported to be the result of proper comparative scientific tests circulated to persons who had an obvious interest in them as such.

Cases subsequent to *De Beers*[38] agree that a material representation for **7–181** the purposes of injurious falsehood may be established from the fact that the reasonable addressee would assume that serious and substantiated claims were being made, and that he was not simply being subjected to a flood of self-serving hyperbole. However, apart from *Compaq v Dell* and *DSG v Comet*, below, the majority of the reported decisions have been in favour of the defendant.

In *Compaq v Dell*[39] the defendants published two press advertisements in which their personal computers were compared in price to those of Compaq under the headings *It Doesn't Compute* and *Spot the Flaw in Compaq's Logic*. Both advertisements presented in adjacent columns photographs of several of the defendants' desktop or portable computer systems opposite supposedly comparable systems of the plaintiffs. The photographs were accompanied with prices and designations of the systems. On motion for an interlocutory injunction the defendants submitted that the advertisements

---

[36] [1975] 1 W.L.R. 972; [1975] 2 All E.R. 599; [1975] F.S.R. 323 (Walton J.).
[37] And for unlawful interference with trade and unfair competition, as to which Walton J. expressed no opinion.
[38] *De Beers Abrasive Products Ltd v International General Electric of New York Ltd* [1975] 1 W.L.R. 972; [1975] 2 All E.R. 599; [1975] F.S.R. 323.
[39] [1992] F.S.R. 93 (Aldous J.).

were true, so as to bring the case within the principle of *Bestobell Paints v Bigg*,[40] but Aldous J. held that there were misrepresentations in the advertisements which were incapable of being justified. The theme of the advertisements was that the computers whose prices were compared were basically and essentially the same, and no reasonable jury could come to that conclusion. There were too many instances where like was not being compared with like, or where the *Dell* systems were illustrated with optional equipment which was not included in the quoted price.

7–182   A useful and systematic application of the reasoning of Walton J. in *De Beers*[41] has recently been given in *DSG Retail v Comet Group*,[42] in which the claimants (trading as *Currys*) and the defendants competed as retailers of electrical goods. Currys initiated two heavily advertised promotions under one of which their ticket prices were discounted by 10 per cent, while under the other they offered to beat Comet's local price by £10 on goods marked at over £300. Shortly afterwards, Currys noticed a shop-front poster at Comet's Mansfield store which advertised "The Comet price is lower than competitors' 10% off promotions and £10 price cuts. That's Comet sense". This poster, or a variation on it, was subsequently rolled out to other Comet stores, and in the case of Comet's Bedford store (and elsewhere) three Currys press advertisements were taped alongside it. Currys initially obtained an interim injunction on short notice, and after argument this was continued by Owen J.

After reciting statements of the general law from *Kaye v Robertson*[43] and *Bestobell v Bigg*,[44] Owen J. extracted from *De Beers v General Electric*[45] and *Jupiter v Johnson Fry*[46] six questions which were relevant to whether the specific facts of the case amounted to injurious falsehood: (a) whether the statements complained of were directed at Currys; (b) what was their meaning; (c) were they false in that meaning; (d) were they actionable in the sense of being likely to be taken seriously; (e) were they published maliciously; and (f) was there a likelihood of Currys sustaining actual damage (taking into account s.3(1)(a), Defamation Act 1952)?

As to (a) there was no doubt both from the terms of the posters, the use of Currys' own advertisements next to them, and Comet's internal documents referring to the likes of "Anti-Currys weekend activity" that Currys was indeed the target. As to (b) and (c), the posters were to be read as a whole through the eyes of the ordinary man. Notwithstanding various arguments to the contrary, their plain meaning was that Comet's ordinary ticketed prices were lower than Currys' promotional prices for equivalent goods. The statements understood in that sense were false, and Comet must have known it. (In fact, Comet staff were only authorised to match the Currys promo-

---

[40] [1975] F.S.R. 421 (Oliver J.).
[41] *De Beers Abrasive Products Ltd v International General Electric of New York Ltd* [1975] 1 W.L.R. 972; [1975] 2 All E.R. 599; [1975] F.S.R. 323.
[42] [2002] F.S.R. 58 (Owen J., QBD).
[43] [1981] F.S.R. 62, CA.
[44] [1975] F.S.R. 421 (Oliver J.).
[45] [1975] 1 W.L.R. 972; [1975] 2 All E.R. 599; [1975] F.S.R. 323.
[46] *Jupiter Unit Trust Managers Ltd v Johnson Fry Asset Managers plc* (Morland J, QBD, April 19, 2000, unreported.).

tional prices for a limited time, on a limited range of goods, and only when challenged to do so.) The price comparison was inherently one which customers would take at its face value, and amounted to a disparagement of Currys' goods. The requirement of malice was satisfied by the conclusion that Comet knew of the falsity of their statements; and since the whole purpose of the posters was to lure customers from Currys to Comet, at the busiest time of year, the requirement of damage was also self-evidently met. There was every reason to think that a continuing interim injunction was necessary under *American Cyanamid*, and fact that the original interim injunction had not fully been complied with was a further reason for doubting Comet's good faith.

Head-to-head comparisons: defendant successful

In *McDonald's v Burgerking*,[47] the defendants' advertising for its *Whopper* **7–183** burger used the slogan *Its Not Just Big, Mac*, with the associated copy stating "[u]nlike some burgers, it is 100 per cent pure beef, flame-grilled never fried, with a unique choice of toppings". There can have been little doubt that the plaintiffs and their "flagship" *Big Mac* burger were being referred to, but the alleged implication that the *Big Mac* burger was not 100 per cent pure beef failed on the facts.

In *Ciba-Geigy v Parke Davis*[48] the defendants promoted their branded generic substitute for the plaintiffs' *Voltarol Retard* with advertisements in the medical press having a picture of an apple with a bite taken out of it and the copy "*Diclomax Retard* takes a chunk out of your prescribing costs"; "*Diclomax Retard* offers everything you'd expect from diclofenac retard with one crucial difference. The price." and "Cost savings of around 25% compared to the leading dicolfenac retard cost. . . ." The plaintiffs' registered trade mark *Volatarol* was not mentioned; and although a picture of a (whole) apple was recognised by the medical profession as denoting the plaintiffs' products, the latter was not registered. Aldous J. refused an interlocutory injunction: the majority of the plaintiffs' arguments fell under passing-off and are considered elsewhere,[49] but so far as the accusation of "knocking copy" was concerned the advertisements fell on the legitimate side of the line:

"Finally, I record the submission made by the plaintiff that the defendant's advertisements were knocking advertisements of the type which wrongly appropriated the plaintiff's goodwill. I believe the advertisements are examples of comparative advertising. Such advertisements are perfectly proper unless registered trademarks are used. They are not knocking advertisements in that they do not suggest that the plaintiff's product is a bad product; they only seek to suggest the defendant's product is as good a product. Such statements are not actionable according

---

[47] [1986] F.S.R. 45 (Whitford J.). The appeal at [1987] F.S.R. 112 was not concerned with this issue.
[48] [1994] F.S.R. 8 (Aldous J.).
[49] See para.5–31, above.

to common law. A party who wishes to protect a mark such as a picture of an apple must apply for and obtain registration under the Trade Marks Act 1938, as amended."

7–184   In *Vodafone v Orange*[50] the parties competed in offering mobile telephone services. Vodafone sued for trade mark infringement and injurious false-hood after Orange published an advertisement with the slogan "On average, Orange users save £20 every month" compared to the "equivalent tariffs" of Vodafone and Cellnet, who were both identified by name. At the trial of the action, Jacob J. conventionally identified the requirements of the action for malicious falsehood as the falsity of the words complained of, that they were published maliciously, and that they were calculated to cause the plaintiff pecuniary damage. The first matter was to interpret the words in question, which was not a question of construing them in any legal sense but of identifying the meaning they would convey to the ordinary man. This was a "jury question" for the judge to decide, and evidence of the meaning of the words to others was inadmissible. This generalisation was subject to one important qualification, which was that in contrast to passing-off the court had to proceed on the basis that the words had a single meaning to all who read them, and only that meaning was relevant. The truth or falsity of the statement had to be judged, for all purposes, against a single standard. Finally, in considering what the ordinary meaning might be, it was relevant to take account of the fact that the public were used to knocking copy and extravagant claims to savings: the test (following *De Beers*[51]) was "whether a reasonable would take the claim being made as one made seriously: the more precise the claim the more likely to be so taken–the more general or fuzzy the less so".

In the present case, there was fundamental disagreement as to what the words of the slogan meant. Jacob J. agreed with Orange that they meant precisely what they said: on average, Orange users would have paid £20 per month more if they had been on Vodafone (or Cellnet) and had made the same usage of the service. The slogan did not mean, and would not be read as implying, that existing Vodafone subscribers would (even on average) save £20 per month by transferring to Orange. Before dealing with the truth or falsity of the slogan, Jacob J. addressed the case on malice and described it as hopeless. Sometimes malice might be deduced from the self-evident falsity of the statement, but this was not remotely such a case. There was no evidence that any of the individuals who gave evidence disbelieved the truth of the slogan, or had concocted their evidence. As to falsity, the comparison was substantially true on the preferred construction, and would still have been true on Vodafone's construction.

7–185   In *Schulke & Mayr v Alkapharm*[52] the parties competed in selling cleaning and disinfecting agents for dentists. The defendants published an adver-tisement for their product *Alkazyme* which claimed that it was "the most

[50] [1997] F.S.R. 34 (Jacob J.).
[51] *De Beers Abrasive Products Ltd v International General Electric of New York Ltd* [1975] 1 W.L.R. 972; [1975] 2 All E.R. 599; [1975] F.S.R. 323.
[52] [1999] F.S.R. 161 (Jacob J.).

powerful; the most stable" such product, identifying the plaintiff's product *Gigasept* by name and referring to some independent tests. The defendants offered interim undertakings not to infringe the *Gigasept* trade mark and not to repeat the claims to superiority, whether in absolute or relative terms, but the plaintiffs applied for interim injunctions to restrain two statements which the defendants wanted to continue using: "Cleans dental instruments quickly and completely without the need for manual cleaning. Enzymes dissolve proteinaceous matter and have detergents which effectively carry it away even in small crevices and areas such as lumens and channels" and "Disinfects. The *Alkazyme* formula also contains a powerful disinfectant compound active against bacteria, fungi and viruses including HIV and HBV". The plaintiffs claimed that both these claims were false. Jacob J. held that even assuming their falsity, neither statement was actionable as injurious falsehood (or as passing-off). The law required the allegedly false statement to be made "of and concerning the plaintiff's goods, that they were in disparagement of his goods and untrue". Here, there was nothing to connect the remaining statements (even if untrue) with the plaintiffs' goods, and there was therefore no question of liability for injurious falsehood.

In *British Airways v Ryanair*[53] press advertisements comparing the prices **7–186** of the claimants and defendants to various destinations under the headings EXPENSIVE BA ... DS or EXPENSIVE BA were held not to be actionable: the first was merely vulgar abuse, and neither advertisement was misleading in fact.

> "Accordingly, I do not think that the average consumer would find the price comparison misleading. He would expect there to be some sort of conditions (and indeed the small print makes that clear). In substance the advertisements were true. The fact that no-one has complained, not even travel agents who might perhaps have lost commission and thus [be] keen to complain, confirms me in my view.
>
> Even if that were wrong however, and fair comparison was for fares staying over a weekend, the substance of the price comparison is sufficiently true. I return to the Frankfurt fares. Ryanair's price is quoted at £69.00, about one fifth of BA's quoted price. If you take BA's suggested comparison–a ticket including a Saturday night–Ryanair's is about one-third. There is still a saving of £123.00...
>
> Accordingly in my view the use was honest comparative advertising. I suspect the real reason BA do not like it is precisely because it is true."

In *Emaco v Dyson*[54] both parties had published unsubstantiated but purportedly scientific comparisons of the performance of their vacuum cleaners with those of the other, which on both sides were sufficiently inaccurate for there to be liability under s.10(6) of the Trade Marks Act 1994. However, the various inaccuracies on each side could be traced to an

---

[53] [2001] F.S.R. 32 (Jacob J.).
[54] [1999] E.T.M.R. 903 (Jonathan Parker J.). The report is confined to the issue of registered trade mark infringement.

accumulation of careless but honest mistakes, and it could not be said that either party had acted maliciously–either in the sense of reckless disregard for the truth, or of being driven by an improper motive. The action and counterclaim for injurious falsehood therefore failed.

Circulation cases

7–187 Claims by newspaper or magazine publishers to have a higher circulation than rivals provide enough decisions to fill a short paragraph. In *Heriot v Stuart*[55] the publishers of the *True Briton* sued for libel in respect of a paragraph in a rival paper, the *Oracle*, reading:

> "Times *versus* True Briton. / In a morning paper of yesterday was given the following character of the True Briton: that it was 'the most vulgar, ignorant and scurrilous journal ever published in Great Britain.' To the above assertion we assent; and to this account we add, that the first proprietors abandoned it, and that it is the lowest now in circulation; and we submit the fact to the consideration of advertisers."

Lord Kenyon L.C.J. agreed that though the accusation of scurrility was not actionable, the latter accusations were, as affecting profits from advertising, but the action failed on a technicality.

In *Lyne v Nicholls*[56] statements by the defendant that the circulation of his newspaper was "20 to 1 of any other weekly paper" in the part of Cornwall where the parties competed, and that "where others count by the dozen, we count by the hundred" were held to be not a mere puff, but an actionable disparagement of the plaintiff's newspaper, and were wholly untrue. The defendants' circulation was in fact far less everywhere than that of the plaintiff, by a margin varying from two to one at the most favourable to the defendant to over 10 to one, depending on location. However the action failed for lack of proof of special damage.

7–188 In *MacMillan Magazines v RCN Publishing*[57] Neuberger J. refused an interlocutory injunction against the publishers of the *Nursing Standard* in respect of an advertisement comparing their circulation with that of the plaintiffs' *Nursing Times*. The basis of the comparison was contested, and it was not possible on an interlocutory application to say whether the comparison was accurate or not.

In the Singapore case of *Integrated Information v CD-Biz Directories*[58] damages of S$80,000 were awarded for various statements to prospective advertisers that the defendants' CD ROM directory would have a circulation of 200,000 compared to 180,000 or 200,000 for the plaintiffs' competitive *Yellow Pages* directory. The latter in fact had a circulation of at least 300,000.

---

[55] (1796) 170 E.R. 411; 1 Esp. 437.
[56] (1906) 23 T.L.R. 86 (Swinfen Eady J.).
[57] [1998] F.S.R. 9 (Neuberger J.).
[58] [2000] 3 S.L.R. 457. Only quantification of damages is reported.

O. Disparagements Relating to Intellectual Property Rights

Assertion that competitor's goods infringe; threats actions

Assertions of infringement were the subject of a substantial number of **7–189** actions for injurious falsehood in the second half of the nineteenth century and afterwards, some of which contributed significantly to the development of the law. However, few were successful and the body of law they represent is of declining relevance compared to the statutory "threats actions". The statutory actions are available in respect of unjustified threats of proceedings for alleged infringement of patents,[59] registered trade marks,[60] registered designs,[61] and design right.[62] They are not further considered here. In exceptional circumstances, proceedings for infringement undertaken in bad faith may constitute an abuse of process;[63] and threats of infringement proceedings may also amount to abuse of process,[64] or contempt of court.[65]

The existence of the statutory causes of action does not preclude that for injurious falsehood, but the improbability of being able to prove malice in all but the most extreme cases means that the latter is of little residual importance.[66] In the present state of the law, the common law actions for injurious falsehood (or, more rarely, for intimidation or interference with contract) remain the only remedies for unjustified assertions of infringement of copyright, breach of confidence, or passing-off; but no matter how the action may be framed there is no common law liability for honestly asserting one's claim to a legal right and threatening (or taking) proceedings to enforce it, even if the claim turns out to be unfounded and damage results: *Granby Marketing Services v Interlego.*[67]

As a separate matter, the tactical reason for an action may be to enable the natural defendant to obtain a judicial determination of whether or not he infringes, without waiting to be sued. In these circumstances an action for a declaration of non-infringement,[68] which only requires the defendant to

---

[59] Patents Act 1977, s.70.
[60] Trade Marks Act 1994, s.21.
[61] Registered Designs Act 1949, s.26.
[62] Copyright, Designs and Patents Act 1988, s.253.
[63] *Landi den Hartog NV v Sea Bird (Clean Air Fuel Systems) Ltd* [1976] F.S.R. 489; *Jacey (Printers) v Norton & Wright Group Ltd* [1977] F.S.R. 475.
[64] *Essex Electric (Pte) Ltd v IPC Computers (UK) Ltd* [1991] F.S.R. 690.
[65] See para.7–204, below.
[66] A rare example of both causes of action succeeding is to be found in *Cars v Bland Light Syndicate Ltd* (1911) 28 R.P.C. 33, below. Both failed in *Olin Matheson Chemical Corp v Biorex Laboratories Ltd* [1970] R.P.C. 157, below. In *Selsdon Fountain Pen Co Ltd v Miles Martin Pen Co Ltd* (1948) 65 R.P.C. 365 an unsuccessful application for an interim injunction against statutory threats was not strengthened by unsubstantiated assertions of libel and contempt of court.
[67] [1984] R.P.C. 209 (Vinelott J.). See also *Ripley v Arthur & Co* (1900) 18 R.P.C. 82. *Olin Matheson Chemical Corp v Biorex Laboratories Ltd* [1970] R.P.C. 157, seemingly to the contrary, is wrong. See below para.7–193.
[68] *Bulmer (HP) Ltd v J Bollinger SA* [1972] F.S.R. 119; [1973] R.P.C. 439 (passing-off); *Leco Instruments (UK) Ltd v Land Pyrometers Ltd* [1982] R.P.C. 133, CA (copyright).

have asserted a claim of right,[69] and for which malice is not required, may provide an alternative.

Patents

7–190 The first relevant case is *Wren v Weild*[70] in which the proprietor of a patent wrote to customers of the plaintiff asserting that certain spooling machines they had purchased from him were infringements, and demanding royalties under threat of legal proceedings. At the trial of the action the plaintiffs offered to prove that their machines did not infringe, and that the defendant's patent was invalid in the light of prior art known to him. The trial judge held that the proposed evidence was immaterial and directed a nonsuit. The plaintiff applied for a new trial and the Divisional Court upheld the decision below. In principle an action lay in respect of threats falsely and maliciously made which had caused them to lose business, but to maintain it they would have had to have proved that the defendant had made the threats *mala fide* in the sense of knowing that they were without foundation, but that state of mind could not have been made out even if the contested evidence had been admitted. The result and reasoning were the same in *Halsey v Brotherhood*.[71] The proprietor of a patent whose validity had not been challenged was liable neither for damages nor to an injunction for issuing circulars warning purchasers of the plaintiff's steam engines that they infringed, and would be the subject of legal proceedings.

"It seems to be clear law that in an action in the High Court in the nature of slander of title, where the defendant has property of his own in defence of which the supposed slander of the plaintiff's title is uttered, it is not enough that the statement should be untrue, but there must be some evidence, either from the nature of the statement itself or otherwise, to satisfy the Court or the jury that the statement was not only untrue, but was made *mala fide* for the purpose of injuring the plaintiff, and not in the *bona fide* defence of the defendant's own property. It seems to be clear that if a statement is made in defence of the defendant's own property, although it injures and is untrue, it is still what the law calls a privileged statement: it is a statement that the defendant has a right to make, unless, besides its untruth and besides its injury, express malice is proved, that is to say, want of *bona fides* or the presence of *mala fides*."[72]

7–191 The statutory "threats action" was originally introduced (for patents only) by s.32 of the Patents, Designs and Trade Marks Act 1883. The "threats action" as such is outside the scope of the present work but some

---

[69] *In re Clay, Clay v Booth* [1919] 1 Ch. 66, CA; *Barclays Bank plc v Homan* [1993] B.C.L.C. 680 (neither intellectual property cases); *Plastus Creativ AB v Minnesota Mining and Manufacturing Co* [1995] R.P.C. 438 (foreign patents–not justiciable); *Wyco Group plc v Cooper Roller Bearings Co Ltd* [1996] F.S.R. 126 (copyright).
[70] (1869) 4 Q.B. 730 (Divisional Court, QBD).
[71] (1881) 19 Ch. D. 386, CA, affirming (1880) 15 Ch. D. 514 (Jessel M.R.).
[72] *per* Lord Coleridge L.C.J.

useful *dicta* about the previous state of the law are to be found in the threats case of *Skinner v Shew*[73]:

"An inquiry into the state of the law before the statute was passed will enable us to see what the statute meant. At Common Law there was a cause of action whenever one person did damage to another willfully and intentionally, and without just cause or excuse.[74] Under the head of that class of action came the action of slander of title, whether the subject of the slander was real or personal property. If a man falsely and maliciously—because the malice would shew there was no just cause—made a statement about the property of another which was calculated to do, and which did do, damage to the other in the management of that property, an action would lie at Common Law, and damages would be recoverable; and in Chancery, I suppose that even if you could not prove that actual damage had occurred, the Court might, if actual damage was likely to occur, prevent the wrongful act by injunction. The cases on the Chancery side and on the Common Law side which occurred before the Act, and which make it clear what the state of the law was, are *Halsey v Brotherhood*, on the Chancery side, and *Wren v Weild*, on the Common Law side. The law is laid down in an unmistakeable manner. Nor does it require elaboration to shew that, if I make a mis-statement falsely and maliciously about the property of another which does him damage, the Common Law would take cognisance of such an action. It is to be observed, that in order to make good such a cause of action at Common Law, or to make good such an application for interference by a Court of Equity, you must shew that the statement was false and malicious, a wilful act done without just cause or excuse. And in the case of a person putting forward in the maintenance of what he conceived to be his rights, a false statement which was not in itself defamatory believing it to be true, even if the statement did damage to another person, an action would not lie at Common Law, and the Court of Equity would not interfere. Why? Because he would be acting upon his rights in putting forward his own case. The law would not accordingly interfere, and a threat about an infringement, or alleged infringement, could not therefore be made the subject of an action or a suit unless the plaintiff was prepared to shew that it was made *mala fide*, and that there was no reasonable excuse for it. But it is to be observed that such a state of the law threw an *onus* on those who were in fact aggrieved, which made almost nugatory the remedy in a case of assertions of patent right, the effect of which was to paralyse the trade of others. Because it would be extremely difficult to prove that the persons complained of had put forward these assertions of patent right maliciously, or without just cause or excuse. And apparently the Legislature were of opinion that there was a mischief which was not touched by the Common Law and which they should cure. Then came the statute, and we

[73] [1893] 1 Ch. 413; *sub nom. Skinner v Perry* (1893) 10 R.P.C. 1, CA, *per* Bowen L.J. *Sugg v Bray* (1885) 2 R.P.C. 223 decided that the 1883 Act did not apply to threats made before its commencement, and well illustrates the deficiencies of the old law.
[74] This sentence needs to be read in the light of *Allen v Flood* [1898] A.C. 1, HL.

must see by the section itself what the mischief was and how far the section has cured it."

7–192   In *Dunlop Pneumatic Tyre Co v Maison Talbot*[75] the plaintiffs were the patentees of a method for making pneumatic tires. There were a total of three English licensees under the patent, one of whom (the North British Rubber Company) supplied the defendants with tires. Tires made by Michelin in France (where the plaintiffs had no rights) were said to infringe the patent, but had previously been imported into England by a company licensed by the plaintiffs for that purpose.[76] Michelin terminated this state of affairs in favour of an exclusive agreement with the defendants, and the defendants wrote to a customer stating that *Michelin* tires would no longer be obtainable in England from the plaintiffs or their former licensee, and that they could not be obtained from third parties without infringing the rights of the North British Rubber Company. Dunlop alleged slander of title in relation to their patent, in so far as they could lawfully buy *Michelin* tires in the open market in France and import them. The Court of Appeal (reversing the trial judge) held that the defendants' statement was not made maliciously, since the writer had honestly misunderstood the legal effect of the complicated licensing and contractual arrangements, and that no damage had been proved.

A relatively rare example of the common law action for injurious falsehood being combined with the statutory threats action may be found in *Cars v Bland Light Syndicate*,[77] where both claims succeeded. An advertisement issued by the defendants suggested that they had successfully prosecuted patent infringement proceedings when in fact the only action had been for passing-off, and a letter by their patent agents had been circulated stating that copies of the defendants' burners were being imported and that the grant of two unspecified patents and three registered designs under the Patents and Designs Act 1907 was "the strongest possible proof (apart from actual legal action) of their validity has been established". In fact, the patents were for minor improvements to an existing design of burner which the defendants had previously imported themselves, and which was then being imported by the plaintiffs. The plaintiffs (who, though not identified by name, were the only competitors) had not copied or infringed, and the defendant had no basis on which to say otherwise.

7–193   In *Mentmore Manufacturing v Fomento*[78] an interlocutory injunction was granted against the defendants stating (correctly) that a patent of theirs had been upheld in the Court of Appeal without also stating that leave to appeal to the House of Lords had been given and the injunction stayed. The defendants' Chief Legal Adviser (a solicitor) had apparently told trade buyers at Selfridges and other stores that the defendants' pens should be taken off sale immediately and that the defendants were entitled to impound them. The action, originally framed as one for statutory threats, had been

---

[75] (1904) 20 T.L.R. 579, CA.
[76] The *Clipper Pneumatic Tyre Co*, plaintiffs in a second action.
[77] (1911) 28 R.P.C. 33 (Warrington J.).
[78] (1955) 72 R.P.C. 157, CA.

amended to include a claim for injurious falsehood, and the status of the solicitor as an officer of the court may also have been relevant.

In *British and International Proprietaries v Selcol*[79] both parties claimed to be exclusive licensees under a patent. The patentee had originally orally agreed to grant an exclusive licence to the defendants, but had subsequently purported to repudiate it and had granted an exclusive licence to the plaintiffs instead. The defendants marked goods manufactured and sold by them as licensed under the patent. Upjohn J. refused an interlocutory injunction enjoining the defendants from representing that they were licensed: there was no tenable allegation of malice against the defendants, the plaintiffs' own title to sue was not beyond doubt, passing-off was not suggested, and the *status quo* was that only the defendants were already on the market.

In *Olin Matheson v Biorex*[80] the defendants to a *quia timet* action for patent infringement counterclaimed for statutory threats and malicious falsehood. Graham J. found the patent valid and infringed. His statement that the plaintiffs' good faith in asserting the patent would have been no defence to the action for injurious falsehood had the patent been invalid or not infringed is therefore *obiter* as well as being *per incuriam* and plainly wrong, being based on a misunderstanding of *Skinner v Perry*,[81] a pure statutory threats action.

Trade marks and passing-off

Assertions of trade mark infringement or passing-off may carry the impli- **7–194** cation that the person accused is dealing in spurious or counterfeit goods, which may amount to either or both of defamation or injurious falsehood. As a practical matter even an action for injurious falsehood is unlikely to succeed unless this is a fair reading of the matter complained of,[82] or the allegation of infringement is as self-evidently hopeless as that in *Greers v Pearman & Corder*[83] where the defendants asserted infringement of part of a registered trade mark which had been disclaimed. Examples (further considered at para.7–165 above) are *Thorley's Cattle Food Co v Massam*[84]; *Thomas v Williams*[85] and *Hatchard v Mège*.[86]

In *Ripley v Arthur*[87] the defendant in an action for trade mark infringement and passing-off counterclaimed for threats to his customers. Farwell J. struck out the counterclaim and refused an application to amend it by pleading malice: without malice the unamended counterclaim disclosed no cause of action, and the fact that the action was being pursued against

[79] [1957] R.P.C. 3 (Upjohn J.).
[80] [1970] R.P.C. 157 at p. 195 (Graham J.).
[81] *Skinner v Shew* [1893] 1 Ch. 413; *sub nom. Skinner v Perry* (1893) 10 R.P.C. 1, CA.
[82] *Thomas Withers & Sons Ltd v Samuel Withers & Co Ltd* (1926) 44 R.P.C. 19 (KBD).
[83] (1922) 39 R.P.C. 406, CA, below.
[84] (1879) 14 Ch. D. 763, CA.
[85] (1880) 14 Ch. D. 864.
[86] (1887) 18 Q.B. 771.
[87] (1900) 18 R.P.C. 82 (Farwell J.).

Arthur demonstrated that the plaintiff was not acting maliciously but vindicating his legal rights as he perceived them.[88]

7–195   In *Royal Baking Powder v Wright Crossley*[89] the defendants successfully revoked the plaintiffs' registered device marks incorporating the words *Royal Baking Powder* and published advertisements stating that they would take legal action against any future use of the marks. The plaintiffs' action for injurious falsehood was dismissed by the House of Lords because the plaintiffs could not prove special damage (except possibly in respect of some lost sales which would have been illegal in the sense that their labels still bore the word "registered" after the marks had been revoked) and their Lordships were therefore absolved from having to agree on whether the defendants' threats would otherwise have been actionable. One school of thought was that the defendants had merely asserted that use of the precise marks revoked might expose the user to some kind of legal action,[90] which was even if untrue in fact was not self-evidently malicious; the other was that the defendants were making a totally unfounded claim to exclusive rights in the word *Royal* in order to interfere with the plaintiffs' legitimate trade.[91]

7–196   In *Greers v Pearman & Corder*[92] the defendants were the registered proprietors of a trade mark for chocolates which included the words *Banquet Brand*, but the word *Banquet* was disclaimed. Their solicitors wrote to trade customers of the plaintiffs asserting that the latter's *Banquet* chocolate assortment infringed the mark. The jury awarded damages of £300, and the Court of Appeal held that there was sufficient evidence on which they could have held that the statement was made maliciously.

In the *Harris Tweed* case, *Argyllshire Weavers v Macaulay*[93] the pursuers objected, *inter alia*, to various statements made by the defenders to the Lyon King of Arms in Scotland, the United States Patent and Trade Mark Office, the United States Customs Service,[94] and the English High Court in the course of protecting or asserting their common law rights and certification trade mark for *Harris Tweed*. All the claims failed on the facts, since none of the cloth manufactured by the pursuers was actually entitled to call itself *Harris Tweed*; in no case were the relevant allegations made maliciously; and in the case of the English action no satisfactory objection to what the defenders had done was advanced.

7–197   In *Essex Electric v IPC Computers*[95] the individual defendant was restrained from commencing or threatening to commence proceedings for passing-off against customers of the plaintiffs. There was a dispute as to which of the parties had the better claim to the mark *IPC* for computers in the United Kingdom–the defendant's case being thin but not quite hopeless–

---

[88] The plaintiffs subsequently obtained a default judgment. See *Ripley v John Arthur & Co* (1902) 19 R.P.C. 443, CA (reported on an application to commit).

[89] (1900) 18 R.P.C. 95, HL.

[90] Lords James and Morris.

[91] Lords Davey and Robertson.

[92] (1922) 39 R.P.C. 406, CA.

[93] [1964] R.P.C. 477 (Lord Hunter, OH).

[94] In the absence of evidence as to United States law the judge reluctantly assumed the latter to correspond to Scots law.

[95] [1991] F.S.R. 690 (Ferris J.).

but the defendant's threats of proceedings against customers were not necessary to vindicate his rights, if any, and his real motive seems to have been to apply improper pressure on the plaintiffs. The plaintiffs acknowledged (in deference to *Bestobell v Bigg*[96]) that no interlocutory injunction could be granted on their claim for injurious falsehood, but the balance of convenience was strongly in their favour and an injunction based on abuse of process and interference with contractual relations was not precluded by *Bestobell*.[97]

In *Ciba-Geigy v Parke Davis*[98] there was neither passing-off, nor injurious falsehood, by the use in a comparative advertising campaign of the device of a green apple with a bite taken out of it to attract attention to the defendants' claim that their generic substitute for the plaintiffs' brand of diclofenac was cheaper. The plaintiffs' own advertising consistently used a similar (whole) apple as a kind of *de facto* trade mark, and although the apple was widely recognised as denoting the plaintiffs, the apple device was not registered. Aldous J. acknowledged that the balance of convenience favoured restraining conduct which might have destroyed the distinctiveness of the apple mark pending trial, but this was impossible when there was no serious issue to be tried.

Copyright

In *Hart v Wall*[99] the *Hartridge Sisters*, two music hall vocalists, had published an advertisement in a trade paper saying that they had permission to sing any works published by Chappell, Metzler and others. The defendant, a musical agent, wrote to the proprietors of two music halls disputing this and implying that the proprietors might find themselves liable to penalties. The trial judge non-suited the plaintiffs, but the Divisional Court ordered a retrial since the letters were capable of an interpretation which was defamatory, and the issue of construction should have been left to the jury. Though the distinction between libel and injurious falsehood was not yet very well developed and some of the arguments are ambiguous, the case does appear to be one of libel properly so called. Lindley J. mentioned the relevance of the defendant's motives, but this would have been equally relevant to rebut a defence of qualified privilege. **7–198**

In *Dicks v Brooks*[1] Millais' painting, *The Hugenot*, had been widely reproduced as a print, and the defendant owned the copyright in the original engraving. The plaintiffs, magazine publishers, distributed as part of the Christmas issue of their magazine *Bow Bells* a pattern for woolwork in which the two central figures from Millais' work were reproduced, though with a different background. It was to be assumed that the figures on the pattern had been copied from the print, rather than the original painting. The defendant issued a circular warning that all copies of *The Hugenot* not

---

[96] [1975] F.S.R. 421 (Oliver J.).
[97] Applying *Microdata Information Services Ltd v Rivendale Ltd* (1984) [1991] F.S.R. 681, CA.
[98] [1994] F.S.R. 8 (Aldous J.).
[99] (1877) 2 C.P.D. 146 (Divisional Court).
[1] (1879) 15 Ch. D 22, CA.

marked as licensed by his firm were infringements, the plaintiff sued for slander of title, and the defendant counterclaimed for copyright infringement. The Court of Appeal initially held that the woolwork pattern was not an infringement of the copyright in the print (since it was too crude to have reproduced the individual contribution of the engraver, as opposed to that of the original artist) but refused the plaintiff an enquiry as to damages because only three copies of the circular had been issued and no appreciable damage had been proved to have been caused. *Dicta* suggested that if damage could have been proved then the defendant's exaggerated assertion of his rights would have been actionable, but *Wren v Weild*[2] was not cited and in *Halsey v Brotherhood*[3] *Dicks v Brooks* received a restricted interpretation.

7–199   In *Jaybeam v Abru*[4] the proprietors of copyright in drawings for a lightweight aluminium step ladder wrote a letter before action to a magazine which was promoting a similar ladder made by the plaintiffs. The letter concluded with a sentence notifying the existence of a registered design.[5] Whitford J. granted interlocutory injunctions against threatening proceedings for infringement of registered design, and from deliberately or recklessly interfering with the plaintiffs' business by threatening customers or potential customers with copyright infringement proceedings. Though injurious falsehood was argued (and was conceded to have some prospect of success for the purposes of *American Cyanamid*[6]) no injunction was granted under that head. Perhaps the best justification for the result is that the defendants had not stopped short of claiming an absolute monopoly in lightweight metal step ladders regardless of whether there had been copying, so that the claims which purported to be in response to the alleged copyright infringement were to that extent either wholly unjustified, or incapable of being separated from the final and otherwise innocuous paragraph notifying the existence of the registered design.

Much more in line with the mainstream of authority is *Granby Marketing Services v Interlego*[7] in which Vinelott J. struck out a claim for unlawful interference with contractual relations arising from the defendants' threat of copyright infringement proceedings in relation to kits of children's plastic building bricks offered in a promotion for a breakfast cereal. No action for wrongful interference with contractual relations arose if all the defendant had done was to assert in good faith a legal right claimed by him, and to threaten proceedings if the right was infringed.

7–200   In *Microdata Information Services v Rivendale*[8] the plaintiffs obtained a

---

[2] (1869) 4 Q.B. 730 (Divisional Court).
[3] (1881) 19 Ch. D. 386, CA, affirming (1880) 15 Ch. D. 514 (Jessel M.R.).
[4] [1975] F.S.R. 334 (Whitford J.).
[5] By s.26(3) of the Registered Designs Act 1949 mere notification of the existence of a registered design is not actionable as a threat.
[6] *American Cyanamid Co v Ethicon Ltd* [1975] A.C. 396; [1975] 1 All E.R. 504; [1975] F.S.R. 101; [1975] R.P.C. 513, HL.
[7] [1984] R.P.C. 209 (Vinelott J.). *Tyburn Productions Ltd v Conan Doyle* [1991] Ch. 75; [1990] R.P.C. 195 turned almost entirely on the fact that infringement of United States copyright and unfair competition laws was not justiciable in England.
[8] (1984) [1991] F.S.R. 681, CA.

licence to market the defendants' computer software, but the parties almost immediately fell out and the corporate defendant purported to terminate the agreement. The individual defendant then threatened to sabotage a promising and extremely lucrative contract between the plaintiffs and the RAF unless he was given a consultancy agreement, and paid £60,000 and 10 per cent royalties on any hardware sold. The plaintiffs obtained *ex parte* and *inter partes* interlocutory injunctions against the defendants representing that the plaintiffs had no right to license or use the software. The Court of Appeal held that because the plaintiffs' claim was not framed in defamation or slander of title, but for interference with contractual relations, they were not bound by the practice in defamation actions which had been applied to injurious falsehood by Oliver J. in *Bestobell v Bigg*,[9] and continued the injunction.

In *Western Front v Vestron*[10] the defendants claimed to have an equitable interest in the copyright for the plaintiffs' film *Gunbus* as a result of a concluded oral contract giving them exclusive home video distribution rights, but on the plaintiffs' version of events there had never been any binding agreement. The plaintiffs applied for summary judgement, or an interlocutory injunction, against the defendants for interference with contractual relations, but both were refused. Although Peter Gibson J. reluctantly held that the existence of a defence of justification was not conclusive,[11] the balance of convenience favoured the defendants and the latter's claim to have an equitable interest in the film was not self-evidently hopeless or made other than *bona fide*.

CHC Software Care v. Hopkins & Wood[12] is reported for two applications in an action for injurious falsehood against the defendant firm of solicitors, in respect of letters before action asserting copyright infringement and breach of confidence on behalf of clients who subsequently agreed to a consent order acknowledging that the CHC program did not infringe any of their rights. Mummery J. refused to transfer the action to the Queen's Bench Division for jury trial, and made an interim order for discovery of the identity of persons to whom such letters had been sent.

Claims to authorship or inventorship

There are statutory regimes for allowing the author of a copyright work, or **7–201** the inventor of a granted patent, to assert his right be identified as such. Sections 77 to 79 of the Copyright, Designs and Patents Act 1988 protect the moral right of an author or director to be identified as such, and s.84 protects against false attribution of authorship. Section 13 of the Patents Act 1977 provides for an inventor to have the right to be identified as such in

[9] [1975] F.S.R. 421 (Oliver J.).
[10] [1987] F.S.R. 66 (Peter Gibson J.). The judgment is heavily edited. A claim for injurious falsehood does appear to have been pleaded, but presumably was not directly relied on to support the interlocutory injunction.
[11] On the authority of *Microdata Information Services Ltd v Rivendale Ltd* (1984) [1991] F.S.R. 681, CA, above.
[12] [1993] F.S.R. 241 (Mummery J.).

any patent granted for that invention (the right is independent of any claim to proprietorship or employee compensation) and there is a corresponding Patent Office procedure.[13]

In the past disputes as to the credit due to a person as an author, inventor or performer have sometimes been litigated as injurious falsehood, defamation or passing-off,[14] and these may remain of marginal relevance.

7–202 In *Reichardt v Sapte*[15] a charge of plagiarism in the writing of a play amounted to libel, the defence of justification having been withdrawn. In *New Musical Express v Cardfont Publishers*[16] one of two complaints about the relative merits of *Top Ten* lists compiled by rival popular music magazines was that sales of records of a song sung by one artist (for whom the second plaintiffs were agents) had been deliberately misattributed in the defendants' list to another singer. Harman J. found it impossible to resolve the allegations on motion, and refused an interlocutory injunction. In *Eothen Films v Industrial and Commercial Education-Macmillan*[17] the plaintiffs initially obtained an *ex parte* injunction against the defendants distributing a brochure in which they supposedly claimed to have produced various films which were in fact the plaintiffs' work, but the injunction was discharged on appeal as the evidence of imminent or irreparable damage was inadequate, and the case on the merits less than overwhelming. The defendants had truthfully claimed to have devised the basic concept of the films, and the proposition that they had also produced them had to be "wrung out of the brochure" if it was to be found there at all. Of course the defendants knew that they had not produced the films, but unless there was evidence that that was what they had intended to say, then there was nothing from which to infer malice.

In *Customglass Boats v Salthouse*[18] advertisements issued by the plaintiffs asserted that two models of yachts in their *Cavalier* range had been designed by them, when in fact they had been designed by the second defendant. Damages of NZ$500 were awarded on his counterclaim, with the judge finding that although the misstatement had originally been issued carelessly rather than maliciously, the plaintiffs had failed to withdraw it promptly once they had been made aware of its falsity.

7–203 In *Wilde v Thompson*[19] the Court of Appeal acknowledged that a libel action might lie for depriving an inventor of the credit for his invention, but ordered the plaintiff's action to be struck out. The book complained of was accurate and indeed complimentary in its treatment of the plaintiff's contribution to the invention of a workable "Dynamo", and the only possible complaint was that the parties differed as to whether that word properly

---

[13] Patents Rules 1995, r.14.
[14] As to which see para.7–152 above.
[15] [1893] 2 Q.B. 308; 9 T.L.R. 604 (Hawkins J., QBD). The libel claims are only reported in the T.L.R.
[16] [1956] R.P.C. 211 (Harman J.).
[17] [1966] F.S.R. 35, CA.
[18] [1976] N.Z.L.R. 36; [1976] R.P.C. 589 (Mahon J., HC of NZ).
[19] (1903) 20 R.P.C. 775, CA, affirming (1903) 20 R.P.C. 361 (Buckley J.).

denoted the plaintiff's invention alone or a wider category embracing earlier attempts. In neither case did the plaintiff have any exclusive right to the word, which had been coined by a third party, or any cause for complaint when it was applied to the inventions of others such as Faraday.

In *Nicrotherm Electrical Co v Percy*[20] a dispute as to whether a loss-making design of pig-rearer had been invented by the (individual) plaintiffs, or by the personal defendant, originally included a claim for passing-off, which appears to have been abandoned, and one for injurious falsehood, which failed at trial for absence of proof of malice. A counterclaim by the defendant for a declaration that he was the inventor was dismissed. The machine had in fact been invented by the individual plaintiffs, and although he may have contributed details to its design he was neither the sole nor even a joint inventor.

In *Easycare v Lawrence*[21] an interlocutory injunction against (*inter alia*) alleged injurious falsehood was refused because the defendant intended to justify his allegations that the plaintiffs' *Easyboot* was a new and inferior copy of his original *Equiboot*. The product underlying the dispute (a plastic boot for horses' hooves) had in fact been invented in the United States by an individual connected with the plaintiffs, and for a while the defendant had distributed it for them in the United Kingdom before parting company and introducing his own close copy, for which he had previously obtained a patent (by importation) under the Patents Act 1949. Both parties claimed the credit for inventing the device and having introduced it to the United Kingdom, but any patents must have expired before 1994.

Contempt of court

In the past, exaggerated public claims by either party of past[22] or pro- **7–204** spective[23] success in litigation have sometimes been treated as contempt of court, but in principle such claims would have to prejudice the proper administration of justice for contempt to be committed,[24] for instance by

---

[20] [1957] R.P.C. 207, CA, affirming [1956] R.P.C. 272 (Harman J.). The judgment on appeal is concerned only with breach of confidence and copyright.
[21] [1996] F.S.R. 597 (Aldous J.).
[22] *Edlin & Co v Pneumatic Tyre and Booth's Cycle Agency Ltd* (1893) 10 R.P.C. 317 and *Gillette Safety Razor Co Ltd v Gamage Ltd* (1906) 24 R.P.C. 1 (both patent cases); *Gillette Safety Razor Co Ltd v Pellett Ltd* (1909) 26 R.P.C. 558 (passing-off).
[23] *Daw v Eley* (1868) L.R. 7 Eq. 49; *Goulard and Gibbs v Sir Coutts Lindsay & Co Ltd* (1887) 4 R.P.C. 189 (both patent cases); *J & P Coates v Chadwick* [1894] 1 Ch. 347 (trade mark and passing-off–but a much criticised decision); *St Mungo Manufacturing Co v Hutchinson, Main & Co Ltd* (1908) 25 R.P.C. 356 (registered design, Scotland).
[24] *Reg. v Payne & Cooper* [1896] 1 Q.B. 577 (Divisional Court); *Fenner v Wilson & Co Ltd* (1893) 10 R.P.C. 283, CA; (patent); *Gaskell & Chambers Ltd v Hudson Dodsworth & Co* [1936] 2 K.B. 595 (Divisional Court–injurious falsehood); *Carl-Zeiss-Stiftung v Rayner & Keeler Ltd* [1961] R.P.C. 1 (trade marks and passing-off). The latter contains a particularly comprehensive review of the authorities by Russell J.

poisoning the minds of jurors or witnesses, and such relief has more often been refused.[25]

An issue of principle arises as to whether post-judgment misrepresentations can ever amount to a contempt, the logical conclusion being that in *Dunn v Bevan*[26] to the effect that if there are no longer any proceedings pending, then there can be no prejudice and no liability for contempt, no matter how outrageous the misrepresentation. It may therefore be significant that the three cases cited above[27] as misstatements of past successes all misrepresented the outcome of interlocutory hearings, so that there was at least the theoretical possibility of the rest of the action being prejudiced. Prejudice might also arise in the not uncommon case of several actions being pending at the same time, in which misrepresenting the outcome of one (even after final judgment) might be thought to prejudice one or more of the others.

In *Hayward v Hayward*[28] the defendant was liable for libel, injurious falsehood or both by implying that judgment had been entered against the plaintiffs for serious and fraudulent passing-off, when in fact the plaintiff (defendant in the passing-off action) had been substantially vindicated but had given certain voluntary undertakings because of a few isolated and unauthorised misrepresentations by an agent.

P. Conclusions

Passing-off and injurious falsehood revisited

7–205 It will be clear from this chapter as a whole that a wide and diverse class of misrepresentations are actionable as passing-off, injurious falsehood, or occasionally as both. Can the recognised categories and instances of misrepresentation be accommodated under a general rule for each, or, preferably, for both together? The purpose of the rule would be to determine those categories of misrepresentation which are capable, in principle, of amounting to passing-off or injurious falsehood as the case may be; to distinguish them from those which are actionable only under some other head of law or not at all; and to identify the class of persons who are entitled to sue. The latter is an important and often overlooked aspect of the problem. Some attempts have been made to define passing-off, at least, in terms

---

[25] *Fenner v Wilson & Co Ltd* (1893) 10 R.P.C. 283, CA (reversing Kekewich J., *ibid.*); *Dunlop Pneumatic Tyre Co Ltd v Clifton Rubber Co Ltd* (1902) 19 R.P.C. 527; *British Vacuum Cleaner Co Ltd v Suction Cleaners Ltd* (1904) 21 R.P.C. 300; *Haskell Golf Ball Co Ltd v Hutchinson* (1904) 21 R.P.C. 487; *Mullard Radio Valve Co Ltd v Rothermell Corp* (1934) 51 R.P.C. 1; *Selsdon Fountain Pen Co Ltd v Miles Martin Pen Co Ltd* (1948) 65 R.P.C. 365 (all patent cases); *Gaskell & Chambers Ltd v Hudson Dodsworth & Co* [1936] 2 KB 595 (Divisional Court–injurious falsehood); *Carl-Zeiss-Stiftung v Rayner & Keeler Ltd* [1961] R.P.C. 1 (trade marks and passing-off); *Easipower Appliances Ltd v Gordon Moore (Electrical) Ltd* [1963] R.P.C. 8 (passing-off).
[26] [1922] 1 Ch. 276 (Sarjant J.), not an intellectual property case.
[27] At fn.22.
[28] (1886) 34 Ch. D. 198

of the representations a prospective defendant may or may not make,[29] but this is futile. No one, trader or not, can be said to have the right to make any misrepresentation about himself, his goods or his business; or about the person, goods or business of a rival; but whether any such misrepresentation is civilly actionable or not, and if so by whom, is another matter altogether. One and the same misrepresentation may be actionable by one person though not by another, and may give rise to liability under one head of law though tolerated elsewhere.

In the present state of the law's development it is probably too ambitious to attempt to propose a single formulation for both passing-off and injurious falsehood (even if the latter were confined to a business context), although it is possible to identify some features that they have in common, and to say how the two are distinguished from one another. The first thing passing-off and injurious falsehood have in common is that they are both torts of misrepresentation in which a material deception of the misrepresentee foreseeably causes economic loss to another party, the claimant. In Sir John Salmond's words the two together constitute[30] "the wrong of deceiving other persons, so that they by their mistaken acts cause harm to the plaintiff". Another feature which passing-off and injurious falsehood have in common is that neither of them provides a remedy for "floating" misrepresentations, for which a proper contradictor cannot be identified.

As Jacob J. said in *Schulke & Mayr v Alkapharm*,[31] where the complaint **7–206** was that the defendants were making unjustified claims for the efficacy of their dentists' disinfectants:

"The plaintiffs say that both of these statements are false and that they accordingly have a cause of action. I will assume that the statements are false. Does the mere publication of such statements by the defendants about their own product without any reference to the plaintiffs or their products give the plaintiffs a cause of action either for malicious falsehood or passing off?

First, malicious falsehood. Mr Arnold says that the authorities establish that all you need for this cause of action is to prove the following three things: (1) that the statements complained of were untrue; (2) that they were made maliciously, that is to say without just cause or excuse; and, (3), that the plaintiff has suffered special damage thereby, or apart from that it is sufficient for them to prove that the words are calculated to cause pecuniary damage to the plaintiffs.

Mr Arnold says that therefore this tort is available to any trader against any trade rival who publishes a false advertisement, thereby affecting the first trader's sales by way of diversion. The only qualification he accepts is that the statement must be specifically false, that is to say a statement likely to be taken seriously as opposed to a mere puff of the sort that 'my goods are better than anybody else's'. It is a far-reaching and bold sub-

---

[29] Lord Halsbury in *Reddaway (Frank) & Co Ltd v George Banham & Co Ltd* [1896] A.C. 199; [1895–9] All E.R. 313; 13 R.P.C. 218, HL, provides the classic example.
[30] Salmond, *The Law of Torts* (1st ed., 1907) p.417.
[31] [1999] F.S.R. 161 (Jacob J.).

mission. It would mean that many aspects of the law of passing off would become unnecessary and, by implication, have been unnecessary for some time. It would mean, and would involve, a very considerable extension by the common law into a field mainly regulated by statutes. ... Is there any warrant in English common law for extending the tort this far? I do not think so."

And in relation to passing-off[32]:

"Passing off involves not only a false representation but a false representation related to the plaintiffs' product or goodwill, not a false representation in the air. This false representation does not depend, on the plaintiffs' case, on any representation concerning the plaintiffs' product at all; it is false (if it is in fact false) not because of the plaintiffs' product or goodwill but because it is inherently false. I do not think that there is a cause of action in passing off. It follows that the plaintiffs' claim will fail."

7–207   Where passing-off and injurious falsehood differ, apart from extraneous factors such as the requirement for malice and (formerly) proof of special damage, is in the type of misrepresentation which is addressed by each. Injurious falsehood, though not strictly confined to disparaging misrepresentations, is only concerned with misrepresentations which are made about an identifiable claimant and which reflect disadvantageously on that claimant in so far as his pecuniary interests are concerned. It is probably not necessary to define the misrepresentation in injurious falsehood any more precisely than that. Provided the misrepresentation is a negative one, and provided the interest adversely affected is economic, then there is at least the theoretical possibility of an action for injurious falsehood lying. The practical shortcomings of the action for injurious falsehood do not stem from any lack of generality in the kinds misrepresentation which it addresses, but principally from the near-impossibility in practice of proving malice and materiality when the alleged misrepresentation is made by a commercial competitor.

Passing-off, though not strictly confined to misrepresentations that the defendant is the claimant or closely connected with the claimant, is only concerned with certain kinds of positive misrepresentation which the defendant makes about himself; but the representation must still be such as to have a connection of some kind with the claimant, in a way which is examined in the reminder of the present section.

In what follows it should be borne in mind that no misrepresentation, whatever its nature, is actionable as passing-off by a particular trader unless it is really likely to cause damage to the goodwill of that trader. Put another way, the misrepresentation must be a material one, which normally means that it must be relied upon by the relevant public and acted upon to the detriment of the claimant. The purpose of this section is only to identify those misrepresentations which are capable in principle of amounting to

---

[32] See further para.7–211, below.

passing-off if they cause damage, and to distinguish them from those that cannot amount to passing-off even if they are damaging. To say, for instance, that a misrepresentation that one is licensed by the claimant is capable of amounting to passing-off is very different to saying that such a misrepresentation is actionable as passing-off regardless of the surrounding circumstances.

The generality of passing-off

Although the scope of passing-off has expanded enormously in the decades **7–208** since the *Champagne* case, *Bollinger v Costa Brava Wine Co*,[33] there is no reason to believe that passing-off has become as sweeping as some continental notions of unfair competition, in which any trader damaged by a misrepresentation may sue whatever its content or character. The nature of such a wide tort may be illustrated by *Koñl ⲻ Ringelhan & Rennett*[34] in the European Court of Justice. In the German courts the plaintiffs applied to have the French defendants restrained from using the name and logo they had inherited from a distinguished, but now defunct, German parent. If the plaintiffs had themselves been the successors to the former German company's goodwill then the case would have been unremarkable, but what makes it so surprising to English eyes is that the plaintiffs were simply competitors with no claim to any rights in the name or mark themselves. In principle, their cause of action was simply that the defendants were not entitled to an unfair competitive advantage through making any misrepresentations about themselves.

Passing-off in English law would not go that far. In the *Advocaat* case, *Erven Warnink v Townend*,[35] Lord Diplock placed only three express restrictions on what misrepresentations by a trader might be actionable as passing-off. The misrepresentation must be made in the course of trade; it must be made to prospective customers or ultimate consumers of the defendant and it must be calculated to damage the goodwill or business of another trader. However, Lord Diplock himself made it clear that he did not intend to exclude the existence of other conditions:

> "[O]ne must be particularly careful to be aware of the fallacy of the undistributed middle. It does not follow that because all passing-off actions can be shown to present these characteristics, all factual situations which present these characteristics give rise to an action for passing-off."

Lord Diplock went on to cite with apparent approval the case of *London* **7–209** *Armoury v Ever Ready*[36] in which the plaintiffs and the defendants were both importers of batteries. The plaintiffs complied with the Merchandise Marks Acts by indicating that their batteries were imported but the defendants did

[33] [1960] Ch. 262; [1959] 3 All E.R. 800; [1960] R.P.C. 16 for the preliminary point of law. At trial [1961] 1 W.L.R. 277; [1961] 1 All E.R. 561; [1961] R.P.C. 116.
[34] Case 177/83; [1984] E.C.R. 3551; [1985] 3 C.M.L.R. 340, ECJ.
[35] [1979] A.C. 731; [1979] 2 All E.R. 927; [1980] R.P.C. 31, HL.
[36] [1941] 1 K.B. 742.

not. Indirectly, the defendants therefore misrepresented their batteries as being of domestic manufacture. The plaintiffs considered that this gave the defendants an unfair and illegal advantage and sued for breach of the statutory duty they claimed was owed to them under the Acts. The Court construed the Acts as not creating any private right of action for competitors, but also indicated that even if the Acts had done so it could not have been invoked by the plaintiffs in the instant case. The plaintiffs themselves imported, and it was not enough that they carried on their own business legally and marked their goods appropriately. To have succeeded, had there been a statutory cause of action, they would have had to have manufactured in Britain themselves.

Lord Diplock's broad statement of principles in *Advocaat* does not have to be stretched to cover the facts of *Kohl v Ringelhan*. The plaintiffs and the defendants were competitors in the laboratory equipment market, and the advantage that the defendants obtained by misrepresenting to that market generally that they were a well-known company could hardly fail to damage the business of the plaintiff, though in common with any other competitors there might have been. All the same, there is something repugnant to the common law in giving a cause of action to all the competitors of the defendant based on a course of dishonest conduct which does not affect some or one of them more directly than the others. One expects such cases to be dealt with by criminal prosecution or a relator action.[37] In *Advocaat* itself Lord Diplock continued the passage cited above by saying:

> "True it is that their presence indicates what a moral code would censure as dishonest trading, based as it is upon deception of consumers of a trader's wares, but in an economic system which has relied on competition to keep down prices and to improve products there may be practical reasons not to run the risk of hampering competition by providing civil remedies to every one competing in the market who has suffered damage to his business or goodwill in consequence of inaccurate statements of whatever kind that may be made by rival traders about their own wares."

Advocaat showed that the previously understood limits of the tort of passing-off were too restrictive, but there is no reason to doubt that the principle behind *Cundey v Lerwill & Pike* and *London Armoury v Every-Ready* remains sound, and that a trader injured by the dishonest or even illegal conduct of a competitor has to show some additional reason for allowing him in particular, though not necessarily him alone, to sue.

The common principle

7–210 It is suggested that a misrepresentation may be actionable as passing-off at the suit of a particular claimant to the extent that it would be justified if made by, about or with the authority of that claimant individually or as a

---

[37] See the passage from the judgment of Parker J. in *Cundey v Lerwill & Pike* (1908) 99 L.T. 273; 24 T.L.R. 584 quoted at para.3–188 above.

member of a distinct class. There is no need for the category of potentially actionable misrepresentations to be defined any more narrowly than this. If there is no such connection between the misrepresentation and the claimant then there is no right to sue. In more colloquial terms, the misrepresentation must have the effect of attracting to the defendant business, custom or some other advantage which properly belongs to the claimant. To this extent, passing-off is concerned with misappropriation, although the existence of misappropriation on its own is insufficient.

On this basis it is suggested that *Schulke & Mayr v Alkapharm*[38] was very **7–211** much closer to the line than Jacob J. would have acknowledged. If the claim to effectiveness against HIV, for instance, had been established as true for the claimants' disinfectant and untrue for the defendants' then there would have been at least an arguable case of passing-off by analogy with *SDS Biotech v Power*[39] and *Hodge Clemco v Airblast*,[40] though an interlocutory injunction would still have been refused unless the defendants' claims were demonstrably false beyond any possibility of contradiction.

The suggested dichotomy in *Schulke & Mayr* between false representations "related to the plaintiffs' product or goodwill", and false representations "in the air" is substantially correct; but not the identification of the latter with "inherently false" misrepresentations or the implication that if a representation can be identified as false without reference to a particular claimant, then it cannot be actionable by him. It is true that in the majority of passing-off cases the defendant can only be convicted of making a misrepresentation by reference to something previously done by the claimant, typically because the claimant has rendered distinctive of himself an arbitrary sign which would otherwise mean nothing, but these cases are not exhaustive. A misrepresentation may be "inherently false" and still have sufficient connection with the claimant, his products, or his goodwill to be actionable. It is inherently false to say or to suggest that insoles for shoes are made with activated charcoal when they are not;[41] or that "Elderflower Champagne" is anything other than flavoured fizzy water;[42] or that "Swiss chocolate" made in Birmingham;[43] or that egg flip is Advocaat.[44] In none of these cases is the falsity as such dependent on anything done by the claimant, although one may readily understand that if no chocolate had ever been made in Switzerland, for instance, then there would have been no one with any commercial interest in restraining the relevant misrepresentation by Cadbury, and no obvious reason for Cadbury to make it in the first place.

[38] [1999] F.S.R. 161 (Jacob J.).

[39] (1989) [1995] F.S.R. 797 (Aldous J.).

[40] [1995] F.S.R. 806 (Jacob J.).

[41] *Combe International Ltd v Scholl (UK) Ltd* [1980] R P.C. 1, distinguished in *Schulke & Mayr v Alkapharm*. In *Combe v Scholl* the misrepresentation as to quality was implicit in copying the plaintiffs' get-up; but would an express misrepresentation have been any less actionable?

[42] *Taittinger SA v Allbev Ltd* [1994] 4 All E.R. 75; [1993] 2 C.M.L.R. 741; [1993] F.S.R. 641, CA.

[43] *Chocosuisse Union des Fabricants Suisse de Chocolat v Cadbury Ltd* [2000] R.P.C. 826, CA.

[44] *Erven Warnink BV v J Townend & Sons (Hull) Ltd* [1979] A.C. 731; [1979] 2 All E.R. 927; [1980] R.P.C. 31, HL.

What was sufficient in all these cases was that there was a distinct class of those with goodwill in relation to the genuine article, which could be defined as including the claimant, and excluding the defendant. Nor would it be right to say that in all these cases the respective claimants had earned a share of the goodwill in the relevant names and products by contributing to their reputation for excellence. The terms in which *locus standi* was defined in *Advocaat* are more than wide enough to include mere importers as well as producers, and there is no probationary period which a new entrant has to serve before he is admitted to the relevant class. By parity of reasoning, if there is a sufficiently distinct and recognised category of dental disinfectants effective against HIV, allowing for any difficulties in definition, and if *Schulke & Mayr* make such a disinfectant and *Alkapharm* do not, then there should be no conceptual difficulty in allowing *Schulke & Mayr* a cause of action for passing-off.

7–212   The broad principle may be recognised in the following quotations from several landmark cases from the late nineteenth century, though at that time the authors were commenting on the underlying nature and rationale of passing-off rather than attempting a definition. Though the law no longer assumes that the claimant and the defendant need be in competition, the tenor of the misrepresentation remains the same.

"[T]he rule of law has been that, if you choose to state that which is false, and induce another person to deal with you by that falsehood and so deprive the original maker of the trade which otherwise he would get, that is an actionable wrong, and gives rise to the right to an injunction."[45]

"I am unable to see why a man should be allowed *in this way more than in any other* to deceive purchasers into the belief that they are getting what they are not, and thus to filch the business of a rival."[46]

"A man shall not by misrepresentation appropriate to himself business which belongs to his neighbour."[47]

7–213   The most common misrepresentation in passing-off is that the goods or business of the defendant are those of the claimant. This is the clearest example of a representation the claimant may justifiably make. His goods or business are his own. If the passing-off is alleged to involve different classes of goods, then it is for the claimant to show that there are two or more such classes and to appropriate his goods to one or the other. If the defendant claims some connection with the claimant then the representation is one

---

[45] *per* Lord Halsbury LC in *Powell v Birmingham Vinegar Brewery Co* [1897] A.C. 710; 14 R.P.C. 721, HL.
[46] *per* Lord Herschell in *Reddaway (Frank) & Co Ltd v George Banham & Co Ltd* [1896] A.C. 199; [1895–9] All E.R. 313; 13 R.P.C. 218, HL. This passage was cited by Lord Diplock in *Erven Warnink BV v J Townend & Sons (Hull) Ltd* [1979] A.C. 731; [1979] 2 All E.R. 927; [1980] R.P.C. 31, HL (with the emphasis added by him) as "a premonitory hint" of what was to come.
[47] *per* Lord Davey in *Cellular Clothing Co v Maxton & Murray* [1899] A.C. 326; 16 R.P.C. 397, HL.

which would be justified had the claimant allowed such a connection to exist. There are also cases in which the representation is such that the claimant might never have made it about himself, but where he was in a position to determine whether the representation would be true or false when made by others. A good example is given in the Australian case of *Scott v Tuff-Kote*[48] where the defendants were restrained from advertising that their rust-proofing service was insured at Lloyd's. The plaintiff did not provide any sort of insured rust-proofing service himself,[49] but had *locus standi* by virtue of being an underwriter in a syndicate which offered such insurance policies to rust-proofing businesses.

Scott v Tuff-Kote was innovatory in allowing a cause of action to an individual plaintiff who was only one of many persons able to have made the defendants' misrepresentation true, but in other respects it may be regarded as following long-standing authority. It is established that it may be passing-off to represent that one is the licensee of another business. Although such a misrepresentation may shade into a suggestion that the two businesses are one and the same, if the misrepresentation is made expressly then it is inherently one which the claimant could not meaningfully have made about himself. Another line of cases consists of those in which unqualified individuals have been restrained by professional associations from using distinctive combinations of letters to misrepresent that they were members or had some particular qualification. In such cases there was no representation that the defendant was the claimant, merely that he was a member and entitled or authorised to use those initials.

In the extended form of passing-off which consists of misrepresenting the character or quality of the defendant's goods, *Advocaat*[50] demolished the fallacy that the law was confined to misrepresentations of geographical origin, but Lord Fraser in that case made it clear that the right to sue for misdescription was confined to those who sold the genuine product in England. Honest sellers of egg flip as such would have no right to sue Townend for selling egg flip as *Advocaat* even if they had lost business to the latter's unfair and deceptive competition. On the facts of the *Champagne Cider* case, *Bulmer v Bollinger*[51] Bulmer would not have been liable to competing cider manufacturers or to businesses selling cheap Spanish sparkling wines of the sort formerly described as *Spanish Champagne*. Given the differences between *Pomagne* and genuine *Champagne* in terms of price, quality and type of customers the latter businesses probably lost far more sales to Bulmer than did the Champagne houses. **7–214**

Finally, "inverse" passing-off needs no separate treatment but reveals itself as a special instance of the general rule. The defendant has claimed

[48] [1975] N.S.W.L.R. 537. Mentioned with approval by Lord Fraser in *Erven Warnink BV v J Townend & Sons (Hull) Ltd* [1979] A.C. 731; [1979] 2 All E.R. 927; [1980] R.P.C. 31, HL.

[49] It is implicit that in cases such as *Scott v Tuff-Kote* any rust-proofing business which was indeed insured at Lloyds and which stood to be damaged would also have had a cause of action.

[50] *Erven Warnink BV v J Townend & Sons (Hull) Ltd* [1979] A.C. 731; [1979] 2 All E.R. 927; [1980] R.P.C. 31, HL.

[51] [1978] 2 C.M.L.R. 625; [1978] R.P.C. 79, CA. The action was for a declaration and the roles of the parties were reversed. Bulmer were restrained from selling *Pomagne* as *Champagne Cider*.

some quality or credit that properly belongs to the claimant, and *ex hypothesi* has made a representation which is false when applied to himself but which the claimant could properly make about his own goods or business.

CHAPTER 8

SIGNS

A. SIGNS, MARKS AND DISTINCTIVENESS

How passing-off is normally established

8–1 The essential elements of passing-off are a misrepresentation causing damage to the business or goodwill of the claimant.[1] The most common form the misrepresentation takes is to the effect that the goods or business of the defendant are those of the claimant, or are associated with the clai-

---

[1] *Spalding (AG) & Bros v A W Gamage Ltd* (1915) 32 R.P.C. 273, HL; *Erven Warnink BV v J Townend & Sons (Hull) Ltd* [1979] A.C. 731; [1979] 2 All E.R. 927; [1980] R.P.C. 31, HL; *Cadbury Schweppes Pty Ltd v Pub Squash Co Pty Ltd* [1981] 1 All E.R. 213; [1981] R.P.C. 429, PC; *Reckitt & Colman Products Ltd v Borden Inc* [1990] 1 W.L.R. 491; [1990] 1 All E.R. 873; [1990] R.P.C. 340, HL.

mant in some sense likely to cause damage.[2] In turn, the misrepresentation is almost always made, or alleged to be made, by the defendant using in relation to his goods or business some matter such as a name, word, device, get-up or other mark or sign which is deceptively similar to matter which the claimant claims to be distinctive of himself. If the claimant cannot prove the distinctiveness of the matter relied on then a passing-off action based on it must fail *in limine*.

> "Even in the case of what are sometimes referred to as Common Law Trade Marks the property, if any, of the so-called owner is in its nature transitory, and only exists so long as the mark is distinctive of his own goods in the eyes of the public or a class of the public. Indeed, the necessity of proving this distinctiveness in each case as a step in the proof of the false representation relied on was one of the evils sought to be remedied by the Trade Marks Act of 1875 ..."[3]

> "It is, of course, essential to the success of any claim in respect of passing-off based on the use of a given mark or get-up that the plaintiff should be able to show that the disputed mark or get-up has become by user in this country distinctive of the plaintiff's goods so that the use in relation to any goods of the kind dealt in by the plaintiff or [*sc* of] that mark or get-up will be understood by the trade and public in this country as meaning that the goods are the plaintiff's goods."[4]

In law, the single question to be answered is whether the defendant is to **8–2** be found liable for making a material misrepresentation, and in answering that question all the relevant circumstances are to be taken into account. In this respect, passing-off differs substantially from the law of registered trade marks. In that field the question of the distinctiveness of the claimant's mark arises as a separate issue; the test for confusing similarity relates only to the claimant's mark as registered and the defendant's corresponding "sign", ignoring any other matter which might be distinctive of the claimant in fact or any other circumstances which might contribute to deception; and the defendant cannot escape liability by using any amount of distinctive matter of his own, although that may effectively remove whatever risk of deception might have arisen from closeness to the claimant's mark alone. In passing-off it is often convenient to divide the question of misrepresentation into the same three issues of the distinctiveness of the claimant's mark, the degree of resemblance with the defendant's, and the presence or absence of other confusing or distinguishing features, but the three issues are not separated in the way they are in trade mark law and are always capable of interacting with one another.

In particular, the claimant in a passing-off case is given complete freedom in asserting what distinguishes his goods from others in the market. He is

---

[2] See Chapter 5.
[3] *per* Lord Parker in *Spalding (AG) & Bros v A W Gamage Ltd* (1915) 32 R.P.C. 273, HL.
[4] *per* Jenkins L.J. in *Gertli (T) AG v E J Bowman (London) Ltd* [1957] R.P.C. 388, 397, CA affirmed [1959] R.P.C. 1, HL.

not put to an election, as in the case of registered trade marks, which has to be made before any individual competitor is in his sights. There are few restrictions in passing-off as to what can be distinctive and the claimant can claim distinctiveness for matter which would never have been registrable under the Trade Marks Act 1994; or which would have been refused registration or made the subject of a disclaimer under previous Acts. This freedom is open to misuse. Allegations of how the claimant's goods are distinguished in the market tend to be drawn so as to fit the facts of the case in hand rather than to identify the features which either the public or the claimant really regard as most significant.

8–3   In what follows, it should be borne in mind that the question of whether a particular mark is distinctive of a certain trader is only one aspect of the wider question of whether there has been a misrepresentation. If the claimant in a typical case is successful it may be assumed that the mark relied on was distinctive of him, that the defendant's corresponding mark was confusingly similar, and that there were no other factors to prevent deception. To this rule there is one very important qualification, which is that if the defendant intended to deceive then the court will be unsympathetic to arguments that he has failed in his purpose, even if that means protecting a mark which *prima facie* is very far from distinctive.[5] On the other hand, if the claimant fails, then it does not necessarily mean that his mark (as pleaded) was not distinctive at all, still less that it was in law incapable of distinguishing his goods. It may have been that the defendant took adequate steps to differentiate his goods, or simply that his own mark was sufficiently different.

Distinctiveness is a matter of degree, and marks of low inherent distinctiveness may be protected against precise copying but not against slight variations. In most cases where the claimant fails it is because of a combination of factors: the points of resemblance between his goods and the defendant's are so slight that he is driven to assert distinctiveness in the trivial or commonplace, or the points of difference are marked enough to outweigh the effect of any similarities.

The concept of distinctiveness

8–4 "Distinctive" is a term of art in the law of passing-off and bears a meaning at variance with that in everyday use. Matter such as a name, mark or get-up is said to be distinctive if it denotes the goods of the claimant to the exclusion of other traders. It is the significance which the relevant public attaches to the supposed mark which is all-important. Matter which is not relied on by the public in this way is not in law distinctive, irrespective of how novel, striking or different it may be. Such matter probably does not serve as a sign at all, and certainly not as a sign performing the functions of a trade mark. Conversely, matter may be distinctive in the legal sense

---

[5] *Reddaway (Frank) & Co Ltd v George Banham & Co Ltd* [1896] A.C. 199; [1895–9] All E.R. 313; 13 R.P.C. 218, HL.

although it is altogether unremarkable in its own right. What is important is the function the mark serves, rather than how well it is adapted to serve it.

In considering whether a mark is distinctive for the purposes of passing-off it is important to bear in mind that the matter relied on may be distinctive in the everyday sense but not in law. This arises particularly often in get-up cases, but is not confined to them. The appearance of the furniture in *Jarman & Platt v Barget*[6] was "distinctive" in the sense that the plaintiffs had virtually created the market for furniture of a striking design, but that appearance did not denote the trade source of the goods, so it was not distinctive in the legal sense. Conversely, in *Sodastream v Thorn Cascade*[7] the colour grey was (arguably) distinctive of the plaintiffs' gas cylinders. In *Hoffman-La Roche v DDSA*[8] the plaintiffs' black and green capsules were also novel, unique and eye-catching. The defendants' case, which was sound in law although it failed on the facts, was that they were not distinctive because to patients they denoted the chemical composition of the drug they contained rather than the identity of the manufacturer. In cases based on word marks too, even an invented and arbitrary term such as *linoleum*[9] is not distinctive in law if its true meaning is as the generic name of the product.

Passing-off is relatively unconcerned with the distinction drawn in trade mark law between inherent capacity to distinguish and distinctiveness in fact. If factual distinctiveness exists, then it does not matter whether it was achieved with ease for a mark well adapted to distinguish or with difficulty for a mark of the opposite kind. If factual distinctiveness does not exist a traditional passing-off case must fail.[10] Passing-off never has to deal with the common situation in trade mark law of deciding how readily a mark not yet in use may become distinctive: the question is always whether an existing mark is distinctive in fact. Because of this, and because there are few *a priori* restrictions on what may be considered distinctive, the supposed inherent capacity of a mark to distinguish is only one factor among many. If the claimant adopts a mark which is obviously descriptive or otherwise of low capacity to distinguish then the evidential burden on him becomes higher, but never impossible. The other effect of low inherent distinctiveness is that smaller differences will serve to differentiate the defendant's goods when the claimant's mark is only marginally distinctive, but this is true if the mark is weakly distinctive for whatever reason.

Burberrys v Cording

The classic explanation of the principles on which the use of a particular **8–5** word or other mark may be restrained as passing-off is that of Parker J. in *Burberrys v Cording*[11]:

---

[6] [1977] F.S.R. 260, CA.
[7] [1982] R.P.C. 459, CA.
[8] [1969] F.S.R. 416, CA.
[9] *Linoleum Manufacturing Co v Nairn* (1878) 7 Ch.D. 834 (Fry J.).
[10] One based on one of the other categories of misrepresentation may still succeed. See Chapter 7.
[11] (1909) 26 R.P.C. 693. Paragraph breaks supplied.

"The principles of law applicable to a case of this sort are well known. On the one hand, apart from the law as to trade marks, no one can claim monopoly rights in the use of a word or name. On the other hand, no one is entitled by the use of any word or name, or, indeed, in any other way, to represent his own goods as being the goods of another to that other's injury. If an injunction be granted restraining the use of a word or name, it is no doubt granted to protect property, but the property to protect which it is granted is not property in the word or name, but property in the trade or goodwill which will be injured by its use. If the use of a word or name be restrained, it can only be on the ground that such use involves a misrepresentation, and that such misrepresentation has injured, or it calculated to injure, another in his trade or business.

If no case of deception by means of such misrepresentation can be proved, it is sufficient to prove the probability of such deception, and the court will readily infer such probability if it be shown that the word or name has been adopted with any intention to deceive. In the absence of such intention, the degree of readiness with which the court will infer the probability of deception must depend on the circumstances of each particular case, including the nature of the word or name the use of which is sought to be restrained.

It is important for this purpose to consider whether the word or name is *prima facie* in the nature of a fancy word or name, or whether it is *prima facie* descriptive of the articles in respect of which it is used. It is also important for the same purpose to consider its history, the nature of its use by the person who seeks the injunction, and the extent to which it is or has been used by others. If the word or name is *prima facie* descriptive, or be in general use, the difficulty of establishing the probability of deception is greatly increased, and again, if the person who seeks the injunction has not used the word or name simply for the purpose of distinguishing his own goods from the goods of others, but primarily for the purpose of denoting or describing the particular kind of article to which he has applied it, and only secondarily, if at all, for the purposes of distinguishing his own goods, it will be more difficult for him to establish the probability of deception.

But whatever be the nature of [*sc* or] history of the word or name, in whatever way it has been used, either by the person seeking the injunction or by others, it is necessary, where there has been no actual deception to establish at least a reasonable probability of deception. In such cases the action is, in effect a quia timet action, and unless such reasonable probability be established, the proper course is, in my opinion, to refuse an injunction, leaving the plaintiff to his remedy if cases of actual deception afterwards occur."

What can be distinctive?

8–6 The traditional compendious formula for what may be distinctive in passing-off is "name, mark or get-up", but as well as using "mark" ambiguously this is unduly narrow. In practice, passing-off tends to be concerned with marks or signs (in the broadest sense) which fall into a few specific categories: verbal marks as such, including personal and geographical names and descriptive or suggestive terms; words written in a special manner, including signatures and logos; purely visual marks such as labels, symbols, devices and pictures; get-up of packaging or goods; and composite marks including more than one of these elements. Marks protected have also included initials, numerals, and shape, size and colour, at least in combination. There is no reason to doubt that other kinds of mark or sign may also be distinctive, although they may fall on the boundaries of, or even outside, the traditional concept of a trade mark. Distinctiveness has been urged for an actor's voice,[12] the get-up of business premises, slogans, pattern, advertising style or themes and the very manner of doing business. Although the majority of such cases have failed on the facts, only in the latter case may this reflect a rule of law that the matter is incapable of being distinctive.

The general rule is that the law of passing-off is free of the doctrine that some indicia such as common personal or geographical names, laudatory terms and highly descriptive terms are incapable of being distinctive and ought to remain open to use by all. Even generic names can lose that character and become distinctive of a particular trader.

Public policy has more influence on the law of passing-off when what is in issue is the right to compete itself. The fact that the law has almost consistently refused to protect get-up alleged to consist of the appearance of the goods themselves (as opposed to their packaging) has undoubtedly been influenced by reluctance to give functional or aesthetic elements an indefinite protection potentially longer than for patents, registered designs or copyright. Likewise, the law has refused to prevent the copying of a new line of business or method of trading. The rule that slight differences are adequate to distinguish one descriptive name from another also reflects public policy, but it does not go so far as to refuse protection altogether even to highly descriptive names.

A law of signs

Consistently with modern usage elsewhere[13] and with its breadth of scope **8–7** after *Advocaat*,[14] one may describe the action for passing-off in terms of the use and misuse of *signs*. Passing-off protects against misrepresentation, and the misrepresentation is invariably conveyed by way of signs of some kind. In what is still by far the most typical case, the sign misused by the defendant (whether or not deliberately or precisely) is one which is distinctive of the claimant: in other words the sign is the claimant's trade mark in fact, even if it may not be registered as such. Though the word "sign" has not often been used in this context, that is simply a matter of preference and tradition: the principle has been stated in terms of signs as long ago as the nineteenth century, in a passage that has often been approved since:

---

[12] *Sim v H J Heinz Co Ltd* [1959] 1 W.L.R. 313; [1959] 1 All E.R. 547; [1959] R.P.C. 80, CA.

[13] Under the Trade Marks Act 1994 and the Community Trade Mark Regulation.

[14] *Erven Warnink BV v J Townend & Sons (Hull) Ltd* [1979] A.C. 731; [1979] 2 All E.R. 927; [1980] R.P.C. 31, HL.

"I have often endeavoured to express what I am going to express now (and probably I have said it in the same words, because it is very difficult to find other words in which to express it)–that is, that no man is entitled to represent his goods as being the goods of another man; and no man is permitted to use any *mark, sign* or *symbol, device* or *other means*, whereby, without making a direct false representation himself to a purchaser who purchases from him, he enables such purchaser to tell a lie or to make a false representation to somebody else who is the ultimate customer."[15]

8–8   Of course the consequence of misuse of the claimant's distinctive *sign*, in this sense, by the defendant, is very likely to amount to passing-off in the classic sense of misrepresenting the defendant's goods, services or business as those of the claimant. However, passing-off is not only concerned with signs which function as trade marks. The relevant sign may be a geographical indication such as *Champagne, Scotch whisky*, or *Swiss chocolate*. It may be a descriptive term with a precise meaning, such as *Advocaat*. It may be a composite expression. Whether the context be that of classic passing-off or one of its extended forms, the relevant sign need not be a word or a combination of words, but may be some essentially visual material such as a logo, device or get-up. The sign may be implicit in the defendant's conduct, or even in his silence, as with passing off by substitution. In theory, at least, if not yet to any significant extent in practice, the sign may be one which appeals to one of the senses other than hearing and sight, such as a word written in Braille, or may appeal to either or both of those without falling into the familiar rubric of "name, mark or get-up". Indeed, there may be no inherent reason to confine signs to those perceptible to the human senses–if, for instance, they are capable of affecting choices which humans delegate to machines or computers. Passing off by use of deceptive metatags may already be an example of the latter.

For all these reasons, it might be appropriate to dispense with tradition and prefer the term "sign" to more restrictive alternatives such as "name, mark or get-up," "trade mark," or even "mark" alone. The word "sign" is perfectly neutral as to what information is conveyed and the medium for conveying it. All that need be said of a sign is that it signifies something. Since the information so signified may be true or false, and since passing-off is concerned with wider categories of misrepresentation than trade mark law properly so called, it may be said that passing-off is in a general sense a law of signs.

B. Establishing Distinctiveness

Time factor and extent of use

8–9 A mark can only become distinctive by user, but there is no rule of law as to what kind or amount of user is necessary or sufficient to found the action.

---

[15] *per* James L.J. in *Singer v Loog* (1880) 18 Ch.D. 395, CA affirmed (1882) 8 App.Cas 15, HL, emphasis added.

What is in issue is whether there has been a material misrepresentation, which in turn depends on whether the mark has become distinctive to a sufficient proportion of the public. In general, the claimant's case will be strengthened by user which has lasted a long time and been on a large scale, but neither is essential. Cases in which the claimant has failed solely because of inadequate user have been rare in modern times. What is rather more common is that relatively small differences in the defendant's own mark, or field of business, will be held to afford a defence when the claimant's user has been slight. Occasionally, older decisions have referred to periods of several months, or even years, as being inadequate to appropriate marks of very low inherent capacity to distinguish.[16] Although inherently distinctive marks will be protected after a shorter period than ones which are descriptive or otherwise non-distinctive, it may be doubted if the supposed marks in question would have been protected whatever the length of use.

Certain types of user may be insufficient to create goodwill. Distinctiveness (or reputation) is a pure matter of fact and a mark may become distinctive through user which is insufficient in law to create goodwill. If so, an action must fail, but for lack of goodwill, not for absence of a misrepresentation. It is possible for advertising to render a mark distinctive even before the goods or services in question are available, as in *W H Allen v Brown Watson*[17] and *BBC v Talbot*.[18] Two issues are involved: whether the claimant has goodwill to protect before business commences and whether there is a misrepresentation to restrain. Advertising is also important in that without it the claimant's trade is likely to build up only slowly, and this in itself may delay the date at which the claimant's mark can be said to be distinctive of his business. With advertising or without, it is a matter of fact and degree how much user is required to render the mark distinctive. No minimum period of use can be set *a priori* because intensive user for a short period is as effective as longer but less concentrated use.

In *Licensed Victuallers Newspaper Co v Bingham*[19] the plaintiffs, without **8–10** any preliminary advertising of the name, published the first number of a new paper named The *Licensed Victuallers' Mirror*. Three days later the defendants published a competing paper under the same name. Sales of the plaintiffs' paper in the intervening period had been less than 100 copies, although afterwards they rose considerably. The Court of Appeal refused an injunction. The fact that sales of the plaintiffs' paper had subsequently risen could not help.

Sales of 50 dozen bottles of Champagne bearing the name *Court & Cie* was insufficient to make the name or label distinctive in *Goodfellow v Prince*,[20] even supposing the shippers had been the plaintiffs rather than the distributors, who had no *locus standi* to sue.

---

[16] 25 years in *Horlicks Malted Milk Co v Summerskill* (1916) 34 R.P.C. 63, HL, but the plaintiffs had used *Malted Milk* in a generic sense.
[17] [1965] R.P.C. 191 (Pennycuick J.).
[18] [1981] F.S.R. 228 (Megarry V.C.).
[19] (1888) 38 Ch.D. 139, CA.
[20] (1887) 35 Ch.D. 9, CA.

In *Compatibility Research v Computer Psyche*[21] the plaintiffs were the first to introduce a computer dating service to the United Kingdom. They adopted a symbol consisting of a heart linked with the male and female symbols on either side. The defendants started business shortly afterwards with a symbol consisting of a single circle, the top and bottom halves of which formed the male and female symbols, with a heart in the middle. Stamp J. refused an interlocutory injunction. The symbols were essentially descriptive of the service offered, were in common use, and could not have become distinctive of the plaintiffs in the three or four weeks' priority the plaintiffs enjoyed over the defendants.

Six months' use of the title *Gold AM* for a radio programme was not sufficient to make it distinctive when it was *prima facie* descriptive of the music played ("Golden Oldies") and the method of transmission by amplitude modulation in *County Sound v Ocean Sound*.[22]

8–11 It can still happen that the parties both start business so close together that the name in question does not have time to become distinctive of either. In the Canadian case of *Cira v Karmanoff*[23] two restaurants independently opened as *Capri* seven miles apart within three weeks of one another. An injunction was refused. An injunction was also refused to one restaurant against another 30 miles away, the plaintiffs having only a few months' priority, and the nature and customers of the parties' restaurants differing: *Blades Enterprises v Thibault*.[24] In *Isaccson v Nationwide News*[25] the parties launched competing newspapers in the Northern Territory of Australia under the name *Sunday Territorian* within a week of one another. Even within advertising and media circles neither could establish priority. On passing-off there was a stalemate. A similar result was reached in England in *Marcus Publishing v Hutton-Wild*[26] where both parties had conducted some promotion of their rival publications in the trade press but neither publication had been launched or even advertised to the public. In the circumstances, the name *Leisure News* cannot have been distinctive of either.

Slight use may be protected

8–12 Signs have been protected although the use made of them has been relatively slight. In *Weingarten v Boyer*,[27] the plaintiffs and defendants were respectively the largest corset manufacturers in the United States and in England, but until a year before the action the plaintiffs had no business here. They introduced a new design of corset called *Erect Form* and had sold 24,000 before the defendants copied it and sold theirs under the same mark, their sales rapidly surpassing those of the plaintiffs. The House of Lords held that the words *Erect Form* themselves had not acquired a secondary meaning,

[21] [1967] R.P.C. 201 (Stamp J.).
[22] [1991] F.S.R. 367, CA.
[23] [1955] O.R. 250; 23 C.P.R. 17; 15 Fox P.C. 90; [1955] 2 D.L.R. 337 (Ferguson J., Ontario).
[24] (1975) 65 D.L.R. (3d) 378, 24 C.P.R. (2d) 288 (Anderson J., British Columbia).
[25] (1984) 56 A.L.R. 595 6 F.C.R. 289; 3 I.P.R. 255 (Beaumont J., Federal Court of Australia).
[26] [1990] R.P.C. 576, CA.
[27] [1904–7] All E.R. 877; (1903) 22 R.P.C. 341, HL.

but that the defendants were liable for passing-off for having copied the precise and distinctive manner in which it was written. The commanding position of the defendants did not allow them to trespass on a new and smaller business.

In *Penney v Penneys*,[28] the plaintiffs were American manufacturers who had exported a variety of clothing and textile goods to England, retail sales amounting to about £1 million in total for the years 1970–73. The goods had been sold through department stores scattered about the country. £15,000 spent advertising Penney's goods in 1970 by department stores themselves was described as "considerable", less was spent in later years and none by the plaintiffs themselves. Graham J. held that there was sufficient reputation to justify an interlocutory injunction against retail shops in Bristol and Cirencester, and was upheld by the Court of Appeal.

The plaintiffs in *Chelsea Man v Chelsea Girl*[29] operated four retail shops as **8–13** *Nickelby* in London and the Midlands. Clothing of their own manufacture was sold in the shops under the mark *Chelsea Man*, which the defendants adopted as a trading name. About 58,000 items so marked had been sold, which was about 20 per cent of the plaintiffs' turnover. The defendants argued that these sales were *de minimis*, but Whitford J. held that the plaintiffs had established their reputation and was upheld by the Court of Appeal. A trader operating through a relatively small number of outlets selling articles of high quality (and price) was as much entitled to protect his brands as any large concern. In *Stacey v 2020 Communications*[30] an individual working from home for two years with a turnover rising to £140,000 per annum had probably made *20/20 Telecom* distinctive of himself, though an interlocutory injunction was refused on the balance of convenience. The claimant's business was not much bigger in *Teleworks v Telework Group*,[31] though it had traded since 1996 (the action being commenced in 2000), but the defendant operated in a different field, the claimant's name was at least partly descriptive and there was no evidence of actual deception. The action failed.[32]

Nature of use

Only use in a trade mark sense can contribute to a name, mark or get-up **8–14** becoming distinctive. In particular, if a word mark is used in a descriptive or generic sense then no amount of such use can make it distinctive. On the contrary, it only contributes to its descriptive or generic quality. Whenever a word of undoubted distinctiveness is coupled with one which is apparently descriptive or generic, then the natural inference is that the former serves as

---

[28] [1975] F.S.R. 367, CA.
[29] [1987] R.P.C. 189, CA.
[30] [1991] F.S.R. 49 (Millett J.).
[31] [2002] R.P.C. 27 (Christopher Floyd Q.C., Deputy Judge).
[32] Other examples are *Stannard v Reay* [1967] R.P.C 589; *Fletcher Challenge Ltd v Fletcher Challenge Pty Ltd* [1982] 1 N.S.W.L.R. 196; [1982] F.S.R. 1; *Elida Gibbs Ltd v Colgate Palmolive Ltd* [1982] F.S.R. 95.

a trade mark and the latter does not. Examples are *Parsons* Flaked Oat-meal,[33] *Horlicks* Malted Milk,[34] and *McCains* Oven Chips.[35] It does not avail the plaintiff that the descriptive element in these names may receive as much use and publicity as the other.

In *Cellular Clothing v Maxton & Murray*[36] the plaintiffs claimed that *Cellular* was distinctive of their cloth and put advertisements in evidence but the House of Lords found

"[T]he clearest evidence of its being simply a descriptive term in the advertisements and price lists which the plaintiffs themselves circulated. In the price lists they expressly say, 'Cellular cloth is so woven that it consists of an infinite number of small cells.' And in the advertisements, as the Lord Chancellor observed, the appellants have made it quite clear that they were merely adopting this word as properly describing their goods."

In *Horlicks Malted Milk v Summerskill*[37] the plaintiffs claimed *Malted Milk* as distinctive of them by virtue of 25 years' exclusive user. However, they had never used the term as a trade mark on its own, but always prefaced by *Horlicks*. They had also used "malted milk" as the description of goods in a trade mark application and in advertising in expressions such as "there is no malted milk as good as *Horlick's*".

Public need not know claimant by name

8–15 It is unnecessary for the claimant in a passing-off action to show that any members of the public can identify him by name. In the majority of cases that would be impossible. What is necessary in the typical case is that the public should recognise the claimant's mark as denoting a particular trade source, and should be misled by the defendant's use of that or a similar mark into believing that the defendants' goods are from that same source or from one associated with it:

"A fancy name ... can only indicate that the product bearing that name is, or is licensed by, or is derived from one and the same supplier."[38]

As Robert Walker L.J. observed in *United Biscuits v Asda*,[39] in which the name and get-up of the plaintiffs' *Penguin* chocolate biscuits had been taken as a reference point for the defendants' competitive *Puffin* brand:

"The third point calling for special mention is as to customers' knowledge of the identity of the company which makes Penguins and owns goodwill

---

[33] *Parsons v Gillespie* [1898] A.C. 239; 15 R.P.C. 57, PC.
[34] *Horlicks Malted Milk Co v Summerskill* (1916) 34 R.P.C. 63, HL.
[35] *McCain International Ltd v Country Fair Foods Ltd* [1981] R.P.C. 69, CA.
[36] [1899] A.C. 326; 16 R.P.C. 397, HL, *per* Lord Shand.
[37] (1915) 33 R.P.C. 1, affirmed (1916) 33 R.P.C. 108, CA and (1916) 34 R.P.C. 63, HL.
[38] *per* Templeman L.J. in *McCain International Ltd v Country Fair Foods Ltd* [1981] R.P.C. 69, CA.
[39] [1997] R.P.C. 513.

reflecting its reputation in those goods. That company is the plaintiff, United Biscuits. McVities is, it seems, now used as the name of a division...

There is authority that a customer need not know or care about the name of the manufacturer who owns the goodwill, provided that the customer knows that there is such a person and cares that goods which he buys are made by that person. This point was clearly expressed by a famous American judge, Learned Hand J., in a passage in *Crescent Tool Co v Kilborn & Bishop Co* (1917) 247 F. 290 at page 300 quoted by Jacob J. in *Hodgkinson & Corby Ltd v Wards Mobility Services Ltd* [1994] 1 W.L.R. 1564 at page 1573,

> 'It is an absolute condition to any relief whatever that the plaintiff in such cases show that the appearance of his wares has in fact come to mean that some particular person–the plaintiff may not be individually known–makes them, and the public cares who does make them.'

That was said in the special context of the appearance of a product, but the point is of more general application. When witnesses called on behalf of United Biscuits said that they did not know or care who made Penguins, I did not understand them to be saying or implying that they did not expect Penguins to be of consistently high quality because of their origin from a particular source."

The original authority normally cited for this rule is the *Yorkshire Relish* **8–16** case, *Powell v Birmingham Vinegar Brewery*,[40] although the principle had been accepted far earlier. It was typical in the nineteenth century for businesses to be carried on by individual sole traders or partnerships, so that the ownership of the business would change from time to time and the names of the owners would normally cease to correspond to the trading name after the founders had retired. In these circumstances, it could hardly be expected that the public would know the plaintiff's real identity. Furthermore, the reason for the public being unable to identify the claimant by name is irrelevant, and a claimant may succeed even if he has deliberately refrained from putting his name before the public in any way.[41]

A fortiori, it does not matter if the public can identify the claimant only by an assumed trading name which is not his real name. In the *Yorkshire Relish* case itself the plaintiff *Powell* would have been known, if at all, by the trading name *Goodall Backhouse* which was conspicuously displayed on his bottles. Likewise, in another classic case:

> "It may very well be that hundreds of people like *Glenfield Starch* and order it because they think it is the best starch they have ever used, without having heard of the name of Mr. Wotherspoon, and without

[40] [1897] A.C. 710; 14 R.P.C. 721, HL.

[41] *Edge (William) & Sons Ltd v William Niccolls & Sons Ltd* [1911] A.C. 693. 28 R.P.C. 582, HL. See also *Reckitt & Colman Products Ltd v Borden Inc* [1990] 1 W.L.R. 491; [1990] 1 All E.R. 873; [1990] R.P.C. 340, HL, *per* Lord Oliver.

knowing him at all. They say, 'I want the thing that bears that name, the thing made in a particular way, made by the manufacturer who makes it in that way, and, there being only one manufacturer who makes it in that way, I want the article made by that manufacturer'."[42]

In *Wotherspoon v Currie* the plaintiff's name had been on the packets, although it was less conspicuous than the mark *Glenfield*. In *Edge v Niccolls*[43] the plaintiffs sold washing blue in packets which had no label, name or other identification, so that the public recognised them solely by get-up. The defendants were restrained from selling blue in the same get-up, notwithstanding that they used a label with their own name on it:

"No name or description appears upon the wrapper containing the plaintiffs' blues and tints, and to many of such persons [washerwomen, etc.] the plaintiffs' name is unknown ... It is not necessary, in my opinion, for the plaintiffs to prove that the ultimate purchasers, who are likely to be misled, know the name of the plaintiffs' firm."[44]

Spontaneous public adoption; abbreviations and variations

8–17 It is not essential for the claimant deliberately to set out to appropriate some name, mark or get-up as his. Although his intentions and the manner in which he may use various words are given weight they are not conclusive. It is possible for a term to become distinctive of the claimant's goods by virtue of spontaneous public adoption. In *Siegert v Findlater*[45] the plaintiff had manufactured in the town of Angostura a flavouring which he sold under the name *Aromatic Bitters* but which was popularly known as *Angostura Bitters*. The defendants were restrained from using the latter name.[46] The plaintiff began to use *Angostura Bitters* on his bottles only after the defendant commenced to do so. The *Stone Ales* case, *Montgomery v Thompson*[47] may also be one where the name protected was coined by the public rather than the plaintiff. *Siegert v Findlater* was followed in Australia in *Neylan v Toison*[48] where a newspaper, *The Suburban*, was popularly known by the name of its *de facto* predecessor, *The Express*.

In South Africa the nickname of the plaintiffs' football team *The Birds* was protected in *Moroka Swallows Football Club v The Birds Football Club*.[49] In *Arsenal v Reed*[50] the club's official name *Arsenal* and its popular nickname *The Gunners* were treated on the same basis, but claims for passing-off

---

[42] *per* Lord Hatherley L.C. in *Wotherspoon v Currie* (1872) L.R. 5 H.L. 508, HL.

[43] [1911] A.C. 693; 28 R.P.C. 582, HL.

[44] *per* Lord Gorell see also *Hoffman-La Roche & Co AG v DDSA Pharmaceuticals Ltd* [1969] F.S.R. 416, CA.

[45] (1878) 7 Ch.D. 801 (Fry J.).

[46] Compare *Edge & Sons Ltd v Gallon & Son* (1900) 17 R.P.C. 557, HL where the nickname of the defendants' goods anticipated the name chosen by plaintiffs.

[47] [1891] A.C. 217; 8 R.P.C. 361, HL.

[48] [1983] 1 Qd. 600 (Williams A.J.).

[49] 1987 (2) SA 511 (Stegmann J., Witwatersrand).

[50] [2001] E.T.M.R. 77, [2001] R.P.C. 46 (Laddie J.), on appeal [2003] EWCA Civ 696.

against a seller of unlicensed merchandise failed in respect of both. The *Manchester United* football club had no such rights in *United* on its own so as to allow them to oppose an application to register UNITED for beer under s.5(4)(a) of the Trade Marks Act 1994: *Rygrange Ltd's Trade Mark Applications.*[51]

In *Pete Waterman v CBS,*[52] *Hit Factory* was widely used as the nickname of the plaintiffs' recording studio in London, and, by derivation, for his whole organisation. However, it was not the plaintiffs' trading style and had not become distinctive of his business alone. On the facts there was no likelihood of substantial damage arising from the defendants using the same name for a London studio under licence from the American *Hit Factory*.

More commonly, the public may come to refer to the claimant's goods **8–18** through terms which are derived from the claimant's chosen mark,[53] but which thereby become distinctive of the claimant's goods in their own right. This has been particularly important with pictorial marks in illiterate communities, and raises similar issues to the "idea of the mark".

In *Lee Kar Choo v Lee Lian Choon*[54] the plaintiff's mark for tea was a red-coloured goldfish.

"As might well be expected and as the learned judge of first instance found, the label not only became itself distinctive of the appellant's tea and tea dust, but that commodity sold in packages so labelled came to be dealt in by the public as red fish or gold fish or simply fish brand tea."[55]

Likewise, in *White Hudson v Asian Organisation*[56] the plaintiffs' cough sweets became known in Singapore as "red paper cough sweets" as they were the only ones on the market so wrapped. The verbal mark *Hacks* was incomprehensible and irrelevant to native purchasers.

If the public is in the habit of abbreviating the claimant's chosen verbal **8–19** mark then the abbreviated version should be considered with regard both to distinctiveness and likelihood of deception. In *Daimler Chrysler v Alavi*[57] Pumfrey J. accepted evidence that the names of the claimant's *Mercedes* and *Mercedes-Benz* cars were frequently abbreviated to *Merc* (although the claimants had until recently discouraged this), but held that there was no passing-off by the defendant's use of the latter name in his retail clothing business. In *Associated Newspapers v Express Newspapers*[58] the fact that the claimants' daily and Sunday titles (the *Daily Mail* and the *Mail on Sunday*) were both commonly abbreviated to *The Mail* contributed significantly to a finding that any of the defendants' proposed titles (*The Mail*, the *Evening Mail* or the *London Evening Mail*) would deceive; likewise the fact that the

---

[51] [2001] E.T.M.R. 78 (Mr M. Reynolds, Trade Mark Registry).
[52] [1993] E.M.L.R. 27 (Browne-Wilkinson V.C.)
[53] As in *Seixo v Provezende* (1865) L.R. 1 Ch. 192 (Lord Cranworth L.C.) *Crown Seixo*.
[54] [1967] 1 A.C. 602; [1966] 3 All E.R. 1000, PC.
[55] *per* Sir Garfield Barwick.
[56] [1964] 1 W.L.R. 1466; [1965] 1 All E.R. 1040; [1965] R.P.C. 45, PC.
[57] [2001] R.P.C. 42 (Pumfrey J.).
[58] [2003] EWHC 1322, (Laddie J.).

latter two titles would almost inevitably be abbreviated to *The Mail*. Various other newspapers incorporated *Mail* into their titles, but none had a significant circulation in the London area, where *Mail* on its own was sufficiently distinctive of the claimants. Conversely, in *United Biscuits v Asda*[59] the "official name" of the defendant's chocolate coated biscuits was said to be *ASDA Puffin*, but *ASDA* was indistinct and to all intents and purposes it was referred to simply as *Puffin*, thereby increasing the possibility of confusion with the plaintiffs' *Penguin*.

Previously, in *British Vacuum Cleaner Co v New Vacuum Cleaner Co*,[60] Parker J. had taken into account the fact that "British" was normally dropped from *British Vacuum Cleaner*, but as "vacuum cleaner" itself was generic the additional confusion which might have resulted was irrelevant. Compare *Associated Newspapers v Express Newspapers*[61] where Laddie J. expressly rejected the argument that "(the) Mail" was either generic or descriptive for newspapers. In *Fialho v Simond*[62] the brand *Marie Elizabeth* for sardines was commonly abbreviated to *Maries* and the defendants were restrained at trial from using *Marie* (or *Maria*) *Lisette*. In *Macleans v Lightbrown*[63] *Macs* had been used by the plaintiffs for throat lozenges as well as *Maclean's* for stomach powder. *Maclean's* itself had started as the generic name for a stomach remedy invented by a doctor of that name but had become at least partly distinctive of the plaintiffs. The defendants were permanently restrained from selling sweets called *Merrimacs*, which contained a small amount of Professor Maclean's powder.

Conversely, the claimant's name may be extended or elaborated by the public or varied in some other way. In *Heels v Stafford Heels*[64] the plaintiffs' case was assisted by the fact that although *Heels* was their full firm name, they were quite frequently referred to in the trade as *Heels, Stafford*. *Heels v Stafford Heels* was cited by Robert Walker J. in *British Diabetic Association v The Diabetic Society*[65] where, however, neither *British Diabetic Society* nor *Diabetic Society* had become the *de facto* alternative name of the plaintiffs. In Scotland, an interim interdict was granted in *Thistle Communications v Thistle Telecom*.[66] There was evidence that although *Thistle Communications* was the pursuer's trading name, his business was quite frequently referred to simply as *Thistle* or as *Thistle Telecom* or *Thistle Telecoms*.

Use of the same mark by others

8–20 It often happens that one and the same sign, or two closely similar, may be in use by more than one business. On the traditional understanding of the tort, it was necessary for the claimant to prove that the sign relied on was

---

[59] [1997] R.P.C. 513 (Robert Walker J.).
[60] [1907] 2 Ch. 312; 24 R.P.C. 641 (Parker J.).
[61] [2003] EWHC 1322, (Laddie J.).
[62] (1937) 54 R.P.C. 193 (Farwell J.).
[63] (1937) 54 R.P.C. 230 (Farwell J.).
[64] (1927) 44 R.P.C. 299 (Romer J.).
[65] [1996] F.S.R. 1 (Robert Walker J.).
[66] 2000 SLT 262 (Lord Hamilton, OH).

distinctive of him alone in whatever might be defined as his field of business. The modern definition of the law is based on misrepresentation. If the sign is used by the claimant alone, then the likelihood is that it is distinctive of him and adoption of it by a competitor raises a *prima facie* case of passing-off. If this is not the case, then one must look beyond the sign itself at all the relevant circumstances to see if the defendant is making a misrepresentation that his goods or business are those of the claimant. If so, it need not matter that the claimant's case may rely to some extent on a sign which is not unique to him. So in *Parker & Son (Reading) v Parker*[67] the common surname *Parker* was used by several estate agents in or near Reading, but it was abundantly clear that the defendant was passing himself off as the plaintiffs; and in *Mappin & Webb v Leapman*[68] the defendant claimed that *Mappins' A1 Quality* on his goods denoted a separate business carried on as *Mappin & Sons*, but he too was clearly passing them off as the plaintiffs'.

It is no valid objection that a particular mark (or ones confusingly similar to that in respect of which distinctiveness is claimed) may have been used by others locally, at distant times or on too small a scale to compromise the distinctiveness of the claimant's mark. In *Sutherland v V2 Music*[69] two pop groups other than the claimants and defendants were supposed to have released records in the past under the name *Liberty*, but no details were forthcoming and Laddie J. dismissed their relevance as "unexplained footprints in time." Much the same might have been said about the *Puffin* and *Pelican* bars which had transiently appeared on the shelves of two supermarket chains prior to the launch of Asda's *Puffin* bar, in *United Biscuits v Asda*.[70] In *Asprey & Garrard v WRA (Guns) Ltd and Asprey*[71] Jacob J. was criticised in the Court of Appeal for ignoring the fact that two businesses other than the claimants had briefly traded in the luxury goods market, in London, under names incorporating *Asprey*, but their only relevance was to prove that this could be done without confusion being caused, and the final outcome was not affected.

In *Associated Newspapers v Express Newspapers*[72] the claimants' assertion of distinctiveness in the abbreviation *The Mail* for their national daily and Sunday titles the *Daily Mail* and the *Mail on Sunday* was challenged on the basis that there were three important regional newspapers incorporating "Mail" into their mastheads (the Scottish *Sunday Mail*, the *Birmingham Evening Mail* and the *Western Mail* in Wales) and several small local ones in the Southeast, such as the *Alton Times and Mail*, the *Aldershot Mail* and the *Molesey News and Mail*. None of these prevented *Mail* on its own being distinctive of the claimants in and around London, which was where the defendants' projected newspaper was to be distributed as *The Mail*, the

---

[67] [1965] R.P.C. 323 (Plowman J.).
[68] (1905) 22 R.P.C. 398.
[69] [2002] E.M.L.R. 28 (Laddie J.).
[70] [1997] R.P.C. 513 (Robert Walker J.).
[71] [2002] F.S.R. 30 (Jacob J.) affirmed [2001] EWCA Civ 1499; [2002] E.T.M.R. 47; [2002] F.S.R. 31, CA.
[72] [2003] EWHC 1322, (Laddie J.).

Evening Mail or the *London Evening Mail*. Laddie J. granted a permanent injunction.

8–21   If two unconnected businesses in competition with one another already use the same sign on a substantial scale then that sign, on its own, can hardly be distinctive of either of them. This may be illustrated by the judgment of Parker J. in *Hopton Wood v Gething*[73] where the fact that three unconnected businesses had once used *Hopton* indicated that it could not have had trade mark significance. The situation was not affected by the fact that one of the three had gone out of business and the other two had merged. In such circumstances, a newcomer may adopt the same sign without being guilty of passing-off. There must be more than coincidental and uncoordinated use of the same sign to give rise to a case of joint ownership. If the sign is in use by more than two competitors then the case can be no stronger, but the crucial difference is between a sign which is unique in its field and one which is not.

In *Lee v Haley*[74] an interlocutory injunction was granted against the defendant calling himself the *Guinea Coal Company*. More than one coal company in London used that name (alluding to the price charged) but it was clear from the defendant's choice of address that he intended to pass himself off as the plaintiff specifically.

In *Jamieson v Jamieson*[75] there were four manufacturers of harness composition named *Jamieson* in Aberdeen, including the plaintiffs and the defendant. The defendant's tins resembled the plaintiffs' only in the surname and matters which were common to the trade. The Court of Appeal discharged an injunction. If the plaintiffs had been the only Jamieson then identity of names would have sufficed. Conversely, the number of Jamiesons in the business would have been irrelevant if the distinctive aspects of the plaintiffs' get-up had been copied or something else had pointed to the defendant passing his goods off as those of the plaintiff specifically.

In *Attenborough v Jay*,[76] decided in the same year as *Jamieson v Jamieson*, six London pawnbrokers who were members of the same family but otherwise unconnected all traded under the family name *Attenborough*. They failed to prevent the defendant company adopting that as part of its registered name and an appeal was dismissed. In *Harding v Smilecare*[77] the two claimants (who had formerly been in partnership, and were still joint proprietors of a registered trade mark) practised separately as *Smilecare* in different areas of London, and a third person (not a claimant) had purchased their former practice at another location, with the right to use the name. The case seems to have proceeded on the basis that each of the two claimants had a several right of action, but failed for lack of any risk of confusion.

8–22   The distinctiveness of the claimant's mark in his chosen field of business is not destroyed by use of the same or a similar mark in other fields. To some extent this is the converse doctrine to that of the common field of activity,

---

[73] (1910) 27 R.P.C. 605 (Parker J.).
[74] (1869) L.R. 5 Ch. 155 (L.JJ.).
[75] (1898) 15 R.P.C. 169, CA.
[76] (1898) 14 T.L.R. 365 affirmed (1898) 14 T.L.R. 439, CA.
[77] [2002] F.S.R. 37 (P.W. Smith Q.C., Deputy Judge).

but unlike that doctrine it has continuing vitality. In *Somerville v Schembri*[78] the Privy Council dismissed an argument that the mark *Kaisar-i-Hind* could not be distinctive of the plaintiff's cigarettes because it was already used by others for hats, umbrellas, soap, pickles and as a name for ships.

> "[I]t would hardly have been necessary for their Lordships to observe that the acquisition of an exclusive right to a mark or name in connection with a particular article of commerce cannot entitle the owner of that right to prohibit the use by others of such mark or name in connection with goods of a totally different character, and that use by others can as little interfere with his acquisition of the right."[79]

More generally, two or more businesses may use the same mark even in closely allied fields, and it may be distinctive of each in its chosen sphere. If so, each business may have a several right of action for passing-off and it is a matter of fact whether a business which adopts that name is liable to be taken for the one, the other or even both. In *Brittain Publishing Co v Trade & Commercial Press*[80] the plaintiffs published the *London Weekly Advertiser* and the *National Advertiser*, both of which essentially consisted of small classified advertisements. The defendants submitted to an injunction (in the *Corona* form) against calling a similar paper the *National Weekly*. In two separate cases decided in the same year as one another *Lloyd's of London* obtained an interlocutory injunction in the Court of Appeal against a firm of yacht brokers using their name,[81] and *Lloyds Bank* obtained an interlocutory injunction against an investment trust.[82] In the former case, especially, there could be no doubt that the defendants' conduct was deliberately calculated to suggest an association with the corporation rather than the bank.

Mere association with claimant

The fact that the claimant's mark may be very well known, and may even be **8–23** associated with the goods in question by most customers, does not necessarily mean that it is distinctive.

> "Probably to the large majority of persons who require light rain-proof overcoats for use while shooting, or fishing, or riding on bicycles, or in motors, or playing golf, the word 'slip-on' will at once suggest not only the cut and material of the garment, but the name of the firm which advertises these garments so largely and has been so successful in satisfying the needs of the sporting sections of the community. So far as the trade is concerned, the plaintiffs have contributed to the same result by continually insisting on their right to the exclusive use of the word as

---

[78] (1887) 12 App.Cas. 453, PC.
[79] *per* Lord Watson.
[80] [1957] R.P.C. 134 (Harman J.).
[81] *Lloyd's & Dawson Bros v Lloyd's, Southampton Ltd* (1912) 29 R.P.C. 433, CA.
[82] *Lloyd's Bank Ltd v Lloyd's Investment Trust Co Ltd* (1912) 29 R.P.C. 545 (Neville J.).

distinctive of goods of their manufacture, and threatening other traders, who have attempted to use to word, with legal proceedings.

Summing up what the plaintiffs have done, I think it may be stated as follows: First, they have adopted, as the name of a particular kind of coat which they intended to introduce to the trade and to the public, a name which aptly described, and which they intended to describe, one of the chief characteristics of the article to which it was applied. Secondly, by their advertisements, catalogues and trade circulars, they have identified the name so chosen with the article to which it was applied in such a manner that, besides describing the chief characteristic of the coat, it has come to connote also the cut and material. Thirdly, by these same advertisements, catalogues and trade circulars, by the consequent world-wide development of their business, by their labels, and by their claim to monopoly rights in the word, they have associated this name with the name of their firm n the minds both of the trade and of that section of the public which requires coats of that class to which they applied the word . . .

The real question is whether under the circumstances above described there is any reasonable probability of deception if the defendants continue to use the word 'slip-on' in the way they have done and are doing. In considering this question it must be borne in mind that, upon the facts as I have found them, the word 'slip-on' is and has always been used by the plaintiffs, primarily as a word describing the article, and that the word does in fact describe the article in the minds of both the trade and the public. The word has never been used by the plaintiffs primarily as a word distinctive of goods of their own manufacture. If it has come to distinguish their goods from those of others, it has done so by acquiring a secondary meaning without losing its descriptive character.

Though I do not agree with the argument that a word cannot be at the same time descriptive and distinctive, I think that fact that it retains its *prima facie* descriptive signification increases the difficulty of proving that it is distinctive of the goods of any particular manufacturer. If a word is *prima facie* the name of or description of an article, evidence that it is also generally associated with the name of a particular manufacturer is, in my opinion, by no means conclusive that it has become a distinctive word which cannot be used of the same article when made by others without the risk of deception. If the article in question is made exclusively or mainly by a particular manufacturer, it is almost bound to be associated with the name of that manufacturer by the trade and the public, for each trader and each member of the public will naturally associated the article with the name of the manufacturer who supplies it to him and who may possibly be, in his opinion, the only person who supplies it at all."[83]

8–24   The principle applies whether it is a name, mark, or get-up, or some other type of sign, which is supposed to be associated with the claimant. In

---

[83] *per* Parker J. in *Burberrys v J C Cording & Co Ltd* (1909) 26 R.P.C. 693. Paragraph breaks supplied.

Imperial Tobacco Co v Purnell[84] the plaintiffs failed to prove that a narrow red band was distinctive of their cigars, although they had made more use of that feature than any other manufacturer and some customers asked for "narrow red band" cigars instead of the brand. In *Imperial Group v Philip Morris*[85] the plaintiffs' black pack for *John Player Special* cigarette was well known but not distinctive of Players. The plaintiffs were simply the best known of several who used such a pack. When the claimant has had a legal or *de facto* monopoly in certain goods it is likely that they will become associated with him even under their generic name, but that state of affairs does not prove that the name (or the appearance of the goods) has become distinctive.[86]

Primary association not with claimant

The sign complained of may in fact suggest a connection with a business, or, **8–25** for instance, with a person,[87] or a place,[88] other than the claimant.

In *Barnsley Brewery v RBNB*[89] three years' exclusive use, an annual turnover rising to £400,000, and advertising expenditure of £25,000 p.a. might otherwise have been enough to make the name *Barnsley Bitter* distinctive of the plaintiffs, but the name had been used for almost 100 years (until 1976) for beer brewed in Barnsley, by a company unconnected to either party, which had acquired and to some extent retained a high local reputation. The plaintiffs' advertising exploited this (non-existent) connection, so that there was only a barely arguable case of passing-off when the defendants proposed to use the same name for beer brewed at the original, reopened, brewery. An interlocutory injunction was refused.

In *French Connection v Sutton*[90] the initials or near-acronym *FCUK* had been adopted as the trading style of the claimants (conveniently corresponding to *French Connection UK*); but anyone seeing *fcuk.com* as an internet domain name would recognise it as anagrammatic for a site of appropriately pornographic content, though in the case of the defendant's site they would be disappointed. Summary judgment was refused: "secondary meaning" requires more than that an association with the claimant should be the second idea to enter one's head.

In *Rolls Razor v Rolls Lighters*[91] the plaintiffs were razor manufacturers. **8–26**

---

[84] (1904) 21 R.P.C. 598, CA.

[85] [1984] R.P.C. 293 (Whitford J.).

[86] *Canadian Shredded Wheat Co Ltd v Kellogg Co of Canada Ltd* [1938] 1 All E.R. 618; 55 R.P.C. 125, PC.

[87] As in *Poister Ltd v Marcel Fenez Ltd* [1965] R.P.C. 187 where the use of the name *Guy Laroche* truthfully denoted that the goods were designed by him. The plaintiffs, as exclusive distributors of his dresses, had no cause of action. See also *MID Sydney Pty Ltd v Australian Tourism Co Ltd* (1998) 40 I.P.R. 20, in which *Chifley* was the surname of a former Australian Prime Minister, Ben Chifley, and equally arbitrary for both parties.

[88] *Angoves Pty Ltd v Johnson* (1982) 66 F.L.R. 216; 43 A.L.R. 349 (Federal Court of Australia, Full Court), below.

[89] [1997] F.S.R. 462 (Robert Walker J.).

[90] [2000] E.T.M.R. 341 (Rattee J.). The domain name is now in the ownership of the claimants.

[91] (1949) 66 R.P.C. 299, CA.

They failed to obtain an injunction against the use of *Rolls* for cigarette lighters, the likelihood being that if the word "Rolls" caused the defendants to be associated with any other business it would be with Rolls-Royce and not with them.[92]

In *Evian v Bowles*[93] the plaintiffs imported various cycling accessories under the name *Evian*. These had included plastic water bottles for racing cyclists which originated from the suppliers of *Evian* mineral water, and were advertised as such. The plaintiffs were refused an injunction against defendants who imported similar bottles. In connection with water bottles specifically, *Evian* was likely to be taken as denoting the owners of the mineral water source, and the plaintiffs therefore had no *locus standi*.

In *Harrods v Harrodian School*[94] it was conceivable that any confusion arising from the defendants' name would be with Harrow School, the famous boys' public school whose pupils are *Harrovians*, rather than with the plaintiff department store.

8–27 In *Gilbey v Continental Liqueurs*[95] the plaintiffs were undoubtedly the first to use *Smirnoff* for Vodka in Australia. However, in Europe *Smirnoff* was already well known as a brand of vodka and had nothing to do with the plaintiffs. In Australia vodka was drunk mainly by recent immigrants from Europe. Immigrants as a class would be familiar with the worldwide reputation of the name, and would not associate it with the plaintiffs. The plaintiffs' use of *Smirnoff* had been slight, and in the circumstances was insufficient to make it distinctive of them among the vodka-consuming public, especially as the plaintiffs' advertisements had sought to trade off the European and world-wide reputation. Note that the defendants failed to prove any trade connection between themselves and the "original" *Smirnoff* known in Europe.

In *Angoves v Johnson*[96] the plaintiffs objected to the defendants calling themselves the *St Agnes Liquor Store*, *St Agnes* being the plaintiff's brand of brandy. However, *St Agnes* was also the name of the suburb in which the store was located and the name would be understood as indicating the location rather than any association with the plaintiffs.

An argument by the defenders that *Thistle* would simply be taken as denoting Scottish-ness failed in *Thistle Communications v Thistle Telecom*,[97] where the pursuers had used their trading name since 1983.

8–28 In an extreme case the mark claimed to be distinctive of the claimant may in fact denote the goods or business of the defendant or a connected party.[98]

In *Brewster Transport v Rocky Mountain Tours & Transport*[99] the Canadian Supreme Court refused an injunction to a Canadian company which had adopted the well-known name and livery of a United States rival, the

---

[92] The name *Rolls Razor* itself was supposed to have been adopted with this in mind.
[93] [1965] R.P.C. 327; [1965] F.S.R. 86 (Stamp J.).
[94] [1996] R.P.C. 697, CA.
[95] (1959–60) 103 C.L.R. 406 (High Court of Australia).
[96] (1982) 66 F.L.R. 216; 43 A.L.R. 349 (Federal Court of Australia, Full Court).
[97] 2000 SLT 262 (Lord Hamilton, OH).
[98] See also *Edge & Sons Ltd v Gallon & Son* (1900) 17 R.P.C. 557, HL. The argument failed in *Penney (JC) Co Inc v Penneys Ltd* [1975] F.S.R. 367, CA.
[99] [1931] S.C.R. 336; [1931] 1 D.L.R. 713 (Supreme Court of Canada).

defendants. The plaintiffs had not come to court with clean hands, and it did not matter that the defendants, as an American company, might not originally have had a cause of action against the plaintiffs' own imitation.

In a Singapore case, *Malaysia Daily Industries v Yakult*[1] the plaintiffs failed in an action based on the shape of a bottle because it was actually distinctive of the company supplying the defendants and had been copied by the plaintiffs.

Brewster Transport v Rocky Mountain Tours & Transport ought to be of general application in passing-off cases where a claimant with reputation fails solely on the technical ground that he has no relevant goodwill. Examples might include well-known foreign claimants with no local trade and perhaps claimants in personality merchandising cases. If there has been a misrepresentation by the defendant, then although the claimant may be unable to restrain it, it would be inequitable to assist the defendant if he brought a counterclaim based on his own misleading use. More fundamentally, the claimant is guilty of no misrepresentation if the sign in question is in fact distinctive of him.

Local distinctiveness

It is possible for a sign such as a name, mark or get-up to be distinctive of a **8–29** particular person only in a limited geographical area. Some businesses, such as car dealerships,[2] or dentists,[3] and all but the most famous shops and restaurants, are likely to draw their customers only from their immediate surrounding area and it is only in that area that their name will be distinctive of them.[4] Though the claimant's business may be confined to a particular locality, there is still passing-off if another business adopts the same name, mark or get-up in or near that locality. The claimant does not have to prove nationwide distinctiveness.[5] Despite this, there is a noticeable tendency to award injunctions which cover the whole jurisdiction, or at any rate the largest possible area in which it can be said that the claimant has any reputation at all.[6]

Associated Newspapers v Express Newspapers[7] is best understood as a case of local distinctiveness rather than one of local goodwill. The claimants' daily and Sunday titles, the *Daily Mail* and the *Mail on Sunday*, were sold throughout the United Kingdom and both were commonly abbreviated to *The Mail*. Other newspapers of regional importance outside London and the Southeast incorporated *Mail* into their titles, but none had a significant

---

[1] [1980] F.S.R. 43 (Chua J.).
[2] *Bushbury Land Rover v Bushbury Ltd* [1997] F.S.R. 709 (CA, on appeal from Rattee J.).
[3] *Harding v Smilecare* [2002] F.S.R. 37 (P.W. Smith Q.C., Deputy Judge).
[4] *Jay's Ltd v Jacobi* [1933] Ch. 411; [1933] All E.R. 690; 50 R.P.C. 132, as explained in *Wright, Layman & Umney Ltd v Wright* (1949) 66 R.P.C. 149, CA, is regarded as an example of this.
[5] *Paine & Co v Daniells & Sons Breweries* [1893] 2 Ch. 567; 10 R.P.C. 217, CA. *Dicta* apparently to the contrary in *Chivers (S) & Sons v S Chivers & Co Ltd* (1900) 17 R.P.C. 420 are too strict, although the decision itself need not be doubted on its facts.
[6] *Brestian v Try* [1958] R.P.C. 161, CA; *Chelsea Man Menswear Ltd v Chelsea Girl Ltd* [1987] R.P.C. 189, CA.
[7] [2003] EWHC 1322, (Laddie J.).

circulation in the London area, where *Mail* on its own was sufficiently distinctive of the claimants for Laddie J. to hold that any of the defendants' proposed titles for a proposed giveaway evening newspaper (*The Mail*, the *Evening Mail* or the *London Evening Mail*) would deceive. In Scotland, Birmingham or Wales the analysis would have been that the *Daily Mail* and the *Mail on Sunday* had ample goodwill, but that only their full names were distinctive of them. In the London area, they could also claim distinctiveness for the abbreviated form.

Effect of legal or *de facto monopoly*

8–30 It is more difficult for a claimant to prove that a mark has become distinctive of him when he has enjoyed a legal, natural or *de facto* monopoly of the goods in question. The rule was originally stated in relation to goods in which the plaintiff had introduced under patent[8] or secret process, but it is not confined to that situation. It is wrong to say that distinctiveness cannot be acquired during a period of monopoly, but proof of acquired distinctiveness may be harder to come by, especially for a mark which has a low inherent capacity to distinguish. There is no rule of law that because goods were formerly (or recently) patented the name or get-up given to them by the patentee can be copied with impunity.[9]

The rule has two separate explanations, one of which applies only to verbal marks and the other of which ought to apply also to visual marks such as get-up. The first is that the inventor or introducer of new goods acts at his own risk if he does not confer on them a generic name by which the public and competitors can refer to the goods as such without reference to their source. This is true whether or not a period of monopoly is involved. A generic name does not become distinctive simply because for many years there was only manufacturer in the market and so no need to distinguish between species and genus.

The second, and more basic, reason is that while there is no competition the public need not trouble to distinguish the goods of the claimant from any others, and indeed have no opportunity to do so. If, as is often the case, those goods bear several potentially distinctive signs then it is impossible to say from experience which are important and which are not. It may be correspondingly difficult to identify the paramount idea inherent in the claimant's mark when, as is normal, several different expressions of it are possible. Once a reasonable number of competitors are on the market it will be easier to say which particular features distinguish the claimant's goods in fact, but until then one has to rely predominantly on common sense.

8–31 As Lord Davey observed in *Cellular Clothing v Maxton & Murray*:

---

[8] For example, *Linoleum Manufacturing Co v Nairn* (1878) 7 Ch.D. 834; *Magnolia Metal Co v Atlas Metal Co* (1897) 14 R.P.C. 389, CA; *British Vacuum Cleaner Co Ltd v New Vacuum Cleaner Co Ltd* [1907] 2 Ch. 312; 24 R.P.C. 641; *Bowden Wire Ltd v Bowden Brake Co Ltd (No.2)* (1913) 30 R.P.C. 609; *Canadian Shredded Wheat Co Ltd v Kellogg Co of Canada Ltd* [1938] All E.R. 618; 55 R.P.C. 125, PC.

[9] *Slazenger & Sons v Feltham & Co* (1889) 6 R.P.C. 531, CA and *Edge (William) & Sons Ltd v William Niccolls & Sons Ltd* [1911] A.C. 693; 28 R.P.C. 582, HL.

"[W]here a man produces, or invents if you please, a new article, and attaches a descriptive name to it, a name which, as the article has not been produced before, has of course not been used in connection with the article, and secures for himself either the legal monopoly or a monopoly in fact of the sale of that article for a certain time, the evidence of persons who come forward to say that the name in question suggests to their minds and is associated by them with the plaintiff's goods alone is of a very slender character, for the simple reason that the plaintiff was the only maker of the goods during the time that his monopoly lasted, and therefore there was nothing to compare with it, and anybody who wanted the goods had no shop to go to ... except the plaintiff."[10]

To the same effect there is the judgment of Parker J. in *British Vacuum Cleaner v New Vacuum Cleaner*:

"I think that the evidence ... really points to the fact that the public have understood 'Vacuum Cleaner' and the 'Vacuum Cleaning Process' to be descriptive of a particular kind of cleaner and a particular process, a cleaner, namely, which operates by means of a nozzle applied to the furniture, and the suction in the pipes caused by the vacuum created by the machine. As long as the plaintiff company was the only manufacturer who manufactured, and dealt with, and went from house to house with a machine of that sort no doubt, in the mind of the public, there would be a connotation of the fact that the machine was the machine of the plaintiff company. But I do not think that primarily the words have ever been, in the mind of the public, anything else than descriptive words and, if that be so, then it appears to me that the case falls for this purpose within what was said by Lord Davey, namely, that no great inference can be drawn from the fact that, during the period when the patentee has had a monopoly, or the manufacturer has had a monopoly, either at law, or in fact, words primarily descriptive of an article have become associated with the patentee or manufacturer. There is nothing, and there was nothing, as he said, for the public to contrast it with, so that it is impossible to say that the public understood by those words a machine dealt in, or brought round, by any one person or company as distinguished from any other person or company."[11]

An erroneous public opinion that the claimant has a monopoly in a **8–32** certain field may create the belief that the defendant must be licensed, but that does not in itself make him liable for passing-off:

---

[10] *per* Lord Davey in *Cellular Clothing Co v Maxton & Murray* [1899] A.C. 326, 343; 16 R.P.C. 397, HL.

[11] *per* Parker J. in *British Vacuum Cleaner Co Ltd v New Vacuum Cleaner Co Ltd* [1907] 2 Ch. 312; 24 R.P.C. 641.

"[I]f a consumer has an erroneous preconceived belief that the first manufacturer has a monopoly, a false assumption by the consumer as to the source of the latter manufacturer's goods is self-induced."[12]

Although such monopoly rights as the claimant may have in a mark will lapse if not enforced rigorously, the converse is not true. Monopolies are not to be created through ignorance or intimidation. The fact that the claimant may have been successful in getting others to discontinue use of what he claims as his mark is slight evidence, at best, that it is really distinctive.[13]

Legal or *de facto* monopoly in get-up

8–33 Some cases subsequent to *Cellular Clothing v Maxton & Murray*[14] and *British Vacuum Cleaner v New Vacuum Cleaner*[15] may have drawn too much of a distinction between verbal marks, which cannot readily acquire distinctiveness during a period of monopoly if they are *prima facie* descriptive, and non-verbal marks such as get-up. It is true that with get-up no question of descriptive or generic meaning is likely to arise,[16] but the other of Lord Davey's objections still holds good: a witness asked if the supposedly distinctive get-up suggested the claimant's goods to him may answer "yes" for no other reason than because the claimant was the only source of those goods. If a witness is used to buying *Shredded Wheat* shaped like a small pillow then he may truthfully say that if he asked for "Shredded Wheat" *simpliciter*, or if it was shaped like a small pillow, he would expect it to be the plaintiffs'. That does not mean that either *Shredded Wheat* or the shape of the biscuit is distinctive.[17] In *Rizla v Bryant & May*[18] the plaintiffs' case based on the defendants adopting the same colour coding for three different qualities of cigarette paper was undermined by the fact that they had enjoyed a virtual monopoly in the cigarette paper market for many years. Though customers were used to asking tobacconists for a packet of *reds*, *blues*, or *greens*, it was not established that they used the colours to denote the plaintiffs' brand, as opposed to the type of paper, and the defendants' brand name *Swan* was distinct.

The implications of over 30 years' *de facto* monopoly in the sale of lemon juice packaged in life-like plastic lemons were considered by the House of

---

[12] *per* Brennan J. in *Parkdale Custom Built Furniture v Puxu* (1982) 42 A.L.R. 1; 149 C.L.R. 191 (Trade Practices Act 1974); see also *My Kinda Town Ltd v Soll* [1983] R.P.C. 407, CA and *Ciba-Geigy plc v Parke Davis & Co Ltd* [1994] F.S.R. 8.

[13] *Cellular Clothing Co v Maxton & Murray* [1899] A.C. 326; 16 R.P.C. 397, HL; *Hennessy (James) & Co Ltd v Keating* (1908) 25 R.P.C. 361, HL; *Burberrys v J C Cording & Co Ltd* (1909) 26 R.P.C. 693.

[14] [1899] A.C. 326; 16 R.P.C. 397, HL.

[15] [1907] 2 Ch. 312; 24 R.P.C. 641 (Parker J.).

[16] Though the *Jif Lemon* case, *Reckitt & Colman Products Ltd v Borden Inc* [1990] 1 W.L.R. 491; [1990] 1 All E.R. 873; [1990] R.P.C. 340, HL, may be regarded as one in which a descriptive get-up acquired secondary meaning.

[17] *Canadian Shredded Wheat Co Ltd v Kellogg Co of Canada Ltd* [1938] All E.R. 618; 55 R.P.C. 125, PC; see also *Hodgkinson and Corby Ltd v Wards Mobility Services Ltd* [1998] F.S.R. 530.

[18] [1986] R.P.C. 389 (Walton J.).

Lords in *Reckitt & Colman v Borden*.[19] The defendants' "monopoly assumption" argument in the House of Lords was to the effect that the plaintiffs' evidence of confusion was undermined by the fact that Reckitt & Colman had enjoyed a *de facto* monopoly in lemon juice packed in lemon-shaped squeeze packs. The argument failed to find favour, and Lord Oliver demonstrated its *reductio ad absurdum*: it is the monopoly the plaintiff has in his marks or signs which makes them distinctive and ultimately gives rise to his legal right to restrain others from using them. The fallacy of the monopoly assumption argument was closely bound up to another which failed. If it had been true that plastic lemons were articles of commerce in their own right then the analogy with the *Cellular Clothing* case would have been a fair one. However, once it was accepted that the relevant market was for lemon juice no matter how packaged the argument rebounded on the defendants. Lemon juice was available in plain glass bottles, squeeze packs of various designs, and two squeeze packs which resembled real lemons rather more distantly than did *Jif*. Out of all the competing products, *Jif* alone imitated a real lemon reasonably accurately in terms of size, shape and colour. The uniqueness of this get-up in a competitive market was itself an indication that the get-up was distinctive in the legal sense.

Conversely, in *Philips v Remington*[20] the Federal Court of Australia gave **8–34** short shrift to an argument that the introduction of *Remington* electric shavers with three rotary cutting heads into a market previously dominated by Philips would lead to passing-off, despite the Remington product being clearly branded as such:

"The appellants presented a number of arguments the common theme of which was that some persons might have built up in the past a favourable impression of triple rotary shavers without connecting them with the name Philips; if contemplating a purchase, they might assume the Remington is the shaver they had in mind (which, of course, would not have been a Remington), despite the prominence of the Remington brand. But arguments of this kind could always be raised when an incoming competitor seeks to break a monopoly. Of course, some people might, probably unjustifiably, and probably transiently, associate the new product in some way with the only product of that sort previously available. However, if anyone were misled as a result, it would not be by the conduct of the intruder upon the monopoly, but by virtue of an inherent problem of the situation. Nor is such a difficulty to be attributed to passing off, provided the goods in question are appropriately and clearly branded. Here, the Remington brand is prominent and virtually ubiquitous.

In any case, arguments of this kind float, dreamlike, in an atmosphere of unreality. It is not to be assumed that actual purchasers will, other than exceptionally, see the Remington shaver in circumstances so insulated from information that the suggested misconception might be nourished. Generally, Philips shavers (holding 30% of the world market for electric

---

[19] [1990] 1 W.L.R. 491; [1990] 1 All E.R. 873; [1990] R.P.C. 340, HL.
[20] [2000] FCA 876; 48 I.P.R. 257 (Federal Court of Australia).

shavers and, up to now, 100% of the Australian market for rotary shavers) will be displayed in shops and stores alongside the newcomer. It will
be plain to anyone that here are two rival brands."

At least two English cases, *Hoffman-La Roche v DDSA Pharmaceuticals*[21]
and *Sodastream v Thorn Cascade*[22] are open to criticism for supposing that
the absence of any competition contributed to making the get-up of the
plaintiffs' goods distinctive. In those cases, the plaintiffs had faced no
competition at all in their respective markets. However, if there is competition for the product as such then the importance of the claimant's get-up as
a badge for distinguishing the claimant's goods from competitors is not to
be undermined by describing it, inappropriately, as a monopoly.

Loss of distinctiveness

8–35 The distinctiveness of the claimant's chosen name, mark or get-up may be
lost in a variety of circumstances. Use of the mark, *etc*, may be discontinued,
in which case it is a matter of fact and degree as to what length of time may
elapse before the mark ceases to denote the claimant.[23] This raises the same
issues as extinction of goodwill, and the same cases are relevant. Distinctiveness may also be lost through licensing or assigning the mark in gross,[24]
or by issuing goods bearing it which appear to be the goods of others.[25]

Distinctiveness may also be destroyed through unchecked passing off.
"The very life of a trade mark depends on the promptitude with which it is
vindicated".[26] However, it is not infringement *per se* which destroys the
distinctiveness of the mark. What matters is whether the public have ceased
to rely on the mark as denoting one trade source.[27] If the infringement is
covert, then it may occur on a considerable scale without the public
appreciating that the mark does not any longer reliably denote the goods or
business of the claimant. As long as this remains the case, it is not too late to
restore the situation. In *Manus v Fullwood & Bland*[28] the whole of the
plaintiffs' trade was for a time usurped by the defendants. The contention
that the mark had ceased to be distinctive of the plaintiffs, and perhaps
become distinctive of the defendants, failed. In *In Things v Leather Garments*[29] the plaintiffs had had two successive suppliers, both of whom had
been guilty of passing-off. They still obtained an interlocutory injunction. In
United Biscuits v Asda,[30] the distinctiveness of *Penguin* for chocolate sand-

---

[21] [1969] F.S.R. 416, CA.

[22] [1982] R.P.C. 459, CA.

[23] *Ad-Lib Club Ltd v Granville* [1971] 2 All E.R. 300; [1972] R.P.C. 673; *Kark (Norman)
Publications Ltd v Odhams Press Ltd* [1962] R.P.C. 163.

[24] *Thorneloe v Hill* [1894] 1 Ch. 569; [1891–4] All E.R. 1263.

[25] *Wolff & Son v Nopitsch* (1900) 18 R.P.C. 27, CA.

[26] *Johnston v Orr-Ewing* (1882) 7 App.Cas. 219, HL *per* Lord Blackburn.

[27] *Ford v Foster* (1872) L.R. 7 Ch. 611, CA; see also *Treasure Cot Co Ltd v Hamley Bros Ltd*
(1950) 67 R.P.C. 89.

[28] (1949) 66 R.P.C. 71, CA.

[29] [1974] F.S.R. 35 (Walton J.).

wich biscuits was unaffected by the fact that *Puffin* and *Pelican* bars had transiently appeared on the shelves of two supermarket chains some years prior to the launch of Asda's *Puffin*.

In *Ford v Foster*[31] it was suggested that *Eureka* no longer denoted shirts of the plaintiff's manufacture. Although that might have been true in the trade, **8–36** the term was still distinctive to the general shirt-buying public:

"Then the question is, has it become *publici juris*? And there is no doubt, I think, that a word which was originally a trade mark, to the exclusive use of which a particular trader, or his successors in trade, may have been entitled, may subsequently become *publici juris*, as in the case ... of *Harvey's* Sauce ... Then what is the test by which a decision is to be arrived at whether a word which was originally a trade mark has become *publici juris*? I think the test must be, whether the use of it by other persons is still calculated to deceive the public, whether it may still have the effect of inducing the public to buy goods not made by the original owner of the trade mark as if they were his goods. If the mark has come to be so public and in such universal use that nobody can be deceived by the use of it, and can be induced from the use of it to believe that he is buying the goods of the original trader, it appears to me, however hard to some extent it may appear on the trader, yet practically, as the right to a trade mark is simply a right to prevent the trader from being cheated by other persons' goods being sold as his goods through the fraudulent use of the trade mark, the right to the trade mark must be gone."

In *Van Zeller v Mason Catteley*[32] the owners of a port vineyard and the English consignees of the wine each claimed that *Kopke Roriz* was dis- **8–37** tinctive of themselves. Joyce J. held that the name denoted the vineyard, and that the defendants' case was not assisted by the fact that in some years they had sold other wine under the mark.

In the *Harris Tweed* case, *Argyllshire Weavers v Macaulay Tweeds*[33] the pursuers in an action for a declarator argued that *Harris Tweed* could properly be used for tweed partly made by machinery on the Scottish mainland and partly by the crofters of Harris. Perhaps the greater part of the so-called Harris Tweed on the market had been of this kind. The Court of Session held that the term still denoted tweed wholly made on the island. The meaning of the term had not been destroyed by widespread but covert use for mainland, machine-made, cloth.

[1] [1997] R.P.C. 513 (Robert Walker J.).
[31] (1872) L.R. 7 Ch. 611, 628, CA, *per* Mellish L.J.
[32] (1907) 25 R.P.C. 37 (Joyce J.).
[33] [1964] R.P.C. 477 (Lord Hunter).

C. Assessing the Probability of Deception

Introduction

8–38 By far the most common way in which goods or businesses are passed off is by the adoption by the defendant of a sign or signs, of some kind, already distinctive of the claimant. Ultimately, the question is the single one of whether in all the circumstances there has been a misrepresentation as to the source of the goods or the identity of the business, but it is often convenient to break this down into specific questions: in terms of goods, what features of the claimant's goods are distinctive of him, to what extent and for what reasons? Are the defendant's goods sufficiently similar in those features to be taken for the claimant's? And has the defendant taken other measures, or are there other factors, which effectively eliminate the possibility of confusion?

These are questions of fact, which depend as much on the surrounding circumstances as on comparison of the respective signs themselves. It is impossible to give an *a priori* definition of what degree of resemblance will be sufficient to mislead, and every case has to be treated on its own merits.[34] The standard adopted is realistic. The public at large is not particularly careful or knowledgeable and a proportion may be deceived by ambivalent matter which would not mislead in every case.

> "The real question I have to ask myself is whether there is anything in the words *Iron Oxide* Tablets which would lead persons of average intelligence, in that class of the public likely to buy proprietary articles of that sort, into accepting the goods of the defendants as and for the goods of the plaintiffs that is to say, under the impression that they were getting *Iron-Ox* Tablets. I have to consider not only the case of a person who has been accustomed to buy the plaintiffs' goods and might, therefore, having regard to the difference in get-up, be unlikely to be deceived, but I have also to consider the case of a person who has, for example, seen an advertisement of, or has otherwise been told of *Iron-Ox* Tablets and who goes into a retail shop with the intention of buying them."[35]

> "The imitation of a man's trade mark, in a manner liable to mislead the unwary, cannot be justified by showing, either that the device or inscription upon the imitated mark is ambiguous, and capable of being understood by different persons in different ways, or that a person who carefully and intelligently examined and studied it might not be misled."[36]

---

[34] *Seixo v Provezende* (1865) L.R. 1 Ch. 192, *per* Lord Cranworth L.C.
[35] *per* Parker J. in *Iron-Ox Remedy Co Ltd v Co-op Wholesale Society Ltd* (1907) 24 R.P.C. 425.
[36] *per* Lord Selborne L.C. in *Singer v Loog* (1882) 8 App. Cas. 15, 18, HL.

The persons to consider

The persons to consider are ordinary, sensible members of the public[37] **8–39** representative of consumers of the goods or services in question. In most cases this means that the standard to apply is that of the public at large, but for goods with a narrower market the relevant standard may be different. So in *Asprey & Garrard v WRA (Guns) Ltd and Asprey*[38] it was relevant that the customers of both parties were likely to be extremely rich; but also that many of them would be foreign, and unfamiliar with London and the English language. "If you have an international trade, you must take your international customers as you find them".[39] At the other end of the social scale, in *Edge v Niccolls*[40] the goods in question were bought mainly by cottagers, washerwomen and the like who at that time would often have been illiterate. The fact that the defendants had copied the plaintiffs' get-up therefore outweighed their use of their own name. There are many older cases on passing-off in the former Empire in which it was highly relevant that purchasers were either wholly illiterate or were unable to read English.[41] Conversely, if the only relevant customers are traders then they are likely to be more knowledgeable and exercise more care, especially if expensive goods such as machinery are involved. Professional persons such as dentists[42] and pharmacists[43] are less likely to be misled by similar names than the general public.[44]

With the relevant public defined, the standard to adopt is that of purchasers using ordinary caution,[45] which in practice is likely to tend towards the incautious or unwary[46] unless the goods are major purchases. It is no defence that careful customers would not be deceived, even if they are likely to be numerous. However, the fact that a "moron in a hurry"[47] might be deceived is insufficient, the customer is assumed to be of average intelligence. The hypothetical purchaser should also be assumed to be aware of what makes the claimant's mark distinctive in the market,[48] and to be alive

---

[37] *Newsweek Inc v British Broadcasting Corporation* [1979] R.P.C. 441, CA. approving *Morning Star Co-operative Society Ltd v Express Newspapers Ltd* [1979] F.S.R. 113.

[38] [2002] F.S.R. 30 (Jacob J.) affirmed [2001] EWCA Civ 1499; [2002] E.T.M.R. 47; [2002] F.S.R. 31, CA.

[39] *per* Jacob J.

[40] [1911] A.C. 693; 28 R.P.C. 582, HL.

[41] *Johnston v Orr-Ewing* (1882) 7 App. Cas. 219, HL; *White Hudson & Co Ltd v Asian Organisation Ltd* [1964] 1 W.L.R. 1466; [1965] 1 All E.R. 1040; [1965] R.P.C. 45, PC.

[42] *Ash (Claudius) & Sons Ltd v Invicta Manufacturing Co Ltd* (1911) 28 R.P.C. 597, HL.

[43] *Sterwin AG v Brocades (Great Britain) Ltd* [1979] R.P.C. 481; pharmacists are assumed to exercise reasonable care even when buying biscuits: *Blue Lion v National Brands* 2001 (3) SA 885 (SCA).

[44] Lloyds brokers in *Hayter (John) Motor Underwriting Agencies Ltd v RBHS Agencies Ltd* [1977] F.S.R. 285; [1977] 2 Lloyd's Rep. 105, CA.

[45] *Seixo v Provezende* (1865) L.R. 1 Ch. 192, *per* Lord Cranworth L.C.

[46] *Singer v Loog* (1882) 8 App.Cas. 15, HL.

[47] *Morning Star Co-operative Society Ltd v Express Newspapers Ltd* [1979] F.S.R. 113, *per* Foster J.

[48] *Payton & Co v Snelling, Lampard & Co* [1901] A.C. 308; 17 R.P.C. 628, HL.

to the possibility that the claimant is not or will not always be the only supplier of the goods or services in question.

> "Now when one talks about the ordinary purchaser being deceived or being induced to accept one manufacturer's goods as the goods of another there is some difficulty perhaps in understanding exactly what that means. An ordinary purchaser certainly does not mean the very careful man who knows exactly what he wants and takes very good care when he is buying an article that he gets what he actually wants, who looks closely at the article he is buying, and who would detect any striking difference between the article he is purchasing and the article he intended to purchase. Nor does it mean the very careless man who does not know the peculiar characteristics of the article he wants to buy, and who is not at all particular about what he gets, but who when he asks for an article accepts what is given him as being the article he requires, and therefore does not look at it and does not very much care whether he is getting the article he asked for or not. The ordinary purchaser does not mean either the very careful or the very careless and ignorant man. I think it must mean someone between the two. I take it the ordinary purchaser is a man who knows more or less the peculiar characteristics of the article he wants; he has in his mind's eye a general idea of the appearance of the article, and he looks at the article not closely, but sufficiently to take in its general appearance."[49]

Where the claimant has enjoyed a monopoly, or where a consumer knows only of the claimant's goods, there is a tendency for a part of the public to assume that any unfamiliar goods are the claimant's under a new guise, irrespective of how readily they may be distinguished.[50] No weight should be given indifferent customers who do not bother to distinguish brands and will happily take either: they are not deceived.[51] Persons who are particularly knowledgeable[52] or closely connected with the claimant[53] are apt to be put in mind of him by factors which would not have the same effect on the public at large.

Proportion of public that matters

8–40 The claimant need not show that the name, mark or get-up in issue is distinctive to all, or even the majority, of the customers in the relevant market. It is sufficient that a substantial proportion would be deceived.

---

[49] per Solomon J. in *Pasquali Cigarette Co Ltd v Diaconicolas & Capsopolus* [1905] T.S. 472 (South Africa), a case on the get-up of cigarette packets.
[50] *My Kinda Town Ltd v Soll* [1983] R.P.C. 407, CA.
[51] *Schweppes Ltd v Gibbens* (1905) 22 R.P.C. 601, HL, per Lord Halsbury and *Kark (Norman) Publications Ltd v Odhams Press Ltd* [1962] R.P.C. 163.
[52] *T & C Associated Industries Ltd v Victoria Wagon Works Ltd* (1931) 48 R.P.C. 148.
[53] *Saper (M) Ltd v Specter's Ltd* (1953) 70 R.P.C. 173.

"[The appellants] contended that in a passing-off action the plaintiff, in order to prove the association of the goods with his mark or get-up must establish that all persons or substantially all persons in the market are aware of his mark or get-up. There is no authority for this view and, if adopted, it would make it almost impossible to succeed in such an action. The actionable wrong in a passing-off action is the representation by the defendant in the course of his trade that his goods are those of the plaintiff. It is not a defence to prove that there are persons who purchase the goods of the defendant who are not misled, if it established that there are a large number of persons who are."[54]

"[I]t is enough to show that a substantial number of persons likely to become purchasers of the goods are liable to be deceived by the defendant's use of the name. On the one hand it is not necessary to show that all, or substantially all, persons in the market associated the name with the plaintiff's goods, if this can be shown of a substantial proportion of persons who are probably purchasers of the goods in question. On the other hand, that careless or indifferent persons may be led into error is not enough."[55]

It is impossible to give an *a priori* definition of what number or proportion of the market counts as substantial. The standard varies from case to case, but two contrasting situations may be distinguished. If the mark is arbitrary, then provided it means something to a proportion of the public which is not trivial then it probably does not matter that to the majority it conveys nothing at all. Arbitrary marks have been protected despite user being on such a small scale that they can have been distinctive to very few. On the other hand, if the mark is *prima facie* ill-adapted to distinguish the claimant's goods, for instance because it is descriptive, distinctive of a third party in another field, or very simple, then a much larger proportion are required to use or recognise it in a trade mark sense. Relief has been refused although a mark which was descriptive in its origins had almost certainly become distinctive to the majority of purchasers.[56]

Imperfect recollection

It is not to be supposed that the typical customer can precisely remember **8–41** every detail of the name, mark or get-up of the goods he intends to buy. It is therefore inappropriate to compare the marks or signs side-by-side.[57] Allowance has to be made for the imperfect recollection of the purchaser.

[54] *per* Viscount Maugham in *Saville Perfumery Ltd v June Perfect* (1941) 58 R.P.C. 147 at 175, HL.
[55] *per* Wilberforce J. in *Kark (Norman) Publications Ltd v Odhams Press Ltd* [1962] R.P.C. 163.
[56] *Burberrys v J C Cording & Co Ltd* (1909) 26 R.P.C. 693 (Parker J.).
[57] *De Cordova v Vick Chemical Co* (1951) 68 R.P.C. 103, PC. Which is not to say it never happens: see Lord Halsbury in *Schweppes Ltd v Gibbens* (1905) 22 R.P.C. 601, HL.

"What degree of resemblance is necessary from the nature of things, is a matter incapable of definition a priori. All that courts of justice can do is to say that no trader can adopt a trade mark so resembling that of a rival, as that ordinary purchasers, purchasing with ordinary caution, are likely to be misled.

It would be a mistake, however, to suppose that the resemblance must be such as would deceive persons who should see the two marks placed side by side. The rule so restricted would be of no practical use.

If a purchaser looking at the article offered to him would naturally be led, from the mark impressed on it, to suppose it to be the production of the rival manufacturer, and would purchase it in that belief, the court considers the use of such a mark to be fraudulent. But I go further. I do not consider the actual physical resemblance of the two marks to be the sole question for consideration. If the goods of a manufacturer have, from the mark or device he has used, become known in the market by a particular name, I think that the adoption by a rival trader of any mark which will cause his goods to bear the same name in the market, may be as much a violation of the rights of that rival as the actual copy of his device."[58]

"[T]he marks ought not, of course, to be compared side by side. An attempt should be made to estimate the effect or impression produced on the mind of potential customers by the mark or device for which the protection of an injunction is sought. The impression or recollection which is carried away and retained is necessarily the basis of any mistaken belief that the challenged mark or device is the same. If a mark is in fact or from its nature likely to be the source of some name or verbal description by which buyers will express their desire to have the goods, then similarities both of sound and of meaning may play an important part. The usual manner in which ordinary people behave must be the test of what confusion or deception must be expected. Potential buyers of goods are not to be credited with any high perception or habitual caution. On the other hand, exceptional carelessness or stupidity may be disregarded. The course of business and the way in which the particular class of goods are sold gives, it may be said, the setting and the habits and observation of men considered in the mass affords the standard."[59]

The idea of the mark

8–42 The respective signs of the claimant and defendant may be so different that even after invoking the doctrine of imperfect recollection there is no reason to conclude that the signs as such would be confused with one another. It does not follow from this that there can be no passing-off. If the central or prominent feature of the claimant's sign is embodied in the defendant's, if the "idea of the mark", or sign, is the same in both cases, then the public

---

[58] *per* Lord Cranworth L.C. in *Seixo v Provezende* (1865) L.R. 1 Ch. 192, 196.
[59] *per* Dixon and McTiernan JJ. in *Australian Woollen Mills Ltd v F S Walton & Co Ltd* (1937) 58 C.L.R. 641.

may be led to believe that there is or may be a relevant connection between the two parties. The public is used to marks and signs with a common theme being used on different goods from the same source, and to traders modifying them in their less essential details.

The plaintiffs in *Johnston v Orr-Ewing*[60] exported yarn to India and Aden under a mark the essential feature of which was a pair of elephants supporting a banner between them, so that the goods became known simply as *Two Elephants* in the local language. The defendants adopted a label with two elephants in different postures, with a different banner, and other distinctions. The House of Lords found for the plaintiffs.

"[A]lthough the mere appearance of these two tickets could not lead anyone to mistake one of them for the other, it might easily happen that they might both be taken by natives of Aden or of India unable to read and understand the English language, as equally symbolical of the plaintiffs' goods. To such persons, or at least to many of them, even if they took notice of the differences between the two labels, it might probably appear that these were only differences of ornamentation, posture, and other accessories, leaving the distinctive and characteristic symbol substantially unchanged."

Though the concept itself is as old as the ninetheenth century, it has made **8–43** a reappearance in modern law, in certain common law jurisdictions, under the name of the "gestalt" or "gestalt impression".[61] In *Sydneywide Distributors v Red Bull Australia*[62] the Federal Court of Australia recited a dictionary definition, in the context of summarising the evidence of a marketing expert.

"Dr Beaton focused on what was described as the gestalt of the [Red Bull] brand. According to the Shorter Oxford Dictionary this word means 'An integrated perceptual structure or unity conceived, as functionally more than the sum of its parts'. Dr Beaton described the notion as 'the overall identify of a brand as it relates to consumers', including 'not only the name, colour, physical properties and packaging but also associations with the brand and branding devices used to create associations, including its advertising and the "channels" through which it is sold' ... He considered that many buyers of packaged goods recognize and differentiate between brands on the basis of the overall look and feel of the product and its total image, particularly where no single brand identity element is dominant, and where the whole is greater than the sum of the parts. Dr Beaton said that where the gestalts of two products are almost identical, then without more information about the 'look alike' products, some consumers are likely to perceive them as comprising the same brand and/ or as derived from the same source."

[60] (1882) 7 App.Cas. 219, HL, *per* Lord Selborne at 225.
[61] See *Hoechst Pharmaceuticals v The Beauty Box* 1987 (2) SA 600 (Appellate Division); *Sydneywide Distributors Pty Ltd v Red Bull Australia Pty Ltd* [2002] FCAFC 157; 55 I.P.R. 354.
[62] Above.

8–44   In *United Biscuits v Asda*,[63] in which the name and get-up of the plaintiffs'
Penguin chocolate biscuits had been taken as a reference point for the
defendants' own-brand *Puffin*, Robert Walker J. held that the words *Penguin* and *Puffin* were too distinct for *Puffin* to be an infringement of a trade
mark registration for *Penguin*, but that the defendants' combination of
name and get-up was deceptive. The reasoning acknowledges the importance of a common idea to the two marks (supported rather than contradicted by the degree of visual and aural similarity) in so far as penguins and
puffins are seabirds with several common attributes of appearance and
habit, and neither is remotely apt for a chocolate covered biscuit.[64]

> "Penguin and Puffin, by contrast,[65] are words denoting real creatures, and
> they appear on packing designed for self-service shopping in a super-
> market. However they are artificial or 'fancy' names in the sense that an
> unpalatable seabird has no obvious connection with a chocolate-coated
> sandwich biscuit; and Puffin is, as a word, not wholly dissimilar from
> Penguin. It was to the seabird, and the names in black lettering, that
> almost all the witnesses referred in their explanations (some more
> articulate than others) of why they had been led to suppose, or assume, or
> guess at a common manufacturer."[66]

8–45   Although it is normal to speak of the idea of the mark as if it could be
uniquely defined, in reality the distinctiveness of a mark can be expressed in
many different ways, depending on the features identified as crucial and the
degree of abstraction allowed. Defining the idea of a mark allows at least as
much freedom as drafting a patent claim and the basic techniques are
similar: to decide which integers to include, individually or in combination,
and how precisely each is to be constrained.

In *Johnston v Orr-Ewing*[67] the idea of the mark was two elephants holding
a banner. In other circumstances the idea of the mark might have been said
to have embraced any two animals, but similar marks with animals other
than elephants were in common use and such a broad formulation of the
idea of the mark could not have been distinctive. The mark might equally
well have been defined more narrowly in terms of a crown as the or an
essential element, but the defendants had not copied the crown so the
plaintiffs ignored it. It is not entirely speculative to wonder if either or both
of *Pelican* and *Peregrine* would have been actionable by the proprietors of
Penguin. The former had transiently been used for a chocolate biscuit in the
past, both are of about the right length, and both have a degree of visual and
aural similarity from the initial "P" and the final "n" phoneme; but a
pelican is an ungainly and predominantly white water bird, and a peregrine

---

[63] [1997] R.P.C. 513 (Robert Walker J.).
[64] One might add (though the judge did not) that *Puffin* had long ago been chosen as an
appropriate name for the children's imprint of *Penguin* books.
[65] With *Ravenhead Brick Co Ltd v. Ruabon Brick & Terra Cota Co Ltd* (1937) 54 R.P.C. 341
and *Wagamama Ltd v City Centre Restaurants Ltd* [1995] F.S.R. 713.
[66] *per* Robert Walker J., above.
[67] (1882) 7 App. Cas. 219, HL.

is a kind of falcon. In *Juggi Lal-Kamlapat v Swadeshi Co*[68] the idea of a mark consisting of a lotus flower was wide enough to cover a rose, whereas in *Noordin v Abdul Kareem*[69] one consisting of a fez was not protected against a mark embodying a hat of a different design, still less against one of a glass tumbler the same shape as the fez. In *Parker-Knoll v Knoll International*[70] the plaintiffs successfully argued that *Knoll* was the truly distinctive half of their name *Parker-Knoll*, but in other circumstances can it be doubted that *Parker*, or its double-barrelled nature, would have been emphasised?

Because there can be so many different expressions of the idea underlying a mark or sign care must be taken on two counts. The first is that it is not sufficient for the claimant's sign in the precise form used to be *prima facie* distinctive. What matters is whether the central feature or idea remains distinctive at whatever degree of abstraction is contemplated. As well as the pictorial mark cases this can arise for verbal marks. In the *Office Cleaning*[71] case the plaintiffs traded as *Office Cleaning Services* and the defendants as *Office Cleaning Association*. It could be said that there was no real distinction between the names at all, as both provided services and neither was an association. If the names had been arbitrary then the difference in the third word could hardly have outweighed the identity of the first two. But the only "idea of the mark" the plaintiffs could claim was that of cleaning offices, and that was wholly descriptive of the work both performed. What distinctiveness there was could lie only in the precise form of words used, and in that respect there was sufficient distinction. The second point is that the absence of circumstances which would destroy its distinctiveness does not prove that any particular expression of the idea behind a mark actually corresponds to what the public recognise as distinctive in the mark, and it is the state of the public mind that matters.

Examples

In *Hodgson & Simpson v Kynock*[72] the plaintiffs sold soap under various **8–46** marks incorporating the word *Lion* and in some cases the device of a lion.[73] The most popular grade, *Red Lion Soap* was habitually ordered simply as *Lion Soap*. The defendants were restrained from selling various brands of soap (such as *Victory*) in wrappers which were generally dissimilar to those of the plaintiffs but on which pictures of lions' heads were prominent.

In *Juggi Lal-Kamlapat v Swadeshi*[74] the plaintiffs used a lotus flower and the words *Lotus Brand* for their cloth. They complained of two labels of the defendants. One had a lotus flower as a prominent feature. The other included a rose instead of a lotus and the words *Flower Brand*. The Privy

[68] (1928) 46 R.P.C. 74, PC.
[69] (1931) 48 R.P.C. 491, PC.
[70] [1962] R.P.C. 265, HL.
[71] *Office Cleaning Services Ltd v Westminster Office Cleaning Association* [1946] 1 All E.R. 320; 63 R.P.C. 39, HL.
[72] (1898) 15 R.P.C. 465 (Romer J.).
[73] The plaintiffs' wrappers are not illustrated in the report, and it is the word mark to which attention was given.
[74] (1928) 46 R.P.C. 74, PC, *per* Lord Dunedin.

Council upheld injunctions on both counts. The defendants' marks "though if critically looked at by a person of such literacy as to have critical powers of observation, would not be confused, yet would be apt to be confused by the illiterate and unobservant".

The plaintiffs in *Noordin v Kareem*[75] imported sarongs which they sold under a label carrying a picture of a fez and the words *Chop Topi*, meaning hat brand. The plaintiffs sought, but failed, to prove that "their goods were known and asked for as *Chop Topi* goods . . . so that sarongs offered for sale under any label which contained, or contained as its distinctive feature, a hat or cap, would be confused with and taken for sarongs of the plaintiff".

8–47   In *Australian Woollen Mills v Walton*[76] *Caesar* and the device of a Roman soldier on horseback facing the reader were not likely to be confused with *Crusader* and the device of a crusader on a horse sideways on. The plaintiffs failed to show that the idea of the mark was simply that of a man or soldier on a horse.

In *Subbiah Nadar v Kumavaral Nadar*[77] the plaintiff claimed that cheap cigarettes whose label consisted of a picture of him were known as *Photo Mark*. The defendant's mark was a generally similar portrait of the defendant himself. A defence of antecedent or concurrent user failed on the facts, the only possible inference being that the defendants were guilty of deliberate copying. The Privy Council held that there was infringement of the plaintiffs' trade mark but that the evidence fell far short of showing that *Photo Mark* exclusively denoted the plaintiffs. The refusal to grant an injunction against passing-off is surprising when the labels were deliberately made deceptively similar. The plaintiffs seem to have set too high a target for themselves and suffered accordingly.

The circumstances of the sale

8–48   The way in which goods or services are supplied has a major effect on the likelihood of deception occurring. More generally, so does any other context in which the parties' respective names or marks will come to the attention of those likely to be influenced by them. Different issues may arise according to whether the goods are bought in person, by telephone or post, or by messengers such as children or (formerly) servants. Other circumstances are also to be taken into account. For instance pubs are crowded, noisy and busy, so mistakes are more likely to be made and less likely to be noticed.[78] Cases involving newspapers and magazines show a tendency towards the belief that readers will distinguish between the parties through content and appearance despite strong similarities in name. This may probably be justified in so far as readers have strong loyalties, and buy each title so often as to recognise even small details.

[75] (1931) 48 R.P.C. 491, PC, *per* Lord Russell of Killowen.
[76] (1937) 58 C.L.R. 641 (High Court of Australia).
[77] (1946) 63 R.P.C. 187, PC.
[78] *Montgomery v Thompson* [1891] A.C. 217; 8 R.P.C. 361, HL, *per* Lord Macnaghten; *Lowenbrau Munchen v Grunhalle Lager International Ltd* [1974] R.P.C. 492; [1974] F.S.R. 1; [1974] 1 C.M.L.R. 1. Quotation marks around "mistakes" may be implicit.

If the goods are bought over the counter from an assistant then they are likely to be requested by name, so that aural similarity assumes importance. Get-up and essentially visual marks are likely to be relevant only to the extent they would obviate deception, and that depends on the customer having and exercising the opportunity to examine the goods. This is even more so if the purchaser is buying on behalf of another or on recommendation. If self-service predominates then get-up and visual marks assume greater importance, but without altogether displacing the brand name. In the *Jif Lemon* case, *Reckitt & Colman v Borden*,[79] it was relevant that the competing brands of plastic lemon would not often be stocked side by side because supermarkets normally carried only one brand of lemon juice. Consumers would therefore have no opportunity to compare one brand to the other to refresh their memory. It was also relevant that the distinguishing feature between the two brands was a label, which was in the form of an easily detachable collar. By the time a customer came to replace an empty *Jif* lemon, the collar would probably have disappeared and the immediate point of comparison would be a bare plastic lemon without its label.

Sales assistants are in a position to substitute the defendant's goods for those asked for, and if the goods are inherently deceptive or the defendant lacked *bona fides* this may be taken into account. If orders are placed by telephone then the importance of aural similarity is increased,[80] but an ambiguous order can be clarified at once, which is not the case if the order is by post. In all cases of sales responding to postal or telephone orders the customer is put to major inconvenience in returning goods which are not what he wanted, even if he recognises the fact.

The defendant may attempt to rely on the fact that his goods are suffi- **8–49** ciently distinct for customers to recognise them before consuming them or putting them into use, but if there was deception at the time of sale the possibility of the goods being returned is no defence. This applies with special force to mail order,[81] but it can also be true for ordinary retail sales. "Who would kick up a fuss over a 4d loaf which was to all intents and purposes what they wanted" asked Roxburgh J. in a case where loaves of bread clearly marked *Nutrex* were substituted in response to orders for the plaintiffs' *Procea*.[82] In *Kimberley-Clark v Fort Sterling*[83] what mattered was that at the point of sale the slogan "Softness guaranteed (or we'll exchange it for Andrex®)" on promotional packs of the defendants' *Nouvelle* brand of toilet tissue was likely to deceive significant numbers of consumers. Many would simply notice the prominent use of *Andrex*, and pay little or no attention either to the implication that *Nouvelle* and *Andrex* were rival

---

[79] [1990] 1 W.L.R. 491; [1990] 1 All E.R. 873; [1990] R.P.C. 340, HL.

[80] As in *Morcream Products Ltd v Heatherfresh (Foods) Ltd* [1972] R.P.C. 799 (*Everfresh, Heatherfresh*).

[81] *Pearson Bros v Valentine & Co* (1917) 34 R.P.C. 267; *Purefoy Engineering Co Ltd v Sykes Boxall & Co Ltd* (1954) 72 R.P.C. 89, CA.

[82] *Procea Products Ltd v Evans & Sons Ltd* (1951) 68 R.P.C. 210. See also *Montgomery v Thompson* [1891] A.C. 217; 8 R.P.C. 361, HL and *Du Cross v Gold* (1912) 30 R.P.C. 117.

[83] [1997] F.S.R. 877 (Laddie J.).

brands, or to a disclaimer in very small type. There was uncontradicted evidence that the time taken by a consumer to select goods such as toilet paper in a supermarket was about 10 seconds.

Defendant's goods or business distinguished

8–50 The law of passing-off does not create a monopoly in any name, mark or get-up, no matter how prestigious or distinctive. In theory, it is always open to a competitor to use the claimant's mark but to avoid liability by adequately distinguishing his own goods, services or business.[84] Whether this is possible in practice is another matter,[85] and an injunction may be granted in unqualified form if the court is convinced that any attempt to distinguish would be insincere or doomed to failure.[86] In *Asprey & Garrard v WRA (Guns) Ltd and Asprey*[87] the Court of Appeal observed of an express disclaiming notice that Jacob J. "was entitled to draw on his considerable experience in this field to say that such disclaimers hardly ever work".

If the claimant relies primarily on verbal or device marks then it is common for the defendant to claim that his get-up or the appearance of the goods themselves is sufficiently distinctive to avoid liability, but not often with success.[88] The converse argument more often prevails, in that differences in brand name are more likely to outweigh similarities in get-up. Whether the distinguishing matter is effective or not depends on all the circumstances in which it is alleged passing-off is liable to take place.[89]

The misrepresentation in the traditional form of passing-off is that there is some connection between the claimant and defendant which is likely to cause damage to the claimant. The strongest example of this is where the public believe the parties to be one and the same. What steps the defendant must take to distinguish himself depends on this. If the public fail to distinguish the parties at all, then it must be idle for the defendant to give his full name[90] or to use forms of words such as "no connection with any other business", because the public do not recognise that more than one business exists. Conversely, if the tenor of the misrepresentation is that there is a

---

[84] See Lord Greene in *Saville Perfumery Ltd v June Perfect* (1941) 58 R.P.C. 147, CA, affirmed *ibid.*, HL.

[85] See *Powell v Birmingham Vinegar Brewery Co* [1897] A.C. 710; 14 R.P.C. 721, HL, where a business which had successfully revoked the plaintiff's trade mark and had been warned it could hardly use it without passing-off, was in due course enjoined.

[86] *Montgomery v Thompson* [1891] A.C. 217; 8 R.P.C. 361, HL.

[87] [2002] F.S.R. 30 (Jacob J.) affirmed [2001] EWCA Civ 1499; [2002] E.T.M.R. 47; [2002] F.S.R. 31, CA.

[88] An unusual exception is *TGI Friday's Australia v TGI Friday's Inc* [1999] FCA 304, 45 I.P.R. 43 (Federal Court of Australia, Full Court) in which dissimilarities in get-up of premises outweighed near identity of names.

[89] See the judgment of Parker J. in *Iron-Ox Remedy Co Ltd v Co-op Wholesale Society Ltd* (1907) 24 R.P.C. 425; compare *World Athletics and Sporting Publications Ltd v ACM Webb (Publishing) Co Ltd* [1981] F.S.R. 27, CA.

[90] As in *Edge (William) & Sons Ltd v William Niccolls & Sons Ltd* [1911] A.C. 693; 28 R.P.C. 582, HL and *Saville Perfumery Ltd v June Perfect* (1941) 58 R.P.C. 147, HL. Far from removing the cause of the misrepresentation, this may lead the public to believe that the person they know only by reputation is at last revealing himself under his true colours.

connection between two separate businesses then use of the defendant's own name, mark or get-up will not necessarily correct the situation: the public already appreciate the defendant's separate identity and no amount of emphasis of that will necessarily rebut the belief that there exists a link with the claimant.

If goods are not always collected by the customer in person, then even **8–51** radically different appearance or get-up will not necessarily suffice to distinguish if the brand names are identical.[91] The same applies if the claimant's goods are well-known by name but not by appearance, as may be the case for exotic or luxury goods infrequently purchased by any individual, or where the goods are purchased on recommendation. For appearance or get-up to distinguish effectively three requirements must be met: the claimant's get-up must be sufficiently well-known to the customer in advance, the defendant's get-up must be sufficiently different for it to be obvious that the goods are not those of the claimant, allowing for imperfect recollection, and the sale must take place in circumstances where the difference will come to the attention of the purchaser in time.

In *Fisons v Godwin*[92] Brightman J. observed

"If the *Fisons* 'Gro-bag' had not contained the name '*Fisons*' or if the name '*Godwins*' had not been so prominently displayed, I might well have reached a different conclusion, but I doubt whether the defendants could have done much more to signify to a buyer that he was looking at a product of Godwins and not at a product of Fisons."

When what is in issue is the get-up or trade dress of the goods themselves, **8–52** as opposed to their packaging, then there are strong policy reasons for recognising the distinguishing value of brand names or other marks, since otherwise the claimant may obtain a *de facto* monopoly in a useful or attractive design or feature. In this respect the Australian decisions in *Parkdale v Puxu*,[93] and *Philips v Remington*[94] are to be preferred to that of the South African Supreme Court in *Weber-Stephen Products Co v Alrite Engineering*.[95]

Comparative advertising, which is permitted by the law of passing-off, more often involves use of the claimant's name or mark in the defendant's advertising than on the defendant's goods themselves. Once again, an issue of policy is involved although not to the point of creating an absolute right to use the claimant's name or mark regardless of the consequences. In *Kimberley-Clark v Fort Sterling*[96] the defendants' use of the plaintiffs' mark *Andrex* on promotional packs of their toilet paper, though it may have been legitimate in principle, amounted to passing-off because a significant num-

---

[91] *Powell v Birmingham Vinegar Brewery Co* [1897] A.C. 710; 14 R.P.C. 721, HL.
[92] [1976] R.P.C. 563.
[93] (1982) 149 C.L.R. 191, a decision under the Trades Practices Act 1974.
[94] [2000] FCA 876; 48 I.P.R. 257 (Federal Court of Australia).
[95] [1992] R.P.C. 549; 1992 (2) S.A. 489.
[96] [1997] F.S.R. 877 (Laddie J.).

ber of consumers would have assumed that the defendants' *Nouvelle* brand
was one of the plaintiffs' products.

D. Descriptive and Generic Terms

Introduction

8–53 The authorities on descriptive terms, which may be single words or whole
phrases, constitute one of the largest individual categories of reported cases
in the law of passing-off. Many are of interest only on their specific facts or
as illustrating their historical context. Since at least as early as *Reddaway v
Banham*[97] the law has recognised that a word or phrase which is apparently
descriptive may acquire what is called secondary meaning and become
distinctive of the claimant's goods, services or business. However, there are
important differences in the way the law treats descriptive terms as opposed
to arbitrary marks such as "fancy" words, visual marks and get-up.

1. A mark which is *prima facie* descriptive will only be protected if it can
   be shown to have acquired secondary meaning: that is to say, if it has
   become distinctive of the claimant. Of course, distinctiveness is an
   essential precondition for all marks, whether initially descriptive or
   "fancy", but the burden of proof is significantly higher for *prima facie*
   descriptive terms. So much so, that the decision to categorise a term
   as "descriptive" or "fancy" has often been treated as virtually
   determinative of the whole action, with the predictable consequence
   that the decision may be taken with one eye on the final result. Many
   obviously descriptive terms have been labelled "fancy" so as not to let
   an unmeritorious defendant off the hook. It is arguable that the law
   has sometimes been too ready to attribute distinctiveness to fancy
   terms on the strength of very slight user, and too slow to protect those
   which are descriptive in origin.

2. As an entirely separate matter, a term may be descriptive in the sense
   that it is the name of the goods themselves. In other words, it is
   generic, although that word is not often used in the older decided
   cases. Generic names are often also *prima facie* descriptive, but this is
   no more than a coincidence arising from the tendency of traders in
   many fields of business to favour descriptive or suggestive terms. If a
   term is the name of the goods as such, it cannot simultaneously
   denote any particular trade source. It may therefore be used in respect
   of goods of that sort by any competing trader without there being
   passing-off.

3. The defendant likewise cannot be prevented from unambiguously
   using a descriptive term in its original descriptive sense, unless it has

---

[97] [1896] A.C. 199; [1895–9] All E.R. 313; 13 R.P.C. 218, HL.

wholly lost that descriptive sense and become distinctive of the claimant in every context. More usually, some vestige of descriptive meaning remains even after the term has acquired enough secondary meaning to be protected as the claimant's trade mark. Equivocal or ambiguous use will be restrained, and often indicates lack of good faith, but if the defendant's use of the term is clearly and accurately in a descriptive rather than a trade mark sense then there is no misrepresentation to restrain. Passing-off gives no monopoly rights to words or marks of any sort, and this is all the more important when the term is (or was once) in common use outside its capacity as the claimant's trade mark.

4.   Even if the claimant succeeds in proving that a *prima facie* descriptive term has acquired some degree of secondary meaning, he will find that the scope of protection for his mark is narrower than for a wholly arbitrary term. There is a rule of law that relatively minor differences will suffice to distinguish the defendant's goods or business when both use a mark which is descriptive of the goods or services they provide. This applies even though the defendant is using the closely similar term in a trade mark sense. *Office Cleaning Association* was sufficiently different to *Office Cleaning Services* even though it was the trading name of the defendant.[98] The plaintiff was free to choose a name of higher inherent distinctiveness, and the penalty for his failing to do so was that a degree of confusion would be tolerated as the only alternative to giving him an unfair monopoly.

The term "secondary meaning" is often used as synonymous with "distinctiveness" and to that extent is a term of art. However, it is potentially misleading, especially when the sign in issue never had any, or any relevant, primary meaning, as with "fancy" words and most visual marks. In this work its use is avoided where possible except in the context of *prima facie* descriptive terms.

Generic terms: the name of the goods

A trader who introduces goods or services which are novel enough for the **8–54** English language not already to have a word to describe them does so at his own risk if he fails to provide the public with a suitable generic term for identifying the new goods or services without implicitly referring to their source. This is not to say that such failure is necessarily fatal. The public may invent a generic name for themselves, or may manage without, or it may be a rival whose chosen mark suffers the fate of generic status. The rule was first applied in respect of goods which were formerly patented, but the proposition applies equally to unpatented goods and patented or unpatented services. In his own interest, the introducer should adopt both a brand name and a generic name, and should use each consistently.

[98] *Office Cleaning Services Ltd v Westminster Office Cleaning Association* [1946] 1 All E.R. 320; 63 R.P.C. 39, HL.

"[The inventor] has sworn, that having invented a new substance, namely the solidified or oxidised oil, he gave to it the name of '*Linoleum*', and it does not appear that any other name has ever been given to this substance. It appears that the defendants are now minded to make, as it is admitted they may make, that substance. I want to know what they are to call it. That is a question I have asked, but I have received no answer; and for this simple reason, that no answer could be given, except that they must invent a new name. I do not take that to be the law. I think that if '*Linoleum*' means a substance which may be made by the defendants, the defendants may sell it by the name which that substance bears.

But then it is said that although the substance bears this name, the name has always meant the manufacture of the plaintiffs. In a certain sense that is true. Anyone who knew the substance, and knew that the plaintiffs were the only makers of this substance, would, in using the word, know he was speaking of a substance made by the plaintiffs. But nevertheless, the word directly or primarily means solidified oil. It only secondarily means the manufacture of the plaintiffs, and has that meaning only as long as the plaintiffs are the sole manufacturers. In my opinion, it would be extremely difficult for a person who has been by right of some monopoly the sole manufacturer of a new article, and has given a new name to the new article, meaning that new article and nothing more, to claim that the name is to be attributed to his manufacture alone after his competitors are at liberty to make the same article."[99]

8–55 The treatment of new generic names in English law has been confused by two factors. One is that traders have failed to give new products generic names, or have treated the generic and brand names interchangeably, or have claimed exclusivity in what must objectively have been a generic name at its adoption. The other is that for brand and generic names alike traders have a strong preference for the highly descriptive. In consequence, the courts have quite often had to deal with allegations of passing-off based on the use of a word which appears to have been both generic in its meaning and descriptive in its origins. Such cases have tended to concentrate on the *prima facie* descriptive quality of the term.

In cases of passing-off involving verbal marks the converse of "distinctive" is often taken to be "descriptive". Unfortunately, there are really two different concepts behind that word, since "descriptive" is often used when "generic" would be more appropriate. In English legal usage it is more consistent with the older authorities to use "descriptive" as a term of art embracing "generic" as well as its natural meaning.[1] The fact that one word has been used to cover two concepts which are related but not identical has resulted in some confusion of thought, especially in respect of arbitrary

---

[99] *per* Fry J. in *Linoleum Manufacturing Co v Nairn* (1878) 7 Ch.D. 834 at 836.

[1] Of the older passing-off cases, the very few to use the word "generic" at all do so interchangeably with "descriptive": see *British Vacuum Cleaner Co Ltd v New Vacuum Cleaner Co Ltd* [1907] 2 Ch. 312; 24 R.P.C. 641; *Electromobile Co Ltd v British Electromobile Co Ltd* (1907) 25 R.P.C. 149, CA and *De Cordova v Vick Chemical Co* (1951) 68 R.P.C. 103, PC. In recent cases the distinction is more likely to be made expressly.

generic names for new goods or services. Words such as *paraffin*,[2] *linoleum*[3] and *magnolia*[4] are wholly arbitrary in relation to oil, floor coverings and alloys, but that does not stop them being descriptive in the sense that they are the name of the article as such. With terms such as *malted milk*,[5] *shredded wheat*[6] or *oven chips*[7] the objection to distinctiveness is twofold. Those terms indicate clearly enough what the product is and how it is made or may be used, but the more fundamental objection is that they are the generic names of those products, and this does not depend at all on anyone recognising the descriptive message they were also designed to convey. Arguments that the public would not realise "oven chips" were potato chips for cooking in the oven, even if made out, are beside the point.

In *Associated Newspapers v Express Newspapers*[8] the defendants alleged that "mail" was generic, descriptive, or both for newspapers. Both contentions rightly failed, but both were logically separate from the rather stronger submission that there were sufficient newspapers with names including "Mail" for the latter on its own to be incapable of denoting the claimants. The argument that "Mail" must be generic because the word could be found in 781 newspaper titles published since 1800 (almost all of them either defunct, foreign, or both) was not only absurd, but provided its own *reductio ad absurdum*: on the same argument, neither *Daily Mail* nor *Mail on Sunday* could possibly be distinctive, although their distinctiveness had been conceded.

The two usages were recognised and identified by Lord Davey in *Cellular* **8–56** *Clothing v Maxton & Murray*:[9]

"[A] man who takes upon himself to prove that words, which are merely descriptive or expressive of the quality of the goods, have acquired the secondary sense to which I have referred, assumes a much greater burden ... than that of a man who undertakes to prove the same thing of a word not significant and not descriptive, but what has been compendiously called a 'fancy' word.

The other observation which occurs to me is this, that where a man produces, or invents if you please, a new article, and attaches a descriptive name to it, a name which, as the article has not been produced before, has of course not been used in connection with the article, and secures for himself either the legal monopoly or a monopoly in fact of the sale of that article for a certain time, the evidence of persons who come forward and say that the name in question suggests to their minds and is associated by

[2] *Young v Macrae* (1862) 9 Jur.N.S. 322.
[3] *Linoleum Manufacturing Co v Nairn* (1878) 7 Ch.d. 834 (Fry J.).
[4] *Magnolia Metal Co v Atlas Metal Co* (1897) 14 R.P.C. 389, CA.
[5] *Horlicks Malted Milk Co v Summerskill* (1916) 34 R.P.C. 63, HL.
[6] *Canadian Shredded Wheat Co Ltd v Kellogg Co of Canada Ltd* [1938] All E.R. 618; 55 R.P.C. 125, PC.
[7] *McCain International Ltd v Country Fair Foods Ltd* [1981] R.P.C. 69, CA.
[8] [2003] EWHC 1322 (Laddie J.).
[9] [1899] A.C. 326, 343; 16 R.P.C. 397, HL, *per* Lord Davey. The majority of the House seemed to concentrate on the fact that the word was *prima facie* descriptive. The passage deleted from the first paragraph would now be considered obsolete.

them with the plaintiff's goods along, is of a very slender character ... He brings the article before the world, he gives it a name descriptive of the article all the world may make the article, and all the world may tell the public what article it is they make, and for that purpose they may prima facie use the name by which the article is known in the market."

8–57   Lord Davey's speech was followed by Parker J. in *British Vacuum Cleaner Co v New Vacuum Cleaner Co*[10] in which the plaintiffs had obtained a patent for cleaning articles by suction. He called the apparatus a vacuum cleaner and the process vacuum cleaning. Once again the term was *prima facie* descriptive, but Parker J. expressly referred to its generic nature as well.

> "The name which he chose, however, for his machinery, and for the process of cleansing by means of such machinery was not a specific name denoting in any way the essential feature of his patent, but was a generic name applicable to all processes of cleaning by means of the creation of a vacuum and of suction caused by means of such vacuum through pipes, and [he] must have known when he applied a generic description to his machinery and his process that other people might devise, and bring upon the market, other means of vacuum cleaning not protected by his patent, in fact different species of the same genus...
>
> [I]t appears to me that there is nothing, in principle, to prevent the defendant company from using the words 'Vacuum Cleaner' as part of its name. Having a new species of vacuum cleaner which it proposes to bring before the public, it desires, in order to bring itself before the public as dealing with that article, to use a name involving a description of that article distinguishing it from all other articles of the same genus by using the term 'New'."

Generic names: examples

8–58 It is not easy to be confident in giving examples of cases which turned on the claimant's alleged mark being the generic name of the goods, as opposed to those in which it was simply a *prima facie* descriptive term which might in principle have acquired secondary meaning with more intensive or extended use of the same kind. The problem arises from the habit of concentrating on the self-evidently descriptive character of most of the terms in issue and the fact that neither "generic" nor any cognate term has been used more than occasionally. The most telling expression to look for is that the term is "the name of the article", but even this is often subordinated to its inherent descriptiveness. With this reservation, it is suggested that the following are some instances of generic names which the respective defendants were entitled to use.

---

[10] [1907] 2 Ch. 312; 24 R.P.C. 641 (Parker J.).

Paraffin in *Young v Macrae*[11]; *James's Blister* in *James v James*[12]; *Linoleum* in *Linoleum Manufacturing Co v Nairn*[13]; *Liebig's Extract of Meat* in *Liebig's Extract of Meat Co v Anderson*[14]; and *Liebig's Extract of Meat Co v Hanbury*[15]; *Native Guano* in *Native Guano Co v Sewage Manure Co*[16]; *Maizena* in *National Starch Manufacturing Co v Munn's Patent Maizena & Starch Co*[17]; *Flaked Oatmeal* in *Parsons v Gillespie*[18]; *Magnolia* in a group of cases[19]; *Aerator* in *Aerators v Tollit*[20]; *Haematogen* in *Hommel v Bauer*[21]; *Vacuum Cleaner* in *British Vacuum Cleaner Co v New Vacuum Cleaner Co*[22]; *Electromobile* in *Electromobile Co v British Electromobile Co*[23]; *Diabolo* in *Philippart v William Whiteley*[24]; *Slip-on* in *Burberrys v Cording*[25]; *Malted Milk* in *Horlicks Malted Milk Co v Summerskill*[26]; *Shredded Wheat* in *Canadian Shredded Wheat Co v Kellogg Co of Canada*[27]; *Vapour Rub* (in England, but not in Jamaica) in *De Cordova v Vick Chemical Co*[28]; *Oven Chips* in *McCain International v Country Fair Foods*[29]; *Chicago Pizza* in *My Kinda Town v Soll*[30]; and *Jaffa Cakes* in *United Biscuits v Burtons Biscuits*.[31]

In addition, *Siegert v Findlater*[32] (*Angostura Bitters*) and *Powell v Birmingham Vinegar Brewery Co*[33] (*Yorkshire Relish*) may be early examples of cases in which those terms were generic but relief was granted on the basis that the defendant was misrepresenting the character or quality of his goods. The *Yorkshire Relish* case is hard to reconcile with *Horlicks Malted Milk Co v Summerskill*,[34] among others, on any other basis. The *Drinks Cases*   **8–59**

[11] (1862) 9 Jur. N.S. 322. Strictly, "*paraffine oil*"; "*paraffin*" was already in use for wax.
[12] (1872) L.R. 13 Eq. 421 (Romilly M.R.). The name of the inventor, patentee or introducer of new goods was once a prime candidate for generic status, but the cases are now of historical interest only.
[13] (1878) 7 Ch. D. 834 (Fry J.).
[14] (1886) 55 L.T. 206 (Chitty J.).
[15] (1867) 17 L.T. (N.S.) 298 (Page-Wood V.C.). But there was passing-off by imitation of get-up and substitution in *Liebig's Extract of Meat Co Ltd v Chemists Co-op Society Ltd* (1896) 13 R.P.C. 736, CA. The three cases are not entirely consistent.
[16] (1891) 8 R.P.C. 125, HL.
[17] [1894] A.C. 275; 11 R.P.C. 281, PC.
[18] [1898] A.C. 239; 15 R.P.C. 57, PC.
[19] Of which the last was *Magnolia Metal Co v Tandem Smelting Syndicate Ltd* (1900) 17 R.P.C. 477, HL. The decision holding that *Magnolia* described the metal as such irrespective of manufacturer is *Magnolia Metal Co v Atlas Metal Co* (1897) 14 R.P.C. 389, CA.
[20] [1902] 2 Ch. 319; 19 R.P.C. 418 (Farwell J.).
[21] (1904) 22 R.P.C. 43, CA.
[22] [1907] 2 Ch. 312; 24 R.P.C. 641 (Parker J.). The word "genus" was used.
[23] (1907) 25 R.P.C. 149, CA. It was admitted that the word had been generic five years previously.
[24] [1908] 2 Ch. 274; 25 R.P.C. 565 (Parker J.).
[25] (1909) 26 R.P.C. 693 (Parker J.).
[26] (1916) 34 R.P.C. 63, HL.
[27] [1938] All E.R. 618; 55 R.P.C. 125, PC.
[28] (1951) 68 R.P.C. 103, PC.
[29] [1981] R.P.C. 69, CA.
[30] [1983] R.P.C. 407, CA.
[31] [1992] F.S.R. 14 (Vinelott J.). The case was argued on get-up, the defendants' right to use the name not being challenged.
[32] (1878) 7 Ch.D. 801 (Fry J.).
[33] [1897] A.C. 710; 14 R.P.C. 721, HL.
[34] (1916) 34 R.P.C. 63, HL.

provide clearer examples of the inaccurate use of generic names such as *Champagne* in *Bollinger v Costa Brava Wine Co*[35]; *Scotch Whisky* in *John Walker v Henry Ost*[36]; and *Advocaat* in *Erven Warnink v Townend.*[37]

A special class of case exists in which the name of the claimant (or a predecessor) has itself come to be used as the generic name of the product.[38] This situation is so obviously disadvantageous that in modern conditions few traders are likely to allow themselves to fall into the trap, and the authorities are therefore of little more than historical interest. Examples are *James's Blister* in *James v James*[39]; *Cheavin's Patent* in *Cheavin v Walker*[40]; *Liebig's Extract of Meat* in *Liebig's Extract of Meat Co v Anderson*[41] and *Liebig's Extract of Meat Co v Hanbury*[42]; *Winser Interceptors* in *Winser v Armstrong*[43]; *Daimler* in *Daimler Motor Car Co v British Motor Traction Co*[44]; Bowden in *Bowden Wire v Bowden Brake Co (No.2)*[45]; and possibly *Universal* in *Universal Winding Co v George Hattersley.*[46] However, there is no rule of law that the name of an inventor, introducer or patentee is open to use by all, and there are probably at least as many examples of such use being restrained.[47]

8–60   A different issue arises when the defendant uses expressions such as "similar to",[48] "as",[49] "pattern",[50] "type",[51] "model"[52] or "system"[53] in conjunction with the claimant's name or mark. Cases in which relief has been refused are still consistent with the name or mark being distinctive of the claimant. If it is clear that the defendant will supply his own goods, then

[35] [1960] Ch. 262; [1959] 3 All E.R. 800; [1960] R.P.C. 16 (Danckwerts J.).

[36] [1970] 1 W.L.R. 917; [1970] 2 All E.R. 106; [1970] R.P.C. 489 (Foster J.)

[37] [1979] A.C. 731; [1979] 2 All E.R. 927; [1980] R.P.C. 31, HL.

[38] It can also happen that the claimant, if a company, chooses to name itself after the product, as in *Canadian Shredded Wheat Co Ltd v Kellogg Co of Canada Ltd* [1938] All E.R. 618; 55 R.P.C. 125, PC.

[39] Above.

[40] (1877) 5 Ch.D. 850, CA.

[41] Above.

[42] Above.

[43] (1899) 16 R.P.C. 167 (Byrne J.).

[44] (1901) 18 R.P.C. 465 (Buckley J.). But by 1907 it had become distinctive: *Daimler Motor Co (1904) Ltd v London Daimler Co Ltd* (1907) 24 R.P.C. 379, CA.

[45] (1913) 30 R.P.C. 609 (Warrington J.).

[46] (1915) 32 R.P.C. 479 (Joyce J.).

[47] For example *Massam v Thorley's Cattle Food Co* (1880) 14 Ch.D. 748, CA; *Edison Storage Battery Co v Britannia Batteries Ltd* (1931) 48 R.P.C. 350.

[48] *Broad & Co Ltd v Cast Iron Drainage Co Ltd* [1970] F.S.R. 363.

[49] *Broad & Co Ltd v Graham Building Supplies Ltd* [1969] R.P.C. 285; [1969] F.S.R. 153: "As *Broadstel*" not passing-off when it was clear the defendant was supplying his own goods.

[50] *Armstrong Pattern* was allowed in *Armstrong Oiler Co Ltd v Patent Axelbox and Foundry Co Ltd* (1910) 27 R.P.C. 362. Customers knew the defendants would supply their own goods and the meaning of *Armstrong* on its own was left undecided. *Alligator Pattern* was restrained as trade mark infringement in *Stone (JB) & Co Ltd v Steelace Mfg Co Ltd* (1929) 46 R.P.C. 406, CA but the action was held to have been rightly dismissed as regards passing-off.

[51] *Roe (AV) & Co Ltd v Aircraft Disposal Co Ltd* (1920) 37 R.P.C. 249. "*Avro* type" was allowed, but not "*Avro*" on its own.

[52] Though in *Bechstein v Barker & Barker* (1910) 27 R.P.C. 484. "*Bechstein* model" was restrained. There was trade evidence that "*X* model" for pianos meant a piano manufactured by X.

[53] See the various *Singer* cases, below.

there is no misrepresentation as to source. There may be one as to quality, but it is only recently that such a misrepresentation would have been considered actionable.

It is possible for a generic term to lose that status and become distinctive of one manufacturer, as may have happened to *Singer*[54] and certainly happened to *Daimler*.[55] Although these cases are explained as turning on a change in the way those terms were understood, there seems to be underlying them a change in the law's attitude to what constituted a genus deserving a name of its own. In the earlier cases, the genus was not sewing machines or motor cars, but specific models of each. In the later ones, the need for a generic name for every particular design had implicitly been abandoned.

Descriptive terms and secondary meaning

As an entirely separate matter, a trader who chooses to use a name or mark **8–61** which is *prima facie* descriptive of his goods, services or business runs the risk that the public will continue to use the term in its descriptive sense rather than identifying it with him. He must prove that the mark has acquired a secondary meaning as denoting his goods, and the burden of doing so is higher in proportion to the descriptive quality of the mark. Even if secondary meaning is proved two problems remain. One is that no trader can be prevented from using the word in its old descriptive sense if he avoids misrepresentation. The second is that other traders may use similar and equally descriptive names or marks as their own and will be allowed to do so even if a degree of confusion results.

Although there are practical difficulties confronting the trader who chooses a descriptive word or phrase, there is no rule of law that marks which are descriptive in their literal meaning can be used with impunity by other traders. In *Reddaway v Banham*[56] *Camel Hair Belting* was held by the House of Lords to be distinctive of the plaintiffs, although the belting of both parties was predominantly composed of camel hair. The Court of Appeal had held that in those circumstances the defendant could not be restrained from using it, even in bad faith. Lord Hershell replied:

---

[54] The authorities are inconclusive. In *Singer Machine Manufacturers v Wilson* (1877) 3 App.Cas. 376, HL, the House of Lords was unable to say whether or not *Singer* was distinctive because Jessel M.R. had wrongly dismissed the plaintiffs' case before hearing the defendant's evidence. In *Singer v Loog* (1882) 8 App.Cas. 15, HL the defendant was allowed to use *Singer* to describe the system of operation of his machines but in a context in which it could not have deceived. He did not resist an injunction against using *Singer* on brass plates on the machines themselves. *Singer Manufacturing Co v Spence* (1893) 10 R.P.C. 297 and *Singer Manufacturing Co v British Empire Manufacturing Co Ltd* (1903) 20 R.P.C. 313 clearly went in the plaintiffs' favour.

[55] Compare *Daimler Motor Car Co Ltd v British Motor Traction Co Ltd* (1901) 18 R.P.C. 465 with *Daimler Motor Co (1904) Ltd v London Daimler Co Ltd* (1907) 24 R.P.C. 379, CA. And see *Woodward Ltd v Boulton Macro Ltd* (1915) 32 R.P.C. 173 where the wheel turned full circle.

[56] [1896] A.C. 199; [1895–9] All E.R. 313; 13 R.P.C. 218, HL.

"I think the fallacy lies in overlooking the fact that a word may acquire in a trade a secondary signification differing from its primary one, and that if it is used, to persons in the trade who will understand it, and be known and intended to understand it in its secondary sense, it will, none the less be a falsehood that in its primary sense it may be true. A man who uses language which will convey to persons reading or hearing it a particular idea which is false, and who knows and intends this to be the case, is surely not to be absolved from a charge of falsehood because in another sense, which will not be conveyed and is not intended to be conveyed, it is true. In the present case the jury have found ... that the words 'Camel Hair' had in the trade acquired a secondary signification in connection with belting; that they did not convey to persons dealing in belting the idea that it was made of camel hair, but that it was belting manufactured by the plaintiffs. They have found that the effect of using the words in the manner in which they were used by the defendants would be to lead purchasers to believe that they were obtaining goods manufactured by the plaintiffs, and thus both to deceive them and to injure the plaintiffs."

8–62   In the absence of proof that the term chosen by the claimant has become distinctive of him by acquiring a secondary meaning, there is no reason why the use of that or a similar term by another trader should involve any misrepresentation as to source. Thus *Cellular* was descriptive rather than distinctive in *Cellular Clothing Co v Maxton & Murray*.[57] In addition to the fact that it was *prima facie* descriptive of the plaintiffs' cloth, the plaintiffs had used it descriptively in advertisements and had very little trade in Scotland, which was the relevant market. *Flaked Oatmeal* was descriptive of a cereal in *Parsons v Gillespie*.[58] *Slip-on* was held descriptive of a type of coat by Parker J. in *Burberrys v Cording*,[59] it having been in use on a small scale before the plaintiffs adopted it. As passing-off was formerly understood, absence of secondary meaning was necessarily fatal to the plaintiff's case, whether the defendant was using the descriptive term accurately or not. In the modern form of the tort, an action may lie for misuse of a descriptive or generic term for goods or services which do not deserve it, though it is uncertain how far the law has developed.

A term does not have to be a literal or accurate description of the goods or services to which it applies for it to be descriptive for the purposes of passing-off. Nor is it necessary for the term to be the only one which could be applied.[60] In *Parsons v Gillespie*[61] the plaintiffs unsuccessfully argued that *Flaked Oatmeal* was not properly descriptive of a breakfast cereal consisting of oats which had been ground and flattened. The Privy Council held that it was "a natural and obvious term for oats so treated; one which everybody would accept at once as appropriate enough". There was insufficient evi-

[57] [1899] A.C. 326; 16 R.P.C., HL.
[58] [1898] A.C. 239; 15 R.P.C. 57, PC.
[59] (1909) 26 R.P.C. 693 (Parker J.).
[60] See *Aerators Ltd v Tollit* [1902] 2 Ch. 319; 19 R.P.C. 418 and *Horlicks Malted Milk Co v Summerskill* (1916) 34 R.P.C. 63, HL.
[61] [1898] A.C. 239; 15 R.P.C. 57, PC, *per* Lord Hobhouse.

dence that the primary descriptive meaning had been displaced and the defendants' goods were clearly distinguished. The plaintiffs in *Horlicks Malted Milk Co v Summerskill*[62] likewise failed to persuade the House of Lords that Malted Milk could not be descriptive because it was impossible to malt milk. As they had enjoyed a *de facto* monopoly of milk combined with malt, and had always described it as *Horlicks Malted Milk, malted milk* must also have been the generic name of the product.

In *McCain v Country Fair*[63] the plaintiffs had introduced potato chips which could be cooked in the oven and had called them *Oven Chips*, always prefaced with their name. The Court of Appeal held there was no arguable case of passing-off against defendants who sold *Country Fair Oven Chips* and *Birds Eye Oven Chips*. *Oven Chips* might be ungrammatical and meaningless in the absence of a product to which it related, but it was an ingenious and apt description of that product which informed the customer of what it was. Neither the nature of the use of the term nor its duration were consistent with its acquiring secondary meaning.

Descriptive and "fancy" words compared

A distinction is sometimes drawn in which "fancy" words are contrasted **8–63** with those which are *prima facie* descriptive. A fancy word is one which has no obvious relevance to the character or quality of the goods or business in relation to which it is used, such as *Eureka* for shirts,[64] *June* for toiletries,[65] and *Puffin* or *Penguin* (names of unpalatable seabirds both) for chocolate-coated sandwich biscuits.[65a] It is "of an arbitrary and fanciful nature"[66] in that context.

Whether a word is fancy or descriptive may depend on how it is used. *Health* may plausibly be called a fancy word in respect of fishing gear but not for cocoa.[67] The significance of the difference is that distinctiveness is very much more easily acquired for fancy words, and it is inappropriate to speak of secondary meaning when the word has no primary meaning to displace.[68] Some authorities, such as *Parsons v Gillespie*, almost appear to treat fancy words as if the mere fact of adoption were sufficient for protection by virtue of the plaintiffs having invented or appropriated the word, but this cannot be correct. Others, including *Cellular Clothing v Maxton & Murray* perhaps go too far in creating difficulties when the words in issue are not fancy. It is not the law that *prima facie* descriptive words are distinctive only as against fraudulent defendants. The decision to categorise a

---

[62] (1916) 34 R.P.C. 63, HL.

[63] [1981] R.P.C. 69, CA.

[64] *Ford v Foster* (1872) L.R. 7 Ch. 611, CA.

[65] *Saville Perfumery Ltd v June Perfect* (1941) 58 R.P.C. 147, HL.

[65a] *United Biscuits (UK) Ltd v Auda Stores Ltd* [1997] R.P.C. 513.

[66] *Parsons v Gillespie* [1898] A.C. 239; 15 R.P.C. 57, PC per Lord Hobhouse. See also *Cellular Clothing Co v Maxton & Murray* [1899] A.C. 326; 16 R.P.C. 397, HL, especially the speeches of Lord Shand and Lord Davey.

[67] *Dictum* of Neville J. in *Thorne & Co v Sandow* (1912) 29 R.P.C. 440.

[68] *per* Lord Shand in *Cellular Clothing Co v Maxton & Murray* [1899] A.C. 326; 16 R.P.C. 397, HL.

word as fancy or descriptive is only one part of the wider issue of whether there is a material representation to restrain. Inherent ability to distinguish is always a matter of degree with there being a continuous spectrum between the highly fanciful and the obviously descriptive. Wherever the name may fall on that range, what matters is whether the name is distinctive in fact.

8–64   A slightly different distinction was drawn by Templeman L.J. in *McCain International v Country Fair Foods*[69] in which he put weight on the information the names impart as well as on the way they first strike the reader. This change in emphasis is in keeping with the modern understanding of the tort.

> "[T]here is a very real difference in passing-off litigation between a fancy name and a descriptive name. A fancy name which is not descriptive of a product can only indicate that the product bearing that name is, or is licensed by, or is derived from one and the same supplier. Thus in *Spalding v Gamage*[70] the plaintiffs described their football as '*Orb* Football' ... in my judgment it was a fancy name in that nobody would have dreamed of connecting a football with an orb in normal speech, and if it was a fancy name the defendants could not use the same fancy name without thereby representing that their goods were the goods of the plaintiff. In my judgment a fancy name is an indication of a single source and that is why it is impossible, generally speaking, for a defendant to appropriate the same fancy name without committing the tort of passing off.
>
> A descriptive name, on the other hand, does not indicate the source of the goods, but the nature of the goods."

This is reminiscent of the way Parker J. had already treated the distinction between fancy and descriptive words in *British Vacuum Cleaner Co v New Vacuum Cleaner Co*[71]

> "Now with regard to questions such as arose in *Reddaway v Banham and Cellular Clothing Co v Maxton* and *Chivers & Sons v Chivers* I think a distinction must always be drawn between cases in which the word in question the word which it is proposed to restrain the defendant from using is a word of ordinary use, descriptive of an article, and cases in which the word complained of more or less, partakes of the character of a 'fancy word', or, primarily, does not relate to the article but to the person who makes the article."

Prima facie descriptive terms: examples

8–65   The authorities on *prima facie* descriptive terms are very numerous, what they have in common being that each one turned on its own set of facts. To give an exhaustive list would be neither practical nor useful. The following is

---

[69] [1981] R.P.C. 69, CA.
[70] (1915) 32 R.P.C. 273, HL.
[71] [1907] 2 Ch. 312, 321; 24 R.P.C. 641 (Parker J.).

a summary of some of the more influential or illustrative cases. Cases listed below as those in which the claimant prevailed include some in which the term in issue was distinctive, but the action failed on other grounds.

Cases in which the claimant prevailed

Exactly twelve yards written in Greek, Turkish and Armenian was dis- **8–66** tinctive for being in three foreign languages, even though the goods were exported: *Broadhurst v Barlow*.[72] *Camel Hair Belting* was protected both before[73] and after it was realised that the belting in question really was made of camel hair: *Reddaway v Banham*.[74] Several other cases by the same plaintiffs on the same mark culminated in *Reddaway v Hartley*[75] in which the Court of Appeal affirmed that the words had never been used descriptively and held that *Lechat's Camel Hair Belting* was calculated to deceive. *Silverpan* was distinctive for jam in *Faulder v Rushton*[76] although the jam was boiled in silver pans and the plaintiffs' advertisements drew attention to the fact. *Incorporated Accountant* meant a member of the plaintiff society in *Society of Accountants & Auditors v Goodway*.[77] *Iron-Ox* was distinctive of the plaintiffs' medicine in *Iron Ox Remedy Co v Co-op Wholesale Society*[78] and the defendants were restrained from selling *Iron Oxide* tablets, Parker J. holding that they were not using the term in a descriptive sense. The plaintiffs' tablets were not made from iron oxide, which had no medical value. There was passing-off when the defendants sold oil out of a barrel marked *Vacuum Motor Oil A Quality* despite an argument that *Vacuum Quality* denoted quality and would not deceive: *Vacuum Oil Co v Gooch & Tarrant*.[79]

Minties for mint-flavoured sweets was distinctive in *Angelides v James Steadman Henderson Sweets*[80] and infringed by *Mentes*. *Radio Rentals* restrained *Rentals* on its own in *Radio Rentals v Rentals*.[81] *Brine Baths* meant the plaintiffs' in *Hesketh Estates, Southport v Droitwich Brine Baths*[82] and an interlocutory injunction was granted against *Droitwich Brine Baths*. In

---

[72] Unreported. Summarised and commented on in *Kaggett v Findlater* (1873) L.R. 17 Eq. 29.

[73] *Reddaway (F) & Co v Bentham Hemp Spinning Co Ltd* [1892] 2 Q.B. 639; 9 R.P.C. 503, CA. The Court of Appeal ordered a new trial when the judge withdrew the case from the jury. The defendants thereupon submitted to an injunction: see the headnote to *Reddaway (Frank) & Co Ltd v George Banham & Co Ltd, infra.*

[74] [1896] A.C. 199; [1895–9] All E.R. 313; 13 R.P.C. 218, HL.

[75] (1930) 48 R.P.C. 283, CA. The other cases are *Reddaway (F) & Co Ltd v Ahlers* (1901) 19 R.P.C. 12; *Reddaway (F) & Co Ltd v Frictionless Engine Packing Co Ltd* (1902) 19 R.P.C. 505; *Reddaway (F) & Co Ltd v Stevenson & Brother Ltd* (1902) 20 R.P.C. 276.

[76] (1903) 20 R.P.C. 477, CA.

[77] [1907] 1 Ch. 489; 24 R.P.C. 159 (Warrington J.).

[78] (1907) 24 R.P.C. 425 (Parker J.).

[79] (1909) 27 R.P.C. 76 (Neville J.).

[80] (1927) 40 C.L.R. 43 (High Court of Australia, Full Court).

[81] (1934) 51 R.P.C. 407 (Clauson J.).

[82] (1934) 52 R.P.C. 39 (Farwell J.).

Delavelle v Stanley[83] *Blue Orchid* meant the plaintiffs' brilliantine (and a wider range of toilet goods) and was not used descriptively by either party. Although the brilliantine was coloured blue it did not smell of orchids. Many orchids had no smell at all, and those that did ranged in fragrance from "sugary sweet" to "the smell of a dead rat" by way of "new mown hay" and "freshly cut cucumbers". *Vapour Rub* was not descriptive in Jamaica, though in England it was generic.[84] *VapoRub* was distinctive of the plaintiffs, and the defendants were guilty of passing-off by using *Vapour Rub* even with the preface *Karsote: De Cordova v Vick Chemical Co.*[85]

8–67   The *Legal and General Assurance Society* obtained an interlocutory injunction in the Court of Appeal against a detective agency in *Legal & General Assurance Society v Daniel.*[86] The combination of the two words was unusual, and distinctive of the plaintiffs. A New Zealand court granted an injunction against *Wellington Pest Control* in *Pest Control Service v McClelland*[87] but left open the question of whether an order of mandamus could issue against the Registrar of Companies. An injunction was also granted in *Effluent Disposal v Midlands Effluent Disposal,*[88] *Midlands* being said to be insufficient distinction. *Top of the Pops* was distinctive for records and *Pick of the Pops* restrained in *Pickwick International v Multiple Sound Distributors.*[89] *Style* was distinctive of the plaintiffs' dress-making patterns and *Style'n Fit* restrained in *Style Patterns v K-Tel.*[90] *Brasserie* for a restaurant was not descriptive in British Columbia in *Blades Enterprises v Thibault.*[91] *Budget Rent-a-Car* for car hire was distinctive in the Australian case of *BM Auto Sales v Budget Rent-a-Car Systems.*[92] *Hikers* for shoes was restrained in *Boot Tree v Robinson.*[93] The Court of Appeal in *Mothercare v Penguin Books*[94] allowed that *Mothercare* was distinctive of the plaintiffs in their field of business although relief was refused because the defendants had not used it in a trade mark sense.

Farm Fluid for an agricultural liquid disinfectant was protected both on an application for an interim injunction, and subsequently at trial, in *Antec International v South Western Chicks.*[95] *Denim Company* (for denim jeans) as well as *Primark* were the subject of summary judgment for the claimant in

---

[83] (1946) 63 R.P.C. 103 (Evershed J.). an Earlier Australian case, *Helena Rubenstein Pty Ltd v Von Bronneck* (1943) S.R. (N.S.W.) 283 (*Apple Blossom*) is comparable in result and the arguments raised.
[84] A rare example of that word actually being used, and making it clear that the term "descriptive" may embrace "generic".
[85] (1951) 68 R.P.C. 103, PC.
[86] [1968] R.P.C. 255, CA.
[87] [1968] N.Z.L.R. 482 (Wild C.J.). Following *National Timber Co Ltd v National Hardware Timber and Machinery Co Ltd* [1923] N.Z.L.R. 1258, CA.
[88] [1970] R.P.C. 238; [1969] F.S.R. 468 (Stamp J.).
[89] [1972] R.P.C. 786 (CA opposed *ex parte*; Megarry J. *inter partes*).
[90] [1974] F.S.R. 499 (Graham J.).
[91] (1975) 65 D.L.R. (3d) 378 (Anderson J.). The plaintiff failed on other grounds.
[92] (1977) 12 A.L.R. 363; 51 A.L.J.R. 254 (High Court of Australia, Full Court).
[93] [1984] F.S.R. 545 (Nourse J.).
[94] [1988] R.P.C. 113, CA.
[95] [1997] F.S.R. 278 (Laddie J.); [1998] F.S.R. 738 (Michael Hart Q.C., Deputy Judge). The products were respectively marketed as *Antec Farm Fluid S* and *SWC Super Farm Fluid.*

Primark Stores v Lollypop Clothing,[96] but the only defence argued with any vigour was that the defendant had obtained the goods from one of the claimant's suppliers. In *Temporary Roadways and Access Co v Trax Portable Access*[97] a case based on the similarity between the trading names *TRAC* and *TRAX* (in both cases, for the provision of temporary road surfaces at events) was strengthened by the "remarkably close" similarity of the appearance of the defendants' vehicles to those of the claimants. An interim injunction was granted in terms directed both to the name and the livery of the vehicles.

In Australia, the former *Western Mining* company and a subsidiary **8–68** obtained a permanent injunction against another mining company using the same name,[98] despite having formally changed their names in 1995 or 1996. They were still well known under the old name: *WMC v Westgold Resources*.[99] Also in Australia, a mortgage lender trading as *Aussie Home Loans* was granted a final injunction against the use of *Aussie Home Builders* (with a very similar stylised design of a house) in *Australian Home Loans v Phillips*.[1] The defendant had previously briefly acted as an agent for the plaintiffs, and intended to arrange home loans as well as constructing houses.

Cases in which the claimant has failed

Nourishing Stout for beer could not be monopolised by the plaintiff, the **8–69** defendant's label being quite distinct: *Raggett v Findlater*.[2] *Flaked Oatmeal* for cereal and *Cellular* cloth were not distinctive of the respective plaintiffs in *Parsons v Gillespie*[3] and *Cellular Clothing Co v Maxton & Murray*.[4] *Aerator* had been in common use for 30 years and aptly and rightly described the devices in question, so the plaintiffs were not entitled to monopolise it in their company name: *Aerators v Tollit*.[5] *Naptha* for soap meant soap containing naptha, whether or not the soap was of the plaintiffs' manufacture, in various cases brought by *Fels* over a short period of time. The earlier ones established that if Naptha was descriptive the defendants could not be restrained from using it whether or not their soap contained any of that ingredient.[6] Later the plaintiff tried and failed to prove secondary meaning.[7]

---

[96] [2001] F.S.R. 37 (John Martin Q.C., Deputy Judge). The defendant abbreviated *Denim Company* to *Denim Co*

[97] [2002] EWHC 1728 (Blackburne J.)

[98] The second defendant, Western Mining NL.

[99] (1997) 39 I.P.R. 319 (North J., Federal Court of Australia).

[1] (1998) 40 I.P.R. 392 (Lehane J., Federal Court of Australia).

[2] (1873) L.R. 17 Eq. 29 (Malins V.C.).

[3] [1898] A.C. 239; 15 R.P.C. 57, PC.

[4] [1899] A.C. 326; 16 R.P.C. 397, HL.

[5] [1902] 2 Ch. 319; 19 R.P.C. 418 (Farwell J.).

[6] *Fels v Christopher Thomas & Bros Ltd* (1903) 21 R.P.C. 85, CA; *Fels v Stephenson Bros Ltd* (1903) 21 R.P.C. 89 (appeal on similar issues to preceding case dismissed by consent). These cases may no longer represent the law.

[7] *Fels v Thomas Hedley & Co Ltd* (1903) 21 R.P.C. 91. CA *Fels v Hodgson* (1903) 21 R.P.C. 95 (action on similar facts dismissed).

The following cases carry the authority of Parker J.: *Vacuum Cleaner* was the name of the article as such and its use in the name of the defendant company legitimate in *British Vacuum Cleaner Co v New Vacuum Cleaner Co*[8] In *Philippart v William Whiteley*[9] the name *Diabolo* was coined by the plaintiff as a new name for the old game known as "The Devil on Two Sticks". It was therefore open to the defendants to sell any suitable equipment (though not of the plaintiffs' manufacture) when *Diabolo* sets were asked for, and to advertise their sets under that name. The plaintiff had invited the world at large to do just that. In *Burberrys v Cording*[10] *Slip-on* for coats, though widely associated with the plaintiffs, was not distinctive of them.

8–70 *Haematogen* was descriptive of a medicine for improving the blood, and the term had been invented by a scientist before the plaintiff adopted it for his specific product in the form *Hommel's Haematogen: Hommel v Bauer*.[11] *Anglo-American* for retail shoe stores meant American-style goods made in Britain, and could be used by the defendants without liability: *Randall v Bradley & Son*.[12] *Electromobile* was descriptive of a motor car driven by electricity in *Electromobile Co v British Electromobile Co*.[13] *Erect Form* for a novel design of corset was too descriptive to be distinctive *per se* in *Weingarten Bros v Bayer*,[14] but the special manner in which it was written was protected.[15] *Universal* denoted a particular type of machinery formerly manufactured under patent, and not necessarily of the plaintiffs' manufacture, in *Universal Winding Co v George Hattersley & Sons*.[16] *Malted Milk* was descriptive in *Horlicks Malted Milk Co v Summerskill*.[17]

In *T & C Associated Industries v Victoria Wagon Works*[18] *Chequerboard* for fence panels was descriptive. *Shredded Wheat* was both the name for, and descriptive of, a breakfast cereal in *Canadian Shredded Wheat Co v Kellogg Co of Canada*.[19] *Office Cleaning Services* was so descriptive that *Office Cleaning Association* was a sufficient distinction in *Office Cleaning Services v Westminster Office Cleaning Assn*.[20] The makers of a carpet cleaning device sold as the *Countess Shampoomatic* were refused an inter-

---

[8] [1907] 2 Ch. 312; 24 R.P.C. 641 (Parker J.),
[9] [1908] 2 Ch. 274; 25 R.P.C. 565 (Parker J.).
[10] (1909) 26 R.P.C. 693 (Parker J.). Extensive quotations are given above.
[11] (1904) 22 R.P.C. 43, CA.
[12] (1907) 24 R.P.C. 773, CA.
[13] (1907) 25 R.P.C. 149, CA.
[14] [1904–7] All E.R. 877; (1903) 22 R.P.C. 341, HL.
[15] Compare *Weingarten Bros v Rosental, Weingarten Bros v Sherwood & Co* (1904) 21 R.P.C. 212 in which the same plaintiffs failed because user had been too slight to make *Erect Form* distinctive. Total sales before action brought had only been 28, and Farwell J. held that the defendants in the second action had used the term before the plaintiffs. Neither defendant had apparently copied the "scroll" device on which the case against Bayer had turned.
[16] (1915) 32 R.P.C. 479 (Joyce J.)
[17] (1916) 34 R.P.C. 63, HL. The facts, which could hardly have been less favourable to the plaintiffs, are set out more fully in the first instance of judgment of Joyce J. at (1916) 33 R.P.C. 1.
[18] (1931) 48 R.P.C. 148 (Maugham J.).
[19] [1938] All E.R. 618; 55 R.P.C. 125, PC.
[20] [1946] All E.R. 320; 63 R.P.C. 39, HL.

locutory injunction against *Addis Shampoomatic* in *Countess Housewares v Addis*.[21] *International* was descriptive for an hotel: *Park Court Hotel v Trans World Hotels*.[22] *Bullet* for darts meant shaped like a bullet to the public even though it was distinctive to the trade: *Unicorn Products v Roban Jig & Tool Co*.[23] *Newsweek* for a weekly news magazine was descriptive, or very nearly so, and an injunction refused against a television current affairs programme in *Newsweek Inc v BBC*.[24] *Oven Chips* was not distinctive in *McCain International v Country Fair Foods*[25] nor *Chicago Pizza* in *My Kinda Town v Soll*.[26]

Gold AM for a radio program of "Golden Oldies" broadcast by ampli- **8–71** tude modulation was too descriptive for the plaintiffs to have an arguable case when the name had only been in use for six months. It made no difference that the defendants had copied: *County Sound v Ocean Sound*.[27] In *Teleworks v Telework Group*[28] the different fields of business of the parties, and the relatively slight and local reputation of the claimant, were the main reasons for a finding that there was no serious prospect of deception; but it was also relevant that "teleworking" was descriptive, and the fact that both parties capitalized the middle "W" did not tip the balance against the defendant.

In Australia, the words *Dry-Fry Convection Oven Pan with Lid* for a cooking utensil had not acquired secondary meaning in *Telemak Teleproducts v Coles Myer*[29] but the manner in which they were written had been copied closely, as had other aspects of get-up. An injunction was granted against using those words in lettering substantially similar to that of the plaintiffs. A case based on the name *Fish Caf* for the defendants' fish restaurant was said to be highly speculative but rescued from striking out by similarities in get-up: *The Last Aussie Fish Caf v Almove*.[30] *Flexibond* for a single premium life assurance policy was too descriptive to be protected in *Lumley Life v IOOF of Victoria Friendly Society*.[31] Both parties prefaced the name of the policy with their own name, *Lumley* or *IOOF*. and *IOOF* spelt theirs as two words. The *Lumley Life* case was followed in *Equity Access v Westpac Banking Corp*,[32] where, in addition, the plaintiffs' use of the name in issue had been very slight. Both parties used *Equity Access* for a type of mortgage promoted to homeowners with substantial equity of redemption in their homes. In *Guide Dog Owners & Friends Association v Guide Dogs Association of NSW and ACT*[33] *Seeing Eye* and *Seeing Eye Dogs* were held

[21] [1964] R.P.C. 251 (Pennycuick J.).
[22] [1972] R.P.C. 27 (Ungoed-Thomas J.).
[23] [1976] F.S.R. 169 (Whitford J.).
[24] [1979] R.P.C. 441, CA.
[25] [1981] R.P.C. 69, CA.
[26] [1983] R.P.C. 407, CA.
[27] [1991] F.S.R. 367, CA.
[28] [2002] R.P.C. 27 (Christopher Floyd Q.C., Deputy Judge).
[29] (1989) 89 A.L.R. 48 (Federal Court of Australia, on appeal).
[30] (1990) 16 I.P.R. 376 (French J., Federal Court of Australia).
[31] (1989) 16 I.P.R. 316 (Lockhart J., Federal Court of Australia).
[32] (1989) 16 I.P.R. 431 (Hill, J., Federal Court of Australia).
[33] [1999] FCA 316, 43 I.P.R. 531 (Federal Court of Australia).

to be generic terms for guide dogs for blind people, and the plaintiff charity had no right to prevent two other charities using them to advertise their services.

8–72   In Canada, the words *Permanent Discount* were equally descriptive of the trading policies of rival chain stores and an interlocutory injunction was refused: *Westfair Foods v Jim Pattison Industries.*[34] In the Singapore case of *S$1.99 Private Ltd v Lifestyle 1.99 Private Ltd*[35] both parties operated shops where the majority of goods were priced at S$1.99. Variants on "1.99" were the only common element between the trading styles of the claimant and defendant, it was equally descriptive of both, and the defendants' name and logo were adequately distinct. The action therefore failed.

Many cases involving newspapers or magazines have seen relief refused because the title of the claimant's publication was too descriptive.

Minor differences sufficient to distinguish

8–73 A descriptive term may be sufficiently distinctive to be protected against precise copying, but may still not enjoy protection of such wide scope as a term which is wholly arbitrary. Other traders are free to use similar descriptive expressions as their own trade names or marks, and smaller differences will suffice to distinguish them than in the case of fancy words. This may be expressed in terms of "the idea of the mark". When an arbitrary mark is in use by the claimant, deception can occur by the defendant adopting a mark which incorporates the same predominant idea even if the expression differs. If, however, the only idea which can be identified is wholly descriptive then such distinctiveness as exists can only lie in the precise form of words used, or something even more specific, such as the manner in which they are written.[36] As may be seen from the *Office Cleaning*[37] case, there is an element of public policy here, in that a degree of confusion is held to be an acceptable price for keeping descriptive terms open to fair use by all.

> "Foremost I put the fact that the Appellants chose to adopt as part of their title the words 'Office Cleaning' which are English words in common use, apt and more apt than any other words to describe the service they render. This is a trade name, not a trade mark, case, but I would remind your Lordships of the close analogy between the two classes of case found by Farwell J. in *Aerators v Tollit*[38] and by Parker J. in the *Vacuum Cleaner* case.[39] So it is that, just as in the case of a trade mark the use of descriptive words is jealously safeguarded, so in the case of trade names the Courts

---

[34] (1900) 30 C.P.R. (3d) 174 (British Columbia Court of Appeal).

[35] [2001] F.S.R. 10, CA of Singapore.

[36] *Weingarten Bros v Bayer & Co* [1904–7] All E.R. 877; (1903) 22 R.P.C. 341, HL.

[37] *Office Cleaning Services Ltd v Westminster Office Cleaning Association* [1946] 1 All E.R. 320; 63 R.P.C. 39, HL. See also *Motor Manufacturers' and Traders' Society v Motor Manufacturers' & Traders' Insurance Co* [1925] Ch. 675; [1925] All E.R. 616; 42 R.P.C. 307, CA.

[38] [1902] 2 Ch. 319; 19 R.P.C. 418 (Farwell J.).

[39] *British Vacuum Cleaner Co Ltd v New Vacuum Cleaner Co Ltd* [1907] 2 Ch. 312; 24 R.P.C. 641 (Parker J.).

will not readily assume that the use by a trader as part of his trade name of descriptive words already used by another trader as part of his trade name is likely to cause confusion and will easily accept small differences as adequate to avoid it. It is otherwise when a fancy word has been chosen as part of the name...

It comes in the end, I think, to no more than this, that where a trader adopts words in common use for his trade name, some risk of confusion is inevitable. But that risk must be run unless the first user is allowed unfairly to monopolise the words. The Court will accept comparatively small differences as sufficient to avert confusion. A greater degree of discrimination may fairly be expected from the public where a trade name consists wholly or in part of words descriptive of the articles to be sold or the services to be rendered."[40]

The same principles were stated by Stephen J. in the High Court of **8-74** Australia (Full Court), in a passage which was quoted and approved by Lord Scarman in *Cadbury Schweppes v Pub Squash Co.*[41]

"There is a price to be paid for the advantages flowing from the possession of an eloquently descriptive trade name. Because it is descriptive it is equally applicable to any business of a like kind, its very descriptiveness ensures that it is not distinctive of any particular business and hence its application to other like businesses will not ordinarily mislead the public. In cases of passing-off, where it is the wrongful appropriation of the reputation of another or that of his goods that is in question, a plaintiff which uses descriptive words in its trade name will find comparatively small differences in a competitor's trade name will render the latter immune from action: *Office Cleaning Services v Westminster Office Cleaning Assn* per Lord Simonds. As his Lordship said, the possibility of blunders by members of the public will always be present when names consist of descriptive words. 'So long as descriptive words are used by two traders as part of their respective trade names, it is possible that some members of the public will be confused whatever the differentiating words may be.' The risk of confusion must be accepted, to do otherwise is to give to one who appropriates to himself descriptive words an unfair monopoly in those words and might even deter others from pursuing the occupation which the words describe."[42]

The *Office Cleaning* case notwithstanding, the courts have not been **8-75** entirely consistent in applying the principle that small differences are suffi-

---

[40] *per* Lord Simonds in *Office Cleaning Services Ltd v Westminster Office Cleaning Association* [1946] 1 All E.R. 320; 63 R.P.C. 39, HL.

[41] [1981] R.P.C. 429; [1981] 1 All E.R. 213, PC.

[42] *Hornsby Building Information Centre Pty Ltd v Sydney Building Information Centre Pty Ltd* (1978) 140 C.L.R. 216; 52 A.L.J.R. 392; 18 A.L.R. 639.

cient to distinguish businesses using descriptive names or marks.[43] The *Music Corporation of America* was granted an injunction against *Music Corporation (Great Britain)*, both acting as agents for musicians and entertainers.[44] The *Associated Booking Corporation* restrained the *Associated Booking Agency*, both parties acting as theatrical booking agencies for artistes.[45] In *Effluent Disposal v Midlands Effluent Disposal* the addition of *Midlands* to *Effluent Disposal* was "no distinction at all" when that was the area both parties traded in.[46] *Pick of the Pops* was too similar to *Top of the Pops* in *Pickwick International v Multiple Sound Distributors*.[47] *Chill Foods* and *Cool Foods* were too close in *Chill Foods (Scotland) v Cool Foods*, although all they seem to have in common is the idea of refrigerating food.[48] Small differences may suffice, but minimal ones will not. It would have been surprising if the difference between *Computervision* and *Computer Vision* had been conclusive: *Computervision Corp v Computer Vision*.[49] In New Zealand, an operator of a tourist jet boat service on the Shotover River under the name *Shotover Jet* was awarded an interlocutory injunction[50] against a rival using *Lower Shotover Jet* with the word "Lower" relatively inconspicuous:[51] *Shotover Gorge Jet Boats v Marine Enterprises*.[52]

8–76 Cases in which injunctions have been refused are generally the more obviously consistent with the general principle.[53] In South Africa, *Truck and Car* and *Kar-n-Truk* were different enough: *Truck and Car Co v Kar-N-Truk Auctions*.[54] The addition of the letter "s" at the end of "egg" in *Egg and Bacon* was more than sufficient to distinguish the defendants' restaurant from *Bacon and Egg* in *Lyons v G & K Restaurants*.[55] A retail mail order

---

[43] Several of the decisions which follow denied that the name in issue was descriptive at all. Others distinguish *Office Cleaning Services Ltd v Westminster Office Cleaning Association* [1946] 1 All E.R. 320; 63 R.P.C. 39, HL on the basis that the name in issue, unlike *Office Cleaning* had acquired secondary meaning, but that is to ignore the special sense in which the term was used by Lord Simonds.

[44] *Music Corporation of America v Music Corporation (Great Britain) Ltd* (1947) 64 R.P.C. 48 (Wynn Parry J.).

[45] *Associated Booking Corp v Associated Booking Agency* [1964] R.P.C. 372 (Pennycuick J.).

[46] [1970] R.P.C. 238; [1969] F.S.R. 468 (Stamp J.)

[47] [1972] R.P.C. 786 (CA opposed *ex parte*; Megarry J. *inter partes*).

[48] [1977] R.P.C. 522 (Lord Maxwell, Court of Session). Compare *Technical Productions Ltd v Contemporary Exhibitions Ltd* [1961] R.P.C. 242, below.

[49] [1975] R.P.C. 171; [1974] F.S.R. 206 (Plowman J.).

[50] Following *American Cyanamid Co v Ethicon Ltd* [1975] A.C. 396; [1975] 1 All E.R. 504; [1975] R.P.C. 513; [1975] F.S.R. 101, HL.

[51] The defendants had used that name on a different stretch of the river since 1977.

[52] [1984] 2 N.Z.L.R. 154 (Hardie Boys J.). Injunctions were also granted in the earlier cases of *National Timber Co Ltd v National Hardware, Timber and Machinery Co Ltd* [1923] N.Z.L.R. 1258, CA and *New Zealand Insurance Co Ltd v New Zealand Insurance Brokers Ltd* [1976] 2 N.Z.L.R. 40.

[53] As well as *Office Cleaning* above, and those that follow, see *British Vacuum Cleaner Co Ltd v New Vacuum Cleaner Co Ltd* [1907] 2 Ch. 312; 24 R.P.C. 641 and *Motor Manufacturers' & Traders' Society v Motor Manufacturers' & Traders' Insurance Co* [1925] Ch. 657; [1925] All E.R. 616; 42 R.P.C. 307, CA.

[54] 1954 (4) SA 552 (Appellate Division).

[55] (1955) 72 R.P.C. 259. The change was offered by the defendants. Roxburgh J. would not have required it.

business trading as *The Tape Recorder Centre* was refused an interlocutory injunction against a wholesale business using and advertising that name for a stand at a show in *Syphia Sound Sales v Tape Recorders (Electronics)*.[56] *Credit Management Co Ltd v Credit Management*[57] in which the only difference in the names was the words "Co Ltd" might have gone too far but for the fact that the customers of both parties were traders. In *Technical Productions v Contemporary Exhibitions*[58] rival exhibitions were both allowed to use *Refrigeration* in their titles. A child minding business called the *Under Six Club* was refused interlocutory relief against a similar business called the *Over Six Club* in *Deane v Schofield*.[59] *Salaried Persons Postal Loans v Postal & Salaried Loans of Glasgow*[60] is another example of names being sufficiently different. In *Coral Index v Regent Index*[61] the only similarity was the word *Index*, which was accounted for by the fact that both parties accepted bets on The *Financial Times Index*. In *Industrial Furnaces v Reaves*[62] the addition of *Reaves* to *Industrial Furnaces* was sufficient. *International* was descriptive of a class of hotels so the defendants' name *London International Hotel* was sufficiently different to *Hotel International* in *Park Court Hotel v Trans-World Hotels*.[63] *Furniture City* was sufficiently different to *Furnitureland* for there to be no serious issue to be tried in *Furnitureland v Harris*.[64] Such confusion as might arise was the direct result of the plaintiffs' choice of a very descriptive name.

In *Australian Marketing Development v Australian Interstate Marketing*[65] not only the names but the ideas behind them differed. In South Africa, *Hans's* before *Bar-B-Que Steakhouse* was sufficient distinction to discharge an interim interdict when the competing restaurants were in different suburbs four kilometres apart: *Burnkloof Caterers v Horseshoe Caterers*.[66] *Hornsby Building Information Centre v Sydney Building Information Centre*[67] is mentioned above. In Ontario, *Kopy Kwik* was so descriptive that *Kwik-copy* was sufficient distinction: *Anacona Printing v Kwik-Kopy Corp*[68] In Singapore, differences in name and logo were sufficient to distinguish in *S$1.99 Private Ltd v Lifestyle 1.99 Private Ltd*.[69] Both parties operated

[56] [1961] R.P.C. 27 (Buckley J.).
[57] [1961] R.P.C. 157 (Cross J.).
[58] [1961] R.P.C. 242 (Wilberforce J.). Compare *Associated Newspapers Ltd v Lew Barclay Exhibitions Ltd* (1955) 72 R.P.C. 278 (*Ideal Home*).
[59] [1962] R.P.C. (Plowman J.).
[60] [1966] R.P.C. 24 (Lord Cameron, Court of Session).
[61] [1970] R.P.C. 147; [1970] F.S.R. 13 (Stamp J.). The plaintiffs' literature had been copied, but this was not relied on for passing-off.
[62] [1970] R.P.C. 605 (Graham J.).
[63] [1972] R.P.C. 27 (Ungoed-Thomas J.). Contrast *Berkeley Hotel Co Ltd v Berkeley International (Mayfair) Ltd* [1972] R.P.C. 237 where the descriptive nature of the word *International* and the high acquired distinctiveness of *Berkeley* meant that it was inadequate to distinguish.
[64] [1989] 1 F.S.R. 536 (Browne-Wilkinson V.C.).
[65] [1972] V.R. 219.
[66] 1976 (2) SA 930 (Appellate Division): even though the defendants' neon sign omitted *Hans's* and was very similar to that of the plaintiffs.
[67] (1978) 140 C.L.R. 216; 52 A.L.J.R. 392; 18 A.L.R. 639.
[68] (1983) 73 C.P.R. (2d) 122 (White J.).
[69] [2001] F.S.R. 10, CA of Singapore.

shops where the majority of goods were priced at S$1.99, those of the claimant being branded *ONE.99 Shop* and those of the defendant *LIFE-STYLE 1.99* with the logos also differing in shape and colour.

Many further examples of small differences serving to distinguish the defendant's goods are to be found in the field of periodical titles, which are often highly descriptive.

8–77   The principle is only applicable if the defendant is using words which are descriptive of the business he carries on. Words which are descriptive in the claimant's field of business may yet be quite inappropriate to describe the business of the defendant. In one South African case, *Capital Estate & General Agencies v Holiday Inns*,[70] the *Holiday Inn* chain of hotels prevented the use of that name for a shopping centre: a context in which Lord Simonds' question "Why else did he adopt it?"[71] is just as devastating as if *Holiday Inn* had no descriptive character at all. In England, *Midland Counties Dairy v Midland Dairies*[72] may be regarded as an application of this principle if one accepts that "dairy" is an inappropriate term for an ice-cream factory.

Whether used as trademark by defendant or customer

8–78 It is not passing-off for the defendant to use a descriptive or generic term accurately and unambiguously in its descriptive significance. Even if the term has acquired a degree of secondary meaning, there is no mis-representation as to source unless the defendant will be understood as using it in a trade mark sense.[73] Nor is there passing-off if the defendant supplies goods not of the claimant's manufacture in response to an order in which the customer uses an ambiguous term in a descriptive or generic sense rather than as indicating a desire for the claimant's goods.[74]

In *Mothercare v Penguin Books*[75] the plaintiffs owned a chain of shops catering for mothers and young children. They complained of an academic book on child care published under the title *Mother Care/Other Care*. The Court of Appeal held that the title, taken as a whole, did not begin to suggest that the book had been issued or sponsored by, or was in any way associated with, *Mothercare*, the plaintiffs. There was no serious issue to be tried.

"The name *Mothercare* is made up of two common words in the English language, 'mother' and 'care'. The name is not used in a strictly

---

[70] 1977 (2) SA 916 (Appellate Division).
[71] From *Office Cleaning Services Ltd v Westminster Office Cleaning Association* [1946] 1 All E.R. 320; 63 R.P.C. 39, HL.
[72] (1948) 65 R.P.C. 429 (Harman J.).
[73] *Unidoor Ltd v Marks & Spencer plc* [1988] R.P.C. 275.
[74] *Cellular Clothing Co v G White & Co Ltd* (1952) 70 R.P.C. 9 (Harman J.), which perhaps goes too far in absolving the trader of the need to enquire what it is the customer wants. The same judge found for the plaintiffs in *Treasure Cot Co Ltd v Hamley Bros Ltd* (1950) 67 R.P.C. 89 despite the fact that the mark was descriptive to some customers. Compare *Havana Cigar & Tobacco Factories Ltd v Oddenino* [1924] 1 Ch. 179; 41 R.P.C. 47, CA.
[75] [1988] R.P.C. 113, CA.

descriptive sense as describing the business of the company, but it has a descriptive flavour in that it creates at once in the mind of the reader or hearer an impression of the sort of things that the business of Mothercare is about. Descriptive or not, however, its name is now a household name and it has established ample goodwill in the name to support a passing-off action if, for instance, some third party were to seek to trade on the name of Mothercare within the field of Mothercare's established activities...

[S]o far as the title is concerned, it is fair to say that the title '*Mother Care/Other Care*' chosen by the American publishers is such an obviously good descriptive title of what the book is about that it is not at all easy to think of an equally good alternative."[76]

Though the defendant may claim to be using a term similar to the claimant's mark in a descriptive sense, there will be passing-off if this is no more than a pretence. Ambiguous or unduly prominent use is an indication that deception was intended. **8–79**

"The [plaintiffs] concede they cannot, indeed, any longer dispute that everyone who makes belting of camel hair is entitled to describe his belting as '*Camel-hair belting*', provided he does so fairly. But they contend, and I think with reason, that neither *Banham* nor anybody else is entitled to steal Reddaway's trade under colour of imparting accurate and possibly interesting information." [77]

Iron-Ox was distinctive of the plaintiffs' medicine in *Iron Ox Remedy Co v Co-op Wholesale Soc*[78] and the defendants were restrained from selling *Iron Oxide* tablets. The defendants' motives had clearly been to commission a commercial substitute for goods the plaintiffs were no longer willing to supply to them. Parker J. held that they were not using the term in a descriptive sense. The plaintiffs' tablets were not made from iron oxide, which had no medical value and for which there was no demand as such.

In *In Things v Leather Garments*[79] the plaintiffs used *Skinners* for denim jeans and an injunction was granted against *Skins* for similar goods sold by their subcontractors in their own right. The defendants claimed that *Skins* simply referred to the dress favoured by the "Skinhead" cult, but the Skinheads had (supposedly) become extinct by 1972. Walton J. concluded that the motives and evidence of the defendants were not to be trusted.

Where the claimant's distinctive name or mark was also a personal name, it was formerly quite common for defendants to hire an individual of that name in, literally, a nominal capacity. This has continued to occur occasionally even in recent times. Far from providing a defence, this is one of the recognised "badges of fraud" and an indication that the defendant intended to have his goods or business passed off. The same may apply when the **8–80**

---

defendant sets up in business at the place from which the name of the claimant's business may have been derived, as in *Wotherspoon v Currie*.[80] The two occurred together in *Southorn v Reynolds*.[81]

In an appropriate case, an injunction may be qualified to make it clear that the defendant may use a term descriptively.[82] In *Bewlay v Hughes*[83] the word *Dinigul* was distinctive of the plaintiffs' cigars despite being the name of an area where tobacco was produced. An injunction was granted, but the defendants were to be allowed to say where their tobacco came from. In *Banbury Buildings v Sectional Concrete Buildings*[84] the defendants offered an undertaking not to use *Banbury* for advertising sectional concrete garages except *bona fide* as part of their address, which was in that town. The plaintiffs moved for an interlocutory injunction which would have prevented even this. Pennycuick J. held that the undertaking was sufficient.

Distinctive term becoming descriptive

8–81 Just as a descriptive term may acquire secondary meaning and become distinctive, so a term which was once distinctive of the claimant's goods or business may lose that status and become purely descriptive or generic. There are not many examples of this having happened, and some of the cases often given as illustrations are ambiguous because at the time the term was supposed to have been distinctive there was no competition to distinguish. Cases such as *Linoleum Manufacturing Co v Nairn*[85] and *British Vacuum Cleaner Co v New Vacuum Cleaner Co*[86] are better understood as ones in which the word was descriptive (or generic) from the very beginning, although while the plaintiff had a legal or *de facto* monopoly the difference hardly mattered. Others are not properly examples of a formerly distinctive name acquiring any recognisable descriptive meaning, as opposed to merely becoming *publici juris* and devoid of meaning of any sort. As the law was formerly understood, all that mattered was that the term was no longer distinctive, because misuse of a descriptive or generic term was no more actionable than use of a meaningless one. In the modern state of the law, misuse of a descriptive or generic term may be actionable.

Reading Sauce had probably once been distinctive of the plaintiff in *Cocks v Chandler*,[87] but had come through acquiescence to denote no more than a recipe. However, the defendant was not entitled to described his sauce as *The Original Reading Sauce*. *Eureka* was used by the trade to denote a design of shirt in *Ford v Foster*[88] though to the general public it was distinctive of the plaintiff. An injunction was granted. In *Wolff v Nopitsch*[89]

---

[80] (1872) L.R. 5 H.L. 508, HL.
[81] (1865) 12 L.T. 75 (Page-Wood V.C.).
[82] The principle was approved in *Bach & Jackson Ltd v Cowan* [1969] R.P.C. 156.
[83] (1898) 15 R.P.C. 290 (North J.).
[84] [1970] R.P.C. 463 (Pennycuick J.).
[85] (1878) 7 Ch. D. 834 (Fry J.).
[86] [1907] 2 Ch. 312; 24 R.P.C. 641 (Parker J.).
[87] (1871) L.R. 11 Eq. 466 (Romilly M.R.).
[88] (1872) L.R. 7 Ch. 611, CA.
[89] (1901) 18 R.P.C. 27, CA.

Spanish Graphite had apparently once been distinctive of the plaintiff's pencils. Its use by other traders (sometimes on pencils actually supplied by the plaintiffs, but not identifiable as such) cost it its distinctiveness,[90] but that is not to say it acquired any descriptive meaning instead. It simply became a term in common use which conveyed little or no information as to quality, nature or source. *Gledhill Coils* had supposedly once been distinctive of the plaintiffs' rolls of cash-register paper but had come to mean rolls of anyone's manufacture for that machine in *Gledhill v British Perforated Toilet Paper Co.*[91] An equally valid explanation is that the defendants were only making fair use of *Gledhill* to indicate which machine their coils were for. The Court of Appeal found it unnecessary to say whether use of the term could ever have been restrained.

In *Woodward v Boulton Macro*[92] the term *Gripe Water* had certainly been descriptive when the plaintiff started business in the 1850s, had acquired some degree of distinctiveness since that time, but had then been used by too many unconnected traders still to be distinctive at the date of the action. Eve J. refused an injunction against passing-off. An example of a mark in the transition between distinctive and descriptive status is to be found in *Havana Cigar and Tobacco Factories v Oddenino.*[93] *Corona* for cigars was distinctive of the plaintiffs to some smokers but only denoted a cigar of a certain size to others. An injunction in special form was granted.

E. Problem Verbal Marks by Category

Place names

Examples of place names becoming distinctive of one trader are numerous. **8–82** The place may be large or small, famous or obscure, in this country or abroad. The claimant's goods may actually originate from the place in question, may have some other affinity with it, or the place name may be quite arbitrary in relation to them. The question is purely the factual one of whether the name has come to denote the goods or business of the claimant. This is most easily shown if the name is arbitrary and unfamiliar,[94] but there is no doctrine that some place names are incapable of being distinctive.

If the place name in question has become distinctive of the claimant then it cannot be used in a trade mark sense by others. The claimant may not be entitled to restrain the use of the term in its original descriptive sense, to the extent that it still retains it, but it is passing-off to use the term ambiguously or with undue prominence, and both of these may indicate a lack of good faith. It is no defence that the defendant may operate from the place in

---

[90] Compare *Wood v Lambert* (1886) 32 Ch.D. 247; 3 R.P.C. 81.
[91] (1911) 28 R.P.C. 714, CA.
[92] (1915) 32 R.P.C. 173 (Eve J.).
[93] [1924] 1 Ch. 179; 41 R.P.C. 47, CA.
[94] So *Bristol* was not distinctive of the American plaintiffs in *Bristol-Myers Co Ltd v Bristol Pharmaceutical Co Ltd* [1968] R.P.C. 259, they being relatively unknown in England at the time.

question, or that the claimant may not.[95] In *Provident Financial v Halifax Building Society*[96] both parties were based in the Yorkshire town of Halifax and the defendant was much the larger and better known; but the plaintiffs had prior rights to *Halifax* for insurance services, and an interim injunction was granted.

8–83   The authorities may be said to begin with *McAndrew v Basset*[97] in 1864, in which Lord Westbury granted an injunction against the defendant's use of *Anatolia* for liquorice. *Anatolia* was the name of a large province of Turkey where liquorice came from, but in England the name was virtually unknown. Three cases decided in 1872 consolidated this. In *Wotherspoon v Currie*[98] the plaintiff had manufactured starch at a tiny hamlet called *Glenfield* and it had become famous under that name. The defendant set up in *Glenfield* and put the name conspicuously on his own packets of starch. The House of Lords found for the plaintiff. In *Radde v Norman*[99] the plaintiffs proved that the name *Leopoldshall* was distinctive of them, notwithstanding that the goods were a natural product of a place of that name. In *Hirst v Denham*[1] the plaintiff's marks included *Liverpool* and *Turin*.[2] Any final doubts must have been laid to rest in *Montgomery v Thompson*.[3] The plaintiff was the only brewer in the small town of *Stone*. His beers were known as *Stone Ales*. A former customer, a Liverpool publican, built a brewery in *Stone* and proposed to call the beer brewed there *Stone Ales*. The House of Lords found for the plaintiff.

Other examples of familiar geographical terms which have been held to be distinctive include *London* in respect of candles exported from Scotland to Morocco in *Price's Patent Candle Co v Ogston & Tennant*[4] and as the composite phrases *Charles of London* for a hairdresser with shops in London and the South East in *Brestain v Try*[5] and *London Olympia* for a circus in *Mills v Chapman*.[6] *Chelsea Man* was distinctive for menswear in *Chelsea Man Menswear v Chelsea Girl*.[7] *Manchester* as part of the name of a brewery was restrained in *North Cheshire & Manchester Brewery Co v Manchester Brewery Co*[8]; likewise *Yorkshire* for bottled sauce in *Powell v Birmingham*

---

[95] The facts of *Wotherspoon v Currie* (1872) L.R. 5 H.L. 508, HL, and *Siegert v Findlater* (1878) 7 Ch.D. 801.
[96] [1994] F.S.R. 81 (Aldous J.).
[97] (1864) 46 E.R. 965 (Lord Westbury L.C.).
[98] (1872) L.R. 5 H.L. 508, HL.
[99] (1872) L.R. 14 Eq. 348 (Wickens V.C.).
[1] (1872) L.R. 14 Eq. 542 (Bacon V.C.).
[2] In relation to the goods in question they were quite arbitrary.
[3] [1891] A.C. 217; 8 R.P.C. 361, HL.
[4] (1909) 26 R.P.C. 797 (Lord Johnston, Court of Session).
[5] [1958] R.P.C. 161, CA.
[6] (1930) 47 R.P.C. 115 (Farwell J.). An injunction against *London simpliciter* was refused on the evidence. The plaintiff's circus was in fact held at Olympia, London. See also *Associated Newspapers Ltd v Lew Barclay Exhibitions Ltd* (1955) 72 R.P.C. 278.
[7] [1987] R.P.C. 189, CA.
[8] [1899] A.C. 83, HL.

Vinegar Brewery Co;[9] *Reading* for biscuits in *Huntley & Palmer v Reading Biscuit Co*[10]; *Worcester* for china in *Worcester Royal Porcelain Co v Locke*[11] and *Waterford* for glassware in *Waterford Wedgewood v David Nagli.*[12] *Oxford* was distinctive for marmalade *in CPC v Keenan*[13] and *Cambridge* for a system of dieting in a South African case: *Cambridge Plan AG v Moore.*[14]

The name may be that of (or derived from) the name of a country, as with **8–84** *British* in *British Bond* for paper in *Spicer Bros v Spalding & Hodge*[15]; *Local Ireland* for an internet search service in *Local Ireland v Local Ireland-Online*[16] or *Aussie* in *Australian Home Loans v Phillips*[17]. Even *Globe* (for furniture) in *Grant v Levitt*[18] and *Universe* for an assurance company in *Hendriks v Montague*[19] have been protected; likewise *Southern* for music publishing in *Southern Music Publishing Co v Southern Songs*[20] and *Western* for a mining company in *WMC v Westgold Resources.*[21]

However, the fact that the claimant may have been the only trader to have used in particular geographical term does not mean that it is necessarily distinctive of him, especially if he enjoyed a legal or *de facto* monopoly in the goods in question. If it retains its geographical meaning to the relevant public then any other trader remains free to use it accurately. In particular, if the goods are the natural produce of the place in question then the likelihood is that the word remains primarily descriptive.[22] It is even possible for a name which was once distinctive to become a geographical term open to general use.[23] An argument that the name of the plaintiffs' *Millenia* complex

---

[9] [1897] A.C. 710; 14 R.P.C. 721, HL. And *Halifax* for motor insurance in *Provident Financial v Halifax Building Society* [1994] F.S.R. 81.

[10] (1893) 10 R.P.C. 277 (Chitty J.). *Reading Sauce* had become generic: *Cocks v Chandler* (1871) L.R. 11 Eq. 446.

[11] (1902) 19 R.P.C. 479 (Byrne J.).

[12] [1998] F.S.R. 92 (Scott V.-C.). Not all the plaintiffs' *Waterford* crystal was made in Waterford, nor even in Ireland.

[13] [1986] F.S.R. 527 (Peter Gibson J.). The defendant used *Oxbridge*.

[14] 1987 (4) SA 821 (Page J., Durban).

[15] (1914) 32 R.P.C. 52 (Joyce J.). The words appeared in the watermark of the paper. The plaintiffs' monogram was also copied.

[16] [2001] E.T.M.R. 42 (Herbert J., High Court, Dublin).

[17] (1998) 40 I.P.R. 392 (Lehane J., Federal Court of Australia). (*Aussie Home Loans* and *Aussie Home Builders*).

[18] (1901) 18 R.P.C. 361 (Porter M.R., Ireland).

[19] (1881) 17 Ch.D. 638, CA: *Universal Life Assurance Society* and *Universe Life Assurance Association.*

[20] [1966] R.P.C. 137 (Buckley J.).

[21] (1997) 39 I.P.R. 319 (North J, Federal Court of Australia). The plaintiffs had quite recently changed their name from *Western Mining* (by which they were still known). The second defendant was Western Mining NL.

[22] *Radde v Norman* (1872) L.R. 14 Eq. 348 (*Leopoldshall*) is a rare exception.

[23] *Tigon Mining & Finance Corp Ltd v South Tigon Mining Co Ltd* (1931) 48 R.P.C. 526. Cases such as *Rickerby v Reay* (1903) 20 R.P.C. 380 (*Crown Works*) in which the name of a business has become the address of specific premises are an illustration of this on a smaller scale.

of offices, shops and hotels (including the *Ritz-Carlton, Millenia Singapore*) was merely geographical failed in *Pontiac Marina v CDL Hotels*.[24]

Cases in which geographical names have become distinctive should not be confused with those in which the name has retained its geographical connotation but has been misapplied by the defendant. In the former case the misrepresentation is that the defendant's goods are those of the claimant, and it is coincidental that the claimant's mark happens also to be a geographical term. In the latter, the misrepresentation is that the defendant's goods are associated with a certain place when they are not. The distinction has not always been observed, and there are some cases which may not fit precisely into either category,[25] but these should be seen in their historical context.

Personal names

8–85 Personal names have often acquired distinctiveness and been protected by the action for passing-off. This was one of the most common forms the action took in the nineteenth century, when most businesses traded under the name of the proprietor or founder. So far as the existence of a cause of action is concerned, there is no distinction between personal names used as business names and those used as trade marks on goods. The name may be the real name of the claimant or a predecessor in business, or an assumed name, or a quite arbitrary choice. Most of the cases concern surnames (with or without forenames or initials), but forenames alone can also be distinctive. The name may be foreign or English, as famous as *Gucci*,[26] as unusual as *Jaeger*[27] or *Teofani*,[28] or as common as *Reed*,[29] *Wright*,[30] *Rodgers*[31] or *Roberts*.[32] It may be harder to prove distinctiveness for a common name, but there is no rule of law that certain names are incapable ever of being distinctive. The question is purely one of fact.

Examples of surnames being distinctive may be found in *Tussaud (Madame) & Sons v Tussaud*,[33] *Pullman v Pullman*,[34] *Joseph Rodgers v*

---

[24] [1998] F.S.R. 839 (CA, Singapore) affirming [1997] F.S.R. 725 (Chao Hick Tin J.). Compare *MID Sydney Pty Ltd v Australian Tourism Co Ltd* (1998) 40 I.P.R. 20 (Hill J., Federal Court of Australia) in which *Chifley Tower, Chifley Plaza* and *Chifley Square* (named after a former Prime Minister, Ben Chifley) were primarily the address of a location, rather than the brand name of the plaintiff property developer which owned it. There was no liability for passing off when the defendants proposed to use *Chifley* in place of *Country Comfort* for their chain of hotels.

[25] *Braham v Beachim* (1878) 7 Ch.D. 848; and perhaps *Smith (Arthur) (S & B Foundry Sands) Ltd v George Fieldhouse Ltd* [1961] R.P.C. 110.

[26] *Guccio Gucci SpA v Paolo Gucci* [1991] F.S.R. 89 (Browne-Wilkinson V.-C.).

[27] *Jaeger v Jaeger & Co Ltd* (1927) 44 R.P.C., CA.

[28] *Teofani & Co Ltd v Teofani* [1913] 2 Ch. 545; 30 R.P.C. 446, CA.

[29] *Reed Executive plc v Reed Business Information Ltd* [2002] EWHC 1015; [2003] R.P.C. 12 (Pumfrey J.).

[30] *Wright, Layman & Umney Ltd v Wright* (1949) 66 R.P.C. 149, CA.

[31] *Joseph Rodgers & Sons Ltd v W N Rodgers & Co* (1924) 41 R.P.C. 277 (Romer J.).

[32] *Roberts Numbering Machine Co v Davis* (1935) 53 R.P.C. 79 (Luxmoore J.).

[33] (1890) 44 Ch.D. 678 (Stirling J.).

[34] (1919) 36 R.P.C. 240 (P. O. Lawrence J.).

Rodgers,[35] *Poiret v Jules Poiret,*[36] *Roberts Numbering Machine Co v Davis,*[37] *Goddard v Watford,*[38] *Wright, Layman & Umney v Wright,*[39] *Parker-Knoll v Knoll International,*[40] *Ballantine (George) & Son v Ballantyne,*[41] *Parker & Sons (Reading) v Parker,*[42] *Alfred Dunhill v Sunoptic,*[43] *Guccio Gucci v Paulo Gucci,*[44] *Asprey & Garrard v WRA (Guns) Ltd and Asprey*[45] and *Reed Executive v Reed Business Information.*[46] There are many others. In *Thistle Communications v Thistle Telecom*[47] the pursuer was a sole trader whose surname was *Thistle.* That this was also a Scottish emblem was coincidental, and did not prevent the grant of an interim interdict.

Forenames on their own have been protected in *Annabel's v Schock*[48] where *Annabel* was equally arbitrary for the plaintiffs' night club and the defendant's escort agency, and *Globelegance v Sarkissian*[49] where *Valentino* was the real Christian name of the individual who designed for the plaintiffs. *Maxim's* restaurant in Paris was given an injunction in default of appearance in *Maxim's v Dye.*[50] *Biba* was restrained in *Biba Group v Biba Boutique.*[51] In *Bresian v Try*[52] *Charles of London* was distinctive of the plaintiff hairdresser whose real name was *Karl Brestian.* *Nicola* was probably distinctive in Australia in *Ramsay v Nicol*[53] but the defendant had a concurrent right to use it. In Canada, *Mario* for an Italian restaurant was restrained on an interlocutory appeal in *Mario's Spaghetti House & Pizzeria v Italian Village.*[54] The common Spanish Christian name *Mercedes* was undoubtedly distinctive of the claimants' range of motor vehicles in *Daimler-Chrysler v* **8–86**

---

[35] (1924) 41 R.P.C. 277 (Romer J.).

[36] (1920) 37 R.P.C. 177 (P. O. Lawrence J.).

[37] (1935) 53 R.P.C. 79 (Luxmoore J.).

[38] (1924) 41 R.P.C. 218 (Astbury J.), despite another Goddard (the supplier to the defendants) having some sort of concurrent right to use the name.

[39] (1949) 66 R.P.C. 149, CA.

[40] [1962] R.P.C. 265, HL.

[41] [1959] R.P.C. 273, CA.

[42] [1965] R.P.C. 323 (Plowman J.).

[43] [1979] F.S.R. 337, CA.

[44] [1991] F.S.R. 89 (Browne-Wilkinson V.C.).

[45] [2002] F.S.R. 30 (Jacob J.) affirmed [2001] EWCA Civ 1499; [2002] E.T.M.R. 47; [2002] F.S.R. 31, CA.

[46] [2002] EWHC 1015; [2003] R.P.C. 12 (Pumfrey J.).

[47] 2000 SLT 262 (Lord Hamilton, OH)

[48] [1972] R.P.C. 838, CA.

[49] [1974] R.P.C. 603 (Templeman J.).

[50] [1977] 1 W.L.R. 1155; [1978] 2 All E.R. 55; [1977] F.S.R. 364 (Graham J.).

[51] [1980] R.P.C. 413 (Whitford J.). The personal defendant claimed it was her nickname. Compare *Jay's Ltd v Jacobi* [1933] Ch. 411; [1933] All E R. 690; 50 R.P.C. 132 (as explained in *Wright, Layman & Umney Ltd v Wright* (1949) 66 R.P.C. 149, CA) which is better regarded as turning on insufficient reputation.

[52] [1958] R.P.C. 161, CA.

[53] [1939] V.L.R. 330 (O'Bryan A.-J.).

[54] (1976) 29 C.P.R. (2d) 257 (Nova Scotia, Appeal Division). But an action for passing off based on the name *Giovanni* for restaurants failed on the facts in *Hammond (Marc A) Pty Ltd v Papa Carmine Pty Ltd* (1976) 28 F.L.R. 160; 15 A.L.R. 179; [1976] 2 N.S.W.L.R. 124; [1978] R.P.C. 697.

Alavi,[55] but not to the extent that *Merc* for fashion clothing would be restrained.

8–87   Some early cases treated the name of the inventor, patentee or introducer of a new product as the generic name for that product. Examples are *James's Blister*[56] and *Cheavin's Patent*.[57] This may have corresponded to nineteenth century trade usage but it is obsolete today. There is no rule of law that the name of an inventor or patentee cannot be distinctive. Thus *Thorley's Food for Cattle* could not be used by the defendants, although they made their preparation to the same recipe as *Joseph Thorley*, the originator.[58] *Edison* was distinctive of batteries manufactured by the plaintiff company in *Edison Storage Battery Co v Britannia Batteries*,[59] even though the principle of operation had been invented and patented by *Thomas Alva Edison*. *Jaeger* for a new system of clothing, far from being descriptive, became distinctive of former licensees of Professor Jaeger who were able to enforce their exclusivity against the successors of the Professor.[60] In *Macleans v Lightbrown & Sons*[61] *Macleans* had at least to some extent lost its original meaning of a composition created by a doctor of that name and had become distinctive of the plaintiffs.[62] Conversely, it is possible for a product to be named after a famous person and for that person's name to become descriptive of it even though he did not introduce or patent it, as in *Gamage v Randall*[63] (*Shorland* for cycling shoes) and *Jaques v Chess*[64] (*Staunton* for chess men). In both the name was taken as indicating the design rather than the manufacturer. Examples not actually litigated might include *Wellington* for boots and *Gladstone* for a type of bag.[65]

Names of authors, artists, performers, etc.

8–88   Authors, artists, performers and the like are entitled to protect themselves against work being passed off as theirs by the use of their real or assumed names. An early example occurs in *Byron v Johnson*.[66] In *Martin v Wright*[67] relief was refused to an artist in respect of a diorama copied from one of his pictures and exhibited (arguably) as his original work. The reasoning was that the plaintiff's only cause of action was in libel, which the court would not restrain, but this is obsolete. Shadwell V.C. might have granted relief if

---

[55] [2001] R.P.C. 42 (Pumfrey J.).
[56] *James v James* (1872) L.R. 13 Eq. 421 (Romilly M.R.).
[57] *Cheavin v Walker* (1877) 5 Ch.D. 850, CA.
[58] *Massam v Thorley's Cattle Food Co* (1880) 14 Ch.D. 748, CA. The defendants' food was made by Joseph Thorley's brother, who knew the formula.
[59] (1931) 48 R.P.C. 350 (Bennett J.). See also *W H Dorman & Co Ltd v Henry Meadows Ltd* [1922] 2 Ch. 332.
[60] *Jaeger v Jaeger & Co Ltd* (1927) 44 R.P.C. 437, CA.
[61] (1937) 54 R.P.C. 230 (Farwell J.).
[62] See also *Cambridge Plan AG v Moore* (*Dr Howard's Cambridge Diet*) 1987 (4) SA 821 (Page J., Durban).
[63] (1899) 16 R.P.C. 185, CA. The decision is open to criticism on its facts.
[64] [1940] 2 All E.R. 285; 57 R.P.C. 77, CA.
[65] See the observations of Eve J. in *Imperial Tobacco Co's TMs* (1914) 32 R.P.C. 40.
[66] (1816) 35 E.R. 851 (L.C.).
[67] (1833) 58 E.R. 605 (Shadwell V.C.).

the plaintiff had himself exhibited a diorama of the work. In *Marengo v Daily Sketch*[68] the House of Lords granted the cartoonist *Kem* an injunction against a paper publishing another cartoonist who signed his work *Kim*. In *Clark v Associated Newspapers*[69] a satirical column in the *Evening Standard* entitled *Alan Clark's Secret Political Diary* was held to amount to passing-off, despite its obviously satirical content and attribution (less prominently) to the real author, Peter Bradshaw. The decision is hard to justify. Further examples are to be found at para.3–148 where they are discussed under the question of whether an assumed name may be said to belong to the individual author, *etc.* or to the publisher, employer or other business through which his works reach the public.

It is also, at least in principle, actionable as passing-off to publish as the work of an identified author and without further explanation work which has been revised by another, or altered,[70] distorted or mutilated.[71] In *Sweeney v Macmillan Publishers*[72] the trustees of James Joyce's estate sued the publisher and compiler of what the defendants called a "Reader's Edition" of *Ulysses*. *Ulysses* had originally been published in 1922, but the published text had never been accepted as definitive. The second defendant produced, and the first defendant published, a version of *Ulysses* compiled from the 1922 text and other authentic materials. The trustees alleged that the Reader's Edition was so different to what Joyce intended that it could not properly be described as his *Ulysses* at all. Although Lloyd J. would not have rejected "the possibility that there could, in theory, be a publication passed off as James Joyce's *Ulysses* which did fall outside some clearly and objectively defined class, and could possibly be the subject of a passing-off claim" the action failed because there was no such class of which it could be said that the Reader's Edition fell outside it.[73] Despite the tentative language of the passage quoted, liability should be open and shut for selling as Joyce's *Ulysses* a work which was not *Ulysses* or even by Joyce at all–Homer's *Odyssey*, perhaps.

It would also be passing-off to misrepresent old or poor quality work as **8–89** current work of the author's normal standard, but the existence of such a misrepresentation is inevitably hard to make out. Such a claim failed in *Harris v Warren & Phillips*[74] but an undertaking was offered by the defendants in *Beecham v British Lion*.[75] *Coogan v Odhams Press*[76] is either an example of this being made out or of passing-off by false attribution of authorship.

In addition to passing-off, there is a statutory cause of action for false

---

[68] [1948] 1 All E.R. 406; 65 R.P.C. 242, HL.

[69] [1998] 1 W.L.R. 1558; [1998] 1 All E.R. 959; [1998] R.P.C. 261 (Lightman J.).

[70] See *Humphreys v Thompson & Co Ltd* [1905–10] M.C.C. 148 though it is inconclusive. See also *Archbold v Sweet* (1832) 172 E.R. 947.

[71] *Lee v Gibbings* (1892) 67 L.T. N.S. 263 (Kekewich J.) would have treated this solely as libel, but is too restrictive.

[72] [2002] R.P.C. 35 (Lloyd J.).

[73] Compare *Harris v Warren & Phillips* (1918) 35 R.P.C. 217.

[74] (1918) 35 R.P.C. 217.

[75] (1900) 68 R.P.C. 111.

[76] [1928–35] M.C.C. 1.

attribution of a literary, dramatic, musical or artistic work, or of a film, under s.84 of the Copyright, Designs and Patents Act 1988.[77] The claimant need not be an author or in business at all, which makes the statutory action wider than that at common law. If the work falsely attributed is of such a nature as to reflect adversely on the reputation of the purported author then there may also be a cause of action for defamation.[78] The moral rights of paternity and integrity protected under ss.77–83 of the Copyright, Designs and Patents Act 1988 may also be relevant.

Laudatory terms

8–90 There is no rule of law in passing-off that laudatory terms cannot become distinctive but examples are few. A greater practical difficulty with laudatory terms is that they are so popular. Words such as *Ideal* or *Standard* are in such widespread use that if they are to be distinctive of a particular business at all it is likely to be within a very narrowly defined field.

The title of *The Wonderful Magazine* was protected in *Hogg v Kirby*,[79] but there were also express misrepresentations that the defendant's magazine was a continuation of the plaintiff's title. In another early case, *Braham v Bustard*,[80] *Excelsior* for soap was distinctive although this has been explained in terms of its being fanciful, despite its derivation, to the majority of the public.[81] *Eureka* for shirts was distinctive in *Ford v Foster*[82] although part of the trade used it descriptively. *IXL* (a pun on I excel) was probably distinctive in *Marshall v Sidebotham*.[83] *Standard* was restrained in *Standard Book of South Africa v Standard Bank*[84] but had failed to acquire secondary meaning in *Standard Ideal Co v Standard Sanitary Manufacturing Co*.[85] *Health* for cocoa was too commendatory for Neville J. to be prepared to restrain its use in *Thorne v Sandow*,[86] but the plaintiffs had no reputation in the defendants' territory anyway. *Classic* was not distinctive of the plaintiffs' greetings cards in *Sharpe v Solomon Bros*.[87] *Universal* was not distinctive in

---

[77] *Moore v News of the World* [1972] 1 Q.B. 441, CA; *Noah v Shuba* [1991] F.S.R. 15 (Mummery J.); *Alan Clark v Associated Newspapers Ltd* [1998] 1 W.L.R. 1558, [1998] 1 All E.R. 959, [1998] R.P.C. 261 (Lightman J.).

[78] *Ridge v English Illustrated Magazine Ltd* [1911–16] M.C.C. 91; (1913) 29 T.L.R. 592. See also *Moore v News of the World*, above.

[79] (1803) 8 Ves. Jun. 215; 32 E.R. 336 (Lord Eldon L.C.).

[80] (1863) 71 E.R. 195 (Page Wood V.C.).

[81] In *Raggett v Findlater* (1873) L.R. 17 Eq. 29. The plaintiff in *Griffiths v Frankenberg* (1910) 27 R.P.C. 733 failed, on the facts, to restrain the same word for tyre covers.

[82] (1872) L.R. 7 Ch. 611, CA.

[83] (1900) 18 R.P.C. 43 (Kekewich J.). This was the one part of the plaintiff's mark the defendant had not taken. *Excel* itself (for carpet cleaning) was protected against use by a former franchisee in *Ariaans v Hastings* (1996) 36 I.P.R. 211.

[84] (1909) 26 R.P.C. 310 (Eve J.).

[85] [1911] A.C. 78, PC.

[86] (1912) 29 R.P.C. 440 (Neville J.). The observation that *Health* was laudatory or commendatory occurred in connection with a motion to rectify the register of trade marks. Passing-off did not necessarily raise the same issue.

[87] (1914) 32 R.P.C. 15, CA. Distinguished in *Pickwick International (GB) Ltd v Multiple Sound Distributors Ltd* [1972] R.P.C. 786, CA.

Universal Winding Co v George Hattersley & Sons,[88] but that was probably because it denoted a particular type of machinery formerly manufactured under patent.[89] More recently, *Ideal* for trading cheques has been restrained in *Ideal General Supply Co v Edelston*[90] and as *Ideal Home* in *Associated Newspapers v Lew Barclay Exhibitions.*[91] *Treasure* was distinctive in *Treasure Cot Co v Hamley Bros.*[92] *Premier* was not restrained on an application for an interlocutory injunction in *Premier Motor Co v Premier Driving School,*[93] but the primary reason was that the parties were not in competition. The plaintiffs were motor distributors and the defendants a driving school. In Scotland the brewers of *Special Brew* lager were granted an interim interdict in *Carlsberg v Tennent Caledonian Breweries.*[94] *Top of the Pops* was sufficiently distinctive for an interlocutory injunction to be granted against *Pick of the Pops* in *Pickwick International (GB) v Multiple Sound Distributors.*[95]

Hit Factory for a recording studio had not become distinctive in *Pete* **8–91** *Waterman v CBS*[96] where it was essentially a nickname or accolade rather than the plaintiffs' trading style. In Australia, whatever rights the plaintiff had for *Betta* in relation to ice cream cones did not justify an interlocutory injunction against *Betta* for fruit bars: *Betta Foods Australia v Betta Fruit Bars.*[97] In *Premier Luggage and Bags v Premier Co*[98] (where the parties were in the same field of business) the Court of Appeal also held that there was no passing-off. There was a single example of actual confusion, but on balance use of the defendant's corporate name in oral statements by its sales staff and on swing tags attached to the goods was not likely to deceive. The dominant element of the defendant's tag was the mark or logo *PCL*, and *Premier* appeared only as part of the full corporate name, which was not prominent or conspicuous. The trial judge accepted that *Premier* had become distinctive of the claimant's goods, notwithstanding its laudatory character, and the reasoning of the Court of Appeal does not criticise this.

In *Easyjet v Dainty*[99] the claimants operated an airline, a chain of internet cafes, and a car hire business under the names *easyJet, easyEverything* and *easyRentacar.* They obtained summary judgment against registration of the domain name *easyRealestate.co.uk* by a cybersquatter, but the defendant's motives were transparent, and the judgment turned on the fact that get-up

[88] (1915) 32 R.P.C. 479 (Joyce J.).

[89] Contrast *Hendriks v Montague* (1881) 17 Ch.D. 638, CA: *Universal Life Assurance Society* and *Universe Life Assurance Association.*

[90] [1957] R.P.C. 252 (Diplock J.). However, the same authority was not prepared to accept the slogan *York's popular store* as distinctive.

[91] (1955) 72 R.P.C. 278 (Harman J.). The defendants' misuse of *Olympia* turned the case against him.

[92] (1950) 67 R.P.C. 89 (Harman J.).

[93] [1962] R.P.C. 222 (Plowman J.). The local telephone directory listed 15 to 20 businesses called *Premier.*

[94] [1972] R.P.C. 847 (Lord Hunter).

[95] [1972] R.P.C. 786, CA.

[96] [1993] E.M.L.R. 27 (Browne-Wilkinson V.C.)

[97] [1987] FCA 257; (1998) 41 I.P.R. 347 (Goldberg J., Federal Court of Australia).

[98] [2002] EWCA Civ 387; [2002] E.T.M.R. 69; [2003] F.S.R. 5, CA; reversing [2001] E.T.M.R. 6, [2001] F.S.R. 29.

[99] [2002] F.S.R. 6 (Bernard Livesey Q.C., Deputy Judge).

had also been copied. The claimants could not assert exclusive rights to the word or prefix "easy-" in every field of business.

Initials

8–92 There is ample authority that initials or arbitrary combinations of letters may be distinctive, and that the use of confusingly similar letters will be restrained. As early as 1872 the Court of Appeal in *Ford v Foster*[1] approved an Irish case, *Kinahan v Bolton*,[2] in which the defendants' use of the initials *LL*[3] was restrained. The plaintiffs failed to restrain the use of *WR* for corsets in *Rosenthan v Reynolds*,[4] but that was because they had disclaimed them in their trade mark registration. The reasoning, if ever correct, was overruled by the proviso to s.14 of the Trade Marks Act 1938; and is inapplicable under the Trade Marks Act 1994. The Court of Session refused to follow *Rosenthal v Reynolds* in *Bayer v Baird*[5] and granted an interdict against use of *CB* for corsets despite a disclaimer. The plaintiffs in *Findlater, Mackie, Todd v Henry Newman*[6] were granted a declaration and an account of profits over the use of the initials *F, M, T and Company*.[7]

In *Birmingham Small Arms v Webb*[8] Parker J. held that *BSA* was distinctive of the plaintiffs in respect of spanners and had innocently been infringed by the defendant using *BAS*. In *Boake Roberts v Wayland*[9] the initials *KMS* were distinctive of the plaintiffs, even though the full name *Kalium Meta Sulphite* of which they were an abbreviation was one chemical name of the substance. In *Du Cros v Gold*[10] *W & G* (specially written) on the doors of taxicabs was infringed by *M & G* written in the same way with the *M* imitating the *W* and a flourish between the two letters. *ABC* enclosed in a device representing interlocking steel sections was not too similar to the plaintiffs' marks *A, B, C* and *AB* (all enclosed in diamonds) in *Andrew v Kuenhrich*.[11] The marks denoted quality, were always used with the plaintiffs' house mark, and the "C" mark had fallen in disuse. In *AGS Manufacturing Co v Aeroplane General Sundries*[12] the initials *AGS* could not have been distinctive of the plaintiffs *per se*, because they primarily denoted a Government specification. However, the defendants were guilty of an express misrepresentation in advertising that *AGS* denoted or stood for their company.

8–93 *RAA* for a garage was restrained in *Royal Automobile Association of South Australia v Hancock*,[13] but an injunction was refused in *FMC Engi-*

---

[1] (1872) L.R. 7 Ch. 611, CA.
[2] 15 Ir. Ch. Rep. 75.
[3] *Kinahan's LL Whisky* and *Bolton's LL Whisky*.
[4] [1892] 2 Ch. 301; 9 R.P.C. 189 (North J.).
[5] (1898) 15 R.P.C. 615 (Court of Session, Inner House).
[6] (1902) 19 R.P.C. 235 (Kekewich J.).
[7] On corks in bottles of wine and spirits, which is interesting in its own right.
[8] (1906) 24 R.P.C. 7 (Parker J.).
[9] (1909) 26 R.P.C. 249 (Neville J.).
[10] (1912) 30 R.P.C. 117 (Swinfen Eady J.).
[11] (1913) 30 R.P.C. 677, CA.
[12] (1918) 35 R.P.C. 127, CA.
[13] [1939] S.A.S.R. 60.

neering Pty Ltd v FMC (Aust) Ltd[14] because the parties operated in sufficiently different fields of business. In more recent times an Australian totalisator board popularly known as *The TAB* obtained an injunction against the use of those initials as the title of a racing tip-sheet in *Totalizator Agency Board v Turf News*.[15] A company which had used the initials *H & C* or *H + C* for lifts was awarded an interlocutory injunction against *HAC: Hammond & Champness v HAC Lifts*.[16] The Irish Supreme Court granted an injunction against *C & A* in *C & A Modes v C & A (Waterford)*.[17] In *Century Electronics v CVS Enterprises*[18] the plaintiffs failed to obtain an interlocutory injunction against the use of *CVS* on various grounds including delay and the balance of convenience, although they had an arguable case. The Court of Appeal in *John Hayter Motor Underwriting Agencies v RBHS Agencies*[19] also refused an interlocutory injunction in a case where two Lloyds' syndicates used *JSB* and *BJS* respectively.

In *Nice and Safe Attitude v Flook*[20] the reputation of *NASA* (the American *National Aeronautics and Space Administration*) extended in a general sense to Britain, but not so as to create trading goodwill which could be licensed to a third party, the defendant. In *NAD Electronics v NAD Computer Systems*[21] the defendant company was restrained after trial from using *NAD* in respect of computers, the plaintiffs using *NAD* or *N-A-D* (originally derived from New Acoustic Dimension) for audio equipment. Summary judgment was granted for British Telecom against (*inter alia*) use of *BT* in the form of the domain name *bt.org* in *British Telecommunications v One in a Million*[22]; though not against *fcuk.com* in *French Connection v Sutton*.[23] Adoption of *FCUK* as the plaintiffs' trading style may have been too recent to have made the letters distinctive of them in the retail clothing trade, and in any event that is not how *fcuk.com* would necessarily be understood when standing on its own as an internet domain name.

In *HFC Bank v HSBC Bank*,[24] the defendants were in the process of rebranding themselves from *Midland Bank* to *HSBC*. Lloyd J. held on the facts that reasonably perspicacious borrowers who knew of the plaintiffs would not be confused by the defendants' new style. In *Dawnay, Day v Cantor Fitzgerald*[25] the main dispute was over the name *Dawnay, Day Securities*, but the injunction granted extended to the initials *DD* and *DDS*. In *Temporary Roadways and Access Co v Trax Portable Access*[26] the parties

---

[14] [1966] V.R. 529.
[15] [1967] V.R. 605; [1972] R.P.C. 579 (Smith J.).
[16] [1975] F.S.R. 131 (Templeman J.).
[17] [1978] F.S.R. (Irish Supreme Court). In England a qualified injunction against *CP Modes* or *C A P Modes* had been granted in *C & A Modes Ltd v Central Purchasing Association Ltd* (1930) 48 R.P.C. 163 (Humphreys J.).
[18] [1983] F.S.R. 1 (Dillon J.).
[19] [1977] F.S.R. 285; [1977] 2 Lloyd's Rep. 105, CA.
[20] [1997] F.S.R. 14 (Robert Walker J.).
[21] [1997] F.S.R. 380 (Ferris J.).
[22] [1999] 1 W.L.R. 903; [1999] 4 All E.R. 476; [1999] E.T.M.R. 61; [1999] F.S.R. 1, CA.
[23] [2000] E.T.M.R. 341 (Rattee J.).
[24] [2000] F.S.R. 176 (Lloyd J.). An appeal was compromised.
[25] [2000] R.P.C. 669, CA (affirming Lloyd J., *ibid.*).
[26] [2002] EWHC 1728 (Blackburne J.).

respectively traded as *TRAC* and *TRAX*, and the claimants' case was strengthened by close similarities in the appearance of the defendants' vehicles and livery. An interim injunction was granted. In New Zealand, there was no doubt that the initials *P & N* were distinctive in the cutting tool industry, and the question was which party was entitled to them. The New Zealand Court of Appeal held in favour of the local company: *Cyclone Hardware v Patience & Nicholson.*[27]

8–94   In the foregoing examples the claimant and the defendant both used the initials as such in their respective names or as their marks. Different issues arise if the only potential cause of deception is the fact that the parties trade under names which are different but which share common initial letters. According to Megarry J. in *I D W Superstores v Duncan Harris*[28] the court should be very slow to restrain the use of a trading name merely because the words comprising the name bear initials which make up the name under which the claimant trades. In the intermediate case, a trader who trades under a set of initials cannot ordinarily restrain a competitor from trading under a particular name because that name has the same initial letters, unless they are displayed so prominently that in substance the defendant is trading under the initials themselves.[29] Such an example occurred in *Liquid Veneer Co v Scott*[30] in which fraudulent defendants who had left the plaintiffs' employment were restrained from using *Elve* for a competing product.[31] The plaintiffs' product was habitually abbreviated to *LV*. The initials *HQ* were held to be arguably distinctive of the American plaintiffs in a Canadian case, *HQ Network Systems, Inc v HQ Office Supplies Warehouse, Inc*[32] and an interlocutory injunction was granted extending to the use of the word *HeadQuarters* by the defendants, as it would inevitably be abbreviated. In Australia, an injunction was granted against the defendants' use of the initials or acronym *ABT* in *Applied Business Technology v Grandmaster Computers.*[33]

Actions brought by professional associations against non-members frequently involve the misuse of initials which imply membership or a particular qualification. Thus, the use of *BMA* was restrained in *BMA v Marsh*,[34] *FSAA* in *Society of Incorporated Accountants v Vincent*[35] and *MIEE* in *Electrical Engineers v Emerson.*[36] Several of the cases are open to the criticism that the distinctiveness of the initials in question may have been assumed rather than proved. However, in *Att-Gen v Barrett Proprietaries*[37] the action failed because *BP* was not recognised or understood by the public.

---

[27] [2002] F.S.R. 41.
[28] [1975] R.P.C. 178; [1974] F.S.R. 114 (Megarry J.).
[29] Compare *AGS Manufacturing Co Ltd v Aeroplane General Sundries Ltd, above.*
[30] (1912) 29 R.P.C. 639 (Swinfen Eady J.).
[31] They also used *Ellvee* in their company name, but the plaintiffs seem not to have requested an interlocutory injunction directed to that.
[32] (1990) 30 C.P.R. (3d) 558 (Reed J., Federal Court).
[33] [1999] FCA 36; 44 I.P.R. 131 (Katz J., Federal Court of Australia).
[34] *British Medical Association v Marsh* (1931) 48 R.P.C. 565 (Maugham J.).
[35] (1954) 71 R.P.C. 325 (Vaisey J.).
[36] (1950) 67 R.P.C. 167 (Danckwerts J.).
[37] (1932) 50 R.P.C. 45 (Bennett J.).

Slogans

There is no reason in principle why a slogan should not be capable of being **8–95** distinctive, and the proposition that the tort of passing-off is wide enough to protect distinctive slogans has been accepted by the Privy Council.[38] The few cases in which slogans have been in issue have failed on the facts, with the equivocal exception of *United Biscuits v Asda*[39] in which the plaintiffs' slogan *P ... P ... P ... Pick up a Penguin* had been transiently parodied by the defendants with *P ... P ... P ... Pick up a Puffin*, resulting in a finding of trade mark infringement (the slogan being registered) and the likelihood that this also constituted, or would have contributed to, passing off. The point seems not to have been separately argued.

In *Midgley v Morris*[40] the plaintiff claimed *Fair Wear or a Free Pair* for shoes but the defendants had used it first. In *Cordes v Addis*[41] the slogan *A Clean Tooth Never Decays* was alleged to be distinctive but Eve J. found for the defendants. Diplock J. refused to accept *York's Popular Store* as distinctive in *Ideal General Supply Co v Edelson*,[42] but found for the plaintiff on other issues. In Canada, *Sugar and Spice and Everything Nice* for dolls was not distinctive *per se* and had not acquired secondary meaning, although the court found for the plaintiffs on the mark *Star Doll: Regal Toy v Goodtime Toys Inc.*[43]

In *Cadbury Schweppes v Pub Squash Co*[44] itself the plaintiffs unsuccessfully argued that various slogans to the effect that their lemon drink was *Like Those Great Old Squashes the Pubs Used to Make* were distinctive of them, but they were held to be essentially descriptive. *Browns, Seasons and Thickens* was claimed to be distinctive of the plaintiffs' gravy mix in *RHM Foods v Bovril*,[45] but the issue was never decided. The Court of Appeal accepted the plaintiffs' contention as arguable but not strong.

F. TITLES

Titles of newspapers and periodicals

The titles of newspapers, magazines and other periodical publications **8–96** undoubtedly have trade mark significance. Liability for passing-off may therefore arise from using the same title, or one confusingly similar, for

---

[38] In *Cadbury Schweppes Pty Ltd v Pub Squash Co Pty Ltd* [1981] R.P.C. 429; [1981] 1 All E.R. 213, PC.
[39] [1997] R.P.C. 513 (Robert Walker J.).
[40] (1904) 21 R.P.C. 314 (Farwell J.).
[41] (1923) 40 R.P.C. 133 (Eve J.).
[42] [1957] R.P.C. 252 (Diplock J.).
[43] (1974) 19 C P.R. (2d) 98 (Federal Court, Trial Division, Heald J.).
[44] [1981] R.P.C. 429; [1981] 1 All E.R. 213, PC.
[45] [1983] R.P.C. 275, CA.

another publication or even in a totally different field of business.[46] In practice, successful actions are rare. Proprietors do not help their case by choosing titles which are self-evidently descriptive of content, area or frequency of publication; or are made up of words such as *Star, Post, Advertiser*, etc. which may not strictly be descriptive but which are too hackneyed to be distinctive in this field. The usual rule applies that where a name is *prima facie* descriptive or otherwise of low inherent distinctiveness then relatively small differences will suffice to distinguish.

In *World Athletics and Sporting Publications v Webb*[47] the plaintiffs had published *Athletics Weekly* for 30 years. They objected to the defendants' *Athletics Monthly*. An injunction was granted at first instance but discharged on appeal. The magazines were entirely different in size, cover, price, frequency and content. No one comparing them could be confused. If the plaintiffs were not to monopolise the word "athletics" it was necessary to take comparatively small differences in name as sufficient. To grant an injunction because a few purchasers buying on recommendation might forget the full name would be unfair to the defendants.

8–97 A common theme in many of the decided cases is that the respective periodicals were too different in terms of appearance, presentation, content, price, readership or other matters for either deception or damage to occur.

> "The plaintiff's is a quality production, selling at 3/-, published monthly, or bi-monthly, using (even when picturing the nude) art paper, with serious articles requiring or meriting careful reading, appealing to a select type of reader, and likely to be limited in circulation to numbers of the order of 20,000. The defendants' is a weekly production, sold for 5d, printed on ordinary paper, with articles on popular and ephemeral subjects, aimed at achieving a mass circulation of the order of three-quarters of a million."[48]

Two other factors deserve mention as helping to explain why so few cases are successful. One is that readers tend to show great loyalty to their preferred newspaper or (at least in some cases) magazine. In contrast to many other fields of business, they are likely to take whatever trouble is necessary to buy that in preference to others which might be very similar in name or get-up. The second, and related, reason is that periodicals are bought regularly and frequently, perhaps every day, week or month. Even if a reader of The *Morning Star* should once buy The *Daily Star* in error, he will take whatever care is necessary to avoid repeating the mistake. The damage from such infrequent mistakes to a newspaper published every day, year in and year out, is slight.

---

[46] As in *Walter v Ashton* [1902] 2 Ch. 282 (*Times* bicycles) and *Hulton Press Ltd v White Eagle Youth Holiday Camp Ltd* (1951) 68 R.P.C. 126 (*White Eagle* holiday camp); though not in *Marie Claire Album SA v Hartstone Hosiery Ltd* [1993] F.S.R. 692 (*Marie Claire* hosiery), nor *ELLE TMs* [2000] E.T.M.R. 311 (*ELLE* tampons).

[47] [1981] F.S.R. 27, CA.

[48] *per* Wilberforce J. in *Kark (Norman) Publications Ltd v Odhams Press Ltd* [1962] R.P.C. 163.

Taken as a whole, the cases are open to criticism once they cease to be **8–98** based on the very descriptive nature of many of the titles in issue. Differences in the goods themselves are given far more weight here than is usual in any other field of business. Many border on suggesting that there can be passing-off only if the parties' publications compete for the same readers, and those readers would not readily distinguish them as alternatives. If this were true for passing-off as a whole then the tort would be confined to counterfeiting. The familiar argument that there can be deception and damage if similarity of names causes two businesses or their goods to be associated with one another in the public mind despite obvious differences between them has been very hard to make out in this context, although *Associated Newspapers v Express Newspapers*[49] may mark a change of direction. Even the more modern cases tend specifically to cite previous cases on newspaper or magazine titles, as if they defined a separate body of law, and the result is that a characteristically nineteenth century approach has been preserved here although discarded as obsolete in the mainstream of the tort.

Newspapers: examples

In *Maxwell v Hogg*[50] the plaintiff failed to restrain piracy of the title *Bel-* **8–99** *gravia* for a paper he had advertised but not yet launched. In *Walter v Emmot*[51] the proprietor of *The Times* published a summary of its contents every other day as *The Mail*. It was mainly sold in the provinces. He failed on the facts to restrain *The Morning Mail* for an ordinary daily newspaper. The plaintiffs in *Licensed Victuallers' Newspaper Co v Bingham*[52] beat the defendant to the market by a few days, but the sale of no more than a few tens of copies was insufficient to make *The Licensed Victuallers' Mirror* distinctive and an injunction was refused. In *Borthwick v Evening Post*[53] the plaintiff owned the long-established *Morning Post*. The Court of Appeal refused to infer any damage on the defendant launching the *Evening Post*, despite fraud,[54] evidence of actual deception and the fact that *Evening Post* was the obvious and only title for an evening edition of the *Morning Post*.[55] In *Outram v London Evening Newspaper Co*[56] the publishers of the *Evening Times* in Glasgow with a small readership in London failed to restrain the use of the same name for a London paper.

In *Britain Publishing Co v Trade & Commercial Press*[57] the two plaintiffs respectively published the *London Weekly Advertiser* and the *National Advertiser*, both of which essentially consisted of small classified advertise-

---

[49] [2003] EWHC 1322 (Laddie J.).
[50] (1867) L.R. 2 Ch. 307, CA.
[51] (1885) 54 L.J. Ch. 1059; 53 L.T. 437, CA.
[52] (1888) 38 Ch.D. 139, CA.
[53] (1888) 37 Ch.D. 449, CA.
[54] The defendant was refused his costs.
[55] Compare *Associated Newspapers Ltd v Express Newspapers* [2003] EWHC 1322 (Laddie J.), below.
[56] (1911) 28 R.P.C. 308 (Warrington J.).
[57] [1957] R.P.C. 134 (Harman J.).

ments. The defendants submitted to an injunction (in the *Corona* form[58]) against calling a similar paper the *National Weekly. In D C Thomson v Kent Messenger*[59] the proprietors of *The Sunday Post* failed to obtain an interlocutory injunction against *The South East Sunday Post*. The plaintiffs' newspaper circulated mainly in Scotland and the North of England with about 2,000 purchasers in the area where the defendants intended to publish. The proprietors of *The Maidenhead Advertiser* (known simply as *The Advertiser*) failed to prevent a free newspaper in the same area calling itself *The New Advertiser* in *Baylis (The Maidenhead Advertiser) v DarlenCo*[60]

8–100   In *Morning Star Co-operative Society v Express Newspapers*[61] Foster J. concluded that only "a moron in a hurry" would confuse *The Morning Star* with *The (Daily) Star*, the papers differing in almost every imaginable respect. Aldous J. refused the publishers of the *Tamworth Herald* an interlocutory injunction against the *Tamworth Herald and Post* in *Tamworth Herald Co v Thomson Free Newspapers.*[62] In *Associated Newspapers v Express Newspapers*[63] the publishers of the *Daily Mail* and the *Mail on Sunday* were granted permanent *quia timet* injunctions against the threatened launch of a giveaway London evening paper under a name which might have been *The Mail*, the *Evening Mail* or the *London Evening Mail*, but which would almost inevitably have been abbreviated to *The Mail*. Various other newspapers incorporated *Mail* into their titles, but none had a significant circulation in the London area, where *Mail* on its own was sufficiently distinctive of the claimants. The defendants' reticence as to the precise title of their paper did not help their case.

Another example of relief being granted comes from Australia. In *Neylan v Toison Holdings*[64] a newspaper had been published in the suburb of Nundah as *The Nundah Express*, then *The Express* until September 1980 when it was closed down. Thereafter the defendants (there were cross applications) had published a free newspaper under the name *The Suburban* from the same premises and it was widely regarded as the *de facto* successor to *The Express*. The defendants took over some of the staff and assets of the defunct paper but not its goodwill or masthead, which the former proprietors intended to keep. In November 1981 the plaintiffs announced plans to publish a paper to be called *The Nundah Express*. In December the defendants renamed their paper *The Suburban Express* and in January 1982 the plaintiffs' paper was first published. Williams A.J. refused an injunction to the plaintiffs and granted one to the defendants.

8–101   Two cases deserve mention in this paragraph for convenience, although they do not deal with newspaper titles as such. In *Financial Times v Evening Standard*[65] Aldous J. refused an interlocutory injunction against the defen-

---

[58] *Havana Cigar & Tobacco Factories Ltd v Oddenino* [1924] 1 Ch. 179; 41 R.P.C. 47, CA.
[59] [1975] R.P.C. 191; [1975] F.S.R. 485 (Megarry J.).
[60] [1974] F.S.R. 284 (Plowman J.).
[61] [1979] F.S.R. 113 (Foster J.).
[62] [1991] F.S.R. 337 (Aldous J.).
[63] [2003] EWHC 1322 (Laddie J.).
[64] [1983] 1 Qd. 600 (Williams A.J.).
[65] [1991] F.S.R. 7 (Aldous J.).

dant newspaper publishing its business pages on pink paper similar to that used by the plaintiffs. In *Associated Newspapers v Insert Media*[66] the Court of Appeal granted an injunction against the insertion of advertising supplements into the plaintiffs' papers imitating their presentation and style.

Magazines: examples

In *Hogg v Kirby*[67] the defendant was enjoined from using the title *The* **8–102** *Wonderful Magazine* and misrepresenting his magazine as a continuation of the plaintiff's. In *Bradbury v Beeton*[68] the publishers of *Punch* failed to restrain *Punch & Judy* at one-third the price despite deliberately deceptive similarities in get-up. The publishers of *The Magazine of Fiction* failed to restrain *Cassell's Magazine of Fiction and Popular Literature* in *Stevens v Cassell*.[69] In *Ridgeway Co v Amalgamated Press*[70] the publishers of *Everybody's Magazine*, published monthly at one shilling, failed to prevent *Everybody's Weekly* at one penny. The plaintiffs' magazine was imported from America and had only a trifling circulation here. The same plaintiffs as publishers of another American magazine, *Adventure*, failed to restrain *Hutchinson's Adventure Story Magazine* in *Ridgway Co v Hutchinson*.[71] As well as *Adventure* being used descriptively by the defendants, circulation of the plaintiffs' magazine in Britain had virtually been confined to American troops taking part in the First World War.

In *Pearl Cooper v Richmond Hill Press*[72] *Sports Car & Lotus Owner* was refused an injunction against *Sports Car Illustrated*. In *Rubber & Technical Press v MacClaren & Sons*[73] Cross J. refused the publishers of the monthly magazine *Rubber and Plastics Age* an interlocutory injunction against *Rubber and Plastics Weekly*. Confusion was likely but not to the extent of causing damage to goodwill or custom. Wilberforce J. in *Kark (Norman) Publications v Odhams Press*[74] refused the former publisher of *Today* an injunction against the defendants using the same title. The main ground was that the goodwill had been extinguished by seven years' disuse,[75] but differences between the two publications would apparently have been sufficient to avoid confusion, identity of name notwithstanding. The Court of Appeal has refused *Newsweek* magazine an interlocutory injunction against the use of that name for a current affairs programme on television in *Newsweek Inc v British Broadcasting Corporation*,[76] and *Athletics Weekly* one against

---

[66] [1991] F.S.R. 380, CA.
[67] (1803) 8 Ves. Jun. 215; 32 E.R. 336 (Lord Eldon L.C.).
[68] (1869) 39 L.J. Ch. 348. Cited in *Kark (Norman) Publications Ltd v Odhams Press Ltd* [1962] R.P.C. 163.
[69] (1913) 29 R.P.C. 199 (Neville J.).
[70] (1911) 29 R.P.C. 130 (Warrington J.).
[71] (1923) 40 R.P.C. 335 (Sarjeant J.).
[72] [1957] R.P.C. 363 (Upjohn J.).
[73] [1961] R.P.C. 264 (Cross J.).
[74] [1962] R.P.C. 163 (Wilberforce J.).
[75] *Today* had been incorporated into another title, *Courier*. Compare *EMAP National Publications v Security Publications* [1997] F.S.R. 891 (Lloyd J.), *below*, where another otherwise discontinued title was still used sufficiently prominently to assist the plaintiffs' case.
[76] [1979] R.P.C. 441, CA.

Athletics Monthly in *World Athletics and Sporting Publications v ACM Webb*.[77] In an Australian case, *Cricketer v Newspress*,[78] an English magazine called *The Cricketer* was refused relief against a new Australian magazine under the name *Cricketer*. Although the plaintiffs' sales in Australia were not large, the main reason for refusing relief was that no one familiar with the plaintiffs' magazine would be confused.

8–103   *Leisure News* could not have become distinctive of either party as a result of minimal pre-launch publicity in *Marcus Publishing v Hutton-Wild*[79] and the Court of Appeal discharged an interlocutory injunction granted in favour of the defendants in the Queen's Bench Division. In *Management Publications v Blenheim Exhibitions Group*[80] the Court of Appeal held there to be an arguable case that *Security Management Today* would be taken as connected in some way with the plaintiffs' long-established *Management Today*, but the balance of convenience favoured refusing an injunction. In *Morgan-Grampian v Training Personnel*[81] the plaintiffs published a series of ten magazines with titles commencing "*What's new in ...*". Mummery J. granted an interlocutory injunction against the defendants re-naming an existing title, *Training Personnel*, as *What's New in Training*. There was a risk that advertisers would be confused. Like the two preceding cases, this one was to do with controlled circulation magazines which were distributed free and which relied entirely on advertising for their income. While confusion of readers might be relevant, confusion of advertisers was the main source of complaint. Rather more typical both in facts and result is *Advance Magazine Publishing v Redwood Publishing*[82] in which the publishers of the American magazine *Gourmet* failed to restrain the launch of *BBC Gourmet Good Food*. Their circulation was only some 2,300 copies per month in the United Kingdom, but the main reason was the descriptiveness of the title, in which they could claim no monopoly.

In *EMAP National Publications v Security Publications*[83] the respective titles *Practical Classics* and *Classics*, both for magazines for classic car enthusiasts, were too descriptive to be the basis of a passing-off claim in their own right, but the publishers of *Practical Classics* were still granted an interlocutory injunction. The risk of actionable confusion arose from similarities in get-up and partially rested on the presentation of the *Classics* title in an oval badge, which was similar in format to that of the plaintiffs' former publication *Popular Classics*. The latter had been discontinued and incorporated into *Practical Classics*, but the *Popular Classics* "badge" was still retained on the front cover of *Practical Classics*.

8–104   In Australia, a first instance finding that the defendants' *Triathlon & Multisport Magazine* would be confused with the plaintiffs' established title *Triathlon Sports* (both titles having *Triathlon* as the prominent element) was

---

[77] [1981] F.S.R. 27, CA.
[78] [1974] V.R. 477 (Supreme Court of Victoria, Kaye J.).
[79] [1990] R.P.C. 576, CA.
[80] [1991] F.S.R. 550, CA.
[81] [1992] F.S.R. 267 (Mummery J.).
[82] [1993] F.S.R. 449 (Harman J.).
[83] [1997] F.S.R. 891 (Lloyd J.).

reversed on appeal: *S & I Publishing v Australian Surf Life Saver*.[84] It was insufficient that readers might merely be caused to wonder if the titles came from the same publisher; it was barely conceivable that the name of the sport could have acquired secondary meaning in its own right; and an objective comparison showed that the defendants' masthead was well differentiated from that of the plaintiffs. In *Rumcoast Holdings v Prospero Publishing*[85] the plaintiffs' regional up-market lifestyle magazine *Scoop* was protected against *The Scoop* for a national magazine with a blue-collar readership and pornographic content.

Television and radio

Two Australian cases have dealt with the titles, content and presentation of **8–105** rival television series.[86] In *Willard King Organisation v United Telecasters Sydney*[87] the plaintiffs had produced in Victoria a television quiz programme entitled *It's Academic*. They licensed the name and format of the programme to the defendants for broadcasting in New South Wales. On expiry of the licence the defendants proposed to produce a similar programme under the name *John Bailey's It's Academic* without the participation of the plaintiffs. Else-Mitchell J. granted an injunction on the grounds of passing-off, unfair competition and breach of confidence.[88] The opposite result was reached in *South Australian Telecasters v Southern Television Corp*.[89] The plaintiffs broadcast a programme called *Adelaide's New Faces* which was a showpiece for new talent. They failed to stop a similar programme being broadcast by another station as *Australia's New Faces*. In a New Zealand case, *Greene v Broadcasting Corp of New Zealand*,[90] the originator and presenter of the British television programme *Opportunity Knocks* failed principally because he had no goodwill in New Zealand. Nor was there any evidence that anyone in New Zealand had been deceived into thinking that the defendants' programme of the same name and format was even so much as approved by the plaintiff.

The name *Gold AM* for a radio programme of "Golden Oldies" broadcast by amplitude modulation was too descriptive for the plaintiffs to have an arguable case when the name had only been in use for six months. It made no difference that the defendants had copied: *County Sound v Ocean Sound*.[91] In an Australian case, the English television station *TV AM* had insufficient reputation for that name to be distinctive of it locally in *TV AM v Amalgamated Television Services*.[92] In contrast to the *TV-AM* case, the

---

[84] (1998) 00 I.P.R. 581 (Federal Court of Australia; Hill, Nicholson and Emmett JJ.).

[85] [1999] W.A.S.C. 176; 00 I.P.R. 75 (Templeman J., SC of Western Australia).

[86] It is suggested that television series have more in common with periodicals than with one-off publications such as books, plays or films.

[87] (1970) [1981] 2 N.S.W.L.R. 547 (Else-Mitchell J.).

[88] See also *Hexagon Pty Ltd v Australian Broadcasting Commission* (1975) 7 A.L.R. 233; [1976] R.P.C. 628.

[89] [1970] S.A.S.R. 207 (Walters J.).

[90] [1988] 2 N.Z.L.R. 490; [1989] R.P.C. 469 (CA of NZ).

[91] [1991] F.S.R. 367, CA.

[92] (1988) 12 I.P.R. 85.

defendants in *Jelly's Music Hall v Triple-M Broadcasting*[93] were restrained from using the name *Radio Free* on the application of the American plaintiffs who already used that name for a service broadcast in Hawaii. There had been abortive discussions to licence the name and format to the defendants.

In the Hong Kong case of *Television Broadcasts v Home Guide Publication Co*[94] Macdougall J. granted the broadcasters of a television programme *New Looks of Women* an interlocutory injunction against the defendants using that name for a magazine aimed at a similar market. However, in England the producers of the television series *Neighbours* failed to obtain an interlocutory injunction against a magazine entitled *Neighbours Who's Who* dealing with characters in the series: *Grundy Television v Startrain*.[95] The *Neighbours* decision is probably more representative of English law than the opposite result reached in a case on very similar facts involving the BBC series *EastEnders*.[96]

Titles of books (etc.); publishing

8–106 Cases on the title of an individual book, or that of a play, film or similar work, raise an issue which is fundamentally different to that of the title of a periodical such as a magazine. When many different issues of a work have a common title then that title may properly be regarded as having trade mark significance. The same applies to works such as legal or medical textbooks which go into many editions, perhaps under different editors. The same conclusion does not apply to a single work. The distinction has often been overlooked, and discussion of the titles of books (and of plays, films and the like) has often proceeded on the assumption that the title is either descriptive or is distinctive of the publisher in the same way as for periodicals. It is possible for an action based on the title of a book to fail because the title is not exclusively associated with the claimants' work, for instance because it is *prima facie* descriptive, or hackneyed, or used by others, or used on too small a scale or too long ago to be remembered. However, even a title which is novel, striking, arbitrary and universally known cannot normally be said to be distinctive of the publisher of that book. If it is distinctive at all, it is distinctive of the book itself.

It is not easy to apply the normal terminology of passing-off to the titles of individual literary works. It is sometimes said that a title is descriptive, but this does not depend on the title recognisably indicating what the book contains. A title such as *How to Appeal Against Your Rates*[97] is self-evidently descriptive of what the book deals with, as, to a lesser extent, is *Mother Care/Other Care*.[98] However, a wholly arbitrary title still denotes nothing

---

[93] (1993) 26 I.P.R. 127 (Einfield J.)

[94] [1982] F.S.R. 505 (Macdougall J.).

[95] [1988] F.S.R. 581 (Millett J.).

[96] *BBC v Celebrity Centre* (1988) 15 I.P.R. 333 in which Falconer J. granted an interlocutory injunction against the *A to Z of EastEnders*.

[97] *Mathieson v Sir Isaac Pitman & Sons Ltd* (1930) 47 R.P.C. 541.

[98] *Mothercare UK Ltd v Penguin Books Ltd* [1988] R.P.C. 113, CA.

but the book itself and perhaps its author. It does not in general denote or carry any reference to the publisher. The title denotes more than just authorship, so it is not right to treat it simply as distinctive of the author. There can be passing-off by publishing one work of an author so as to be taken for another by the same person, as in *Metzler v Wood*.[99] Nor does it matter that during the subsistence of copyright the book may have been published only by one publisher, or by that one and under licence to others. If it were otherwise then the publishers of a work with a "fancy" name such a Kipling's *Rewards and Fairies*[1] would be able to prevent any other person publishing it under that name when the copyright in it expired. What the publisher is able to restrain is the publication of one book under a name which is already recognised by the public as denoting another. This is not because there is any misrepresentation as to source, but because there is a misrepresentation as to the book's content or nature.[2] The title of a book is comparable in this respect to a term such as *Champagne* or *Advocaat*.

This may be illustrated from the facts of *W H Allen v Brown Watson*,[3] **8-107** although the decision itself does not analyse in detail where the defendants' misrepresentation lay. The autobiography of Frank Harris had previously been published in expurgated form as *My Life and Adventures*. The plaintiffs intended to publish the unexpurgated version and advertised it as *My Life and Loves*. The defendants were restrained from issuing the old, expurgated, version under the new title. If the defendants had published the full text under the latter title, they would have been guilty of copyright infringement but not passing-off. What *My Life and Loves* meant to the public was the complete version, no matter by whom published. If they got that, they were satisfied. If they bought the defendants' version their complaint would be that it was incomplete, not that it was published without the *imprimatur* of the plaintiffs. Similar (but infinitely more complicated) issues arose in respect of James Joyce's novel *Ulysses* in *Sweeny v Macmillan Publishers*,[4] discussed above.

The principles to apply in cases turning on the distinctiveness of titles of books were explained by Maugham J. in *Mathieson v Sir Isaac Pitman*.[5] The parties published books of which the titles of both began *How to Appeal Against Your Rates*. There were no similarities beyond the titles and subject matter. Maugham J. drew a distinction between titles which were arbitrary, such as *Rewards and Fairies*, those which were descriptive but capable of acquiring secondary meaning, and those such as *Bills of Exchange* or *Heat*

---

[99] (1876) 8 Ch.D. 606, CA.

[1] The example given in *Mathieson v Sir Isaac Pitman & Sons Ltd* (1930) 47 R.P.C. 541.

[2] The principle may be detected in two early cases on song titles: *Chappell v Sheard* (1855) 69 E.R. 717 (Page-Wood V.C.) and *Chappell v Davidson* (1855) 69 E.R. 719 (Page-Wood V.C.), order varied (1856) 44 E.R. 289 (L.JJ.). Though the publisher's main complaint was imitation of the title of his successful song *Minnie* by *Minnie Dale* and *Minnie, dear Minnie*, there were express misrepresentations in both cases that the defendants' songs had achieved popular success which in fact belonged only to the plaintiff's song.

[3] [1965] R.P.C. 191 (Pennycuick J.). See Anthony Walton "A Pervasive but not Often Explicitly Characterised Aspect of Passing-off" [1987] E.I.P.R. 159.

[4] [2002] R.P.C. 35 (Lloyd J.).

[5] (1930) 47 R.P.C. 541 (Maugham J.).

which were so inherently descriptive that they could never be distinctive. He held that the title of the plaintiffs' book came in the middle category, but that the evidence failed to show it had acquired secondary meaning. Sales had been small and it had been the only one on the subject on the market. The defendant could not therefore be prevented from using an equally descriptive and almost indistinguishable title, notwithstanding that other equally appropriate titles could have been devised.

8–108   Publishers' names and imprints are capable of being trade marks like any others and protection depends on their being distinctive in fact. In *Blacklock v Bradshaws Publishing Co*[6] Astbury J. granted an interlocutory injunction in favour of the publishers of *Bradshaws Railway Guide* against a defendant soliciting business for a *Bradshaws Directory*. The case was one of gross fraud. A similar example is to be found in *RAC Motoring Services v RAC (Publishing)*[7] in which the defendants were committed for contempt by Browne-Wilkinson V.-C. after fraudulently inviting hoteliers to pay for inclusion in the *RAC Handbook*. A more conventional case is *Pan Books v World Distributors*[8] in which Upjohn J. granted an interlocutory injunction against *Pem Books*. In *Minerva TM, Reed Consumer Books v Pomaco*[9] three weeks' use of *Minerva* as a publisher's imprint, with considerable launch publicity, would have given the opponents prior rights in respect of literary matter of the under s.5(4)(a) Trade Marks Act 1994.

The same principle would apply to a recognisable series of books issued under a common mark or incorporating a distinctive idea into the titles of all. However, in *Pet Library v Ellason*[10] Megarry J. refused an interlocutory injunction to the publishers of *The Pet Library* because the phrase was descriptive and the defendants had distinguished themselves adequately. In *Games Workshop v Transworld Publishers*[11] the defendants' use of *Dark Future* as a common element in the titles of a series of four science fiction books was probably passing-off, but an interlocutory injunction was granted solely on the basis of trade mark infringement. Get up can also cause or contribute to a book being taken to be the work of another author or publisher.[12]

Plays and films

8–109   In two Australian cases injunctions have been granted against producing one play under the same name as another. In *Broadhurst v Nicholls*[13] the producers of a comedy *The Wrong Mr Wright* obtained an injunction against a different play being re-named and produced as *The Wrong Mrs*

---

[6] (1926) 43 R.P.C. 97 (Astbury J.).
[7] [1988] R.P.C. 321 (Browne-Wilkinson V.C.).
[8] [1957] R.P.C. 366 (Upjohn J.).
[9] [2000] F.S.R. 734 (Jacob J.)
[10] [1968] F.S.R. 359 (Megarry J.).
[11] [1993] F.S.R. 705, CA.
[12] *Biddulph v De Vries* (1998) 43 I.P.R. 144 (Emmett J, Federal Court of Australia): *Raising Boys* and *Raising Girls*. An interlocutory injunction was granted.
[13] (1903) 3 S.R. (N.S.W.) Eq. 147 (Simpson C.J. in Eq).

Wright. In *Meynell v Pearce*[14] the producers of a play called *The Fatal Wedding* were granted an injunction against another play being advertised as *The Fatal Wedding Day* with *Day* written inconspicuously. In *Loewe's Inc v Littler*[15] the plaintiffs failed to prove that *The Merry Widow* denoted their particular translation of Lehar's operetta. The defendants were therefore free to perform another translation under that name.

The title of a film can become distinctive, as apparently happened in *Twentieth Century Fox Corp v Gala Film Distributors*[16] where the defendants undertook to change the title of their film from *Anastasia*. It is clear Roxburgh J. would have granted an interlocutory injunction on the merits if necessary. The plaintiffs had acquired the film rights to a play of that name dealing with the supposed surviving daughter of the Tzar. They had made and advertised it, but its premiere had not yet taken place. In *Hexagon v Australian Broadcasting Commission*[17] the producers of two films called *Alvin Purple* and *Alvin Rides Again* would (but for acquiescence) have obtained relief against a television series based on the same character and entitled *Alvin*.[18]

There are several cases dealing with films having the same title as existing **8–110** literary or dramatic works, but most have failed on the facts. An injunction was conceded in *Raleigh v Kinematograph Trading Co.*[19] An equivocal exception is *Twentieth Century Fox Corp v Gala Film Distributors*[20] where a film of the play had already been advertised by the plaintiffs. *Samuelson v Producers Distributing Co*[21] turned on express misrepresentations rather than on whatever similarity there was between the titles of the film and the sketch it was rather distantly derived from. One decision of the Privy Council would apparently have refused relief as a matter of principle, but this would be going too far.[22] It is interesting that (long before "inverse" passing-off was recognised) argument has often dwelt on the play and film being quite different in content, implicitly recognising that the alleged misrepresentation was really one of quality rather than source.

In *Raleigh v Kinematograph Trading Co*[23] the defendants reluctantly submitted to an injunction against using the title *Sealed Orders* for a film, that being the name of a well-known play the plaintiffs had written and produced successfully the previous season. The plaintiffs in *Houghton v Film Booking Offices*[24] failed to establish sufficient reputation in the name *The*

[14] [1906] V.L.R. 447 (Cussen J.).
[15] (1955) 72 R.P.C. 166 (Upjohn J.).
[16] [1957] R.P.C. 105 (Roxburgh J.).
[17] (1975) 7 A.L.R. 233; [1976] R.P.C. 628 (Needham J.).
[18] See also the Hong Kong case *Shaw Bros (Hong Kong) Ltd v Golden Harvest (HK) Ltd* [1971] H.K.L.R. 167; [1972] R.P.C. 559 in which it is unclear how much similarity there was in the titles of the respective films.
[19] (1914) 31 R.P.C. 143 (Eve J.).
[20] [1957] R.P.C. 105 (Roxburgh J.): *Anastasia*.
[21] (1931) 48 R.P.C. 580, CA.
[22] *Francis Day & Hunter Ltd v Twentieth-Century Fox Co Ltd* [1940] A.C. 112; [1939] All E.R. 192, PC.
[23] (1914) 31 R.P.C. 143 (Eve J.).
[24] (1931) 48 R.P.C. 329 (Bennett J.).

Younger Generation to restrain a film appearing under the same name. The play had been performed in London in 1910 and 1912–13, and occasionally thereafter by amateurs and provincial touring companies. Three unrelated films with the same title had been shown in 1913, 1915 and 1926 without evidence of confusion and the title had also been used for other works. In *O'Gorman v Paramount Film Service*[25] it was held that the public would not think that *Irish and Proud of It* was a film version of a musical play of the same name last produced 13 years before, and an argument that the film copyright was depreciated by another film having the same title was rejected.[26] The Privy Council in *Francis Day & Hunter v Twentieth Century Fox Co*[27] held that there was no passing-off by calling a film *The Man Who Broke the Bank at Monte Carlo*, the song and the film being too different to admit of comparison.

Titles of events

8–111 The titles of beauty contests were in issue in *Morecambe & Heysham v Mecca*[28] and *Miss World (Jersey) v James St Productions*.[29] In both cases the plaintiffs failed on the facts. In the former, *Miss Britain* for the defendants' contest was sufficiently different to the plaintiffs' *Miss Great Britain* in the absence of evidence of actual confusion among potential entrants, spectators or the public at large. In the latter, a grotesque and satirical X-rated film entitled *Miss Alternative World* would not have been taken as produced by the promoters of the *Miss World* contest.

The title of an exhibition may be distinctive, as with *Ideal Home* in *Associated Newspapers v Lew Barclay Exhibitions*[30] and *Long Point* in *Artistic Upholstery v Art Forma (Furniture)*.[31] In the first, the exhibition and its name were, so to speak, proprietary to a single commercial promoter; in the second the exhibition was promoted by an unincorporated trade association to which the representative claimant belonged and from which the defendant company had been expelled. In *Technical Productions v Contemporary Exhibitions*[32] the plaintiffs failed to prevent a rival exhibition using the word *Refrigeration* in its title as it was descriptive of the subject matter of both.

---

[25] [1937] 3 All E.R. 113 (Clauson J.).
[26] Based on the judgment of Romer L.J. in *Samuelson v Producers Distributing Co Ltd* (1931) 48 R.P.C. 580, CA.
[27] [1940] A.C. 112; [1939] All E.R. 192, PC.
[28] [1962] R.P.C. 145 (Wilberforce J.); [1966] R.P.C. 423 (Buckley J.).
[29] [1981] F.S.R. 309, CA.
[30] (1955) 72 R.P.C. 278 (Harman J.).
[31] [1999] 4 All E.R. 277; [2000] F.S.R. 311 (Lawrence Collins Q.C., Deputy Judge).
[32] [1961] R.P.C. 242 (Wilberforce J.).

G. DISTINCTIVENESS OF GET-UP

Introduction

The term "get-up" is normally used in passing-off to mean the whole visible **8–112**
external appearance of goods in the form in which they are likely to be seen
by the public before purchase.[33] If the goods are sold in packages, then their
get-up means the appearance of the pack taken as a whole. If they are sold
or displayed unpackaged, then the get-up relied on can only be that inherent
in the goods themselves. Intermediate cases exist where both the goods
themselves and their packaging contribute to what the customer sees: for
instance where the goods are mounted on cards,[34] or in transparent plastic,[35]
or are liquids in bottles. However, there can be few cases, if any, in which
passing-off results from the adoption by the defendant of so-called "get-up"
which is only apparent to the consumer after purchase of the defendants'
goods.[36] There are also cases where the get-up said to be distinctive is that of
advertisements, literature,[37] premises or almost anything used in the conduct
of the claimant's business.

Get-up is not only of importance when it is of itself distinctive of the
claimant. Similarity in general appearance (even if the appearance does not
legally qualify as get-up) may enable dishonest traders to substitute the
defendant's product when asked for that of the claimant, even if the claimant's get-up is not distinctive on its own. Whether the defendant is liable
for this depends on intention and knowledge.[38] Similarity or dissimilarity of
get-up may also influence the result of a case based mainly on brand names
or other marks if the likelihood of deception is finely balanced, or if the
similarities constitute a "badge of fraud" indicating an intention to deceive.

The difficulty confronting the claimant in all actions for passing-off based
on get-up is that it is unusual for one trader's goods to be distinguished from
those of his competitors exclusively, or even primarily, by their get-up.
Normally a brand name or other mark is chosen and given prominence and
it is this on which consumers are expected and encouraged to rely.[39] To
make out a case based solely on similarities of get-up the claimant must

---

[33] This passage was approved by the Supreme Court of Canada in *Ciba-Geigy Canada Ltd v
Apotex Inc* (1992) 95 D.L.R. (4th) 385; 44 C.P.R. (3d) 289; 24 I.P.R. 652 (Supreme Court of
Canada).

[34] As in *Parker & Smith v Satchwell & Co Ltd* (1901) 18 R.P.C. 299. Compare *De Long Hook
& Eye Co v Newey Bros Ltd* (1911) 29 R.P.C. 49 where the get-up of the cards was very simple
and the defendants' were adequately distinguished.

[35] As in *New Way Packaged Products Ltd v Lucking (S) Ltd* [1960] R.P.C. 147; compare
Politechnika Ipari Szovertkezet v Dallas Print Transfers [1982] F.S.R. 529.

[36] *Bostik Ltd v Sellotape GB Ltd* [1994] R.P.C. 556.

[37] Copying literature contributed to passing-off in *Masson, Seeley & Co Ltd v Embossotype
Manufacturing Co* (1924) 41 R.P.C. 160, but not in *Terrapin Ltd v Ariston Buildings Ltd* [1964]
F.S.R. 218, CA where the only similarities arose from the fact that the defendants had legiti-
mately imitated the appearance of the plaintiffs' goods.

[38] *Cadbury Ltd v Ulmer GmbH* [1988] F.S.R. 385.

[39] *Edge (William) & Sons Ltd v William Niccolls & Sons Ltd* [1911] A.C. 693; 28 R.P.C. 582,
HL, is a rare exception.

show that deception is likely notwithstanding the absence of his own brand name on the defendant's goods and the likely presence there of the defendant's brand name and perhaps other distinguishing matter.[40] Not surprisingly, the cases in which passing-off has been found have predominantly been ones of deliberate deception.

8–113   Although passing-off uses the single term "get-up" for the two cases, there is a fundamental difference between the get-up of packaging and get-up which involves the appearance of the goods themselves. It is not passing-off to copy, even precisely, the construction or appearance of goods if what is copied is valued by the customer for practical, functional or aesthetic reasons rather than as an indication of origin. This is sometimes expressed by saying that such aspects do not form part of the get-up at all.[41] Even if the appearance of the goods is completely arbitrary in some respect, it is still particularly difficult for the claimant to establish that a feature inherent in the goods themselves has trade mark significance.[42]

The decision of the House of Lords in the *Jif Lemon* case, *Reckitt & Colman v Borden*[43] has not affected this crucial distinction in get-up cases, which is between features appreciated for their own sakes and those which serve as an indication of source, quality or whatever else may be valued in its own right. As a practical matter, it is relatively easy to show that an arbitrary feature of packaging is distinctive, and relatively hard to show the same for a feature embodied in the article itself. Lord Oliver deliberately did not address the question of whether features forming part of the article itself could ever be protected, because he dismissed the argument that the items traded in were plastic lemons. The parties sold lemon juice, and the get-up of the plaintiffs' containers concurrently signified the nature of the contents and their source. Lord Jauncey, *obiter*, was prepared to say that features embodied in the shape or configuration of an article could be the subject of a passing-off action, provided they were distinctive in the legal sense.

History and importance of get-up

8–114   The earliest reported cases of passing-off include examples of what would now be called counterfeiting in which the plaintiff's goods were copied in every respect which might have attracted the attention of the purchaser.[44] Thereafter, get-up seem to have played no more than a subordinate role in

---

[40] Compare the *Jif Lemon* case, *Reckitt & Colman v Borden* [1990] 1 W.L.R. 491; [1990] 1 All E.R. 873; [1990] R.P.C. 340, HL, where the defendants' brand name *ReaLemon* was likely to be taken as merely descriptive of the contents.

[41] *per* Fletcher Moulton L.J. in *Williams (JB) Co v H. Bronnley & Co Ltd* (1909) 26 R.P.C. 765, CA.

[42] *Dunhill v Bartlett & Bickley* (1922) 39 R.P.C. 426 is a rare example, but although the feature in question (a white spot on the stem of the plaintiff's pipes) was arbitrary and undoubtedly distinctive, the defendant did not infringe by using a red spot.

[43] Above.

[44] *Blofeld v Payne* (1833) 110 E.R. 509.

passing-off until the late nineteenth century.[45] The leading cases, which remain authoritative to this day, were decided in the last decade of the nineteenth century and the first of the twentieth.[46]

A number of trends since that time have affected the practical importance of get-up in actions for passing-off. The possibilities open to a trader in adopting a get-up have increased enormously. In the early to mid nineteenth century, packaging, if any was used at all, tended to be of the simplest kind. There was very little practical choice as to material or even colour. Wrappers could be printed, but even as late as the 1900s the choice of colour was dictated by the limited number of permanent dyes.[47] Trade in the nineteenth century was very fragmented. Many businesses were local and many more brands, and variations of get-up, seem to have been in use then than now. Much of the population had a low standard of literacy. Finally, retail trade was carried on differently to the present day. There were no supermarkets, customers asked for goods by name rather than picking them from the shelves, and it was common for goods to be collected by servants as well as children.

These trends should be taken into account, and they are not exclusively to the advantage of either claimants or defendants. On the one hand, it is now much easier for each trader in the market to create a get-up well adapted to distinguish his own goods without undue cost or inconvenience.[48] On the other hand, the old test of whether some aspect of get-up is "common to the trade" becomes unworkable in an oligopolistic market, and is no guide to whether a particular feature, though unique in fact, is distinctive of the claimant. The latter factors have changed the relative importance of get-up and brand names. It can no longer as readily be said that no amount of distinguishing get-up can undo the effect of identity of names, but get-up itself probably deserves to be taken more seriously as an indication of origin and perhaps sometimes as of comparable importance to the brand. The illiteracy of purchasers, it is to be hoped, is now only relevant in some less developed jurisdictions, or if the goods are sold to children or exported. **8–115**

It is arguable that there has been a preconception that consumers rely so strongly on verbal, rather than visual marks, that faced with a conflict between the two they will ignore all but the strongest similarities in get-up. If such a preconception has existed, the decision of the House of Lords in *Reckitt & Colman v Borden*[49] should have gone some way to disposing of it.

---

[45] The first major case to turn on get-up seems to have been *Lever v Goodwin* [1887] 36 Ch.D. 1; 4 R.P.C. 492, CA. The plaintiff sued on the mark *Self-Washer*, but that was held to be descriptive for soap and only the get-up of the wrappers remained. The term "get-up" itself was apparently familiar to the witnesses but new to the court.

[46] In particular, *Lever Bros Ltd v Bedingfield* (1898) 16 R.P.C. 3, CA; *Payton & Co v Snelling, Lampard & Co* [1901] A.C. 308; 17 R.P.C. 628, HL; *Schweppes Ltd v Gibbens* (1905) 22 R.P.C. 601, HL; *Williams (JB) Co v H Bronnley & Co Ltd* (1909) 26 R.P.C. 765, CA, and *Edge (William) & Sons Ltd v William Niccolls & Sons Ltd* [1911] A.C. 693; 28 R.P.C. 582, HL.

[47] See *Williams (JB) Co v H Bronnley & Co Ltd* (1909) 26 R.P.C. 765, CA, accounting for the frequency with which one comes across brown and maroon in get-up cases around that time.

[48] Including the claimant, who has less excuse for choosing get-up of low inherent distinctiveness.

[49] Above.

All the judges in that case were persuaded, despite sometimes strong first impressions to the contrary, that shoppers purchased the *Jif* brand of lemon juice specifically in reliance on the get-up of the container and that they would disregard a recognisably different label without the word *Jif* on it.

The *Jif Lemon* case: *Reckitt & Colman v Borden*

8–116 The leading modern case on get-up is now the decision of the House of Lords in *Reckitt & Colman v Borden*.[50] The background to the litigation was that since 1956 the plaintiffs' *Jif* had been the only brand of lemon juice on the United Kingdom market which was packaged in a plastic squeeze pack imitating a real lemon in size, shape and colour. The defendants proposed to introduce lemon juice packed in one of three versions of a similar pack, which were distinguished mainly by having a collar with the name *ReaLemon* around the neck. The *Jif* container also had a collar, which was leaf-shaped and bore the name *Jif*.

The trial judge's findings of fact were that a careful shopper would have no difficulty in concluding from reading the respective labels that none of the three Borden lemons was a *Jif* lemon; that but many housewives would purchase the Borden lemons in the belief they were buying *Jif. Jif* was and had been the only lemon-sized squeeze pack of lemon juice on the market. *Jif* as a brand name, that is to say as a specific make of lemon juice, was well known and shoppers were well aware of other brands. Shoppers wishing to purchase *Jif* crucially relied on the lemon shape itself and ignored the label. The label would be removed and discarded after purchase so that when a replacement was eventually required the unadorned lemon would be the point of reference. In conclusion all three Borden lemons would cause confusion with *Jif* and none of the labels would sufficiently dispel it.

8–117 The arguments for the defendants were that the plaintiffs could have no monopoly in plastic lemons as such; that such confusion as existed was the excusable result of breaking the plaintiffs' former monopoly in plastic lemons; and that the appearance of the plaintiffs' containers was descriptive and could not denote the source of the containers or their contents. The defendants' first argument was dismissed on the ground that the parties were dealing in lemon juice, not plastic lemons as such, and the so-called "monopoly assumption" argument fell with it. The third argument was rejected on the facts: even get-up which was *prima facie* descriptive could acquire secondary meaning in much the same way as a descriptive word. In the result the House of Lords upheld the injunction and dismissed the defendants' appeal.

> "I find it, however, unnecessary to pursue the question [whether shape or configuration of the very object sold can be distinctive] further because there is, to my mind, a fallacy in the argument which begins by identifying the contents with the container and is summarised in the central proposition that 'you cannot claim a monopoly in selling plastic lemons'. Well,

---

[50] [1990] 1 W.L.R. 491; [1990] 1 All E.R. 873; [1990] R.P.C. 340, HL.

of course you cannot any more than you can claim a monopoly in the sale of dimpled bottles. The deception alleged lies not in the sale of the plastic lemons or the dimpled bottles, but in the sale of the lemon juice or whisky as the case may be, in the containers so fashioned as to suggest that the juice or the whisky emanates from the source with which the containers of those particular configurations have become associated in the public mind. ... It is, no doubt, true that the plastic lemon shaped container serves, as indeed does a bottle of any design, a functional purpose in the sale of lemon juice. Apart from being a container *simpliciter*, it is a convenient size; it is capable of convenient use by squeezing; and it is so designed as conveniently to suggest the nature of its contents without the necessity for further labelling or other identification. But those purposes are capable of being and indeed are served by a variety of distinctive containers of configurations other than those of a lemon-sized lemon. Neither the appellants nor the respondents are in the business of selling plastic lemons. Both are makers and vendors of lemon juice and the only question is whether the respondents ... can legitimately complain of the sale by the appellants of similar produce in containers of similar, though not identical, size, shape and colouring."[51]

"Common to the trade"

The issue of the distinctiveness of those elements of the claimant's get-up **8–118** taken by the defendant has often been approached by way of asking whether they are "common to the trade". The expression is normally used to mean that the elements of the get-up are in common use, but it has sometimes carried the overtone that those elements are somehow inherently *res communis*, so as to be incapable of appropriation by any one trader. The latter meaning was expressly rejected by the House of Lords in *Reckitt & Colman v Borden*,[52] and get-up can only be said to be common to the trade if it is not in fact distinctive of the claimant or some other trader.

If the features of the claimant's get-up are also in use by others in the same trade then it is tempting, though not always strictly correct, to dispose of the case on that ground, since features of get-up which are in use by competitors of the claimant in general can hardly be distinctive of him. This approach may be convenient but it offers, at best, no more than a short cut to determining the real question, which is whether there has been a material misrepresentation. It is of declining usefulness as the possibility of varying get-up increases and the number of competitors in any given market falls, though supermarket own-brands are a fruitful source of comparison for some consumer goods. It is never true to say that because get-up is not "common to the trade" copying it must result in passing-off.

There are two objections to approaching the issue of passing-off by way **8–119** of asking whether the claimant's get-up is common to the trade. The first is that the get-up, or individual features of it, may not be distinctive in fact

[51] *per* Lord Oliver in *Reckitt & Colman Products Ltd v Borden Inc* [1990] 1 W.L.R. 491; [1990] 1 All E.R. 873; [1990] R.P.C. 340, HL.
[52] Above.

even though it is not "common to the trade" at all. Use of closely similar get-up by even a single major competitor is likely to disprove distinctiveness, although this hardly makes the get-up common in any normal sense. It is not even conclusive that the claimant may be the only trader to use a particular feature in his get-up, otherwise any aspect of get-up would *ipso facto* be distinctive of a claimant who had a monopoly. It is always difficult to identify precisely where the distinctiveness of a trader's get-up lies, especially in the absence of rival goods to which a comparison may be made.

The second objection is that the test has to be applied carefully if it is not to be unfair to the claimant. It is possible for a combination of features to be distinctive, even though the features individually are in common use. Moreover, distinctiveness of get-up in fact need not be compromised because that get-up or similar has been used by others on a small scale, abroad, locally, or at distant times. Get-up need not be novel to be distinctive.[53] There seems to have been a tendency, at least in pleadings, to treat examples of get-up supposedly common to the trade as if one were giving particulars of objections to a patent.

Functional or aesthetic appearance

8–120 Passing-off in its traditional form only protects get-up, as with any other kind of sign, to the extent that it is distinctive of a particular claimant. Features of an article which are valued for their own sake rather than as an indication of origin are not protected, and are best not regarded as part of the get-up at all:

> "When a member of the public purchases goods on the market believing them to be goods of *A*, it is *A*'s goods that he wants, not the name, mark or get-up, which is no more than a label or badge which signifies that the goods are A's goods. It is the reputation of the goods that matters: it is the association of the name, mark or get-up with those goods distinguishing them from other men's goods, which makes the name, mark or get-up important, serving as a vehicle of the information that the goods are the goods of the kind which had the reputation."[54]

> "The get-up of an article means a capricious addition to the article itself ... but I strongly object to look at anything, that has a value in use, as part of the get-up of the article."[55]

Get-up is therefore only protected if and to the extent that it serves as the badge of a particular trader. Put the other way round, if the customer wants goods with a particular construction or appearance primarily because he

---

[53] *White Hudson & Co Ltd v Asian Organisation Ltd* [1964] 1 W.L.R. 1466; [1965] 1 All E.R. 1040; [1965] R.P.C. 45, PC.

[54] *per* Buckley L.J. in *Bulmer (HP) Ltd v J Bollinger SA* [1978] R.P.C. 79; [1978] 2 C.M.L.R. 625, CA.

[55] *per* Fletcher Moulton L.J. in *Williams (JB) Co v H Bronnley & Co Ltd* (1909) 26 R.P.C. 765, CA.

believes such goods to be functional, practical or aesthetically pleasing then the appearance of the goods, or their get-up if it may be so called, is not being relied on to identify them as coming from a particular trade source. If so, it is hard to say that offering goods indistinguishable from those of the claimant involves any misrepresentation at all. It does not even matter if the claimant's goods are unique and the customer happens to believe or assume that all such goods came from a common source, provided his choice is made without reliance on that belief. At most, any misrepresentation (or misconception on the part of the customer) is an irrelevant one because it does not damage the claimant: the customer would not have bought the claimant's goods in preference to those of the defendant even if he had known of the difference.

In *Hodgkinson and Corby v Wards Mobility Services*[56] Jacob J. (after **8–121** considering the English authorities) commended the classic judgment of Judge Learned Hand in *Crescent Tool v Kilborn & Bishop*[57]:

"Exactly the same thought is so clearly expressed by Judge Learned Hand in *Crescent Tool v Kilborn & Bishop* (1917) 247 F. 299, a case about a copy of an adjustable wrench widely sold and trademarked 'Crescent.' He said, after finding that no adjustable wrench of precisely the same character had ever appeared upon the market:

'...all of these (*i.e.* cases where a secondary meaning has been shown) presuppose that the appearance of the article like its descriptive title in the true cases of 'secondary' meaning has become associated in the public mind with the first comer as manufacturer or source, and, if a second comer imitates the article exactly, that the public will believe his goods have come from the first, and will buy, in part, at least, because of that deception. Therefore it is apparent that it is an absolute condition to any relief whatever that the plaintiff show that the appearance of his wares has in fact come to mean that some particular person–the plaintiff may not be individually known–makes them, and the public cares who does make them, and not merely for their appearance and structure. It will not be enough only to show how pleasing they are, because all the features of beauty or utility which commend them to the public are by hypothesis already in the public domain...

The critical question of fact at the outset always is whether the public is moved in any degree to buy the article because of its source and what are the features by which it distinguishes that source. Unless the plaintiff can answer this question he can take no step forward. No degree of imitation of detail is actionable in its absence...

It is not enough to show the wrench became popular under the name 'Crescent'; the plaintiff must prove that before 1910 the public had already established the habit of buying it, not solely because they wanted that kind of wrench, but because they also wanted a *Crescent* and thought that all such wrenches were *Crescents*...'

[56] [1994] 1 W.L.R. 1564; [1995] F.S.R. 169 (Jacob J.)
[57] (1917) 247 F. 299.

I believe that exactly encapsulates what must be shown when the plaintiff is complaining, in a passing off action, about a copy of his product as such. Is the public 'moved to buy by source'?"

H. Get-up by Category

Get-up of packaging

8–122 A passing-off action based on similarities of get-up of packaging depends, like all others, on proof that the defendant has made a misrepresentation damaging to the claimant.[58] In theory, this means that the claimant must prove that his get-up is distinctive of him and that the defendant's get-up is similar enough to deceive, notwithstanding any other differences between the two sets of goods. In practice, get-up cases where there is no close copying or other evidence of an intention to deceive are often decided in the defendant's favour on the ground that such similarities as exist are insufficient to cause confusion. If so, then there is no need to consider whether the claimant's get-up as a whole is distinctive. The most that need be said is that those features of get-up which are common to the claimant and defendant are not so overwhelmingly distinctive of the claimant as to outweigh the differences. In the reported cases on get-up the issue of distinctiveness is even more difficult to disentangle from the issue of deceptive similarity than is the case for other types of mark.

8–123 What the claimant has to prove has been stated by Lindley M.R. as follows[59]:

"What is it that the plaintiffs must make out in order to entitle them to succeed in this action? They must make out that the defendant's goods are calculated to be mistaken for the plaintiff's, and, where, as in this case, the goods of the plaintiff and the goods of the defendants unquestionably resemble each other, but where the features in which they resemble each other are common to the trade, what has the plaintiff to make out? He must make out not that the defendant's are like his by reason of those features which are common to them and other people, but he must make out that the defendant's are like his by reason of something peculiar to him, and by reason of the defendant having adopted some mark, or device, or label, or something of that kind, which distinguishes the

---

[58] Cases earlier than the end of the first decade of the twentieth century are to be treated with caution. There is sometimes a tendency to treat the question almost as one of copyright infringement, with the issues being the originality of the plaintiff's get-up and whether the defendant copied. This fallacy should have been laid to rest by *Payton & Co v Snelling, Lampard & Co* [1901] A.C. 308; 17 R.P.C. 628, HL and *Williams (JB) Co v H Bronnley & Co Ltd* (1909) 26 R.P.C. 765, CA, but it still occasionally recurs.

[59] *per* Lindley M.R. in *Payton & Co v Snelling, Lampard & Co* (1899) 17 R.P.C. 48 affirmed [1901] A.C. 308; 17 R.P.C. 628.

plaintiff's from other goods which have, like his, the features common to the trade."

It is not sufficient for the claimant to show that he has adopted some novel, original and striking features for his get-up and that the defendant has copied them or innocently adopted similar features. That is to understand the term "distinctive" as if it meant the same as eye-catching.[60] The test for distinctiveness is the function the get-up actually serves, rather than how well it is adapted to serve it. The colour grey is properly said to be distinctive if it serves to identify the goods of one particular manufacturer, although no colour could be said to be less distinctive in the popular sense. Despite some statements apparently to the contrary,[61] it is not necessary for the get-up relied on to have been novel when it was adopted if it is distinctive in fact, although it is easier to prove distinctiveness for get-up which was totally new.[62] Conversely, if the get-up does not distinguish the claimant's goods from those of actual or prospective rivals then however remarkable it may be it is not distinctive in the legal sense.

"Too often it is supposed that the trial of that issue [whether the get-up is calculated to deceive] is the same thing as trying another question, namely, whether the plaintiff has not been the first person to adopt a novel get-up, and it seems to be supposed by some that, if the plaintiff establishes in a case like this, that he is the first person to adopt what is called a new get-up or a novel get-up, then the defendant could be restrained if the defendant being in the same trade adopts that novel get-up. Of course the two questions are really quite-distinct. A trader by adopting a novel get-up does not thereby acquire a monopoly in that get-up. Of course it may well be that if a plaintiff has adopted a novel get-up for his goods that fact has to be borne in mind in considering, if the defendant adopts it, whether or not what the defendant is doing is calculated to deceive. It is a notion that runs through the minds of a great many persons in trades that, if a trader once adopts a novel get-up, he acquires some proprietary right in that get-up. Of course he does not do anything of the kind."[63]

Nor is it sufficient for the claimant to show that the defendant's goods are easily confused with his when they are placed side by side, still less when the doctrine of imperfect recollection is relied on. He must show that the confusion arises from those features of the get-up which are distinctive of him,

---

[60] *New Way Packaged Products Ltd v Lucking (S.) Ltd* [1960] R.P.C. 147 is open to criticism on this point.

[61] Notably Cozens-Hardy M.R. in *Williams (JB) Co v H Bronnley & Co Ltd* (1909) 26 R.P.C. 765, CA.

[62] *White Hudson & Co Ltd v Asian Organisation Ltd* [1964] 1 W.L.R. 1466; [1965] 1 All E.R. 1040; [1965] R.P.C. 45, PC.

[63] *per* Romer L.J. in *Payton & Co v Snelling, Lampard & Co* (1899) 17 R.P.C. 48, CA affirmed [1901] A.C. 308; 17 R.P.C. 628, HL.

at least in combination, and features which are common to the trade or otherwise not distinctive are to be disregarded:

> "[T]he mere fact that the produce of the appellants and that of the respondents may be confused by members of the public is not of itself sufficient. There is no 'property' in the accepted sense of the word in a get-up."[64]

8–124   Finally, the claimant cannot pick and choose those elements of his get-up which find counterparts in the defendant's get-up and rely on those alone. It is tempting for the claimant to suggest that the only features of his get-up which matter are those which are also to be found in the defendant's get-up, or to describe the distinctiveness of his get-up in vague terms which are wide enough to embrace that of both parties. The get-up of the claimant's goods as a whole has to be compared to that of the defendant's as a whole, including features which are not to be found in the claimant's get-up. Weight also has to be given to differences in brand names or other marks.

In *Schweppes v Gibbens* the plaintiffs and the defendant both marked their soda water bottles with a brown label with a red disc in the centre. These features, individually and in combination, were alleged to be common to the trade but the House of Lords did not find it necessary to decide that point. The labels bore the respective names *Schweppes* and *Gibbens*. This, and the fact that the plaintiffs' bottle had two labels and the defendant's only one meant there was no likelihood of deception.

> "It appears to me that the real answer to the appellants' case is this–that they invite your Lordships to look, not at the whole get-up, but at that part of the get-up which suits their case. The resemblances here are obvious enough, but, unfortunately for the appellants, so are the differences. The differences are not concealed; they are quite as conspicuous as the resemblances. If you look at the whole get-up, and not only at that part of it in which the resemblances are to be found, the whole get-up does not deceive."[65]

Own brands and look-alikes

8–125 An increasing number of cases deal with products which have had their get-up, and sometimes also their names, artfully designed to resemble the market leader, or an innovator, sufficiently closely to identify themselves as alternatives or close competitors, but not necessarily so closely as to deceive or cause confusion in sense of being effectively indistinguishable, whether when placed side-by-side, or after the application of the doctrines of imperfect recollection and the "idea of the mark". The legal analysis for this situation is deceptively simple: there is passing-off in the traditional sense if and only if the defendant's get-up in its totality (allowing for the impact of

---

[64] *per* Lord Oliver in *Reckitt & Colman v Borden* [1990] 1 W.L.R. 491; [1990] 1 All E.R. 873; [1990] R.P.C. 340, HL.
[65] *per* Lord Lindley in *Schweppes Ltd v Gibbens* (1905) 22 R.P.C. 601, HL.

any brand name or other word marks) is such as to give the impression to a substantial number of purchasers or ultimate consumers that the defendant's product has the same trade origin as the claimant's, or is something for which the claimant has made himself responsible. Problems of exposition and analysis arise from the difficulty of describing and comparing get-up in print, but above all from the fact that the effect of the crucial first visual impression is all too easily lost when one attempts to recreate or analyse it in words:

"It may indeed be that the eye's perception is insusceptible of clear statement in words. ... '[T]he eye, like the heart according to Pascal, has its reasons that reason does not know.' "[66]

It is probably still true to say that very few traders deliberately use get-up as the sole or primary means of identification of their goods. That is given to verbal marks, and especially brand names. However, what matters is how customers distinguish competing goods in fact. It is quite normal for customers selecting goods from supermarket shelves to go by some aspect of the overall appearance as much as by the name. What is more difficult is to identify the precise visual cues on which the customer relies. Despite the fact that many of the brands of any particular commodity often bear an overall resemblance to one another, the eye seems to be able to distinguish them and select one without any conscious reference to the brand names as such. Unfortunately, there has been little objective analysis of this effect in the reported cases, and self-serving assertions of what is or is not distinctive do not always help.[67]

One of relatively few cases to go to trial is *United Biscuits v Asda*.[68] The **8–126** plaintiffs' *Penguin* brand had been a market leader in chocolate-coated sandwich biscuits for several decades. The precise get-up of the Penguin bar had changed from time to time (with the incidental consequence that there was no granted registered trade mark protection for the current get-up) but the name and essential features of the get-up had remained: the wrapper was predominantly red, with a horizontal yellow band, the word PENGUIN in black or dark blue capital letters, at least one picture of a penguin, and the slogan "P ... P ... Pick up a Penguin". The supermarket chain Asda, like all its major competitors, sold their own brand of biscuits in competition with Penguin. Initially this was a product named *Take a Break* with no allusions to the Penguin get-up, but in 1995 Asda decided to replace the latter with a "brand beater" matching the design "cues" of *Penguin*.

---

[66] *per* Burchett J. in *Koninklijke Philips Electronics NV v Remington Consumer Products Australia Pty Ltd* [2000] F.C.A. 876; 48 I.P.R. 257; quoting Kitto J. in *Wolanski's Registered Design* (1953) 88 C.L.R. 278 and referring to Pascal, *Pensées* (1670) Section IV, number 277. The context was infringement of a registered design, but the comment is equally apposite to passing-off.

[67] The most interesting treatment in terms of "gestalt" is probably that in *Sydneywide Distributors Pty Ltd v Red Bull Australia Pty Ltd* [2002] FCAFC 157; 55 I.P.R. 354.

[68] [1997] R.P.C. 513 (Robert Walker J.).

"These passages [from cross-examination] are a reflection of a general theme in the evidence of Mr. Blundell and Mr. McLeod, amounting to a frank recognition that a redesigning and relaunching the Asda competitor to Penguin they were entitled (and even, by their own lights, bound) to 'match' Penguin, to 'position themselves' against Penguin or to establish themselves as the competitor to Penguin. There is a good deal of authority for the proposition that long use of a particularly distinctive getup does (without creating a monopoly) place on a new competitor (minded to use a similar get-up) a special obligation to avoid confusion: see for instance what was said by Lord Jauncey in the *Jif Lemon* case, *Reckitt & Colman Products Ltd v Borden Inc.* [1990] 1 W.L.R. 491 at page 515 F-G. The evidence of Asda's senior employees suggested a different approach, that is that the brand leader is to some extent 'fair game' to be matched, parodied or challenged–so long as it is not actually copied. I shall have to come back to that point in discussing the law."[69]

The first draft artwork was too obviously copied from Penguin to be acceptable, and the product as launched had predominantly red packaging (with no yellow band), the word PUFFIN in black capitals, and a cartoon picture of a puffin. The word ASDA was so small as to be barely noticeable. Summarising the initial effect of these differences and similarities, Robert Walker J. observed:

"I am of the clear view that with the very important exception of the name and the bird picture, there is nothing in the Puffin get-up that is deceptively similar to Penguin. With the name and the bird picture I have no such clear conviction. The cartoon puffin (whose multicoloured beak is reproduced, but not very clearly) could, I am inclined to think, be mistaken for a cartoon penguin. The word PUFFIN is not very different from PENGUIN. Forty per cent of Penguins are eaten by children, and children often help with the shopping even though they do not pay for it.

Had the Asda product been called for example BISON (to take another name from the original list of possibilities) with a cartoon picture of a brown woolly bison on the packaging, these proceedings could not possibly succeed. Almost certainly they would never have been brought. But the name PUFFIN and the prominent picture of an upright dark-coloured bird with a white front gives me the expectation, as a matter of first impression, that a substantial part of the public who shop in supermarkets would see an association between the Asda product and McVities Penguin. Whether that association would be sufficient to amount to deception is a matter that I shall have to come back to."

8–127   And after a review of the evidence he concluded:

"To succeed in passing off, United Biscuits must establish the 'classic trinity' of reputation (or goodwill), deception and damage. Goodwill is

[69] *per* Robert Walker J.

admitted on the pleadings, and is in any case amply established by the evidence ...

Judicial first impression is of some importance, especially where the goods in question are familiar and inexpensive ... My impression of the Puffin packaging (in all four colours or varieties) is that it would cause a substantial number of members of the public to suppose that there was a connection between the Puffin biscuit and the Penguin biscuit. Despite the evidence of isolated mistakes, I do not consider that a substantial number would believe that the Asda Puffin is the McVities Penguin. But many would believe that the two must be made by the same manufacturer.

That judicial first impression was largely confirmed by the oral evidence. Witnesses repeatedly referred to the dark seabird, the black lettering and the similarity of names as the features which together induced that belief. One or two came close to saying that the Puffin biscuit must be produced by the manufacturer of the Penguin, because otherwise it would not be allowed (there is here some hint of a self-fulfilling prophecy, and this point must not be given any more weight than it merits)."

In the result, liability for passing off was established.

The relevance of copying

Although the claimant's case is greatly strengthened by proof of an intention **8–128** on the defendant's part to deceive, it should be remembered that any trader is free to copy a rival's goods in respects which are not distinctive. In *Payton v Snelling Lampard*,[70] *King v Gillard*[71] and *Williams v Bronnley*[72] there was documentary evidence that the defendants had designed some aspects of their own packaging with reference to that of the plaintiffs, but this did not weigh against them. In *Tavener Rutledge v Specters*[73] a clear case of copyright infringement translated into a weak one of passing-off; and in *Scott v Nice-Pak*[74] a memorandum of the defendants' proposing a "knockoff that is as close as possible to the Scott BABY FRESH WIPES product" was not enough to swing the case in the plaintiffs' favour when the products were compared, especially as there was a history of co-existence without confusion in another market.

On the other hand, in *United Biscuits v Asda*[75] the defendants' admitted **8–129** and undeniable intention of sailing as close to the wind as they dared was one of a number of factors which tipped a finely balanced case in favour of the plaintiffs. Asda had originally issued a design brief which resulted in a very close match of the plaintiffs' *Penguin* get-up, and though this had subsequently been modified, several resemblances, including the name *Puffin*, remained:

[70] [1901] A.C. 308; 17 R.P.C. 628, HL.
[71] [1905] 2 Ch. 7; 22 R.P.C. 327, CA.
[72] (1909) 26 R.P.C. 765, CA.
[73] [1959] R.P.C. 355, CA.
[74] [1989] 1 F.S.R. 100, CA.
[75] [1997] R.P.C. 513 (Robert Walker J.).

"In the *Harrods* case[76] Millett L.J. said at page 706,

'Deception is the gist of the tort of passing off, but it is not necessary for a plaintiff to establish that the defendant consciously intended to deceive the public if that is the probable result of his conduct. Nevertheless, the question why the defendant chose to adopt a particular name or get up is always highly relevant. It is 'a question which falls to be asked and answered': see *Sodastream Ltd v Thorn Cascade Co Ltd* [1982] R.P.C. 459 at page 466 per Kerr L.J. If it is shown that the defendant deliberately sought to take the benefit of the plaintiff's goodwill for himself, the court will not 'be astute to say that he cannot succeed in doing that which he is straining every nerve to do': see *Slazenger & Sons v Feltham & Co* (1889) 6 R.P.C. 531 at page 538 per Lindley L.J.'

Mr. Pollock accepted this as a matter of principle but said that it could have no application to this case. He stressed that Mr. Blundell had readily accepted that the original artwork was 'too close' to the Penguin get-up and that it had been changed in order to avoid confusion, which the defendant (as well as the plaintiff) wanted to avoid. The evidence did not explore fully how the original artwork came to be so obviously 'too close'; apart from Mr. Branckston's design brief, there were very few extant documents (and none as to the reasons for adoption of the name Puffin). It is certainly true that changes were made in the first design so as to lessen the risk (initially more or less a certainty) of confusion. But it seems to me likely that Mr. McLeod, Mr. Blundell and their subordinates and independent designers were, under advice, seeking to make only such changes as were needed in order to avoid what they judged to be an unacceptable risk of being attacked for copying, while maintaining Puffin's position as an obvious competitor and parody, and (they hoped) a 'brand beater'. I cannot escape the conclusion that, while aiming to avoid what the law would characterise as deception, they were taking a conscious decision to live dangerously. That is not in my judgment something that the court is bound to disregard."[77]

And in the result:

"I conclude that the Puffin packaging and get-up was, in the material sense, deceptively similar to those of the penguin. In reaching this conclusion I do not find that it was intended to be deceptively similar; I accept the evidence of Mr. McLeod and Mr. Blundell that they intended to avoid deception. But plainly they had that risk in mind, and in my judgment they miscalculated the degree of 'challenge' or 'matching' or 'parody' that was tolerable without the product being actually deceptive (in the material sense)."

[76] *Harrods Ltd v Harrodian School Ltd* [1996] R.P.C. 697, CA.
[77] *per* Robert Walker J., above.

676

To the same effect there is the decision of the Federal Court of Australia **8–130** in *Sydneywide Distributors v Red Bull Australia*[78]:

"Without wishing to labour the point unduly, we again point out that where a trader, having knowledge of a particular market, borrows aspects of a competitor's get-up, it is a reasonable inference that he or she believes that there will be a market benefit in so doing. Often, the obvious benefit will be the attraction of custom which would otherwise have gone to the competitor. It is an available inference from those propositions that the trader, with knowledge of the market, considered that such borrowing was 'fitted for the purpose and therefore likely to deceive or confuse ...'. Of course, the trader may explain his or her conduct in such a way as to undermine the availability of that inference..."

Get-up of packaging: examples

Whereas cases on the appearance or get-up of goods raise an issue of **8–131** principle, those on the get-up of packaging tend to turn primarily on the facts of each case, and do not readily lend themselves to further analysis, or even a concise written summary. Evidence from actual consumers is important and may be determinative, and much depends on visual appreciation of the get-up used by the claimant, the defendant and others in the market. Cases in which the defendant was successful predominate, often because get-up is subordinated to word marks. Several cases in which the claimant prevailed turned on the illiteracy of purchasers, which is still a factor in some jurisdictions. The other factor capable of tilting the balance towards the claimant is *mala fides*, but it is notable that even intrinsic, or extrinsic evidence of copying is far from conclusive.

As the Supreme Court of Appeal of South Africa has commented[79]:

"A record of 720 pages and heads of argument totalling 57 pages have been placed before us in order to allow us to decide whether the wrapping of its coconut biscuits used by one manufacturer passes itself off as the wrapping of another manufacturer of similar biscuits. I acknowledge, of course, that an applicant in a passing-off case must prove his reputation and that may require a considerable body of evidence, that it behoves him to prove instances of actual deception or confusion if such evidence may be found ..., and that the applicant sought to prove fraudulent intent, as it was entitled to do. But for the rest the case was essentially one of first impression of the two wrappers."

Get-up protected

In *Blofeld v Payne*[80] the plaintiff alleged that the defendant sold hones in **8–132**

---

[78] [2002] FCAFC 157; 55 I.P.R. 354 *per* Weinberg and Dowsett JJ.
[79] *Blue Lion Manufacturing (Pty) Ltd v National Brands Ltd* 2001 (3) SA 885 (SCA), *per* Schultz J.A.
[80] (1833) 110 E.R. 509.

envelopes resembling his. Apparently, the defendant had obtained some of the plaintiff's wrappers and put his own hones in them. The jury awarded nominal damages and an appeal by the defendant was dismissed. In *Lever v Goodwin*[81] the defendant was restrained from using wrappers for soap which imitated the material, layout and print of the plaintiff. The wording differed, but many purchasers would have been illiterate. Stirling J. granted an injunction against labels covering tins of mustard in *Coleman v Farrow*.[82] In *Parker & Smith v Satchwell*[83] the plaintiffs sold a novel (patented) hair comb mounted on a showcard. The defendants produced an identical comb mounted on a card which had clearly been copied in general layout and many details. The Court of Appeal granted an injunction.[84] The get-up of cycle repair kits was copied almost precisely in *County Chemical Co v Frankenberg*.[85] The defendant in *Frankau v Pflueger*[86] was restrained from almost precise copying of the plaintiff's boxes, his unsuccessful defence being that as licensor of a patent he had joint rights in it.

Get-up of bottles contributed to deception in *PC Products v Dalton*,[87] but the mark *1001* was also copied and was of more significance. In *Travener Rutledge v Specters*[88] there was passing-off by imitation of the plaintiffs' sweet tins.[89] Most of the tin was covered with pictures of sweets, the arrangement of which had been copied precisely. The defendants' background was purple rather than black; and although the central medallion was not the same shape it had many similarities in wording, colour and typeface. Even so, Lord Evershed M.R. had great difficulty in concluding that there was passing-off, because of the weakness of the evidence that the plaintiffs' tin was distinctive in the American market.[90] A blister pack was said to be distinctive in *New Way Packaged Products v Lucking*.[91] In *White Hudson v Asian Organisation*[92] red and orange cellophane wrappers for cough sweets were distinctive in Singapore, native customers being unable to read the brand name *Hacks* and calling them *Red Paper Cough Sweets*. Because of this, the name *Pecto* was inadequate to distinguish the defendants' goods. Labels contributing to the general get-up of bottles for flavourings were distinctive in the New Zealand case of *Hensells v Baillie*.[93] In *Coombe International v Scholl*[94] similarities in the get-up of the parties' boxes

---

[81] [1887] 36 Ch.D. 1; 4 R.P.C. 492, CA. The first major get-up case.
[82] (1897) 15 R.P.C. 198 (Stirling J.).
[83] (1900) 17 R.P.C. 713, CA.
[84] Compare *De Long Hook & Eye Co v Newey Bros Ltd* (1911) 29 R.P.C. 49 (Warrington J.) where the get-up of the plaintiffs' cards was very simple and the action was dismissed.
[85] (1904) 21 R.P.C. 722 (Lord Alverstone L.C.J.).
[86] (1910) 28 R.P.C. 130 (Eve J.).
[87] [1957] R.P.C. 199 (Lord Hill Watson, Court of Session).
[88] [1959] R.P.C. 355, CA.
[89] There was also copyright infringement.
[90] This was a case of "instruments of deception" being exported.
[91] [1960] R.P.C. 147 (Cross J.). The reasoning is dubious.
[92] [1964] 1 W.L.R. 1466; [1965] 1 All E.R. 1040; [1965] R.P.C. 45, PC.
[93] [1967] N.Z.L.R. 774 (Haslam J.). Compare *Waiwai Ltd v Grey & Menzies Ltd* [1957] N.Z.L.R. 70 and *Bar's Leaks (NZ) Ltd v Motor Specialties Ltd* [1970] N.Z.L.R. 826; [1973] R.P.C. 21 where claims based on bottles failed.
[94] [1977] F.S.R. 464; [1980] R.P.C. 1 (Fox J.).

as well as the goods themselves contributed to a misrepresentation as to quality.

In *Reckitt & Colman v Borden*[95] the House of Lords granted an injunction **8–133** against the copying of a container for lemon juice which imitated the size, shape and colour of a real lemon. In *United Biscuits v Burtons Biscuits*[96] an interlocutory injunction was refused on the balance of convenience, but it was said that the get-up of the defendants' packaging for their lemon and lime *Jaffa Cakes* might mislead shoppers into the belief that they were a brand extension of the plaintiffs, McVities There was no corresponding risk for their orange *Jaffa Cakes*. In *United Biscuits v Asda*[97] similarities in get-up between the plaintiffs' *Penguin* chocolate biscuit bars and the defendants' *Puffin* bars tipped the balance in a case in which the mark-for-sign comparison between the respective word marks had gone in the defendants' favour. In the Australian case of *Sydneywide Distributors v Red Bull Australia*[98] deliberate imitation of the predominant colours of the cans containing the plaintiffs' *Red Bull* energy drink, blue, silver and red, combined with the "strong diagonal thrust" of both designs, resulted in liability for passing off despite several differences in get-up and the use of a different name, *Live Wire*. However, the same drink in bottles was sufficiently distinct.

In the South African case of *Blue Lion v National Brands*[99] the defendants (appellants) were held to have deliberately adopted packaging for their *Tea Lovers* biscuits which was confusingly similar to the get-up of the plaintiffs' *Tennis* biscuits. Both packages had a lustrous white background, a small picture of a baker in the top right hand corner, and a representation of a scattering of biscuits. The word marks *Tennis* and *Tea Lovers* were both in red, edged with gold, and the lettering was similar. Less prominent text was also imitated in layout, style and colour. Having regard to the whole of the get-up, including the colours, arrangement of matter, and lettering, there was an immediate and striking similarity. There was also evidence of actual confusion, it was an obvious inference that the defendants had set out to copy, and they had refused to disclose or adequately explain the design brief for the packaging. The different word marks were inadequate to distinguish in the circumstances, and were even a further example of sailing too close to the wind.

Get-up not protected

In contrast to *Lever v Goodwin*[1] the same plaintiff was unsuccessful in the **8–134** Court of Appeal in *Lever Bros v Bedingfield*.[2] The defendants had undoubtedly taken the plaintiffs' wrapper as the starting point for the design

[95] [1990] 1 All E.R. 865; [1990] R.P.C. 340, HL.
[96] [1992] F.S.R. 14 (Vinelott J.).
[97] [1997] R.P.C. 513 (Robert Walker J.), above.
[98] [2002] FCAFC 157; 55 I.P.R. 354.
[99] 2001 (3) SA 885 (SCA).
[1] [1887] 36 Ch.D. 1; 4 R.P.C. 492, CA.
[2] (1898) 16 R.P.C. 3, CA.

of their own, and some features remained, but taken as a whole the get-up would not deceive. It was the differences rather than the similarities which caught the eye. A previous wrapper, abandoned before action, would have been too close. In *Clark v Sharp*[3] the similarity between the parties' packets of lemonade powder was that both used gold lettering on a white background, although this had been unique to the plaintiffs. In *Payton v Snelling Lampard*[4] and *Payton v Titus Ward*[5] the colour and other aspects of the get-up of the plaintiffs' coffee tins were claimed to be distinctive but the only resemblances were in matters common to the trade and injunctions were refused. The defendants' tins were easily distinguishable. The get-up of the defendants' wine bottles and their paper wrappers were not calculated to deceive in *Coleman v Stephen Smith*.[6]

A narrow red band round cigars was not distinctive in *Imperial Tobacco Co v Purnell*.[7] That the plaintiffs had used such a band more than any other manufacturer and the public sometimes asked for "narrow red band" cigars (instead of for the brand, *Marcella*), was not enough. Other traders had used a similar band and the plaintiffs themselves emphasised the brand name. Get-up of the parties' soda water bottles was too different to cause deception in *Schweppes v Gibbens*.[8] The tins and packets used for the plaintiffs' dried soups were not protected against a degree of admitted imitation in *King v Gillard*.[9] There was also evidence of copying in *Williams v Bronnley*,[10] but the relevant aspects of the get-up of the plaintiffs' containers for shaving sticks were common to the trade. In *Burford v Mowling*[11] the High Court of Australia held that the defendants were entitled to copy the size, shape, material and colour of the boxes in which the plaintiffs sold soap, there being sufficient differences in name. Hooks and eyes were mounted on cards in *De Long Hook & Eye Co v Newey Bros*,[12] but the get-up of the plaintiffs' cards was very simple, the defendants had not copied, and the action was dismissed. In *Perry v Hessin*[13] the plaintiffs argued that their pens and the boxes they were sold in had been copied but failed on both counts.

8–135   In *Smith's Potato Crisps v Paige's Potato Crisps*[14] the bags for the parties' potato crisps were fairly similar except for the parties' names, but were different enough for the Court of Appeal to dismiss an appeal by the plaintiffs. Harman J. refused an injunction in *Saper v Specters*[15] where the shared aspect of the get-up was that both parties used striped boxes for their sweets. There would have been passing-off by similar get-up for plant

---

[3] (1898) 15 R.P.C. 141 (Byrne J.).
[4] [1901] A.C. 308; 17 R.P.C. 628, HL.
[5] (1899) 17 R.P.C. 58, CA.
[6] (1911) 29 R.P.C. 81, CA.
[7] (1904) 21 R.P.C. 598, CA.
[8] (1905) 22 R.P.C. 601, HL.
[9] [1905] 2 Ch. 7; 22 R.P.C. 327, CA.
[10] (1909) 26 R.P.C. 765, CA.
[11] (1908) 8 C.L.R. 212 (High Court of Australia).
[12] (1911) 29 R.P.C. 49 (Warrington J.).
[13] (1912) 29 R.P.C. 509, CA.
[14] (1928) 45 R.P.C. 132, CA.
[15] (1953) 70 R.P.C. 173 (Harman J.).

growing bags in *Fisons v Godwin*[16] but for the fact that the brand names were dissimilar. A domed top for an aerosol was not distinctive in *Adcock-Ingram Products v Beecham*[17] and other differences removed any remaining danger of confusion. Tubs for domestic filler were not too similar in *Tetrosyl v Silver Paint & Lacquer Co*[18] In *Imperial Group v Philip Morris*[19] Whitford J. held that a black pack with gold lettering for cigarettes was not distinctive in itself. At best, the plaintiffs' was the best known brand so packaged. The defendants' pack was easily distinguishable. In *Rizla v Bryant & May*[20] the only significant similarities between the parties' packs of cigarette papers were in colour, in which the plaintiffs had no monopoly.

In *Scott v Nice-Pak*[21] the Court of Appeal acknowledged that similarities between the respective tubs in which the parties packed their baby wipes could not be brushed aside, but the defendants' labels were sufficiently distinct, and there was no confusion in fact. An interlocutory injunction was refused. In *United Biscuits v Burtons Biscuits*[22] the get-up of the packaging for the defendants' lemon and lime *Jaffa Cakes* might have misled shoppers into the belief that it was a brand extension of the plaintiffs, McVities; but the getup of their orange *Jaffa Cakes* was too distinct for there to be an arguable case in respect of that product. In *Dalgety v Food Brokers*[23] the plastic containers for the plaintiffs' *Pot Noodles* and the defendants' *Cup Noodles* were similar in terms of size, colour and shape, but were otherwise visually distinct. It could not be said that there was no serious issue to be tried, but an interlocutory injunction was refused on the balance of convenience. Although the appearance of the product itself was imitated in *Bostik v Sellotape GB*,[24] this was not apparent until after purchase, and the defendants' packaging was distinct. In the Irish case of *SmithKline Beecham v Antigen Pharmaceuticals*[25] an interim injunction was refused (on the balance of convenience) in a case in which the package for the defendants *Solfen* painkiller had certain similarities of colouring and design to that of the plaintiff's *Solpadeine*.

In Australia, an interlocutory injunction was refused in *Simplot v McCain*.[26] The plaintiffs, effectively *Birds Eye*, had introduced a new frozen potato product under the name *Hash Brown Triangles* packaged in a polythene envelope coloured pillar-box red, and McCain had subsequently introduced a competing product, in a cherry red envelope. It could not be said that Birds Eye had any proprietary rights in the name or shape of the product, and the brand name *McCain* was sufficient distinction.

---

[16] [1976] R.P.C. 653 (Brightman J.).
[17] 1977 (4) SA 434; [1978] R.P.C. 232 (Nicholas J., South Africa).
[18] [1980] F.S.R. 68, CA.
[19] [1984] R.P.C. 293 (Whitford J.).
[20] [1986] R.P.C. 389 (Walton J.).
[21] [1989] 1 F.S.R. 100, CA.
[22] [1992] F.S.R. 14 (Vinelott J.).
[23] [1994] F.S.R. 504 (Blackburne J.).
[24] [1994] R.P.C. 556 (Blackburne J.).
[25] [1999] E.T.M.R. 512 (McCracken J., HC Ireland).
[26] [2001] FCA 518; 52 I.P.R. 539.

Get-up of goods

8–136 The cases in which imitation of the actual appearance of goods has been restrained as passing-off are very few, and although they include decisions of the House of Lords and Court of Appeal, all those in England have been on motion for interlocutory injunctions.[27] The *Jif Lemon* case, *Reckitt & Colman v Borden*,[28] is not one in which the appearance of the goods themselves was protected against copying, though there is a danger of misinterpreting it in this way because of the way the case was argued by the defendants and a mistaken tendency in a line of cases[29] to treat bottles and certain other containers not as packaging for their contents, but as the very goods which the customer is interested in purchasing. The fundamental point made in *Jif* was that the lemon juice was the article of commerce and the plastic lemon merely the container for it. However, although Lord Oliver declined to speculate on the situation which would have arisen if the get-up of the goods themselves had been in issue, Lord Jauncey was prepared to go further with a hypothetical example:

> "*A* markets a ratchet screwdriver with a distinctively shaped handle. The screwdriver has acquired a reputation for reliability and utility and is generally recognised by the public as being the product of *A* because of its handle. *A* would be entitled to protection against *B* if the latter sought to market a ratchet screwdriver with a similarly shaped handle without taking sufficient steps to see that the public were not misled into thinking that his product was that of *A*. It is important to remember that such protection does not confer on *A* a monopoly in the sale of ratchet screwdrivers nor even in the sale of such screwdrivers with similarly distinctive handles if other appropriate means can be found to distinguish the two products."[30]

8–137 In Australia, the *Philips v Remington*[31] litigation in relation to electric shavers with three rotary cutting heads included claims for passing-off and under the Trade Practices Act 1974. Both were dismissed: although it was incumbent on Remington to distinguish their shavers from those of Philips they had done so effectively by the use of their own brand name.

> "The appellants also relied on causes of action under s 52 of the Trade Practices Act 1974 and for passing off. These were argued together, reliance being placed on the same evidentiary material. The foundation of Philips' contentions was the long period of effective monopoly it had

---

[27] See J.M. Evans "Passing-off and the Problem of Product Simulation" (1968) 31 M.L.R. 642.

[28] [1990] 1 All E.R. 865; [1990] R.P.C. 340, HL.

[29] Culminating in *Coca-Cola TMs* [1986] 1 W.L.R. 695; [1986] R.P.C. 421, HL.

[30] *per* Lord Jauncey in *Reckitt & Colman Products Ltd v Borden Inc* [1990] 1 W.L.R. 491; [1990] 1 All E.R. 873; [1990] R.P.C. 340, HL.

[31] [2000] F.C.A. 876; 48 I.P.R. 257, (Federal Court of Australia). The case principally concerned trade mark and registered design infringement.

enjoyed in respect of the production and sale of triple rotary shavers. There is no doubt this has led to an association between Philips and triple headed rotary shavers in the minds of many persons. That association has been assiduously cultivated by advertising images and marketing campaigns, in which the configuration of the head of the shaver has been emphasized (as one might expect, since it distinguishes the type of shaver from foil shavers, and constitutes a visible working feature), though always the shaver has been held up to the public as an appealing *Philips* product, not simply as an appealing product...[32]

Remington's response robustly asserted its right to produce a proven product in all its features–including its technology and anything belonging to the public's perception of the product itself. What Remington could not and did not do was to suggest that its triple rotary shaver was in any sense a *Philips* shaver. On the contrary, the Remington shaver was very clearly marked with the *Remington* name, a well-known brand. In practice, it was to be expected that the rival shavers would be displayed in shops as competing products, each plainly identified as a *Philips* or as a *Remington* ...

I accept that, in view of the similarity of the Remington triple rotary to the Philips, and in view of the similarity of the image each competitor sought to project for its product, it was incumbent upon Remington to distinguish the shaver it was putting on the market from the rival shaver that was already there: *Reckitt & Colman Products Ltd v Borden Inc* [1990] 1 WLR 491 at 507–508, 515; *United Biscuits (UK) Ltd v Asda Stores Ltd* [1997] RPC 513 at 524. However, I can see no error in the trial judge's approach to this issue, or in his conclusion in Remington's favour. Given that Remington desired to produce a shaver like the Philips shaver in most respects not the exclusive property of Philips by virtue of some right of intellectual property, it is difficult to see what more Remington could reasonably be expected to have done to emphasize that the product was its own triple rotary shaver. And what it did, on the judge's findings which I think should stand, was in fact sufficient to achieve the purpose."[33]

The leading English case prior to *Reckitt & Colman v Borden* is *Edge v Niccolls*[34] in which the House of Lords held that a distinction was to be drawn between the functional features of an article, which might be copied, and capricious detail, which might not. The plaintiffs had for 20 years sold washing blue in unlabelled and unmarked bags with a stick protruding from the top. The stick was functional, in that the bag of blue could be agitated in the water without scalding or staining the fingers, but it was conceded by the defendants for the purposes of the motion to be distinctive of the plaintiffs' manufacture. The defendants relied on the use of a label carrying their own name to distinguish, and on the fact that a patent for the stick had been granted and revoked. Apart from the addition of their label, they had copied **8–138**

---

[32] Passages relevant to alleged passing-off by imitating the themes of Philips' advertising, omitted here, are quoted at para.8–187 below.

[33] *per* Burchett J.

[34] [1911] A.C. 693; 28 R.P.C. 582, HL.

the plaintiffs' bag and stick almost precisely and they had claimed the get-up as a registered design of their own. By the time the case reached the House of Lords the plaintiffs had abandoned an argument that the use of any kind of stick would be passing-off. The House of Lords held that the defendants' label was ineffective to distinguish their goods in view of the fact that the plaintiffs' name was unknown to most purchasers, many of whom were illiterate. However, they made it clear that the injunction they granted was not intended to prevent the defendant using any sort of stick, and that what was being restrained was the precise and unnecessary copying of the plaintiffs' get-up in detail.

In *Elliot v Hodgson*[35] Buckley J. granted an interlocutory injunction restraining the defendant from selling cigars made in the same shape as those of the plaintiffs without clearly distinguishing them. The cigars of both parties were often sold loose, the plaintiffs' shape was unique and had no functional or aesthetic significance, and the court accepted that a band on the defendant's cigars would adequately distinguish them.[36]

In *Hoffman-La Roche v DDSA Pharmaceuticals*[37] the plaintiffs and patentees had supplied the drug chlordiazepoxide to the National Health Service in green and black capsules. The defendants obtained a compulsory patent licence and adopted the same get-up, except that their initials appeared inconspicuously instead of the equally inconspicuous name of the plaintiffs. The Court of Appeal granted an interlocutory injunction.

Edge v Niccolls and *Roche v DDSA* are treated here, as is usual, as cases of the get-up of the goods themselves. However, it could equally well be said that the "goods" in each case were the blue and the chlordiazepoxide respectively, and that the get-up was that of their packaging, with the qualification that the packaging served more of a functional purpose than usual and was not removed before the goods were used.

8–139   An example of a feature which was intrinsic to the goods but wholly arbitrary may be found in *Dunhill v Bartlett & Bickley*.[38] The plaintiff marked his pipes with a white spot on the mouthpiece and gave prominence to it in his advertising. Russell J. found for the defendants on the ground that the red spot they used was sufficiently different, but he acknowledged that the white spot itself was distinctive.[39]

The characteristic radiator grille on *Rolls-Royce* cars may serve as another example of a feature, neither functional nor mechanically useful, which has acquired trade mark significance by virtue of consistent use on different

---

[35] (1902) 19 R.P.C. 518.
[36] *Elliot v Hodgson* is more often distinguished than followed.
[37] [1969] F.S.R. 416, CA.
[38] (1922) 39 R.P.C. 426 (Russell J.).
[39] See also *Ideal Werke AG v Willesden & District Light Supply Co Ltd* (1930) 48 R.P.C. 123 (*Blue Spot, Navy Spot*). An uncontested injunction was granted, partly on the get-up of the goods themselves, but the report is very brief and the name and the get-up of cartons were also relevant.

models since 1906. In Australia an interlocutory injunction was granted against a car which used a similar grille and emblem, and the name *Phaeton: Rolls-Royce Motors v DIA (Engineering)*.[40]

In *Charles Church Developments v Cronin*[41] an allegation of passing-off based on copying the appearance of a house, in terms of overall design and the use of flint facing, was struck out as disclosing no cause of action. Nothing in the appearance of the design of house copied could be said to be "a capricious addition" or distinctive in the legal sense. It was not even clearly alleged that any part of the appearance of the plaintiffs' design of house was identified with one particular builder.

In *Adidas v O'Neill & Co*[42] the plaintiffs failed to prove that the device of **8-140** three parallel stripes on their shoes and sportswear was distinctive of them in Ireland. They had enjoyed relatively little reputation or trade in Ireland until after the defendants had established themselves. Apart from the stripes, there were no other features in common and the defendants' goods were distinguished by brand name. To the majority of the Supreme Court the stripes were no more than a fashionable decoration, even if the plaintiffs had started the trend. In South Africa, on the other hand, Adidas had convinced Botha J. that three such stripes on shoes were distinctive of them and that there was passing-off by selling sports shoes bearing four stripes although the brand name *Beaver* differed: *Adidas v Henry Walt*.[43] In the Canadian case of *Adidas (Canada) v Collins*[44] the Federal Court came to a decision mid-way between the Irish and South African decisions.[45] The defendants were enjoined from passing-off by close copying of the plaintiffs' garments, but the use of three stripes was not *per se* distinctive and the plaintiffs' registered marks were revoked. As in the South African case, the defendants' goods bore four parallel stripes, but the use of a maple leaf in the same position as the Adidas trefoil mark disclosed their intentions.

An interesting return to the marketing concept of *Edge v Niccolls* arose in the Canadian case of *Westfair Foods v Canada Safeway*[46] in which the plaintiff chain of retailers introduced a wide range of *No Name* products, unbranded but heavily advertised and identifiable by get-up. The plaintiffs were refused an interlocutory injunction on the balance of convenience, but were said to have a strong case.

Get-up or appearance of goods: examples

Other cases of passing-off by get-up allegedly consisting of the appearance **8-141** of the goods themselves are very few. Kekewich J. granted an injunction

---

[40] (1981) 50 F.L.R. 340 (Lockhart J., Federal Court of Australia). The English cases, *Rolls-Royce Motors Ltd v Zanelli* [1979] R.P.C. 148, CA and *Rolls-Royce Motors Ltd v Dodd* [1981] F.S.R. 517 are consistent with this but less explicit. In Australia, the plaintiffs still had to make out a *prima facie* case.

[41] [1990] F.S.R. 1 (Edward Nugee Q.C.).

[42] [1983] F.S.R. 76 (Irish Supreme Court).

[43] 1976 (1) SA 531 (Botha J., Transvaal).

[44] (1978) 38 C.P.R. 145 (Federal Court, Walsh J.).

[45] The South African *Adidas* case was cited with approval by Walsh J.

[46] (1986) 7 C.P.R. (3d) 368 (Wright J., Saskatchewan.)

where the "get-up" essentially consisted of the colour, size and material of a polishing cloth for glasses and some very simple markings on it,[47] but in an almost identical case against a subsequent defendant the Court of Appeal found against the same plaintiffs.[48] In *Combe v Scholl*[49] the fact that the defendants' insoles were the same colour and carried the same markings as those of the plaintiffs may have contributed to an interlocutory injunction being granted, but there were other matters in the plaintiffs' favour, and the relevant misrepresentation may have been as to quality, rather than source.[50]

Some foreign courts have gone further in preventing copying of articles with a greater degree of precision than is necessary to reproduce their function. In the Australian case of *Kettles & Gas Appliances v Anthony Horden & Sons*[51] Long Innes J. held that the shape of the plaintiffs' kettle was distinctive in the legal sense and would have granted relief but for a misrepresentation by the plaintiffs that it was patented. In Hong Kong, an interlocutory injunction was granted against the precise copying of an electric fan in *Kemtron Properties v Jimmy's Co*,[52] on the ground that the features copied in combination were not wholly dictated by utilitarian considerations. However, the Court was only applying the *Cyanamid*[53] test of a serious issue to be tried.

8–142 In South Africa the precise copying of a meat cutting machine was held to amount to passing-off,[54] and this has been explained[55] as meaning that there were distinctive non-functional elements which were copied. To this extent, neither case is necessarily wrong, but there is a very wide gap between proving that certain details are non-functional and proving that it is those details specifically which serve to distinguish the plaintiff's goods in the market. In *Agriplas v Andrag*[56] itself an interdict was refused on reasoning consistent with English law. In a more recent South African case, *Weber-Stephen v Alrite*,[57] the goods in question were rival kettle-shaped barbecues. Although the injunction granted at trial was qualified to allow the defendants to sell their barbecue if it could be distinguished, this proved impossible in fact because the plaintiffs were not known by name and the defendants were found to be in contempt. One is left wondering whether even the qualified injunction should have been granted. The trial judge had

---

[47] *Jones v Hallworth* (1897) 14 R.P.C. 225 (Kekewich J.).
[48] *Jones Bros Ltd v Anglo-American Optical Co* (1912) 29 R.P.C. 361, CA.
[49] [1980] R.P.C. 1; [1977] F.S.R. 464 (Fox J.).
[50] Another case is *New Way Packaged Products Ltd v Lucking (S) Ltd* [1960] R.P.C. 147 where the goods were similar and could be seen through their transparent packaging.
[51] (1934) 35 S.R. (N.S.W.) 108 (Long Innes J.).
[52] [1979] F.S.R. 86 (Leonard J.).
[53] *American Cyanamid Co v Ethicon Ltd* [1975] A.C. 396; [1975] 1 All E.R. 504; [1975] R.P.C. 513; [1975] F.S.R. 101, HL.
[54] *William Lasar v Sabon Precision Machine Co Ltd* not fully reported. Noted at 1952 (2) P.H. A. 37 and commented upon in the following case.
[55] *Agriplas (Pty) Ltd v Andrag & Sons (Pty) Ltd* 1981 (4) SA 873 (Burger J., Cape) which contains a comprehensive review of South African, Commonwealth and even American decisions. The goods copied were "a plastic irrigation device known as a Lego dripper" from Israel.
[56] Above.
[57] [1992] R.P.C. 549; 1992 (2) SA 489.

not intended the qualification to be a trap. In *Caterham Car Sales v Birkin Cars*[58] allegations that the shape of the *Lotus Seven Series III* sports car was distinctive of Caterham were abandoned on appeal, being obviously untenable in view of the fact that Lotus themselves had tolerated widespread copying of the design both by individual enthusiasts and replica manufacturers such as Birkin and even Caterham themselves.

In Australia again, an interlocutory injunction was granted in *United Pacific Industries v Madison Sports*[59] in which the colours and surface appearance of the plaintiffs' *Thermoskin* heat retaining products for sportspeople were copied, though the respective logos and packaging were different. The facts are reminiscent of *Reckitt & Colman v Borden*[60]: in the first place because the "point of reference" for a new purchaser was quite likely to be one of the plaintiffs' products being worn on someone else's body, perhaps on television, rather than in its packaging; and secondly because the plaintiff was not generally known by name, and the respective logos were inconspicuous.

Cases of alleged passing-off based on the appearance or get-up of goods **8–143** as such have failed far more often than they have succeeded. In *Blundell v Sidney Margolis*[51] an interlocutory injunction was refused to a plaintiff whose idea of producing bubble gum in the shape of a set of false teeth had been copied by the defendants. Dankwerts J. dismissed an action in which the plaintiffs imported a corkscrew in the shape of a lady's head and the defendant one in the shape of a clown's: *Universal Agencies London v Swolf*.[62] In *British American Glass Co v Winton Products*[63] the defendants had copied the shape of the plaintiffs' ornamental glass dogs, which were novel. Pennycuick J., refusing an interlocutory injunction, observed that "a member of the public buying an ornamental trinket of this nature is concerned only with what it looks like and is unlikely to care by whom it is made".

The Court of Appeal in *Terrapin v Ariston Buildings*[64] refused an interlocutory injunction when the only case that could be made of passing-off rested on the fact that the defendants had very closely copied the plaintiffs' collapsible buildings. Strictly, what was complained of was not the buildings themselves but illustrations of them in the defendants' catalogue. In *Gordon Fraser Gallery v Tatt*[65] Buckley J. refused an interlocutory injunction against copying the artistic style of the plaintiffs' greetings cards. In South Africa, the producers of *Monopoly* were refused an interim interdict against a game called *Big Deal* which used a closely similar lay-out of board: *Waddington v Harris*.[66] In *Lyngstad v Annabas Products*[67] Oliver J. doubted whether the

---

[58] 1998 (3) SA 938 (SCA).
[59] (1998) 41 I.P.R. 546 (Finkelstein J., Federal Court of Australia).
[60] [1990] 1 All E.R. 865; [1990] R.P.C. 340, HL.
[61] (1951) 68 R P.C. 71 (Harman J.).
[62] [1959] R.P.C. 247 (Dankwerts J.).
[63] [1962] R.P.C. 230 (Pennycuick J.).
[64] [1964] F.S.R. 218, CA.
[65] [1966] F.S.R. 250; [1966] R.P.C. 505 (Buckley J.).
[66] 1968 (1) SA 38 (Galgut J., Transvaal).
[67] [1977] F.S.R. 62 (Oliver J.).

plaintiff pop group could restrain the sale of badges, *etc.* bearing their photographs. Similarities in the appearance, size and texture of rival brands of biscuits did not amount to passing-off when the get-up of the packaging of the defendants' biscuits was distinct: *United Biscuits v Irish Biscuits.*[68] In *Drayton Controls v Honeywell Control Systems*[69] an interlocutory injunction was refused in respect of the appearance of radiator valves.

8–144   The authorities are not all interlocutory. At trial in *Politechnika Ipari Szovertkezet v Dallas Print Transfers*[70] Dillon J. held that there had been no passing-off by the defendants copying the structure and even the precise colouring of the heavily advertised and enormously popular *Rubik's Cube*. Most people at that time "wanted the cube as a puzzle to enjoy or try their wits on, without regard to what source it came from". In the corresponding (interlocutory) Australian case *John Engelander v Ideal Toy Corp*[71] it was decided that *Rubik's cube* was the name of the article and that the copied cube was sufficiently distinguished from the original by the get-up of its packaging. Fox J. would apparently have regarded the *Ideal* cube in its plastic container as having a distinctive combination of features. In *Cadbury v Ulmer GmbH*[72] Falconer J. held that there was no passing-off by imitation of the shape of the plaintiffs' *Flake* chocolate bars, and that the defendants were not obliged to distinguish their goods or take steps to prevent substitution by retailers. In *Bostik v Sellotape*[73] the plaintiffs did not even have an arguable case as a result of the defendants having copied the blue colour of their *Blu-tac* adhesive putty. The defendants' product was clearly distinguished both by the brand name *SelloTak* and by its get-up. In *Hodgkinson and Corby v Wards Mobility Services*[74] Jacob J. at trial held that there was no liability for passing-off by the defendants copying a cushion for use by wheelchair-bound patients. The shape of the plaintiffs' *Roho* cushion was not the crucial point of reference for customers (principally the NHS) and persons wishing to buy it were unlikely to be misled.

8–145   In the Canadian case of *Sheres v Texpol*[75] the plaintiffs had imported sewing boxes. The defendants commenced to import exact replicas. The Exchequer Court refused an interlocutory injunction. There was no reason to believe that the public identified the appearance of the boxes with any trade source at all, still less with the plaintiffs as importer. In *Oxford Pendaflex Canada v Korr Marketing*[76] the Supreme Court of Canada held there was no passing-off when the defendants copied the plaintiffs' desk tray. The appearance of the tray was not distinctive. An interlocutory injunction was refused where the defendant intended to sell a Christmas tree-stand identical

---

[68] [1971] I.R. 16 (Kenny J.).
[69] [1992] F.S.R. 245 (Knox J.).
[70] [1982] F.S.R. 529 (Dillon J.).
[71] (1981) 54 F.L.R. 227 (Fox J., Federal Court of Australia). The position of the parties was reversed.
[72] [1988] F.S.R. 385 (Falconer J.).
[73] [1994] R.P.C. 556 (Blackburne J.).
[74] [1998] F.S.R. 530 (Jacob J.).
[75] (1969) 58 C.P.R. 136 (Jackett P., Exchequer Court).
[76] [1982] 1 S.C.R. 494; 134 D.L.R. (3d) 270 (Supreme Court of Canada).

to that of the plaintiffs: *Gunnard v Regal Home Products.*[77] The plaintiffs in *Ganz Bros Toys v Irwin Toy*[78] marketed a *Wrinklies* puppet dog. They failed to obtain an interlocutory injunction against the defendants' *Pound Puppies* dog which was similar to that of the plaintiffs but not to such a degree that even a careless shopper would fail to distinguish them. One month after *Ganz*, the same court refused an interlocutory injunction to the defendants in that case in another action involving the appearance and packaging of more toy dogs: *Irwin Toy v Marie-Anne Novelties.*[79]

In the Australian case of *Dr Martens Australia v Rivers*[80] claims against four unconnected defendants based on the appearance, get-up or trade dress of *Doc Martens* Z-welt footwear were dismissed: although the defendants' boots and shoes were similar in appearance to *Doc Martens* products (and had obviously been copied) they were all adequately distinguished by brand name and there was no substantial risk of deception or confusion. On appeal, the Federal Court refused to find that the alleged features of trade dress were so distinctive on their own that the parties' brand names did not enter into consideration. In *Philips v Remington*[81] the appearance of the plaintiff's three-headed rotary electric shavers may have been sufficiently distinctive for the defendants to be under an obligation to distinguish their own product, but they were not liable for passing-off by launching a shaver with a similar configuration, clearly branded as their own.

A number of cases to the same effect come from the furniture and fur- **8–146** nishing industries. In *Hawkins & Tipson v Fludes Carpets*[82] Dankwerts J. held that the pattern on the plaintiffs' coir matting was not distinctive. In *Benchairs v Chair Centre*[83] Graham J. refused an interlocutory injunction based on the supposedly confusing similarity of two designs of chairs. Graham J. reached the same conclusion at trial in *Hensher v Restawhile Upholstery,*[84] holding that there was no evidence that the appearance of the plaintiffs' furniture was associated by the public with any particular manufacturer. The Court of Appeal approved the latter judgment in *Jarman & Platt v Barget*[85] and allowed an appeal by the defendants. The trial judge had fallen into the trap of taking rather slight evidence of confusion as evidence of distinctiveness. Once again, the public wanted the furniture for its appearance, not its source. The same principles have been applied in *Parkdale Custom Built v Puxu,*[86] an Australian case under the Trade Practices Act.

---

[77] (1986) 13 C.P.R. (3d) 335 (Henry J., Ontario).
[78] (1986) 12 C.P.R. (3d) 434 (Houston D.C.J., Ontario).
[79] (1986) 12 C.P.R. (3d) 145 (Trainor J.).
[80] [1999] FCA 1655; 47 I.P.R. 499 (Federal Court of Australia).
[81] [2000] FCA 876; 48 I.P.R. 257 (Federal Court of Australia).
[82] [1957] R.P.C. 8 (Dankwerts J.).
[83] [1972] F.S.R. 397 (Graham J.).
[84] [1975] R.P.C. 31 (Graham J.). The case went to the House of Lords on the issue of copyright infringement, but the plaintiffs did not appeal on passing-off.
[85] [1977] F.S.R. 260, CA.
[86] (1982) 149 C.L.R. 191; 56 A.L.J.R. 715; 1 T.P.R. 282; A.L.R. 1 (Full Court).

Get-up of business premises

8–147 There is no reason in principle why the misrepresentation in passing-off should not be found in the adoption of get-up for business premises which is confusingly similar to that used by the claimant, and the issue is increasingly likely to arise with franchised businesses, for which the get-up of the premises and their contents is often important. Several cases exist in which passing off on this basis has been alleged, but all those in Britain have failed on the facts. Ironically, the case which has probably gone furthest in attaching importance to the get-up of premises did so by holding that dissimilarities in get-up outweighed near-identity of names: *TGI Friday's Australia v TGI Friday's Inc.*[87]

In *Plotzker v Lucas*[88] the plaintiffs failed to prove that the adoption by the defendant of get-up similar to that of their shops would deceive or cause them damage when the defendant's shop was in Edinburgh and the only Scottish shop of the plaintiffs was in Glasgow.[89] The plaintiffs in *Coleman v Stephen Smith*[90] alleged as evidence of fraudulent intent that the defendants had copied their stall at an exhibition, but the defendants' stall had been completed before work on the plaintiffs' had begun. In an Australian case, *Wilson v Samuels*,[91] the defendant closely copied the window dressing of the plaintiff's nearby shop as well as adopting a deliberately similar name. The two together were actionable. An English action based on alleged similarities in name and get-up failed in *Société Nildé v Erndalé*[92] and the fact that the shops were opposite one another would have dispelled confusion, rather than creating it. The plaintiffs were perfumiers and the defendants hairdressers.

In *Laraine Day v Kennedy*[93] the plaintiffs failed at trial to prove that the defendant's shop front and window dressings were deceptively similar to theirs. An interlocutory injunction was refused in *Bravingtons v Barrington Tennant*[94] where both similarity of names and of the shops themselves was relied on. Deception was not inevitable and there had been delay. The increasing importance of get-up of premises is to some extent reflected in *My Kinda Town v Soll*.[95] The plaintiffs and defendant both gave their restaurants a theme based on the city of Chicago, and the plaintiffs alleged that this and other similarities strengthened a case of passing-off based mainly in similarity of names. The Court of Appeal found for the defendants, but the state

---

[87] [1999] FCA 304, 45 I.P.R. 43 (Federal Court of Australia, Full Court). Despite its corporate name, the defendant actually traded without the final apostrophised "s".
[88] (1907) 24 R.P.C. 551 (MacKenzie, Court of Session, Outer House).
[89] The reasoning is obsolete. Compare *C & A Modes Ltd v C & A (Waterford) Ltd* [1978] F.S.R. 126 (Irish Supreme Court) and *Chelsea Man Menswear Ltd v Chelsea Girl Ltd* [1987] R.P.C. 189, CA.
[90] (1911) 29 R.P.C. 81, CA.
[91] (1913) 13 S.R. (N.S.W.) 394 (Simpson C.J. in Eq.).
[92] (1929) 46 R.P.C. 453 (Eve J.).
[93] (1952) 70 R.P.C. 19 (Roxburgh J.).
[94] [1957] R.P.C. 183 (Upjohn J.).
[95] [1983] R.P.C. 407, CA.

of the pleadings meant that the similarities in get-up were not fully taken into account.

In *Carless Capel v Pilmore*[96] it was unsuccessfully argued that the defendants were liable for passing-off by dispensing petrol from pumps shaped like a lighthouse. The plaintiffs' mark for heating and lighting oils had a lighthouse as a prominent component, but neither the idea nor the representation of a lighthouse had come to be distinctive of them for petrol. On the facts, the defendants had not misrepresented the origin of the petrol they sold. In *BP Amoco v John Kelly*,[97] BP's green and yellow livery for its petrol stations was held to be distinctive in Northern Ireland, but although the defendant employed a similar shade of green his stations traded under the name *TOP* and there was no likelihood of confusion.

The clearest examples of the get-up of retail premises being distinctive **8–148** come from a series of related cases in Canada. In *Mr Submarine v Voultsos*[98] the plaintiffs operated a franchise of about 80 sandwich bars under the name Mr Submarine with a distinctive get-up for the premises. The defendant was a former franchisee who opened sandwich bars with similar get-up as *Mrs Submarine* and *Ace Submarine*, with similar lettering for the names. The Court granted permanent injunctions against the use of *Mr* or *Mrs* with *Submarine*, the precise scope depending on the specific colour and typeface used. The decor of the shops was also held to be distinctive, although no injunction directed to it alone was granted. An account of profits was awarded. In *Mr Submarine v Bikas*[99] an interlocutory injunction was granted to the same plaintiffs specifically in respect of the get-up of the shops and in *Mr Submarine v Emma Foods*[1] the plaintiffs were granted an interlocutory injunction against the defendants operating a sandwich booth at an exhibition with a sign similar in colour and typography to theirs.

Allegations that a fish restaurant in Western Australia had copied the name, style, get-up, trade methods, menu documentation, advertising materials, design, decor, entertainment and general appearance and operations of the plaintiffs' two restaurants in Sydney and Melbourne were not so hopeless as to justify striking out the action in *The Last Aussie Fish Caf v Almove*.[2] So far as the case rested on the descriptive words *Fish Caf* it was highly speculative, but comparison of the get-up of the respective restaurants suggested that the possibility of deception could not be ruled out. Similar allegations, though, fell well short of the standard required to justify an interlocutory injunction in *Fernwood Fitness Centre v Today's Woman Health and Fitness*.[3] Neither the name *Today's Woman*, not the decor, fixtures, fittings and colour schemes of the plaintiffs' franchised health and fitness centres were distinctive; and even if any of them were, the defendants'

---

[96] (1928) 45 R.P.C. 205 (Tomlin J.).
[97] [2002] F.S.R. 5, CA of Northern Ireland.
[98] (1977) 36 C.P.R. (2d) 270 (Osler J., Ontario High Court).
[99] (1975) 24 C.P.R. (2d) 135 (Cory J., Ontario High Court).
[1] (1976) 34 C.P.R. (2d) 177 (Estey C.J.H.C., Ontario). *Mr Submarine Ltd v Amandista Investments Ltd* (1987) 19 C.P.R. (3d) (Federal Court of Appeal) was decided solely on the basis of trade mark infringement.
[2] (1990) 16 I.P.R. 376, (French J., Federal Court of Australia).
[3] (1998) 41 I.P.R. 78 (Goldberg J., Federal Court of Australia).

business was sufficiently distinguished. In the Canadian case of *Edmonds v Kealy*[4] the plaintiff had a better than arguable case based on the get-up of a lemonade stand, but an interlocutory injunction was refused on the balance of convenience. In South Africa, a case based on an accumulation of supposed similarities between the trade dress or get-up of the plaintiffs' *Spur* steak house restaurants and two of the *Saddles* restaurants of the defendants did not justify an interim interdict against unlawful competition, the plaintiffs' trade dress not being sufficiently distinctive to be protected: *Spur Steak Ranches v Saddles Steak Ranch.*[5] In Australia again, the get-up of the defendant's *Thomas Shop* contributed to a finding of passing off in *Miller v Britt Allcroft,*[6] where the complaint was that customers would believe that the shop as such (and not just the *Thomas the Tank Engine* merchandise on sale) was licensed by the plaintiffs.

8–149 Conversely, having consistent and highly distinctive get-up for its business premises can work to the disadvantage of the claimant. Striking dissimilarities in the get-up of premises may weaken a case primarily based on similarity of trading names, as in *Furnitureland v Harris.*[7] In *TGI Friday's Australia v TGI Friday's Inc*[8] the "instantly recognisable" get-up of the plaintiffs' brand of bars and restaurants was so well known internationally (despite there only being two in Australia) that the complete dissimilarity of the design of the defendants' *TGI Friday* hotel and tavern would disabuse customers of the possibility of any connection. The differences in get-up were so striking and substantial that patrons would assume that the near-identity of name was simply coincidental.

Get-up of items used in trade

8–150 Get-up may be protected even though the items for which the distinctive get-up is claimed are not sold to the public. As always, the question is whether the use of the claimant's get-up or get-up similar to it by the defendant involves the making of a material misrepresentation. In *Easyjet v Dainty*[9] the colours orange and white, and a certain style of lettering, were used consistently for the claimants' budget airline, chain of internet cafes, and car hire business. Though they had no exclusive rights to the word "easy," the claimants obtained summary judgment against a cybersquatter who had registered the domain name *easyRealestate.co.uk* and copied the claimants' get-up. In *Temporary Roadways and Access v Trax Portable Access*[10] a case based on the similarity between the trading names *TRAC* and *TRAX* was strengthened by the "remarkably close" similarity of the appearance of the defendants' vehicles to those of the claimants. Both were dark blue overall with TRAC or TRAX in bold upper case lettering in an orange or gold

---

[4] (1989) 27 C.P.R. (3d) 434 (Pinard J., Federal Court).
[5] 1996 (3) SA 706 (CPD).
[6] [2000] FCA 1724, 52 I.P.R. 419 (Federal Court of Australia).
[7] [1989] 1 F.S.R. 536 (Browne-Wilkinson V.C.).
[8] [1999] FCA 304, 00 I.P.R. 43 (Federal Court of Australia, Full Court).
[9] [2002] F.S.R. 6 (Bernard Livesey Q.C., Deputy Judge).
[10] [2002] E.W.H.C. 1728 (Blackburne J.)

colour. An interim injunction was granted in terms directed both to the name and the livery. In *Sydneywide Distributors v Red Bull Australia*[11] it was relevant that the get-up of the cans of the plaintiffs' *Red Bull* energy drink was also employed for dedicated barrel fridges in retail establishments.

In the very early case of *Knott v Morgan*[12] the defendant was restrained from passing-off by copying the name and get-up of the plaintiff's omnibuses and the uniforms of the crew. Get-up of buses was also in issue in *London General Omnibus Co v Felton*[13] and *London General Omnibus Co v Lavell*.[14] *Du Cross v Gold*[15] is sometimes cited as a case where get-up of vehicles was distinctive but it does not quite bear that interpretation. The defendant copied the get-up and colour scheme of the plaintiffs' taxi cabs, but those were common to the trade. The plaintiff's cabs were identified by the letters *W & G* in script on the doors. The defendant used his initials *MG* in the same place, in similar script and with a flourish instead of the ampersand. This was intended to deceive and an injunction was granted, with an order to obliterate the offending initials. Two clearer examples of the get-up of taxi cabs being protected come from New Zealand: *Black & White Cabs Co v Hagen*[16] and *Black & White Cabs Co v McEneany*.[17] However, the same plaintiffs went too far in trying to restrain the use of blue and white: *Black & White Cabs Co v Nicholson*.[18] In Australia the plaintiffs in *Blue and White Cabs v Bowerin*[19] failed to restrain the use of cabs coloured white and the same shade of pale blue but with no white band round the body and with black spots instead of the plaintiff's blue spots. This might have seemed too close but for the fact that the two had been in competition for two years with no evidence of confusion. In *Smith's Potato Crisps v Paige's Potato Crisps*[20] the plaintiffs claimed that the defendants had systematically copied not only the plaintiffs' bags, but also the tins in which the bags of crisps were delivered to retailers and the vans used to carry them. The case collapsed on the evidence.

In South Africa, the maroon and white colours in which the members of the plaintiffs' football team played were distinctive in *Moroka Swallows Football Club v The Birds Football Club*[21] and an interim interdict was granted against a rival team using those colours. In England Harman J. was perhaps too indulgent in refusing an interlocutory injunction in *Dagenham Girl Pipers v Vishnu Pather*[22] where one of the complaints was that the defendant had copied the plaintiffs' uniforms.

---

[11] [2002] FCAFC 157; [*other cites*].
[12] (1836) 48 E.R. 610 (Lord Langdale M.R.).
[13] (1896) 12 T.L.R. 213.
[14] [1901] 1 Ch. 105; 18 R.P.C. 74, CA.
[15] (1912) 30 R.P.C. 117 (Swinfen Eady J.).
[16] [1927] N.Z.L.R. 535 (Alfers J.).
[17] [1927] N.Z.L.R. 862, CA.
[18] [1928] N.Z.L.R. 273, CA.
[19] [1937] S.R. (Qd) 339 (Douglas J.).
[20] (1928) 45 R.P.C. 132, CA.
[21] 1987 (2) SA 511 (Stegmann J.).
[22] (1951) 69 R.P.C. 1 (Harman J.).

I. VISUAL MARKS AND ASPECTS OF GET-UP

Labels and pictures

8–151 Labels and pictorial marks may be distinctive taken as a whole or because of some prominent feature:

> "[T]he eye is not an accurate recorder of visual detail, and ... marks are remembered rather by general impressions or by some significant detail than by any photographic recollection of the whole."[23]

In the former case, there may be passing-off by the adoption of a label which is similar in overall effect, although the individual elements are all different. The issues which arise are very similar to those in respect of get-up of packaging, and there is no fast division between a label as such and the wrapping of goods as a whole. Examples are *Lever v Goodwin*,[24] *Coleman v Farrow*,[25] *Wright, Crossley v Blezard*[26] and *Bryant & May v United Match Industries*.[27] Liability depends very much on visual appreciation of the competing labels, and the authorities do not lend themselves to further analysis. As with get-up,[28] similarities which lie only in matter which is common to the trade or otherwise non-distinctive are to be ignored,[29] and the labels must be compared fairly giving weight to the differences as well as to the similarities.

In *Hennessy v Keating*[30] the plaintiffs' label for brandy was printed in gold on white, with a border of vine leaves, a device of an arm grasping a battle-axe, and the name Hennessy prominently in the centre. Their advertisements drew attention to these features. The defendant sold brandy under labels in which the only similar features were the colours and the use of vine leaves for the border, which was common to the trade. The House of Lords found for the defendant.

8–152 Alternatively, there may be a prominent feature which is likely to define "the idea of the mark" and if that feature is distinctive of the plaintiff there is passing-off if it is copied. However, matter which is given prominence in a label may serve the purpose of indicating what the goods are, or what they are for, rather than denoting their trade source. If so, that matter is essentially descriptive in its nature and there will not necessarily be passing-off if another trader adopts a similar device.

In *White, Tomkins & Courage v United Confectionery Co*[31] the plaintiffs

---

[23] *per* Lord Radcliffe in *De Cordova v Vick Chemical Co* (1951) 68 R.P.C. 103, PC.
[24] [1887] 36 Ch.D. 1; 4 R.P.C. 492, CA. Compare *Lever Bros Ltd v Bedingfield* (1898) 16 R.P.C. 3, CA.
[25] (1897) 15 R.P.C. 198 (Stirling J.).
[26] (1910) 27 R.P.C. 299 (Leigh Clare V.C., Palatine Court).
[27] (1932) 50 R.P.C. 12 (Clauson J.).
[28] *Schweppes Ltd v Gibbens* (1905) 22 R.P.C. 601, HL.
[29] *Hennessy (James) & Co Ltd v Keating* (1908) 25 R.P.C. 361, HL.
[30] (1908) 25 R.P.C. 361, HL.
[31] (1914) 31 R.P.C. 430 (Warrington J.).

claimed that they were the only manufacturers of jelly to use a picture of the fruit with which each jelly was flavoured. The defendants had previously used a mixture of fruit to illustrate the labels of their jellies, but now followed the plaintiffs' example of matching the picture of the fruit to the flavour. The packets were readily distinguishable and there was no evidence from customers. Relief was refused.

In a Canadian case, *Prairie Maid Cereals v Christie, Brown*,[32] the idea of selling a party snack food in the shape of nuts and bolts was admittedly not distinctive, so the defendants were not guilty of passing-off by using packaging in which the main element of get-up matching that of the plaintiffs was a picture of a bowl of the snack at a party: "[A] manufacturer, it seems to me, is entitled to display a pictorial representation of his product in his promotional literature, and he is also entitled to display in pictorial form the circumstances under which the product can, or is intended to, be used".[33] It was not sufficient that a customer with only "a vague recollection" of the plaintiffs' pack might be confused by the resemblances.

Symbols, devices, logos

Marks which comprise devices such as symbols, pictures, photographs, **8–153** portraits, logos or words written in a special manner present no theoretical difficulty. The issues are whether the device is distinctive, and whether the defendant's corresponding device is calculated to deceive after taking into account the doctrine of imperfect recollection, the idea of the mark, and the surrounding circumstances. A device mark may be essentially descriptive, as in *White, Tomkins & Courage v United Confectionery Co*[34] and *Prairie Maid Cereals v Christie, Brown*,[35] discussed above.

In *Leather Cloth Co v American Leather Cloth Co*[36] the plaintiffs' mark was circular with an eagle in the centre. The defendants' was semi-circular with an eagle in a different posture. The similarities were sufficient for Page-Wood V.-C. to grant an injunction but on appeal Lord Westbury L.C. and the House of Lords refused relief, partly because the defendants' mark was sufficiently different to that of the plaintiffs, and partly because the plaintiffs had misrepresented their goods as patented.

Likewise in *Hubbuck v William Brown*[37] the similarities were that both parties used circular marks with writing going round the edge of the Royal Arms in the centre. The Court of Appeal (with some hesitation) held that there was no likelihood of deception.

In *Smith's Potato Crisps v Paige's Potato Crisps*[38] the plaintiffs' mark was the device of a diamond containing the words Potato Smith's Crisps with the

---

[32] (1966) 58 D.L.R. (2d) 186 (British Columbia Court of Appeal).
[33] *per* Maclean J.A. This raises similar issues to *Terrapin Ltd v Ariston Buildings Ltd* [1964] F.S.R. 218, CA.
[34] (1914) 31 R.P.C. 430 (Warrington J.).
[35] (1966) 58 D.L.R. (2d) 186.
[36] (1865) 11 E.R. 1435, HL.
[37] (1900) 17 R.P.C. 638, CA.
[38] (1928) 45 R.P.C. 132, CA.

IT of *Smith's* emphasised as a visual pun. There was no passing-off by the defendants using a generally similar mark with their own name instead of Smith's, and the *AI* of *Paige's* emphasised in a similar way.

8–154   In *Compatibility Research v Computer Psyche Co*[39] the plaintiffs were the first to introduce a computer dating service to the United Kingdom. They adopted a symbol consisting of a heart linked with the male and female symbols on either side. The defendants started business shortly afterwards with a symbol consisting of a single circle, the top and bottom halves of which formed the male and female symbols, with a heart in the middle. Stamp J. refused an interlocutory injunction. The symbols were essentially descriptive of the service offered, were in common use, and could not have become distinctive of the plaintiffs in the three or four weeks priority the plaintiffs enjoyed over the defendants. In *Ciba-Geigy v Parke Davis*[40] the device of an apple was probably distinctive of the plaintiffs, but the defendants had used it for comparative advertising in a way which could not deceive.

In *EMAP National Publications v Security Publications*[41] the presentation of the defendant's magazine title *Classics* in an oval badge, similar in format to that of the plaintiffs' former publication *Popular Classics*,[42] sufficiently strengthened a case which could not have been won on the very descriptive titles themselves.

Words specially written; signatures

8–155 Words or phrases which are not distinctive in their own right, for instance because of their descriptive nature, may yet be protected in respect of the manner in which they are written. In *Weingarten v Bayer*[43] the House of Lords held that the words *Erect Form* for corsets had not acquired secondary meaning, but that the defendants were liable for passing-off by having copied the precise and distinctive scroll effect in which they were written. In *Telemak v Coles Myer*[44] the words "dry-fry convection oven pan with lid" for a type of frying pan could not have been distinctive as such, but the style in which they were written had been copied and an injunction directed specifically to the lettering used for those words was granted by a majority of the Federal Court of Australia, even though other aspects of the defendants' get-up were not such as to cause confusion.

Signatures as such are of relatively little importance in passing-off because, in comparison to the law of registered trade marks, there is no policy against protecting personal names as such. If the name is distinctive, then the manner in which it is written would normally only be relevant as a "badge of fraud" or in the rare case of the defendant using a signature

---

[39] [1967] R.P.C. 201 (Stamp J.).
[40] [1994] F.S.R. 8 (Aldous J.).
[41] [1997] F.S.R. 891 (Lloyd J.).
[42] The latter had been discontinued and incorporated into *Practical Classics*, but the *Popular Classics* "badge" was still retained on the front cover of *Practical Classics*.
[43] [1904–7] All E.R. 877; (1903) 22 R.P.C. 341, HL.
[44] (1989) 89 A.L.R. 48 (Federal Court).

visually similar to that of the plaintiff though the name as such was dissimilar if considered in the abstract. In *Marengo v Daily Sketch*[45] the House of Lords granted a cartoonist who signed his work *Kem* an injunction against a paper publishing another cartoonist who signed his work *Kim*. Argument in the House of Lords and below turned mainly on the issue of whether the manner in which the defendant's signature was written, without a dot over the letter "i", was capable of being mistaken for *Kem*. The likelihood is that if the words *Kim* and *Kem* had both been printed, the difference in spelling would have been held to be sufficient.

Colour, shape and size

The distinctiveness of colour, shape and size individually or in combination **8–156** raises similar issues to the distinctiveness of get-up. In accordance with normal principles, the colour, shape or size relied on may be that of the goods themselves, or of their packaging, provided that in either case the feature has trade mark significance in the sense of being the or a point of reference for customers. The decision of the House of Lords in *Reckitt & Colman v Borden*[46] affirms that the colour, shape and size of containers may be distinctive in their own right.

Where the shape or size of the goods themselves is said to be distinctive then the public interest in allowing free competition is likely to weigh against the plaintiff, but this is not the only factor and it applies with much less force where packaging is concerned. There is also a public interest in preventing appropriation of an established trader's custom by deceit. Choice of colour for packaging is also essentially arbitrary, and the live issues tend to be whether a mark as simple as a single colour is sufficiently distinctive, and whether the colour truly denotes trade origin. It is increasingly recognised that certain colours are more appropriate than others for the packaging of particular goods. Yellow is obviously appropriate for a lemon-flavoured drink, brown for potato products, and green for vegetables such as peas and beans.

Colour may also have more subtle connotations which are inconsistent with its serving as a trade mark *simpliciter*. In *Scott v Nice-Pak*[47] Walton J. referred to evidence that the colour blue denoted freshness and cleanliness and was therefore a preferred colour for all kinds of baby goods; though he may have overlooked *Delavell v Stanley*[48] in which Evershed J. had taken notice that the colour blue "has a somewhat romantic significance, so as to give, when properly dealt with, a more than usually rare and rich and haunting ... flavour to the substance offered".

Individual colours or colours in combination may be distinctive. In **8–157** *Sodastream v Thorn Cascade*[49] the Court of Appeal was prepared to say on an application for an interlocutory injunction that grey was distinctive of the

---

[45] [1948] 1 All E.R. 406; 65 R.P.C. 242, HL.
[46] [1990] 1 W.L.R. 491; [1990] 1 All E.R. 873; [1990] R.P.C. 340, HL.
[47] [1988] F.S.R. 125 (Walton J.), affirmed [1989] F.S.R. 100, CA.
[48] (1946) 63 R.P.C. 103 (Evershed J.).
[49] [1982] R.P.C. 459, CA.

plaintiffs' gas cylinders. In *Bostik v Sellotape*[50] Blackburne J. would have allowed that the blue colour of the plaintiffs' BLU-TACK product had become distinctive (likewise the name), but that did not avail the plaintiffs because the colour of the defendants' product was hidden until after sale, and the name SELLO-TAK was distinct. An interlocutory injunction was refused, there being no arguable case. In Australia, an interlocutory injunction was granted in *United Pacific Industries v Madison Sports*[51] where the colour blue was the main component of the get-up of the plaintiffs' *Thermoskin* heat retaining products for sportspeople.

The *Pink Paraffin* case, *Shell-Mex & BP and Aladdin Industries v Holmes*,[52] is sometimes given as an example of a colour being distinctive, but although the pinkness of the paraffin and the nickname *Pink Paraffin* both seem to have been distinctive in fact, the decision rests on substitution in filling orders for the brand *Aladdin*.[53] If the defendant's paraffin had not been pink, this would have been detected. At trial in *Imperial Group v Philip Morris*[54] Whitford J. held that the colour black *per se* was not distinctive of the plaintiffs' cigarettes and that there was no passing-off by the defendants introducing cigarettes in a black pack which was clearly distinguishable by brand name and other aspects of get-up.[55] In *Financial Times v Evening Standard*[56] the plaintiffs' newspaper had been published since 1893 on pink paper. The defendants proposed to introduce pink paper for the business section of the *Evening Standard*. The balance of convenience and delay were against granting an *ex parte* interlocutory injunction, but in addition the risk of confusion and consequent damage would be slight. In Northern Ireland, the green component of BP's green and yellow livery for its petrol stations had become distinctive, and the defendant employed a similar shade of green, but the defendant's stations were clearly not selling the products of BP so there was no likelihood of confusion: *BP Amoco v John Kelly*[57].

8–158   Some marks are on the borderline between colours as such and verbal marks. The *Pink Paraffin* and *BLU-TACK* cases were mentioned above. Other examples are *White Spot* for pipes and *Blue Spot* for loudspeakers in *Dunhill v Bartlett & Bickley*[58] and *Ideal Werke v Willesden & District Light Supply Co*[59] respectively[60]; *REDEX* for an oil additive in *Wayne v Fields Auto Services*[61] and *Blue Orchid* Brilliantine in *Delavelle v Stanley*.[62] In *White Hudson v Asian Organisation*[63] the plaintiffs' goods became known in Sin-

---

[50] [1994] R.P.C. 556 (Blackburne J.).
[51] (1998) 41 I.P.R. 546 (Finkelstein J., Federal Court of Australia).
[52] (1937) 54 R.P.C. 287 (Luxmoore J.).
[53] Compare *Bostik Ltd v Sellotape GB Ltd* above, where the blue colour of both parties' products was not part of the get-up because it was invisible until after purchase.
[54] [1984] R.P.C. 293 (Whitford J.).
[55] See also *Williams (J B) Co v H Bronnley & Co Ltd* (1909) 26 R.P.C. 765, CA
[56] [1991] F.S.R. 7 (Aldous J.).
[57] [2002] F.S.R. 5, CA of Northern Ireland.
[58] (1922) 39 R.P.C. 426 (Russell J.).
[59] (1930) 48 R.P.C. 123 (Clauson J.).
[60] A pink spot did not infringe the former but *Navy Spot* infringed the latter.
[61] (1954) 71 R.P.C. 435 (Vaisey J.).
[62] (1946) 63 R.P.C. 103 (Evershed J.).
[63] [1964] 1 W.L.R. 1466; [1965] 1 All E.R. 1040; [1965] R.P.C. 45, PC.

gapore as *Red Paper Cough Sweets* on account of their wrapping. In *John Walker v Rothmans International*[64] Brightman J. accepted that the plaintiffs had an arguable case that the defendants' *Red Label* cigarettes would be taken as connected with the plaintiffs' *Red Label* whisky, but refused an interlocutory injunction on the balance of convenience. In *Silicon Graphics v Indigo Graphic Systems*[65] there was a triable issue as to whether it was the plaintiffs or the defendants who had first used the mark *Indigo* in the United Kingdom in the field where computers and printing equipment met. An interlocutory injunction was refused.

Combinations of colours are more likely to be distinctive than single colours. In *Hoffman-La Roche v DDSA Pharmaceuticals*[66] pharmaceutical capsules coloured green and black were sufficiently distinctive of the plaintiffs for an interlocutory injunction to be granted. In contrast, cases based on uniformly coloured capsules or tablets have failed. A tag in red, white and green sewn into the seam of pairs of jeans was distinctive in the Canadian case of *Caron v US Dungaree Seafarers*,[67] and confusion was not avoided by moving the tag or by the use of a red, white and blue tag in the original position. However, the latter tag in a different position to the plaintiffs' was allowed. In another Canadian case, *VISA International Service Association v Visa Motel Corp*[68] the plaintiffs authorised member banks to use the word *VISA* and three coloured bands for credit cards. The defendant supplied portable buildings to construction sites. It used *VISA* in its corporate name and the coloured bands on the portable buildings themselves. An injunction and damages were granted.

Where two or more colours are used separately for goods from the same manufacturer, the natural inference may be that the colours serve to differentiate different kinds or qualities rather than to denote the trade source.[69] This was the conclusion reached by Walton J. in refusing an interlocutory injunction in *Rizla v Bryant & May*.[70] The plaintiffs sold *Rizla* papers for rolling cigarettes with the three colours blue, green and red corresponding to the weight of the paper and whether it was cut at the corners. The defendants introduced corresponding packets of papers under those colours, but with otherwise distinct get-up and under the brand name *Swan*.[71]

It must be rare for an attribute as simple and functional as the shape of **8–159** goods to be distinctive in its own right. In *Ripley v Bandey*[72] Kekewich J. was prepared to hold that the oval shape of the plaintiff's blue was distinctive, as

---

[64] [1978] F.S.R. 357 (Brightman J.).
[65] [1994] F.S.R. 403 (Knox J.).
[66] [1969] F.S.R. 416, CA.
[67] (1978) 40 C.P.R. (2d) 245 (British Columbia Supreme Court, Bouck J.).
[68] (1984) 1 C.P.R. (3d) 109 (British Columbia Court of Appeal).
[69] *Roche Products Ltd v Berk Pharmaceuticals Ltd* [1973] R.P.C. 473, CA and *Wyeth (John) & Brother Ltd v M & A Pharmachem Ltd* [1988] F.S.R. 26.
[70] [1986] R.P.C. 389 (Walton J.).
[71] The use of three colours to distinguish different qualities recalls *Payton & Co v Snelling Lampard & Co* [1901] A.C. 308; 17 R.P.C. 628, HL, but although in that case the defendants used the same colours, it was in a different order.
[72] (1897) 14 R.P.C. 591 (Kekewich J.).

well as the name *Oval Blue* itself. However, he refused relief because the plaintiff had allowed his rights to lapse. Compare *Ripley v Griffiths*[73] in which the same plaintiff failed to satisfy Farwell J. that there was passing-off by substitution when blue not of his manufacture was supplied in response to trap orders for *Oval Blue*. The shape of cigars was distinctive enough for an interlocutory injunction to be awarded in *Elliott v Hodgson*,[74] but the case has subsequently been doubted[75] and a band with the defendant's mark on it would have distinguished. In the Australian case of *Simplot v McCain*[76] the plaintiffs (effectively Birds Eye) had introduced a new frozen potato product under the name of *Hash Brown Triangles* but could claim no proprietary rights in either the name or shape of the product, and the defendants' brand name *McCain* was sufficient distinction.

Colour and shape of bottles and containers

8–160 Cases on the get-up of bottles and similar containers taken as a whole, including their labels and wrapping, are fairly numerous and are discussed above under get-up of packaging. It is also possible for bottles and the like to be distinctive in their size, shape or colour (or a combination of these) independently of any markings or labels, although differences in those must be taken into account on the question of deceptive similarity. The leading case is now *Reckitt & Colman v Borden*[77] in which the House of Lords upheld relief against the copying of a container for lemon juice which imitated the size, shape and colour of a real lemon. However, every case still has to be considered on its own facts. In *Ty-Nant Spring Water v Simon Feeney*[78] an application for an interlocutory injunction based solely on the cobalt blue colour of the plaintiffs' mineral water bottles was described as "hopeless" when the defendants' bottles, though of the same colour, were entirely distinct in terms of shape, label and brand name.

In an early Australian case, *Champion v Smith*[79] the plaintiffs sold vinegar in bottles of a peculiar shape, embossed with their name and bearing labels. The defendant obtained a second-hand supply of those bottles, filled them with vinegar of his own, and sold them with labels covering the plaintiffs' name. He was found liable for passing-off despite the labels being dissimilar. In England, *Cusenier v Gaiety Bars & Restaurant Co*[80] turned on substitution when the brand was asked for. Similarities in the shapes of the respective bottles may have facilitated this, but only the bar proprietor was sued.

In *Haig v Forth Blending Co*[81] the Court of Session granted an interim interdict against the use of bottles for whisky similar in shape to those used

---

[73] (1902) 19 R.P.C. 590 (Farwell J.).
[74] (1902) 19 R.P.C. 518 (Buckley J.).
[75] *Hawkins & Tipson Ltd v Fludes Carpets Ltd* [1957] R.P.C. 8 and *Cadbury Ltd v Ulmer GmbH* [1988] F.S.R. 385.
[76] [2001] FCA 518; 52 I.P.R. 539.
[77] [1990] 1 W.L.R. 491; [1990] 1 All E.R. 873; [1990] R.P.C. 340, HL.
[78] [2000] R.P.C. 55 (Scott V.-C.).
[79] (1900) 21 L.R. (N.S.W.) Eq. 110 (Simpson C.J. in Eq.).
[80] (1902) 19 R.P.C. 357 (Buckley J.).
[81] (1952) 69 R.P.C. 323 *per* Lords Birnham and Sorn.

for the pursuers' *Dimple* brand, and a permanent interdict was granted at trial.[82] However, in England the same plaintiffs were refused an interlocutory injunction against bottles which were said to reproduce a similar effect by an optical illusion.[83] The plaintiffs' case was really that the bottles were similar enough to encourage substitution in bars abroad. That a sober and knowledgeable customer would not be deceived misses the point. In New Zealand, both parties used unlabelled bottles of similar shape for cola drinks in *Waiwai v Grey & Menzies*.[84] Relief was refused on various grounds: customers selected the drinks by name rather than by get-up; the crown caps were of different colours; the principal similarity in shape was a raised central band, but that was functional in that it was there to keep the bottles steady in the filling machine; the patterned mouldings on the bottles differed and there was acquiescence. In another Scottish case, *Coca-Cola Co v Barr*,[85] there was a *prima facie* case of passing-off in respect of bottles the same size and shape as *Coca-Cola* bottles if they were filled with brown liquid, but not if the contents were another colour.[86] Bottles have also been protected in terms of shape and colour in Canada. In *Jay-Zee Food Products Inc v Home Juice Co*[87] a bottle with handles at the neck resembling ears was held to be distinctive of the plaintiffs and an interlocutory injunction granted. In *Source Perrier v Canada Dry*[88] the plaintiffs were granted an interlocutory injunction against imitation of their mineral water bottle which was shaped like an Indian club and made of green glass. A competitor already used a bottle of the same shape in blue glass. In a Singapore case, *Malaysia Dairy Industries v Yakult*[89] the plaintiffs failed in an action based on the shape of a bottle because it was distinctive of the company supplying the defendants and had been copied by the plaintiff.

In all the foregoing cases the claimant's bottle or container had a shape of **8–161** relatively high inherent distinctiveness, sometimes reinforced by choice of colour. In other cases it has been argued that passing-off has been committed or facilitated by the use of quite ordinary cans, tubs or other containers too similar in size, shape or colour to those of the claimant. Where the claimant's containers are unremarkable in these respects the defendant is under no obligation to avoid such standard features if he distinguishes his goods adequately in other respects.[90] In the New Zealand case of *Bar's*

---

[82] [1953] R.P.C. 259; [1954] S.C. 35, *per* Lord Hill Watson. In *Reckitt & Colman v Borden,* above, Lord Oliver approved the *Dimple* case.

[83] *Haig (John) & Co Ltd v Brooks & Bohm (Wineshippers) Ltd* (1955) 72 R.P.C. 247 (Roxburgh J.).

[84] [1957] N.Z.L.R. 70 (Turner J.).

[85] [1961] R.P.C. 387 (Lord Walker).

[86] In *Coca-Cola Co v All-Fect Distributors Ltd* (1998) 43 I.P.R. 47 (Merkel J., Federal Court of Australia) there was no liability for passing off by importing and selling cola-flavoured confectionery in the same shape as the contoured *Coca-Cola* bottle.

[87] (1977) 32 C.P.R. (2d) 265 (Ontario High Court, Grange J.).

[88] (1982) 64 C.P.R. (2d) 116 (Ontario High Court, Anderson J.).

[89] [1980] F.S.R. 43 (Chua J., Singapore).

[90] *Cadbury Schweppes Pty Ltd v Pub Squash Co Pty Ltd* [1981] R.P.C. 429; [1981] 1 All E.R. 213, PC. But if the claimant's container is not distinctive in the first place, it is hard to see how any obligation to distinguish can arise. Compare *Cadbury Ltd v Ulmer GmbH* [1988] F.S.R. 385.

Leaks v Motor Specialities[91] the use of a wide-mouthed 5 oz. bottle was dictated by necessity and the defendant had distinguished his adequately. In *Tetrosyl v Silver Paint & Lacquer*[92] the parties sold household filler in white tubs of the same shape and size, obtained from the same supplier. Others in the field also used these tubs. The get-up differed in other respects. The Court of Appeal refused an interlocutory injunction, holding that there was no serious issue to be tried. A similar result was reached in *Scott v Nice-Pak*[93] in which the plaintiffs and defendants sold baby-wipes in blue tubs of similar size but differing in shade and labelling. Similarities confined to the use of similar white plastic tubs with a ribbed band round the top were not particularly confusing once conspicuous differences in get-up as a whole were taken into account in *Dalgety Spillers v Food Brokers*[94] and an interlocutory injunction was refused.

In *Cadbury Schweppes v Pub Squash Co*[95] Powell J. at first instance held that by putting their lemon drink in a can of the same size, shape and colour as the plaintiffs, the defendants had made it incumbent to distinguish it by other means. They had done so by the brand name and the rest of the get-up generally. That cans came in certain standard shapes and sizes was notorious, but a submission that drinks were "colour-coded" to correspond to flavour was not made out on the evidence. The Privy Council upheld his decision.

Colour and shape of capsules and tablets

8–162 Several cases have dealt with the colouring and sometimes the shape of pharmaceutical capsules and tablets. Pharmaceutical companies face difficulties in the choice of distinguishing features because pharmacists buy in bulk and dispense to the public in standard containers which may not carry the brand name at all, or may do so inconspicuously. Any indication of origin which is to come to the attention of the patient must therefore be carried by the capsules or tablets themselves. Word marks and even initials are likely to be too small to be legible, which leaves colour and shape as almost the only options.[96] What is perhaps surprising is that relatively few manufacturers have favoured two-colour capsules, or non-standard shapes, or have attempted to reinforce the trade mark significance of their get-up through adopting a consistent house style. In *Hoffman-La Roche v DDSA Pharmaceuticals*[97] the Court of Appeal granted an interlocutory injunction against the copying of chlordiazepoxide capsules coloured green and black. However, where the pill or capsule has borne only one colour relief has always been refused, even where shape was also relied on: in *Roche Products v*

---

[91] [1970] N.Z.L.R. 826; [1973] R.P.C. 21 (Richmond J.).
[92] [1980] F.S.R. 68, CA.
[93] [1989] F.S.R. 100, CA.
[94] [1994] F.S.R. 504 (Blackburne J.). (*Pot Noodles* and *Cup Noodles*).
[95] [1981] R.P.C. 429; [1981] 1 All E.R. 213, PC.
[96] This passage was approved in *Ciba-Geigy v Apotex, infra.*
[97] [1969] F.S.R. 416, CA.

Berk Pharmaceuticals[98] (diazepam) where different dosages were presented as white and yellow tablets, magenta in *Boots Co v Approved Prescription Services*[99] (ibuprufen), and blue and yellow for different dosages in *Wyeth v M & A Pharmachem*[1] (lorazepam).

Cases on pharmaceutical get-up are more numerous in Canada. Until 1992, the Canadian authorities differed from the English in defining the relevant public for prescription medicines as doctors and pharmacists, rather than including patients themselves. However, the Supreme Court of Canada has now held in *Ciba-Geigy v Apotex*[2] that patients as the ultimate consumers of medicines are part of the relevant public for the purposes of passing-off, so that their evidence should not be excluded. The previous Canadian decisions must now be regarded as having been decided on wrong principles, although some might have been justified on the ground that even patients themselves chiefly associated the colour or shape of the capsule with the therapeutic effect of the medicine rather than its trade source, especially where different dosage strengths were distinguished by different colours. Ultimately, this is a matter of fact and evidence.

Many of the Canadian passing-off cases refer to the trade mark case of **8–163** *Parke Davis v Empire Laboratories*[3] before the Supreme Court of Canada, in which the get-up of the plaintiffs' capsules had failed to acquire secondary meaning. Although the get-up was not distinctive, this case is one of the few which is not inconsistent with treating patients as part of the relevant public. An interlocutory injunction was refused in *Hoffman-La Roche v Rocke-William*[4] in respect of the same black and green capsule for chlordiazepoxide as was in issue in *Hoffman-La Roche v DDSA Pharmaceuticals.*[5]

A new trial was ordered in *Ayerst McKenna & Harrison v Apotex*[6] because the trial judge had been biased against the plaintiffs, but the Ontario Court of Appeal described the plaintiffs' case as "tenuous at best". The plaintiffs' drug, propranolol, was in four dosage forms, each with a different colour, and the tablets were of typical bi-convex shape. An interlocutory injunction was refused in *Syntex Inc v Novopharm.*[7] Patients identified the trade dress with the kind of medication, not with the supplier. Doctors and pharmacists were the relevant public. Injunctions were also refused in *Hoffman-La Roche v Apotex*[8] and *Smith Kline & French Canada v Novopharm.*[9] Likewise, in

---

[98] [1973] R.P.C. 473, CA.
[99] (1980) [1988] F.S.R. 44, CA.
[1] [1988] F.S.R. 26 (Whitford J.).
[2] *Ciba-Geigy Canada Ltd v Apotex Inc* (1992) 95 D.L.R. (4th) 385; 44 C.P.R. (3d) 289; 24 I.P.R. 652 (Supreme Court of Canada). Gonthier J., delivering the judgment of the Court, quoted with approval a passage from the first edition of the present work criticising the Ontario authorities.
[3] [1964] S.C.R. 351; 45 D.L.R. (2d) 97; 43 C.P.R. 1; 27 Fox Pat. Cas. 67 (Supreme Court of Canada).
[4] (1970) 44 Fox (Pat. Cas.) 163; 62 C.P.R. 233 (Dumoulin J., Exchequer Court).
[5] [1969] F.S.R. 416, CA.
[6] (1983) 41 O.R. (2d) 366; 146 D.L.R. (3d) 93; 72 C.P.R. (2d) 57 Ontario Court of Appeal.
[7] (1983) 74 C.P.R. 110 (Walsh J., Ontario); (naproxen).
[8] (1983) 72 C.P.R. (2d) 183 (White J., Ontario); (flurazepam).
[9] (1983) 72 C.P.R. (2d) 197 (McRae J., Ontario); (cimetidine).

Smith Kline & French Canada v Apotex[10] doctors and pharmacists were said to be "the true customers" for prescription pharmaceuticals and an interlocutory injunction was again refused. The same result was reached in *Ciba-Geigy v Novopharm*.[11] There was not even a serious issue to be tried.

A rare exception prior to *Ciba-Geigy v Apotex* is *Hoffman-La Roche v Novopharm*[12] in which an interlocutory injunction was granted in respect of bi-coloured capsules of flurazepam, orange and ivory for 15 mg and red and ivory for 30 mg.[13] In *Ciba-Geigy v Apotex* itself, the plaintiffs claimed that the size, shape and colour (blue) of their *Lopresor* brand metoprolol tablets were distinctive of them. The trial court refused to give summary judgment for the defendants but decided as a point of law that the plaintiffs must establish confusion of physicians or pharmacists, and the Ontario Court of Appeal affirmed. The Supreme Court of Canada overruled *Ayerst, McKena & Harrison v Apotex* and allowed the appeal by the plaintiffs. *Ciba-Geigy v Apotex* was immediately followed in *Ciba-Geigy v Novopharm*[14] where an interlocutory injunction was granted restraining the defendants from selling generic diclofenac tablets with the same pink colour and shape as the plaintiffs' brand *Voltarol*.[15] One reason was that loss of distinctiveness of the get-up would result and would be impossible to compensate in money.

In South Africa, neither imitation of the elliptical bi-convex shape of tablets of the antibiotic *Augmentin*, nor the name *Augmaxcil*, amounted to passing-off in *Triomed v Beecham Group*.[16]

Pattern

8–164   In principle, there is no reason why pattern as such should not be distinctive: even the simplest pattern has, after all, greater inherent capacity to distinguish than one or two plain colours. In practice, pattern is normally relevant as one component of a get-up which may or may not be distinctive when taken as a whole. The few cases in which pattern on its own has been in issue have failed on the facts. Stripes were found not to be distinctive in *Saper v Specter's*,[17] *Baskin-Robbins v Gutman*[18] and *Adidas v O'Neill*.[19] In *Klissers*

---

[10] (1985) 12 C.P.R. (3d) 479 (Callon J., Ontario); (cimetidine).

[11] (1986) 12 C.P.R. (3d) 76 (Holland J., Ontario).

[12] (1980) 51 C.P.R. (2d) 40 (O'Driscoll J., Ontario).

[13] Not followed in *Hoffman-La Roche Ltd v Apotex Inc* (1983) 72 C.P.R. (2d) 183 (White J., Ontario) in which an interlocutory injunction was refused on almost identical facts.

[14] (1994) 52 C.P.R. (3d) 497 (Gibson J., Federal Court).

[15] The plaintiffs' 75 mg tablets were triangular bi-convex; the 100 mg ones, round bi-convex and a darker pink. The plaintiffs' literature emphasised the trade mark significance of these features.

[16] [2001] F.S.R. 34 (Smit J., Transvaal Provincial Division). The case was principally argued and decided on an application to expunge a registered trade mark for the tablet shape, irrespective of colour.

[17] (1953) 70 R.P.C. 173 (Harman J.).

[18] [1977] F.S.R. 545 (Graham J.).

[19] [1983] F.S.R. 76 (Irish Supreme Court). It was accepted that the familiar three stripes would have been distinctive of Adidas had there been more use in the jurisdiction. Compare *Adidas Sportschuenfabriken Adi Dassler KG v Henry Walt & Co Ltd* 1976 (1) SA 531.

Bakeries v Harvest Bakeries[20] the checked gingham wrapping for the plaintiffs' brand of sliced bread (which differed in detail from product to product) was not sufficiently distinctive on the facts for there to be passing-off when the brand names were distinct. Checks were a common feature of packaging in the bread trade and the plaintiffs' case was not rescued by the supposedly distinctive ponytail effect with which their bags were sealed.

While pattern applied to wrapping may form part of the get-up of the product in the legal sense, pattern applied to the goods themselves is more likely to be appreciated for its own sake than as an indication of origin. The pattern on a mat was held not to be distinctive in *Hawkins & Tipson v Fludes*.[21]

J. DOMAIN NAMES AND THE INTERNET

The nature of the problem

Businesses and other organisations are known to users of the internet **8–165** principally by their domain names. Their importance and manner of allocation and operation were explained in the first instance judgment of Jonathan Sumption Q.C. in *British Telecommunications v One in a Million*,[22] in a passage which was adopted by the Court of Appeal.

"The Internet is increasingly used by commercial organisations to promote themselves and their products and in some cases to buy and sell. For these purposes they need a domain name identifying the computer which they are using. A domain name comprises groups of alphanumeric characters separated by dots. A first group commonly comprises the name of the enterprise or a brand name or trading name associated with it, followed by a 'top level' name identifying the nature and sometimes the location of the organisation. Marks & Spencer, for example, have a number of domain names, including *marks-and-spencer.co.uk, marks-and-spencer.com* and *stmichael.com*. The domain name *marks-and-spencer. co.uk*, for example, will enable them to have an e-mail address in the form *johnsmith@marks-and-spencer.co.uk* and a web site address in the form *http://www.marks-and-spencer.co.uk*. The top level suffix *co.uk* indicates a United Kingdom company. Other top level names bear conventional meanings as follows:

    .com International commercial organisations
    .edu Educational organisation
    .gov Government organisation
    .org Miscellaneous organisations

[20] [1988] 1 N.Z.L.R. 16; [1989] R.P.C. 27 (CA, New Zealand).
[21] [1957] R.P.C. 8 (Dankwerts J.).
[22] [1999] 1 W.L.R. 903, [1999] 4 All E.R. 476, [1999] E.T.M.R. 61; [1999] F.S.R. 1, CA, affirming [1998] F.S.R. 265.

There is an argument, which does not matter, about whether this last designation is confined to non-profit-making organisations. There is no central authority regulating the Internet, which is almost entirely governed by convention. But registration services in respect of domain names are provided by a number of organisations. Network Solutions Inc. of Virginia in the United States is the organisation generally recognised as responsible for allocating domain names with the top level suffixes 'com' and 'edu.' In the United Kingdom a company called Nominet U.K. provides a registration service in respect of domain names ending with the geographical suffix *uk* preceded by functional suffixes such as *co, org, gov* or *edu*."

8–166   Problems capable of being addressed by passing-off most obviously arise when two or more persons claim the right to a domain name or a component of it.[23] Where the incumbent has no obvious interest in using the name other than inconveniencing an person with a better right to it, generally with the intention of being bought out, then the practice is known as cybersquatting. For most practical purposes, all that need be said about cybersquatting following *British Telecommunications v One in a Million* was said by Deputy Judge Jonathan Sumption Q.C. at first instance:

> "Any person who deliberately registers a domain name on account of its similarity to the name, brand name or trade mark of an unconnected commercial organisation must expect to find himself on the receiving end of an injunction to restrain the threat of passing off, and the injunction will be in terms which will make the name commercially useless to the dealer."

However, while cybersquatting has perhaps attracted the most attention, it is not necessarily the most representative or important situation in the long term. Passing off also has to deal with the conceptually simpler, but probably more important, case of defendants using a particular domain name in such a way as actually to divert business intended for the claimant, whether inadvertently or not[24]; and with use of the plaintiff's distinctive signs either visibly in the defendant's own site, or (as "metatags") in a manner only perceptible to search engines.[25]

Cybersquatting: *BT v One in a Million*

8–167   The leading case on passing-off by the deliberate and dishonest adoption of a domain name distinctive of another business is now *British Telecommunications v One in a Million*.[26] The problem of cybersquatting (or mis-

---

[23] As in *Pitman Training Ltd v Nominet UK* [1997] F.S.R. 797 and *Prince plc v Prince Sports Group Inc* [1998] F.S.R. 21.

[24] *Musical Fidelity Ltd v Vickers* [2002] EWCA Civ 1989.

[25] *Reed Executive plc v Reed Business Information Ltd* [2002] EWHC 1015; [2003] R.P.C. 12 (Pumfrey J.).

[26] [1999] 1 W.L.R. 903; [1999] 4 All E.R. 476; [1999] E.T.M.R. 61; [1999] F.S.R. 1, CA.

registration of internet domain names) was not entirely new in *One in a Million*, but its treatment in that case must be taken as superceding previous authorities, which are now of no more than residual interest.

The facts of *British Telecommunications v One in a Million* were that the defendants[27] had made a practice of registering internet domain names corresponding to the corporate names or trade marks of well-known companies, and subsequently offering those names for sale to the same companies at what might be thought to be an extortionate price, with the implicit (and in some cases explicit) threat that they would otherwise be offered for sale to the highest bidder on the open market. Six plaintiffs in all[28] sued for passing-off and trade mark infringement and obtained summary judgment at first instance,[29] and on appeal. The five actions consolidated into a single hearing and appeal concerned the domain names *bt.org, cellnet.net, sainsbury.com, sainsburys.com, j-sainsbury.com, ladbrokes.com, marksandspencer.com*, and *virgin.org*, (all registered by One in a Million); *marksandspencer.co.uk, britishtelecom.co.uk* and *britishtelecom.net* (registered by Global Media Communications); and *britishtelecom.com* (registered by Junic). It may be noted that all these domain names were inactive, and that all the plaintiffs had web sites (such as *marks-and-spencer.co.uk* as well *marks-and-spencer.com* and *stmichael.com*) operating under appropriate names.

At first instance, the Deputy Judge (Jonathan Sumption Q.C.) granted **8–168** summary judgment in all five actions requiring the defendants to assign the domain names to the respective plaintiffs. The defendants had not yet committed any acts of actual passing off in relation to those names, but the domain names constituted "instruments of deception" which the defendants expressly proposed to dispose of to the highest bidder, and their actions to date unequivocally amounted to threatened passing off, which the court would restrain *quia timet*:

"The mere creation of an 'instrument of deception', without either using it for deception or putting it into the hands of someone else to do so, is not passing off. There is no such tort as going equipped for passing off. It follows that the mere registration of a deceptive company name or a deceptive Internet domain name is not passing off. In both of these cases [*GlaxoWellcome* and *Direct Line*] the court granted what amounted to a *quia timet* injunction to restrain a threatened rather than an actual tort. In both cases, the injunctions were interlocutory rather than final, and the threat is no doubt easier to establish in that context. But even a final injunction does not require proof that damage will certainly occur. It is enough that what is going on is calculated to infringe the plaintiff's rights in future."

---

[27] The company One in a Million Ltd, the two individuals who controlled it, and two other firms (Global Media Communications and Junic) through which they conducted business.

[28] British Telecommunications plc and Telecom Securicor Cellular Radio Ltd, Virgin Enterprises Ltd, J Sainsbury plc, Marks and Spencer plc and Ladbroke Group plc.

[29] [1998] F.S.R. 265.

Consistently with this analysis, Jonathan Sumption Q.C. considered whether there was a more than theoretical possibility that the names might be retained, used, or disposed of by the defendants without there being any passing off; and concluded that although this was valid in point of legal analysis, the possible legitimate uses were simply irrelevant to the defendants' scheme. This was clearest in the case of the Marks and Spencer action:

> "The only point made by the defendants which is worthy of any attention is that there are uses to which they can put the domain name which would not involve passing off by them or anyone else, namely (i) the sale of the domain name to Marks & Spencer themselves, and (ii) its simple retention with a view to blocking the use of the same name by Marks & Spencer in order to induce them to pay. I would accept that neither of these activities in themselves constitutes passing off. But that is not the point. The point is that the names are only saleable to Marks & Spencer and blocking their use by Marks & Spencer is only a useful negotiating tactic on the footing that they are names which it is dangerous for Marks & Spencer to allow to remain out of their control. The danger arises from the risk of deception which their existence necessarily presents. The allegation that this was the defendants' object in this case is fairly made, supported by overwhelming evidence, and is left wholly unanswered by the defendants' affidavits."

8–169   For the other four plaintiffs, the same result was reached after disposing of a further argument:

> "In the four other cases, the facts relevant to both causes of action are substantially the same in all relevant respects save one. The difference is that in the other four cases, it is somewhat less absurd for the defendants to suggest the names which they have registered have an innocent use. It is impossible to imagine any unconnected party using the phrase 'Marks and Spencer' in his name or address if not to deceive, and the same may well be true of Cellnet. But the possibility is not so far-fetched in the case of the words 'Sainsbury', 'Ladbroke', 'Virgin' or 'BT'. . . . The defendants make much of this point, but I am not impressed by it for the simple reason that although the words are probably capable of an innocent use, that is not the use that these defendants intend. The history of the defendants' activities shows a deliberate practice followed over a substantial period of time of registering domain names which are chosen to resemble the names and marks of other people and are plainly intended to deceive. The threat of passing off and trade mark infringement, and the likelihood of confusion arising from the infringement of the mark are made out beyond argument in this case, even in which it is possible to imagine other cases in which the issue would be more nicely balanced."

In the result, summary judgment would be granted:

> "The result is that the plaintiffs in all five actions are entitled to final injunctions *quia timet* . . . I accept that an order in the form of paragraph 2

(which requires the defendants to take steps to have the disputed names assigned to the plaintiffs) goes rather further than the negative form of injunctions normally appropriate *quia timet*. But it seems to me to be the most completely effective remedy, and one which does no injustice to the defendants, for these names are of no value to them otherwise than as a means of threatening unlawful acts. It is the equivalent, in this rather arcane context, of the delivery up of infringing goods..."

One in a Million on appeal

The judgment of the Deputy Judge in *British Telecommunications v One in a* **8–170**
Million was upheld in the Court of Appeal, but on considerably broader grounds, so much so that it is not altogether easy to say how much of the judgment is truly its *ratio decidendi*.[30] Logically, the first basis of liability to consider is whether the tort of passing off was complete–in the sense of a present misrepresentation actually causing damage to the plaintiffs' good-will–either by virtue of the defendants being entered in the relevant register as owners of the contested domain names, or by their offers to dispose of the names. This had been decided against the plaintiffs at first instance. By respondents' notices, the plaintiffs argued on appeal that the decision below should be affirmed on the additional grounds that the registration of a deceptive Internet domain name in a publicly accessible register did constitute passing-off, or at least amounted to a sufficient threat of passing-off to warrant the intervention of the court.[31] This was decided in favour of Marks & Spencer, at least, as giving rise to both complete and *quia timet* liability:

"The judge considered first the action brought by Marks & Spencer Plc. and then went on to deal with the other actions. I will adopt the same approach as the *Marks & Spencer* case raises slightly different issues from those raised in the other cases.

It is accepted that the name Marks & Spencer denotes Marks & Spencer Plc. and nobody else. Thus anybody seeing or hearing the name realises that what is being referred to is the business of Marks & Spencer Plc. It follows that registration by the defendants of a domain name including the name Marks & Spencer makes a false representation that they are associated or connected with Marks & Spencer Plc. This can be demonstrated by considering the reaction of a person who taps into his computer the domain name marksandspencer.co.uk and presses a button to execute a 'Whois' search. He will be told that the registrant is One In A Million Ltd. A substantial number of persons will conclude that One In A Million Ltd must be connected or associated with Marks & Spencer Plc. That amounts to a false representation which constitutes passing off.

Mr. Wilson submitted that mere registration did not amount to passing

---

[30] [1999] 1 W.L.R. 903; [1999] 4 All E.R. 476; [1999] E.T.M.R. 61; [1999] F.S.R. 1, CA.
[31] See [1999] 1 W.L.R. 903 at 906. A further argument raised by the respondents' notices was that the creation or initial acquisition of an "instrument of deception" sufficiently constituted passing-off or a threat to pass off.

off. Further, Marks & Spencer Plc. had not established any damage or likelihood of damage. I cannot accept those submissions. The placing on a register of a distinctive name such as 'marksandspencer' makes a representation to persons who consult the register that the registrant is connected or associated with the name registered and thus the owner of the goodwill in the name. Such persons would not know of One In A Million Ltd and would believe that they were connected or associated with the owner of the goodwill in the domain name they had registered. Further, registration of the domain name including the words 'Marks & Spencer' is an erosion of the exclusive goodwill in the name which damages or is likely to damage Marks & Spencer Plc."[32]

8–171 The logically separate analysis of the defendants' conduct in *One in a Million* in terms of "instruments of deception" was also addressed. This had been the only basis for the decision at first instance, and it was upheld on appeal in respect of the all the names and all the plaintiffs, and for substantially the same reasons:

"I also believe that domain names comprising the name 'Marks & Spencer' are instruments of fraud. Any realistic use of them as domain names would result in passing off and there was ample evidence to justify the injunctive relief granted by the judge to prevent them being used for a fraudulent purpose and to prevent them being transferred to others.

The other cases are slightly different. Mr. Wilson pointed to the fact that there are people called Sainsbury and Ladbroke and companies, other than Virgin Enterprises Ltd, who have as part of their name the word Virgin and also people or firms whose initials would be B.T. He went on to submit that it followed that the domain names which the defendants had registered were not inherently deceptive. They were not instruments of fraud. Further there had been no passing off and none was threatened and a transfer to a third party would not result in the defendants becoming joint tortfeasors in any passing off carried out by the person to whom the registrations were transferred. Thus, he submitted, there was no foundation for the injunctive relief in the actions brought by four of the plaintiffs.

I believe that, for the same reasons I have expressed in relation to the Marks & Spencer Plc. action, passing off and threatened passing off has been demonstrated....

I also believe that the names registered by the defendants were instruments of fraud and that injunctive relief was appropriate upon this basis as well. The trade names were well known 'household names' denoting in ordinary usage the respective plaintiff. The defendants registered them without any distinguishing word because of the goodwill attaching to those names. It was the value of that goodwill, not the fact that they could perhaps be used in some way by a third party without deception, which caused them to register the names. The motive of the defendants was to

[32] *per* Aldous L.J., above.

use that goodwill and threaten to sell it to another who might use it for passing off to obtain money from the plaintiffs. The value of the names lay in the threat that they would be used in a fraudulent way. The registrations were made with the purpose of appropriating the plaintiffs' property, their goodwill, and with an intention of threatening dishonest use by them or another. The registrations were instruments of fraud and injunctive relief was appropriate just as much as it was in those cases where persons registered company names for a similar purpose."[33]

Finally, there is the doctrine of the equitable protective jurisdiction, which **8–172** had not been mentioned below. Nonetheless, it was expressly invoked by Aldous L.J. after he had reviewed the major authorities on the classic doctrine of instruments of deception, as well as the cases on company names:

"The ability to restrain dissemination of an instrument of fraud was recognised by the Court of Appeal in *Norwich Pharmacal Co v Customs and Excise Commissioners* [1974] A.C. 133. That was an action in which the plaintiffs sought discovery of the names of patent infringers. The plaintiffs submitted, by analogy to trade mark and passing off cases, that the customs could be ordered to give discovery of the names. The most pertinent passage to the issue in this case is in the judgment of Buckley L.J., at pp. 145–146:

'If a man has in his possession or control goods the dissemination of which, whether in the way of trade or, possibly, merely by way of gifts (see *Upmann v Forester* (1883) 24 Ch.D. 231) will infringe another's patent or trade mark, he becomes, as soon as he is aware of this fact, subject to a duty, an equitable duty, not to allow those goods to pass out of his possession or control at any rate in circumstances in which the proprietor of the patent or mark might be injured by infringement ensuing. The man having the goods in his possession or control must not aid the infringement by letting the goods get into the hands of those who may use them or deal with them in a way which will invade the proprietor's rights. Even though by doing so he might not himself infringe the patent or trade mark, he would be in dereliction of his duty to the proprietor. This duty is one which will, if necessary, be enforced in equity by way of injunction: see *Upmann v Elkan* (1871) L.R. 12 Eq. 140; L.R. 7 Ch. App. 130. The man having possession or control may also be under a duty to give information in relation to the goods to the proprietor of the patent or mark: *Upmann v Elkan*.'"[34]

[33] *per* Aldous L.J., above.
[34] *per* Aldous L.J., above.

One in a Million criticised

8–173 The Court of Appeal judgment in *British Telecommunications v One in a Million* includes a coded message which should warn the reader that legal certainty is about to be sacrificed:

"His [Lord Diplock's] five characteristics were those he identified in 1980 from previously decided cases, but I do not believe that he was thereby confining for ever the cause of action to every detail of such characteristics, as to do so would prevent the common law evolving to meet changes in methods of trade and communication as it had in the past."

True to this promise, much of the reasoning of *British Telecommunications v One in a Million* is confused and fails to convince–once one's instinctive emotional response to the defendants' combination of greed, dishonesty and hypocrisy has cooled. This might not matter if, or to the extent, that an entirely new situation required an equally unconventional legal response. But this is hardly the case given the way the action progressed: the judgment at first instance had given the plaintiffs all the relief they really needed, on the basis of a uncontested extension to a long-known and entirely orthodox doctrine, that of "instruments of deception". The judgment on appeal not only upheld this, but did so on the basis of some distinctly old case law. Not the least striking thing about the *One in a Million* judgment is the use it makes of cases decided before the telephone was invented. Far from being an advance on passing-off as understood in *Advocaat* and *Jif*, much of the reasoning *One in a Million* is shockingly regressive.[35]

8–174 The most questionable conclusion of *One in a Million* is the proposition that the mere entry of any of the domain names in the relevant directory in the name of the defendants constituted actual passing off. An argument of such condensed circularity, if generally applicable, would render most of the accumulated learning on passing-off entirely redundant. Why bother to prove that the existence of the *Harrodian School* in Barnes would or might cause damaging confusion with *Harrods* department store across the River, if the reasoning of *One in a Million* applies *mutatis mutantur* to the entry for the former in the Register of Companies?[36] The objection is twofold: in all cases, the *Marks & Spencer* names as well as the others, it is contrary to both principle and authority, and not remotely necessary in order to do justice between the parties. If it be right that mere registration of *marksand spencer.co.uk* in the defendants' name (in a register accessible to the public, but not likely to be used for directing business to anyone) amounted to actual passing-off in fact, then what does one make of the general situation in which defendant D registers in his own name a trade mark which is in fact

---

[35] See Hazel Carty, "Passing off and Instruments of Deception: the Need for Clarity" (2003) 25 E.I.P.R. 188.

[36] *Harrods Ltd v Harrodian School Ltd* [1996] R.P.C. 697, CA. The final "Ltd" in the defendants' name is dropped in the heading of the report in the R.P.C.s, but the full name in the Court of Appeal transcript is *Harrodian School Ltd*.

distinctive of claimant C, whether in the official Trade Marks Registry, or even, for instance, in an ordinary trade directory? The first practice is as old as the Trade Mark Acts, but previously it has been dealt with in a perfectly satisfactory way within the registered trade mark system itself, and no one has suggested that this kind of situation inherently amounted to passing-off regardless of actual use,[37] although an unjustified attempt at registration made in bad faith might well constitute or involve injurious falsehood in the sub-species known as slander of title. But if anything the trade mark scenario is the stronger one, since (in contrast to an unused domain name) there will be little doubt as to the goods or services in respect of which the defendant intends to use the mark, and for which he implicitly asserts that it belongs to him.[37a]

So far as the names other than those of Marks & Spencer were concerned, a further objection is that the judgment is too Delphic. At first sight, the passage reading "... for the same reasons I have expressed in relation to the Marks & Spencer Plc. action, passing off and threatened passing off has been demonstrated" suggests that the tort was considered to be complete with the very act of registration of names such as *virgin.org* or *bt.org*. However the reasoning for Marks & Spencer had proceeded on the concession that the likes of *marksandspencer.com* were so strongly distinctive of the plaintiff that no manner of use could fail to deceive. This was the express difference between the Marks and Spencer cases and the others, the very point which called for separate analysis. Names such as *Virgin, BT, Ladbroke* or *Sainsbury* are only distinctive of their respective "owners" in a legally relevant sense once an appropriate business context has been defined, and perhaps also an appropriate geographical area. Absent such a context, the first two are not unambiguously names at all, and the latter two need not denote the relevant plaintiffs. Either that distinction was being abandoned, or there has to be some other basis for the finding that passing-off was complete in all cases and not just for Marks and Spencer. The only credible basis for that distinction in the judgment is fraud, which implies once again that the Court of Appeal was contemplating reversing a century of authority to the contrary and reviving the pre-Judicature Act common law tort of fraudulent passing-off.

In terms of passing-off as currently understood, any misrepresentation **8–175** inherent in registration of the names fails most of Lord Diplock's five express tests in *Advocaat*,[38] and one which is unstated by him but no less important for that: the representation is not necessarily made in the course of any trade; it is not directed at customers or consumers, and certainly not in a medium in which it would likely to be noticed or acted upon by them;

---

[37] In *Reality Group Ltd v Chance* [2002] F.S.R. 13 it was asserted, expressly in reliance upon *One in a Million*, that an application for a Community Trade Mark did amount to passing-off. Rimer J. refused to strike out the claim, but was clearly unsympathetic to the way it was put.

[37a] Compare *Inter Lotto (UK) Ltd v Camelot Group plc* [2003] EWCA Civ 1132; [2003] 4 All E.R. 575, CA, where the argument, if valid, would surely have decided the preliminary issue in the defendants' favour.

[38] *Erven Warnink BV v J Townend & Sons (Hull) Ltd* [1979] A.C. 731; [1979] 2 All E.R. 927; [1980] R.P.C. 31. HL.

and any damage calculated to result is not to the plaintiffs' goodwill in any recognisable sense. No one wishing to direct their custom to Marks & Spencers over the internet would be in any way diverted, deterred or discouraged by the mere existence of any of the registrations complained of. At most, they would be subjected to the minor inconvenience of using a search engine or retyping the domain name in one of Marks & Spencers' preferred forms, with the internal hyphens.

More fundamentally, perhaps, any such misrepresentation is not of the kind which passing-off addresses. As Lord Diplock acknowledged in *Advocaat*, immediately after proposing his five characteristics making up the cause of action:

> "In seeking to formulate general propositions of English law, however, one must be particularly careful to beware of the logical fallacy of the undistributed middle. It does not follow that because all passing off actions can be shown to present these characteristics, all factual situations which present these characteristics give rise to a cause of action for passing off."

At the very least, Lord Diplock must have had in mind the entirely separate torts concerned with disparaging misrepresentations in business. So far as *One in a Million* is concerned, it is much more appropriate to treat any misrepresentation inherent in registration as injurious falsehood rather than passing off. In injurious falsehood the relevant addressees and the pecuniary interest protected are much more broadly defined than in passing-off; there is no requirement for the misrepresentation to be made in the course of any trade; and the misrepresentation may be a statement of any kind provided that it can be said that it was made of and concerning the claimant, was calculated to cause pecuniary damage, and was made maliciously. The misrepresentation that a name such as *marksandspencer.com* is in some sense the property of, or under the control of, any company other than Marks & Spencer plc fits the tort of injurious falsehood very well: it is a classic example of slander of title updated to apply to a kind of asset which could not have existed before the late twentieth century. A policy advantage is that the maker of the entry or the keeper of the register will be liable only if acting "maliciously", a concept which is more than wide enough to apply all the *One in a Million* defendants but which avoids creating difficulties for *bona fide* registrants and the likes of Nominet. For registrants not acting *bona fide*, inferences of malice and damage are amplified, if that be necessary, in the common case of linking the domain name to a pornographic or otherwise undesirable website, or threatening to do so.

8–176 The next issue to address is that of "instruments of fraud" or "instruments of deception". It will be noted that as regards the *marksandspencer* names, the doctrine of instruments of deception might be applied without reference to the state of mind of the defendants or their prospective assignees since it was conceded (rightly or wrongly) that "Marks and Spencer" was so distinctive that no use of it was possible without referring to the plaintiffs. However with regard to the other names, it is impossible to read the judgment without concluding that it turned once again on the defendants' bad faith: not only is their dishonesty constantly reiterated, but it is expressly made the touchstone to distinguish their situation from that of persons who might have had a legitimate interest in using, acquiring, or transferring names which were not uniquely and invariably distinctive of the respective plaintiffs.

The attractions of invoking the doctrine of "instruments of fraud" in this context are considered in more detail elsewhere,[39] but they may be described as rhetorical rather than substantial. The disadvantages to the approach are threefold: in its classic form it has long since ceased to be dependent on fraudulent intent, and it applies irrespective of the defendant's state of mind–which may be too strict a standard in the present context; in its classic form again, it applies only to tangible deceptive goods which will inevitably deceive once placed in circulation; and although there may be an extended form which may be dependent on fraudulent intent, the latter is anomalous and of uncertain scope. It is noticeable that the authorities relied on by the Court of Appeal all seem to have been chosen because their language is permeated by references to fraud. For the older cases this is not surprising, since prior to the Judicature Act 1873 passing-off (as opposed the emerging doctrine of trade mark infringement) knew no juridical basis other than fraud of some kind, in either the legal or equitable senses of the word. But since the decision of the House of Lords in *Spalding v Gamage*,[40] the action for passing-off has been understood as having no mental element and turning solely on goodwill, misrepresentation and damage. There is ample authority from the late nineteenth century onwards that liability under the doctrine of instruments of deception in its original form applies irrespective of the defendant's state of mind, as for the rest of passing-off. It was only when the doctrine was (rather dubiously) extended to components, rather than complete goods, that courts once again tried to invoke fraud as the cornerstone for liability, as in the *Scotch Whisky* cases cited in the Court of Appeal.

The final possible basis for the *One in a Million* decision is the equitable **8–177** protective jurisdiction and this, it is suggested, is the most satisfactory of those expressly considered in the Court of Appeal. The equitable protective jurisdiction is not tied to any individual cause of action, it is not confined to the delivery up of tangible things, and it applies flexibly (with different consequences in costs) to innocent as well as fraudulent defendants. Like the doctrine of instruments of deception (with which it overlaps to a considerable extent in practice) the equitable protective jurisdiction has always applied to the kind of tangible things which will give rise to a cause of action if released by their holder to a third party. Unlike the doctrine of instruments of deception, the equitable protective jurisdiction is not confined to that situation and has already been applied in a case of high authority to one kind of intangible, namely knowledge of the identify of an infringer.[41] To

---

[39] See para.5–122.
[40] (1915) 32 R.P.C. 273, HL.
[41] *Norwich Pharmacal Co v Customs and Excise Commissioners* [1974] A.C. 133; [1973] 2 All E.R. 943; [1973] F.S.R. 365; [1974] R.P.C. 101, HL.

extend the equitable doctrine to a new kind of deceptive intangible more resembles addressing an intermediate situation, rather than extending the doctrine to an entirely new one.

Domain names: examples

8–178 The *One in a Million*[42] decision apart, subsequent cases on cybersquatting or other alleged misuses of the domain name system are not entirely without legal interest. *One in a Million* was distinguished and summary judgment refused in *French Connection v Sutton*.[43] Use of *fcuk.com* for the defendant's internet site could not be said to constitute an unambiguous assertion of connection with the claimants, when it was doubtful that their recently adopted trading style *FCUK* had become distinctive of them at the relevant time; "fcuk" was used and widely recognised on the internet as an obvious anagram for the expletive; and the defendant claimed to be using the name to draw attention to his own business and not for overt extortion or disposal to others. Neither actual passing off, nor allegations based on instruments of fraud, were made out with sufficient certainty for summary judgment. In *Roadtech v Mandata*[44] liability was all but conceded in respect of discontinued use of the claimants' marks *Roadrunner* and *Roadtech* as metatags on the defendants' site, and summary judgment for damages of £15,000 was awarded. In *W H Smith v Colman*[45] the defendant had registered *WHSmith.com* as a domain name. On an application for summary judgment (including transfer the domain name) the claimant put in evidence a letter from the defendant which was marked "without prejudice". The first instance judge admitted the letter, but the Court of Appeal held that the "without prejudice" rule applied unless there was "unambiguous impropriety", which had not been made out. The appeal was allowed.

In *Easyjet v Dainty*[46] the claimants operated an airline, a chain of internet cafes, and a car hire business under the names *easyJet, easyEverything* and *easyRentacar*. All three used a common get-up with white and orange predominating and all did a substantial amount of business over the internet. The defendant–a civil engineer with no experience in either computing or estate agency–purported to set up a cut-price internet estate agency under the name *easyRealestate.co.uk* with the website adopting the claimants' features of get-up. He was restrained from operating under the name, and ordered to transfer it to the claimants. In *Metalrax Group v Vanci*[47] the defendant's registration of *metalrax.co.uk* had already been suspended by Nominet, but an injunction was granted restraining him from reacquiring or

[42] *British Telecommunications v One in a Million Ltd* [1999] 1 W.L.R. 903; [1999] 4 All E.R. 476; [1999] E.T.M.R. 61; [1999] F.S.R. 1, CA.
[43] [2000] E.T.M.R. 341 (Rattee J.).
[44] [2000] E.T.M.R. 970.
[45] [2001] F.S.R. 9, CA. The appeal only concerned the preliminary question of the admission of "without prejudice" correspondence.
[46] [2002] F.S.R. 6 (Bernard Livesey Q.C., Deputy Judge).
[47] [2002] EWHC 167 (Lawrence Collins J.).

reregistering the name. This was a case in which at attempt at extortion had been buttressed by linking the name to pornography.

In *Musical Fidelity v Vickers*[48] the internet was being used to assist actual passing off in one of its classic forms. The claimant had used the trade name *Musical Fidelity* since 1982, and the defendant had previously been one of its authorised distributors. Summary judgment was granted in respect of his use of *musicalfidelity.co.uk* for his own business, with the description on its home page as "one of Musical Fidelity's oldest retailers", and was upheld on appeal. In *Reed Executive v Reed Business Information*[49] the defendants were liable for using the name *Reed* on the pages and metatags of a web site (*totaljobs.com*) which aimed to match job applicants to vacancies. This had been discontinued, but the claimants were entitled to an inquiry as to damages.

In New Zealand, the *One in a Million* decision was considered in *New* **8–179** *Zealand Post v Leng*,[50] and an interlocutory injunction was granted against use of *nzpost.com*. The domain name was active in the sense that it connected to a site with pornographic content. *British Telecommunications v One in a Million* was also followed in Scotland in *Bonnier Media v Smith*,[51] in which the Scottish publishers of the *business a.m.* newspaper (associated with the website *businessam.co.uk*, as well as a number of variant names) obtained interim interdict in the Court of Session against a *businessam.com* website, hosted at an uncertain offshore location, and run by a Mauritius company and an individual who might have been domiciled in either Greece or England. There was an express, if barely plausible, intention to offer an advisory service under the name, but the personal defendant had a history of bad faith registrations and had demanded $25,000 for the name.

The Irish case of *Local Ireland v Local-Ireland Online*[52] belongs rather to the category of cases in which the defendant really intended to offer a service under the name, and the question was which party had priority. Herbert J. found for the plaintiffs. Another case which may not have been an example of pure cybersquatting (although it was argued as such) comes from India. In *Yahoo! v Akash Arora*[53] the Indian High Court at Delhi granted the owners of the search engine *yahoo.com* an interlocutory injunction against a site providing a competitive service under the name *yahooindia.com*. The plaintiffs' *yahoo.com* website already had an Indian regional section, the get-up of which had been copied by the defendants.

---

[48] [2002] EWCA Civ 1989; [2003] F.S.R. 50, CA.
[49] [2002] EWHC 1015, [2003] R.P.C. 12 (Pumfrey J.-liability); [2003] EWHC 2772 (Pumfrey J.-damages).
[50] (1998) 45 I.P.R. 263.
[51] 2003 S.C. 36; [2002] E.T.M.R. 86 (Lord Drummond Young, OM).
[52] [2001] E.T.M.R. 42 (Herbert J., HC of Ireland).
[53] [1999] F.S.R. 931 (Sharma J., HC of India).

K. MISCELLANIA

Numerals

8–180   Numerals are capable of being distinctive, although there are relatively few authorities in point. The plaintiffs failed in *Perry v Hessin*,[54] although the defendants had copied the numbers *341* and *335* which the plaintiffs used on their boxes of pens, but the case was argued almost entirely on get-up and there were sufficient dissimilarities. In *Reuter v Muhlens*[55] *4711* was almost certainly distinctive in respect of Eau de Cologne, but the case turned on which party owned the English goodwill. In the Scottish case of *PC Products v Dalton*[56] *1001* was distinctive of the pursuer's carpet cleaning solution and the defender was restrained from using that number in words or figures, even after he had changed his get-up. He was allowed *2002*, which seems unduly generous given his record.

In *Hymac v Priestman Bros*[57] Walton J. granted an interlocutory injunction against the use of *580* for a mechanical excavator. The mark was derived from the fact that the plaintiffs' digger in question had a capacity of five eighths of a cubic yard, but that did not render it descriptive. In a Canadian County Court, the numerals *501* in *501 Video* were held to be distinctive of the plaintiff's video arcade and an injunction granted at trial against *501 Arcade: Joseph v Lee*.[58] In *Stacey v 2020 Communications Ltd*[59] there was a better than arguable case that the plaintiff's trading name *20/20 Telecom* was distinctive, despite the relatively small scale of the plaintiff's business, but an interlocutory injunction was refused on the balance of convenience.

8–181   If the defendant's choice of numerals is not identical to that of the claimant, then the scope of protection for the claimant's mark has to be identified by reference to what makes it distinctive.

In *Leahy, Kelly & Leahy v Glover*[60] the plaintiffs claimed that *The Great Two D Brand* was distinctive of them, but the House of Lords held that on the most favourable assumptions in their favour they were not entitled to monopolise the expression *2d*, that being the actual price of the cigars sold by both parties.

Similar issues arose in the case of *United Kingdom Tobacco Co v Malayan Tobacco Distributors*[61] where the plaintiffs sold cigarettes in tins bearing the numbers *2 for 1* on the tins and *2 1* on the cigarettes themselves, in both cases with an additional mark of *Golden Sword* as a device or phrase. The cigarettes were normally sold loose at two for one cent. The defendants adopted a mark consisting of the number *21* with the device of playing cards

---

[54] (1912) 29 R.P.C. 509, CA.
[55] (1953) 70 R.P.C. 235, CA.
[56] [1957] R.P.C. 199 (Lord Hill Watson, Court of Session).
[57] [1978] R.P.C. 495 (Walton J.).
[58] (1984) 78 C.P.R. (2d) 159 (Campbell Co Ct J., Ontario).
[59] [1991] F.S.R. 49 (Millett J.).
[60] (1893) 10 R.P.C. 141, HL.
[61] (1933) 51 R.P.C. 11, PC.

making up that number. The Privy Council found for the defendants. In *Ardath Tobacco Co v Sandorides*[62] the plaintiffs sold *State Express* cigarettes with the marks *999* and *555* distinguishing their two qualities. They had registered various other triple digit marks. They failed to restrain use of *99* by the defendants, their essential distinctive feature being triplication. *Baskin-Robins Ice Cream v Gutman*[63] (*31* and *32* flavours) was decided against the plaintiffs on the balance of convenience.

In South Africa the numeral *Seven*, either as a word or as the figure *7*, was claimed to be distinctive of the plaintiff's replica version of the *Lotus Seven Series III* sports car in *Caterham Car Sales v Birkin Cars*.[64] The action failed on other grounds, but it seems that *Seven*, if ever distinctive at all, had only ever been distinctive of the Lotus range (rather than any single model), and must have subsequently have become *publici juris* for the Series III by virtue of widespread unrestrained and unlicensed use.

Part Numbers

In contrast to numerals used as trade marks, part numbers and the like have **8–182** generally not been protected against copying.[65] If the defendant competes with the claimant and supplies alternatives to the claimant's parts, then use of the claimant's numbers is often the only effective way to identify them.[66] The question is whether the customer is misled into believing that the defendant's goods are those of the claimant. If it is clear that the defendant is using the numbers in respect of his own goods, then there is no passing-off. However, a customer placing an order by reference to the claimant's part numbers on their own may or may not expect to receive the claimant's goods, and the defendant risks a finding of passing-off if he does not enquire. In *Purefoy Engineering Co v Sykes Boxall*[67] the Court of Appeal drew a distinction between orders from unknown customers where the defendants were liable for passing-off by substitution, and orders from existing customers who must have known that the defendants would supply their own goods.

Telephone numbers

In *Law Society of England and Wales v Griffiths*[58] the plaintiffs were awarded **8–183** an interlocutory injunction to protect the freephone number of their *Accident Line* referral service 0500 192939 against the use of 0800 192939 by the defendant firm of solicitors. Mention may also be made of *British Tele-*

---

[62] (1924) 42 R.P.C. 50 (Tomlin J.).

[63] [1977] F.S.R. 545 (Graham J.).

[64] 1998 (3) SA 938 (SCA).

[65] *Hilti AG v Ucan Development Ltd* [1964] R.P.C. 206; *British Northrop Ltd v Texteam Blackburn Ltd* [1974] R.P.C. 57. *Perry & Co Ltd v T Hessin & Co* (1912) 29 R.P.C. 509, CA has some affinity with part number cases.

[66] See also *Toshiba Europe GmbH v Katun Germany GmbH*, Case C112/99; [2001] E.C.R. I–7945; [2002] 3 C.M.L.R. 7; [2002] E.T.M.R. 26; [2002] F.S.R. 39, ECJ.

[67] (1954) 72 R.P.C. 89, CA.

[68] [1995] R.P.C. 16 (Aldous J.).

communications v Planet Telecom,[69] in which the defendants were restrained from representing that questionnaires sent out by them (for return *via* a premium rate fax service, on machines set to receive at the slowest possible rate) were required by BT to maintain the accuracy of its *192* directory enquiries service.

In a Canadian case, *Pizza Pizza v 528635 Ontario Inc*[70] the plaintiffs undertook an advertising campaign emphasising the figures *1111* in their telephone number. An interlocutory injunction was granted against the defendants using the same figures in theirs. In Canada again an interlocutory injunction against passing-off by use of a telephone number was granted in *241 Pizza v Pizza Pizza*[71] where the defendants' telephone number *527–0241* was confusingly similar to that of the plaintiffs' local franchise: *526–0241*. The plaintiffs made a point of their outlets having telephone numbers ending in –241, alluding to their two-for-one marketing plan, and had registered *241–0–241* as their trade mark.

In a South African case, *Truth Verification Testing Centre v PSE Truth Detection*,[72] the personal defendant caused her home telephone number to be inserted in the telephone directory against the trading name of the plaintiff. The defendants had previously been in negotiations to become a franchisee of the plaintiffs, but these had been abortive. A final interdict was granted, extending to stopping all use of the number in question.

8–184   As another separate matter, it may be passing-off for a business formerly connected with the claimant, for instance by franchising, to continue using its former telephone number after the connection has ceased. This does not depend on the number being distinctive in the sense considered above. The reason is that telephone directories and advertisements will continue to circulate with the number listed under the name of the franchisor, and new customers may phone the defendant under the impression that they are still dealing with a branch of the claimant's. There will be passing-off if the defendant does not explain the true state of affairs.

In *Canren Systems v British Columbia Telephone Co*[73] the individual defendants had formerly been contractors of the plaintiffs, who operated a referral service for home repairs as *The Blue Army*. They set up in competition with it, and took over its telephone number in Vancouver when the plaintiffs failed to pay the bill. Bouck J. granted an interlocutory injunction against the defendants trading as *A–1 Army Trades* on that number. The plaintiffs had nothing corresponding to a property right in the number, and the defendants were, in principle, free to use it if they could do so without passing-off. However, the defendants' suspicious choice of name combined with the use of the old number tipped the scales in the plaintiffs' favour.

In *Goliger's Travel v Gilway Maritimes*[74] the plaintiffs were granted an

[69] [2002] EWHC 553 (Patten J.).
[70] (1986) 10 C.P.R. (3d) 139 (Galligan J., Ontario).
[71] (1992) 43 C.P.R. (3d) 523 (MacDonald J., Ontario).
[72] 1998 (2) SA 689 (Witwatersrand).
[73] (1983) 74 C.P.R. (2d) 48 (British Columbia, Bouck J.). Compare *241 Pizza v Pizza Pizza* (1992) 43 C.P.R. (3d) 523 (MacDonald J., Ontario), above.
[74] (1987) 17 C.P.R. (3d) 380 (Nova Scotia, Hall L.J.S.C.).

interlocutory injunction against the defendants, a former franchisee, continuing to use the same telephone number as when it had been franchised. The ordinary and Yellow Pages telephone directories listed the number under the name of the franchisor, and there would be passing-off if a proportion of prospective customers of the franchisor were misled.[75]

Independent Locksmiths v Aardvark Master Locksmiths[76] was concerned with a name rather than a telephone number as such, though the name *Interdependent Locksmiths* had been entered in the telephone directory with the defendants' number before the plaintiffs could act. The defendants were not ordered to disconnect their telephone but they were ordered to arrange an explanatory recorded message.

Scent and smell

There does not yet appear to be any authority dealing with the possibility of **8–185** a scent or smell being distinctive for the purposes of passing-off. In the New Zealand case of *Yves St Laurent Parfums v Louden Cosmetics*[77] it was alleged that the defendants' suppliers had closely copied the smell of the plaintiffs' *Kouros, Jazz, Paris* and *Opium* brands of perfume[78]; but the decision turned entirely on similarities of get-up and the corresponding names *Kosmos, Java, Paradise* and *Optimism*. The claims for passing off against the copies of *Kouros, Jazz* and *Paris* succeeded. That against *Optimism* failed, its get-up being very dissimilar to that of *Opium* and the respective names conveying entirely different associations. It may be noted that the only claim which failed was against a perfume which was a very close copy in terms of smell, whereas one of those which succeeded was against the poorest imitation. More general questions of unfair competition, unjust enrichment and misappropriation of property were left unanswered.

Manner of advertising

Cases have occasionally arisen in which the defendant has allegedly copied **8–186** the claimant's advertising themes or style or whole manner of doing business. If what has been copied is indeed distinctive of the claimant and the defendant's conduct is calculated to deceive and cause damage then there is passing-off, despite the fact that the copied matter may be outside the familiar categories of name, mark or get-up.[79] However, passing-off depends on misrepresentation rather than misappropriation, and in the absence of a general tort of unfair competition such copying is unlikely to be actionable even if its existence cannot be denied. It is not passing-off to seek to benefit

---

[75] See also *Daily Leasing v De Graw* (1976) 28 C.P.R. (2d) 241 and *Texaco Canada v Keith* (1983) 40 Nfld. & P.E.I.R. 247.

[76] (1986) 7 I.P.R. 432 (Federal Court, Full Court).

[77] (1997) 39 I.P.R. 11 (HC of NZ).

[78] In one case alone (*Java*) the smell of the imitation was only "slightly similar" to its assumed comparator, *Jazz*. The other matches were "virtually identical" (*Paradise–Paris*); "very close" (*Kosmos–Kouros*) and "a convincing substitute" (*Optimism–Opium*).

[79] *Cadbury Schweppes Pty Ltd v Pub Squash Co Pty Ltd* [1981] R.P.C. 429; [1981] 1 All E.R. 213, PC.

from material, ideas or demand created by another.[80] When advertising themes are in issue a further consideration is that the defendant's advertisements are useless if they do not attract custom to him specifically, and if they do that successfully then they can hardly be mistaken for advertisements issued by the claimant. The argument that the claimant is damaged if the defendant's advertisements are confused with his own may apply in rare cases,[81] but Parker J. in *Burberrys v Cording*[82] authoritatively disposed of most of the arguments which can be raised.

There was copying of the plaintiffs' advertisements and more in *Standard Ideal Co v Standard Sanitary Manufacturing Co*,[83] but although the defendant had "availed itself unscrupulously, if not unfairly, of the labour, ingenuity, and expenditure of the plaintiff company in preparing the ground and educating the public on sanitary matters"[84] there was no liability for passing-off. In the *Pub Squash* case itself, *Cadbury Schweppes v Pub Squash Co*[85] the plaintiffs introduced a lemon drink which was novel in that it was specifically aimed at the adult male market. The themes of its advertising were vigorously manly sports and nostalgia for the old Australian pubs. The defendants copied the taste of the drink itself and both promotional themes, but their product and the advertising for it were readily distinguishable. The Supreme Court of New South Wales found for the defendants despite uncandid evidence and the Privy Council rejected an appeal. Similar issues were left unresolved in *RHM Foods v Bovril*[86] in which the plaintiffs alleged that the defendants had deliberately copied the theme of their television advertisements involving the wives of celebrities using *Bisto* to make gravy. The Court of Appeal, *obiter*, accepted that this could amount to passing-off but was unimpressed with its factual basis.

In the South African case of *Hoechst Pharmaceuticals v Beauty Box*[87] the plaintiffs alleged that the defendants' pack for a fibre-based slimming aid should be compared with the whole "gestalt impression" conveyed by the plaintiffs' own pack and their advertising themes in combination: specifically, a leotard-clad blonde and a yellow tape measure. In more familiar terms the two were supposedly distinctive *per se* of Hoechst. The defendants used both components on their pack, and the plaintiffs used both in advertising, but the blonde did not appear on their own pack. The Court, following *Cadbury Schweppes v Pub Squash Co*[88] and *Oertli v Bowman*,[89] did not agree. Both were clichés in the context of slimming products and the packs themselves were readily distinguishable. Allegations that the defendants had copied the plaintiffs' advertisements, along with their name, logo,

[80] *Cadbury Schweppes Pty Ltd v Pub Squash Co Pty Ltd*, above.
[81] *Macdonald's Hamburgers Ltd v Burgerking (U.K.) Ltd* [1987] F.S.R. 112, CA.
[82] (1909) 26 R.P.C. 693 (Parker J.).
[83] [1911] A.C. 78, PC.
[84] *per* Lord Macnaghten.
[85] [1981] 1 All E.R. 213: [1981] R.P.C. 429, PC.
[86] [1983] R.P.C. 275, CA.
[87] 1987 (2) SA 600 (Appellate Division).
[88] [1981] 1 All E.R. 213; [1981] R.P.C. 429, PC.
[89] [1959] R.P.C. 1, HL; affirming [1957] R.P.C. 388, CA.

and manner of doing business also failed on the facts in *William Bartfield v Job Hypermarket*.[90]

In the Australian *Philips v Remington*[91] case the passing-off claim against **8–187** Remington was based partly on similarity of the parties' goods (electric shavers with three rotary cutting heads) and partly on allegations that Remington had copied the themes of Philips' advertising. Both received short shrift:

> "Attempts have been made, in [Philips'] advertising, to heighten the appeal by a 'masculine' association with a fantasy world of fast sports cars–Jaguars and Porsches.
>
> One of Philips' most strongly urged contentions centred upon the complaint that Remington had taken up the motoring theme, by referring to the three heads as three wheels, and generally. According to Philips, this associated the Remington shaver with the Philips, so as to deceive purchasers and appropriate Philips' goodwill.
>
> Remington's response robustly asserted its right to produce a proven product in all its features–including its technology and anything belonging to the public's perception of the product itself. What Remington could not and did not do was to suggest that its triple rotary shaver was in any sense a *Philips* shaver. On the contrary, the Remington shaver was very clearly marked with the *Remington* name, a well-known brand. In practice, it was to be expected that the rival shavers would be displayed in shops as competing products, each plainly identified as a *Philips* or as a *Remington*..."

This led to the conclusion that the *Remington* and *Philips* shavers were adequately distinguished at the point of sale. A final argument based on the alleged similarities of the products and the advertising for them also failed:

> "Nor is there any more reality to the suggestion that the mere similarity of the goods, combined with a similar 'masculine' tone pervading the advertising of each, might lead some persons to assume the Remington shaver is produced under licence, or is a sub-brand of Philips. The Remington brand is well known in its own right, and, in Australia, sells more personal care products, though fewer electric shavers, than Philips. The public is thoroughly accustomed to competing brands of almost identical products, which may or may not have some link–or may not today, but may tomorrow, share an over-all owner, by virtue of a take-over or purchase. A similar suggestion, made in the *Dr Martens* case, was there described (at 148) as 'fanciful' and 'bizarre'."

Whole manner of trading

If what is allegedly copied is the claimant's whole manner of doing business **8–188**

---

[90] 1976 (3) SA 157 (Transvaal Provincial Division).
[91] [2000] FCA 876; 48 I.P.R. 257 (Federal Court of Australia).

then there is the further difficulty that to restrain the defendant would give the claimant a *de facto* monopoly inconsistent with the policy of the common law:

"[I]f a trader sets up a new business and carries it on by startling new methods which become well known to the public, confusion is likely to be caused when another trader establishes a similar sort of business and carries it on by methods which have become well known to the public as the plaintiffs' methods; but a trader who sets up a new trade has no monopoly of that trade or of the manner of carrying it on, and he cannot prevent a rival trader copying his ideas, notwithstanding that confusion will be caused."[92]

In *Wertheimer v Stewart Cooper*[93] the plaintiff had adopted a novel method of trading by offering prizes for selling certain quantities of seeds. The defendants copied this idea as such and virtually every detail of the plaintiff's advertisements. Kekewich J. held that there was no passing-off. Harman J. refused an interlocutory injunction in *Dagenham Girl Pipers v Vishnu Pather*[94] where one of the plaintiffs' complaints was that the defendant had copied the performance they gave. In *Lyons v G & K Restaurants*[95] the plaintiffs had introduced a restaurant with supposedly distinctive features in that it specialised in bacon and eggs, the kitchen was separated from the restaurant only by a large plate glass window, and the food was served in the same stainless steel utensil in which it had been cooked. Roxburgh J. was clearly unimpressed with the argument that any of this was distinctive.

8–189 An interlocutory injunction was granted in an Australian case, *Con-Stan Industries v Satinique Corp*,[96] in which the defendants were guilty of wholesale copying of the plaintiffs' way of doing business, but the decision is hard to justify except in so far as the get-up of containers was concerned.[97] A somewhat similar case from South Africa is *Easyfind International v Instaplan Holdings*.[98] The plaintiffs introduced the idea of distributing free of charge in areas of about 10,000 homes a time planner containing advertisements by local businesses. The defendants copied the idea and much of the layout of the time planner itself, but so far as the goods themselves were concerned the defendants distinguished theirs as well as could be expected. It was even less likely that advertisers would be deceived. There was no case of passing-off but the plaintiffs had made out a case of unlawful competition, based largely on misuse of confidential information. In Australia

---

[92] *per* Stamp J. in *Compatibility Research Ltd v Computer Psyche Co Ltd* [1967] R.P.C. 201. See also *My Kinda Town Ltd v Soll* [1983] R.P.C. 407, CA.
[93] (1906) 23 R.P.C. 481 (Kekewich J.).
[94] (1951) 69 R.P.C. 1 (Harman J.).
[95] (1955) 72 R.P.C. 259 (Roxburgh J.).
[96] (1969) 91 W.N. (N.S.W.) 563 (Hope J.).
[97] Compare *Amway Corp v Eurway International Ltd* [1974] R.P.C. 82; [1972] F.S.R. 213 in which the plaintiffs had conceded that anyone might copy their way of doing business.
[98] 1983 (3) SA 917 (Schutz A.J.). The defendants' conduct was dishonest. There was also wholesale copying of the plaintiffs' manner of doing business in *Cambridge Plan AG v Moore* 1987 (4) SA 821 (Page J.), but the decision only relies on similarities in name.

again, allegations that one fish restaurant had copied the name, style, get-up, trade methods, menu documentation, advertising materials, design, decor, entertainment and general appearance and operations of the plaintiffs were not so hopeless as to justify striking out the action in *The Last Aussie Fish Caf v Almove*.[99]

Characters and themes

This paragraph deals with the situation in which a fictional character, **8–190** storyline, theme, or some other literary creation is adopted by another author or publisher without the consent of the originator. This differs from character merchandising in that the character, etc., is not being used to promote goods which have some independent existence and value of their own. Rather, the defendant creates a comparable work of his own around the character. Passing-off deals only with misrepresentation, not with misappropriation, and it would not normally be supposed that there is any misrepresentation implicit in works such as George Macdonald Fraser's *Flashman* series, Tom Stoppard's *Rosencranz and Guildenstern are Dead* or Shakespeare's *King Lear*, notwithstanding that all are written around characters recognisably derived from other authors. What little authority there is in English law confirms that copying of this sort is not inherently actionable as passing-off.

In *Conan Doyle v London Mystery Magazine*[1] Wynn-Parry J. refused the executor of Sir Arthur Conan Doyle an interlocutory injunction against the proprietors of a detective magazine which referred to *Sherlock Holmes* and purported to be published from 221B Baker Street. The plaintiff's goodwill in the *Sherlock Holmes* stories did not stand to suffer any damage from what was no more than a boast that the magazine would be worthy of the standards set by Holmes. If *Sherlock Holmes* had been a real person Wynn-Parry J. would have intervened.

The plaintiffs in *Hospital for Sick Children v Walt Disney Productions*[2] were the owners of the copyright in J. M. Barrie's *Peter Pan*. The defendants were licensed to make animated cartoons of it. The Hospital sought an interlocutory injunction to restrain the defendants from advertising their film in such a manner as to imply that it was a film with real actors. Plowman J. refused the injunction on the ground that none of the defendants' publicity material was capable of bearing that meaning.

In *Grundy Television v Startrain*[3] the plaintiffs were the producers of the television soap opera *Neighbours*. The defendants published a magazine called *Neighbours Who's Who*, which was written around the series and the characters and performers in it. The defendants offered not to use the same form of script as was used for the title of the programme and Millett J. refused any further interlocutory relief. There was no implicit misrepresentation that the magazine was connected with the plaintiffs: it

---

[99] (1990) 16 I.P.R. 376 (French J., Federal Court of Australia).
[1] (1949) 66 R.P.C. 312 (Wynn-Parry J.).
[2] [1966] R.P.C. 246 (Plowman J.).
[3] [1988] F.S.R. 581 (Millett J.).

derived its name from the subject matter it dealt with and referred only to its contents. Inaccuracies and errors in the publication had nothing to do with passing-off, and the only damage the plaintiffs stood to suffer was loss of potential merchandising profits.

8–191   Some foreign courts have gone further than this, but the reasoning often shades over into the broader concept of unfair competition based on misappropriation of trade values.

In the Hong Kong case of *Shaw Bros v Golden Harvest*[4] the plaintiffs claimed to have established a right of property in a film character *Fang Kang*, or *The One Armed Swordsman*. It is unclear precisely what use the defendants were making of this name or character, but it appears to have involved a film of their own. Huggins J. concluded that the author had a right of property in the character, and that the producer of the films was entitled to protect it. The reasoning is confused and scarcely consistent with passing-off. The supposed right of property in the character is neither goodwill nor copyright, and the defendants' conduct is treated wholly in terms of misappropriation rather than misrepresentation.

In *Hexagon v Australian Broadcasting Commission*[5] the plaintiffs had made two films featuring the character *Alvin Purple*, and had entered into negotiations with the defendants for production of a television series. The negotiations broke down and the defendants proposed to continue with the series based on the character, employing the leading actor from the films, and entitled *Alvin*. Needham J., following the *Its Academic* case[6] held that there was passing-off, but that the defendants were not guilty of such underhand or sharp conduct as to amount to unfair competition. However, the plaintiffs were estopped from preventing the defendants going ahead with the series.

[4] [1971] H.K.L.R. 167; [1972] R.P.C. 559.
[5] (1975) 7 A.L.R. 233; [1976] R.P.C. 628.
[6] *Willard King Organisation Pty Ltd v United Telecasters Sydney Ltd* (1970) [1981] 2 N.S.W.L.R. 547 (Else-Mitchell J.).

CHAPTER 9

DEFENCES IN EUROPEAN AND NATIONAL LAW

A. INTRODUCTION

Passing-off and injurious falsehood

9–1 The various defences addressed in the present Chapter have different degrees of relevance to claims for passing-off and injurious falsehood.

The section on the European Convention on Human Rights applies equally to both causes of action, although one might expect its implications to be felt more readily in the field of injurious falsehood, where the right to free expression under Art.10 has more potential for conflict with the proprietary rights of the claimant. The section on European Community law, conversely, is more likely to be relevant in passing-off cases, although there is at least a theoretical possibility of Community law impinging on a claim for injurious falsehood, for instance if cross-border advertising were involved. In practice, the scope for conflict between European law in either of these manifestations and the common law of unfair competition is rather slight, since the interests protected by the latter rarely conflict even superficially with the values of the former.

9–2 So far as defences in national law are concerned, the defence that the claimant is carrying on an illegal or deceptive trade applies equally to injurious falsehood and to passing-off, and indeed one of the most extreme examples is to be found in a case of alleged injurious falsehood. The defence of honest use of one's own name only arises, if at all, in passing-off; and injurious falsehood has no need for the almost equally nebulous partial defence of innocence. Innocence is hardly consistent with malice, and the latter is an essential component of the cause of action. The defence of antecedent or concurrent user is also relevant only in passing-off. Defences of delay, acquiescence and estoppel might conceivably arise in injurious falsehood, although there are no obvious examples. In the context of delay, it should be noted that the limitation period in injurious falsehood is only one year,[1] compared to six years for passing-off.

---

[1] Defamation Act 1996, s.5(2), amending Limitation Act 1980, s.4A.

The impact of European law: the EC treaty...

National laws of unfair competition are of course subordinate to European **9–3**
Community law, in particular, the laws on competition and the free
movement of goods. It is therefore a defence to an action for passing-off or
for injurious falsehood that to enforce otherwise valid rights of the claimant
would be to interfere with competition or free movement in a manner
inconsistent with Community law. To this extent, Community law wholly
overrides English law so far as the two are inconsistent.

In practice, Community law has little impact on the everyday conduct of
passing-off actions, and still less on the action for injurious falsehood. Both
these bodies of law are concerned with misrepresentation, and are consistent
with an underlying principle of Community law that customers and consumers are best protected by providing them with accurate and adequate
information, rather than banning outright products which might possibly
confuse the uninformed or unwary.[2] The main thrust of Community law in
this field has been to prevent the owners of intellectual property rights using
them to hinder international trade in goods after they have been put on the
market: the rights of the proprietor are deemed to be exhausted on first sale
in the Community or European Economic Area. Unlike some of the statutory intellectual property rights, passing-off does not create monopoly
rights which would lend themselves to this sort of abuse. Passing-off
requires a misrepresentation, and as a matter of long-standing English law
there is in general no misrepresentation implicit in buying goods on the
market in one country and selling them in competition with the original
supplier or an exclusive distributor of his in another.[3]

It has also been suggested that Community law may require relief to be **9–4**
granted in circumstances where under English law it would have been
refused.[4] It is undoubtedly true that the English courts ought not to treat an
English claimant any more favourably than one from another member
state.[5] That, however, is a situation which does not arise in passing-off
because the law does not discriminate. The case which supposed otherwise
did so on the erroneous assumption that passing-off would protect the
reputation of an English business (but not a foreign one) even if that
business had no goodwill. In law, English and foreign businesses are treated
identically in this respect: the existence of a goodwill in England is essential
and mere reputation always insufficient. The argument contemplated by
Graham J. in *Maxim's v Dye*[6] received a clear, though implicit, repudiation
in the judgment of Aldous J. *in British Sky Broadcasting v David Lyons*[7]

---

[2] Case 120/78 *Rewe v Bundesmonopolverwaltung fur Branntwein* (*"Cassis de Dijon"*) [1979]
E.C.R. 649; [1979] 1 C.M.L.R. 494.
[3] *Imperial Tobacco Co of India Ltd v Bonnan* [1924] A.C. 755; 41 R.P.C. 44, PC.
[4] *per* Graham J. in *Maxim's Ltd v Dye* [1977] 1 W.L.R. 1155; [1978] 2 All E.R. 55; [1977]
F.S.R. 364.
[5] Case 92/92 *Phil Collins v Imrat Handelsgesellschaft mbH* [1993] E.C.R. I–5145; [1993] 3
C.M.L.R. 773; [1994] E.M.L.R. 108; [1994] F.S.R. 166 relying on former Art.7 (now Art.12) of
the Treaty of Rome.
[6] [1977] 1 W.L.R. 1155, [1978] 2 All E.R. 55, [1977] F.S.R. 364.
[7] [1995] F.S.R. 357 (Aldous J.), not a passing-off case.

where the defendant argued that the plaintiffs' statutory transmission rights could not be enforced because the UK legislation conferred such rights only in respect of transmissions originating in the United Kingdom. In rejecting this submission, Aldous J. drew an analogy with passing-off:

> "Similarly, the right to restrain passing off is only available to traders with goodwill in the United Kingdom. Thus the condition for obtaining the right to restrain passing off is local trade, but that does not amount to illegal discrimination or a disguised restriction on trade between member states."

...and the European Convention on Human Rights

9-5 The European Convention on Human Rights was adopted in 1950, and since October 2, 2000 has been given effect in English domestic law by the Human Rights Act 1998, s.1 and 6. In the event of a conflict between the common law and the Convention, the Convention would now prevail. The subject matter of the present work might appear very far removed from that of the Convention, but in several respects the Convention is much wider in its application than may appear at first sight, and the possibility of a conflict between the Convention and the common law of passing-off or injurious falsehood needs to be considered, if only to be dismissed.

So Art.10 (freedom of expression) applies to commercial speech as well as to political controversy; Art.8 (right to private life) protects a lawyer's offices; and Art.6 (right to a fair trial) applies to all kinds of civil and commercial litigation and not just to the determination of an individual's "civil rights" in the American sense. Art.1 of the First Protocol (right to one's possessions) applies to intellectual property, whether owned by a legal or natural person. To summarise the section which follows, there is no reason to believe that either the substantive law of passing-off or injurious falsehood, or its practical application, is likely to require consideration of any provision of the Convention; but that if it did, then the wide "margin of appreciation" which is allowed to the member states in this field means that it is extremely unlikely that any systematic inconsistencies with Convention rights would be found.[8]

---

[8] In *Hart v Relentless Records Ltd* [2002] EWHC 1984; [2003] F.S.R. 36 the Human Rights Act 1998 and Art.6 of the Convention were unsuccessfully invoked on an application for the trial judge to recuse himself for appearance of bias. In *Asprey & Garrard v WRA (Guns) Ltd and Asprey* [2001] EWCA Civ 1499; [2002] E.T.M.R. 47; [2002] F.S.R. 31, CA, Convention defences were described as "highly optimistic" in the Court of Appeal, but did not require decision. The possibility that the Convention might have assisted the claimant was raised by the trial judge in *Irvine v Talksport Ltd* [2002] EWHC 367; [2002] 1 W.L.R. 2355; [2002] 2 All E.R. 414; [2002] E.M.L.R. 32; [2002] F.S.R. 60; affirmed [2003] EWCA Civ 423; [2003] 2 All E.R. 881; [2003] E.M.L.R. 26; [2003] F.S.R. 35, CA, but again did not require decision. In the trade mark case of *Levi Strauss & Co v Tesco Stores Ltd* [2002] EWHC 1625; [2002] 3 C.M.L.R. 11; [2002] E.T.M.R. 95; [2003] R.P.C. 18 human rights defences raised by parallel importers were described as being without substance.

B. The European Convention on Human Rights

Sources of law

The ultimate arbiter of Convention rights is the European Court of Human **9–6** Rights in Strasbourg. Until 1998–9, applications to the Court were initially examined by the European Commission of Human Rights, which would issue a reasoned decision stating whether or not the complaint was *prima facie* admissible or not.[9] If the Commission decided against the applicant, then the case terminated. If not, then the Commission would ascertain the relevant facts (including provisions of national law), attempt to promote a friendly settlement, and issue a report. A case declared admissible would be heard by the European Court of Human Rights which would deliver a reasoned judgment, possibly with dissents by any minority.

There are no decisions of the European Court of Human Rights (or the Commission) dealing specifically with passing-off or other aspects of unfair competition in English law, but the relevant principles can be deduced from the way in which the Convention has been applied to Continental laws of unfair competition. Admissibility decisions of the Commission are also treated as having precedential value, though to a lesser degree than decisions of the Court. It will be seen that the majority of cases in the field of unfair competition have been decisions by the Commission declaring the application to be "manifestly inadmissible". The Human Rights Act 1988, s.2(1), obliges the courts of the United Kingdom to take account of the decisions of both the Court and the Commission.[10]

The right to receive and impart information

A number of decided cases in the European Court of Human Rights have **9–7** dealt with the relationship between the Convention and national laws of unfair competition, most frequently in the context of Art.10 which provides:

> Everyone has the right to freedom of expression. This right shall include freedom to hold opinions and to receive and impart information and ideas without interference by public authority and regardless of frontiers. This Article shall not prevent States from requiring the licensing of broadcasting, television or cinema enterprises.
>
> The exercise of these freedoms, since it carries with it duties and responsibilities, may be subject to such formalities, conditions, restrictions or penalties as are prescribed by law and are necessary in a democratic society, in the interests of national security, territorial integrity or public safety, for the prevention of disorder or crime, for the protection of health or morals, for the protection of the reputation or the rights of others, for

---

[9] Most of the cases which follow were decided under this procedure.

[10] The Court maintains an excellent online database of both kinds of decision at *http://hudoc.coe.int*.

preventing the disclosure of information received in confidence, or for maintaining the authority and impartiality of the judiciary.

Complaints under Art.10 are analysed according to a logical progression through the relevant provisions of these paragraphs. First, is Art.10 applicable? This depends on whether there has been an interference with freedom of expression and whether that interference was by a public authority. At this stage, Art.10 is interpreted generously to the applicant, and anything which can fairly be described as a restraint by a public authority is likely to give rise to an issue under Art.10. An adverse court judgment, especially an injunction with penal sanctions, can hardly fail to be an interference by a public authority if the applicant's freedom of expression is restrained in any degree. The second group of questions asks whether the interference is one which is prescribed by law, necessary in a democratic society, necessary for the protection of one or more of the listed interests, and no more than proportionate to the need for the restraint. It is at this stage that the interference is most likely to find its justification, although the questions are cumulative and it is important not to overlook any of them. For instance, an interference which was not "prescribed by law" could never pass the test of para. (2), even it could otherwise be said to be justified.

9–8   The attitude of the European Court of Human Rights to national laws of unfair competition differs markedly between the two stages. At the first stage, it will be seen that the Court applies the jurisprudence developed in cases of political or artistic expression so that the terms of para. (1) are given an autonomous interpretation and little or no margin of appreciation is left to the member states as to what constitutes an interference by a public authority. It is at the second stage that treatment of commercial expression departs from the treatment of political and artistic expression, and a wide margin of appreciation is allowed to the member states. At least two reasons are given for this: the absence of any generally accepted international norms as to what ought to be permitted or prohibited, and the fact that national legislatures and courts are better equipped than the Court itself to respond to local conditions. A strong dissenting minority in the leading case has objected that this is to reverse the normal rule that it is exceptions to the Convention freedoms which are to be construed narrowly.

It is noticeable that the truth or falsehood of the information sought to be imparted seems to be of little or no relevance as a matter of Convention law, even in commercial expression cases, and even allowing for the Court's self-imposed reluctance to re-open questions of fact decided in the courts below. Several cases rejected as inadmissible by the Commission have involved the restraint of factual statements whose accuracy was never in question. Of the few cases in this field actually decided by the Court, two have found no violation of Art.10 although the respective defendants were restrained from publishing matters of undisputed fact; while one—admittedly on the borderline between commercial and political speech—has held that Art.10 was violated when the defendant was prohibited from publishing absurd and unfounded attacks on the safety of microwave ovens, which the relevant national courts had held to be without scientific basis.

Art.10 in unfair competition cases

The right to impart and receive information is particularly likely to conflict **9–9** with national unfair competition laws when the latter restrict commercial speech, for example by a blanket prohibition on advertising in certain industries or professions; or by specific prohibition of, for instance, comparative advertising or advertisements considered to be disparaging. It is fundamental to both passing-off and injurious falsehood that only conduct amounting to a misrepresentation is actionable, but the margin of appreciation allowed under Art.10 in the past has been wide enough even to allow restraint of true statements made in apparently justifiable situations. It will be seen that legal rules and court decisions far more intrusive on freedom of expression than those permitted under English common law have been upheld by both the Court and the Commission.

There is no doubt that the right to impart information extends not just to natural persons but to businesses, including ordinary commercial enterprises imparting business information as well as publishers or media interests imparting politically contentious or otherwise controversial material.[11] Likewise, advertising is protected by Art.10:

> "The Court would first point out that Article 10 guarantees freedom of expression to 'everyone.' No distinction is made in it according to whether the type of aim pursued is profit-making or not (see, *mutatis mutandis*, the *Autronic AG v Switzerland* judgment ...) and a difference in treatment in this sphere might fall foul of Article 14. In its *Barthold v Germany* judgment ... the Court left open the question whether commercial advertising as such came within the scope of the guarantees under Article 10, but its later case-law provides guidance on this matter. Article 10 does not apply solely to certain types of information or ideas or forms of expression (see the *markt intern Verlag GmbH and Klaus Beermann v Germany* judgment ...), in particular those of a political nature; it also encompasses artistic expression (see the *Müller and others v Switzerland judgment* ...), information of a commercial nature (see the *markt intern Verlag GmbH and Klaus Beermann* judgment previously cited, *ibid.*)—as the Commission rightly pointed out—and even light music and commercials transmitted by cable (see the *Groppera Radio AG and Others v Switzerland* judgment ...).
>
> In the instant case the impugned notices merely gave the applicant's name, profession, address and telephone number. They were clearly published with the aim of advertising, but they provided persons requiring legal assistance with information that was of definite use and likely to facilitate their access to justice."[12]

Conversely, there is authority that "reputation" in para. (2) of Art.10 **9–10** includes the commercial reputation of businesses as well as the personal

---

[11] *markt intern Verlag GmbH v Germany* Series A/164; (1990) 12 E.H.R R. 161, ECHR.
[12] *Casado Coea v Spain* Series A/285; (1994) 18 E.H R.R. 1, ECHR, below, paras 35 and 36 (citations omitted). Art.10 was held applicable, but not infringed.

reputation of natural persons,[13] but rights other than reputation may also be taken into account. In any event, there is a balance to be struck under para. (2) between the interests of the party claiming the benefit of Art.10 and the party claiming the benefit of the allegedly inconsistent national law; and both the Court and the Commission have allowed the legislatures and courts of member states a considerable margin of appreciation in framing their unfair competition laws and in applying them in practice. Laws of unfair competition which impede free expression may also be justified by reference to the protection of consumers and members of the public generally. Again, there is a considerable margin of appreciation.

9–11   As the Court observed in *Stambuk v Germany*[14]:

> "The Court recalls that, for the citizen, advertising is a means of discovering the characteristics of services and goods offered to him. Nevertheless, it may sometimes be restricted, especially to prevent unfair competition and untruthful or misleading advertising. In some contexts, the publication of even objective, truthful advertisements might be restricted in order to ensure respect for the rights of others or owing to the special circumstances of particular business activities and professions. Any such restrictions must, however, be closely scrutinised by the Court, which must weigh the requirements of those particular features against the advertising in question; to this end, the Court must look at the impugned penalty in the light of the case as a whole."

The *markt intern* decision

9–12   The leading case on the application of Art.10 to unfair competition laws is *markt intern and Beerman v Germany*.[15] The first applicants (defendants in Germany) were a company run by journalists, including the personal applicant, which supported the interests of small and medium-sized traders, *inter alia* by publishing newsletters as well as by lobbying and assisting with test cases on their behalf. One such newsletter was aimed at chemists and beauty product retailers. In it, the applicants published an article critical of an English mail order firm, *Cosmetic Club International*, accusing it of failing to reimburse a named customer who had returned goods as unsatisfactory, inviting readers to supply further examples, and insinuating that the complaint might reflect official policy rather than being an isolated occurrence. Cosmetic Club sued markt intern for breach of s.1 of the German Unfair Competition Act 1909 and obtained an injunction which

---

[13] *markt intern Verlag GmbH v Germany*, below; *Gretch and Montanaro v Malta* (Application 29473/95). For the separate proposition that goodwill is protected by Art.1 of the First Protocol, see below.

[14] Application 37928/97; unreported judgment of October 17, 2002, former Third Chamber; referring to *Casado Coca*, above.

[15] Series A/164; (1990) 12 E.H.R.R. 161, ECHR. The applicants' name is conventionally spelled without initial capitals. There is a second *markt intern* case, on different facts, which was held inadmissible.

was eventually confirmed by the German Federal Supreme Court and the Federal Constitutional Court.

The European Court of Human Rights, sitting in plenary session, unanimously rejected arguments by the German Government that Art.10 had no application in a case where the information was not intended to influence or mobilise public opinion, but to promote the economic interests of a given group of undertakings, and held that the injunction was an interference by a public authority with the right of free expression, so as to require justification as being prescribed by law, necessary and proportionate. However, on the Chairman's casting vote, an equally divided Court held that the application of the German Unfair Competition Act in the instant case was within the margin of appreciation allowed to Germany:

"The national courts did weigh the competing interests at stake. In their judgments of 2 July 1976 and 31 March 1977, the Hamburg Regional Court and the Hanseatic Court of Appeal explicitly referred to the right to freedom of expression and of the press, as guaranteed by Article 5 of the Basic Law (...) and the Federal Constitutional Court, in its decision of 9 February 1983, considered the case under that provision...

The Federal Court of Justice based its judgment of 16 January 1980 on the premature nature of the disputed publication and on the lack of sufficient grounds for publicising in the information bulletin an isolated incident and, in doing so, took into consideration the rights and legal interests meriting protection ... In a market economy an undertaking which seeks to set up a business inevitably exposes itself to close scrutiny of its practices by its competitors. Its commercial strategy and the manner in which it honours its commitments may give rise to criticism on the part of consumers and the specialised press. In order to carry out this task, the specialised press must be able to disclose facts which could be of interest to its readers and thereby contribute to the openness of business activities.

However, even the publication of items which are true and describe real events may under certain circumstances be prohibited: the obligation to respect the privacy of others or the duty to respect the confidentiality of certain commercial information are examples. In addition, a correct statement can be and often is qualified by additional remarks, by value judgments, by suppositions or even insinuations. It must also be recognised that an isolated incident may deserve closer scrutiny before being made public; otherwise an accurate description of one such incident can give the false impression that the incident is evidence of a general practice. All these factors can legitimately contribute to the assessment of statements made in a commercial context, and it is primarily for the national courts to decide which statements are permissible and which are not.

In the present case, the article was written in a commercial context; markt intern was not itself a competitor in relation to the Club but it intended—legitimately—to protect the interests of chemists and beauty product retailers. The article itself undoubtedly contained some true statements, but it also expressed doubts about the reliability of the Club, and it asked the readers to report "similar experiences" at a moment when the Club had promised to carry out a prompt investigation of the one reported case. According to the Federal Court of Justice . . ., there was not sufficient cause to report the incident at the time of the publication. The Club had agreed to undertake an immediate investigation in order to clarify the position. Furthermore, the applicants had been aware that criticisms of the Club could not be fully justified before further clarification had been sought, as they themselves had described the reply of the Club as a provisional answer. In the opinion of the Federal Court they should therefore have taken into consideration that any such premature publication of the incident was bound to have adverse effects on the Club's business because it gave the specialised retailers an effective argument capable of being used against the Club with their customers, and one which could be used even if the incident should turn out to be an isolated mishap from which no conclusion could be drawn as to the Club's business policy.

In the light of these findings and having regard to the duties and responsibilities attaching to the freedoms guaranteed by Article 10, it cannot be said that the final decision of the Federal Court of Justice— confirmed from the constitutional point of view by the Federal Constitutional Court—went beyond the margin of appreciation left to the national authorities. It is obvious that opinions may differ as to whether the Federal Court's reaction was appropriate or whether the statements made in the specific case by markt intern should be permitted or tolerated. However, the European Court of Human Rights should not substitute its own evaluation for that of the national courts in the instant case, where those courts, on reasonable grounds, had considered the restrictions to be necessary."

A significant minority of the Court dissented and would have allowed the complaint.

Other art.10 cases before the Court and Commission

9–13 Apart from the *markt intern* decision,[16] the Court itself has considered unfair competition laws in a number of cases. The first (preceding *markt intern*) was the *Barthold*[17] case, in which a veterinary surgeon was subjected to interim and final injunctions under ss. 1 and 13(1) of the German Unfair Competition Act 1909, as a result of being identified and favourably commented upon in an unsolicited newspaper article about the limited availability of late-night veterinary care in Hamburg. The court held[18] that the injunctions were disproportionate to the legitimate aim of the legislation and that there was a breach of Art.10. In *Cascado Coca v Spain*[19] the Court unanimously held that enforcement of a ban on advertising by lawyers was

---

[16] *markt intern Verlag GmbH v Germany* Series A/164; (1990) 12 E.H.R.R. 161, ECHR, above.
[17] *Barthold v Germany* Series A/90; (1985) 7 E.H.R.R. 383, ECHR.
[18] By a majority of five votes to two.
[19] Series A/285; (1994) 18 E.H.R.R. 1, ECHR.

an interference with the applicant's right to impart information, but was proportionate to the pursuit of legitimate objectives. The Court rejected an argument that the prohibition (by the local Bar) was not one imposed by a public authority.

In *Jacubowski v Germany*[20] the applicant, who had been dismissed by his former employers and publicly blamed by them for incompetence and mismanagement, was restrained under s.1 of the German Unfair Competition Act 1909 from circulating copies of published newspaper articles which supported his version of events. The Court held[21] that this restraint did not overstep the permitted margin of appreciation. Most recently, in *Hertel v Switzerland*,[22] the application of the Swiss Federal Unfair Competition Act 1986 to prohibit further publication by a private individual of the results of his purported scientific research into the allegedly harmful effects of food cooked in microwave ovens, was held[23] to be a violation of Art.10.

Before the Commission, the following applications invoking Art.10 have **9–14** been held to be inadmissible:[24] by *markt intern* and two of its journalists against an injunction under s.1 of the German Unfair Competition Act 1909, restraining them from publishing a statement by a retailer critical of Sony's handling of the marketing of its Beta system;[25] by a German generic pharmaceutical company which had been enjoined under the same Act from advertising its generic nifedipine as bio-equivalent,[26] and from circulating to insurance companies lists comparing its prices to those of a competitor;[27] by a Dutch broadcasting company fined for allowing brand names to be used with excessive prominence in two children's television programmes;[28] by the German proprietor of a dance school in Ludwigshafen, who had been restrained at the suit of a competitor from using the slogan *Die Ludwigshafener Tanzschule* on the basis that this misrepresented his school as the only, best, or most important dance school in the town;[29] and by two Maltese newspaper editors successfully sued for libel after publishing a reader's letter complaining of passing-off, which they had not verified and which turned out to be fabricated.[30] The letter had complained that a

---

[20] Series A/291; (1995) 19 E.H.R.R. 64, ECHR.
[21] By a majority of six votes to three.
[22] (1999) 28 E.H.R.R. 534; 5 B.H.R.C. 260; [1998] H.R.C.D. 817, ECHR.
[23] By a majority of six votes to three again.
[24] Generally with reference to the margin of appreciation allowed to national law and practice by the *markt intern* decision.
[25] *markt intern Verlag GmbH, Weber and Beyen v Germany* (Application 12278/86). At the time the preliminary injunction was granted, markt intern had not published the quotation, but had only submitted it to "S." for comment. It is to be assumed that the party identified only as "S." in the decision was Sony.
[26] *R (sc. Ratiofarm) GmbH v Germany* (Application 16555/90). Note that the advertisement restrained by the Cologne courts had made no express reference to the plaintiffs (Bayer) or to their brand *Adaiat*, and there was no suggestion that the claim to bio-equivalence was untrue.
[27] This was restrained by trial and appellate courts in Hamburg. Again, it was not suggested that the comparison was inaccurate or misleading.
[28] *Nederlandse Omroepprogramma Stichting v Netherlands* (Application 16844/90).
[29] *K v Germany* (Application 17006/90).
[30] *Gretch and Montanaro v Malta* (Application 29473/95).

company which could be identified as the plaintiffs in the libel action was guilty of selling tuna in tins labelled as sardines.[31]

9–15　Also declared inadmissible was an application by an Austrian association opposed to smoking, which had been restrained from publishing a parody of an advertisement for *Camel* cigarettes, and from any use of the words *Camel* or *Kamel*.[32] The advertisements parodied had the slogan "I walk miles for a CAMEL". The parody, distributed on pamphlets, stickers and posters, showed a skeleton riding a camel and holding a cigarette in front of it, with the slogan "Only a camel would walk miles for a cigarette".[33]

In comparison to the *Hertel* case, the application in *Schweitzerische Radio- und Fernsehgesellschaft v Switzerland*[34] was declared inadmissible. The applicants had been restrained from broadcasting an item in a consumer affairs programme critical of a named painkilling medicine as representative of a class, but they could have made the same point without identifying an individual brand.

9–16　Complaints by members of the liberal professions restricted from advertising or soliciting for business have attracted mixed results before the Commission.[35] The Commission has refused to admit a complaint by Austrian newspaper publishers who were successfully sued by a competitor after publishing paid-for articles without identifying them as advertisements, and subsequently fined for breaches of the earlier injunctions.[36] The Commission did declare admissible an application by Austrian publishers who had been subjected to an injunction under the Austrian Unfair Competition Act after involving themselves in a tasteless war of words between two other papers.[37]

9–17　In *Krone Verlag v Austria*[38] the applicant newspaper publishers complained that they had been restrained, under the Austrian Unfair Compe-

---

[31] Since tuna was expensive and in short supply, and sardines were relatively cheap and plentiful, the gravamen of the complaint was not that the importers were cheating their customers but that they were evading Government regulations which applied only to tuna. After publication, the importers had their import licence suspended by the Maltese Government and they successfully sued the newspaper.

[32] *Osterreicher Schutzgemeinschaft fur Nichtraucher and Rockenbauer v Austria* (Application 17200/91).

[33] The Commission explains that "In the German language, 'kamel' is a pejorative term for a person acting in a foolish or stupid manner".

[34] (Application 43524/98).

[35] Declared inadmissible: *Janssen v Germany* (Application 21554/93—German freelance non-medical therapist featured in a newspaper article); *Lindner v Germany* (Application 32813/96—German lawyer offering copyright clearance service). *Colman v United Kingdom* (Application 16632/90—English medical practitioner offering holistic health care) was declared admissible without prejudice to the merits. The relevant restrictions were relaxed while the application was pending and the case settled after the Commission issued a majority report (October 19, 1992) unfavourable to the applicant.

[36] *Krone-Verlag GmbH and Mediaprint Anzeigen GmbH & Co KG v Austria* (Application 28977/95). The complaints (which turned mainly on the liability of one group company for breaches of injunctions by others) were based on Arts 6, 7 and Art.1 of the First Protocol. Art.10 was not in issue.

[37] *Familiapress Zeitungs-GmbH v Austria* (Application 20915/92).

[38] (Application 39069/97). *Krone-Verlag GmbH and Mediaprint Anzeigen GmbH & Co KG v Austria* (Application 42429/98), declared inadmissible, was essentially a case of political controversy over World War II revisionism pursued between rival newspapers under the Austrian Unfair Competition Act.

tition Act, from publishing advertisements comparing their subscription rates to those of a rival paper in which they described their paper as "the best" and their rival as "expensive"; and from publishing any kind of price comparison without disclosing the differences in the respective reporting styles as regarded coverage of foreign and domestic politics, economy, culture, science, health, environmental issues and law. The application was declared admissible.

Other relevant Convention provisions

Apart from Art.10, articles of the Human Rights Convention potentially **9–18** relevant in the context of the present work are Art.6 (right to a fair trial), Art.8 (right to private life) and Art.1 of the First Protocol (right to one's possessions). The latter provides:

> Every natural or legal person is entitled to the peaceful enjoyment of his possessions. No one shall be deprived of his possessions except in the public interest and subject to the conditions provided for by law and by the general principles of international law.[39]

Art.1 of the First Protocol only applies where there has been an illegal deprivation of a person's property by the state or one of its agencies, which may be total or partial. It is not applicable where the deprivation has been effected by a private person, nor to the extent that the state may be involved in the adjudication or enforcement of competing claims to property by private parties, in accordance with the relevant law,[40] unless the purported decision is so arbitrary and unjust as to amount to an expropriation. Subject to that, the term "possessions" is interpreted widely and includes subsisting intellectual property rights, and goodwill.

In *van Marle v Netherlands*[41] some Dutch accountants whose right to **9–19** practise had been curtailed alleged, *inter alia*, partial deprivation of their possessions in breach of Art.1 in so far as the goodwill of their practices had been diminished. The Dutch Government argued that goodwill was not a "possession" within the meaning of Art.1, nor capable of being legal property as a matter of Dutch law. The Court held[42] that Art.1 was applicable, but (unanimously) that the interference was justified. Whilst the mere use of "goodwill" in the judgment is potentially ambiguous because of the range of meanings which the word can bear, it is clear that the Court did use the term in much the same sense as it is used in passing-off:

> "[T]he right relied on by the applicants may be likened to the right of property embodied in Article 1: by dint of their own work, the applicants

---

[39] The second paragraph, relating to control of the use of property and to taxes, *etc.* is omitted.

[40] *Aral, Tekin and Aral v Turkey* (Application 24563/94)—ruling by Turkish courts as to ownership of copyright in cartoon characters did not give rise to admissible complaint.

[41] Series A/101; (1986) 18 E.H.R.R. 483, ECHR.

[42] By a majority of 16 to two.

had built up a clientele; this had in many respects the nature of a private right and constituted an asset and, hence, a possession within the meaning of the first sentence of Article 1."

There is some authority that damage to professional reputation may also amount to an infringement of Art.1.[43]

9–20 Art.6 of the Convention, and to a lesser extent Art.8, are capable of applying to unfair competition litigation. Art.6, so far as relevant, provides:

> In the determination of his civil rights and obligations ... everyone is entitled to a fair and public hearing within a reasonable time by an independent and impartial tribunal established by law.[44]

The term "civil rights and obligations" is understood widely, and includes all kinds of private law rights enforced in civil litigation between private persons, whether natural or legal. Several decisions of the Court and the Commission have held Art.6 to be applicable to cases of unfair competition, or other aspects of intellectual property, though generally without finding any violation.[45]

One specific context in which issues under Art.6 might arise concerns interim measures of all kids, especially those imposed without notice or without giving the defendant an adequate opportunity to defend himself at that stage. Measures of this kind are not inherently inconsistent with Art.6, provided that they are necessary and proportionate to the interest protected. *Chappell v United Kingdom*[46] decided that *Anton Piller* orders, obtained and executed *ex parte*, were not inconsistent with Art.6 or 8.

C. Defences under European Community Law

Introduction

9–21 There are two main sources of Community law potentially relevant to actions for passing-off or injurious falsehood. The more important consists of Arts 28 to 30 (formerly 30 to 36) of the amended EC treaty, abolishing quantitative restrictions on the free movement of goods and measures having equivalent effect. Other similar freedoms which may be relevant, and which raise comparable issues, are freedom of establishment under Art.43

---

[43] *Niemietz v Germany* Series A/251B; (1993) 16 E.H.R.R. 97, ECHR. Damage to the professional reputation of a German lawyer (both with regard to his existing clients, and the public at large) as a result of a disproportionately intrusive police search of his office premises contributed to a finding of violation of Art.8; but *held* that no separate issue arose under Art.1 of the First Protocol.

[44] Provisions relating to criminal prosecutions are omitted.

[45] In particular *markt intern Verlag GmbH v Germany* Series A/164; (1990) 12 E.H.R.R. 161, ECHR.

[46] Series A/152; (1990) 12 E.H.R.R. 1; [1989] 1 F.S.R. 617, ECHR.

(formerly Art.52) of the EC Treaty and the freedom to provide services under Art.49 (formerly Art.59). Freedom for the cross-border dissemination of advertising or other forms of commercial information is not separately addressed in the Treaty, but restrictions on advertising may directly or indirectly contravene one or more of the other freedoms.[47] The other relevant treaty provisions consist of Arts 81 and 82 (formerly 85 and 86), which form the basis of Community competition law.

There is an extensive body of law from the European Court of Justice and national courts on the application of these provisions to intellectual property rights in general, but only a few decisions of the English courts deal specifically with passing-off, and then only incidentally, with passing-off generally being subordinated to issues of registered trade mark infringement.[48] Passing-off as English law understands it is a concept unique, within the Community, to the United Kingdom and the Republic of Ireland. Consequently, one has to deduce the likely application of Community law from first principles and from decisions on registered trade marks, unfair competition and (to a certain extent) consumer protection. There is even less material, whether at Community or national level, from which to derive the treatment of injurious falsehood in Community law, but the same sources and principles may be expected to apply.

Free movement of goods: general principles

It is a basic principle of Community law that once goods have been released **9–22** into free circulation in one member state they should enjoy unimpeded entry into the markets of every other member state.[49] The basic rule is subject to derogations in favour, *inter alia*, of the protection of industrial property rights and the protection of consumers. However, the benefit of the derogations is lost if they are discriminatory, unnecessary or disproportionate. This three-layered approach is reflected in the provisions of the EC treaty establishing the principle of free movement

Art.28 (formerly Art.30)

Quantitative restrictions on imports and all measures having equivalent effect shall be prohibited between Member States.

---

[47] Case C-262/88 *GB-INNO-BM v Confederation du Commerce Luxembourgeois ASBL* [1990] E.C.R. I-667; [1991] 2 C.M.L.R. 801; Joined Cases C-34/95, C-35/95 and 36/95 *Konsumentombudsmannen v De Agostini (Svenska) Forlag AB* [1997] E.C.R. I-3843; [1998] 1 C.M.L.R. 32; [1998] E.T.M.R. 44; [1998] E.M.L.R. 43.

[48] *Imperial Chemical Industries Ltd v Berk Pharmaceuticals Ltd* [1981] F.S.R. 1, a pleading point; *Bulmer (HP) Ltd v J Bollinger SA* [1978] R.P.C. 79; [1978] 2 C.M.L.R. 625, C.A.; *Lowenbrau Munchen v Grunhalle Lager International Ltd* [1974] R.P.C. 492; [1974] F.S.R. 1; [1974] 1 C.M.L.R. 1; *Tayto (Northern Ireland) Ltd v McKee* [1991] 3 C.M.L.R. 269 (HC of Northern Ireland); *Glaxo Group Ltd v Dowelhurst Ltd* [2000] 2 C.M.L.R. 571; [2000] E.T.M.R. 415; [2000] F.S.R. 529.

[49] Case 120/78 *Rewe v Bundesmonopolverwaltung fur Branntwein ("Cassis de Dijon")* [1979] E.C.R. 649; [1979] 1 C.M.L.R. 494.

Art.29 (formerly Art.34)

Quantitative restrictions on exports, and all measures having equivalent effect, shall be prohibited between Member States.

Art.30 (formerly Art.36)

The provisions of Articles 28 and 29 shall not preclude prohibitions or restrictions on imports, exports or goods in transit justified on grounds of public morality, public policy or public security; the protection of health and life of humans, animals or plants; the protection of national treasures possessing artistic, historic or archaeological value; or the protection of industrial and commercial property. Such prohibitions or restrictions shall not, however, constitute a means of arbitrary discrimination or a disguised restriction on trade between Member States.

9–23   Art.28 (formerly Art.30) turns on the concept of quantitative restrictions and measures having equivalent effect. The term "quantitative restriction" is itself a wide one and not confined to quotas or outright import bans. However, it is unnecessary to define quantitative restrictions as such because almost any measure which hinders imports to any extent is *prima facie* equivalent to a quantitative restriction. A straightforward interpretation of Arts 28 and 30 (formerly Art.36) would be to say that any rule of law which impedes the importation of goods in free circulation in another member state is a measure equivalent to a quantitative restriction, but that it may be justified under Art.30 (formerly Art.36) if it serves one of the purposes listed and is not discriminatory or unduly restrictive.

This interpretation came to give difficulties because the European Court of Justice had insisted that Art.30 (in the original numbering) should be interpreted very widely, and Art.36 correspondingly narrowly because it was a derogation from a fundamental principle. To restore some balance between the competing principles of free trade and justifiable restrictions on it, the Court invented the further concept of "mandatory requirements" as an additional qualification to Art.30. According to the judgment in the *Cassis de Dijon* case:[50]

"Obstacles to movement within the Community resulting from disparities between the national laws relating to the marketing of the products in question must be accepted in so far as those provisions may be recognised as being necessary in order to satisfy mandatory requirements relating in particular to the effectiveness of fiscal supervision, the protection of public health, the fairness of commercial transactions and the defence of the consumer."

Passing-off and injurious falsehood post *Keck*

9–24 Even after the invention of the "mandatory requirements" in *Cassis de*

[50] Above.

Dijon[51] the disparity between the apparent breadth of what might constitute a measure equivalent to a quantitative restriction, and the grounds on which the latter could be justified in national law, continued to generate problems. To address these the European Court of Justice in *Keck and Mithouard*[52] invented a further distinction, between laws relating to the "product characteristics"[53] of the goods themselves, and those relating to mere "selling arrangements" regulating how goods were sold or marketed. In the result, a French law prohibiting the practice of loss leaders was upheld, although it would have been struck down under the unqualified doctrine of *Cassis de Dijon*.

"In view of the increasing tendency of traders to invoke Article 30 of the Treaty as a means of challenging any rules whose effect is to limit their commercial freedom even where such rules are not aimed at products from other Member States, the Court considers it necessary to re-examine and clarify its case law on this matter.

It is established by the case law beginning with '*Cassis de Dijon*' (Case 120/78, *Rewe-Zentral v Bundesmonopolverwaltung für Branntwein*) that, in the absence of harmonisation of legislation, obstacles to free movement of goods which are the consequence of applying, to goods coming from other Member States where they are lawfully manufactured and marketed, rules that lay down requirements to be met by such goods (such as those relating to designation, form, size, weight, composition, presentation, labelling, packaging) constitute measures of equivalent effect prohibited by Article 30. This is so even if those rules apply without distinction to all products unless their application can be justified by a public-interest objective taking precedence over the free movement of goods.

By contrast, contrary to what has previously been decided, the application to products from other Member States of national provisions restricting or prohibiting certain selling arrangements is not such as to hinder directly or indirectly, actually or potentially, trade between Member States within the meaning of *Dassonville* (Case 8/74) so long as those provisions apply to all relevant traders operating within the national territory and so long as they affect in the same manner, in law and in fact, the marketing of domestic products and of those from other Member States.

Provided that those conditions are fulfilled, the application of such rules to the sale of products from another Member State meeting the requirements laid down by that State is not by nature such as to prevent their access to the market or to impede access any more than it impedes the access of domestic products. Such rules therefore fall outside the scope of Article 30 of the Treaty."

---

[51] Above.
[52] Cases C-267/91 *Criminal Proceedings against Keck* and C-268/91 *Criminal Proceedings against Mithouard* [1993] E.C.R. I-6097; [1995] 1 C.M.L.R. 101.
[53] This phrase (unlike "selling arrangements") was not used in *Keck* itself, but is a convenient antithesis to the latter.

9–25   *Keck*[54] probably has little effect on the application of settled jurisprudence to passing-off, although its implications may be rather greater for injurious falsehood and for Continental laws of unfair competition which regulate business conduct to a much greater extent than does English law. So far as passing-off is concerned, the matter complained of is almost always intimately connected with the goods themselves: typically a name, mark, label, description or get-up which can only be dissociated from the goods by physically interfering with them or their packaging. These are precisely the kind of "product characteristics" for which *Keck* expressly leaves *Cassis de Dijon*[55] in full force and effect. In comparison, injurious falsehood typically deals with misrepresentations conveyed by some kind of advertising, and so is more likely to involve so-called "selling arrangements" which (in principle) can be regulated without adversely affecting the free movement of the goods themselves. Of course, the dividing line is not hard and fast, and has to be determined on a case-by-case basis.[56] Passing-off may arise from the terms in which a competitor advertises;[57] there may be liability for injurious falsehood arising directly from trading in goods, without any separate representation;[58] and goods or their packaging may be customised for a promotional campaign.[59]

Exhaustion of rights and "specific subject matter"

9–26 Prior to *Keck*[60] the general principles as to exhaustion of rights under former Arts 30 and 36 (now 28 and 30) were summarised by Jacobs A.-G. in *CNL-Sucal v Hag (HAG II)*[61] in terms that are still relevant:

> "In view of the modest scale of legislative activity in relation to trade marks and to intellectual property in general, the task of reconciling the competing interests enshrined in Articles 30 and 36 of the Treaty has fallen mainly to the Court. It has worked out three fundamental principles, which have played a central part in the entire field of intellectual property, and all of which have their origin in Case 78/70 *Deutsche Grammophon v Metro.*

[54] Cases C-267/91 *Criminal Proceedings against Keck* and C-268/91 *Criminal Proceedings against Mithouard* [1993] E.C.R. I-6097; [1995] 1 C.M.L.R. 101.

[55] Case 120/78 *Rewe v Bundesmonopolverwaltung fur Branntwein* [1979] E.C.R. 649; [1979] 1 C.M.L.R. 494.

[56] As is demonstrated by Case C-255/97 *Pfeiffer Grosshandel GmbH v Lowa Warenhandel GmbH* [1999] E.C.R. I-2835; [2001] 1 C.M.L.R. 7; [1999] E.T.M.R. 603, below.

[57] As in *McDonald's Hamburgers Ltd v Burger King Ltd* [1986] F.S.R. 45, CA.

[58] As in *Wilts United Dairies Ltd v Thomas Robinson Sons & Co Ltd* [1958] R.P.C. 94, CA.

[59] As in Case C-344/98 *Verein gegen Unwesen in Handel und Gewerbe Koln eV v Mars GmbH* [1995] E.C.R. I-1923; [1995] 3 C.M.L.R. 1, where the wrapping of ice cream bars was modified for a "10 per cent extra" promotion.

[60] Cases C-267/91 *Criminal Proceedings against Keck* and C-268/91 *Criminal Proceedings against Mithouard* [1993] E.C.R. I-6097; [1995] 1 C.M.L.R. 101.

[61] Case C-10/89 [1990] E.C.R. I-3711; [1990] 3 C.M.L.R. 571; [1991] F.S.R. 99. Citations and references to the former "common origin" doctrine of *Café Hag* are omitted.

(i) While the Treaty does not affect the existence of intellectual property rights, there are none the less circumstances in which the exercise of such rights may be restricted by the prohibitions laid down in the Treaty (see, for example, *Deutsche Grammophon* at para. 11).

(ii) Article 36 permits exceptions to the free movement of goods only to the extent to which such exceptions are necessary for the purpose of safeguarding the rights that constitute the specific subject-matter of the type of intellectual property in question (*Deutsche Grammophon, loc. cit*). Perhaps the main advantage of this formula, apart from the fact that it narrows the scope of the exceptions permitted by Article 36, is that it allows subtle distinctions to be made depending on the type of intellectual property in issue.

(iii) The exclusive right conferred on the owner of intellectual property is exhausted in relation to the products in question when he puts them into circulation anywhere within the Common Market. Spelt out more fully, 'the proprietor of an industrial or commercial property right protected by the legislation of a Member-State may not rely on that legislation in order to oppose the importation of a product which has lawfully been marketed in another Member-State by, or with the consent of, the proprietor of the right himself or a person legally or economically dependent on him' (see, for example, Case 144/81 *Keurkoop v Nancy Kean Gifts* one of many cases confirming a principle first developed in the *Deutsche Grammophon* case).

In addition, the Court has developed the principle that the rights conferred under national law by a trade mark (or presumably by any other form of intellectual property) cannot be exercised in such a way as to frustrate the competition rules of the Treaty."

Trade marks are like other intellectual property rights in being subject to **9–27** the doctrine of exhaustion of rights. Consequently, a trade mark owner cannot prevent the importation, etc., of goods previously marketed in the common market with his consent or with the consent of a connected party such as a licensee, subsidiary, parent or sister company. This applies equally whether the mark is registered or unregistered, and whether the cause of action is formally for trade mark infringement, passing-off, or unfair competition. The decided cases are overwhelmingly concerned with the first.

In *Centrafarm v Winthrop*[62] the defendants (Centrafarm) imported into **9–28** the Netherlands drugs which had been marketed in the United Kingdom or Germany by members of the Sterling Drug group. The Sterling subsidiary in the Netherlands, Winthrop, sued for infringement of the trade mark *Negram* of which it was the registered proprietor.[63] On a reference under the former Art. 177 of the EEC Treaty the European Court held that it was inconsistent

---

[62] Case 16/74 [1974] E.C.R. 1183; [1974] 2 C.M.L.R. 480.
[63] In a parallel case *Centrafarm B.V. v Sterling Drug Inc.* (Case 15/74) *ubi supra* Sterling sued for patent infringement. The European Court treated the two as raising the same issues.

with the rules on the free movement of goods for the holder of a trade mark to prohibit the marketing in one state of goods put on the market in another member state by the proprietor or with his consent. Former Art.36 only permitted derogations from the principle of free movement to the extent necessary to protect "the specific subject matter" of the rights in question. The latter concept was defined as follows:

> "In relation to trade marks, the specific subject matter of the industrial property is the guarantee that the owner of the trade mark has the exclusive right to use that trade mark, for the purpose of putting products protected by the trade mark into circulation for the first time, and is therefore intended to protect him against competitors wishing to take advantage of the status and reputation of the trade mark by selling products illegally bearing that trade mark."

9–29   The specific subject matter of trade marks has been further explained to the effect that in specified circumstances third parties may if necessary re-pack goods to which a trade mark owner has applied a mark, and may apply that mark or (in more limited circumstances) an equivalent one, to the re-packaged goods. The law is principally to be found in *Hoffman-La Roche v Centrafarm*,[64] *Centrafarm v American Home Products*,[65] *Pfizer v Eurimpharm*,[66] *Bristol Myers Squibb v Paranova*,[67] *Pharmacia & Upjohn v Paranova*[68] and *Boehringer Ingelheim v Swingward*.[69] All of these concerned pharmaceuticals, but the law is of general application.[70] Broadly speaking, the importer may re-pack the claimant's goods and affix the claimant's mark under which they were originally sold, provided that the re-packing cannot affect the condition of the product, the proprietor is notified in advance and the packs state by whom the goods have been repacked. It can happen that identical goods are sold under different marks in different member states. If the importer is to be entitled to affix a different mark, it must be shown that the proprietor had used the two marks so as to partition the market.

9–30   As the law stands, in any other circumstances a trade mark proprietor may *prima facie* enforce his rights against infringement of his trade mark unaffected by the rules on the free movement of goods. In general, therefore, nothing in these provisions affects the right of a trade mark owner to prevent the importation from another member state of goods which infringe his mark, provided the goods were not put into circulation by him or with his consent. In particular, the fact that goods may lawfully be marketed in one

---

[64] Case 102/77 [1978] E.C.R. 1139; [1978] 3 C.M.L.R. 217.
[65] Case 3/78 [1978] E.C.R. 1823; [1979] 1 C.M.L.R. 326.
[66] Case 1/81 [1981] E.C.R. 2913; [1982] 1 C.M.L.R. 406.
[67] Cases C-427/93 *Bristol Myers Squibb v Paranova S/A*; C-436/93 *Bayer AG v Paranova S/A*; C-429/93 *CH Boehringer Sohn v Paranova S/A* [1996] E.C.R. I-3457; [1997] 1 C.M.L.R. 1151; [1996] E.T.M.R. 1; [1996] F.S.R. 102.
[68] Case C-379/97 [1999] E.C.R. I-6927; [2000] 1 C.M.L.R. 51; [1999] E.T.M.R. 937; [2000] F.S.R. 621.
[69] Case C-143/00 [2002] 2 C.M.L.R. 26; [2002] E.T.M.R. 78]; [2002] F.S.R. 61.
[70] Case C-349/95 *Loendersloot v George Ballantine & Son Ltd* [1997] E.C.R. I-6227; [1998] 1 C.M.L.R. 1015; [1998] E.T.M.R. 10; [1998] F.S.R. 544.

member state does not mean that they can be imported into another member state in defiance of private rights.

In *Terrapin v Terranova*[71] the German plaintiffs were the owners of the mark *Terranova*. The English defendants independently owned the mark *Terrapin* in England. The German *Bundesgerischthof* considered that the marks were close enough to deceive and that Terrapin were infringers. The European Court of Justice held that the rules on free movement did not prevent Terranova exercising its right under German law to restrain the importation of Terrapin goods in these circumstances. Otherwise, the specific object of the rights would have been undermined. The Court refused to subject different national laws to an overriding Community definition of what resemblance was close enough to cause confusion.

In *Pfeiffer v Löwa*[72] the plaintiffs, Pfeiffer, operated a supermarket in **9–31** Austria under the name *Plus KAUF PARK*, which was registered as a trade name and as a trade mark for various classes of goods. The defendants, who already operated 139 supermarkets in Austria under the name *Zielpunkt*, decided to re-brand themselves in Austria as *Plus prima leben und sparen* to correspond to the trading style of the group elsewhere in Germany and Europe. Löwa were sued by Pfeiffer, and the referring Austrian court held that *Plus* was sufficiently distinctive, that there was a substantial risk of confusion between the two trading styles, and that the defendants were therefore infringing the Austrian Unfair Competition Act subject to any overriding defences. The European Court of Justice held that an order restraining Löwa from trading as *Plus* in Austria was capable of affecting their right of establishment under Art.52, since it impeded them from trading and advertising in a uniform manner throughout the Community, but that the relevant Austrian law was non-discriminatory and justified for the protection of industrial property. The argument based on Art.30 added nothing.

None of the foregoing restrictions on the trade mark owner's rights **9–32** applies when goods are imported into the common market from a third country. Arts 28 and 30 are only applicable to trade between member states, including the EEA. It follows that Art.28 does not apply (and Art.30 need not be invoked) when a trade mark owner seeks to prevent the importation of infringing goods from outside the EEC. If imports are to be allowed under these circumstances, it must be as a result of the application of Art.81, or purely national law.

In *EMI v CBS*[73] the trade mark *Columbia* for records had once been in common ownership for America and Europe, but had subsequently become vested in CBS for the United States and EMI for the whole of the EEC. EMI sued CBS for importing records bearing the mark and courts in England, Denmark and Germany made references to the European Court of Justice. The Court ruled that neither former Art.30 itself, nor the former

---

[71] Case 119/75 [1976] E.C.R. 1039; C.M.L.R. 482.
[72] Case C-255/97 *Pfeiffer Grosshandel GmbH v Löwa Warenhandel GmbH* [1999] E.C.R. I-2835; [2001] 1 C.M.L.R. 7; [1999] E.T.M.R. 603.
[73] Case 5/71 [1975] E.C.R. 811; [1976] 2 C.M.L.R. 235.

common origin doctrine of *Cafe Hag*,[74] applied to imports from outside the EEC.

Unfair competition

9–33 Relatively few cases before the European Court of Justice have dealt with aspects of unfair competition analogous to passing-off or injurious false-hood but unconnected with registered trade marks or trade names. The starting point is *Cassis de Dijon*,[75] in which the European Court included measures to ensure "the fairness of commercial transactions", as well as those for consumer protection, among the "mandatory requirements" which exempt what would otherwise be quantitative restrictions from the impact of Art.28 (formerly Art.30), provided they are necessary, proportionate and non-discriminatory. Since consumer protection is separately identified, it must be assumed that "the fairness of commercial transactions" was intended to refer to fairness between traders, and specifically to laws for the repression of unfair competition. The latter interpretation is confirmed by subsequent authority[76] as well as by the French text of *Cassis de Dijon* itself, which speaks of *"la loyauté des transactions commerciales"*,[77] supporting the conclusion that laws of *concurrence déloyale* were being referred to as among the mandatory requirements.

On this basis, there is strictly no need to invoke Art.30 (formerly 36) to justify such laws. However, it would seem that the prevention of unfair competition may also fall within the concept of "the protection of industrial and commercial property" for the purposes of Art.30, though this is undecided. The Court has referred approvingly to the fact that Art.10*bis* of the Paris Convention for the Protection of Industrial Property obliges all member states to assure effective protection against unfair competition as there defined,[78] and copyright has been treated as industrial property although it is subject to a different international regime. Despite the existence of Art.10*bis* the Court has not attempted a definition of the specific subject matter of unfair competition law.

9–34 In *Dansk Supermerked v Imerco*[79] the plaintiffs (Imerco) commissioned English china manufacturers to produce a commemorative service for their

---

[74] Case 192/73 *Van Zuylen v Hag* [1974] E.C.R. 731; [1974] 2 C.M.L.R. 127; reversed by Case C-10/89 *CNL-Sucal v Hag (HAG II)* [1990] I E.C.R. 3711; [1990] 3 C.M.L.R. 571, [1991] F.S.R. 99.

[75] Case 120/78 *Rewe v Bundesmonopolverwaltung fur Branntwein ("Cassis de Dijon")* [1979] E.C.R. 649; [1979] 1 C.M.L.R. 494.

[76] Specifically Case 6/81 *Industrie Diensten Group v Beele* [1982] E.C.R. 707; [1982] 3 C.M.L.R. 102.

[77] Compare the Fourth preamble to the EC Treaty, the French text of which refers to *"la loyauté dans la concurrence"*. Perhaps unwittingly, *Cassis de Dijon* more closely tracks the language of the Preamble to the original 1883 text of the Paris Convention, referring to the desire of the original 11 contracting states *"... de contribuer a la guarantie ... de la loyauté des transactions commerciales ..."*

[78] Case 6/81 *Industrie Diensten Group v Beele* [1982] E.C.R. 707; [1982] 3 C.M.L.R. 102, but this was only to support its conclusion that the relevant Dutch law was justified under the "mandatory requirements".

[79] Case 58/80 [1981] E.C.R. 181; [1981] 3 C.M.L.R. 590.

fiftieth anniversary. About 1,000 services failed to meet Imerco's standard of quality. Imerco agreed that the manufacturers could sell these services in England subject to a prohibition on their being exported to Scandinavia. The defendants managed to buy 300 substandard services and put them on sale in Denmark. The packaging was different and the price lower, but customers of the defendants appear not to have been notified that the goods were seconds. The Danish court granted an interlocutory injunction. The European Court of Justice dealt with the case solely under former Arts 30 and 36. They ruled that Imerco could not rely on its copyright or trade marks because those rights had been exhausted on the sale in England. The actual importation of goods marketed in another member state could not, as a matter of interpretation of Art.30, be treated as an unfair commercial practice. Nor could the existence of an agreement intended to prohibit importation be relied on or taken into account in characterising the subsequent marketing as an unfair commercial practice: a conclusion the Court drew from Art.30 itself and not from former Article 85 which it had dismissed as irrelevant. However, the Court allowed that Art.30 did not prevent the application of the law of consumer protection or unfair competition to the manner in which the goods were actually marketed.

In *Industrie Diensten Group v Beele*[80] the plaintiffs (Beele) were the distributors in the Netherlands of a system of cable ducts which had formerly been patented. The defendants imported from a third party in Germany cable ducts based on the same design. The Dutch court granted an interlocutory injunction on the basis that the defendants were guilty of unfair competition since the imported ducts were slavish copies of those distributed by the plaintiffs, the similarities being closer than functional equivalence required. The European Court ruled that national laws prohibiting slavish imitation fell within the mandatory requirements of *Cassis de Dijon* and that there was therefore no contravention of former Art.30. The law did not discriminate against imports and was not disproportionate to the need to prevent unfair competition and protect consumers. The Court expressly left open the application of former Arts 30 and 36 to spare parts.

However one may characterise national law, it cannot be enforced if it is **9–35** discriminatory in fact, even if it is expressed in terms which do not appear to bear any more heavily on importers as opposed to native businesses.

The plaintiffs in *Theodor Kohl v Ringelhaan & Rennett*[81] applied for an injunction under the German Unfair Competition Act 1909 against the defendants using the symbol "r & r" in relation to pharmacy equipment imported from France. Ringelhaan & Rennett had been an old-established German concern which had been wound up and its French subsidiary (the defendant) sold off. The plaintiffs had no claim to the mark themselves nor any interest in the goodwill of the former German company. Their argument under German law was that the use of the mark was deceptive as implying that the goods were German. The European Court ruled that to enforce the German Unfair Competition Act in these circumstances would infringe

---

[80] Case 6/81 [1982] E.C.R. 707; [1982] 3 C.M.L.R. 102.
[81] Case 177/83 [1984] E.C.R. 3651; [1985] 3 C.M.L.R. 340.

former Art.30 and was not justified by former Art.36. It appeared that despite the very wide and non-discriminatory wording of the section of the Act in question, it had, in practice, never been used against purely domestic competition.

Competition law: Art.81

9–36 The doctrines of exhaustion of rights and of specific subject matter were originally evolved in the context of market-sharing and price maintenance agreements which misused intellectual property rights to partition the common market or regulate terms of trade. The reason for this is largely historical. Infringements of former Arts 85 and 86 were justiciable by the European Court from a much earlier date than former Arts 30 to 36. Art.85 proved to be a useful weapon in this context but an imperfect one, since it was inapplicable to purely unilateral abuses. Since the early 1970s such restrictions on free trade within the Community have been dealt with almost entirely under what is now Art.28, which is not restricted by the need to find or postulate some offending agreement.[82] It should be remembered that trade mark delimitation agreements,[83] including agreements settling litigation, may come within Art.81 if they are unduly restrictive and affect trade between member states.[84]

Art.81 prohibits in general terms all agreements and concerted practices

Which may affect trade between member states and which have as their object or effect the prevention, restriction or distortion of competition within the common market.

Price fixing and market sharing are mentioned as specific examples. Art.81 does not in terms refer to intellectual property or to litigation, its concern being with restrictive agreements and the like. However, the European Court of Justice has held that what is now Art.81 provides a defence to an action for infringement of an intellectual property right where the action tends to partition the common market and is "the subject, the means or the result"[85] or an agreement prohibited under Art.81. These two requirements are cumulative. If there is no such connection between the right, the infringement action, and a prohibited agreement or concerted practice then there is no breach of Art.81 on which to base a defence. Purely unilateral

---

[82] Compare Case 58/80 *Dansk Supermerked A/S v Imerco A/S* [1981] E.C.R. 181; [1981] 3 C.M.L.R. 590, decided solely under Art.30 with Art.85 being dismissed as irrelevant despite the existence of a blatant contractual export ban, with Case 40/70 *Sirena SRL v Eda SRL* [1971] E.C.R. 69; [1971] C.M.L.R. 260; [1971] F.S.R. 666.

[83] See *Apple Corps Ltd v Apple Computer Inc* [1992] F.S.R. 431 and *Fyffes plc v Chiquita Brands International Inc* [1993] F.S.R. 83 in both of which delimination agreements were upheld.

[84] *Penneys* [1978] 2 C.M.L.R. 100; Case 35/83 *B.A.T. v Commission ("Toltecs")* [1985] E.C.R. 363; [1985] 2 C.M.L.R. 470.

[85] Case 40/70 *Sirena SRL v Eda SRL* [1971] E.C.R. 69; [1971] C.M.L.R. 260; [1971] F.S.R. 666.

attempts to partition the common market are the exclusive preserve of Art.28.[86]

The first decision of the European Court of Justice applying former **9–37** Article 85 to intellectual property actions was *Consten & Grundig v Commission*[87] Consten was the exclusive distributor for France of Grundig goods. Consten registered the mark *GINT* (for Grundig International) in France in its own name but agreed to assign it to Grundig if the distributorship ended. All Grundig goods were marked with the *GINT*, as well as the Grundig mark. Consten used its registration of *GINT* to prevent parallel imports of genuine Grundig goods from Germany. The Commission ordered Consten to desist and was upheld by the European court of Justice. The exercise of the trademark by Consten to maintain a system of contractual territorial protection was an infringement of Art.85.[88]

Sirena v Eda[89] marks the high water mark of the application of the competition rules to ensure free movements of goods in the face of conflicting trade mark rights. Sirena was the owner in Italy of trade marks assigned to it by an American company, Mark Allen, well before the establishment of the EEC. The defendant, Novimpex, imported goods under those marks into Italy from a German licensee of Mark Allen. On a reference under Art.177 from the Italian court, the Court ruled that Art.85 was applicable to trade mark rights when their exercise was "the subject, the means or the result, of a restrictive practice". This being an Art.177 reference, it did not fall to the Court to decide whether any breach of Art.85 had actually taken place. The Court ruled that Art.85 would apply to these agreements from the 1930s and 1940s if they continued to produce effects after the EEC treaty entered into force, but this has been explained on the basis that there must have been continuing collusion after the assignments.

EMI v CBS[90] gave a clearer, more restrictive, and more logical account of **9–38** the application of Art.85 to trade marks than did *Sirena v Eda*, and implicitly withdrew from the wider implications of that case. The trade mark *Columbia* for records had once been in common ownership for America and Europe, but had subsequently become vested in CBS for the United States and EMI for the whole of the common market. EMI sued CBS for importing records bearing the mark and courts in England, Denmark and Germany made references to the European Court of Justice. On former Art.85, the Court affirmed that a trade mark right as such did not possess the necessary element of contract or concerted practice but that the exercise of the right might be prohibited if it was the subject, means or consequence of a restrictive contract or practice. To that extent, the Court affirmed *Sirena v Eda*, but ruled that it did not extend to completed assignments where the only continuing effects were those flowing from the exercise of the marks themselves.

---

[86] Unless there is an abuse of a dominant position contrary to Article 82.
[87] Cases 56 and 58/64 [1966] E.C.R. 299.
[88] Followed in *Mantruck Services Ltd v Ballinlough Electrical Refrigeration Co Ltd* [1992] 1 C.M.L.R. 325; [1993] E.C.C. 295 (Irish Supreme Court).
[89] Case 40/70 [1971] E.C.R. 69; [1971] C.M.L.R. 260; [1971] F.S.R. 666.
[90] Case 5/71 [1976] E.C.R. 811; [1976] 2 C.M.L.R. 235.

This interpretation of *Sirena v Eda* was affirmed by the Court of Justice in *IHT v Ideal Standard*,[91] where the principal issue was whether the doctrines of common origin (now abolished) or exhaustion of rights applied to a completed, arm's length, voluntary assignment of a trade mark in one country of the common market:

"It should be added that, where undertakings independent of each other make trade mark assignments following a market sharing agreement, the prohibition of anti-competitive agreements under Article 85 applies and assignments which give effect to that agreement are consequently void. However ... that rule and the accompanying sanction cannot be applied mechanically to every assignment. Before a trade mark assignment can be treated as giving effect to an agreement prohibited under Article 85, it is necessary to analyse the context, the commitments underlying the assignment, the intention of the parties and the consideration for the assignment."

9–39   Despite the greater importance of Art.28 (formerly Art.30) in recent times, there are still circumstances in which a defence based on Art.81 or 82 may be worth raising. The most important of these is that Art.81, unlike Art.28, is capable of applying to restrictions on trade between the Community and non-member states, on the ground that preventing imports into the common market may indirectly affect trade within it. This doctrine does not apply to Art.28. A defendant importing into the Community from a third state may therefore have a defence under Art.81 when none would exist under Art.28. In addition, breaches of Art.81 may be investigated, restrained and penalised by the Commission, so that the importer has the option of applying additional pressure at little additional expense to himself. The Commission has no such jurisdiction under Art.28. A breach of Art.81 is probably more convincing than one of Art.28 as the basis for a defence of unclean hands or illegality, as in the latter case it is not the owner of the right who is in the wrong, but the legal system which purports to benefit him.

Art.82

9–40   Art.82 (formerly Art.86) is of comparatively little importance in this field, even in comparison to the reduced role of Art.81. Art.82 prohibits any abuse of a dominant position within the common market so far as it may affect trade between member states. Unlike Art.85, this Article is applicable to unilateral conduct, but there must be both a dominant position and an abuse thereof. It has consistently been denied that ownership of trade marks or other intellectual property rights constitutes a dominant position *per se* or that enforcing such rights is abusive. In *Imperial Chemical Industries v Berk*[92] a plea that the plaintiffs were abusing a dominant position by overcharging

---

[91] Case C-9/93 [1994] E.C.R. I-2789; [1994] 3 C.M.L.R. 857; [1995] F.S.R. 59.
[92] [1981] F.S.R. 1 (Megarry V.C.).

was struck out as having no connection with the allegation that the defendants were passing off. This decision was distinguished by the Court of Appeal in the industrial copyright case of *Lansing Bagnall v Buccaneer*[93] where the defence was allowed to stand, with Lawton L.J. observing: "There is nothing in Article 86 of the Treaty of Rome which allows passing-off. Passing-off is essentially misrepresentation. It cannot be an abuse of a dominant position to stop someone passing off your goods".

ICI v Berk and *Lansing Bagnall v Buccaneer* were followed by Ferris J. in *IBM v Phoenix*[94] where he struck out an Art.86 defence alleging that the plaintiffs had abused a dominant position by refusing to maintain IBM computers containing the defendants' substitute parts, the description of which by the defendants as *IBM Manufactured* was the subject of the passing-off action. If the action failed on the ground that there had been no misrepresentation then the defence would be unnecessary. On the other hand, if the action succeeded then even the existence of a positive legal duty on IBM to service computers fitted with the defendants' parts would not absolve the defendants from liability for passing-off by describing as *IBM Manufactured* parts which *ex hypothesi* were nothing of the sort. There was no nexus between the alleged abuse and the action. A counterclaim for breach of Community competition law was not struck out, but was stayed pending proceedings before the EC Commission. A stay of the action pending a decision by the Commission was refused.

D. Illegal or Deceptive Mark or Trade

The basis and effect of the doctrine

The claimant in an action for passing-off or injurious falsehood cannot **9–41** claim the protection of a court of justice for whatever is illegal, fraudulent or deceptive. As the property protected by a passing-off action is the goodwill the claimant has in his business, and as injurious falsehood also protects pecuniary or economic interests, the rule applies where the relevant class of the claimant's business is illegal or a fraud upon the public.[95] More commonly, it applies where the business itself is lawful but where the mark or other sign alleged to have taken by the defendant contains a material misrepresentation. It is no answer to the defence that the defendant may be *in pari delictu* with the claimant.

> "Nobody doubts that a trader may be guilty of such misrepresentations with regard to his goods, as to amount to a fraud upon the public, and to disentitle him on that ground, as against a rival trader, to the relief in a

---

[93] [1984] F.S.R. 241, CA.
[94] [1994] R.P.C. 252 (Ferris J.).
[95] For instance in *Estcourt v Estcourt Hop Essence Co.* (1875) L.R. 10 Ch. 276, CA, where, *inter alia*, the parties competed in selling an adulterant for beer; *Caterham Car Sales v Birkin Cars* 1998 (3) SA 938 (SCA), below.

court of equity which he might otherwise claim. What would constitute a misrepresentation of this description, may in particular cases be a reasonable subject of doubt, and it was in the present case the ground of the difference between the two judgments under consideration.

The general rule seems to be that the mis-statement of any material fact calculated to deceive the public, will be sufficient for this purpose."[96]

9–42   There have been differences of judicial opinion as to whether the defence in passing-off cases is purely an equitable one, based on the doctrine of unclean hands, or whether it also exists at common law. The two extremes of opinion are represented by *obiter dicta* of Vaughan Williams L.J. in *Jamieson v Jamieson*[97] to the effect that such misrepresentations were not a defence to a claim for damages at common law; and of Mellish L.J. in *Ford v Foster*[98] that if the defence did not succeed at common law then a court of equity would be obliged to grant an injunction. The question is not entirely an academic one, because if the defence is merely an equitable one then it would not prevent the claimant recovering damages and, perhaps, costs.

Despite some judicial opinions to the contrary, the better view is that the defence exists at common law as well as in equity, so that a claimant guilty of a fraudulent trade or sufficiently material misrepresentations may be refused all relief, and have his action dismissed with costs. This would be more consistent with the grounds on which the plaintiffs failed in *Royal Baking Powder v Wright Crossley*,[99] a common law action for injurious falsehood, although the reasoning is complicated by the relationship between a superficially trivial illegality and the plaintiffs' consequent inability to prove special damage. It remains the case, however, that all equitable remedies are discretionary so that in appropriate circumstances the court might withhold or limit equitable relief, particularly the grant of an injunction, because of conduct by the claimant which fell short of that establishing a complete defence: "[T]he proper course is for a court of law, and much more a court of equity, to refuse to interfere to protect a trade which is assisted or supposed to be assisted by misrepresentations".[1]

9–43   The defence is rare in modern law, but that it continues to exist is confirmed by the South African case of *Caterham Car Sales v Birkin Cars*,[2] which concerned Caterham's claim to exclusive rights in South Africa in relation to the Lotus Super Seven Series III sports car and replicas of it.

"I am prepared to accept that Caterham had a reputation during the 1980s in South Africa. It was reputed to be the exclusive successor to Lotus in relation to the Series III and properly licensed. The prime cause

---

[96] *per* Lord Kingsdown in *Leather Cloth Co Ltd v American Leather Cloth Co Ltd* (1865) 11 E.R. 1435, HL.

[97] (1898) 15 R.P.C. 169, CA.

[98] (1872) L.R. 7 Ch. 611, CA.

[99] (1900) 18 R.P.C. 95, HL.

[1] *per* Cotton L.J. in *Newman v Pinto* (1887) 4 R.P.C. 508, CA.

[2] 1998 (3) SA 938, SCA.

of this was the belief that the 1973 Agreement[3] had given it those rights. Caterham, directly and indirectly, nurtured this notion. In addition, Howard JP held that for many years Caterham had been sedulously passing off its product as that of Lotus by the improper and unauthorised use of the trade mark 'Lotus' in relation to the Caterham Seven or Super Seven and that this course of conduct was deliberate and dishonest ...

Whether a passing-off action can be used to protect a misapprehension or a false reputation appears to me to open to serious doubt but since it was not argued it need not be decided. However, to the extent that a reputation is founded on a conscious falsehood, public policy demands that legal protection should be withheld ... Caterham cannot be permitted to benefit from its own wrong."[4]

In *Inter Lotto v Camelot*[5] it was argued that the claimants' action for **9-44** passing-off might be defeated by the defendants' pending trade mark application, by virtue of which the claimants' goodwill was supposedly unlawfully acquired, in the sense of predominantly being based on user which would prospectively have infringed the trade mark once registered. The practical effect of this argument, if successful, would have been that the claimants would have had to have proved sufficient goodwill to prevail in a notional passing-off action at the trade mark filing date, rather than the later date on which the defendants actually launched their rival game. The Court of Appeal held as a preliminary point that the defence was bound to fail. The alleged defence fell far short of imputing illegality or fraud to the claimants so as to bring the defence of *ex turpi causa non oritur actio* into play, and s.2(2) of the Trade Marks Act 1994 was fatal to the argument that the claimants' rights in the passing-off action could be affected at all by the defendants' trade mark application. The relevant date for ascertaining whether the claimants had sufficient goodwill to support the action was therefore the date the defendants commenced the conduct complained of, not the date on which the latter had applied for registration of their mark.

Material and immaterial misrepresentations

Not all misrepresentations by the claimant are of equal significance. For the **9-45** defence to be made out two criteria must be satisfied. One is that the misrepresentation must be one which would come to the attention of the relevant public, or in some cases competitors, and be really likely to deceive. If the misrepresentation is that a trade mark is registered then competitors would be the only relevant misrepresentees, and similar issues apply to some extent with a misrepresentation that goods are patented. The other is that there must be a close connection between the rights the claimant seeks to protect and the conduct said to disentitle him to protection. Mere "puffing" has been treated as innocuous.

---

[3] An agreement between Lotus and Caterham relating only to the Model IV, and to spare parts for previous models.
[4] *per* Harms J.A.
[5] [2003] EWCA Civ 1132, CA, affirming [2003] EWHC 1256; [2003] 3 All E.R. 191 (Laddie J.).

Misrepresentations which are inherent in the claimant's own name, mark or get-up have been considered to be the most serious. One reason is that they are bound to come to the attention of everyone familiar with the mark, *etc.* and can therefore be said to be immaterial only if they would not be taken at face value. The other is that in practice, if not in legal theory, adoption of the claimant's mark or part of it is the normal ground for complaint in passing-off, so that the claimant's own misrepresentations cannot easily be dismissed as collateral or dissociated from that of the defendant.

9–46   The claimant's mark must be considered as a whole, and in all the circumstances surrounding how it is used. It is no answer to the defence that the existence of a misrepresentation in the mark can only be established if reference is made to the goods on which it is used or to other material for which the claimant is responsible. Thus, there is nothing *prima facie* misleading in the mark *Charles Forde's Bile Beans*, for pills,[6] whether or not it is appreciated that the name of the person is fictitious; nor in the use of Spanish and Cuban indicia on a cigar box.[7] However, when the name *Charles Forde* is linked to an imaginary account of how he discovered a miraculous panacea from the aborigines of Australia, or the cigars in the box turn out to be German, then the defence is made out.

The fact that a mark may be misdescriptive is not fatal to its owner.[8] In this respect, passing-off may protect a mark which would not have been allowed registration under the Trade Marks Act 1994 or previously. The law also distinguishes between misrepresentations contained in the mark itself, or very closely associated with it, and those which are collateral, the latter not normally providing a defence. The law allows the claimant a *locus poenitentiae*, so that a misrepresentation which has been discontinued need not disentitle him to relief in the future.[9] It has been said that a misrepresentation commenced after action brought is irrelevant,[10] but this is *obiter* and contrary to basic principles. The better view is that equity looks at the claimant's conduct as a whole, up to the time of granting or refusing the injunction.

Whether misrepresentation is collateral

9–47 A claimant will not be deprived of relief as a result of having made misrepresentations which are merely collateral to the trade sought to be protected.[11] The normal dividing line drawn by the courts has been that a misrepresentation inherent in the mark sought to be protected is material,

---

[6] *Bile Bean Manufacturing Co. v Davidson* (1906) 23 R.P.C. 725 (Court of Session, Inner House).

[7] *Newman v Pinto* (1887) 4 R.P.C. 508, CA.

[8] The plaintiff in *Reddaway (Frank) & Co. Ltd v George Banham & Co. Ltd* [1896] A.C. 199; [1895–9] All E.R. 313; 13 R.P.C. 218, HL., had no problems until it was realised that his *Camel Hair Belting* really was made of camel hair.

[9] *Ford v Foster* (1872) L.R. 7 Ch. 611, C.A.; *Mrs Pomeroy Ltd v Scalé* (1906) 24 R.P.C. 177; *Coles (JH) Pty Ltd v Need* [1934] A.C. 82; 50 R.P.C. 379, PC.

[10] *Siegert v Findlater* (1878) 7 Ch.D. 801.

[11] *Ford v Foster* (1872) L.R. 7 Ch. 611, CA.

whereas one altogether extraneous to the mark is collateral. However, this is not a hard and fast rule. In any event, a part of a mark which at first sight appears to be no more than an unobjectionable fancy word may reflect a systematic policy of misrepresentation carried on through advertisements or elsewhere, so as to form the whole substratum of the claimant's business. The fundamental question in every case is whether the claimant is attempting to protect a part of his trade based on a misrepresentation of his own.

The extent to which the claimant's mark itself incorporates or refers to a misrepresentation is one relevant factor. Others are the extent to which the misrepresentation has been circulated; whether to those likely to be influenced by it or only to those, such as trade customers, unlikely to rely on it; and whether it is of such a kind as to influence the scale of the claimant's trade. Examples of cases in which misrepresentations by the plaintiff were disregarded include *Hogg v Kirby*[12] in which the plaintiff misstated the authorship of his magazine; *Holloway v Holloway*[13] in which the plaintiff called himself a professor and claimed his pills would cure all the diseases in the world; *Metzler v Wood*[14] in which the plaintiff's work was described as "600th edition, specially revised by Hemy"[15] and *Perry v Hessin*[16] in which the misrepresentation was that the goods were patented.

In *Ford v Foster*[17] the plaintiff had incorrectly described himself as **9-48** "patentee" in some advertisements, invoices and bill-heads. However, the advertisements had been few in number, and the other documents had gone only to trade customers and not to the general public. The Court of Appeal held that such misrepresentations did not provide a defence:

"[W]here the trade is, as in this case, a perfectly honest trade, and where the trade mark is, as in this case, a perfectly honest trade mark, I am clearly of the opinion that there is no common law principle upon which it is possible to hold that the fact of the plaintiff having been guilty of some collateral fraud would be an answer to the action."[18]

According to Lord Diplock in *G.E. Trade Mark*[19] misrepresentations as to **9-49** the character of goods or their origin were the most common reason for refusing injunctions in passing-off cases prior to 1875. Be that as it may, this defence was frequently raised in the nineteenth century, was quite often successful, and was almost always taken seriously even when relied on by the

---

[12] (1803) 32 E.R. 336 (Lord Eldon L.C.). Though "the false colours under which the original publication appear[ed]" troubled Lord Eldon.
[13] (1850) 51 E.R. 81 (Lord Langdale M.R.). The defence was clearly raised in argument but not even referred to in the judgment.
[14] (1878) 8 Ch.D. 606 (Mallins V.-C.) affirmed *ibid.*, CA.
[15] Hemy himself had not revised the work since 1867. 190,000 copies had been sold and the plaintiffs claimed that every 250 copies constituted an edition.
[16] (1912) 29 R.P.C. 101 (Eve J., *obiter*) affirmed without reference to this point *ibid.* at 509, CA.
[17] (1872) L.R. 7 Ch. 611, CA.
[18] *per* Mellish L.J.
[19] [1972] 1 W.L.R. 729; [1972] 2 All E.R. 507; [1973] R.P.C. 297, HL.

most unmeritorious defendant. Towards the end of the century a change took place and the courts became very much more reluctant to refuse relief solely on this ground. This was given effect by an increasing willingness to categorise all but the most flagrant misrepresentations as "collateral", although the difference between collateral and material misrepresentations in the decided cases defies objective analysis. In particular, the defence that the plaintiff had misrepresented his goods as patented virtually fell into disuse. Despite *dicta* that the courts expect a higher standard of commercial honesty in the late twentieth century than in the nineteenth,[20] and that trading must be honest and not even unintentionally unfair,[21] it is notable that the standard of fairness and honesty actually demanded of the claimant is far lower now than one hundred years ago. Consequently, the older cases which follow should be viewed with caution.

Examples

9–50 In the very early common law case of *Sykes v Sykes*[22] the plaintiff obtained damages for passing-off notwithstanding that he had continued to sell his goods as *Sykes Patent* after the patent had expired. Subsequent cases always treated *Sykes v Sykes* as being a decision on its own facts, not as illustrating or establishing a general rule that damages could not have been withheld. In *Perry v Truefitt*[23] the plaintiff advertised his *Medicated Mexican Balm* under a false claim that it was to the recipe of a named distinguished scientist and incorporated vegetable balsams from Mexico. Lord Langdale M.R. refused an injunction, referring both to the lack of any connection with Mexico and to the admittedly false story of the inventor. The plaintiff was given liberty to bring an action at law, but failed to do so and the bill in equity was dismissed with costs.

9–51 In *Pidding v Howe*[24] the plaintiff had introduced a blend of tea called *Howqua's Mixture*. The plaintiff's advertisements claimed that the blend had been invented by a Chinese merchant *Howqua*, was supplied by him directly to the plaintiff, and used particularly rare and expensive ingredients. Without deciding whether a person called *Howqua* had communicated the blend to the plaintiff, Shadwell V.C. held that there were sufficient misrepresentations in the advertisements to refuse an injunction.

In *Ford v Foster*[25] the Court of Appeal, though *obiter*, was of the opinion that a misrepresentation in the mark itself would have been a defence to an action at common law under the rule *ex turpi causa non oritur actio*, and that the same would apply if the plaintiff's trade was fraudulent. Although misrepresentation by the plaintiff was proved (and had been discontinued) the court held it to be collateral and not to disentitle him to an injunction.

---

[20] *per* Lord Diplock in *Erven Warnink B V v J Townend & Sons (Hull) Ltd* [1979] A.C. 731; [1979] 2 All E.R. 927; [1980] R.P.C. 31, HL.
[21] *per* Lord Morris in *Parker-Knoll Ltd v Knoll International Ltd* [1962] R.P.C. 265, HL.
[22] (1824) 107 E.R. 834 (Abbott C.J.).
[23] (1842) 49 E.R. 749 (Lord Langdale M.R.).
[24] (1837) 59 E.R. 190 (Shadwell V.C.).
[25] (1872) L.R. 7 Ch. 611, CA.

However, the account of profits requested by the plaintiff was limited in time to the period since the filing of his bill, partly because of the misrepresentation and partly because of delay.

In *Newman v Pinto*[26] the plaintiffs sued for infringement of a registered trade mark. The Court of Appeal described the mark as used as "an elaborate concatenation of pictorial lies",[27] intended to give the impression that the plaintiff's cigars were from Havana. They dismissed the action, though without costs as the defendant's conduct was no less fraudulent. Two members of the Court were prepared to state that the defence prevented recovery of damages, although at first instance the plaintiff had elected to take an account of profits. Passing-off was not pleaded, but the Court of Appeal regarded themselves as following *Ford v Foster*, and the principle stated would appear to apply *a fortioti* to non-statutory rights.[28] **9-52**

In *Mrs Pommeroy v Scalé*[29] the plaintiff was not debarred from relief although continuing to use advertisements to the effect that the defendant was connected with them after she had left to set up in competition. The advertisements had been continued inadvertently after ceasing to be true and had been withdrawn, though not as quickly as they might have been.

In the Australian *Bayer* case, *Bayer Pharma v Henry Yorke*,[30] the local subsidiary of *Bayer* had been taken over by Sterling as a result of wartime expropriation and all contact with the German company had ceased. Systematic and persistent misrepresentations that *Sterling* aspirin was the original aspirin, and that the Australian company was part of the world-wide group, were serious enough for the court to have been prepared to refuse relief on those grounds. However, there was no misrepresentation by the defendants to restrain, this being a case of legitimate parallel imports. **9-53**

In the South African case of *Caterham Car Sales v Birkin Cars*,[31] one reason for refusing Caterham any relief was that they had systematically misrepresented themselves as the holders of exclusive rights in South Africa in relation to the Lotus Super Seven Series III sports car and replicas of it.

False claim to patent

A relatively numerous category of reported cases in which relief has been refused on account of misrepresentation concerns marks embodying a false claim that the goods to which they are applied were patented.[32] Such claims were formerly regarded as being likely to deceive both the public, who might be prepared to pay more for patented goods, and competing traders who might be deterred from copying what was really in the public domain. **9-54**

---

[26] (1887) 4 R.P.C. 508, CA.
[27] *per* Bowen L.J.
[28] The decision was not based on the statutory prohibition against the registration of deceptive matter.
[29] (1906) 24 R.P.C. 177 (Parker J.).
[30] [1964] F.S.R. 143 (Myers J., Supreme Court of NSW).
[31] 1998 (3) SA 938, SCA.
[32] A few cases, summarised below, apply the same principle to false claims to registration of a trade mark: *Intercontex v Schmidt* [1988] F.S.R. 575. No doubt claims to other legal monopolies such as copyright or registered or unregistered design rights would raise the same issues.

Although this defence was not uncommon in the nineteenth century there appears to be no recent case of its being raised successfully. The public no longer appears to be greatly impressed by goods being patented, and it is no longer common for the words "patent" or "patented" to be given any prominence or incorporated into the claimant's mark. Moreover, the importance attached to the defence in the nineteenth century was in part explained by what now seems to have been an excessive fear of trade mark rights being used to extend the 14 year patent term in perpetuity.[33] Around the turn of the century, one finds judges more and more inclined to treat untrue claims to patent rights as collateral.[34] Consequently, although the cases to be discussed are still good law in one sense, it is increasingly likely that inaccurate claims to patent rights would be taken as involving only a collateral misrepresentation, not disentitling the claimant to relief.

9–55   In *Leather Cloth Co v American Leather Cloth Co*[35] the House of Lords refused relief to the plaintiffs, who had described their goods as patented in what they claimed as their trade mark.[36]

"If a trade mark represents an article as being protected by a patent, when in fact it is not so protected, it seems to me that such a statement *prima facie* amounts to a misrepresentation of an important fact, which would disentitle the owner of the trade mark to relief in a court of equity against anyone who pirated it.

In *Flavel v Harrison*,[37] Vice-Chancellor Wood intimated his opinion that this would be so where there had never been any patent at all; but in the subsequent case of *Edelsten v Vick*[38] he seems to doubt whether the rule would be the same if there had originally been a patent, and the statement in the trade mark, being true when first introduced, had been continued after it had ceased to be true. I confess that I should have great difficulty in assenting to that distinction. If the word patent be not used so as to indicate the existing protection of a patent, but merely as part of the designation of an article known in the market by that term (and this I collect to have been the main ground of his Honour's decision), then I quite agree with his view. In such case nobody is meant to be deceived, or is deceived; a patent may have expired, and be known to have expired fifty years ago, and yet the name of patent may have become attached to the

---

[33] Compare the reluctance of the courts to allow words to acquire secondary meaning during the existence of a patent, which was probably motivated by the same fears and likewise was greatly moderated early in the present century. *Edge (William) & Sons Ltd v William Niccolls & Sons Ltd* [1911] A.C. 693; 28 R.P.C. 582, HL, shows the same tendency at work.

[34] *Ingram & Sons v The India Rubber, Gutta Percha, and Telegraph Co. Ltd* (1902) 29 V.L.R. 172 is a striking example. Putting the (expired) patent number on the goods made the use of "patent" acceptable! *Perry & Co Ltd v T Hessin & Co* (1912) 29 R.P.C. 101 (*dictum* of Eve J.) affirmed *ibid.* 509, CA, perhaps marks the end of the defence in England.

[35] (1865) 11 E.R. 1435, HL.

[36] The House of Lords also held that the defendants had sufficiently distinguished their goods, and this may be the predominant ratio of the case. The defendants did not use "patent" in their mark.

[37] (1853) 68 E.R. 1010.

[38] (1853) 68 E.R. 1194.

article and be used in the trade as designating it; but if the trade mark represents the article as protected by a patent, when it is in fact not so protected, I cannot think that it can make any difference whether the protection never existed or has ceased to exist."[39]

In *Cheavin v Walker*[40] the defendant's use of the words *Cheavin's Patent* was held to be acceptable, as being an accurate description of the goods. However, the plaintiff, but not the defendant, also used the Royal Arms in his mark and this was taken as a misrepresentation that a patent still subsisted, which would have disentitled the plaintiff to relief had a case otherwise been made out. In *Hubbuck v William Brown*[41] Rigby L.J. would have disentitled the plaintiffs to protection of a mark for white zinc in which the word "patent" appeared. The word did not appear in the defendant's mark, which the plaintiff unsuccessfully argued showed a sufficient overall resemblance for there to be passing-off.

The cases which provide the basis of this defence are not entirely con- **9–56** sistent in the rationale they attribute to it. In *Ford v Foster*[42] the Court of Appeal granted an injunction despite a misrepresentation by the plaintiff that he was the patentee of the design of shirt in issue. One reason given for not refusing relief was that the misrepresentation had only come to the attention of the trade, not the public at large. However, in *Flavel v Harrison*[43] Page-Wood V.-C., refusing an injunction to the maker of *Flavel's Patent Kitchener* stove, had alluded both to public willingness to pay more for patented articles and to the fact that competitors would be deterred from copying the article. Moreover, it is settled law that a misrepresentation that a trade mark is registered may also provide a defence, although no member of the public could conceivably be influenced by it in making his purchase. *Ford v Foster* is therefore better understood as turning on the fact that the plaintiff had discontinued the misrepresentation in question.

In the Australian case of *Kettles & Gas Appliances v Anthony Horden & Sons*[44] relief was refused because of a misrepresentation by the plaintiffs that their kettle was patented. The plaintiffs' case was that the shape of the kettle was distinctive in the legal sense. It was significant that "patented" may have put competitors off copying the kettle and therefore may have contributed to *de facto* distinctiveness.

There are two elements to the defence. The first is that the use of the word **9–57** "patent", *etc.* must be understood as implying that the goods are, in some sense, produced under patent. The second is that this representation must be

[39] *per* Lord Kingsdown in *Leather Cloth Co. Ltd v American Leather Cloth Co. Ltd* (1865) 11 E.R. 1435, HL.
[40] (1877) 5 Ch.D. 850, CA.
[41] (1900) 17 R.P.C. 638, CA.
[42] (1872) L.R. 7 Ch. 611, CA.
[43] (1853) 68 E.R. 1010 (Page-Wood V.C.). Approved in *Leather Cloth Co Ltd v American Leather Cloth Co Ltd* (1865) 11 E.R. 1435, HL.
[44] (1934) 35 S.R. (NSW) 108 (Long Innes J.).

unjustified. If the use of the word is otherwise ambiguous, then other parts of the mark may indicate how it would be understood.[45] Where "patent" or a similar word appears as part of the claimant's mark the use of it may be true in the sense that the goods themselves are patented, or even that their production involved the working of a subsisting patent. In either of these cases there is no misrepresentation and the defence is not made out. The very nature of the goods may be such that no reasonable person could suppose them to be patented, in which case the misrepresentation, if any, would seem to be immaterial.[46] Finally, the defence is normally regarded as an equitable one, which means that the court always has a discretion to grant an injunction notwithstanding that the claimant may have been guilty of a misrepresentation in the past.

9–58　　The word "patent" has borne a surprisingly wide number of interpretations in the decided cases. The most natural is that the article itself is a patented product or the product of a patented process. Next, "patent" may be understood as referring to a former patent which has expired or been revoked. It is also possible for "patent", on its own or in combination, to acquire a distinctive secondary meaning. In *Sykes v Sykes*[47] the term *Sykes Patent* was distinctive of the plaintiff, the patent in question having expired. In *Lawrie v Baker*[48] the defendant was restrained from selling his own goods in response to orders for "Patent cups".[49] On the other hand, "patent" may have an essentially descriptive connotation as with *Cheavin's Patent* in *Cheavin v Walker*[50] which could legitimately be used by the defendants to describe filters constructed according to a patent granted to one Cheavin.[51] Finally, the word "patent" may have come to be understood as part of the generic name of the article, as in "patent medicine" or "patent leather". Such examples are obvious, but trade evidence is admissible, as in *Marshall v Ross*: "Patent Thread".[52]

False claim to trade mark registration

9–59　It may also be a defence that the claimant has misrepresented his mark, *etc.* as registered. This is a criminal offence under s.95 of the Trade Marks Act 1994, but the defence does not depend on the criminality of the misrepresentation.[53] The cases are fewer in number than those dealing with

---

[45] In *Cheavin v Walker* (1877) 5 Ch.D. 850, CA, use of the Royal Arms confirmed the implication that the product was still patented. Use of a serial number might serve as a more typical but hypothetical example.
[46] *Cochrane v Macnish* [1896] A.C. 225; 13 R.P.C. 100, PC: no one would suppose soda water to be patented.
[47] (1824) 107 E.R. 834 (Abbott C.J.).
[48] (1885) 2 R.P.C. 213 (Day J.).
[49] The case is open to two explanations. One is that it is an early example of inverse passing-off by misrepresenting the defendant's goods as falling within the plaintiff's patent. The other is that "Patent Cups" had acquired secondary meaning.
[50] (1877) 5 Ch.D. 850, CA.
[51] This usage of the plaintiff's name is obsolete.
[52] (1869) L.R. 8 Eq. 651.
[53] *Dictum* of Stirling J. in *Sen Sen Co v Britten* [1899] 1 Ch. 692; 16 R.P.C. 137.

claims to patent rights, but they include a modern example of relief being refused. In at least one respect a false claim to registered trade mark rights is actually more material than one to patent rights, even though it is even less likely to influence any purchaser. This is because success in a passing-off action almost always depends on factual distinctiveness of the claimant's name, mark or get-up, and distinctiveness is likely to be destroyed or pre-empted by concurrent use of the same mark, *etc.* by others. However, the use of the words "trade mark" or the like on their own for a common-law mark need not imply that the mark is registered, and is therefore unobjectionable.[54]

In *Royal Baking Powder v Wright Crossley*[55] the plaintiffs' action for malicious falsehood failed because they were unable to prove special damage. They might have lost some individual sales as a result of the defendants' campaign, but in every such case the product they would have sold would still have carried the word "registered" after the relevant trade mark had been expunged, and they were therefore seeking to protect an "illegal trade".

In *Intercontex v Schmidt*[56] the plaintiffs had misrepresented that the titles of their directories were registered trade marks by putting the device of the letter "R" in a circle after the name on invoices and other literature. This was one reason for refusing interlocutory relief. An interlocutory injunction was also refused in *Johnson & Son v Puffer*[57] where the plaintiffs had marked their stockings *Trinity Street Brand Registered 321,009* although that registration was actually for a device in which the words were not the most important component.

Other aspects of "clean hands" defence

The "clean hands" defence is not confined to cases of misrepresentations **9–60** associated with the claimant's mark itself, although those are the most common. In *Lee v Haley*[58] it was said that an injunction would have been refused if the defendant had made good an accusation that the plaintiff habitually sold short weight, although by modern standards this would at first sight be going too far.[59] There must be a connection of some sort between the plaintiff's misconduct and the cause of action. However, the name in dispute was *The Guinea Coal Co* which alluded to the price charged, so selling short weight would have rendered the name deceptive. In recent times, the defence was recognised as existing by the Privy Council in *New Zealand Netherlands Society "Oranje" v Kuys*[60] but again was not made out

---

[54] *Sen Sen Co v Britten* [1899] 1 Ch. 692; 16 R.P.C. 137.
[55] (1900) 18 R.P.C. 95, HL.
[56] [1988] F.S.R. 575 (Peter Gibson J.).
[57] (1930) 47 R.P.C. 95 (Bennett J.).
[58] (1869) L.R. 5 Ch. 155 (L.JJ.).
[59] In *Ad-Lib Club Ltd v Granville* [1971] 2 All E.R. 300 [1972] R.P.C. 673 there was no adverse comment on the fact that the plaintiff night club had been forced to close because it had been committing a nuisance. It obtained an injunction despite not having found new premises.
[60] [1974] R.P.C. 272, PC.

on the facts. There were some irregularities in the plaintiff's conduct but none sufficiently grave or relevant.

9–61   In *Brewster Transport Co. v Rocky Mountain Tours & Transport Co.*[61] the Canadian Supreme Court refused an injunction to a Canadian company which had adopted the well-known name and livery of a United States rival, the defendants. The plaintiffs had not come to the court with clean hands, and it did not matter whether the defendants would originally have had a cause of action against the plaintiffs.[62]

In the South African case of *Scott and Leisure Research and Design v Watermaid*[63] an interdict was refused because of unclean hands. The plaintiffs purported to be selling a single type of swimming pool chlorinator which had gained world-wide acceptance, but actually used the mark for a variety of different systems. This false representation by the plaintiffs was deliberate and material, being at the forefront of their marketing strategy.

9–62   However, there must be a connection between the misconduct or illegality and the claim for passing-off (or injurious falsehood) itself.

In *Seagoing Uniform Corp. v U.S. Dungaree Seafarers (No. 2)*[64] the failure of the plaintiffs to mark some of their jeans with information required by statute, such as the country of origin, did not entitle the defendants to an order dissolving an interlocutory injunction because it did not relate to the issue between the parties.

In *Imperial Chemical Industries v Berk Pharmaceuticals*[65] the plaintiffs sued for passing-off by imitation of the get-up of *Inderal* tablets.[66] One paragraph of the defence pleaded that ICI had a dominant position which they had abused by charging excessive prices.[67] Megarry V.-C. ordered the paragraph to be struck out. There was no nexus between the alleged breach of former Art.86 of the EEC treaty and the rights of the parties *inter se*.

E. *Bona Fide* use of Defendant's Own Name

Summary and rationale

9–63   It has widely been accepted that in certain circumstances an individual trader may make *bona fide* use of his own name in circumstances which would otherwise amount to passing-off.[68] The defence is primarily one for

---

[61] [1931] S.C.R. 336; [1931] 1 D.L.R. 713 (Supreme Court of Canada).

[62] Distinguished in *Jumbo Seafood v Hong Kong Jumbo Seafood Restaurant* [1998] 1 S.L.R. 860 (HC of Singapore).

[63] 1985 (1) SA 209 (Friedman J.).

[64] (1975) 20 C.P.R. (2d) 113 (British Columbia Supreme Court, Hutcheon J.).

[65] [1981] F.S.R. 1 (Megarry V.C.).

[66] A motion for an interlocutory injunction was refused. Unreported judgment of Whitford J. (November 27, 1979). The balance of convenience was inconclusive and the plaintiffs not likely to succeed.

[67] In the South African case of *Cambridge Plan AG v Moore* 1987 (4) SA 821 a defence of unclean hands because of illegal resale price maintenance was not made out on the facts.

[68] The defence has no relevance to injurious falsehood.

individual traders, and appears to be available to a corporation only in limited circumstances, if at all. Whether there is any longer a rule of law to this effect may be doubted, but it is convenient to summarise the scope of the alleged defence before considering what basis it has in authority. If the defence does exist, there is no doubt that it is a complete one entitling the defendant to judgment in the action, with costs, and to continue using the name indefinitely.

The most widely adopted summary of the defence is that of Romer J. in *Rodgers v Rodgers*:[69]

"To the proposition of law that no man is entitled to carry on his business in such a way as to represent that it is the business of another, or is in any way connected with the business of another, there is an exception, that a man is entitled to carry on his business in his own name so long as he does not do anything more than that to cause confusion with the business of another, and so long as he does it honestly. To the proposition of law that no man is entitled so to describe his goods as to represent that the goods are the goods of another, there is no exception."

The second head of Romer J.'s formulation has been approved in subsequent cases of undoubted authority,[70] although it has been criticised as having no basis in antecedent case law and as contradicting a number of authorities normally cited as examples of defendants using their own names with impunity. The first head has been doubted as possibly being too favourable to the defendant.[71]

Applying *Rodgers v Rodgers*,[72] there are five elements to the supposed **9–64** defence: the defendant must be using his own full name; he must do nothing more that causes confusion with the claimant; he must act honestly; he must in general be a natural person; and he must not be using the name so as to describe his goods. Even without considering these requirements in detail and despite doubts that Romer J. may even have framed the defence too widely, it will be seen that the defence is at best a very narrow one, and hardly relevant to modern trading conditions.

Moreover, as *bona fides* are an essential requirement, it would be an extremely unwise individual who deliberately set up in business under his own name in reliance upon the defence and knowing of the likelihood of confusion with the claimant. If the first instance judgment of Jacob J. in *Asprey & Garrard v WRA (Guns) Ltd and Asprey*[73] had stood in its entirety,

---

[69] (1924) 41 R.P.C. 277.

[70] *Parker-Knoll Ltd v Knoll International Ltd* [1962] R.P.C. 265, HL; *Asprey & Garrard v WRA (Guns) Ltd and Asprey* [2002] F.S.R. 30 (Jacob J.) affirmed [2001] EWCA 1499; [2002] E.T.M.R. 47; [2002] F.S.R. 31, CA.

[71] *Rodgers v Rodgers* received such criticism from the House of Lords in *Parker-Knoll Ltd v Knoll International Ltd* [1962] R.P.C. 265 (H.L.); but the most recent decision, *Asprey & Garrard v WRA (Guns) Ltd and Asprey* [2001] EWCA 1499; [2002] E.T.M.R. 47; [2002] F.S.R. 31, CA, proceeded on the concession by counsel that *Rodgers v Rodgers* was correct.

[72] Above.

[73] [2002] F.S.R. 30 (Jacob J.) affirmed in part [2001] EWCA 1499; [2002] E.T.M.R. 47; [2002] F.S.R. 31, CA.

then it would have been clear beyond argument that the relevant issue is not the personal defendant's ethical standards, but whether he knew (or should have known) that damaging confusion with the claimant would result. With that decided against him, it could not matter that he genuinely intended to remedy any confusion as and when it occurred, or that he honestly believed he was acting within his rights. In *Reed Executive v Reed Business Information*[74] Pumfrey J. would have adopted the same objective criteria as Jacob J. did in *Asprey*, but on that point the former judgment is *obiter*, and no useful generalisations can be made from the Court of Appeal's hesitant treatment of the defence in *Asprey* itself.

9-65 It seems that the defence may be lost if the defendant does not use his own name in full without abbreviations or embellishments.[75] In particular, an individual may not in general claim any right to trade under his surname alone, or as part of a trading style, where to do so would involve passing-off. Failure to use one's full name may itself indicate a lack of *bona fides*, but the proposition does not appear to rest on this alone. Finally, there are a few cases where an individual claims to be known by a nickname or an abbreviation of his own name. The better view is that names in the latter category do not benefit from the defence.[76] In *NAD Electronics v NAD Computer Systems*[77] the defence failed on several grounds: the corporate defendant was using *NAD* in respect of goods, NAD was not its full corporate name, and Nad (for *Nader*) was at most a nickname of the defendants' owner, whose real name was Aghda.

The defence should not be confused with that available under s.11(2)(a) of the Trade Marks Act 1994. The statutory defence extends to use of the defendant's name as a mark on goods and is unaffected by whether the defendant is an individual or not. However, the statutory defence is only relevant in so far as infringement of registered trade marks is alleged, and would not prevent a passing-off action succeeding on the same facts.

Does the defence exist?

9-66 If the claimant in a passing-off action fails to make out even one of the essential elements of the tort then his case must fail, without the defendant having to raise or prove any of the specific defences discussed here. Conversely, if a case is won on the "own name" defence then it follows that the defendant is relieved from the normal consequences of making a misrepresentation damaging to the claimant, albeit innocently, and the claimant suffers a corresponding diminution in his right to vindicate his goodwill. Not all courts and commentators have been willing to accept this conclusion, and it is necessary to consider whether the defence exists as such,

---

[74] [2002] EWHC 1015; [2003] R.P.C. 12 (Pumfrey J.).

[75] *Rodgers (Joseph) & Sons Ltd v W N Rodgers & Co.* (1924) 41 R.P.C. 277.

[76] *Jay's Ltd v Jacobi* [1933] Ch. 411; [1933] All E.R. 690; 50 R.P.C. 132 as explained in *Wright, Layman & Umney Ltd v Wright* (1949) 66 R.P.C. 149, CA; *Biba Group Ltd v Biba Boutique* [1980] R.P.C. 413.

[77] [1997] F.S.R. 380 (Ferris J.).

whether it is better regarded as affecting the burden of proof, or even if it is no more than a long-standing misconception.

There are numerous older English explanations of the defence which pay lip service to it but which are really inconsistent with its having any independent existence. Thus, it has been said that the defendant *bona fide* using his own name may do so, but only if the plaintiff's name has no secondary meaning, or if nothing more damaging than mere confusion arises, or if the defendant's business is adequately distinguished. All these explanations are open to two criticisms. One is that such factors apply equally whether the defendant is using his own name or an assumed one, and whether *bona fide* or not; let alone whether he is an individual or a company and whether or not the name is used on goods. The second is that they describe as a defence what is really a failure, and sometimes a very basic one, to make out a cause of action. Nor can it be suggested that the only effect of the defence is to increase the burden of proof on the claimant, because that explanation was rejected by the House of Lords in *Parker-Knoll v Knoll International*.[78]

It may be surprising to suggest that the defence of honest use of one's own **9-67** name does not exist, even in respect of trade names, when so much discussion has been devoted to it and so many decisions have purported to give it effect. However, the suggestion is less radical than it seems, because following *Parker-Knoll v Knoll International* all cases purportedly applying the defence to use of a name on goods are either wrong or must be justified on other grounds. On closer analysis the cases acknowledging the defence in whatever context all seem to fall into one of three categories. There are those which purport to give effect to it and which do indeed find in favour of the defendant, but which are equally explicable on some other basis, generally that the defendant had adequately distinguished his goods or business.[79] Then there are cases in which the defendant fails to make out the defence, often because he lacks *bona fides* but sometimes because of its many technical pitfalls. Sometimes the defence is defined in terms a defendant could hardly ever satisfy. Finally there are cases such as *Marengo v Daily Sketch & Sunday Graphic*[80] in which the existence of the defence is acknowledged in a context which makes the observation wholly *obiter*. What is lacking in recent case law is a decision unequivocally allowing an honest defendant to go on making use of his own name, though acknowledging that deception and damage will result.[81] Anything short of this is insufficient to prove that the defence has any real existence.

---

[78] [1962] R.P.C. 265, HL. A rather similar suggestion was rejected by Jacob J. in *Asprey & Garrard v WRA (Guns) Ltd and Asprey* [2002] F.S.R. 30; affirmed [2001] EWCA 1499; [2002] E.T.M.R. 47; [2002] F.S.R. 31, CA, and was not revisited on appeal.

[79] Notably *Brinsmead (John) & Sons Ltd v Brinsmead & Waddington & Sons Ltd* (1913) 30 R.P.C. 493, CA. And compare *Parker-Knoll Ltd v Knoll International Ltd* [1962] R.P.C. 265, HL with *Parker Knoll plc v Knoll Overseas Ltd* [1985] F.S.R. 349, showing how failure to make good the defence can be more than compensated for by a generous attitude to what is sufficient to distinguish.

[80] [1948] 1 All E.R. 406; 65 R.P.C. 242, HL *per* Lord Simonds.

[81] At first instance in *Asprey & Garrard v WRA (Guns) Ltd and Asprey* [2002] F.S.R. 30; affirmed [2001] EWCA 1499; [2002] E.T.M.R. 47; [2002] F.S.R. 31, CA, Jacob J. assumed exactly these facts, but still decided against the personal defendant.

The own name defence after *Asprey* and *Reed*

9–68 In South Africa it has been said at first instance[82] that the own-name defence does not exist at all, that early cases to the contrary were overruled by *Reddaway v Banham*,[83] and that subsequent cases recognising it were few and open to criticism. On appeal the judgment was affirmed on the facts in terms that leave open almost any interpretation of the defence.[84]

9–69 A similar result may now have been reached in England, although it is too early to say whether or not it will prevail. In *Reed Executive v Reed Business Information*[85] Pumfrey J. examined the scope of the defence in the context of its use for service businesses and concluded: "In other words, the only defence is 'no passing off' . . ." However, a previous first instance attempt to lay the defence to rest had recently failed in *Asprey & Garrard v WRA (Guns) Ltd and Asprey*,[86] and the comments of Pumfrey J. in *Reed* are *obiter*, since he also held that the defendants' conduct was not sufficiently honest, so that the statutory defence to trade mark infringement failed. That being the case, there was strictly no need to re-open the vexed question of whether the House of Lords in *Parker-Knoll v Knoll International*[87] had intended to preserve any distinction between goods and services, with the defence surviving in some attenuated form only for the latter. It is also far from obvious how the common law defence could ever have availed the corporate defendants (even the two which had "Reed" in their full corporate names), when their choice of name was voluntary and no material connection with any individual named Reed was adverted to in the judgment. The conclusion that s.11(2)(a) of the Trade Marks Act 1994 applied to corporations as well as to individuals because of the gloss placed on "person" by Schedule 1 to the Interpretation Act 1978 is obviously inapplicable to passing-off.

9–70 In *Asprey & Garrard v WRA (Guns) Ltd and Asprey*[88] William Asprey, the second defendant and the moving spirit of the first, was a member of the family which had formerly owned the World-famous *Asprey* luxury goods business. He had previously worked for *Asprey's* in their gun room, but had become disaffected and left to set up his own business competing with the claimant in selling luxury goods, and especially sporting firearms. The new business traded as *William R. Asprey Esquire*, and was owned by the corporate defendant. At first instance Jacob J. granted summary judgment against both defendants for passing-off: the individual defendant was an honest and honourable man, but none the less his choice of trading style had

---

[82] *Boswell-Wilkie Circus Pty Ltd v Brian Boswell Circus Pty Ltd* [1985] F.S.R. 434, affirmed [1986] F.S.R. 479.

[83] [1896] A.C. 199; [1895–9] All E.R. 313; 13 R.P.C. 218, HL.

[84] [1986] F.S.R. 479.

[85] [2002] EWHC 1015; [2003] R.P.C. 12 (Pumfrey J.); referring to *dicta* of Lord Greene M.R. in *Marengo v Daily Sketch* (1946) [1992] F.S.R. 1, themselves commenting on Romer J. in *Rodgers (Joseph) & Sons Ltd v W. N. Rodgers & Co.* (1924) 41 R.P.C. 277.

[86] [2002] F.S.R. 30; affirmed in part [2001] EWCA 1499; [2002] E.T.M.R. 47; [2002] F.S.R. 31, CA.

[87] [1962] R.P.C. 265, HL.

[88] Above.

caused, and would continue to cause, numerous instances of confusion with the claimant, and damage to the latter's goodwill was inevitable.

Turning to the own name defence, "if defence it be", Jacob J. identified three situations: there was the use of *William R. Asprey Esquire* as a mark on some (but not all) of the defendant's goods, especially guns. This was clearly outside the defence as defined by Romer J. in *Rodgers v Rodgers*,[89] regardless of the identity of the defendant. There was the existing use by the company of *William R Asprey Esquire* as its trading name, for instance on the shop front.[90] The defence was not available to the company because its choice of name was entirely voluntary. As against the personal defendant, Jacob J. proceeded as if William Asprey might take over the business himself and run it as a sole trader, with everything else unchanged. On this (hypothetical) basis, and despite his *bona fides*, he would have no defence and would still be liable.

The Court of Appeal affirmed summary judgment against the corporate **9–71** defendant and William Asprey in his capacity as its moving spirit, but declined to consider his prospective liability or immunity if he were to trade in his personal capacity. It was plain beyond argument that *WRA (Guns) Ltd* could not avail itself of the own name defence, both because the trading style *William R Asprey Esquire* was not its name at all, and because the defence did not apply to the names of new companies or those newly adopted by existing ones: "otherwise, a route to piracy would be obvious, [and] because a company can chose to adopt any trading name, there could be an own name defence in almost every case ..." As to whether William Asprey himself would have had a defence if he had set up in business as a sole trader in place of the corporate defendant (as the judge, with the consent of the parties, had been prepared to assume) the Court of Appeal declined to decide whether the defence would arise or not. Romer J.'s criteria were sensitive to precisely what an individual defendant might do (over and above using his own name) to cause or dispel confusion, and it was wrong in principle to decide hypothetical future questions on an inadequate foundation of existing facts. Since there was no such existing factual situation to address, and since the terms of the injunction against the first defendant in his personal capacity were extremely wide and might inhibit lawful conduct, the Court discharged it. Those against the corporate defendant and the individual defendant in his capacity as joint tortfeasor were upheld.

Whether or not Jacob J.'s "pragmatic approach to anticipatory relief" **9–72** was justified—and it was not obviously any more speculative than what is standard practice in *quia timet* actions—it is suggested that his treatment of the "so-called defence" for the individual defendant was substantially right in law.

---

[89] (1924) 41 R.P.C. 277.
[90] The company's name was actually *WRA (Guns) Ltd*. It had been incorporated as *William Asprey (Guns) Ltd*, but it, and a sister company, had already been re-named in response to complaints by the claimant.

"Mr Thorley [counsel for the claimant], who was not interested in a detailed discussion of the limits or otherwise of the own-name defence, simply put his case on the crude and, to my mind, correct basis that once the defendant is shown to be causing deception, then the balance between the right of the trader to use his name and the right of the public and of the owner of the goodwill to stop that use of name tips in favour of the latter.

If one looks at Romer J.'s judgment in more detail, one sees several references to necessity. The basis of his exception is necessity. There is nothing necessary about the way that Mr William Asprey is actually trading. If the company had a different name that was the name of the company and he simply indicated that he was the managing director, that would be a very different matter because a man must use his name."

So, if and to the extent that the defence has any continuing existence in modern law, it is based on the defendant actually needing to use his own name in some way in the course of business, and not on any supposed right to invoke his "ancestral heritage", as Chadwick L.J. described it. The supposed primacy of the latter, which provides some of the rationale and most of the rhetoric for cases in the mould of *Burgess v Burgess*,[91] was disowned by the Court of Appeal even more emphatically than by Jacob J. William Asprey might trade on his own skills and his own personal connections, but any attempt by him to obtain some of the benefit of *Asprey's* past glory was an aggravating, not a mitigating, factor. Taking this reasoning into account, there may still be one situation in which the defence might serve a valid purpose in modern law, which is in certain of the liberal professions (such as medicine, or the Bar) where individuals still practise in their capacity as such and under their own names. No question of using a mark on goods arises, the problems of incorporation and succession do not arise, and use of an individual's proper name is normal if not actually compulsory. Be that as it may, passing-off actions between fellow professionals are vanishingly rare, and a defence confined to these circumstances is of little more than academic interest.

Early history of the defence...

9–73 There is no doubt that in the nineteenth century and even later the courts sometimes showed a strong reluctance to restrain defendants from trading under their own names. There was a feeling that every person was entitled to trade under his own name, and that the adoption of any other name called for explanation. The cases in which relief was granted were ones of obvious fraud,[92] but also mostly involved copying other matter or garnishing the name in such a way that the probability of deception was increased well beyond what would have occurred simply from the use of a similar name.

---

[91] (1853) 43 E.R. 90; [1843–60] All E.R. 90 (L.JJ.), below.
[92] Such as *Sykes v Sykes* (1824) 107 E.R. 834, the earliest case of passing-off at common law, and *Croft v Day* (1843) 49 E.R. 994.

When a defendant in a nineteenth century case is accused of lacking *bona fides* it often refers to the manner of his use of the name as much as to his motives.

In *Burgess v Burgess*[93] an injunction was refused in a case in which the **9–74** defendant, the son of the plaintiff, was selling a sauce for fish as *Burgess's Essence of Anchovies*, which had become famous as the name used by the plaintiff. The reasoning is inconsistent. Knight Bruce L.J. asserted that every subject had the right to trade and sell goods under his own name. Turner L.J. based his judgment on the fact that the defendant's goods were adequately distinguished so that there was no false representation to restrain. In *Turton v Turton*[94] the Court of Appeal followed *Burgess v Burgess* and discharged an injunction which *Thomas Turton and Sons* had obtained against *John Turton and Sons*, both being steel makers in Sheffield. Lord Esher put the defendants' right to trade in the family name in the strongest possible terms. "Therefore upon principle, I should say it is perfectly clear that if all that a man does is to carry on the same business, and to state how he is carrying it on—that statement being the simple truth—he is doing no wrong. He is doing what he has an absolute right by the law of England to do..."[95]

However, the plaintiffs' case was factually weak, because the two businesses had co-existed for several years without confusion while the defendants had traded as *John Turton and Co.*, and the change of the last word to *Sons* was all the plaintiffs could rely on. Lord Esher's judgment must also be taken as discredited by the fact that in *Reddaway v Banham*[96] a judgment of his displaying a similar sense of priorities was to be reversed by the House of Lords. To Lord Esher, an objectively true statement could not be restrained, whether it was one as to the nature of the goods or the identity of the maker. The "absolute right" was qualified neither by the need to act in good faith nor by requiring that the statement should not deceive in fact. This supposed right to tell the "simple truth", even at the cost of deception, recurred using that very phrase in *Reddaway v Banham* and was exploded.

Towards the end of the nineteenth century the courts were moving away **9–75** from the paramountcy of the right to trade under one's own name. The Court of Appeal in *Massam v Thorley's*[97] explained *Burgess v Burgess* in terms of the absence of any misrepresentation, as did the House of Lords in *Reddaway v Banham*.[98] In the latter, those Lords who referred to *Burgess v Burgess* treated it as a decision on its facts, preferring the judgment of Turner L.J. to that of Knight Bruce L.J. Lord Macnaughten described the plaintiff's case in *Turton v Turton* as "extravagant and absurd". Several cases decided immediately after *Reddaway v Banham* treated the use by a defendant of his own name as raising nothing more than a question of fact:

---

[93] (1853) 43 E.R. 90; [1843–60] All E.R. 90 (L.JJ.).
[94] (1889) 42 Ch.D. 128, CA.
[95] *per* Lord Esher.
[96] [1896] A.C. 199; [1895–9] All E.R. 313; 13 R.P.C. 218, HL.
[97] (1880) 14 Ch.D. 748, CA.
[98] Above.

whether in all the circumstances the defendant had adequately distinguished his goods from those of the plaintiff.

In retrospect, the own-name cases prior to *Reddaway v Banham* may be regarded as special instances of two general rules which did not survive the end of the nineteenth century. One was that fraud was the essential basis of the action for passing-off, the other that a representation had to be objectively false if it was to be restrained. A defendant making *bona fide* use of his own name therefore had a twofold defence under the general law without needing to invoke any special rule in his favour. It was not until *Reddaway v Banham* that it was finally decided that the defendant could be restrained from making a representation which was apparently justified in the sense of being objectively true, but likely to deceive for all that. From *Reddaway v Banham* to *Spalding v Gamage*,[99] the basis of the action was still generally said to be fraud, in that even if the defendant commenced his conduct innocently it was considered fraudulent for him to continue once he had been put on notice of the existence of confusion with the plaintiff. This may have been reasonable for arbitrary marks, but there were obvious difficulties in pressing the doctrine to the point of saying that it was so much as constructively fraudulent for a person to continue trading under his own name after being put on notice. It was not until after damage to goodwill became identified as the basis of the action that the defendant's state of mind could safely be ignored.

...to Parker-Knoll v Knoll international

9–76 The major cases on the defence following *Reddaway v Banham*[1] are listed in the first instance judgment of Didcott J. in *Boswell-Wilkie Circus v Brian Boswell Circus*[2] with extensive quotations. That judgment perhaps overstates the extent to which purely objective criteria were applied in the early twentieth century, but it is a useful collection of source material and the general tenor is sound. The important cases from this period may be regarded as subsumed into the decision of the House of Lords in *Parker-Knoll v Knoll International*.[3] Those which continue to deserve mention by name are *Brinsmead v Brinsmead*,[4] which is better regarded as a case in which the defendant's goods were adequately distinguished; *Rodgers v Rodgers*,[5] quoted from above; *Marengo v Daily Sketch & Sunday Graphic*,[6] in which an *obiter dictum* of Lord Simonds acknowledged the existence of the defence in the terms stated by Romer J. in *Rodgers v Rodgers*; and

---

[99] (1915) 32 R.P.C. 273, HL.
[1] [1896] A.C. 199; [1895–9] All E.R. 313; 13 R.P.C. 218, HL.
[2] [1895] F.S.R. 434, *per* Didcott J. (Natal) affirmed [1986] F.S.R. 479.
[3] [1962] R.P.C. 265, HL.
[4] (1913) 30 R.P.C. 493, CA.
[5] (1924) 41 R.P.C. 277 (Romer J.).
[6] [1948] 1 All E.R. 406; 65 R.P.C. 242, HL.

Wright, Layman & Umney Ltd v Wright[7] which produced an uncharacter-istically inconsistent judgment from Lord Greene.[8]

Parker-Knoll v Knoll International[9] itself was an action for trade mark **9–77** infringement and passing-off brought by the English furniture manu-facturers against the subsidiary of an American company. In the House of Lords, the passing-off aspect of the case was virtually confined to the single issue of whether the defendants were entitled to use *Knoll International* as a trade mark on their furniture. It was undisputed that they had acted in good faith. All five law lords delivered reasoned speeches, and the House was divided both in terms of the final result and in their expositions of the law applicable.

The majority[10] upheld the injunction granted by the Court of Appeal[11] and approved the statement by Romer J. in *Rodgers v Rodgers*[12] to the effect that honest use of one's own name was never a defence to passing-off if the name was used on goods. The majority thus adopted an entirely objective test in respect of goods: the defendant would be restrained if the use of any name, including his own, was calculated to deceive. Intention was only relevant to the extent that intent to deceive was of evidential weight against him. They left open the question of whether, or in what circumstances, the defence existed in respect of use as a business name.

The minority[13] would have allowed the defendants to use the name *Knoll* **9–78** *International* on their goods. Lord Denning refused to draw any distinction between use as a trade mark and use as a trade name:

> "I would agree at once that, if the use by the defendants of their own name were likely to deceive, they would have no defence, no matter how honest and *bona fide* they were. For I fully agree with what Buckley [L].J. said in *Brinsmead v Brinsmead*, that if a man uses his own name as to be likely to deceive and so to divert business from the plaintiffs to the defendants, he will be restrained. ... But here the use of the defendants' name is not likely to deceive but only to cause confusion. And when that is the case, the authorities all show that he is not to be prevented from *bona fide* using his own name...
>
> It was said that this right of a man *bona fide* to use his own name is confined to his using it as the name of his business (as a trade name) and does not extend to his using it to describe or mark his goods (as a trade mark): and this suggestion was supported by the observations of Romer J. in *Rodgers v Rodgers* at p.291, which were approved by Lord Simonds in

---

[7] (1949) 66 R.P.C. 149, CA.

[8] Lord Greene's attitude to the defence emerges more clearly from his judgment in *Marengo v Daily Sketch & Sunday Graphic* (1946) [1992] F.S.R. 1, CA, reversed [1948] 1 All E.R. 406; 65 R.P.C. 242, HL.

[9] [1962] R.P.C. 265, HL.

[10] Lords Morris, Hodson and Guest.

[11] The injunction against passing-off was qualified with the words "without clearly distin-guishing their goods from the goods of the plaintiffs" but was not qualified so as to allow the defendants to use the name "*Knoll International*".

[12] Above.

[13] Lords Denning and Devlin.

Marengo v Daily Sketch & Sunday Graphic at p.251. I confess that I see no good ground for the distinction...

Apart from the two *dicta* I have mentioned, I find no support in the cases for the distinction. Both *Burgess's case* and *Brinsmead's case* go to refute it, for they were both cases where a man was using his very own name upon goods and he was held entitled to do so, even if it was likely to cause confusion. The judgment of Lord Greene in *Wright, Layman & Umney v Wright* at pp.151–2, is also opposed to it. He had *Rodgers v Rodgers* before him and yet he said: 'If a man uses his own name, and uses it honestly and fairly, and is doing nothing more, he cannot be restrained, even if confusion results,' and he made it clear that this applies to the use of it as a trade mark as well as a trade name.

Seeing that the supposed distinction has no foundation, I hope your Lordships will reject it and law down the principle which ought to govern the courts in this important matter: and I suggest that it is simply this, that the law of passing-off does not interfere with any *bona fide* use by a person of his own name, so long as he does nothing more than that to cause confusion."

Lord Devlin, on the other hand, may be regarded as agreeing with the majority on the central point of law but reaching the opposite conclusion on the facts. For him, *Knoll International* was sufficiently different. He too left open the question of whether trade names constituted an exception. In what is probably the most cogent and perceptive speech in the case he said:

"Where there is no question of fraud, where the question is whether the statement is literally true but whether it carries with it a false representation, I cannot see how it can matter whether or not the name whose use is capable of being misunderstood is an actual or a fictitious one. Buckley L.J. said categorically in his third proposition:[14] 'There is, in my opinion no difference whatever where the true statement consists in an accurate statement of the defendant's name as distinguished from any other true statement of fact if of course you have evidence that from the use of his own name deception results.'"

9–79   In the last analysis, *Parker-Knoll v Knoll International*[15] is inconclusive. It is clear authority that use of one's own name as a trade mark on goods is no defence, even if *bona fide*, and in that context personal names are no different to marks of any other nature. However, the majority failed to answer the question of whether use as a trade name was any different. It is suggested that Lord Denning was right to say that there was no distinction, and that despite the fact that he would have found for the defendants his speech does not give such overriding importance to the defence as might appear. The passage quoted above begins by saying that if the defendants' conduct had

[14] From *Brinsmead (John) & Sons Ltd v Brinsmead & Waddington & Sons Ltd* (1913) 30 R.P.C. 493, CA.
[15] [1962] R.P.C. 265, HL.

deceived they would have had no defence, though they were using their own name honestly. But confusion, on its own, is never sufficient for there to be passing-off. Lord Denning's speech might have been open to the criticism that he was contemplating a half-way house, in which mere confusion was actionable as against defendants generally but not against those making honest use of their own names. That, however, would be to ignore the fact that he relied on the *Office Cleaning*[16] case, in which confusion went unrestrained although the own name defence was not in issue.

The real difference of opinion between the majority and the minority was not on the law, but on whether the differences in name, market and type of goods were sufficient to distinguish the defendants. When the same plaintiffs applied to commit the defendants for breach of the injunction some two decades later,[17] Whitford J. held that the use of *Knoll International* and even *Knoll* alone did not infringe the passing-off injunction because the defendants' goods were adequately distinguished.[18]

Corporations

Unlike an individual, a newly formed company has an almost infinite choice **9–80** of names to adopt. Consequently, the choice of the promoters, even if made *bona fide*, cannot confer on the company whatever rights an individual of that name might have had.[19]

One instance in which it has been said that a company can have the same rights as an individual is when the company is the assignee of subsisting goodwill transferred to it by an individual trader of that name.[20] It has been said in South Africa that a company founded from scratch by an individual should have the same rights as the individual would have had to trade under his own name, but this was in the context of holding that there were no such rights.[21] The decision of the House of Lords in *Parker-Knoll v Knoll International*[22] is problematical, because, although finding for the plaintiff, it did not distinguish between the rights of corporations and individuals as defendants. The corporate defendant was only distantly connected with

---

[16] *Office Cleaning Services Ltd v Westminster Office Cleaning Association* [1946] 1 All E.R. 320; 63 R.P.C. 39, HL.
[17] *Parker Knoll plc v Knoll Overseas Ltd* [1985] F.S.R. 349. Both parties had changed their names.
[18] This borders on saying that the decision of the House of Lords was wrong on the facts. The argument that these matters were *res judicata* (subject to any changes in circumstances) seems to have been overlooked.
[19] *Asprey & Garrard v WRA (Guns) Ltd and Asprey* [2001] EWCA 1499; [2002] E.T.M.R. 47; [2002] F.S.R. 31, CA.
[20] *Fine Cotton Spinners Ltd v Harwood Cash & Co. Ltd* [1907] 2 Ch. 184; 24 R.P.C. 533 and *Kingston Miller & Co. Ltd v Kingston (Thomas) & Co. Ltd* [1912] 1 Ch. 575; 29 R.P.C. 289, neither of which is conclusive.
[21] *Boswell-Wilkie Circus Pty Ltd v Brian Boswell Circus Pty Ltd* [1985] F.S.R. 434, affirmed [1986] F.S.R. 479.
[22] [1962] R.P.C. 265, HL.

anyone called *Knoll*.[23] Likewise in *Reed Executive v Reed Business Information*[24] Pumfrey J. may have contemplated extending the benefit of the defence to two companies whose connection to any individual named "Reed" was at best tenuous and obscure, but he doubted whether the defence existed, and held on the facts that it was not made out.

To the extent that the defence is available to a company, it may be lost by abbreviating the company's full name or giving undue prominence to any part. It is an open question whether the omission of the final word "limited" is significant.

F. INNOCENCE

Introduction

9–81 The right to an injunction in a passing-off action does not depend in any way on the state of mind of the defendant.[25] In this sense, fraud is not an essential component of the cause of action, nor is innocence a defence. Innocence is, however, a partial defence in that it is almost certainly a defence to the remedy of an account of profits, and may be a defence to damages.[26]

It has to be said that there is very little modern authority on innocence as a defence to either damages or profits, and what there is suggests that if the defence continues to exist at all it is confined to the equitable remedy of an account.[27] If so, however, this would not mean that an arcane or irrelevant distinction has been removed, but rather that a distinction has been invented which has no historical basis, and in which the normal roles of law and equity have been reversed.

9–82 In the nineteenth century the common law and equity were at one in refusing pecuniary relief of any sort against a wholly innocent defendant. The common law reached this result by saying that *mala fides* was an essential part of the cause of action, equity by saying that the right to equitable relief arose on an otherwise innocent defendant being put on notice of the plaintiff's rights. The only material difference between law and equity concerned the defendant who knew of the plaintiff but honestly and wrongly believed he was acting within his rights. Equity would award an account of profits in these circumstances,[28] but there was authority that damages at common law could not be recovered.[29] Even this distinction,

---

[23] Nor was it suggested that the defendants could trade as *Knoll simpliciter*. The live issue was whether they could use the full name *Knoll International*.

[24] [2002] EWHC 1015; [2003] R.P.C. 12 (Pumfrey J.).

[25] Malice is an essential element of the action for injurious falsehood, so an innocent defendant requires no further defence.

[26] See Catherine Best, "Damages Against the Innocent Infringer in Passing Off and Trade Mark Infringement" (1985) 1 *Intellectual Property Journal* (Canada) 205.

[27] *Gillette (UK) Ltd v Edenwest Ltd* [1994] R.P.C. 279 (Blackburne J.).

[28] *Millington v Fox* (1838) 40 E.R. 956.

[29] *Crawshay v Thompson* (1842) 134 E.R. 146.

which rested on an isolated first instance decision, showed signs of disappearing with the common law adopting the stricter approach of equity.[30]

In *Spalding v Gamage*[31] Lord Parker confirmed that at common law the misrepresentation must have been fraudulently made, and that in equity the complete innocence of the party making the misrepresentation was a reason for limiting the account of profits to the period after the defendant became aware of the true facts.[32] *Draper v Trist*[33] and *Marengo v Daily Sketch & Sunday Graphic*[34] considered the question but did not decide whether more than nominal damages could be awarded in respect of innocent passing-off.

Does the defence still exist in respect of damages?

There can be no doubt that inquiries as to damages are frequently awarded **9–83** against defendants in passing-off actions although no charge of deliberate dishonesty was ever made.[35] It can hardly be said that so many cases are wrong, so it remains to be seen if the modern practice can be reconciled with the continuing existence of the defence. In *John Walker v Henry Ost*[36] the defendants unsuccessfully objected to an enquiry as to damages being taken, specifically on the ground that fraud had not been pleaded, but this is not conclusive since Foster J. had made an express finding of fraud notwithstanding its absence from the pleadings.

If the strict nineteenth century common law position still held good, then an enquiry as to damages (*quaere* substantial damages) should only be ordered if the claimant proved fraud, and fraud must be specifically pleaded. However, awarding an enquiry as to damages against a defendant who acted innocently is not inconsistent with the continuing existence of the defence if it is allowed that the common law has become assimilated to the equitable doctrine that pecuniary remedies are available after the defendant has been put on notice. The letter before action, or at latest the writ or claim form itself, would serve as notice of the claimant's rights and start liability to damages or profits running after the defendant had had a reasonable period to consider his position. On this basis, an enquiry would only be refused if the defendant ceased the conduct complained of within a reasonable time after being put on notice, as appears to have happened in *Vokes v Evans*.[37] If the defendant persists, then there is necessarily a right to recover damages thereafter even if the conduct had been started innocently. This analysis is

---

[30] See Lord Blackburn in *Singer Manufacturing Co. v Loog* (1882) 8 App.Cas. 15, HL.

[31] (1915) 32 R.P.C. 273, HL.

[32] See also *Birmingham Small Arms Co. Ltd v Webb & Co.* (1906) 24 R.P.C. 27, a decision of Parker J. where the defendant was admittedly innocent and the plaintiffs did not press for damages.

[33] [1939] 3 All E.R. 513; 56 R.P.C. 429, CA.

[34] [1948] 1 All E.R. 406; 65 R.P.C. 242, HL.

[35] For example *Illustrated Newspapers Ltd v Publicity Services (London) Ltd* [1938] Ch. 414; [1938] 1 All E.R. 321; 55 R.P.C. 172 and *Baume & Co Ltd v AH Moore Ltd* [1958] Ch. 907; [1958] 2 All E.R. 113; [1958] R.P.C. 226, CA. In the latter the defendants made out a defence of *bona fide* use in respect of trade mark infringement.

[36] [1970] 1 W.L.R. 917; [1970] 2 All E.R. 106; [1970] R.P.C. 489 (Foster J.).

[37] (1931) 49 R.P.C. 140 (Farwell J.). An enquiry was refused.

settled law in Australia, following *Turner v General Motors*[38] and *B M Auto Sales v Budget Rent A Car*.[39]

9–84 In *Gillette v Edenwest*[40] Blackburne J., after considering the authorities, went further than this and ordered an inquiry as to damages for trade mark infringement and passing-off against dealers in counterfeit razor cartridges whom the plaintiffs accepted had acted innocently, in respect of only one purchase and two sales, all of which had occurred before the defendants had notice of their nature. However, the reasoning of *Gillette v Edenwest* is not entirely convincing so far as passing-off is concerned. In the first place, the defendants' liability to pay substantial damages for trade mark infringement was unaffected by their innocence; and once this had been decided in favour of the plaintiffs, concurrent liability for damages for passing-off was of no further practical importance to either party. Secondly, the analogy drawn by the judge between statutory trade mark infringement and passing-off may be misleading because the two torts are not entirely comparable: trade mark infringement, for instance, has a much more generous defence of *bona fide* use of one's own name, and for registered trade marks alone the existence of a public register means that there is nothing unfair in fixing the defendant with constructive notice of the claimant's name or mark. In general, it is much easier to protect oneself in advance against a claim for trade mark infringement than one for passing-off.

Neither of these two factors applies directly to the facts of *Gillette v Edenwest*,[41] but they do illustrate that "innocence" has several possible meanings which do not necessarily deserve to be treated alike: first, the defendant may not have actual or constructive notice of the existence of the claimant or his name or mark, the situation discussed in *Young v Holt*, below; secondly, the defendant may know of the claimant but may honestly (but wrongly) believe that his own name, mark or line of trade is sufficiently distinct; thirdly, there is the case of unrecognised counterfeit goods represented by *Gillette v Edenwest* itself; finally, the defendant may have a personal defence for which absence of *male fides* is an essential component. Since each of these possibilities raises different issues, and need not receive the same treatment in passing-off as in registered trade mark infringement, it is suggested that *Gillette v Edenwest* need not be the final word.

Effect of the defence

9–85 To the extent that the defence exists at all, its effect is limited. The claimant's right to an injunction is not affected. Nor is the right to damages or profits arising from a reasonable time after putting the defendant on notice, supposing he does not discontinue the conduct complained of. In the context of

---

[38] (1929) 42 C.L.R. 352 (High Court of Australia).
[39] (1976) 12 A.L.R. 363; 51 A.L.J.R. 254 (High Court of Australia). See also Gummow J. in *10th Cantanae Pty Ltd v Shoshana Pty Ltd* (1987) 10 I.P.R. 289; (1989) A.T.P.R. 40–833 (Federal Court of Australia, Full Court) and *Hogan v Pacific Dunlop* (1988) I.P.R. 225.
[40] [1994] R.P.C. 279 (Blackburne J.).
[41] Above.

an account of profits, it has effectively been held that constructive notice of the claimant's rights is sufficient to defeat the defence.

In *Vokes v Evans*[42] Farwell J. granted an injunction against the defendants but refused an enquiry as to damages. The defendants had acted innocently until the plaintiffs had written to them; and although the defendants had not conceded, there was no evidence that they had any dealings in the goods concerned after that date.

In *Young v Holt*[43] Wynn-Parry J. had to consider what Lord Parker had meant by "complete innocence". The defendant had adopted the name *Mencoza* as a brand for Sherry, not knowing that the plaintiffs already used *Mendoza*. He persisted in using it after a customer had drawn his attention to the plaintiffs' brand. Clearly this was sufficient to put him on notice, but the judge ordered the account to run from the original adoption of the name. The defendant was experienced in the wine and spirits trade, and was culpable in not using one of the readily available reference books which would have told him of the plaintiffs' brand.

In *Myers v Fields Auto Services*[44] there had been both passing-off and trade mark infringement, both inadvertent. Vaisey J. granted the plaintiffs a declaration on both heads but confined the inquiry as to damages to trade mark infringement.

G. Concurrent and Antecedent Rights

The problem stated

The present section deals with situations in which two or more traders may **9–86** concurrently enjoy the right to use the same or a similar name, mark or get-up.[45] This can occur when a single business or a corporate group is split without one part acquiring exclusive rights to the name; or when a name, *etc.* is adopted independently by two businesses which come into conflict with one another. Even a business which adopts a name, mark or get-up in circumstances which would originally have been actionable may acquire, for instance by acquiescence, a concurrent right to continue using it. The analysis applies *a fortiori* if, with the passage of time, the public come to distinguish two businesses which they might originally have confused.

In *Daimler Chrysler v Alavi*,[46] Pumfrey J. observed:

[42] (1931) 49 R.P.C. 140 (Farwell J.).
[43] (1948) 65 R.P.C. 25 (Wynn-Parry J.).
[44] (1954) 71 R.P.C. 435 (Vaisey J.).
[45] This section is therefore only directly relevant to claims for passing-off.
[46] [2001] R.P.C. 42 (Pumfrey J.). The passage quoted is *obiter*, as there had never been any passing off. In *Arsenal v Reed* [2001] R.P.C. 46 the defendant had also been trading for 30-odd years, but Laddie J. held that his present activities did not amount to passing off, so no question arose as to acquiescence or accrued rights. The allegations of passing off were not pursued on appeal.

"I should just add that there must come a time after which the court would not interfere with a continued course of trading which might have involved passing off at its inception but no longer did so: logically this point would come six years after it could safely be said that there was no deception and independent goodwill had been established in the market by the protagonists."

That was a case in which many years trading as *Merc* in the retail clothing business had given the defendants a goodwill and reputation independent of that of *Mercedes-Benz* for motor vehicles.

9–87 The present section is only concerned with rights of antecedent or concurrent user so far as they provide a defence. The circumstances in which either party may have a cause of action against others are dealt with elsewhere. The term "honest concurrent use" derived from successive Trade Marks Acts[47] is inappropriate in passing-off.[48] If there has been concurrent user in fact, then it cannot be conclusive whether or not it was honest. The distinctiveness of marks is frequently destroyed by conduct which would have been actionable, even fraudulent, had the claimant acted in time. *A fortiori*, a concurrent right to use the mark, or more properly an immunity, can be obtained by use which was less than honest in its inception. In all that follows, it is assumed that despite the concurrent user the mark has not become *publici juris*. It is possible for the distinctiveness of a mark to survive a degree of concurrent user by others,[49] and to remain enforceable against third parties with no such rights.

Antecedent rights

9–88 The definition of passing-off in terms of misrepresentation makes it necessary to deal with the case where the defendant claims to have anticipated the claimant in the course of conduct complained of. As the tort was formerly understood, it would normally be said that the sign in issue could not be distinctive of the claimant if they were already in use by another, but this is not necessarily true. If the senior user in time is a small or local business, and the junior user a large one advertising heavily, then the public may soon come to associate the sign in question so strongly with the larger party as to lead to the belief that the senior user is the interloper.[50] It is self-evident that the senior user is entitled to continue with conduct which was innocent in its inception notwithstanding that it might later be said to convey a misrepresentation to the majority of the public. Thus, in *Stacey v 2020 Communications*[51] the evidence was that customers confused the plaintiff's small

---

[47] See now Trade Marks Act 1994, s.7; formerly Trade Marks Act 1938, s.12(2).

[48] *Habib Bank Ltd v Habib Bank A G Zurich* [1981] 1 W.L.R. 1265; [1981] 2 All E.R. 650; [1982] R.P.C. 1, CA. The Act is equally concerned with whether the party relying on concurrent user should be allowed the positive benefits of registration.

[49] *Star Cycle Co Ltd v Frankenbergs* (1907) 24 R.P.C. 405, CA.

[50] As might have happened, but for the injunction, in *Chelsea Man Menswear Ltd v Chelsea Girl Ltd* [1987] R.P.C. 189, CA, or *Provident Financial v Halifax Building Society* [1994] F.S.R. 81.

[51] [1991] F.S.R. 49 (Millett J.).

but longer established business for a branch of the defendants. Millet J., though refusing the plaintiff an interlocutory injunction, pointed out that the defendants plainly could not prevent the plaintiff from continuing to use the name *2020*, nor could they complain about third-party recommendations intended for them which accidentally benefited the plaintiff instead.

In *Midgley v Morris & Cowdery*[52] the plaintiffs claimed that the slogan **9–89** *Fair Wear or a Free Pair* for shoes was distinctive of them but their case collapsed when it was proved that the defendants had used it first. In *Payton v Titus Ward*[53] the plaintiffs complained of the get-up of the defendants' coffee tins (which was common to the trade) and the name *Palais Royal*, but the defendants had used the name for 22 years which was far longer than the plaintiffs had used their mark *Royal*. In *Edge v Gallon*[54] the plaintiffs alleged that the term *Dolly Blue* was distinctive of them, but it was proved that before the plaintiffs adopted that as their mark the blue of a much smaller manufacturer (Ripley) was already colloquially known as *Dolly Blue* by purchasers in the North of England.[55] The House of Lords found for the defendants, who as retailers had supplied *Ripley's* blue in response to orders for *Dolly Blue*.

In *Pitman Training v Nominet*[56] both the plaintiffs and the second **9–90** defendants (Pearson) had concurrent rights to use the name *Pitman* in the UK, the latter for publishing and the former for training, the respective businesses having been sold off to separate owners in 1985. A delimitation agreement executed at the time regulated the rights of the parties to the name. The domain names *pitman.com* and *pitman.co.uk* were originally delegated to the second defendants, but *pitman.co.uk* was reallocated by mistake to the (second) plaintiffs, and reallocated again to the second defendants when the mistake was realised. So far as passing-off was concerned,[57] Scott V.C. held that the plaintiffs had no viable claim against the defendants for use of the domain name *pitman.co.uk*. The defendants had traded as *Pitman* for nearly 150 years, their use of *Pitman* alone was consistent with the 1985 agreement, and there was no evidence that the public associated the domain name with the plaintiffs.

In *Barnsley Brewery Co Ltd v RBNB*[58] it was relevant that the defendants were proposing to reopen the defunct *Barnsley Brewery*, but the underlying reason for refusing an interlocutory injunction was that the manner and extent of the plaintiff's use of the name had not eradicated the memory of the former business and made *Barnsley Brewery* distinctive of them. Neither party could claim to be successors to the former reputation and goodwill.[59]

---

[52] (1904) 21 R.P.C. 314 (Farwell J.).
[53] (1899) 17 R.P.C. 58, CA.
[54] (1900) 17 R.P.C. 557, HL.
[55] Although that was not the name actually given to it by Ripley. He called it *Oval Blue*.
[56] [1997] F.S.R. 797 (Scott V.C.).
[57] There were also claims, held to be unarguable, for interference with contract and abuse of process.
[58] [1997] F.S.R. 462 (Robert Walker J.).
[59] A purported assignment to the plaintiffs, 20 years after the business had ceased to trade, was ineffective to transfer any rights.

Antecedent rights: exceptions

9–91 However, it is not legitimate for the defendant to expand from his existing business into a different field of business or geographical area already occupied by the claimant, or to recommence an abandoned business under a name or mark which has meanwhile become distinctive of the claimant. Nor does an defence of antecedent user arise from mere preparations for trading (even if costly) which are not such as to generate goodwill.[60]

In *Daniel & Arter v Whitehouse*[61] the defendant had (perhaps) anticipated the plaintiffs in using the term *Brazilian Silver* for cutlery but had ceased his user and it was held distinctive of the plaintiffs. Conversely, in *Macmillan v Ehrmann Bros*[62] the plaintiffs were a firm of whisky merchants based in Paisley. In 1899 they began to trade in England under the name *Macfarlane*, The defendants had independently adopted *Macfarlane* as a brand name for whisky in 1897, but discontinued it and reintroduced it in 1902. Buckley J. and the Court of Appeal found for the defendants.[63] In *Rugby Football Union v Cotton Traders*[64] the defendants had started selling the "classic" English rugby jersey in 1987, but between 1991 and 1997 only sold newly designed versions under the licence of the claimants. After 1997 the defendants had reverted to selling the classic version without the benefit of any licence. Lloyd J. held that the defendants were not able to rely on their business prior to 1991. What happened on expiry of the licence in 1997 was a new business, not a revival of the discontinued pre-1991 one. However, even judged at the later date the design of the classic jersey was not distinctive of the claimants, so there was no passing-off.

9–92 In the New Zealand case of *Stanley Works v Stanley Ironworks*[65] the plaintiffs were the well known American tool company. The defendants claimed to be entitled to trade as *Stanley Ironworks* by virtue of having taken over the business of a long established engineering firm of that name in Auckland. The court held that the defendants' predecessors had not traded as *Stanley* and that they had not succeeded to any pre-existing goodwill in the name. A defence of antecedent user failed in *Fraser Taxi v Reid*[66] because the user relied on was illegal. It was also colourable and very slight.[67] In *Isaacson v Nationwide News*[68] the parties launched competing newspapers under the name *Sunday Territorian* within a week of one

---

[60] *Barnsley Brewery Co. Ltd v RBNB* [1997] F.S.R. 462, above.
[61] [1898] 1 Ch. 685; 16 R.P.C. 71 (Barnes J.).
[62] (1904) 21 R.P.C. 647, CA.
[63] The plaintiffs' case was weak on other grounds: their English trade even after 1899 was slight and their *locus standi* rested on an assignment executed after action brought, which was probably colourable as well.
[64] [2002] E.T.M.R. 76 (Lloyd J.).
[65] [1935] N.Z.L.R. 865 (Smith J.).
[66] [1949] 2 D.L.R. 846; [1949] 1 W.W.R. 457; 10 C.P.R. 49; 8 Fox Pat. C. 253 (Can.).
[67] See also *Rubenstein (Helena) Pty Ltd v Von Bronneck* (1943) S.R. (N.S.W.) 283.
[68] (1984) 6 F.C.R. 289; 3 I.P.R. 255; 56 A.L.R. 595 (Federal Court of Australia).

another. Even within advertising and media circles neither could establish priority. On passing-off there was a stalemate.[69]

New departure: expansion of geographical area

It quite frequently happens that two or more businesses may use the same **9–93** name, mark or get-up in different geographical areas without difficulties arising, but may come into conflict when one or both of them expands. The basic rule is that each may use that name, *etc.*, in its home territory, but that established rights of use in one area do not provide a defence should one business expand into an area where the name denotes the other. There is little authority on what happens when two parties simultaneously expand into an area where the name is distinctive of neither of them,[70] but it should be borne in mind that user which has been relatively localised or otherwise limited has still been found to justify an injunction covering an area much wider than that in which the claimant has actually traded.[71]

In *Cavendish House v Cavendish-Woodhouse*[72] the plaintiffs were a long- **9–94** established department store in Cheltenham. The defendants had a furniture shop in Cheltenham and had recently changed its name to *Cavendish*, that name being in use by other shops in the chain all over the country on a large scale. The Court of Appeal granted an injunction against the use of the name for the Cheltenham shop, despite nine months' delay. Similarly, in *Levey v Henderson-Kenton*[73] a department store in Newcastle (which had been out of business for two years but hoped to reopen) obtained an interlocutory injunction against the defendants opening a furniture shop in Newcastle under the same name. The defendants had about thirty shops already trading as *Kentons*, but most were in the South of England or the Midlands and the nearest was 120 miles from Newcastle.

In *Taylor Bros v Taylor Group*[74] a linen hire business which was well-established elsewhere in New Zealand was liable for passing-off when it began trading in Wellington, where the plaintiffs were already in business as dry cleaners. In *Greyhound Pioneer Australia v Pioneer Motor Service*[75] the parties had both used the name *Pioneer* for bus services, the latter only in areas to the south of Sydney, but came into conflict when the defendants started to compete with the plaintiffs' established Sydney to Brisbane service. The plaintiffs were said to have a strong arguable case, but an interlocutory injunction was refused for delay and on the balance of convenience.

Expansion in both the geographic and economic senses was in issue in

---

[69] For the same situation in an English context see *Marcus Publishing plc v Hutton-Wild Communications Ltd* [1990] R.P.C. 576, CA (*Leisure News*).

[70] The question arose, but was not answered, in *Evans v Eradicure Ltd* [1972] R.P.C. 808.

[71] For example *Ewing v Buttercup Margarine Co. Ltd* [1917] 2 Ch. 1; [1916–17] All E.R. 1012; 34 R.P.C. 232, CA; *Brestian v Try* [1958] R.P.C. 161, CA; *Chelsea Man Menswear Ltd v Chelsea Girl Ltd* [1987] R.P.C. 189, CA.

[72] [1970] R.P.C. 234, CA.

[73] [1974] R.P.C. 617 (Foster J.).

[74] [1988] 2 N.Z.L.R. 1, CA of NZ.

[75] (1997) 38 IPR 385 (Drummond J. Federal Court of Australia).

Silicon Graphics v Indigo Graphic Systems[76] where there was a triable issue as to whether it was the American plaintiffs or the Israeli defendants who had first used the mark *Indigo* in the UK in the field where graphic computer workstations and computer-controlled printing equipment collided. An interlocutory injunction was refused on the balance of convenience.

New departure: expansion in field of business

9–95 Similar issues arise in the increasingly common situation of conflict occurring as a result of expansion in one or both parties' fields of business. As in the previous case, the basic rule is that each party may use its established name, *etc.*, for its established business; but that established rights of use in one field of business do not provide a defence should one party expand into a field of business where the name denotes the other. This is not to say that the expanding business cannot make honest efforts to exploit its existing goodwill and connections in the new field, but it must take care not to encroach on the established goodwill of its new competitor, and in this respect its conduct is judged by exactly the same standards as for any other interloper.

> "To anticipate, when two traders with confusingly similar marks operate in fields which are sufficiently different that neither substantially affects the other (or shows up on the other's radar, to use a metaphor employed by one of the witnesses) it goes without saying that if one of them expands its activities with the result that there could be a risk that what was previously mere confusion becomes deception causing damage to goodwill there is a positive duty upon that trader to take such steps as may be necessary to reduce that risk to zero."[77]

9–96 In *Reed Executive v Reed Business Information*,[78] from which the foregoing quotation is taken, the facts were that the claimants had operated a chain of High Street employment agencies, starting in 1960. Since 1969 the defendants had published numerous business and professional magazines, many of which carried recruitment advertisements. At this stage, they co-existed with no suggestion of passing off on either side. The conduct complained of began in 1999 with the setting up by the defendants of a recruitment-orientated website *totaljobs.com*, which initially included various references to the two defendant Reed companies and their group, so that *totaljobs.com* was likely to be returned by internet search engines in response to searches for terms such as "Reed jobs." Pumfrey J. held that there had been passing-off, although it had been discontinued sufficiently promptly for an injunction to be inappropriate. It made no difference that:

---

[76] [1994] F.S.R. 403 (Knox J.).
[77] *per* Pumfrey J. in *Reed Executive plc v Reed Business Information Ltd* [2002] EWHC 1015; [2003] R.P.C. 12, below.
[78] Above.

"This is not a case of deliberate passing off in the sense that the defendants were willing to accept confusion in the hope that it would bring them more business than would otherwise be the case. All the defendants were emphatic that they were aware of the possibility of confusion and did not want to contribute to it. I accept this evidence...

The defendants insist that totaljobs.com represents a natural development of their recruitment-associated publishing business in the light of the vast potential of the internet as a medium both for publication of the vacancies and for processing the responses of candidates. I have no doubt that this is correct. It is, however, a different business, and to move into it involves moving towards the business conducted by the claimants in such a way that the claimants and defendants become competitors."

And he went on to conclude that the defendants were not entitled to the defence of honest use of their name in the new field.

Expansion of business: examples

Earlier cases are consistent with this analysis in principle, always subject to their individual facts. In *Everest v Camm*[79] the plaintiffs and defendant had both used the mark *Everest* for their chairs for many years. Historically, the plaintiffs made fully upholstered chairs and the defendant wicker chairs. The defendant introduced a partially upholstered wicker chair. In the Court of Appeal the plaintiffs succeeded on the issue of trade mark infringement but failed on passing-off. In *Sterwin v Brocades*[80] the plaintiffs had introduced a medicine in 1974 under the name *DANOL*, knowing that the defendants already used *DE-NOL* for a totally different medicine, in fact since about 1947. The plaintiffs' medicine was a capsule, the defendants' a liquid. The defendants now intended to introduce a solid formulation of *DE-NOL*. Whitford J. held that there had been no confusion to date, but there would be a likelihood of it if solid *DE-NOL* were introduced. He granted the plaintiffs a declaration (there being no immediate threat) and dismissed the defendants' counterclaim that the plaintiffs were themselves passing off.

In *Provident Financial v Halifax Building Society*[81] there was a serious issue to be tried as to whether the defendants' expansion into motor insurance would misrepresent that they were connected with the plaintiffs in such a way as to cause damage. The parties had both traded under the name *Halifax* without confusion for many years, the plaintiffs as motor insurance underwriters since 1966 and the defendants as a building society since 1928. The defendants' enormous reputation in financial services was one reason for supposing that the more specialised reputation of the plaintiffs might be altogether swamped.

9–97

[79] (1950) 67 R.P.C. 200, CA.
[80] [1979] R.P.C. 481 (Whitford J.).
[81] [1994] F.S.R. 81 (Aldous J.). The case subsequently settled with the plaintiffs' rights being bought out for £2 million: see *Halifax Building Society v Urquart-Dykes and Lord* [1997] R.P.C. 55.

9–98   In *HFC Bank v HSBC*[82] Lloyd J. held that although the *Hongkong and Shanghai Banking Corporation* had a long history of trading in England as well as the far East, it no established goodwill in the retail banking sector in the United Kingdom so as to allow it to confer the right to use the initials *HSBC* on its subsidiary, *Midland Bank*. The proposed change of name by the latter was a new departure, not a continuation of an existing business. However, the action failed on other grounds.

In *Premier Luggage and Bags v Premier Co*[83] the defendants came into conflict with the claimants when they expanded their business from Christmas decorations to luggage and travel goods. It was not suggested that their previous use in a different field gave them any immunity in the new one, but it was relevant that the trade buyers to whom the defendant's sales staff introduced themselves as *Premier* (or the like) were already customers of the older sister company, and would have associated the new company with them, rather than the claimants. The possibility of confusion at retail level was discounted for other reasons.

9–99   However, while threatened expansion by the defendant into a new field can and must be taken into account as conduct actionable *quia timet*, there is no scope for arguing that the claimant can assert any kind of "future goodwill" in relation to a field of business it has not yet actually entered.[84] All that can be said is that well-publicised plans by the claimant to expand into a particular field, may make it more probable as a matter of fact that expansion into the same field by the defendant will deceive.

Antecedent or concurrent use abroad

9–100   It was formerly suggested that an established foreign company has the right to expand its trade to this country under its own name.[85] However the *dictum* is an old one, taken from a case decided before the crucial decision of the House of Lords in *Reddaway v Banham*,[86] and it is hard to reconcile with later authority.[87] The defence would also treat a foreign company better than an English one: *Levy v Henderson-Kenton*[88] and *Cavendish House v Cavendish-Woodhouse*.[89] As Oliver L.J. observed in *Anheuser-Busch v Budejovicky Budvar*,[90] where the supposed defence was combined with an additional submission as to their name's descriptiveness in its country of origin:

---

[82] [2000] F.S.R. 176 (Lloyd J.). An appeal was compromised.

[83] [2002] EWCA Civ 387; [2002] E.T.M.R. 69; [2003] F.S.R. 5, CA; reversing [2001] E.T.M.R. 6, [2001] F.S.R. 29.

[84] *Teleworks Ltd v Telework Group plc* [2002] R.P.C. 27 (Christopher Floyd Q.C., Deputy Judge).

[85] *Saunders v Sun Life Assurance Co. of Canada* [1894] 1 Ch. 537.

[86] [1896] A.C. 199; [1896] A.C. 199; [1895–9] All E.R. 313; 13 R.P.C. 218, HL.

[87] If it is right, the injunction granted in *Penny (JC) Co Inc v Penneys Ltd* [1975] F.S.R. 367, CA, was too wide.

[88] [1974] R.P.C. 617 (Foster J.).

[89] [1970] R.P.C. 234, CA.

[90] [1984] F.S.R. 413, CA. The defendants succeeded on other grounds.

"The first defendants, he submits, were doing no more than honestly using their own business name, in which there was no monopoly and which in any event signified no more than a geographical origin. I am certainly prepared to accept that the first defendants were acting honestly, but the proposition that because they were doing no more than using their own business name which they had previously used in Europe, there was no misrepresentation, begs the question. If the plaintiffs had in fact an established reputation and goodwill in the name in England, the use of the same name by the first defendants, however honest and however much used elsewhere, constitutes a misrepresentation if it leads people to believe that their goods are the goods of the plaintiffs."

The result is not entirely fortunate, because under modern trading con- **9–101** ditions this situation is probably that in which the greatest damage is done to the defendant if he is prevented from trading under a uniform style or exploiting an existing foreign reputation here.[91] It is also the case in which it is perhaps easiest to believe the *bona fides* of the defendant. Nonetheless, it is suggested that the true state of the law is that stated by Oliver L.J. above and by Knox J. in *Island Trading v Anchor Brewing*[92] where the defendants, who were brewers in San Francisco, claimed to have a reputation among beer connoisseurs in England, although their beer was not available here:

"I accept Mr. Wilson's submission that what Oliver L.J. said there[93] makes untenable the proposition that a reputation without goodwill to support it is a good defence to an action for passing-off, notwithstanding the decision of Whitford J. on the counterclaim in the Budweiser action. In my judgment, it follows from the well-established proposition that no intent to deceive is needed to establish a claim in passing off, that a defendant's state of mind is not the relevant subject of inquiry. What matters is whether there is deception of the public or relevant section of the public through misrepresentation. The existence of a reputation without supporting goodwill will doubtless make any misrepresentation innocent as opposed to fraudulent, but it will only be if the defendant's reputation is such as to negative the plaintiffs' claim that the trade mark distinguishes the class of goods in which he deals in England, that a defendant's reputation without goodwill will, in my judgment, avail him."

In more general terms, there is a two-stage test, and it applies equally **9–102** whether what is in issue is a trading name, a mark used on goods, or get-up. If a foreign defendant has no goodwill in the jurisdiction then he can rely on bare reputation only if his reputation is strong enough to negative that of the claimant. In that case, the claimant's name or mark will lack exclusive

[91] As in Case C-255/97 *Pfeiffer Grosshandel GmbH v Lowa Warenhandel GmbH* [1999] E.C.R. I-2835; [2001] 1 C.M.L.R. 7; [1999] E.T.M.R. 603.
[92] [1989] R.P.C. 287a (Knox J.). The issue was also addressed but left unresolved in the *Hit Factory* case, *Pete Waterman Ltd v CBS United Kingdom Ltd* [1933] E.M.L.R. 27 (Browne-Wilkinson V.-C.).
[93] In *Anheuser Busch Inc. v Budejovicky Budvar NP* [1984] F.S.R. 413, CA.

distinctiveness, there will be no misrepresentation to restrain and no need to invoke a specific defence as such. This is the situation exemplified by *Brewster Transport v Rocky Mountain Tours & Transport*.[94] Otherwise, the defendant may have a defence properly so called if, and only if, he can claim an antecedent or concurrent goodwill in the jurisdiction, which will only be the case if he has customers here in the sense contemplated by *Budweiser*.[95] *A fortiori*, if he has neither reputation nor goodwill in the jurisdiction then despite the fact that he may be making honest use of his own name the defence does not arise at all. In *HFC Bank v HSBC*[96] the *Hongkong and Shanghai Banking Corporation* (the defendants' parent company) was very well known under its initials *HSBC* to financial professionals in the City of London, as well as in the Far East, but that was barely relevant because such professionals did not constitute the relevant sector of the public for whom the parties competed at the retail banking level.

9–103   In *Pontiac Marina v CDL Hotels*[97] the defendants (appellants) adopted *Millennium* as a global brand for their hotel business, but were held to have no goodwill in Singapore antedating that of the plaintiffs' hotel, the *Ritz Carlton Millenia Singapore*. The defendants were a Singapore company themselves, but had previously only used the *Millennium* name in respect of three hotels in the United States and New Zealand. In *Jumbo Seafood v Hong Kong Jumbo Seafood Restaurant*[98] the defendants purported to be connected with the famous *Jumbo* floating restaurant in Hong Kong, but any connections with the Hong Kong restaurant were tenuous, the plaintiffs had not acted with unclean hands in adopting the name, and in any event the Hong Kong *Jumbo* restaurant was held to have no goodwill in Singapore under which it could confer any immunity on the defendants.

H. DELAY, ACQUIESCENCE AND ESTOPPEL

Delay and limitation

9–104   It is doubtful if delay on its own is ever sufficient to extinguish the right to an injunction.[99] However, delay is relevant in a number of ways in passing-off. At its most serious, delay in suing infringers may contribute to a mark losing its distinctiveness. In that case the plaintiff's right to restrain the use of that mark is wholly destroyed and all that remains is the right to past damages up to the date when the mark ceased to be distinctive. It does not matter that the defendant may be relying on his own wrongful conduct to defeat the plaintiff's case. As a lesser danger, and especially if the parties are

---

[94] [1931] S.C.R. 336; [1931] 1 D.L.R. 713 (Supreme Court of Canada).
[95] See also *Business Depot v Canadian Office Depot* (1993) 49 C.P.R. (3d) 230 (Rouleau J., Federal Court) and *Silicon Graphics v Indigo Graphic Systems* [1994] F.S.R. 403 (Knox J.).
[96] [2000] F.S.R. 176 (Lloyd J.).
[97] [1998] F.S.R. 839 (CA, Singapore).
[98] [1998] 1 S.L.R. 860 (HC of Singapore).
[99] *Fullwood v Fullwood* (1878) 9 Ch.D. 176, not a passing-off case.

not in direct competition, then the defendant may establish an independent reputation and goodwill of his own.[1] However, it is not delay as such that causes the loss of distinctiveness, and the claimant's cause of action remains if the mark is still distinctive of him despite the presence of infringers.

Delay is also relevant as a component to defences of acquiescence and estoppel, described below. Delay is likely to defeat an application for an interlocutory injunction, even though delay of the same order would not influence final relief. The presence of delay affects the evidential burden on the claimant, in that if the conduct of the defendant has been going on for some time adverse conclusions may be drawn if the claimant fails to provide evidence of actual deception and damage.[2] If the defendant's conduct is recent it is more reasonable to leave these to inference, which will normally favour the claimant.

The limitation period in passing-off is the normal one of six years before the date of issue of the claim form. Damages and profits cannot be recovered in respect of acts of passing-off committed outside this period, but the right to an injunction if passing-off is continuing is not affected. For injurious falsehood the limitation period is one year.[3]

Acquiescence and estoppel

In the context of passing-off, defences of acquiescence and estoppel raise the **9–105** same issue, which is whether it would be unconscionable for the claimant to enforce his rights against the defendant. In *Willmot v Barber*[4] Fry J. identified five *probanda* to be satisfied if acquiescence were to be made out. The law is now more flexible, but the five factors all continue to be relevant though they may no longer deserve the original name. In terms of the situations likely to arise in passing-off they are:

1. The defendant must have mistaken his legal rights;

2. He must have altered his position on the strength of his mistaken belief;

3. The claimant must have known of his right to restrain the defendant;

4. The claimant must have known of the defendant's mistaken belief; and

5. The defendant, in altering his position, must have been directly or indirectly encouraged by the claimant.

---

[1] *Daimler Chrysler AG v Alavi* [2001] R.P.C. 42 (Pumfrey J.).
[2] *Bulmer (HP) Ltd v J Bollinger SA* [1978] R.P.C. 79; [1978] 2 C.M.L.R. 625, CA; *Habib Bank Ltd v Habib Bank AG Zurich* [1981] 1 W.L.R. 1265; [1981] 2 All E.R. 650; [1982] R.P.C. 1, CA.
[3] Defamation Act 1996, s.5(2), amending Limitation Act 1980, s.4A.
[4] (1880) 15 Ch.D 96 (Fry J.).

9–106   Modern authority on acquiescence and estoppel in passing-off begins with the decision of the Court of Appeal in *Habib Bank v Habib Bank AG Zurich*.[5] The plaintiffs' predecessors had formed the defendants as a subsidiary and had assisted it to start business. Nationalisation of the plaintiffs resulted in the defendants becoming independent, but the plaintiffs' own staff assisted the defendants to set up in new premises and over a period of years the parties had benefited from agency arrangements with one another. The Court of Appeal found for the defendants on the issue of passing-off, but would have allowed the defence of acquiescence had that been necessary. The plaintiffs could hardly have done more to encourage the defendants to continue using the *Habib* name, and it was a legitimate inference that the defendants had relied on this.

In *My Kinda Town v Soll*[6] it was held at first instance that the plaintiffs had not disentitled themselves to relief, although they had actively assisted the defendant in setting up his restaurant knowing of almost all the circumstances likely to cause confusion. However, they had not realised that there would be confusion until after the defendant's restaurant opened. The Court of Appeal agreed that there had been no acquiescence, although this was obiter as the defendant's appeal on the merits succeeded. In *Anheuser Busch v Budvar*[7] the trial judge would have found acquiescence (had the plaintiffs otherwise made out their case), in the fact that the defendants had mistakenly believed themselves to have a contractual right to use the mark in question. The Court of Appeal found for the defendants on the merits, but rejected the defence of acquiescence. The defendants had acted on a unilateral misconception of their own making, and had not altered their position in reliance of any act or default of the plaintiffs.

9–107   In the Scottish case of *William Grant v Glen Catrine Bonded Warehouse*[8] there had been delay in suing from at least as early as 1986 to 1992, but the defenders had never relied on the alleged acquiescence and believed they had a valid independent claim to use the name *Grant*. Nor was there any inference that the pursuers had abandoned their rights. In *Daimler Chrysler v Alavi*[9] Pumfrey J. held a defence of acquiescence did not arise because the defendant had never relied on the claimants' failure to act earlier, and the claimants had been unaware of the defendant's activities until quite late.[10] There was, in any event, no *prima facie* liability for passing off.

The present state of the law appears to be this. The irreducible minimum of the defence is that the defendant must have altered his position on the

---

[5] [1981] 1 W.L.R. 1265; [1981] 2 All E.R. 650; [1982] R.P.C. 1, CA. Followed in *IBM Corp v Phoenix International (Computers) Ltd* [1994] R.P.C. 252 (Ferris J.).

[6] [1983] R.P.C. 407, CA.

[7] [1984] F.S.R. 413, CA.

[8] *William Grant v Glen Catrine Bonded Warehouse (No. 3)* 2001 S.C. 901; 2001 S.L.T. 1419 (Inner House).

[9] [2001] R.P.C. 42 (Pumfrey J.).

[10] The claimant only became aware of the defendant in 1997, but Pumfrey J. found that he had been trading continuously under the contested name since at least as early as 1985, and probably earlier.

basis of an act, omission or representation of the claimant in such circumstances as to make it inequitable for the claimant to enforce his rights. The second and last of Fry L.J.'s *probanda* probably remain essential, the others are relevant but not individually necessary.

CHAPTER 10

ENFORCEMENT

A. ENFORCEMENT AFTER THE CPR REFORMS

Scope of chapter

The major change to the procedural aspects of the actions for passing-off or   **10–1** injurious falsehood since the previous edition is, of course, the replacement of the former Rules of the Supreme Court with the Civil Procedure Rules (CPR). Individually, relatively few Parts of the CPR call for specific comment in the context of a passing-off action or one for injurious falsehood, and there is as yet little case law on how the CPR apply, whether for passing-off and injurious falsehood specifically, or for analogous causes of action in the field of intellectual property as a whole. In this edition, it has been assumed that pre-CPR authorities on purely procedural matters are of little or no continuing relevance and references to them have been deleted, except to a certain extent in relation to evidence and remedies, which are less affected by the CPR reforms.

The treatment of interim injunctions has also been much abbreviated. So far as ordinary interim injunctions are concerned, these are now of less paramount importance than previously, for reasons discussed in the following section, and for the same reasons pre-CPR decisions to grant or refuse an interim injunction are of decreasing relevance, even by analogy.

Finally, the Chapter now includes a section on the treatment of actions for unfair competition in private international law.

The CPR and the action

10–2 Pre-action protocols for intellectual property actions, including passing-off, are under discussion but have not been adopted at the time of writing.[1]

CPR Pt 63 applies to actions for passing off by virtue of the definition contained in CPR Pt 63 r.1(1)(b)(iii). Practice Direction 63—Patents and other Intellectual Property Claims also applies by virtue of the latter definition, and specifically mentions passing-off at para.18.1(13). Actions for passing-off must be commenced in the Chancery Division, a Patents County Court, or a county court where there is also a Chancery District Registry.[2] The claim form must be marked in the top right hand corner "Chancery Division, Intellectual Property" below the title of the court in which it is issued.[3] There are no specific rules or practice directions for injurious falsehood,[4] and actions have previously been brought in the Chancery or

---

[1] There is a pre-action protocol for defamation, but the likelihood is that it and the corresponding CPR Pt 53 and Practice Direction are not intended to apply to the action for injurious falsehood, and this would be consistent with previous practice and the normal meaning of "defamation".

[2] CPR Pt 63 r.13(3); Practice Direction—Patents and other Intellectual Property Claims, paras 18.1 and 18.2. Chancery district registries are at Birmingham, Bristol, Cardiff, Leeds, Liverpool, Manchester and Newcastle upon Tyne. Although not stated in the Practice Direction, the Patents County Court judge (HH Michael Fysh Q.C.) enjoys a peripatetic jurisdiction and can hear actions outside London.

[3] Practice Direction—Patents and other Intellectual Property Claims, para.19.1. Passing-off actions are not allocated to the Patents Court.

[4] Assuming that CPR Pt 53 and the corresponding Practice Direction apply only to "defamation claims" in the sense of libel and slander. This is consistent with the usual (though not invariable) usage of "defamation", and with their respective provisions, most of which are obviously inapplicable to injurious falsehood. The Practice Direction to CPR Pt 63 (Patents and other Intellectual Property Claims) does not mention injurious falsehood in the listing of causes of action at para.18.1.

Queen's Bench divisions at the claimant's option. If the claim for injurious falsehood is combined with another, such as trade mark infringement or passing-off, then the latter will determine which court or division is properly seized.

No other provisions of CPR Pt 63 or the Practice Direction are specifically relevant to passing-off, and the normal provisions of the CPR apply. By CPR Pt 16 and para.8.2 of the corresponding Practice Direction, the statement of case must set out any allegation of fraud and details of any misrepresentation relied on.[5]

B. Interim Remedies

Final, interim or summary relief?

The main effect of the CPR in the context of the present work is an indirect **10-3** one. Prior to the CPR, very few passing-off actions were commenced with no thought of an interlocutory injunction, and fewer still were actually prosecuted to trial after an interlocutory injunction had been granted or refused. Under the CPR it is noticeable that the situation is almost precisely reversed. Full trials in passing-off actions are now commonplace, and although applications for interim injunctions continue to be made, often with success, they do not dominate as they previously did.[6] Applications for summary judgment have also become much more common since the introduction of the CPR, and this only partly reflects the probably transient phenomena of cybersquatting and opportunist registrations of company names.[7]

The main reason for this change is that it is now assumed that even a substantial passing-off action can be brought to trial within a few months from issue of the claim form, rather than the two or three years which might have been typical previously. Trial of a major passing-off or trade mark action within six months of issue of the claim form would have excited comment four or five years ago, but is now almost taken for granted in urgent cases, and the period to trial may be even less.[8] One result of this is that a claimant seeking an interim injunction has to convince the court of two propositions which will not easily be satisfied: first, that the damage he will suffer over a period measured in weeks or months, rather than years,

---

[5] Practice Direction—Statements of Case, para.8.2(1) and (3).
[6] Post-CPR examples are *Temporary Roadways and Access Co Ltd v Trax Portable Access Ltd* [2002] EWHC 1728 (injunction granted); *Weight Watchers UK Ltd v Tesco Stores Ltd* [2003] EWHC 1109 (injunction refused).
[7] For example, *British Telecommunications plc v One in a Million Ltd* [1999] 1 W.L.R. 903; [1998] 4 All E.R. 476; [1999] E.T.M.R. 61; [1999] F.S.R. 1, CA; *Asprey & Garrard Ltd v WRA (Guns) Ltd and Asprey* [2001] EWCA Civ 1499; [2002] E.T.M.R. 47; [2002] F.S.R. 31, CA; *Musical Fidelity Ltd v Vickers* [2002] EWCA 1989, CA. The procedure is governed by CPR Pt 24.
[8] Three months in *Associated Newspapers Ltd v Express Newspapers* [2003] EWHC 1322, interim undertakings having been given by the defendants.

will truly be irreparable in the sense of *American Cyanamid*; and secondly that the effort expended on both sides on the application for the interim injunction, including evidence on the balance of convenience, would not have been better spent in going to full trial on an expedited basis.[10] The very real prospect of a trial actually taking place at a fixed date in the near future also discourages applications for interim injunctions in cases which may be thought to clear the *American Cyanamid* criterion of an arguable case, but which fall short of even a 50:50 prospect of success on the merits.

10-4 Another result has been to discourage applications for interim injunctions except in cases of genuine urgency, and to see a corresponding increase in the number of cases being disposed of at trial. From the defendant's point of view too, the prospect of having an interim injunction or undertaking discharged in a few months time, and of being able to recover on the cross-undertaking in damages, means that interim undertakings are likely to be offered more willingly, though no longer with the thought that they are final in all but name, and the offer of an undertaking or the grant of an interim injunction are not the near-certain conclusion of the litigation which they were previously. A second effect is that when contested applications for interim injunctions do take place, then it is likely to be on a much abbreviated timetable compared to practice before the CPR, so that everything about them is several degrees more rough and ready than was previously the case. For all these reasons, individual pre-CPR decisions awarding or refusing interim injunctions are no longer of much value, even analogically.

The importance of interim remedies in passing-off

10-5 It is still true to say that any business which suspects passing-off should urgently consider applying for interlocutory relief. If the defendant can be sued before his business actually commences, then the odds are heavily on the claimant's side and the incentive for the defendant to resist is not great. If this opportunity is not taken, then the claimant has to consider whether the uncertain prospect of an injunction in perhaps a year's time justifies the cost of a full scale action. Claimants are increasingly willing to commit themselves to such action, but if an interim injunction can be obtained then that is almost always preferable.

The most important form of interim relief in passing-off is the ordinary interlocutory injunction obtained after hearing evidence and argument from both parties. The circumstances in which an interim injunction can be obtained continue to be governed in principle by the decision of the House of Lords in *American Cyanamid v Ethicon*,[11] below. Interim injunctions in general are intended to preserve the position of the claimant until the action can be heard, and for the reasons given in the previous numbered paragraph this is no longer the legal fiction it was for most of the lifetime of *Cyanamid*.

---

[9] *American Cyanamid Co v Ethicon Ltd* [1975] A.C. 396; [1975] 1 All E.R. 504; [1975] F.S.R. 101; [1975] R.P.C. 513, HL.
[10] This was noticeable even before formal introduction of the CPR, *e.g. Bushbury Land Rover Ltd v Bushbury Ltd* [1997] F.S.R. 709, CA.
[11] [1975] A.C. 396; [1975] 1 All E.R. 504; [1975] F.S.R. 101; [1975] R.P.C. 513, HL.

It follows that the interim injunction need not necessarily be as wide as that to which the claimant would be entitled if successful at trial. Interim injunctions are preferably expressed in terms as objective as possible so that there can be no doubt what has to be done so as to comply. Injunctions in such a form as to prohibit "passing-off" are open to the objection that it is only after trial that one will know whether the conduct complained of amounts to passing-off or not.

As an alternative to an injunction, the defendant may offer to submit to **10-6** an interim undertaking without admitting liability. The consequences are almost identical, with the claimant being entitled to commit the defendant for breach and the defendant being entitled to a cross-undertaking. It is also quite common for defendants to offer more limited undertakings, for instance by keeping an account, or limiting sales, or paying a proportion of turnover into a joint account by way of security.

Procedure on an application for an interim injunction is governed by CPR Pt 25 rr.1 to 4 and the Practice Direction—Interim Injunctions. Interim injunctions may be in mandatory form, such as those requiring corporate defendants to change their names in *Nishika Corp v Goodchild*[12] and *Glaxo Group v Glaxowellcome*.[13]

The *Cyanamid* principles set out...

The principles which the court is supposed to follow in granting or with- **10-7** holding interlocutory relief are the same whatever the nature of the cause of action. They were set out by Lord Diplock in *American Cyanamid v Ethicon*,[14] in a speech with which all the other members of the House of Lords concurred. The decision in *American Cyanamid* overruled the previously widely held view that the plaintiff had to make out a *prima facie* case, and earlier decisions granting or refusing interlocutory relief in passing-off cases must therefore be treated with caution.

"The use of such expressions as 'a probability', a '*prima facie* case', or 'a strong *prima facie* case' in the context of the exercise of a discretionary power to grant an interlocutory injunction leads to confusion as to the object sought to be achieved by this form of temporary relief. The court no doubt must be satisfied that the claim is not frivolous or vexatious; in other words, that there is a serious question to be tried.

It is no part of the court's function at this stage of the litigation to try to resolve conflicts of evidence on affidavit as to facts on which the claims of either party may ultimately depend nor to decide difficult questions of law which call for detailed argument and mature considerations. These are matters to be dealt with at the trial ... So unless the material available to the court at the hearing of the application for an interlocutory injunction fails to disclose that the plaintiff has any real prospect of succeeding in his

---

[12] [1990] F.S.R. 371 (Knox J.).
[13] [1996] F.S.R. 388 (Lightman J.).
[14] [1975] A.C. 396; [1975] 1 All E.R. 504; [1975] F.S.R. 101; [1975] R.P.C. 513, HL.

claim for a permanent injunction at the trial, the court should go on to consider whether the balance of convenience lies in favour of granting or refusing the interlocutory relief that is sought.

As to that, the governing principle is that the court should first consider whether if the plaintiff were to succeed at the trial in establishing his right to a permanent injunction he would be adequately compensated by an award of damages for the loss he would have sustained as a result of the defendant's continuing to do what was sought to be enjoined between the time of the application and the time of the trial. If damages in the measure recoverable at common law would be an adequate remedy and the defendant would be in a financial position to pay them, no interlocutory injunction should normally be granted, however strong the plaintiff's claim appeared to be at that stage. If, on the other hand, damages would not provide an adequate remedy for the plaintiff in the event of his succeeding at trial, the court should then consider whether, on the contrary hypothesis that the defendant were to succeed at the trial in establishing his right to do that which was sought to be enjoined, he would be adequately compensated under the plaintiff's undertaking as to damages for the loss he would have sustained by being prevented from doing so between the time of the application and the time of trial. If damages in the measure recoverable under such an undertaking would be an adequate remedy and the plaintiff would be in a financial position to pay them, there would be no reason upon this ground to refuse an interlocutory injunction.

It is where there is doubt as to the adequacy of the respective remedies in damages available to either party or to both, that the question of balance of convenience arises. It would be unwise to attempt even to list all the various matters which may need to be taken into consideration in deciding where the balance lies, let alone to suggest the relative weight to be attached to them. These will vary from case to case.

Where other factors appear to be evenly balanced it is a counsel of prudence to take such measures as are calculated to preserve the *status quo*. If the defendant is enjoined temporarily from doing something that he has not done before, the only effect of the interlocutory injunction in the event of his succeeding at the trial is to postpone the date at which he is able to embark upon a course of action which he has not previously found it necessary to undertake; whereas to interrupt him in the conduct of an established enterprise would cause much greater inconvenience to him since he would have to start again to establish it in the event of his succeeding at the trial.

Save in the simplest cases, the decision to grant or refuse an interlocutory injunction will cause to whichever party is unsuccessful on the application some disadvantages which his ultimate success at the trial may show he ought to have been spared and the disadvantages may be such that the recovery of damages to which he would then be entitled either in the action or under the plaintiff's undertaking would not be sufficient to compensate him fully for all of them. The extent to which the disadvantages to each party would be incapable of being compensated in damages in the event of his succeeding at the trial is always a significant factor in assessing where the balance of convenience lies; and if the extent of the uncompensatable disadvantage to each party would not differ widely, it may not be improper to take into account in tipping the balance the relative strength of each party's case as revealed by the affidavit evidence adduced on the hearing of the application. This, however, should be done only where it is apparent upon the facts disclosed by evidence as to which there is no credible dispute that the strength of one party's case is disproportionate to that of the other party. The court is not justified in embarking upon anything resembling a trial of the action upon conflicting affidavits in order to evaluate the strength of either party's case.

I would reiterate that, in addition to those to which I have referred, there may be many other special factors to be taken into consideration in the particular circumstances of individual cases."[15]

... and summarised

To summarise the *American Cyanamid* criteria as they apply to passing-off: **10–8**

1. Applications for interim injunctions should be decided primarily on the balance of convenience, in the wider sense of that phrase, rather than on the relative strength of the parties' substantive cases as they may then appear.

2. There is no rule of law that the court may consider the balance of convenience only if satisfied that the claimant has made out a *prima facie* case.

3. The court must, however, satisfy itself that there is a serious question to be tried.

4. An interim injunction should be refused if damages awarded at trial would adequately compensate the claimant and the defendant will be able to pay.

5. But should be granted if the claimant's cross-undertaking in damages would adequately compensate the defendant if successful at trial, and the claimant would be able to pay.

6. If, as will normally be the case, damages would not fully compensate either party, then the issue depends of the balance of convenience.

7. If other factors are finely balanced, the *status quo* should be maintained;

8. If the balance of convenience favours neither party, then the relative strengths of the parties' respective cases on the merits may be taken into account if one case is disproportionately stronger.

[15] *per* Lord Diplock in *American Cyanamid Co v Ethicon Ltd* [1975] A.C. 396; [1975] 1 All E.R. 504; [1975] F.S.R. 101; [1975] R.P.C. 513, HL.

Cyanamid and injurious falsehood actions

10–9 Interim injunctions in actions for injurious falsehood are subject to a different set of principles intended to give paramount weight to freedom of expression. By analogy with the practice in defamation cases, no interim injunction will be granted, regardless of the balance of convenience, if the defendant intends to justify the statement complained of, and the statement is not so self-evidently false that no reasonable jury could find otherwise. Other issues, if they arise, as subject to the normal *Cyanamid* criteria. The principle was established by Oliver J. in *Bestobell v Bigg*[16] and was approved by the Court of Appeal in *Crest Homes v Ascott*.[17] Examples of interim injunctions being granted despite the rule are to be found in *Compaq v Dell*,[18] *Kaye v Robertson*[19] and *DSG Retail v Comet Group*.[20] The same principle has been applied in passing-off, in a rare case where the truth or falsehood of an express representation was the central issue: *Bradbourne (Lord) v Hough*.[21]

Search orders

10–10 Under the Civil Procedure Act 1997, s.7, the court has jurisdiction to make "search orders" obliging defendants and others to permit specified persons to enter premises to search for, and take away for safe keeping, such things as counterfeit products and evidence relating to them.[22] Section 7 provides:

(1) The court may make an order under this section for the purpose of securing, in the case of any existing or proposed proceedings in the court—

(a) the preservation of evidence which is or may be relevant, or
(b) the preservation of property which is or may be the subject-matter of the proceedings or as to which any question arises or may arise in the proceedings.

(2) A person who is, or appears to the court likely to be, a party to proceedings in the court may make an application for such an order.
(3) Such an order may direct any person to permit any person described in the order, or secure that any person so described is permitted—

(a) to enter premises in England and Wales, and
(b) while on the premises, to take in accordance with the terms of the order any of the following steps.

---

[16] [1975] F.S.R. 421 (Oliver J.).
[17] [1980] F.S.R. 396, CA.
[18] [1992] F.S.R. 93 (Aldous J.).
[19] [1981] F.S.R. 62, CA.
[20] [2002] F.S.R. 58 (Owen J., QBD).
[21] [1981] F.S.R. 79 (Slade J.).
[22] The statutory Search Order effectively supercedes the former common law *Anton Piller* order, named after *Anton Piller KG v Manufacturing Processes Ltd* [1976] Ch. 55; [1976] 1 All E.R. 779; [1976] F.S.R. 129; [1976] R.P.C. 719, CA.

(4) Those steps are—

(a) to carry out a search for or inspection of anything described in the order, and

(b) to make or obtain a copy, photograph, sample or other record of anything so described.

(5) The order may also direct the person concerned—

(a) to provide any person described in the order, or secure that any person so described is provided, with any information or article described in the order, and

(b) to allow any person described in the order, or secure that any person so described is allowed, to retain for safe keeping anything described in the order.

(6) An order under this section is to have effect subject to such conditions as are specified in the order.

(7) This section does not affect any right of a person to refuse to do anything on the ground that to do so might tend to expose him or his spouse to proceedings for an offence or for the recovery of a penalty.

(8) In this section—

"court" means the High Court, and
"premises" includes any vehicle;

and an order under this section may describe anything generally, whether by reference to a class or otherwise.

10–11 Procedure on the application and execution of search orders is governed by CPR Pt 25 and the Practice Direction—Interim Injunctions, paras 7 and 8. The Annex to the Practice Direction contains the standard form Search Order and related undertakings.

C. Evidence

Introduction

10–12 The basic rule in passing-off is that it is for the judge to decide if the behaviour of the defendant is calculated to deceive and in so doing "he must not surrender his own independent judgment to any witness whatever."[23] In the words of Lord Parker in *Spalding v Gamage*[24]:

"It was also contended that the question whether the advertisements were calculated to deceive was not one which your Lordships could yourselves

[23] *per* Lord Macnaghten in *Payton & Co v Snelling, Lampard & Co* [1901] A.C. 308; 17 R.P.C. 628.
[24] *per* Lord Parker in *Spalding (AG) & Bros v AW Gamage Ltd* (1915) 32 R.P.C. 273, HL.

determine by considering the purport of the advertisements themselves, having regard to the surrounding circumstances, but was one which your Lordships were bound to determine upon evidence directed to the question itself. I do not take this view of the law. There may, of course, be cases of so doubtful a nature that a judge cannot properly come to any conclusion without evidence directed to the point, but there can be no doubt that in a passing-off action the question whether the matter complained of is calculated to deceive, in other words, whether it amounts to a misrepresentation, is a matter for the judge, who, looking at the documents and evidence before him, comes to his own conclusion, and to use the words of Lord Macnaghten in *Payton v Snelling Lampard* 'must not surrender his own independent judgment to any witness whatever.' "

10–13   To similar effect there is the speech of Lord Devlin in *Parker Knoll v Knoll International*:[25]

"[W]hat the judge has to decide in a passing-off case is whether the public at large is likely to be deceived. What would the effect of the representation be upon the reasonable prospective purchaser? Instances of actual deception may be useful as examples, and evidence of persons experienced in the ways of purchasers of a particular class of goods will assist the judge. But his decision does not depend solely or even primarily on the evaluation of such evidence. The court must in the end trust to its own perception into the mind of the reasonable man."

As Lord Devlin indicated, evidence of actual deception is helpful, but such evidence is not conclusive. Nor is the absence of evidence of actual deception conclusive in the defendant's favour, although it may reflect adversely on the claimant's case if the defendant has openly been on the market for a long time. If the action is *quia timet* or effectively so then it would be unreasonable to expect evidence of actual deception.[26]

10–14   The basic rule in injurious falsehood is rather stricter: as an aspect of the "single meaning rule", the statement complained of must be interpreted by the court and evidence is inadmissible as to how it was, or would have been, understood by its intended recipients.[27] There are the usual exceptions for technical terms and the like, and for legal innuendoes where the real meaning is determined in the light of extrinsic facts not generally known.

10–15   The CPR do not directly affect the question of admissibility of evidence in actions for passing-off or injurious falsehood. Evidence from traders and the like, below, is likely to constitute or comprise expert evidence and if so must comply with CPR Pt 35 and its Practice Direction—Experts and Assessors. Evidence from ordinary members of the public or other consumers of the goods or services in question, and other evidence of fact, is governed by

---

[25] *per* Lord Devlin in *Parker-Knoll Ltd v Knoll International Ltd* [1962] R.P.C. 265, HL.
[26] *Sodastream Ltd v Thorn Cascade Ltd* [1982] R.P.C. 459, CA; *Harrods Ltd v Harrodian School Ltd* [1996] R.P.C. 697, CA, below.
[27] See para.6–43 and *Royal Baking Powder Co v Wright Crossley & Co* (1900) 18 R.P.C. 95, HL.

CPR Pt 32 and Practice Direction—Written Evidence. The evidence of market researchers has traditionally been classified as expert evidence, not least to circumvent the former severity of the hearsay rule. With hearsay now readily admitted under the Civil Evidence Act 1995, and all kinds of expert evidence under increasingly restrictive Court control, litigants wishing to adduce survey evidence may find it expedient to re-examine the reasoning by which the latter has come to be held admissible over the past 25 years; but until the point is decided it must be assumed that survey evidence, unless consisting of a bare "witness collection programme", falls within CPR Pt 35.

Trade and retail evidence

There has been considerable dispute as to whether, or to what extent, opinion evidence is admissible from retailers, traders or other suitably qualified experts to the effect that the relevant public would or would not be likely to be deceived by the name, mark or get-up used by the defendant. If the market is highly specialised then there is no doubt that such evidence is admissible, but the typical situation in passing-off involves everyday consumer goods with which the court is more likely than not to have at least some familiarity. It has long been acceptable to ask a witness if he himself would be deceived,[28] but not whether the public at large would be deceived,[29] as that is the very question the court has to decide.[30] Short of this, evidence from the trade as to the way business is carried on and the likely reaction of consumer is admissible.[31] The practical difficulty is where to draw the line, and the authorities are not easy to reconcile. **10–16**

In *Dalgety Spillers v Food Brokers*[32] Blackburne J. reviewed the two **10–17** streams of authority and concluded:

"(1) There is no absolute bar against admitting evidence directed to the question whether the matter complained of is calculated to deceive.

(2) In cases where the goods are of a kind not normally sold to the general public for consumption or domestic use but are sold in a specialist market, evidence of persons accustomed to deal in that market as to the likelihood of deception or confusion is admissible.

(3) In cases where the goods are of a kind which are sold to the general public for consumption or domestic use evidence of persons accustomed to deal in that market as to the likelihood of deception of confusion may be admissible. Whether in any case such evidence will be admissible will depend upon a variety of factors which it is neither possible nor desirable

[28] *Ash (Claudius) & Sons Ltd v Invicta Manufacturing Co Ltd* (1911) 28 R.P.C. 597, HL.

[29] *Payton & Co v Snelling, Lampard & Co* [1901] A.C. 308; 17 R.P.C. 628, HL.

[30] *North Cheshire & Manchester Brewery Co Ltd v Manchester Brewery Co Ltd* [1899] A.C. 83, HL.; *Mothercare UK Ltd v Robson Books Ltd* [1988] R.P.C. 113, CA.

[31] *Ballantine (George) & Son Ltd v Ballantyne* [1959] R.P.C. 273, CA; *Sodastream Ltd v Thorn Cascade Ltd* [1982] R.P.C. 459, CA. In *White Hudson & Co Ltd v Asian Organisation Ltd* [1964] 1 W.L.R. 1466; [1965] 1 All E.R. 1040; [1965] R.P.C. 45, PC, the Privy Council criticised the court *a quo* for rejecting such evidence as hearsay.

[32] [1994] F.S.R. 504 (Blackburne J.).

to define. Broadly, the test in such cases must be whether the experience which a judge must be taken to possess as an ordinary shopper or consumer will enable him, just as well as any other, to assess the likelihood of confusion. If it will, then the evidence will not be admissible. If, for whatever reason, it will not, then such evidence will be admissible. What, if any, weight the court then attaches to such evidence will, of course, depend on its nature and quality . . .[33]

(4) In all cases evidence will be admissible to prove the circumstances and the places in which the goods are sold, the kind of persons who buy them and the manner in which the public are accustomed to ask for those goods."

Goods for specialised markets

10–18 A distinction is to be drawn between goods sold to the general public and those which have a specialised market. In the former case, the judge's own experience is a sound basis for deciding if deception is likely. In the latter, it needs to be supplemented by evidence, and opinion evidence is admissible:

"[W]here goods are of a kind which are not normally sold to the general public for consumption or domestic use but are sold in a specialised market consisting of persons engaged in a particular trade, evidence of persons accustomed to dealing in that market as to the likelihood of deception or confusion is essential. A judge, though he must use his common sense in assessing the credibility and probative value of that evidence is not entitled to supplement any deficiency in evidence of this kind by giving effect to his own subjective view as to whether or not he himself would be likely to be deceived or confused . . . But where goods are sold to the general public for consumption or domestic use, the question whether such buyers would be likely to be deceived or confused by the use of the trade mark is a 'jury question'. By that I mean: that if the issue had now, as formerly, to be tried by a jury, who as members of the general public would themselves be potential buyers of the goods, they would be required not only to consider any evidence of other members of the public which had been adduced but also to use their own common sense and to consider whether they would themselves be likely to be deceived or confused.

The question does not cease to be a 'jury question' when the issue is tried by a judge alone or on appeal by a plurality of judges. The judge's approach to the question should be the same as that of a jury. He too, would be a potential buyer of the goods. He should, of course, be alert to the danger of allowing his own idiosyncratic knowledge or temperament to influence his decision, but the whole of his training in the practice of the

---

[33] Citing *Guccio Gucci SpA v Paolo Gucci* [1991] F.S.R. 89; and *Taittinger SA v Allbev Ltd* [1994] 4 All E.R. 75; [1993] 2 C.M.L.R. 641; [1993] F.S.R. 641, CA.

law should have accustomed him to this, and this should provide the safety which in the case of a jury is provided by their number."[34]

Trade evidence—examples

In *Sodastream v Thorn Cascade*[35] Kerr L.J. would have admitted affidavit **10–19** evidence as to what would happen in the event of the defendants marketing carbon dioxide in the same grey cylinders as the plaintiffs and remarked:

> "It seems to me that it is perfectly proper and admissible for someone in the trade to express opinions about the likely reaction of others in relation to matters which are within his or her sphere of work; indeed, it is part of their responsibility to form a view on such matters. In particular it seems to me that this kind of evidence must be admissible in affidavits in interlocutory proceedings, although at the trial the witness will of course be cross-examined about the opinions expressed in them."[36]

A less accommodating view was expressed by Mummery J. in *Associated Newspapers v Insert Media*[37] but his views on the admissibility of expert evidence were *obiter* because the plaintiffs had failed to give proper notice that they intended to adduce it and the defendants would have been prejudiced by giving leave at trial. In *Island Trading v Anchor Brewing*[38] Knox J. disregarded as inadmissible direct statements by witnesses that in their opinion it was possible or probable that the public would confuse the defendants' *Anchor Steam Beer* for the plaintiffs' *Newquay Steam Beer*. However, evidence was admissible to show that the public identified the plaintiffs' beer as *Steam Beer* and ordered it as such. Evidence was also admissible from publicans who said they would not stock the defendants' beer because of the risk of confusion, and this included hearsay evidence by a private detective posing as a member of the public who reported a conversation with bar staff.

Trade evidence of customer behaviour and likelihood of confusion was **10–20** admitted by Browne-Wilkinson V.C. in *Guccio Gucci v Paolo Gucci* where he said:[39]

> "The trade witnesses also expressed the view that if Mr Paolo Gucci were to market in the way that he proposed, the average customer—or a substantial number of them—would be confused into thinking that the goods were of Gucci origin. This is the one point on which there is any

---

[34] *per* Lord Diplock in *GE Trade Mark* [1972] 1 W.L.R. 729; [1972] 2 All E.R. 507; [1973] R.P.C. 297, HL. A registered trade mark case, but the issue being one of fact the same principles apply in passing-off.
[35] [1982] R.P.C. 459, CA.
[36] *Sodastream Ltd v Thorn Cascade Ltd* [1982] R.P.C. 459, CA, *per* Kerr L.J. Described as "the high water mark in favour of the admissibility of such evidence" by Knox J. in *Island Trading Co v Anchor Brewing Co* [1989] R.P.C. 287a.
[37] [1990] 2 All E.R. 803 (Mummery J.), affirmed [1991] F.S.R. 380, CA.
[38] [1989] R.P.C. 287 (Knox J.).
[39] [1991] F.S.R. 89 (Browne-Wilkinson V.C.).

issue of law. I am not myself a buyer of designer label goods; I do not know the habits of designer label buyers. I do not know what it is that influences them or what they are looking for. It might be said that I ought to have knowledge of ordinary shopping for an ordinary product, but in the designer label field I do not myself actually have that knowledge. Plainly, it is my decision as to whether or not people will be confused but why I should be required to make that decision on the basis of my own lack of information, rather than on the basis of expert evidence from those who can tell me what the experience in that market is, I do not understand...

In my judgment the distinction is this. If you ask an ordinary witness with no trade expertise what he thinks other people will do, he has no specific knowledge greater than anyone else as to what other people's reaction will be. Those cases relied on by Mr Beloff are all cases where it either is not clear who the witnesses were, or it is clear that they were not expert witnesses in any ordinary sense. If on the other hand you are in an area which requires specialist knowledge, it is the function of the expert to instruct and inform the court as to those things which the court would otherwise not know, and in the process of so doing the expert is frequently asked the very question which the court has to answer. In my judgment where you have a specific area of the market of which the judge is ignorant ... it is legitimate to produce evidence from amongst those who are skilled in that market and know of it, and likelihood of confusion amongst customers in the same market. For those reasons I think I am entitled to look at the evidence."

10–21   In direct contrast to *Gucci v Gucci, Taittinger v Allbev*[40] involved confusion of a class of the public far less knowledgeable about the goods in question than the court itself. The Court of Appeal, though *obiter*, would apparently have approved the admission of trade evidence as to whether a sufficient number of members of the public were undiscerning enough not to appreciate that the defendants' *Elderflower Champagne* was not the same as the famous French wine. The evidence was not essential, because the trial judge independently reached the same conclusions as the plaintiffs' witnesses, but Peter Gibson L.J. would have been inclined to agree with Kerr L.J. in *Sodastream* and Browne-Wilkinson V.C. in *Gucci*. In *IBM v Phoenix*[41] one reason for not striking out part of the defence was that in the specialised market for computer components expert evidence from persons in the market was essential to determine the issues of passing-off and trade mark infringement. The court could not decide such issues uninstructed. In *Dalgety Spillers v Food Brokers*[42] itself Blackburne J. ruled that the disputed and contradictory evidence of retailers and marketing experts was inadmissible: bare assertions of the likelihood of confusion did not assist the

[40] [1994] 4 All E.R. 75; [1993] 2 C.M.L.R. 641; [1993] F.S.R. 641, CA.
[41] [1994] R.P.C. 252 (Ferris J.).
[42] [1994] F.S.R. 504 (Blackburne J.).

court in the case of an ordinary food product, *Pot Noodles*, sold in vast quantities throughout the United Kingdom.

Trade evidence of likely confusion (as opposed to opinion evidence from **10–22** members of the public) was treated as admissible and relevant by Knox J. in *Jian Tools for Sales v Roderick Manhattan Group*[43] where the market was for computer software for generating business plans. In *Neutrogena v Golden*[44] the evidence of shopkeepers that they had not observed confusion between *Neutrogena* and *Neutralia* and were willing to stock the two side by side was allowed to be relevant but given little weight by Jacob J. or the Court of Appeal: shopkeepers would not be aware of the sort of confusion otherwise proved to exist and the name was not self-evidently deceptive. Expert evidence on brand-switching by a professor of marketing was admitted, but given no weight. In *Chocosuisse v Cadbury*[45] trade and consumer evidence were vital to proving that "Swiss chocolate" was a premium product with a distinctive reputation of its own.

Consumer evidence and actual deception

There is no doubt that evidence is admissible in passing-off actions from **10–23** actual consumers as to whether they would be deceived, and this applies *a fortiori* to evidence of actual deception. Conversely, absence of evidence of actual deception when the defendants' conduct has persisted openly for a substantial period of time may justify the inference that such deception has not occurred on any significant scale.[46] This obviously does not apply if the action is *quia timet* or effectively so,[47] and the speed with which passing-off actions may now be brought to trial also provides a reason why evidence of actual confusion may not be forthcoming.[48]

The general principle was stated by Millett L.J. in *Harrods v Harrodian* **10–24** *School*[49]:

"Evidence of actual confusion is always relevant and may be decisive. Absence of such evidence may often be readily explained and is rarely decisive. Its weight is a matter for the judge."

The absence of evidence of actual confusion in that case was regarded as "compelling" by Harman J. at trial, and as "not without significance" by Millett L.J. in the Court of Appeal. The defendant school had been announced in February 1993 and had opened in September 1993 with 70 pupils, rising to 100 at the date of trial. The writ was issued in April 1993,

---

[43] [1995] F.S.R. 924 (Knox J.).

[44] [1996] R.P.C. 473, C.A. affirming Jacob J. *ibid.*

[45] [1999] E.T.M.R. 1020; [1999] R.P.C. 826, CA, affirming [1998] E.T.M.R. 205; [1998] R.P.C. 117 (Laddie J.).

[46] *Bulmer (HP) Ltd v J Bollinger SA* [1978] R.P.C. 79; [1978] 2 C.M.L.R. 625, CA.

[47] *Reckitt & Colman Products Ltd v Borden Inc.* [1990] 1 W.L.R. 491; [1990] 1 All E.R. 873; [1990] R.P.C. 340, HL.

[48] *Harrods Ltd v Harrodian School Ltd* [1996] R.P.C. 697, CA, below. Likewise *Kimberly Clark Ltd v Fort Sterling Ltd* [1997] F.S.R. 877.

[49] [1996] R.P.C. 697, CA.

and the trial was in May 1994. The dissenting judgment of Sir Michael Kerr expresses the same principle as Millett L.J. but is rather more realistic in its emphasis, and doubly so now that the passage of thirteen months from claim form to trial would not be regarded as exceptionally fast:

"Even if there is no evidence of confusion whatever, the court must decide for itself, and may conclude that passing-off has been established: see e.g. per Sir Raymond Evershed M.R. in *Electrolux Ltd v Electrix Ltd* (1953) 71 R.P.C. 23 (CA) at p. 31. Thus, it has often been said that the availability of such evidence is important, but not its absence, because it is notoriously difficult to procure such evidence. In the present case, given the recency of the start-up of the school, this is even less surprising."

10–25   Several categories of consumer and trade evidence were examined in *Neutrogena v Golden*.[50] The case was a marginal one on first impression and consumer evidence was crucial. As Jacob J. put it:

"If the judge's own opinion is that the case is marginal, one where he cannot be sure whether there is a likelihood of sufficient deception, the case will fail in the absence of enough evidence of the likelihood of deception. But if that opinion of the judge is supplemented by such evidence then it will succeed. And even if one's own opinion is that deception is unlikely though possible, convincing evidence of deception will carry the day. It was certainly my experience in practice that my own view as to the likelihood of deception was not always reliable. As I grew more experienced I said more and more 'it depends on the evidence'."

The categories of evidence relied on were: First, that a television advertisement for *Neutralia*, showing a woman's bare nipple, had produced numerous complaints to the Independent Television Commission, some of them attributing the advertisement to *Neutrogena*. Secondly, there were members of the public who had communicated with the plaintiffs or defendants, including one who had bought *Neutralia* in the belief it was made by *Neutrogena*. An e-mail message around the plaintiffs' solicitors asking if anyone had bought or used *Neutralia* products produced instances of confusion; and finally a "witness collection programme" at chemists' shops produced 11 members of the public who gave evidence in person or by witness statement, as did some of the interviewers. Attacks on the inferences drawn from all these categories of evidence failed on appeal.

10–26   The judgment of Jacob J. in *Neutrogena* was also approved by the Court of Appeal in *Premier Luggage and Bags v Premier Co*,[51] although in that case the trial judge was criticised for attaching too much significance to a single instance of actual confusion, and failing to provide any other justification for his conclusion that confusion was likely. In the result, the judge's finding

---

[50] [1996] R.P.C. 473, CA, affirming Jacob J. *ibid.*
[51] [2002] EWCA Civ 387; [2002] E.T.M.R. 69; [2003] F.S.R. 5, CA; reversing [2001] E.T.M.R. 6, [2001] F.S.R. 29.

for the claimants was reversed, notwithstanding submissions that to do so was contrary to *Norowzian v Arks (No. 2)*[52] and *Designers Guild v Russell Williams*.[53] The trial judge had made an error of principle in not forming his own independent judgment as to whether the defendants' swing tag was really likely to mislead—perhaps compounded by the assumption that his decision as to registered trade mark infringement disposed of the corresponding issue for passing-off.

Evidence of passing-off by substitution may depend on trap orders, which **10–27** must be scrupulously fair and representative of actual business conditions. In *Marie Claire v Hartstone*[54] it was decided that there was nothing improper or unprofessional in trap orders being placed by the plaintiffs' solicitors, even though this involved an implicit misrepresentation that they were *bona fide* customers.

Survey evidence and witness collection programmes

The former tendency to put in evidence formal opinion surveys[55] by pro- **10–28** fessional market researchers acting as experts has predominantly been superceded, over the past decade, by more limited exercises under the name of "witness collection programmes". The latter do not typically present a statistical analysis of the responses of what is supposed to be a statistically significant cross-section of anonymous members of the relevant public to pre-formulated questions, but have the more modest objective of providing the court with first-hand evidence from a moderate number of members of the public in such circumstances that the party tendering the evidence cannot be accused of hand-picking his witnesses to support his case. This is not to say that the process by which formal surveys came to be regarded as admissible has been subjected to any fundamental reconsideration, and any former objections to survey evidence as hearsay are much reduced by the Civil Evidence Act 1995, but for the most part practical experience has been unfavourable to the older kind of survey.[55] Witnesses in the real world do not fit neatly into pre-determined boxes, and without seeing and hearing a witness in person it is typically impossible to tell whether he or she was really deceived or confused at all, let alone for what reason. In the result, formal surveys, even if properly designed and conducted, have a tendency to unravel under sustained criticism.

Witness collection programmes and surveys of the less ambitious kind **10–29** have undoubtedly proved their evidential value. Older cases aside,[57] in *Reckitt & Colman v Borden*[58] Walton J. admitted the plaintiffs' surveys at trial and found them helpful, at least when taken in conjunction with live

---

[52] [2000] E.M.L.R. 67; [2000] E.C.D.R. 205; [2000] F.S.R. 363, CA.
[53] [2000] 1 W.L.R. 2416; [2001] 1 All E.R. 700; [2001] E.C.D.R. 10; [2001] F.S.R. 11, HL.
[54] [1993] F.S.R. 692 (Chadwick J.).
[55] See generally Gary Lea, "Masters of All They Survey?" [1999] I.P.Q. 191.
[56] For instance, *Weight Watchers UK Ltd v Tesco Stores Ltd* [2003] EWHC 1109.
[57] *Customglass Boats Ltd v Salthouse Bros. Ltd* [1976] N.Z.L.R. 36; [1976] R.P.C. 589; *Lego System A/S v Lego M Lemelstrich Ltd* [1983] F.S.R. 135; *Imperial Group Ltd v Philip Morris Ltd* [1984] R.P.C. 293.
[58] [1990] 1 W.L.R. 491; [1990] 1 All E.R. 873; [1990] R.P.C. 340, HL.

evidence. The Court of Appeal deliberately put the surveys on one side and decided the case solely on the more conventional forms of evidence. The House of Lords favoured the approach of Walton J., and in referring to the evidence which led him to find for the plaintiffs did not draw any distinction between the different forms of evidence adduced.

"Because of the *quia timet* nature of the proceedings there was, in the nature of things, little opportunity for either side to observe the reaction of the public to the appellants' products in normal market conditions and the evidence before the court was, inevitably, in the main the result of surveys carried out in somewhat artificial conditions. Judges accustomed to trying cases of this nature are rightly somewhat suspicious of evidence obtained in this way, for so much can depend upon the conditions in which the surveys are conducted, the format of the questions posed and the manner in which they are asked. It is clear, however, that Walton J., who was a very experienced judge in this field, had well in mind the limitations and possible defects of such evidence, and he had before him not just the results of the surveys conducted by market researchers on both sides but the *viva voce* evidence of a substantial number of the members of the public interviewed which he was able to observe tested in cross-examination. In particular he had the evidence of the reaction of shoppers to the appellants' products when they were displayed experimentally in a co-operating supermarket. His findings, therefore, although they may appear at first sight a little surprising in the light of a close comparison and inspection of the products with their labels, are quite unassailable."[59]

10–30 For the time being, and regardless of strict legal theory, it is probably most realistic to regard surveys conducted for trial, under whatever name, primarily as a means of producing live witnesses who can give evidence in chief and have that evidence tested by cross-examination. The value of the survey lies principally in the fact that the witnesses so produced are demonstrably representative of the relevant public by virtue of having been chosen at random instead of by an unascertained, and possibly unobjective, process controlled by the party calling them. If the survey was originally more ambitious than a simple witness collection programme, then calling a number of individual respondents as witnesses may be regarded as a sort of survey-within-a-survey, partly intended to verify that the survey as a whole is reliable and partly to allow both parties to go into issues which interviewers cannot reasonably be expected to address in the street. However, once first hand evidence has been taken from a reasonable number of the respondents to the survey, the survey as such may quietly be allowed to drop out of sight, even if its methodology and conclusions are vindicated in the process.

10–31 The "witness collection programme" in *Neutrogena v Golden*[60] was not a

[59] *per* Lord Oliver, *ibid.*
[60] [1996] R.P.C. 473, CA, affirming Jacob J. *ibid.*

survey in the normal sense, and it was not relied on its totality to show what proportion of customers would be confused. Although the plaintiffs were ordered to produce all their questionnaires, they offered no expert statistical analysis. The purpose was simply to identify suitable witnesses who were called for cross-examination, a procedure of which Jacob J. approved:[61]

"This was rather different from an ordinary market survey of the kind which has sometimes been before the courts. In a normal market survey the members of the public are interviewed according to a set pattern of questions and their answers recorded on forms. The answers are classified according to a code and then analysed. Often statisticians come along and give evidence, based upon collation of data from surveys as to the statistical validity of conclusions. The evidence often contains long explanations from statisticians of things like 'confidence limits.' I have long thought that sort of exercise as such is unnecessarily elaborate in a passing off action. The court in a passing off case is not concerned with statistical precision. What it wants to know is whether or not there is a substantial degree of deception or confusion. Moreover pure questionnaire evidence is seldom helpful—there are almost inevitable faults with the questions or the recordal of the answers as well as in later stages of the processing. Of course the court needs to know how the evidence was collected, and needs to have the full picture, including particularly what failed surveys, if any, there were. But unless one can have some real evidence, tested in cross-examination, one cannot really be sure of what was passing through people's minds. Those cases where surveys have proved to be useful have all involved some of the 'pollees' coming to court."

An informal telephone survey without expert statistical analysis was **10–32** conducted for the plaintiffs in *Wagamama v City Centre Restaurants*[62] and some respondents gave oral evidence. Other cases in which witness collection programmes or similar exercises have been conducted include *Chocosuisse v Cadbury*[63] and *Daimler Chrysler v Alavi*.[64]

Conduct of the survey: the *Raffles* criteria

In the *Raffles* case, *Imperial Group v Philip Morris*[65] Whitford J. set out the **10–33** following criteria for surveys, which have generally continued to be required since, in so far as the survey itself has been relied on:

1. The interviewees must be selected to represent a relevant cross-section of the public.

---

[61] Above. Three routine surveys by the defendants were also regarded as relevant in the Court of Appeal.
[62] [1995] F.S.R. 713 (Laddie J.).
[63] [1998] E.T.M.R. 205; [1998] R.P.C. 117 (Laddie J.) affirmed [1999] E.T.M.R. 205; [1999] R.P.C. 826, CA.
[64] [2001] E.T.M.R. 98; [2001] R.P.C. 42 (Pumfrey J.).
[65] [1984] R.P.C. 293 (Whitford J.).

2. The size of the sample must be statistically significant.

3. The survey must be conducted fairly.

4. All the surveys carried out must be disclosed including the number carried out, how they were conducted, and the totality of the persons involved

5. The totality of the answers given (and the other requisite details) must be made available to the opposite party before trial.

6. The questions must not be leading nor should they lead the person answering into a field of speculation he would never have embarked upon had the question not been put.

7. The exact answers and not some abbreviated form must be recorded.

8. The instructions to the interviewers as to how to carry out the survey must be disclosed.

9. Where the answers are coded for computer input, the coding instructions must be disclosed.

10–34 Several of these either correspond to the Civil Evidence Acts or draw on experience with earlier cases where survey evidence was admitted only to be discredited on cross-examination. Some contemplate the production of material which might be privileged, in the sense that although production cannot be compelled, the survey may be disregarded if the disclosure is not made. In particular, item (4) causes problems. Normally, it would be good practice in preparation for a major survey to carry out a small-scale trial survey to identify unforeseen problems and refine the protocols for the full scale survey in the light of experience. On one reading of *Raffles* this creates a trap. If the trial survey has to be disclosed then differences between it and the full-scale one may be seized upon to attack the latter.

Even if the survey is not relied upon as such, the *Raffles* criteria may still be applicable in part, as in *Neutrogena v Golden*[66] where the plaintiffs were ordered to disclose all their questionnaires.

The Civil Evidence Act 1995

10–35 The Civil Evidence Act 1995 abolishes the common law rule against the admission of hearsay evidence in civil proceedings and supersedes the hearsay provisions of 1968 and 1972 Civil Evidence Acts. Section 1 provides:

(1) In civil proceedings evidence shall not be excluded on the ground that it is hearsay.
(2) In this Act—

(a) "hearsay" means a statement made otherwise than by a person

[66] [1996] R.P.C. 473, CA.

while giving oral evidence in the proceedings which is tendered as evidence of the matters stated and

(b) references to hearsay include hearsay of whatever degree.

(3) Nothing in this Act affects the admissibility of evidence admissible apart from this section.

(4) The provisions of sections 2 to 6 (safeguards and supplementary provisions relating to hearsay evidence) do not apply in relation to hearsay evidence admissible apart from this section, notwithstanding that it may also be admissible by virtue of this section.

Supplementary provisions and CPR Pt 33[67] require advance written notice **10–36** of proposed hearsay evidence to be given[68] and provide for the giver of the evidence to be called and cross-examined by the opposite party if necessary.[69] Section 4 of the 1995 Act lists a number of factors the court is to take into account in estimating the weight to be given to hearsay.

D. Final Remedies

Injunctions and delivery up

If the claimant is successful then a permanent injunction is, in practice, **10–37** normally granted as a matter of course, although a declaration is sometimes given in lieu of an injunction if the defendant has voluntarily discontinued the conduct complained of.[70] The form of injunction granted in a passing-off action depends on the circumstances of the case, and is necessarily to some extent a compromise between protecting the rights of the claimant and allowing the defendant to trade legitimately. On a strict analysis, the injunction granted sometimes covers acts which might not be passing-off at all, but this may be inevitable if the claimant is to be given adequate protection. It may be impossible to produce a form of words which is simple and workable but still precisely tailored to what the claimant is entitled to restrain. If the choice is between giving the claimant rather more than he is entitled to or rather less, the court at this stage of the action is likely to be more sympathetic towards the claimant.[71] If an injunction is granted, it is normal to order delivery up or destruction upon oath of items the disposal of which would infringe the injunction.

In *British Telecommunications v Nextcall Telecom*[72] Jacob J. refused to

---

[67] The Practice Direction—Civil Evidence Act 1995 relates only to transitional provisions.
[68] s.2 and CPR Pt 33.2, subject to exceptions in r.3.
[69] s.3 and CPR Pt 33 r.4.
[70] As in *Reed Executive Plc v Reed Business Information Ltd* [2002] EWHC 1015; [2003] R.P.C. 12 (Pumfrey J.); subsequent proceedings [2002] EWHC 2772.
[71] See *Chelsea Man Menswear Ltd v Chelsea Girl Ltd* [1987] R.P.C. 189. CA, where the defendants failed to have the injunction limited by geographical area.
[72] [2000] F.S.R. 679 (Jacob J.).

qualify an injunction which was being broken because of inadequate supervision of junior staff.

10–38   Mandatory injunctions requiring a change of name are more readily given now than previously, even at the interlocutory stage, in comparison to the old and convoluted practice of granting a prohibitory injunction against the defendant continuing to exist under the disputed name. The defendant charity was ordered to change its name after trial in *British Diabetic Association v Diabetic Society*.[73] In *Glaxo v Glaxowellcome*[74] Lightman J. granted interlocutory mandatory injunctions requiring the defendant company and its promoters to change its name, but the reasoning is not entirely satisfactory. Rimer J. also made an interlocutory order for the defendant to change its name in *Law Society v Society of Lawyers*.[75]

In *Havana Cigar & Tobacco v Oddenino*[76] the word *Corona* denoted the plaintiffs' brand of cigar to the majority of smokers but others used it for a cigar of a certain shape and size. The context in which passing-off had taken place was the supply of cigars which were not the plaintiffs' to diners who asked for "a *Corona* cigar" or similar. An injunction against passing-off by substitution was granted, with the qualification: "unless it be made clear by word of mouth or otherwise that the cigar or cigars supplied is or are of a brand other than the plaintiffs' ".

Corrective statements

10–39   The claimant himself may publish advertisements intended to correct the effect of the defendant's passing-off, and it would appear from *Spalding v Gamage*[77] that the cost of doing so may be recovered as damages in the action. This raises the question of whether the defendant himself could be compelled to undo the effect of his misrepresentation. There does not appear to be a case of such an order being made. In the main action in *Spalding v Gamage* Lord Sumner observed in a slightly different context that the defendants could not fairly be required to "advertise their penitence", notwithstanding that fair and honest traders would have set out to correct the effect of the first misleading advertisement.

In *Fisher v Apollinaris*[78] the plaintiff unsuccessfully objected to publicity given by the defendants to an apology he had given them in settlement of proceedings against him. It was held that on the terms of the settlement the Apollinaris Co were entitled to make what use of it they pleased.

In *Independent Locksmiths v Aardvark Master Locksmiths*[79] the defendants were ordered to arrange an explanatory recorded message on their telephone to correct the effect of a misleading name (*Interdependent Lock-*

---

[73] [1996] F.S.R. 1 (Robert Walker J.).
[74] [1996] F.S.R. 388 (Lightman J.).
[75] [1996] F.S.R. 739 (Rimer J.).
[76] [1924] 1 Ch. 179; 41 R.P.C. 47, CA.
[77] (1915) 32 R.P.C. 273, HL.
[78] (1875) L.R. 10 Ch. 297, CA.
[79] (1986) 7 I.P.R. 432 (Federal Court, Full Court).

smiths) which had been entered in the telephone directory with the defendants' number before the plaintiffs could act.

In an action for injurious falsehood, *CHC Software Care v Hopkins &* **10–40**
Wood,[80] Mummery J. ordered a firm of solicitors to disclose the names and addresses of the persons to whom they had sent certain allegedly inaccurate letters, so that corrective statements might be sent to them.

In *Law Society v Griffiths*[8] the defendants were ordered not to answer their telephone number 0800 192939 except by way of a pre-recorded message stating that theirs was not the *Law Society Accident Line* which was available on 0500 192939. They were also ordered to procure British Telecom to re-direct calls from the 0800 number to the Law Society's 0500 number. In *Roadtech v Mandata*[82] an otherwise successful application for summary judgment was refused in so far as damages for corrective advertising were concerned, since the conduct complained of had ceased too long ago for the proposed advertisements to be of any use.

Inquiry as to damages

If the claimant in a passing-off action is successful it is normal (unless the **10–41**
claimant elects for an account of profits) to order an inquiry as to damages at the claimant's risk as to costs. In principle, there would be no right to damages in a case which was wholly *quia timet*, but in passing-off it is not always possible to distinguish between true *quia timet* actions and those in which a certain amount of damage might have been caused. The question which sometimes arises is whether the court ought to order an enquiry as to damages if the likelihood is that the actual damage suffered by the claimant would have been very slight. The principle is that the court has a discretion to refuse an inquiry (and award nominal damages instead) if satisfied that the inquiry would be futile,[83] but should exercise this discretion against the claimant only in the clearest cases: "[T]he improbability of [the plaintiffs] proving much is not the same as the legal certainty that they can prove nothing".[84] The defendant can always protect himself against the cost of the inquiry by making a payment into court. It should be remembered that disclosure in the action does not cover quantum of damage, and the claimant does not come to court prepared to prove how much damage he may have suffered.

The circumstances in which the court might refuse an inquiry were considered by the Court of Appeal in *McDonald's v Burger King*.[85] The defendants had displayed on London Underground trains for a few months several hundred advertisements with the slogan *It's Not Just Big, Mac, Big Mac* being a product of the plaintiffs. The trial judge held that this was

[80] [1993] F.S.R. 241 (Mummery J.).
[81] [1995] R.P.C. 16 (Aldous J.).
[82] [2000] E.T.M.R. 970 (Master Bowman).
[83] In *Samuelson v Producers Distributing Co. Ltd* (1931) 48 R.P.C. 580, CA, the Court of Appeal awarded nominal damages of £5 instead of ordering an inquiry.
[84] *per* Lord Sumner in *Spalding (A G) & Bros v A W Gamage Ltd* (1915) 32 R.P.C. 273, HL.
[85] [1987] F.S.R. 112, CA.

passing-off and granted an injunction, but refused an inquiry as to damages. The Court of Appeal held that it was impossible to say that there was no prospect of the plaintiffs recovering any damages and awarded an inquiry.

10–42   In *Reed Executive v Reed Business Information*[86] Pumfrey J. found at trial that the defendants were liable for passing-off as a result of various uses of the word *Reed* on or in relation to their recruitment website *totaljobs.com*. At a subsequent hearing, he held that there was negligible evidence of diversion of trade but that other heads of damage not dependent on diversion might be made out. He granted an inquiry limited to the three issues of visible use of *Reed* on the site, a single example of banner advertising by the defendants in response to using *Reed* as a search term in *Yahoo!*, and invisible use of the word in metatags. All these were to be assessed on the basis of a reasonable royalty.

Measure of damages

10–43 Damages for passing-off are inherently very difficult to quantify, which is one reason why interlocutory relief is so important. The basic rule is that the claimant is entitled to recover

> "[S]uch damages as naturally flow from [the defendants'] unlawful act ... there is no artificial limitation in the case of passing-off actions."[87]

This was amplified by the Court of Appeal in the inquiry as to damages which followed in the same case:

> "The decision of the House of Lords in the present case determines that the defendants have infringed a right of property in the plaintiffs' business or goodwill, which was likely to be injured by the misrepresentation; and the defendants are liable, in my opinion, for all the loss actually sustained by the plaintiffs, which is the natural and direct consequence of the unlawful acts of the defendants. This will include any loss of trade actually suffered by the plaintiffs, either directly from the acts complained of, or properly attributable to the injury to the plaintiffs' reputation, business, goodwill and trade and business connection caused by the acts complained of; in other words, such damages as flow directly and in the usual course of things, from the wrongful acts, and excluding any speculative and unproven damages."[88]

10–44   Damage usually arises under two heads: loss of sales, especially if the parties are in actual competition, and general damage to goodwill. Under the first head it is not to be supposed that all the sales made by the defendant are necessarily at the claimant's expense. Although the defendant's goods

---

[86] [2002] EWHC 1015; [2003] R.P.C. 12 (Pumfrey J.); subsequent proceedings [2002] EWHC 2772.

[87] *per* Lord Parmoor in *Spalding (AG) & Bros v AW Gamage Ltd* (1915) 32 R.P.C. 273, HL.

[88] *per* Swinfen Eady L.J. in *Spalding (AG) & Bros v AW Gamage Ltd* (1918) 32 R.P.C. 101, CA.

may be inherently deceptive, the claimant is only entitled to damages under this head to the extent that his own sales have suffered:

> "[T]he court is not entitled to assume that every one of those sales would have been obtained by the plaintiff. For obvious reasons that is an assumption which is quite unwarranted."[89]

An estimate has to be made, at least implicitly, of what proportion of the goods put into circulation by the defendant will ultimately be sold at the expense of the claimant. This is necessarily an approximate exercise. Evidence of a general falling off in the claimant's level of sales may be helpful but is not necessarily conclusive. Substantial damages have been awarded in the absence of evidence that any customer has actually been deceived.

In this respect there is an important difference between an inquiry as to damages and an account of profits:

> "A tortious act, therefore, in the case of a sale to a middleman, is committed by selling the deceptive goods to that middleman, and if the relief given is an account of profits you stop there and find out the profits on those sales. If, on the other hand, what is being asked for is damages, obviously the profit made on those sales is not the relevant consideration, and the further enquiry falls to be made, what is the damage which is fairly to be attributed to that initial wrongful act of selling deceptive goods to the middleman, and that will appear on the consideration of all the circumstances and the probabilities of the case."[90]

Under the second head it must always be reasonable to suppose that there **10–45** is some general damage to business if there has been passing-off on a significant sale:

> "[Y]ou cannot have deceptive trading of a considerable volume without inflicting, at any rate, some measure of damage on the goodwill. How long that will last, what its extent will be, is a thing which no evidence except in the most exceptional case could satisfactorily define, and the matter is reduced, as many of these matters are reduced, to forming a rough estimate in a way that a jury could properly form it."[91]

General damage to goodwill is even more difficult to quantify than loss of sales, and all that can normally be done is to award a round sum which seems reasonable.

In *Spalding v Gamage*[92] the defendants obtained and advertised as the **10–46** current model a stock of footballs which the plaintiffs had discontinued. The House of Lords[93] held this to be actionable, and an enquiry as to damages

---

[89] *per* Lord Greene in *Draper v Trist* [1939] 3 All E.R. 513; 56 R.P.C. 429, CA.
[90] *ibid. per* Lord Greene.
[91] *ibid. per* Lord Greene.
[92] (1918) 35 R.P.C. 101, CA.
[93] (1915) 32 R.P.C. 273, HL.

was held before an Official Referee. The Official Referee awarded £2,000 for general damage to reputation and £5,000 for loss of profits on projected lost sales of the improved ball. On appeal to the High Court Younger J. reduced the award to £100, calculated as the cost of counter-advertisements. The Court of Appeal raised the award to £250: there had been some damage to the plaintiffs' general goodwill from some of their trade customers supposing that they had given the defendants unduly favourable treatment. The claim that the defendants' advertisements had destroyed a profitable new venture in its infancy was dismissed as extravagant and absurd.

Juggi Lal-Kamlapat v Swadeshi[94] was an appeal to the Privy Council from India. The Indian court awarded damages by assuming that 60 per cent of the defendants' goods had been sold on the strength of the plaintiff's copied mark and that the profit margin was nine per cent. As the defendants had sold goods to the value of Rs. 3,200,000 damages came to Rs. 172,800. The Privy Council held it was speculative to say what proportion of the defendants' sales was attributable to passing-off. Instead, they took as their starting point the fall in the plaintiffs' sales which was Rs. 1,000,000. They were prepared to assume that all of this was due to passing-off, and to increase it by just under 10 per cent to allow for the likelihood of the plaintiff's trade increasing. At a profit of 9 per cent damages came to Rs. 67,000.

10–47 In *Draper v Trist*[95] the Court of Appeal increased damages for passing-off from £2 to £2,000. The only sales of deceptive goods proved were to middlemen who were not deceived, but there was evidence that some ultimate customers would be likely to be deceived and there would inevitably be some general damage to goodwill.

In *Plomien Fuel Economiser v National School of Salesmanship*[96] £750 was awarded by the Official Referee and upheld on appeal to the High Court and the Court of Appeal. There was no evidence of actual purchasers being deceived but it was legitimate to draw such an inference from the fact that the defendants had deliberately issued misleading literature claiming advantages belonging to the plaintiffs. There was no evidence of falling off in the plaintiffs' trade. The plaintiffs claimed damages of around £7,400 based on the profits made by the defendants in all the cases in which the sale of an economiser could be associated with the deceptive literature. This was rejected by the Official Referee and on appeal. The defendants' offer of a free trial had probably swayed more customers than the deceptive material.

10–48 In *Manus v Fullwood & Bland*[97] damages of £10,000 were awarded in a case in which the defendants' conduct had prevented the resumption of the plaintiffs' business (halted by the war) for several years as well as causing serious damage to their goodwill.

In *Baume v Moore*[98] the defendants sought clarification of the terms on which the inquiry was to be held. All the defendants' sales had been to

[94] (1928) 45 R.P.C. 74, PC.
[95] [1939] 3 All E.R. 513; 56 R.P.C. 429, CA.
[96] (1943) 60 R.P.C. 209, CA.
[97] [1958] R.P.C. 319, CA.
[98] (1954) 71 R.P.C. 243, CA.

middlemen. The Court of Appeal indicated that only damages due to passing-off could be recovered, and not injury resulting from competition as such.

In *Unik Time v Unik Time*[99] the defendants submitted to a consent order providing for an account to be taken of the damages to be paid by them for passing-off and conspiracy. The master made an award of £34,000 (corresponding to a profit of 20 per cent. on lost turnover of £170,000) which Warner J. upheld. He refused to award exemplary damages, partly because of delay.

The background to *Dormeuil Freres v Feraglow*[1] was unusual, in that the **10–49** defendant company had gone into liquidation after submitting to an enquiry and the live issue was whether the plaintiffs were entitled to an interim payment under R.S.C., Ord.29, rr.10 and 11 from out of a sum £50,000 previously paid into court in lieu of a *Mareva* injunction.[2] The plaintiffs argued that they were entitled, at least to damages on a royalty basis; to recovery of legal costs incurred in pursuing the defendants' foreign suppliers; and to interest. As well as resisting these, the defendants argued that a settlement in another action in respect of goods supplied by them had been unduly generous to those defendants and had therefore increased the liability of the defendants in the present action. On the question of whether damages could be awarded on a royalty basis, Knox J. observed that there was no reported instance of this having been done in a passing-off or trade mark action.[3] In the result, it was an open question whether damages should ultimately be calculated on this basis or in terms of lost profits and general damage to goodwill. It could not be said in advance that the plaintiffs were bound to recover at least as much as they claimed on the royalty basis. On the other points, the plaintiffs were entitled to recover as damages their unrecovered legal costs in putting the foreign suppliers of the defendants on notice. Costs incurred in litigation against those defendants after that stage were probably too remote to attribute to the defendants. There was no answer to the claim for interest and there was no reason to doubt that the settlement in the previous action had been at arm's length and had adequately protected the plaintiff's interests. In the result the interim payment was increased to £20,000.

In *Roadtech v Mandata*[4] summary judgment for damages of £15,000 for **10–50** trade mark infringement and passing-off was granted in respect of the use of the claimants' marks *Roadrunner* and *Roadtech* as metatags on the defen-

---

[99] [1983] F.S.R. 121 (Warner J.).

[1] [1990] R.P.C. 449 (Knox J.).

[2] The defendants had conceded that general damages would amount to at least £10,000 and the Master had ordered an interim payment of this sum.

[3] See now *Reed Executive plc v Reed Business Information Ltd (costs)* [2002] EWHC 2772 (Pumfrey J.) and *Roadtech Computer Systems Ltd v Mandata (Management and Data Services) Ltd* [2000] E.T.M.R. 970 (Master Bowman), although both are complicated by the existence of claims for trade mark infringement.

[4] [2000] E.T.M.R. 970 (Master Bowman).

dants' website so as to divert enquiries intended for the claimants, although there had probably been no actual diversion of trade. In *Irving v Talksport*[5] the Court of Appeal increased from £2,000 to £25,000 the damages awarded to Eddie Irving, a motor racing driver, for the use of his photograph in a promotional mailshot so as to give the impression that he was endorsing the defendants' radio station. There was evidence that Mr Irving's popularity at the time was such that he would not even bother to consider deals for any less than this, and the trial judge had been wrong to attach any significance to the fact that the defendants would not voluntarily have paid so much.

Account of profits

10–51 A successful claimant is *prima facie* entitled to elect for an account of profits as an alternative to an enquiry as to damages.[6] An account of profits is an equitable remedy and there is a discretion to refuse it altogether or to limit it to take account of such factors as the defendant's innocence, inequitable conduct by the claimant, or delay prejudicial to the defendant.[7] As with all equitable discretions, it must be exercised judicially.

There are, in effect, two separate sets of rules for evaluating the profits for which the defendant must account to the claimant. One set applies where the defendant is a manufacturer, importer or dealer who puts into circulation "instruments of deception" which bear indicia deceptively similar to those of the claimant and are therefore calculated to be passed-off to ultimate customers as the claimant's goods. The other set of rules applies in every other case and in particular where the defendant is a retailer, or deals directly with ultimate consumers or the passing-off does not involve the use of the claimant's indicia on goods so as to make the goods inherently deceptive.

The common principle is that the defendant is only obliged to account for his profits on so much of his trade is wrongful. The difference arises from the fact that disposing of instruments of deception to a middleman is deemed to be wrongful whether or not anyone is or will ever be deceived. Apart from this it is a question of fact and degree whether and to what extent the defendant's trade is attributable to improper means.

10–52 The rule of law that a trader is liable to account for his profits on all inherently deceptive goods disposed of by him to middlemen dates back to the decision of Lord Westbury L.C. in *Edelsten v Edelsten*[8] which was followed in *Lever v Goodwin*[9] in which the Court of Appeal affirmed that the defendant's liability on the account could not depend on whether the mid-

---

[5] [2003] EWCA Civ 423; [2003] 2 All E.R. 881; [2003] E.M.L.R. 26; [2003] F.S.R. 35, CA, reversing (on quantum) [2002] EWHC 367; [2002] 1 W.L.R. 2355; [2002] 2 All E.R. 414; [2002] E.M.L.R. 32; [2002] F.S.R. 60 (Laddie J.).

[6] *Weingarten Bros v Bayer & Co* [1904–7] All E.R. 877; (1903) R.P.C. 341, HL.

[7] *Ford v Foster* (1872) L.R. 7 Ch. 611, CA; *Young (Edward) & Co Ltd v Holt* (1947) 65 R.P.C. 25.

[8] (1863) 46 E.R. 72 (Lord Westbury L.C.).

[9] [1887] 36 Ch.D. 1; 4 R.P.C. 492, CA.

dlemen to whom goods bearing a deceptive get-up were consigned were themselves guilty of passing-off in their dealings with the general public.

In *Weingarten v Bayer*[10] the parties were both firms of corset manu-facturers. The trial judge ordered an account of all profits made by the defendants "by reason of the sale by them of corsets ... under the name *Erect Form Corsets*". The Court of Appeal allowed an appeal by the defendants. The House of Lords held that only the device of a "scroll" in which *Erect Form* was written was distinctive of the plaintiffs and ordered an account of the profits derived by the defendants from the sale of corsets in boxes bearing an imitation of the scroll. In this case too, the sales appear to have been to middlemen rather than to the general public. It is note-worthy that the defendants were the leading British corset manufacturers and had enormous goodwill of their own. The proportion of their profits on the infringing goods attributable to copying the scroll as such (as opposed to copying the words *Erect Form* and the design of the corsets, both of which were legitimate) must have been tiny, but that was not the basis on which the order for the account was made. Every sale of goods bearing the scroll was tortious and therefore the whole of the profit on every such sale had to be accounted for.

The logic of the foregoing cases is that the tort of passing-off is complete **10–53** upon a trader putting deceptive goods into the hands of middlemen. In general, however, an act cannot constitute passing-off unless there is both a misrepresentation and damage. To this extent the law stated in the foregoing section is anomalous, but some such rule is necessary if passing-off actions are to be brought against traders other than retailers, and the authority for the rule cannot be denied. However, if the defendant is dealing directly with the consuming public then it is possible even for goods which are inherently deceptive to be disposed of in a manner which does not mislead the pur-chaser[11] or damage the claimant. The defendant may recognise the possi-bility of confusion, and take special steps to see it does not take place.[12] So far as this is the case, the retailer is not guilty of passing-off and ought not to be obliged to account for his profits. The same principle applies when deceptive goods are not involved at all, for instance because the passing-off alleged arises from the use of a business name.

In *My Kinda Town v Soll*[13] Slade J. found at trial that the defendants had passed off their restaurant as a branch of the plaintiffs by the inclusion of the term *Chicago Pizza* in its name, reinforced by similarities in get-up and trading style. The plaintiffs elected to take an account of profits and claimed they were entitled to all the profits of the defendants' restaurant,[14] irre-spective of the proportion of customers who had believed there to have been a connection between the parties. Slade J. rejected this argument after careful consideration of the principles and authorities. He directed that the account should cover only the profits attributable to the use of the term

---

[10] [1904–7] All E.R. 877; (1903) 33 R.P.C. 341, H.L.
[11] *Lever v Goodwin* [1887] 36 Ch.D. 1; 4 R.P.C. 492, CA.
[12] *Draper v Trist* [1939] 3 All E.R. 513; 56 R.P.C. 429, CA.
[13] [1983] R.P.C. 15 (Slade J.).
[14] Subsequent to receipt of the letter before action.

Chicago Pizza in the name. Although this is *obiter*, since the Court of Appeal subsequently found for the defendants on liability, it is submitted that the principle is correct.

10–54   An unusual situation arose in Australia in *Apand v Kettle Chip Co*,[15] in that the defendants (appellants) sold off the whole division responsible for their infringing *Country Kettle* product before trial. The Federal Court,[16] affirming Birkett J., held that the defendants were liable for the capital profit attributable to the infringing brand and goodwill as part of the business sold, determined at A\$5,590, 800. In addition, the defendants were liable on normal principles for their trading profits prior to the sale, less an allocation of fixed costs.

Orders for accounts of profits have been limited in time to the period after the letter before action, or the writ, giving effect to the rule that an account is not available in respect of innocent passing-off. Delay may also limit the right to an account of profits even if it is not serious enough to prevent the grant of an injunction. For this to happen it is necessary for the claimant to be at fault, and for the defendant to have been placed at a disadvantage, as would be the case if the defendant would have ceased the conduct complained of on being given notice of the claimant's claim.[17]

The equitable protective jurisdiction

10–55 Under a doctrine known as the equitable protective jurisdiction, an innocent person who becomes involved in the commission of a tort is under an obligation to provide the victim of the tort with the information necessary to identify and sue the tortfeasor. The principle has been extended to persons whose involvement was not innocent, and the same doctrine sometimes provides the claimant with a qualified right to delivery up of infringing goods even though the holder of the goods is not committing any wrong.

In a patent case, the plaintiffs were aware that infringement was occurring because statistical summaries published by the Customs and Excise showed that a certain chemical was being imported. The Customs refused to identify the importer, but the House of Lord ruled that they were under an equitable obligation to do so at the request (and cost) of the patentee.

> "[I]f through no fault of his own a person gets mixed up in the tortious acts of others so as to facilitate their wrong-doing he may incur no personal liability but he comes under a duty to assist the person who has been wronged by giving him full information and disclosing the identity of the wrongdoers. I do not think that it matters whether he became so mixed up by voluntary action on his part or because it was his duty to do what he

---

[15] [1999] FCA 483; 43 I.P.R. 225, affirming (1998) 40 I.P.R. 481.
[16] Beaumont and Heerey JJ., Emmett J. dissenting.
[17] *Young (Edward) & Co Ltd v Holt* (1947) 65 R.P.C. 25.

did. It may be that if this causes him expense the person seeking the information ought to reimburse him. But justice requires that he should co-operate in righting the wrong if he unwittingly facilitated its perpetration."[18]

As part of the equitable protective jurisdiction, the court may therefore **10–56** order the disclosure of information which is necessary to enable the claimant to identify tortfeasors or to trace infringing goods.[19] This was formerly referred to as discovery, which is historically justified although such disclosure is to be distinguished from disclosure of documents relevant to the issues in the passing-off action as such. Although this form of disclosure is better regarded as a final, rather than interlocutory, remedy, it can be made at an interlocutory stage.[20] An order for disclosure may be made against wholly innocent parties who have become mixed up in wrongdoing by others, and *a fortiori* it may be made against tortfeasors themselves, whether innocent or deliberate.

The normal use of such orders is to trace the source of infringing goods so as to identify the person responsible for manufacturing, importing or putting them into circulation. An action against him is likely to be far more effective, and more just, than numerous actions against retailers. *Dormeuil Freres v Feraglow*[21] contains a discussion of the extent to which the costs of pursuing foreign suppliers of infringing goods can be recovered from an English importer. It was held that the legal costs incurred by the plaintiffs in putting the foreign suppliers on notice of their rights were recoverable as damages from the English defendants, who had procured the infringing goods to be made and who must have foreseen that the plaintiffs would have to take such steps. Thereafter, however, the costs of pursuing the foreign suppliers were too remote to attribute to the English defendants. It is also possible to obtain discovery of the identity of customers, but this is ordered less readily.[22] In *Levi Strauss v Barclays*[23] the defendants made, by consent, an affidavit disclosing the names of their suppliers and customers for counterfeit jeans, and were subsequently refused an order which would have prevented the plaintiffs from using that information in further proceedings. In *Coca Cola Company and Schweppes v Gilbey*[24] the defendant was ordered to comply with an order to disclose the identities of others involved in large-

[18] per Lord Reid in *Norwich Pharmacal Co v Commissioners of Customs and Excise* [1974] A.C. 133; [1974] R.P.C. 101, HL. This decision largely supersedes the historical authorities, including several on the border between trade mark infringement and passing-off, which are cited in the report.
[19] An early example, approved in *Norwich Pharmacal* [1974] A.C. 133 was *Orr v Diaper* (1876) 4 L.R. Ch. 92.
[20] *RCA Corporation of America v Reddingtons Rare Records* [1975] 1 All E.R. 38; [1975] R.P.C. 95, *EMI Ltd v Sarwar* [1977] F.S.R. 146, CA.
[21] [1990] R.P.C. 449 (Knox J.).
[22] See *Freedman (Harry) v Hillingdon Shirts Co Ltd* [1975] F.S.R. 449; *Sega Enterprises Ltd v Alca Electronics* [1982] F.S.R. 516, CA; *Intelsec Systems Ltd v Grech-Cini* [2000] 1 W.L.R. 1190; [1999] 4 All E.R. 11, below.
[23] [1993] F.S.R. 179 (Judge Bromley Q.C., Deputy Judge).
[24] [1996] F.S.R. 23 (Lightman J.).

scale counterfeiting, despite a fear of violence towards himself. In *Intelsec v Grech-Cini*[25] former employees of the plaintiff against whom there were claims for passing off and breach of confidence were ordered to disclose the identity of all persons with whom they had been in written contact with a view to supplying or soliciting orders for the smoke detection equipment in issue.

10–57 The obligation to assist in putting right wrongful acts in which one may have participated may go even further. In *CHC Software Care v Hopkins & Wood*,[26] where there was an allegation of injurious falsehood, Mummery J. ordered a firm of solicitors to disclose the names of all recipients of a threatening letter they had sent, so that corrective statements might be sent to them. The same principle might sometimes usefully be applied in passing-off, especially in the case of customers who needed to be notified of dangerous counterfeit goods.

The equitable protective jurisdiction can also be used to obtain possession of infringing goods from carriers, warehousemen and the like.[27] Even though they are not liable as tortfeasors in their own right, they are obliged to surrender such goods to the claimant rather than deliver them to their owner and so allow them to be passed off at retail level. This right of the claimant does not override any lien on the goods. The carrier or warehouseman is not committing any wrong, and cannot be penalised or exposed to liability for his involvement. If a dispute arises between the warehouseman or carrier, his customer, and the claimant, the former may take interpleader proceedings.

E. Unfair Competition in Private International Law

Introduction: issues arising

10–58 A claim brought in England in respect of acts of passing off or unfair competition taking place overseas is likely to involve at least the following issues: personal jurisdiction over the proposed defendant(s), including the grounds under which the claim form may be served out of the jurisdiction if necessary, and whether with or without leave; subject matter jurisdiction or justiciability of the claim, and the possibility of arguments of *forum non conveniens*; identification of the applicable law for the claim; ascertainment by expert evidence of the requirements of that law; and evidence of liability or not in fact.[28]

So far as personal and subject matter jurisdiction are concerned, there are

---

[25] [2000] 1 W.L.R. 1190; [1999] 4 All E.R. 11 (Nichols Warren Q.C., Deputy Judge).
[26] [1993] F.S.R. 241 (Mummery J.).
[27] See *Smith, Kline and French Laboratories Ltd v RD Harbottle (Mercantile) Ltd* [1979] F.S.R. 555; [1980] R.P.C. 363, another patent case.
[28] For a more detailed treatment of the private international law of infringement actions in general see Wadlow, *Enforcement of Intellectual Property in European and International Law* (1998), on which the present Section draws.

now two regimes to consider: that for defendants domiciled in the EU and
EEA, which is governed by European law;[29] and that that existing at
common law which applies to defendants from the rest of the World.

So far as the applicable law is concerned, all cases are now governed by **10–59**
the Private International Law (Miscellaneous Provisions) Act 1995 regardless of the domicile of any party, although the Act creates two different
regimes according to whether the act of unfair competition under the relevant foreign law is for passing-off or injurious falsehood as English law
would understand it. In the case of injurious falsehood alone, so far as the
present work is concerned, the Act continues to apply the former rule of
double actionability of *Phillips v Eyre*.[30]

Older cases are still relevant to a certain extent. First, the doctrine of
"instruments of deception" is wholly a doctrine of domestic law, not of
private international law, so it is unaffected by the 1995 Act. Secondly, any
action for passing off abroad which succeeded or would have succeeded
under the former double actionability rule prior to the 1995 Act must succeed *a fortiori* under the new law, as must any action which would have
failed only because the conduct complained of would not have been
actionable in England. Next, as already stated, the 1995 Act expressly saves
the former double actionability rule for actions for injurious falsehood.
Finally, although the old and new codes for jurisdiction are very different,
the practical results are rather similar. Both at common law and under the
Jurisdiction Regulation or one of the conventions, the English courts are
likely to have jurisdiction over acts of unfair competition committed by any
person in England, or by English-based defendants anywhere abroad, but
generally not otherwise.

The older cases: passing-off

10–60

In contrast to other fields of intellectual property, actions in respect of acts
of passing-off or injurious falsehood committed abroad are by no means a
novelty. So far as passing-off is concerned, since the late nineteenth century
the common law has given effect to a doctrine under which it is actionable as
passing-off to export goods which will cause deception in the ultimate
market to which they are consigned, regardless of whether or not there
would be any legal liability under the law of that place. The tort is complete,
at the latest, when the deceptive goods leave the jurisdiction, and no issues
of liability or non-liability under any foreign system of law arise. The only
enquiry which has to be made abroad concerns the circumstances of the
relevant foreign market, since it is by those standards that the question of
deception is to be judged. Deceptiveness or not by domestic standards is not
relevant.

---

[29] Council Regulation 44/2001 of December 22, 2000 on Jurisdiction and the Recognition and
Enforcement of Judgments in Civil and Commercial Matters; the Brussels and Lugano Conventions, below.
[30] (1870) L.R. 6 Q.B. 1 (Exchequer Chamber).

If the case can be framed as one of export of instruments of deception, then an extra-territorial claim on that basis is attractively simple—especially if many different foreign markets are involved,[31] or the relevant local law is difficult of proof, or is ineffective.

10–61   More recently, it came to be recognised that conduct in a foreign country which would have been actionable as passing-off had it occurred in England could be restrained by the English courts, and damages awarded, if the latter had personal jurisdiction over the defendant, quite irrespective of whether instruments of deception are involved or whether it could be said that a tort had actually been committed under English law. This formerly arose from application of the rule in *Phillips v Eyre*,[32] but the same result may now be achieved under the Private International Law (Miscellaneous Provisions) Act 1995, below.

The first such case was *John Walker v Ost*[33] in which exporters of Scotch Whisky sued in respect of a blend of Scotch malt whisky and local cane spirit sold as *Scotch* in Ecuador. Foster J. held that the defendants had committed passing-off in England by selling instruments of deception knowing and intending that they would be used deceptively in Ecuador, and also that the plaintiffs had proved that the sale of the mixture as Scotch Whisky was actionable under Ecuadorian law. He awarded damages under the latter head, and a number of injunctions which were qualified to apply only to acts done within the jurisdiction.[34]

In *Alfred Dunhill v Sunoptic*[35] the Court of Appeal went one step further by granting an interlocutory injunction against passing off sunglasses and spectacle frames in Switzerland as well as Britain. This was not an instruments of deception case, as the defendants' sunglasses and frames were manufactured by a contractor in Italy and had no connection with the United Kingdom. The plaintiffs had asked for a world-wide injunction, but Switzerland (where the defendant company was incorporated) was the only country for which they had adduced satisfactory evidence of local law. The court rejected the argument that the plaintiffs could rely on the presumption that foreign law corresponds to English. If the plaintiffs wanted more extensive injunctions, they could come back to the court with evidence of reputation, confusion, and consequent legal liability in those countries. In *James Burrough v Speymalt*[36] the pursuers were able to maintain an action for alleged passing off in Italy, although claims for registered trade mark infringement were struck out as not being justiciable in Scotland.

---

[31] For example *William Grant v Glen Catrine Bonded Warehouse. William Grant v Glen Catrine Bonded Warehouse (No. 1)* was an unsuccessful interim application to strike the claim in so far as it related to exports: 1995 S.L.T. 936 (Lord Abernethy, Outer House); *(No. 2)* at trial (Lord Cameron, August 18,1999, unreported); *(No. 3)* on reclaiming motion to the Inner House 2001 S.C. 901; 2001 S.L.T. 1419 (Inner House).

[32] (1870) L.R. 6 Q.B. 1 (Exchequer Chamber).

[33] [1970] 1 W.L.R. 917; [1970] 2 All E.R. 106; [1970] R.P.C. 489 (Foster J.).

[34] It is suggested there would have been nothing improper in restraining conduct in Ecuador provided it was shown to be actionable there and here, and the court had personal jurisdiction over the defendant. See *Alfred Dunhill Ltd v Sunoptic SA* [1979] F.S.R. 337, CA, below.

[35] [1979] F.S.R. 337, CA.

[36] [1991] R.P.C. 130 (Court of Session, Outer House).

Dunhill v Sunoptic was followed in *An Bord Trachtala v Waterford Foods*[37] **10–62** where the plaintiffs were an Irish statutory body established to promote the export of Irish foods. Their logo was extensively used and advertised in Ireland and abroad. They complained of the use by the defendants, principally in England, of an allegedly similar logo in relation to food products they had not endorsed. Applying *Phillips v Eyre*, Keane J. found that a cause of action would have been available in principle to the plaintiffs under both Irish and English law so that both heads of *Phillips v Eyre* were satisfied and the court had jurisdiction, even though the doctrine of "instruments of deception" was inapplicable. On the facts, however, the *Food Ireland* logo was not distinctive of the plaintiffs, the defendants' logo was sufficiently distinct, and the probability of confusion remote. An interlocutory injunction was refused.

In *IBM v Phoenix*[38] there were three pleaded (and admitted) sales of computer memory cards described as *IBM Manufactured* respectively in England, Denmark and Portugal. In refusing to strike out the defence Ferris J. observed:

"This conclusion [not to strike out] is strengthened by the fact that, of the three sales relied upon by IBM, only one took place in England. While IBM may be entitled to rely upon a misrepresentation made abroad this raises issues of foreign law and thus of fact. It is pleaded in the statement of claim that the sales alleged in Portugal and Denmark are unlawful but no particulars of foreign law have been given and in its defence Phoenix has not admitted this allegation. There is no evidence before me concerning the relevant foreign law and even if there were this would, it seems to me, be inappropriate to be explored on an application to strike out. Thus for present purposes IBM's case depends upon a single case of a sale effected in England."

Where no goods are involved, liability for passing-off abroad can only **10–63** arise from the application of general principles of private international law, there being no instruments of deception through which the tort might be deemed to be committed in England. In *Intercontex v Schmidt*[39] the plaintiffs complained that the defendants sent invoices from West Germany to business in various countries (not including England) in such a manner as to misrepresent that they were the publishers of the plaintiffs' directories. The only connection with England was that remittances were received here. Peter Gibson J. held[40] that in the absence of any evidence of foreign law the plaintiffs had failed to make out an arguable case. The reasoning (if not necessarily the result) of *Intercontex v Schmidt* is to be preferred to that in *Fleetwood Mac v Clifford David Management*,[41] in which an interlocutory injunction was granted against the defendants touring the United States

---

[37] [1994] F.S.R. 316 (Keane J., Ireland).
[38] [1994] R.P.C. 252 (Ferris J.).
[39] [1988] F.S.R. 575 (Peter Gibson J.).
[40] Following *Alfred Dunhill Ltd v Sunoptic SA* [1979] F.S.R. 337, CA.
[41] [1975] F.S.R. 150 (Goff J.).

under the name of the plaintiff pop group on the ground that "the passing-off originated in and was engineered from England". So it had been, but only if it deserved to be called passing-off at all, and there was no evidence that the defendants' tour was actionable under American law. If the tour would be lawful in the country where it took place, why should the defendants be restrained from carrying it out because it was planned from here?

The foregoing cases in which the respective plaintiffs failed, and *Alfred Dunhill v Sunoptic* in so far as it concerned foreign countries other than Switzerland, should be taken solely as illustrating the importance of giving evidence of the relevant foreign law if an injunction is to be awarded in respect of conduct abroad.

Older cases: injurious falsehood

10–64 A number of actions for injurious falsehood have also involved alleged misrepresentations whose effect, if any, would wholly or predominantly have been felt in a foreign market. The doctrine of instruments of deception is inapplicable to the action for injurious falsehood, and although there are a number of cases in which the relevant misrepresentation was made abroad there is very little discussion of private international law principles in the judgments.

In *Thomas v Williams*[42] both parties were British, and they competed in exporting needles to Australia. Fry J. granted a perpetual injunction against the defendants re-issuing a circular, entirely distributed in Australia, in terms implying that the plaintiff's needles were counterfeit. The case appears to have been argued as if it were purely a domestic one and without any reference to private international law. Conversely in the result, but consistently in its reasoning, the Court of Appeal in *Hubbuck v Wilkinson Heywood*[43] struck out an action for injurious falsehood in which the advertisements complained of were published entirely in China and Japan, those countries being the market to which both parties exported their respective brands of white zinc paint. Although neither of these cases expressly alluded to *Philips v Eyre*,[44] neither is inconsistent with the latter: so far as *Thomas v Williams* was concerned the substantive common law of injurious falsehood was certainly the same in Australia as in England,[45] and in *Hubbuck v Wilkinson Heywood* it mattered not at all whether the conduct of the defendants would have been actionable in China and Japan, since once it was decided that the advertisements were innocent under English law, then the double actionability rule meant that the action was bound to fail.

10–65 In *Fielding v Variety*[46] one of two heads of damage alleged by the plaintiff

---

[42] (1880) 14 Ch. D. 864 (Fry J.).

[43] [1899] 1 Q.B. 86, CA,

[44] (1870) L.R. 6 Q.B. 1 (Exchequer Chamber).

[45] Though not so for procedural law. Fry J.'s ability to grant an injunction against a "trade libel" crucially depended on the Judicature Act 1873, and Australia had no Judicature Act(s) of its own until much later.

[46] [1967] 2 Q.B. 841, CA.

was that the defendants' description of his musical *Charlie Girl* as "a disastrous flop" had destroyed his chance of finding American backers for an adaptation for the United States. The argument succeed at first instance to the extent of damages of £10,000 being awarded, but failed (on the facts) on appeal, with damages being reduced to £100. The Court of Appeal treated the issue purely as one of causation: there was little or no evidence that the prospect of such a production had been adversely affected. In the *Harris Tweed* case, *Argyllshire Weavers v Macaulay*[47] the Lord Ordinary was clearly troubled by the fact that no evidence had been given of American law, but reluctantly applied the presumption that the latter corresponded to Scots law so far as relevant. In the result the pursuers failed on the facts on all their claims, including those in relation to certain statements made by the defenders to the United States Customs Service and Patent and Trademark Office.

Jurisdiction at common law...

The same rules as to jurisdiction apply to both passing-off and injurious **10–66** falsehood, but differ according to whether or not the defendant is domiciled in a European state to which the Brussels or Lugano conventions, or the EC Jurisdiction Regulation,[48] apply. Prior to January 1, 1987, when the Civil Jurisdiction and Judgments Act 1982 came into force, jurisdiction over actions for passing-off, injurious falsehood, or other acts of unfair competition committed abroad was wholly governed by the common law and the former RSC Ord.11. The pre-1987 common law rules as to jurisdiction continue to apply to non-European defendants and are now to be found in CPR Pt 6 Section III and Practice Direction 6B, which together substantially correspond to the former RSC Ord.11.

As a practical matter, the only relevant bases of jurisdiction at common law are or were that if the High Court had personal jurisdiction over the defendant (typically by virtue of the latter being a UK-incorporated company with its registered office in England and Wales, or by carrying on business in the jurisdiction) then the latter could in principle be sued for acts of passing off, *etc.* committed anywhere in the World; and if a foreign defendant had committed, or was otherwise liable for, acts of passing-off or injurious falsehood within the jurisdiction then service on him would be permitted outside the jurisdiction under the former RSC Ord.11 r.1(1)(h)—tort committed within the jurisdiction.[49] In the former respect, there was and is a recognised and well-established distinction between passing-off and the proprietary intellectual property torts, such as patent, copyright and even trade mark infringement. Unlike the latter, neither the former "double

---

[47] [1964] R.P.C. 477 (Lord Hunter, Outer House).
[48] Council Regulation 44/2001 of December 22, 2000 on Jurisdiction and the Recognition and Enforcement of Judgments in Civil and Commercial Matters.
[49] *e.g. James North & Sons Ltd v North Cape Textiles Ltd* [1984] 1 W.L.R. 1428; [1985] E.C.C. 541; [1984] F.S.R. 28, CA.

actionability" rule of *Phillips v Eyre*,[50] nor the rule in the *Mocambique* case,[51] ever prevented a foreign cause of action being entertained. The leading cases deciding against the common law justiciability in the United Kingdom of infringements of foreign proprietary intellectual rights expressly distinguished, and approved, the separate treatment of passing-off.[52]

...and after the 1982 Act

10–67 Jurisdiction over defendants domiciled in Europe is now governed by the relevant provisions of the Jurisdiction Regulation,[53] the Brussels Convention,[54] or the Lugano Convention,[55] as the case may be. The Brussels Convention (as amended by various Accession conventions) was originally given effect by the Civil Jurisdiction and Judgments Act 1982, s.2, which came into force on January 1, 1987. The Lugano Convention is also given legal effect by the 1982 Act, s.3A, whereas the Jurisdiction Regulation is directly applicable by virtue of its status as such. The practical effects under all three instruments are very much the same: if the defendant is domiciled in a relevant contracting state then he may be sued in the courts of that state for causes of action accruing anywhere in the World.[56] A UK-domiciled defendant may therefore be sued in the United Kingdom for acts of unfair competition committed (or threatened) anywhere. The other head of jurisdiction likely to be of relevance in the context of the present work is the special jurisdiction in cases of tort.[57] In tort cases, the defendant, if domiciled in Europe, may also be sued in the place where the "harmful event" occurred. The latter phrase has been explained so that if direct (as opposed to merely consequential) damage is suffered in one member state as a result of a harmful event occurring in another, then the courts of both states have

---

[50] (1870) L.R. 6 Q.B. 1 (Exchequer Chamber).

[51] *British South Africa Co v Companhia do Mocambique* [1893] A.C. 602, HL.

[52] *Tyburn Productions Ltd v Conan Doyle* [1991] Ch. 75; [1990] 1 All E.R. 909; [1990] R.P.C. 185 distinguished *Alfred Dunhill Ltd v Sunoptic SA* [1979] F.S.R. 337, CA. In *Def Lepp Music v Stuart Brown* [1986] R.P.C. 273 claims for passing-off were struck out, but for being inadequately particularised and for not pleading the relevant foreign law. In the Scottish case of *James Burrough Distillers Ltd v Speymalt Whisky Distributors Ltd* 1989 S.L.T. 561; 1989 S.C.L.R. 255; [1991] R.P.C. 130 claims for alleged passing-off in Italy were allowed to go to proof, although those for registered trade mark infringement were struck out.

[53] Council Regulation 44/2001 of December 22, 2000 on Jurisdiction and the Recognition and Enforcement of Judgments in Civil and Commercial Matters. The Regulation applies to all EU member states except Denmark.

[54] The 1968 Brussels Convention (as amended) on Jurisdiction and the Recognition and Enforcement of Judgments in Civil and Commercial Matters. The Brussels Convention formerly applied to all EU Member States but has been superceded, except for Denmark, by the Jurisdiction Regulation, above.

[55] The 1988 Lugano Convention on Jurisdiction and the Recognition and Enforcement of Judgments in Civil and Commercial Matters. The Lugano Convention applies to relations between the EU and remaining EFTA states, Iceland, Norway and Switzerland. It has also been adopted by Poland.

[56] Art.2(1) of the Jurisdiction Regulation. Numbering is unaltered from the Brussels and Lugano Conventions.

[57] Art.5(3) of the Jurisdiction Regulation. Numbering is unaltered from the Brussels and Lugano Conventions.

jurisdiction, but the jurisdiction of those of the place where the damage is felt is confined to the state in question, whereas the courts of the place where the causative event originated have unlimited jurisdiction.[58]

Although causes of action for trade mark infringement and passing-off are quite likely to arise on the same underlying facts and to require similar issues to be addressed, they are completely separate and governed by entirely different principles. Registered trade mark infringement actions are covered by the exclusive jurisdiction provisions of Art.22.4 of the Jurisdiction Regulation,[59] but the latter is inapplicable to actions not involving registered intellectual property rights, such as those for passing-off or injurious falsehood, or unfair competition generally. The latter are therefore unaffected by the continuing debate about the impact of Art.22.4 on extraterritorial actions for infringement of registered intellectual property rights. In *LA Gear v Whelan*[60] and *Mecklermedia v DC Congress*,[61] Arts 21 and 22 of the Brussels Convention[62] were held not to apply as between trade mark infringement actions in one jurisdiction and passing-off actions in another.

In *Modus Vivendi v British Products Sanmex*[63] the plaintiffs alleged that **10–68** butane gas refills manufactured by the defendants in Scotland were shipped to China where they were passed off as the plaintiffs' refills, so as to make the defendants liable for passing-off by the export of "instruments of deception". However, both the corporate and personal defendants were domiciled in Scotland and the question therefore arose of whether the English or Scottish courts had jurisdiction under the modified Brussels Convention scheme which applies between the parts of the United Kingdom.[64] The plaintiffs' claim was that although the refills had been manufactured in Scotland, England was the "place where the harmful event occurred" in the sense of *Shevill v Presse Alliance*,[65] either because that was where they suffered damage, or because the refills had been shipped from English ports. Knox J. held that such connections as there were with England were insufficient to found jurisdiction in England, and struck the action out. The two places contemplated by the *Shevill* case were China, to which the goods were exported and where the plaintiffs' relevant goodwill stood to suffer damage, and Scotland, which was where they were manufactured and packed in their offending livery.

---

[58] Case C–68/93 *Shevill v Press Alliance SA* [1995] 2 A.C. 18; [1995] E C.R. I–415; [1995] I.L.Pr. 267; [1995] E.M.L.R. 543; explaining Case 21/76 *Handelswerkerij GJ Bier BV v Mines de Potasse d'Alscace SA* [1978] Q.B. 708; [1976] E.C.R. 1735; [1977] 1 C.M.L.R. 284.
[59] Corresponding to Art.16(4) of the Brussels and Lugano Conventions.
[60] [1991] F.S.R. 670 (Mummery J.).
[61] [1997] F.S.R. 627 (Jacob J.), below.
[62] Dealing respectively with *lis alibi pendens* and "related actions"; Arts 27 and 28 of the Jurisdiction Regulation correspond.
[63] [1997] I.L.Pr. 654; [1996] F.S.R. 790 (Knox J.).
[64] Civil Jurisdiction and Judgments Act 1982, s.16 and Sch. 4.
[65] Case C–68/93; [1995] 2 A.C. 18; [1995] E.C.R. I–415; [1995] I.L.Pr. 267; [1995] E.M.L.R. 543.

"The problem before me is to transpose these principles [of *Shevill*] into a passing off claim where there is a geographical separation between the place of the action of the defendant giving rise to and at the origin of the damage—in the present case somewhere in the United Kingdom, whether Scotland or England is disputed—and the place where the misrepresentation involved in the passing off took effect—in the present case Hong Kong and the People's Republic of China—and the place where economic loss was suffered by the plaintiff, a drop in sales by the plaintiff...

If one supposes that the passing off in the present case was effected in a Convention country, say, for example, France, rather than in distant Hong Kong or the People's Republic of China, there would in my view be seen to be close connecting factors with France where, to put it neutrally, the illicit incursion into the plaintiff's goodwill, whether by way of impairment through the sale of shoddy goods or of misappropriation through the misrepresentation that perfectly adequate goods were those of the plaintiff rather than those of the defendant, occurred.

I have therefore reached the conclusion that England, for all that it was apparently where the plaintiff claims to have suffered loss, is not the place within the meaning of Article 5(3) where the harmful event occurred as the place where the damage occurred."

10–69 Turning to the other head of *Shevill*, Knox J. concluded that Scotland rather than England was the place where the harmful event originated, so that the Scots courts had jurisdiction:

"I can deal more shortly with the question whether England was the place where the event giving rise to and at the origin of the damage occurred. This of course turns upon the geographical location of what the defendant company did. So far as its own manufacturing can filling process is concerned there is no doubt that that occurred in Scotland. The plaintiff relies on the fact, which it claims is at least arguably shown, that the transaction whereby the cans were exported in the plaintiff's livery were set up by a Mr Phelan, an English resident, whom the plaintiffs allege to have acted as the defendants' agent. This is disputed by the first defendant which claims that Mr Phelan was acting for the dishonest Chinese-based buyer.

Secondly, the plaintiff relies on the fact that the offending cans were printed on the first defendant's order by an English resident company and the cans, with the infringing material upon it, were then sent to Scotland where they were filled by the defendant and exported, it is claimed, via England. The point of export is not established firmly probably largely because the first defendant's records have, as the evidence has shown, been damaged by a flood in December 1994. I assume, for present purposes, that the goods did travel through England on their way to Hong Kong. They were sent c.i.f. but that is about all that is known about the terms on which the carriers operated by whom the goods were transported.

Whether one looks at it narrowly or, as I would prefer to do, broadly, it seems to me that the event which gave rise to the damage relied upon should be placed in Scotland. A broad approach is in my view to be preferred because I respectfully agree with what Steyn J. said in *Minster Investments Ltd v Hyundai Precision and Industry Co. Ltd* [1988] 2 Lloyd's Rep. 621 at 624 after the *Mines de potasse* case which was quoted by him but obviously before the *Dumez, Marinari* and *Shevill* cases which had not yet been decided. He said this at page 624:

> 'In my judgment, common sense and policy considerations require one to ask where in substance the cause of action in tort arises, or what the tort is most closely connected with.''

In *Mecklermedia v DC Congress*[66] Jacob J. held that an action for passing- **10–70** off in England should not be struck out or stayed as a result of the existence of a trade mark infringement action in Germany, in which the positions of the parties were nearly reversed. The facts were that the plaintiffs claimed goodwill in England in relation to various publishing activities and organising trade shows under the name *Internet World*. The defendants DC had also organised shows under the name *Internet World*, in Düsseldorf in 1996 and in Vienna in 1997, and they had promoted their shows in the United Kingdom. Some of the promotional activity had been directed towards exhibitors at, or visitors to, the plaintiffs' shows. Although the defendants' activities actually took place abroad, the plaintiffs' United Kingdom goodwill stood to be damaged by promotion of the shows in the United Kingdom so there was a serious question of passing-off to be tried. Jacob J. held that the passing-off action fell within Art.5(3) of the Brussels Convention in that the "place where the harmful event occurred" was England, where the plaintiffs' goodwill and reputation existed. All the elements of the tort—goodwill, misrepresentation and damage—would have to be made out in England.

In the Scots case of *Bonnier Media v Smith*[67] the first (individual) defender **10–71** lived in Greece and the second defenders were incorporated in Mauritius. They obtained registration of the domain name *businessam.com* which the pursuers alleged would be used for passing themselves off as connected with the latter's *business a.m.* newspaper and its *businessam.co.uk* website. The pursuers obtained an *ex parte* interim interdict and the defenders applied to set it aside, *inter alia* for want of jurisdiction. The Court of Session held that regardless of the defenders' domicile, there was jurisdiction under Art.5(3) of the Brussels Convention by virtue of the defenders threatening to commit acts of passing-off and trade mark in Scotland, and the interim interdict would be continued.

---

[66] [1998] Ch. 40; [1998] 1 All E.R. 148; [1997] E.T.M.R. 265; [1997] I.L.Pr. 629; [1997] F.S.R. 627 (Jacob J.).

[67] 2002 S.C. 36; 2002 S.C.L.R. 977; [2002] E.T.M.R. 86 (Lord Drummond Young, Outer House).

Applicable law under the 1995 Act

10–72 The law applicable to an action in the United Kingdom for acts of unfair competition committed abroad is now determined by the Private International Law (Miscellaneous Provisions) Act 1995, which so far as relevant came into force on May 1, 1996. In contrast to issues of jurisdiction, in matters of applicable law there is a significant distinction to be drawn between passing-off and injurious falsehood; but the same rules for determination of the applicable law apply to all defendants, wherever domiciled, and regardless of whether jurisdiction is governed by European law or by the common law.

Actions in England for passing-off abroad are now governed by the general provisions of Part III of the Private International Law (Miscellaneous Provisions) Act 1995. The Act abolishes the former rule of "double actionability", otherwise known as the rule in *Phillips v Eyre*,[68] in favour of the application in most cases of the law of the place where the tort occurred. Although the latter may be displaced in favour of another system of law if there are sufficiently important factors connecting the tort with another country,[69] in the application of the Act to passing-off the normal and perhaps invariable rule will be that the *lex loci delicti commissi* applies unmodified.

10–73 The principal sections of the 1995 Act potentially relevant to passing-off are sections 9 and 11:

Section 9: Purpose of Part III

(1) The rules in this Part apply for choosing the law (in this Part referred to as "the applicable law") to be used for determining issues relating to tort or (for the purposes of the law of Scotland) delict.

(2) The characterisation for the purposes of private international law of issues arising in a claim as issues relating to tort or delict is a matter for the courts of the forum.

(3) The rules in this Part do not apply in relation to issues arising in any claim excluded from the operation of this Part by section 13 below.[70]

(4) The applicable law shall be used for determining the issues arising in a claim, including in particular the question whether an actionable tort or delict has occurred.

(5) The applicable law to be used for determining the issues arising in a claim shall exclude any choice of law rules forming part of the law of the country or countries concerned.

. . .

---

[68] (1870) L.R. 6 Q.B. 1 (Exchequer Chamber), abolished (except for defamation and injurious falsehood) by s.10.

[69] s.12, not reproduced here.

[70] Principally defamation claims, but including injurious falsehood.

Section 11. Choice of applicable law: the general rule

(1) The general rule is that the applicable law is the law of the country in which the events constituting the tort or delict in question occur.

(2) Where elements of those events occur in different countries, the applicable law under the general rule is to be taken as being—

. . .

    (c) in any other case, the law of the country in which the most significant element or elements of those events occurred.

The practical effect of the Act in the context of passing-off is that in future **10–74** actions in England for unfair competition abroad will continue to be possible, provided there is personal jurisdiction over the defendant, but the applicable law under the 1995 Act will be the *lex loci delicti commissi* and English law as the *lex fori* will cease to have any relevance to such claims. There is an exception to the foregoing if the act of unfair competition is characterised as analogous to defamation or injurious falsehood, in which case ss.9(3), 10 and 13 preserve the old double actionability rule of *Philips v Eyre*.[71]

Actions for unfair competition under systems of law where the latter is a nominate tort in its own right may involve claims for commercial disparagement or inaccurate comparative advertising which might be said to correspond to injurious falsehood in English law. To that extent, s.13 would apply. The latter provides:

Section 13. Exclusion of defamation claims from Part III.

(1) Nothing in this Part applies to affect the determination of issues arising in any defamation claim.

(2) For the purposes of this section "defamation claim" means:—

    (a) any claim under the law of any part of the United Kingdom for libel or slander or for slander of title, slander of goods, or other malicious falsehood and any claim under the law of Scotland for verbal injury; and

    (b) any claim under the law of any other country corresponding to or otherwise in the nature of a claim mentioned in paragraph (a) above.

The 1995 Act in practice

To date, only one reported case has applied s.11 of the Private International **10–75** Law (Miscellaneous Provisions) Act 1995 to passing-off. In *Waterford Wedgwood v David Nagli*[72] Irish plaintiffs sued for trade mark infringement and passing-off in respect of dealings by the defendants in counterfeit

---

[71] Above.
[72] [1998] F.S.R. 92 (Scott V.-C.). For subsequent proceedings see [1999] I.L.Pr. 9 (third party notice) and [1999] 3 All E.R. 185 (costs).

Waterford crystal, and applied for summary judgment. The defendants (an English company and its managing director) had purchased the counterfeit crystal from an intermediary for sale to an American company and it was shipped from Ireland to Spain, where it was repackaged, and then shipped onwards from Bilbao to the United States, but via Felixstowe. The purchasers inspected the goods at Bilbao and on arrival at New York, and on each occasion were assured that the goods, their packaging and marks, were genuine.

On the passing-off claims, the Vice-Chancellor described the facts as showing the clearest case of passing off imaginable. Though the individual defendant was conceded to have acted innocently, he had expressly represented to his own customers and to their intended customers that the counterfeit goods were genuine. The terms of certain invoices and letters describing the goods as "Waterford" were not conclusive, because at their dates the counterfeit goods had not been appropriated to the contract, but clear misrepresentations had been made in this respect when the goods were at Bilbao and later in New York. The question therefore arose as to the law to apply to these misrepresentations:

> "This raises the question whether the passing off is a tort to which English law is applicable. If it is not, if the applicable law is the law of Spain or the law of New York, evidence of the requisite foreign law would be necessary in order to establish that the acts relied on as constituting the tort were indeed tortious under the foreign law in question. Since there is no evidence of foreign law before the Court, the case would not be one for summary judgment. This proper law difficulty seems to me to be the only point standing in the way of summary judgment for the plaintiffs on their passing-off claim.
>
> The identification of the country whose law is applicable to the alleged tortious acts of which a plaintiff complains is often a matter of difficulty. The rules to be applied are now to be found in sections 11 and 12 of the Private International Law (Miscellaneous Provisions) Act 1995."

10–76 The Vice-Chancellor went on to hold that the events constituting the tort had occurred in Spain and New York, but not in England. Although there were some connections with England and with English law, it would not have been right to give summary judgment on the basis that English law applied. Nor was it possible to give summary judgment under Spanish and/or New York law, when the relevant foreign law had not been pleaded or put in evidence. In the result, the application for summary judgment on the passing-off claim failed, although that on the trade mark claim had succeeded:

> "It seems to me that 'the events constituting the tort or delict' (see section 11 of the 1995 Act) occurred in Spain and in New York but not in England. Under the section 11 general rule, therefore, the applicable law would not be the law of England. It might, however, be argued that because the crystal was passed off in Spain for the purpose of satisfying

the purchaser under an English contract, and was appropriated to the English contract before being exported to and passed off in New York, it would be 'substantially more appropriate for the applicable law ...' to be the law of England (see section 12 *ibid.*). However, neither counsel has addressed me on the effect of sections 11 and 12 of the 1995 Act on the facts of this case. A conclusion that the law of this country is the proper law applicable to the passing off that took place in Spain and in New York cannot possibly be reached on this summary judgment application. For these reasons I have come to the conclusion that the plaintiffs' application for summary judgment for passing off must fail. This is, in many ways, an unfortunate conclusion. It seems to me almost certain that the events in Bilbao whereby the counterfeit crystal was represented to be genuine crystal would be as delictual in Spain as they would have been tortious in England. The same applies to the passing-off that took place in New York. But the plaintiffs have not pleaded any reliance on foreign law and have not placed before me any evidence of the relevant rules of Spanish or New York law. It would not be right for me to give summary judgment against the defendants on a point of foreign law neither pleaded nor supported by evidence."

INDEX

[all references are to paragraph number]